# IMPORTANT:

## HERE IS YOUR REGISTRATION CODE TO ACCESS
## YOUR PREMIUM McGRAW-HILL ONLINE RESOURCES.

For key premium online resources you need THIS CODE to gain access. Once the code is entered, you will be able to use the Web resources for the length of your course.

If your course is using **WebCT** or **Blackboard**, you'll be able to use this code to access the McGraw-Hill content within your instructor's online course.

Access is provided if you have purchased a new book. If the registration code is missing from this book, the registration screen on our Website, and within your WebCT or Blackboard course, will tell you how to obtain your new code.

## Registering for McGraw-Hill Online Resources

TO gain access to your McGraw-Hill web resources simply follow the steps below:

1. USE YOUR WEB BROWSER TO GO TO: **http://www.mhhe.com/lahey8/**

2. CLICK ON **FIRST TIME USER**.

3. ENTER THE REGISTRATION CODE* PRINTED ON THE TEAR-OFF BOOKMARK ON THE RIGHT.

4. AFTER YOU HAVE ENTERED YOUR REGISTRATION CODE, CLICK **REGISTER**.

5. FOLLOW THE INSTRUCTIONS TO SET-UP YOUR PERSONAL UserID AND PASSWORD.

6. WRITE YOUR UserID AND PASSWORD DOWN FOR FUTURE REFERENCE. KEEP IT IN A SAFE PLACE.

**TO GAIN ACCESS** to the McGraw-Hill content in your instructor's **WebCT** or **Blackboard** course simply log in to the course with the UserID and Password provided by your instructor. Enter the registration code exactly as it appears in the box to the right when prompted by the system. You will only need to use the code the first time you click on McGraw-Hill content.

Thank you, and welcome to your McGraw-Hill online Resources!

**0-07-294311-4 LAHEY: PSYCHOLOGY, 8E**

---

W9-BMO-399

MCGRAW-HILL
ONLINE RESOURCES

**REGISTRATION CODE**

**SH49-EXYM-FIT0-XNAR-F99Z**

# PSYCHOLOGY

## An Introduction

# PSYCHOLOGY
## An Introduction

### EIGHTH EDITION

**Benjamin B. Lahey**

*University of Chicago*

Boston   Burr Ridge, IL   Dubuque, IA   Madison, WI   New York   San Francisco   St. Louis
Bangkok   Bogotá   Caracas   Kuala Lumpur   Lisbon   London   Madrid   Mexico City
Milan   Montreal   New Delhi   Santiago   Seoul   Singapore   Sydney   Taipei   Toronto

The McGraw·Hill Companies

# Higher Education

PSYCHOLOGY: AN INTRODUCTION
Published by McGraw-Hill, a business unit of The McGraw-Hill Companies, Inc., 1221 Avenue of the
Americas, New York, NY 10020. Copyright © 2004, 2001, 1998 by The McGraw-Hill Companies, Inc.
All rights reserved. No part of this publication may be reproduced or distributed in any form or by any
means, or stored in a database or retrieval system, without the prior written consent of The McGraw-
Hill Companies, Inc., including, but not limited to, in any network or other electronic storage or
transmission, or broadcast for distance learning.
Some ancillaries, including electronic and print components, may not be available to customers
outside the United States.

This book is printed on acid-free paper.

2  3  4  5  6  7  8  9  0  QPD/QPD  0  9  8  7  6  5  4  3

ISBN 0–07–256314–1

Publisher: *Steven Rutter*
Sponsoring editor: *Ken King*
Developmental editor I: *Cheri A. Dellelo*
Marketing manager: *Melissa S. Caughlin*
Senior media producer: *Sean Crowley*
Senior project manager: *Rebecca Nordbrock*
Production supervisor: *Enboge Chong*
Art director: *Jeanne M. Schreiber*
Designer: *Sharon Spurlock*
Interior and cover design: *Claire Seng-Niemoeller*
Lead supplement producer: *Marc Mattson*
Photo research coordinator: *Alexandra Ambrose*
Art manager: *Robin Mouat*
Illustrators: *John and Judy Waller*
Photo researcher: *David Tietz*
Typeface: *9.5/12 New Baskerville*
Compositor: *GAC Indianapolis*
Printer: *Quebecor World Dubuque Inc.*

Cover image: *Frida Kahlo,* Self-Portrait with Necklace, *1933, oil on metal, 35 x 30 cm.*

*© 2003 Banco de México Diego & Frida Kahlo Museums Trust. Av. Cinco de Mayo No. 2, Col. Centro,
Del. Cuauhtémoc 06059, México, D.F. y Instituto Nacional de Bellas Artes y Literatura, Edificio "La Nacional"
8 Piso, Av. Jurárez No. 4 esq. Eje Central Lázaro Cárdenas, Colonia Centro 06050, México, D.F. Photo courtesy
of The Vergel Foundation, New York*

**Library of Congress Cataloging-in-Publication Data**

Lahey, Benjamin B.
    Psychology : an introduction / Benjamin B. Lahey.—8th ed.
      p.  cm.
    Includes bibliographical references and indexes.
    ISBN 0–07–256314–1 (softcover : alk. paper)
    1. Psychology.  I. Title.
  BF121 .L214 2004
  150—dc21

                        2002043140
                        CIP

www.mhhe.com

# Lahey's Learning System

## ● Effective Learning

This book contains several proven features to help you turn your study time into effective learning. These features:

1. Focus your attention on the subject of the chapter

2. Give you an advance view of what you are about to learn

3. Show you how each fact and concept are related to the theme of the chapter

4. Help you review, so you can be sure that you understood the material and so you can strengthen your newly formed memories

5. Help you think critically about information and relate what you have learned to your life

**1** **Chapter Outline** Each chapter begins with an outline that organizes the key ideas of the chapter. Examine the outline carefully to see which topic will be studied, but also notice how the topics are arranged. Studying the outline for a few minutes will give you an advance look at the material and will reinforce relationships among topics.

**2** **Chapter Prologue** Each chapter begins with a high-interest essay that briefly introduces you to the content of the chapter. Research shows that having a general understanding of what is going to be learned improves learning and memory of the new information.

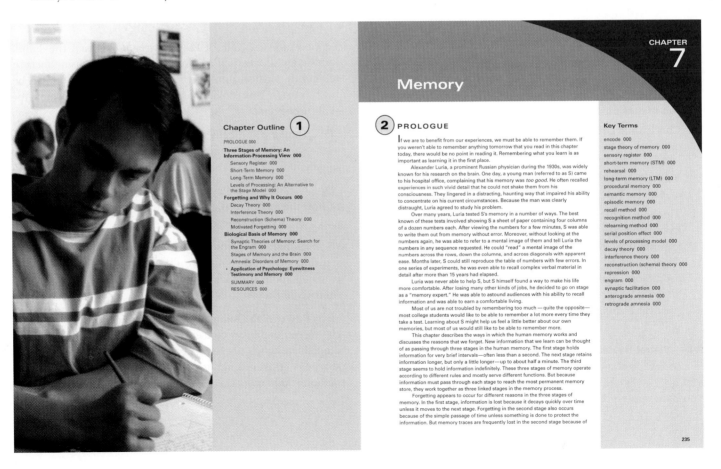

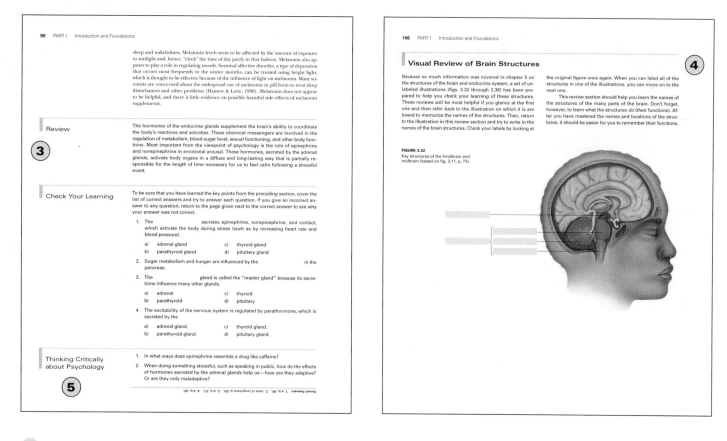

**3   Section Reviews**  Within each chapter you will find reviews at the end of each major section. The review is made up of three separate parts:

1. The **Review** paragraph summarizes the main ideas introduced in the section. This will help you keep the overall organization of the new material in your mind as you master the details.

2. **Check Your Learning** questions are multiple-choice questions designed to test your mastery of the material before you move on. The answers are provided to give you immediate feedback and guide you to the page where the material is covered if you need additional review.

3. **Thinking Critically about Psychology** is designed to stimulate more than just memorizing new ideas. The few minutes of active thought that each question provokes should help you personalize your new knowledge of psychology, making it "your own" to keep and use for a lifetime. Be sure to read the section in the preface entitled "Critical Thinking" to help you sharpen this important skill.

**4   Visual Reviews**  end many of the chapters in this book. These key illustrations are reprinted from the chapter, this time without the labels. This is a final check for you to ensure that you have mastered the material before you start a new chapter.

## ● Critical Thinking

Success in every walk of life requires more than the simple knowledge of facts—it requires evaluating and using facts intelligently. Critical thinking is the skill that allows human beings to make this transition, and this text helps develop this skill throughout.

**5   Thinking Critically about Psychology**  questions appear at the end of each major section to actively engage you in thinking about what you have just read.

**6   Application of Psychology**  boxes provide rich examples of how the facts and theories from the chapter can be applied and used in the real world.

**7   Human Diversity**  boxes give special emphasis to understanding and respecting the differences among people and learning about the sociocultural factors that contribute to the diversity of human lives.

**8   PowerWeb Online Reader**  is a collection of online articles linked to the key concepts in each chapter. Read and complete the assignments associated with each article. This exercise sharpens critical thinking skills and shows you how the information you have learned can be applied to your life.

## application of psychology ⑥

### The Legal Consciousness-Altering Drugs

Each day, many of us use consciousness-altering drugs, usually without even being aware that we are taking "drugs." Coffee contains the stimulant drug caffeine, cigarettes contain the stimulant drug nicotine, and alcohol is a powerful depressant drug. Millions of individuals who would never consider using "drugs" use, abuse, or are addicted to these drugs. What are these drugs' consciousness-altering effects (and side effects)?

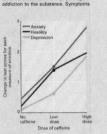

The average American drinks 36 gallons of coffee each year.

**Caffeine**

Eighty-five percent of Americans ingest caffeine daily (Hughes, Oliveto, Helzer, Higgins, & Bickel, 1992). Indeed, each year the average person in the United States drinks 36 gallons of coffee, 7 gallons of tea, and 30 gallons of cola and uses untold amounts of over-the-counter drugs containing caffeine (Ray, 1974). At approximately 125 milligrams (mg) per cup of coffee, that is an enormous consumption of caffeine.

You've seen the ads on television: The attractive woman, frazzled by the day's hassles, is restored to peaceful balance with a cup of coffee. Is that a good way to cope with our emotions when they have been bent and abused by life? Is caffeine good medicine for our nerves? Because caffeine is a stimulant, it does produce an increase in alertness, which helps explain the popularity of coffee, tea, colas, and other beverages that contain caffeine. But does it make you feel *better*?

Physicians and psychologists have long suspected that caffeine actually produces negative changes in emotions in many persons. David Veleber and Donald Templer (1984) conducted a study of the effects of caffeine on emotions using volunteer college students and businesspeople in the San Joaquin Valley of California. The participants completed a psychological test that measured the degree of depression, anxiety, and hostility that the individual was experiencing at the time of the test.

They took the test before and 1 hour after drinking a cup of coffee. Some of the participants drank decaffeinated coffee, whereas others received a low or high dose of caffeine in their coffee (the individuals did not know how much caffeine they were drinking, if any). The amount of caffeine was adjusted for the individual's body weight, with a 100-pound person receiving the equivalent of either one cup (low dose) or two cups (high dose) of strong brewed coffee.

As shown in figure 5.7, the caffeine produced small but significant changes in all three emotions. Most of us feel no ill effects from small amounts of coffee, but a large amount of caffeine is an invitation to lousy moods for all of us, and even small amounts may cause distress for sensitive individuals.

Unfortunately, serious health risks are associated with the overuse of caffeine. Although caffeine produces relatively small changes in consciousness, it has powerful effects on the body. It has long been known that consumption of eight or more cups of caffeinated coffee per day (1,000 mg) constitutes a dangerously high level of intake (Greden, 1974). Common effects of such consumption for a prolonged period of time include excessive stomach acid and ulcers, abnormal heart rhythms and accelerated heart rate, increased kidney activity, anxiety, irritability, insomnia, sensory disturbances, and definite physiological addiction with intense withdrawal symptoms when caffeine is not consumed (Greden, 1974; Hughes & others, 1992). Prolonged use of caffeine at even moderate levels can also result in a physiological addiction to the substance. Symptoms

**FIGURE 5.7**
Change in measures of emotion after drinking either decaffeinated coffee or coffee containing small or large amounts of caffeine.
Source: Data from D. M. Veleber and D. T. Templer, "Effects of Caffeine on Anxiety and Depression," *Journal of Abnormal Psychology*, 93, 120–122, 1984. © 1984 by the American Psychological Association.

---

### ⑦ HUMAN DIVERSITY

**Culture and Pain**

In this chapter, we examine the ways in which neural impulses from the sense organs are experienced as sensations and perceptions. Although much of this process is determined by the biological nature of the sense organs and neurons, learning experiences in our cultures apparently can influence even basic sensations such as pain.

Let's consider an example of the impact of culture on the perception of pain. Members of the Bariba society in Benin, West Africa, appear to be able to tolerate pain more easily than members of most cultures. Bariba folklore includes many examples of honored people who showed strength in the face of pain, and this calm response to pain is seen as an integral part of Bariba pride (Sargent, 1984). For example, pregnant women are expected not to let the fact that they are experiencing labor pains show to others. When labor becomes advanced, they leave the company of others to go through labor and childbirth alone, only calling for help with cutting the umbilical cord.

To the Bariba, letting other people see that they are in pain is cause for great shame. When discussing pain, many Bariba quote a Bariba proverb that translates to "Between death and shame, death has the greater beauty." According to a Bariba physician, an individual who displays pain lacks courage, and cowardice is the essence of shame. Rather than live in shame, a Bariba would rather die (Sargent, 1984). In this cultural context, one would do everything possible to avoid displaying signs of pain.

Do Bariba women who are in labor actually experience less pain than women in other cultures, or have they simply learned not to let the pain show? It is difficult to answer such questions, partly because of the difficulties involved in describing pain to another person. Because pain is a private experience, language must be used to communicate the experience to others, and language is shaped by culture. It is not surprising that there is a more limited vocabulary for describing pain in the Bariba language than in most other languages. When the Bariba discuss the experience of pain, therefore, it is difficult to know how much their description is influenced by their language.

But there is some reason to believe that the cultural emphasis on not showing reactions to pain might actually reduce the amount of pain that the Bariba experience. As noted on page 000 of chapter 10, there is evidence that facial expressions are an important part of the experience of pain (Izard, 1977). Apparently, sensory feedback to the brain from facial muscles supplies part of the neural input for the perception of pain (along with input from the part of the body that is cramped or injured). Indeed, persons who were given electrical shocks reported less pain when they were told to make no facial reactions than when they let their emotions show in their faces (Colby, Lanzetta, & Kleck, 1977). Maybe the calm face of a Bariba woman in labor results in the experience of less pain than does the agonized grimace of women in other cultures.

According to Linda Garro (1990), it is important for medical professionals who work with people in pain to understand the impact of culture on the expression of pain. If culture is not taken into account, the physician may overestimate or underestimate the amount of pain experienced by the patient. On the other hand, it is important to remember that not all members of a culture are the same. In all other aspects of human diversity, it is important to be aware of variation within cultures.

What did you learn about pain in your own culture? Were you taught to minimize pain because it is important to be tough? Did you learn that no one will pay attention to your pain unless you exaggerate it? How do you respond when your parent or friends are in pain? Such questions will help you think about cultural influences on perception. ▪

Amazingly, many amputees experience their missing arm or leg as if it were still there. They feel a missing arm, for example, as if it were hanging by their side when they sit still, and swinging in coordination with their other arm and legs when they walk. This "phantom limb" is experienced not as a memory of the lost limb but as a clear and realistic sensation that the missing limb is actually there. Ronald Melzack (1992) wrote about a man who experienced his missing arm as sticking straight out to the side, so he turned sideways when he walked through doorways to avoid bumping his arm, even though he knew perfectly well that the arm was not really there.

The sadder part is that as many as 70 percent of amputees experience a disturbing pain in the phantom limb. The pain is often a burning sensation, with many persons

---

### Support for Learning

In addition to the in-text learning devices that will reinforce your learning, the text has a *full complement* of ancillary resources to help you learn about psychology.

**⑨   Online Learning Center**

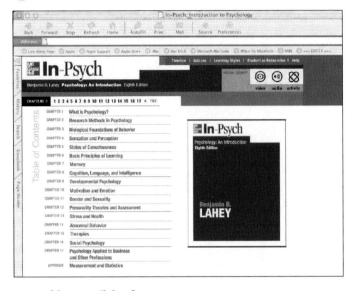

**www.mhhe.com/lahey8**

1. **Student Resources**  Chapter outlines and practice quizzes are keyed to the text Learning Goals. The student section of the Web site also contains flashcards, interactive review exercises, and access, via **PowerWeb,** to current news about psychology, research tools, and many other valuable study tools.

2. **PowerWeb**  This unique online tool provides you with current articles, curriculum-based materials, weekly updates with assessment, informative and timely world news, refereed Web links, research tools, study tools, and interactive exercises. A PowerWeb access card is packaged FREE with each new copy of the text. PowerWeb is integrated into the Online Learning Center. Each chapter ends with an exercise to help integrate this valuable tool.

**⑩   In-Psych CD-ROM**    Packaged FREE with the text, In-Psych features more than 60 interactive exercises chosen to illustrate especially difficult core introductory psychology concepts. It also includes Web resources, chapter quizzes, a research guide, and much more!

**⑪   Student Practice Test Booklet**  Each copy of the text is packaged with a student practice test booklet to help you prepare for exams. The multiple-choice questions focus on the key concepts from the chapter to ensure that you understand the material at a conceptual level. This paper supplement is ideal for studying on the go.

For Megan, Ted, Erin,
Clare, Eamonn, and Kate

# Contents in Brief

# Contents

# Part II    Awareness    111

# Part III:    Learning and Cognition    195

## 6    Basic Principles of Learning    196

# Part IV:    Developmental Psychology    317

# Part VI:  Health and Adjustment  497

# Part VII:    Social Context    603

## 16  Social Psychology    604

# Preface

Although the preface is the first part of the book that you read, it is the last part that I write. It is my opportunity to reflect on the completed project in the hope that these reflections will help introduce you to the text. Over eight editions, the unchanging goal of *Psychology: An Introduction* has been to *teach*. We (referring to the large group of talented psychologists, editors, consultants, and reviewers who have worked with me) have centered our efforts on giving you a text that fully captures the immense importance and fascination of the scientific study of ourselves. You have my pledge that I have done my best to teach the concepts and facts of psychology in the clearest and most exciting manner possible. The gratifying responses of both instructors and students to the first seven editions of this textbook have been a wonderful source of encouragement for these efforts.

Overall, the time-tested format of the book has not changed in the eighth edition. Students continue to like the format, and research continues to support its use. As before, the book enhances learning and memory by using advance organizers followed by clearly written text (with explicit organizational cues) and repeated reviews. An additional advance organizer was added to the eighth edition, however, to help you see the "forest" before you begin to read about the "trees." The opening page to each major section of the text now contains a visual overview of the conceptual organization of the information presented in that section. This should help you use the prologue to each chapter to create a cognitive structure to organize your learning.

It has only been three years since the last revision of this text, but the thousands of psychologists at work in research these days have given us rapid scientific progress. The rapidity of scientific advance is striking when I read the wide range of psychological literatures needed to keep up with the field. This progress is reflected in many changes in the content of the text. Most of these changes reflect confirmations and relatively minor modifications of existing hypotheses, but there have been some notable advances in knowledge and theory. The major content changes in the eighth edition include

1. New information on *positive psychology*—the study of happiness, productiveness, and other aspects of successful adjustment in addition to the study of maladjustment.

2. Expanded coverage of *evolutionary psychology*, particularly its application to theories of gender differences.

3. New information on *developmental changes in the brain* and their relation to changes in behavior and mental processes —it is now clear that the brain is a dynamic organ that changes in response to the environment.

4. Expanded coverage of how the *genome* influences behavior and mental processes.

5. Enhanced coverage of the modern version of the *reconstruction theory of forgetting*, which has received substantial support in recent years, and discussion of its relation to *false memories*.

6. New information on the role of psychological research in improving the validity of *eyewitness testimony* in legal proceedings.

7. Increased inclusion of brain imaging findings related to *cognitive neuroscience* and *affective neuroscience* when discussing cognition, emotion, and personality.

8. New information on *cultural influences* on psychological processes such as inferential reasoning and on mental health problems.

9. Studies of the emotional effects of the *terrorist attacks* on September 11, 2001, and effective coping responses to such traumatic stress.

10. New information on *individual differences in response to stress*, particularly the new hypothesis that the notion of the fight-or-flight syndrome may be more applicable to men than to women.

11. New coverage of the applications of psychological principles to *safety management* in the workplace and in automobiles.

12. Coverage of recent research on the *psychology of the entrepreneur*.

13. Discussion of recent applications of cognitive neuroscience to the field of *human factors engineering*, particularly the development of methods to help persons with health problems interact safely and productively with their environments.

14. Use of recent research on the psychology of *racial prejudice* to improve this section.

15. Expanded coverage of psychology's role in *environmental protection*.

I hope you enjoy reading about these advances in psychology as much as I enjoyed writing about them!

## ● Reviewers

The following individuals have helped tremendously by reviewing this or previous editions of *Psychology: An Introduction;* their helpful guidance has been carried forward into the current edition.

Edward Brady
*Southwestern Illinois College*

Gary Caldwell
*John A. Logan College*

James Carroll
*Central Michigan University*

Richard X. Chandler
*Itawamba Community College*

Joan Cook
*Community College of Morris*

Brenda K. Davis
*South Georgia College*

Randall D. Gold
*Cuesta College*

Terri Heck
*Macomb Community College*

Benetha Jackson
*Angelina Junior College*

Charmaine E. Jake-Matthews
*Prairie State College*

Diana Kyle
*Fullerton College*

Velton Lacefield-Cole
*Prairie State College*

R. Eric Landrum
*Boise State University*

Callista Lee
*Fullerton College*

Giovanni Misceo
*Benedictine College*

Donald Nichols
*Oakland Community College*

James E. Oliver
*Henry Ford Community College*

Jeanne Porcelli
*Florida Community College of Jacksonville*

Amy Posey
*Benedictine College*

Charles N. Riley
*Itawamba Community College*

Deanna Riveira
*College of the Canyons*

Mark Silkey
*Northern Oklahoma College*

Christine M. Vanchella
*South Georgia College*

Jean P. Volckmann
*Pasadena City College*

Special thanks to Dr. J. W. Selgas and the Harrisburg Area Community College Student Advisory Review Committee, chaired by Abigail Miller, for providing detailed and thoughtful feedback on the seventh edition.

Many talented editors and illustrators also played essential roles. The results of that combined effort are before you, and I hope that it will serve the needs of students and instructors even better than did the previous edition.

**Benjamin B. Lahey**

# To the Instructor

*Psychology: An Introduction* offers thorough topic coverage and standard organization designed to fit courses as they are most commonly taught. But it differs significantly from other textbooks in two main ways. First, every effort has been made to create a writing style that is—as one former student kindly described it—"friendly." This book does not attempt to impress students with the arcane complexities of the science of psychology. It was written to provide a clear, informative, challenging, exciting, and personal introduction to psychology. All of the necessary complexities are taught, but in the clearest manner possible.

Second, *Psychology: An Introduction* differs from other textbooks in its emphasis on meaningful learning. This book contains many elements designed to enhance learning and remembering based on an organizational model of semantic memory. The content of the first course in psychology can be thought of as a *hierarchical organization* of concepts and facts. Quite simply, this means that information about psychology is not a disorganized jumble of new facts. Some information "goes with" other information, some concepts are detailed elaborations of more general concepts, and so on. To improve learning and memory, it is as important for students to understand the overall organization of new information as it is for them to understand the individual concepts and facts themselves.

Based on what is well known about learning from textbooks, this book helps the student understand how new information about psychology is organized and to process that information more deeply in five primary ways:

1. *Advance organizers.* Considerable research indicates that students learn and retain information better when they have an advance understanding of the hierarchical organization of the information being learned. To accomplish this, the student is given two kinds of advance organizers before reading the main body of the text. The student is first presented with a **chapter outline** of the major topics covered within the chapter, a device common to many textbooks. But to add to the effectiveness of this bare-bones overview, a prose organizer, called the **prologue,** both piques the student's interest with exciting information and highlights the major concepts in the

forthcoming chapter. Thus, the student is provided with two forward looks at the chapter to create a cognitive organization on which to "hang" new facts and concepts. The prologues in this edition combine the best features of both the prologue and preview sections of previous editions by fusing high-interest material with an advance organizer.

2. *Questions to stimulate critical thinking.* An important feature of the book is the set of questions designed to stimulate critical thinking (Baron & Sternberg, 1987). These critical thinking questions appear at the end of each section. They are designed to catch the student's attention and stimulate thought for two reasons. First, it is important that students not passively absorb new information but, rather, critically evaluate and ponder what they are learning. Moreover, it may be more effective to teach critical thinking skills through the content of a specific course than in the abstract. And what course is more appropriate than psychology—in which human beings ponder themselves? Second, current research suggests that thinking about what you have just learned leads to deeper semantic processing and better retention. Thus, both as an aid to student reading and as a stimulus for classroom discussion, these high-interest questions at the end of each section are important pedagogical tools. To help students prepare to use these critical thinking questions, a discussion on critical thinking appears in the "Before You Begin" section. In addition, the *Instructor's Course Planner* includes pertinent information to help the instructor.

3. *Nested hierarchical reviews.* The interrelationships among new concepts are highlighted further in **review** and **summary** sections. Following each major section within each chapter, the content of that section is briefly reviewed in prose. In addition, the student can test his or her knowledge of each section in the **check your learning** sections. At the end of each chapter, the main content of the chapter is again summarized, but this time in a hierarchical outline that visually highlights the organization of the material.

4. *Visual organizational cues.* Using hierarchical outlines in the end-of-chapter summaries is only one way in which the

student is actually shown the organization of the new material. Close attention has been paid to the use of visual cues—such as typeface, type size, color of type, and indentations—to indicate the organization of the text. The difference between this book and others is intentionally subtle in this respect, but students should have little trouble distinguishing the superordinate-subordinate structure of A, B, and C levels of headings. In diagrams and figures, colors were chosen not to be decorative but to show students which elements are related and which are different. In addition, lists—like the one you are reading now—have been frequently (but not excessively) used to show that each element in the list is at the same level of organization and subordinate to the title of the list ("five ways to help students understand organizational structure," in the case of the list you are reading now).

5. *Verbal cues to organization.* Another important way to help readers see how concepts and facts are related is simply to tell them in words. Therefore, this textbook makes many references to the organization of the new information. This is done in two main ways. First, when a newly introduced concept is related to another concept that was discussed in an earlier section, this fact is specifically pointed out. Second, information that is subordinate to a concept is frequently introduced in a way that makes that relationship very clear (e.g., "The two factors that cause forgetting in short-term memory are . . ."). Although these cues are subtle so as not to interrupt the flow of the discussion, they have been added to help improve the student's comprehension and memory.

The use of these pedagogical devices was chosen over two other pedagogical approaches after much consideration. I chose not to use the SQ3R (survey, question, read, recite, review) method of organizing the text because the author, not the student, must ask the questions, which reduces student involvement and discourages the student from critically evaluating and deeply processing the new information. It is much better for the *student* to use SQ3R than for the *author* to use it. Therefore, instructions to the student on the use of SQ3R are included in the **study skills** section, which follows the preface. For those instructors who wish to use instructional objectives, we have included them in the *Student Study Guide* and the *Instructor's Course Planner* that accompany this book.

## ● Print and Media Supplements

### For the Student

#### PowerWeb

This unique online tool provides you with current articles, curriculum-based materials, weekly updates with assessment, informative and timely world news, refereed Web links, research

tools, study tools, and interactive exercises. A PowerWeb access card is packaged FREE with each new copy of the text. This is a great way to hone critical thinking skills and stay up to date on current events related to core concepts in the course.

#### Student Practice Tests

Each copy of the text is packaged with a student practice test booklet to help you prepare for exams. This paper supplement is ideal for students who study on the go. The multiple-choice questions focus on the key concepts from the chapter to ensure that you understand the material at a conceptual level.

#### Making the Grade Student CD-ROM

Packaged FREE with the text, this user-friendly CD-ROM gives you an opportunity to test your comprehension of the course material in a manner that is comfortable and beneficial. The CD-ROM opens with a Learning Style/Study Skills questionnaire that you can use to identify the best way for you to study. Also included are practice tests that cover topics in the introductory psychology course, an Internet primer, and a statistics primer.

#### New! In-Psych Student CD-ROM

In-Psych sets a new standard for introductory psychology multimedia. The CD-ROM is organized according to the text chapter outlines and features more than 60 interactive exercises chosen to illustrate especially difficult core introductory psychology concepts. Each exercise showcases one of three types of media assets—an audio clip, a video clip, or a simulation/lab—and includes a pre-test, follow-up assignments, and Web resources. In-Psych also includes chapter quizzes, a student research guide, and an interactive timeline that puts events, key figures, and research in psychology in historical perspective. (Available in Fall 2003)

#### Student Study Guide

Designed to reinforce the key ideas in the text, the student study guide contains the following features for each chapter of the text: learning objectives, detailed chapter outline, guided review of terms and concepts, a section that promotes students' understanding of human diversity, and a practice quiz that tests students' mastery of the chapter's key concepts and ideas.

#### Online Learning Center for Students

The official Web site for the text contains PowerWeb articles, *New York Times* news feeds, chapter outlines, practice quizzes that can be e-mailed to the professor, key term flashcards, interactive exercises, Internet activities, Web links to relevant psychology sites, drag-and-drop labeling exercises, Internet primer, a career appendix, and a statistics primer: http://www.mhhe.com/Lahey8.

# For the Instructor

## Instructor's Manual

This manual provides many useful tools to enhance your teaching. For each chapter you will find teaching objectives, chapter outlines, suggestions for teaching the chapter, lecture/discussion suggestions, critical thinking questions, in-class activities, public policy and current controversies discussion launchers, applications questions, and a media integrator with helpful suggestions for how to link the electronic resources to your syllabus.

## Test Item Files

*Three* Test Item Files provide you with the widest variety of questions to last the life of this edition. The questions in the Test Item Files are also available on *Brownstone,* a powerful but easy-to-use test-generating program that McGraw-Hill offers on a hybrid CD-ROM. With Brownstone, you can easily select questions and print tests and answer keys. You can also customize questions, headings, and instructions; add or import your own questions; and print tests in a choice of printer-supported fonts. In addition, the questions from the first two test banks are available in Rich Text Format (RTF) on the Enhanced Instructor's Resource CD-ROM.

## Enhanced Instructor's Resource CD-ROM

This two–CD-ROM set includes a DVD that features 25 video clips to be used in class to illustrate key concepts in the course. Included in the collection of clips are animations designed to bring complex processes to life. The CD-ROM features the Instructor's Manual, Test Item Files, and PowerPoint lectures.

## In-Class Activities Manual

By Patricia A. Jarvis, Cynthia R. Nordstrom, and Karen B. Williams, Illinois State University. Geared to instructors of large introductory psychology courses, this activities manual covers every major topic in the course. Nineteen chapters include 58 separate activities, all of which have been used successfully in the authors' classes. Each activity includes a short description of the demonstration, the approximate time needed to complete the activity, the materials needed, step-by-step procedures, practical tips, and suggested readings related to the activity. The manual also includes advice and teaching tips—for the novice and experienced instructor—on how to prepare an effective syllabus, what to consider when structuring a large section, how to select and manage a teaching assistant, and other key topics.

## PowerPoint Lectures

Available on the Internet and on the Enhanced Instructor's Resource CD-ROM, these presentations cover the key points of each chapter and include charts and graphs from the text. Helpful lecture guidelines are provided in the notes section for each slide. They can be used as-is or modified to meet your needs.

## Overhead Transparencies

More than 100 key images from the text are available to you upon adoption.

## Online Learning Center for Instructors

The password-protected instructor side of the text Web site contains the Instructor's Manual, a sample chapter from the text, PowerPoint Presentations, Web links, *New York Times* news feeds, and other teaching resources: http://www.mhhe.com/lahey8.

## PageOut™

Build your own course Web site in less than an hour. You don't have to be a computer whiz to create a Web site, especially with an exclusive McGraw-Hill product called PageOut™. It requires no prior knowledge of HTML, no long hours of coding, and no design skills on your part. With PageOut™, even the most inexperienced computer user can quickly and easily create a professional-looking course Web site. Simply fill in templates with your information and with content provided by McGraw-Hill, choose a design, and you've got a Web site specifically designed for your course. Best of all, it's FREE! Visit us at http://www.pageout.net to find out more.

Populated WebCT and Blackboard course cartridges are available. Contact your McGraw-Hill sales representative for details.

## Instructor's Resource CD-ROM

This comprehensive CD-ROM includes the contents of the Instructor's Manual, Test Item Files (in RTF format), an image gallery, and PowerPoint slides. An easy-to-use interface is provided for the design and delivery of multimedia classroom presentations.

# Before You Begin:
## A Primer on Study Skills

You are about to begin your introduction to the science of psychology. Before you do, I would like to offer you some suggestions that are based on psychological principles. Psychology is a science that addresses a great many topics, most of which have some direct relevance to our lives. One topic that has long been of interest to psychologists is human learning—the ways in which we learn and remember new information, such as the new information that you are learning about the field of psychology. Much has been discovered about learning and memory that can be translated into suggestions for more efficient learning in this course and all of your other courses.

People do not absorb information as a sponge absorbs water; we have to *work* at learning new information in college courses. Human beings are highly effective learners, but we learn better in some ways than we do in others. If we understand the characteristics and quirks of the human learner, we can make better use of our study time. These characteristics will be discussed in some detail in chapters 6 and 7 on learning and memory, but before you begin to study the science of psychology, it may be useful to summarize some of the more helpful hints provided by psychologists for more effective learning and recall.

I have kept this section brief because I know how busy the beginning of the term can be, but the information contained in this section is worth your attention. From my own experience as a student, and from working with many students since that time, I know that learning better ways to study can make the learning process more enjoyable, can increase the amount of information that you learn and retain, and can improve your grades. I hope that the following suggestions will help you.

## ● The SQ3R Method

Francis Robinson of Ohio State University suggested a method for studying textbooks known as the SQ3R method. These initials stand for the five steps in effective textbook study outlined by Robinson:

S: *Survey.* Look ahead at the content of the text before you begin to read.

Q: *Question.* Ask yourself questions about the material you are reading before and as you read.

R: *Read.* Read through the material in the normal way.

R: *Recite.* Recite the new information that you are learning out loud or silently.

R: *Review.* Go over the material that you have learned several times before you are tested on it.

Let's go through these steps in more detail to better understand them.

### Survey

Most of us think there is just one way to read—you start at the beginning and read to the end. That is the best way to read a novel because you don't want to know about the next plot twist or the surprise ending until you get there. But a very different strategy is needed when reading a textbook. It's important to survey, or look ahead, at what you are going to read. In fact, you should try to find out as much as possible about the text material you are going to read *before* you read it.

The reason behind this strategy of surveying before reading is based on the way humans learn and store new information in memory. Speaking loosely, we "hang" new information on what we already know. If we learn a new fact about marijuana, we hang that information on what we already know about mind-altering drugs; and, the more organized knowledge we have of a topic, the better we are able to learn and remember new

Human beings are highly effective learners, but we learn better in some ways than we do in others. If we understand the characteristics and quirks of the human learner, we can make better use of our study time.

*Where is the thyroid gland located? What role does the thyroid gland play in Metabolism? What are the effects of thyroxin?*

The **thyroid gland,** located just below the larynx, or voice box, plays an important role in the regulation of **metabolism.** It does so by secreting a hormone called **thyroxin.** The level of thyroxin in a person's bloodstream and the resulting metabolic rate are important in many ways. In children, proper functioning of the thyroid is necessary for proper mental development. A serious thyroid deficiency in childhood will produce sluggishness, poor muscle tone, and a type of mental retardation called **cretinism.**

information about it. In particular, the more general information we possess about a topic, the easier it is to learn and remember new specific information about the topic (Ausubel, 1960; Deese & Deese, 1979).

There are several effective ways to survey this textbook. As in studying any text, you should look at the general content of each chapter by reading the headings within it. For your convenience, the headings within each chapter of this text are placed in an outline on the chapter opening page. Novels do not have headings because there is no reason to survey their content in advance; textbooks have them because they greatly aid surveying and reviewing. For example, did you look ahead at the headings in this section before beginning to read it? If you did, you developed an overall view of its content.

Next, look at the prologue section at the beginning of each chapter. It gives you an advance look at the main points of the content you will be reading. Study this section carefully before going on, and it will improve the amount of information you learn as you read. When surveying some textbooks, you may need to add to what you learn from the headings by briefly skimming sections and looking at illustrations, but in this text, the chapter outlines and prologues provide the best sources of advance information. Is it really worth the time and effort to read the prologue section of each chapter to get an overview of what is ahead? Actually, I spent a considerable amount of time researching this question before I started writing this book. I didn't want to waste my time in writing the prologues—and your time in reading them—unless they would actually increase what you learn. The value of prologues was tested by David Ausubel (1960) in a classic experiment conducted at the University of Illinois. One hundred twenty students were divided into two groups that read a long passage with and without a prologue section preceding it. The passage covered the properties of carbon steel and contained many facts that were new to the students. After both groups had read the passage on carbon steel, they took a brief multiple-choice test covering the facts presented in the passage. As predicted, the group that read the prologue first correctly answered approximately 20 percent more of the questions (the difference between an *F* and a *B* in most courses). That is why a prologue was written to precede each chapter in this text—and that is why giving them your close attention is worth the effort.

### Question

After you have surveyed the material you will be reading by reading the prologue and looking over the headings, Robinson suggests that you ask questions. Do this before and as you are reading. These questions should be those raised during your survey and first reading. They should reflect your own personal struggle to understand and digest the contents of this book. For example, included here are sample questions that you might ask while studying the thyroid gland in chapter 3, page 89. Asking such questions will help you become actively involved in the learning process and will focus your attention on relevant information. As you locate the information that answers your questions, you may find it helpful to underline or highlight such information with a felt-tip pen.

### Read

After the *S* and *Q* steps, you are ready to begin reading in the usual way. Although you have put in a lot of time preparing for this step, your reading probably will be so much more efficient that it's worth the extra time. In fact, if you have the time to invest, you could improve the efficiency of your reading even more by skimming the material quickly before reading it more closely.

### Recite

When studying, is it more beneficial to spend your time reading the material over and over again, or to read it and then practice reciting it (repeating it to yourself)? Reciting is definitely the most useful part of the study process. If nothing else, it alerts you to those things you do not really know yet (the things you cannot recite), and it may actually make learning more efficient. Regardless of how recitation works, it works. A. I. Gates (1917) found that individuals who spent 80 percent of their time reciting lists and only 20 percent reading them recalled twice as much as those who spent all of their time reading. This seems to be especially true of students who take the time to understand the meaning of what they are learning rather than memorizing it in rote fashion (Honeck, 1973). The "Check Your Learning" questions at the end of each section will help you "recite" what you have learned. In addition, the list of key terms at the beginning of each chapter and the marginal glossary can help you with this recitation. If you can recite the basic definitions of these terms, you will have learned the most important material.

### Review

After you have learned the new information in the text by reading and reciting, you will need to add one final step that most students neglect: Review what you have learned several times

When you study, really study. Don't just go through the motions.

before you are tested on it. The goal of the review process is to overlearn the material, which means to continue studying material after you have first mastered it. The learning process is not over when you can first recite the new information to yourself without error. Your ability to recall this information can be significantly strengthened later by reciting it several more times before you are tested (Krueger, 1929). To aid you with the review step, this text provides you with a review section following each major heading within the chapter and a sentence outline summary at the end of each chapter.

## Strategies for Studying

The SQ3R method can improve your ability to learn information from textbooks. Several other study strategies may help you make even more efficient use of your study time.

### Be Sure That You Are Actually Learning

The most common reason students "forget" information when taking tests is that they did not actually learn it in the first place. Because studying is an effort, even when you are efficient at it, it's far too easy to act as if you are studying when, in fact, you are really listening to the radio, thinking about your sweetheart, or clipping your nails. If you are good at acting as if you were studying—I was a master of it during my first two years of college—you can easily fool your roommate, your best friend, and even yourself. Fooling yourself is the most dangerous possibility; do not fool yourself into thinking that you are studying when you are not really exerting the effort to become absorbed in the material. When you study, really study.

### Find a Good Place to Study and Only Study There

One way to help you really study during your study periods is to find a good place to study, and only study in that place. The goal is to associate that place only with effective studying. Begin by choosing a spot that is free from distractions. Some places in libraries are ideal for studying, but other places in libraries are great for talking and making new friends. Avoid the latter when you are studying, but feel free to visit these places when you are taking breaks. After you find a good place to study, never do anything there except study. If a friend comes over for conversation, get up and move to another area to talk. Return only when you are ready to study. Similarly, if you are in your study place and find that your mind is wandering, leave it until you are ready to study again. If you do this consistently —if you only study when you are in your study place—this spot will "feel" like a place to study, and you will be more apt to study efficiently while you are there. This doesn't mean that you cannot also study in other places—such as on the bus when you have a 20-minute ride—but having a good place to study that becomes associated only with studying will help you study efficiently when you are there.

### Space Out Your Study Time

As long ago as 1885, Hermann Ebbinghaus found that studying a list of new information once a day for several days resulted in better recall of that information than studying the list several

Spaced practice or study is much more efficient than massed practice (cramming).

times in one day. Since then, a great deal of research has shown that spaced practice often results in better learning and memory than massed practice (Bahrick, Bahrick, Bahrick, & Bahrick, 1993). This is especially true in learning motor skills (such as learning to play a musical instrument or learning large amounts of unfamiliar verbal material, such as studying for a psychology test). This is why cramming (massing all your study time into one long session) is terribly inefficient. You can get much better grades by spacing the same amount of study time over a longer period.

## Use Mnemonic Devices

The suggestions given thus far concern how to study. The following suggestions are about how to memorize information when you are studying. Mnemonic devices are methods for storing memories so that they will be easier to recall. In each mnemonic device, an additional indexing cue is memorized along with the material to be learned. More is less with mnemonics; memorizing something more will result in less forgetting.

1. *Method of loci.* *Loci* is the Latin word for "places." In this method, the items in a list are mentally placed in a series of logically connected places. For example, if you are trying to remember a grocery list, you might think of a bag of sugar hanging on your garage door, a gallon of milk sitting in the front seat of your car, a carton of eggs perched on your steering wheel, and a box of donuts sitting in front of the grocery store door. Stanford University psychologist Gordon Bower (1973) found that persons who used the method of loci were able to recall almost three times as many words from lists as those who did not.

2. *Acronym method.* My favorite mnemonic device is the method of acronyms. Nearly every list of facts in psychology that I successfully memorized in college was memorized in terms of acronyms. In this simple method,

the first letters of each word in a list are combined to form an acronym. For example, the four stages of alcoholism, which are prealcoholic, prodromal, crucial, and chronic, can be memorized using the acronym PPCC. Acronyms are even more useful if they form a real word. For most people, the word *ape* means an animal in a zoo, but the acronym APE helps me remember the names of the three subscales of the psychological test called the Semantic Differential Scale: activity, potency, and evaluation.

A system closely related to acronyms takes the first letter of each word in an ordered series but uses them in a new sentence. My high school biology teacher taught me to remember the hierarchy of biological classification using the sentence "Kathy pulls candy on Friday, good stuff." Notice that the first letter in each word of this sentence is the same as in kingdom, phylum, class, order, family, genus, species. As with acronyms, memory of a phrase or sentence is likely to spark recall of an entire list.

3. *Keyword method.* We will see later in chapter 7 when we look at the psychology of memory that it is easier to memorize information that you understand than information that you do not. Some of the things that you need to memorize for college courses will be meaningful to you if you take the time to think about them before you try to memorize them, but sometimes you will have to give additional meaning to the things you are memorizing. Raugh and Atkinson (1975) demonstrated the value of teaching students to do this in memorizing Spanish vocabulary words, using what they called the *keyword method.* They asked one group of students to memorize English translations in the standard way of rotely associating the English word with the unknown Spanish word. Another group was taught to increase the meaningfulness of the association between the English and Spanish word pairs. As shown in figure 1, students were told to think of an English word that sounded like the Spanish word (such as *charcoal* for the Spanish word

**FIGURE 1**
In the keyword method of learning Spanish vocabulary, the student visualizes the Spanish noun with a noun that sounds like it in English. For example, the Spanish word for *puddle, lizard,* and *clown* sound similar to the English words for *charcoal, log,* and *pie.*

for puddle, *charco*) and to form a mental image of the English sound-alike word and the actual English translation (charcoal grill sitting in a puddle). Students who learned the Spanish vocabulary in this more meaningful fashion were able to recall an average of 88 percent of the words, whereas the students who used rote memorization were able to recall an average of only 28 percent when tested later. By actively enhancing the meaningfulness of what was learned using the keyword method, the students were able to greatly improve its storage in memory.

Try some of these prescriptions for better learning and memory; they could make a big difference.

## ● Critical Thinking

Like most college courses, the goal of this course is to teach you a great deal of new information. But there is a second goal even more important than the first—to teach you to *think critically about human beings*. You are enrolled in a college or university to become well educated. That means, of course, that you want to learn more information, but it also means that you want to be better prepared to make decisions, plan for the future, and realize your goals. If we human beings are to be able to continue to inhabit this fragile planet, and if we are to make the most of our time here, we must all try to hone our intellectual skills.

Psychology provides an excellent vehicle for teaching critical thinking skills. By its very nature—as a *science* of human behavior—we will be looking critically at ourselves. As we discuss the many new facts and concepts that make up this course, we will describe many of the experiments that have helped psychologists reach tentative conclusions about the nature of our behavior and experience. *Psychological research is critical thinking in practice.* As you read about each experiment, take a moment to consider the logic that went into its design. Think for a moment about the thinking that helped the researcher decide between rival explanations for that facet of human life.

But more important than seeing how scientists use their critical thinking skills, a major goal of this course is to encourage *you* to improve your own critical thinking skills. Success in every walk of life and meaningful participation in democratic society require more than the simple knowledge of facts—they require using facts intelligently.

What, then, is critical thinking? There are many aspects of critical thinking, but the steps that I will describe are a good start. As you read this textbook or approach any other source of new information—from political speeches to newspaper articles—try the following steps:

1. *What is the evidence?* I will present you with many statements in this textbook, and I expect you to demand that I back up my statements with evidence. When I tell you that, unlike 20 years ago, women and men now place the same importance on love in marriage, you should look to see if I present evidence to support that conclusion. If

I make a statement without supporting evidence, you should strongly question my statement.

2. *How good is the evidence?* Suppose I tell you that the reason that I believe that women and men place the same value on romance today is because my wife and my daughters say so. My wife and daughters happen to be very smart people, but would you believe the opinions of just three people? Would you be more convinced if I cite a study of 20,000 men and women? Not only should we demand evidence to support statements of fact, we also should examine the quality of that evidence. In this book, I can tell you that I have thought carefully about the quality of evidence that supports every statement. But you should completely disregard my reassurances and think critically about the evidence yourself. You might very well decide that I am wrong on some key issues, but at the very least, you will sharpen your critical thinking skills.

3. *What are the alternative interpretations of the evidence?* Even if I do provide you with solid evidence to support every conclusion, critical thinking cannot stop there. Facts are meaningless until they are *interpreted,* and there is almost always more than one interpretation of every set of facts in psychology.

Let's think about an example. There is strong evidence that, other things being equal, women tend to be attracted to men as marriage partners if they are more intelligent, hardworking, and successful. Those are the "facts," but what do they mean? One group of scholars believe that women have an *innate* need (part of every female in the human species) to guarantee the well-being of their children that leads them to prefer successful husbands who can help them provide for their children. Do you agree? Even if you agree, are there alternative explanations of these facts that would make just as much sense? Take a moment now to think about alternative explanations for these facts (really—I hope you will stop reading and try to think of alternative interpretations of these facts for a moment). Did you come up with any alternative explanations? It doesn't matter if you didn't come up with a brilliant explanation, but it is important that you see that alternative explanations of almost any set of facts are possible.

So what do we do with facts that can be interpreted in several different ways? Critical thinking requires two approaches to this situation. The first and most important step is to look for *more facts* that will help you choose between the alternative explanations. For example, do women in *all* cultures find successful men to be attractive? Do highly successful women in our culture find the man's success to be unimportant? Do women who do not want to have children still find successful men to be attractive? If the answers to these questions are not all yes, you might be less likely to believe that the preference for successful men reflects an innate need shared by all women. There are many ways in which new facts can be sought that might allow you to decide between alternative explanations for facts. Indeed, that is what science is all about.

The other way in which the critical thinker deals with alternative explanations of facts, however, is to learn to live with alternative explanations. At this point in the history of the science of psychology, there are many alternative explanations of facts that we cannot yet choose among. Indeed, one of the things that makes psychology exciting is that there is so much yet to learn. Many of the current disagreements among psychologists will be resolved ultimately through better experiments—the use of critical thinking to plan the logic of scientific studies. But in other cases, the different ways of viewing the same phenomena will prove to be equally valid conceptions. Therefore, the ability to consider more than one perspective on issues in psychology—as in all walks of life—is important. Moreover, the discussion of these differing views will help refine your critical thinking about yourself and the human race in general.

4. *Go beyond the book.* This book only scratches the surface of psychology, and it provides only a few examples of how the facts and concepts of psychology might apply to your life. The final step in critical thinking is to ask questions about the information given in the textbook to expand its application to your experience. Each section of a chapter ends with critical thinking questions. These questions have no right or wrong answers but are designed to stimulate and challenge you as you read the book. (The *Student Study Guide* contains more of these kinds of questions in the sections titled "Encouraging Critical Thinking: Beyond the Text.") But these questions are just a start. The most important critical thinking questions that you ask will be your own.

Critical thinking is not only an academic exercise—it is a part of living. The thinking and evaluative skills that you develop in this and other courses will also serve you well as you solve problems and confront the challenges of daily life.

If you are concerned that critical thinking takes time and might detract from your ability to memorize information that will be on tests, I have good news for you. Thinking critically about the information that you have just read will improve your memory for that information. In chapter 7, we will discuss the "deep processing" of information and present evidence that the more you think about information the more information you will remember. So although you will still need to use the strategies presented in this study skills section, critical thinking will improve your memory for information presented in this book. But don't take my word for it. Read the section on levels of processing in chapter 7 and think about it critically. Better yet, try your own experiment to see if thinking critically about the information presented in this book makes this course a better learning experience.

## ● Additional Information on Study Skills

If you are interested in learning more about study skills, you might want to consult five books that deal with the topic in more depth:

Ellis, D. B. (1994). *Becoming a master student* (7th ed.), Rapid City SD: College Survival, Inc.

Hettich, P. I. (1992). *Learning skills for college and career.* Pacific Grove, CA: Brooks/Cole.

Higgins, R. D. (Ed.). (1993). *The black student's guide to college success.* Westport, CT: Greenwood Press.

Parrott, L. (1994). *How to write psychology papers.* New York: HarperCollins.

Weinstein, C. E., & Hume, L. M. (1998). *Strategies for lifelong learning.* Washington, DC: APA Books.

# PART I

# Introduction and Foundations

In the first three chapters of this book, you will master the basic concepts and facts that form the foundation of the science of psychology. You will be given a definition of psychology and learn about psychology's goals and scientific methods. You will see that psychology was founded only a little over 120 years ago by many people working independently. These founders had very different interests and ideas about psychology, and these differences are still reflected in the diversity of today's field of psychology. Psychology is united, however, by its reliance on scientific methods to answer questions about behavior and mental processes. In part, psychology grew out of the science of biology, and an interest in the brain and other aspects of biology remains an important part of contemporary psychology. In the last chapter in this section, you will learn about the biological foundations of behavior and mental processes.

Here is a visual overview of what you will learn in this section of the text.

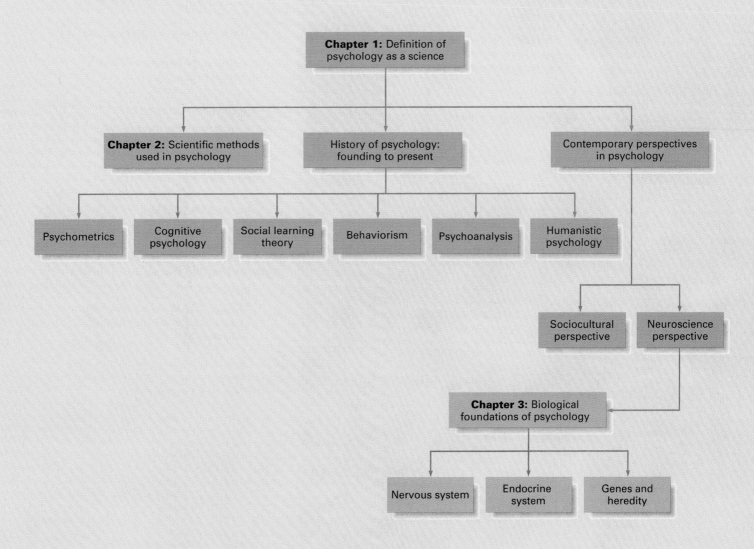

## Chapter Outline

# What Is Psychology?

## PROLOGUE

What will this course in psychology be about? You may have already glanced through the book and noticed the illustrations of nerve cells, the discussion of color vision, and the story of the dogs that were taught to salivate to the sound of a bell. This is psychology?! Are you getting worried that you signed up for the wrong course? If you're like me when I opened my first psychology textbook, you were surprised to see such topics in a book about psychology. I had expected to read tales of madness, love, and social ills, but instead I saw illustrations of brain structures, salivating dogs, and odor receptors.

I hope you looked through the book long enough to see that love, violence, mental disorders, and sexuality are in here, too. Almost everything that you expected is in this course, but a lot of topics that you probably didn't expect also will be covered. If I hadn't had an instructor who explained how all of these topics related to people, I think I would have changed majors. Why on earth would I want to know how to teach dogs to salivate on command? Why did I need to know how a taste bud works? Because I remember very clearly what it was like to take my first psychology course, I wrote this book to help your instructor explain to you how all of these topics fit together to make up the field of psychology.

This text surveys the basic principles of psychology and shows you how these principles can be applied to solve some significant human problems. Because this is a first course in psychology, we cover more basic facts and principles than applications. But to help you make better sense of the fundamental concepts, this book describes applications throughout the course to illustrate the abstract principles in a concrete way.

All of the material in this book, even the most basic material, is relevant to human lives. Many topics relate directly to everyone's personal efforts to make sense out of life. In this text, we discuss emotions, ways of improving memory, relationships between employers and employees, and other important topics. Topics such as the meaning of dreams, compulsive gambling, and hypnosis are also covered. We discuss such topics partly because they are fun to learn about—and fun is one of the legitimate goals of education. But we also study such topics because they can teach us about more basic psychological principles. Ultimately, a firm understanding of the basic concepts will be useful because they can be applied to any issue or situation you might encounter.

A huge amount of basic information must be surveyed in a brief span of time in an introductory psychology course, but we will try not to let you miss the forest for the trees. As you study the way nerve cells influence one another, for instance, you will be reminded that knowledge of this mechanism led to the development of modern psychiatric drugs. When you study the way the eyes sense color, it will be pointed out that such knowledge led to the invention of color television. In psychology you are never far from an application to a human problem, no matter how technical the subject matter.

In this first chapter, you will begin your study of psychology by exploring the things psychologists study and how they study them. You will be struck by the fact

## Key Terms

that psychology is a very broad field. Psychologists use the methods of science to study these things. They learn about behavior, thoughts, and feelings by systematically *observing* them. Certainly, psychologists *think* about human behavior, but, as scientists, they believe that people always learn more by actually *seeing* how people behave than from speculating about it.

Observation is the heart of the scientific method of all the sciences, including psychology. Psychologists use a variety of methods of scientific observation, ranging from surveys to laboratory experiments. Each method of observation is valuable in helping us fit new pieces into the puzzle of human behavior and mental processes. The goal of all of this scientific observation is to describe behavior with enough precision that we can predict it better, understand it more fully, and learn how to influence human behavior in positive ways.

Although the first systematic writings about human behavior date back to the time of Aristotle, psychology did not become an independent science until 1879, when Wilhelm Wundt founded the first laboratory of psychology in Germany. Psychology actually had many other "beginnings" in the late 1800s, led by a number of scientists who were interested in very different aspects of human behavior and mental processes. These were exciting times for the early psychologists, filled with intense disagreements, sharp remarks, and occasional scandals. As you will soon see, psychology is still a very broad field today in which different theories abound and many facets of the human condition are studied. But we are making good progress toward our goal of using observation to describe, predict, and understand human behavior. ■

## ● Psyche + Science = Psychology

Welcome to psychology! You are invited to learn about one of life's most interesting subjects—yourself. You enrolled in this course knowing that it had something to do with people. But what exactly is psychology?

The earliest origins of psychology are in the writings of the ancient Greek philosophers about the nature of life, particularly the writings of Aristotle. Aristotle, who was born in 384 B.C., was interested in learning about the nature of life itself. He collected and dissected plants and animals in an attempt to see how their organs sustained life. He studied reproduction to see how life was re-created in each generation, and he studied the everyday actions of living people as they reasoned, spoke, remembered, and learned.

Philosopher and early scientist Aristotle.

It was Aristotle's habit in his later years to discuss philosophy with his students as they strolled the covered walks of his school, the Lyceum. Imagine what he might have said to them about the nature of life:

> You'll understand what life is if you think about the act of dying. When I die, how will I be different from the way I am right now? In the first moments after death, my body will be scarcely different in physical terms than it was in the last seconds of life, but I will no longer move, no longer sense, nor speak, nor feel, nor care. It's these things that are life. At that moment, the psyche takes flight in the last breath.

Aristotle used the term *psyche* to refer to the essence of life. This term is translated from Greek to mean "mind," but it is closely linked in meaning to the word *breath*. Aristotle believed that psyche escaped in the last dying breath that was exhaled. Modern psychologists are interested in the same actions, thoughts, and feelings of human beings as Aristotle. Indeed, the term *psychology* comes from Aristotle's word *psyche* plus the Greek word *logos*, which means "the study of."

Aristotle received his training in philosophical methods from famous philosopher Plato, but he disagreed with Plato's belief that one could achieve a full understanding of anything simply by *thinking* about it. Aristotle felt that one must also *observe* the thing being studied—look at it, listen to it, touch it. Although he was not a scientist in the modern sense of the word, Aristotle's emphasis on observation is the basis for the methods of contemporary science. Progress in scientific methods from Aristotle to the present has involved no basic changes in this idea; scientists have only developed more precise and efficient ways of observing. Thus, Aristotle launched the study of life that eventually evolved into the modern science of psychology.

## Definition of Psychology

In some ways, it would be correct to say that psychologists still define psychology as the "study of life." The only thing that would be incorrect about this definition is that it is not specific enough to distinguish the modern discipline of psychology from other sciences, such as biology, that also study life. Today, therefore, **psychology** is defined as the *science of behavior and mental processes.*

Notice that this definition contains three key terms—*science, behavior,* and *mental processes.* Let's look at each of these terms separately. Psychology is considered to be a **science** because psychologists attempt to understand people through careful, controlled observation. This reliance on rigorous scientific methods of observation is the basis of all sciences, including psychology. The term **behavior** refers to all of a person's overt actions that others can directly observe. When you walk, speak, throw a Frisbee, or show a facial expression, you are behaving in this sense. The term **mental processes** refers to the *private* thoughts, emotions, feelings, and motives that others cannot directly observe. Your private thoughts and feelings about your dog catching a Frisbee in midair are examples of mental processes. Because mental processes are private and cannot be observed by others, psychologists use observations of public behavior to draw inferences about mental processes.

## Goals of Psychology

What are the goals of the science of psychology? What are psychologists trying to accomplish? Psychologists study people by using scientific methods. The goals of this scientific enterprise are to describe, predict, understand, and influence behavior and mental processes:

1. *Describe.* The information gathered through scientific research helps psychologists describe psychological phenomena more accurately and completely. For example, information gathered in a survey on the frequency of sexual behavior among college students without the protection of a condom would be an important first step in designing a program to prevent the spread of sexually transmitted diseases such as AIDS.

2. *Predict.* In some cases, psychologists are able to predict future behavior. For example, psychologists have developed tests that enable employers to improve their prediction of which job applicants will perform well.

3. *Understand.* We understand behavior and mental processes when we can explain why they happen. Because there is still much more to learn, however, our current explanations are always tentative. In other words, our explanations are **theories,** not truths. Theories are tentative explanations of facts and relationships in sciences. It's essential that you understand this basic fact about science as you read this textbook. The knowledge that we can offer you is always tentative. As the science of psychology progresses through research, our theories are always subject to revision.

4. *Influence.* Finally, psychologists hope to go beyond description, understanding, and prediction to influence behavior in beneficial ways. What can we do to help a teenage boy climb out of a period of severe depression? How can we help parents raise their rambunctious children better? What is the best way to help college students select a career? It's not until we have identified ways to intentionally influence behavior that psychology completely fulfills its promise.

The term *behavior* refers to all of a person's overt actions that others can directly observe. When you walk, speak, throw a Frisbee, or show facial expression, you are behaving in this sense.

The goals of psychology are to describe, predict, understand, and influence human behavior.

**psychology**
The science of behavior and mental processes.

**science**
Approach to knowledge based on systematic observation.

**behavior**
Directly observable and measurable actions.

**mental processes**
Private psychological activities that include thinking, perceiving, and feeling.

**theories**
Tentative explanations of facts and relationships in sciences.

## Review

We have defined psychology as the science of behavior and mental processes. Behavior refers to all of your actions that other people can directly observe. Mental processes, in contrast, are private events, such as thinking and feeling. The goals of psychology are to describe, predict, understand, and influence behavior and mental processes. Using the methods of science, we gather information through systematic observation, which enables us to accurately describe psychological facts and relationships. When adequate descriptive information has been acquired, reasonably accurate predictions can be made and explanations proposed to help us understand these facts and relationships. Finally, when enough understanding and ability to predict have been acquired, we can sometimes intentionally influence people in ways that improve and enrich their lives.

## Check Your Learning

One efficient way to learn information from textbooks is to be sure that you have mastered the key points in each major section before moving on to the next one. You can do this by asking yourself questions about the material you have just read. If you cannot answer some of the questions, you can easily go back to that part of the section and reread it. Then, when you can answer all of your questions, it will be time to move on to the next part of the chapter. This step of asking and answering questions will take a little time, but you will learn and remember much more information.

To make it easier for you to check your learning in this way, I have written some questions at the end of each section. If you give an incorrect answer to any question, return to the page number given next to the correct answer to see why your answer was not correct. When you have mastered the information in this section, you will be ready to move on to the next section.

It is important for you also to ask *your own* questions, however, for two reasons. First, asking your own questions will help you personalize the course and make it a more worthwhile learning experience for you. Second, I have asked you questions only about some of the key points in each section. If you learn only what is emphasized in these few questions, you will miss a great deal of information. Therefore, it is best to use these questions only as a starting point in checking your learning.

1. The ancient Greek philosopher who wrote about "psyche" and first broadly defined the subject matter was

   a) Plato.      c) Hippocrates.
   b) Aristotle.      d) Epicurus.

2. The modern definition of psychology is "the science of _____ and _____."

3. Mental processes are

   a) directly observable.
   b) private.

4. The four goals of the science of psychology are to _____ behavior.

   a) _____
   b) _____
   c) _____
   d) _____

1. What do you personally want to learn in this course?

2. How do your personal goals as a student of psychology relate to the four goals of the science of psychology?

**Correct Answers:** 1. b (p. 4).    2. behavior and mental processes (p. 5).    3. b (p. 5).    4. a. describe, b. predict, c. understand, d. influence (p. 5).

## The Many Viewpoints in Psychology and Their Origins

A psychologist could spend an entire career studying the causes of emotional disorders, or the way we recall facts, or methods of improving job satisfaction among employees, or the role of the brain in emotions, or the nature of racial prejudice, or any of a variety of topics within psychology. When we consider the range of possibilities, it's not surprising that the science of psychology is a very broad field with many divisions, each focusing on a different facet of human behavior. To better understand this diversity in the field of psychology, we need to look back again through the history of its development.

There was no formal discipline of psychology during the time of Aristotle and for 2,200 years after he lived. Like the other sciences, psychology was a part of philosophy. It wasn't until modern times that the sciences emerged from the general field of philosophy. In the seventeenth and eighteenth centuries, physics, biology, medicine, and other disciplines began to accumulate knowledge that set each somewhat apart from the others. Also, each science developed distinct ways of viewing nature. Eventually, psychology also developed its own distinct subject matter and scientific methods.

The launching of the separate field of psychology is usually credited to Wilhelm Wundt for establishing the first Laboratory of Psychology in Leipzig, Germany, in 1879. Some historians feel that William James deserves the honor for a less-publicized laboratory at Harvard University, however, which opened in 1875. Actually, many people "founded" psychology. Their varied interests and talents laid the foundations for the diverse field surveyed in this text. As you read about some of the most influential early psychologists, imagine how different their answers would be if you asked each of them, "What is the most important question for psychology?"

Wilhelm Wundt (1832–1920).

### Nature of Conscious Experience

The first topic studied by psychologists was private conscious experience. What are you thinking and feeling right now? Everything that you are aware of right now is part of your conscious experience. The first psychologists wanted to understand the basic elements of consciousness and how they worked together to create the experience of being alive.

#### Wundt, Titchener, and Structuralism

Wilhelm Wundt was a professor of biology in Germany who was fascinated by human consciousness. His work was expanded by his student Edward Titchener, who later taught in the United States at Cornell University. Just as chemists seek to discover the basic elements that make up physical substances, Wundt and Titchener wanted to identify the basic elements of conscious experience. Indeed, sometimes their work is referred to as "mental chemistry." Wundt and Titchener studied the elements of consciousness using a method of looking inward at one's own conscious experiences, called **introspection.** Wundt and Titchener trained themselves to observe the contents of their own minds as accurately and unemotionally as possible in an attempt to isolate the basic elements of the mind. What does that mean exactly?

Suppose that I visit your school some day and your instructor asks me to give a guest lecture on the history of psychology. Suppose also that I am in a particularly

Edward Titchener (1867–1927).

**introspection**
(in´tro-spek´shun) The process of looking inward at one's own consciousness.

J. Henry Alston.

Warm  Cold
water  water

**FIGURE 1.1**
When you grasp a coil made up of two twisted pipes, one carrying cold water and the other carrying moderately warm water, the sensation is one of extreme heat because the receptors for both cold and heat are stimulated.

**structuralism**
(struk′tūr-al-izm)  The nineteenth-century school of psychology that sought to determine the structure of the mind through controlled introspection.

**Gestalt psychology**
The school of thought based on the belief that human consciousness cannot be broken down into its elements.

**gestalt**
(ges-tawlt′)  An organized or unified whole.

dramatic mood and decide to give the lecture playing the role of Edward Titchener. I arrive wearing a fake beard and the flowing black academic robes that he always wore, and I choose you to be the subject of a demonstration of introspection. I ask you to close your eyes and I place a bit of apple in your mouth that you have not seen. Then I ask you to describe to me the raw *sensations* that this physical stimulus creates in your mind.

You hesitate a moment, then announce with a smile, "It's an apple!"

"Nein! Nein! Nein!" I shout, using the only word I can remember from German 101. "I asked you to tell me what you *sense,* not what the stimulus is. Don't tell me what the thing is on your tongue. Describe the sensations that you experience!"

You hesitate again, regain your composure, and say, "Sweet?"

"Yes! Yes!" I cry. "What else do you sense?"

"A little bit of sourness, a grainy texture, and a wetness."

"Wonderful!" I shout, leading you to break into a grin. "Now you're introspecting. Now you're describing the elemental contents of your mind. Sweet, sour, grainy . . . those are a few of the building blocks from which consciousness is structured. Everything that you experience in life is based on a small number of these basic elements."

Because Wundt and Titchener were interested in the basic elements of the conscious experience and how those elements are organized, their viewpoint is known as **structuralism.** That is, they sought to determine the *structure* of the mind through controlled introspection.

### J. Henry Alston

Although Wundt and Titchener were the first psychologists to study conscious experience, other scientists soon joined the effort. One notable early structuralist was J. Henry Alston. Alston is best known for his studies of the sensations of heat and cold. Alston discovered that we feel cold when one kind of nerve ending in the skin is stimulated, and we feel warm when a different kind of nerve ending is stimulated. Most interestingly, he found that we feel intense heat only when *both* the warmth and cold receptors in the skin are stimulated at the same time. Very hot objects—such as a hot iron—not only stimulate the warmth receptors, but they also stimulate the nerve endings that ordinarily respond only when it is cold.

Alston demonstrated this fact in a simple but elegant experiment in 1920. He constructed the apparatus shown in figure 1.1 by wrapping two water pipes together, one carrying moderately warm water and the other carrying cold water. When people grasped these pipes, they felt the sensation of intense heat! Because both the warmth and the cold receptors in the skin were stimulated by the twisted pipes, the individual in the experiment felt the sensation of intense heat.

J. Henry Alston is a notable figure in the history of psychology for another reason as well. The first research article published by an African American psychologist in a journal of the American Psychological Association was written by J. Henry Alston.

### Max Wertheimer and Gestalt Psychology

Max Wertheimer, a professor of psychology at the University of Frankfurt in the early 1900s, also was interested in the nature of conscious experience. His ideas about consciousness were quite different from those of the structuralists, however. Wertheimer led a group of psychologists known as **Gestalt psychologists.** Their approach to psychology was founded on the concept of the **gestalt,** or *whole*. The Gestalt psychologists felt that human consciousness could not be meaningfully broken down into raw elements, as the structuralists tried to do. As they were fond of saying, "The whole is different from the sum of its parts." To illustrate, the two examples in figure 1.2 are drawn from exactly the same angled lines, but their organization greatly changes our perception of them. Although the parts are the same in each example, the whole is seen as a triangle in one example and arrows in the other. Similarly, the second element in the two rows in figure 1.2 is exactly the same each time, but it is perceived as a "13" in the first row and as a "B" in the second.

**FIGURE 1.2**
The organization of the lines in these two illustrations shows that only "whole" perceptions have meaning. The lines do not change, but their meaning does.

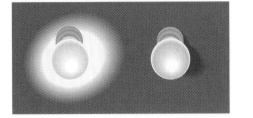

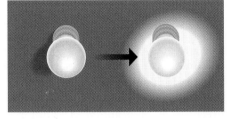

**FIGURE 1.3**
Although these lights are stationary, the rapid, consecutive lighting of them creates an illusion of motion.

Max Wertheimer (1880–1943).

Gestalt psychologists also used the **phi phenomenon** to demonstrate that the whole is different from the sum of its parts (see fig. 1.3). When two lights are presented in rapid sequence, the viewer sees an apparent movement in the stimuli. That is, rather than perceiving two stationary lights, the viewer sees one light moving from one position to another. This is a highly important phenomenon to Gestalt psychologists, because what is seen—a moving light—is not present in the two parts of the stimulus at all. Movement is a property of the whole perception—the gestalt—but movement is not part of the stimulus. Motion pictures are based on the phi phenomenon. A series of still images that change slightly in each frame is projected on the screen so quickly that the image appears to be moving. The Gestalt psychologists used such examples to make their point that perception has meaning only when it's seen as a whole, rather than as a simple collection of elements, as the structuralists implied.

## Functions of the Conscious Mind

While many of the early psychologists were studying the nature of conscious experience, another group was trying to understand the *value* of consciousness to us as a species. What useful *functions* does consciousness serve?

### William James and Functionalism

In 1875, a young professor of biology and philosophy at Harvard University named William James taught the first course on "psychology," and in 1890 he published an influential early textbook of psychology. James was impressed with the work of biologist Charles Darwin, who suggested in his theory of evolution that every physical characteristic evolved in a species because it served a purpose. James suspected that the same thing could be said about the human mind. He speculated that thinking, feeling, learning, remembering, and other processes of human consciousness existed only because they helped us survive as a species. Because we can think, for example, we are better able to find food, avoid danger, and care for our children—all of which help the human species survive. Because of its emphasis on the *functions* of consciousness, the school of thought known as **functionalism** emerged from the work of William James.

James was particularly interested in topics he considered to be evolutionarily important: conscious awareness, voluntary action (free will), habits, and emotions. Because James was concerned with what the mind could do rather than its structure, he criticized the structuralists for creating a barren approach to psychology. He compared human

William James (1842–1910).

**phi phenomenon**
(fī fe-nom′ĕ-non) The perception of apparent movement between two stationary stimuli.

**functionalism**
(funk′shun-al-izm) The nineteenth-century school of psychology that emphasized the useful functions of consciousness.

Hermann Ebbinghaus (1850–1909).

Mary Whiton Calkins (1863–1930).

consciousness to a flowing stream: We could study that stream by isolating single molecules of water like the structuralists, but by doing so we would miss the nature and beauty of the whole stream. Moreover, studying the water molecules in a stream would tell us nothing about what the stream *does*—that it erodes riverbanks, provides a home for fish, carries barges, and so on. Similarly, studying the elements of the mind tells us nothing about how it helps us adapt to the demands of life. The functions of the mind, not its raw elements, were the subject matter of psychology to the functionalists.

### Studies of Memory: Hermann Ebbinghaus and Mary Whiton Calkins

One of the most important cognitive processes is memory. Because of memory, the lessons that we learn today can be remembered tomorrow. In 1885, Germany's Hermann Ebbinghaus published a book titled *On Memory*. This remarkable book described the first extensive set of experiments on a useful function of the mind. Ebbinghaus gave a detailed account of a series of studies spanning 6 years in which he served both as the scientist and the only subject. He memorized lists of information and measured his memory for them after different intervals of time. To be sure that the material he was learning was not affected by his prior experience with it, Ebbinghaus invented an entirely new set of meaningless items for his experiments called *nonsense syllables*, such as KEB and MUZ.

In a typical experiment, Ebbinghaus sat alone in his study, listening to a metronome that clicked every few seconds. At the first click, he tried to say aloud the first nonsense syllable in the list. At the next click, he turned the card containing the first nonsense syllable and tried to recall the next syllable, and so on. He then tested his ability to recall the syllables. Ebbinghaus found that forgetting is very rapid at first but proceeds slowly thereafter. Almost half of his original learning was lost within 20 minutes, and almost all of the forgetting that was going to occur had occurred within about 9 hours (see fig. 1.4). We now know that memories for more meaningful information are not always forgotten in the same way as nonsense syllables, but Ebbinghaus' careful and detailed studies set an important example of how rigorous experimental methods could be used to study functions of human consciousness.

Mary Whiton Calkins was another early pioneer in the study of memory. Calkins was a student of William James at Harvard University in the late 1800s. Calkins presented her subjects with a series of numbers, each paired with a different color. Later she showed the subjects the colors alone to see how many of the numbers they could recall. When physicians memorize the best medicines to prescribe for various illnesses, they are

**FIGURE 1.4**

Hermann Ebbinghaus published these findings in 1885 showing that most forgetting of nonsense syllables occurs rapidly, with almost half of the original learning being lost within 20 minutes.
**Source:** Data from R. M. Tarpy and R. E. Mayer, *Foundations of Learning and Memory*, 1978, Scott, Foresman and Company.

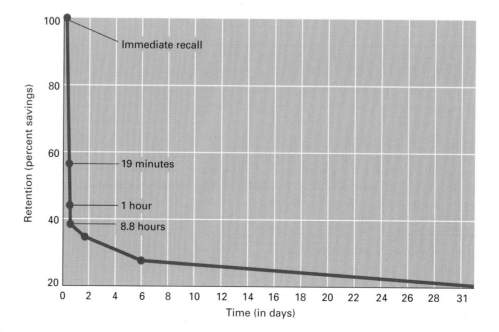

using the same kind of memorization. Variations on this method, called the *paired associates* method, dominated research on memory in the United States for more than 50 years (Madigan & O'Hara, 1992).

### Contemporary Cognitive Psychology

Functionalism continues to have a strong influence on contemporary psychology, but the terminology has changed. Rather than speaking about the functions of human consciousness, psychologists now use the term *cognitive processes*. **Cognition** is a broad term that refers to all intellectual processes—perceiving, believing, thinking, remembering, knowing, deciding, and so on. Contemporary **cognitive psychology** is a modern version of functionalism, but with some key ideas from Gestalt psychology and structuralism thrown in for good measure. A recent analysis of trends in the content of leading psychology journals and dissertation research in psychology found that cognitive psychology is by far the dominant perspective in North American psychology and probably in most of the world (Robins, Goslin, & Clark, 1999).

### Psychometrics: Alfred Binet

In France a notable early psychologist by the name of Alfred Binet took the study of the useful functions of conscious mental processes in a very different but very practical direction—he developed a way to measure intelligence. In the 1890s, the members of the Paris Ministry of Education were faced with a problem. They wanted to provide extensive education for all "intelligent" children and more practical, less academic kinds of schooling for less intelligent children. They wanted to be fair about choosing the children who would be given advanced academic training, but they also wanted to make the decision when the children were still young. How could they measure something so intangible as a child's intelligence?

The Ministry of Education turned for advice to a professor at the University of the Sorbonne who had just founded the first psychology laboratory in France. By experimenting with a large number of test items, Binet and his collaborators were able to find a set of questions (e.g., arithmetic problems, word definitions, memory tasks) that could be answered by most children of a given age, but not by children who were younger or who had low intelligence. These questions were used to create an intelligence test that was later revised and translated in the United States to become the still widely used Stanford-Binet Intelligence Scale. Binet's work led to the modern branch of psychology that specializes in the measurement of intelligence, personality, job aptitude, and so on. Binet's approach is known as **psychometrics,** meaning the measurement (*metric*) of mental functions (*psycho*). It continues to be an important and practical viewpoint in modern psychology.

### Behaviorism and Social Learning Theory

While Wundt and his followers studied the nature of conscious experience and James, Binet, and others examined the usefulness of the conscious mental processes, another group of founders of the science of psychology was getting started in Russia. Like James, this group was influenced by Darwin to study psychological processes that are useful in the struggle to survive. In this case, their emphasis was on *learning* from experience.

### Ivan Pavlov

In the 1890s, Russian psychologist Ivan Pavlov and his coworkers were conducting research on digestion in dogs when they noticed a curious thing. They had surgically implanted tubes in the cheeks of the dogs to study the reflexive secretion of saliva during eating. Pavlov noticed that after several feedings the dogs started salivating when they saw food being brought to them, not just when the food was placed in their mouths. He recognized that the dogs had learned to associate the sight of the food being brought with the food itself. Because the sight had immediately preceded the food on many

**cognition**
(kog-nish′un)  Mental processes of perceiving, believing, thinking, remembering, knowing, deciding, and so on.

**cognitive psychology**
The viewpoint in psychology that emphasizes the importance of cognitive processes, such as perception, memory, and thinking.

**psychometrics**
The perspective in psychology founded by Binet that focuses on the measurement of mental functions.

Ivan Pavlov (1849–1936).

John B. Watson (1878–1958).

Margaret Floy Washburn (1871–1939).

B. F. Skinner (1904–1990).

occasions, the dogs came to respond to the sight of food by salivating. He demonstrated that this interpretation was correct by conducting careful experiments using a clicking metronome instead of the sight of food and small quantities of powdered meat. When the metronome and the meat powder were presented together, the dogs quickly learned to salivate to the metronome alone.

Although teaching dogs to salivate to the sound of the metronome certainly is not important in its own right, Pavlov's accidental discovery was of tremendous importance to the new field of psychology. He had identified a simple form of learning—or *conditioning*, to use his term—in which an inherited reflex (salivating) comes to be triggered by a stimulus that has nothing to do with that reflex (the metronome). Pavlov had shown that even inherited reflexes could be influenced dramatically by learning experiences.

Pavlov also developed a precise scientific way to study learning. By measuring the number of drops of saliva produced by a dog hearing the metronome, Pavlov was able to study many aspects of the learning process, such as the time interval between the sound and the food that produced the most rapid conditioning (one-half second in his studies). Pavlov felt that the study of conditioning was such an important breakthrough that he abandoned his research on digestion, for which he would later win the Nobel Prize, and spent the rest of his career studying his new discovery.

### John B. Watson and Margaret Floy Washburn

Pavlov's research and theories were not immediately accepted in the United States, but in the 1920s the concepts were taken up in the writings of John B. Watson and Margaret Floy Washburn. They were deeply impressed by Pavlov's work on conditioning because of its scientific precision. Watson and Washburn agreed with Pavlov that the importance of conditioning went far beyond salivating dogs and that most human behavior was learned through classical conditioning. Watson felt that it was impossible to study private mental processes because only outward behavior could be measured and scientifically understood. Because he felt that psychologists should study only overt behavior, Watson called the school of thought that was founded on Pavlov's work **behaviorism.**

### Contemporary Behaviorism and Social Learning Theory

Behaviorism has survived as a distinct school of thought in contemporary psychology. Some psychologists are strict adherents of behaviorism and rule out the study of mental processes. Until his death in 1990, B. F. Skinner of Harvard University was the leading exponent of this strict form of behaviorism. Most contemporary behavioral psychologists

**behaviorism**
(be-hāv´yor-izm)  The school of psychology that emphasizes the process of learning and the measurement of overt behavior.

Sigmund Freud (1856–1939).

Carl Rogers (1902–1987).

endorse a broader version of behaviorism, which integrates the study of behavior with the study of cognition. Albert Bandura of Stanford University is the leading spokesperson for this broader viewpoint, which is often referred to as **social learning theory.** This viewpoint states that the most important aspects of our behavior are learned from other persons in society—we learn to be who we are from our family, friends, and culture. As judged by the number of publications in key journals and dissertation research over the past 20 years, the influence of the strict behavioral approach has declined considerably (Robins & others, 1999), but the broader social learning viewpoint, which integrates aspects of behaviorism and the cognitive perspective, is an important theoretical perspective today.

## The Nature of the "Unconscious Mind"

While most of the founders of psychology were focusing on either conscious mental processes or overt behavior, others were moving in a very different direction. They believed that the most important aspect of human psychology was neither the mental processes nor the behavior that we are aware of but, rather, the mental processes that we are *unaware* of. Thus, this group of pioneers in psychology focused on the so-called unconscious mind.

### Sigmund Freud and Psychoanalysis

Sigmund Freud was an Austrian physician who practiced neurology, the treatment of diseases of the nervous system. Unlike the other founders of psychology, he was responsible for the day-to-day care of a large number of patients, many of whom had serious psychological problems. This fact, perhaps more than anything else, explains the enormous differences between his view of psychology and those of the other founders.

Freud believed conscious mental processes were of trivial importance compared with the workings of the **unconscious mind.** Sensation, learning, memory, and other cognitive processes so important to the other founding psychologists were of little interest to Freud. Freud felt that the roots of the psychological problems that he tried to treat were innate **motives,** particularly sexual and aggressive ones, that reside in an unconscious part of the mind. He believed that these unconscious motives and the conflicts that surround them influenced our behavior, even though we do not know they exist.

Freud's theory of **psychoanalysis** has been subjected to a number of revisions since his death. Modern psychoanalysts still adhere to Freud's view that conflicts in the unconscious mind are the chief source of psychological problems. However, there are few "orthodox" psychoanalysts today. Most feel that Freud made an important contribution

**social learning theory**
The viewpoint that the most important aspects of our behavior are learned from other persons in society—family, friends, and culture.

**unconscious mind**
All mental activity of which we are unaware.

**motives**
Internal states or conditions that activate behavior and give it direction.

**psychoanalysis**
(sī″kō-ah-nal′i-sis) The technique of helping persons with emotional problems based on Sigmund Freud's theory of the unconscious mind.

in calling our attention to the role often played by unconscious sexual and aggressive motives in our emotional conflicts but feel that other motives, such as the need to feel adequate in social relationships, are of even greater importance (Westen, 1998). In terms of publications in core journals and dissertation research, the psychoanalytic perspective is not a dominant force in mainstream North American psychology today (Robins & others, 1999).

### Humanistic Psychology and the Unconscious Mind

**humanistic psychology**
The psychological view that human beings possess an innate tendency to improve and determine their lives by the decisions they make.

During the 1950s, another movement that focused on the role of the unconscious in psychological problems emerged, known as **humanistic psychology.** Leading humanists such as Abraham Maslow and Carl Rogers did not agree with Freud that conscious processes were unimportant, however. Indeed, the humanists believe that human beings determine their own fates through the conscious decisions they make. Like Freud, however, the humanists believe that the unconscious mind often defeats efforts to make good decisions.

The humanists see society as being the cause of our self-defeating unconscious minds. To the humanists, the most important aspect of people is our view of what we are like—our *self-concept.* If you think that you are intelligent, you may sign up for a difficult college course. If you think that you are caring and helpful, you might volunteer to work on a telephone crisis line. These are examples of aspects of how a person's self-concept can influence important decisions.

The humanists believe, however, that society often makes it difficult to have an *accurate* self-concept. For example, we are constantly bombarded with information that says that only witty, athletic, and attractive people are worth loving. So, what if you are like most of us and are a little dull, slightly clumsy, and not so attractive? The humanists believe that we often push such upsetting information about ourselves into the unconscious. This causes two kinds of problems. First, it means that most of us have an inaccurate self-concept—because we push out of consciousness information about ourselves that doesn't match what society values. Second, the negative unconscious information sometimes threatens our self-concept and makes us anxious. Thus, although the psychoanalysts and humanists view the unconscious mind in very different ways, they both see it as the most important cause of human problems. Like the psychoanalytic perspective, few current dissertations and papers in core journals are on humanistic themes (Robins & others, 1999).

## Review

There was no formal science of psychology for 2,200 years after the time of Aristotle. Then, in the late nineteenth century, a number of events led to the emergence of an independent discipline. Wilhelm Wundt founded his psychology laboratory in 1879. Wundt and his followers Edward Titchener and J. Henry Alston engaged in controlled introspective studies of human consciousness. Max Wertheimer and his associates in Germany developed Gestalt psychology, which emphasized the need to study consciousness in whole, meaningful units rather than the artificial elements studied by the structuralists. William James taught the first psychology course and published an influential early textbook stressing the evolutionary significance of consciousness. Hermann Ebbinghaus and Mary Whiton Calkins published influential studies of memory that showed how experimental methods could be used to study the functions of consciousness. Alfred Binet developed a useful intelligence test for selecting children for advanced education in Paris. John B. Watson and Margaret Floy Washburn introduced the United States to the research on classical conditioning conducted by Russian biologist Ivan Pavlov. Based on Pavlov's work, Watson advocated a science of psychology that included only overt behavior and made no attempt to study mental processes. Physician Sigmund Freud published his observations on psychoanalysis and the unconscious, which were followed half a century later by the different perspective on the unconscious of the humanists. Together these many founders of psychology launched a diverse science amid a storm of energetic controversy.

**Check Your Learning**

To be sure that you have learned the key points from the preceding section, cover the list of correct answers and try to answer each question. If you give an incorrect answer to any question, return to the page given next to the correct answer to see why your answer was not correct.

1. The early psychologist who first pioneered the introspective study of human consciousness and who is generally credited with founding the first laboratory of psychology in 1879 was

   a)   Ivan Pavlov.                    c)   Hermann Ebbinghaus.
   b)   William James.                  d)   Wilhelm Wundt.

2. The early American psychologist who founded the school of "functionalism," which emphasized the evolutionary importance of human consciousness, and who taught the first psychology course in a college was

   a)   Sigmund Freud.                  c)   Alfred Binet.
   b)   William James.                  d)   Wilhelm Wundt.

3. The functionalist who developed the paired associates method to study memory was

   a)   Alfred Binet.                   c)   Mary Whiton Calkins.
   b)   Max Wertheimer.                 d)   Margaret Floy Washburn.

4. The physician who founded psychoanalysis and its study of the unconscious mind and abnormal behavior was

   a)   Sigmund Freud.                  c)   Alfred Binet.
   b)   William James.                  d)   Max Wertheimer.

**Thinking Critically about Psychology**

1. Each founder of psychology focused on a different aspect of behavior and mental processes. If you had been one of the founders, on what topic do you think you would have focused?

2. Can you think of barriers that exist today to the success of women and minorities in scientific and professional fields that psychologists could study and help eliminate?

Correct Answers:  1. d (p. 7),  2. b (p. 9),  3. c (p. 10),  4. a (p. 13).

## ● Contemporary Perspectives in Psychology

We have just looked at several viewpoints in psychology that emerged in the work of a number of turn-of-the-century scientists. Each perspective had different interests and assumptions about human nature, so each defined the methods and subject matter of psychology in a different way. As you can imagine, the debates between adherents of these different points of view were often very heated in the early days of psychology.

Where are we today in psychology? No single point of view from the early days has emerged as the correct way of viewing human behavior and mental processes. Although there are some strict adherents of some of the traditional schools of thought—such as behaviorism and psychoanalysis—contemporary psychology could be said to combine

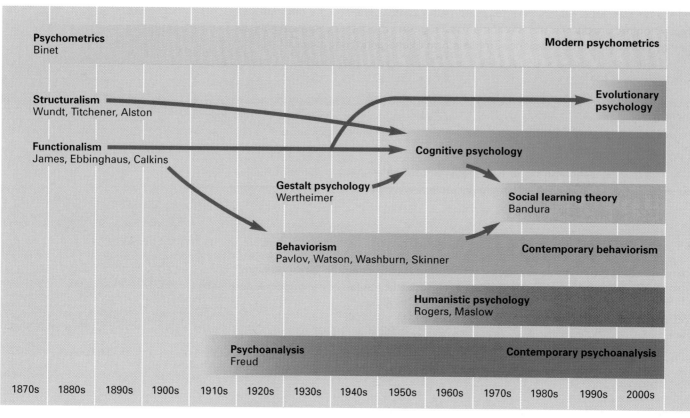

**FIGURE 1.5**

Historical time line describing the major schools of thought that have influenced psychology in the past and continue to directly or indirectly influence psychological thinking today. In addition, the neuroscience and sociocultural perspectives are increasingly integrated into current psychological theory and practice.

Santiago Ramón y Cajal (1852–1934).

**neuroscience perspective**
The viewpoint in psychology that focuses on the nervous system in explaining behavior and mental processes.

the best ideas from all of its founders. In some ways, the impact of their intermingled ideas is even more important than the original schools of thought.

Before we begin studying the methods and findings of psychology, it is important for us to look at three other perspectives that strongly influence contemporary psychology, the neuroscience perspective, the sociocultural perspective, and the evolutionary perspective.

## Neuroscience Perspective

Psychologists have long been interested in the relationship between our psychological nature and our biological nature, particularly our brains. Spanish scientist Santiago Ramón y Cajal first identified *neurons*—the cells that make up the brain and nervous system—in the early 1900s. His view that the brain was made up of a network of interacting neural cells laid the foundation for our modern understanding of the role of the brain in psychology.

Psychologists who approach the science from the **neuroscience perspective** are interested in the structures of the brain that play roles in emotion, reasoning, speaking, and other psychological processes. They seek to determine the extent to which our psychological characteristics, such as intelligence and emotional stability, are influenced by heredity. Neuroscientists study the chemical substances that carry messages in the nervous system from one neuron to another, and they examine how some drugs, such as cocaine and marijuana, alter the action of these important brain chemicals. Similarly, neuroscientists conduct experiments on the role of hormones in the regulation of behavior.

Enormous progress has been made in unraveling the functions of the nervous system, heredity, and the hormonal systems, but understanding the connection between the brain and behavior is a problem that dwarfs any other problem facing science in its scale. The complexity of the brain alone is almost too staggering to comprehend. Its 100 billion neurons form more than 100 *trillion* connections with other neurons. Since each of these connections can be either active or inactive at any moment in time, that means there are *far more* possible states of a single human brain than the estimated total number of all of the electrons and protons in all of the atoms in the universe (Sagan, 1979). We have just scratched the surface of this fascinatingly complex subject.

## Sociocultural Perspective

An important perspective that has emerged in psychology in recent years is termed the **sociocultural perspective.** Like social learning theory, the sociocultural approach is based on the assumption that our personalities, beliefs, attitudes, and skills are learned from others. The sociocultural approach goes further, however, in stating that it is impossible to fully understand a person without understanding his or her culture, ethnic identity, gender identity, and other important sociocultural factors (Miller, 1999; Phinney, 1996).

*Ethnic identity* refers to each person's sense of belonging to a particular ethnic group and of sharing that group's beliefs, attitudes, dress, music, ceremonies, and the like.

For example, we are all shaped by our culture and must be understood in that context. **Culture** is defined as the patterns of behavior, beliefs, and values that are shared by a group of people. Culture includes everything—from language and superstitions to moral beliefs and food preferences—that we learn from the people with whom we live. When I worked in Miami for 3 years, I met many persons who were born in Cuba and had moved to the United States. They brought with them all of the beliefs, attitudes, and ways of Cuban culture, but they are now part of the culture of the United States. To fully understand my Miami friends, you would need to understand the ways in which Cuban and U.S. cultures are similar and different and how each has influenced their lives.

In addition, we must all be understood in terms of our ethnic group and ethnic identity. An **ethnic group** is a group of persons who are descendants of a common group of ancestors, usually from a particular country or area. **Ethnic identity** refers to each person's sense of belonging to a particular ethnic group and of sharing that group's beliefs, attitudes, skills, music, ceremonies, and the like. Members of less powerful ethnic groups in a country also often share a history of discrimination and repression by more powerful ethnic groups.

Members of an ethnic group often share similar racial characteristics. Knowing a person's race is often less informative than knowing his or her ethnic identity, however. For example, my friend Maria is an immigrant to the United States from the Dominican Republic. She grew up speaking Spanish and learned English only after moving to the United States as a teenager. She sees herself as a Hispanic, but she is of African descent and also identifies strongly with her fellow African Americans. Her racial heritage, then, reveals only part of her sense of ethnic identity.

A third term that is important to the sociocultural perspective is **gender identity.** This term refers to one's view of oneself as male or female. As boys and girls interact with their parents, siblings, teachers, and friends, they learn what it means to be a male or female in their society.

According to the sociocultural perspective, all of us can be fully understood only if our culture, ethnic identity, and gender identity are taken into consideration. Other sociocultural factors must be considered as well. For example, gay men and lesbian

**sociocultural perspective**
The theory of psychology that states that it is necessary to understand one's culture, ethnic identity, and other sociocultural factors to fully understand a person.

**culture**
The patterns of behavior, beliefs, and values shared by a group of people.

**ethnic group**
A group of persons who are descendants of a common group of ancestors.

**ethnic identity**
Each person's sense of belonging to a particular ethnic group.

**gender identity**
One's view of oneself as male or female.

# HUMAN DIVERSITY

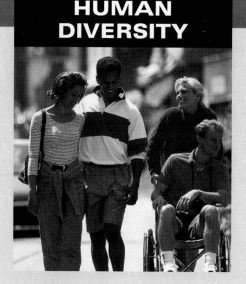

## Different Yet the Same

As will be said often throughout this book, all people are the same in some fundamentally important ways and yet different in other equally important ways. We are the same in the sense that the principles of psychology apply equally to all of us. Your brain has the same working parts whether you are a woman of Chinese descent who was raised in Holland or a man of Swedish descent raised in Minneapolis. In the same sense, the principles of perception, motivation, learning, and personality also apply to all human beings. But people are also different from one another. Their gender, cultural heritage, age, sexual orientation, and unique experiences all contribute to these differences. What is your age, gender, and ethnic heritage? How well educated are the members of your family? What is your political philosophy and your sexual orientation? If all of these things about you were different, would you be a different person in any important ways? I am not asking if you would be a better or a worse person, because we are not talking of value judgments here. I am only asking if you would be psychologically *different*.

What are the factors that must be understood to understand people? We will look at many such factors throughout this text, but one sociocultural factor that will be discussed in many contexts is the differences between persons raised in individualistic and collectivistic cultures (Kitayama & others, 1997; Miller, 1999). Persons raised in these differing types of cultures are taught different views of the world and habits of thought from birth (Nisbett, Peng, Choi & Norenzayan, 2001; Tomasello, 2000). As the name implies, highly individualistic cultures (such as the mainstream U.S. culture) emphasize the importance of individual rights, goals, and accomplishments. Persons in such cultures tend to feel good about themselves if they believe that they are smarter, stronger, richer, funnier, better looking, and more successful than other people. They believe that it is perfectly acceptable to make a profit by selling something to another person for more than they paid for it (free enterprise).

People raised in highly collectivistic cultures such as China, however, place much greater emphasis on performing the expected role in the family, company, and broader society. The focus is not on individual accomplishment but on the individual's contributions and obligations to the group. In collectivistic countries, equal sharing of resources seems more appropriate than making a profit off a fellow citizen. While North Americans are likely to compliment themselves on a job well done, the Japanese are likely to criticize themselves after the same good performance to help themselves better play the role expected by the group in the future (Kitayama & others, 1997; Miller, 1999). Although not everyone holds the same views in individualistic and collectivistic nations, it is not possible to understand people of different cultures without understanding these marked differences.

During the past decade, many psychologists have come to believe that the basic course in psychology overemphasizes the ways in which people are the same and neglects the important message that the human race comes in a rainbow of sociocultural varieties. Therefore, a boxed feature termed *Human Diversity* appears in every chapter in this edition to further counteract the false impression that all human beings are the same in the eyes of psychology. These boxed statements will explore differences related to gender, ethnicity, age, physical disability, and other factors.

Therefore, it would be fair to say that this text takes a "sociocultural" approach, as described in this chapter. As you read this text, please keep in mind that human diversity is discussed in every chapter to help us understand the broad natural range of differences among human beings. Those differences are never discussed in evaluative terms, but simply as elements of the human condition. While it will be said, for example, that males and females are different in some ways, those differences will never be taken to mean that one gender is superior to the other. The same holds for differences associated with ethnic groups and all other sociocultural factors.  ■

women have identities as homosexuals that shape their lives. Similarly, women and men who have integrated a feminist perspective into their lives must be understood partly in that context. Any social or cultural force that influences human lives is important to the sociocultural perspective.

The sociocultural perspective not only encourages us to consider cultural and social factors when attempting to understand a neighbor or coworker but also requires that we not *misuse* that information. Two aspects of this perspective are particularly rele-

3. ***People can be understood fully only in the context of their culture, ethnic identity, and gender identity.*** We are shaped by our learning experiences with other members of our culture. Our beliefs about right and wrong, our food preferences, our language, our religious beliefs, and many other facets of our lives come from cultural learning experiences. Among the most important things that we learn from others is our understanding of what it means to be male or female and a member of our own ethnic group. It is impossible to understand a person fully without understanding the sociocultural forces (such as culture, ethnicity, and gender) that influence them.

4. ***Human lives are a continuous process of change.*** From birth to death, humans are changing, developing organisms. We grow from helpless infancy through the time of playing with toys, through the time of adult work and rearing children, to the age of retirement. Change is almost continuous; standing still is rare in human lives. Much of this developmental change is inevitably the result of our biological nature: Unless the process is disturbed, all creatures grow from infancy to old age. Other aspects of change come from our experiences in life. Every time we learn a new concept from a college course, make a new friend, or adjust to a tragedy in our lives, we change in some way.

5. ***Behavior is motivated.*** Human behavior is not aimless. Rather, most of our actions can be viewed as attempts to meet our needs. We work to earn money for food, shelter, and clothing. We go on dates for companionship and perhaps to satisfy our sexual needs. We tell a joke at a party because of the sweet feeling of approval that laughter brings. However, not all of our motives are simple and selfish. Some of us are willing to spend long hours tutoring children with physical challenges just to see the joy of accomplishment in the children's faces. Others are internally motivated to express themselves in a painting or poem.

6. ***Humans are social animals.*** Like hives of bees and flocks of geese, people gather in social groups. The progress of modern civilization, and indeed the very survival of the human species, has been possible only because people work together in groups for the mutual benefit of all. From hunting large animals in the jungle to operating an assembly line, social groups are able to accomplish things that single individuals cannot.

    The social nature of human lives extends beyond mutual benefit, however. People need to have contact and relationships with one another. People seek out social support, friendships, and romantic relationships. When deprived of these social relationships for even short periods of time, we know the pain that loneliness brings.

7. ***People play an active part in creating their experiences.*** Aristotle compared the mind of an infant to a blank clay tablet on which experiences leave their mark. In his view,

we passively let experiences teach us about the world and become the person that they lead us to become. This is one of the few ideas of Aristotle that almost all contemporary psychologists have rejected. It seems to us today that people play a more active role in creating their experiences. The phi phenomenon discussed earlier was used by Gestalt psychologists to make this point: Often what we see —motion, in this case—is not in the outside world at all; the human nervous system creates it.

At a different level, it's clear that people play an active role in determining what kinds of experiences they will have by seeking out particular kinds of situations. Some people regularly choose relaxed, low-pressure situations; others get themselves into frenetic, exciting circumstances. We are shaped by these experiences, to be sure, but we play a role in choosing the experiences to which we will be exposed. We are active participants in the flow of life, not passive, blank tablets.

8. ***Behavior can be adaptive or maladaptive.*** Humans have an amazing ability to adapt to the demands of life. We are flexible, capable creatures who generally use our wits to adjust to whatever life dishes out in the way of challenges or pressures. Sometimes, however, we deal with life in ways that are harmful to us or to others. For example, some of us are excessively aggressive or much too timid, whereas others use a clinging dependency to get their way. These maladaptive ways of living can result from a combination of biological influences, excessive stress, or improper learning experiences. They are correctable, however, under the right conditions—such as good advice from friends, a change in life circumstances that encourages more adaptive ways to behave, or professional help.

These ideas serve as starting places for our study of psychology. As you read the following chapters, you may find it useful to glance back to these ideas to see how they relate to what you are studying.

Chapter 1 defines psychology and previews what psychologists have learned about human behavior.

**Summary**

I.   Psychology is defined as "the science of behavior and mental processes."

   A.   Psychology is considered to be a science because—like all sciences—knowledge is acquired through systematic observation.

   B.   The goals of psychology are to
      1.   describe,
      2.   predict,
      3.   understand,
      4.   and influence behavior and mental processes.

II.  Modern psychology developed from the pioneering work of many individuals during the late nineteenth and early twentieth centuries.

   A.   Early psychologists who studied the nature of conscious experience included
      1.   Wilhelm Wundt (structuralism)
      2.   Edward Titchener (structuralism)
      3.   J. Henry Alston (structuralism)
      4.   Max Wertheimer (Gestalt psychology)

   B.   Founders of psychology who focused on the useful functions of conscious mental processes (functionalism) included
      1.   William James
      2.   Hermann Ebbinghaus
      3.   Mary Whiton Calkins

   C.   Alfred Binet founded the practical perspective in psychology known as psychometrics, which focuses on the measurement of intelligence and other mental functions.

   D.   Early psychologists who focused on observable behavior and the importance of learning (behaviorism) were
      1.   Ivan Pavlov
      2.   John B. Watson
      3.   Margaret Floy Washburn

   E.   Pioneers of psychology who examined the "unconscious mind" were
      1.   Sigmund Freud (psychoanalysis)
      2.   Carl Rogers (humanistic psychology)

   F.   Three modern perspectives that strongly influence contemporary psychology are
      1.   The sociocultural perspective, which states that people can be understood only in terms of their culture, gender, and other sociocultural factors.
      2.   The neuroscience perspective, which states that we must understand the nature of the nervous system and other biological systems to understand our psychological nature.
      3.   Evolutionary psychology, which hypothesizes that many of our psychological characteristics evolved through natural selection.

   G.   Modern psychology can be divided into basic and applied areas.
      1.   Psychologists working in the basic areas teach and conduct research on the biological basis of behavior, the processes of sensation and perception, learning and memory, cognition, human

development, emotion, personality, social behavior, ethnic and gender identity, and sexual orientation.

2. Applied psychologists put the basic knowledge of psychology to work in helping people. Then they specialize in applied fields, such as clinical treatment, personal or marital counseling, industrial or educational applications, or health psychology.

III. Most psychologists would agree that the following statements accurately describe human behavior and mental processes.

A. Human beings are biological creatures whose structure and physiology influence and limit behavior.

B. Each person is unique, yet enough similarities exist among individuals to allow a true science of behavior.

C. People can be fully understood only in the context of their culture, ethnic identity, and gender identity.

D. Human lives are a continuous process of change, evolving from birth to death.

E. Behavior is motivated, not random or aimless.

F. Humans are social animals who prefer to interact with others.

G. People play an active part in choosing their experiences and constructing perceptions.

H. Behavior can be either adaptive or maladaptive.

## Resources

1. The following three books provide more on the people who founded psychology and their ideas. Kimble, G. A., Wertheimer, M., & White, C. L. (Eds.). (1991). *Portraits of pioneers in psychology*. Washington, DC: American Psychological Association. Benjamin, L. (1997). *A history of psychology* (2nd ed.). Boston: McGraw-Hill. Pickren, W. E., & Dewsbury, D. A. (2002). *Evolving perspectives on the history of psychology*. Washington, DC. American Psychological Association.

2. Although there are fewer intense debates among psychologists today than in the past, there are still many controversial issues. A fascinating guide to these debates that is designed to encourage critical thinking in students is Slife, B. (1998). *Taking sides: Clashing views on controversial psychological issues* (10th ed.). Boston: McGraw-Hill.

3. For more on the psychological importance of gender, race, and ethnicity, see Garcia, J., & Keough, K. (2000). *Social psychology of gender, race, and ethnicity*. Boston: McGraw-Hill.

4. For an important and fascinating history of the psychologist Helen Bradford Thompson, who began the scientific study of psychological gender differences, see Milar, K. S. (2000). The first generation of women psychologists and the psychology of women. *American Psychologist, 55,* 616–619.

5. For an excellent discussion of the psychology of women, along with brief biographies of many women who are prominent in contemporary psychology, see Paludi, M. (1992). *The psychology of women*. Dubuque, IA: Brown & Benchmark.

6. The following are two readable and thought-provoking sources on the psychological forces that influence men in U.S. culture. Graham, S. R. (1992). What does a man want? *American Psychologist, 47,* 837–841. Kilmartin, C. (2000). *The masculine self* (2nd ed.). Boston: McGraw-Hill.

7. For more on the sociocultural perspective, see Triandis, H. C. (1994). *Culture and social behavior.* Boston: McGraw-Hill. Betancourt, H., & Lopez, S. R. (1993). The

study of culture, ethnicity, and race in American psychology. *American Psychologist, 48,* 629–637. Kitayama, S., Markus, H. R., Masumoto, H., & Norasakkunkit, V. (1997). Individual and collective processes in the construction of the self: Self-enhancement in the United States and self-criticism in Japan. *Journal of Personality and Social Psychology, 72,* 1245–1267. Nisbett, R. E., Peng, K., Choi, I., & Norenzayan, A. (2001). Culture and systems of thought: Holistic versus analytic cognition. *Psychological Review, 108,* 291–310.

8. For information on career opportunities in psychology, see American Psychological Association. *A career in psychology.* This can be obtained free from the American Psychological Association, 750 First Street, N.E., Washington, DC 20002–4242, www.apa.org. More detailed information is found in Sternberg, R. J. (1997). *Career paths in psychology: Where your degree can take you.* Washington, DC: APA Books.

# Visual Review of Historical Time Line

This visual review is designed to help you check your learning of the historical influences on modern psychology. Fill in the blanks with the names of the various historical and contemporary perspectives, schools of thought, or movements within psychology. This information is summarized in figure 1.5. Once you have the historical time line in mind, it is easier to organize additional ideas and facts within that structure. Be sure to ask your instructor how much of the historical information he or she expects you to learn. The names and dates are not the most important historical information in this chapter. Rather, the key point is that many psychologists with very different viewpoints founded the science of psychology. Beyond that concept, different instructors expect students to memorize different amounts of detailed historical information.

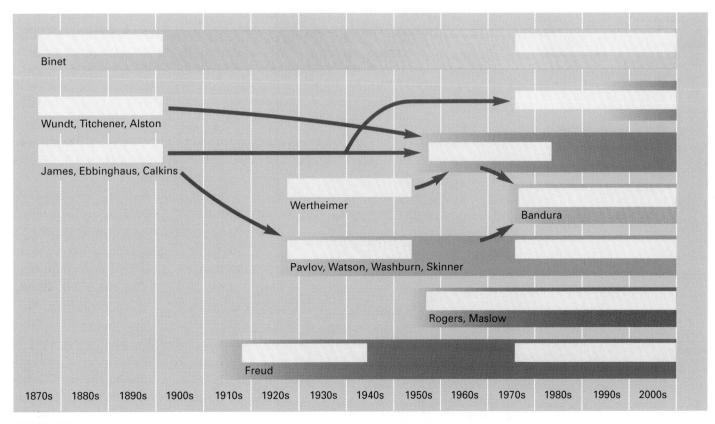

**FIGURE 1.7**

# Chapter Outline

# Research Methods in Psychology

## PROLOGUE

In this chapter, we will discuss how psychologists study human behavior and mental processes scientifically. We will examine two general types of scientific methods used by psychologists—descriptive methods and formal experiments—and some of the specific strategies researchers use in applying these methods. In many ways, this chapter covers the most important concepts in this course. Whereas the other chapters present some of what has been learned about behavior and mental processes, this chapter describes *how* we learn about ourselves in scientific terms. This is of fundamental importance because it is the use of the scientific methods presented in this chapter that allows psychology to move beyond mere speculation about the human condition. Science provides a set of methods for asking questions and rules for using evidence to reach conclusions. These methods give us a framework for answering fundamentally important questions about human existence. Although scientific methods cannot settle all disputes about issues important to the human race, they help tremendously. To fully appreciate the value of scientific methods in psychology, however, you must understand those methods.

All scientists believe that the part of nature they study is orderly and lawful before they begin their research. If astronomers were to feel that the planets wandered aimlessly and randomly through space, they would have little reason to study their paths. The same is true of people. To have a science of psychology, we must believe that human behavior is at least somewhat predictable. Often, though, we see ourselves as capable of doing whatever we choose without being subject to the laws of nature. Although there may be some truth to that, psychologists believe that our behavior is much more orderly and predictable than most of us think.

I regularly begin teaching my own course in psychology with a disguised demonstration that human behavior is actually fairly predictable under some circumstances. It's a little corny, but it makes the point. After telling the students that I'm a very democratic fellow, I ask the class to decide how they want to be evaluated in the course. I tell them that I require a cumulative final examination, but that everything else is open to a vote. I give them the option of doing a term paper (to give them a way of being evaluated that is free from the pressure of classroom testing), and I give them the options of having one, two, or three tests plus the final examination, or no tests plus the final examination. Then I take votes.

In every class, a couple of students vote for the term paper (one student who writes well and one who thinks I'm too lazy to read the papers), but that option is always soundly defeated. A few students vote for no tests or one test, and about 20 percent vote for two tests, but about three-quarters always choose three tests plus the final.

When the voting is over, I thank the students for their judicious decisions and hand out the course syllabus. Then I point out that I correctly predicted their behavior—that 250 copies of the syllabus have already been printed that include no requirement of a term paper and give the dates of three tests plus the final examination. After the laughing, booing, and hissing have subsided, I say something like, "The science of psychology rests on the assumption that your behavior is a good

## Key Terms

empirical evidence 34
operational definition 34
replication 35
survey method 36
naturalistic observation 37
clinical method 37
correlational method 38
coefficient of correlation 39
formal experiment 42
independent variable 44
dependent variable 44
experimental group 44
control group 44
random assignment 44
experimental control 44
placebo effect 45
blind experiment 45
experimenter bias 45

deal more predictable than you might think. That's not to take anything away from the mysteries and complexities of human existence; it's just to say that we aren't immune to the laws of nature. We're predictable enough to study scientifically." ■

## Basic Concepts of Research

**scientific method**
Method of studying nature based on systematic observation and rules of evidence.

**empirical evidence**
Evidence based on observations of publicly observable phenomena, such as behavior, that can be confirmed by other observers.

**operational definition**
A definition used in science that is explicitly based on the procedures, or operations, used to measure a scientific phenomenon, including behavior.

**theories**
Tentative explanations of facts and relationships in sciences.

The basis of the **scientific method** in all of the sciences is making observations in a systematic way, following strict rules of evidence, and thinking critically about that evidence. As was stated in the "Lahey's Learning System" section at the beginning of this book, psychological research is critical thinking in action. The psychological scientist asks: What is the evidence? How good is the evidence? What are the alternative explanations for the evidence? What needs to be learned next? In this chapter, we will discuss several of the most important aspects of the scientific method in psychology.

### Empirical Evidence and Operational Definitions

Like other scientists, psychologists work with **empirical evidence**—evidence from *observations* of publicly observable behavior. All sciences require that their evidence come from observations of *public* phenomena so other scientists can confirm the observations. In the case of psychology, we observe public behavior (and then, in many cases, draw inferences about private mental processes that are not publicly observable).

When scientists describe their empirical evidence, they are careful to use **operational definitions**. This means that they describe their observations in terms of the *operations of measurement*. This arcane-sounding phrase has a simple but important meaning that will be clear if we consider a hypothetical example. Let's say a team of psychologists studied the causes of fatal accidents involving city buses. One of the following conclusions of this hypothetical study uses an operational definition and the other does not:

A. Sixty percent of Chicago bus drivers daydream while driving their buses.

B. Sixty percent of Chicago bus drivers answered "yes" to the question "Do you ever daydream when driving your bus?

Which statement uses an operational definition? Version B does, because it explicitly refers to the operation of measuring daydreaming (the question that was asked), whereas version A does not. Why is this important? Again, this is an issue of critical thinking in action. When you know the operation of measurement, you can easily evaluate the quality of the evidence and the alternative interpretations of the evidence. Are people (including bus drivers) able to accurately recall if they daydream? Would bus drivers be honest in reporting daydreaming while driving to a researcher? Would they believe the researcher's promise of confidentiality? Would some bus drivers be too embarrassed to admit daydreaming even if they thought the researcher would keep their answer private? Is there a more accurate way to studying daydreaming by bus drivers?

If another team of researchers repeated the study and found that about 60 percent of bus drivers answered the question about daydreaming in the same way, we could be more confident about the number of bus drivers who answered yes to the daydreaming question. We would still need to ask critical questions about the best interpretation of the finding, however. Science often moves slowly because the strict rules of science take time. This is often time well spent, however, because it reduces the number of hasty conclusions. By the way, remember that this study about bus drivers was hypothetical; I just made up the 60 percent figure. But now I'm curious about those daydreaming bus drivers . . .

### Theories and Hypotheses

It is important to recognize that science deals in theories and not in "truths." **Theories** are tentative explanations of facts and relationships in sciences. The knowledge that any science provides is tentative because our theories are always subject to revision. Theories are frequently revised because scientists are constantly testing them. A theory is tested by making a prediction based on that theory—called a **hypothesis**—and by conducting a study to see if the hypothesis is confirmed. For example, psychologist Terrie Moffitt (1993) has published an influential theory that states that youths who become juvenile delinquents *before* puberty differ in many ways from individuals who do not commit any crimes until *after* puberty. I have tested a specific hypothesis based on that theory that states that juvenile delinquents who begin committing crimes during childhood are more likely to commit violent crimes than are juvenile delinquents who do not commit their first crime until after puberty. My study confirmed Moffitt's hypothesis (Lahey & others, 1998). This means that, like many other studies, my study provides additional reason for the field to continue to use Moffitt's theory. Confirming a hypothesis based on a theory does not mean that the theory is "true," however. It is always possible that other studies will test Moffitt's theory and fail to support it. If this were to happen often, her theory would be either revised or abandoned.

## Representativeness of Samples

In psychology, studies use human beings or nonhuman animals as the research participants. A relatively small group of participants—called the **sample**—is studied in hopes of learning something that applies to other human beings or animals. This means that studies are valid only if we select a sample that is *representative*, or typical of all humans or animals. For example, suppose a psychologist wanted to test the hypothesis that people who are happy in their work tend to be happy in their marriages. If that psychologist worked in a marital therapy clinic, he or she might be tempted to use the clinic's clients as the sample. Because many people come to the clinic, it would be convenient to ask them to complete some questionnaires about their happiness at work and in marriage. People who seek help for marital problems are hardly representative of all married persons, however. Using such an unrepresentative sample could lead to a very biased and misleading test of the hypothesis.

Psychologists have not always used representative samples in their research. Unfortunately, psychologists have too often used samples that contained too few women, too few persons of color, and too few persons of lower income to be representative. This is partly because they have too frequently used college students as research participants. There is nothing wrong with college students, but they are not representative of the general population of adults in North America. On the average, they are younger and more intelligent and atypical in many other ways. It is only in recent years that psychologists have begun to use more representative samples.

## Importance of Replication in Research

If I were to tell you that a hypothesis had been confirmed by five studies, would you be more convinced that it is a sound hypothesis than if it had been confirmed by only one study? Researchers also are influenced by the **replication** of the findings in many separate experiments. Indeed, the replication of studies by other researchers is an essential principle of science. You should doubt every finding until it has been replicated (and not abandon *all* doubt *after* it has been replicated).

## ● Research Methods

Many kinds of scientific methods are used in psychology, each with its own advantages and disadvantages. Each type of scientific method is best suited for answering unique kinds of questions, so they tend to be relied upon to varying extents by different specialties within psychology. All research methods are based on the same general concepts of systematic observation and rules of evidence, however.

**hypothesis**
A prediction based on a theory that is tested in a study.

**sample**
A group of human or nonhuman research participants studied to learn about an entire population of human beings or animals.

**replication**
Repeating studies based on the scientific principle that the results of studies should be doubted until the same results have been found in similar studies by other researchers.

**descriptive studies**
Methods of observation used to describe predictable behavior and mental processes.

**survey method**
A research method that uses interviews and questionnaires with individuals.

## Descriptive Studies

The simplest methods of scientific inquiry are the **descriptive studies.** These involve studying people as they live their lives, so that we can *describe* their behavior and mental processes. We watch them shop in stores, listen to them during psychotherapy sessions, and observe them in many other ways. Three descriptive methods are widely used in psychology today: the survey method, naturalistic observation, and the clinical method.

### Survey Method

One of the most direct ways to obtain information that will allow us to describe human behavior or mental processes is simply to ask people questions. This approach is called the **survey method.** Surveys are perhaps most widely used today by psychologists who want to describe people's opinions about television programs, soft drinks, political candidates, and similar subjects. Surveys are frequently used for other purposes as well. For example, the myth-shattering surveys of sex researcher Alfred Kinsey (Kinsey, Pomeroy, & Martin, 1948) revealed that the number of people who engaged in masturbation was much higher in the general population than expected at the time.

A survey conducted by a group of researchers at the National Institute of Mental Health (Kasper, Wehr, Bartko, Gaist, & Rosenthal, 1989) provides another excellent example of the use of the survey method in psychology. They were interested in describing variations in people's moods. Are you more likely to have bad moods during certain times of the year? Do they occur during the winter? A lot has been written in the popular press about "winter blahs" and "cabin fever"—periods of depression experienced during the short, cold days of the winter—but, until recently, there was little hard evidence to support this idea (Wehr & others, 2001). These researchers conducted a random telephone survey of 416 persons living in Maryland and Virginia. They asked an adult in each household to name the month during which he or she "felt worst" during the past year. As shown in the top section of figure 2.1, there was a strong tendency for the winter months, particularly January and February, to be the times people reported

**FIGURE 2.1**
Results of a telephone survey of 416 adults living in Virginia and Maryland who were asked the month during which they "felt worst" during the previous year. The authors plotted the 12 months twice to show more clearly the seasonal patterns of depressed feeling.
**Source:** Data from S. Kasper et al. (1989). "Epidemiological Findings of Seasonal Changes in Mood and Behavior" in *Archives of General Psychiatry, 46,* 823–833.

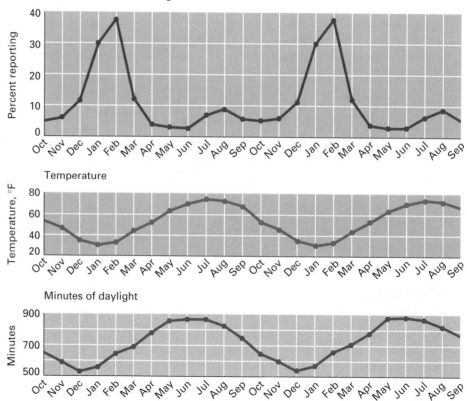

that they felt worst. The bottom sections show that moods tend to be worse when the temperature is the lowest and the number of minutes of sunlight each day is the shortest. Keep in mind as you read about this study that it does not imply that everyone feels depressed during the winter. It simply suggests that more people feel lousy during the winter than during the summer.

The primary advantage of the survey method is that you can gather a great deal of information in a relatively short period of time. The main disadvantage is that the accuracy of information obtained in surveys may be questionable. You cannot always be sure that the answers are completely honest, especially to questions about such sensitive topics as sex and drug use. In addition, a number of very subtle factors have been found to influence the results of surveys. For example, people are more likely to endorse feminist views when the interviewer is a woman than a man (Huddy, Billig, Bracciodieta, Heoffler, Moynihan, & Pugliani, 1997). In addition, subtle differences in how questions are worded can influence answers (Waenke, Schwarz, & Noelle-Neumann, 1995; Schwarz, 1999). This does not mean that surveys are not valuable, but like all other methods of research, survey findings must be very carefully considered.

## Naturalistic Observation

Another straightforward way to learn about behavior is simply to watch and describe it as it naturally occurs. The careful observation and recording of behavior in real-life settings is called **naturalistic observation.** When internationally known scientist Jane Goodall goes to Africa, sits down in the jungle, and watches a troop of apes, she is using naturalistic observation. She watches the apes in their natural habitat over long periods of time, taking careful notes of what she sees until specific patterns of behavior become evident. Using this method, she and her coworkers have learned that the social behavior and use of some tools by apes are often strikingly similar to that of humans. She has discovered, though, that apes are also capable of murder—ambushing and killing other apes in a way that looks "intentional."

The method of naturalistic observation is not restricted to the study of animal behavior. It's a method also used to study such topics as the play and friendship patterns of young children, the leadership tactics of effective business managers, and the ways in which juvenile delinquents encourage antisocial behavior in one another.

## Clinical Method

An important variation on naturalistic observation is the **clinical method,** which simply involves observing people while they receive help from a mental health professional for

**naturalistic observation**
A research method based on recording behavior as it occurs in natural life settings.

**clinical method**
The method of studying people while they are receiving psychological help from a mental health professional.

Jane Goodall.

## THE FAR SIDE® By GARY LARSON

**"Don't shush me — and I don't care if she *is* writing in her little notebook; just tell me where you were last night!"**

their psychological problems. Although clinical observation is not as useful as observing people in the natural situations where they encounter problems—at home, school, or work—it does provide useful information. Sigmund Freud, for example, developed his theories of abnormal behavior from years of intensive work with patients in his "consulting room." He was able to observe their behavior in this situation over long periods of time until he felt he saw consistent patterns in what they did, thought, and felt. The clinical method is also often used today for the preliminary evaluation of clinical treatment methods. For example, daily measures of anxiety might be taken on an individual before, during, and after treatment to evaluate a new method of treating excessive anxiety.

### Correlational Studies

We'll use a topic that is often in the news—the possible effects of media violence on children and adolescents—as an example that will help us understand the correlational method of psychological research and compare correlational studies to formal experiments. Over the past 20 years, scientists and politicians have debated the effects of children's exposure to violence in television, movies, and electronic games. Does watching violence in the media make children and adolescents more likely to engage in real-life violence themselves? This is a controversial topic, because many psychologists feel that the large increases in the amount of violence viewed by children during the twentieth century may have caused an increase in violent crime (Anderson & others, 2001). Many of those who believe that media violence causes real-life violence support legislation to curb violence in the media. Such legislation is often strongly opposed by the producers of violent television shows and films, by people who don't believe that media violence leads to real-life violence, and by others who feel that any form of censorship is a threat to the First Amendment right of free speech. This complex topic involves much more than just scientific issues, but psychological research methods can play an essential role in this and other similar debates by evaluating claims that viewing violence in the media causes real-life violence.

*Correlation: Statistical Relations between Quantitative Variables.* Well over 200 studies have been published in psychological journals on exposure to media violence (Anderson and others, 2001; Huesmann, Moise, & Podolski, 1997). Many of these studies used the **correlational method.** In such studies, researchers simply measure the two variables (viewing media violence and engaging in real-life violence, in this example) and see if they are statistically related. A **variable** is anything whose *numerical* value can be measured. The primary difference between naturalistic observation and correlational studies is the use of **quantitative measures** in correlational studies. This means that numerical values can be assigned to each variable. One quantitative variable in the studies of media violence is the *amount* of violent movies or television programs viewed by each child (measured as the number of hours per week, for example). The other quantitative variable is the amount of violent behavior engaged in by the child (measured as the number of verbally or physically aggressive acts per week, for example). Most published studies show that children who watch more violence in movies and television are more likely to be violent themselves in real life. That is, these two variables are *correlated.*

Does this mean that viewing media violence makes children more violent? Not necessarily. We must consider two issues as we attempt to make sense of correlational

**correlational method**
(kor˝ĕ-lā´shun-al) A research method that measures the strength of the relation between variables.

**variable**
A factor whose numerical value can vary.

**quantitative measures**
(kwon´ti-tā-tiv) Capable of being measured in numerical terms.

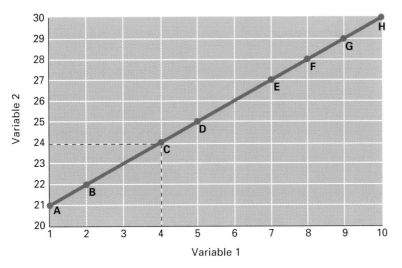

**FIGURE 2.2**
Hypothetical data illustrating a correlation coefficient of +1.00.

studies: How *strong* is the relationship between watching media violence and engaging in violent behavior? And what do correlational studies tell us about cause-and-effect?

*Coefficient of Correlation.* Not only do correlational studies use quantitative measures of each variable, but they also measure the strength and direction of the relationship between the two variables. For example, how strongly is watching media violence correlated with engaging in violent behavior? If the *correlation* is strong, it tells us a great deal about the relationship between the two variables. If the correlation is weak, however, it is not very informative. Researchers in psychology and other fields use the **coefficient of correlation** to measure the strength of the correlation between two quantitative variables in *statistical* terms. You can see how this coefficient is calculated by turning to the appendix on statistics at the end of this book.

The coefficient of correlation can range from −1.00 through zero to +1.00. A correlation coefficient of zero means that there is no relationship between the two variables at all. A coefficient of +1.00 means that there is a perfect *positive correlation* between the two variables, and a coefficient of −1.00 means that there is a perfect *negative correlation* between the two variables. What does that mean?

If two variables are *positively correlated,* participants who have lower scores on one variable will have lower scores on the other variable, and participants who have higher scores on one variable will have higher scores on the other variable. If the correlation coefficient is +1.00, then we can predict with total accuracy each participant's score on one variable by knowing each participant's score on the other variable—they would be perfectly related in the positive direction. Look for a moment at figure 2.2. I have used hypothetical data to illustrate a perfect positive correlation (coefficient of +1.00) between variable 1 and variable 2. Each participant in the study is represented by a dot and a letter of the alphabet in this figure. The dots are positioned at the points that represent each participant's score on the two variables. For example, the dotted lines show that participant C has a score of 4 on variable 1 and a score of 24 on variable 2. Because the correlation between these two variables is perfect, all of the dots representing each participant lie on a straight line.

If two variables are *negatively correlated,* participants who have lower scores on one variable will have *higher* scores on the other variable, and participants who have higher scores on one variable will have *lower* scores on the other variable. If the correlation coefficient is −1.00, then we can still predict with total accuracy each participant's score on one variable by knowing each participant's score on the other variable—they would just

**coefficient of correlation**
The numerical expression of the strength and direction of a relationship between two variables.

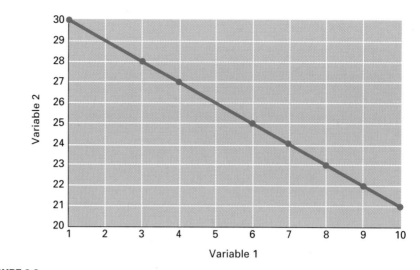

**FIGURE 2.3**
Hypothetical data illustrating a correlation coefficient of −1.00.

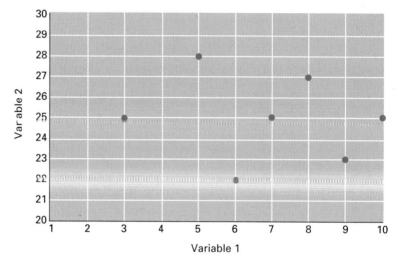

**FIGURE 2.4**
Hypothetical data illustrating a correlation coefficient of zero.

be related in the negative direction. Look for a moment at figure 2.3. I have used hypothetical data again to illustrate a perfect negative correlation (coefficient of −1.00) between variable 1 and variable 2. Again, all of the dots representing each participant's score on each variable lie on the straight line. Because the correlation is negative in this case, however, the direction of the line is opposite that of a positive correlation.

It is common for students to be confused at this point and to think that a coefficient of correlation of +1.00 is better than a coefficient of −1.00. Both are perfect correlations of equal strength—one just predicts in the positive direction and the other in the negative direction.

A correlation coefficient of zero, on the other hand, means that there is absolutely no relationship between the two variables in either the positive or the negative direction. Again, I have used hypothetical data in figure 2.4 to illustrate a correlation coefficient of zero. Note that knowing a participant's score on one variable does not allow us to predict that participant's score on the other variable at all—they are completely unrelated.

Very few correlation coefficients are perfect in actual correlational studies. Therefore, I have used hypothetical data to illustrate a correlation coefficient of −.68 in

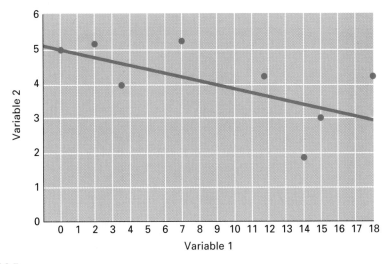

**FIGURE 2.5**
Hypothetical data illustrating a correlation coefficient of −.68.

figure 2.5, which would be considered a fairly high correlation in most studies. Keep in mind that the fact that it is negative implies nothing about how large the correlation is, just the direction of the relationship. In this case, the negative correlation tells us that participants with higher scores on variable 1 tend to have lower scores on variable 2. Notice, however, that some of these data points lie quite far from the line that comes closest to connecting the dots representing each participant's scores. This means that we can only roughly predict each participant's score on one variable by knowing the other score.

Let's return to our example of media violence. Correlations between watching violence in the media and engaging in violence oneself tend to be relatively small, in the range of +.20 to +.30 (Anderson & Bushman, 2001; Paiko & Comstock, 1994). However, these small correlations *could* mean that 8 out of every 100 children are influenced by viewing media violence to be more violent (Paik & Comstock). A 10 percent increase in the number of violent children could be of great importance to society—particularly if you are one of their victims.

***Correlation Does Not Necessarily Mean Causation.*** Finding that two variables are correlated tells us that they are related, but it is essential to understand that it does *not* necessarily mean that one of the variables influences the other variable in a causal way. For example, it is possible that viewing violence in the media causes some children and adolescents to become more violent, but it is equally likely that the *opposite* is true. That is, it is possible that youths who engage in more violence are more likely to enjoy violent shows than do less aggressive children. Correlations do not tell us which variable is the cause in cause-and-effect relationships. In fact, correlations can exist between variables that are not causally related in either direction. For example, it is possible that viewing violence and engaging in violence are both the result of another variable (such as having parents who do not supervise either the child's television viewing or the child's behavior) and are not causally related.

Therefore, we must not reach conclusions about cause-and-effect based on correlational studies alone. They tell us only how strongly two variables are related. How, then, do we decide if one variable *causes* another? In our example, how do we decide if watching violence on television increases violence in real life? The next section will describe another way to study the relationships between variables that can help us answer such questions.

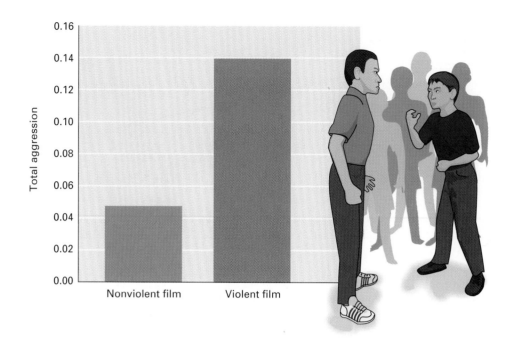

**FIGURE 2.6**

Example of a formal experiment. Incarcerated delinquent boys who were shown films depicting high levels of violence engaged in more verbal and physical aggression over the next 2 weeks than did boys in the same juvenile detention facility who were shown nonviolent films.

## Formal Experiments

**formal experiment**
A research method that allows the researcher to manipulate the independent variable to study its effect on the dependent variable.

**Formal experiments** are particularly helpful in reaching the goals of understanding and influencing behavior. Like the correlational method, experiments are designed to tell us about the relationship between two or more variables. Unlike other methods, however, the experiment involves deliberate arrangement of the variables involved. And, unlike the correlational method, a carefully conducted experiment allows the researcher to draw conclusions about cause-and-effect relationships with more confidence.

In formal experiments, quantitative measures of behavior are compared in different conditions that the researchers create. For example, over 20 years ago, French psychologist Jean-Pierre Leyens conducted a formal experiment of the effects of viewing violent films on the behavior of adolescent boys (Leyens & others, 1975). Boys who were incarcerated in a juvenile detention facility for criminal behavior participated in the study. Over several days, half of the boys were shown several violent films (Westerns and war films), and half of the boys were shown neutral films that contained no violence. During lunch time and during the boys' evening recreation period, observers (who did not know which films the boys had seen) recorded every instance of verbal or physical aggression among the boys. As shown in figure 2.6, the boys who viewed violent films engaged in more verbal and physical aggression over the next 2 weeks than did the boys who viewed the neutral films.

Later, psychologist Wendy Josephson (1987) conducted a similar formal experiment on the effects of media violence. In this case, 400 second- and third-grade boys participated from a public elementary school. Prior to playing floor hockey, the boys were shown films. Half of the boys were shown a highly violent film depicting a police officer being murdered by a sniper and the police officers' vengeful beating and shooting of the sniper and his fellow criminals. The other half of the boys viewed a nonviolent film. To increase the boys' level of anger, they were all frustrated by telling them that they would also see a "really neat" cartoon, but the television monitor did not work. Later, when the boys played hockey, observers who did not know which film the boys had seen counted the number of acts of verbal and physical aggression. As with Leyens' study, the

First **randomly select** a group of potential participants from the full population of interest and ask them to give informed consent to participate.

Randomly **assign** the participants to the experimental group and the control group.

Expose the two groups of participants to different conditions of the **independent variable**. **Control** other factors to keep the conditions of the two groups the same *except* for the independent variable.

**View violent film**          **View nonviolent film**

Measure the **dependent variable** (in this example, violent behavior by the participants) to see if the groups differ.

**Experimental group**          **Control group**

**FIGURE 2.7**
Steps in conducting a formal experiment.

boys who had seen the violent film were more aggressive than the boys who had seen the nonviolent film. Thus, Josephson's study replicated Leyen's study, increasing our confidence in the finding.

These two formal experiments support the hypothesis that viewing media violence *causes* increases in real-life violence (at least in boys, who, unfortunately, have been studied more than girls). Does this surprise you? After all, most college students have viewed a lot of violence in the media, and most have never committed a violent act. If media violence causes real-life violence, why hasn't it affected you? Both of these formal experiments looked at this question. In both studies, boys were divided into two groups on the basis of their levels of aggression *prior* to the study to see if the violent films affected the aggressive boys more than the nonaggressive boys. In both studies, the effect of the violent films was stronger on the boys who were characteristically aggressive, suggesting that media violence does not affect everyone in the same way. Rather, media violence appears to exert its strongest effect on boys who are already aggressive.

Over the years, many other formal experiments have been conducted on this topic, almost always supporting the hypothesis that media violence causes real-life violence, at least among youths with a predisposition to violence (Anderson & others, 2001;

Anderson, Lindsay, & Bushman, 1999; Paik & Comstock, 1994). If we have good evidence that viewing violence in the media increases real-life violence, why haven't we done something to reduce the amount of violence on television, in films, and in electronic games? As I said at the beginning of the section on correlational methods, the scientific question is only part of this issue. Many political, philosophical, legal, and economic issues greatly complicate the debate. However, if we the voters learn to understand the scientific evidence better, we can influence political debates about public policy more effectively. These studies of media violence are important in their own right, but they are presented here only to illustrate the nature of formal experiments.

### Elements and Logic of Formal Experiments

In every formal experiment, there are at least two variables. The **independent variable** is what the researcher arranges to allow a comparison of the participants' behavior under two or more conditions. In the case of the two formal experiments on media violence, the independent variable was the type of film (violent or nonviolent). It is called the independent variable because the researcher has independent control over it—in this example, the researcher can choose any type of film and choose which participants are shown each film. The **dependent variable** is the measure of behavior that is contrasted in the two or more conditions. In these examples, the dependent variable was the amount of aggression engaged in by the boys. It is called the dependent variable because its quantitative value is expected to *depend* on which condition the participant is in.

In simple formal experiments, like the two studies of media violence presented as examples, one group receives the condition of the independent variable that is hypothesized to influence the behavior of the participants (watches the violent film, in this case), and it is called the **experimental group.** A second group receives none of the supposedly "active" condition of the independent variable (watches a film containing no violence), and is called the **control group.** If the behavior of the participants in the experimental group differs from the behavior of the participants in the control group, the hypothesis that differences in the independent variable cause differences in the dependent variable is supported, but only under the following two circumstances.

First, the participants must be assigned *randomly* to the experimental or the control group. That is, the experimenter must follow a random procedure such as putting the names of all participants in a hat and drawing the names of the participants in the two groups without looking. If the researcher uses any other method of assigning participants to the experimental and control groups, the experiment is invalid. If, for example, boys were shown a violent film and girls were shown a nonviolent film, the researcher could not know if any differences in the behavior of the participants in the two groups were due to the violence in the films or the gender of the participants. Hence, formal experiments require **random assignment** to experimental conditions to roughly equalize the groups on all factors except the independent variable.

Second, formal experiments are only valid if all alternative explanations for the findings have been ruled out through strict **experimental control.** For example, in both of the formal experiments on media violence, both groups of boys were shown a film. If half of the boys had been shown a violent film and half of the boys had been shown no film, the unlikely possibility that watching *any* type of film causes increased aggression could not be ruled out. The boys in the control group had to be shown a nonviolent film to rule out this alternative. In all ways, alternative explanations must be controlled. For example, if one film had been shown in the morning and the other film had been shown in the afternoon, the researchers wouldn't know for sure if the content of the film or the time of day was important. Even unlikely alternative explanations have to be controlled in formal experiments. This is because the goal of a formal experiment is to make sure that differences in the *dependent variable* between groups can be traced to just one factor—the *independent variable.*

**independent variable**
The variable whose quantitative value is independently controlled by the researcher.

**dependent variable**
The variable whose quantitative value is expected to depend on the effects of the independent variable.

**experimental group**
The group in an experiment that receives some value of the independent variable.

**control group**
The group in simple experiments that is not exposed to any level of the independent variable and is used for comparisons with the treatment group.

**random assignment**
The requirement that participants be assigned randomly to experimental conditions in formal experiments rather than in a systematic way.

**experimental control**
The requirement that all explanations for differences in the dependent variable are controlled in formal experiments, except for differences in conditions of the independent variable.

**Placebo Control in Formal Experiments**

In this section, we will focus on a type of experimental control that is of great importance in psychological research. The simplest case of this type of control comes from studies of medications. Suppose that after graduation you take a job with a pharmaceutical firm that wants to test a new medication for the treatment of anxiety. You might conduct a formal experiment by randomly assigning participants with high levels of chronic anxiety to two conditions of the independent variable (the medication). The experimental group would receive the medication each day for 5 days, and the control group would not receive the medication. On each of the 5 days, the participants would fill out a questionnaire on their anxiety symptoms. The hypothesis that you are testing is that the participants who receive the medication will show greater reductions in anxiety over the 5 days than the participants who do not receive the medication.

Researchers have known for many years, however, that this kind of formal experiment will not yield valid findings. The problem is that many people who are given pills feel better in such studies even when the pills contain no active ingredients at all. This is known as the **placebo effect.** To control the placebo effect in medication studies, participants in the control group are always given *placebo pills*, which are pills that are exactly like the active medication but contain no active ingredients.

In psychology, it is important to know that placebo effects are not restricted to pills. Suppose you take a job as a research assistant in a study of the effectiveness of a new kind of psychotherapy for treating anxiety. The new psychotherapy involves talking about the irrationality of anxiety in a certain way. If the experimental group is given this new form of psychotherapy, the control group must be given "placebo" psychotherapy. In this case, the control group members should meet with a therapist and talk about their anxiety in a way that seems like psychotherapy but lacks the specific way of focusing on the irrationality of anxiety that is believed to cause improvement in anxiety. In other words, the placebo is not psychotherapy but *seems* like psychotherapy to the participants. If this is not done, it would be impossible to know if any improvements in anxiety in the experimental group were the result of the particular way of discussing the irrationality of anxiety or of just participation in something that seems like psychotherapy. In general, researchers must always create conditions in the experimental and control groups that are identical in every way, except for the active ingredient that is the independent variable. This is the only way that valid conclusions can be reached about the effects of the independent variable on the dependent variable.

**Blind Formal Experiments**

Let's return to the examples of formal experiments on the effects of media violence. Did you notice that the persons who rated the aggressiveness of the boys in the experimental and control groups did not know which boys were in which group? This is called a **blind experiment** because the researchers who were recording the data (the dependent variable) did not know which participants had received which condition of the independent variable. Experimenters who measure the dependent variable are kept blind to control two factors that could contaminate the logic of the experiment. First, researchers are kept blind in the best studies to avoid their unintentionally recording the data in a way that would favor their hypothesis. In the studies of media violence, the researchers who rated boys on their verbal and physical aggression might be more likely to decide erroneously that ambiguous behaviors were aggressive among boys whom they knew had seen the violent films—without knowing that they were doing so.

Second, researchers are kept blind to rule out the possibility of **experimenter bias.** A number of studies show that researchers who are not blind can behave differently toward participants in the experimental and control groups in ways that subtly but powerfully influence their behavior (Basoglu, Marks, Livanou, & Swinson, 1997). If researchers are not kept blind, it is possible that differences in the dependent variable between the experimental and control groups are due to the different ways in which the researchers

**placebo effect**
Changes in behavior produced by a condition in a formal experiment thought to be inert or inactive, such as a placebo pill.

**blind experiment**
A formal experiment in which the researcher who measures the dependent variable does not know which participants are in the experimental group or the control group. In double-blind experiments, the participants also do not know if they are in the experimental or the control group.

**experimenter bias**
Subtle but potentially powerful unintentional influences on the dependent variable caused by experimenters' interacting differently with participants in the experimental and control groups.

interacted with the groups (such as small differences in posture or tone of voice) rather than to the independent variable. Because the logic of formal experiments requires that all alternative explanations for differences between the groups on the dependent variables be controlled, it is essential to keep the researchers who measure the dependent variable blind. This generally means that some researchers will assign the participants to the experimental or control group and expose them to the different conditions of the independent variable, whereas other researchers (who are blind) measure the dependent variable.

The strongest formal experiments are said to be *double blind*. This means that both the researchers who measure the dependent variable and the participants themselves do not know who is in the experimental group and who is in the control group. Researchers can keep participants unaware in this way only if the control group is exactly like the experimental group in every way, except for the condition of the independent variable, and if excellent placebo controls are used. In a following section, we will discuss ethical limits on keeping research participants blind to their condition in some kinds of studies.

## Manipulation Checks

The conditions of the independent variable are arranged by the researcher in formal experiments. It is often wise, however, to conduct *manipulation checks* to see if the arrangement of the independent variable has accomplished what the researcher thought it would. For example, it would have been helpful if the researchers who conducted the two formal experiments on exposure to media violence had asked independent judges to rate the films on their level of violent content. If a panel of judges had agreed that the violent films the researchers had selected were actually violent, that would have increased confidence in the findings. It might have been even better to have the films rated by teenagers similar to the participants. Often, manipulation checks reveal that participants do not find the different conditions of the independent variable to be as violent (or scary, depressing, or stressful) as the researchers thought they would.

## Review

Psychology is a science, which means that it uses scientific methods to gather information and test hypotheses. Psychologists acquire new information through systematic observation and follow logical rules of evidence. All of the scientific methods are based on the assumption that behavior is lawful, orderly, and capable of being understood in scientific terms. Each scientific method has advantages and disadvantages and is best suited to answering unique types of questions. The simplest scientific methods are descriptive methods. Information that allows us to describe a psychological phenomenon can be gathered by asking questions about it in surveys, by observing it in natural settings, or by acquiring extensive experience with it in clinical cases. When the scientific question concerns the relationship between two variables, correlational methods are often used. Two variables are measured quantitatively, and the strength of the relationship between the two is noted. Correlational studies are useful, but they do not tell us if one variable causes the other to change. To determine whether cause-and-effect relationships exist, formal experiments must be conducted.

In formal experiments, scientists arrange conditions of the independent variable and rigorously control other aspects of the experiment, so that only one explanation for the results is likely. In the simplest formal experiments, one factor—the independent variable—is artificially manipulated by the experimenter to see what effect it has on another variable—the dependent variable. Often, one group of participants—control group—is not exposed to any level of the independent variable, whereas the independent variable is present in another group—the experimental group. In a study of the effects of alcohol on the memory of a list of words, for example, the alcohol is the independent variable. Alcohol is given to participants in the experimental group and not given to those in the control group, so its effects on the dependent variable, memory of the list, can be determined. In such a study, both groups of participants would need to be given drinks that look, taste, and smell identical, except that one contains alcohol and the other does not, to rule out placebo effects. In the most completely controlled studies, called double-blind studies, neither the participants nor the researchers who measure the dependent variable know which condition of the independent variable each participant receives.

Check Your Learning

To be sure that you have learned the key points from the preceding section, cover the list of correct answers and try to answer each question. If you give an incorrect answer to any question, return to the page given next to the correct answer to see why your answer was not correct.

1. The basis of all scientific methods is systematic _____ and _____ .

2. A study that simply measured the strength of the quantitative relationship between intelligence scores and the number of illegal acts committed by teenagers would use which method?

   a) naturalistic

   b) clinical

   c) correlational

   d) formal experimental

3. The scientific method that allows the researcher to reach the strongest conclusions about cause-and-effect is

   a) naturalistic.

   b) clinical.

   c) correlational.

   d) formal experimental.

4. In a double-blind study, who does not know which condition of the independent variable each participant received?

   a) the researchers who measure the dependent variable

   c) both a and b

   b) the research participants

---

Thinking Critically about Psychology

1. In what ways is research in psychology similar to research in biology, chemistry, or other fields? How is it distinctive?

2. Are there some aspects of human behavior and mental processes that cannot be studied scientifically?

Correct Answers:   1.  observation, rules of evidence (p. 34),    2.  c (p. 38),    3.  d (p. 42),    4.  c (p. 46).

## ● Ethical Principles of Research

Psychological research is conducted to advance knowledge and improve the lives of all living things. It is a noble goal, but not so noble that any method of conducting research would be justifiable. To be considered ethical, research conducted with people and with nonhuman animals must follow the ethical principles described in the next two sections.

### Ethics of Research with Human Participants

Psychology depends heavily on research conducted with human participants for its database. Although researchers have an obligation to collect meaningful information through research, they also have an ethical responsibility to protect the welfare of their participants by judging the study's risks and potential benefits. Often, the ethics of research with humans poses complicated issues for the researcher—issues that do not have simple solutions. As a human being, and especially as one who may be asked to serve as a participant in psychological research, you may wish to review some of the key ethical issues involved in psychological research with humans. A more complete discussion of these issues can be found in the American Psychological Association's *Ethics in Research with Human Participants* (Sales & Folkman, 2000) and the other resources listed at the end of this chapter.

1. ***Freedom from coercion.*** It's not ethical to coerce or pressure an individual into participating in an experiment. Students in college courses, for example, cannot be required to participate. They must be given an alternative way to meet any course requirement. Similarly, it is considered unethical to offer strong special consideration in parole hearings to prisoners who volunteer to participate in psychological studies, because the promise of special considerations might constitute coercion.

2. ***Informed consent.*** The experimenter must, under most circumstances, give potential participants a full description of the procedures of the study and its risks and benefits in language they can understand before they are asked to participate. It's not ethical to allow individuals to participate in an experiment without knowing what they are getting into. Furthermore, once the experiment has begun, it must be made clear to participants that they are fully free to change their minds and withdraw from the experiment without penalty, such as embarrassment or loss of course credit.

3. ***Limited deception.*** Sometimes it's necessary to conduct experiments without the participant's knowing the true purpose of the study. For example, chapter 16 discusses a study in which individuals were asked to make judgments about the relative lengths of three lines after other individuals (actually, employees of the experimenter who were acting out parts in the experiment) had given an obviously wrong answer. The question was, would the real participants give the wrong answer, too, under these conditions? Obviously, it was necessary to deceive the participants into thinking that the other individuals really believed their erroneous judgments about the lines. Is it ethical to deceive participants in this manner? The current guidelines suggest that deceptions can be used only if two conditions are met. First, the potential participants must be told everything they could reasonably be expected to need to know to make an informed decision about participation. That is, the deception can involve only aspects of the study that do not influence the decision to participate. Second, the nature of the deception must be fully revealed to individuals immediately after their participation in the experiment. Only under these conditions is it considered ethical to deceive research participants.

4. ***Adequate debriefing.*** Research participants have a right to know the results of the study. Current practice dictates that all persons be provided with a summary of the study in language they can understand. If the results are not immediately available, the participants have a right to receive them when they are available.

5. ***Confidentiality.*** Researchers have an obligation to keep everything they learn about the research participants absolutely confidential. This means that data from the study must be published in a way that protects the anonymity of the participants (no names or detailed descriptions of individuals). In addition, data must be stored without names attached, in most cases, to protect against future abuses of the information.

These are not all of the ethical issues raised by psychological research with humans, but they are some of the major ones. All institutions where research is conducted now require that proposals for human experimentation be approved by a board of other scientists to protect individuals from potential abuses.

## Ethics of Research with Nonhuman Animals

A great deal of research is also carried out using nonhuman animals as subjects. Why would some psychologists study animals when they could be studying people? Psychologists study animal behavior for a number of important reasons.

Some kinds of studies are conducted using nonhuman animals because it would be unethical to do the research with humans. Studies of the brain, for example, sometimes require surgically removing a part of the brain to discover its precise role in behavior. For similar reasons, studies in which infants are isolated from all social contact to study the absence of parental and peer relationships on development must be conducted with animals rather than humans. Although we must be very careful not to assume automatically that what is learned about animal behavior will apply to human behavior, much useful information has been learned from such animal research.

In addition, it's possible to conduct experiments that are far more precisely controlled if animals rather than humans are used. A researcher can know and control almost every detail of a laboratory animal's life from birth: its environment, diet, and social experiences. This makes it possible to control a multiplicity of factors that must be left uncontrolled when using humans.

A great deal can be learned also by comparing the behavior of animals of different species. For example, a number of insights into human aggression have come from studies of aggression in other animal species. Similarly, much has been learned about the brain structures involved in sleep by identifying animals that have differing sleep patterns and by comparing the evolutionary development of the sleep centers in these different species. Furthermore, many psychologists study animal behavior not to learn about humans but to learn more about other animal species. If we are going to protect endangered species, we must understand their patterns of behavior. We must know, for example, how an endangered species hunts, mates, and raises its young before we can protect its ability to survive.

As with human participants, a number of principles govern the ethical conduct of research with nonhuman animal subjects in psychology. Research with animals is considered ethical by the American Psychological Association only when all of the following conditions are met:

1. **Necessity.** Studies of nonhuman animals are considered to be ethical only when they are necessary to significantly advance the understanding of human or animal behavior and mental processes.

2. **Health.** All animal subjects must be cared for in a manner that ensures good health.

3. **Humane treatment.** Every effort must be made to minimize the discomfort of the animal subject. Necessary surgery must be performed under anesthesia, and the animal's death must be as painless as possible. Studies that inflict pain or stress are considered ethical only when they are considered essential to worthwhile scientific aims.

The use of nonhuman animals in research has received a great deal of public attention in recent years due to the activities of animal rights groups. Humans have long been concerned with the protection of their fellow animals, however. The Society for the Prevention of Cruelty to Animals was founded in 1824 in London, for example, and the American Psychological Association formed its Committee on Precautions in Animal Experimentation in 1925 (Dewsbury, 1990). Today, oversight committees at all research universities closely monitor all uses of laboratory animals.

The use of animals in research has received a great deal of public attention in recent years due to the activities of animal rights groups.

## Review

Although it is very important to conduct psychological research, it is essential that we protect the rights of research participants. Human research participants must not be coerced in any way into participating and must be informed about the nature of the study before they are asked for their consent to participate. Human research participants may be deceived about a study only if (1) the information withheld is not relevant to their decision to participate, and (2) they are informed about the true nature of the study immediately after it's over. Furthermore, the experimenter has an obligation to keep all information learned about human research participants confidential. Research with nonhuman animals is considered to be ethical only when (1) the research is necessary, (2) the health of the animal is protected, and (3) pain and suffering are minimized.

## Check Your Learning

To be sure that you have learned the key points from the preceding section, cover the list of correct answers and try to answer each question. If you give an incorrect answer to any question, return to the page given next to the correct answer to see why your answer was not correct.

1. Research on humans is considered to be ethical only when the following five conditions are met:

   a) _____

   b) _____

   c) _____

   d) _____

   e) _____

2. Research with nonhuman animals is considered to be ethical only when the following three conditions are met:

   a) _____

   b) _____

   c) _____

## Thinking Critically about Psychology

1. Although research on nonhuman animals has produced many findings that are beneficial to humans, not everyone agrees that it should be allowed. How do you think we should balance the welfare of animals against benefits to human society?

2. Are there some aspects of human behavior and mental processes that would not be ethical to study even if the participants freely consented to be studied?

**Correct Answers:** **1.** freedom from coercion, informed consent, limited deception, adequate debriefing, and confidentiality (p. 48). **2.** the research is necessary, the health of the animal is protected, pain and suffering are minimized (p. 49).

# application of psychology

## Design Your Own Formal Experiment

Now that we have gone over the basic principles of scientific research in psychology, it's time for you to be the researcher. I will suggest a research question and you will design a formal experiment to answer that question. To help you along, I will pose a series of questions and you will make decisions. I hope this will be fun and will give you a chance to review what you have just learned in a new context. Because books do not allow for much interaction between the author and the reader, I will have to guide you more than I would like. I hope, however, you will think about each of the questions on your own before you read my suggested answers.

Here is the general topic for your study: For a long time, psychologists have thought that the simple act of telling someone about your private worries, disappointments, and agonies makes you feel better. In general, it often seems to help get negative feelings off your chest, whether you are venting your emotions to a friend, a relative, or a therapist.[1] More recently, psychologists have suspected that expressing your negative emotions can even improve your physical health. So here is the hypothesis for your study: Expressing negative emotions improves a person's physical health over the next 6 months.

## Who Will Be Your Research Participants?

If you were going to conduct a study during the next year, who would be your research participants? In order for the conclusions of a study to be valid, the sample of subjects needs to be representative of some meaningful population of human beings. Because you are a student and have limited financial resources for conducting this study, you are going to have to use introductory psychology students as your partici-

pants. This means that you cannot be certain that your findings apply to anyone other than introductory psychology students at your school. What should you do to ensure the representativeness of your sample? For starters, include approximately equal numbers of women and men and select a sample that is typical in terms of the race and ethnic composition of college students in your college.

## What Is the Independent Variable?

You are designing a study to test the hypothesis that expressing negative emotions improves physical health, so the independent variable is whether or not a person expresses her or his negative emotions. How could you arrange the conditions of this independent variable? Take a moment to imagine how you would do it if you were really designing this formal experiment.

One convenient way would be to ask a group of introductory psychology students to volunteer for the study. Half of them could be asked to express their feelings about the *saddest* thing that ever happened to them—they would be encouraged to get their negative feelings off their chests. This would be the *experimental group* because they receive the active condition of the independent variable. The other half of the participants would be asked to describe the architecture of the buildings at their college. This would be the *control group* because they get none of the active condition of the independent variable—that is, they do not express their negative emotions. In this way, you could independently arrange for some participants to express their negative emotions and for other participants not to express negative emotions (unless the buildings at your college are really ugly). In order to protect everyone's confidentiality, you could ask all of the participants to write a letter to someone they know. In this way, they

could express their emotions (or describe the buildings) in a way that no one else hears. You could tell them that they will be asked to destroy the letters at the end of the session, so that there is no risk that the letters would upset someone who read them or that some of your research participants would reveal some hidden feelings that they later wished they had kept private. The idea is to have half of the participants *express* their negative feelings, even if no one reads the letters. There are stronger ways of arranging this independent variable (you could actually have each person speak to a therapist a number of times), but writing this kind of letter typically leads to some pretty intense expression of emotions.

## What Is the Dependent Variable?

Your study will test the hypothesis that expressing negative emotions improves physical health, so the physical health of the participants is the dependent variable. If you ask the research participants to write the letters during the fall, you could measure their health over the next 6 months. How do you want to measure their physical health?

There are many ways to measure health. If you had a large research grant, you could draw blood samples every month and directly measure a number of aspects of participants' immune systems. Let's assume that you are doing this study on a shoestring budget, however, and just ask all of the participants each month if they have had a cold during the past month. Then your quantitative dependent variable is the number of months in which each participant had a cold. Therefore, you can make your hypothesis more specific: Writing a letter that expresses your emotions about the worst thing that had ever happened to you reduces your number of colds over 6 months relative to persons who wrote a letter on a neutral topic.

*(continued)*

---

[1]Of course, we always have to balance the benefits of expressing our negative feelings against the risks of hurting other people's feelings and alienating ourselves from friends and family members. There is a right time and situation for everything.

## How Do You Decide Which Participants Will Be in the Experimental or Control Groups?

Randomly! Remember that formal experiments lead to valid conclusions only if the participants are *randomly assigned* to the different conditions of the independent variable. If you were to ask the students sitting in the front half of the classroom to express their negative emotions and the students sitting in the back half of the classroom to write neutral letters, these two groups of students might differ in a systematic way. It is possible that students with better health tend to sit in the front (or the back). If so, this would invalidate your experiment because the health of the participants in the experimental and control groups would differ prior to the start of the study. Therefore, you will need to do something like assigning an identification number to every participant and then using a computer to randomly assign each identification number to one of the two groups.

## What Kinds of Experimental Control Should You Use?

So far you have designed a formal experiment in which the participants will be randomly assigned to the conditions of the independent variable, and you have treated them in the same way, except for the conditions of the independent variable. Both groups of participants will write a letter, and both groups will be asked about their colds monthly for 6 months. The only way in which your procedures are different for the two groups is that one group will write letters that will evoke negative emotions and the other group will write letters that should contain much less negative emotion. To be certain that the groups are treated in the same way, what else should you think about controlling to rule out alternative explanations? Consider that question for a moment.

Because you will ask the participants in the two groups to write letters about different topics, you cannot keep them all in one room and state the instructions out loud. If you separate the groups and have them write their letters in different rooms, what should you control? Would it be okay to have a female give the instructions about the negative emotions letter to the participants in one room while a male gives the instructions for the architecture let-

ter in another room? Is it okay to have one group in a cheerful, well-lighted room and the other group in a cold, messy, dim room? If you treat the participants in the two groups differently in any way, you will not be able to conclude that any differences in the dependent variable are due to the independent variable or the other factors. Maybe the participants who wrote their letters in the cold, messy room caught colds while they were there!

So is that everything? Have you ruled out all possible alternative explanations for differences between the experimental and control groups on the dependent variable?

## Can You Make Your Study Double Blind?

Recall what it means for a study to be double blind. In a double-blind experiment, neither the participants nor the researchers who measure the dependent variable know which participants received which condition of the independent variable. This is the same as saying that they do not know who was in the experimental or the control groups. It would be an easy matter to keep the researchers who measure the dependent variable (ask the questions about having colds, in this case) unaware of which participants were in the experimental and control groups. It is not clear that you could keep the participants completely unaware of who was in the experimental and control groups. You would not tell them, of course, what your hypothesis was, but each participant would know if he or she wrote a letter about negative feelings or not. When you obtained informed consent from the participants who volunteered for the study, you would have needed to tell them that you were studying the relationship between "communicating with others through letters and physical health." So that they would know exactly what they were consenting to participate in, you would have had to tell them that they would be asked to write a letter either about the worst thing that happened to them or about their college's architecture and that they would be asked every month for 6 months if they had had a cold. Therefore, it is likely that some of the participants would guess the hypothesis. Although most people would probably be skeptical about *either* kind of letter writing's actually influencing

their health, very few participants would think that jotting off a note to Dad about the Greek revival columns on the Social Sciences building would have much impact on their health.

Why is it a problem that some of the participants might guess your hypothesis? If the experimental group that wrote letters about negative emotions reported fewer colds over the next 6 months, that might be because getting negative emotions off their chests changed their immune systems in a beneficial way and that reduced their colds. On the other hand, the participants who guessed your hypothesis might intentionally or unintentionally tell you about fewer colds because they think that is what you want to hear. Alternatively, they might think your hypothesis is correct and intentionally or unintentionally remember fewer colds because they expect to be healthier.

How could you deal with these big problems of experimental control? This is the type of issue faced by research psychologists on a daily basis. It is tough to control for every alternative explanation in every experiment. You may decide that this is just a preliminary study to see if writing the different kinds of letters is associated with differences in numbers of colds. If it is, then someone else could design a stronger experiment to figure out exactly why the two groups differed in their rates of colds. But how could you make the study stronger if you wanted to rule out some of these alternative explanations yourself?

There is not a single correct way to design this experiment, but one possibility is to add a third group. It is perfectly okay to have more than one control group to rule out other explanations. For example, your hypothesis is that expression of *negative* emotions improves health. Therefore, you could add an additional control group whose members write a letter about the *happiest* thing that ever happened to them. This could make it less likely that participants would guess your hypothesis. Although most participants would guess that you did not think that writing about college architecture would improve health, they probably would not know if you had hypothesized that expressing negative emotions or positive emotions would improve health. If your hypothesis were correct, then the experimental group that wrote about negative emotions would report fewer colds over the

# Biological Foundations of Behavior

## PROLOGUE

Psychological life depends on biological life for its very existence. This means that the way we behave is influenced to a great extent by the nature of the body. If humans did not have hands that grasp, we might never have learned to write, paint, or play racquetball. If we did not have eyes that could see color, we would see a world that existed only in shades of black and white.

The brain is the part of the body that is most intimately linked to psychological life. A simple experiment conducted by Canadian brain surgeon Wilder Penfield in the 1930s dramatically illustrates the key role played by the brain. Dr. Penfield was conducting surgery on the surface layer of the brain known as the cerebral cortex while the patient was awake during local anesthesia. When Penfield placed a small rod that carried a mild electric current against the brain, there were astonishing results. The patient began to recall in vivid detail an incident from years before. She was in her kitchen, listening to the voice of her little boy playing in the yard. In the background, she could hear the noises of the neighborhood, the cars passing in the street. Penfield was amazed to discover that stimulation of particular spots on the brain could produce experiences of sights and sounds. Another patient recalled a small-town baseball game that included a boy trying to crawl under a fence. Another woman recalled a melody each time a certain point on the cortex was stimulated. The lesson of Penfield's experiments is clear—the brain and our psychological lives are intimately connected.

This chapter is about topics that you would expect to find in a biology course, but it was written to help you understand psychology better. We will discuss only those aspects of human biology that are directly relevant to understanding behavior: the brain and nervous system, endocrine glands, and genetic mechanisms. Without these biological systems, psychological life could not exist.

When we look at ourselves in this way, we see that we are psychological beings living in biological "machines." Just as electronic machines are built from wires, transistors, and other components, the nervous system is built from specialized cells called neurons. Billions of neurons in your nervous system transmit messages to one another in complex ways that make the nervous system both the computer and communication network of the body. The biological control center of the nervous system is the brain. It has many parts that carry out different functions, but the many parts of the brain operate together in an integrated way.

The nervous system can be thought of as consisting of two large parts. One part consists of the brain and the bundle of nerves that run through the spinal column. Because it is located within the skull and spine, this part is called the central nervous system. The many nerves that lie outside of the skull and spine comprise the second part of the nervous system. Because it reaches the periphery of the body, this part is called the peripheral nervous system.

The brain communicates with the body through an intricate network of neurons that fan out to every part of the body. But the brain also uses the endocrine glands to communicate with the body. These glands secrete chemical messengers, called hormones, that travel to the body through the bloodstream. Hormones

## KEY TERMS

brain 58
neuron 58
dendrites 59
axons 59
nerve 59
myelin sheath 61
synapse 62
neurotransmitters 62
neuropeptides 64
central nervous system 65
peripheral nervous system 65
afferent neurons 65
efferent neurons 65
interneuron 65
somatic nervous system 66
autonomic nervous system 67
sympathetic nervous system 67
parasympathetic nervous system 69
hindbrain 72
medulla 72
pons 72
cerebellum 72
midbrain 72
forebrain 72
thalamus 74
hypothalamus 74
limbic system 74
cerebral cortex 74
frontal lobes 76
parietal lobes 78
temporal lobes 78
occipital lobes 79
endocrine system 86
hormones 86
pituitary gland 87
adrenal glands 88
islets of Langerhans 88
gonads 88
thyroid gland 89
parathyroid glands 89
pineal gland 89
chromosomes 91
genes 92

regulate the functions of many parts of the body and influence our behavior and experience. Hormones are powerful tools of the brain, but they influence us in diffuse rather than precise ways.

The fact that the nature of the nervous and endocrine systems influences our psychological functioning means that heredity can influence our behavior by shaping our nervous and endocrine systems. Heredity operates through genes in the nucleus of the body's cells. These genes contain codes that allow heredity to influence the development of our bodies. We do not inherit specific behaviors in the same way that we inherit eye color, though. Instead, the genes influence the development of the brain, endocrine glands, and other body structures in ways that influence our behavior in very *broad* ways. For example, we do not inherit the ability to read, but it appears that heredity is one of the factors that influences how quickly a child learns to read. This is because heredity seems to be one of the factors that determines our intelligence. Similarly, it appears that heredity influences broad aspects of personality. ■

## ● Nervous System: Biological Control Center

The nervous system is both a powerful computer and a complex communication network. But unlike any computer, the complex mass of nerve cells called the **brain** not only thinks and calculates but also feels and controls motivation. The brain is connected to a thick bundle of long nerves running through the spine, called the **spinal cord.** Individual nerves exit or enter the spinal cord and brain, linking every part of the body to the brain. Some of these nerves carry messages from the body to the brain to keep the brain informed about what is going on in the body. Other nerves carry messages from the brain to the body to regulate the body's functions and the person's behavior. Without the nervous system, the body would be no more than a mass of uncoordinated parts that could not act, reason, or experience emotions. In other words, without a nervous system, there would be no psychological life.

### Neurons: The Units of the Nervous System

Computers, telephone systems, and other electronic systems are made of individual wires, transistors, microchips, and other components that transmit and regulate electricity. These components are arranged in complex patterns to create functioning systems. The nervous system is similarly made up of components. The most important unit of the nervous system is the individual nerve cell, or **neuron.** We will begin our discussion of the nervous system with the neuron and then progress to a discussion of the larger parts of the nervous system. As we discuss the neuron in technical, biological terms, try not to forget its importance to consciousness and behavior.

In the early 1900s, Santiago Ramón y Cajal, the scientist who first discovered neurons, described them as "the mysterious butterflies of the soul, the beating of whose wings may someday—who knows?—clarify the secret of mental life." Since his time, much has been learned about these building blocks of the brain. Much remains to be learned about neurons, but some current research is so advanced that it sounds more like science fiction than reality. For example, Masuo Aizawa (1994) has used specially treated living nerve cells outside of the body to construct a simple "living computer" that processes information much like the nervous system does. In time, research like Aizawa's may lead to the ability to repair damaged nerves, like those of actor Christopher Reeve, who was paralyzed by a fall from a horse.

#### Parts of Neurons

Neurons range in length from less than a millimeter to more than a meter in length, yet all neurons are made up of essentially the same parts (see fig. 3.1). The **cell body** is the

**brain**
The complex mass of neural cells and related cells encased in the skull.

**spinal cord**
The nerve fibers in the spinal column.

**neuron**
(nu´ron) An individual nerve cell.

**cell body**
The central part of the neuron that includes the nucleus.

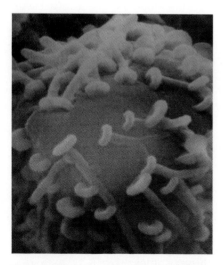

The knoblike tips of the axons transmit messages to the next nerve cell.

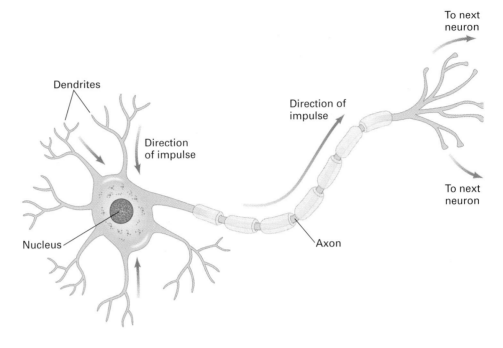

Dendrites

Direction
of impulse

Nucleus

Direction of
impulse

Axon

To next
neuron

To next
neuron

**FIGURE 3.1**
Neurons are typically composed of a cell
body, which contains the nucleus of the
cell, dendrites that typically receive
impulses from other neurons, and an
axon that passes the neural impulse on
to the next neuron.

central part of the nerve cell. It contains the cell's control center, or *nucleus*, and other components of the cell necessary for the cell's preservation and nourishment. **Dendrites** are small branches that extend out from the cell body and receive messages from other neurons. Other parts of the neuron play a role in receiving messages from other neurons, but the dendrite is the specialized part of the neuron that plays the greatest role in receiving neural messages.

The **axons** are small branches at the other end of the neuron that perform a function opposite that of the dendrites. They carry messages away from the cell body and transmit these messages to the next neuron. (It's easy to remember the difference between the functions of the dendrites and axons by remembering that the axon "acts on" the next cell.) The message transmitted along the axon may be picked up by the dendrites of one or more other neurons. Neurons, then, have a cell body, dendrites, and an axon. The shape and size of these parts can vary greatly, depending on what function the neuron serves.

Neurons are grouped in complex networks that make the largest computer seem like a child's toy. The nervous system is composed of 100 billion neurons (Kandel, Schwartz, & Jessel, 1995), about as many as the number of stars in our galaxy. Each neuron can receive messages from or transmit messages to 1,000 to 10,000 other neural cells. All told, your body contains trillions of neural connections, most of them in the brain. These numbers are not important in their own right, but they may help us understand the incredibly rich network of neural interconnections that makes us humans. Incidentally, be careful not to confuse the term *neuron* with the term **nerve;** they are not synonyms. A nerve is a bundle of many long neurons—sometimes thousands of them— outside the brain and spinal cord.

As described in the next two sections, neurons transmit messages in the nervous system in two steps: the transmission of the message from one end of the neuron to the other end (neural transmission) and transmission from one neuron to the next neuron (synaptic transmission).

**dendrites**
(den′ drīts) Extensions of the cell body that usually serve as receiving areas for messages from other neurons.

**axons**
(ak′sonz) Neuron branches that transmit messages to other neurons.

**nerve**
A bundle of long neurons outside the brain and spinal cord.

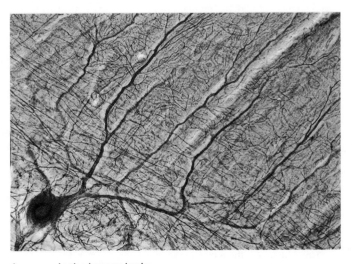

A neuron in the human brain.

**ions**
(i´ons) Electrically charged particles.

**cell membrane**
The covering of a neuron or another cell.

**semipermeable**
(sem´´ē-per´-mē-ah-b´l) A surface that allows some, but not all, particles to pass through.

**polarized**
(pō´lar-īz´d) The resting state of a neuron, when more negative ions are inside and more positive ions are outside the cell membrane.

### Neural Transmission

Neurons are the "wires" of the nervous system—messages are transmitted over the neuron much like your voice is transmitted over a telephone line. But neurons are living wires, with their own built-in supplies of electrical power—they are the "batteries" of the nervous system, too.

Neurons can take on the functions of wires and batteries because, like all living cells, they are wet. Neurons are sacs filled with one type of fluid on the inside and bathed in a different type of fluid on the outside. This is an important fact. Both types of fluid are thick "soups" of dissolved chemicals, including **ions,** which are particles that carry either a positive or negative electrical charge. More of the ions inside neurons are negatively rather than positively charged, making the overall charge of the cell a negative one. This negative charge attracts positively charged ions, just as the negative pole of a magnet attracts the positive pole of another magnet. Thus, the outside of the cell membrane becomes cloaked in positive ions, particularly sodium (Na+). In the resting state, there are 10 times as many positively charged sodium ions outside the membrane of the neuron than inside. This is the source of the neuron's electrical energy—it is electrically positive on one side of the membrane and negative on the other.

If you have trouble remembering which side of the membrane has most of the positive sodium ions, keep in mind that there is a lot of sodium in salty seawater. The fluid on the *outside* of neurons is almost identical to seawater in its chemical contents, including the high amounts of sodium. Why is this so? According to the theory of evolution, as animals evolved and moved from the oceans onto the land, they brought seawater with them *in their bodies*. This seawater-like liquid fills the space between the body's cells. Therefore, it makes sense that the fluid bathing the neural cells is rich in sodium ions.

Many ions are able to move freely through the **cell membrane** of the neuron, but other ions cannot, including the sodium ions. For this reason, the membrane is said to be **semipermeable**—only some chemicals can permeate, or pass through, "holes" in the membrane. When the neuron is in its normal resting state, the membrane is semipermeable and does not let positive sodium ions into the cell. Therefore, a balance exists between the mostly negative ions on the inside and the mostly positive ions on the outside. In this condition, the neuron is said to be electrically **polarized** (see fig. 3.2).

**FIGURE 3.2**
Short sections of an axon illustrating neural transmission (an action potential). (a) When an axon is in its resting state, there is a balance between the number of positively and negatively charged ions along the membrane. (b) When the axon is sufficiently stimulated, the membrane allows positively charged sodium ions to pass into the cell, depolarizing that spot on the membrane. (c) This depolarization disturbs the adjacent section of the membrane, allowing sodium ions to flow in again while sodium ions are being pumped back out of the first section. (d) This process continues as the swirling storm of depolarization continues to the end of the axon.

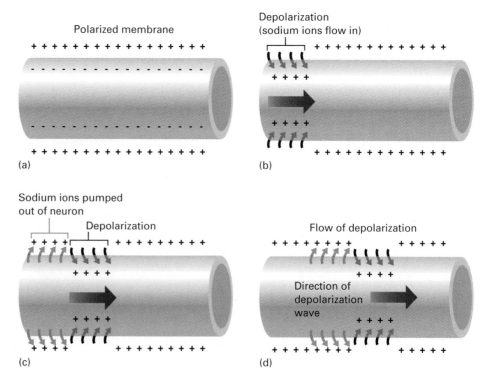

When the membrane is stimulated by an adjacent neuron, however, the semipermeability of the membrane is changed. Positively charged ions, including the important sodium ions, are then allowed to enter the neuron, making the inside less negative. This process is called **depolarization.**

Neural transmission operates according to the **all-or-none principle.** This means that a small amount of depolarization will not affect the neuron. A larger depolarization, however, will trigger a dramatic chain of events known as the **action potential.** It is the action potential that transmits the neural message. The depolarization must be strong enough to trigger an action potential, but the strength of the action potential does not depend on the strength of the depolarization. They are all the same once they get started. In a sense, then, our nervous systems are more like digital electronic systems (that transmit either 1s or 0s) than analog systems (that transmit signals of different strengths). If the depolarization is strong enough to fire the neuron, it is a "1." If not, no transmission occurs at all (it is a "0").

During an action potential, a small section of the axon adjacent to the cell body becomes more permeable to the positive sodium ions. The sodium ions rush in, producing a dramatic depolarization in that part of the axon. Very quickly, however, the membrane regains its semipermeability and "pumps" the positive sodium ions back out, reestablishing the neuron's polarization. This tiny electrical storm of sodium ions flowing in and out of the neuron—which lasts approximately one-thousandth of a second—does not stop there, however. It disturbs the adjacent section of the membrane of the axon, so that it depolarizes, which in turn disturbs the next section of the membrane, and so on. Thus, the action potential—the flowing storm of ions rushing in and out—travels the length of the axon. Local anesthetics, such as the Novocain that your dentist injects, stop pain by chemically interrupting this flowing process of depolarization in the axons of nerves that carry pain messages to the brain.

Many axons are encased in a white, fatty coating called the **myelin sheath.** This sheath, which is wrapped around the axon like the layers of a jelly roll, insulates the axon and greatly increases the speed at which the axon conducts neural impulses (see fig. 3.3).

The myelin sheath continues to grow in thickness into late adulthood. Interestingly, from early childhood to late adulthood, the average thickness of myelin is greater in females than males in some areas of the brain (Benes, 1998). This may indicate more efficient neural processing of some kinds of information by females. Sadly, the importance of the myelin sheath in neural transmission can be seen in victims of multiple sclerosis. This disease destroys the myelin sheath of many neurons, leaving them unable to

**depolarization**
The process during which positively charged ions flow into the axon, making it less negatively charged inside.

**all-or-none principle**
The law that states that once a neural action potential is produced, its magnitude is always the same.

**action potential**
A brief electrical signal that travels the length of the axon.

**myelin sheath**
(mī´ e-lin) The insulating fatty covering wrapped around the axon that speeds the transmission of neural messages.

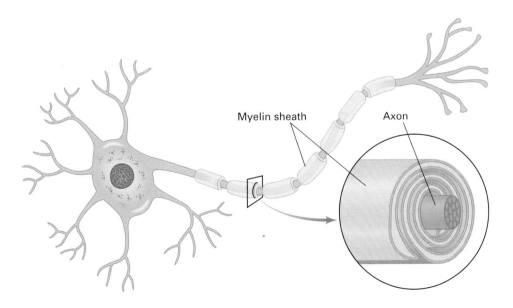

Myelin sheath            Axon

**FIGURE 3.3**
Many neurons are wrapped like a jelly roll in a white, fatty substance called myelin. The myelin sheath insulates the axon and speeds neural transmission.

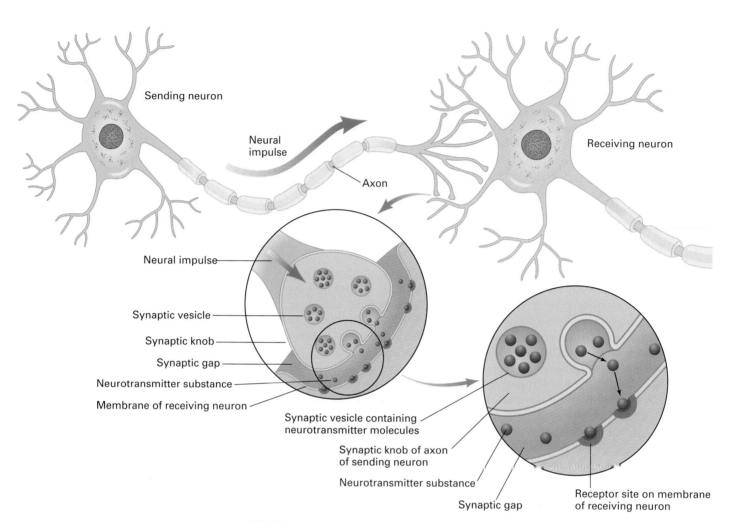

Sending neuron

Neural impulse

Axon

Receiving neuron

Neural impulse

Synaptic vesicle

Synaptic knob

Synaptic gap

Neurotransmitter substance

Membrane of receiving neuron

Synaptic vesicle containing
neurotransmitter molecules

Synaptic knob of axon
of sending neuron

Neurotransmitter substance

Synaptic gap

Receptor site on membrane
of receiving neuron

**FIGURE 3.4**

Neural messages are transmitted chemically from the axon of the sending neuron to the receiving neuron. The neurotransmitter substance contained in the synaptic vesicles is secreted across the synaptic gap. The neurotransmitter is able to stimulate the receiving neuron because its chemical "shape" matches that of receptor sites on the receiving neuron.

operate at normal efficiency. As a result, individuals with multiple sclerosis have severe difficulties controlling their muscles; experience fatigue, dizziness, and pain; and suffer serious vision problems (Morell & Norton, 1980).

**Neurotransmitters and Synaptic Transmission**

Neurons are linked together in complex chains, but they are not directly connected to each other. The junction between one neuron and another is called the **synapse.** The small space between two neurons is known as the **synaptic gap.** The electrical action potential cannot jump across this gap, however. Instead, the neural message is carried across the gap by chemical substances called **neurotransmitters.** The capacity of the brain to process information is multiplied many times by the fact that not all neurotransmitters are *excitatory.* Some axons transmit *inhibitory* substances across synapses, which makes it more difficult for the next neuron to fire. Thus, the brain is composed of a staggering network of "yes" and "no" circuits that process and create our experiences (Kandel & others, 1995).

Most neurotransmitters are stored in tiny packets called **synaptic vesicles** located in the knoblike ends of the axons—called **synaptic knobs.** When an action potential reaches the axon knob, it stimulates the vesicles to release the neurotransmitter into the

**synapse**
(sin-aps´) The space between the axon of one neuron and another neuron.

**synaptic gap**
The small space between two neurons at a synapse.

**neurotransmitters**
(nu´´rō-tranz´-mit-erz) Chemical substances, produced by axons, that transmit messages across the synapse.

**synaptic vesicles**
Tiny vessels containing stored quantities of the neurotransmitter substance held in the synaptic knobs of the axon.

**synaptic knobs**
(si-nap´tik) The knoblike tips of axons.

gap. The neurotransmitter floats across the gap and "fits" into **receptor sites** on the adjacent neuron's membrane like keys fitting into locks. This changes the polarity of the receiving neuron, which either causes an action potential that continues the neural message on its way (see fig. 3.4) or inhibits the receiving neuron from firing.

Many different neurotransmitter substances operate in different parts of the brain, carrying out different functions—probably as many as 50 different neurotransmitters (Kandel & others, 1995). Because of this fact, the process of synaptic transmission in a particular portion of the brain can be altered through the use of drugs that chemically alter the function of one of these neurotransmitters. Thus, emerging knowledge about neurotransmitters has made possible the use of psychiatric drugs to help control anxiety, depression, and other psychological problems. These drugs operate by increasing or decreasing the effectiveness of a specific neurotransmitter. Most drugs that have psychological effects influence neural transmission at the synapse. Some drugs have a chemical structure that is similar enough to a neurotransmitter to fit the receptor sites on the receiving neuron and cause an action potential. Other drugs are similar in chemical structure to a neurotransmitter, but they block the receptor site and reduce the likelihood of neural transmission. Still another class of drugs reduces the amount of neurotransmitter that is reabsorbed by the axon, keeping it active in the synapse longer and increasing the likelihood of neural transmission. The drug Prozac, which is widely used for depression, operates by reducing the reabsorption of a neurotransmitter. (See table 3.1.)

**receptor sites**
Sites on the neuron that receive the neurotransmitter substance.

**acetylcholine**
(a″suh-teel′ koh″leen) A neurotransmitter used by somatic neurons that contract the body's large muscles. Acetylcholine also plays a role in memory and is thought to help regulate dreaming.

**dopamine**
(do″pah′meen) A neurotransmitter substance used by neurons in the brain that control large muscle movements and by neurons in pleasure and reward systems in the brain.

**serotonin**
(ser′uh-to″nin) A neurotransmitter used by systems of neurons believed to regulate sleep, dreaming, appetite, anxiety, depression, and the inhibition of violence.

---

### TABLE 3.1 Selected Neurotransmitters

The neurons of the brain and nervous system use a large number of different neurotransmitters to intricately manage its complex functions. Each year, new neurotransmitters are discovered and more is learned about their biological and psychological functions. A few of the many neurotransmitters are described here to provide examples of their diversity and to lay a foundation for more detailed discussions in later chapters (Cooper, Blum, & Roth, 1996).

*Acetylcholine*

**Acetylcholine** is used by the somatic neurons that contract the body's large muscles. Some poisonous snakes and spiders secrete venoms that disrupt the action of acetylcholine in the synapse, suffocating their prey by interfering with the muscular control of breathing. Similarly, some native peoples of South America put *curare* on the tips of blowgun darts to paralyze animals by blocking the action of acetylcholine. Acetylcholine also plays a role in regulating wakefulness in the brain, is one of the neurotransmitters believed to play a role in dreaming, and plays a role in memory.

*Dopamine*

One large group of neurons in the brain that uses **dopamine** as the neurotransmitter is involved in the control of large muscle movements. Persons with Parkinson's disease experience uncontrollable muscle tremors and other movement problems because of the depletion of dopamine in these neural circuits. A second group of dopamine neurons appears to play a central role in pleasure and reward systems in the brain and may be involved in the mental disorders of schizophrenia and attention-deficit hyperactivity disorder. This second group of neurons appears to be stimulated by cocaine and other drugs of abuse.

*Serotonin*

**Serotonin** plays an important role in a number of seemingly unrelated psychological processes. Serotonin is one of the brain neurotransmitters that is believed to regulate sleep cycles and dreaming, appetite, anxiety, depression, and the inhibition of violence. The widely discussed drug Prozac increases the action of serotonin by keeping it active in the synapse longer.

*(continued on page 64)*

**norepinephrine**
(nor´ep-i-nef´rin) A neurotransmitter believed to be involved in vigilance and attention and released by sympathetic autonomic neurons and the adrenal glands.

**glutamate**
(gloo-tuh-māt) The most widespread excitatory neurotransmitter in the brain.

**neuropeptides**
(nur-o-pep-tidz) A large group of neurotransmitters sometimes referred to as neuromodulators, as they appear to broadly influence the action of the other neurotransmitters.

| Table 3.1 continued |
| --- |

### Norepinephrine

Systems of neurons in the brain that use **norepinephrine** (also known as *noradrenaline*) as the neurotransmitter are believed to play a role in vigilance and attention to important events, such as the presence of rewards or dangers in the environment. It is also thought to be one of the neurotransmitters involved in anxiety and depression. Norepinephrine is also the neurotransmitter in many neurons of the sympathetic division of the autonomic nervous system and plays the role of a hormone when it is released by the adrenal glands.

### Glutamate

**Glutamate** is the major excitatory neurotransmitter in the central nervous system, with virtually every neuron in the brain containing glutamate receptors. Glutamate is thought to play a key role in the regulation of cognition and emotion (and their serious dysfunction in schizophrenia) and is believed to play a key role in the development and shaping of the neural structure of the brain over the life span.

### Neuropeptides

The **neuropeptides** are a broad class of neurotransmitters that differ considerably in chemical composition from other transmitters. They often are secreted by the same neurons that secrete other neurotransmitters. Neuropeptides are sometimes referred to as neuromodulators, because they influence the action of the other neurotransmitters released by their neuron in broad ways. For example, some neurons that release acetylcholine into their synapses also release one or more neuropeptides. When the neuropeptide is released, it can increase or decrease the normal effects of the acetylcholine. Neuropeptides have longer-lasting effects than other neurotransmitters, are released through parts of the neuron other than the axon in many instances, and diffusely affect other nearby neurons. As will be discussed later in this chapter, some neuropeptides are also secreted by some endocrine glands.

## Review

The nervous system is a highly effective living computer and communication system built of neurons. These specialized cells transmit neural messages from their dendrites to their axons in a flowing swirl of electrically charged molecules produced by the changing semipermeability of their membranes. When the neural message reaches the tip of the axon, it is transmitted across the synaptic gap to the next neuron by a neurotransmitter substance. Many of the longer neurons are wrapped in an insulating layer called the myelin sheath, which increases the speed of transmission of neural messages.

## Check Your Learning

To be sure that you have learned the key points from the preceding section, cover the list of correct answers and try to answer each question. If you give an incorrect answer to any question, return to the page given next to the correct answer to see why your answer was not correct. Remember that these questions cover only some of the important information in this section; it is important that you make up your own questions to check your learning of other facts and concepts.

1. The part of the neuron that most often receives messages from other neurons is called the

   a) axon.                    c) dendrite.
   b) cell body.               d) myelin sheath.

2. The part of the neuron that transmits the neural message to the next neuron by releasing a neurotransmitter across the synaptic gap is called the

   a)  axon.                    c)  dendrite.

   b)  cell body.               d)  myelin sheath.

3. During the process of conducting an action potential down the length of the neuron's membrane, the balance of positive ions on the outside of the neuron and negative ions on the inside is disturbed for a moment (called "depolarization") when the _____ are allowed to rush into the neuron through the semipermeable membrane of the cell.

   a)  sodium ions              c)  LSD

   b)  neurotransmitters        d)  negative ions

4. The fatty covering of some long neurons that insulates them and allows them to carry messages more rapidly is called the _____.

---

1. The neurons in the nervous system are not directly connected to one another, and messages must be transmitted across the synaptic gap using neurotransmitters. How would we be different if the neurons were simply connected like wires?

2. Some drugs that affect the nervous system are thought of as useful medications, whereas others are illegal because they are thought to be harmful. Why do such drugs have the potential to harm or help?

**Thinking Critically about Psychology**

Correct Answers:  1. c (p. 59),  2. a (p. 59),  3. a (p. 60),  4. myelin sheath (p. 61).

---

## ● Divisions of the Nervous System

Our complex nervous systems have many different parts, or divisions. The major divisions of the nervous system are the central nervous system and the peripheral nervous system. The **central nervous system** consists of the brain and the spinal cord. The **peripheral nervous system** is composed of the nerves that branch from the brain and the spinal cord to all parts of the body (see fig. 3.5). Nerves of the peripheral nervous system transmit messages from the body to the central nervous system. They also transmit messages from the central nervous system to the muscles, glands, and organs that put the messages into action.

Messages can travel across the synapse in only one direction. So messages coming from the body into the central nervous system are carried by one set of neurons, the **afferent neurons.** Messages going out from the central nervous system to the organs and muscles are carried by another set, the **efferent neurons.**

The spinal cord's primary function is to relay messages between the brain and the body, but it also does some rudimentary processing of information on its own. A simple reflex, such as the reflexive withdrawal from a hot object, is a good example. The impulse caused by the hot object travels up an afferent nerve to the spinal cord. Here a neuron, called an **interneuron,** transmits the message to an efferent neuron that, in turn, stimulates the muscles of the limb to contract (see fig. 3.6). Any behavior more complicated than a simple reflex, however, usually requires processing within the mass of interneurons that makes up the brain.

**central nervous system**
The brain and the spinal cord.

**peripheral nervous system**
(pĕ-rif′ er-al) The network of nerves that branches from the brain and spinal cord to all parts of the body.

**afferent neurons**
(af′er-ent) Neurons that transmit messages from sense organs to the central nervous system.

**efferent neurons**
(ef′er-ent) Neurons that transmit messages from the central nervous system to organs and muscles.

**interneuron**
Neurons in the central nervous system that connect other neurons.

**FIGURE 3.5**
Organization of the human nervous
system.

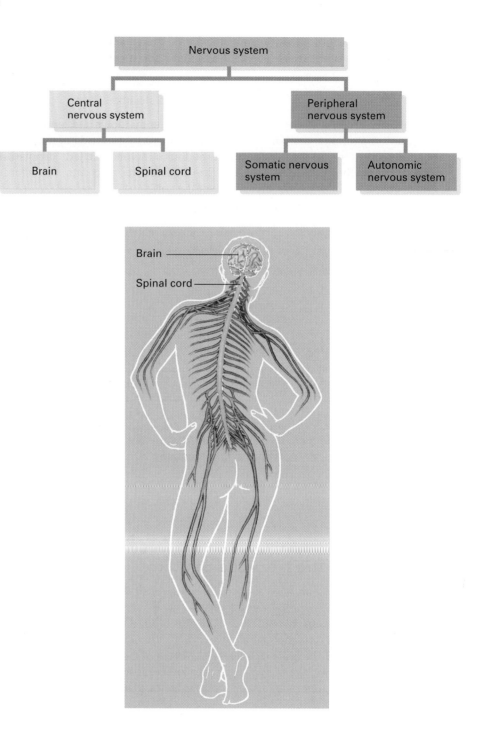

### Divisions of the Peripheral Nervous System

The peripheral nervous system is further divided into the somatic and autonomic nervous systems. The **somatic nervous system** carries messages from the central nervous system to the skeletal muscles that control movements of the body. These include voluntary movements, as when I type the words on a manuscript page, and involuntary movements, as when my eyes maintain fixation on the screen of my word processor in spite of small but frequent changes in the position of my head as I type. The somatic nervous system also receives incoming messages from the sense organs, muscles, joints, and skin and transmits them to the central nervous system.

**somatic nervous system**
(sō-mat′ik) The division of the peripheral nervous system that carries messages from the sense organs to the central nervous system and from the central nervous system to the skeletal muscles.

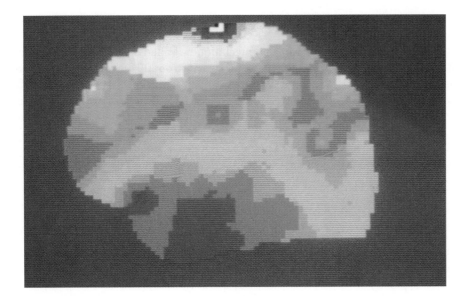

**FIGURE 3.8**
Image of the brain at work created by a computer from electrical recordings (EEG) of the activity of the brain. The image shows the activation of areas of the cerebral cortex of Dr. Monte Buchsbaum immediately after he administered a mild electric shock to his own arm.

imaging techniques is as important to the development of psychology and medicine's understanding of the brain as the invention of the telescope was to astronomy.

A traditional method of studying the brain's activity is the **electroencephalogram, or EEG.** Electrodes are placed on the surface of the person's scalp, and electrical activity from the brain is recorded. The EEG is commonly used to study the sleep cycle and to diagnose medical conditions, such as seizure disorder. One brain-imaging technique converts EEG recordings into computer-generated "maps" of brain activity. The head is covered with closely spaced electrodes to record brain activity. The computer converts these recordings into color images of the brain. The image in figure 3.8 shows the pattern of activity in the brain of psychiatric researcher Monte Buchsbaum moments after he administered a mild electrical shock to his own arm. The area of greatest neural activity (red and orange) is at the top of the brain. We will see later in this section that this is the area of the brain that receives skin sensations (Buchsbaum, 1983).

A different kind of image is shown in figure 3.9. These images were created by computer interpretation of the activity of the brain obtained by **positron emission tomography,** or **PET** scanning. We see reduced activity in the outer portions of the brain beginning in image H and moving through image K as the powerful drug morphine (related to heroin) takes effect (London & others, 1990). In many similar experiments,

**electroencephalogram (EEG)**
(e-lek″trō-en-sef′ah-lo-gram)  A recording of the electrical activity of the brain obtained through electrodes placed on the scalp.

**positron emission tomography (PET)**
An imaging technique that reveals the functions of the brain.

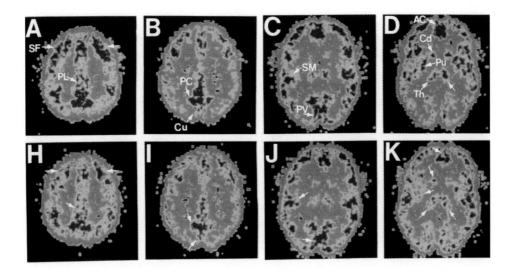

**FIGURE 3.9**
Color-coded PET scans showing rates of glucose use, a measure of brain activity, in a human volunteer who received placebo (A–D) and then morphine, a drug related to heroin (H–K). These images are displayed in sequence from upper to lower levels of the brain (left to right). The lower images (H–K) show a reduction in brain activity in key areas when the subject received the drug.

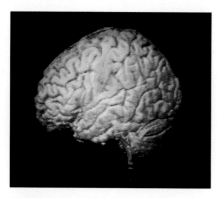

**FIGURE 3.10**
Three-dimensional image of the living brain based on computer-enhanced MRI.

**magnetic resonance imaging (MRI)**
An imaging technique using magnetic resonance to obtain detailed views of the brain structure and function.

**functional MRI**
A type of MRI that measures the activity of parts of the brain by measuring the use of oxygen by groups of neurons.

**hindbrain**
The lowest part of the brain, located at the base of the skull.

**medulla**
(mĕ-dul′ah) The swelling just above the spinal cord within the hindbrain responsible for controlling breathing and a variety of reflexes.

**pons**
(ponz) The part of the hindbrain that is involved in balance, hearing, and some parasympathetic functions.

**cerebellum**
(ser″e-bel′um) Two rounded structures behind the pons involved in the coordination of muscle movements, learning, and memory.

**reticular formation**
(reh-tik′u-lur′) Sets of neurons that project from the medulla and pons downward into the spinal cord to play a role in maintaining muscle tone and cardiac reflexes and upward throughout the cerebral cortex where they influence wakefulness, arousal level, and attention.

**midbrain**
The small area at the top of the hindbrain that serves primarily as a reflex center for orienting the eyes and ears.

**forebrain**
The parts of the brain, including the thalamus, hypothalamus, and cerebral cortex, that cover the hindbrain and midbrain and fill much of the skull.

the PET scan has given brain researchers extraordinary "photographs" of the living brain at work.

Perhaps the most amazing imaging technique is called **magnetic resonance imaging,** or **MRI.** This technique detects magnetic activity from the nuclei of atoms in living cells and creates visual images of the anatomy of the brain. Figure 3.10 shows an MRI of a living brain. Notice the amazingly accurate picture of the anatomy of the brain provided by MRI. More recently, a type of MRI has been developed that allows researchers not only to image the anatomy of the brain but also to measure the *activity* of specific parts of the brain. **Functional MRI** measures changes in the use of oxygen by neurons that reflect their levels of activity. This technique is safer than PET because it does not involve exposure to radiation.

## Hindbrain and Midbrain: Housekeeping Chores and Reflexes

All mental functions require the integrated functioning of many parts of the brain; no function of the brain is carried out solely in one part. Still, the brain does have many specialized parts, each bearing primary responsibility for certain activities. The brain's many and complex structures can be classified in various ways. The most convenient classification divides the brain into three major parts: the hindbrain, the midbrain, and the forebrain. The major structures and functions of each part are described on the following pages. As we look at the brain, we will start at the bottom and work our way up.

The **hindbrain** is the lowest part of the brain, located at the rear base of the skull. Its primary responsibility is to perform routine "housekeeping" functions that keep the body working properly. The hindbrain has three principal parts: the medulla, the pons, and the cerebellum (see fig. 3.11). The **medulla** is a swelling just above the top of the spinal cord, where the cord enters the brain. It controls breathing and a variety of reflexes, including those that enable you to maintain an upright posture. The **pons** is concerned with balance, hearing, and some parasympathetic functions. It is located just above the medulla. The **cerebellum** consists of two rounded structures with a complex architecture located to the rear of the pons. It has long been known that the cerebellum plays a key role in the coordination of complex muscle movements, but it has become clear in recent years that it also plays an important role in types of learning and memory that involve coordinated sequences of information (Andreasen, 1999; Woodruff-Pak, 1999).

The **reticular formation** spans the medulla and pons. Neurons project from the reticular formation down the spinal cord and play a role in maintaining muscle tone and cardiac responsiveness to changing circumstances. More interesting to psychologists, rich networks of neurons arise in the reticular formation and end throughout the cerebral cortex. These networks play very important general roles in influencing wakefulness, arousal level, and attention. Although the reticular formation was originally thought of as a single neural system, it is now clear that it is composed of many neural systems that primarily use different neurotransmitters, including serotonin, norepinephrine, and acetycholine. These parts of the reticular formation influence somewhat different functions of the brain (Guillery & others, 1998; Mesulam, 1995).

The **midbrain** is a small area at the top of the hindbrain that serves primarily as a center for several postural reflexes, particularly those associated with the senses. For example, the automatic movement of the eyes to keep them fixed on an object as the head moves and the reflexive movement of the head to better orient the ears to a sound are both controlled in the midbrain.

## Forebrain: Cognition, Motivation, Emotion, and Action

By far the most interesting part of the brain to psychologists is the **forebrain.** Structurally, the forebrain consists of two distinct areas. One area, which contains the thalamus, hypothalamus, and most of the limbic system, rests at the top of the hindbrain and midbrain (see fig. 3.12). The other area, made up primarily of the cerebral cortex, sits

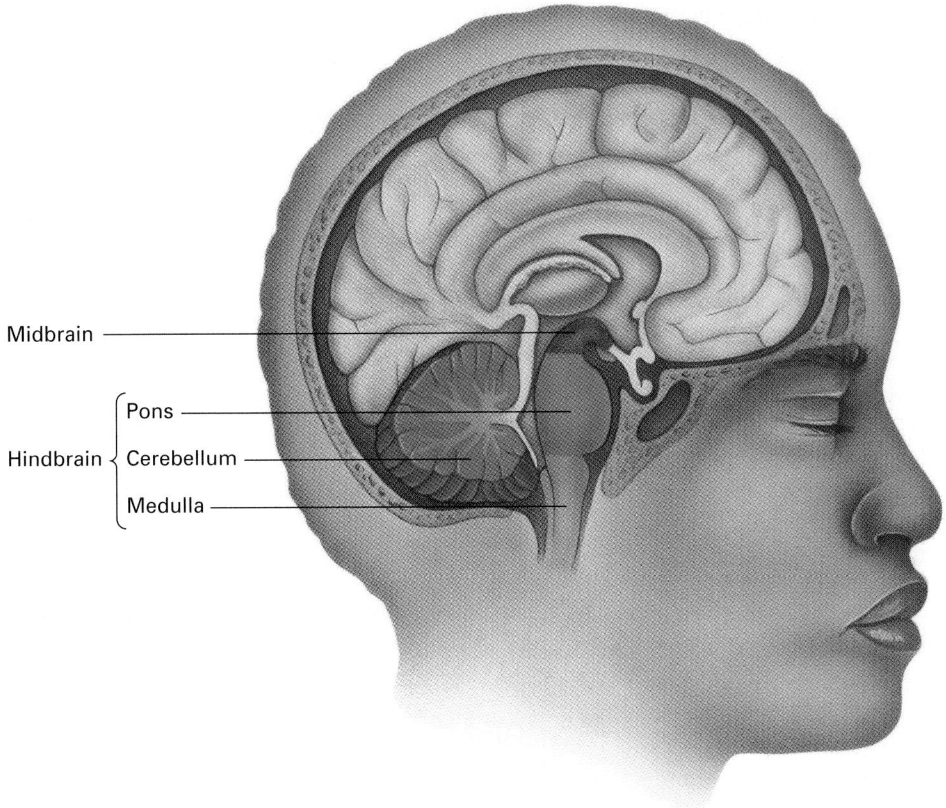

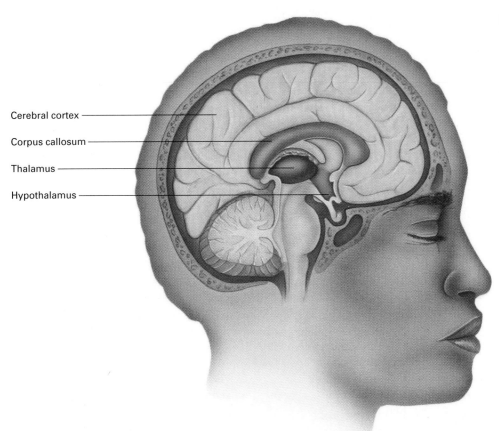

**FIGURE 3.11**
Important structures of the hindbrain
and midbrain.

Midbrain

Hindbrain
Pons
Cerebellum
Medulla

**FIGURE 3.12**
Key structures of the forebrain.

Cerebral cortex

Corpus callosum

Thalamus

Hypothalamus

over the lower parts of the brain like the fat cap of an acorn covering its kernel. Not only are these two areas distinctly different in terms of structure, but they control very different functions as well.

### Thalamus, Hypothalamus, and Limbic System

The **thalamus** is a switching station for messages going to and from the brain. It routes incoming stimuli from the sense organs to the appropriate parts of the brain and links the upper and lower centers of the brain. It also plays an important role in the filtering and preliminary processing of sensory information.

The **hypothalamus** is a small, but vitally important, part of the brain. It lies underneath the thalamus, just in front of the midbrain. The hypothalamus is intimately involved in our motives and emotions. It also plays a key role in regulating body temperature, sleep, endocrine gland activity, and resistance to disease; controlling glandular secretions of the stomach and intestines; and maintaining the normal pace and rhythm of such body functions as blood pressure and heartbeat (Brooks, 1988). Thus, the hypothalamus is the brain center most directly linked to the functions of the autonomic nervous system.

The hypothalamus also appears to contain specific pleasure centers. Rats will repeatedly press a lever for hours to receive electrical stimulation in certain parts of the hypothalamus (Olds & Milner, 1954). Jose Delgado (1969), working with humans, appears to have identified parts of the hypothalamus where electrical stimulation produces intense, generalized sensations of pleasure and parts where electrical stimulation produces strong, specific sensations of sexual pleasure. Apparently, these parts of the hypothalamus and related brain structures are active when we experience pleasure in our daily lives.

The hypothalamus plays its role in emotional arousal by working in close harmony with the **limbic system.** This complex neural system is composed of the parts shown in figure 3.13. The **amygdala** plays a key role in aggression and in processing information about stimuli (Canli & others, 2001; Hamann & others, 2002; Tillfors & others, 2001). Because the amygdala is involved in processing emotions, it plays a key role in the formation of memories about emotionally charged events (Adolph, Tranel, & Denburg, 2000; Kandel, 1999).

The **hippocampus** is also involved in the formation of new memories. The hippocampus is believed to "tie together" the elements of memories (their sights, sounds, meaning, etc.) that are stored in various parts of the cerebral cortex (Nadel & Jacobs, 1998). The memory loss experienced by patients suffering from Alzheimer's disease (see p. 102) results in part from damage to the hippocampus. Along with the **septal area** and the **cingulate cortex**, the hippocampus also brings important cognitive elements to the processing of emotion-related information. All three areas play a role in comparing current emotion-related information to information stored in memory.

### Cerebral Cortex: Sensory, Cognitive, and Motor Functions

The largest structure in the forebrain is called the **cerebral cortex.** It is involved in conscious experience, voluntary actions, language, and intelligence—many of the things that make us human (Gazzaniga, 2000). As such, it is the primary brain structure related to the somatic nervous system. The word *cortex* means "bark," referring to the fact that the thin outer surface of the cerebrum is a densely packed mass of billions of neurons. The cortex has a gray appearance due to the presence of the cell bodies of the neurons and is often called the gray matter of the brain. The area of the cerebrum beneath the quarter inch of cortex is often referred to as the white matter, because it is composed primarily of the axons of the cortical neurons. The fatty myelin coating of these neurons gives them their white appearance. The gray and white areas of the cerebrum work together, but because of its rich interconnections, it is often said that the "business" of the cerebrum is mostly conducted in the cortex. Hence, we often say that an intelligent per-

---

**thalamus**
(thal′-a-mus) The part of the forebrain that primarily routes sensory messages to appropriate parts of the brain.

**hypothalamus**
(hī″po-thal′ah-mus) The small part of the forebrain involved with motives, emotions, and the functions of the autonomic nervous system.

**limbic system**
A complex brain system, composed of the amygdala, hippocampus, septal area, and cingulate cortex, that works with the hypothalamus in emotional arousal.

**amygdala**
(ah-mig′dah-lah) A part of the limbic system that plays a role in emotion.

**hippocampus**
(hip″o-kam′pus) The part of the limbic system that plays a role in emotional arousal and memory.

**septal area**
A part of the limbic system that processes cognitive information in emotion.

**cingulate cortex**
A part of the limbic system lying in the cerebral cortex that processes cognitive information in emotion.

**cerebral cortex**
(ser′ĕ-bral) The largest structure in the forebrain, controlling conscious experience and intelligence and being involved with the somatic nervous system.

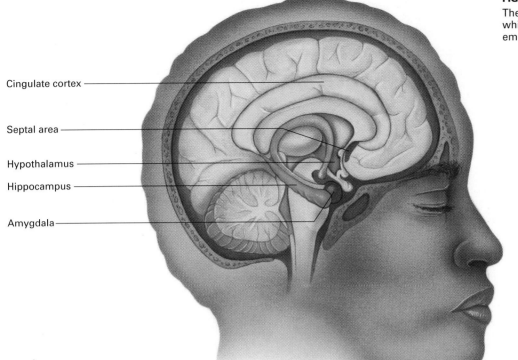

**FIGURE 3.13**
The structures of the limbic system, which play an important role in emotional arousal.

Cingulate cortex

Septal area

Hypothalamus

Hippocampus

Amygdala

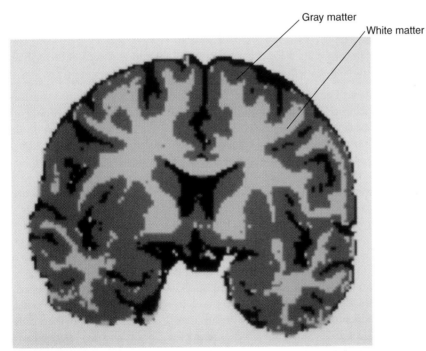

Gray matter

White matter

**FIGURE 3.14**
The gray matter and white matter of the cerebral cortex.

son "has a lot of gray matter." The gray and white matter of the cerebral cortex can be seen clearly in the MRI image in figure 3.14.

## Lobes of the Cerebral Cortex

Because of the importance of the cerebral cortex to our psychological functioning, let's look at it in more detail. The cerebral cortex can be thought of as being composed of

**FIGURE 3.15**
The four lobes of the cerebral cortex and the functions of key areas of the cerebral cortex.

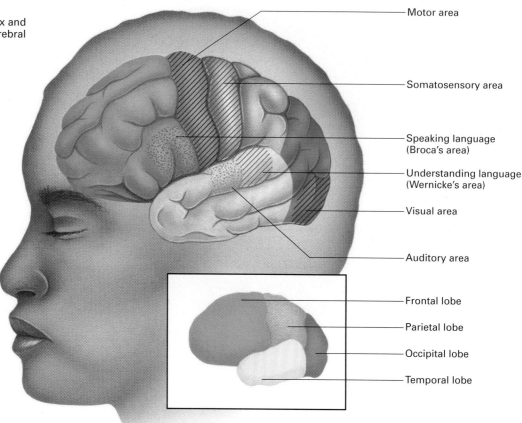

**FIGURE 3.15**
The four lobes of the cerebral cortex and the functions of key areas of the cerebral cortex.

**frontal lobes**
This part of the cerebral cortex in the front of the skull involved in planning, organization, thinking, decision making, memory, voluntary motor movements, and speech.

**Broca's area**
An area of the frontal lobe of the left cerebral hemisphere that plays a role in speaking language.

**stroke**
A rupture or blockage of a blood vessel in the brain that interrupts blood flow and often results in the destruction of a part of the brain.

**expressive aphasia**
(ah-fāˊze-ah) An impairment of the ability to generate spoken language, but not in the comprehension of language.

four sections, or *lobes* (see fig. 3.15). Learning the names and locations of these lobes will help us discuss the major functions of the cerebral cortex.

1. **Frontal lobes.** The frontal lobes occupy the part of the skull behind your forehead and extend back to the middle of the top of your head. The frontal cortex has a wide variety of functions. The frontal lobes play an important role in thinking, decision making, memory, organizing our behavior, and predicting the consequences of our actions (Kimberg, Esposito, & Farah, 1998; Lewis, 2000; Schachter, 1999).

The frontal lobe of the left cerebral hemisphere also contains **Broca's area,** which plays a very specific role in our ability to speak language. This area is named for French neurologist Paul Broca, who discovered its function in the late 1800s. He performed autopsies on persons who had earlier had a nonfatal **stroke** that damaged parts of the cerebral cortex and left them with a specific type of language disorder called **expressive aphasia.** Persons with expressive aphasia are able to understand what is said to them but have difficulty speaking. The strokes of persons with expressive aphasia occurred in what is now known as Broca's area. He concluded from his early studies that Broca's area was involved only in generating language and that another area of the brain must have been involved in understanding language.

The frontal lobes also are the major center for the control of voluntary movements of the limbs and the body. Near the middle of the top of the head, a strip called the motor area runs across the back portion of the frontal lobes. Damage to this area of the cortex from strokes and other causes can result in paralysis and loss of motor control. Not surprisingly, the part of the motor area that serves the mouth, throat, and tongue is located near Broca's area and controls the motor movements required by speech.

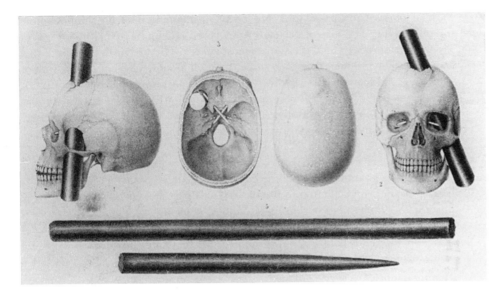

**FIGURE 3.16**
A drawing of Phineas Gage's skull and the tamping rod that passed through his brain.

In addition, the frontal lobes are believed to play a role in the inhibition of socially inappropriate behavior (Pietrini & others, 2000). This function of the frontal lobes is revealed by the dramatic case of Phineas Gage. In 1848, Gage was excavating rock to make way for a new section of track for the Rutland and Burlington Railroad in Vermont. Gage, known as a reasonable, polite, and hard-working man, had been made a foreman by the railroad. On one particular afternoon, he was hard at work preparing to blast a section of rock when an accident happened. Gage was packing blasting powder into a hole with a long tamping rod when a spark ignited the powder. The explosion shot the rod up through his upper left jaw and completely through his skull. As you can see in figure 3.16, the damage from the rod was to the frontal lobes on his left side (close enough to the front to miss the Broca language area). When Gage's coworkers reached him, he was conscious and able to tell them what had happened. He was rushed to a physician, who was able to stop the bleeding and save his life, but the destruction of such a large amount of his left frontal lobe took a terrific toll on him. Gage became irritable, publicly profane, and impossible to reason with. He also seemed to lose much of his ability to think rationally and plan. As a result, he had trouble holding a job and was regarded as a "totally changed" man by his former friends (Bigelow, 1850).

Nearly 150 years later, psychologist Christina Meyers and her colleagues (1992) at the University of Texas Medical Center described a case that is strikingly similar to Phineas Gage. A 33-year-old man, known to us as J.Z., had surgery to remove a tumor from the same area of the left frontal lobe that was destroyed in Phineas Gage. The lesion is shown clearly in an MRI image of his brain (fig. 3.17). Before the surgery, J.Z. was an "honest, stable and reliable worker and husband" (p. 122). His personality changed dramatically after the surgery, however. Like Phineas Gage, he became irritable, dishonest, irresponsible, and grandiose. In spite of no apparent changes in his intellectual skills, he was no longer employable, and he created serious legal and financial problems for his family. The dramatic changes in the behavior of Phineas Gage and J.Z. tell us that the frontal lobes play an important role in the control of complex aspects of our behavior.

Right                    Left

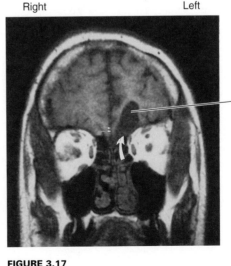

Area of damage to left frontal lobe

**FIGURE 3.17**
An MRI image of the brain of J.Z. (viewed from the front) shows the damage to the frontal lobe created when a tumor was removed.

**parietal lobes**
(pah-ri´e-tal) The part of the cerebral cortex that is located behind the frontal lobes at the top of the skull and that contains the somatosensory area.

**somatosensory area**
The strip of parietal cortex running parallel to the motor area of the frontal lobes that plays a role in body senses.

**temporal lobes**
The part of the cerebral cortex that extends back from the area of the temples beneath the frontal and parietal lobes and that contains areas involved in the sense of hearing and understanding language.

**Wernicke's area**
The language area of the cortex that plays an essential role in understanding spoken language.

2. **Parietal lobes.** The parietal lobes are located just behind the frontal lobes at the top of the skull. The strip of parietal cortex running parallel to the motor area of the frontal lobes is termed the **somatosensory area.** This area is important in the sense of touch and the other body senses that tell us, among other things, where our hands and feet are and what they are doing. It is not surprising, then, that the somatosensory area is located next to the motor area, because their functions clearly go hand in hand. As noted earlier when we discussed brain imaging, the area that was activated when Monte Buchsbaum received a mild shock to his arm was the somatosensory area of the cerebral cortex (see fig. 3.8).

Different areas of the somatosensory and motor areas serve different parts of the body. The amount of area of the cortex devoted to a particular part of the body is not in proportion to the size of that body part, however. Rather, it is proportional to the number of sensory and motor neurons going to and from that part of the body. Brain scientists have created amusing yet informative drawings of people with body features proportional to the space allocated to them in the somatosensory and motor areas (see fig. 3.18).

3. **Temporal lobes.** As suggested by their name, the temporal lobes extend backward from the area of the temples, occupying the middle area at the base of the brain beneath the frontal and parietal lobes. In both hemispheres, the temporal lobes contain the auditory areas. These areas are located just inside the skull near the ears, immediately below the somatosensory area of the parietal lobes, and are involved in the sense of hearing.

**Wernicke's area** is located just behind the auditory area in the left hemisphere. This is the other language area of the cortex, the one that plays an essential role in the understanding of spoken language. In this sense, Wernicke's area further processes the messages arriving from the ears, which are first processed in its next-door neighbor, the auditory area. Damage from strokes and

**FIGURE 3.18**

A cross section of the cerebral cortex in the motor control area and the skin sense area showing the areas in the cortex serving each part of the body. The size of the body feature in the drawing is proportional to the size of the related brain area.
**Source:** Data from W. Penfield and T. Rasmussen, *The Cerebral Cortex of Man.* Copyright © 1950 Macmillan Publishing Co., New York.

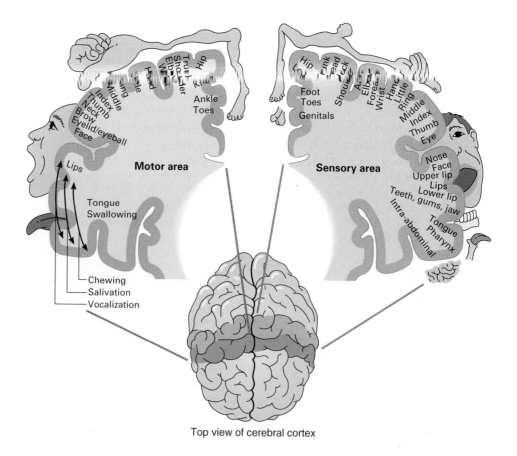

Top view of cerebral cortex

other sources of injury to this area of the cortex result in **Wernicke's aphasia.** Persons with this form of aphasia cannot make sense out of language that is spoken to them by others. In addition, they can make speech sounds normally, but what they say typically makes little sense.

4. **Occipital lobes.**  The occipital lobes are located at the base of the back of the head. Although it is the part of the brain that is located farthest from the eyes, the most important part of the occipital lobes is the visual area. The visual area plays an essential role in the processing of sensory information from the eyes. Damage to the visual area of the occipital lobes can result in partial or complete blindness, even though the eyes are able to function normally.

Notice in figure 3.15 that the specific functions of some areas of each of the four lobes of the cerebral hemispheres have been labeled, but many areas of each lobe have been left unlabeled. These unlabeled parts of the cerebral cortex are known as the **association areas.** The association areas play more general roles in cerebral activities, but they often work in close coordination with one of the nearby specific ability areas. This can be seen in the series of PET scan images presented in figure 3.19. The areas of the cerebral cortex that are yellow and red have the greatest amount of neural activity. Notice that, when the person is hearing words, there is activity in and around Wernicke's area and in the association areas just behind it. When the person is seeing words, the visual area in the occipital lobe is activated, along with part of the nearby association area. In contrast, when the person is speaking words, activation is found only in Broca's area and the motor area of the frontal lobes that controls speech movements; when the person is thinking, the frontal lobes are active.

Neurologists sometimes call the association areas the "silent areas" of the cortex because strokes and other damage to them produce no permanent loss of motor control, language, or other specific abilities. They apparently serve the areas of the cortex

**Wernicke's aphasia**
A form of aphasia in which persons can speak fluently (but nonsensically) and cannot make sense out of language spoken to them by others.

**occipital lobes**
(ok-sip′ĭ-tal)  The part of the cerebral cortex, located at the base of the back of the head, that plays an essential role in the processing of sensory information from the eyes.

**association areas**
Areas within each lobe of the cerebral cortex believed to play general rather than specific roles.

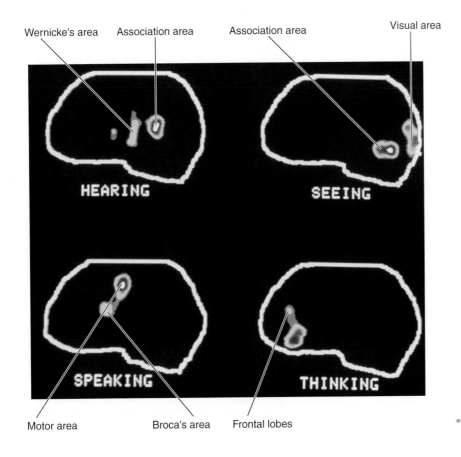

**FIGURE 3.19**
PET images of the brain at work on four different tasks.

that control specific abilities, but we can function quite adequately after the loss of considerable amounts of the association areas.

## Functions of the Hemispheres of the Cerebral Cortex

We just saw that the cerebral cortex is composed of four lobes—each of which is involved in different psychological functions. If we look down at the cerebral cortex from the top, however, we can see that it also is made up of two halves called the **cerebral hemispheres.** These two separate hemispheres are linked by the **corpus callosum,** allowing communication between the two halves of the cortex (see fig. 3.12). Many of the functions of the cerebral cortex are shared by both hemispheres. However, the two hemispheres work together in a way that is different from what we might think. Although there are some exceptions to this rule, input from the senses of vision and touch, for example, generally goes to the *opposite* hemisphere. Stimulation of the skin on the left hand typically goes to the right cerebral hemisphere, visual stimulation falling on the right visual field of each eye goes to the left hemisphere, and wiggling the toes on your left foot is controlled by the right hemisphere. To accomplish this, the major sensory and motor nerves entering and leaving the brain twist and almost completely cross over each other.

### Functions of the Left and Right Cerebral Hemispheres

The left and right cerebral hemispheres play different but complementary roles in processing information. For example, strong evidence suggests that the areas that exercise the greatest control over language are located in the left cerebral hemisphere in over 90 percent of the population (Banich & Heller, 1998; Milner, 1974). The right hemisphere plays a role in processing language, but the left hemisphere is better suited to analyzing logical verbal information (Beeman & Chiarello, 1998). The right cerebral hemisphere, in contrast, appears to play a greater role in processing information about the shapes and locations of things in space. For example, when you study a list of verbal items—such as memorizing the names of the four lobes of the cerebrum—there will be more activity in your left frontal lobe than in your right frontal lobe. On the other hand, if you study a drawing to memorize the shapes and locations of the lobes of the cerebrum, the right side of your frontal lobes will be more involved (Craik & others, 1999; Wheeler, Stuss & Tulving, 1997). The left side of the cerebral cortex tends to handle verbal information, and the right side tends to handle visual and spatial information.

### Split Brains

Coordination of the shared functions of the two cerebral hemispheres is possible because they communicate through structures that connect them. The largest and most important bridge between the two cerebral hemispheres is the *corpus callosum.* It is sometimes necessary, however, to control the neurological disease of epilepsy by surgically cutting the corpus callosum to prevent seizures from spreading from one cerebral hemisphere to the other. When this is done, the right and left hemispheres have much less capacity to exchange information; to a great extent, the left brain does not know what the right brain is doing and vice versa. Experiments performed on these patients (referred to as "split-brain" patients) provide a major source of our knowledge about the different functions of the two cerebral hemispheres (Franz & others, 2000; Gazzaniga, 1967, 1998, 2000).

What would be the result of cutting the primary line of communication between the two cerebral hemispheres? Surprisingly, a patient with a severed corpus callosum changes very little at first glance. But, although it would be difficult for you—or even for the patient—to notice any difference in daily living, clever psychological experiments have revealed the effects of cutting the major connection between the cerebral hemispheres. In one experiment, the split-brain patient was seated in front of a screen and asked to stare at a spot in the middle. A slide projector briefly flashed a word on one side

---

**cerebral hemispheres**
The two main parts of the cerebral cortex, divided into left and right hemispheres.

**corpus callosum**
(kor´pus kah-lo´-sum) The major neural structure connecting the left and right cerebral hemispheres.

of the screen, so that it was seen by only the left or only the right visual field of the eye. This was done because the left visual field sends information only to the right cerebral hemisphere, and the right visual field sends information only to the left cerebral hemisphere. The nerves from the eyes cross at the optic chiasm (see fig. 3.20 on page 82), which is left uncut.

If the word *pencil* is presented in the right visual field of each eye, the information travels to the language control areas in the left hemisphere. In this situation, the patient has no difficulty reading aloud the word *pencil*. But, if the same word is presented to the left visual field of each eye, the split-brain patient would typically not be able to respond when asked what word had been presented. This does not mean that the right side of the brain does not receive or understand the word *pencil*. Rather, it means that the patient cannot verbalize what she sees. Using the sense of touch, the split-brain patient can easily pick out a pencil as the object that matches the word from among a number of unseen objects—but only if she uses her left hand, which has received the message from the right cerebral cortex.

However, if the split-brain patient holds an unseen pencil in her left hand, she cannot tell you what she is holding. It's not that the right cortex does not know, but because it has no area controlling verbal expression, it cannot tell you what it knows. The left cortex that is "talking" to you cannot tell you either, because information in the right cortex often cannot reach it in the split-brain patient. Such studies with split-brain patients clearly reveal the localization of language expression abilities in the left cerebral hemisphere (Gazzaniga, 1967, 1998).

It is interesting to note that these conclusions apply to right-handed persons but do not always apply to left-handed persons. The language functions of the cerebral hemispheres are often reversed in left-handed persons.

### Hemispheres of the Cerebral Cortex and Emotion

In addition to the cerebral cortex's role in sensory, motor, and cognitive processes, it plays a key role in the processing of emotional information. As we have seen, there are marked differences in the cognitive functions of the two cerebral hemispheres. It is of great interest to psychologists, therefore, that the cerebral hemispheres also appear to play different roles in emotion (Davidson, 1992; Voelz & others, 2001).

In general, the right hemisphere plays a greater role in both the expression and perception of emotions. The left side of the face, which is primarily controlled by the right cerebral hemisphere, makes stronger expressions of emotion (Moscovitch & Olds, 1982). In other words, the left side of our mouth "smiles" and "frowns" more dramatically than the right side. One possible reason for our fascination with Da Vinci's painting of "Mona Lisa" is that she smiles more on her right side. We're not used to seeing people smile that way, and it catches our attention. Art historians tell us that Da Vinci finished some features of this painting while studying his own expressions in a mirror. Perhaps the reversed smile that he saw in the mirror became the Mona Lisa's intriguing "right-sided" smile.

In addition to its role in the expression of emotion, the right hemisphere is also essential for understanding the emotions expressed by others (Blonder, Bowers, & Heilman, 1991; Adolph & others, 2000). Beatty (1995) described how patients with right-hemisphere damage failed to match emotional tones of voice to pictures of people expressing anger, happiness, sadness, and

Leonardo da Vinci (1452–1519).

*Mona Lisa* by Leonardo da Vinci.

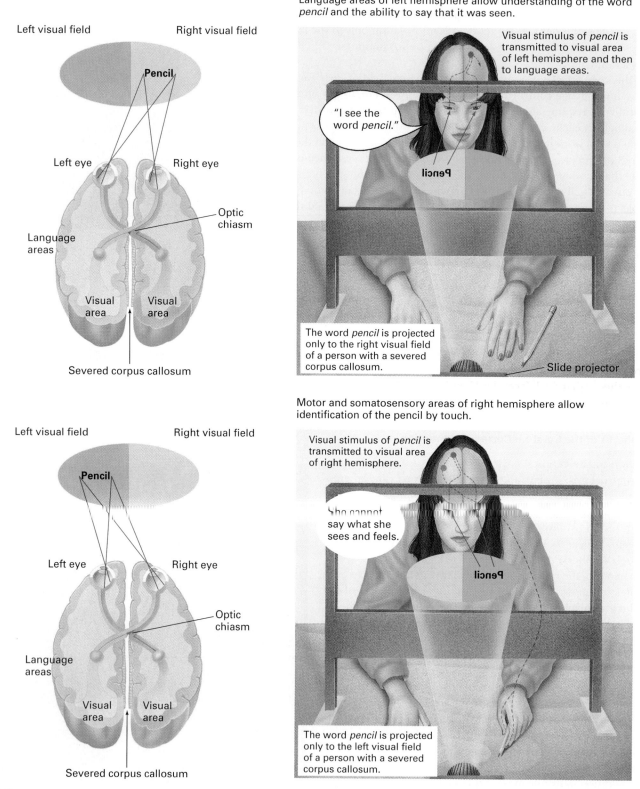

**FIGURE 3.20**

Studies of persons whose corpus callosum has been surgically cut to treat epilepsy tell us much about the different functions of the cerebral hemispheres and the important role that the corpus callosum normally plays in allowing communication between the hemispheres. When the word *pencil* is shown only to the right visual field, the information is sent only to the left cerebral hemisphere. The language areas in the left hemisphere allow the person to say that the word *pencil* has been seen. But, when the stimulus is shown only to the left visual field, the information is sent only to the right hemisphere, which does not have language areas. In this case, the person cannot confirm verbally that the word has been seen but can identify the pencil as the correct stimulus by the sense of touch.

indifference. Patients with left-hemisphere damage, although they had difficulty under-standing the meaning of what was said, had no problems identifying the emotions.

Does this mean that there is no role for the left hemisphere in emotion? Not at all. Think about the implications of the following observation. As long ago as 1861, physician Paul Broca noticed that patients who had suffered strokes in the left cerebral hemisphere often became depressed, whereas patients with right hemisphere strokes were much less likely to do so. Since Broca's time, his observation has been repeated many times (Kinsbourne, 1988; Robinson & Starkstein, 1990; Vataja & others, 2001). For example, the images of the brains shown in figure 3.21 (obtained using computerized X rays) of persons who developed depression following strokes show clearly that the damage to their brains was primarily on the left side of the cortex (Starkstein & others, 1988).

In striking contrast, many patients with right-hemisphere damage are cheerful, happy, and not at all depressed by their disability (Kinsbourne, 1988). It appears that the reason left-hemisphere strokes cause depression has to do with the way in which the two hemispheres process emotional information. The right hemisphere appears to be more involved with the processing of negative emotions, whereas the left hemisphere plays a greater role in the processing of positive emotions. Some theorists believe that, when the left hemisphere is damaged by a stroke, the negative emotions processed in the right hemisphere become dominant and cause depression (Starkstein & Robinson, 1988). This theory is strongly supported by studies in which a sedative injected directly into the artery supplying only the left side of the brain results in a sudden and unexplained sadness. The left side of the brain is sedated, but the "gloomy" right side still functions (Kinsbourne, 1988).

The theory that the left cerebral hemisphere plays a greater role in processing pos-itive emotions, whereas the right cerebral hemisphere is more involved with negative emotions, has been strengthened by findings reported by Richard Davidson of the Uni-versity of Wisconsin (Davidson, Ekman, Saron, Senulis, & Friesen, 1990). In this study, several short films were shown to college students—some entertaining films of playful animals and some "quite gruesome" films of amputations and burn victims. As the stu-dents watched the films, their facial expressions were monitored. When they were smil-ing, EEG recordings indicated more activity in the left cerebral hemisphere, but when

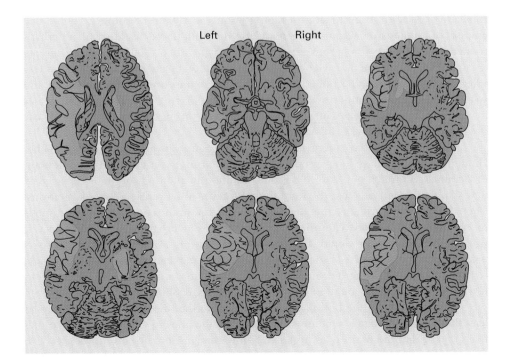

Left          Right

**FIGURE 3.21**
Drawings from computerized X rays of the brains of individuals who became depressed following a stroke. The shaded areas show the damaged cerebral tissue.

they showed disgust, their right hemisphere was more active. Apparently, positive emotions are processed more in the left hemisphere and negative emotions in the right hemisphere (Heller, Nitscke, & Miller, 1998).

### Plasticity of the Cortex

**plasticity**
The ability of parts of the brain, particularly the cerebral cortex, to acquire new functions that partly or completely replace the functions of a damaged part of the brain.

**neural pruning**
The normal process of selective loss of gray matter in the brain over time, which is thought to improve the efficiency of neural systems by eliminating unnecessary cells.

**neurogenesis**
(nu´rō jen´ĭ sis) The hypothesized growth of new neurons in adult mammals.

Severe damage to the cerebral cortex often results in the loss of important psychological functions. Fortunately, many of these functions can be recovered partially or fully, particularly if the damage occurs early in life. This is because the cortex, and some other parts of the brain, show a high degree of **plasticity,** which means that, over time, other areas of the cortex can take over the functions of the damaged area (Garraghty, Churchill, & Banks, 1998). For example, children with damage to the language areas of the left hemisphere can often relearn language because areas in the right hemisphere take over the functions of the damaged area (Gazzaniga, 1992). Although many areas of the brain are specialized to perform certain tasks, they are not completely dedicated to those tasks. For example, blind individuals who read Braille show activation in the visual cortex when they "read" with their fingers (Cohen & others, 1997). Instead of using areas of the brain that usually serve the sense of touch, the tactile stimuli are interpreted in the area of the cortex that normally interprets visual stimuli.

## The Brain Is a Developing System

Although it has long been known that areas of the brain often take on the functions of other damaged areas (brain plasticity), the prevailing view until recently was that the anatomy of the brain changed little from birth through middle adulthood. If the brain changed at all, it declined as the result of trauma, disease, or old age. Dramatic evidence from MRI and other neuroimaging studies have radically changed our view of the brain, however. It is now abundantly clear that the brain continues to change in structure well into the fifth decade of life (Bartzokis & others, 2001; Durston & others, 2001). One reason that scientists were slow to recognize this fact is that the total weight of the brain does not change after 5 years of age. However, this hides the fact that white matter increases in the cerebral cortex (especially the frontal lobes and the corpus callosum that links the right and left hemispheres) from childhood through middle age, while gray matter decreases in the cortex and some subcortical areas at about the same rate. The increase in white matter is due to the continued growth of myelin, which insulates neurons and speeds the transmission of neural impulses (Durston & others, 2001). The amount of white matter begins to decrease after the fifth decade of life, which perhaps reduces some aspects of cognitive speed (Bartzokis & others, 2001). Much of the decrease in gray matter (neural cell bodies) from childhood through middle adulthood results from selective **neural pruning,** which is thought to improve the efficiency of neural systems by eliminating unnecessary cells (Durston & others, 2001). Thus, the increases in white matter and decreases in gray matter that occur through middle age both appear to increase the efficiency of the brain.

Other evidence has emerged that challenges an even more deeply held belief about the brain. We have long accepted that new neurons never grow in the adult brain of mammals. Although new skin cells grow continuously, allowing cuts to be replaced by new skin tissue, neurons that die were thought never to be replaced by new neurons. There is now strong evidence that new neurons do grow in the cortex and hippocampus in rodents and monkeys, a process referred to as **neurogenesis** (Gould, Reeves, Graziano, & Gross, 1999; Gould, Tanapat, Rydel, & Hastings, 2000). Although neurogenesis remains a controversial issue, it appears that the brain can renew itself under some circumstances by growing new neurons and that the new neurons may play a role in learning and memory (Gould, Beylin, Tanapat, Reeves, & Shors, 1999).

This new view of the brain as a dynamic system that develops in healthy ways at least through middle age is a bit unnerving (pardon the pun) to scientists who have long been taught that the brain is an organ that only changes in a negative direction. The new view of the healthy developing brain alters our entire conception of what it means to mature into middle adulthood (the brain may continue to improve) and will undoubtedly open new doors to the prevention and treatment of disorders of the brain.

## The Brain Is an Interacting System

Even though it is convenient to think of the brain as being divided into many separate parts, you should know that the parts commonly work together in intellectual and emotional functioning. Consider, for example, your reaction in the following situation. You are waiting at a bus stop late at night. A poorly dressed man approaches, smelling of alcohol. He asks if you can spare five dollars. In his pocket, you see the outline of what might be a gun. Your reaction to this scene would involve many parts of your brain working together. Parts of your cerebral cortex evaluate the possible threat to you and the alternative courses of action open to you. Your limbic system is involved in a process of emotional arousal. If you fight, run, or reach into your pocket to hand over the money, the motor areas of your cortex will work with your hindbrain and midbrain to coordinate the muscular movements involved. The many parts of the brain work together.

Sometimes the many parts of the brain interact because one part of the brain sends a message to another part, which then sends it on to a third part of the brain, and so on. More often, however, several parts of the brain process different kinds of related information at the same time. To use computer language, the brain often uses "parallel" processing (handling different information at the same time) rather than "serial" processing (handling one kind of information at a time) (Rumelhart & McClelland, 1986). The brain's amazing capacity for parallel processing magnifies its ability to use its 100 billion neurons and their trillions of connections to produce our complex actions, emotions, and thoughts.

---

## Review

The brain is a complex system composed of many parts that carry out different functions but work together in an integrated fashion. The hindbrain and midbrain mostly handle the housekeeping responsibilities of the body, such as breathing, posture, reflexes, and other basic processes. The larger forebrain area carries out the more "psychological" functions of the brain: The thalamus integrates sensory input, and the hypothalamus controls motivation, emotion, sleep, and other basic bodily processes. Both the thalamus and the hypothalamus lie beneath the cap of the cerebral cortex. Most of the limbic system, which plays an important role in emotional arousal, is located below the cortex, but lower cortical structures are involved as well. The cerebral cortex provides the neural basis for thinking, language, control of motor movements, perception, and other cognitive processes, but it also processes emotional information. The cortex is composed of two halves, the cerebral hemispheres, which are connected to each other primarily by the corpus callosum. The two cerebral hemispheres are involved in somewhat different aspects of these cognitive processes. The right hemisphere plays a role in spatial and artistic cognitive processes, whereas the left hemisphere is more involved in logical, mathematical, and language-based processes. The two cerebral hemispheres also appear to process different aspects of emotion, with the left hemisphere being more involved in positive emotion and the right hemisphere playing a greater role in negative emotion. Recent evidence shows that the brain continues to develop until middle age and may even be capable of growing new neurons during adulthood.

---

## Check Your Learning

To be sure that you have learned the key points from the preceding section, cover the list of correct answers and try to answer each question. If you give an incorrect answer to any question, return to the page given next to the correct answer to see why your answer was not correct.

1. The midbrain and hindbrain play the greatest role in which functions?

   a) motivation and emotion
   c) planning for the future
   b) learning and thinking
   d) bodily housekeeping and reflexes

2. The small but vitally important part of the forebrain that plays a key role in the control of emotion, endocrine gland activity, blood pressure, and heartbeat (because it is the brain center most linked to the autonomic nervous system) is the

   a) cerebrum.
   c) hypothalamus.
   b) cerebellum.
   d) thalamus.

3. Broca's area, which controls speaking, is located in the _____ lobe of the left cerebral hemisphere.

   a) frontal
   c) parietal
   b) temporal
   d) occipital

4. The area of the cerebral cortex that is primarily involved in vision is the _____ lobe.

   a) frontal
   c) parietal
   b) temporal
   d) occipital

5. Positive emotions are processed more by the _____ cerebral hemisphere.

## Thinking Critically about Psychology

1. Imagine that you have put down this book and are taking a huge bite of your favorite kind of pizza. Think of the role that each part of the brain plays in this simple act.

2. Does what you have learned about the two cerebral hemispheres suggest that we should think of ourselves as having "two brains" or one? How about the autonomic nervous system—is that "another brain with a mind of its own"?

Correct Answers: 1. d (p. 72), 2. c (p. 74), 3. a (p. 76), 4. d (p. 79), 5. left (p. 83).

## ● Endocrine System: Chemical Messengers of the Body

As we have just seen, the nervous system is the vital computer and communication system that forms the biological basis for behavior and conscious experience. Another biological system also plays an important role in communication and the regulation of bodily processes—the **endocrine system.** This system consists of a number of **glands** that secrete two kinds of chemical messengers. Many endocrine glands secrete *neuropeptides* into the bloodstream. When these neuropeptides reach other endocrine glands, they influence their functions, providing communication and coordination among the endocrine glands. In addition, some neuropeptides secreted by the endocrine glands reach the brain and influence neural systems. Thus, although the brain influences all of the endocrine glands either directly or indirectly, the endocrine glands influence the brain in return. Indeed, as we will see later in this book, some neuropeptides play important roles in the mechanisms underlying stress, emotion, and memory (Izquierdo & Medina, 1997; Kandel & Abel, 1995; Panskepp, 1993).

In addition, the endocrine glands secrete **hormones** into the bloodstream, where they are carried throughout the body. Hormones influence a wide variety of organ systems. The action of hormones is closely related to that of the nervous system in three

**endocrine system**
(en'dō-krin) The system of glands that secretes hormones.

**glands**
Structures in the body that secrete substances.

**hormones**
(hor'mōnz) Chemical substances, produced by endocrine glands, that influence internal organs.

ways. First, the hormones are directly regulated by the brain, particularly the hypothalamus. Second, some of the hormones are chemically identical to some of the neurotransmitters. Third, the hormones aid the nervous system's ability to control the body by activating many organs during physical stress or emotional arousal and by influencing such things as metabolism, blood-sugar level, and sexual functioning. Hormones affect target organs by passing into the body of cells and influencing the way in which genetic codes in their nuclei are translated. Let's look briefly at the seven endocrine glands that are most important to our psychological lives (see fig. 3.22).

## Pituitary Gland

The **pituitary gland** is located near the bottom of the brain, connected to and largely controlled by the hypothalamus. It is sometimes thought of as the body's master gland because its secretions help regulate the activity of the other glands in the endocrine system. Perhaps its most important function is regulating the body's reactions to stress and resistance to disease (Muller & Nistico, 1989). The pituitary gland secretes hormones that have important effects on the body—notably, in controlling blood pressure, thirst, and body growth. Too little or too much of the pituitary's growth hormone will make a person develop into a "dwarf" or "giant." One special function of the pituitary gland is of particular importance to newborns. When the infant sucks the mother's nipples, a neural message is sent to the mother's hypothalamus, which sends a message to the pituitary gland through a neuropeptide. This causes the pituitary to secrete a hormone that releases breast milk for the baby.

**pituitary gland**
(pǐ-tu′i-tār″ē)  The body's master gland, located near the bottom of the brain, whose secretions help regulate the activity of the other glands in the endocrine system.

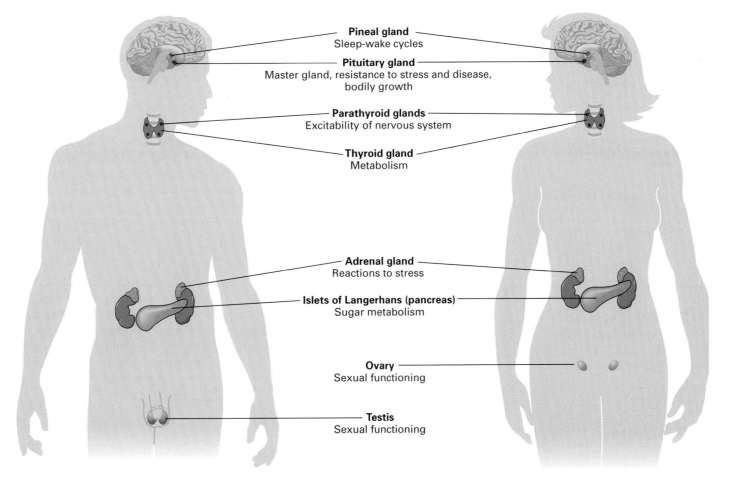

**Pineal gland**
Sleep-wake cycles

**Pituitary gland**
Master gland, resistance to stress and disease, bodily growth

**Parathyroid glands**
Excitability of nervous system

**Thyroid gland**
Metabolism

**Adrenal gland**
Reactions to stress

**Islets of Langerhans (pancreas)**
Sugar metabolism

**Ovary**
Sexual functioning

**Testis**
Sexual functioning

**FIGURE 3.22**
Locations of major endocrine glands and their principal functions.

**adrenal glands**
(ah-drē'nal) Two glands on the kidneys that are involved in physical and emotional arousal.

**epinephrine**
(ep"i-nef'rin) A hormone produced by the adrenal glands.

**norepinephrine**
(nor"ep-i-nef'rin) A hormone produced by the adrenal glands.

**cortisol**
A stress hormone produced by the adrenal glands.

**islets of Langerhans**
(i'lets *of* lahng'er-hanz) Endocrine cells in the pancreas that regulate the level of sugar in the blood.

**pancreas**
(pan'krē-as) The organ near the stomach that contains the islets of Langerhans.

**glucagon**
(gloo'kah-gon) A hormone produced by the islets of Langerhans that causes the liver to release sugar into the bloodstream.

**insulin**
(in'su-lin) A hormone produced by the islets of Langerhans that reduces the amount of sugar in the bloodstream.

**ovaries**
(o'vah-rēz) Female endocrine glands that secrete sex-related hormones and produce ova, or eggs.

**testes**
(tes'tēz) Male endocrine glands that secrete sex-related hormones and produce sperm cells.

**gonads**
(gō'nadz) The glands that produce sex cells and hormones important in sexual arousal and that contribute to the development of secondary sex characteristics.

## Adrenal Glands

The **adrenal glands** are a pair of glands that sit atop the two kidneys. They play an important role in emotional arousal and secrete a variety of hormones important to metabolism. When stimulated either by a hormone from the pituitary gland or by the sympathetic division of the autonomic nervous system, the adrenal glands secrete three hormones, among others, that are particularly important in reactions to stress. **Epinephrine** and **norepinephrine** (which are also neurotransmitters) stimulate changes to prepare the body to deal with physical demands that require intense body activity, including psychological threats or danger (even when the danger cannot be dealt with physically). The effects of these two adrenal hormones are quite similar, but they can be distinguished in terms of their most potent effects. Epinephrine increases blood pressure by increasing heart rate and blood flow, causes the liver to convert and release some of its supply of stored sugar into the bloodstream, and increases the rate at which the body uses energy (i.e., metabolism), sometimes by as much as 100 percent over normal. Norepinephrine also increases blood pressure, but it does this by constricting the diameter of blood vessels in the body's muscles and by reducing the activity of the digestive system (Groves & Rebec, 1988; Hole, 1990). The adrenal glands also secrete the hormone **cortisol,** which also activates the body in terms of stress (Bandelow & others, 2000) and plays a particularly important role in the regulation of immunity to disease.

Let's look at an example of the action of the adrenal glands during stress. Does giving a speech in public make you tense? Most people find public speaking to be at least mildly stressful. German scientist Ulrich Bolm-Andorff collected blood and urine from 10 physicians and psychologists at two different times: (a) just after they gave an important public speech to their colleagues and (b) at the same time on another day when they were not speaking (Bolm-Andorff, Schwämmle, Ehlenz, Koop, & Kaffarnik, 1986). Three adrenal hormones (epinephrine, norepinephrine, and cortisol) were measured in these fluids. Look at figure 3.23 to see the dramatic increase in the secretion of adrenal hormones during the speech. Notice, too, the corresponding increase in heart rate and blood pressure.

The changes in heart rate and blood pressure were caused by the action of epinephrine and norepinephrine on the heart and blood vessels, but also by the direct action of the autonomic nervous system on these organs. Thus, the autonomic nervous system has two ways of activating the internal organs: (1) by directly affecting the organs and (2) by stimulating the adrenals and other endocrine glands that then influence the organs with their hormones. One reason it takes so long to feel calm after a stressful event has passed is because of this second route to activating the body. It takes quite a while for the hormones to leave the bloodstream, so their effects are rather long lasting.

## Islets of Langerhans

The **islets of Langerhans,** which are embedded in the **pancreas,** regulate the level of sugar in the blood by secreting two hormones that have opposing actions. **Glucagon** causes the liver to convert its stored sugar into blood sugar and to dump it into the bloodstream. **Insulin,** in contrast, reduces the amount of blood sugar by helping the body's cells absorb sugar in the form of fat. Blood sugar level is important psychologically because it's one of the factors in the hunger motive, and it helps determine how energetic a person feels.

## Gonads

There are two sex glands—the **ovaries** in females, the **testes** in males. The **gonads** produce the sex cells—ova in females, sperm in males. They also secrete hormones that are important in sexual arousal and contribute to the development of so-called secondary sex characteristics (e.g., breast development in women, growth of chest hair in men, deepening of the voice in males at adolescence, and growth of pubic hair in both sexes).

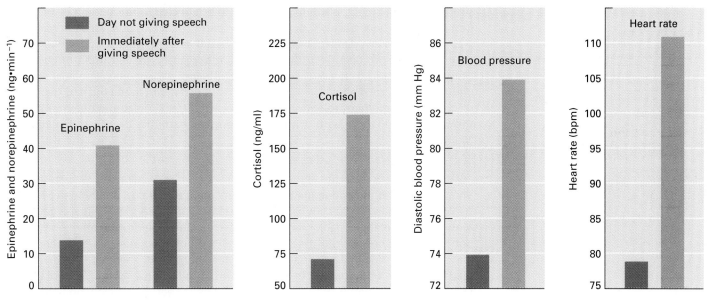

**FIGURE 3.23**

The effects of the stress of giving a public speech on hormones secreted by the adrenal glands and on heart rate and blood pressure.

**Source:** Data from V. Bolm-Andorff, et al., "Hormonal and Cardiovascular Variations During a Public Lecture" in *European Journal of Applied Physiology,* 54:669–674. Copyright 1986 Springer-Verlag, New York, NY.

The most important sex hormones are **estrogen** in females and **testosterone** in males. There is emerging evidence that sex hormones play a role in guiding the development of the brain.

## Thyroid Gland

The **thyroid gland,** located just below the larynx, or voice box, plays an important role in the regulation of **metabolism.** It does so by secreting a hormone called **thyroxin.** The level of thyroxin in a person's bloodstream and the resulting metabolic rate are important in many ways. In children, proper functioning of the thyroid is necessary for proper mental development. A serious thyroid deficiency in childhood produces sluggishness, poor muscle tone, and a rare type of mental retardation called **cretinism.**

In adults, the thyroxin level helps determine one's weight and level of activity. People whose thyroid glands secrete unusually large amounts of thyroxin are typically very active. They may eat large amounts of food but still not gain weight because their rapid metabolic rate burns off calories so quickly. Conversely, people with low thyroxin levels tend to be inactive and overweight. A "thyroid problem" is rarely the main cause of a weight problem, however. Thyroid disturbances can also lead to depression in adults. But, as with weight problems, most depression is not caused by a malfunctioning thyroid.

## Parathyroid Glands

The four small glands embedded in the thyroid gland are the **parathyroid glands.** They secrete **parathormone,** which is important in the functioning of the nervous system. Parathormone controls the excitability of the nervous system by regulating ion levels in the neurons. Too much parathormone inhibits nervous activity and leads to lethargy; too little of it may lead to excessive nervous activity and tension.

## Pineal Gland

The **pineal gland** is located between the cerebral hemispheres, attached to the top of the thalamus. Its primary secretion is *melatonin.* Melatonin is important in the regulation of biological rhythms, including the menstrual cycles in females and the daily regulation of

**estrogen**
(es´tro-jen) A female sex hormone.

**testosterone**
(tes-tos´ter-ōn) A male sex hormone.

**thyroid gland**
(thī´roid) The gland below the voice box that regulates metabolism.

**metabolism**
(me-tab´o-lizm) The process through which the body uses energy.

**thyroxin**
(thīrok´sin) A hormone produced by the thyroid that is necessary for proper mental development in children and helps determind weight and level of activity in adults.

**cretinism**
(krē´tin-izm) A type of mental retardation in children caused by a deficiency of thyroxin.

**parathyroid glands**
(par´´ah-thī´roid) Four glands embedded in the thyroid that produce parathormone.

**parathormone**
(par´´ah-thor´mōn) A hormone that regulates ion levels in neurons and controls excitability of the nervous system.

**pineal gland**
(pin´e-al) The endocrine gland that is largely responsible for the regulation of biological rhythms.

sleep and wakefulness. Melatonin levels seem to be affected by the amount of exposure to sunlight and, hence, "clock" the time of day partly in that fashion. Melatonin also appears to play a role in regulating moods. Seasonal affective disorder, a type of depression that occurs most frequently in the winter months, can be treated using bright light, which is thought to be effective because of the influence of light on melatonin. Many scientists are concerned about the widespread use of melatonin in pill form to treat sleep disturbances and other problems (Haimov & Lavie, 1996). Melatonin does not appear to be helpful, and there is little evidence on possible harmful side effects of melatonin supplements.

## Review

The hormones of the endocrine glands supplement the brain's ability to coordinate the body's reactions and activities. These chemical messengers are involved in the regulation of metabolism, blood-sugar level, sexual functioning, and other body functions. Most important from the viewpoint of psychology is the role of epinephrine and norepinephrine in emotional arousal. These hormones, secreted by the adrenal glands, activate body organs in a diffuse and long-lasting way that is partially responsible for the length of time necessary for us to feel calm following a stressful event.

## Check Your Learning

To be sure that you have learned the key points from the preceding section, cover the list of correct answers and try to answer each question. If you give an incorrect answer to any question, return to the page given next to the correct answer to see why your answer was not correct.

1. The _____ secretes epinephrine, norepinephrine, and cortisol, which activate the body during stress (such as by increasing heart rate and blood pressure).

   a)   adrenal gland                     c)   thyroid gland
   b)   parathyroid gland                 d)   pituitary gland

2. Sugar metabolism and hunger are influenced by the _____ in the pancreas.

3. The _____ gland is called the "master gland" because its secretions influence many other glands.

   a)   adrenal                           c)   thyroid
   b)   parathyroid                       d)   pituitary

4. The excitability of the nervous system is regulated by parathormone, which is secreted by the

   a)   adrenal gland.                    c)   thyroid gland.
   b)   parathyroid gland.                d)   pituitary gland.

## Thinking Critically about Psychology

1. In what ways does epinephrine resemble a drug like caffeine?

2. When doing something stressful, such as speaking in public, how do the effects of hormones secreted by the adrenal glands help us—how are they adaptive? Or are they only maladaptive?

Correct Answers:   1. a (p. 88).   2. islets of Langerhans (p. 88).   3. d (p. 87).   4. b (p. 89).

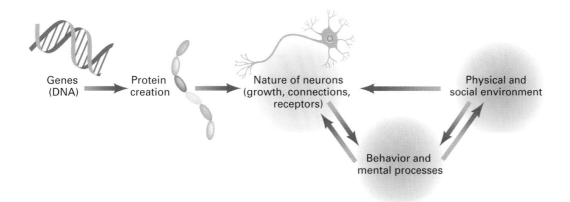

**FIGURE 3.25**
Genes work with the environment to influence our psychological lives by influencing the synthesis (or creation) of proteins, which influences the nature of neurons. The nature of our neurons (which is also influenced by our experiences in the environment) works with the environment to shape our behavior and mental processes. Our behavior and mental processes often shape our physical and social environment.

about 9 months until it emerges as a baby. Monozygotic twins are formed, however, when that cluster of cells breaks apart into two clusters early in the growth process. If conditions are right, each of these clusters grows into a baby. These infants are "identical" not only in appearance but also identical in genetic structure, since they came from the same fertilized egg.

**Dizygotic twins,** in contrast, are formed when the female produces two separate eggs that are fertilized by two different sperm cells. These two fertilized eggs grow into two babies that are born at about the same time, but they are not genetically identical. Dizygotic twins are no more alike genetically than are siblings born at different times. Like other siblings, dizygotic twins share 50 percent of their genes on average.

The natural experiment comes from the fact that both types of twins provide us with pairs of children who grow up in essentially the same home environment. They have the same parents, they are reared during the same time period, and they have the same sisters and brothers. On the other hand, the two kinds of twins differ genetically. If a characteristic of behavior is influenced to some degree by heredity, therefore, monozygotic twin pairs will be more similar to one another than would dizygotic twin pairs.

The many experiments conducted using twins have revealed the influence of heredity on behavior (Angoff, 1988). For example, studies of twins have suggested that intelligence, or IQ, is partly determined by heredity (Bartels & others, 2002; Plomin, 1999; Plomin & Petrill, 1997). Figure 3.26 summarizes the findings of a number of studies indicating the degree of similarity in the intelligence test scores among various types of twins and siblings (Bouchard & McGue, 1981). Monozygotic twins who share both identical genetic structure and common environments have almost identical IQ scores. Dizygotic twins, on the other hand, are only slightly more similar in their IQ scores than are other pairs of siblings who are not twins.

### Studies of Adopted Children

Studies of adopted children have also shown that inheritance influences behavior (Angoff, 1988; Plomin, 1994). Take the case of IQ again. It's well known that the IQs of children are pretty similar to those of their parents. But why is this so? Is it because bright parents provide a stimulating intellectual environment that makes their children bright like them, whereas unintelligent parents do just the opposite? Or is it because the children inherit their intellectual potential from their parents? As it turns out, *both* heredity and environment work together to influence IQ, but studies of adopted

Identical, or monozygotic, twins are formed when a single fertilized egg breaks apart into two clusters of cells, each growing into a separate person.

**dizygotic twins**
(dī″zi-got′ik) Twins formed from the fertilization of two ova by two sperm.

**FIGURE 3.26**

The degree of similarity among monozygotic twins, dizygotic twins, and other siblings on measures of intelligence.

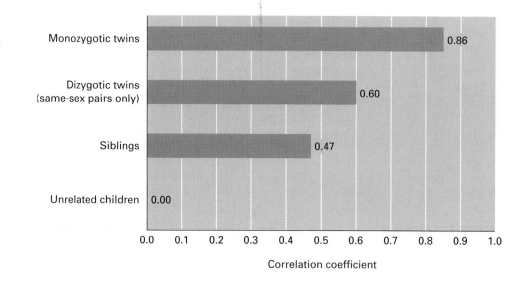

children have helped show us that the role played by heredity is a strong one. These studies have shown that the IQs of adopted children are more similar to those of their biological parents than to those of the adoptive parents who raised them since infancy (Plomin, 1994). Because the children spent no time living with their biological parents, the only explanation for the similarity in IQs is the link of inheritance.

### Genetic Influences on Complex Human Behavior

I have a friend who has an outgoing, dominant personality that makes her the "leader" of almost any group she is in. And her mother is just like her. Does this dominant young woman resemble her mother because she imitated her mother and learned to deal with others in the same dominant way, or did she inherit this personality characteristic in the same way that she inherited her mother's green eyes? Since the time of Plato, it has been suspected that positive and negative characteristics of our personalities—and even psychological disorders—might be influenced by genetic factors. Until recently, however, little solid evidence has been available to test this genetic hypothesis. In recent years, strong evidence from a number of studies from several countries suggests that *both* heredity and experience work together to influence normal and abnormal aspects of personality, including sociability, aggressiveness, alcohol and drug use, kindness, depression, and anxiousness (Dick & others, 2001; Kendler, 2001; Plomin, 1989, 1995).

The fact that an aspect of our physical or psychological selves is influenced by heredity does not mean that it is etched in stone. Even highly heritable characteristics can be influenced to some extent by environmental factors. William Angoff (1988) reminds us that, even though height is strongly influenced by heredity, the average height in some countries has increased by over 3 inches since World War II. He believes that the characteristic of intelligence, in the right circumstances, has the same potential for change over time. Notice, too, that even the strongest estimate of the role of genetics in the formation of our personalities leaves a major role to be played by our child rearing, the stresses and strains of our lives, our social relationships, and other psychological factors. Heredity and experience always work together to influence our psychological characteristics.

Specific patterns of behavior are not inherited by humans, but heredity does influence broad dimensions of behavior. Among the characteristics that appear to be influenced to some degree by inheritance are intelligence, several aspects of personality, and some aspects of abnormal behavior. The hereditary blueprints that exert this influence are coded in thousands of genes arranged on pairs of chromosome strips in the nuclei of cells. One member of each chromosome pair comes from each parent, giving each individual two sets of genes. Sometimes these genes are in conflict, as when a person inherits a gene for blue eyes from the mother and brown eyes from the father. When this happens, some genes are dominant because they suppress the influence of the other conflicting gene for the same trait; other genes are recessive and have an effect only when the same recessive gene is inherited from both parents.

The effects of heredity on human behavior have been examined in studies using twins and adopted children. For example, the fact that monozygotic (identical) twins have exactly the same genes, whereas dizygotic twins share only about 50 percent of their genes, can be used to study the role of heredity. Even though both kinds of twins grow up in comparably similar environments, monozygotic twins are more similar than dizygotic twins on several dimensions of behavior, suggesting that genetics plays some role in behavior. In addition, studies showing that adopted children resemble their biological parents in some ways more than they resemble the adoptive parents who reared them indicate the role of inheritance. Although the influence of heredity on behavior is significant, many other factors influence behavior as well. We are far from being as rigidly programmed by our inheritance as some species of animals are.

**Review**

To be sure that you have learned the key points from the preceding section, cover the list of correct answers and try to answer each question. If you give an incorrect answer to any question, return to the page given next to the correct answer to see why your answer was not correct.

**Check Your Learning**

1. The genetic code is contained in segments of DNA called

   a) genes.  c) neurons.

   b) mitochondria.  d) hormones.

2. A trait that will be found in a child only when the child receives the same gene for the same trait from both parents is a _____ trait.

   a) recessive  c) Mendelian

   b) dominant  d) dizygotic

3. To study inheritance in humans, scientists often study twins because one type of twins is genetically identical, whereas the other type shares only about 50 percent of the same genes; the type of twin that is genetically identical is called

   a) Mendelian.  c) monozygotic.

   b) adopted.  d) dizygotic.

4. The results of a study of adopted children would indicate that a characteristic was influenced by inheritance if the children resembled more their _____ parents.

   a) adoptive  c) nonparous

   b) biological  d) dizygotic

## Thinking Critically about Psychology

1. What are the social implications of research suggesting that intelligence and some personality traits are, to a considerable extent, inherited?

2. What are the advantages of studying twins who have been raised apart? Can such studies give us a complete answer about the influence of heredity on human behavior?

**Correct Answers: 1.** a (p. 92), **2.** a (p. 93), **3.** c (p. 94), **4.** b (p. 95).

## Madness and the Brain

We began this chapter by stating the obvious fact that the brain is the most important biological organ to psychology. We will end the chapter by looking at two striking and sad examples in which the psychological lives of some people are seriously disturbed because the brain does not function normally—schizophrenia and Alzheimer's disease.

## Schizophrenia and the Brain

Schizophrenia is an uncommon disorder that affects a little less than 1 percent of the general population. However, it's a severe psychological disorder that, unless successfully treated, renders normal patterns of living impossible. The central feature of schizophrenia is a marked abnormality in thought processes that leaves the person with schizophrenia "out of touch with reality." Persons with schizophrenia often hold strange and disturbing beliefs (such as believing that they receive telepathic messages from devils in another universe). They also often have strangely distorted perceptual experiences (such as hearing voices that are not really there that tell them to do dangerous things) and think in fragmented and illogical ways. At the same time, the emotions and social relationships of the person with schizophrenia are often severely disturbed.

Great strides have been made recently in understanding the link between schizophrenia and the brain. Although this evidence is strong and impressive, a word of caution might be wise before we look at this topic. Researchers tend to study very severe cases of any disorder, including schizophrenia, to make the difficult task of finding the cause of the disorder a little easier. Therefore, when we look at the striking images in this section of the very abnormal brains of persons with schizophrenia, keep in mind that these are the brains of severe cases. Individuals with milder schizophrenia may have more normal brains.

Remember that there is strong evidence that a predisposition to schizophrenia is inherited. As discussed earlier in this chapter (p. 94), the role of genetics can be examined in studies comparing identical twins (who have identical genes) with fraternal twins (who share only about half of their genes). The fact that about 50 percent of identical twins both have schizophrenia if one has schizophrenia, compared with only about 10 percent of fraternal twins, is strong evidence for a genetic factor in the disorder. However, the fact that not *all* of the identical twins of persons with schizophrenia also have the disorder clearly shows that more than just heredity is involved. Some other factor or factors must play key roles in the cause of schizophrenia (Fowles, 1992).

### Images of the Brains of Persons with Schizophrenia

Whatever those factors are that work along with heredity to cause schizophrenia, they produce marked changes in the brains of persons with severe schizophrenia. An impressive number of studies using magnetic resonance imaging (MRI), PET, and other brain-imaging techniques show that the cerebral cortex and key structures of the limbic system are literally "shrunken" in persons with schizophrenia (Andreasen, 1999; Byne & others, 2001; Mathalon, Sullivan, Lim, & Pfefferbaum, 2001; Cannon & others, 1998). The easiest way to see the reduced size of the brain in persons with schizophrenia using MRI is to measure the size of structures called the *ventricles*. The ventricles are fluid-filled passageways located near the center of the brain that bathe the brain in fluid. If the underside of the cortex and nearby structures are shrunken, the ventricles are enlarged.

The enlargement of the ventricles in persons with schizophrenia is shown clearly in the two striking brain images in figure 3.27. These are MRI images of the brains of two identical twins,

*(continued)*

Ventricles
Ventricles

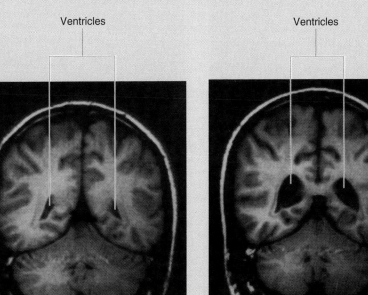
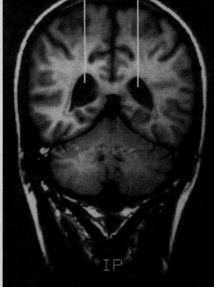

**FIGURE 3.27**
These are MRI images of the brains of two identical twins viewed from the back. The twin on the right has schizophrenia, but the twin on the left does not. Notice that the open spaces inside the brain, called the ventricles, are enlarged in the schizophrenic because the interior regions of the brain are reduced in size.

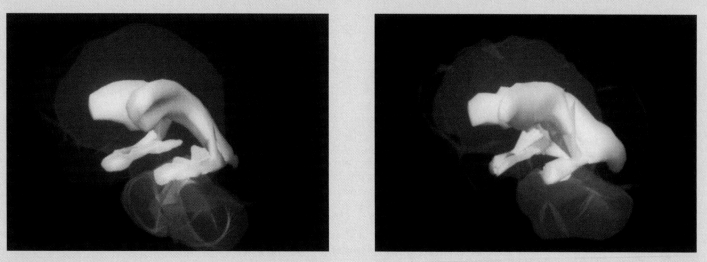

**FIGURE 3.28**

The brain of a person with schizophrenia (right) shows a shrunken hippocampus (in yellow) and enlarged, fluid-filled ventricles (gray) in comparison with the brain of a person without schizophrenia (left).

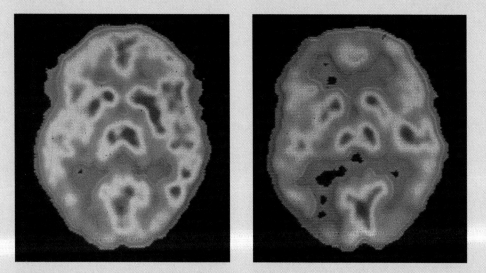

**FIGURE 3.29**

These PET scans demonstrate how functioning of the cerebral cortex can be affected in schizophrenia. The level of activity in the brain is indicated by the colors on the scan. Yellow and red indicate high levels, whereas green signifies a low activity level. During a task that requires close attention, the frontal lobes of the cerebral cortex (at the top of each scan) are highly active in a person without schizophrenia (left). In contrast, a person with schizophrenia, shown on the right, has little activity in the same area during the same task.

has colored the ventricle closer to us in silver and the ventricle in the cerebral hemisphere that is farther away from us in white. Both the cerebral cortex and the cerebellum are colored in red. The image at the left is of a person with schizophrenia, whereas the image at the right is of a normal person. Notice that the ventricles of the person with schizophrenia are enlarged in the middle and rear portions of the brain, showing reductions in size of the interior portions of the brain in these areas. Perhaps more interestingly, these color images also allow us to directly measure a key structure in the limbic system, the hippocampus, which is color-coded in yellow. Recall that the hippocampus plays a key role in the regulation of both emotion and memory (see p. 74). In this image, the person with schizophrenia has a markedly smaller hippocampus.

The parts of the brain surrounding the ventricles are important in their own right, but they also are the source of neurons that activate the frontal lobes of the cerebral cortex (p. 75). The frontal lobes play important roles in emotional control and logical planning—two qualities that are quite disturbed in schizophrenia. Look at the two PET images of the cerebral cortex shown in figure 3.29 that reveal more about the level of brain activity than the size of the structures. We are looking at the brain from the top, with the frontal lobes shown at the top of these images. High levels of activity in an area of the brain are shown in yellow and red, whereas cool greens

only one of whom has schizophrenia (Horgan, 1993). These images were made looking at the *back* of the head. The two lobes of the cerebral cortex can be seen at the top of the head, with the slightly darker cerebellum clearly visible at the base of the skull. The ventricles are two dark spots toward the bottom of the two hemispheres of cerebral cortex. Which identical twin has schizophrenia—can you tell? The brain of the twin with schizophrenia is shown on the right. Notice that the ventricles are greatly enlarged because

the interior portions of the cerebral cortex and limbic system are reduced in size.

An even more dramatic set of images is shown in figure 3.28. These three-dimensional color photographs were constructed from computer-enhanced MRI images in the laboratory of Nancy Andreasen at the University of Iowa School of Medicine (from Gershon & Rieder, 1992). In these images, the brain is seen from an angle, looking at the head from the front on the left side. In these images, the computer program indicate low levels of brain activity. Notice that the level of activity in the frontal lobes of the normal person (the left image) is high during a task that requires close attention. In contrast, the person with schizophrenia in the image on the right shows little activity in the frontal lobes—they appear to be "turned off."

More recent findings indicate that the thalamus may not function normally in individuals with schizophrenia (Hazlett & others, 1999). This is important because, as mentioned earlier in this chapter, the thalamus routes incoming sensory information. Perhaps the hallucinations experienced by schizophrenics result in part because the thalamus does not function normally.

### Neurotransmitters and Schizophrenia

These images, and many similar ones from other studies using brain imaging and autopsy studies of schizophrenics who have died, strongly suggest that persons with schizophrenia experience life in abnormal ways partly because they have abnormalities in the hippocampus, the cerebral cortex, and other key brain structures. Interestingly, evidence shows that these abnormalities in brain structure are also reflected in abnormal levels of the neurotransmitter *dopamine* (Albert & others, 2002; Berman & others, 1988; Conklin & Iacono, 2002). This neurotransmitter is involved in the activities of many parts of the brain, including the frontal lobe of the cerebral cortex. For a variety of reasons, researchers have long suspected that dopamine is involved in schizophrenia. For example, great strides were made in the treatment of schizophrenia in the 1950s with the introduction of the *phenothiazine* drugs. The first clue to the specific effects of these drugs on the body was that phenothiazines often produced the serious side effect of muscular control problems such as those found in Parkinson's disease. Since Parkinson's disease is caused by a deterioration of the parts of the brain that use the neurotransmitter dopamine to transmit neural messages, it was hypothesized that the phenothiazine drugs operated by interfering with dopamine. Thus, if drugs that produce improvements alter dopamine transmission, it makes sense to theorize that schizophrenia is caused by abnormal dopamine transmission.

Another sort of evidence that supports the dopamine hypothesis comes from experience with the side effects of the stimulant drugs called *amphetamines*. These drugs are widely abused because of the intense high and feelings of energy they produce. Excessive use of amphetamines, however, can lead to a condition called *amphetamine psychosis,* which closely resembles paranoid schizophrenia. The fact that this condition resembles schizophrenia is important because amphetamines produce this psychotic reaction by altering dopamine transmission (Snyder, 1974). Furthermore, the best treatment for amphetamine psychosis is phenothiazine medication, which is also the best treatment for schizophrenia.

### Causes of Schizophrenia

A great deal of evidence suggests that the brains of persons with schizophrenia are abnormal in structure and function. There is evidence that a predisposition to schizophrenia is inherited, but it is also clear that some other factor or factors must play a role in causing schizophrenia because not even all identical twins both exhibit schizophrenia. What might be the other factor or factors that can cause schizophrenia in genetically predisposed persons? For one thing, there is evidence that *stress* causes persons who are genetically predisposed to have episodes of schizophrenia (Ventura, Neuchterlein, Lukoff, & Hardesty, 1989). However, because this chapter covers the biological foundations of behavior, we focus on evidence that the genetic predisposition is most likely to lead to schizophrenia if the predisposed person suffered some disturbance of the development of the *brain* before birth or during birth (Barre & others, 2001; McNeil, Cantor-Graae, & Weinberger, 2000; Mednick, Machon, Huttunen, & Bonett, 1988; Wyatt, 1996).

Studies by Sarnoff Mednick and others (Barr, Mednick, & Munk-Jorgensen, 1990; Cannon, Mednick & others, 1993; Conklin & Iacono, 2002; Mednick & others, 1988) support the so-called *double strike theory* of schizophrenia. Mednick hypothesizes that schizophrenia is most likely in persons with (a) a genetic predisposition to schizophrenia and (b) some form of complication during pregnancy that alters the brains of individuals who are genetically predisposed to schizophrenia. According to this theory, a genetically predisposed individual who has no complications during pregnancy or birth would be unlikely to develop schizophrenia. Similarly, pregnancy complications would be unlikely to cause schizophrenia in individuals who are not genetically predisposed to it.

Emerging evidence suggests that brain development in genetically predisposed infants can be damaged by dehydration of the mother when she contracts influenza during pregnancy, by severe malnutrition of the mother during pregnancy, by an uncommon Rh incompatibility between the blood of the mother and the fetus, and by birth complications that deprive the newborn of oxygen during birth (Kunugi & others, 1995; Susser & others, 1996; van Err & others, 2002; Wyatt, 1996).

For example, studies of large samples suggest that schizophrenia is more common in children whose mothers were pregnant during periods of influenza epidemics. Figure 3.30 on page 102 shows the rates of schizophrenia in the offspring of women whose pregnancies occurred during periods of low, medium, or high rates of influenza. Notice that the highest rates of schizophrenia are for the children of women who were exposed to influenza during the fifth through the seventh months of pregnancy, which is during the period of the most rapid development of the nervous system in the fetus. Other studies show that severe malnutrition of the mother during pregnancy and other pregnancy complications can also cause the same damage to the developing brain that influenza does (Bracha, Torrey, Gottesman, Bigelow, & Cunniff, 1992; Marenco & Weinberger, 2001; McGlashan & Hoffman, 2000; Susser & Lin, 1992).

The clearest evidence in support of Mednick's double strike theory of schizophrenia comes from a long-term study (Cannon & others, 1993). Mednick's research team has been following a group of children of parents with schizophrenia in Denmark for many years and has detailed information on them from birth to adulthood. Some of the children had two schizophrenic parents (and are considered to have an increased genetic predisposition to schizophrenia), whereas others had only one schizophrenic parent. In contrast, a third group of children has been studied who have no schizophrenic parents (and,

*(continued)*

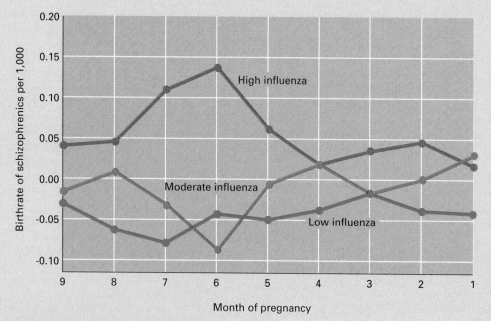

**FIGURE 3.30**

The average birthrate of persons who later develop schizophrenia when mothers were exposed to low, medium, or high levels of influenza during each month of their pregnancy. Negative birthrates are lower than average; positive birthrates are higher than average.

**Source:** Data from C. E. Barr, S. A. Mednick, and P. Munk-Jorgensen, "Exposure to Influenza Epidemics during Gestation and Adult Schizophrenia" in *Archives of General Psychiatry,* 47:869–874, 1990.

therefore, are thought to be at low risk for schizophrenia).

Mednick's research team later obtained brain images of these children at age 29 years using computerized X rays and looked to see whether the persons with the highest genetic predisposition were most likely to have one of the kinds of brain abnormalites associated with schizophrenia (enlarged ventricles). But, because Mednick believes that a person with a genetic predisposition to schizophrenia will develop the disorder only if a pregnancy or birth complication occurred, the researchers looked at birth complications as well.

Mednick found that the ventricles in the children of one parent with schizophrenia were significantly larger than those of the children of no schizophrenic parents, and the ventricles of the children with two schizophrenic parents were significantly larger than those of the children in either of the other two groups, but *only* when a birth complication had occurred. More recently, Mednick's double strike hypothesis of the origins of schizophrenia has been confirmed by a number of independent studies (Dalman & others, 1999; Kinney & others, 1998; Kirkpatrick & others, 1998). Thus, these studies provide strong support for the idea that both genetic predisposition and pregnancy and

birth complications operate together to cause schizophrenia.

## Alzheimer's Disease and the Brain

Few facts portray the intimate relationship between the brain and our psychological selves more vividly or more sadly than the decline of an individual with Alzheimer's disease. Fully functioning individuals who develop this disorder often fade rapidly in emotional and intellectual functioning, until they are "no longer themselves." Like schizophrenia, Alzheimer's disease results from the deterioration of the cerebral cortex, the hippocampus, and other structures. In Alzheimer's disease, this deterioration is due to the death of neurons, the accumulation of protein deposits, and the development of tangles of neuronal fibers. In most cases, this deterioration can be seen clearly using brain-imaging techniques. Alzheimer's disease is a principal cause of what we commonly refer to as senility.

The loss of brain function results in loss of memory for recent and past events, confusion, and errors in judgment. The individual may no longer recognize close relatives, may forget to turn off the stove, may become lost in a familiar supermarket, and may often lose objects such as keys. Changes in personality are also common. A person who was formerly thought of as polite and socially inhibited may make coarse remarks, lewd jokes, and insulting sexual advances. A formerly shrewd businessperson may make extremely unwise investments. And a happy and loving parent may become apathetic, withdrawn, and unaffectionate.

Individuals who develop Alzheimer's disease often rapidly fade, particularly in intellectual capacity, until they are "no longer themselves."

Alzheimer's disease is uncommon before age 75, but it can develop as early as middle age. The cause of this massive deterioration of the brain is not presently known, but apparently there is an inherited predisposition to develop it. Close relatives of persons with Alzheimer's disease are four times as likely to develop the disorder by age 86 than are individuals without a relative with the disorder (Mohs, Breitner, Silverman, & Davis, 1987). Recent advances in brain-imaging technology using magnetic resonance imaging make it possible to see the deterioration of portions of the cerebral cortex that results in Alzheimer's disease. The image on the left in figure 3.31 is of an older adult with few symptoms; the image on the right shows the dramatic deterioration in both hemispheres of the cortex that accompanies severe symptoms of Alzheimer's disease (Bondareff, Raval, Woo, Hauser, & Colletti, 1990).

I hope this detailed discussion of two ways in which disorders of the brain can alter psychological lives will help give you a better understanding of why we must understand the brain to understand psychology. Also, this discussion will give you a more informed perspective on these two conditions. ■

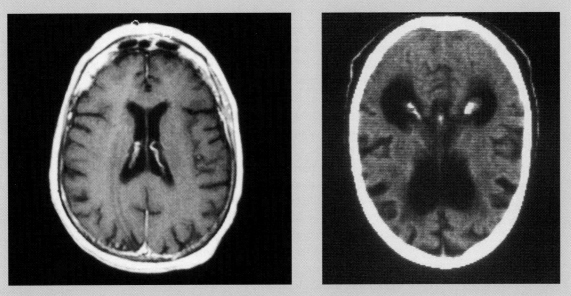

**FIGURE 3.31**
(Left) MRI scan of a normal older adult. (Right) MRI scan showing the deterioration of the cerebral cortex in both hemispheres (viewed from the top) in a patient with severe Alzheimer's disease.

## Summary

Chapter 3 describes people as psychological beings who live in biological bodies; it looks at the role played by the nervous system, the endocrine system, and genetic mechanisms in our behavior and mental processes.

I. The nervous system is a complex network of neural cells that carry messages and regulate body functions and personal behavior.

  A. The individual cells of the nervous system (neurons) transmit electrical signals along their length.

  B. Chemical substances called neurotransmitters transmit neural messages from the axon of one neuron across the gap (synapse) to the next neuron.

  C. The central nervous system is composed of the brain and spinal cord. The peripheral nervous system carries messages between the central nervous system and the rest of the body. It consists of the somatic and autonomic nervous systems.

    1. The somatic nervous system carries messages from the sense organs to the central nervous system, and it carries messages from the central nervous system to the skeletal muscles.

2. The autonomic nervous system regulates the visceral organs and other body functions and plays a role in emotional activity.

II. The brain has three basic parts: the hindbrain, the midbrain, and the forebrain.

  A. The hindbrain consists of the medulla, the pons, and the cerebellum.

   1. The medulla controls breathing and a variety of reflexes.

   2. The pons regulates balance, hearing, and several parasympathetic functions.

   3. The cerebellum is chiefly responsible for maintaining muscle tone and coordination of muscular movements but also plays a role in learning and memory involving sequenced events.

  B. The midbrain is a center for reflexes related to vision and hearing.

  C. Most cognitive, motivational, and emotional activity is controlled by the forebrain, which includes the thalamus, hypothalamus, limbic system, and cerebral cortex.

   1. The thalamus is a switching station for routing sensory information to appropriate areas of the brain.

   2. The hypothalamus and limbic system are involved with motives and emotions.

   3. The largest part of the brain is the cerebral cortex, made up of two cerebral hemispheres, which are primarily connected by the corpus callosum. The cortex controls conscious experience, intellectual activities, the senses, and voluntary functions.

  D. Each part of the brain interacts with the entire nervous system, and the parts work together in intellectual, physical, and emotional functions.

  E. The brain is an organ that is plastic to some degree—it changes over the course of development.

III. Whereas the nervous system forms the primary biological basis for behavior and mental processes, the endocrine system of hormone secreting glands influences emotional arousal, metabolism, sexual functioning, and other body processes.

  A. Adrenal glands secrete epinephrine and norepinephrine, which are involved in emotional arousal, heart rate, and metabolism.

  B. Islets of Langerhans secrete glucagon and insulin, which control blood-sugar and energy levels.

  C. Gonads produce sex cells (ova and sperm) for human reproduction and estrogen and testosterone, which are hormones important to sexual functioning and the development of secondary sex characteristics.

  D. The thyroid gland secretes thyroxin, which controls the rate of metabolism.

  E. Parathyroid glands secrete parathormone, which controls the level of nervous activity.

  F. The pituitary gland secretes various hormones that control the activities of other endocrine glands and have important effects on general body processes.

IV. Some human characteristics and behaviors are influenced by genetic inheritance.

  A. Inherited characteristics are passed on through genes, which are segments of DNA on the chromosomes.

  B. Most normal human cells contain 46 chromosomes (23 pairs).

  C. The sex cells (sperm and ova) contain only 23 chromosomes each; they are capable of combining into a new zygote during fertilization.

D.   Research has shown that inheritance plays a significant role in influencing behavior—including intelligence, some aspects of personality, and some aspects of abnormal behavior—but environmental and other personal factors are very important as well. Genetic and environmental factors always operate together to influence psychological characteristics.

**Resources**

1.   For a very readable discussion of the relationship between brain and behavior written for the intelligent public, see LeDoux, J. (1996). *The emotional brain.* New York: Touchstone. A more sophisticated summary for college students is provided by Beatty, J. (1995). *Principles of behavioral neuroscience.* Boston: McGraw-Hill.

2.   The classic studies of patients with split brains are described in readable detail in Gazzaniga, M. S. (1992). *Nature's mind: The biological roots of thinking, emotion, sexuality, language, and intelligence.* Boston: Houghton Mifflin. A great collection of papers on the relationship between brain and cognition is found in Gazzaniga, M. S. (2000). *Cognitive neuroscience: A reader.* Malden, MA: Blackwell.

3.   A fascinating look at the possible role played by neural factors in mental disorders is provided by Andreasen, N. C. (1983). *The broken brain: The biological revolution in psychiatry.* New York: Harper & Row. She has also published an updated report of such research in Andreasen, N. C. (1999). A unitary model of schizophrenia: Bleuler's "fragmented phrene" as schizoencephaly. *Archives of General Psychiatry, 56,* 781–787.

4.   For an elegantly written description of the use of functional magnetic resonance imaging (MRI) in the study of the human brain, see D'Esposito, M. (2000). *Seminars in Neurology, 20,* 487–498.

5.   For more on the interplay of genetic and environmental influences on behavior and mental processes, see Plomin, R. (1994). *Genetics and experience.* Thousand Oaks, CA: Sage.

6.   For an easy-to-understand discussion of genetic influences on intelligence and learning problems, see Plomin, R., & DeFries, J. C. (1998, May). The genetics of cognitive abilities and disabilities. *Scientific American,* pp. 62–69.

# Visual Review of Brain Structures

Because so much information was covered in chapter 3 on the structures of the brain and endocrine system, a set of unlabeled illustrations (figs. 3.32 through 3.36) has been prepared to help you check your learning of these structures. These reviews will be most helpful if you glance at the first one and then refer back to the illustration on which it is are based to memorize the names of the structures. Then, return to the illustration in this review section and try to write in the names of the brain structures. Check your labels by looking at the original figure once again. When you can label all of the structures in one of the illustrations, you can move on to the next one.

This review section should help you learn the names of the structures of the many parts of the brain. Don't forget, however, to learn what the structures *do* (their functions). After you have mastered the names and locations of the structures, it should be easier for you to remember their functions.

**FIGURE 3.32**
Key structures of the hindbrain and midbrain (based on fig. 3.11, p. 73).

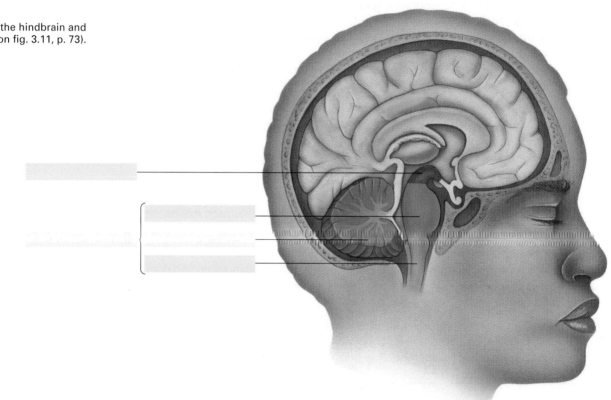

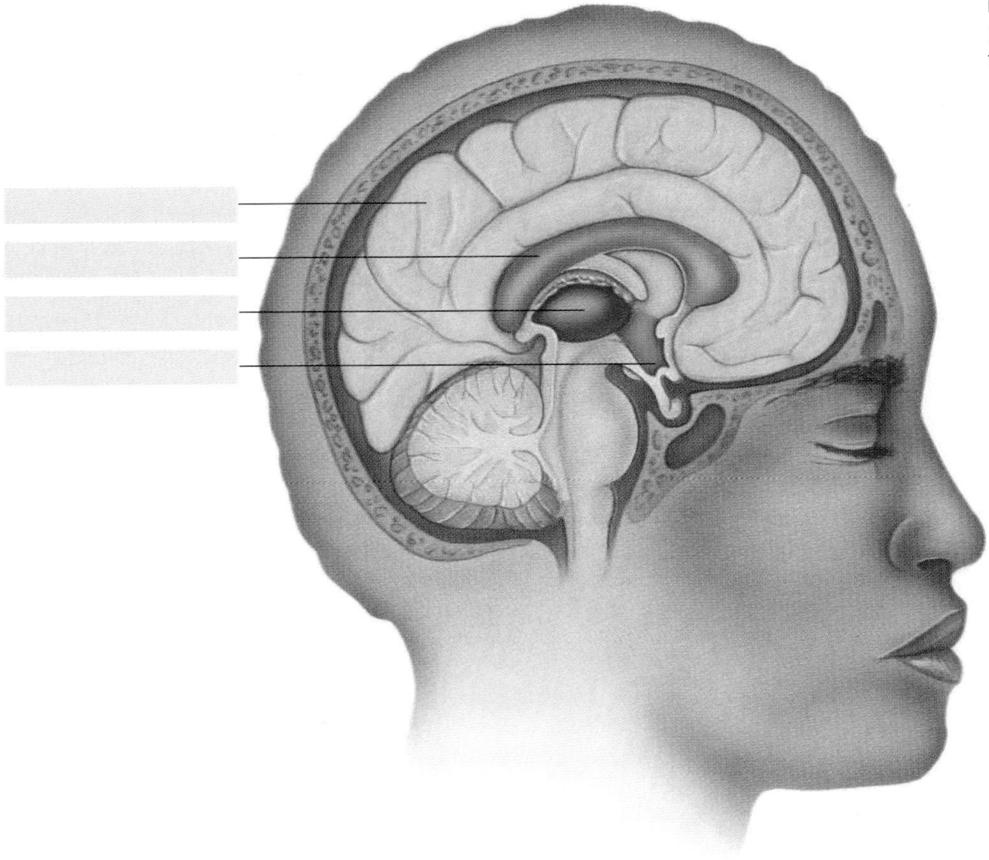

**FIGURE 3.33**
Key structures of the forebrain (based on
fig. 3.12, p. 73).

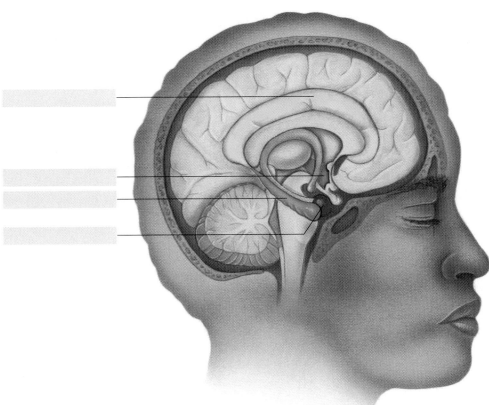

**FIGURE 3.34**
Key structures of the limbic system
(based on fig. 3.13, p. 75).

**FIGURE 3.35**

The four lobes of the cerebral cortex (box on lower right) and areas with specific functions (top area of illustration) in the cerebral cortex (based on fig. 3.15, p. 76).

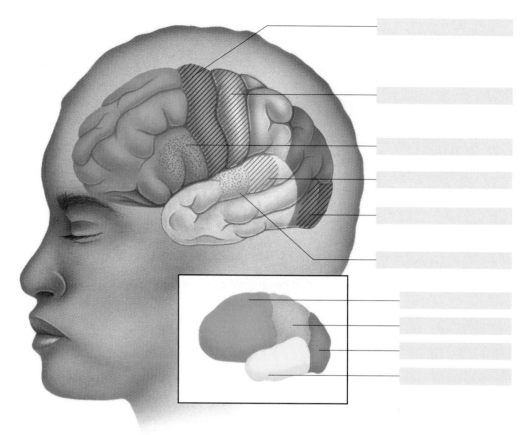

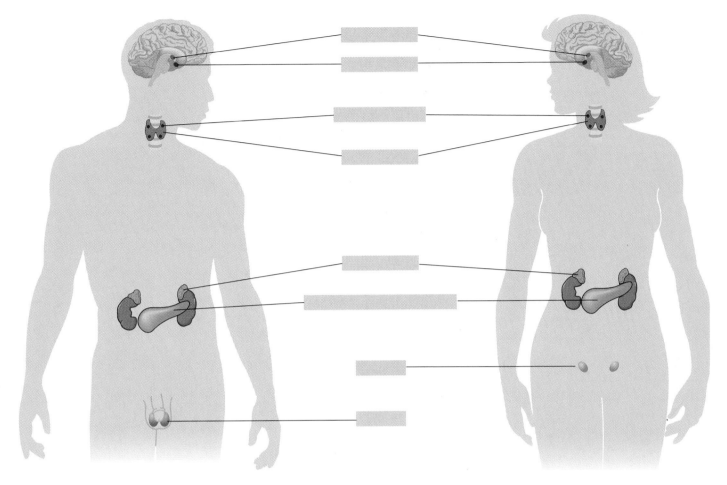

**FIGURE 3.36**
Endocrine glands (based on fig. 3.22, p. 87).

# PART II

# Awareness

In chapters 4 and 5, you will learn about awareness. In chapter 4, you will see how the sense organs transduce energy in the environment into neural signals that are sent to the brain—sights, sounds, tastes, odors, and bodily sensations. You will learn how this basic sensory information is integrated and interpreted in the sensory systems and the brain as meaningful perceptions. In chapter 5, we explore the many states of consciousness—wakefulness, sleep, dreams, and altered states of consciousness.

Here is a visual overview of what you will learn in the second section of the text.

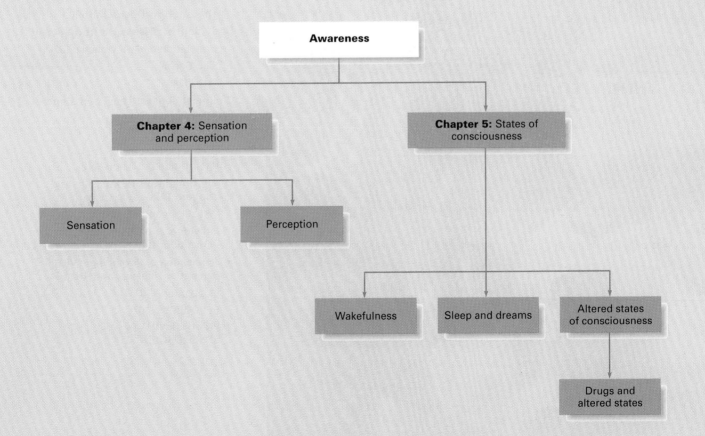

## Chapter Outline

# Sensation and Perception

## PROLOGUE

Last night I "saw" the University of North Carolina play Notre Dame in basketball—by listening to the radio. The play-by-play announcer watched the game, and he translated what he saw into a kind of information (words) that could be transmitted over the radio. Then I used that information to form a mental picture of the game. I did not see with my eyes, yet I was able to "watch" the game in my head.

I realized this morning that my way of seeing the game last night was not very different from how I see games in person. We never really "see" with our eyes alone. We use our eyes to gather information and translate it into a form that can be transmitted to the brain. It's in the brain that visual perception is created out of the incoming sensory information.

We usually assume that we simply "see" what is "out there." The processes of seeing, smelling, or touching seem so straightforward. In reality, however, perception is based on a complex chain of receiving, transmitting, and interpreting sensory information. Each step of this process actively changes the information in significant ways. Because we know "reality" only through our sensations and perceptions, we must understand the sense organs and the ways in which the processes of sensation and perception change sensory information.

In this chapter, we will study the five major senses: vision, hearing, the body senses, taste, and smell. In vision, the eye collects, translates, and transmits energy from light to the brain. The ear—the sense organ for hearing—accomplishes the same for the energy in vibrating molecules of air. The body senses provide the brain with information from the skin about temperature, touch, and pain; and information from receptors in the inner ear, joints, and muscles tells us about the position and movement of the body—where we are and where we are going. The chemical senses use receptor cells in the nose and on the tongue to provide information to the brain about the chemicals in the air we breathe and in the things we drink and eat.

Raw sensations have little meaning until they are organized and interpreted in the process of perception. Perception is an active process that changes sensory information. As we discussed in chapter 1, we perceive actors as moving when we watch a motion picture. In reality, however, the sensory information is just a series of rapidly changing *still photographs*. The people on the movie screen don't actually move at all. We perceive them as moving only because the process of perception often goes well beyond the immediate sensory information. The brain creates the perception of motion in a movie that the sensory information only hints at.

In most cases, the ways in which the brain interprets information in the process of perception appear to be inborn. Our perceptions of reality are also colored by individual expectations, cultural learning experiences, and needs, however. As a result, different people sometimes have rather different views of the same world.

Human life would be very different without our ability to sense and perceive. Take friendships as an example. How could we have friends if we could not

## Key Terms

distinguish one person from another by sensing their differences? How could we communicate with our friends if we could not hear their words properly or read their notes accurately or notice the expressions on their faces? How could we let them know that we cared if they could not feel a pat on the back? ■

## ● Sensation: Receiving Messages about the World

We are aware of an outside world and the internal world of our own bodies only because we have a number of **sense organs** able to receive messages. These organs enable us to see, hear, taste, smell, touch, balance, and experience such feelings as body stiffness, soreness, fullness, warmth, pleasure, pain, and movement. Sense organs operate through **sensory receptor cells,** which *receive* outside forms of energy (light, vibrations, heat) and *translate* them into *neural impulses* that can be *transmitted* to the brain for interpretation. Sense organs do the job of the basketball announcer who translates what he or she sees into words that can be transmitted on the radio. The process of receiving information from the outside world, translating it, and transmitting it to the brain is called **sensation.** The process of interpreting that information and forming images of the world is called **perception.**

### Stimuli: What Messages Can Be Received?

A key concept you will run into frequently throughout this text is **stimulus,** which refers to any aspect of the outside world that directly influences our behavior or conscious experience. The term *stimulus* comes from the action of *stimulating* sensory receptor cells.

Virtually anything that can excite receptor cells can be a stimulus. When you take a seat at a dinner party, the chair is a stimulus through your senses of sight and touch. When you begin to eat, the food becomes a stimulus through your senses of taste, smell, and sight. If the room is too hot, the temperature acts as a stimulus through the sensory receptors in your skin. The compliments you lavish on your hosts are also stimuli, which increase your chances of being invited for dinner again. Whenever a person is aware of, or in some other way responds to, a part of the outside world, she or he receives a stimulus.

When I say that any part of the outside world can be a stimulus, I am using the term *outside* broadly. Even parts of the internal world of the body can be stimuli. If you eat too much at the dinner party, the bloated stretching of your stomach is a very noticeable stimulus.

### Transduction: Translating Messages for the Brain

Energy from stimuli cannot go directly to the brain. Light, sound, and other kinds of energy from the outside world are not able to travel through the nerves, and the brain cannot "understand" what they mean. To be useful to the brain, sensory messages must be translated into neural impulses that the neurons carry and the brain understands. The translation of one form of energy into another is called **transduction.**

Sense organs transduce sensory energy into neural energy. This is accomplished in the sense organ by the sensory receptor cells, which are specialized neurons that are excited by specific kinds of sensory energy and give off neural impulses from their axons. Some sensory receptor cells are sensitive to sound, some to light, some to chemicals, and so on. But in every case, the receptor cells give off coded neural impulses that carry the transduced sensory message to one of the sensory areas of the brain. The sense organs themselves (such as the ear, eye, and nose) are constructed in special ways that expose the receptor cells to sensory energy and help them transduce it into neural impulses. At the center of every sense organ are receptor cells that do the transducing.

Note that we can be aware of a stimulus only if we have receptor cells that can transduce it. For example, we cannot see radio waves or hear some high-frequency tones, and we find some chemicals to be "tasteless" and "odorless" because we do not have

**sense organs**
Organs that receive stimuli.

**sensory receptor cells**
Cells in sense organs that translate messages into neural impulses that are sent to the brain.

**sensation**
(sen-sā´-shun) The process of receiving, translating, and transmitting messages from the outside world to the brain.

**perception**
(per-sep´-shun) The process of organizing and interpreting information received from the outside world.

**stimulus**
(stim´ ū-lus) Any aspect of the outside world that directly influences our behavior or conscious experience.

**transduction**
(trans-duk´shun) The translation of energy from one form to another.

At first, cold water bombards us with sensations. After being in cold water for a while, receptors in the skin adapt to changes in temperature and lessen the sensation of coldness.

receptors that can transduce these kinds of stimuli. Although a radio wave is just as real as the light reflected to our eyes from an apple, we cannot transduce the radio wave. We know that radio waves exist only because radios physically transduce them into sound waves, which are in turn transduced by our ears into neural messages to the brain. There are many forms of energy in the world that we are not aware of because we do not have receptor cells that can transduce them (see fig. 4.1). If our planet were visited by aliens with sensory receptors sensitive *only* to forms of energy different from our own sensory receptors, they would experience a world entirely different from the one we experience.

## Sensory Limits: How Strong Must Messages Be?

Even when we have receptor cells that can transduce a kind of sensory message, not every message will be strong enough to be detected. The term *threshold* refers to the lower limits of sensory experience. The two primary kinds of thresholds are (a) the smallest *magnitude* of a stimulus that can be detected and (b) the smallest *difference* between two stimuli that can be detected.

The **absolute threshold** is the smallest magnitude of a stimulus that can be detected. Look at the absolute thresholds for a number of common stimuli shown in figure 4.2 to gain a fuller appreciation of your remarkably sensitive receptor cells. Measuring such thresholds is no simple matter. People differ considerably in their sensitivity to weak stimuli, and the sensitivity of each of us differs from time to time. For this reason, absolute thresholds are defined as the magnitude of a stimulus that subjects can detect *half the time.* The smallest difference between two stimuli that can be detected half the time is called the **difference threshold.** For example, the smallest change in intensity of your stereo that you can distinguish as "louder" 50 percent of the time is your difference threshold for that stimulus. Detailed knowledge of absolute and difference thresholds has, in fact, been used by the electronics industry to design better stereo systems.

### Sensory Adaptation

Recall that an individual's sensitivity to a stimulus differs from time to time. There are many reasons why this happens, such as fatigue or inattention, but **sensory adaptation** is one of the major causes. When a stimulus is continuously present or repeated at short intervals, the sensation that the same amount of sensory energy causes becomes gradually weaker, in part because the receptor cells become fatigued. When I was a teenager, I frequently went skin diving in an extremely cold spring in central Florida. At first the water was almost unbearably cold; when I jumped in from the dock, the intensity of the cold grabbed my attention so totally that for a moment I felt like only the cold skin of a person rather than a whole person. But after a few minutes the water felt comfortably cool. The water did not change in temperature, of course, but the sensation changed considerably because the temperature receptors in the skin adapted to the temperature of the water. This is sensory adaptation. It happens to some extent in all the senses; loud sounds and offensive odors, fortunately, also seem less intense as time goes by.

### Psychophysics

The specialty area within the field of psychology that studies sensory limits, sensory adaptation, and related topics is called **psychophysics.** The subject matter of this field is the relationship between the *physical* properties of stimuli and the *psychological* sensations they produce. Psychophysics is an important field because frequently there is *not* a direct or simple relationship between stimuli and sensations. Because our knowledge of the outside world is limited to what our sensations tell us, we need to understand under what conditions our sensations do not directly reflect the physical nature of the stimulus. Sensory adaptation is a process that alters the relationship between stimuli and sensations, but numerous other circumstances provide examples of this lack of a one-to-one relationship. The concept of the difference threshold provides another good example.

What humans see    What bees "see"

**FIGURE 4.1**
The visual receptor cells of bees allow them to transduce ultraviolet light better than we can with our normal visual receptor cells. Therefore, bees "see" more of this form of energy. The flower on the left is as the human sees it; the bee, however, is able to see an ultraviolet "landing strip" on the flower that we do not see.

**absolute threshold**
The smallest magnitude of a stimulus that can be detected half the time.

**difference threshold**
The smallest difference between two stimuli that can be detected half the time.

**sensory adaptation**
Weakened magnitude of a sensation resulting from prolonged presentation of the stimulus.

**psychophysics**
(sī″kō-fiz′iks) A specialty area of psychology that studies sensory limits, sensory adaptation, and related topics.

**Weber's law**
A law stating that the amount of change in a stimulus needed to detect a difference is in direct proportion to the intensity of the original stimulus.

A candle flame seen at 30 miles on a clear, dark night

The tick of a watch under quiet conditions at 20 feet

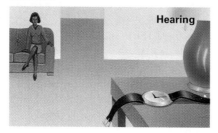

One teaspoon of sugar in 2 gallons of water

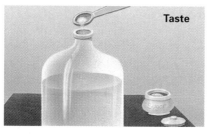

One drop of perfume diffused into the entire volume of a 3-room apartment

The wing of a bee falling on your cheek from a height of 1 centimeter

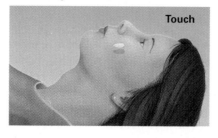

A fact about difference thresholds that has captured the attention of psychophysicists since the nineteenth century is that the size of the difference threshold increases as the strength of the stimulus increases. When a stimulus is strong, changes in it must be bigger to be noticed than when the stimulus is weak. You can see this for yourself the next time you turn on a three-way light in a dark room. Most three-way bulbs provide light energy in three approximately equal steps (such as a 50-, 100-, and 150-watt bulb), but the greatest difference in brightness in the room is noticeable after the first click of the switch—the sofa that you just tripped over in the darkness is now plainly visible. Turning up the light to the next level adds a less noticeable increase in perceived brightness, and the third level adds even less in apparent brightness. At each level of increasing illumination, the difference threshold is greater, so the perceived increase in brightness is less. If you were to turn on another 50-watt bulb at this point—with the three-way bulb at its highest illumination—you might not see any increase in apparent brightness because your difference threshold is so high.

The ability to detect small changes in the intensity of weak stimuli, but only large changes in the intensity of strong stimuli, was first formally noted by German psychophysicist Ernst Weber. Today this phenomenon is known as **Weber's law.** Interestingly, the amount of the change needed to be detected half the time (the difference threshold) is almost always in direct proportion to the intensity of the original stimulus. Thus, if a waiter holding a tray on which four glasses had been placed were just able to detect the added weight of one glass, he would just be able to feel the added weight from *two* more glasses if the tray were already holding eight glasses. The amount of detectable added weight would always be in the same proportion, in this case 1/4.

What is the relevance of this bit of information? Weber's law tells us that what we sense is not always the same as the energy that enters the sense organ. The same magnitude of physical change in intensity can be obvious one time, yet would go undetected under different circumstances. This fact has important practical implications. Suppose, for example, that you are chosen to help design the instruments for a new airplane. The pilot wants an easier way to monitor the plane's altitude, so you put in a light that increases in intensity as the plane nears the earth—the lower the altitude, the more intense the light. That way, you assume, the pilot can easily monitor changes in altitude by seeing changes in brightness. Right? According to Weber's law, this would be a dangerous way to monitor altitude. At high altitudes, the intensity of the light would be low, so small changes could be detected easily; at low altitudes, however, the intensity would be so great that large changes in altitude—even fatal ones—might not be noticed. That is why the people who design instruments for airplanes, cars, and the like need to know about psychophysics.

## Review

The world is known to us only indirectly because our brains are not in direct contact with the outside world. But sensory receptor cells have the ability to transduce physical energy into coded neural messages that are sent to the brain (sensation), where they are interpreted (perception). Not all forms of physical energy can become part of our perception of the world: We must have sensory receptor cells that can transduce that form of energy and the stimulation must be strong enough to exceed the sensory threshold. Our perception of external reality is complicated because there is no simple and direct relationship between the properties of physical stimuli and our conscious sensations. For example, a small change in the intensity of sound from a stereo is noticeable when the stereo is being played softly, but the same size change would go unnoticed if the stereo were at high volume. The complicated relationship between physical stimuli and conscious sensations is the subject matter of psychophysics.

## Check Your Learning

To be sure that you have learned the key points from the preceding section, cover the list of correct answers and try to answer each question. If you give an incorrect answer to any question, return to the page given next to the correct answer to see why your answer was not correct. Remember that these questions cover only some of the important information in this section; it is important that you make up your own questions to check your learning of other facts and concepts.

1. The _____ is the smallest magnitude of a stimulus that can be detected half the time.

   a) absolute threshold       c) difference threshold
   b) visual threshold         d) relative threshold

2. When a stimulus is continuously present or repeated at short intervals, the sensation gradually becomes weaker. This is termed

   a) sensory adaptation.      c) desensitization.
   b) psychophysics.

3. According to _____, the amount of the change in a stimulus needed to be detected half the time is almost always in direct proportion to the intensity of the original stimulus.

   a) psychophysical dualism    c) Weber's law
   b) McGurty's law             d) threshold variation

4. The specialty area within the field of psychology that studies sensory limits, sensory adaptation, and related topics is called _____.

## Thinking Critically about Psychology

1.  How would life be different if human beings had a lower absolute threshold for the sense of sound? How about a higher absolute threshold for taste?

2.  What is the difference between sensation and perception? Can you have a perception without a sensation?

Correct Answers:  **1.** a (p. 115),  **2.** a (p. 115),  **3.** c (p. 116),  **4.** psychophysics (p. 115).

## Vision: Your Human Camera

In 1950, psychologist George Wald wrote an important paper comparing the eye to a camera. In many ways, this is still a good analogy. Both the eye and a camera are instruments that use a lens to focus light onto a light-sensitive surface on which the visual image is registered. The gross anatomy of the human eye shown in figure 4.3 makes the resemblance to a camera very apparent. This intricate and efficient instrument transduces the physical properties of light into elaborately coded neural messages.

### Light: What Is It?

We need to have some knowledge of the nature of light to understand vision. Light is one small part of the form of energy known as **electromagnetic radiation,** which also includes radio waves and X rays. Only a small portion of this radiation is visible—that is, our senses can transduce only a small part of it. We can best think of light as being composed of *waves* that vary in *frequency* and *intensity.* These two properties of light waves provide us with most of our information about vision.

**electromagnetic radiation**
(e-lek″trō-mag-net′ik)  A form of energy including electricity, radio waves, and X rays, of which visible light is a part.

**FIGURE 4.3**

Optical similarities between an eye and a camera are apparent in their cross sections. Both use a lens to focus an inverted image onto a light-sensitive surface. Both possess an iris to adjust to various intensities of light.

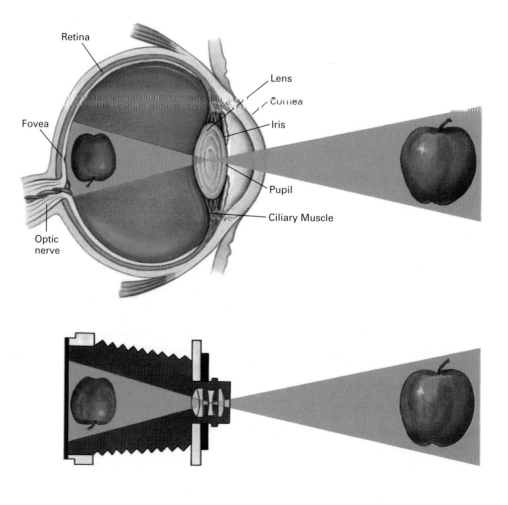

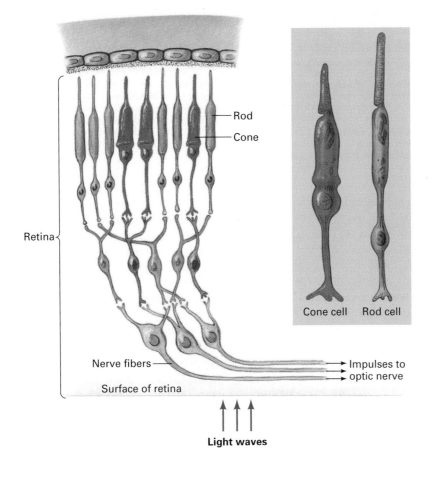

Cone cell   Rod cell

**FIGURE 4.4**
Diagram of the microscopic structure of a section of the retina showing the rods and cones and their principal neural interconnections. The blowup shows individual rod and cone cells.

Rod
Cone
Retina
Nerve fibers
Impulses to optic nerve
Surface of retina
**Light waves**

The *intensity* of the light wave largely determines the *brightness* of the visual sensation. The light reflected by an apple that is lighted by a single candle is low in intensity, so we see the red of the apple as a dim rather than a bright sensation. The **wavelength** of the light largely determines the *hue* that we see—that is, light waves of different wavelengths are seen as different colors. But most light waves are not made up of a single wavelength and are therefore not seen as a pure hue. Rather, they are made up of light waves of more than one wavelength. The more wavelengths in a light, the less *saturated* (or pure) its hue is. The relationship between the physical properties of light and what is seen is not always simple and direct, however.

## The Eye: How Does It Work?

The eye is an almost perfect sphere composed of two fluid-filled chambers. Light passes through the clear **cornea** into the first chamber. At the back of this chamber, the colored **iris** opens and closes to regulate how much light passes through the **pupil** into the **lens.** The lens is held in place by ligaments attached to the **ciliary muscle.** This muscle focuses images by controlling the thickness of the lens, so that a clear image falls onto the light-sensitive **retina** at the back of the second chamber (see fig. 4.3). When the ciliary muscle is uncontracted, the tension of the ligaments stretches the lens relatively flat. When the ciliary muscle contracts, it lessens the tension of the ligaments and the lens thickens. The lens must be thickened to focus on close objects; that is why reading for long periods—which involves prolonged contraction of the ciliary muscle—makes your eyes feel tired.

The real business of transducing light waves is carried out in the retina by two types of receptor cells named the **rods** and the **cones** because of their shape (see fig. 4.4). The cones are far less numerous than the rods—about 6 million cones compared

**wavelength**
The frequency of light waves, which determines the hue we perceive.

**cornea**
(kor′nē-ah)  The protective coating on the surface of the eye through which light passes.

**iris**
(ī′ris)  The colored part of the eye behind the cornea that regulates the amount of light that enters.

**pupil**
(pyoo′pil)  The opening of the iris.

**lens**
The transparent portion of the eye that adjusts to focus light on the retina.

**ciliary muscle**
(sil′ē-ar″e)  The muscle in the eye that controls the shape of the lens.

**retina**
(ret′i-nah)  The area at the back of the eye on which images are formed and that contains the rods and cones.

**rods**
The 125 million cells located outside the center of the retina that transduce light waves into neural impulses, thereby coding information about light and dark.

**cones**
The 6 million receptor cells located mostly in the center of the retina that transduce light waves into neural impulses, thereby coding information about light, dark, and color.

**FIGURE 4.5**

You can demonstrate to yourself the existence of the "blind spot" in the following way. Hold your book at about arm's length with the word *Spot* in front of your eyes. Close your right eye and stare at the word *Spot*. Move the book in slowly until the word *Blind* disappears. At this point, its image is falling on the spot in the retina where the optic nerve is attached and there are no receptors. We are not normally aware of the existence of this blind spot because we "fill in" our perceptions to compensate for the missing information. In this case, we see the dotted line as continuous after the word *Blind* disappears.

**fovea**

(fō′vē-ah) The central spot of the retina, which contains the greatest concentration of cones.

**visual acuity**

(vizh′u-al ah-ku′i-tē) Clarity and sharpness of vision.

**optic nerve**

The nerve that carries neural messages about vision to the brain.

**blind spot**

The spot where the optic nerve attaches to the retina; it contains no rods or cones.

**optic chiasm**

The area in the brain where half of the optic nerve fibers from each eye cross to the opposite side of the brain.

with 125 million rods in each eye (Pugh, 1988). Cones are concentrated in the center of the retina, with the greatest concentration at a central spot called the **fovea.** In good light, **visual acuity** (the clarity and sharpness of vision) is best for images that are focused directly on the fovea, largely because of the high concentration of cones.

The rods are located throughout the retina, except in the center (the fovea). Their role in vision differs from that of the cones in four main ways. First, because of their location, they are largely responsible for peripheral vision—vision at the top, bottom, and sides of the visual field—whereas the cones play little role in this aspect of seeing. Second, the rods are hundreds of times more sensitive to light than the cones. This means that they play a far more important role in vision in dim light than do the cones. Third, the rods produce images that are perceived with less visual acuity than do cones. This is largely because neurons leading from several rods often converge, so that their impulses are sent to the brain on a single nerve fiber (shown in fig. 4.4). In contrast, cones more commonly send their messages to the brain along separate nerve fibers, giving the brain more precise information about the location of the stimulation on the retina.

The fourth difference between the rods and cones concerns color vision. Both types of receptors respond to variations in light and dark (in terms of the number of receptors that fire and the frequency with which they fire), but only the cones can code information about color. Because the rods do not detect color, and because the cones can respond only in bright light, we can see only indistinct forms of black and gray in an almost dark room.

Would you be surprised to learn that you are partially blind in each eye? The spot near the center of the retina where the **optic nerve** is attached contains no rods or cones. Because there is no visual reception at this point, it is known as the **blind spot.** We are not normally aware of this blind spot because we "fill in" the missing information during the process of seeing by using information coming in from the other parts of the retina. However, look at figure 4.5 for a demonstration of its existence.

Coded messages from the rods and cones are processed in a preliminary way in the neurons of the retina and are then sent to the visual areas of the left and right occipital lobe of the cerebral cortex for interpretation. Recall from chapter 3 that the information from the eyes is transmitted to the visual areas in a complicated fashion. As shown in figure 4.6, stimuli that are on your right fall on the left side of each eye. Information from the right visual field of both eyes is sent to the visual area in the occipital lobe of the left visual hemisphere after the optic nerves cross over at the **optic chiasm** in the brain. Information from stimuli on your left falls on the right side of each eye and is sent to the visual area in the right cerebral hemisphere. It's a bit confusing when you read about it for the first time, but the brain manages to keep it all straight.

## Dark and Light Adaptation

When you walk into a dark movie theater from the daylight, you are "blind" at first; your eyes can pick up very little visual information. Within about 5 minutes, however, your vision in the darkened room has improved considerably, and very slowly it improves over

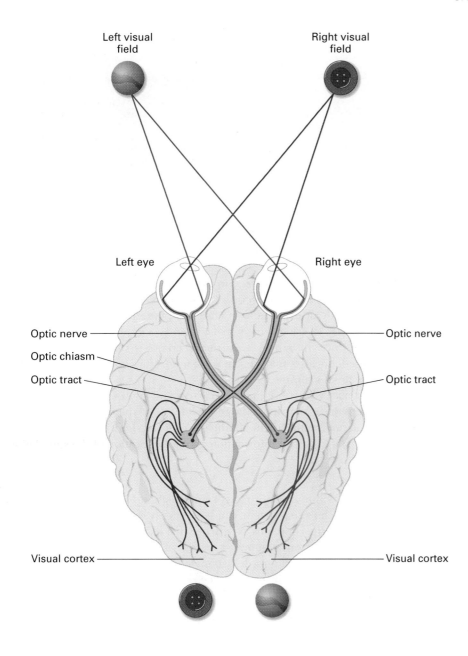

Left visual
field

Right visual
field

Left eye

Right eye

Optic nerve

Optic nerve

Optic chiasm

Optic tract

Optic tract

Visual cortex

Visual cortex

**FIGURE 4.6**
Images of objects in the right visual field
are focused on the left side of each
retina, and images of objects in the left
visual field are focused on the right side
of each retina. This information is
conveyed along the optic nerves to the
optic chiasm and the thalamus. The
thalamus then relays the information to
the visual cortex of the occipital lobes.
Note that images of objects in the right
visual field are processed by the left
occipital lobe and images of objects in
the left visual field are processed by the
right occipital lobe.

the next 25 minutes until you can see fairly well. When you exit the theater from the matinee performance, you have the opposite experience. At first the intense light "blinds" you. You squint and block out the painful light, but in a little while you can see normally again. What is going on? How can you be sighted one moment and blind the next just because the intensity of light has suddenly changed?

The phenomena are called *dark adaptation* and *light adaptation*. Here is what happens in the retina during **dark adaptation.** In a lighted room, the rods and cones are being used frequently, so they are not very sensitive. When we enter darkness, the rods and cones are not sensitive enough to be stimulated by the low-intensity light. This gives the receptors a "rest," so they begin to gain sensitivity by making a fresh supply of the chemicals used in light reception, which have been literally "bleached out" by the intense light.

At first, both the rods and the cones are recovering their sensitivity, so improvement is fairly rapid. But the cones become fully sensitive (remember, they are not very sensitive in weak light) within about 5 minutes, so the rate of improvement slows after

**dark adaptation**
Increased sensitivity of the eye in semidarkness following a reduction in overall
illumination.

In dim light, the color of this red apple hasn't changed, but its color appears to fade. Cones in the eye pick up color, but they work well only in bright light.

**light adaptation**
Regaining sensitivity of the eye to bright light following an increase in overall illumination.

**trichromatic theory**
(trī″krō-mat′ik) The theory of color vision contending that the eye has three different kinds of cones, each of which responds to light of one range of wavelength.

that. The rods continue to improve in sensitivity slowly, reaching a level of sensitivity to light that is an amazing *100,000 times greater* than in bright illumination after about 30 minutes in the dark.

In **light adaptation,** eyes that have been in the dark for a while become very sensitive to light, partly because they have built up a full supply of chemicals used in light reception. When we are suddenly exposed to intense light, the rods and cones are highly responsive and, in essence, "overload" the visual circuits. It's not until the intense light has had a chance to reduce the sensitivity of the receptors—partly by bleaching out some of the receptor chemicals—that we can see comfortably again. Fortunately, this process takes place in about a minute.

By the way, your parents were right about carrots and good vision. The chemical involved in light reception in the rods is largely made up of vitamin A. This is why a deficiency of vitamin A can lead to "night blindness." And yes, there is a lot of vitamin A in carrots.

## Color Vision

Energy of any wavelength within the spectrum of visible light evokes a sensation of color when it stimulates the human visual system. But light energy is just that—energy; it has no color of its own. Color is the conscious experience that results from the processing of light energy by the eye and nervous system.

It's obviously useful to be able to discriminate among lights of different wavelengths: "Blue" berries are ready to be eaten; "green" berries are not. But how does the human visual system produce the sensation of color? It has taken psychologists and other scientists more than a hundred years to reach the current understanding of the complex mechanisms of color vision.

In the early 1800s, Thomas Young and Hermann von Helmholz made the observation that any color can be created by shining different combinations of the wavelengths of light for red, blue, and green on a single spot. For example, as illustrated in figure 4.7, the combination of red and green light produces yellow. Based on this observation, Young and Helmholz guessed that there are three kinds of cones in the retina that respond mostly to light in either the red, green, or blue range of wavelengths. Their theory is referred to as the **trichromatic theory** of color vision. According to this theory, all sensations of colors result from different levels of stimulation of the red, green, and blue receptors.

Over the years, many types of studies have confirmed that there are indeed three kinds of cones. As shown in figure 4.8, each kind of cone contains pigments that mostly absorb light of the wavelengths that correspond to red, green, and blue. Does that mean that the trichromatic theory of Young and Helmholz was correct? Yes and no. Color vision is fascinatingly complex.

Soon after Young and Helmholz stated the trichromatic theory, other scientists pointed out that it could not explain three intriguing phenomena:

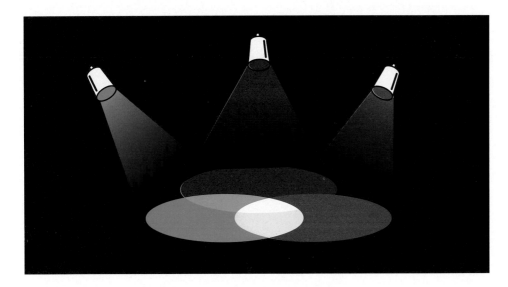

**FIGURE 4.7**
The trichromatic theory of color vision is based on the observation that all colors can be produced by various combinations of red, blue, and green light (and that all three lights together create white).

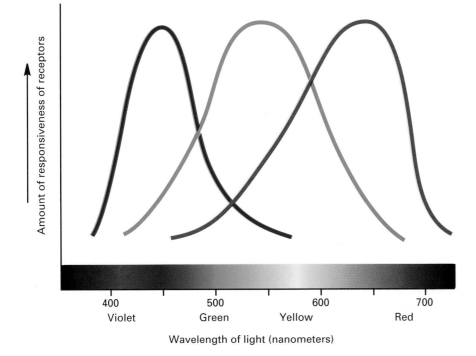

**FIGURE 4.8**
Our ability to see color is partly based on the fact that three kinds of cones contain pigments that respond mostly to light in the wavelengths for blue, green, and red. Note, however, that each type of cone also responds to other nearby wavelengths of light. This means, for example, that light in the yellow range stimulates both the red and the green cone receptors, but not as strongly as light in the red or green ranges, respectively.

1. ***Complementary colors.*** Artists know that yellow and blue, as well as red and green, are complementary colors. You cannot mix lights of these colors to produce a yellowish-blue or a reddish-green. If color vision is simply a matter of combinations of impulses from cones that are mostly sensitive to red, green, and blue, how could some colors be complementary in this sense?

2. ***Color afterimages.*** If you stare at a patch of color for a while and then shift your eyes to a white surface, you will see a ghostly "afterimage" of the patch in the color that is *complementary* to that of the original patch. For example, stare intensely for about 30 seconds at the white dot in the center of the word *red* that is printed in the color red in figure 4.9. Then stare at the blank white space above it. You will see an afterimage of the word *red,* but it will be *green.* The same thing occurs for all four of the complementary colors.

**FIGURE 4.9**
Stimulus used in the demonstration of afterimages. Stare at the white dot in the center of the word *red* for 30 seconds. Then look at the white space above the word. What do you see?

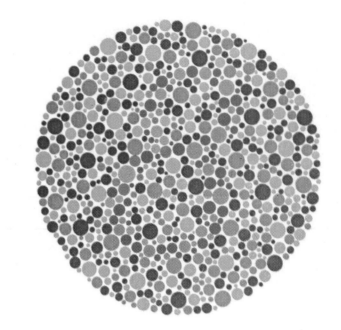

**opponent-process theory**
The theory of color vision contending that the visual system has two kinds of color processors, which respond to light in either the red-green or yellow-blue ranges of wavelength.

3. ***Partial color blindness.*** Partial color blindness affects about 8 percent of males and 1 percent of females. Most people with partial color blindness seem to see the world *almost* normally but have difficulty distinguishing between two colors. Usually, color-blind individuals cannot tell the difference between red and green, but they see yellow and blue normally (in fewer cases, they cannot distinguish yellow from blue but can see red and green normally). Note that the colors that look the same to a color-blind person are always complementary colors (see figure 4.10)

Color blindness does not make sense in the trichromatic theory. You can explain why a person cannot distinguish between red and green by hypothesizing that something is wrong with either the red or the green receptors or both. But, according to the trichromatic theory, a person sees yellow because light of this wavelength stimulates both the red and the green receptors. If a person is color blind to red and green because there is something wrong with the red and green receptors, how can that person still see yellow? Psychologists soon realized that something more than three kinds of cones was involved in color vision.

The **opponent-process theory** was developed to explain the three phenomena that cannot be explained just by the existence of three kinds of cones. The opponent-process theory states that there are also two kinds of *color-processing mechanisms*, which receive messages from the three kinds of cones (see fig. 4.11). These two color-processing mechanisms respond in *opposite* ways that correspond to the two pairs of complementary colors. For example, suppose you look at a lemon (and light in the yellow range of wavelength reflects from the lemon onto your retinas). Light of this wavelength stimulates both the red and green receptors, but not the blue receptors (see figure 4.8). The rate of firing of the *yellow-blue (Y-B) processing mechanism* is *increased* by signals from the red and green receptors but is *slowed down* by inhibitory signals from the blue receptors. Therefore, light in the yellow wavelengths leads the Y-B mechanism to send a high-frequency message along the visual system to the brain. This signal is the primary information used by the brain to produce the sensation of yellow on the peel of the lemon. On the other hand, the rate of firing of the *red-green (R-G) processing mechanism* is increased by signals from the red receptors but is slowed by signals from the green receptors. When light in the green wavelengths stimulates the green receptors, the receptors send a strong inhibitory message to the red-green (R-G) opponent mechanism, which causes it to send low-frequency neural signals to the brain. In similar ways, combinations

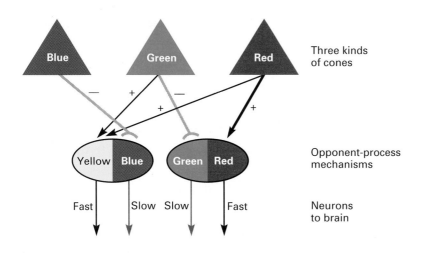

**FIGURE 4.11**
The modern theory of color vision combines the three kinds of cone color receptors of trichromatic theory with the two processing mechanisms of opponent-process theory. When light in the red wavelengths stimulates the red receptors, the receptors send a strong excitatory message to the red-green (R-G) opponent mechanism, which stimulates rapid firing of neural signals to the brain. Light in the yellow wavelengths stimulates both the red and the green receptors somewhat. They both send weak excitatory messages to the yellow-blue (Y-B) opponent mechanism, but together they are strong enough to stimulate it to send fast signals to the brain. When light is in the blue wavelengths, it stimulates the blue receptors, which send strong inhibitory messages to the Y-B opponent mechanism, leading it to fire slowly. Light in the green wavelengths leads to slow firing of the R-G opponent mechanism in a similar fashion.

of signals from the opponent-processing mechanisms supply the brain with the information necessary for all color sensations.

Notice that opponent-process theory explains the phenomenon of complementary colors because the R-G and Y-B mechanisms cannot signal both of their opponent colors at the same time. It also explains why afterimages are always in the opposite complementary color to the original stimulus. Staring at the red stimulus reduces the sensitivity of the red receptors (through sensory adaptation), leading the R-G system to send a signal to the brain that is interpreted as the sensation of green. The opponent-process theory also explains color blindness as an abnormality in one of the opponent-process mechanisms. Perhaps the strongest evidence for the opponent-process theory, however, is that neurons throughout the visual system and cerebral cortex respond to light in an opponent-process fashion (Engle, 1999). For example, if a specific neuron in the retina is excited by green light, then it is inhibited from firing by red light.

Thus, the trichromatic theory accurately describes events very well at the first level of neurons in the visual system—the cones within the retina—but the opponent-process theory best describes the activities of neurons in the rest of the visual system. They are both correct, in other words, when combined (Pugh, 1988).

---

The eye is much like a human camera. The lens focuses a visual image on the retina of the eye, which contains two kinds of sensory receptor cells, the rods and cones. These transduce the wavelength, amplitude, and complexity of the light waves into neural messages. The two kinds of receptor cells perform their jobs somewhat differently. Cones work best in intense light, provide good visual acuity, and transduce information about color. Rods work well in weak light, do not provide good acuity, and do not code information about color. The eye does not function well when the intensity of light suddenly changes, but it quickly regains its sensitivity through the processes of light and dark adaptation. There are two major theoretical explanations of how the visual system transduces color. One states that three different kinds of cones are most sensitive to light of different wavelengths. The other suggests that two kinds of color-processing mechanisms in the visual system process complementary colors. Each theory is "correct" at different stages of the information processing about the wavelength of light.

**Review**

---

To be sure that you have learned the key points from the preceding section, cover the list of correct answers and try to answer each question. If you give an incorrect

**Check Your Learning**

answer to any question, return to the page given next to the correct answer to see why your answer was not correct.

1. The hue that we see is largely determined by the _____ of the light.

   a) intensity
   b) amplitude
   c) saturation
   d) wavelength

2. Light waves are transduced into neural messages by two types of receptor cells, named rods and cones, in the _____ of the eye.

   a) ciliary structure
   b) pupil
   c) retina
   d) iris

3. Cones are concentrated in the

   a) periphery of the eye.
   b) fovea.
   c) iris.
   d) blind spot.

4. The theory of color vision that there are three kinds of cones in the retina, which respond primarily to light in either the red, green, or blue range of wavelengths, is the _____ theory.

   a) opponent-process
   b) trichromatic
   c) psychophysical
   d) sensory adaptation

---

## Thinking Critically about Psychology

1. If cones give us the best visual acuity, what is the advantage of having rods as well?

2. How can two different theories of color vision both be "correct"?

---

**Correct Answers: 1.** d (p. 119), **2.** c (p. 119), **3.** b (p. 120), **4.** b (p. 122).

---

## ● Hearing: Sensing Sound Waves

Without hearing and vision, there probably would be no spoken or written languages, and without language most of the cultural and scientific accomplishments of human beings probably would have been impossible. The sense of hearing depends on the ear, a complex sensory instrument that transduces the physical properties of sound waves into neural messages that can be sent to the brain. Neural messages from the ears are first interpreted in the temporal lobe's auditory area and then forwarded to other parts of the brain for additional interpretation.

### Sound: What Is It?

Hearing, or **audition,** is the sense that detects the vibratory changes in the air known as **sound waves.** When an object, such as a tuning fork, vibrates back and forth, it sets in motion successive waves of *compression* (increased density) and *rarefaction* (reduced density) of the molecules of the air (see fig. 4.12). When the waves reach the ear, the reception of sound begins. As we will see, the sound waves in the air cause a chain of small structures in the ear to vibrate in a way that is eventually translated into a neural message to the brain.

Not all sound waves are alike, however, and the nature of a sound wave determines to a great extent how we will sense it. For one thing, sound waves differ in the **frequency of cycles** of compression and rarefaction of the air (see fig. 4.12). Objects that vibrate slowly create low-frequency sound waves, whereas rapidly vibrating objects produce high-frequency sound waves. The frequency of sound waves is measured in **hertz (Hz)** units,

**audition**
(aw-dish'un) The sense of hearing.

**sound waves**
Cyclical changes in air pressure that constitute the stimulus for hearing.

**frequency of cycles**
The rate of vibration of sound waves; determines pitch.

**hertz (Hz)**
The measurement of the frequency of sound waves in cycles per second.

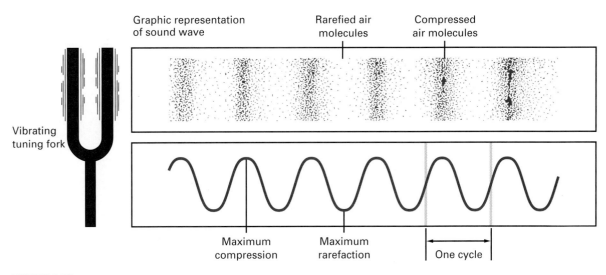

**FIGURE 4.12**

Vibrating objects, such as a tuning fork, create a sound wave of successive compression and rarefaction (expansion) in the air, which can be represented graphically as shown.

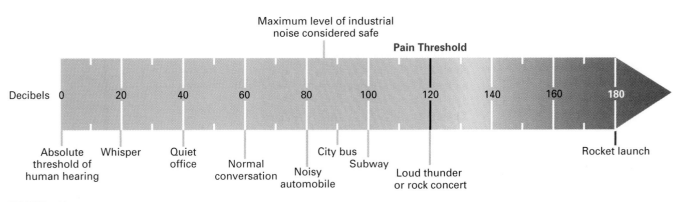

**FIGURE 4.13**

The loudness of common sounds as measured in decibel units.

**Note:** Prolonged exposure to sounds over 85 decibels can lead to permanent hearing loss. Even brief exposure to loudness of 150 decibels (being close to an explosion or the speakers at some rock concerts) can permanently damage hearing.

the number of vibratory cycles per second. The human ear is sensitive to sound waves in the range of 20 to 20,000 Hz. Sound waves also differ in terms of **intensity,** or how densely compacted the air molecules are in the sound wave.

The frequency of a sound wave largely determines its **pitch,** or how high or low it sounds to us. For example, striking a glass with a spoon causes a higher-frequency sound wave—which we hear as a higher pitch—than striking a bass drum. The loudness of a sound is largely determined by its intensity. Gently tapping a bass drum produces less dense compression and rarefaction, and a quieter sound, than striking it hard. Intensity is measured in **decibel (db)** units. This scale begins at zero at the absolute threshold for detecting a 1,000 Hz tone (and increases by 20 db as the intensity of the stimulus is multiplied by 10). Normal conversation averages about 60 db, whereas sounds of 120 db or more are quite painful (see fig. 4.13). The **timbre** of a sound (its characteristic quality) is determined by the complexity of the sound wave—that is, the extent to which it is composed of many waves of different frequency and intensity. The voices of different people sound different to us largely because of their unique timbres.

The relationship between the physical properties of sound waves and the sensation of sound is not as simple as I have just made it seem, however. Take loudness, for

**intensity**
The density of vibrating air molecules, which determines the loudness of sound.

**pitch**
The experience of sound vibrations sensed as high or low.

**decibel (db)**
(des′i-bel) Measurement of the intensity of perceived sound.

**timbre**
(tim′ber, tam′br) The characteristic quality of a sound as determined by the complexity of the sound wave.

**FIGURE 4.14**
Major structures of the ear.

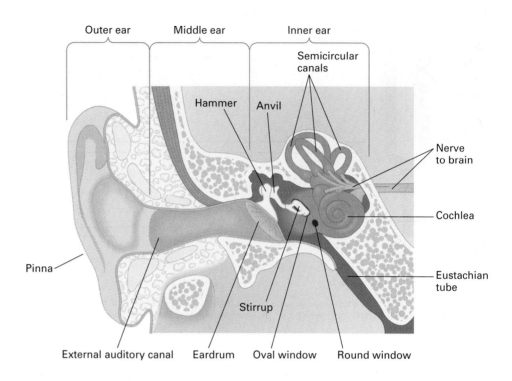

example. Two tones of equal intensity may not be heard as equally loud if they are not equal in frequency. Loudness seems greatest for tones of about 3,000 to 4,000 Hz; higher- or lower-frequency sounds of the same intensity seem less loud to us.

## The Ear: How Does It Work?

The ear is a sensitive sensory instrument that transduces sound waves into neural impulses to the brain. It is composed of three major sections: the outer ear, middle ear, and inner ear (see Fig. 4.14).

### Outer Ear

The external part of the ear, or **pinna,** which we think of as the "ear," is useful as a sound collector, and it plays an important role in locating the origins of sounds. The shape of the pinna is especially important in sound localization, as shown by the fact that temporarily smoothing the pinna with putty impairs sound localization. Connecting the outer and middle ear is the hollow **external auditory canal.** It's the part that gets waxy and the part through which sound waves reach the eardrum, the first structure of the middle ear.

### Middle Ear

The outermost structure of the middle ear is a thin membrane that is known as the **eardrum** because it resembles the skin on a drum. Sound waves in the air cause the eardrum to vibrate. The vibrating eardrum passes the vibration on to a series of three movable, interconnected bones: the **hammer,** the **anvil,** and the **stirrup,** so named because of their shapes. These middle-ear structures amplify the vibrations and pass them on to the inner ear.

### Inner Ear

The vibrating stirrup shakes another eardrumlike structure called the **oval window** into motion. This membrane is at the end of a long, curled structure called the **cochlea,** which is filled with fluid. The vibrating oval window creates waves in the fluid of the

**pinna**
(pin′nah) The external part of the ear.

**external auditory canal**
The tube connecting the pinna to the middle ear.

**eardrum**
A thin membrane that sound waves cause to vibrate; a structure of the middle ear.

**hammer, anvil, stirrup**
Three linked bones of the middle ear, which pass sound waves to the inner ear.

**oval window**
The membrane of the inner ear that vibrates in response to movement of the stirrup, creating waves in the fluid of the cochlea.

**cochlea**
(cok′lē-ah) A spiral structure of the inner ear that is filled with fluid and contains the receptors for hearing.

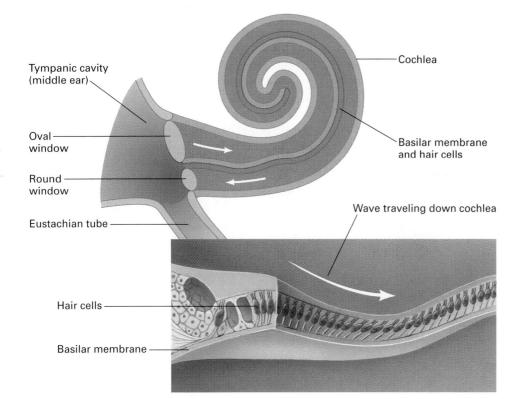

Tympanic cavity
(middle ear)

Oval
window

Round
window

Eustachian tube

Hair cells

Basilar membrane

Cochlea

Basilar membrane
and hair cells

Wave traveling down cochlea

**FIGURE 4.15**
Vibrations from sound waves enter the
cochlea through the oval window and
travel the length of the cochlea, where
they are transduced into neural
messages by hair cell receptors in the
organ of Corti.

Two factors tell the listener the location
of sounds. First, a sound wave that
originates from the side reaches the
closer ear slightly sooner than it reaches
the farther ear. Second, the head blocks
some of the sound wave that reaches the
farther ear, reducing the intensity of
stimulation to the ear that is farther away
from the source of the sound.

Sound wave

cochlea (see fig. 4.15). The cochlea contains two long tubes that double back on themselves and are connected only at the tip end of the spiral. The pressure of the vibrating
waves is relieved by a third eardrumlike membrane at the other end of the cochlea
called the **round window.** Running almost the entire length of the cochlea are several
layers of membranes that separate the two tubes. The lower membrane, called the

**round window**
The membrane that relieves pressure
from the vibrating waves in the cochlear
fluid.

The barn owl hunts at night, often inside dark barns and other structures that block the light. It uses its extraordinary sense of hearing to locate its prey in the darkness. The same cues used by humans to localize the source of sounds (differences in sounds reaching the two ears) enable the barn owl to find its scampering prey.

**basilar membrane**
(bas´ĭ-lar)  One of the membranes that separate the two tubes of the cochlea and on which the organ of Corti rests.

**organ of Corti**
(kor´tē)  A sensory receptor in the cochlea that transduces sound waves into coded neural impulses.

**bone conduction hearing**
Hearing accomplished through sounds transmitted through the bones of the head directly to the cochlear fluid.

basilar membrane, forms a floor on which the ear's sensory receptors sit. Hairlike receptor cells are contained in the **organ of Corti.** Vibrations in the cochlear fluid set the basilar membrane in motion. This movement, in turn, moves the organ of Corti and stimulates the receptor cells it contains. These receptors transduce the sound waves in the cochlear fluid into coded neural impulses, which are sent to the brain.

How does the organ of Corti code neural messages for the brain? The *intensity* of a sound wave is coded by the number of receptors in the organ of Corti that fire. Low-intensity sounds stimulate only a few receptors; high-intensity sounds stimulate many receptors.

The *frequency* of the sound wave is apparently coded in at least two ways. First, sound waves of different frequencies stimulate receptor cells at different *places* along the organ of Corti. Higher-frequency waves stimulate the organ of Corti close to the oval window; lower-frequency waves stimulate it farther along the cochlea (except for very low frequencies). Second, the frequency of the sound waves is duplicated to some extent in the *frequency* of the signals sent to the brain by the auditory receptors. Only at lower frequencies is each neuron able to signal at the same frequency as the sound wave. At higher frequencies, the coding of frequency is achieved by *volleys* of neural impulses by different groups of neurons, which reflect the frequency of the sound wave.

Not all sounds travel this complete route from outer ear to cochlea. Some sounds are transmitted through the bones of the head directly to the cochlear fluid. We hear ourselves speak (and eat) largely through **bone conduction hearing.** This is an important consideration in diagnosing hearing problems. People who have suffered damage to the hearing apparatus of the middle ear can hear bone-conducted sounds fairly well, but not airborne sounds. People with damage to the auditory nerve—nerve deafness—have difficulty hearing either type of sound.

One more thing about ears deserves mentioning. Ever wonder why people have two of them? For one thing, a pair of ears gives us a spare in case something goes wrong with one, but the fact that we have two ears also serves an important function in *locating* the origin of sounds. The ears locate sounds in two ways. First, when a sound wave is coming from straight ahead or from straight behind us, the sound reaches both ears simultaneously. But, when a sound is coming from the sides or from an angle, it reaches each ear at a slightly different time. The ears are sensitive enough to this difference that they allow us to locate the direction of sounds, especially high-frequency sounds. The reason you know that the person to the left of you is blowing her nose again is because your left ear hears it before your right ear does. Second, cues for the location of high-frequency sounds are also produced by the fact that your head dampens some of the sound reaching the more distant ear, creating a difference in the intensity of the sound waves that reach each of the ears.

## Review

Sound is a physical stimulus made up of successive waves of densely and sparsely compressed air. The ear is composed of a series of structures that transmit the sound wave from the outer ear to the inner ear, where it produces vibrations in the fluid of the cochlea. The vibrations of the cochlear fluid are transduced by the ear's receptor cells in the organ of Corti. Coded neural messages are sent to the auditory sensory areas of the brain, where frequency, intensity, and complexity are interpreted as pitch, loudness, and timbre. Differences in the timing and intensity of sound waves reaching the two ears allow us to determine the location of the source of the sound.

To be sure that you have learned the key points from the preceding section, cover the list of correct answers and try to answer each question. If you give an incorrect answer to any question, return to the page given next to the correct answer to see why your answer was not correct.

1. Objects that vibrate slowly create low-frequency sound waves, which we hear as having

   a)   low pitch.              c)   simple timbre.
   b)   high pitch.             d)   complex timbre.

2. The sound wave is amplified by the hammer, anvil, and stirrup in the

   a)   outer ear.             c)   inner ear.
   b)   middle ear.            d)   pinna.

3. The sound wave is transduced into neural impulses in the _____, which is located in the cochlea in the inner ear.

   a)   auditory nerve         c)   organ of Corti
   b)   cochlear fluid         d)   pinna

4. You know that the person speaking to you is on your left because

   a)   the sound reaches your left ear slightly before it reaches your right ear.
   b)   the sound wave that reaches your left ear is slightly more intense than the sound wave that reaches your right ear.
   c)   both of the above.
   d)   neither of the above.

1. In terms of human adaptation and survival, what are the advantages and disadvantages of having our ears located on the sides of our heads rather than somewhere else on the body?

2. Juan and Patrick are close friends. Juan hears normally, but Patrick is totally deaf. How might this difference in the way they experience life influence their friendship?

Correct Answers: 1. a (p. 127),  2. b (p. 128),  3. c (p. 130),  4. c (p. 130).

## ● Body Senses: Messages from Myself

The body senses tell us how the body is oriented, where it moves, what it touches, and so on. Information about orientation and movement comes from a sense organ located in the inner ear and from individual receptors spread throughout the body. Information about touch and temperature is provided by a variety of receptors located below the surface of the skin. Information about pain comes from receptors in the skin and inside the body. Although we usually are not aware that we are using this information, the body senses play an important role in keeping us standing upright, moving straight ahead, and literally out of hot water. Information from all of the body senses is sent to the somatosensory area of the parietal lobe of the cerebral cortex.

**FIGURE 4.16**
Major structures of the vestibular organ.

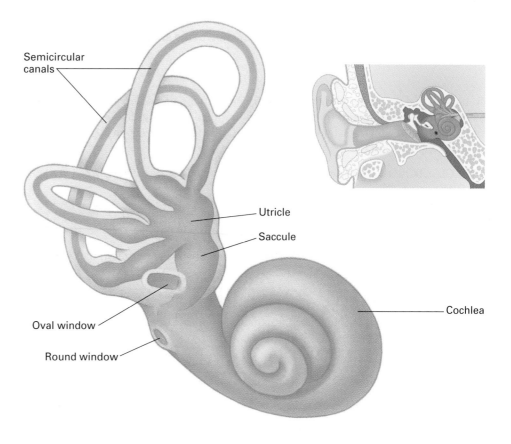

Semicircular
canals

Utricle

Saccule

Cochlea

Oval window

Round window

**vestibular organ**
(ves-tib´u-lar) The sensory structures in
the inner ear that provide the brain with
information about orientation and movement of the head and body.

**kinesthetic receptors**
(kin´´es-thet´ik) Receptors in the muscles,
joints, and skin that provide information about movement, posture, and
orientation.

**saccule, utricle**
(sak´ul u´tre-k´l) Fluid-filled sacs of the
vestibular organ that inform the brain
about the body's orientation.

**semicircular canals**
(sem´´e-ser´ku-lar) Three nearly circular
tubes in the vestibular organ that inform
the brain about tilts of the head and
body.

**cupula**
(ku´-pu-lah) A gelatin-like structure containing a tuft of hairlike sensory receptor
cells in the semicircular canals.

## Orientation and Movement

Messages about the orientation, balance, and movement of the body come to us from
two kinds of sense organs. A complicated set of sensory structures called the **vestibular
organ** is located in the inner section of the ear, where it provides the cerebral cortex with
information about orientation and movement. Individual sensory receptors, called
**kinesthetic receptors,** located in the muscles, joints, and skin provide additional messages about movement, posture, and orientation.

### Vestibular Organ

The vestibular organ is composed of two sets of small sensory structures: the *semicircular
canals* and the linked *saccule* and *utricle* (see fig. 4.16). The **saccule** and **utricle** are fluid-
filled sacs in the inner ear that contain sensory receptors that keep the brain informed
about the body's orientation. The part of the vestibular organ that provides the most
sensitive messages to the brain about orientation, however, is the **semicircular canals.**
This organ constitutes a marvelous bit of natural engineering perfectly suited to its purpose. The semicircular canals are composed of three nearly circular tubes (canals) that
lie at right angles to one another, providing information on orientation of the body in
three planes—left and right, up and down, and front to back. Think of the semicircular
canals as the corner of a room, with one in the plane of the floor and the other two in
the planes of the walls. At the base of each canal is an enlargement that holds the sensory receptors. A tuft of these hairlike receptor cells is formed in a gelatin-like structure
called the **cupula,** which sticks out into the enlargement of the canal. As the head is
tilted, the fluid flows through the canal in the opposite direction. This bends the cupula
and causes its receptors to fire, sending a message of "tilt" to the brain. Although the
vestibular organ provides the brain with vital information about orientation and movement, it can turn from a friend to an enemy at times. When confused by rocking boats,
bumping airplanes, or twisting circus rides, it can produce nausea. Why does that

happen? Why would tilting the vestibular organ cause nausea and vomiting—as in seasickness? Experts think it is because the disorientation and dizziness of seasickness resemble the dizziness caused by poisoning. The body apparently vomits in response to dizziness regardless of the cause, just in case it is due to poisoning (Stern & Koch, 1996).

### Kinesthetic Sense

Throughout the skin, muscles, joints, and tendons are kinesthetic receptors, which signal when they are moved. As the body walks, bends, writes, and so on, these receptors provide information about the location and movement of each part of the body. Close your eyes, take off your shoes, and wiggle your toes. You can tell they are wiggling because of your kinesthetic sense. Unlike the vestibular organ, the kinesthetic receptors are individual receptors that are not clumped together into sense organs. But, as reflected in the skilled movements of a musician, painter, or discus thrower, they are remarkably sensitive, allowing fine and complicated patterns of movement.

The vestibular organ and kinesthic receptors help orient us, even in unusual situations.

## Skin Senses

We usually do not think of the skin as a sense organ, yet it's capable of picking up many different kinds of sensory information. The skin can detect *pressure, temperature,* and *pain.* Feeling a kiss on the cheek, cold in the winter, getting hit by a rock, and all other sensations involving the skin are made up of combinations of these three skin sensations.

Although the skin can detect only three kinds of sensory information, there are at least four types of receptors in the skin: the **free nerve endings,** the **basket cells** wound around the base of hairs, the **tactile discs,** and the **specialized end bulbs.** These are shown in figure 4.17. It appears that all four play a role in the sense of touch (pressure), with the free nerve endings being the primary receptors for temperature and pain (Groves & Rebec, 1988; Hole, 1990).

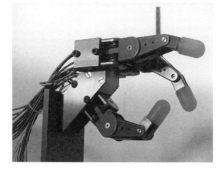

Robots are important to the safe handling of hazardous materials. Using what is known about the sense of touch, the inventors of the "Salisbury Hand" have given it kinesthetic sensors that simulate tension on the tendons of the hand and stimulation of the fingertips.
(Photo of Salisbury Hand at MI TAI lab courtesy of David Lampe, MIT)

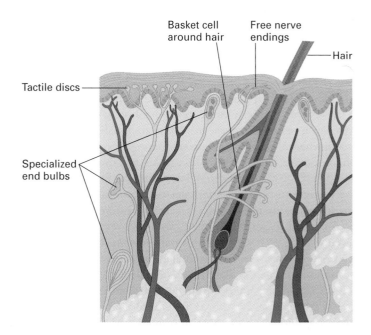

**FIGURE 4.17**
Diagram of the skin showing the major skin receptor cells.

**free nerve endings**
Sensory receptor cells in the skin that detect pressure, temperature, and pain.

**basket cells**
Sensory receptor cells at the base of hairs that detect pressure.

**tactile discs**
(tak′til) Sensory receptor cells that detect pressure.

**specialized end bulbs**
Sensory receptor cells that detect pressure.

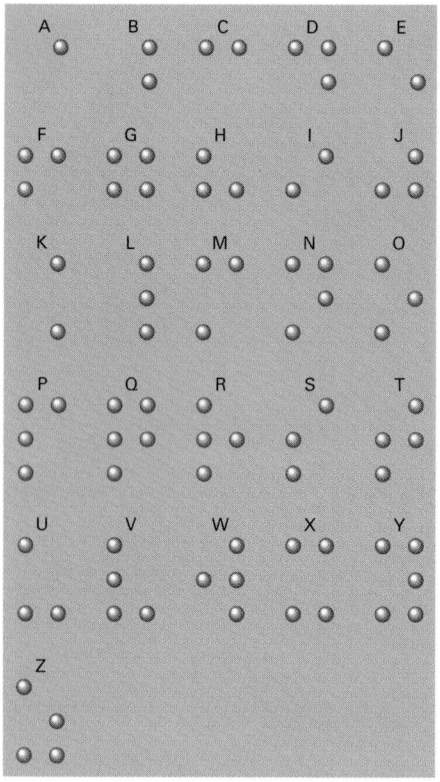

**FIGURE 4.18**
Raised dots used in the Braille alphabet are "read" with the fingertips.

**nocioceptors**
(nō″-see-oh-sep′-turs) Receptors for stimuli that are experienced as painful.

## Pressure

The skin is amazingly sensitive to pressure, but sensitivity differs considerably from one region of the skin to another depending on how many skin receptors are present. In the most sensitive regions—the fingertips, the lips, and the genitals—a pressure that pushes in the skin less than 0.001 mm can be felt, but sensitivity in other areas is considerably less (Schiffman, 1976). Perhaps the most striking example of the sensitivity of the skin is its ability to "read." Many blind people can read books using the Braille alphabet, patterns of small raised dots that stand for the letters of the alphabet. An experienced Braille user can read up to 300 words per minute using the sensitive skin of the fingertips (see fig. 4.18).

## Temperature

When the air outside is hot or cold, how do you sense this fact? It seems to most of us that the entire surface of the skin is able to detect temperature, but we actually sense skin temperature only through sensory receptors located in rather widely spaced "spots" on the skin. One set of spots detects warmth and one detects coldness. The information sent to the brain by these spots creates the feeling of temperature across the entire skin surface.

When the skin is warmed (for example, by air, sunlight, or water), the receptors in the warm spots send messages about warmness to the brain; when the skin is cooled, the cold spots send messages about coldness. Recall from chapter 1 (p. 8) that the sensation of intense heat is created by stimulation of *both* the warm and cold spots. Although the cold receptors are generally responsive only to cold temperatures, extreme heat also makes them fire. Therefore, high temperatures stimulate the receptors in both sets of spots to send messages simultaneously to the brain, which are interpreted as hotness.

## Pain

Everyone experiences some pain. Toes get stepped on, fingers are cut, and ankles are twisted from time to time. Even though it is unpleasant, pain is the useful signal that something bad has happened to a part of the body and it needs our attention. What are the neural systems that underlie the experience of pain?

Free nerve endings throughout the body serve as **nocioceptors**—receptors for stimuli that are experienced as painful. Neural messages from the nocioceptors are transmitted to the brain along two distinct nerve pathways—*rapid* and *slow* neural pathways. This is why we often experience "first and second pain" (Melzack & Wall, 1983; Sternbach, 1978). The first pain sensation is a clear, localized feeling that does not "hurt" much, but it tells us what part of the body has been hurt and what kind of injury has occurred. The second pain is a more diffuse, long-lasting pain that hurts in the emotional sense. When you cut your finger with a knife, an initial sensation tells you that you have been cut and where the cut has occurred, followed a moment later by a more diffuse and painful sensation. The first sensation makes you drop the knife and grab your finger; the second makes you jump up and down and scream!

There are two reasons that we experience these two somewhat separate pain sensations in sequence. First, the two sensations travel on different neural pathways, which have different speeds of transmission. The rapid pathway neurons are thicker and sheathed in myelin (see p. 61), which speeds transmission. The slow pathway neurons, in contrast, are smaller and slower, unmyelinated neurons. The second reason that we experience first and second pain is that the two neural pathways travel to different parts of the brain. The rapid pathway travels through the thalamus to the somatosensory area. If you recall from chapter 3 (p. 78), this is the part of the parietal lobe of the cerebral cortex that receives and interprets sensory information from the skin and body. When the information transmitted to this area on the rapid pathway is interpreted, we know what has happened and where it has happened, but the somatosensory area does not

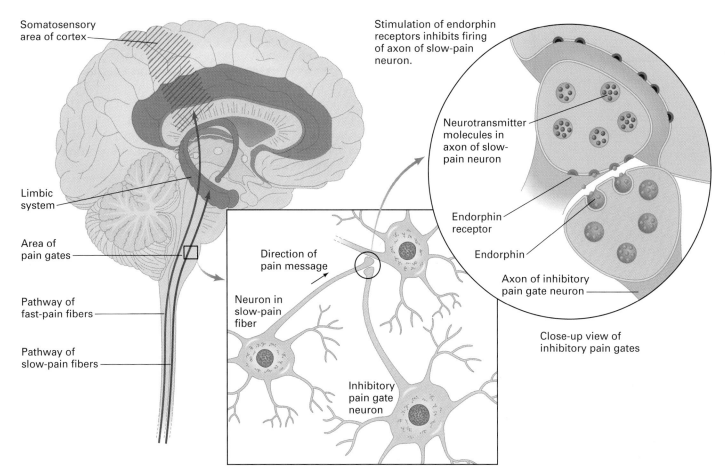

**FIGURE 4.19**

The operation of inhibitory pain gates. Secretion of endorphins by inhibitory gate neurons inhibits the firing of the axon of the neuron that transmits the pain message. Pain gate neurons regulate only the transmission of "slow-pain" fibers and are located primarily in the brain stem and spinal cord. Unfortunately, other pain gate neurons can make transmission of "slow-pain" messages to the limbic system more likely under some circumstances.

process the emotional aspects of the experience of "pain." Information that travels on the slower pathway is routed to the limbic system (p. 74). It is here, in the brain system that mediates emotion, that the emotional "ouch" part of the experience of pain is processed.

### Pain Gates

Pain involves much more than the transmission of neural messages from nocioceptors to the brain, however (Keefe & France, 1999). There is not a direct relationship between the stimulus and the amount of pain experienced. Under certain circumstances, pain messages can even be blocked out of the brain. For example, a football player whose attention is focused on a big game may not notice a painful cut until after the game is over. The pain receptors transmit the pain message during the game, but the message is not fully processed by the brain until the player is no longer concentrating on the game (Keefe & France, 1999).

Psychologist Ronald Melzack of McGill University proposed the *gate-control theory of pain* to explain such phenomena (Melzack & Wall, 1983). According to this theory, neural "gates" regulate the transmission of impulses from the nocioceptors to the brain (see fig. 4.19). All messages from nocioceptors from the body travel to the brain through the brain stem. The slow-pain neural fibers pass through neural gates in the brain stem that can be either "opened" or "closed." That is, the pain gates can make us more or less sensitive to stimulation of the nocioceptors. The pain gates can be influenced to allow more slow-pain neural transmission along the slow-pain pathways to the limbic system in two ways. First, when pain messages are received from nocioceptors—say, from a bruised toe—they sensitize the pain gates and make them transmit slow-pain impulses more readily. This is because the neuropeptide involved in slow-pain transmission—called *substance P* (for pain)—sometimes diffuses across to nearby neurons in the brain stem that ordinarily do not carry pain messages, causing them to transmit pain impulses too (Hopkins, 1997). Second, messages down from the midbrain make the pain gates more likely to allow slow-pain impulses through to the limbic system.

Fortunately, the pain gates also can be "closed" to make them less likely to transmit slow-pain impulses to the limbic system. For example, placing a sore foot in warm water helps close the gate on pain from the toe. The warm sensations block some of the pain sensations by closing the neural gates. Apparently, the rapid-pain pathways do not pass through the pain gates and cannot be blocked. The slow-pain pathways that carry the most distressing pain messages can be regulated by the pain gates under some circumstances, however (Melzack & Wall, 1983).

The pain gates appear to be operated by specialized neurons that block transmission in the neurons that carry "second pain" messages to the brain. As shown in figure 4.19, the *gate neurons* inhibit the pain neurons using substances called *endorphins*. When signaled by other sensory neurons or by neural fibers from the cortex to close the pain gate, the gate neuron inhibits the pain neuron and stops the pain message from reaching the brain.

Interestingly, women have a second pain-gate mechanism, based on the hormone estrogen, that males do not have (Mogil, Sternberg, Kest, Marek, & Liebeskind, 1993). This additional pain gate may help women deal with the pain experienced in childbirth, and its discovery may explain differences between males and females in their experience of pain and lead to more effective pain-controlling medications for women.

The discovery of a second substance that regulates the pain gates does not reduce the importance of the endorphins in both men and women, however. The discovery of the endorphins in 1973 by Candace Pert and Solomon Snyder has helped explain several mysteries about pain. First, a number of pain-killing drugs, such as the opiate morphine, clearly operate by duplicating the effects of the endorphins in inhibiting pain neurons. Indeed, the term *endorphin* means *endogenous* (produced inside the body) *morphine*. Second, the "high" that many runners feel during and right after endurance runs appears to be the result of the release of high levels of endorphins (Harte, Eifert, & Smith, 1995). Endorphins are released not only by specialized neurons in the spinal cord and brain stem but also by the hypothalamus and pituitary gland under times of physical or psychological stress, including the stress of endurance running. Apparently, runners are slightly high on the body's own supply of morphine.

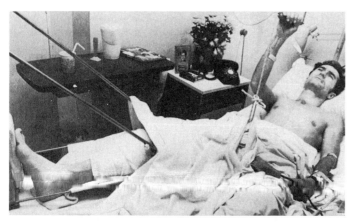

Guy Gertsch, who finished the 1982 Boston Marathon in a respectable 2 hours and 47 minutes, discovered at the finish line that he had run the last 19 miles with a broken thigh bone.

In addition, two medical mysteries apparently can be explained by the endorphins—the effects of acupuncture and placebo medications. Pain can often be reduced by the procedure of *acupuncture*. In this procedure, needles are inserted in the skin at special points and then twirled or heated. There is little doubt that some persons receiving acupuncture experience less pain, but the question is why. One possibility is that the needles stimulate the production of endorphins, which block the pain in the pain gates. To test this hypothesis, a drug that blocks the action of the endorphins (naloxone) was administered to persons undergoing acupuncture. While the endorphin-blocking drug was active, the person receiving acupuncture experienced the normal level of pain (Price, 1988). This suggests that acupuncture may close the pain gates by stimulating the endorphins.

*Placebo* medications are inactive substances, such as sugar pills or injections of saline solution, that are given during studies of new medications. The effects of the actual medication are compared with those of the placebo to see whether the medication is truly effective. Physicians have long been puzzled by the fact that placebos often make patients with a wide range of discomforts feel better. It now appears that endorphins also mediate the effects of placebos. As with the acupuncture studies, giving the endorphin-blocking drug naloxone eliminates the pain-killing effects of placebos (Levine, Gordon, & Fields, 1979). Apparently, being told that you have been given a medication that will help you stimulates the release of endorphins, and you really do feel better. This raises the possibility that acupuncture is effective not because of the placement of the needles but because of the placebo effect of believing that it will work.

In one sense, endorphins are wonderful things. They block pain, give runners a sense of euphoria, and make you feel better even when the doctor gives you a sugar pill. Endorphins undoubtedly play a positive role in lessening the aches and pains of everyday life. But there is a downside of endorphins, too. Endorphins probably have a negative effect on the immune system of the body (Calabrese, Kling, & Gold, 1987). This may be one reason marathon runners often experience the paradox of being in very good physical condition, yet being prone to catching colds and the flu.

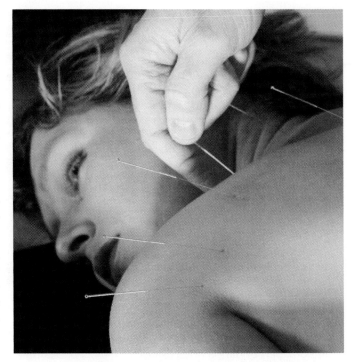

A woman is being treated for pain by an acupuncturist. One theory for the effectiveness of acupuncture is that the needles stimulate the release of pain-blocking endorphins.

### Peripheral Sensitization

There is another way in which there is not a direct one-to-one relationship between a magnitude of the painful stimulus and the amount of pain that a person experiences. Unfortunately, the nociceptors outside of the spinal column can be made more sensitive under some circumstances. If you have been cut on the hand, you may notice that even a light touch near the cut feels painful. When you think about it, that doesn't make sense. Why would lightly touching the skin near the wound (not touching the wound itself) hurt? The reason is that inflammation (swelling) leads to the sensitization of nociceptors near the cut, which results in the light touch being experienced as painful. This occurs in two ways. First, inflammation makes nociceptors so sensitive that they fire even when stimulated by a light touch. Second, just as substance P can permeate nonpain fibers in the spinal cord and make them transmit pain messages, substance P can turn nerve endings that normally play a role in the sense of touch into nociceptors (Hopkins, 1997). Usually, this sensitization of nerve endings reverses itself as the wound or bruise heals, but for persons with arthritis and other chronic inflammatory diseases, the phenomenon of peripheral sensitization can be debilitating. Hopefully, our growing understanding of pain will lead to new ways to control it for these individuals.

### Phantom Limbs

Suzanne Vega recorded a striking song in 1990 about lingering feelings for a lost love by drawing an analogy to a sad and curious phenomenon that often occurs to persons who have lost a limb:

> Men in a war
>
> If they've lost a limb
>
> Still feel that limb
>
> As they did before

## HUMAN DIVERSITY

### Culture and Pain

In this chapter, we examine the ways in which neural impulses from the sense organs are experienced as sensations and perceptions. Although much of this process is determined by the biological nature of the sense organs and neurons, learning experiences in our cultures apparently can influence even basic sensations such as pain.

Let's consider an example of the impact of culture on the perception of pain. Members of the Bariba society in Benin, West Africa, appear to be able to tolerate pain more easily than members of most cultures. Bariba folklore includes many examples of honored people who showed strength in the face of pain, and this calm response to pain is seen as an integral part of Bariba pride (Sargent, 1984). For example, pregnant women are expected not to let the fact that they are experiencing labor pains show to others. When labor becomes advanced, they leave the company of others to go through labor and childbirth alone, only calling for help with cutting the umbilical cord.

To the Bariba, letting other people see that they are in pain is cause for great shame. When discussing pain, many Bariba quote a Bariba proverb that translates to "Between death and shame, death has the greater beauty." According to a Bariba physician, an individual who displays pain lacks courage, and cowardice is the essence of shame. Rather than live in shame, a Bariba would rather die (Sargent, 1984). In this cultural context, one would do everything possible to avoid displaying signs of pain.

Do Bariba women who are in labor actually experience less pain than women in other cultures, or have they simply learned not to let the pain show? It is difficult to answer such questions, partly because of the difficulties involved in describing pain to another person. Because pain is a private experience, language must be used to communicate the experience to others, and language is shaped by culture. It is not surprising that there is a more limited vocabulary for describing pain in the Bariba language than in most other languages. When the Bariba discuss the experience of pain, therefore, it is difficult to know how much their description is influenced by their language.

But there is some reason to believe that the cultural emphasis on not showing reactions to pain might actually reduce the amount of pain that the Bariba experience. As noted on page 390 of chapter 10, there is evidence that facial expressions are an important part of the experience of pain (Izard, 1977). Apparently, sensory feedback to the brain from facial muscles supplies part of the neural input for the perception of pain (along with input from the part of the body that is cramped or injured). Indeed, persons who were given electrical shocks reported less pain when they were told to make no facial reactions than when they let their emotions show in their faces (Colby, Lanzetta, & Kleck, 1977). Maybe the calm face of a Bariba woman in labor results in the experience of less pain than does the agonized grimace of women in other cultures.

According to Linda Garro (1990), it is important for medical professionals who work with people in pain to understand the impact of culture on the expression of pain. If culture is not taken into account, the physician may overestimate or underestimate the amount of pain experienced by the patient. On the other hand, it is important to remember that not all members of a culture are the same. As in all other aspects of human diversity, it is important to be aware of variation within cultures.

What did you learn about pain in your own culture? Were you taught to minimize pain because it is important to be tough? Did you learn that no one will pay attention to your pain unless you exaggerate it? How do you respond when your parent or friends are in pain? Such questions will help you think about cultural influences on perception. ■

Amazingly, many amputees experience their missing arm or leg as if it were still there. They feel a missing arm, for example, as if it were hanging by their side when they sit still, and swinging in coordination with their other arm and legs when they walk. This "phantom limb" is experienced not as a memory of the lost limb but as a clear and realistic sensation that the missing limb is actually there. Ronald Melzack (1992) wrote about a man who experienced his missing arm as sticking straight out to the side, so he turned sideways when he walked through doorways to avoid bumping his arm, even though he knew perfectly well that the arm was not really there.

The sadder part is that as many as 70 percent of amputees experience a disturbing pain in the phantom limb. The pain is often a burning sensation, with many persons with amputated legs reporting that their nonexistent toes feel as if they are being seared by a hot fireplace poker. Similarly, persons with amputated arms often say that they feel their phantom hand is tightly clenched, with the fingernails digging painfully into their palms. A friend of mine recently wrote to say, "My mother, who lost her left leg to polio in her early 20s, is now 73, and sometimes when I ask how her arthritis is, she often responds, 'The foot I don't have aches as much as my good one.'" Amputees are not the only persons who experience such sensations. Persons with spinal cord injuries can experience no true sensations from the parts of their body below the break in the neural pathways in the spinal cord, but they sometimes experience phantom sensations in their limbs or genitals. Similarly, persons born without arms or legs often experience phantom sensations in the missing limb (Melzack, 1992).

How is it possible to "feel" sensations from a limb that does not exist and, therefore, cannot be transmitting sensations to the brain? A team of researchers from Germany and the United States appears to have provided the answer (Flor & others, 1995). Using brain-imaging techniques, they found that, when sensory and pain neurons from one part of the body have been cut, the area of the somatosensory cortex that served that part of the body becomes sensitive to input from parts of the body that activate *nearby* portions of the somatosensory cortex. For example, in the case of a woman who has lost her left arm through amputation, the portion of somatosensory cortex that formerly served her left arm may begin to receive input from her face (look back to figure 3.18, p. 78, to see that the area of the somatosensory cortex that serves the face is next to the area that receives input from the arm). In addition, cutting sensory neurons from one part of the body tends to reduce the efficiency of the pain gates. This suggests that phantom pain that is perceived as being in a missing arm may come from minor irritations to the face that are allowed through the pain gate and are perceived to be pain in the missing limb because the neural message stimulates the part of the cortex that used to serve input from the arm.

The phantom limb experience is another excellent illustration of the fact that our conscious experience is not always a direct and simple representation of the sensory information that reaches the brain. Sometimes, an individual experiences sensations and pains as if they arise in limbs that do not exist. As mentioned at the start of this section, Suzanne Vega's song used the phenomenon of phantom limbs as an analogy for lost love. Sometimes we experience lost friends or loves as if they were still there, somewhat like the experience of a phantom limb. One difference is that we usually get over the lost love, especially if we are lucky enough to move on to a better relationship. In contrast, even with treatment, some persons with phantom limb pain never stop experiencing pain in the missing limb.

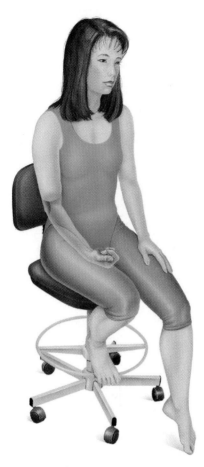

Some persons who have had limbs amputated still feel "phantom limbs" in place of the missing limbs. Often, they feel pain in the phantom limbs.

## Review

The body contains a number of sense organs that provide vital information about the body's movement and orientation in space and about the world as it contacts our skin. Information about posture, movement, and orientation is coded and sent to the somatic sensory area of the cortex by the vestibular organ in the inner ear and by kinesthetic receptors spread throughout the body. Skin receptors send information about temperature, pressure, and pain to the same area of the brain. We experience the pain from cuts and other injuries in two steps (a first pain that tells us what has happened and where it has happened, followed by a second, more emotional pain) because these two aspects of the pain experience travel on different neural pathways to different parts of the brain. The phenomenon of pain provides a good example of the lack of direct relationship between physical stimuli and conscious sensations in that a number of factors increase or decrease the experience of pain. The phantom limb experience also provides compelling evidence that conscious experiences are constructed in the brain and do not always have a direct relationship to incoming sensations.

## Check Your Learning

To be sure that you have learned the key points from the preceding section, cover the list of correct answers and try to answer each question. If you give an incorrect answer to any question, return to the page given next to the correct answer to see why your answer was not correct.

1. Sensory receptors located in the muscles, joints, and skin provide the brain with messages about movement, posture, and orientation of the body. These are called _____ receptors.

   a) vestibular                    c)    ciliary
   b) semicircular                  d)    kinesthetic

2. Which is *not* one of the four types of receptors in the skin?

   a)    vestibular cells          c)    tactile discs
   b)    basket cells              d)    specialized end bulbs

3. The sensation of intense heat is created by the stimulation of _____ on the skin.

   a)    warm spots               c)    both warm and cold spots
   b)    cold spots               d)    vestibular cells

4. Placing a sore foot in warm water blocks pain signals on the slow-pain pathway by closing neural "gates" in the spinal cord and brain stem, according to the _____ theory of pain.

## Thinking Critically about Psychology

1. In what ways is the experience of pain both a psychological and a physical event?

2. Have you had experiences in your own life that would support the gate-control theory of pain?

Correct Answers    1. d (p. 133),  2. a (p. 133),  3. c (p. 134),  4. gate control (p. 135)

### ● Chemical Senses: The Flavors and Aromas of Life

The senses of **gustation** (taste) and **olfaction** (smell) differ from the other senses in that they respond to chemicals. The chemical senses tell us about the things we eat, drink, and breathe.

### Taste

We are able to taste food and other things because of the 10,000 *taste buds* on the tongue. Each taste bud contains approximately a dozen sensory receptors, called **taste cells,** grouped together much like the segments of an orange (fig. 4.20). It is the taste cells that are sensitive to chemicals in our food and drink (Bartoshuk, 1988). The taste buds are further bunched together in bumps, called **papillae,** that can easily be seen on the tongue.

Collectively, the taste buds respond to thousands of chemicals, but all of our sensations of taste apparently result from the stimulation of different *combinations* of a small number of different types of taste receptors, which are most responsive to only one class of chemicals each. There are taste buds that respond primarily to chemicals that give rise to the sensations of *sweetness* (mostly sugars), *sourness* (mostly acids), *saltiness* (mostly salts), and *bitterness* (in response to a variety of chemicals that have no food value or are toxic). Recently, enough evidence has been accumulated to conclude that there is a fifth

**gustation**
(gus-tā′-shun) The sense of taste.

**olfaction**
(ōl-fak′-shun) The sense of smell.

**taste cells**
The sensory receptor cells for gustation located in the taste buds.

**papillae**
(pah-pil′ē) Clusters of taste buds on the tongue.

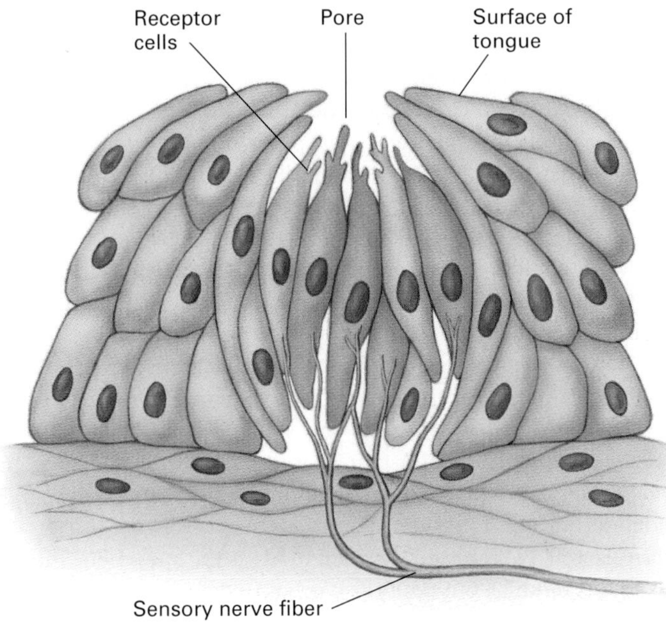

Receptor cells    Pore    Surface of tongue

Sensory nerve fiber

**FIGURE 4.20**
Taste buds contain clusters of taste (gustatory) receptor cells.

type of taste bud, which gives rise to the sensation of *fattiness* in response to fats (Schiffman, Graham, Sattely-Miller, & Warwick, 1998).

Interestingly, the taste buds that are most sensitive to these five classes of chemicals are not evenly distributed over the tongue. They are bunched together in different parts of the tongue, as shown in figure 4.21. This means that different parts of the tongue are sensitive to different tastes. We do not usually notice this because the differences in sensitivity are not great and because our food usually reaches all parts of the tongue during the chewing process anyway. But, if you ever have to swallow a truly bitter pill, try placing it in the exact middle of the tongue, where there are no taste receptors at all.

We lose taste buds as we age, especially over 45 years of age. Babies have the most taste buds and are very sensitive, whereas older adults are less sensitive to the chemicals that give rise to taste sensations (Schiffman & others, 1998).

Our perception of food also includes sensations from the skin surfaces of the tongue and mouth: touch (food texture and thickness), temperature (cold coffee tastes very different from hot coffee), and pain (as in Jalapeño peppers). The sight and aroma of food also greatly affect our perception of food.

## Smell

Chemicals in the air we breathe pass by the olfactory receptors on their way to the lungs. These receptor cells are located in a dime-sized, mucous-coated sheet at the top of the nasal cavity called the **olfactory epithelium** (see fig. 4.22). As with taste, we seem to be able to smell only a limited number of primary odors. There is much less agreement among psychologists about primary odors than about primary tastes, but one widely used system of classifying odors divides all of the complex aromas and odors of life into combinations of seven primary qualities (Ackerman, 1991; Amoore, Johnston, & Rubin, 1964): *resinous* (camphor), *floral* (roses), *minty* (peppermint), *ethereal* (pears), *musky* (musk oil), *acrid* (vinegar), and *putrid* (rotten eggs). However, professionals who create perfumes and other aromas distinguish 146 distinct odors (Dravnieks, 1983).

Interestingly, nearly all of the chemicals that humans can detect as odors are organic compounds, meaning they come from living things. In contrast, we can smell very few inorganic compounds like rocks and sand. Thus, our noses are useful tools for sensing the qualities of plants and animals—necessary, among other things, to distinguish between poisonous and edible things (Cain, 1988).

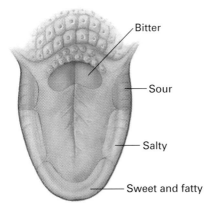

**FIGURE 4.21**
Areas of the tongue that are most sensitive to the five primary qualities of taste: sweet, fatty, salty, sour, and bitter.

**olfactory epithelium**
(ōl-fak′to-rē ep″i-thē′lē-um)  The sheet of receptor cells at the top of the nasal cavity.

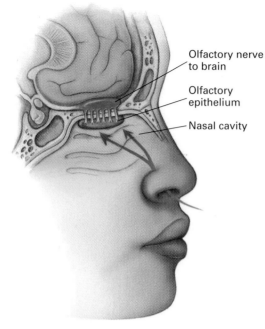

**FIGURE 4.22**
Olfactory receptor cells are located in the olfactory epithelium at the top of the nasal cavity.

Olfactory nerve to brain

Olfactory epithelium

Nasal cavity

Although we can smell only compounds derived from living things, chemists have long known how to create these organic compounds in test tubes. This means that any aroma can be custom-created and no longer has to be painstakingly extracted from flower petals and spices. One of the first perfumes created entirely in a laboratory was also one of the most successful fragrances ever made, Chanel No. 5. Once Marilyn Monroe boasted that she wore only Chanel No. 5 to bed, cloaking herself in a romantic blend of organic compounds created in a chemistry laboratory in 1922 (Ackerman, 1991).

How do we smell these organic molecules? According to the **stereochemical theory,** the complex molecules responsible for each of these primary odors have a specific shape that will "fit" into only one type of receptor cell, like a key into a lock. Only when molecules of a particular shape are present will the corresponding olfactory receptor send its distinctive message to the brain (Cain, 1988).

The sense of smell is important in and of itself, of course, sometimes bringing joyous messages of sweet perfumes to the brain and other times warning us of dangerous and foul odors. But the sense of smell contributes to the sense of taste as well. Not only do we smell foods as they pass beneath our noses on the way to our mouths, but odors also rise into the nasal passage as we chew. We are usually unaware of the impact of smell on the sense of taste, until a head cold makes everything taste like paste. The contribution of smell to taste is important partly because of the greater sensitivity of the sense of smell. The nose can detect the smell of cherry pie in the air that is 1/25,000th of the amount that is required for the taste buds to identify (Ackerman, 1991).

## Pheromone Detection

In many animal species, an additional chemical sense plays an important role in the regulation of reproductive behavior. Animals such as opossums and rabbits have an organ behind their olfactory epithelium known as the **vomeronasal organ.** This organ contains receptors for chemicals known as **pheromones.** Pheromones released in the sweat and urine of one animal are sensed by the vomeronasal organs of other animals. The receptor cells in the vomeronasal organ send neural messages to the hypothalamus and limbic system, which stimulate the release of sex hormones, ovulation, sexual behavior, and sometimes aggression toward rivals.

Do pheromones influence the reproductive behavior of humans? Researchers at the University of Chicago have discovered pheromones that influence human female reproductive cycles (Stern & McClintock, 1998). It has been known for some time that women who live together, such as in military barracks, soon find that they are on similarly timed menstrual cycles. It was not clear until recently, however, that this was due to the influence of pheromones. Psychologists Kathleen Stern and Martha McClintock (1998) collected sweat from women at different times in their menstrual cycles and identified at least two distinct pheromones. When other women inhaled sweat collected during the early phase of the menstrual cycle, lutenizing hormone was secreted by most of the women, and their menstrual cycles were accelerated. When sweat collected during the later stages of the menstrual cycle was inhaled by other women, it had the opposite effect. Because these pheromones have no odor (that is, they do not stimulate receptors in the olfactory epithelium itself), and because the receptors for pheromones send their neural messages to subcortical structures rather than to the cortex, the women were not consciously aware of their influence.

In addition, two laboratories have found evidence that when women inhale adrostadienone, a male sex hormone found in high concentrations on the skin, their mood improves (Grosser, Monti-Bloch, Jennings-White, & Berliner, 2000; Jacob & others, 2001). PET imaging shows that brain activity in regions associated with mood also change, even when the women are unaware of the hormone. Males may also respond to sex hormones, but less has been learned on this response to date.

**stereochemical theory**
The theory that different odor receptors can be stimulated only by molecules of a specific size and shape that fit them like a key in a lock.

**vomeronasal organ**
An organ in the nasal cavity of many animals that contains receptors for pheromones.

**pheromones**
Chemicals that stimulate receptors in the vomeronasal organ in some animals, influencing some aspects of reproductive behavior.

Chemicals in the air we breathe and in the things we eat and drink are sensed by the gustatory receptors (taste buds) on the tongue and the olfactory receptors in the nose. For both chemical senses, combinations of a relatively small number of primary sensations apparently make up the entire variety of our experiences of taste and smell. Pheromones influence reproductive behavior in many animal species. It is not known if pheromones influence sexual behavior in humans, but they appear to influence human menstrual cycles and mood.

To be sure that you have learned the key points from the preceding section, cover the list of correct answers and try to answer each question. If you give an incorrect answer to any question, return to the page given next to the correct answer to see why your answer was not correct.

1. Approximately a dozen sensory receptors called taste cells are found on each of the 10,000 _____ on the tongue.

2. All of our sensations of taste appear to result from five basic sensations of taste: sweetness, fattiness, sourness, saltiness, and _____ .

3. The olfactory receptors are located in a dime-sized, mucous-coated sheet at the top of the nasal cavity called the

   a) gustatory center.          c) olfactory cortex.
   b) olfactory epithelium.       d) thalamus.

4. The molecules responsible for each of the primary odors have a specific shape that will fit into only one type of olfactory receptor cell, according to the _____ theory.

   a) opponent-process          c) stereochemical
   b) trichromatic               d) camphoraceous

5. Chemicals that influence reproductive behavior in many animals are called

   a) pheromones.               c) astringents.
   b) olfactory bulbs.           d) stereochemicals.

1. Why do you think some people love the smell of coffee, but other people dislike it?

2. Why do you think there is an uneven distribution of the five types of taste buds on the tongue?

**Correct Answers:** 1. taste buds (p. 140), 2. bitterness (p. 140), 3. b (p. 141), 4. c (p. 142), 5. a (p. 142).

## ● Perception: Interpreting Sensory Messages

Sensations that are transmitted to the brain have little "meaning" of their own. They are in the form of raw neural energy that must be organized and interpreted in the process we call *perception*. The process is pretty much the same in all of us. If this were not the case—if each of us were to interpret sensory input in a unique way—there would be no common "reality" in the sense of a perceived world that we all share. However, some aspects of perception are unique to members of different cultures. The specific learning experiences, memories, motives, and emotions of the individual also can influence perception. For example, we all perceive the visual stimuli of a knife in pretty much the same way because of the inborn ways we organize visual information. But a knife also has

**figure-ground principle**
The Gestalt principle of perception that states that part of a visual stimulus will be the center of our attention (figure) and the rest will be the indistinct ground. In many cases, the figure and ground can be reversed in our perception of the same stimulus.

**FIGURE 4.23**
The distinction between figure and ground in visual perception is clearly illustrated by this vase prepared for Queen Elizabeth of England. Do you see a vase, or do you see the profiles of Queen Elizabeth and Prince Philip looking at one another? It depends on whether the dark space on each side of the vase is the figure or the ground in your perceptual organization of the stimuli.

**FIGURE 4.24**
This drawing can be viewed as a younger or an older woman, depending on the viewer's figure-ground organization.

unique perceptual meaning to each individual, depending on whether the person has been cut by a similar knife.

In this section, we will examine the inborn organizational properties that all humans share and will briefly discuss some of the ways in which each individual's perceptions are unique. Keep in mind as we discuss perception that, although it's easy to distinguish between sensation and perception in theory, it's very difficult to do so in practice. Visual perception, for example, begins in the complex neural structures of the eye before sensory messages are transmitted to the brain (Hochberg, 1988). The distinction between sensation and perception, then, is largely an arbitrary one, but it makes our discussion of information processing by the sense organs and brain easier to understand.

## Visual Perception

In the discussion that follows, we will look at the major ways in which sensory information is interpreted into meaningful perceptions, including both those that are common to us all and those that are unique to each individual. This discussion focuses on visual perception, rather than on all of the perceptual systems, for several reasons: Visual perception is a highly important sensing system; scientists understand how it works better than they do other systems; and it is representative enough of other systems to tell us something about the process of perception in general.

### Perceptual Organization

Raw visual sensations are like the unassembled parts of a washing machine: they must be put together in an organized way before they are useful to us. Some of the fundamental ways in which the eye and brain organize visual sensations were described about 75 years ago by Gestalt psychologists in their pioneering writings on perception (see chapter 1). These principles of perceptual organization are still worthy of our attention (Palmer, 2002; Prinzmetal, 1995). The following are five of the so-called Gestalt principles of perception:

1. **Figure-ground.** When we perceive a visual stimulus, part of what we see is the center of our attention, the figure, and the rest is the indistinct ground. The vase in figure 4.23 shows that this way of seeing can reorganize the nature of "reality." The figure and ground of this photo can be reversed to perceive either a vase or two opposing faces. In the same way, the woman in figure 4.24 could be viewed as a young woman facing away or as an older woman facing forward and downward, depending on which parts you perceive as the figure and which parts you perceive as ground. This principle of perception is very useful in showing us that what we perceive is often based more on what goes on in our brains than what is in front of our eyes. The remaining Gestalt principles amplify this point.

2. **Continuity.** We tend to perceive lines or patterns that follow a smooth contour as being part of a single unit. In figure 4.25, at which point did child B start bouncing her pogo stick? We tend to organize our perceptions of the tracks so that it appears that girl B started at point 1, but both girls could have made sharp turns in the center and headed off at right angles. We do not naturally organize sensations in this way, however; we tend to perceive continuity in lines and patterns.

3. **Proximity.** Things that are proximal (close together) are usually perceived as belonging together. In figure 4.26, we see three vertical columns of blocks on the left side and three horizontal rows on the right side, due to proximity.

4. **Similarity.** On the left side of figure 4.27, we perceive two vertical columns of apples and two vertical columns of pears, even though they are evenly spaced. On the right side, in contrast, a different arrangement results in the perception of two horizontal rows of each fruit. Similar things are perceived as being related.

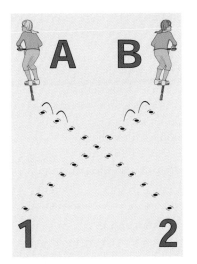

**FIGURE 4.25**
At which point did girl B start jumping on her pogo stick? According to the principle of continuity, we would tend to perceive point 1 as her starting point, although either 1 or 2 would be equally possible.

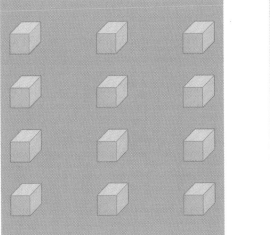

**FIGURE 4.26**
Do you see vertical columns or horizontal rows? The principle of proximity determines how these stimuli are organized perceptually.

**FIGURE 4.27**
Do you see vertical columns or horizontal rows? The principle of similarity suggests that we organize the figure on the left into vertical columns and the one on the right into horizontal rows, even though the objects are equally spaced.

**FIGURE 4.28**
We see a face rather than unrelated lines because of the perceptual principle of closure.

5. **Closure.** Incomplete figures of familiar things, such as in figure 4.28, tend to be perceived as complete wholes. Again, we fill in missing sensory information to create complete and whole perceptions.

Our perceptions are actively organized according to these and other, similar inborn principles.

## Perceptual Constancy

We perceive the world as a fairly constant and unchanging place. Tables, lamps, and people do not change in size, shape, or color from moment to moment. Yet, the sensations that tell us about these things do change considerably from moment to moment. The size of the image that falls on the retina changes as a person walks away from us, but we do not perceive the person as shrinking in size. The shape of a pot seen from different angles is different on the retina, but we do not believe that the pot is changing shape.

**continuity principle**
(kon'ti-noo"i-tee) The Gestalt principle of perception that states that lines or patterns that follow a smooth contour will be perceived as part of a single unit.

**proximity principle**
(prok'sim"-i-tee) The Gestalt principle of perception that states that parts of a visual stimulus that are close together will be perceived as belonging together.

**similarity principle**
The Gestalt principle of perception that states that parts of a visual stimulus that are similar will be perceived as belonging together.

**closure principle**
(klo'zhur) The Gestalt principle of perception that states that incomplete figures of familiar objects will tend to be perceived as wholes.

**perceptual constancy**
The tendency for perceptions of objects to remain relatively unchanged in spite of changes in raw sensations.

**monocular cues**
(mon-ok´ū-lar) Eight visual cues that can be seen with one eye and that allow us to perceive depth.

Perceptual constancy helps us recognize this vase as unchanging, even though we are viewing it from different angles and from different distances.

This characteristic of perception is called **perceptual constancy.** There are several types of perceptual constancy:

1. *Brightness constancy.* A piece of white paper does not change in perceived brightness when it moves from a weakly lit room to a brightly lit room, even though the intensity of the light reaching the eye changes considerably. Fortunately for our ability to cope with the world, our perception corresponds to the unchanging physical properties of the paper rather than to the changing sensory information about its brightness. When you stop to think about it, this is a remarkable accomplishment, but one that we take so much for granted that you may not have been aware that it was happening until you read this paragraph.

2. *Color constancy.* Colors do not appear to change much in spite of different conditions of light and surroundings that change incoming visual information.

3. *Size constancy.* A dollar bill seen from distances of 1 foot and 10 feet casts different-sized images on the retina, but we do not perceive it as changing in size. Familiar objects do not change in perceived size at different distances.

4. *Shape constancy.* A penny seen from straight ahead casts a circular image on the retina. When seen from a slight angle, however, the image it casts is oval, yet we continue to perceive it as circular.

The process of perceptual constancy means that we automatically adjust our perceptions to correspond with what we have learned about the physical world, rather than relying solely on changing stimulus input.

**Depth Perception**

The retina has a two-dimensional surface. It has an up and a down, and a left and a right, but no depth. How is it, then, that we are able to perceive a three-dimensional world using a two-dimensional retina? The eye and brain accomplish this remarkable feat by using a number of two-dimensional cues to create a perceptual distance.

The **monocular cues** to depth perception can be perceived by one eye (see fig. 4.29). The eight monocular cues are:

1. *Texture gradient.* The texture of objects is larger and more visible up close and smaller when far away. On curved surfaces, the elements of texture are also more slanted when they are farther away.

2. *Linear perspective.* Objects cast smaller images on the retina when they are more distant. As a result, parallel lines, such as railroad tracks, appear to grow closer together the farther away they are from us. In paintings, therefore, objects with larger relative size will appear to be closer than will objects with smaller relative size.

3. *Superposition.* Closer objects tend to be partially in front of, or partially cover up, more distant objects.

4. *Shadowing.* The shadows cast by objects suggest their depth.

5. *Speed of movement.* Objects farther away appear to move across the field of vision more slowly than do closer objects. A dog running through a distant field appears to move slowly, but it moves more quickly when the dog runs right in front of us.

6. *Aerial perspective.* Water vapor and pollution in the air scatter light waves, giving distant objects a bluish, hazy appearance compared with nearby objects.

7. *Accommodation.* As discussed earlier in the chapter, the shape of the lens of the eye must change to focus the visual image on the retina from stimuli that are different distances from the eye. This process is called accommodation. Kinesthetic receptors in the ciliary muscle, therefore, provide a source of information about the distance of different objects. This information is useful, however, only for short distances up to about 4 feet.

Texture gradient.

Linear perspective.

Shadowing.

Superposition.

Aerial perspective.

**FIGURE 4.29**
Texture gradient, linear perspective, shadowing, superposition, and aerial perspective are monocular cues used in depth perception.

8. *Vertical position.* When objects are on the ground, the farther they appear to be below the horizon, the closer they appear to be to us. For objects in the air, however, the farther they appear to be above the horizon, the closer they appear to be to us.

**Binocular cues** in depth perception can only be perceived using two eyes. The two binocular cues are:

1. *Convergence.* When both eyes are looking at an object in the center of the visual field, they must angle inward more sharply for a near object than for a distant object (see fig. 4.30). Information from the muscles that move the eyes thus provides a clue as to the distance of an object from the viewer.

2. *Retinal disparity.* Because our two eyes are a couple of inches apart, they do not see the same view of three-dimensional objects, especially when the object is close. This disparity, or difference, between the images on the two retinas is a key

**binocular cues**
(bīn-ok´ū-lar) Two visual cues that require both eyes to allow us to perceive depth.

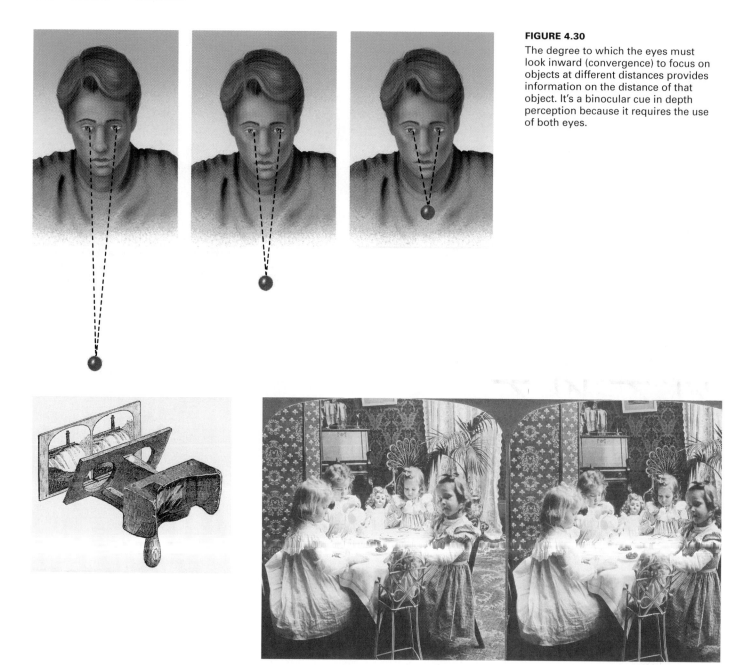

**FIGURE 4.30**
The degree to which the eyes must look inward (convergence) to focus on objects at different distances provides information on the distance of that object. It's a binocular cue in depth perception because it requires the use of both eyes.

**FIGURE 4.31**
Two photos taken from slightly different angles are used in a stereopticon to create an illusion of depth through retinal disparity.

factor in depth perception. Retinal disparity is the principle behind the old-fashioned stereopticon. As shown in figure 4.31, the individual looks at two pictures of the same scene in a viewer that lets each eye see only one of the two images. The images have been photographed from two slightly different spots to duplicate the disparity between two retinal images. When seen in the stereopticon, the two images fuse into a single scene perceived in startlingly good three dimension. Try placing your hand edgewise between the two pictures and the bridge of your nose to allow each eye to see only one of the pictures. Look at them for a while to see if they fuse into a single, three-dimensional scene.

Through a combination of these monocular and binocular cues, we are able to perceive our three-dimensional world using only two-dimensional information.

**FIGURE 4.32**
The Ponzo illusion. Are the horizontal lines the same length?

**FIGURE 4.33**
This figure often produces an illusory judgment of length. Which line is longer, the horizontal or the vertical line? Actually, they are the same length.

**FIGURE 4.34**
Do you see a white square? Most of us perceive the illusory "Kanizsa square" in front of four black circles, in spite of the fact that there is no square actually depicted in the drawing—just four circles with missing quarters. What we see is often not literally what is "out there."

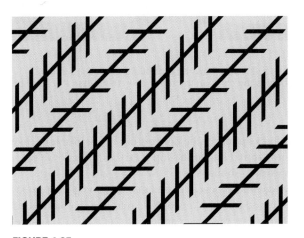

**FIGURE 4.35**
The Zoliner illusion. Are the diagonal lines parallel?

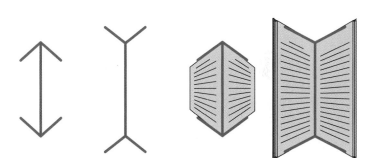

**FIGURE 4.36**
The Müller-Lyer illusion. Most people see the vertical line on the right as being longer, even though they are the same length. The shorter lines give an illusion of depth, as in the two books on the right.

## Visual Illusions

Instructors of introductory psychology have long enjoyed amazing their classes with **visual illusions**. These illusions intentionally manipulate the cues that we use in visual perception to create a false or illusory perception. They are instructive, therefore, in showing us more about the process of perception and for showing us in yet *another* way that what we see is not always the same as the visual information that enters the eyes. For example, are the two horizontal lines in figure 4.32 (the Ponzo illusion) the same size? (They are, even though the upper line looks longer.) How about the two lines in figure 4.33 (the vertical-horizontal illusion)—most people see the vertical line as longer, even though they are the same length. The white square that you see in figure 4.34 does not exist in the drawing, which is just four circles with missing quarters. My personal favorite is the Zoliner illusion, shown in figure 4.35. Believe it or not, the diagonal lines are parallel. Even after you cover all but two lines or measure the distance between the diagonal lines for yourself, this illusion is amazing.

How do these illusions fool us? They do so by using monocular depth cues to create an illusion. Consider the Müller-Lyer illusion: The two vertical lines on the left of figure 4.36 are of different lengths—or are they? Actually, they just look different because of the context they are in. Ordinarily, the short lines at the end of the longer lines would be cues to depth, as in the two booklets shown on the right side of figure 4.36. We see the vertical line as longer when the cues suggest that it is farther away. In the Ponzo

**visual illusion**
Visual stimuli in which the cues uesd in visual perception create a false perception.

**FIGURE 4.37**

The Ames room, which was constructed to illustrate how the monocular cues used in depth perception can be used to create illusions. Is the child on the right really taller than the adult on the left?

illusion (fig. 4.32), the two vertical lines appear to be converging in the distance, like railroad tracks, suggesting that the horizontal line at the top is farther away, so we see it as longer. The other visual illusions work in similar ways.

Perhaps the most impressive visual illusion ever created in a psychology laboratory is the *Ames room*. When this room is viewed through a peephole made in one wall (used to restrict the availability of binocular cues), the room appears to be a normal square. Actually, however, the room is much deeper on one side than the other, but many cues of depth perception have been altered to give the illusion of equal depth for all sides of the back wall. The effect this room has on perception is startling when people are in the room (see figs. 4.37 and 4.38).

Not all visual illusions are laboratory demonstrations, however. They are common in everyday life. Few sights are more beautiful than a huge full moon on the horizon. Have you ever stopped to wonder why it always looks *bigger* on the horizon than overhead? It doesn't really grow, you know; it's an illusion. In fact, it's an illusion that still puzzles scientists. There is no widely accepted theory of the moon illusion (Reed, 1984; Rock & Kaufman, 1972), but it is based partly on the misperception of depth.

As shown in figure 4.39, an object that our senses tell us is *farther away* is perceived as being *larger* than an object that casts the same-size image on the retina but appears to be closer. The two triangles in this figure are the same size, but the one at the top is perceived as larger because it appears to be farther away. Ordinarily, the top triangle *would* be larger if it were farther away, but it could still cast as large a retinal image as a closer object.

The moon illusion is based partly on the same principle. When the moon is overhead, not only does it appear closer due to its vertical position, but we have no distance cues, so depth cues do not accurately influence our perception of the moon's size. When it's near the horizon, however, it appears to be farther away because of its vertical position. In addition, we can see the moon is farther away than objects such as distant trees and buildings, which we know to be large but which cast a small image on the retina. When the size of the moon is perceived in comparison with these objects, it looks much bigger.

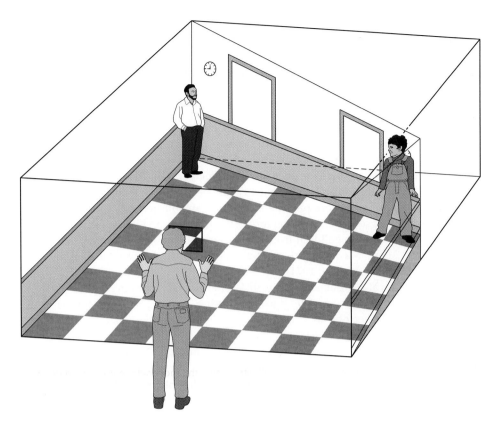

**FIGURE 4.38**
Although not apparent to the viewer, the right side of the Ames room is one-half as deep as the left, the floor is higher and the ceiling is lower on the right, and the window on the right is smaller. All of these cues create the impression that the person on the right is much larger than the person on the left in the Ames room.

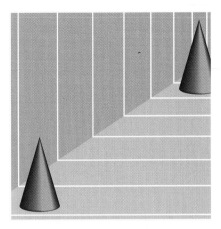

**FIGURE 4.39**
When two objects of the same size are perceived as being at different distances, the one that seems farther away is perceived as being larger.

And then there is the dreaded Poggendorf illusion! Look at the diagonal line that appears to pass behind the green bar in figure 4.40. Which line on the right is the continuation of the diagonal line? Most persons choose the middle line. Now place the edge of a piece of white paper along the line. Which line on the right do you think is the continuation of the line on the left now? In the Poggendorf illusion, lines that appear to pass behind solid objects at an angle appear to be "moved over" when they emerge. You can demonstrate this phenomenon again by drawing a straight line with a ruler on a piece of paper and then covering it with a quarter (25-cent piece). The line now emerges from the quarter in the wrong place.

The Poggendorf illusion is not only interesting, it can be downright *dangerous* (Coren & Girgus, 1978)! Consider the dilemma that might be faced by a surgeon, as illustrated in figure 4.41. Suppose the surgeon views a bullet that lies next to a bone on an X ray and lines up a probe to remove it. Will the probe touch the top of the bullet? Is it lined up correctly? If you place the edge of a piece of paper along the line of the probe, you will see that it will *miss* the bullet. The Poggendorf illusion may even be involved in some air accidents. In 1965, two airplanes heading for a

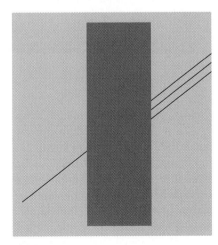

**FIGURE 4.40**
A demonstration of the Poggendorf illusion. Which line on the right is the continuation of the diagonal line on the left?

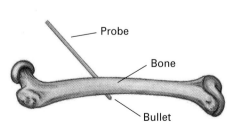

**FIGURE 4.41**
An example of the danger of the Poggendorf illusion. Will the surgeon's probe touch the top of the bullet?

landing field near New York City passed on opposite sides of a cloud. Apparently because of the Poggendorf illusion, their paths seemed to be on line for a collision where they were estimated to emerge from the cloud. Tragically, the pilots changed course and collided, killing 4 persons and injuring 49 more (Matlin, 1988).

## Individual and Cultural Influences on Perception

Up to this point, we have discussed factors that determine perception in the same way for all of us—characteristics of the inborn "wiring" of the human brain and sensory systems. But perception is strongly influenced by other factors as well. For example, a number of studies tell us that *motivation* influences perception: Hungry college students are more likely to interpret ambiguous pictures as being of food; sexually aroused males perceive females as being more physically attractive; anxious persons are more likely to interpret ambiguous sentences as being threatening; and poor children estimate the size of coins as larger than do children from higher income families (Bruner & Goodman, 1947; Eysenck, Mogg, May, Richards, & Mathews, 1991; McClelland & Atkinson, 1948; Stephan, Berscheid, & Walster, 1971).

Perception is also influenced by the different *learning* experiences of people living in different cultures. For example, persons who live in the dense rain forests of the African Congo rarely see objects at long distances. In their world, thick vegetation blocks the sight of distant objects. It is interesting, then, that, if these peoples travel to the African plains, distant buffalo are at first seen as tiny "insects" (Turnbull, 1962). Pictures they draw are flat, two-dimensional renderings without depth cues. Furthermore, when they are shown pictures like figure 4.42 and asked which animal the man is trying to spear, they answer, "The tiny rhinoceros," because they do not perceive the rhinoceros as being in the distance.

**FIGURE 4.42**

One of the drawings used to study depth perception in different cultures. Which animal is the man about to spear?

## Review

Perception is the interpretation of sensations. It's an active process in which perceptions are created that often go beyond the minimal information provided by the senses. Many of the ways in which we organize and interpret sensations are inborn and common to all humans. The Gestalt principles of perceptual organization, perceptual constancies, depth perception, and visual illusions provide examples of the active, creative nature of perception. Other factors that enter into the process of perception are unique to the individual, such as motivational states and cultural learning experiences. These factors ensure that we will perceive the world in a way that is largely universal among humans, but with a great deal of individuality due to differences in motivation, emotion, learning, and other factors.

To be sure that you have learned the key points from the preceding section, cover the list of correct answers and try to answer each question. If you give an incorrect answer to any question, return to the page given next to the correct answer to see why your answer was not correct.

1. When we perceive a visual stimulus, the center of our attention is termed the *figure* and the rest of the visual stimulus is perceived as the indistinct *ground*. Is it possible to change our perception of the same stimulus so that the figure becomes the ground and the ground becomes the figure?

   a)  yes
   b)  no

2. The cues used in depth perception that require both eyes are called

   a)  constant.             c)  binocular.
   b)  monocular.            d)  dichromatics.

3. The shape of the lens of the eye must change to focus the visual image on the retina from stimuli that are different distances from the eye, providing a cue used in depth perception. This process is called

   a)  superposition.        c)  convergence.
   b)  aerial perspective.    d)  accommodation.

4. Visual perception can be influenced by

   a)  motivation.           c)  both a and b.
   b)  learning.             d)  neither a nor b.

1. What is the point of studying perceptual illusions? What can we learn from them?

2. What is the value of knowing that our perception is influenced by our emotions?

**Correct Answers:** 1. a (p. 144),  2. c (p. 147),  3. d (p. 146),  4. c (p. 152).

## Visual Perception, Illusion, and Art

During the winter of 1993, I went to New York with my best friend to see a collection of paintings, drawings, and sculpture by Henri Matisse at the Museum of Modern Art. The sheer beauty and emotional impact of these works was amazing. But, ever being the psychologist, I sometimes found myself thinking about his paintings in terms of the monocular cues to depth perception. And as I thought about it, I found that the way Matisse used monocular cues of depth perception in his art was pretty interesting, too. Maybe looking at some paintings from this perspective will add to our appreciation of the visual arts and teach us something about depth perception.

The artist who paints a landscape, a still life, or a portrait of a person is creating a visual illusion. He or she uses what is known about the monocular cues of depth perception to create the *illusion* of a three-dimensional object (one with height, width, and depth) on a two-dimensional canvas (one with height and width only). No part of the flat canvas is farther away from the viewer than any other part, but the artist creates the illusion of depth—the impression that some parts of the painting are farther away than others—mostly by using the cues of texture gradient, linear perspective, superposition, shadowing, and aerial perspective. Cues based on the way in which the eyes focus on objects that are different distances from the eye and the binocular cues that are based on differences in the alignment of the two eyes cannot be used by the artist, but artists often achieve striking illusions of depth with the few cues at their disposal.

Look at the striking illusions of depth created in two paintings. The painting in figure 4.43 by the Spanish painter Diego Velazquez (*Las Meninas,* 1656) uses four depth perception cues to suggest depth very effectively. Notice that the image of the man standing in the doorway is smaller on the canvas than the man standing on the left (a self-portrait of the artist) and even smaller than the young blonde child who appears to be standing in the front of the painting. Note also that the part of the wall on the right that is meant to be perceived as farther away is shorter on the canvas than the image of the wall meant to be perceived as being in the front of the room. These are uses of the monocular cue of *linear perspective,* and they give a powerful illusion of depth to the room. Notice also that the persons that Velazquez wishes us to perceive as being in the front of the room partially cover the persons portrayed as being at the rear of the room (the cue of *superposition*). The detailed texture of the clothing of the persons in the front of the room is also clearer than that of

**FIGURE 4.43**

*Las Meninas* (1656) by Diego Velazquez.
Erich Lessing/Art Resource, NY.

persons at the rear of the room (the cue of *texture gradient*). Velazquez also uses shadowing effectively to create an illusion of depth, but let's study this cue in the even more effective example by Artemisia Gentileschi (fig. 4.44).

A more subtle, but wonderfully effective, illusion of depth has been created in this extraordinary self-portrait. Gentileschi gives us an amazingly three-dimensional view of herself partly by using linear perspective. Notice, for example, that her right hand appears to be farther away from us partly because it is smaller on the canvas than her left hand, which seems to be very close to us. In addition, her face partially hides the right shoulder, which seems farther away from us (superposition). But, it is Gentileschi's exceptional mastery of shadowing that brings the illusion of subtle depth to life. Her face is painted on a flat canvas, but it seems as rounded as an apple. As a result, her left cheek seems inches closer to us than does her nose.

Sometimes, Matisse was interested in creating a sense of depth, but sometimes he intentionally ignored depth. The reclining nude in figure 4.45 (*L'Atelier du Quai Saint-Michel*), for example, is positioned in a scene painted with powerful depth cues. Notice that the building seen outside the window is shorter on the canvas than the delicate table standing in front of the window. Compare that painting with a later painting in which he has portrayed exactly the same subject in a very different way. In *Grand Nu Couche* (fig. 4.46), Matisse has eliminated most cues of depth from the painting, including depth through shadowing. The woman is mostly a flat surface in a flat room. Matisse eliminated the depth cues intentionally to force us to see only color and form. If he had been a great chef, he might have asked us to focus on the flavors of his creations by wearing a

**FIGURE 4.44**
Self-portrait by Artemisia Gentileschi.
The Royal Collection © 1994 Her Majesty Queen Elizabeth II.

**FIGURE 4.45**
*L'Atelier du Quai Saint-Michel* by Henri Matisse.
Art Resource, NY © 1995 Succession H. Matisse, Paris/Artists Rights Society (ARS), New York.

blindfold during the meal to avoid distractions. By taking depth out of this painting, Matisse leaves us with nothing to perceive but form and color.

## Painting and Depth Cues: Doing It Yourself

A few years ago, I came across some good advice on learning to paint realistic three-dimensional scenes with a good sense of depth on a two-dimensional canvas (Hochberg, 1988). The advice is based on a solid understanding of the cues that we use to create the perception of depth using our own two-dimensional retinas. I would like to be able to attribute this advice to the research of a contemporary psychologist to show you that the science of psychology is useful even to your more artistic side, but the advice comes from the artist Leonardo da Vinci writing in the early sixteenth century. His keen observations will not only help your drawing and your appreciation of the work of other artists but will also help you understand depth perception better.

Da Vinci suggests that we place a pane of clear glass the size of our canvas in front of the objects that we want to draw, as in figure 4.47. As we look at the objects, we should trace them exactly as they appear o*n the flat surface of the glass* (which is how they appear on the surface of the retina and how we should draw them on the flat surface of the canvas). For example, in figure 4.47(a), child 1 and child 2 are actually the same height and are both smaller than adult 3. However, as shown in 4.47(b), child 1 appears much larger on the surface of the glass than child 2 because child 1 is much closer than child 2. In fact, when traced on the flat glass, child 1 is the same size as the much taller adult 3. By drawing these figures as they appear on the glass rather than as they are in reality, an illusion of depth is created on the canvas. Notice that ob-

**FIGURE 4.46**
*Grand Nu Couche* by Henri Matisse.
The Baltimore Museum of Art: The Cone Collection, formed by Dr. Claribel Cone and Miss Etta Cone of Baltimore, Maryland BMA 1950.258. © 1995 Succession H. Matisse, Paris/Artists Rights Society (ARS), New York.

ject 5 looks farther away than object 4, partly because of linear perspective (5 is smaller than 4 on the glass) and partly because of superposition (4 is partially blocking our view of 5). ∎

*(continued)*

**155**

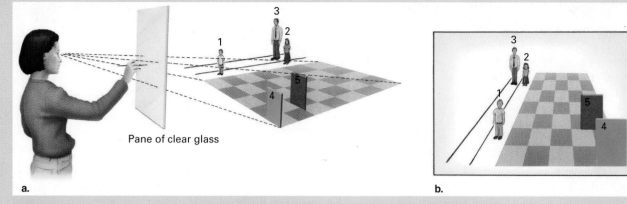

**FIGURE 4.47**
Leonardo da Vinci suggested that we can learn to use the principles of linear perspective and superposition to give depth to our drawings by placing a pane of glass in front of the scene to be drawn. Trace the objects on the flat glass and you will see how to draw them on the flat canvas.

# Summary

Chapter 4 recognizes that we live in a physical world that we experience through our sense organs and interpret (perceive) by means of our nervous systems.

I. We are aware of the outside world because we have specialized sensory receptor cells.

    A.    Sense organs transduce sensory energy into neural impulses and send neural messages to the brain for interpretation.

    B.    Psychophysics is the field of psychology that studies the relationships between physical stimuli and psychological sensations and perceptions.

II. The rods and cones of the eye transduce light energy into neural signals.

    A.    The intensity of light waves largely determines brightness, whereas the wavelength (frequency) largely determines hue.

    B.    The eye, working much as a camera does, is the primary sense organ for seeing.

        1.    Light enters the eye through the cornea (with the iris regulating the size of the pupil) and the lens into the retina.

        2.    Rods and cones transduce light waves into neural impulses for transmission to the brain.

        3.    The 125 million rods, located throughout the retina except for the fovea, are active in peripheral vision and vision in dim light, but they do not play a role in color vision.

        4.    The 6 million cones, clustered mostly near the fovea, code information for color.

        5.    Both trichromatic theory and opponent-process theory are helpful in understanding color vision.

III. The sense of hearing responds to sound waves.

    A.    The frequency of sound waves determines pitch, whereas the intensity determines loudness.

    B.    The ear is the primary sense organ for hearing.

        1.    The outer ear functions as a sound wave collector.

        2.    Sound waves vibrate the eardrum, which is connected to a series of three movable bones (hammer, anvil, stirrup) in the middle ear.

3.  The inner ear, containing the cochlea and the organ of Corti, transduces the sound wave energy into neural impulses for transmission to the brain.

IV.  Chemical senses respond to chemicals in the environment.

   A.  In the sense of taste, different classes of chemicals are experienced as sweet, sour, bitter, salty, and fatty.

   B.  In the sense of smell, different classes of chemicals are experienced as different odors.

V.  Internal stimuli are also received by the sensory system.

   A.  The vestibular organ provides information about the orientation of the body relative to the pull of gravity, whereas the kinesthetic sense reports the position and movement of the limbs and body.

   B.  The various skin senses can detect pressure, temperature, and pain.

   1.  Two sensations of pain reach the brain at slightly different times because they travel on different neural pathways.

      a.  The first sensation reaches the somatosensory area quickly on myelinated neurons.

      b.  The more emotional type of pain reaches the limbic system more slowly on unmyelinated neurons.

   2.  Many factors can block the pain gates for the emotional aspect of pain.

VI.  Sensory neural impulses, when transmitted to the brain, are interpreted in a process called perception; examining visual perception demonstrates the general nature of the process.

   A.  Perception is an active mental process. Gestalt principles explain many of the ways in which humans tend to organize sensory information.

   B.  Individual factors, such as emotion, motivation, and previous learning, also affect our perceptions.

---

**Resources**

1.  If you think of yourself as a sensual person and something of an intellectual, then treat yourself to the most wonderful book ever written about the senses: Ackerman, D. (1991). *A natural history of the senses.* New York: Vintage Books.

2.  A readable but sophisticated examination of classical principles of perception and illusions is supplied by Sekuler, R. (1994). *Perception* (3rd ed.). Boston: McGraw-Hill.

3.  If you are a serious student of visual perception or of the visual arts, you may wish to tackle an excellent in-depth analysis of this subject: Hochberg, J. (1988). Visual perception. In R. C. Atkinson, R. J. Herrnstein, G. Lindzey, & R. D. Luce (Eds.), S*tevens' handbook of experimental psychology: Vol. 1. Perception and motivation.* New York: Wiley-Interscience.

4.  Perhaps the ultimate sensory illusion is experienced by persons who have lost an arm or a leg. If you would like to learn about phantom limbs, read Melzack, R. (1992). Phantom limbs. *Scientific American,* pp. 120–126. Also see Ramachandran, V. S., & Blakeslee, S. (1998). *Phantoms in the brain.* New York: Morrow.

5.  A nice summary of recent concepts and techniques is provided by Keefe, F. J., & France, C. R. (1999). Pain: Biopsychosocial mechanisms and management. *Current Directions in Psychological Science, 5,* 137–141.

# Visual Review of the Sense Organs

A great deal of new information was covered in chapter 4 on the structure of the sense organs. A set of unlabeled illustrations (figs. 4.48 through 4.51) has been prepared to help you check your learning of these structures. These reviews will be most helpful if you glance at the first one and then refer back to the illustration on which it was based to memorize the names of the structures. Next, return to the illustration in this review section and try to write in the names of the key structures of the sense organs. Then check your labels by looking at the original figures once again. When you can label all the structures in one of the illustrations, move on to the next one.

**FIGURE 4.48**
Key structures of the eye (based on fig. 4.3, p. 118).

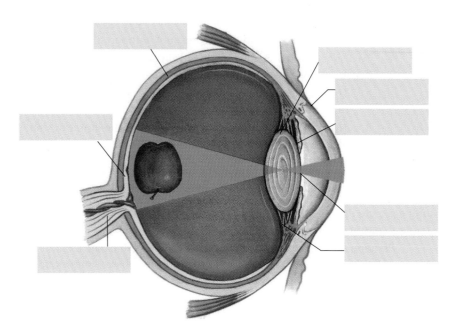

**FIGURE 4.49**
Key structures of the ear (based on fig. 4.14, p. 128).

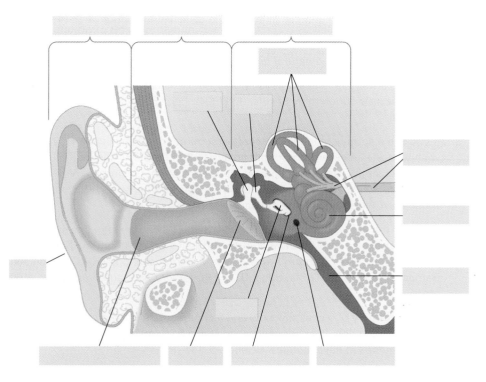

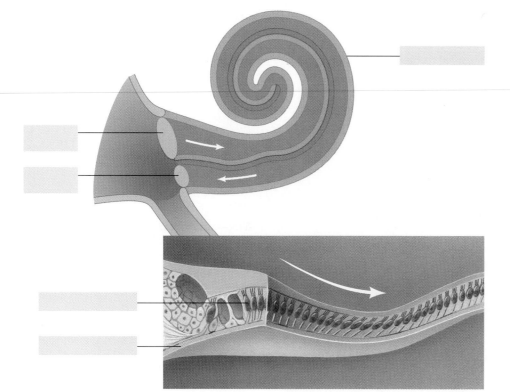

**FIGURE 4.50**
Key structures of the cochlea (based on fig. 4.15, p. 129).

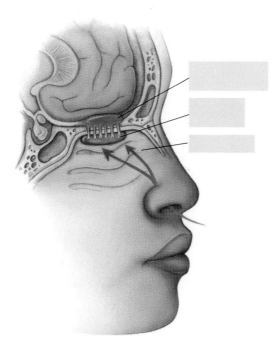

**FIGURE 4.51**
Key structures of the olfactory receptors (based on fig. 4.22, p. 142).

## Chapter Outline

# States of Consciousness

## PROLOGUE

Stop for a moment at the end of this sentence and, with your eyes closed, imagine that your book rises slowly from your lap, drifts to your face, and closes, lightly pinching your nose. Try it—seriously.

Could you see the book rise in your imagination? Did you feel a little pinch on your nose? My point is this: Life is made of many kinds of conscious awareness. Sometimes they are based on what is "out there," as when you are aware of the words in this textbook. But often you create your conscious experiences entirely in your brain—like the floating textbook that rose up and pinched your nose. You create realities in your consciousness that never were and may never be. You do so every time you imagine, daydream, or dream.

Nancy Kerr of the Georgia Mental Health Institute conducted a classic study that illustrates this point beautifully (Foulkes, 1989). Kerr studied the dreams of adult men and women who had lost their eyesight as young children. She found that, when they dreamed about friends, their dreams were very much like those of sighted adults. Indeed, when they dreamed about people they had met as blind adults—friends they had never seen—they dreamed about them in visual images. They could "see" what their friends looked like in their dreams, even though they had never seen them with their eyes. They created these visual images entirely in their brains.

In this chapter, we will define consciousness as a state of awareness—awareness of the outside world, of our own thoughts and feelings, and sometimes even of our own consciousness. Consciousness is not a single state, however. Rather, there are many different states of conscious awareness. When the waking day ends, we do not cease to be aware; rather, we experience other kinds of consciousness. As we drift off to sleep, we pass through a dreamlike "twilight" phase, and even amid the shifting stages of sleep itself we experience the strange reality of dreams. Apparently, these dreams are important to our well-being. Indeed, sleep may not rest and restore us for the next day if we do not dream sufficiently.

Other states of consciousness are experienced much less often. Some states of altered awareness occur spontaneously, as do hallucinations and other distorted perceptual experiences. Other altered states of consciousness are achieved in part through deep concentration and relaxation, such as during meditation and hypnosis. Still other altered states are induced by taking certain kinds of drugs. As you read about each form of consciousness, ask how much of the awareness comes through the sense organs that you studied in chapter 4, and how much comes from within. ■

**consciousness**
(kon'shus-nes) A state of awareness.

**daydreams**
Relatively focused thinking about fantasies.

"I'm sorry dear, I must have lost consciousness. What were you saying?"
© The New Yorker Collection 1982 Chon Day from Cartoonbank.com. All Rights Reserved.

## ● Wide Awake: Normal Waking Consciousness

What does it mean to be conscious? Clearly, it has something to do with awareness. When conscious, we are aware of the sights and sounds of the outside world, of our feelings, our thoughts, and sometimes even our own consciousness. When unconscious, we are not aware of any of these things. **Consciousness,** simply defined, is *a state of awareness.*

However, there is more than one kind of conscious state; it comes in more than the wide-awake-and-thinking variety. The qualities of conscious awareness that people experience when daydreaming, when hypnotized, when high on drugs, or when dreaming are so different from one another that we need to think of consciousness as being many different states of awareness. To understand consciousness fully, we need to explore its many varieties and the conditions under which they occur. In this chapter, we will speak of dreams, trances, highs, and the like, both to understand the nature of these states and to help us better understand the conscious experience of being awake.

We spend our lives passing from one state of consciousness to another. We read a book, we daydream, we drift off to sleep, we dream, and so on. Each of these states of conscious awareness is so different from the next that the very sense of reality it imparts differs. What is logical and possible in a dream may seem absurd when considered the next day. We seldom wonder which state contains the ultimate reality, however. We assume without questioning that the waking state in which we spend most of our lives is the "real" consciousness. It's the standard by which we judge other states and find them to be "distorted" or "unreal."

### Daydreams

Many features of everyday consciousness and dreams are combined in the state of waking consciousness called **daydreams.** They are a period of thinking and feeling that is not bound by what is logical or likely to happen. Daydreams are not a sometime thing; most of us daydream many times each day. Why do we spend time in these dreamlike reveries instead of focusing all of our awareness productively on the concerns of the day?

Sigmund Freud, the Austrian founder of psychoanalysis, believed that daydreams reduced the tension left by our unfulfilled needs and wishes. What we cannot do in reality we accomplish in the fantasy world of daydreams. While daydreaming, we win the race, see our lost love return, and build a rustic home in the country with our own hands.

Was Freud right? Are daydreams a way of reducing the tension of unmet needs and unfulfilled wishes? To answer this question, researchers asked college students to jot down a summary of each of their daydreams for several days (Pope & Singer, 1978). As predicted by Freud, many daydreams involved the fulfilling of a wish. Also consistent with Freud's theory is the fact that most people feel quite relaxed during this type of daydreaming. Contrary to Freud's predictions, however, many daydreams are filled with regret, sorrow, and guilt. Other daydreams are highly sexual, such as those focusing on that gorgeous person you would love to know better. These daydreams *create* rather than release tension, casting doubt on Freud's theory of daydreaming. Instead of reducing tension, daydreams may be merely a slightly distorted reflection of our current concerns and emotions (Pope & Singer, 1978).

### Divided Consciousness: Being Two Places (Mentally) at the Same Time

Last Saturday I was asked to watch a friend record a demonstration tape of a song he had written. It was my first time in a studio and I was fascinated—they even let me record a few bars using my friend's guitar (I was less than excellent). Driving home, my thoughts raced about my own long-forgotten fantasies of making hit records. When I got home, I was horrified to realize that I had no recollection whatsoever of the 5-mile drive. Obviously I had negotiated several stoplights and made a couple of turns, but I was lost in my thoughts and have no recollection of the drive. Stanford University psychologist Ernest Hilgard (1975) describes such phenomena as moments of **divided consciousness.** He believes that our conscious awareness becomes "split" and we simultaneously perform two activities requiring conscious awareness (in my case, driving and thinking about recording songs).

How about driving and talking on a cell phone at the same time? Can people successfully allocate their conscious awareness to these two tasks at the same time? A number of studies strongly suggest that we cannot. Whether the phone is hand-held or hands-free, conversations on cell phones distract drivers and cause driving errors and accidents (Strayer & Johnston, 2001). Listening to the radio or to taped music does not distract us to nearly the same extent.

## The Concept of the Unconscious Mind

In discussing conscious experience, it's important to compare the term *conscious* with the term *unconscious*. Most people beginning to study psychology expect to learn about the **unconscious mind.** It may surprise you to know, then, that until recently the term was not even mentioned in most modern introductory psychology textbooks. Psychology is taught in most American colleges and universities from a scientific viewpoint. The term *unconscious*, in contrast, is used primarily by psychologists who take a more philosophical approach to understanding people and their problems. It would be wrong, however, to dismiss the unconscious simply as "unscientific" and not discuss it at all.

Today, most scientists agree that it's time to apply scientific thinking to the study of the unconscious. For example, when a person is in a room where more than one person is talking, most of the time we can pay attention to one voice and "tune out" the other voice. This has been called the *cocktail party phenomenon* because it happens so often at parties. However, what becomes of the other voice—the one we do not listen to? There is evidence that it reaches the brain, even though we are never *consciously* aware of it. In that sense, the voice is processed *unconsciously* by the brain. Andrew Mathews and Colin MacLeod (1986) studied this phenomenon experimentally. Participants in the study were asked to listen to two messages presented simultaneously over different earphones. They were instructed to ignore one of the messages but to repeat the other message aloud. Some of the time, the words presented to the ignored earphone were nonthreatening words, such as *friend* and *concert,* whereas threatening words, such as *assault* and *emergency,* were presented at other times. As the participants repeated the message, they also kept their eyes on a computer screen and pressed a key as quickly as they could after the word *press* appeared on the screen (see fig. 5.1).

To be sure that the threatening words would have a great deal of emotional impact on the research participants, they were all highly anxious persons who were receiving treatment for their problems. The participants reported that they were not consciously aware of any of the ignored words because they focused all of their attention on the message they had to repeat, yet when threatening words were being presented, the anxious individuals pressed the key significantly less quickly than when nonthreatening words were presented. Apparently, the ignored words were being processed without conscious awareness, and the emotional impact of the threatening words disrupted performance on the reaction time task. Careful experiments of this sort may lead to a better understanding of mental processes that affect us without our being consciously aware of them.

**divided consciousness**
The splitting off of two conscious activities that occur simultaneously.

**unconscious mind**
Mental processes that occur without conscious awareness.

**FIGURE 5.1**

Participants in Mathews and MacLeod's study of unconscious information processing listened to two different messages that were presented simultaneously through different earphones. The participants were able to completely ignore one message and repeat the other one. At the same time, they pressed a key as quickly as they could when the word *press* appeared on the computer screen. Although not consciously heard, threatening words disrupted the reaction time of highly anxious individuals. This suggests that these persons had unconsciously processed the emotional meaning of the threatening words.

Listens to:
"... ran quickly along the beach ..." through left ear

Repeats
"... ran quickly along the beach ..."

Ignores:
"emergency ... assault ..." through right ear

## Review

Consciousness is composed of many different states of awareness. During each day, we shift many times between everyday consciousness and daydreams. At times, our consciousness appears to "do two things at once" in what Hilgard refers to as divided consciousness. At other times, we appear to process information in an entirely unconscious way, opening the door to the possibility of scientific studies of unconscious mental processes.

## Check Your Learning

To be sure that you have learned the key points from the preceding section, cover the list of correct answers and try to answer each question. If you give an incorrect answer to any question, return to the page given next to the correct answer to see why your answer was not correct. Remember that these questions cover only some of the important information in this section; it is important that you make up your own questions to check your learning of other facts and concepts.

Match each definition with one of the following terms:

a) unconscious

b) divided consciousness

_____ 1. Mental processes that occur without conscious awareness

_____ 2. The splitting off of two conscious activities that occur simultaneously

## Thinking Critically about Psychology

1. What is the value of daydreaming? Does it help humans survive as a species or hinder our survival?

2. Can you think of any instances when you've experienced divided consciousness?

## ● Sleep and Dreams: Conscious While Asleep

Most nights, we slip gently from wakefulness into sleep, only to return from our nocturnal vacation the next morning. Is this all there is to sleeping? Is it a mere gap in awareness that consumes one-third of our lives? Sleep is not a single state; instead, it's a complex combination of states, some involving conscious awareness. We do not leave consciousness behind for the entire night when we sleep. Rather, we enter worlds of awareness with properties that are very different from those of the wide-awake world.

## Stages of Sleep

Several states of conscious awareness are a part of the sleep process. As we fall asleep, we pass from waking consciousness into a semiwakeful state, into four states of progressively deeper sleep (all of which contain little or no conscious awareness). Intermittently, we shift from the four stages of sleep into dream sleep, which brings a kind of conscious awareness with a reality all its own. We need to look carefully at each of these parts of the sleep cycle.

### Hypnagogic State

We do not always go directly from wakefulness to sleep. Often, we daydream for a while, then pass into a "twilight" state that is neither daydreaming nor dreaming. This is the **hypnagogic state** (Mavromatis, 1987). We begin to lose voluntary control over our body movements; our sensitivity to outside stimuli diminishes; and our thoughts become more fanciful, less bound by reality. For most people, it's a highly relaxed, enjoyable state. On some occasions, however, we are rudely snapped out of the peaceful hypnagogic state—we suddenly feel as if we are falling and our body experiences a sudden jerk called a **myoclonia.** These jerks are caused by brief (and completely normal) seizure-like states of the brain as sleep commences.

### Stages of Light and Deep Sleep

After making the transition from the hypnagogic state to sleep, we pass through four stages of progressively deeper sleep. Most sleep researchers distinguish among four levels of sleep defined on the basis of **electroencephalogram (EEG)** measures of electrical brain activity (Webb, 1968). The depth of sleep alternates upward and downward many times during the night. Indeed, young adults show an average of 34 shifts in the depth of sleep during the first 6 hours (Webb, 1968). Sleep, then, is not a single, continuous state; it is an almost constantly changing one (see fig. 5.2).

### REM Sleep and Dreams

The year was 1952. University of Chicago graduate student Eugene Aserinsky was spending a sleepless night watching a child sleep in Dr. Nathaniel Kleitman's laboratory. Kleitman, Aserinsky's professor, was interested in the slow, rolling eye movements that occur during sleep in infants. The child was connected to a complicated network of wires that led from instruments to monitor many aspects of the body's functioning (such as brain waves, heartbeat, breathing) and an instrument to measure eye movements.

As Aserinsky dutifully watched the instruments, he was startled to see an unexpected pattern of rapid eye movements. Half a dozen times during the night, the child's eyes darted back and forth rapidly and irregularly under his closed eyelids. At first Aserinsky thought his instruments were not working properly, but he could easily see the child's eye movements. When Aserinsky looked again at his electroencephalograph (EEG), he saw something even more startling: The subject's brain activity looked more like he was awake than asleep. Each time the rapid eye movements returned, the same brain pattern resembling wakefulness returned.

When Aserinsky showed his professor the unexpected findings, the hypothesis was almost inescapable: Was the child **dreaming?** During the next several years, Aserinsky

**hypnagogic state**
(hip′nah-goj′ik) A relaxed state of dreamlike awareness between wakefulness and sleep.

**myoclonia**
(mi′o-klō′nē-ah) An abrupt movement that sometimes occurs during the hypnagogic state in which the sleeper often experiences a sense of falling.

**electroencephalogram (EEG)**
(e-lek′trō-en-sef′ah-lo-gram) A measure of electrical brain activity.

**dreaming**
Conscious awareness during sleep that primarily occurs during rapid-eye-movement (REM) sleep.

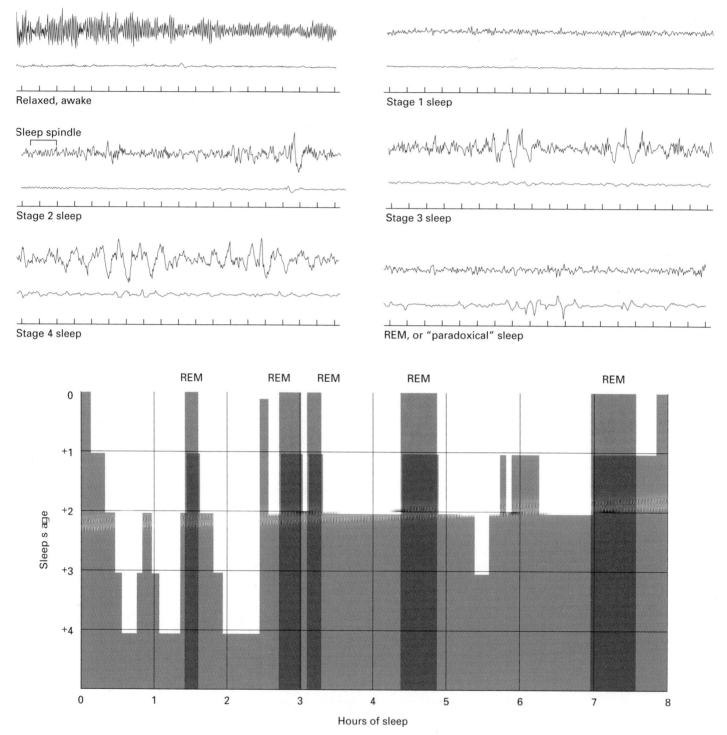

Relaxed, awake

Sleep spindle

Stage 2 sleep

Stage 4 sleep

Stage 1 sleep

Stage 3 sleep

REM, or "paradoxical" sleep

**FIGURE 5.2**

Each night we pass through the four stages of sleep and the phase of rapid eye movement (REM) sleep. The irregular pattern of shifting from one stage or phase of sleep to another is shown in the bottom illustration. The top part of this figure shows records of electroencephalograph (EEG) recordings of brain activity (in purple) and eye movement activity (in red) from one night of sleep of a male college student. Note the slow rolling eye movements that give REM sleep its name. Except for the amplitude of the EEG tracings (displayed as distance up and down the black lines), the EEG during REM sleep paradoxically resembles wakefulness.

**Source:** Records provided by T. E. LeVere. Used by permission.

and Kleitman awakened many sleeping adult and child participants when they entered this peculiar stage of sleep characterized by rapid eye movements. If awakened during rapid-eye-movement sleep and asked if they were dreaming, over 80 percent said yes.

The era of the scientific study of this elusive state of consciousness was ushered in by Aserinsky and Kleitman's surprising discovery of the relationship between dreaming and movements of the eyeballs (Kleitman, 1960). Their discovery that dreams are very common during a period of sleep that is marked by rapid eye movements and brain-wave activity suggesting the presence of conscious awareness provided a convenient way for scientists to know when dreams were occurring so that they could study them. Because of the characteristic eye movements, this phase of sleep is referred to as *rapid-eye-movement sleep,* or **REM sleep.**

## Autonomic Storms

After five decades of study, it's now known that the eyeballs are not the only parts of the body that are busy during dreams. Sleep researcher Wilse Webb (1968) has likened dream sleep to an "autonomic storm." The autonomic nervous system and other parts of the peripheral nervous system (see chapter 3) are very active during dreams, causing noticeable changes in many parts of the body: Blood flow to the brain increases; the heartbeat becomes irregular; the muscles of the face and fingers twitch; and breathing becomes irregular. Interestingly, voluntary control of the large body muscles is largely lost during REM sleep, perhaps to keep us from acting out our dreams. Anyone who has watched a sleeping beagle twitch, make miniature running movements, and rasp muffled barks (at dream rabbits?) knows about these autonomic storms and knows that REM sleep is not limited to humans. This fact has been confirmed in many laboratory studies of sleeping mammals.

In addition, there is vaginal lubrication and erection of the clitoris in females and erection of the penis in males during REM sleep. Because of erections that begin during REM sleep, the penis of an adult male is erect during one-fourth to one-half of an average night's sleep. This fact has led to advances in the diagnosis of conditions in which some males are unable to have an erection (known as *erectile dysfunction*). By having the patient spend a night in a sleep laboratory to see if he has erections during REM sleep, it is possible to determine if the cause of the problem is psychological (he would have erections during REM sleep) or physical (he would not have REM erections).

## Time Spent Dreaming

How often do you dream? In a survey of college-aged adults, about 15 percent said that they dream every night, and another 25 percent said that they dream on most nights. On the other hand, almost a third of young adults said that they rarely or never dream (Strauch & Meier, 1996). How often do you dream? Even if you recall a dream every night, you probably greatly underestimate the frequency of your dreams. We spend much more time in the world of dream consciousness than most of us realize.

Studies of dreaming conducted during the past 30 years show that the average college student spends about 2 hours a night in REM sleep, divided into about four to six separate episodes. Based on the reports of sleepers who were awakened during REM sleep, it is clear that we dream during at least 80 percent of these episodes of REM sleep (Strauch & Meier, 1996). The length of our REM dreams vary, but the longest REM dream, generally about an hour in duration, usually occurs during the last part of the sleep cycle (Hobson, 1989; Webb, 1982).

**REM sleep**
Rapid-eye-movement sleep, characterized by movement of the eyes under the lids; often accompanies dreams.

REM sleep is like an autonomic storm, causing marked changes in many parts of the body—human or animal. Beagles provide an interesting sight during REM sleep as they twitch and sometimes even make muffled howls.

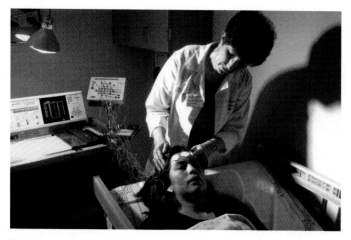

Electroencephalograms and eye muscle monitors allow psychologists to study dreams scientifically.

Therefore, young adults have 30 to 40 REM dreams per week. We do not remember dreaming nearly this often when we are awake because we forget dreams quickly unless we awaken during or soon after the dream. But we spend about 2 hours each night in the conscious state of REM dreams. There is much more to the story of consciousness while sleeping, however. REM sleep is not the only part of the sleep cycle that contains dreams.

## Non-REM Sleep and Dreams

Initially, sleep researchers believed that dreams were uncommon during the non-REM parts of the sleep cycle (Kleitman, 1960). Subsequent studies showed, however, that the number of dreams that occur during non-REM sleep is much higher than suspected (Foulkes, 1962). Many studies have consistently shown that, when participants are awakened during non-REM phases of sleep, they report dreaming about half of the time (Horne, 1988; Strauch & Meier, 1996).

The nature of non-REM dreams is quite different from that of REM dreams, however. Non-REM dreams are more likely to consist of brief, fragmentary impressions that are less emotional and less likely to involve visual images than are REM sleep dreams. Whereas REM dreams are like watching or participating in a play, non-REM dreams resemble the ordinary process of thinking briefly about something during the daytime. In fact, non-REM dreams so resemble fleeting daytime thoughts that individuals awakened during a non-REM dream often deny that they had been asleep at all. Similarly, persons awakened during the non-REM phases of sleep report far more dreams if they are asked "What was going through your head before you were awakened?" instead of "Were you dreaming?" (Foulkes, 1989). Non-REM dreams are so different from REM dreams that they are often not thought of as dreams at all by participants in sleep studies. Perhaps for similar reasons, it appears that non-REM dreams are less likely to be spontaneously recalled after waking than are REM dreams (Foulkes, 1989; Hobson, 1989; Horne, 1988; Strauch & Meier, 1996).

When both REM and non-REM dreams are considered, we spend a surprising amount of time in states of consciousness during sleep. In addition to the 2 hours of REM dreaming per night, non-REM dream activity is occurring during half of the other 4 to 6 hours that we sleep each night. Unlike waking consciousness, most of the hours that we are conscious during sleep do not become part of the permanent records of our lives by being stored in memory, but modern sleep research has revealed that we are consciously aware during sleep much more than we would have ever suspected.

## Circadian Rhythms

When is it time to go to sleep? For some of us, drowsiness takes over not long after sundown. Others are "night owls" who find that they are wide awake until the wee hours of the morning. But all of us—even those who do not sleep well—are on a biological cycle of approximately 24 hours in length that regulates our pattern of sleep, called the **circadian rhythm** (*circa* = about; *dia* = day). Much remains to be learned about the biological basis of circadian rhythms. One part of the hypothalamus has been implicated as a part of the body's internal "clock." Its activity increases and decreases in a regular pattern that lasts about 24 hours. In addition, variations in the hormone *melatonin* that fluctuate on a 24-hour pattern appear to be a key factor in regulating sleepiness (Gilbertini, Graham, & Cook, 1999).

The body has many other circadian rhythms, most of which roughly follow the pattern of the sleep-wake cycle. For example, an important hormone of the pituitary that plays a key role in body growth and repair, *growth hormone,* is secreted mostly during the first 2 hours of sleep, with little secreted during the waking hours of the day. Apparently, this reflects the role that sleep plays in normal growth and the maintenance of health.

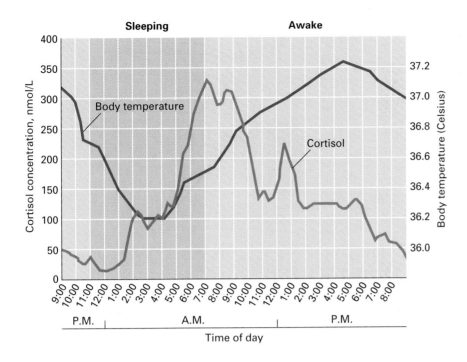

**FIGURE 5.3**

The concentration of the adrenal hormone cortisol in the blood follows a circadian rhythm, reaching its peak just before a person wakes from sleep, whereas the circadian rhythm for body temperature follows a different pattern.
**Source:** Data based in part on J. Puig-Antich, et al., "Cortisol Secretion in Prepubertal Children with Major Depressive Disorder," *Archives of General Psychiatry,* Vol. 46:801–812, 1989.

*Body temperature* also follows a circadian rhythm that is linked to the sleep cycle. As you can see in figure 5.3, body temperature falls just as you are beginning to feel sleepy and continues to fall until the middle of the sleep period. This is why you sometimes want to pull on more covers in the middle of the night, even when the temperature in your room is controlled by a thermostat.

Figure 5.3 also shows that the adrenal stress hormone *cortisol* follows a circadian rhythm that is tied to the sleep period in yet another pattern. Cortisol secretion begins to rise shortly after you fall asleep and continues to rise through the night. This is another indication that REM sleep is not a calm period for the body. The peak of cortisol secretion is just before awakening, the time of the longest period of REM sleep. The autonomic storm (p. 167) that takes place during REM dreams results in the same activation of the adrenal glands that occurs during physical or emotional stress. Ironically, a good night's sleep may be good for you, but not all of it is a "restful" time for the body.

The circadian sleep-wake cycle is obviously influenced to some extent by differences in illumination during the day and night. Although many cultures take "siestas" during the day and cultures living near the North and South poles have long periods without days and nights as we know them, people throughout the world generally are awake when it is light and sleep when it is dark. Some clever experiments have shown that the circadian sleep rhythm continues even when individuals are isolated in chambers that are always kept lighted, but surprisingly, the rhythm quickly changes to a *25-hour cycle* (Aschoff, 1981; Horne, 1988). Apparently, the body's clock runs on a schedule that is a little longer than 24 hours, but is reset each day by daylight.

The most dramatic way that most of us will become aware of circadian rhythms is by disrupting them with long airline flights. If you fly west from Atlanta to Hawaii, for example, you will experience a much longer period of daylight and will generally stay awake longer than usual on the first day. If you fly to Paris, however, you will have a very short first night. Both trips will disrupt your circadian rhythms and make you inefficient and out-of-sorts"—a phenomenon known as "jet lag." People differ in how much they are affected by jet lag, but interestingly, the time required to readjust to local time is generally longer when traveling from west to east (Moore-Ede, Sulzman, & Fuller, 1982; see fig. 5.4). Unfortunately, taking melatonin does nothing to minimize jet lag (Spitzer & others, 1999). Thus, you shouldn't expect to tour the entire Louvre museum the morning after arriving in Paris. You'll be lucky to have the energy to break your French bread.

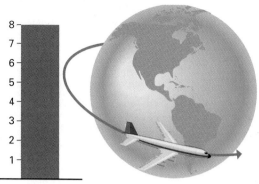

Average number of days to adjust to local sleep schedule

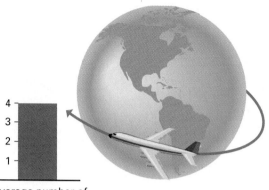

Average number of days to adjust to local sleep schedule

**FIGURE 5.4**

It generally takes longer to adjust to local sleep schedules and get over jet lag when traveling west to east. **Source:** Data from M. C. Moore-Ede, F. M. Sulzman, and C. A. Fuller, *The Clocks That Time Us.* Copyright 1982 Harvard University Press.

The same phenomenon is seen when workers rotate the times of their work shifts (Wilkinson, Allison, Feeney, & Kaminska, 1989). It is less disruptive to rotate from the night shift (midnight to 8 A.M.) to the day shift (8 A.M. to 4 P.M.) or from the day shift to the swing shift (4 P.M. to midnight) than to rotate in the opposite direction. This is because you stay awake longer on the first day of each rotation. It is apparently better to move from night to day shift and to travel from east to west because these changes are consistent with our natural tendency to lengthen our circadian rhythms (Moore-Ede & others, 1982). The topics of jet lag and work-shift rotations are the subject of considerable study, because it is important to the scheduling of airline pilots, nurses, and other key employees as well as to the timing of travel for diplomatic, business, and military purposes.

## Content of Dreams

Dreams are one of the most fascinating aspects of human consciousness. Since at least the time of the Egyptian pharaohs, people have attempted to decipher the meaning of dreams—and some psychologists are still trying. Let's begin our discussion of dreams by looking at psychological studies of what people dream about. Because dreams are private, it is interesting to compare our own dreams with those of others.

The first systematic study of dreams was conducted by Mary Whiton Calkins. You first learned Calkins' name in chapter 1, when we discussed the founders of psychology. Calkins was a pioneer in the study of memory, but she was also the founder of scientific dream research. Over a hundred years ago, Calkins and her partner wrote down a verbatim description of every dream they recalled over several months—often writing by candlelight in the middle of the night (Calkins, 1893). Since the time of Calkins, many researchers have studied thousands of dreams, both spontaneously recalled dreams and dreams that are recalled when research participants are awakened in sleep labs. Therefore, we can now confidently describe the content of human dreams.

### Images and Characters in Dreams

Most of the conscious experience in dreams is visual. If you dream about washing dishes, you will almost always experience a visual image of dishwashing but will be less likely to "hear" the clatter of the dishes or to "feel" the hot, wet dishwater. Only about one-fourth of dream images include auditory sensations, and about 20 percent include body sensations. About half of the dreams that involve body sensations are sexual—10 percent of all dreams. Less than 1 percent of dreams include tastes or smells (Hall, 1951; Strauch & Meier, 1996).

Do you dream in black-and-white or color? Most people dream in something that is in between. The visual images in dreams are usually as bright and clear as waking images, but they are drab in color. Dreams usually include few intense colors, and most have blurry backgrounds (Rechtschaffen & Buchignami, 1983). Who are the characters in your dreams—your friends and family? Are there strangers in your dreams? Are you a character in your own dreams? Because you are always the "author" of your dreams, it is not surprising that you often play a leading role. The dreamer has an active role in nearly three-fourths of dreams, and you are absent from your own dreams only 10 percent of the time (Strauch & Meier, 1996). About half of the other characters in your dreams are friends, acquaintances, or family members, but the other half are people you do not know or cannot recognize—or are animals 4 percent of the time. The characters in dreams are about an even mixture of men and women, with men being slightly more likely to dream about men than women are (Hall, 1951; Strauch & Meier, 1996).

### Sweet Dreams: The Emotional Content of Dreams

Are your dreams mostly happy or sad or scary? Most dreams contain positive emotions (Fosse, Stickgold, & Hobson, 2001), but mother nature plays a little trick on us. When people are asked about the emotional content of their dreams as soon as they spontaneously wake up, about 60 percent of their emotional dreams contain negative emotions (Strauch & Meier, 1996). When researchers wake up people during REM sleep, however, most of the emotional dreams they report are positive (Fosse & others, 2001). What is happening here? Why don't we remember all of our sweet dreams in the morning? It seems that we mostly dream of positive things, but negative dreams late in the sleep cycle are more likely to wake us up. So we forget many of our positive dreams (because they don't wake us up) and are more likely to be aware of the negatively charged dreams that awaken us. It's totally unfair, but it's reassuring to know that we are mostly happy in our dreams.

There are gender differences in the emotional qualities of the dreams that we recall when we spontaneously awake. Overall, men are a little more likely to recall positive dreams than are women. Similarly, the actions of the characters in men's dreams are somewhat more socially restrained than the characters in women's dreams. The people in men's dreams are both less likely to act in friendly ways toward other characters in the dream and less likely to act aggressively toward other dream players. When verbal or physical aggression occurs in dreams, both men and women are more likely to dream that they are the victim than the perpetrator of that aggression, but this tendency is somewhat stronger for women than men (Strauch & Meier, 1996).

### Creative and Bizarre Aspects of Dreams

Dreams fascinate us largely because they can be amazingly creative and bizarre. Most of our dreams actually resemble normal, everyday life, but even our more realistic dreams often contain creative and usual elements. About three-fourths of our dreams contain at least one bizarre and unrealistic element, usually mixed into an otherwise realistic dream. On the other hand, 10 percent of our dreams involve mostly nonsensical story lines, and another 10 percent of dreams are almost completely fantastic and bizarre (Hall, 1951; Strauch & Meier, 1996).

## Meaning of Dreams

Why do we dream about the things that fill our heads during sleep? What is the meaning of dreams? A century of research suggests that some of the content of dreams is easy to understand, but the rest is still a mystery.

**day residue**
Dream content that is similar to events in the person's waking life.

**stimulus incorporation**
Stimuli that occur during sleep that are incorporated into dreams either directly or in altered form.

### Day Residue and Stimulus Incorporation

A large part of the content of dreams is directly related to things that are going on in our lives during the day—which Sigmund Freud called **day residue.** The majority of dreams contain at least one character or event from the preceding day—or, less often, from the preceding week or even earlier in the dreamer's life. The most important characters and events are more likely to reflect day residue than are less central parts. One clear demonstration of the importance of day residue in the content of dreams is that half of all dreams reported by research participants in sleep laboratories include the sleep researchers or parts of the laboratory in the dream (Strauch & Meier, 1996).

The role of day-to-day events and people in our dreams was also demonstrated in a well-designed study conducted at the Max Planck Institute of Psychiatry in Munich, Germany (Lauer, Riemann, Lund, & Berger, 1987). Participants slept in the sleep laboratory after being shown either a neutral film or an upsetting film depicting violence, humiliation, and despair. They were awakened during their first REM stage and asked if they were dreaming. After viewing the upsetting film, the participants' REM dreams were rated as containing considerably more aggressive and anxious content than on the night following the neutral film. Furthermore, about one-third of the dreams contained images or themes directly related to the content of the upsetting film.

Our current concerns are reflected in our dreams. After the 1989 earthquake, students in the San Francisco area reported many upsetting dreams.

A more naturalistic study of the impact of daytime events on the content of dreams was conducted by Wood, Bootzin, Rosenhan, Nolen-Hoeksema, and Jourdon (1992). On October 17, 1989, a major earthquake hit the San Francisco area and caused more than $5 billion in damage and killed 62 people, including 42 who were killed when a freeway collapsed on them. The researchers asked students at two universities in the San Francisco area to keep track of the number of upsetting dreams that they had during a 3-week period immediately following the earthquake. As a control group, students at the University of Arizona who had not been near the earthquake did the same thing. Not surprisingly, the students in the area of the earthquake reported more vivid, upsetting dreams than did the students in Arizona. In addition, 40 percent of the students in the San Francisco area reported at least one dream about earthquakes, compared with 5 percent of the students in Arizona (Wood & others, 1992). Persons exposed to highly stressful events, such as wars, sometimes have nightmarish dreams about them for many years afterwards (Neyland & others, 1998). Clearly, events and concerns in our daily lives are among the most common things that we dream about.

Sometimes the real-world event that is included in the dream is something that is going on while we are asleep. Have you ever had a dream that somehow included the telephone or alarm clock that was ringing in your ear at the time? This phenomenon is called **stimulus incorporation.** Sometimes the stimulus in the real environment is directly incorporated into the dream, but more often it is "transformed" somewhat. In a Swiss study, sleep participants were presented with the recorded sound of a jet plane while asleep. About one-third later reported dreaming about flying or reported hearing something that sounded like a jet plane (such as a sputtering gas stove) in their dream, but the sound was usually not heard in the dream exactly as it actually sounded (Strauch & Meier, 1996).

### Dream Interpretation

We know that some of the content of dreams simply reflects the events and concerns of daily life, but what about the rest? And what is the meaning of the bizarre and fictional images in dreams? Different psychologists have very different views of the meaning of dreams, ranging from the opinion that they mean virtually nothing to the belief that they provide a rich source of information about hidden aspects of our personalities that cannot be gotten easily in other ways.

To followers of Sigmund Freud, dreams are the "royal road to the unconscious." They allow us to travel deep into the unconscious mind and view hidden conflicts and motives cloaked only by the symbols of dreams. To Freud, there are two levels of the content of dreams: manifest and latent. The events that we experience in dreams are their **manifest content.** This level held little interest for Freud; he felt that it was necessary to get beyond the surface and find out what the manifest content of the dream symbolized to discover its true meaning, or **latent content.** For example, the manifest content of a young woman's dream might involve riding on a train and becoming frightened as it enters a tunnel. On the surface, the dream is about trains and tunnels. But what does the manifest content of the dream symbolize? Freud might see the train as symbolizing a penis and the tunnel as symbolizing a vagina. Hence, the hidden, or latent, content of the dream might concern the young woman's conflicts about having sex.

Such interpretations are provocative and fascinating, but are they accurate? Psychologists simply do not agree on this issue. Because symbols can be interpreted in an infinite number of ways, we can never be sure that our interpretations are correct. Perhaps as a result, most contemporary psychologists place much less emphasis on dream interpretation than did Freud.

## Reasons for Sleep and Dreams

Why do we sleep and dream? Do we need to sleep? What effects does a lack of sleep have on us? It is clear that we need sleep in the sense that we apparently create a "sleep debt" that needs to be made up if we miss sleep. College students at the University of Florida who participated in a sleep experiment were limited to 2 hours of sleep for one night. The next day they were irritable, fatigued, and inefficient, and the next night they fell asleep more quickly and slept longer than usual (Webb & Bonnet, 1979).

Longer periods of sleep deprivation produce more pronounced inefficiency and fatigue, but people are remarkably able to do without a lot of sleep. For example, teenager Randy Gardner set a new world record by staying awake for 264 hours as a science project with no serious ill effects, but he felt a great deal of fatigue, sleepiness, and irritability. However, when a group of volunteers gradually reduced their sleep from 8 to 4 hours a night for a period of 2 months, there were no detectable immediate effects (Webb & Bonnet, 1979). It's when we abruptly reduce the amount of sleep, or reduce it to less than 4 hours, that we are most likely to feel ill effects and an intense need for sleep.

Harvard University researcher J. Allan Hobson (1989) has proposed a specific theory in which sleep plays a restorative role. His theory is based on the existence of a center in the brain stem that is active when we are awake (called the **sleep-inhibiting system**) and two other centers in the brain stem that are activated when we are sleeping —especially when we are dreaming (called the **sleep-promoting systems;** see fig. 5.5). Hobson suggests that we need to sleep and dream to give the sleep-inhibiting system a chance to rest and replenish itself.

Researchers have not reached full agreement as to why we sleep but there is considerable evidence that at least some sleep is essential to maintaining good health over the long run. A survey of more than 1 million adults in the United States (ages 30 to 102 years) found that most men and women sleep 7 or 8 hours per night (Kripke & others, 2002). Death rates (controlling for age and other factors) increase slightly as the number of hours of sleep increase or decrease from 7 hours per night. Only extreme deviations from the norms are associated with large differences in death rates, however. For example, sleeping less than 4.5 hours per night for men and less than 3.5 hours per night for women is associated with a 15 percent higher death rate.

**manifest content**
According to Freud, the literal meaning of dreams.

**latent content**
According to Freud, the true meaning of dreams that is found in the symbols in their manifest content.

**sleep-inhibiting system**
An area of the brain stem that inhibits sleep.

**sleep-promoting systems**
Two areas of the brain stem that lead to sleep.

**FIGURE 5.5**
According to Hobson, sleep is controlled by the balance of sleep-promoting and sleep-inhibiting systems in the brain.

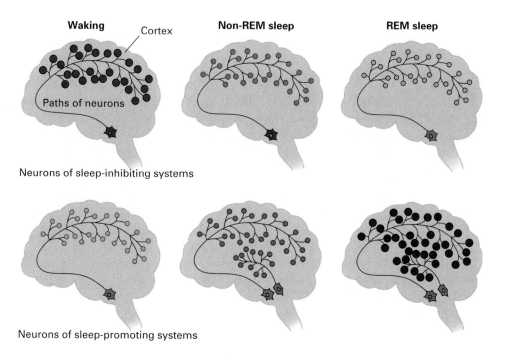

In addition, there is evidence that REM sleep plays an essential role in the consolidation of newly learned information from the day before (Ribeiro, Goyal, Mello, & Pavlides, 1999; Stickgold, Hobson, Fosse, & Fosse, 2001). REM plays this important role by activating the expression of a gene that controls the modification of connections between neurons. So study hard, but leave time to get a good night's sleep (and plenty of REM) before the exam. Seriously—you need to sleep to consolidate your memory of what you learned. This is one reason studying all night before a test is very inefficient.

Sleep researcher Wilse Webb (1975) popularized a very different theory of why we sleep that suggests that sleep serves a protective rather than a restorative role. Webb was not convinced that humans have much of a physiological need for sleep. Because the eyes of animals that sleep at night are not very efficient in low light, he hypothesized that we fall asleep to keep us from moving around in the dark of night. In his view, sleep keeps us from wasting energy, falling off cliffs, and being eaten by animals that hunt at night and have better night vision.

Regardless of why we sleep, it is clear that we have a "need" to dream. In a number of experiments, sleeping individuals were awakened whenever they entered REM sleep. They were otherwise allowed to get a normal amount of sleep each night. Depriving participants of approximately 2 hours of REM sleep each night had the same effects as much longer deprivations of sleep in general. The participants were irritable, inefficient, and fatigued. On subsequent nights, they showed an increase in the amount of REM sleep, suggesting that they had a need to catch up on REM sleep—and perhaps on their vivid dreaming. Other studies have also shown that deprivation of the deepest part of non-REM sleep has much the same effects (Hobson, 1989; Webb & Bonnet, 1979).

Research has shown the importance of REM sleep in another way. When volunteers gradually reduced their nightly sleep by 4 hours, they packed their 2 hours of REM sleep tightly into their shortened sleeping time (Webb & Bonnett, 1979). The amount of non-REM sleep that occurred between REM periods was greatly reduced when total sleep time was cut, but the amount of dream sleep stayed fairly constant.

## Nightmares and Other Sleep Phenomena

We have all had the terrifying kind of dreams known as **nightmares.** These are dreams that occur during REM sleep and whose content is exceptionally frightening, sad, pro-

**nightmares**
Dreams that occur during REM sleep and whose content is exceptionally frightening, sad, angry, or in some other way uncomfortable.

voking, or in some other way uncomfortable. They are upsetting enough to wake us up during the dream, so we can vividly remember our nightmares, even though they account for only a small proportion of the dreams most of us have (Hartmann, Russ, Oldfield, Sivian, & Cooper, 1987).

**Night terrors** are a less common but perhaps even more upsetting nocturnal experience. The individual awakens suddenly in a state of panic, sometimes screaming and usually with no clear recollection of an accompanying dream. A sense of calm usually returns within a few minutes, but these can be terrifying experiences. Unlike nightmares, they do not occur during REM sleep but occur during the deepest phases of non-REM sleep. Night terrors are most common in preschool-age children, but sometimes adults experience them (Hartmann & others, 1987).

**Sleepwalking** is another interesting phenomenon that occurs primarily during the deepest parts of non-REM sleep. Sleepwalkers rise from the bed and carry on complicated activities, such as walking from one room to another, even though they are sound asleep. Sleepwalking is most common in children before the age of puberty but is not particularly unusual in adults. Sleepwalking usually reappears in adults only during periods of stress, but except for the danger of accidents while wandering around in the dark, it's not an abnormal behavior.

**Sleeptalking** is a fairly common phenomenon that can occur during any phase of the sleep cycle. In this, the soundly sleeping person says words, sometimes making fairly coherent statements for a brief period of time. It's most common in young adults but occurs at all ages.

## Sleep Disorders

Although we all sleep, some people sleep more or less than they would prefer or they experience other serious difficulties with the sleep process. The term **sleep disorders** is often used to refer to these troublesome but highly treatable disorders.

**Insomnia** refers to a variety of difficulties in which individuals report that they sleep less than they wish. There are two major varieties of insomnia. In *sleep-onset insomnia,* individuals have difficulty falling asleep at the hour at which they would like, but sleep is normal after it begins. In contrast, *early-awakening insomnia* is characterized by waking up earlier than desired, either several times in the middle of the night or early in the morning. Both are found in individuals experiencing no other psychological problems but are more common in individuals undergoing periods of stress, anxiety, or depression.

**Narcolepsy** is a rare sleep disorder, occurring in less than one-half of 1 percent of the general population, but its impact can be quite serious. The narcoleptic often falls unexpectedly into a deep slumber in the middle of work or even during conversations with others, especially when upset or stressed. Often, the individual experiences loss of muscle tone and shows a lack of body movement, as if she or he has suddenly fallen into dream sleep, but laboratory studies show that narcoleptic sleep is not REM sleep. Narcolepsy is not just intense sleepiness, because it occurs in individuals who get adequate sleep. Narcolepsy often causes serious difficulties with the use of dangerous machines and other job-related activities.

**Sleep apnea** is the sudden, temporary interruption of breathing during sleep. To qualify as sleep apnea, these interruptions of breathing must be longer than 20 seconds, because brief interruptions are normal. Sleep apnea is common, particularly in older adults who snore. It is caused either by too much relaxation of the muscles of the throat or by a temporary cessation of brain signals for breathing. Generally, the individual experiences a few apneas each night, which is not problematic.

**night terrors**
Upsetting nocturnal experiences that occur most often in preschool-age children during deep non-REM sleep.

**sleepwalking**
Waking and carrying on complicated activities during the deepest part of non-REM sleep.

**sleeptalking**
Talking during any phase of the sleep cycle.

**sleep disorders**
Disturbances of sleep.

**insomnia**
A disorder in which the person has difficulty falling asleep or staying asleep.

**narcolepsy**
A sleep disorder in which the person suddenly falls asleep during activities usually performed when fully awake, even when the person has had adequate sleep.

**sleep apnea**
The sudden interruption of breathing during sleep.

People with sleep-onset insomnia have difficulty falling asleep.

## Review

Each night, we depart the world of waking consciousness and enter another world that we scarcely remember the next morning. Alternating among periods of sleep that contain no conscious experience, we live a life of dreams accompanied by a flurry of internal activity in the body. When studied systematically, much of the content of dreams is found to reflect daily events and concerns. Still, the meaning of dreams has long fascinated us and played a major role in Freud's attempts to understand the hidden workings of the mind. Sleep eludes some of us for part of the night, or is troubled in some other way—the sleep disorders. The daily rhythm of sleep and wakefulness is only one of numerous natural rhythms that tend to follow daily, weekly, or annual patterns.

## Check Your Learning

To be sure that you have learned the key points from the preceding section, cover the list of correct answers and try to answer each question. If you give an incorrect answer to any question, return to the page given next to the correct answer to see why your answer was not correct.

1. Research suggests that _____ may be the most important components of sleep because subjects deprived of them were irritable, inefficient, and fatigued.

   a)   hypnagogic sleep
   b)   myoclonia and REM sleep
   c)   REM sleep and deep sleep
   d)   naps

2. According to Freud, the _____, or true meaning of dreams, reveal(s) hidden conflicts and motives in the unconscious mind.

   a)   latent content
   b)   manifest content
   c)   events
   d)   colors

3. _____ is a rare sleep disorder in which the person suddenly falls asleep during activities usually performed when fully awake, such as during conversations with others

   a)   Sleep apnea
   b)   Insomnia
   c)   Epilepsy
   d)   Narcolepsy

4. Body temperature and hormones such as cortisol follow a _____, or daily cycle linked to the sleep cycle.

## Thinking Critically about Psychology

1. In your opinion, why do we sleep? Why do we dream?

2. What does research on sleep-wake cycles suggest about being at your best when taking a test?

Correct Answers:   1. c (p. 167),   2. a (p. 173),   3. d (p. 175),   4. circadian rhythm (p. 168).

## ● Altered States of Consciousness

Thus far, we have talked about states of consciousness with which we are all familiar. We all know what it feels like to think about a problem, to dream, and to let our minds wander. Next we will turn to more unusual and less familiar realms of conscious experience, the so-called altered states of consciousness. We will begin by looking at some general characteristics of altered states of consciousness.

There are many kinds of altered states of consciousness and they differ from one another in important ways, yet these altered states—whether they occur during meditation, during drug use, during an unusually intense sexual orgasm, or during a moment of religious conversion—have been described as having a number of characteristics in common (Deikman, 1980; Pahnke, 1980; Tart, 1975):

1. *Distortions of perception.* In altered states of consciousness, distortions often occur in what is seen, heard, and felt. Time passes differently, and the body may seem distorted—indeed, the body may even seem to have been left behind and is being observed from the outside.

2. *Intense positive emotions.* People who have experienced altered states of consciousness frequently describe them as joyful, ecstatic, loving, and tranquil experiences.

3. *Sense of unity.* Individuals often experience a sense of being unified with nature, blended with the universe, or "one" with a spiritual force.

4. *Illogical.* Many of the experiences and "revelations" of the altered states of consciousness do not make sense by the standards of everyday logic. For example, the experience that "I exist as a separate person, yet I am one with the universe" is typical of altered states.

5. *Indescribable.* Individuals who have experienced altered states of consciousness usually feel that words cannot adequately express the nature of their experience. Our languages may not have words for many of the qualities of the experience, but the difficulty also may come from trying to use language to describe illogical experiences.

6. *Transcendent.* The altered states are experienced as transcending—going beyond—what is normally experienced. In particular, the individual may experience a new perspective that goes beyond ordinary conceptions of space and time limitations.

7. *Self-evident reality.* New revelations and insights are experienced that concern "ultimate reality" and are felt to be "real" in a way that requires no proof. The insight is intuitively and immediately understood as the truth; it requires no explanation or justification.

Given these qualities—particularly the euphoric emotionality of experiencing self-evident revelations—it may be wise to state the obvious here. Our evaluation of the insights obtained through altered states of consciousness clearly depends on the perspective we take. From the standpoint of a logical science, we can say only that altered states of consciousness are different from everyday waking consciousness. No claims can be made that one "reality" is more "real" than another. From the perspective of those who have experienced the self-evident reality of altered states, however, our everyday reality is often seen as false. Who is right? It depends on which perspective we believe is correct; it is a question for philosophy, not science.

## Meditation

Although most of us think of waking consciousness as the normal state, others seek a different, more "perfect" state. One method of searching for an alternative to waking consciousness is **meditation.** This was a popular exercise in the United States during the 1960s and 1970s and continues to be common today. Its popularity in the Western world is dwarfed by its popularity in Asia, however, because meditation is an important part of Zen Buddhism and other religions for many tens of millions of Asians.

There are many varieties of meditation, some very difficult to master and others much simpler. In its simplest form, meditation involves assuming a relaxed sitting or lying position and breathing deeply, slowly, and rhythmically. Attention is directed only at the breathing movements of the diaphragm, and all other thoughts and feelings are

**meditation**
(med″i-tā-shun) Several methods of focusing concentration away from thoughts and feelings and generating a sense of relaxation.

Many persons achieve altered states of consciousness and deep relaxation through meditation.

**mantras**
(man´trahz) Words or sounds containing religious meaning that are used during meditation.

**transcendental state**
An altered state of consciousness, sometimes achieved during meditation, that is said to transcend normal human experience.

**hypnosis**
(hip-nō´sis) An altered state of consciousness in which the individual is highly relaxed and susceptible to suggestions.

gently blocked from consciousness. Although this feat is very difficult to accomplish at first, if you do not pressure yourself, it becomes easier with practice. In some forms of meditation, the individual also repeats a sound or word silently to himself or herself. These words often have special religious meaning (**mantras**), but researchers have found that any pleasant sound or word (such as *calm* or *one*) has the same effect of further focusing attention away from thoughts and feelings (Benson, 1975).

Once mastered, the practice of meditation can produce what many describe as a desirable altered state of consciousness. If nothing else, meditation generally produces a relaxed state (Beiman, Majestic, Johnson, Puente, & Graham, 1976). Some experienced meditators also report achieving an altered state of consciousness—the so-called **transcendental state**—that is very different from normal consciousness.

Because the state of meditation often involves a reduction in sympathetic autonomic arousal (Wallace & Benson, 1972), meditation has been prescribed for more than 90 years as a natural remedy for stress-related medical problems ranging from high blood pressure to insomnia. As a result, thousands of individuals practice meditation in the belief that it counteracts the physiological effects of stress. Is this assumption correct? Does meditation beneficially dampen sympathetic autonomic arousal?

In a cogent review of research on this topic, psychologist David Holmes (1984) argues that teaching individuals to meditate does not lead to greater reductions in blood pressure, heart rate, oxygen consumption, general muscle tension, skin sweat, or any other measure of sympathetic arousal than that produced by simple relaxation. Other researchers, however, suggest that the form of meditation called transcendental meditation produces greater reductions in anxiety and stress-related medical illness than do other forms of meditation or relaxation (Eppley, Abrams, & Spear, 1989; Orme-Johnson, 1987). As a result, there is no consensus in the scientific community regarding the benefits of meditation compared to other forms of relaxation.

## Hypnosis

A person who has been hypnotized can sometimes be so convinced that she is standing in a snowstorm without a coat that she shivers. Similarly, a hypnotist can tell a hypnotized person he is going back to his 4th birthday party and watch him act as if he is playing with other 4-year-olds. People who have been hypnotized like this often tell us that they actually feel the cold wind and believe that they are reexperiencing the birthday party. What is it about this state of **hypnosis** that makes it so fascinatingly different from waking consciousness?

The person becoming hypnotized focuses his or her attention firmly on the hypnotist's voice and is talked and lulled into an altered state of consciousness. This hypnotic state differs from individual to individual but typically has the following characteristics:

1. **Relaxation.** A sense of deep relaxation and peacefulness exists, often accompanied by changes in the way the body feels, such as floating or sinking.

2. **Hypnotic hallucinations.** When told to do so, the person may see, feel, or hear things in altered ways or may even experience things that are not there, such as smelling a flower that does not exist.

3. **Hypnotic analgesia.** When told to do so, the person may lose the sense of touch or pain in some region of the body. This is one of the best validated aspects of hypnosis and has led to the use of hypnosis in surgery, dentistry, and childbirth (Harmon, Hyan, & Tyre, 1990; Hilgard, 1978; Miller & Bowers, 1993; Price & Barber, 1987).

4. **Hypnotic age regression.** The person can sometimes be made to feel that he or she is passing back in time to an earlier stage of life, but most experts do not believe that hypnosis improves the recall of childhood events (Kirsch & Lynn, 1995).

5. **Hypnotic control.** The actions of hypnotized individuals sometimes *seem* as if they are out of their own control. When told that her arm can float, a hypnotized person's arm may seem to float up as if it were lifted by invisible balloons rather than by her own muscles (Bowers, 1976).

A person being hypnotized focuses attention firmly on the hypnotist's voice and is lulled into an altered state of consciousness.

What is the nature of this altered state of consciousness? To understand it best, we should look briefly at the fascinating history of hypnosis.

### Mesmer and Mesmerism

Franz Anton Mesmer was a practicing physician in Paris in the late 1700s. Although he was trained in classical medicine, his medical practice was decidedly unusual—so unusual that he had earlier been driven from his native Austria by the medical establishment for alleged quackery. He treated patients with medical or psychological problems in what he called *magnetic seances*. Mesmer believed that all living bodies were filled with magnetic energy and that diseases resulted when these magnetic forces were out of balance. His treatment, therefore, consisted of passing his hands, which he believed had become magnetized, over the afflicted part of the patient's body and having the patient touch metal rods that protruded from a large tub. The tub was filled with water, chemicals, ground glass, and iron filings—a mixture that Mesmer thought created magnetism.

What Mesmer actually created, however, was something quite different—an atmosphere that induced a mysterious and powerful hypnotic trance. He entered the darkened and silent room wearing flowing lilac-colored robes. He lulled his patients into a deep state of relaxation and made them believe deeply in his healing powers; that is, he *hypnotized* them. He told them that their problems would go away, and some of them did. The process of putting people into hypnotic trances came to be known for many years as *mesmerism*. Only much later was it referred to as hypnosis.

In recent years, hypnotism has been intensively studied, and understood to some extent. It took psychologists a long time to decide that it was respectable to study a phenomenon with such a shady and controversial past, but in the past 30 years, hypnosis has finally seen the hard light of scientific inquiry (Allen, Iacono, Laravuso, & Dunn, 1995; Kirsch & Braffman, 2001; Miller & Bowers, 1993). For example, it is now clear that when

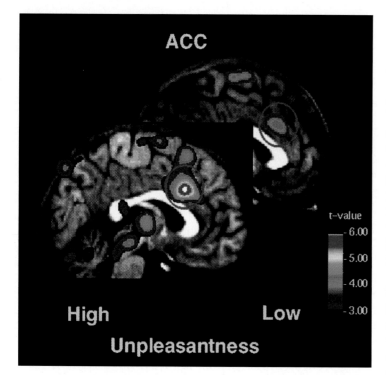

These are PET scan images of the brain of a hypnotized person whose hand is immersed in a hot water bath. When the image on the right was made, the hypnotized person had been told that the water was comfortable. When the image on the left was made, the person had been told that the water was painfully hot. Notice the large differences in activity in the cingulate cortex—a part of the limbic system that plays a key role in the perception of the emotional aspect of pain transmitted by slow-pain fibers. Apparently, hypnosis reduced the emotional experience of pain in this person.

hypnotized persons are told to "see" a gray stimulus as having color, areas of the brain involved in color perception are actually activated (Kosslyn & others, 2000), indicating that they are not merely faking the report of seeing color.

Psychologists are still not in agreement on how to characterize hypnosis, however. Theodore Barber (Barber & Wilson, 1977; Kirsch & Lynn, 1995) suggested that hypnosis should not be thought of as a "trance" but as a highly relaxed state in which the person's conscious awareness is highly focused, the person's imagination is intensified, and the person is highly susceptible to the instructions of the hypnotist. Ernest Hilgard (1975), in contrast, believes that hypnosis is based on divided consciousness. According to Hilgard, individuals can, for example, experience a loss of pain through hypnosis because that part of consciousness can be separated from waking consciousness.

In recent years hypnosis has gained limited acceptance by the medical and dental professions for the relief of pain through hypnotic analgesia (Price & Barber, 1987). For example, patients who cannot use analgesic medications for a variety of reasons have been able to have extensive operations or undergo childbirth under hypnosis with little or no pain (Harmon & others, 1990; Hilgard & Hilgard, 1975).

## Depersonalization

Not all altered states of consciousness occur when we are striving to attain them; some occur spontaneously. This section describes one of the most common of these experiences. The term **depersonalization** refers to the perceptual experience of one's body becoming "distorted" or "unreal" in some way, or the sense of strange distortions in one's surroundings. Although very bizarre, such spontaneous experiences are not necessarily abnormal or even uncommon among young adults. British researchers interviewed 891 university students and found 76 who had experienced depersonalization. Excerpts from the accounts of a number of students help portray these experiences (Myers & Grant, 1972):

> I felt slightly unreal and as though I wasn't part of my surroundings, but watching from a distance; my voice sounded strange to me and did not seem to be part of me.
>
> The feeling of not belonging to my body but being outside it.
>
> I do not feel the sensation of it being my hand; it is something else which is there but nothing to do with me.
>
> I suddenly felt that I was really behind myself, not watching myself but detached from everything including my body to some extent.
>
> My mother and I were walking towards each other from opposite ends of a street, and I suddenly felt an odd sense of estrangement, as if I had never seen her face in my life before.
>
> I felt disembodied . . . only my mind seemed to exist . . . I would have to pinch myself to reassure myself that I did exist. (p. 60)

**depersonalization**
(dē-per´sun-al-i-zā´shun) The perceptual experience of one's body or surroundings becoming distorted or unreal.

**astral projection**
(as´tral) Depersonalization that includes the illusion that the mind has left the body.

Suppose that this afternoon you feel as if your mind is leaving your body and floating up to the ceiling, where it watches you. Does this mean you have gone crazy? Have you had a psychic or religious experience? Depersonalization experiences sometimes include the illusion that the mind has left the body and traveled about in a so-called out-of-body experience, or **astral projection.** When such experiences are recurrent, they may be an indication of psychological problems, but isolated experiences seem to be quite normal, if somewhat unnerving.

Sometimes a kind of consciousness is experienced that is greatly different from normal waking consciousness. Some altered states of consciousness may be unwelcome and upsetting occurrences (as with depersonalization), but others are intentionally induced through meditation and hypnosis. Meditation produces a transcendent sense of relaxation that may be helpful in combating stress, and hypnosis has been found to be useful in relieving pain under some circumstances.

Review

To be sure that you have learned the key points from the preceding section, cover the list of correct answers and try to answer each question. If you give an incorrect answer to any question, return to the page given next to the correct answer to see why your answer was not correct.

**Check Your Learning**

1. _____ is the focusing of conscious awareness away from thoughts and feelings and the generation of a sense of deep relaxation.

   a) Sleep
   b) Depersonalization
   c) Hallucination
   d) Meditation

2. One of the first persons to use what is now called hypnosis was _____, who used it while treating patients in so-called magnetic seances.

   a) Ernest Hilgard
   b) Franz Anton Mesmer
   c) Sigmund Freud
   d) David Holmes

3. _____ is the perceptual experience of one's body becoming "distorted" or "unreal" in some way, or the sense of strange distortions in one's surroundings.

   a) Meditation
   b) Psychosis
   c) Depersonalization
   d) Hypnosis

1. In your opinion, why isn't hypnosis more widely used in our society as a substitute for anesthesia in surgery?

2. What has been your experience with altered states of consciousness? How would you describe them in terms of current scientific explanations?

**Thinking Critically about Psychology**

Correct Answers:  1. d (p. 177),  2. b (p. 179),  3. c (p. 180).

## ● Drugs and Altered Consciousness

Up to this point, we have been discussing altered states of consciousness that are "natural" in the sense that they can be experienced by anyone without artificial inducements. Perhaps the most distinctly different types of altered consciousness, however, involve taking chemicals into the body—using drugs. Specifically, we are talking about **psychotropic drugs,** a class of drugs that alter conscious experience. These drugs exert their effects by influencing specific neurotransmitters in the brain or by chemically altering the action of neurons in other ways. The range of effects of psychotropic drugs is enormous, from mild relaxation to vivid hallucinations. Perhaps even more enormous than the range of their effects, however, is the frequency of their use in contemporary society (Carroll, 2000).

**psychotropic drugs**
(sī″ko-trōp′pik)  The various classes of drugs, including stimulants, depressants, and hallucinagens, that alter conscious experience.

Psychotropic drugs can be divided into four major categories. *Depressants* reduce the activity of inhibitory centers of the central nervous system, leading to a sense of relaxation and lowered inhibitions. *Stimulants* are drugs that increase the activity of the motivational centers and decrease action in inhibitory centers of the central nervous system, providing a sense of energy and well-being. *Hallucinogens* produce dreamlike alterations in perceptual experience. *Inhalants* are common household chemicals that are put to dangerous use by being inhaled, which produces feelings of intoxication. Not fitting easily into this classification is the drug marijuana, which induces a relaxed sense of well-being in most persons. Common members of these classes of drugs are summarized in table 5.1. Their patterns of use will be discussed in the section that follows. We will begin by focusing on illegal drugs and frequently abused prescription drugs. The Application of Psychology section at the end of this chapter will cover the most commonly used legal consciousness-altering drugs: caffeine, nicotine, and alcohol.

## Drug Use: Some Basic Considerations

Although the effects of psychotropic drugs are varied, we need to consider a number of issues that are relevant to all of them. These issues include the wide variation in responses to drugs and the problems that are associated with their use.

**Table 5.1    Commonly Abused Legal and Illegal Psychotropic Drugs**

| Depressants | Stimulants | Hallucinogens |
|---|---|---|
| Tranquilizers | Amphetamines | LSD (lysergic acid diethylamide-25) |
|   Equanil (meprobamate) |   Benzedrine (amphetamine) | Mescaline (peyote) |
|   Librium (chlordiazepoxide) |   Dexedrine (dextroamphetamine) | PCP (phencyclidine hydrochloride) |
|   Miltown (meprobamate) |   Methedrine (methamphetamine) | Psilocybin (psychotogenic mushrooms) |
|   Valium (diazepam) | Cocaine | |
|   Xanax (alprazolam) | MDMA (ecstasy) | |
| Narcotics | Caffeine (in coffee, tea, and colas) | |
|   Opiates (opium and its derivatives) | Nicotine (in tobacco) | |
|     Codeine | | |
|     Heroin | | |
|     Morphine | | |
|     Opium | **Inhalants (Volatile Hydrocarbons)** | **Marijuana Family** |
|   Synthetic narcotics | Cleaning fluids | Marijuana |
|     Demerol | Gasoline | Hashish |
|     Methadone | Glue | |
|     Percodan | Nail polish remover (acetone) | |
| Sedatives | Paint thinner | |
|   Alcohol (ethanol) | | |
|   Barbiturates | | |
|     Nembutal (pentobarbital) | | |
|     Quaalude (methaqualone) | | |
|     Seconal (secobarbital) | | |
|     Tuinal (secobarbital and amobarbital) | | |
|     Veronal (barbital) | | |

**Variable Response to Drugs**

In the sections that follow, we will look at the psychological effects of a number of widely used drugs. In discussing these effects, we must keep in mind that the effects that drugs have on each individual are far from perfectly predictable. Many factors influence the individual's response to a drug; most important among them are:

1. *Dose and purity.* Obviously, the amount of the drug taken influences its effect. Less obvious is the fact that drugs purchased on the street are often cut (mixed) with other substances, which can alter the effects of the drug.

2. *Personal characteristics.* The weight, health, age, and even the personality of the person taking a drug can influence the drug's effect.

3. *Expectations.* The effect that a person expects a drug to have, based on his or her past experiences and what the person has heard from others, partly determines the effect of the drug.

4. *Social situation.* Other people influence a person's response to the drug. The person may respond differently if the drug is taken alone versus in the midst of an upbeat party.

5. *Moods.* The mood that the person is in at the time of taking the drug can dramatically alter its effects. Alcohol, for example, can make a happy person happier or a sad person more depressed, and it can unleash violence in an angry individual.

When you consider the interplay of these factors, it's easy to see how their effects are at least partly unpredictable.

**Problems Associated with Drug Use**

The use of drugs to alter conscious experience carries with it certain risks. These risks differ considerably from drug to drug, but the risks associated with all drugs involve the same basic issues.

1. *Drug abuse.* A drug is being abused if taking it causes physical damage (as in liver damage caused by alcohol) or impairment of psychological or social functioning (as in frequent drinking of alcohol leading to marital conflicts).

2. *Psychological dependence.* A psychological dependence has been developed when the individual needs to use the drug regularly to maintain a comfortable psychological state, as when a person gets edgy if he or she does not smoke marijuana daily.

3. *Physiological addiction, tolerance, and withdrawal.* Many drugs quickly become involved in the chemical functioning of the body. The body adjusts to such a degree that when the drug is not present, the body cannot function properly and the person experiences painful *withdrawal* symptoms. Addictive drugs produce progressively stronger addiction because over time the body learns to adapt more easily to the drug in its system. As *tolerance* for the drug increases, larger doses are needed to produce the same effect on consciousness. Therefore, the addicted person's body chemistry becomes progressively more tied to the drug.

4. *Direct side effects.* The direct dangers of drugs just described are not the only risks associated with their use. Psychotropic drugs rarely have effects that are limited to a single neurotransmitter or organ system. They often have powerful and potentially serious *side effects*. Some of these are merely annoyances, such as the temporary numbness in the throat caused by inhaling cocaine, whereas others are far more serious. Brain damage, heart attacks, loss of control of automobiles, violence, and suicide are only some of the common side effects of psychotropic drugs.

5.  ***Indirect side effects.***  Some psychotropic drugs are dangerous not only because of their direct psychological and medical side effects but because of their indirect effects as well. The obvious example is the greatly increased risk of infection with hepatitis or human immunodeficiency virus (HIV), which causes acquired immune deficiency syndrome (AIDS), as a result of sharing needles used for drug injection. Many drugs, however, result in slower and less immediately obvious impairment of immune system functioning that increases the risk of serious disease.

## Psychotropic Drugs

Many consciousness-altering drugs are used and abused today. The drugs described in the following paragraphs are powerful in their effects, are often powerfully addictive, and are used illegally in most circumstances.

### Stimulants

**stimulants**
Drugs that increase the activity of motivational centers in the brain, providing a sense of energy and well-being.

**amphetamines**
(am-fet′ah-minz) Powerful stimulants that produce a conscious sense of increased energy and euphoria.

**amphetamine psychosis**
(sī-kō′sis) A prolonged reaction to the excessive use of stimulants, characterized by disordered thinking, confused and rapidly changing emotions, and intense suspiciousness.

**Stimulants,** often called *uppers,* are drugs that activate motivational centers and reduce activity in inhibitory centers of the central nervous system. *Caffeine,* which is found in coffee, tea, soft drinks, and some nonprescription medicines, and *nicotine,* which is found in cigarettes and other tobacco products, are by far the most widely used stimulants. As described later, these relatively mild stimulants are, nonetheless, extremely addictive and pose major health risks.

**Amphetamines** (trade names Dexedrine, Benzedrine, and Methedrine) are stimulant drugs that generally produce a conscious sense of increased energy, alertness, enthusiasm, and a euphoric high. They are not physically addictive but produce rapid and intense psychological dependence. Hence, the possibility for abuse is very high. The amphetamines are dangerous physically, particularly in their effects on the heart. Psychologically, the greatest risk is known as **amphetamine psychosis**—a prolonged reaction to excessive use of stimulants characterized by distorted thinking, confused and rapidly changing emotions, and intense suspiciousness.

The use of amphetamines in the United States was on the decline until the late 1980s, particularly use of the dangerous form of amphetamine known as *methamphetamine* or *speed.* Apparently word had gotten around the street that "speed kills." But, unfortunately, when the street name for methamphetamine changed to "crystal" and

Cocaine is a stimulant, which can lead to dependence on the drug whether snorted or smoked in the form of crack.

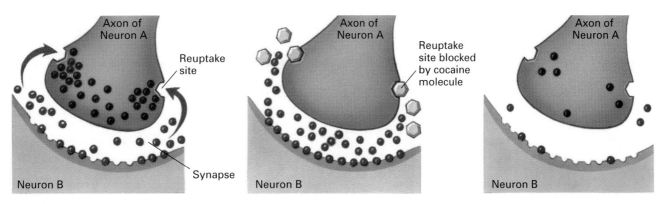

**FIGURE 5.6**
The steps in cocaine dependence looked at from the point of view of changes in the transmission of neural messages across the synapse.

"crystal meth," the bad reputation that speed had earned for serious psychological and medical side effects was lost. Today this white powder—which is usually sniffed but is also swallowed or injected—is used in virtually epidemic proportions in some areas of the country.

*Cocaine* is one of the more widely abused drugs in the United States. Cocaine, a stimulant much like amphetamine, is made from the leaves of the coca plant. It is taken in many forms but is most commonly inhaled as a powder, injected, or smoked in the dangerously powerful form known as crack. Cocaine produces alertness, high energy, optimism, self-confidence, happiness, exhilaration, and talkativeness. It raises body temperature, breathing, and heart rate and reduces the desire for food and sleep.

Because the cocaine high only lasts a matter of minutes, its use is often repeated each time the effect wears off. These binges of repeated cocaine use sometimes last for hours or even days, until a state of exhaustion is reached. At this point, the cocaine user *crashes,* feeling immensely tired, hungry, and in need of long periods of sleep. In the first few days following a cocaine binge, the user is absolutely miserable. Depression, agitation, confusion, paranoia, anger, and exhaustion are all part of the cocaine crash (Weddington et al., 1990).

Repeated cocaine use rapidly leads to addiction because of the way in which it exerts its effect on the brain. Like most consciousness-altering drugs, cocaine passes into the brain in the fluids that bathe the neurons. Here, they alter the functioning of the brain by influencing neurotransmission at the synapse. Cocaine interferes with one part of synaptic transmission for a class of neurotransmitters called *catecholamines* (Pearlson et al., 1993). After the neurotransmitter is secreted from the axon, a large part of it is absorbed back into the axon to be used again—a process called *reuptake* (see fig. 5.6). However, cocaine blocks the reuptake openings and prevents the reabsorption of the neurotransmitter by the axon. This means that the neurotransmitter stays in the synapse longer than normal, setting into motion a series of events that lead to the cocaine "high" (Cooper, Bloom, & Roth, 1996).

Withdrawal from cocaine dependence differs considerably from withdrawal from heroin or nicotine addiction, especially in the absence of changes in heart rate and blood pressure, the absence of chills and sweats, and the absence of physical pain. The intense depression, agitation, and craving for cocaine during withdrawal is a mean and miserable monkey on the back of the cocaine addict, however. Although the craving diminishes as the crash wears off, it returns when the person is exposed to cocaine again, or to the people and places that are associated with cocaine use. Going straight after becoming dependent on cocaine is an enormous challenge, although it is one that can be met by genuinely motivated persons given proper treatment (Weddington & others, 1990).

## HUMAN DIVERSITY

### Substance Abuse and Human Diversity

Without doubt, drug and alcohol abuse is a major problem in the United States. A large-scale study of the U.S. population (Kessler et al., 1993) found that 25 percent of adolescents and adults have had a substance abuse problem at some time in their life—that's one person out of every four! Alcohol abuse alone cost the country an estimated $10 billion in 1991 in terms of lost work time, accidents, increased medical costs, and other economic costs (Heien & Pittman, 1993), but the human cost of drug and alcohol abuse is much greater.

Who abuses drugs and alcohol in our society? Gender, ethnicity, and income level are important factors that influence the likelihood of substance abuse. Men consistently have been found to be twice as likely to abuse substances as women. The problem is very serious among women, but substance abuse is much more widespread among men.

In terms of ethnicity, African Americans have been found to be less likely than whites to abuse drugs, tobacco, and alcohol (Breslau & others, 2001; Kessler et al., 1993). Apparently, there are cultural traditions in the African American community that protect against substance abuse. The lower rates of substance abuse among African Americans—which has been found in several U.S. surveys—are even more striking when findings for education and income level are considered. Persons with less education who earn less money in the United States are more likely to abuse substances than persons with more

money. Thus, even though African Americans tend to earn less money, on the average, than white Americans in the United States at this time in history, their rates of substance abuse are much lower. The protective influence of ethnicity is so strong that it counters the trends associated with income and education.

It is important to understand the ways in which human diversity—gender, ethnicity, and education and income level—are linked to substance abuse. We will not fully understand the causes of substance abuse until we understand why women, African Americans, and the affluent are so much less likely to abuse drugs and alcohol.

It is equally important to remember to treat everyone as an *individual,* however. Although African American women from high-income families are at the lowest risk for substance abuse, some members of this select group have serious substance abuse problems. Similarly, most low-income white males have no difficulties with drugs and alcohol whatsoever.

Why do you think persons with low income and little education are more likely to abuse substances? What makes men more likely than women to abuse drugs and alcohol? In your opinion, why are African Americans at less risk for the abuse of these substances? Could the answers to these questions be used to reduce everyone's risk for substance abuse? Many hundreds of researchers in psychology and psychiatry are actively at work today trying to answer these important questions. ■

---

Cocaine is dangerous even to the occasional user. Even small doses can lead to fatal heart attacks, and because tolerance for cocaine varies considerably, it is dangerously easy for experienced occasional users to overdose accidentally. Ironically, cocaine was once a legal drug in the United States. Coca-Cola, originally marketed as a "nerve tonic," initially contained cocaine as part of its "secret formula." In 1906, the cocaine was replaced by the milder stimulant caffeine.

### Depressants

**depressants**
Drugs that reduce the activity of the central nervous system, leading to a sense of relaxation, drowsiness, and lowered inhibitions.

The **depressants** are a large class of psychotropic drugs that influence conscious experience by depressing parts of the central nervous system. Tranquilizers, sedatives, and narcotics are all depressant drugs, and as we will see at the end of this chapter, alcohol is the most widely used depressant of all.

*Sedatives and tranquilizers.* **Sedatives** are depressants that in mild doses generally produce a state of calm relaxation. They are prescribed in the United States as drugs to aid sleep and sometimes to combat anxiety. Common trade names for these drugs are Seconal, Tuinal, Nembutal, and Quaaludes (which are no longer sold in the United States but are still abused). Because they are highly addictive and dangerous to withdraw from without medical supervision and because overdoses are highly dangerous (and even small doses are dangerous when taken with alcohol), they are prescribed by physicians less frequently now than in the past. However, they are still widely abused through illegal drug markets.

Tranquilizers are milder drugs that are similar to sedatives in that they typically produce a sense of calm relaxation for a period of time. As such, they are often prescribed to reduce anxiety. Common trade names are Xanax, Valium, Librium, Ativan, Miltown, and Equanil. Like sedatives, most are dangerously addictive, often difficult to withdraw from, and are very dangerous when mixed with alcohol; they must be taken with great care. Also like sedatives, these types of downers are widely sold illegally.

*Narcotics.* **Narcotics** are powerful and highly addictive depressants. The use of the narcotic drug opium, derived from the opium poppy, dates back at least 7,000 years in the Middle East. Derivatives of opium, including morphine, heroin, and codeine, are powerful narcotic drugs that dramatically alter consciousness. They generally relieve pain and induce a sudden, rushing high, followed by a relaxed, lethargic drowsiness. Narcotics create a powerful physiological addiction very rapidly. With prolonged addiction, the physical effects on the body are profoundly damaging. Compared with the use of other drugs, narcotics use in the United States is not high, but the drastic effects of opiates, including the crimes that many addicts commit to maintain their increasingly expensive habits, make it an extremely significant drug abuse problem. It became an especially difficult problem during the Vietnam War. Perhaps due to a combination of the availability of heroin and the stress of war, it was estimated that 20 percent of all Vietnam veterans tried heroin at least once (Harris, 1973).

Opium and its derivatives (the **opiates**) are not the only kinds of narcotic drugs. In recent years, synthetic narcotics have been artificially produced in drug laboratories. These synthetic narcotics include widely used painkilling drugs with trade names such as Demerol, Percodan, and Methadone.

## Inhalants

Substances that when inhaled produce a sense of intoxication are called **inhalants.** To produce a "high," toxic (poisonous) substances, such as glue, cleaning fluid, and paint, are typically placed in paper bags and inhaled ("sniffed"). This type of intoxication is common among children because the materials are relatively easy to obtain. Inhalants are highly addictive and extremely dangerous. These toxic fumes often cause permanent brain damage and other serious complications.

## Hallucinogens

The drugs that most powerfully alter consciousness are **hallucinogens,** such as lysergic acid diethylamide (LSD), mescaline (derived from the peyote cactus), and psilocybin (derived from a kind of mushroom). These drugs typically alter perceptual experiences, but only large doses cause vivid hallucinations. In these unusual states, the drugged individual experiences imaginary visions and realities that, ironically, sometimes seem more "real" to the drug user than waking consciousness. This fact, however, may be more attributable to the drug taker's dissatisfaction with everyday life than to the drug itself.

The hallucinogens are generally not physiologically addictive, but individuals can quickly become psychologically dependent on them. In addition, although many of the

**sedatives**
Depressants that in mild doses produce a state of calm relaxation.

**narcotics**
Powerful and highly addictive depressants.

**opiates**
(ō′pē-ats) Narcotic drugs derived from the opium poppy.

**inhalants**
(in-hā′lants) Toxic substances that produce a sense of intoxication when inhaled.

**hallucinogens**
(hah-lū′si′′no-jenz) Drugs that alter perceptual experiences.

drug-induced states (trips) produced by hallucinogens are experienced as pleasant, "bad trips"—frightening and dangerous drug responses—are not uncommon (McWilliams & Tuttle, 1973). Individuals who are frightened about taking a drug but do so because of peer pressure are more likely to experience bad trips. These trips, both good and bad, can sometimes recur in flashbacks without the individual's taking the drug again. About 65 percent of flashbacks are bad trips, apparently being triggered by stress or anxiety. About 25 percent of all regular LSD users experience flashbacks, sometimes several months after the original trip (Matefy & Kroll, 1974).

One other hallucinogenic drug needs to be discussed because of its dangers. The drug phencyclidine, or PCP (angel dust), which was originally developed as an animal tranquilizer, has come into common use, especially among adolescents. The effects of PCP typically last from 4 to 6 hours. In some cases, the individual experiences auditory or visual hallucinations, but more likely the experience includes feelings of numbness, lack of muscular coordination, anxiety, and a sense of detachment from the environment. Euphoria, a sense of strength, and "dreaminess" may also be present. The individual on PCP may also engage in unconventional behavior, such as going into public places nude. Violent behavior toward others, suicide, and psychotic episodes are other possible reactions to this drug. It's generally considered one of the most dangerous drugs on the street (Petersen & Stillman, 1978).

## Marijuana

Not since Prohibition has any drug been as hotly debated as marijuana.

Marijuana is a popular consciousness-altering drug that generally produces a sense of relaxation and well-being. In some cases, the drug alters sensory experiences and the perception of time. Not since Prohibition has any drug been so hotly debated or so widely used in spite of being illegal. It's not physically addictive, but regular users experience uncomfortable withdrawal symptoms when they stop using marijuana (Budney, Hughes, Moore, & Novy, 2001). Although the evidence as to possible physical or psychological harm is not conclusive, there is clear evidence that prolonged marijuana use decreases the efficiency of cognitive processing, weakens the body's immune response, and decreases the action of male sex hormones (Pope & others, 2001; Wallace & Fisher, 1983). Moreover, like smoking any type of cigarette, marijuana greatly increases the risk of lung cancer. Driving an automobile or using any other form of machinery when intoxicated by marijuana (or any other substance) is also obviously dangerous.

## Act-Alike and Designer Drugs

Until the 1980s, it was legal in most states to manufacture and sell drugs that looked and acted like illegal substances, such as amphetamines, but contained only substances that were legal to sell openly. For example, combinations of high doses of powdered caffeine and some over-the-counter decongestants produce some of the effects of amphetamines. Hence, these drugs are sometimes called *act-alike* drugs.

States have had to scramble to find ways to block the sale of act-alike drugs. These drugs are considered dangerous because of their own serious adverse effects. In addition, because the strength of drugs that act as amphetamines varies considerably, the risk of accidental overdose is very high.

Amateur chemists try to stay ahead of the law by designing new drugs that have not yet been classified as illegal—the so-called *designer drugs*. For example, the designer drugs MDA and MDMA (*ecstasy*) are derivatives of amphetamines that produce a dreamlike high lasting for up to 8 hours. The constant push to design new mind-altering drugs to stay ahead of the law means that new drugs are widely sold and used before anyone has a chance to evaluate their potential side effects. This is a major concern because any substance powerful enough to change the functioning of the brain generally carries with it serious medical and psychological risks (Carroll, 1989). For example, there is now strong evidence from studies of humans and other animals that ecstasy, which is one of the most widely used "recreational" drugs in the western hemisphere, causes lasting damage to neurons that use serotonin as the neurotransmitter (Croft, Klugman, Baldeweg, & Gruzelier, 2001; Reneman & others, 2001).

**Review**

Altered states can be induced by taking psychotropic drugs that alter conscious experience by influencing the action of neurons in the brain. These drugs produce changes in consciousness ranging from mild alterations of mood to vivid hallucinations, but they also carry with them the danger of abuse, dependence, addiction, and direct physical damage in some cases. The effect of drugs on consciousness depends on a variety of factors, including dose and purity; the weight, health, age, and personality of the person taking the drug; expectations about the effects of the drug; the social situation; and the mood that the person is in at the time of taking the drug.

**Check Your Learning**

To be sure that you have learned the key points from the preceding section, cover the list of correct answers and try to answer each question. If you give an incorrect answer to any question, return to the page given next to the correct answer to see why your answer was not correct.

1. Many factors influence an individual's response to a drug, such as the dose and purity of the drug, expectations about the drug, and one's mood, making the response somewhat unpredictable.

   a) True                           b) False

2. Psychologically, the greatest risk of amphetamine abuse is known as _____, which is a prolonged reaction to an excessive use of stimulants characterized by distorted thinking, confused and rapidly changing emotions, and intense suspiciousness.

   a) schizophrenia              c) overdose
   b) amphetamine psychosis     d) withdrawal

3. A long-lasting drug, originally developed as an animal tranquilizer, that typically produces numbness, a lack of muscular coordination, a sense of detachment from the environment, euphoria, and a sense of strength and that sometimes results in unconventional, psychotic, or violent behavior is _____.

   a) phencyclidine (PCP)        c) cocaine
   b) amphetamine               d) ecstasy (MDMA)

4. The drugs that most powerfully alter consciousness are _____ such as lysergic acid diethylamide (LSD), mescaline (derived from the peyote cactus), and psilocybin (derived from a kind of mushroom).

   a) inhalants                  c) hallucinogens
   b) stimulants                 d) depressants

**Thinking Critically about Psychology**

1. What social and personal factors induce millions of people to abuse drugs despite the publicity regarding the negative effects of drug abuse?

2. Our society makes a distinction between drugs such as alcohol and caffeine, which are legal to use, and others, such as marijuana and cocaine, that are not. Does this distinction make sense?

**Correct Answers:** 1. a (p. 183),  2. b (p. 184),  3. a (p. 188),  4. c (p. 187).

## The Legal Consciousness-Altering Drugs

Each day, many of us use consciousness-altering drugs, usually without even being aware that we are taking "drugs." Coffee contains the stimulant drug caffeine, cigarettes contain the stimulant drug nicotine, and alcohol is a powerful depressant drug. Millions of individuals who would never consider using "drugs" use, abuse, or are addicted to these drugs. What are these drugs' consciousness-altering effects (and side effects)?

The average American drinks 36 gallons of coffee each year.

### Caffeine

Eighty-five percent of Americans ingest caffeine daily (Hughes, Oliveto, Helzer, Higgins, & Bickel, 1992). Indeed, each year the average person in the United States drinks 36 gallons of coffee, 7 gallons of tea, and 30 gallons of cola and uses untold amounts of over-the-counter drugs containing caffeine (Ray, 1974). At approximately 125 milligrams (mg) per cup of coffee, that is an enormous consumption of caffeine.

You've seen the ads on television: The attractive woman, frazzled by the day's hassles, is restored to peaceful balance with a cup of coffee. Is that a good way to cope with our emotions when they have been bent and abused by life? Is caffeine good medicine for our nerves? Because caffeine is a stimulant, it does produce an increase in alertness, which helps explain the popularity of coffee, tea, colas, and other beverages that contain caffeine. But does it make you feel *better?*

Physicians and psychologists have long suspected that caffeine actually produces negative changes in emotions in many persons. David Veleber and Donald Templer (1984) conducted a study of the effects of caffeine on emotions using volunteer college students and businesspeople in the San Joaquin Valley of California. The participants completed a psychological test that measured the degree of depression, anxiety, and hostility that the individual was experiencing at the time of the test.

They took the test before and 1 hour after drinking a cup of coffee. Some of the participants drank decaffeinated coffee, whereas others received a low or high dose of caffeine in their coffee (the individuals did not know how much caffeine they were drinking, if any). The amount of caffeine was adjusted for the individual's body weight, with a 100-pound person receiving the equivalent of either one cup (low dose) or two cups (high dose) of strong brewed coffee.

As shown in figure 5.7, the caffeine produced small but significant changes in all three emotions. Most of us feel no ill effects from small amounts of coffee, but a large amount of caffeine is an invitation to lousy moods for all of us, and even small amounts may cause distress for sensitive individuals.

Unfortunately, serious health risks are associated with the overuse of caffeine. Although caffeine produces relatively small changes in consciousness, it has powerful effects on the body. It has long been known that consumption of eight or more cups of caffeinated coffee per day (1,000 mg) constitutes a dangerously high level of intake (Greden, 1974). Common effects of such consumption for a prolonged period of time include excessive stomach acid and ulcers, abnormal heart rhythms and accelerated heart rate, increased kidney activity, anxiety, irritability, insomnia, sensory disturbances, and def-

inite physiological addiction with intense withdrawal symptoms when caffeine is not consumed (Greden, 1974; Hughes & others, 1992). Prolonged use of caffeine at even moderate levels can also result in a physiological addiction to the substance. Symptoms

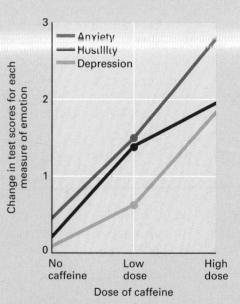

**FIGURE 5.7**

Change in measures of emotion after drinking either decaffeinated coffee or coffee containing small or large amounts of caffeine.

Source: Data from D. M. Veleber and D. T. Templer, "Effects of Caffeine on Anxiety and Depression," *Journal of Abnormal Psychology,* 93, 120–122, 1984. © 1984 by the American Psychological Association.

of withdrawal can be experienced even by moderate caffeine users if they suddenly stop drinking coffee, tea, caffeinated soft drinks, and other sources of caffeine. These withdrawal symptoms include drowsiness, headaches, and mildly depressed mood.

Caffeine also produces marked increases in blood pressure, particularly during times of stress (Pincomb, Lovallo, Passey, Brackett, & Wilson, 1987). Moreover, drinking large amounts of coffee (five or more cups per day) over a period of years is associated with a two to three times greater risk of coronary heart disease, at least in men (LaCroix, Mead, Liang, Thomas, & Pearson, 1986). Drinking excessive amounts of coffee is a behavior that produces serious health risks, but even moderate amounts appear to pose some risk.

A person who never smokes has a life expectancy of 8 years longer than a person who smokes two packs of cigarettes a day. Consequently, the cost of the smoker's life insurance averages 25 percent higher.

## Nicotine

Nicotine found in tobacco is another widely used drug. A survey of over 4,400 individuals in the United States found that half of all persons aged 15 to 54 years of age had smoked daily at some time in their life. Twenty-four percent of these individuals had been, or were currently, dependent on (addicted to) nicotine (Breslau, Johnson, Hiripni, & Kessler, 2001). Persons with problems with depression are especially likely to become dependent on nicotine, but the problem is widespread (Dierker & others, 2001). Although rates of casual smoking have gone down among 15- to 24-year-olds in recent years, their rates of nicotine dependence have declined little (Breslau & others, 2001).

Rates of tobacco use remain surprisingly high, given the clear evidence that cigarette smoking is highly dangerous. The life expectancy of regular smokers is reduced because smoking *greatly* increases the chances of lung and mouth cancer, heart attacks, pneumonia, emphysema, and other life-threatening diseases (Jenkins, 1988). In addition, cigarette smoking during pregnancy greatly increases the risk of lower birthweight, premature delivery, and death of the infant. Each year, approximately 135,000 people die of lung cancer in the United States; of those deaths, 101,000 are directly attributable to smoking (Jeffrey, 1988). A person aged 25 who never smokes has a life expectancy that is more than *8 years longer* than a person who smokes two packs a day. Why, then, do people smoke?

The answer to that question seems to have several parts. First, virtually all smokers begin during their teenage years, when they are especially vulnerable to peer pressure and to advertisements that portray smoking as something that strong, sexy adults do. Second, because teenagers usually know that their parents do not want them to smoke, it becomes attractive forbidden fruit and an easy way to rebel against parents. (Few teenagers are mature enough to realize that there are adults who *want* them to start smoking —the mega-rich owners of tobacco companies, who are happy to sell them an addictive drug that will kill one out of four of them.)

Third, regardless of why smokers begin to smoke, addiction soon takes over for most regular smokers (Russell, 1971; Stein & others, 1998). Nicotine is highly addictive for two primary reasons. It is a mild stimulant of the pleasure centers in the limbic system, and it increases alertness to a small degree by stimulating the frontal lobes of the cerebral cortex (Stein & others, 1998). More important, nicotine soothes the discomfort that it creates. Aftereffects of nicotine increase the smoker's level of irritability and discomfort after a cigarette. The next cigarette is highly reinforcing because it brings the smoker's discomfort back down to a normal level (the level before he or she began smoking), but the discomfort soon rises again after that cigarette, producing the recurrent motive to smoke (Parrott, 1999).

## Alcohol

Are beer, wine, and liquor drugs? Although we do not generally think of alcohol as a drug, it's a powerful and widely abused psychotropic drug that happens to come in liquid form. Alcohol works principally as a depressant, but it is experienced as a drug that "stimulates" sociability and exuberant activity ("partying"). This is because alcohol depresses inhibitory mechanisms in the brain. Thus, alcohol seems to stimulate the person because it makes the drinker less inhibited.

Alcohol also reduces tension and anxiety and increases self-confidence and self-esteem by erasing doubts about ourselves (Steele & Josephs, 1990). Alcohol has other effects as well. It impairs visual judgment and motor control and induces sleepiness (Matthews, Best, White, Vandergriff, & Simpson, 1996). In addition, alcohol can worsen negative moods, particularly deepening depression and making it more likely that anger will result in verbal or physical aggression (Steele & Josephs).

Most states consider an individual legally intoxicated when .10 percent (one-tenth of 1 percent) of the volume of his or her circulating blood is alcohol. At this level, sensory and motor performance are noticeably impaired. Unfortunately, even blood-alcohol levels of .03 percent are sufficient to make driving an automobile or operating other machinery dangerous.

*(continued)*

| Males | Alcohol consumed in 1 hour | |
| --- | --- | --- |
| Weight | (100 proof liquor) | Blood alcohol level |
| 150 lbs | 2 oz | .05 |
| 150 lbs | 4 oz | .10* |

| Females | Alcohol consumed in 1 hour | |
| --- | --- | --- |
| Weight | (100 proof liquor) | Blood alcohol level |
| 100 lbs | 2 oz | .09 |
| 100 lbs | 4 oz | .18 |

*Note: Blood alcohol concentration of .03 can impair automobile driving; concentration of .10 constitutes intoxication according to most state laws.

**FIGURE 5.8**
Average blood-alcohol levels as a result of drinking.

It is not easy to translate blood-alcohol levels into amounts of alcohol consumed because many factors influence blood-alcohol levels. Drinking on an empty stomach, drinking carbonated alcoholic beverages, drinking quickly rather than sipping, and drinking higher proof beverages all lead to higher levels of blood alcohol, even when the same amount of alcohol is consumed under other circumstances (Chruschel, 1982). The principal complicating factor, however, is the amount of fluid in the body, which differs according to body size and sex. The liver can remove from the bloodstream the alcohol in one 12-ounce can of beer (or one glass of wine or 1 ounce of 100-proof liquor) in about 1 hour; the remainder stays in the blood. Figure 5.8 shows the average blood levels that can be expected for males and females of different sizes, but keep in mind that these are merely averages.

Except for nicotine, alcohol is the most widely abused addictive drug in the United States. Assessing the exact extent of alcohol abuse is difficult mainly for two reasons. First, the amount of alcohol consumption that can lead to harmful effects varies markedly from person to person and from situation to situation. An individ-ual who has only four drinks every New Year's Eve is an alcohol abuser if he drives himself home when intoxicated; a surgeon who has two drinks a day may be an alcohol abuser if she drinks them right before performing surgery. Second, the potential harmful effects of alcohol abuse are so varied. Heavy drinking can affect job performance, disrupt marriages, and harm one's health. It is involved in about half of all fatal fire and automobile accidents, one-third of all suicides, and two-thirds of all murders (Marlatt & Rose, 1980). Alcohol abuse frequently leads to highly stressful consequences, such as divorce and loss of employment; these stressful consequences then take a toll on health. In addition, alcohol has directly harmful effects on the liver, brain, and circulatory system.

As a result, the life span of the addicted alcoholic is 12 years shorter than average (National Institute on Alcohol Abuse and Alcoholism, 1987). Even moderately high levels of alcohol consumption create a health risk (Hennekens, Rosner, & Cole, 1978; R. W. Jenkins, 1988).

In addition, drinking during pregnancy has been linked to a form of combined physical defects and mental retardation in the infant known as *fetal alcohol syndrome* (Briggs, Freeman, & Yaffe, 1986). Although heavy drinking is most likely to lead to birth defects, no "safe" level of alcohol consumption during pregnancy has been established —and there may not be one.

In spite of the difficulties involved in defining alcohol abuse, surveys have been taken with eye-opening results. Using a broad definition of alcohol abuse, it has been found that nearly one-third of the individuals surveyed reported at least one serious alcohol-related problem (for 21 percent of females and 41 percent of males; Cahalan, 1970; Cahalan & Room, 1974).

Because of its powerful mood-altering qualities, alcohol can rapidly result in psychological dependence and physiological addiction (*alcoholism*). This is not to say that alcohol is always harmful. In the survey cited (Cahalan & Room, 1974), more than half of all the drinkers reported no harmful side effects. Indeed, under some conditions, small amounts of alcohol may be beneficial to the health of some individuals. Individuals who drink an average of one drink per day or so live longer than individuals who do not drink at all (Dawson, 2000; Jenkins, 1988). ■

Chapter 5 explores human awareness, normal waking consciousness, sleeping and dreaming, and altered states of consciousness.

I. Consciousness is defined as "a state of awareness" and is experienced in a variety of states.

   A. Daydreams combine the features of everyday consciousness and dreamlike fantasies.

   B. At times, consciousness appears to become divided, with different conscious activities occurring simultaneously.

   C. Psychologists have conducted studies that suggest that it makes sense to say that unconscious mental processes operate in our lives.

II. Approximately one-third of our lives is spent in sleep, but not all of sleep is unconscious.

   A. Sleep begins with a semiwakeful, hypnagogic state and moves through stages of progressively deeper sleep.

   B. Dreams occur mostly during the phase of sleep known as REM sleep, but a different type of dream is common in non-REM sleep as well.

   C. Sleeping and dreaming seem important to health, but even extended periods of sleep deprivation have been shown to cause only fatigue, inefficiency, and irritability.

   D. Nightmares, night terrors, sleepwalking, and sleeptalking are fairly common sleep phenomena.

   E. Some persons suffer from the sleep disorders of insomnia (inability to get sufficient sleep), narcolepsy (falling asleep during daily activities), and sleep apnea (breathing stops briefly during sleep).

III. We sometimes experience more unusual altered states of consciousness.

   A. Many individuals practice meditation to achieve a highly relaxed state.

   B. Hypnosis is sometimes used to alter consciousness and to relieve pain.

   C. Altered consciousness is sometimes experienced in the form of depersonalization.

IV. Consciousness can also be altered through the use of various psychotropic drugs.

   A. Psychotropic drugs can be classified as stimulants, depressants, hallucinogens, and inhalants; the drug marijuana does not fit easily into this classification.

   B. Though risks differ from drug to drug, drug use can lead to abuse, dependence, or addiction.

   C. Even the more common legal drugs (caffeine, nicotine, alcohol) produce definite physical and psychological effects and can be quite harmful if used in excess.

   D. The more powerful drugs cause radical changes in consciousness, they can lead to serious physical and psychological problems, and many are illegal.

      1. Stimulants are not physically addictive but produce psychological dependence; they can be dangerous, particularly in their effects on the heart.

      2. Sedatives and tranquilizers are highly addictive and can be highly dangerous, particularly when taken in large doses or with alcohol.

      3. Narcotics are powerful and dangerous depressants; physiological addiction occurs rapidly, and prolonged use has profoundly damaging effects on the body.

**Summary**

4. Inhalants are usually toxic and often cause permanent brain damage.

5. Hallucinogens radically alter perception, cause hallucinations, and are often associated with bizarre or even violent behavior. Although hallucinogens are not physiologically addictive, psychological dependence is common.

6. Marijuana is a drug that produces a sense of well-being in most people and sometimes alters perception.

## Resources

1. For a readable discussion of meditation without its metaphysical or religious trimmings, read Benson, H. (1975). *The relaxation response.* New York: Morrow. For an intelligent discussion of Zen meditation, see Austin, J. H. (1998). *Zen and the brain toward an understanding of meditation and consciousness.* Cambridge, MA: MIT Press.

2. For a fascinating and sensible look at hypnosis, see Bowers, K. S. (1976). *Hypnosis for the seriously curious.* Monterey, CA: Brooks/Cole.

3. For more on the contents of dreams, written by a Freudian psychologist, see Hall, C. S. (1951). What people dream about. *Scientific American, 84:* 60–63. For additional information on the study of sleeping and dreaming, see Webb, W. B., & Agnew, H. W. (1973). *Sleep and dreams.* Dubuque, IA: Wm. C. Brown; Horne, J. (1988). *Why we sleep.* New York: Oxford University Press; Hobson, J. A. (1989). *Sleep.* New York: Scientific American Library; and Stauch, I., & Meier, B. (1996). *In search of dreams: Experimental dream research.* Albany: State University of New York Press.

4. A fascinating and in-depth analysis of the hypnogogic state is Mavromatis, A. (1987). *Hypnogogia.* London: Routledge.

5. For thorough summaries of mind-altering drugs, see Carroll, C. R. (2000). *Drugs in modern society* (5th ed.). Boston: McGraw-Hill; and Julien, R. M. (1002). *A primer of drug addiction* (6th ed.). San Francisco: Freeman.

6. Broad overviews of the topic of consciousness are provided by Wallace, B., & Fisher, L. E. (1991). *Consciousness and behavior,* (3rd ed.). Boston: Allyn & Bacon; Ornstein, R. (1991). *The evolution of consciousness.* New York: Prentice-Hall; and Rychlak, J. F. (1997). *In defense of human consciousness.* Washington, DC: American Psychological Association.

7. If you smoke or use smokeless tobacco and are thinking about quitting, this Web site offers useful information and links to other sites: http://unr.edu/homepage/shubinsk/smoke.html

# PART III

# Learning and Cognition

In chapters 6, 7, and 8, you will learn about learning from experience, the retention of learning in memory, thinking and problem solving, and language. Although not limited to humans, these are the processes that have given humans our adaptive advantage. In the final section of chapter 8, you will learn about intelligence, which can be thought of as the sum total of cognition.

Here is a visual overview of what you will learn in the third section of the text.

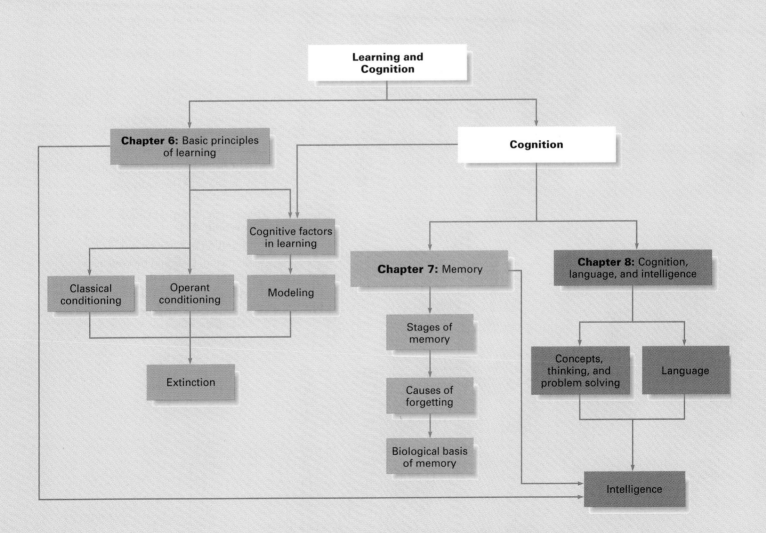

# Chapter Outline

# Basic Principles of Learning

## PROLOGUE

You behave the way you do largely because you *learned* to act that way. Take a moment and think about who you are. Now imagine that you had been adopted as an infant by a family in a distant part of the world. You would now speak a different language, eat different foods, and act in ways that are characteristic of a different culture. You would be a different person in all of these ways simply because your learning experiences were different.

In 1934, a young scientist named Ruth Benedict published a book about remote cultures that were very different from one another. Her book tells a remarkable story about the power of learning experiences in shaping human lives. In the 1930s, the Dobu were a competitive people who generally did everything they could to acquire more possessions than anyone else. Theirs was a very violent culture, with high rates of assault and murder. In a way, they were very much like Americans—only more so. But the Zuñi people (pictured on p. 196), who are native Americans who once flourished in the Southwest, were very different. The Zuñi people found greed and ambition to be repugnant. Instead, they valued generosity and modesty. They shared all wealth equally with one another and actively avoided doing anything that would bring them individual fame. Perhaps as a result, violence among the Zuñi was rare. Benedict argued that if there were some cultures in which greed, ambition, and violence were rare, then it could not be true that these were inborn traits of all humans—they were learned traits that could be changed.

Are you still not convinced of the power of learning in shaping personalities? Benedict used courtship and marriage as another example of the great differences among cultures due to learning. In Zuñi society, male and female children were strictly separated until adolescence, allowing almost no contact before marriage. If a female and a male interacted in any way, their parents quickly arranged their marriage. Courtship often consisted of no more than the male's asking a young woman whom he had never met for a drink of water as she returned from the stream with a water jug. If she gave him a drink, they were soon married.

Courtship among the Dobu was dramatically different than among the Zuñi. In Dobu society, male and female children were not only allowed to play with each other, but sex play among children was common and approved of by adults. When children reached puberty, frequent sex was common among the unmarried males and females, with the lovemaking generally occurring openly in the one-room home of the girl's parents.

By showing scholars in the Western world that not all people were like us, Benedict helped convince many scholars that learning experiences were far more important in shaping human behavior than realized until that point. In this chapter, you will learn about three kinds of learning. In one of these types of learning, parts of the environment that you have hardly noticed before become stimuli that influence your behavior. If your water pipes were to make a groaning sound one morning while you are in the shower, you probably wouldn't pay much attention to it. But if over time the groaning always immediately preceded a sudden change in

## Key Terms

the temperature of your shower—from warm to icy cold—you would soon learn to jump at the sound of the groan. The groan would become a powerful stimulus for you.

Another kind of learning results from the *consequences* of your behavior. If you behave in a way that leads to something positive, you will probably behave that way more often in the future. If your behavior leads to something negative, on the other hand, you will be less likely to behave that way again. For example, let's say you stay up all night studying for a test. The next day, you can hardly stay awake and you can't remember half of what you learned the night before. Those are negative consequences that will lead to learning not to try that again. In contrast, if studying for a few hours each night for five nights before the test results in your first *A*, you are more likely to use that strategy again. The consequences of our behavior are a powerful source of learning.

The third type of learning comes from watching those around you. When you are in a new situation, such as your first day in a college class, you tend to notice how other students are behaving. Everybody else is taking notes—so you decide that you should, too. Instead of always having to learn from the consequences of our own actions, we can benefit from the experience of others.

As you learn about the details of the process of learning, try not to lose sight of the overall importance of the topic. Learning is one of the most important forces that made you the person you are today. ▪

## Definition of Learning

Life is a process of continual change. From infancy to adolescence to adulthood to death, we are changing. Many factors produce those changes, but one of the most important is the process of **learning.** Through our experiences, we learn new information, new attitudes, new fears, and new skills. We also learn to understand new concepts, to solve problems in new ways, and even to develop a personality over a lifetime. And, in the course of reading textbooks, we learn new definitions for words such as *learning:* In psychology, the term *learning* refers to any relatively permanent change in behavior brought about through experience—that is, through interactions with the environment.

**learning**
Any relatively permanent change in behavior brought about through experience.

As the definition states, not *all* changes in behavior are the result of learning. The term is restricted to the relatively permanent, as opposed to temporary, changes that are the result of experience, rather than changes due to biological causes such as drugs, fatigue, maturation, and injury. If a baseball pitcher throws the ball differently this season because his pitching coach has demonstrated a new way to pitch, learning has occurred—a relatively permanent change in pitching due to the experience of the coach's demonstration. But if the pitcher's changed style is due to an injury, fatigue from throwing too much before each game, an arm strengthened by weight lifting, or biological maturation (if he is a 7-year-old Little League pitcher), we would not refer to the change in pitching as learning.

The *change in behavior* is not always immediately obvious, however. If you watch a film on the proper way to hit backhands in tennis this winter, the change will not be evident until you are on the tennis court again next spring. Notice also that the definition of learning does not restrict its usage to intentionally produced changes in behavior or even to desirable changes in behavior. For instance, if you begin to loathe fish sandwiches because you get sick after eating one, learning has occurred. The new disgust for fish sandwiches is undesirable and certainly unintentional, but it's still the result of learning.

Learning is any relatively permanent change in behavior brought about through experience.

Over the years, psychologists have isolated and studied a number of ways that learning takes place. As a result, we now understand a number of different principles of learning. In the following sections, we describe these principles of learning and indicate some of the ways that they can influence us in our daily lives.

## Classical Conditioning: Learning by Association

We will begin our study of specific types of learning with a simple form called *classical conditioning*. The scientific study of classical conditioning began around the turn of the century with an accidental discovery made in the Leningrad laboratory of Ivan Pavlov. Pavlov was a Russian physiologist who was awarded the Nobel Prize for his work on the role of saliva in digestion. To study salivation, Pavlov surgically implanted tubes in the cheeks of his dogs. This allowed him to measure the amount of saliva produced when food was placed in their mouths (see fig. 6.1). Pavlov noticed, however, that dogs that had been in the experiment a few days started salivating when the attendant entered the room with the food dish *before* food was placed in their mouths. The sights (and probably sounds) of the attendant had come to *elicit* (evoke or produce) a reflexive response that only the food had originally elicited. This fact would have gone unnoticed had the saliva-collection tubes not been placed in the dogs' cheeks—that is the accidental part of the discovery. Noticing that a dog salivates whenever it sees the laboratory attendant who brings food may not seem like a great step forward for science at first glance. But Pavlov recognized that an inborn reflexive response to food, which was biologically "wired into" the nervous system, had come under the control of an *arbitrary* stimulus—the sight of the attendant.

Stated in a different way, Pavlov knew he had witnessed a form of learning that was based on nothing more than the repeated association of two stimuli. Remember from chapter 4 that a *stimulus* is anything that can directly influence behavior or conscious experience. Because the dogs' experience of food was linked to the sight of the attendant, the dogs' behavior was changed—the dogs now salivated to the stimuli of the approaching attendant. That is, the stimuli elicited a *response*. When you were born, you could respond to the outside world with only a limited repertoire of inborn reflexes, but

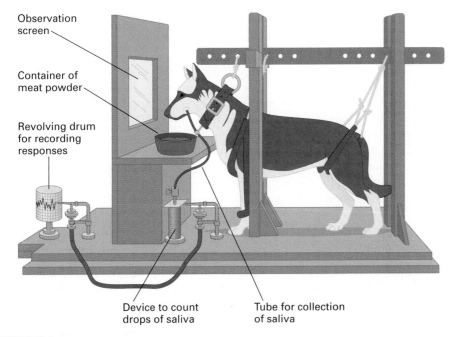

Observation screen

Container of meat powder

Revolving drum for recording responses

Device to count drops of saliva

Tube for collection of saliva

**FIGURE 6.1**

Apparatus originally used by Pavlov to study the role of salivation in digestion, and later in his studies of classical conditioning.

Ivan Pavlov accidentally discovered that dogs learn to associate the sounds of food being prepared with the food itself.

now you are a marvelously complex product of your learning experiences. Pavlov wanted to understand this process of learning, so over his colleagues' objections, he hastily completed his studies of digestion and devoted the rest of his career to the study of learning (Watson, 1971).

## Association: The Key Element in Classical Conditioning

More than 2,000 years before Pavlov, Aristotle noted that two sensations repeatedly experienced together will become *associated*. For example, if you have frequently visited the seashore with a friend, visiting the seashore alone may trigger memories of that friend. If you got sick the last time you ate a hot dog, you will likely feel nauseous the next time you see one. Learning through association is a common part of our lives.

Pavlov considered classical conditioning to be a form of learning through association—the association in time of a neutral stimulus (one that originally does not elicit the response) and a stimulus that does elicit the response. Pavlov used the apparatus that was already constructed in his laboratory to measure the progress of learning, and he used food as the stimulus to elicit the response (of salivation).

Specifically, Pavlov presented (as the neutral stimulus) a clicking metronome that the dog could easily hear. After a precisely measured interval of time, he would blow a small quantity of meat powder into the dog's mouth to elicit salivation. Every 15 minutes, the same procedure was repeated, and soon the dog began salivating to the metronome when it was presented alone. By continuously measuring the amount of saliva drained through the tube in the dog's cheek, the strength of the new learning was accurately monitored throughout the process of classical conditioning.

Keep in mind that the key phrase in classical conditioning is the "association" of the two stimuli. The more *frequently* the metronome and the food are associated, the more often the metronome will come to elicit salivation (see fig. 6.2). The *timing* of the

DENNIS THE MENACE © used by permission of Hank Ketcham and by North America Syndicate.

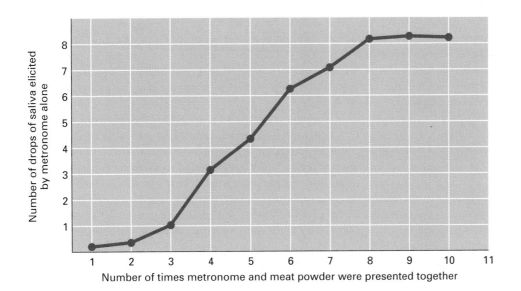

**FIGURE 6.2**
In Pavlov's studies, the more often the metronome was associated in time with meat powder, the more effective it was in eliciting salivation.

association of the two stimuli is also highly important. Pavlov found, for example, that he obtained the best results when the metronome preceded the food powder by about a half a second. Longer time intervals were less effective, and almost no learning occurred when the metronome was presented at the same time as the food or when the food was presented slightly before the metronome.

Thus, Pavlov took advantage of a chance observation and began a systematic study of one aspect of the learning process. Although learning had been studied before Pavlov's time, his experiments were highly influential because of their extensiveness and precision. But perhaps his true genius lay in seeing that this simple form of learning had important implications far beyond clicking metronomes and salivating dogs. Pavlov's writings became an important part of American psychology when they came to the attention of John B. Watson, who expanded upon and popularized Pavlov's views in English.

## Terminology of Classical Conditioning

Before we can proceed much further in our understanding of classical conditioning, we need to learn some new terminology. Although these terms are a bit awkward at first, they will help us expand our discussion of classical conditioning to topics more relevant to your life than salivating dogs. First we use each of these four terms to refer to the specific stimuli and responses in Pavlov's experiments; then we use them with new examples. The terms are as follows:

1. *Unconditioned stimulus.* The meat powder was the **unconditioned stimulus (UCS)** in Pavlov's experiment. This is a stimulus that can elicit the response without any learning. In other words, the response to an unconditioned stimulus is inborn.

2. *Unconditioned response.* Salivation was the **unconditioned response (UCR)**. It's an unlearned, inborn reaction to the unconditioned stimulus.

3. *Conditioned stimulus.* The metronome was originally unable to elicit the response of salivation, but it acquired the ability to elicit the response because it was paired with the unconditioned stimulus. It was the **conditioned stimulus (CS)** in Pavlov's studies.

4. *Conditioned response.* When the dog began salivating to the conditioned stimulus, salivation became the **conditioned response (CR)**. When a response is elicited by the conditioned stimulus, it's referred to as the conditioned response.

**unconditioned stimulus (UCS)**
A stimulus that can elicit a response without any learning.

**unconditioned response (UCR)**
An unlearned, inborn reaction to an unconditioned stimulus.

**conditioned stimulus (CS)**
A stimulus that comes to elicit responses as a result of being paired with an unconditioned stimulus.

**conditioned response (CR)**
A response that is similar or identical to the unconditioned response that comes to be elicited by a conditioned stimulus.

To summarize, the meat powder was the unconditioned stimulus (UCS); the metronome was the neutral stimulus that became the conditioned stimulus (CS); salivation was the unconditioned response (UCR); and when the salivation was elicited by the conditioned stimulus, it became the conditioned response (CR). These are difficult terms to keep straight at first; it may help to read through the diagram in figure 6.3 to review the meaning of these terms.

As a further example of classical conditioning, here's another dog story. One of my all-time best friends was a beagle named Lester. Lester had a number of fine qualities that are not always found in humans; he was affectionate, warm, and genuinely loyal. But, in all candor, Lester was also a profound coward. I will never forget the time I took him to the veterinarian for the first of a weekly series of shots. He stood perfectly still with a friendly beagle smile on his face until the needle was stuck into his hindquarter. At that point, he produced a flinching, lurching, terrified yelp. After a few injections, Lester began yelping before the injection when he saw the vet with the needle in her hand.

Now, to be completely honest, I cannot criticize Lester too much for his cowardly behavior, because I also yelp when I see a needle coming my way. Why do you suppose that is so? Why should both of us, a grown man and a grown dog, react so strongly to the sight of a needle? After all, the sight of the needle cannot hurt you; only its stab can do that. The answer, of course, is that we have been classically conditioned to yelp at needles.

Stop for a minute and read back through the example of Lester's fear of needles and see if you can identify the CS, UCS, UCR, and CR.

The sight of the needle is the CS because it originally did not elicit the yelp; the painful stab of the needle is the UCS because it elicited the yelp; the yelp after the stab is the UCR; and, when the CS comes to elicit yelping, the yelp is the CR. I feel a little better knowing that my yelping at needles is simply a CR to a CS, but not a whole lot better; I still hate the things.

## Definition of Classical Conditioning

**classical conditioning**
A form of learning in which a previously neutral stimulus (CS) is paired with an unconditioned stimulus (UCS) to elicit a conditioned response (CR) that is identical to or very similar to the unconditioned response (UCR).

We have finally covered enough terminology to be able to give a precise definition of classical conditioning. **Classical conditioning** is a form of learning in which a previously neutral stimulus (CS) is followed by a stimulus (UCS) that elicits an unlearned response (UCR). As a result of these pairings of the CS and UCS, the CS comes to elicit a response (CR) that, in most cases, is identical or very similar to the UCR.

For classical conditioning to take place, a CS must also serve as a reliable signal for the occurrence of the UCS (Rescorla, 1967, 1988; Woodruff-Pak, 1999). An emergency siren that goes off only in a real emergency (no routine tests or false alarms) will generate more fear responses than sirens routinely tested once a month. Similarly, if the sound of a metronome is always followed by food, salivation will be stronger than if the metronome is followed by food only some of the time.

Note that classical conditioning is considered to be a form of learning not because a new behavior has been acquired but because old behavior can be elicited by a new stimulus; behavior is "changed" only in that sense. It's important to notice also (for reasons that will be clear to you later in the chapter) that the process of classical conditioning *does not depend on the behavior of the individual* being conditioned. The metronome and the meat powder were paired whether the dog salivated or not, and the sight of the needle was followed by the stab whether Lester yelped or not. The critical elements in classical conditioning are that the CS and UCS be closely associated in time and that the CS be a reliable predictor of the UCS. Our behavior simply provides evidence that conditioning has taken place. As we will see later, if the behavior of the individual can determine whether the stimulus is presented or not, the process is not classical conditioning.

By the way, are you curious as to why it's called *classical* conditioning? This term simply refers to the fact that Pavlov performed the *classic* laboratory studies of learning. For the same reason, classical conditioning is also referred to as *Pavlovian* conditioning.

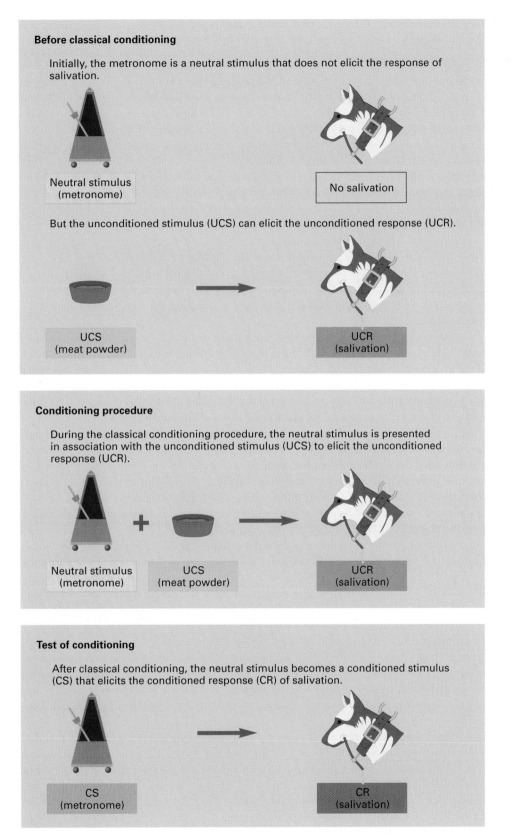

**Before classical conditioning**

Initially, the metronome is a neutral stimulus that does not elicit the response of salivation.

Neutral stimulus
(metronome)

No salivation

But the unconditioned stimulus (UCS) can elicit the unconditioned response (UCR).

UCS
(meat powder)

UCR
(salivation)

**Conditioning procedure**

During the classical conditioning procedure, the neutral stimulus is presented in association with the unconditioned stimulus (UCS) to elicit the unconditioned response (UCR).

Neutral stimulus
(metronome)

UCS
(meat powder)

UCR
(salivation)

**Test of conditioning**

After classical conditioning, the neutral stimulus becomes a conditioned stimulus (CS) that elicits the conditioned response (CR) of salivation.

CS
(metronome)

CR
(salivation)

**FIGURE 6.3**
Diagram of classical conditioning.

This photo shows behaviorist John Watson and his graduate student assistant Rosalie Rayner with Watson's most famous subject—Little Albert. In this early study on the classical conditioning of fear reactions, Watson was able to demonstrate the importance of the environment in the development of human emotions.
Courtesy of Prof. Benjamin Harris, Ph.D., Univ. of New Hampshire.

**counterconditioning**
The process of eliminating a classically conditioned response by pairing the conditioned stimulus (CS) with an unconditioned stimulus (UCS) for a response that is stronger than the conditioned response (CR) and that cannot occur at the same time as the CR.

## Importance of Classical Conditioning

The concept of classical conditioning would not be so widely studied by psychologists if it applied only to salivating dogs. On the contrary, classical conditioning is helpful in understanding a number of important and puzzling issues concerning human behavior.

In 1920, behaviorist John B. Watson and his associate Rosalie Rayner published what is probably the most widely cited example of classical conditioning in psychology. Watson was convinced that many of our fears were acquired through classical conditioning and sought to test this idea by teaching a fear to an 11-month-old child, the now famous "Little Albert." Albert was first allowed to play with a white laboratory rat to find out whether he was afraid of rats: He was not at that time. Then, as he played with the white rat, an iron bar was struck loudly with a hammer behind Albert's head. As might be expected, the noise caused Albert to cry fearfully. After seven such pairings, Albert showed a strong fear response when the rat was placed near him. He had learned to fear the rat through classical conditioning.

Watson's own words provide the best description of the experiment's outcome: "The instant the rat was shown the baby began to cry. Almost instantly he turned sharply to the left, fell over on his left side, raised himself on all fours, and began to crawl away so rapidly that he was caught with difficulty before reaching the edge of the table" (Watson & Rayner, 1920, p. 3).

For understandable reasons, this experiment would not be considered ethical by today's standards. It is particularly distressing that Watson and Rayner chose not to reverse the conditioning of Albert's fear (Watson & Rayner, 1920). In a subsequent study (Jones, 1924), however, Mary Cover Jones and Watson successfully reduced fear of rabbits in another small child by gradually pairing the rabbit (CS) with cookies (UCS). This method of reversing a classically conditioned response by pairing the CS (the rabbit, in this case) with a UCS (cookies, in this case) for a response (eating the cookies) that cannot occur at the same time as the undesirable CR (crying fearfully) is called **counterconditioning.** As in the present example, the UCS for the incompatible response is typically presented first (Mary Cover Jones initially let the child start eating the cookie); then the CS (the rabbit) for the undesirable CR (fearful crying) is introduced only briefly. Over time, the CS for the undesirable response can be presented for longer periods of time, until it no longer elicits the undesirable CR.

Classical conditioning also has proved useful in explaining several questions about our health (Ader & Cohen, 1993). When the body is exposed to threats to health, such as viruses, a number of blood cells that attack the invading germs are produced. The immune system is an amazingly effective defense against disease, but it does not always operate at full capacity. Not only can fatigue and psychological stress adversely affect the functioning of the immune system (Ader, 1981), but it is now clear that immune system responses can be classically conditioned. Robert Ader (Ader & Cohen, 1981) administered a drug (the UCS) to rats that suppressed the activation of their immune system cells (the UCR). The drug was given at the same time that the rats drank saccharin-sweetened water (the CS). After several pairings of the drug and the sweetened water, the rats showed a suppression in immune cell production (the CR) just from drinking the sweetened water.

One particularly important type of cell in the immune system's arsenal is called the *natural killer,* or *NK,* cell. These cells are essential to health because they play a key role in resistance to viruses and tumors. Dennis Dyck and associates at the University of Manitoba (Dyck, Greenberg, & Osachuk, 1986) have shown that suppression of the activity of NK cells can be classically conditioned. The full implications of these studies have not been worked out, but it appears that classical conditioning could play a role in our resistance to disease.

Sexual arousal has also been shown to be influenced by classical conditioning (Zamble, Mitchell, & Findlay, 1986). Male rats were placed in a distinctive cage with a sexually receptive female rat. A screen prevented sexual intercourse, but the presence of the sexually receptive female (UCS) led to sexual arousal (UCR) in the male. The question was, would the pairing of the receptive female with the distinctive cage (CS) lead to classical conditioning of sexual arousal to the cage? This was shown by placing the male rats in the same cage later with another receptive female—but this time without the dividing screen. Compared with male rats who had not had the classical conditioning experience, males for whom the cage was a CS for sexual arousal became aroused and engaged in intercourse considerably more quickly. The fact that sexual arousal can be classically conditioned has been used to explain the origins of unusual *sexual fetishes*. Humans sometimes find that they have become classically conditioned to be sexually aroused by nonsexual objects, such as shoes or leather gloves (Rachman, 1966).

Later in this chapter, we will look at the role of classical conditioning in aversions to specific kinds of food, and in later chapters we will examine its possible role in the origins of our attitudes and the intense fears called *phobias*. Classical conditioning is a simple concept, but it helps us understand some of the complex puzzles of human life.

## Review

Your behavior is not static; it changes from day to day and from year to year as a result of your experiences. This process of behavior change is called learning. Learning is defined as any relatively permanent change in behavior or in the potential for behavior brought about by experience (rather than by biological causes). The prominence of the study of learning in American psychology can be traced in part to studies of a simple but important form of learning launched around the turn of the last century by Russian medical researcher Ivan Pavlov. Pavlov was studying salivary reflexes when he noticed that, after a few days in the study, his dogs began salivating before the food was placed in their mouths. He reasoned that they had learned to salivate at the sight of the attendant bringing the food because this stimulus was always associated with (immediately preceded) the food. Pavlov tested this explanation in a series of studies in which a clicking metronome was repeatedly paired with the presentation of meat powder. As a result, the metronome soon came to elicit the response of salivation. In general, when a neutral stimulus is repeatedly paired with another stimulus that elicits an unlearned response, the previously neutral stimulus will begin to elicit the same or a very similar response. This form of learning is called classical conditioning.

## Check Your Learning

To be sure that you have learned the key points from the preceding section, cover the list of correct answers and try to answer each question. If you give an incorrect answer to any question, return to the page given next to the correct answer to see why your answer was not correct. Remember that these questions cover only some of the important information in this section; it is important that you make up your own questions to check your learning of other facts and concepts.

1. The term *learning* refers to _____.

2. The critical element in classical conditioning is that the UCS and the _____ be closely associated in time.

   a)  CS              c)  UCR

   b)  CR              d)  REM

3. A(n) _____ is a response that is similar or identical to the unconditioned response that comes to be elicited by a conditioned stimulus.

   a)  unconditioned stimulus       c)  conditioned stimulus

   b)  unconditioned response       d)  conditioned response

4.  Ivan Pavlov first studied classical conditioning, but _____ popularized the idea that classical conditioning and other forms of learning were important to the development of our personalities in the United States.

    a)  B. F. Skinner            c)  Albert Bandura
    b)  John B. Watson           d)  Karen Horney

---

## Thinking Critically about Psychology

1.  How might a student develop a classically conditioned fear response to a specific college classroom?

2.  Is our ability to learn through classical conditioning generally an advantage or a disadvantage? How would Little Albert answer that question?

---

**Correct Answers:  1.** any relatively permanent change in behavior brought about through experience (p. 198),  **2. a** (p. 201),  **3. d** (p. 201),  **4. b** (p. 204).

## ● Operant Conditioning: Learning from the Consequences of Your Behavior

If you were to start parking your car in a parking space marked "For the President Only" and your car were towed away every day as a consequence, you would probably stop parking there after a while. Similarly, if you were to move to a new seat in class and suddenly an interesting, attractive person were to start talking to you, you would probably choose to sit in that seat again. To a great extent, the frequency with which people do things increases or decreases depending on the *consequences* of their actions. Learning from the consequences of our behavior is called *operant conditioning*. The term is derived from the word *operate*. When our behavior "operates" on the outside world, it produces consequences for us, and those consequences determine whether we will continue to engage in that behavior. We can define **operant conditioning,** then, as the form of learning in which the consequences of behavior lead to changes in the probability of its occurrence (Dragoi & Staddon, 1999).

Operant conditioning was first described by American psychologist Edward Thorndike (1911). Thorndike was interested in the question of animal intelligence, which he investigated using an apparatus he called a "puzzle box." A hungry cat was placed inside the box, food was placed outside, and the cat's efforts to escape were observed. With each trial, the cat became more efficient at opening the door of the box. Based on these observations, Thorndike formulated the "law of effect," which states that the consequences of a response determine whether the response will be performed in the future. Thorndike's law of effect formed the basis for subsequent study of what is now referred to as *operant conditioning* in contemporary psychology. In the sections that follow, we will examine three ways in which desirable and undesirable consequences influence our behavior: positive reinforcement, negative reinforcement, and punishment.

### Positive Reinforcement

In *positive reinforcement,* the consequences of a behavior are *positive,* so the behavior is engaged in *more frequently.* Simply stated, we say that **positive reinforcement** has occurred whenever a consequence of behavior leads to an increase in the probability of its occurrence.

In the early 1960s, a team of preschool teachers conducted a classic study in which they helped a young girl overcome her shyness in what has become a widely cited example of the principle of positive reinforcement (Allen, Hart, Buell, Harris, & Wolf, 1964). The teachers were worried because the girl spent little time playing with the other children and too much time with her adult teachers. They decided to encourage peer play through positive reinforcement. They knew that she enjoyed receiving praise from the teachers, so they decided to praise her *only* when she was playing with another child. The

---

**operant conditioning**
(op′e-rant)  Learning in which the consequences of behavior lead to changes in the probability of its occurrence.

**positive reinforcement**
(re″in-fors′ment)  Any consequence of behavior that leads to an increase in the probability of its occurrence.

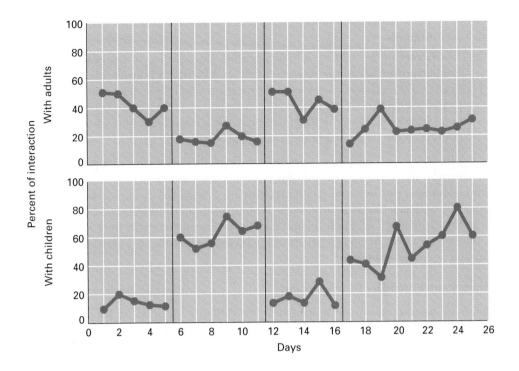

**FIGURE 6.4**
Increasing the amount of time that a
child spends playing with other children
through the use of positive
reinforcement.
**Source:** Data from K. Eileen Allen, et al., "Effects of
Social Reinforcement Isolate Behavior of a Nursery
School Child" in *Child Development,* 35:511–518, 1964.
Copyright © 1964 The Society for Research in Child
Development.

results of this use of positive reinforcement are shown in figure 6.4. To be able to evaluate the results of their positive reinforcement program, the teachers first counted the frequency with which the little girl interacted with other children and with adults before anything was done to help her. Then they started to positively reinforce (praise) her for playing with other children, but otherwise they paid very little attention to her (so that she would get positive reinforcement from her teachers only for playing with peers). As can be seen in the second segment of figure 6.4, the little girl's frequency of playing with peers increased markedly when the teachers reinforced her. To be sure that the positive reinforcement and not some other factor was responsible for the changes, the teachers stopped reinforcing her for playing with peers in the third segment (the *reversal* phase) of figure 6.4 and then reinforced her again during the fourth phase. As can be seen, the frequency of peer play dropped when the positive reinforcement was discontinued but increased again when it was resumed in the fourth phase. Thus, the teachers were able to intentionally teach this child a more adaptive pattern of play by using positive reinforcement.

Many other applications have been made of this principle, ranging from teaching hospitalized schizophrenic adults more normal patterns of behavior to teaching employees to reduce the amount of damage sustained when sorting boxes for airfreight delivery. In each case, the behavior that becomes more frequent is termed the *operant response,* and the positive consequence of that response is called the *positive reinforcer.*

Two important issues in the use of positive reinforcement should be noted:

1. *Timing.* The positive reinforcer must be given within a short amount of time following the response, or learning will progress very slowly, if at all. There are some ways to get around this issue of timing (such as immediately telling an employee that she will get a bonus for making an important sale, even though the bonus will not come until the end of the month), but in general the greater the delay between the response and the reinforcer, the slower the

Secondary reinforcers, such as praise, are learned from primary reinforcers, such as gentle physical contact.

learning. This phenomenon has been referred to as the principle of **delay of reinforcement.**

2. *Consistency in the delivery of reinforcement.* For learning to take place, the individual providing positive reinforcement must consistently give it after every (or nearly every) response. After some learning has taken place, it's not always necessary, or even desirable, to reinforce every response (as we will see later in the section "Schedules of Positive Reinforcement"), but consistency of reinforcement is essential in the beginning of the learning process.

I do not want to give the impression through this discussion that positive reinforcement is something that occurs only when it's intentionally arranged. The natural consequences of our behavior can be reinforcing as well. For example, we learn that some ways of interacting with our friends or supervisors just naturally lead to happier relationships, and that is positively reinforcing. We are *always* affected by the consequences of our behavior and, hence, are always in the process of learning to adjust to our world through operant conditioning.

### Primary and Secondary Reinforcement

Where do positive reinforcers come from? Are they inborn, or do we have to acquire them through learning? Actually, some are inborn and some are learned. There are two types of positive reinforcement, primary and secondary reinforcement. **Primary reinforcers** are ones that are innately reinforcing and do not have to be acquired through learning. Food, water, warmth, novel stimulation, physical activity, and sexual gratification are all examples of primary reinforcers.

**Secondary reinforcers** (which play an important part in operant conditioning) are learned through classical conditioning. Remember that classical conditioning involves the association of two stimuli: A neutral stimulus can be turned into a secondary reinforcer by pairing it repeatedly with a primary reinforcer. Consider an example from dog training. In teaching dogs to perform complex acts, such as those required of Seeing Eye dogs, primary reinforcers such as pieces of food are used extensively. It's much more convenient, however, to reinforce the dog for good behavior simply by saying, "Good dog!" than by lugging around a pocketful of dog biscuits. Unfortunately, dogs do not know what you are saying when you praise them and would not care much if they did—that is, not until you *teach* them to care. So, how would you go about making praise into a secondary reinforcer? Actually, it's quite simple. You would only need to say, "Good dog," to the dog every time you give the dog a biscuit. After enough pairings of these two

**delay of reinforcement**
The passage of time between the response and the positive reinforcement that leads to reduced efficiency of learning.

**primary reinforcers**
Innate positive reinforcers that do not have to be acquired through learning.

**secondary reinforcers**
Learned positive reinforcers.

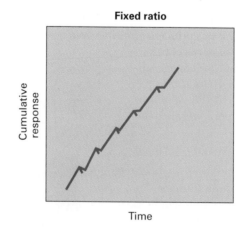

**FIGURE 6.5**
Pattern of behavior typically produced by a fixed ratio schedule of reinforcement. The hash marks show the delivery of reinforcement. In figures 6.5 to 6.8, steeper slopes indicate higher rates of responding.

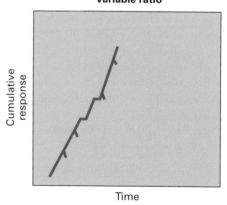

**FIGURE 6.6**
Pattern of behavior typically produced by a variable ratio schedule of reinforcement.

stimuli, the praise will become a secondary reinforcer and will be effective in reinforcing the dog's behavior.

Dogs are not the only creatures that learn secondary reinforcers, however. People do it, too. How many of the things that motivate us—such as school grades, prize ribbons, money, applause—were acquired through pairing with primary reinforcers? Learning undoubtedly plays a key role in turning these things into powerful reinforcers for some people.

### Schedules of Positive Reinforcement

Up to this point, we have talked about positive reinforcement as if every response were always followed by a reinforcer, a situation known as *continuous reinforcement.* The world is not constructed in such a regular and simple way, however. So what happens when reinforcement follows behavior on some other schedule? In addition to continuous reinforcement, psychologists have described four types of schedules of reinforcement and have shown us the effects of each on behavior (Ferster & Skinner, 1957):

1. *Fixed ratio.* On a **fixed ratio schedule** of reinforcement, the reinforcer is given only after a specified number of responses. If sewing machine operators were given a pay slip (to be exchanged for money later) for every six dresses that were sewn, the schedule of reinforcement would be called a fixed ratio schedule. This schedule produces a fairly high rate of response because many responses need to be made to get the reinforcer, but there is typically a pause after each reinforcer is obtained (see fig. 6.5).

2. *Variable ratio.* On a **variable ratio schedule** of reinforcement, the reinforcer is obtained only after a varying number of responses have been made (see fig. 6.6). These schedules produce very high rates of responding, and the learning is rather permanent. For example, why do even successful sales representatives hustle so? They know from experience that, on the average, they will make a sale, for example, after every sixth presentation. But the fact that they cannot predict which presentation will make the sale—this one? the next one?—keeps them hopping. Another good example of reinforcement on a variable ratio is gambling. Slot machine players are reinforced for putting money into the machine and pulling the lever just often enough in an unpredictable fashion to addict many individuals to gambling.

3. *Fixed interval.* In other cases, the schedule of reinforcement is not based on the *number* of responses but on the passage of *time.* The term **fixed interval schedule** is used when the first response that occurs after a predetermined period of time is reinforced. This produces a pattern of behavior in which very few responses are made until the fixed interval of time approaches and then the rate of responding increases rapidly (see fig. 6.7). A fellow psychology professor

Gold medals are powerful secondary reinforcers.

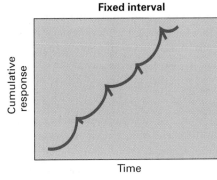

**FIGURE 6.7**
Pattern of behavior typically produced by a fixed interval schedule of reinforcement.

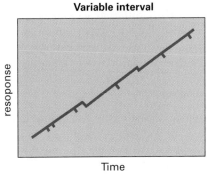

**FIGURE 6.8**
Pattern of behavior typically produced by a variable interval pattern of reinforcement.

**fixed ratio schedule**
A reinforcement schedule in which the reinforcer is given only after a specified number of responses.

**variable ratio schedule**
A reinforcement schedule in which the reinforcer is given after a varying number of responses have been made.

**fixed interval schedule**
A reinforcement schedule in which the reinforcer is given following the first response occurring after a predetermined period of time.

Casino operators may not claim to use variable ratio schedules of reinforcement, but they know that an occasional jackpot will keep players at the slot machines.

**variable interval schedule**
A reinforcement schedule in which the reinforcer is given following the first response occurring after a variable amount of time.

provided this great example of a fixed interval schedule: While in graduate school, he worked as a guard at night in a steel mill. He was paid for walking around the mill each hour and punching in at the time clock each time as he passed it on his rounds. He confessed that this schedule of reinforcement led to 40 minutes of sitting around each hour, followed by a brisk 20-minute walk around the mill to the time clock! Members of Congress also are on a fixed interval schedule for the response of visiting with the voters in their districts. Making a visit back home to talk to the people is of little value to the politicians until the fixed 2-year interval between elections starts to elapse. Then visits back home are reinforced by votes, so the rate of visits rises dramatically.

1. *Variable interval.* Finally, there is a schedule of reinforcement in which the first response made after a variable amount of time is reinforced. Like the variable ratio schedule, this **variable interval schedule** produces high rates of steady response (see fig. 6.8), and although it's not a good schedule for initial learning, it produces highly stable performance when the response has already been partially learned through continuous reinforcement. Where I grew up in Florida, there were lots of people sitting on docks and bridges with fishing poles in their hands because of variable reinforcement. You can't tell when fish are going to bite—they're unpredictable. But, for some people, catching a fish every now and then is strong enough variable interval reinforcement to keep their lines in the water as much as they can.

Thus, different schedules of positive reinforcement result in distinct patterns of behavior. It is very important for anyone responsible for managing another person's behavior, such as teachers, parents, or supervisors, to make informed choices regarding the type of reinforcement schedule to be used.

### Shaping

In many situations, the response that we want to reinforce never occurs. For example, let's say you want to positively reinforce your child for cleaning her or his room. You might have to wait a long time for that behavior to occur! If left to their own devices, most children would spend little if any time cleaning their rooms. What we need to do in this case is to reinforce responses that are progressively more similar to the response that you finally want to reinforce (the "target response"). In doing so, you will gradually increase the probability of the target response and can then rein-force it when it occurs. This is called **shaping,** or the *method of successive approximations,* because we "shape" the target response out of behaviors that successively approximate it.

Before considering the practical applications of the concept of shaping, let's go back to the animal learning laboratory where so many of the principles of learning that are useful to humans were first carefully researched. Suppose you wanted to teach a rat to press a lever in the special kind of learning apparatus called the **Skinner box,** named after its creator, B. F. Skinner of Harvard University (see fig. 6.9). If you continue to take psychology courses, you may be given this assignment in a lab course: "Here's a rat and here's a Skinner box; do not come back until you have taught him to press the lever!" What do you do? If you have not read the section on shaping in your textbook, you might program the Skinner box to drop a little pellet of rat food into the food tray every time the lever is pressed and then wait—and wait and wait—for the rat to press the bar. This strategy might work in time—the rat *might* accidentally press the lever enough times to get reinforced by the food pellets enough to make this a frequent response—but I wouldn't bet on it. Rats generally do not go around pressing levers. When placed in a Skinner box, they groom themselves, bite the Plexiglas walls, urinate, defecate, and sniff a lot, but they do not press levers. How, then, do you teach the uncooperative rodent to press the lever?

You use shaping. First, whenever the rat (we'll call him "B. F." in honor of B. F. Skinner) gets up and *moves toward the lever,* give him a food pellet. After you do that a few times, the rat ought to be moving toward the lever quite a bit. Then you can wait until B. F. *touches* the lever in some way to reinforce him. Do that a few times and then wait until he *touches it with a downward pushing movement* (if at any time you have failed to reinforce him enough, you can go back a step). Then, after he is reliably touching the bar in a downward motion, B. F. should have quite a high probability of *pushing it down enough* to activate the automatic feeder, which will reinforce him for the complete response of lever pressing.

The principle of shaping has great importance outside of the rat lab. For example, most beginning skiers cannot be reinforced for making perfect post turns because they just are not able to do them yet. But they can be reinforced for successive

Reinforcement of successive approximations by a violin teacher who understands shaping will help this girl become a better violinist.

**shaping**
A strategy of positively reinforcing behaviors that are successively more similar to desired behaviors.

**Skinner box**
A cage for animals, equipped with a response lever and a food tray dispenser, used in research on operant conditioning.

**FIGURE 6.9**

In this Skinner box designed for rats, the response under study is lever pressing. Food pellets, which serve as reinforcers, are delivered into the food cup on the left. The speaker and light permit manipulations of visual and auditory stimuli, and the electric grid gives the experimenter control over negative consequences (mild shock) in the box.

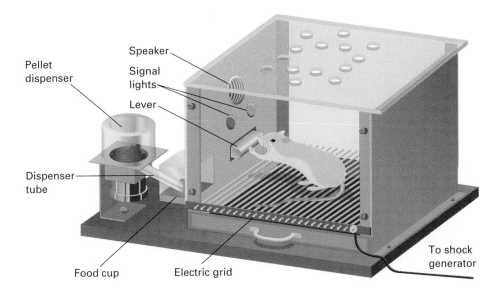

approximations to good turns and thereby shaped into good skiing. In programs for children with developmental handicaps, shaping is used to teach basic skills such as brushing teeth, performing useful jobs, and using public transportation. And how about shaping 3-year-olds to clean their rooms? At first you have to reinforce them for putting one toy away—even though the rest of the room is littered with junk. After doing that a couple of times, reinforce them for putting several toys away, and then for an "approximately" clean room, and so on until the target response occurs.

## Negative Reinforcement

Reinforcers are not always positive events; sometimes the reinforcing consequence is the *removal or avoidance of a negative event.* Suppose the fellow in the apartment next door plays his stereo so loud that it has kept you awake every night this week. If you assertively ask him to turn it down and the loud music stops, that consequence will reinforce your assertive behavior. Operant learning based on negative reinforcement plays an important, but often unnoticed, role in influencing our behavior.

The concept of negative reinforcement is one that students frequently find confusing for two reasons. First, to many students, the name implies that a negative or undesirable behavior—such as a bad habit—is being reinforced. That actually does happen a lot, but the behavior that is negatively reinforced may be either desirable or undesirable. Second, even more students find the term *negative reinforcement* confusing because it sounds like a new term for punishment, which it is not. When we look at the concept of punishment later in this chapter, you will see that it is a quite different phenomenon.

What the term **negative reinforcement** *does* mean is this: A behavior is reinforced (and, therefore, becomes more likely to occur) because something negative (or unpleasant or aversive) *is removed* by the behavior or does not happen at all because of the behavior. In the previous example, the loud music was the negative thing that your assertive behavior got rid of. Your asking him to turn down the volume was reinforced through negative reinforcement (stopping the loud music), and you probably would be more likely to be assertive in the future as a result.

Two types of conditioning are based on negative reinforcement:

1. **Escape Conditioning**

   In **escape conditioning,** the behavior causes the negative event to *stop.* For example, if a young boy has been confined to his room for an hour, that is probably a pretty negative situation to him. If he starts to cry softly and murmur pitifully that no one loves him, and if this causes his parent to relent in a few minutes and let him out of his room, then negative reinforcement has occurred. Which behavior has been strengthened? Probably he will be much more likely to act pitifully the next time he is sent to his room because it made something negative—the confinement—stop. Escape conditioning, therefore, is a form of negative reinforcement because something negative is removed. It's called escape conditioning because the individual *escapes* from something negative (in the sense of causing it to stop).

2. **Avoidance Conditioning**

   In the other form of negative reinforcement, called **avoidance conditioning,** the behavior has the consequence of causing something negative *not to happen* when it otherwise would have happened. Suppose you are terrified of pit bulldogs, but the route that you walk to campus takes you past a yard where a particularly vicious pit bull is penned up. If you find a new route to school that does not take you past a single pit bull, you will probably continue to take this route because it causes the

**negative reinforcement**
Reinforcement that comes about when the removal or avoidance of a negative event is the consequence of behavior.

**escape conditioning**
Operant conditioning in which the behavior is reinforced because it causes a negative event to cease (a form of negative reinforcement).

**avoidance conditioning**
Operant conditioning in which the behavior is reinforced because it prevents something negative from happening (a form of negative reinforcement).

negative event of passing the pit bull not to occur. Even if it does make you feel a bit like a coward, finding a new route is a highly reinforcing consequence. This is an example of avoidance conditioning, because the behavior of taking a new route is reinforced by avoiding something negative (the pit bull).

Negative reinforcement is a very powerful method of reinforcement, so we learn patterns of behavior quickly and easily from it. Unfortunately, what we learn are often immature ways of dealing with unpleasant situations rather than mature ways of facing them directly. The child in our first example would have been better off taking his punishment and learning how not to get into trouble next time, and the college student would have been better off getting over the fear of the penned pit bull. It's often too easy to learn a quick and easy, though inappropriate, solution through negative reinforcement.

Incidentally, when the parent let the child who was acting pitifully out of his room, the parent was probably reinforced for that lapse in discipline, too. Through what principle of operant conditioning was the parent reinforced? Because the act of letting the child out of his room caused the child's unpleasant whining to stop, the parent was reinforced through escape conditioning. Negative reinforcement of inappropriate behavior is a frequent occurrence that we need to avoid.

## Punishment

Sometimes the consequence of behavior is negative, and as a result, the frequency of that behavior will decrease. In other words, the behavior has been *punished*. For example, if you buy a new set of pots and pans with metal handles and pick up a hot pan without a pot holder, a negative consequence will surely occur. And you will probably not try to pick up your new pans in that way again. **Punishment** is a negative consequence that leads to a reduction in the frequency of the behavior that produced it (Church, 1969; Tarpy & Mayer, 1978). When appropriately used, punishment can be an ethical and valuable tool for discouraging inappropriate behavior. In our society, however, *physical* punishment is still used with children by parents, teachers, and others in authority. In addition to the obvious ethical issues in using physical punishment, there are serious dangers inherent in the use of any form of punishment that must be weighed against its potential benefits.

**punishment**
A negative consequence of a behavior, which leads to a decrease in the frequency of the behavior that produces it.

### Dangers of Punishment

The dangers inherent in punishment are as follows:

1. The use of punishment is often *reinforcing to the punisher.* For example, if a parent spanks a child who has been whining and the spanking stops the child from whining, the parent will be reinforced for spanking through negative reinforcement. This, unfortunately, may mean that the frequency of spankings, and perhaps their intensity, will increase, thereby increasing not only the amount of physical pain the child endures but also the dangers of child abuse.

2. Punishment often has a *generalized inhibiting effect* on the individual. Repeatedly spanking a child for "talking back" to you may lead the child to quit talking to you altogether. Similarly, criticizing your bridge partner for mistakes may lead him or her to give up playing the game altogether, or at least to stop playing with you.

3. We commonly react to physical punishment by *learning to dislike* the person who inflicts the pain, and perhaps by *reacting aggressively* toward that person. Sometimes an individual takes out his or her resentment on someone else if it's not possible to react directly against the person who gave the pain. Thus,

punishment may solve one problem but only lead to a worse problem—namely, aggression.

4. What we think is punishment is not always effective in punishing the behavior. In particular, most teachers and parents (and many supervisors, roommates, etc.) think that *criticism* will punish the behavior at which it's aimed. However, in many settings, especially homes and classrooms filled with young children, it has been demonstrated that criticism is often a *positive reinforcer* that increases the rate of whatever behavior the criticism follows. This has been called the **criticism trap** (Madsen, Becker, & Thomas, 1968). For example, some teachers and parents see a behavior they do not like and criticize to get rid of it. But children are sometimes reinforced by the attention they receive when criticized. In this way, the criticism reinforces rather than punishes the behavior, and the criticized behavior increases in frequency. The adult then uses more criticism in an effort to quell this misbehavior. This reinforces the behavior even more and increases its rate in an upwardly spiraling course.

5. Even when punishment is effective in suppressing an inappropriate behavior, it does not teach the individual how to act more appropriately instead. Punishment used by itself may be self-defeating; it may suppress one inappropriate behavior only to be replaced by another one. It's not until appropriate behaviors are taught to the individual to replace the inappropriate ones that any progress can be made.

**criticism trap**
An increase in the frequency of a negative behavior that often follows the use of criticism, reinforcing the behavior it is intended to punish.

## Guidelines for the Use of Punishment

The preceding list is an indictment of punishment as a method of changing behavior in childrearing, industry, education, or any other setting. It should not be considered to be a total condemnation of punishment, however. In some situations, punishment is a necessary method of changing behavior. For example, in teaching a young child not to run out into a busy street, punishment may be the only method that makes sense. In these instances, however, every effort should be made to minimize the negative side effects of punishment by following some guidelines for its use.

1. Do not use *physical* punishment. Taking away TV time from a 10-year-old or placing a 4-year-old in a chair in the corner for 3 minutes is more effective than spankings, and certainly more humane. Indeed, physical punishment usually backfires and causes children to behave worse rather than better (O'Leary, 1995).

2. Make sure that you positively reinforce appropriate behavior to take the place of the inappropriate behavior you are trying to eliminate. Punishment will not be effective in the long run unless you are also reinforcing appropriate behavior.

3. Make it clear to the individual what behavior you are punishing and remove all threat of punishment as soon as that behavior stops. In other words, it might be okay to punish a certain behavior, but it does more harm than good to become generally angry at the other person for doing something inappropriate. *Do not punish people; punish specific behaviors.* And stop punishing when the inappropriate behavior ceases.

4. Do not mix punishment with rewards for the *same* behavior. For example, do not punish a child for fighting and then apologetically hug and kiss the child you have just punished. Mixtures of this sort are confusing and lead to inefficient learning.

5. Once you have begun to punish, do not back down. In other words, do not reinforce begging, pleading, or other inappropriate behavior by letting the individual out of the punishment. It both nullifies the punishment and reinforces the begging and pleading through negative reinforcement.

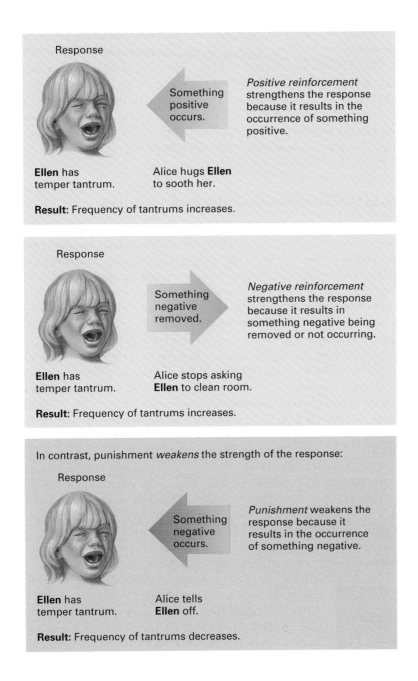

Response

Something positive occurs.

*Positive reinforcement* strengthens the response because it results in the occurrence of something positive.

**Ellen** has temper tantrum.

Alice hugs **Ellen** to sooth her.

**Result:** Frequency of tantrums increases.

Response

Something negative removed.

*Negative reinforcement* strengthens the response because it results in something negative being removed or not occurring.

**Ellen** has temper tantrum.

Alice stops asking **Ellen** to clean room.

**Result:** Frequency of tantrums increases.

In contrast, punishment *weakens* the strength of the response:

Response

Something negative occurs.

*Punishment* weakens the response because it results in the occurrence of something negative.

**Ellen** has temper tantrum.

Alice tells **Ellen** off.

**Result:** Frequency of tantrums decreases.

Comparison of the types of operant conditioning: positive reinforcement, negative reinforcement, and punishment. The two types of reinforcement, positive and negative, are called *reinforcement* because the response is strengthened by the consequence.

Notice that the terms *positive* and *negative reinforcement* and *punishment* have nothing to do with the nature of the response that is strengthened or weakened. This example uses a very "negative" response; however, a "positive" response could have been used to illustrate the same results in each case.

## Contrasting Classical and Operant Conditioning

We have just talked about a number of forms of "conditioning." This blitz of new concepts can be confusing. However, if you can understand the distinction between classical and operant conditioning, the rest will be easy.

Classical and operant conditioning differ from each other in three primary ways:

1.  Classical conditioning involves an association between two stimuli, such as a tone and food. In contrast, operant conditioning involves an association between a response and the resulting consequence, such as studying hard and getting an A.

2.  Classical conditioning usually involves reflexive, involuntary behaviors, which are controlled by the spinal cord or autonomic nervous system. These include fear responses, salivation, and other involuntary behaviors. Operant conditioning, on the other hand, usually involves more complicated voluntary behaviors, which are mediated by the somatic nervous system.

3. The most important difference, however, concerns the way in which the stimulus that makes conditioning "happen" is presented (the unconditioned stimulus, or UCS, in classical conditioning and the reinforcing stimulus in operant conditioning). In classical conditioning, the UCS is paired with the conditioned stimulus (CS) independent of the individual's behavior. The individual does not have to do anything for either the CS or UCS to be presented. In operant conditioning, however, the reinforcing consequence occurs *only if* the response being conditioned has just been emitted; that is, the reinforcing consequence is contingent on the occurrence of the response.

## Stimulus Discrimination and Generalization

Most responses do not have an equal probability of occurring in any situation. They are more likely to occur in some circumstances than in others. For example, schoolchildren are more likely to behave well when the teacher is in the room than when the teacher is not. Similarly, you are more likely to clean up your apartment when your new girlfriend or boyfriend says, "I'll be over after class," than when no one is coming. Most responses are more likely to occur in the presence of some stimuli than in the presence of others. This phenomenon is called **stimulus discrimination,** meaning that we discriminate between appropriate and inappropriate occasions for a response.

**stimulus discrimination**
The tendency for responses to occur more often in the presence of one stimulus than others.

Let's go back to the rat lab and see one way in which stimulus discrimination might be learned. The last time you were in the lab, you taught your rat, B. F., to press the lever through shaping and positive reinforcement for lever pressing. Let's suppose that you want him to press the bar only in the presence of a specific stimulus, such as a light; that is, you want B. F. to learn a stimulus discrimination. We start by turning on a light over the lever, letting B. F. press the lever and receive the reinforcer several times. Then we turn off the light for a little while, and we do *not* reinforce lever presses when the light is out. Then we turn the light back on and reinforce responses, turn it off and do not reinforce responses, and so on many times. The stimulus in which the response is reinforced is called S$^d$ (short for *discriminative stimulus*), and the stimulus in which the response is never reinforced is called S$^{delta}$. Soon, if we follow the teaching program just outlined, B. F. will begin pressing the lever almost every time the light comes on, and almost never press it when the light is off. He will learn a stimulus discrimination.

Humans have to learn stimulus discriminations, too—lots of them. We have to learn to say "Car" only to the stimulus of a car and not to a toy wagon; we have to learn to say "Dog" to the stimulus of the printed letters *D-O-G* and not to other letters; and so on. Many of the stimulus discriminations that we learn are much more subtle than that, however. For example, we must learn to introduce ourselves to others at a party when they are showing interest in us (rather than no interest). We have to learn to express sympathy when a sad thing has been told to us. Responses made during the presence of an S$^d$ for that behavior will lead to favorable consequences, whereas the same behavior made during S$^{delta}$ will often lead to unfavorable consequences. Introducing yourself to a person showing interest in you will lead to a pleasant conversation; introducing yourself to a person showing no interest can make you both feel extremely uncomfortable.

Stimulus discrimination does not occur only in operant conditioning, however. Let's say that your lab instructor wants you to use classical conditioning to teach B. F. to stop moving and to crouch in the presence of a slow-ringing bell but not a fast-ringing bell. First you need to know that rats explore freely in dim light but crouch defensively in bright light. You would start classical conditioning in the normal way, by pairing the slow ring with the

Stopping for a stop sign is one stimulus discrimination drivers must learn.

UCS (bright light) for the response of crouching. After several pairings, B. F. should be crouching whenever the slow-ringing bell is sounded. If we now begin presenting the fast ring sometimes, B. F. will respond to that with the crouch response, too. But, if we continue to present both the slow and fast rings, *but pair the bright light only with the slow ring,* B. F. will respond with the fear response only to the slow ring and not the fast one; he will have learned a stimulus discrimination through classical conditioning.

The opposite of stimulus discrimination is **stimulus generalization.** This term indicates that people (as well as rats and other creatures) do not always discriminate between stimuli that are similar to one another. Stated another way, the more similar two stimuli are, the more likely the individual is to respond to them as if they were the same stimulus. A person who is afraid of Siamese cats is usually also afraid of tabby and alley cats.

As with everything else, let's go back to the lab to demonstrate stimulus generalization based on similarity in the color of the stimulus. This time, however, we will use a pigeon as our laboratory animal instead of a rat, because rats are color blind and pigeons are not. For example, we can reinforce the pigeon only for responding in the presence of a *yellow-green* light whose wavelength is 550 nanometers (a unit used to measure the wavelength of light). In a while, the pigeon will emit lever presses only when the $S^d$ of the light is present. In this part of our study of the pigeon's learning, however, the fact that it presses the lever only in the presence of the light is important to us only because it gives us a tool for carefully studying stimulus generalization. If we begin changing the wavelength of the light stimulus, we will be able to see that the more we change the wavelength, the less likely the pigeon will be to respond to it. If we carefully change the wavelength many times in small gradations, we will be able to make a graph that shows us this fact about stimulus generalization. The results of such a study appear in figure 6.10. Notice that, the more similar stimuli are, the more likely the pigeon is to respond to them as if they were the same; the less similar they are, the less likely they are to be responded to as the same.

Before we leave this concept, let's look at one more example of stimulus generalization—in this case, generalization involving classical conditioning. Recall the famous experiment with Little Albert, in which Albert was classically conditioned to fear a white laboratory rat by pairing a loud noise with the rat. In addition, the fear generalized to other similar objects. Five days later, Albert reacted fearfully to a white rabbit, a white dog, and a white coat. He also showed mildly fearful reactions to balls of cotton and a Santa Claus mask.

**stimulus generalization**
The tendency for similar stimuli to elicit the same response.

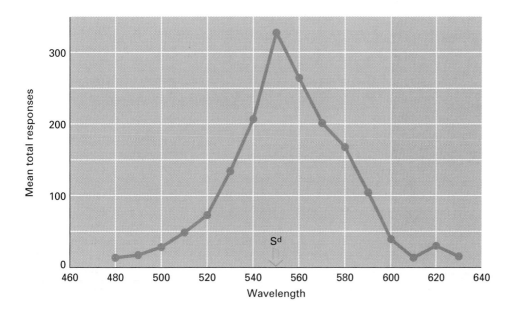

**FIGURE 6.10**
Stimulus generalization means that the more similar stimuli are, the more likely they will be responded to as if they were the same. In this case, a pigeon has been reinforced for pecking when a light measuring 550 nanometers (was measure of wavelength) was present. When lights of other wavelengths were later presented in random order, the pigeon pecked most frequently to lights similar to the $S^d$ (discriminative stimulus of 550 nanometers).

## Review

We learn from the consequences of our behavior. If our behavior leads to a positive consequence, we are more likely to engage in that behavior again, with the specific pattern of behavior depending in part on the schedule with which reinforcement is delivered. The events that serve as positive reinforcers are both inborn (primary reinforcers) and learned (secondary reinforcers). Positive reinforcement can even increase the probability of behaviors that initially never occur by reinforcing successive approximations to that behavior (shaping).

Behavior can be reinforced not only when the consequence is positive but also when the behavior removes or avoids a negative consequence (negative reinforcement). Actually, two slightly different forms of learning are based on negative reinforcement: (a) escape conditioning, in which the behavior removes a negative event, and (b) avoidance conditioning, in which behavior causes the negative event not to occur. Punishment, which is different from negative reinforcement, is a negative consequence of behavior that reduces the probability of its future occurrence.

Behavior that is reinforced only in the presence of a specific stimulus tends to occur only in the presence of that stimulus (stimulus discrimination). On the other hand, there is a strong tendency to respond to similar stimuli as if they were the same (stimulus generalization). The phenomena of stimulus generalization and discrimination also occur in classical conditioning.

## Check Your Learning

To be sure that you have learned the key points from the preceding section, cover the list of correct answers and try to answer each question. If you give an incorrect answer to any question, return to the page given next to the correct answer to see why your answer was not correct.

1. Learning from the consequences of our behavior is called _____.

   a)   operant conditioning        c)   environmental learning

   b)   classical conditioning       d)   cognitive learning

2. Slot machine players are on a _____ of reinforcement.

   a)   variable interval schedule   c)   fixed ratio schedule

   b)   variable ratio schedule      d)   fixed interval schedule

3. Negative reinforcement is another term for punishment.

   a)   True                         b)   False

4. The more similar two stimuli are, the more likely the individual is to respond to them as if they were the same stimulus. This is termed _____.

   a)   stimulus discrimination      c)   stimulus generalization

   b)   generalized responding        d)   stimulus conditioning

## Thinking Critically about Psychology

1. Do your friends ever reinforce you for behaving in ways that are not good for you? In what ways?

2. What kinds of behaviors does our culture encourage? Is this done more through positive reinforcement, negative reinforcement, or punishment?

Correct Answers: 1. a (p. 206), 2. b (p. 209), 3. b (p. 212), 4. c (p. 217).

## ● Extinction: Learning When to Quit

The process of learning is essential to human life. Through it we learn to cope with the demands of the environment. But the world is apt to change at any time, so people have to change, too. If we were able to learn only once and never change, we would not be able to survive changes in the environment. For example, if we were Stone Age people who learned to get oranges from the tops of orange trees by shaking the trees, that learned behavior would be very useful—that is, it would be positively reinforced. But the learned behavior of shaking orange trees would no longer be useful after all the oranges had been shaken out of the tree. At that point, we would need to quit shaking orange trees! If changes in the environment did not lead to changes in our learned behavior, we would be in big trouble.

If a learned response stops occurring because the aspect of the environment that originally caused the learning changes, **extinction** has occurred. The process of extinction is similar in many respects for both classical and operant conditioning.

### Removing the Source of Learning

Extinction occurs because the original source of the learning has been removed. In classical conditioning, learning takes place because two stimuli are repeatedly paired together. If Pavlov's dog were to stop receiving meat powder with the sound of the metronome, the dog would eventually stop salivating to the metronome. Or if you are hurt a couple of times when you are in the dentist's chair, the dentist's chair will come to elicit the response of fear (from the pairing of pain with the previously neutral chair). Let's suppose, however, that the clumsy dentist sells his practice to a new, truly painless dentist and you no longer get hurt in that chair. In this case, the cause of learning to fear the dentist's chair is removed. Eventually (classically conditioned fears are difficult to extinguish), the fact that the conditioned stimulus is presented alone (the dentist's chair is never again paired with pain) will lead to the extinction of the response of fear to the dentist's chair. In essence, you will have learned that the chair no longer predicts pain. Thus, using the terminology of classical conditioning, a CR will be extinguished if the CS for that response is presented repeatedly but the UCS for that stimulus is no longer paired with it.

In the case of operant conditioning, extinction results from a change in the consequences of behavior. If a response is no longer reinforced, then that response will eventually decline in frequency. If Skinner's rat were no longer given food pellets for bar presses, the bar pressing would eventually stop. Similarly, when there are no longer any oranges in the tree, the response of shaking it will no longer be reinforced and shaking will eventually stop.

There is one notable difference between extinction in classical and in operant conditioning. During the early stages of the operant extinction process, "frustration" often occurs. This may lead to a brief, rapid burst of responding before the response finally begins to disappear. When you first discover that no more oranges fall out of the tree, you might shake the tree angrily for a while.

The schedule of reinforcement and the type of reinforcement greatly influence the speed with which the extinction of operant conditioning takes place. This phenomenon is known as the **partial reinforcement effect.** Responses that have been continuously reinforced are extinguished more quickly than responses that have been reinforced on variable ratio or variable interval schedules. Perhaps this is so because it's easier to see that the reinforcement is not going to come again if it used to come after every response. It may not be a bad thing that parents, employers, teachers, and others are often too busy to reinforce every good response; a variable pattern of reinforcement makes the good response more resistant to extinction.

The most difficult responses of all to extinguish, however, are responses learned through avoidance learning. Extinction of an avoidance response should result when the negative event ceases to occur. However, if you continue to perform avoidance

**extinction**
(eks-ting′shun) The process of unlearning a learned response because of the removal of the original source of learning.

**partial reinforcement effect**
The phenomenon that responses that have been reinforced on variable ratio or variable interval schedules are more difficult to extinguish than responses that have been continuously reinforced.

**response prevention**
The prevention of avoidance responses to ensure that the individual sees that the negative consequence will not occur to speed up the extinction of avoidance responses.

**spontaneous recovery**
A temporary increase in the strength of a conditioned response, which is likely to occur during extinction after the passage of time.

**disinhibition**
(dis″in-hi-bish′un) A temporary increase in the strength of an extinguished response caused by an unrelated stimulus event.

responses, you will never see that the situation has changed. For example, if you continue to avoid the pit bull by taking the longer route to school, you will never learn that the owner and his dog have moved to another neighborhood.

Avoidance responses can be extinguished rapidly, however, using a technique called **response prevention.** This technique does exactly what its name implies. Avoidance responses are simply *prevented* to be sure that the individual sees that the negative consequence does not occur. The technique of response prevention has useful applications in treating disorders such as obsessive-compulsive disorder (see chapter 15). When compulsive behaviors, such as frequent hand washing, are physically prevented, the individual has an opportunity to discover that the feared consequences, such as terrible illness, are not really going to happen (Steketee & Cleere, 1990).

## Spontaneous Recovery and Disinhibition

The course of extinction is not always smooth. Normally, the learned response occurs many times before extinction is complete. Consider again the fear of the dental chair: The strength of the response gradually decreases because the CS (chair) is never again paired with the UCS (pain). If, however, there is a long period of time between presentations of the CS (such as a year between visits to the dentist), the fear can reappear the next time the CS is presented (see fig. 6.11). This is termed **spontaneous recovery.** It may occur several times during the course of extinction, but as long as the stimulus continues to be presented alone, the recovered response will be extinguished more quickly each time until the response no longer recovers.

In some cases, the strength of the extinguished response returns for a reason other than spontaneous recovery. If an intense but unrelated stimulus event occurs, it may cause the strength of the extinguished response to return temporarily. For example, if the dentist's assistant drops a tray of dental instruments while you were sitting in the chair, your fear response might come back for a while. This phenomenon is called **disinhibition.** That term will not seem to fit the phenomenon unless you understand that Pavlov, for theoretical reasons, believed that no response was ever really unlearned, just "inhibited" by another part of the brain. He termed this temporary increase in the strength of the response "disinhibition" because he felt that noise temporarily reduced the inhibition of the response. Both spontaneous recovery and disinhibition occur during the course of operant as well as classical extinction.

**FIGURE 6.11**
The course of extinction of a classically conditioned fear of dental chairs.

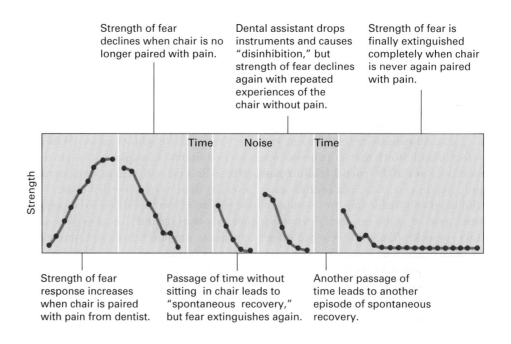

Strength of fear declines when chair is no longer paired with pain.

Dental assistant drops instruments and causes "disinhibition," but strength of fear declines again with repeated experiences of the chair without pain.

Strength of fear is finally extinguished completely when chair is never again paired with pain.

Strength of fear response increases when chair is paired with pain from dentist.

Passage of time without sitting in chair leads to "spontaneous recovery," but fear extinguishes again.

Another passage of time leads to another episode of spontaneous recovery.

To adapt fully to a changing world, we must be able to unlearn as well as learn. The process of extinction begins as soon as the source of the original learning is removed. In classical conditioning, this means that no longer pairing the UCS with the CS will produce extinction of the CR. In operant learning, no longer reinforcing the response will extinguish the response. The course of extinction is often irregular, with the strength of the response often spontaneously recovering after long periods of time or when a strong disinhibiting stimulus occurs.

Review

To be sure that you have learned the key points from the preceding section, cover the list of correct answers and try to answer each question. If you give an incorrect answer to any question, return to the page given next to the correct answer to see why your answer was not correct.

Check Your Learning

1. The process of unlearning a learned response because of a change in the aspect of the environment that originally caused the learning is termed _____.

   a) repression              c) extinction
   b) forgetting              d) terminating

2. The most difficult responses of all to extinguish are responses learned through _____.

   a) avoidance learning      c) classical conditioning
   b) operant conditioning    d) experience

3. _____ is a temporary increase in the strength of an extinguished response caused by an unrelated stimulus event.

   a) Spontaneous recovery    c) Revival
   b) Disinhibition           d) Learning

1. What makes some behaviors more difficult to extinguish than others?

2. Have you personally tried to eliminate unwanted behaviors using extinction?

Thinking Critically about Psychology

Correct Answers:  1. c (p. 219),  2. a (p. 219),  3. b (p. 220).

## ● Theoretical Interpretations of Learning

What is learned? When an individual's behavior changes as the result of classical or operant conditioning, what exactly has happened to the individual? One view dating back at least to the time of Pavlov is that neural *connections* between brain regions associated with specific stimuli and specific responses are acquired during the learning process. For example, when a rat is reinforced for pressing a lever in the presence of a light, a connection is believed to be automatically created between brain regions associated with the light and the specific pattern of muscle movements of the lever press. The next time the light is turned on, the neural connections to the muscles will cause the lever press to occur. Research based on the connection approach emphasized readily observable changes in behavior and basically ignored internal mental processes.

Other psychologists argue that internal mental processes play a central role in the learning process and are therefore deserving of study. For these psychologists, learning involves changes in cognitions rather than specific neural connections. As noted earlier in the text, the term *cognition* refers to the intellectual processes of thinking, expecting, believing, perceiving, and so on. Adherents to this view consider that the individual (rat or human) changes cognitions about a given situation during the learning process. For example, you flinch when a light comes on that has previously been paired with an electric shock, because you *expect* it to be followed by a shock. A rat turns left in a maze because it *knows* that the food was down that way the last 10 times it ran through the maze.

## Cognition or Connection?

A considerable amount of research has been conducted through the years to evaluate the connectionist and cognition theories of learning. Although most of it has been carried out using animals as subjects, what has been learned about the nature of learning is relevant to us human animals, too.

### Place Learning

An ingenious experiment to test the cognitive view of learning was designed by the late Edward C. Tolman of the University of California at Berkeley (Tolman, Ritchie, & Kalish, 1946). Rats were initially trained to run down the elevated path shown in figure 6.12. They started at point A, made a series of turns (left, right, right), and ran to point B, where food was provided. In the connectionist view of learning, the rats learned to do this by learning connections between the stimuli of the alley and the particular muscle movements of running and turning. Tolman took a cognitive view, however. He believed that the rats had learned a **cognitive map** of where the food was located relative to the starting place. They did not acquire a fixed pattern of muscle movements; they acquired knowledge of the location of the food.

How can we distinguish between the cognitive and connectionist interpretations? Tolman's experimental test was ingenious. Suppose we give the rats a chance to take a shortcut directly to the food; will they take it? Or will they be unable to recognize it as a better path, because all they had learned were connections between maze stimuli and patterns of muscle movements? Tolman and his colleagues answered this question by

This young woman has learned that good grooming usually elicits compliments from her friends. Is this a learned behavior involving a new stimulus-response connection or a change in cognition?

**cognitive map**
(kog′ni-tiv) An inferred mental awareness of the structure of a physical space or related elements.

**FIGURE 6.12**

The initial part of the apparatus used in Tolman's study of cognitive aspects of learning in rats. The rat begins at point A and receives food when it has reached point B.
**Source:** E. C. Tolman, B. F. Ritchie, and D. Kalish, "Studies in Spatial Learning I: Orientation and the Short-Cut" in *Journal of Experimental Psychology,* 36:13–25, 1946.

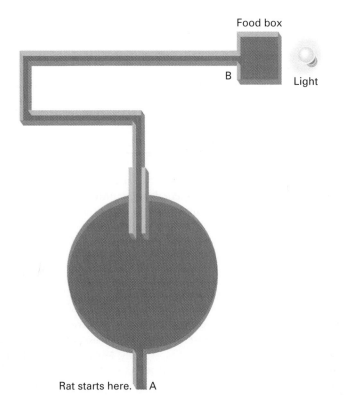

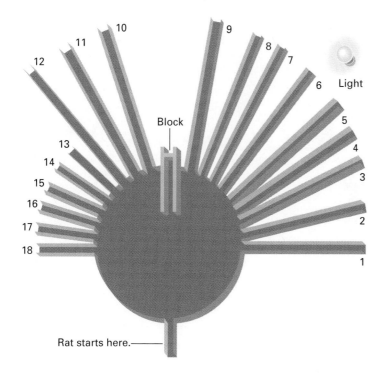

**FIGURE 6.13**
The modified apparatus used in the second part of Tolman's study of cognitive aspects of learning in rats.
**Source:** E. C. Tolman, B. F. Ritchie, and D. Kalish, "Studies in Spatial Learning I: Orientation and the Short-Cut" in *Journal of Experimental Psychology*, 36:13–25, 1946.

blocking the old path (as shown in fig. 6.13) and providing a variety of new choices. Interestingly, the greatest number of rats chose the path that led directly to where the food had been. Tolman interpreted this as meaning that they had learned a new cognition, knowledge of the location of the food.

### Latent Learning

Tolman conducted another informative experiment that evaluated the cognitive interpretation of learning in a rather different way (Tolman & Honzik, 1930). Suppose we allow a rat to run around in a complex maze of alleys, like the one shown in figure 6.14. Would the rat learn anything? The connectionist view would say no: Learning would occur only if reinforcement were delivered at the end of the maze to "stamp in" a connection between the stimuli of the maze and a specific series of movements leading from the starting box to the box containing the food. Tolman, on the other hand, felt that the rat would learn a cognitive map of the maze, but we would not be able to see that the rat had learned it until it was given a good reason (such as food) to run to the food box.

In Tolman's experiment, three groups of hungry rats were placed in the maze and timed to see how long it took them to reach the food box. One group was reinforced each time it reached the food box, so it gradually learned to run to the food box. A second group was never reinforced, so they wandered aimlessly in the maze (never decreasing the time it took to reach the food box). The third group of rats was the interesting one, though. This group was not reinforced for going to the food box for the first 10 days but was reinforced from then on. Look at figure 6.15 to see what happened. This group showed a sudden decrease in the amount of time it took the rats to reach the goal, catching up almost immediately to the group that had been reinforced every time. Tolman interpreted these results as showing that the unreinforced rats had learned just as much about the location of the food box

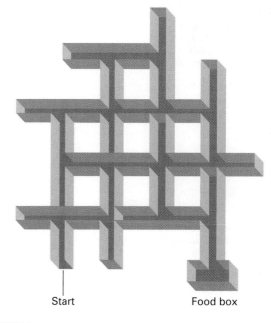

**FIGURE 6.14**

The maze used in Tolman's study of latent learning in rats.
**Source:** E. C. Tolman and C. H. Honzik, "Introduction and Removal of the Reward, and Maze Performance in Rats," *University of California Publications in Psychology*, 4:257–275, 1930.

**FIGURE 6.15**

The results of Tolman's study of latent learning in rats. A group of rats that was never reinforced for reaching the food box did not improve in the amount of time required to reach it. But a group of rats that was reinforced each time gradually improved. A third group of rats was not reinforced for the first 10 days but was reinforced from then on. These rats' rapid improvement indicated that they had "latently" learned about the maze before they were reinforced.

**Source:** E. C. Tolman and C. H. Honzik, "Introduction and Removal of the Reward, and Maze Performance in Rats," *University of California Publications in Psychology,* 4:257–275, 1930.

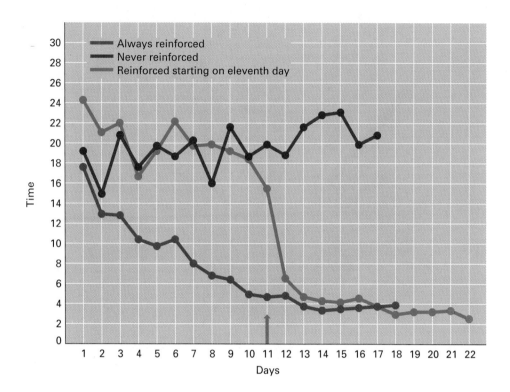

In Köhler's view, this chimp did not learn to reach the bananas on the ceiling through a gradual learning process but, rather, through a process of sudden cognitive change involving a new understanding of the uses of the boxes.

**insight**

(in´sĭt) A form of cognitive change that involves recognition of previously unseen relationships.

as the reinforced group, but they showed their learning only when given a reason to do so (the food). If learning were a matter of reinforcement strengthening connections between stimuli and responses, no learning would have been expected prior to the introduction of reinforcement.

### Insight Learning and Learning Sets

Perhaps the most striking evidence for the cognitive view of learning comes from a series of experiments conducted by a German Gestalt psychologist during World War I. Wolfgang Köhler was visiting the island of Tenerife (in the Canary Islands) when the war broke out, and he found himself interned there for the duration of the war. He took good advantage of a poor situation, however, by conducting learning experiments with chimpanzees that were native to the island. Köhler presented the caged chimps with a number of problems to see how they learned to solve them. For example, he hung a bunch of bananas out of reach on the ceiling. At first, the chimps tried to reach the bananas by jumping. When that failed, they sat down, looking annoyed. In time, however, one of the chimps picked up the wooden boxes that were in the cage, stacked them, and climbed up to reach the bananas. From that time on, the chimps always reached bananas hung from the ceiling of the cage by stacking the boxes.

Köhler conducted many similar experiments with other chimps. For example, he placed another chimp in a cage with bananas hung from the ceiling. In this case, there were no boxes in cage, but there were two bamboo poles, which could be fitted together to make a pole long enough to reach the bananas. At first, the chimp tried to reach the bananas by jumping and then by throwing the bamboo poles at the bananas, but it soon gave up. Later, the chimp suddenly picked up the sticks, put them together, and used the new "pole" to knock down the bananas. Again, when presented with the same problem later, the chimp immediately solved it every time by putting the sticks together.

In both cases, Köhler concluded that the chimps had not learned to solve the problem by gradually strengthening neural connections between stimuli and responses but, rather, had learned through **insight**—a sudden cognitive change that solved the problem. The chimps did not gradually improve their ability to reach the bananas over time but, rather, suddenly went from being unable to reach the bananas to being able to reach them easily using their new solution. Connection theorists have a great deal of difficulty explaining this type of insightful learning, but a series of classic experiments conducted by Harry Harlow (1949) at the University of Wisconsin took some of the mystery out of the chimps' insightful behavior. Harlow showed that the ability to solve problems insightfully is itself partially learned.

The apparatus shown in figure 6.16 was used in Harlow's study. A tray was presented to the monkey with two objects on it. Although the objects differed from problem to problem, food was always located under one of the objects. The monkeys had six chances to solve each problem. The monkeys in Harlow's experiments solved a total of 312 different problems because Harlow's interest was in whether the monkeys' ability to solve the problems improved with experience. As can be seen in figure 6.17, their problem-solving ability improved dramatically. Look first at their performance on the first group of problems (problems 1 through 8). While their percentage of correct performance improved gradually over the six trials, they were still choosing the correct object only about 75 percent of the time by the sixth trial. In contrast, look at their performance on problems 257 through 312. On the first trial, they had to guess which object the food was under, so they were correct only 50 percent of the time. But note that if they did not get it right the first time, they "insightfully knew" that it must be under the other object, and they made the correct choice from the second trial on.

In Harlow's terms, the monkeys had acquired a **learning set;** that is, they had learned to learn insightfully. Harlow's point was that the insightful performance of Köhler's apes was not characteristic of all learning; rather, one must *learn* how to solve a particular class of problems insightfully. Further supporting Harlow's contention is a follow-up study of Köhler's banana-and-stick problem (Birch, 1945). Chimpanzees that had no previous experience playing with sticks could not solve the problem. However, after these chimps had been allowed to play with the sticks for only 3 days, they were able to solve the banana-and-stick problem easily. Evidently, they had learned something in their play that enabled them to learn insightfully.

## Modeling: Learning by Watching Others

Stanford University psychologist Albert Bandura is one of the most influential contemporary proponents of the cognitive view of learning. One of his most important contributions has been to emphasize that people learn not only through classical and operant conditioning but also by observing the behavior of others. Bandura calls this **modeling.** For example, in countries where grasshoppers are considered to be a delicacy, people learn to eat them partly by watching other people enjoy themselves while eating grasshoppers. Similarly, patterns of speech, styles of dress, patterns of energy consumption, methods of rearing children, and myriad other patterns of behavior are taught to us through modeling.

Bandura considers modeling to be an important demonstration of the role of cognition in learning. A child who watches his older sister play baseball for several years will be able to come pretty close to playing the game properly (that is, know how to hold the bat, how to swing, where to run if he hits the ball) the very first time he is allowed to play. In Bandura's view, a great deal of cognitive learning takes place through watching, *before* there is any chance for the behavior to occur and be reinforced. But we can learn more than skills through modeling. Bandura has suggested that modeling can also remind us of appropriate behavior in a given situation, reduce our inhibitions concerning certain behaviors that we see others engaging in, or suggest to us what behaviors will lead to reinforcement.

In Bandura's ground-breaking laboratory studies of modeling, children learned to be more aggressive or less fearful as a result of simply observing the behavior of models in films. In one study (Bandura, Ross, & Ross, 1963), one group of children saw an adult kick, hit, and sit on a blow-up Bobo doll. When these children were placed in a playroom

**learning set**
Improvement in the rate of learning to solve new problems through practice solving similar problems.

**modeling**
Learning based on observation of the behavior of another.

Albert Bandura's views about modeling predict that this boy will learn good work habits from watching his father work on home projects.

**FIGURE 6.16**

The apparatus used by Harlow to study learning sets (learning to learn insightfully) in monkeys.

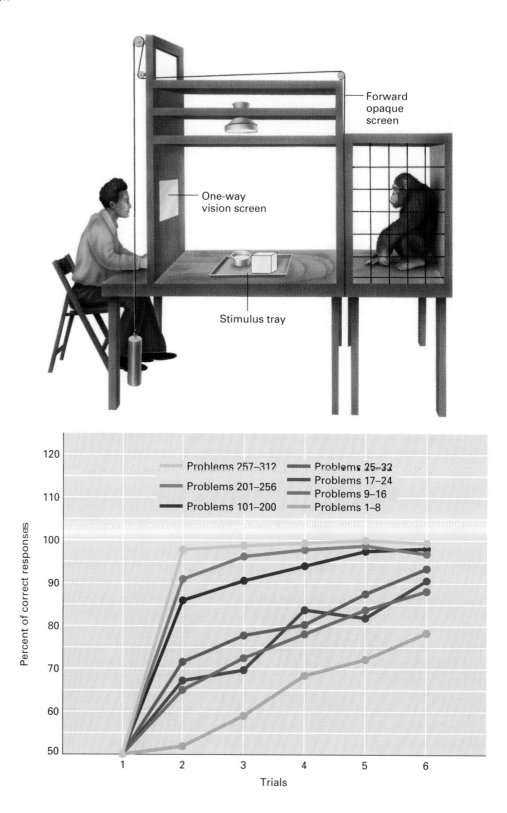

Forward opaque screen

One-way vision screen

Stimulus tray

**FIGURE 6.17**

Monkeys learn which object is hiding food very slowly the first few times they are given this type of problem (problems 1–8). But they learn quickly (insightfully) after they have had a great deal of experience with such problems (problems 257–312).

Source: H. F. Harlow, "The Formation of Learning Sets" in *Psychological Review*, 56:51–56, 1949.

(then frustrated by having all toys except the Bobo doll taken away), they were significantly more aggressive toward the Bobo doll than was a group of children who had not seen the film—they learned to act more aggressively through modeling. In a similar study with a more uplifting conclusion, research participants who were initially strongly afraid of snakes gradually learned to be less fearful by imitating a series of actions of the model, ranging from looking at a caged snake to holding it (Bandura, Blanchard, & Ritter, 1969). Modeling can be an important and powerful form of learning.

A.    Classical conditioning occurs because of the association in time of a neutral stimulus that already elicits the response. The CS becomes a signal that predicts the occurrence of the UCS.

III.  Operant conditioning is a form of learning in which the consequences of behavior lead to a change in the probability of the behavior's occurrence.

A.    In positive reinforcement, a positive consequence of behavior leads to an increase in the probability of the occurrence of the response.

1.    Primary reinforcers are innately reinforcing.

2.    Secondary reinforcers are learned through classical conditioning.

3.    Four schedules of reinforcement that result in different patterns of behavior are fixed ratio, variable ratio, fixed interval, and variable interval.

4.    Shaping is the process of positively reinforcing responses that are progressively more similar to the response that is wanted.

B.    Negative reinforcement occurs when the reinforcing consequence is the removal or avoidance of a negative event.

1.    The type of negative reinforcement in which the response causes an aversive stimulus to cease is called escape conditioning.

2.    The type of negative reinforcement in which the response prevents the occurrence of the aversive stimulus is called avoidance conditioning.

C.    Punishment is the process through which an aversive consequence of behavior reduces the frequency of a behavior.

IV.   New stimuli come to influence behavior through the process of learning.

A.    A stimulus discrimination has been learned when a response is more likely to occur in the presence of a specific stimulus than in its absence.

B.    Stimulus generalization has occurred when an individual responds in the same way to a stimulus that is similar to the original stimulus.

V.    The process of unlearning a learned response because of the removal of the aspect of the environment that originally caused the learning is termed extinction.

A.    During extinction, the strength of the response sometimes increases after a period of time since the last extinction trial; this is termed spontaneous recovery.

B.    An extraneous stimulus sometimes causes an extinguished response to recur; this is called external disinhibition.

VI.   Psychologists disagree about whether learning results from changes in neural connections between specific stimuli and specific responses or whether learning is a change in cognition.

A.    Research that supports the cognitive view includes Tolman's studies of place learning and latent learning, Köhler's studies of insight learning, and Bandura's work on modeling.

B.    The ability of humans to learn from experience is not limitless; it is influenced in a number of ways by biological factors.

---

**Resources**

1.    Excellent summaries for the serious student of learning include: Domjan, M. (1996). *Essentials of conditioning and learning.* Monterey: Brooks-Cole; and Tarpy, R. (1997). *Contemporary learning theory and research.* Boston: McGraw-Hill.

2. For more on modeling, see: Bandura, A. (1977). *Social learning theory.* Englewood Cliffs, NJ: Prentice-Hall.

3. For B. F. Skinner's views on operant conditioning and the science of psychology in general, see: Skinner, B. F. (1974). A*bout behaviorism.* New York: Knopf; and Skinner, B. F. (1971). *Beyond freedom and dignity.* New York: Knopf.

4. For a firsthand account of early research on classical conditioning, see: Pavlov, I. P. (1927). *Conditioned reflexes.* Gloucester, MA: Peter Smith.

5. A still cogent and controversial novel describing the utopia that one psychologist believes could result from our using the principles of learning to design society is Skinner, B. F. (1948). *Walden two.* New York: Macmillan.

# Chapter Outline

# Memory

## PROLOGUE

If we are to benefit from our experiences, we must be able to remember them. If you weren't able to remember anything tomorrow that you read in this chapter today, there would be no point in reading it. Remembering what you learn is as important as learning it in the first place.

Alexander Luria, a prominent Russian physician during the 1930s, was widely known for his research on the brain. One day, a young man (referred to as S) came to his hospital office, complaining that his memory was *too good.* He often recalled experiences in such vivid detail that he could not shake them from his consciousness. They lingered in a distracting, haunting way that impaired his ability to concentrate on his current circumstances. Because the man was clearly distraught, Luria agreed to study his problem.

Over many years, Luria tested S's memory in a number of ways. The best known of these tests involved showing S a sheet of paper containing four columns of a dozen numbers each. After viewing the numbers for a few minutes, S was able to write them out from memory without error. Moreover, without looking at the numbers again, he was able to refer to a mental image of them and tell Luria the numbers in any sequence requested. He could "read" a mental image of the numbers across the rows, down the columns, and across diagonals with apparent ease. Months later, S could still reproduce the table of numbers with few errors. In one series of experiments, he was even able to recall complex verbal material in detail after more than 15 years had elapsed.

Luria was never able to help S, but S himself found a way to make his life more comfortable. After losing many other kinds of jobs, he decided to go on stage as a "memory expert." He was able to astound audiences with his ability to recall information and was able to earn a comfortable living.

Most of us are not troubled by remembering too much—quite the opposite! Most college students would like to be able to remember a lot more every time they take a test. Learning about S might help us feel a little better about our own memories, but most of us would still like to be able to remember more.

This chapter describes the ways in which the human memory works and discusses the reasons that we forget. New information that we learn can be thought of as passing through three stages in the human memory. The first stage holds information for very brief intervals—often less than a second. The next stage retains information longer, but only a little longer—up to about half a minute. The third stage seems to hold information indefinitely. These three stages of memory operate according to different rules and mostly serve different functions. But because information must pass through each stage to reach the most permanent memory store, they work together as three linked stages in the memory process.

Forgetting appears to occur for different reasons in the three stages of memory. In the first stage, information is lost because it decays quickly over time unless it moves to the next stage. Forgetting in the second stage also occurs because of the simple passage of time unless something is done to protect the information. But memory traces are frequently lost in the second stage because of

A postal worker needs a good memory. According to the information-processing model, memory is a process involving attention, encoding, and transfer to storage from which information can be retrieved.

**encode**
(en'cōd)  To represent information in some form in the memory system.

**stage theory of memory**
A model of memory based on the idea that we store information in three separate but linked memories.

**sensory register**
The first stage of memory, in which an exact image of each sensory experience is held briefly until it can be processed.

**short-term memory (STM)**
The second stage of memory, in which five to nine bits of information can be stored for brief periods of time.

interference from other memories. For example, if you look up a number in the telephone book, you may forget it if you try to remember what you planned to say.

The third stage of memory is called long-term memory. Information that reaches this stage seems to stay there permanently. Nonetheless, we are often unable to recall information from long-term memory for several reasons. Interference from similar memories is a common reason for being unable to recall long-term memories. In addition, long-term memories tend to change over time, making the information inaccurate. Finally, we are sometimes unable to recall some very unpleasant or threatening memories.

It's not known yet how the memory trace is stored in the brain, but several theories have been proposed. As you will see, our best clues about the biological basis of memory have come from the study of persons with a severe form of memory loss called amnesia.  ■

## ● Three Stages of Memory: An Information-Processing View

In recent years, psychologists have attempted to develop theories of memory using the computer as a model. These *information-processing* theories of memory are based on the apparent similarities between the operation of the human brain and that of the computer. This is not to say that psychologists believe that brains and computers operate in exactly the same way. Clearly they do not, but enough general similarity exists to make the information-processing model useful. Before looking at specific theories, let's look briefly at the general information-processing model and its terminology.

In the information-processing model, information can be followed as it moves through the following operations: input, storage, and retrieval. At each point in the process, a variety of *control mechanisms* (such as attention, storage, and retrieval) operate. Information enters the memory system through the sensory receptors. This is like your entering a term paper into your computer by typing on the keyboard. Attention operates at this level to select information for further processing. The raw sensory information that is selected is then represented — or **encoded** — in a form (sound, visual image, meaning) that can be used in the next stages of memory.

Other control mechanisms might then transfer selected information into a more permanent memory storage, like saving your term paper on a computer disk. When the stored information is needed, it is *retrieved* from memory. Before printing out your paper, you must first locate your file on the disk and retrieve it. Unfortunately, with both computers and human memory, some information may be lost or become irretrievable.

Some information needs to be stored in memory for only brief periods of time, whereas other information must be tucked away permanently. When we look at a cookbook to see how much tomato paste to add to chicken cacciatore, we need to remember that bit of information for only a few seconds. However, we must remember our social security numbers and our siblings' names for our entire lifetimes. The influential **stage theory of memory** (Atkinson & Shiffrin, 1968; Baddeley, 1999) assumes that we humans have a three-stage memory that meets our need to store information for different lengths of time. We seem to have one memory store that holds information for exceedingly brief intervals, a second memory store that holds information for no more than 30 seconds unless it's "renewed," and a third, more permanent memory store. Each of these memories operates according to a different set of rules and serves a somewhat different purpose. Because information must pass through each stage of memory to get to the next, more permanent one, these memory stores are best thought of as three closely linked "stages" of memory, rather than three separate memories. The three stages are known as the sensory register, short-term memory, and long-term memory (see fig. 7.1).

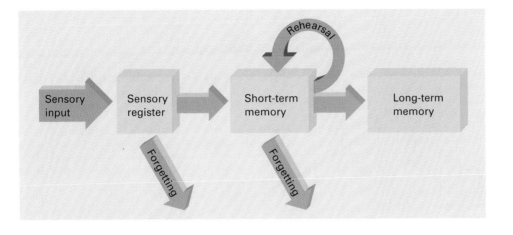

**FIGURE 7.1**
Stage model of memory.

## Sensory Register

The first stage of memory—the **sensory register**—is a very brief one, designed to hold an exact image of each sensory experience until it can be fully processed. We apparently retain a copy of each sensory experience in the sensory register long enough to locate and focus on relevant bits of information and transfer them into the next stage of memory. For visual information, this "snapshot" fades very quickly, probably lasting about one-quarter of a second in most cases. For auditory information, a vivid image of what we hear is retained for about the same length of time, one-quarter of a second (Cowan, 1987), but a weaker "echo" is retained for up to 4 seconds (Tarpy & Mayer, 1978).

The information stored in the sensory register does not last long, but it's apparently a complete replica of the sensory experience. This fact was demonstrated in an important experiment by George Sperling (1960). Sperling presented research participants with an array of 12 letters arranged in three horizontal rows of four letters each (see fig. 7.2). He showed the participants these letters for 1/20 of a second and then asked them to recall all of the letters in one of the three rows. He did not tell them ahead of time which row he would ask them to recall. Instead, he signaled to them using a tone. A high-pitched tone indicated the first row, a medium tone indicated the second row, and a low tone indicated the third row. If the tone was presented very soon after the presentation of the array of letters, the participants could recall most of the letters in the indicated row. But if the delay was more than one-quarter of a second, the participants recalled an average of just over one letter per row, indicating how quickly information is lost in the sensory register.

Visual information in the sensory register is lost and replaced so rapidly with new information that we seldom are aware we even have such a memory store. Sometimes the longer-lasting, echolike traces of auditory information can be noticed, though. Most of us have had the experience of being absorbed in reading when a friend speaks. If we divert our attention from the book quickly enough, we can "hear again" what was said to us by referring to the echo of the auditory sensation stored in the sensory register.

## Short-Term Memory

When a bit of information is selected for further processing, it's transferred from the sensory register into **short-term memory,** or **STM.** It's not necessary to intentionally transfer information to STM; generally, just paying attention to the information is enough to transfer it. You might not intentionally try to memorize the price of your dinner, but you will be able to recognize that you were given the wrong amount of change. Once information has been transferred to short-term memory, a variety of control processes may be applied. Rehearsal and chunking are two important examples of these control processes.

**FIGURE 7.2**
Array of letters like that used in the sensory register experiments conducted by Sperling (1960).

When we dial a number that we have just looked up in the telephone book, we are generally using information that has been stored only in short-term memory.

**FIGURE 7.3**
The accuracy of recall for a single group of three consonants declines rapidly when subjects are prevented from rehearsing by being asked to count backward.
**Source:** R. L. Peterson and M. J. Peterson, "Short Term Retention of Individual Items" in *Journal of Experimental Psychology* 58:193–198, 1959.

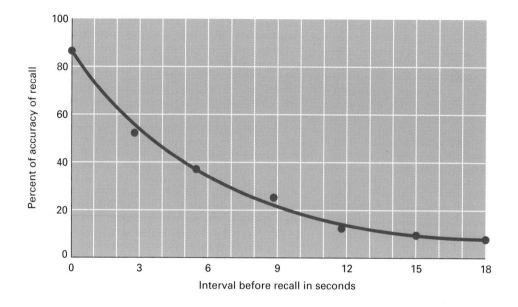

**rehearsal**
Mental repetition of information to retain it longer in short-term memory.

## Rehearsal in Short-Term Memory: Overcoming STM's Limited Life Span

As the name implies, short-term memory (STM) is good for only temporary storage of information. In general, information is lost from STM in less than half a minute unless it's "renewed," and it is often lost in only a few seconds (Ellis & Hunt, 1993). Fortunately, information can be renewed in STM by mental repetition, or **rehearsal,** of the information. When a grocery list is rehearsed regularly in this way, it can be held in STM for relatively long periods of time. If the list is not rehearsed, however, it's soon lost. Rehearsing the information stored in STM has been compared to juggling eggs: The eggs stay in perfect condition as long as you keep juggling them, but as soon as you stop juggling, they are lost.

Our first reliable estimate of the limited life span of information in STM was provided by an experiment conducted by Lloyd and Margaret Peterson (1959). The participants were shown a single combination of three consonants (such as LRP) and asked to remember it as they counted backward by threes to keep them from rehearsing the letters. The individuals counted backward for brief intervals (0 through 18 seconds) and then were asked to recall the letters. As shown in figure 7.3, the participants were able to remember the three consonants less than 20 percent of the time after only 12 seconds had passed. These findings make it clear that memories are impermanent in STM unless kept alive by rehearsal.

The information stored in STM can be of many different types of memories: the smell of a perfume, the notes of a melody, the taste of a fruit, the shape of a nose, the finger positions in a guitar chord, or a list of names. But we humans have a preference for transforming information into sounds, or *acoustic codes,* whenever possible for storage in STM. If I asked you to memorize a list of letters (*B, P, V, R, M, L*), you would most likely memorize them by their "names" (bee, pee, vee, etc.) rather than by the shapes of the letters. We know this because most people say they do it this way and because the errors people make are most likely to be confusions of similar sounds (recalling *zee* instead of *bee*) rather than confusions of similar shapes (recalling *O* instead of *Q*, or *R* instead of *P*) (Reynolds & Flagg, 1983). We probably use acoustic codes in STM as much as possible because it's easier to rehearse by mentally talking to ourselves than by mentally repeating the images of sights, smells, and movements. Nonetheless, STM can store any form of information that can enter the brain through the senses.

### Chunking in Short-Term Memory: Overcoming STM's Limited Capacity

Perhaps the most important thing to know about STM is that its storage capacity is quite limited. The exact capacity differs slightly for different kinds of information, but as psychologist George Miller (1956) put it, it's constant enough to call it the *magic number seven plus or minus (±) two*. Estimates of the span of STM are obtained by asking research participants to memorize simple lists (of randomly ordered numbers, letters, and unrelated words) of different lengths. The length of the list that the participants can recall half the time is considered to represent the capacity of STM (Miller, 1956). Rarely are we able to hold more than five to nine bits of information in STM, regardless of the nature of that information. This is a very limited capacity, indeed.

In addition to temporarily storing information, STM serves another important function, which further limits its already small capacity—it serves as our *working memory* (Baddeley, 1992; 1999). This means that space in STM is used when old memories are temporarily brought out of long-term memory to be used or updated. Space in STM is also used when we think about this information (Morris, 1986). This is why you cannot remember the telephone number of the hardware store, which you just looked up, if you begin thinking about your purchase before you dial—thinking takes up space in STM and forces out the numbers. The fact that thinking uses STM also explains why it's difficult to think about problems that involve more than 7 ± 2 issues. We keep forgetting some of the aspects of complex problems because they exceed the limited capacity of STM. In such situations, writing out all the issues on paper helps keep them straight while you are thinking.

STM holds 7 ± 2 bits of information. This shopper probably needs a written list.

One advantage of the small storage capacity of STM is that it's easy to "search" through it. When we try to remember something in STM, we apparently examine every item that is stored there. Experiments conducted by Saul Sternberg (1969) confirm that we exhaustively search STM every time we try to recall something. Sternberg's experiments even give us an estimate of how long it takes us to examine each bit of stored information. Participants were asked to memorize lists of numbers of different lengths. They were then shown a number and asked if it was in the list they had just memorized. When individuals had just memorized a long list of numbers, it took them longer to respond than when they had memorized a short list. In fact, the amount of time required to respond increased by a rather constant .04 of a second for each item in STM. Apparently, that's how long it takes to examine each item in STM.

Fortunately, there are some effective ways to get around the limited capacity of STM. One way is to learn the information well enough to transfer it into long-term memory, which, as we will see shortly, has no real space limitation. Another way is to put more information into the 7 ± 2 units of STM.

George Miller (1956) calls the units of memory **chunks.** Although it's true that we can hold only five to nine chunks in STM, we can often put more than one bit of information into each chunk. If you were to quickly read the following list of 12 words once,

**chunks**
Units of memory.

| | |
|---|---|
| east | winter |
| spring | lateral |
| fall | north |
| dorsal | ventral |
| west | summer |
| medial | south |

you probably would not be able to recall it perfectly 10 seconds later, because 12 chunks normally exceed the capacity of STM. But, if you reorganized the words into 3 chunks (points of a compass, seasons, and anatomical directions) and memorized those, you could remember the list quite easily. This strategy would work for you only if you were able to regroup the list into meaningful chunks, however. If you did not know the four anatomical directions, it would do you no good to memorize these terms because you could not generate the four directions when you recalled them.

Other chunking strategies can also be used to expand the amount of information that can be stored in STM. It's no accident that social security numbers (as well as bank account numbers and telephone numbers) are broken up by hyphens. Most people find it easier to remember numbers in chunks (319-555-0151) than as a string of single digits.

In summary, STM is a stage of memory with limited capacity in which information —often stored in acoustic codes—is lost rapidly unless it's rehearsed. The capacity of STM can be expanded by increasing the amount of information in each chunk to be learned. But, no matter how good a job we do of chunking and rehearsing, STM is not a good place to store information for long periods of time. Such information must be transferred to long-term memory for more permanent storage.

## Long-Term Memory

**Long-term memory,** or **LTM,** is the storehouse for information that must be kept for long periods of time. But LTM is not just a more durable version of STM; the stage model of memory suggests it's a different kind of memory altogether.

*LTM differs from STM in four major ways:* (1) the way in which information is recalled, (2) the form in which information is stored in memory, (3) the reasons that forgetting occurs, and (4) the physical location of these functions in the brain. Let's look at each of these four differences between STM and LTM separately:

1.  Because the amount of information stored in LTM is so vast, we cannot scan the entire contents of LTM when we are looking for a bit of information, as we do in STM. Instead, LTM has to be *indexed.* We retrieve information from LTM using *cues,* much as we use a call number to locate a book in the library. This retrieval can be an intentional act (such as "What was the name of the secretary in Accounts Receivable?") or an unintentional one, as when hearing a particular song brings back memories of a lost love. In either case, only information relevant to the cue is retrieved, rather than the entire contents of LTM.

2.  LTM differs from STM in the kind of information that is most easily stored. You will recall that information is usually stored in STM in terms of the physical qualities of the experience (what we saw, did, tasted, touched, or heard), with a special emphasis on acoustic codes. Although sensory memories can be stored in LTM, information is stored in LTM primarily in terms of its meaning, or *semantic codes* (Cowan, 1988).

3.  LTM also differs from STM in the way forgetting occurs. Unlike STM, where information that is not rehearsed or processed appears to drop out of the system, information stored in LTM is not just durable but actually appears to be permanent. In a dramatic demonstration of LTM, Bahrick (1984) tested memory for Spanish using individuals who had studied the language in high school 50 years ago. Bahrick's participants retained much of their knowledge of Spanish, even after a period of 50 years. Not all psychologists agree that memories in LTM are permanent, but there is a great deal of evidence supporting this view. If memories in LTM are indeed permanent, this means that "forgetting" occurs in LTM not because the memory is erased but because we are unable to retrieve it for some reason (Baddeley, 1999).

4.  Each stage of memory is handled by a different part of the brain. STM is primarily a function of the frontal lobes of the cerebral cortex (Buckner & Barch, 1999; Fuster, 1995; Williams & Goldman-Rakic, 1995), whereas information that is

Hearing an old favorite song can bring back memories of the earliest times you heard the song. We can use cues like old songs either intentionally or unintentionally to retrieve long-term memories.

**long-term memory (LTM)**
The third stage of memory, involving the storage of information that is kept for long periods of time.

stored in LTM is first integrated in the hippocampus and then transferred to the areas of the cerebral cortex involved in language and perception for permanent storage (Nadel & Jacobs, 1998).

We will describe these differences in more detail in the final section of this chapter.

### Types of Long-Term Memory: Procedural, Episodic, and Semantic

Tulving (1972, 1985, 1987) has proposed the existence of three kinds of long-term memory storage, each with distinctly different properties, and each probably based on different brain mechanisms. I think I can best explain the differences among these kinds of LTM by telling you another one of my stories. Recently, I came across a photograph taken of me on my fourteenth birthday in my home in St. Petersburg, Florida. I was holding my birthday present—my first guitar. I took guitar lessons for a while and played in several mediocre rock bands until my junior year in college. Then I sold my guitar and concentrated on my studies. About 15 years ago, however, I bought another guitar, and playing guitar once again became a part of my life. That's the story; now for the three types of LTM:

1. When I picked up my new guitar in the music store, I found that I could still play the basic chords, even though I had not played them in years. That is a long-term **procedural memory**—memory for skills and other procedures. Memories of how to ride a bicycle, to cook, or to kiss are procedural memories.

2. Although I did not stop to think about it, I also obviously remembered what a guitar was. I knew what it was when I saw it, knew what it was used for, and so on. In other words, I had not forgotten the semantic memory of the meaning of *guitar*. **Semantic memory** is memory for meaning. When you remember what a father is, what pudding is, and what the phrase "peace of mind" means, you are recalling meaning from long-term semantic memory.

3. Until my memory was jogged by finding the old photograph, however, it had been years since I had remembered when and where I had gotten my first guitar. **Episodic memory** is the kind of LTM that stores information about experiences that took place at specific times and in specific places.

The LTM mechanisms are apparently able to store procedural and semantic memories quite effectively, but LTM handles episodic information much less well. I immediately knew what a guitar was (semantic) and how to play it (procedural), but it took a photograph to recall the time and place of getting my first guitar (episodic). A great deal of research has been done to show the greater ability of LTM to store semantic than episodic memories. A clever study of the memorization of sentences by J. D. S. Sachs (1967) clearly illustrates this point. The experimenter had research participants listen to passages containing a number of different sentences. After intervals of different lengths, she asked the individuals to listen to more sentences and tell her whether they were exactly the same as one of the sentences in the passage. Some of the test sentences were the same, but some were changed either in physical form or in meaning. For example, an original sentence in the passage such as "Jenny chased Melissa" might be changed to "Melissa was chased by Jenny" (change in physical structure, but not meaning) or to "Melissa chased Jenny" (change in both physical structure and meaning). Sachs found that the participants could tell quite well if a sentence had been changed in either way, as long as the test interval was within the span of STM (about 30 seconds). However, at longer intervals, they were only accurate in detecting changes in meaning. Apparently, the meaning of the sentences (semantic memory) was held in LTM, whereas details about their physical structure (episodic memory) were forgotten when they were lost from STM.

  In spite of these apparent differences, some psychologists group semantic memory and episodic memory together under the heading **declarative memory** (see fig. 7.4).

**procedural memory**
Memory for motor movements and skills.

**semantic memory**
(se-man′tik) Memory for meaning without reference to the time and place of learning.

**episodic memory**
(epĭ-sod′ik) Memory for specific experiences that can be defined in terms of time and space.

**declarative memory**
Semantic and episodic memory.

**FIGURE 7.4**

Semantic and episodic memory are sometimes grouped together under the term *declarative memory* because both kinds of memory can be easily described (declared) in words. In contrast, procedural memories are difficult to describe in words because they involve such skills as playing the guitar, which can be seen only when the task is performed.

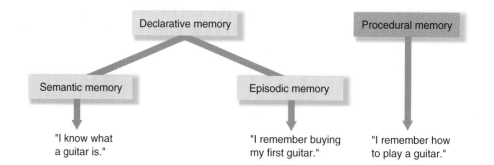

Declarative memory

Semantic memory

Episodic memory

Procedural memory

"I know what a guitar is."

"I remember buying my first guitar."

"I remember how to play a guitar."

Semantic and episodic memories are quite different, but they are alike in an important way as well: They are easily described (declared) in words. For example, I would have no difficulty telling you what a guitar is. This is in contrast to *procedural memory*, which can be accessed only through performance—as in when I play a song on my guitar (Squire, 1987). It is difficult, if not impossible, to describe verbally how to play a song on the guitar without playing it. This distinction between procedural and declarative memories will be important to our discussion of amnesia later in the chapter.

### Organization in Long-Term Memory

We noted earlier that it's possible to make more efficient use of the limited capacity of STM by organizing information into larger chunks (Miller, 1956). Organization of information is also important for LTM, but it's probably not related to a need to save capacity, because LTM has essentially unlimited capacity. Rather, organization helps to facilitate the retrieval of information from the vast amount stored in LTM. The retrieval task in LTM is vastly different from that in STM: Instead of 7 ± 2 items that can be easily searched, LTM stores such an extensive amount of information that it almost certainly must be *organized* in some fashion. For instance, it's sometimes inconvenient that the 60-odd books in my office are not organized on my bookshelves, but I can still find what I am looking for by searching long enough. It would be impossible, on the other hand, to find the same book in the university library if the books were as unorganized and randomly placed on the shelves as mine. Like LTM, the library needs an organized way of storing and retrieving a huge amount of information.

Evidence for the organization of LTM has been available for some time. When research participants memorize new lists of items that could be categorized, they tend to recall them in related groups. For example, Weston Bousfield (1953) asked individuals to memorize a list of 60 words that could be conceptually grouped into four categories: animals, vegetables, names, and professions (*muskrat, blacksmith, panther, baker, wildcat, Howard, Jason, printer,* and so on). Even though the words were presented in random order, participants recalled them in categorical groupings significantly more often than would be expected by chance. Apparently, the words were stored in LTM according to organized categories.

In addition, there is clear evidence that recall from LTM is better when we impose more organization on the information that is stored there. Gordon Bower's Stanford University research group (Bower & Clark, 1969) asked participants to memorize 12 lists of 10 words, such as the following:

| | |
|---|---|
| boy | rag |
| boat | wheel |
| dog | hat |
| wagon | house |
| ghost | milk |

Half of the individuals were given the usual instructions to memorize the lists of words in any order, but the others were asked to "make up stories" containing all of the words

Like a library, LTM organizes information to facilitate retrieval.

in the list—to organize them into a single story. For example, the previous list could be memorized as "The boy with the hat pulled his dog and his boat in his wagon with the crooked wheel. He saw a rag hanging on a house that he thought was a ghost. It scared him so much that he spilled his milk." The group that organized the words into stories recalled an amazing 90 percent of the words, whereas the other group recalled only 15 percent!

The organization of memory in LTM has been characterized as an *associative network* by some theorists (Ellis & Hunt, 1993; Raaijmakers & Shiffrin, 1992). According to this view, memories are associated, or linked together, through experience. Your experience forms links between that special song and memories of your summer vacation, or between algebra and that unbearable teacher. Researchers have studied the operation of associative networks by asking research participants to answer general knowledge questions. For instance, suppose you were asked to answer the question "Is a canary a bird?" How do you access your store of information to answer correctly? An influential network model known as the *spreading activation model* (Collins & Loftus, 1975) attempts to explain this process. According to Collins and Loftus, we form links between various concepts and their characteristics based on our experience. When we are asked a question, representations of the concepts or characteristics are activated. As shown in figure 7.5, the question would activate separate memory representations of *canary* and *bird*. The model then assumes that this activation spreads out along previously formed links to other representations. In the case of *canary* and *bird*, which are very closely associated for many people, the lines of activation spreading from these representations meet quickly, and a decision can be made. If representations are not as closely associated, it takes a longer time to respond. If you were asked whether or not a penguin is a bird, your answer would probably be slower than in the canary example.

Experimental support for the spreading activation model can be seen in a clever study (Meyer & Schvaneveldt, 1971). Research participants watched while groups of letters were flashed on a computer screen. Some of the letter groups spelled out real words, but others (such as *plame* and *blop*) just *looked* like words. The participants were asked to respond by hitting a "yes" button when a real word was shown and a "no" button when a made-up "word" was shown. The important part of this study is the time it took them to hit the button each time a real word was shown. The researchers found that the participants' reaction times were much faster for words that had been shown immediately preceded by a related word (*bread-butter*) than by an unrelated word (*nurse-butter*).

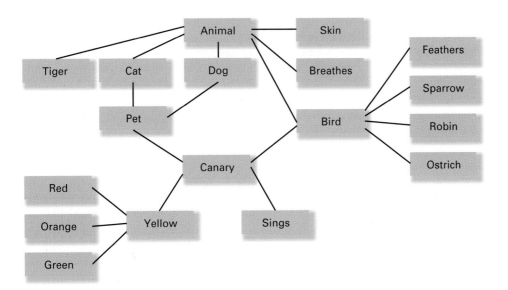

**FIGURE 7.5**

An example of the associative links that are hypothesized to exist among bits of information stored in long-term memory in the spreading activation theory.

What does this mean for the spreading activation model of long-term memory? According to this theory, activation of *bread* would spread along the network to related items, including *butter*. Therefore, *butter* would be partially activated even before the word appeared on the screen, producing a very fast reaction time. Thus, these results support the spreading activation model.

### Retrieval of Long-Term Memories

Students are very familiar with the frustration that comes from knowing that you know something but being totally incapable of retrieving it (until, of course, you step outside the exam room!). Research on types of retrieval, on serial learning, and on the tip-of-the-tongue phenomenon provide us with important insights into the retrieval process in long-term memory.

***Three Ways of Testing Retrieval: Recall, Recognition, and Relearning.*** Psychologists have distinguished three ways of measuring memory retrieval that differ from one another in important ways. In the **recall method,** you are asked to recall information with few, if any, cues: Whom did George W. Bush defeat for the presidency of the United States in 2000? This is a recall method of assessing your memory for that fact.

In the **recognition method,** you are asked to recognize the correct information from among alternatives. The same question could be asked as a recognition question:

In 2000, George W. Bush defeated _____ for the presidency of the United States.

| | | | |
|---|---|---|---|
| a. | Bob Dole | c. | Pat Buchanan |
| b. | Al Gore | d. | Jimmy Carter |

Generally, we can "remember" more when tested by the recognition rather than the recall method, because recognition tasks provide more cues for retrieving information from long-term memory. Our greater ability to recognize rather than to recall remembered information was demonstrated vividly in an experiment on everyday memory to which we are all subject (Bahrick, Bahrick, & Wittlinger, 1975). Two years after graduation from high school, college students were found to be able to *recall* an average of 60 percent of the names of the students in their class when looking at their photographs. However, when they were shown their yearbook pictures and asked to *recognize* the corresponding names from a list, they could match names correctly 90 percent of the time.

The **relearning** (or *savings*) **method** is the most sensitive of all three of the methods of evaluating memory. Even when you can neither recall nor recognize information, it may be possible to measure some memory of the information using the relearning method. In this method, you relearn previously memorized information. If the relearning takes less time than the original learning, then the information has been "remembered" in this sense. For instance, at some point in your life, you probably learned how to find the area of a right triangle. You might be unable to remember how to do that now, but you could relearn the method much faster than it took you to learn it the first time. Your enhanced ability to relearn the technique shows that the memory was never completely "lost."

***Serial Learning.*** In some types of retrieval tasks, the order in which we memorize a list is as important as the items in the list. It would be useless to memorize the steps in defusing a bomb if you were not able to remember them in the right order! When psychologists have studied memory for serial lists (lists of words, numbers, and the like that must be recalled in a certain order), a surprisingly consistent finding has emerged. The recall of items in the serial lists is often better for items at the *beginning* and *end* of the list than in the middle. This is called the **serial position effect.** Many explanations have been

---

**recall method**
A measure of memory based on the ability to retrieve information from long-term memory with few cues.

**recognition method**
A measure of memory based on the ability to select correct information from among the options provided.

**relearning method**
A measure of memory based on the length of time it takes to relearn forgotten material.

**serial position effect**
The finding that immediate recall of items listed in a fixed order is often better for items at the beginning and end of the list than for those in the middle.

It is easier to retrieve long-term memories using recognition than to try to recall the information.

suggested for this effect, but it's perhaps best explained in terms of the differences between short-term and long-term memory. The last items in a list are remembered well because they are still in STM, whereas the first items in a list are remembered well because they can be rehearsed enough times to transfer them firmly into LTM.

Two experiments provide strong support for this explanation. First, Vito Modigliani and Donald Hedges of Simon Fraser University (1987) have shown that better recall for items at the beginning of lists is indeed related to greater opportunities for rehearsal. In a second experiment on the serial position effect (Glanzer & Cunitz, 1966), research participants attempted to memorize a list of 15 items. As shown in figure 7.6, the serial position effect was clearly found when the individuals were asked to recall the list immediately after learning it. That is, recall was better for items at both the beginning and the end of the list. But, when the participants were asked to recall the list after

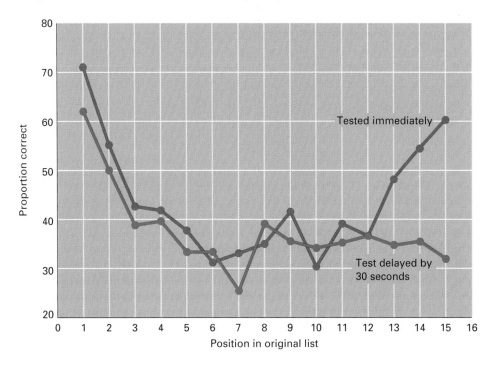

**FIGURE 7.6**

When recall of a serial list of 15 items is tested immediately after the presentation of the last item, participants recall the first and last items better than the middle items. But when the test is delayed by 30 seconds, fewer of the last items are recalled, suggesting that at least some of the last items in the list were stored only in short-term memory.

**Sources:** Data from M. Glanzer and A. R. Cunitz, "Two Storage Mechanisms in Free Recall," *Journal of Verbal Learning and Verbal Behavior*, 5:351–360, 1966 Academic Press; and R. M. Tarpy and R. F. Mayer, *Foundations of Learning & Memory,* © 1978 Scott, Foresman.

# HUMAN DIVERSITY

## Cultural Circumstances and Memory Skills

Does culture influence even basic intellectual skills, such as memory? Some psychologists believe that our cultural circumstances have a powerful impact on many fundamental aspects of intelligence. For example, psychologist Judith Kearins (1986) hypothesized that Australian aboriginal peoples possessed better visual memory skills for objects than white Australian children. She reasoned that excellent visual memory skills had allowed the aboriginal people to thrive in the challenging desert environments in which many of them live.

In Kearins' experiments, aboriginal and white adolescents were given 30 seconds to memorize the location of objects arranged on a rectangular grid. The experimenter then mixed up the objects, and each adolescent was asked to replace them in their original positions. Two of the tasks involved manufactured objects (matchbox, ring, eraser) and two involved natural objects (twig, seed pod, feather, bone, etc.). The aboriginal adolescents performed significantly better than the white Australians on all of the tasks. The white adolescents performed better when the task material was manufactured objects than they did when the objects were natural, but this distinction did not affect the performance of the aboriginal children.

Kearins found that the aboriginal and white Australian adolescents used different memory strategies to approach the task. The aboriginal adolescents sat very still, were silent, and appeared to concentrate deeply. They were slow and methodical in replacing the objects. Most of the white adolescents, on the other hand, tended to fidget and mutter and replaced the first few objects hurriedly. Kearins speculated that the white children were muttering the verbal labels of the objects in an effort to remember them, whereas the aboriginal children were more likely to memorize the arrangement of the objects in visual terms. Perhaps the different cultures emphasized verbal or visual approaches to memorization because of the importance of those skills in each culture.

Think about your own approach to memorization. How would you have approached the memory task in Kearins' experiment? Would you have memorized the placement of the objects in visual terms, or would you have memorized verbal labels for the objects ("The feather in the top-left, then moving clockwise, the stick, the weird-looking bone . . . ")? What type of information is most important for you to remember to survive in your ethnic group? What cultural differences have you noticed between your community and other ethnic communities in terms of their approach to intellectual skills? Finally, has your ethnic community influenced your approach to memorization and other intellectual skills—and, if so, how has it done so? ■

---

a delay of 30 seconds—just beyond the limits of STM—the serial position effect was only half there. Recall was better at the beginning of the list—presumably because those items were rehearsed more and stored in LTM—but not at the end of the list, probably because the participants could not hold the last items in STM that long. The serial position effect shows that we are simultaneously using both STM and LTM in an attempt to soak up and retain as much of what's going on as possible.

***The Tip-of-the-Tongue Phenomenon.*** We have all had the maddening experience of trying to recall a fact that we can *almost* remember—it's on the "tip of my tongue." Fortunately, there is a lesson in this on the nature of retrieval from LTM. The tip-of-the-tongue phenomenon was investigated by Harvard University psychologists Roger Brown and David McNeil (1966) by giving definitions of uncommon words to college students and asking them to recall the words. For example, they might be read the definition of *sampan* ("a small boat used in shallow water in Asia that is rowed from behind using a single oar"). Often, the students could recall the word *sampan*. Sometimes, though, they could not quite recall the word, and the researchers were able to create the tip-of-the-tongue sensation in these students. When this happened, the students found that they were able to recall some information about the word ("It starts with *s*" or "It sounds like *Siam*") or recall something about the thing the word referred to ("It looks a little like a junk"), even when they could not retrieve the word. Then, moments later, the word would pop

"Hey, good buddy!    "Can't kick, big fella.
How you doin'?"      What's shakin'?"

into memory for some students, proving that it was there all the time but just could not be retrieved for the moment. Studies suggest that about half of the things that we can't remember, but are on the tip of our tongues, are recalled within a minute or so (Schachter, 1999), but you can drive yourself nuts for hours trying to remember the other half!

## Levels of Processing: An Alternative to the Stage Model

The model suggesting that there are three separate stages of memory (sensory register, STM, and LTM) has been enormously helpful in making sense of the complex phenomenon of memory. Fergus Craik and Robert Lockhart (1972) have proposed an alternative **levels of processing model,** however, suggesting that the distinction between short-term and long-term memory is a matter of *degree* rather than separate stages. In brief, Craik and Lockhart believe that there is only one memory store beyond the sensory register. The durability of stored information depends on how well it is processed as it is being encoded for memory. Information will be kept only briefly if it's processed at a *shallow* level, but it will be kept much longer if it's processed at a *deeper* level. Thus, the differences that we have just examined between STM and LTM are not, in this view, differences between two different memory systems operating according to different principles. Rather, these differences are the results of different levels of processing during the encoding process. Furthermore, according to Craik and Lockhart, there is a continuum of levels of processing, ranging from very shallow to very deep, rather than just two types of storage (short and long).

What is the difference between deep and shallow processing? One way of putting it is to say that shallow processing involves the encoding of superficial perceptual information, whereas deep processing encodes meaning (Ellis, 1987). Consider the following list of adjectives:

    soft
    swift
    warm
    sharp
    witty
    bright
    clean
    beautiful

If you were to ask 10 acquaintances to process this list in a superficial way ("Look at each word for 5 seconds; then circle the adjectives containing the letter *i*") and ask 10 other acquaintances to process it in a deep way ("Look at each word for 5 seconds; then circle the adjectives that describe you"), which group do you think would remember more of the words if, without warning, you asked them to recall the list 10 minutes later? Craik and Lockhart's levels of processing view correctly predicts that the individuals who processed the words deeply by thinking about their meanings (the second group) will recall more of the words—not because they had stored the words in a different memory (LTM vs. STM) but because information processed more deeply is stored more permanently.

Deep processing also involves greater *elaboration* of memories during the encoding phase than does shallow processing. **Elaboration,** in this sense, means creating more associations between the new memory and existing memories (Ellis, 1987; Ellis & Hunt, 1993). For example, if you read a paragraph in a textbook and spend a few minutes relating its contents to what you had learned in the previous chapters or to your own life, you are elaborating the memory—linking it to existing memories. We have already seen how the associative network model assumes that these links are vital to your ability to use stored information. Therefore, deeply processing the new information in this way will improve your memory of the paragraph and your ability to use the information later. In contrast, simply going through the motions

It is possible that all information stored in long-term memory is still there but cannot always be retrieved.

**levels of processing model**
An alternative to the stage theory of memory stating that the distinction between short-term and long-term memory is a matter of degree rather than different kinds of memory and is based on how incoming information is processed.

**elaboration**
(e-lab″or-rā′shun) The process of creating associations between a new memory and existing memories.

of rereading a paragraph several times without really thinking about it is a much less successful study technique. What is also interesting about this view of deep processing is that even superficial perceptual information can be richly elaborated, such as by relating a new telephone number to existing memories about the person you are calling. Many studies suggest that one of the best ways to promote the elaboration of new memories to improve their later recall is to relate the new information to *yourself* (Symons & Johnson, 1997). Because your perceptions of yourself are well-elaborated and accessible in memory, linking new information to yourself is an excellent way to improve memory through deep processing. The next time you read a textbook (from English literature to physics), try relating every new fact or concept to yourself in some way—it should improve your memory for that information later (Symons & Johnson, 1997).

The levels of processing view probably will not replace the STM/LTM stage model. This is not to say that the levels of processing view of memory is unimportant, however. It is a useful reminder to us that information that is learned in a shallow, rote manner will not be around in our memories very long. If you want to retain information for a long time and have the ability to retrieve it easily, you need to take the time and effort to understand and elaborate the information as you learn it.

## Review

We can think of human memory as being composed of three different, but related, stages of memory. The sensory register holds a replica of the visual, auditory, or other sensory input for a very brief interval while relevant information is selected for further processing. Short-term memory holds information, generally as acoustic codes, for about a half minute unless it's renewed through rehearsal. The capacity of short-term memory is quite limited unless information is organized into larger chunks. Long-term memory stores information primarily in terms of its meaning, or semantic codes. Its capacity is very large, and memories stored there seem to be permanent. The store of information in LTM is so vast that it must be organized to facilitate retrieval of information. Current theories suggest that the organization is primarily in terms of categories of meaning or associative networks.

The division of memory into a distinct STM and LTM has been questioned by some theorists, however. They suggest, instead, that the duration that information can be held in memory depends on the *depth* at which it's processed, not the *stage* of memory in which it's held. Information that is processed deeply—more richly elaborated—during the encoding process is stored more permanently than information that is processed in a shallow way.

## Check Your Learning

To be sure that you have learned the key points from the preceding section, cover the list of correct answers and try to answer each question. If you give an incorrect answer to any question, return to the page given next to the correct answer to see why your answer was not correct. Remember that these questions cover only some of the important information in this section; it is important that you make up your own questions to check your learning of other facts and concepts.

1. The _____ assumes that we humans have a three-stage memory, which meets our need to store information for different lengths of time.

    a) lateral processing theory of memory
    c) psychoanalytic theory of memory
    b) stage theory of memory
    d) progression theory of memory

2. The first stage of memory is the _____, which holds an exact image of each sensory experience for a very brief time until it can be fully processed.

   a)   short-term memory        c)   sensory register

   b)   primary store            d)   initial memory store

3. The _____ is used to store information temporarily and to think while holding information in "working memory."

   a)   short-term memory        c)   sensory register

   b)   long-term memory         d)   primary store

4. Long-term memory is similar to short-term memory in terms of the way in which information is recalled, the reason forgetting occurs, and the form in which information is usually stored.

   a)   True                     b)   False

5. The _____ is a memory model suggesting that the distinction between short-term and long-term memory is a matter of degree rather than separate stages.

---

1. Episodic memories are less durable than semantic memories in long-term memory. This is sometimes inconvenient, but is it also advantageous in some ways?

2. Can you think of some episodic memories that have stayed especially clear through the years? What is it about those events that has caused them to be so durable?

**Thinking Critically about Psychology**

---

**Correct Answers:** 1. **b** (p. 236),   2. **c** (p. 237),   3. **a** (pp. 237–240),   4. **b** (p. 240),   5. levels of processing model (p. 247).

## ● Forgetting and Why It Occurs

So far we have talked about remembering and forgetting in terms of the three stages of memory. We have noted that forgetting is different in STM than in LTM, but we have skirted the issue of the causes of forgetting. Why do some memories become lost or irretrievable? What causes forgetting to occur? There are four major theories of forgetting that should be discussed in some detail: *decay theory*, which states that time alone causes memory traces to fade; *interference theory*, which suggests that other memories interfere with remembering; *reconstruction (schema) theory*, which proposes that memory traces become distorted with time, sometimes to the point of becoming unrecognizable; and the *theory of motivated forgetting*, which suggests that we forget information that is unpleasant or threatening.

### Decay Theory

According to **decay theory,** memories that are not used fade gradually over time. This theory has been around for a long time and fits our commonsense understanding of forgetting. It had been discarded by psychologists as being wholly incorrect until recent years, however. As we will see in a moment, forgetting is more complicated than the mere fading of memory traces and involves factors other than time. The acceptance by most psychologists of some version of the three-stage conception of memory has brought the decay theory back into limited favor, however. It appears that the simple passage of time is a cause of forgetting, both in the sensory register and in STM (White, 2002). It does not appear that decay due to the passage of time is a cause of forgetting in LTM, however. Memory "traces" appear to be "permanent" once they make it into LTM. Forgetting does

**decay theory**
The theory that forgetting occurs as the memory trace fades over time.

Forget the combination? According to the decay theory, forgetting occurs because time passes.

not seem to happen in LTM because of disuse over time but because other factors, particularly *interference*, make memories irretrievable.

## Interference Theory

**Interference theory** is based on strong evidence that forgetting in LTM does not occur because of the passage of time but, rather, because other memories interfere with the retrieval of what you are trying to recall, particularly if the other memories are similar to the one you are trying to remember. Suppose you take an interest in French impressionist painters and you read a book about the painting techniques of Degas, Monet, and Matisse. It would be no great feat to memorize each painter's techniques and keep them straight, but suppose you then learn about the techniques of three more French impressionists, and then three more. Pretty soon, recall becomes difficult, partly because the similar memories interfere with the retrieval of one another. This also happens when you try to remember a lot of telephone numbers, grocery-list items, or math formulas.

The fact that the other memories must be similar to the one you are trying to recall in order to interfere with its retrieval has been shown in a simple experiment by Delos Wickens and his associates (Wickens, Born, & Allen, 1963). Wickens asked one group of research participants to memorize six lists of three-digit combinations (such as 632, 785, 877). As can be seen in figure 7.7, these individuals became progressively worse at recall as they memorized more and more lists. The previously memorized lists interfered with the recall of each new list. By the sixth list, their performance was quite poor. A second group of individuals was asked to memorize five lists of combinations of three letters, and then to memorize a list of three-digit combinations like those used in the first group. As can also be seen in figure 7.7, these participants became progressively less successful at recalling the letter combinations due to the buildup of interference. But when they memorized the list of digit combinations instead of a sixth list of letters, their memory performance shot up, showing that the letters were too dissimilar to the digits to interfere with their recall. Interference comes primarily from *similar* memories.

In the experiment by Wickens and others, the interference came from memories that were formed *before* learning the last list. The prior memorization of similar material caused interference with the recall of newly learned material. Interference can also come from memories that are formed *after* memorizing the material in question. If the individuals in the Wickens study had tried to recall the first digits they had learned after memorizing five additional lists, they would have found that a great deal of interference had been created. Psychologists refer to the interference built up by *prior* learning as **proactive interference** and to interference created by *later* learning as **retroactive interference.**

Suppose you meet two interesting people, Rolf and Kate, on your vacation at the beach. Rolf tells you his room number and you listen carefully and commit it to memory. The next day, Kate tells you her room number and you memorize it. Later, you try to go to Kate's room and, oops, you can't remember the number. You are the victim of *proactive interference.* The recall of Kate's number was blocked by interference from the memorization of the number that *preceded* it.

**interference theory**
The theory that forgetting occurs because similar memories interfere with the storage or retrieval of information.

**proactive interference**
(prō-ak′tiv) Interference created by memories from prior learning.

**retroactive interference**
(ret″rō-ak′tiv) Interference created by memories from later learning.

**Proactive Interference**

Rolf's number

Kate's number    6213

Try to recall Kate's number

**motivated forgetting** in chapter 12 on personality. Freud believed that the conscious mind often dealt with unpleasant or dangerous information by pushing it into unconsciousness, by an act of **repression.** This theory of forgetting has not been extensively tested in the laboratory, but support has come from a number of clinical case studies. There are many well-documented cases of memory loss for highly stressful events, such as auto accidents and crimes (Elliott, 1997; Squire, 1987).

This type of evidence is not strongly supportive of the theory, however, for three reasons. First, because case histories do not involve careful experimental control, other causes of memory loss are often possible, such as a blow to the head in an automobile accident. Second, as we will see in a later section, it may be that the effect of the stressful event is to disrupt the biological process of consolidating the memory trace in LTM rather than to cause the memory to be repressed. And third, this type of evidence makes motivated forgetting seem like something that is not a part of ordinary lives but related only to unusually stressful events.

In recent years, it has become clear that the relationship between emotion and memory is more complex than first assumed by Freud. Emotional arousal does not always lead to poor memory —sometimes emotional arousal improves memory in some ways.

A series of well-controlled laboratory studies by psychologist Michael Bock (1986; Bock & Klinger, 1986) examined the relationship between emotional arousal and memory. When individuals were shown a list of words and asked to recall them later, they were better able to recall words with positive emotional impact (such as *kiss* and *prize*) than words with negative emotional impact (such as *disease* and *loss*). However, words with neutral emotional impact were recalled least well in Bock's studies. In similar studies, the improved recall of positively and negatively emotional words was correlated with increased activation of the amygdala (Hamann & others, 1999). This suggests that, although Freud was correct in saying that negative events are recalled less well than positive events, experiences with any type of emotional impact appear to be easier to recall than neutral experiences.

According to Freud, motivated forgetting can occur as a result of repressing details of stressful events.

Although negative emotional arousal leads to better recall than no emotional arousal, our memories of events that are associated with negative emotional arousal are often rather different from other memories, particularly when the negative emotional arousal is intense. Our memories of intensely negative events tend to be vivid but are often disorganized and confused (Nadel & Jacobs, 1998).

Vivid memories for emotional events have been termed *flashbulb memories* (Brown & Kulik, 1977). I can clearly recall some parts of the day of the assassination of President John Kennedy, and one particularly disturbing newscast describing atrocities committed by American soldiers during the Vietnam War still sticks with me. Both seem like flash photos printed on my brain, but it is likely that some of the elements of these vivid memories are confused or distorted (Nadel & Jacobs, 1998).

Where were you when you first heard about the verdict in the controversial O. J. Simpson murder trial? Were you at home? At school? Did you hear it on television or did someone tell you? Researchers at the University of California in San Diego (Schmolck, Buffalo, & Squire, 2000) asked students in a psychology class similar questions 3 days after the verdict was announced and then asked the same question 1 year and 3 years later. Three days after the verdict, virtually all of the students had a vivid, emotional "flashbulb memory" of learning the verdict. A year later, only 11 percent of the recollections of this event were highly distorted (remembering being told by your father at home instead of

**motivated forgetting**
Forgetting that is believed to be based on the upsetting or threatening nature of the information that is forgotten.

**repression**
Sigmund Freud's theory that forgetting occurs because the conscious mind often deals with unpleasant information by pushing it into unconsciousness.

hearing the verdict on the radio when alone in your car), but after three years, 40 percent of the recollections were highly distorted. The memories remained clear over time, but often became quite inaccurate.

Another interesting aspect of the complicated relationship between emotion and memory is that emotion focuses memory on some aspects of the situation and away from others. For example, many studies show that portraying emotion-laden violence on television programs decreases viewers' recall of the advertisements for those programs (Bushman & Phillips, 2001). Sponsoring violent television programs may not be good business, which is good news to the majority of North Americans who say in surveys that too much violence is portrayed on television.

## Review

There are four major causes of forgetting, each with different relevance to the three stages of memory. Forgetting in the sensory register seems to occur primarily because of simple decay of the memory over time. Forgetting in short-term memory can be attributed to decay over time, but also to interference from other similar information stored in memory. Interference from other memories explains some forgetting in long-term memory, but information also appears to be recalled inaccurately from LTM because it is distorted to be more consistent with our schemas (beliefs, knowledge, and expectations) about that information (reconstruction errors). In addition to forgetting events from the past, we also sometimes have false memories of events that never occurred. This is thought to be caused by reconstruction errors based on the associative nature of LTM. Recall of information about positive events appears to be better than recall of information about negative events. Therefore, Freud may have been partially correct that some memories may be less accessible because they are associated with negative emotions (motivated forgetting). Overall, however, both positive and negative emotional arousal appear to facilitate memory. Memories of intensely emotional events tend to be particularly vivid, but often became distorted over time.

## Check Your Learning

To be sure that you have learned the key points from the preceding section, cover the list of correct answers and try to answer each question. If you give an incorrect answer to any question, return to the page given next to the correct answer to see why your answer was not correct.

1. According to _____ theory, forgetting occurs simply because the memory trace fades as time passes.

   a) decay                     c) diminishing
   b) disintegration            d) decline

2. _____ theory states that forgetting occurs because similar memories block the storage or retrieval of information.

   a) Disruption                c) Disturbance
   b) Interference              d) Freudian

3. _____ theory suggests that some memories become so distorted over time that they are unrecognizable.

   a) Reconstruction (Schema)   c) Retrieval
   b) Destruction               d) Distortion

4. Forgetting that occurs because the memory is upsetting or threatening is termed _____.

5. Remembering an event that never happened is called a _____.

1.  Suppose you have started a company that manufactures cameras. Design an experiment to see if teaching the same employees to do two different assembly tasks produces proactive interference.

2.  Based on your understanding of the four major causes of forgetting, what improvements could you make in your general study habits to improve your test performance?

Correct Answers:  1.  a (p. 249),   2.  b (p. 250),   3.  a (p. 251),   4.  motivated forgetting (p. 254),   5.  false memory (p. 254).

## Biological Basis of Memory

A great deal has been learned about memory in recent years through the study of the role of the brain in the storage and retrieval of information. This boom in knowledge not only gives us a better understanding of the brain, but also helps us understand memory.

### Synaptic Theories of Memory: Search for the Engram

It's obvious that some physical change must take place in the nervous system when we learn something new (Baddeley, 1998; McGaugh, 1983). If some physical change did not occur, how would we be able to recall the new learning at a later time? The "something" that remains after learning—the **engram,** as early memory researcher Karl Lashley called it—is the biological basis of memory. Although neuroscientists have searched for the engram for a long time, there is not yet a full consensus as to what or where it is. However, this is one of the most active areas in psychological research, and much is already known.

A theory stated many years ago by Canadian researcher Donald Hebb (1949) is still considered to provide an accurate model of the physiological processes responsible for learning and memory (Jeffrey & Reid, 1997). According to Hebb, **synaptic facilitation** is the biological basis of learning and memory. Individual experiences result in unique patterns of neural activity, which cause structural changes in the synapses to occur. These changes make firing in the loop more likely in the future. In other words, synapses become more efficient, or facilitated. Thus, for Hebb, changes in the synapses are the biological basis of memory.

In a series of clever experiments conducted on sea snails (*Aplysia*), Eric Kandel and his associates (Dale & Kandel, 1990; Dash, Hochner, & Kandel, 1990; Kandel & Schwartz, 1982) have provided evidence that strongly supports Hebb's synaptic theory. Sea snails were chosen for study because they have very simple nervous systems in which it is easy to study individual neurons. In one key study (Castelluci & Kandel, 1976), the snails were classically conditioned to withdraw their gills and water siphons. First, the snails were prepared for the study by gently touching the siphons many times. Ordinarily, sea snails retract their gills and siphons at the slightest stimulation, but they soon habituate to being touched and stop withdrawing their gills and siphons. Then, the classical conditioning began: Each snail's siphon was touched (CS); then the snail was given a mild electric shock (UCS), which caused the withdrawal of the gill and siphon (UCR). Later, when the snail was touched (CS), the gill and siphon were withdrawn (CR). (See p. 201 if you don't remember what the terms CS, UCS, UCR, and CR mean.)

The change in the synapses was studied by measuring the amount of neurotransmitter in the neuronal connections involved in the withdrawal of the gills and siphons. In the first part of the study, as each sea snail stopped withdrawing its gill and siphon when touched, the amount of neurotransmitter present at the

**engram**
(en´gram)  The partially understood memory trace in the brain that is the biological basis of memory.

**synaptic facilitation**
The process by which neural activity causes structural changes in the synapses that facilitate more efficient learning and memory.

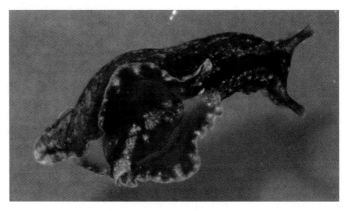

*Aplysia,* the sea snail that opened new vistas to understanding the cellular basis of learning and memory.

synapse *declined;* however, after classical conditioning, the amount of neurotransmitter *increased.* Thus, Hebb appears to be correct—at least for some forms of simple learning, the learning is "remembered" at the synapse. Several groups of scientists have published evidence that indicates that the changes in the synapses are based on changes in their proteins for LTM, but not for STM (Ezell, 1994; Kwon & others, 2001; Milner, Squire, & Kandel, 1998). This finding is important not only for understanding the biological basis of memory but also for indicating that STM and LTM are based on different processes in the brain.

Because the change in synapses that is the basis of LTM is a biological process, it is influenced by the biological state of the brain. Animal research tells us that central nervous system stimulants, such as caffeine, improve retention of learning if injected shortly after learning (McGaugh & Dawson, 1971). How do stimulant drugs enhance memory? When an animal is excited, either by a stimulant drug or by a stressful event, epinephrine is released into the bloodstream (see chapter 3). The epinephrine itself does not affect memory, but it causes an increase in blood sugar. The sugar nourishes the brain and enhances consolidation of memories (McGaugh, 1990). Human research also shows that the accuracy of college students' memories is better when their level of blood sugar is higher (Benton & Sargent, 1992). So don't starve yourself when you're studying.

Research into the causes of Alzheimer's disease has led to the identification of other chemicals that have the potential for enhancing memory. Alzheimer's disease systematically destroys neurons containing the neurotransmitter *acetylcholine.* As a result, neuroscientists have assumed that acetylcholine plays an important role in memory. Studies have shown that drugs that block the action of acetylcholine disrupt the formation of memory. Drugs that facilitate acetylcholine also appear to act as memory enhancers, at least in laboratory animals (Meck, Smith, & Williams, 1989). Recently it has also been shown that drugs that interfere with protein synthesis block the formation of long-term memories (Kandel & others, 1995).

## Stages of Memory and the Brain

Some advances in our understanding of the brain's role in memory in recent years help us understand the different types of memory. I have illustrated the major brain structures involved in the three stages of memory in figure 7.9. As more is learned about the brain, this description will probably prove to be an oversimplification, but it gives you a reasonable overview of current knowledge of how the brain stores information. Consider this example: In 1990, I visited the Rocky Mountains for the first time, and I still have a clear recollection of one part of the trip. As we drove up to the mountain that the Shoshoni people named "Going to the Sun," the amazing visual stimuli from the mountain pass traveled from my eyes to the thalamus, where it was routed to the visual area of the occipital cortex (part 1 of figure 7.9). This neural activity briefly held the trace that we call the sensory register. If I had closed my eyes at that time, I would have been able to recall the visual image from the sensory register and could have kept the memory active in STM for a while in the frontal and parietal lobes of the cerebral cortex (part 2 of fig. 7.9; D'Esposito, 2000; Goldman-Rakic, 1992).

Because I can still recall this scene, it must have been stored temporarily and integrated in the hippocampus (Nadel & Jacobs, 1998). The hippocampus plays a key role in the transfer of information from STM to LTM (Kandel & Hawkins, 1992), but the visual image was stored permanently in the occipital lobe, where it was first processed (part 3 of figure 7.9). As I recall this memory now, my frontal lobes play the key role (part 4 of figure 7.9; Schachter, 1999; Smith, 2000). If my experience in the Rockies had involved a negative emotion—such as my almost driving off the road as I marveled at the gorgeous view—my amygdala would also have played a role in the formation of the memory (Kandel, 1999).

Recent advances in understanding the role of brain structures may help explain why memories for events associated with intense negative emotions (flashbulb memories) tend to be vivid but disorganized (Nadel & Jacobs, 1998). Events that create intense

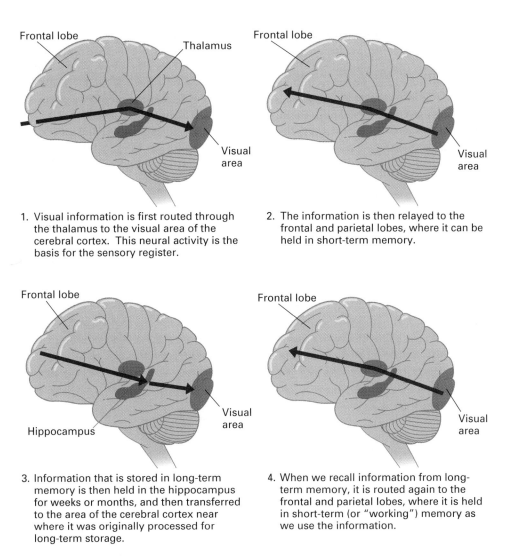

1. Visual information is first routed through the thalamus to the visual area of the cerebral cortex. This neural activity is the basis for the sensory register.

2. The information is then relayed to the frontal and parietal lobes, where it can be held in short-term memory.

3. Information that is stored in long-term memory is then held in the hippocampus for weeks or months, and then transferred to the area of the cerebral cortex near where it was originally processed for long-term storage.

4. When we recall information from long-term memory, it is routed again to the frontal and parietal lobes, where it is held in short-term (or "working") memory as we use the information.

**FIGURE 7.9**
Stages of memory and the brain.

negative emotional arousal activate the amygdala, and its involvement tends to improve recall (Hamann & others, 1999). On the other hand, negative emotional arousal stimulates the release of the adrenal stress hormone cortisol, which inhibits the hippocampus (Nadel & Jacobs, 1998; Newcomer & others, 1999; Schachter, 1999). Because the hippocampus organizes the elements of complex memories that are stored in different parts of the cortex, inhibition of the hippocampus appears to result in a lack of organization in emotionally charged memories, which may make distortions more likely (Nadel & Jacobs, 1998).

## Amnesia: Disorders of Memory

Major disorders of memory deserve our attention, both because they are important conditions in their own right and because of what they tell us about the biological basis of memory. We will begin with a clinical case history describing an individual who suffers from severe memory loss, known as *anterograde amnesia,* as a result of brain surgery. His tragic case tells us much about memory disorders and vividly shows how important an intact memory is for the normal experience of life.

### Anterograde Amnesia

**Anterograde amnesia,** a disorder of memory characterized by an inability to consciously retrieve new information in LTM, is well exemplified in the case history of H. M. (Milner, Corkin, & Teuber, 1968). H. M. began suffering major epileptic seizures at the

**anterograde amnesia**
(an-ter´o-grād) Disorder of memory characterized by an inability to store and/or retrieve new information in long-term memory.

age of 10. The seizures increased in frequency to about once a week by age 27, despite the use of antiseizure medications, leading his neurosurgeon to conclude that surgery must be performed to stop them. The surgery destroyed several brain structures important in memory. The procedure dramatically reduced the incidence of the seizures but left H. M. with severe anterograde amnesia. He retained his above-average intelligence and had nearly normal memory for anything that had been stored in LTM *prior* to the surgery, but he had severe memory deficits for events that occurred *after* the surgery.

H. M.'s short-term memory was generally normal after the surgery. Like most people, he could retain verbal information in STM for about 15 seconds without rehearsal and could retain it for longer intervals if he was allowed to rehearse it. However, H. M. had serious problems in *storing new information* in LTM and then retrieving it. He had almost no knowledge of current events because he forgot the news as soon as it slipped out of STM. He could read the same magazine over and over because it was "new" to him each time. He had no idea what time of day it was unless he had just looked at a clock; and generally he could not remember that his father had died since H. M.'s operation.

The most dramatic disruption caused by his memory problems, however, was to his social life. Although he could recognize friends, tell you their names, and relate stories about them, he could do so only if he had met them before the surgery. People that H. M. met after the surgery remained, in effect, permanent strangers to him. Each time a person came to his house, he had to learn the person's name again, but he could remember it for no more than 15 seconds or so unless he continued to rehearse it. This effectively meant that H. M. was incapable of forming new social relationships—a poignant but dramatic lesson in how important a basic cognitive function such as memory is to our lives.

H. M.'s inability to make new use of LTM was not total, however. His ability to learn and retain perceptual and motor skills in LTM (procedural memory) remained good, allowing him to learn to perform employable skills under supervision. However, he had to be reminded each day what new skills he had learned to perform; if he left his job for a short while, he could not remember what kind of work it was that he did. Similarly, when other individuals with anterograde amnesia have been taught to play a simple tune on the piano, they have been able to play it the next day but are surprised by their inability to do so because they have no recollection of being taught to play the tune the day before (Hirst, 1982). These cases illustrate again the differences between *procedural memory,* on the one hand, and the two kinds of *declarative memory* (episodic and semantic), on the other hand. Anterograde amnesia usually does not affect the ability to acquire procedural memories but disrupts the ability to form new declarative memories. Thus, the difficulties experienced by the anterograde amnesia patient in using LTM are highly selective; some kinds of long-term memories are affected, whereas others are not.

What caused H. M. to have this peculiar and sadly debilitating form of memory disorder? What happened to him during the surgery that damaged his ability to make new use of LTM? The key biological structure that was damaged in H. M.'s surgery, and is often damaged in anterograde amnesia, is the **hippocampus** (Kandel & Hawkins, 1992; Scoville & Milner, 1957). As noted earlier in the chapter, this brain structure is believed to govern the transfer of memories from STM to LTM. The case of H. M. also suggests that the hippocampus plays an important role in declarative memory, but not procedural memory (Squire, 1987; Squire, Knowlton, & Musen, 1993). Persons with anterograde amnesia, like H. M., perform very badly on long-term declarative memory tasks but perform as well as normal individuals on procedural memory tasks (Graf, Squire, & Mandler, 1984; Squire & others, 1993). Damage to the hippocampus spares both new and old procedural memories but prevents the formation of new long-term declarative memories.

Anterograde amnesia also can be caused by brain tumors, lack of oxygen to the brain, damage to blood vessels in the brain, senility, and severe nutritional deficiencies. In addition, hard blows to the head can cause anterograde amnesia, although it's often only a temporary condition (Hirst, 1982).

**hippocampus**
(hip″o-kam′pus) The forebrain structure believed to play a key role in long-term memory.

### Retrograde Amnesia

Some individuals are unable to recall information from the past; that is, they cannot retrieve old long-term memories. **Retrograde amnesia** is just the opposite of anterograde amnesia, then, in that old rather than new long-term memories cannot be recalled. As in anterograde amnesia, however, there is typically little or no disruption of STM. Generally, the period of memory loss is not for the individual's entire lifetime. Rather, it extends back in time from the beginning of the disorder. Memory might be lost for a period of minutes, days, or even years (Kapur, 1999).

Retrograde amnesia can be caused by seizures, brain damage of various sorts, a blow to the head, or highly stressful events. When retrograde amnesia has been caused by seizures or by stress, it generally occurs alone. When it has been caused by brain damage or a blow to the head, however, it generally occurs along with anterograde amnesia. Indeed, most brain-damaged individuals with anterograde amnesia also experience retrograde amnesia for the period of a few days or weeks prior to the onset of their amnesia (Hirst, 1982).

Both anterograde and retrograde amnesia are experienced by individuals with **Korsakoff's syndrome,** a disorder caused by prolonged loss of the vitamin thiamine from the diet of chronic alcoholics. Because of their extreme degree of memory loss, individuals with Korsakoff's syndrome often engage in *confabulation*—when they cannot remember something that is needed to complete a statement, they make it up. Generally, they are not being knowingly dishonest but are engaging in an exaggerated version of normal reconstructive distortion.

Retrograde amnesia has also been cited as further evidence for the stage theory of memory. Electroconvulsive shock (ECS) reliably produces retrograde amnesia. If rats are given ECS following a learning experience, their retention of the learning will be greater as the interval between the learning and the shock increases. The ECS appears to interfere with the biological process of transfer or consolidation of learning from short-term to long-term memory.

**retrograde amnesia**
(ret'rō-grăd) A memory disorder characterized by an inability to retrieve old long-term memories, generally for a specific period of time extending back from the beginning of the disorder.

**Korsakoff's syndrome**
(Kor-sak'ofs) A disorder involving both anterograde and retrograde amnesia caused by excessive use of alcohol.

### Review

The memory trace, or engram, must be stored in the brain in some form after learning; otherwise, recall at a later time would not be possible. Theories have been proposed about the specific nature of the engram, suggesting that it's most likely a change at the level of the neural synapse.

A group of disorders involving memory loss, known as amnesia, is instructive to study. Anterograde amnesia is characterized by a normal STM and normal memory for information that was in LTM prior to the onset of the amnesia, but by an inability to retrieve newly learned information from LTM. This condition is almost always caused by brain damage, generally involving the hippocampus. The memory disorder known as retrograde amnesia involves a loss of memory for old long-term memories, usually for a specific period of time extending back from the cause of the amnesia, such as a blow to the head, a stressful event, or a seizure. Chronic alcoholics sometimes experience such extensive brain damage due to nutritional deficiencies that they develop Korsakoff's syndrome, which is marked by both anterograde and retrograde amnesia.

### Check Your Learning

To be sure that you have learned the key points from the preceding section, cover the list of correct answers and try to answer each question. If you give an incorrect answer to any question, return to the page given next to the correct answer to see why your answer was not correct.

   1.  Scientists study the brain in hopes of discovering the _____, which is the change in the brain that occurs when a memory trace is stored.

2. The neural basis of memory formation may be the process of _____, which can produce long-lasting changes in synapses.

    a) electroconvulsive shock    c) synaptic facilitation

    b) anterograde amnesia    d) operant conditioning

3. A disorder of memory characterized by an inability to store and/or retrieve *new* information in LTM is _____.

4. A memory disorder characterized by an inability to retrieve *old* long-term memories is _____.

---

## Thinking Critically about Psychology

1. What would life be like without your long-term memory? What role do memories play in your life?

2. Why is research on the biological basis of memory important?

---

**Correct Answers:** **1.** engram (p. 257), **2.** c (p. 257), **3.** anterograde amnesia (p. 259), **4.** retrograde amnesia (p. 261).

## Eyewitness Testimony and Memory

No evidence is more convincing to a jury than the testimony of an eyewitness to the crime. If you were a juror and you heard an intelligent, credible witness say that she saw Professor Plum murder the victim in the conservatory with the candlestick, wouldn't you be convinced? In many cases, of course, eyewitnesses provide accurate descriptions of crimes. But eyewitness testimony is based on *memories* of the crime, and as we have seen in this chapter, what goes into memory is not always the same as what comes out.

The three men pictured in figure 7.10 were involved in an actual case of double mistaken identity by eyewitnesses to a crime. Lawrence Benson (left) was mistakenly arrested for rape, and George Morales (right) was erroneously arrested for robbery. Both men were arrested because they had been identified in police lineups by eyewitnesses to the crimes. Benson was cleared of the charges, however, when Richard Carbone (center) was arrested and more convincingly implicated in the rapes. After his conviction for rape, he cleared Morales by confessing to the robbery as well (Buckhout, 1974).

Consider another case of mistaken eyewitness testimony (Thomson, 1988). A woman was raped in her home. Later, she was able to give the police a detailed description of the rapist. Her description led to the arrest of Donald Thompson, who perfectly fit her description. Charges against Thompson were quickly dropped, however, as he had an airtight alibi. He was appearing live on television at the time of the rape and could not have committed the rape. In fact, the victim was watching him on television just before the rape occurred. As discussed earlier in this chapter, events that create intense negative emotional arousal—and few experiences could be more intensely negative than being raped—leave memories that are vivid but very subject to distortion. In this traumatic circumstance, the woman recalled a vivid image of the

**FIGURE 7.10**

Mistakes in eyewitness testimony led to the arrest of the man on the left and the man on the right for separate crimes. Both were cleared following the conviction of the man in the middle for both crimes.

man on the television screen, but her recollection of the event was so distorted that she incorrectly recalled the man on the television as being the rapist. Ironically, Donald Thompson is a respected psychologist known for his research on memory and was discussing memory distortions on television at the time.

It is frightening to think that these mistaken eyewitness identifications could have occurred, but at least these incorrectly accused individuals were not convicted. Now that DNA evidence is routinely used to investigate crimes, a considerable number of imprisoned persons—many on death row—have been found to be innocent on appeals based on DNA evidence. In one study of 40 such individuals, 90 percent of the cases of mistaken conviction involved erroneous eyewitness testimony (Wells & others, 1998).

We certainly should not conclude that eyewitness testimony is always incorrect. Still, it is both important and revealing to consider the conditions under which it is sometimes incorrect. By doing so, psychologists will be able to help law enforcement personnel obtain and use eyewitness testimony in ways that will minimize its inherent flaws (Kassin, Tubb, Hosch, & Memon, 2001; Schachter, 1999; Wells & others, 1998).

### Inaccurate Recall Due to Biased Questioning

Several researchers have looked at factors that lead to inaccurate recall of information by eyewitnesses (Zaragoza & Mitchell, 1996). A number of studies suggest that information contained in questions asked of the eyewitness can be a potent source of distortion. When a lawyer or police investigator asks questions about the crime, the questions may contain cues that influence retrieval to a great extent. Elizabeth Loftus has conducted several important studies that look at the effect of the questions asked of eyewitnesses. In one study (Loftus & Palmer, 1974), individuals were shown a film of an automobile accident. Later, half of the research participants were asked the first question and half were asked the second question:

1. "About how fast were the cars going when they smashed into each other?"

2. "About how fast were the cars going when they hit each other?"

The speed was estimated to be considerably faster by individuals who were asked the first version of the question ("smashed") than by those asked the second question ("hit"). One week later,

*(continued)*

all of the participants were asked the same question:

"Did you see any broken glass?"

Although the film showed no broken glass, 32 percent of the participants who had been asked how fast the cars were going when they "smashed" into each other "remembered" seeing broken glass, compared with only 14 percent of the participants who were asked the more neutral version of the question. The reconstruction theory of forgetting that we studied in this chapter would suggest that they remembered seeing broken glass when it was not there because broken glass would be consistent with two cars "smashing" together. Apparently the memory was reconstructed to include broken glass to make it more consistent.

Another researcher interviewed a large number of people who had witnessed a real-life drama. A high school football player went into cardiac arrest and apparently died (but, fortunately, was revived after he was taken from the field). Later, errors in recalling what had happened were common among the spectators. When some of them were intentionally questioned in a way that suggested that there might have been blood on his jersey, more than 25 percent of the spectators "remembered" seeing it there (Abhold, 1992).

Vicki Smith and Phoebe Ellsworth (1987) of Stanford University conducted a similar experiment, in which college students watched a videotape of a bank robbery in which the robbers were not wearing gloves and did not carry guns. Later, some of the students were asked neutral questions, such as

"Were they wearing gloves?"
"Did the other guy have a gun?"

The other students were asked misleading questions, such as

"What kind of gloves were they wearing?"
"What did the other guy's gun look like?"

As in Loftus' original studies, the misleading questions cued inaccurate recall of nonexistent gloves and guns. Interestingly, this happened only when the questioner was thought to be knowledgeable about the crime. Apparently, the memory was reconstructed to include gloves and guns only when the question implied that gloves and guns

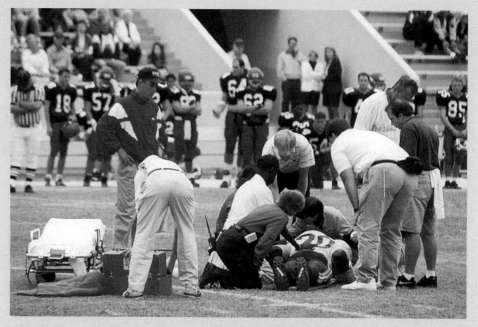

The way questions about a past event are phrased can affect people's memories of the event. For example, after seeing a football player collapse with heart trouble, over a fourth of spectators recalled seeing blood on his jersey when questioned in a way that suggested he had been bloody.

"What did the other guy's gun look like?"

were present. Thus, the way in which an eyewitness is questioned can greatly affect the accuracy of the information recalled. This means that we must be extremely careful to allow only neutral questions in legal proceedings, particularly if the witness believes the questioner has actual knowledge of the crime—as is often the case with attorneys in trials.

Are you losing your confidence in eyewitness testimony? Consider some

more experimental findings. A simulated crime was staged in the early 1970s at California State University at Hayward, in which a student "attacked" a faculty member (Buckhout, 1974). The staged crime was videotaped to have a record of what happened and was then compared with the eyewitness accounts of 141 students who saw the attack. Overall, the witnesses were accurate on an average of only about 25 percent of the facts that they recalled. By now, you know that eyewitness testimony is frequently inaccurate. But the more interesting part of this experiment is that the eyewitnesses were later asked to pick out the "attacker" from a set of six photos of similar-looking college men. Half of the eyewitnesses were shown the photos under unbiased conditions: All of the photos were head shots facing front and the witnesses were asked *if* the attacker was pictured. The other half of the eyewitnesses were shown the photos in a biased fashion: The photo of the actual attacker was different in head angle and was tilted slightly in the presentation. In addition, the eyewitnesses were told that one of the photos *was* the attacker and were asked to pick him out. Under these biased conditions, 50 percent more of the eyewitnesses chose the attacker. In this case, the presentation was biased against the actual attacker, but the same kind of subtle bias could be unintentionally introduced when an investigator was questioning a witness about a suspect that the investigator falsely believed was guilty. Unfortunately, a number of subtle factors in the questioning of eyewitnesses have been shown to influence their testimony (Haney, 1980; Kassin, Ellsworth, & Kassin, 1989).

A growing number of studies indicate that preschool children are particularly suggestible when they are interviewed by adults. Although their memories are often quite accurate, they sometimes provide convincing descriptions of events that never happened. This greatly complicates the investigation of allegations of sexual abuse by parents and day-care workers (Ceci & Bruck, 1995).

## Eyewitnesses Who "Look But Do Not See"

We human beings are often poor eyewitnesses because we too often do not really see what we observe. In one study of this topic, research participants were shown a movie scene. Part of the way through the scene, the actor was replaced by a different actor, but only a third of the participants noticed the change (Levin & Simons, 1997). Even more strikingly, a similar study was conducted on a college campus (Simons & Levin, 1998). A person (who was one of the experimenters) walked up to another person and asked for directions. As they spoke, two men walked between them, carrying a door,

**FIGURE 7.11**
Psychologist Gordon Allport showed individuals this picture for a very brief period of time to test the accuracy of their "eyewitness" testimony in a situation in which racial prejudice might influence their perception.

blocking the person's view of the experimenter for a moment. After the door passed, the conversation about the directions was completed. Less than half of the people noticed that the experimenter changed places with a *different* experimenter behind the door.

These people who looked but did not see would have made very poor eyewitnesses if they were later called on to identify the experimenter in a police lineup. They didn't even notice that the person who began the conversation was not the same person who completed it. How could this have happened? Perhaps we often process what we observe in shallow, rather than deep ways (Schachter, 1999), and because information that is not processed deeply is quickly forgotten, the change in people was not detected. Whatever the explanation, this phenomenon highlights the limits on the validity of eyewitness testimony.

## Stereotypes and Eyewitness Testimony

Do our stereotypes and prejudices influence the accuracy of eyewitness testimony? Unfortunately for the cause of justice, there is considerable reason to believe that they do.

Gordon Allport of Harvard University conducted a classic experiment

some years ago that demonstrated the extent to which our memories can be distorted by our prejudices (cited in Buckhout, 1974). Allport had individuals look briefly at the picture shown in figure 7.11. Look carefully to see who is holding the straight razor. Now be prepared for a shock when you learn that an amazing 50 percent of Allport's subjects later recalled that the African American man was holding the razor. Allport's study was conducted many years ago. Does prejudice play less of a role in the United States today? Sadly, no. In a more recent series of studies, participants were shown a list of male names of famous criminals and were asked if they remembered seeing any of them mentioned in the news media. Half of the names were common names in the African American community and half were typical European names. Although none of the names were actually names of criminals, the research participants "recognized" significantly more African American names as famous criminals in several studies (Banaji & Bhaskar, 1999).

How do our prejudices influence what we remember? This probably represents distortions of memories to fit our schemas. People who believe that African Americans are more likely to

*(continued)*

be criminals will be more likely to "recall" information that is consistent with that schema. In the case of eyewitness testimony in the courtroom, this could lead to inaccurate testimony.

## Inaccurate Recall Due to Characteristics of the Eyewitness

The eyewitness may have been tired, upset, or intoxicated at the time that the crime was observed—what effect, if any, would that have on the accuracy of recall? One study showed that intoxication can reduce the accuracy of recall under some circumstances, but not others (Yuille & Tollestrup, 1990). In this study, some research participants were given enough alcohol to bring their blood-alcohol levels up to .10, the level of legal intoxication for operating an automobile. The other participants were given no alcohol. Both sets of individuals watched a brief videotape of staged theft and were shown photos of possible thieves a week later for identification.

When a photograph of the person who played the role of the thief in the videotape was one of the photographs shown to the participants, there was no difference in the accuracy of the recall of the drunk and sober eyewitnesses. However, when none of the photos were of the actual thief, the intoxicated eyewitnesses falsely identified people who had not been in the videotape as the thief more often than did the sober eyewitnesses.

## Recall of "Repressed Memories" of Sexual and Physical Abuse

The most compelling eyewitness testimony is from victims themselves. Many court cases have been in the news in which women and men recall that they had been abused as children, but they had not been able to remember the abuse for many years. Some psychologists believe that memories of sexual and physical abuse are often suppressed. Other psychologists who specialize in the study of memory believe that it is difficult to know when so called repressed memories of abuse are accurate. This issue poses a serious dilemma for psychologists (Frankel, 1995). On the one hand, no psychologist wants to discourage anyone from reporting sexual abuse. The sexual abuse of children is a sadly common

occurrence, and any victim with the courage to report it should be supported in every way. On the other hand, there is reason to believe that not every adult who recalls that sexual abuse occurred in childhood is recalling something that actually occurred (Clancy & others, 2000; Pope, 1996; Spanos, 1996).

What is the evidence on the repression of upsetting memories, such as sexual abuse? One study of 590 persons who had been in automobile accidents found that 14 percent of the accident victims did not remember being in the accident one year earlier (Loftus, 1993). Similarly, in a study of adult women who reported that they were sexually abused as children, 18 percent reported that they went through a period in which they lost their memory of the sexual abuse and then recovered it later (Loftus, Polonsky, & Fullilove, 1993). These data suggest that it is possible that some people who experienced sexual abuse as a child may not remember it during parts of their adulthood.

On the other hand, it is well known that information that adults recall from childhood can be very inaccurate. The most famous example is that of Jean Piaget's false memory of his childhood "kidnapping." As you will see in chapter 9, Piaget was a well-known Swiss child psychologist. For a large part of his adult life, he remembered in some detail an incident in which someone attempted to kidnap him when he was a young child. His nanny, however, was able to chase off the would-be kidnapper and save young Jean. Many years later, however, the nanny confessed that she had made up the entire incident to gain attention. She confessed because she felt guilty about the watch she had received as a reward. Piaget concluded that he must have heard a description during early childhood of the kidnapping attempt that never occurred and formed a memory from his visual images of what he imagined had taken place. Later those visual images seemed like a memory of a real event to Piaget.

Was Piaget's experience just a fluke, or can anyone remember experiences in childhood that never happened? Ira Hyman and his colleagues conducted a series of studies that sheds light on this question (Hyman & Billings, 1998; Hyman & Pentland, 1996). The research participants were college students

whose parents had agreed to complete a questionnaire about events that had happened in the student's childhood. The researchers told the college students that they had looked over the information about childhood events provided by their parents and asked the college students to attempt to recall and describe several events. Some of the events were ones reported by the parents, but the researchers deceived the participants by asking them to describe some completely fictitious childhood events that their parents confirmed had *not* happened. For example, students were asked if they remembered running around with other kids at age 5 at a wedding reception, bumping into a table and spilling punch on the parents of the bride. In the first interview, the college students remembered almost 90 percent of the events that had actually happened in childhood, but almost no one remembered events that had never happened—not at first. Later, however, when the students were tested again, about a fourth of them "remembered" completely fictitious events from their childhood. The students were particularly likely to remember the false event if they were instructed to try to form mental images of the fictitious childhood event that the researchers led them to believe they had forgotten between testing sessions. They had constructed fictional memories of things that had never happened based on the suggestive questions asked by the researchers.

Many psychologists now believe that some memories of traumatic childhood events that some people "discover" in psychotherapy are false memories created by a combination of suggestive questioning and distortions of actual events (Hyman & Loftus, 1998; Porter & others, 2000). As we struggle to understand our emotional problems, we could be unintentionally influenced to recall ambiguous moments in our childhoods (such as a bath given by a baby-sitter or an accidental encounter with a relative who was changing clothes) as an incident of sexual abuse. A well-meaning psychotherapist might say something like, "There is a lot of evidence that people with problems like yours have been sexually abused as children but have repressed the memory. Do you have any trace of a memory from childhood that might indicate that you were abused?" (Loftus, 1997).

Controversy surrounds the use of hypnosis to aid the recall of eyewitnesses.

Police lineups are often used to test the ability of an eyewitness to identify a suspect by asking the eyewitness if the person who committed the crime is in the lineup. If the police know that the eyewitness said that the perpetrator had a moustache, having only one person in the lineup with a moustache could make a false identification more likely.

Could being asked such a question lead a person to unknowingly construct a distorted memory of an ambiguous event—or even recall an event that never happened?

In summarizing many similar research studies, memory researcher Elizabeth Loftus put it this way:

> There are hundreds of studies to support a high degree of memory distortion. People have recalled nonexistent broken glass and tape recorders, a cleanshaven man as having a mustache, straight hair as curly, and even something as large and conspicuous as a barn in a bucolic scene that contained no buildings at all. Clearly, then, inaccurate memories of traumatic childhood events are possible as well. Perhaps as psychologists learn more about memory we will be able to play a more effective role in helping others distinguish between real and imagined memories. (Loftus, 1993, p. 530)

## Hypnosis and Eyewitness Testimony

Some psychologists believe that hypnosis can be used to help individuals recall the past. Witnesses to crimes are sometimes hypnotized to help them remember details, and individuals who cannot recall traumatic events may be hypnotized to improve their recall dur-

ing psychotherapy. The popular belief that hypnosis improves memory is reinforced frequently by dramatic cases in the news. For instance, in 1976, a school bus driver was able to recall the license plate of the children's kidnappers while under hypnosis (Kroger & Douce, 1979). This type of hypnosis involves what is termed *hypnotic age regression.* In this procedure, hypnotized individuals are told that they are no longer in the present but are in the past —at the scene of a crime that occurred a month ago, or even 20 years ago in their childhoods. The purpose of the procedure is to allow individuals to "relive" parts of their earlier lives and recall important but forgotten experiences.

Can repressed memories of traumatic childhood experiences such as physical or sexual abuse be recalled in this way? Does hypnotic age regression really work? In some ways, it does appear to work. For example, when individuals are regressed to 3 years of age, they clearly act like 3-year-olds (Nash, Drake, Wiley, Khalsa, & Lynn, 1986). But are they actually reliving their third year of life and recalling those forgotten memories? Michael Nash of North Texas State University and his colleagues (1986) conducted a clever experimental test of age regression. Nash hypnotized a group of undergraduate

volunteers and told them that they had regressed to 3 years of age. As in previous studies, most of the participants vividly experienced a sense of being a young child. Nash then asked the students to tell him about any objects they clung to for security as a 3-year-old— such as blankets and teddy bears. Their reports were later compared with those of their parents. Interestingly, the reports of hypnotically age-regressed research participants were accurate about 20 percent of the time, whereas the recall of participants who were not hypnotized was accurate 70 percent of the time. Nash (1987) and others interpret these findings as meaning that the experience of hypnotic age regression is in the heightened *imagination* of the hypnotized individual and that "memories" dredged up during age regression are more erroneous than factual.

Similar controversy surrounds the use of hypnosis to aid the recall of eyewitnesses to more recent crimes. Some studies suggest that hypnotized individuals may actually recall more accurate information (Dywan & Bowers, 1983; Nogrady, McConkey, & Perry, 1985). But this advantage is greatly outweighed for most legal purposes because hypnotized individuals also recall more erroneous information (Lynn, Lock,

*(continued)*

267

Myers, & Payne, 1997). For this and other reasons, a great deal of controversy surrounds testimony obtained under hypnosis, even though it is admissible as evidence in some courts.

## Improving the Accuracy of Eyewitnesses Testimony

Psychologists have conducted more than a thousand experiments since the 1970s to understand why persons who see a crime being committed can be wrong about the perpetrator of the crime (Wells & others, 2000). These psychological studies raised concerns, but little was done to improve the use of eyewitness information in courts until recently. When DNA became accepted as evidence in criminal courts, it led to the overturning of many convictions of innocent persons. These innocent persons—some of whom were on death row awaiting execution—were mostly convicted on the basis of eyewitness testimony. These mistakes created enough concern about the problem of faulty eyewitness testimony to promote attempted solutions. In the late 1990s, the U.S. Department of Justice assembled a group of psychologists, police officers, prosecutors, and defense attorneys to discuss eyewitness testimony. In 1999, their recommendations for obtaining and using eyewitness testimony were released (available at http://www.ojp.usdoj.gov/nij/pubs-sum/178240.htm). This remarkable document is important for its positive approach to the issue. Whereas most of what had been written about eyewitness testimony focused on its shortcomings, these guidelines help police obtain and use information from eyewitnesses in the most accurate ways possible. Here is summary of the recommendations:

1. *Establish good rapport—a friendly and comfortable relationship—with the eyewitness before questioning begins.* Eyewitnesses are more likely to relax and invest their time and effort when this is done, especially if they are frightened or distrustful of the police.

2. *Ask open-ended questions, do not lead the witness, and let the eyewitness speak.* Police investigators tend to ask many questions that have a fixed set of answers—yes or no, red or green, etc. They often interrupt the eyewitness and cut off his or her answer after they have heard what they are seeking. As a result, eyewitnesses rarely have a chance to provide unsolicited information. This information can be critically important because it provides information that the investigator did not even know enough to ask about. It is similarly important for the investigator not to ask leading questions—questions that imply that a certain answer is desired by the police. Such questions may influence some eyewitnesses to be "good citizens" and give the officer the information that is desired (whether it is entirely accurate or not) and may lead some hostile eyewitnesses to withhold information.

3. *"Fillers" in lineups should generally fit the witness's description of the perpetrator.* Police often bring suspects into the police station, where eyewitnesses view them from behind a one-way mirror in a line of persons. Some of the persons in the lineup are called fillers because they are known to be innocent. Fillers who look very different from the suspect—different height, hair color, or race—will increase the likelihood that the eyewitness will identify the suspect (whether the suspect is guilty or not). The same principle applies when eyewitnesses are viewing photographs—mug shots—of potential perpetrators. Defense attorneys often successfully attack photo identifications and lineups as biased if credible fillers were not used.

4. *When conducting lineup identifications of suspects, place only one suspect in each lineup.* If the police have more than one suspect for a crime, they often put all of them in a single lineup. The problem in this common practice can be seen in the simple arithmetic of the process. An eyewitness is more likely to mistakenly identify a suspect if there is more than one suspect in the lineup. If the eyewitness identified perpetrators at random, and half of the people in the lineup were people suspected of committing the crime, the eyewitness would mistakenly select one of the suspects half the time.

5. *Instructions to eyewitnesses before viewing photos and lineups should not bias their choices.* They should be told that the person who committed the crime may or may not be in the photos or lineup. In addition, they should be told that it is just as important to clear innocent suspects as it is to identify the guilty person. This will reduce false identifications by making it clear to the eyewitness that it is okay to fail to select someone.

6. *Avoid giving feedback to eyewitnesses after they identify a photo or a person in a lineup.* Feedback can increase or decrease the eyewitnesses' confidence in their identification. This is important because eyewitnesses are commonly asked how confident they are in their judgment during court proceedings. ■

# Summary

Chapter 7 examines how we process information and how we remember or forget that information.

I. Human memory is composed of three stages of memory.
   A. The sensory register holds an exact image of each sensory experience for a very brief interval until it can be fully processed.
   B. Short-term memory holds information for about half a minute.
      1. Information fades from short-term memory unless it is renewed by rehearsal.
      2. Short-term memory has a limited capacity of 7 ± 2 items.
      3. The capacity of STM can be increased by organizing information into larger chunks.
   C. Long-term memory stores information primarily in terms of its meaning. Information is organized in LTM primarily in categories of related meanings and according to how frequently events have been associated in our experience.
      1. Procedural memory is memory for skills and other procedures.
      2. Episodic memory is memory for specific experiences that can be defined in terms of time and space.
      3. Semantic memory is memory for meaning.
      4. Declarative memory, which includes both episodic and semantic memory, is memory that is described easily in words.
   D. The levels of processing model views the distinction between short-term and long-term memory in terms of degree rather than separate stages.

II. There are four major causes of forgetting, each with different relevance to the three stages of memory.
   A. Decay theory states that forgetting occurs simply because time passes. This occurs in the sensory register and STM but probably does not occur in LTM.
   B. Interference theory states that forgetting occurs when other memories interfere with retrieval. Interference can occur from memories that were formed in prior learning (proactive interference) or from memories that were formed in later learning (retroactive interference).
   C. Reconstruction (schema) theory states that memories can be distorted as they are recalled from LTM to make them more consistent with our beliefs, knowledge, and expectations.
   D. Freud believed that some unpleasant memories could not be recalled because they were repressed. Memory for positive events has been found to be better than for negative events, but memory for events associated with either positive or negative emotional arousal is usually better than for emotionally neutral events, raising questions about Freud's theory. In addition, intense negative emotional arousal can produce memories that are vivid in some ways, but distorted in other ways.

III. Much has been learned in recent years about the role of the brain in memory.
   A. The frontal lobes play a key role in STM, in encoding memories for long-term storage, and in the retrieval of information from LTM into working memory.
   B. The hippocampus is a key structure in the organization and transfer of information between STM and LTM.

C.    When events are accompanied by emotional arousal, the amygdala plays a key role in memory formation. Intense emotional arousal may suppress the organizing role of the hippocampus by releasing cortisol, however.

D.    Synaptic theories view the engram as a change in the pattern or strength of synaptic linkages between neurons.

E.    Amnesia is a major disorder of memory.

1.    An inability to consciously retrieve new information in LTM is anterograde amnesia. Anterograde amnesia is caused by damage in the hippocampus and other brain structures.

2.    The inability to retrieve old, rather than new, long-term memories is known as retrograde amnesia.

## Resources

1.    A scholarly yet very readable analysis of cognition and memory is Ellis, H. C., & Hunt, R. R. (1996). *Fundamentals of cognitive psychology* (6th ed.). Boston: McGraw-Hill.

2.    For a wonderfully well-written synopsis of what psychology has learned about human memory, see Schachter, D. L. (1999). The seven sins of memory: Insights from psychology and cognitive neuroscience. *American Psychologist, 54,* 182–203.

3.    For a detailed look at the relationship between mood and memory, see Bower, G. H. (1981). Mood and memory. *American Psychologist, 36,* 129–148.

4.    For more information on the biological basis of memory, see Squire, L. R. (1987). *Memory and the brain.* New York: Oxford University Press; and D'Esposito, M. (2000). Functional imaging of neurocognition. *Seminars in Neurology, 70,* 487–498.

5.    For more on the debate about false "recovered" memories and related topics, see Lynn, S. J., & McConkey, K. M. (1998). *Truth in memory.* New York: Guilford Press; and Loftus, E. F. (1997). Creating false memories. *Scientific American,* pp. 70–75.

6.    For a discussion of the guidelines for collecting eyewitness testimony issued by the U.S. Department of Justice, see Wells, G. L., & others (2000). From the lab to the police station: A successful application of eyewitness research. *American Psychologist, 55,* 581–598.

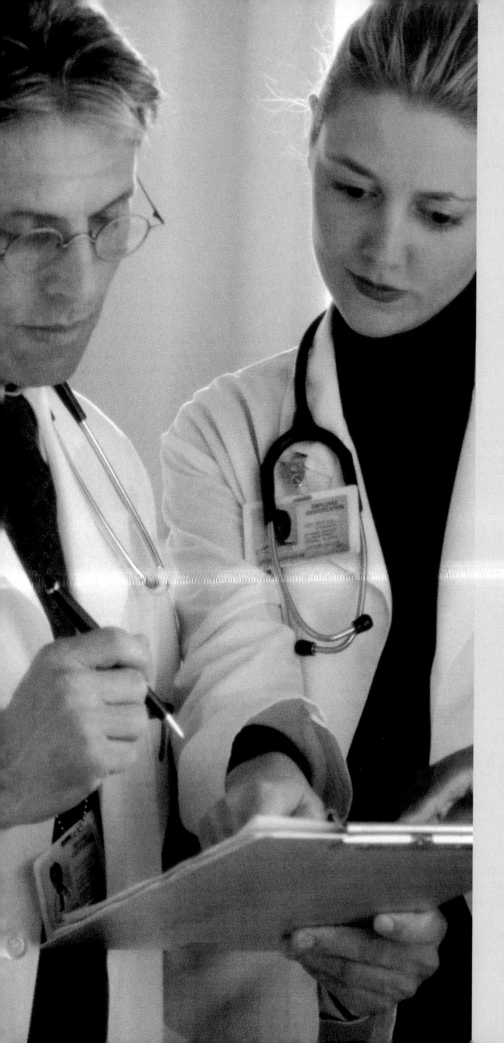

## Chapter Outline

# Cognition, Language, and Intelligence

## PROLOGUE

Perhaps the most important reason that the human race has survived for more than 1.5 million years is that we are intelligent. We aren't the strongest, the fastest, or the most ferocious. But compared with other animal species, we are extremely good at solving problems. We survive cold weather by building shelters and making warm clothing; we invent wheels to move heavy objects; and we develop antibiotics when threatened by disease.

But we speak of human intelligence here not to praise it, but to marvel at its quirks, foibles, and flaws! If human intelligence is a miracle of evolution, it's an amazingly flawed miracle. When our intellectual processes are examined carefully, it's sometimes amazing that we soft-skinned and slow-moving humans have been able to survive by our wits.

To help us understand the sometimes peculiar properties of human reasoning, Daniel Kahneman and Amos Tversky conducted a fascinating series of experiments. In one study, a group of physicians was presented with the following problem:

> Imagine that the United States is preparing for the outbreak of a rare Asian disease, which is expected to kill 600 people. Two alternative programs to combat the disease have been proposed. Assume that the exact scientific estimates of the consequences of the programs are as follows: If Program A is adopted, 200 people will be saved. If Program B is adopted, there is a 1/3 probability that 600 people will be saved and a 2/3 probability that no people will be saved. Which of the two programs would you favor? (Kahneman & Tversky, 1982, p. 163)

What decision would you have made? The majority of physicians polled by Kahneman and Tversky chose Program A. The guarantee of saving 200 lives made it a better alternative than a long shot of saving all of the lives. But a fascinating thing happened when the researchers presented exactly the same problem in a different way. A second group of physicians was presented the following version of the same problem:

> If Program A is adopted, 400 people will die. If Program B is adopted, there is a 1/3 probability that nobody will die and a 2/3 probability that 600 people will die. (pp. 163–164)

Would framing the problem in this different manner have influenced your decision? It did influence the physicians. When presented in the latter way, the majority chose B. The sure death of 400 people was too difficult to accept when stated this way. There is actually no logical difference between the two ways of asking the question. Stated either way, 200 people would live and 400 people would die if Program A were adopted. But the physicians' decision making was strongly influenced by the way the question was framed. Cold logic is sometimes less important than the way in which the problem is framed.

Perhaps the best way to view human intelligence is to recognize its amazing capacity and great importance to our survival, yet to use our intelligence to understand its shortcomings and compensate for them. In this chapter, we will examine both the capacity and the limits of human reasoning.

We will use the term *cognition* in this chapter to refer to all of the intellectual processes through which we obtain information from the world, change it to meet our needs, store it for later use, and use it to solve our problems. Clearly, it's a very broad concept. Cognition is an important topic in nearly every chapter in this book. We first discussed the term in the first chapter and discussed important aspects of cognition when we studied perception, learning, and memory. In later chapters, we will discuss cognition again in other contexts. But in this chapter we will discuss several fundamental aspects of cognition—thinking, language, and intelligence. ■

## Definition of Cognition

**cognition**
The intellectual processes through which information is obtained, transformed, stored, retrieved, and otherwise used.

**concepts**
(kon´septs) Categories of things, events, and qualities that are linked together by a common feature or features in spite of their differences.

**Cognition** can be defined as the intellectual processes (such as perception, memory, thinking, and language) through which information is obtained, transformed, stored, retrieved, and used. Let's analyze this complicated definition and its three primary facets:

1.  *Cognition processes information.*  Information is the stuff of cognition: the stuff that is obtained, transformed, kept, and used. Much of this information is dealt with in the form of categories or concepts, the subject of the next section.

2.  *Cognition is active.*  The information that the world gives us is actively changed, kept, and used in the process of cognition. In cognition, information is

    a) Obtained through the senses

    b) *Transformed* through the interpretive processes of perception and thinking

    c) *Stored and retrieved* through the processes of memory

    d) *Used* in problem solving and language

3.  *Cognition is useful.*  It serves a purpose. We think because there is something we do not understand. We use language when we need to communicate something to others. We create when we need something that does not exist. Humans use cognition to survive physically and to live in a social world.

Cognition involves intellectual processes through which information is obtained, transformed, stored, retrieved, and put to use.

In this chapter, we will survey problem solving, concept formation, language, and general intelligence. Other important aspects of cognition have already been discussed in the chapters on perception, consciousness, learning, and memory. And more aspects of cognition will be mentioned in later chapters on development, emotion, personality, stress, abnormal behavior, and social psychology. Cognition is more than a topic in the science of psychology; it's a theme that cuts across many diverse topics.

## Concepts: The Basic Units of Thinking

**Concepts** are the basic units of thinking. Concepts are general categories of things, events, and qualities that are linked by a common feature or features, in spite of their differences. About an hour ago, I went for a ride on my new bicycle. My bicycle is a specific object, but *bicycle* in general is a concept. I passed several people on bicycles as I rode—each bicycle was different in some ways from every other one, but I knew that they were all bicycles because they shared a list of characteristics (two wheels, pedals, handlebars, etc.) that all bicycles share. I also passed a lot of things that were not bicycles (cars, trucks, barbecue grills, etc.), but being a clever fellow, I knew in a flash that they were not bicycles because they did not have the features shared by all bicycles. Keep in mind that concepts are categories of more than just concrete things—the terms *vacation, romance,* and *generosity* refer to concepts as well.

Nearly all productive thinking would be impossible were it not for concepts. Consider the following syllogism:

All human beings are mortal.

I am a human being.

Therefore, I am mortal.

When I reason in that way, I am using the general concepts of *human beings* and *mortality.* Without concepts, we would be able to think only in terms of specific things and acts. Concepts allow us to process information in more general, efficient ways. In this way, concepts are the basic units of logical thinking.

Adults take for granted that all these objects belong to the concept *bicycle.*

## Simple and Complex Concepts

Some concepts are based on a single common feature, such as the concept *red.* If a thing is red, it belongs to the concept *red* regardless of its other characteristics. Red apples, red balls, and red T-shirts are all examples of the concept *red,* in spite of the other ways in which these objects differ. Other concepts are more complex. **Conjunctive concepts** are defined by the simultaneous presence of two or more common characteristics. The concept of *aunt* is an example of a conjunctive concept because it has two simultaneous defining characteristics (female and sister of one of your parents). To be considered an aunt, a person must have both characteristics. **Disjunctive concepts** are defined by the presence of one common characteristic or another one, *or both.* For example, a person might be considered to be schizophrenic if he persistently has distorted perceptual experiences (such as hearing strange voices that are not there) *or* persistently holds distorted false beliefs (such as believing he is a king or a CIA agent), *or both.* The concept *schizophrenic person* is a disjunctive concept because it is defined by the presence of either of two characteristics or both of them.

Suppose the six cards in figure 8.1 were presented to you in the order shown (left to right). The odd-numbered cards are members of the concept and the even-numbered cards are not. What is the concept—and is it a simple, conjunctive, or disjunctive concept?[1]

**conjunctive concepts**
(kon-junk″tiv′) Concepts defined by the simultaneous presence of two or more common characteristics.

**disjunctive concepts**
(dis-junk″tiv′) Concepts defined by the presence of one of two common characteristics or both.

## Natural Concepts

Eleanor Rosch (1973) has suggested that some concepts are easier for humans to learn than others; some are more *natural* than others. This idea is an important extension of the notion discussed in chapter 6 that we are biologically prepared to learn some things more readily than others. Rosch suggests that, by virtue of being born human beings, we are prepared to learn some concepts more easily than others. According to Rosch, natural concepts have two primary characteristics: They are *basic* and *prototypical.* Let's define these terms.

### Natural Concepts Are Basic

A *basic concept* is one that has a medium degree of *inclusiveness.* Inclusiveness simply refers to the number of members included in a concept. Three levels of inclusiveness have been distinguished by Rosch:

1.  *Superordinate concepts are very inclusive.* Therefore, they contain a great many members. For example, *vehicles* is a superordinate concept that contains all of the many cars, boats, planes, wagons, and so on that carry loads (see fig. 8.2).

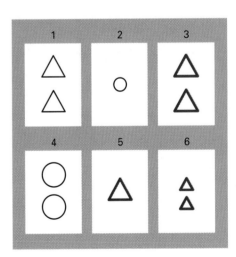

**FIGURE 8.1**
Cards like those used in laboratory studies of concept formation.

---

[1]The concept illustrated in this example is large triangles, which is a conjunctive concept.

**FIGURE 8.2**

Basic concepts, which include neither the most nor the least other concepts under them, are easier to learn than superordinate or subordinate concepts.

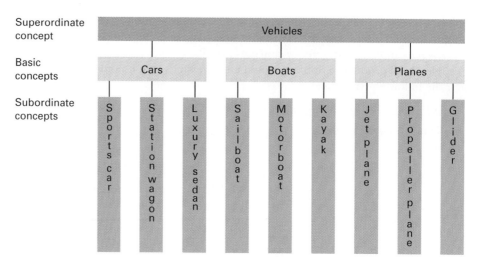

2. **Basic concepts are of a medium degree of inclusiveness.** *Cars* is an example of a basic concept because it is less inclusive than the superordinate concept *vehicles*, yet this category still includes many members.

3. **Subordinate concepts are the least inclusive level of concepts.** For example, the subordinate concept *sports car* includes far fewer members than the basic concept *cars* or the superordinate concept *vehicles*.

Medium-degree inclusive concepts such as *cars* are called basic concepts; the broader concept of *vehicle* is a superordinate concept; and the narrower concept of *luxury sedan* is a subordinate concept.

Rosch suggests that basic concepts are more natural and, hence, easier to learn and use. She offers an observation on the way in which young children learn concepts as evidence. Children generally learn basic concepts, such as *cars,* before they learn superordinate or subordinate concepts, such as *vehicles* or *sports cars.* Why is this so? Why are basic concepts easier to learn than either superordinate or subordinate concepts? Rosch suggests that the explanation lies in several characteristics of basic concepts that "fit" the human intellect very well (Matlin, 1983; Rosch, Mervis, Gray, Johnson, & Boyes-Braem, 1976).

1. **Basic concepts share many attributes.** For example, the members of the basic concept *screwdriver* are all used to turn screws, have a metal protrusion, have a handle, are usually 4 to 10 inches long, and so on. Members of the superordinate category of *tools* have far fewer characteristics in common. Although the members of the subordinate category of chrome-plated screwdrivers have many common characteristics, only a few of them are not also common to the basic concept of screwdrivers (Jones, 1983).

2. **Members of basic concepts share similar shapes.** All screwdrivers (a basic concept) are shaped about the same, but the same cannot be said about all tools (a superordinate concept). The shapes of all chrome-plated screwdrivers (a subordinate concept) are also similar, but they are distinguishable from other screwdrivers on the basis of only one difference—the chrome plating—that has nothing to do with shape.

3. **Members of basic concepts often share motor movements.** The motor movements associated with members of basic-level concepts are similar (turning screwdrivers), but the same cannot be said for superordinate concepts (the motor movements for using different kinds of tools are very different). Members of subordinate concepts like chrome-plated screwdrivers also share motor movements, but they are generally the same as or similar to the basic concept to which they belong (see fig. 8.3).

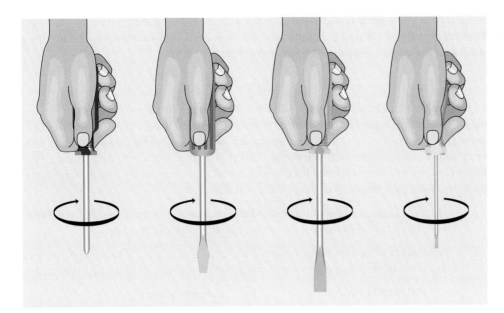

**FIGURE 8.3**
Members of the basic concepts like *screwdrivers* often share the same motor movements in spite of other differences.

4. ***Basic concepts are easily named.*** If you were asked to name a half-dozen objects in your classroom, most of the words that you would use would probably refer to the basic concepts to which the objects belong. When referring to a chrome-plated screwdriver, we tend to say *screwdriver* instead of *tool* or *chrome-plated screwdriver.*

Rosch believes that these four characteristics of basic concepts make them more "natural"—easier to learn and use in the human information-processing system.

### Natural Concepts Are Good Prototypes

The second defining characteristic of natural concepts is that they are good examples, or *prototypes* (Rosch, 1975). If you were asked to give the best example, or the prototype, of the superordinate concept *toy,* you might say *doll* or *toy fire truck,* but you would be unlikely to say *sandbox.* Similarly, you might think of *chair* or *sofa* as prototypes of the superordinate concept of *furniture,* but you would not think of *carpet.* Rosch suggests that natural concepts tend to be both basic and good prototypes.

In her research with the Dani tribe of New Guinea, Rosch (1973) has provided intriguing evidence to support her notion that natural concepts are good prototypes. This tribe, which possessed a very limited technology in the 1970s, has only two color concepts in its vocabulary: *mola* for light colors and *mili* for dark colors. Hence, these people were ideal individuals for research on learning new color concepts.

Rosch's Dani research participants were taught to give a label to members of a color category that corresponded to both "pure" primary colors (wavelengths that are near the middle of the range described as red or blue, for example) and intermediate colors (such as bluish-green). Both kinds of color names are basic concepts (with the superordinate concept being *color*), but the Dani learned the names of the primary colors more easily.

---

Concepts are the basic units of thinking. They allow us to reason because they permit us to think in general categories. Concepts are categories that have one or more features in common in spite of differences among members of that concept. All red things belong to the concept of *red* even though apples, fire trucks, and red balls differ from one another in many ways. Some concepts are defined by a single characteristic, whereas others are defined by multiple characteristics in complex ways. Not

**Review**

all concepts are equally easy to learn; apparently, some concepts are more "natural" than others. These natural concepts are easy to learn because they are of a medium degree of inclusiveness and are good prototypes.

## Check Your Learning

To be sure that you have learned the key points from the preceding section, cover the list of correct answers and try to answer each question. If you give an incorrect answer to any question, return to the page given next to the correct answer to see why your answer was not correct. Remember that these questions cover only some of the important information in this section; it is important that you make up your own questions to check your learning of other facts and concepts.

1. _____ are categories of things, events, or qualities that are linked by some common feature or features in spite of their differences.

2. The concept of *aunt* is an example of a _____ because it has two simultaneous defining characteristics (female and sister of one of your parents).

   a)    disjunctive concept          c)    simple concept
   b)    conjunctive concept          d)    natural concept

3. By virtue of being born human beings, we are prepared to learn some concepts more easily than others. These concepts are termed _____.

   a)    simple concepts             c)    natural concepts
   b)    disjunctive concepts        d)    conjunctive concepts

4. Which of the following statements is *not* true?

   a)    Basic concepts share many attributes.
   b)    Basic concepts share similar shapes.
   c)    Basic concepts often share motor movements.
   d)    Basic concepts are difficult to describe in words.

## Thinking Critically about Psychology

1. What is your favorite kind of thing (think of a concept, not a specific thing)? Try to describe in words the prototype of that concept.

2. Recall what you learned earlier about the role of the cones in color vision. Does this suggest why primary colors are "natural" color concepts?

Correct Answers:  1.  Concepts (p. 274),  2.  b (p. 275),  3.  c (p. 275),  4.  d (p. 277).

### ● Thinking and Problem Solving: Using Information to Reach Goals

Without concepts, sophisticated thinking would be impossible. Understanding concepts gives us insight into the *content* of thinking. Let's look now at an important example of the *process* of thinking—the question of how we use concepts to solve specific problems.

What should you do when you think you have upset your boss with the hotly political statement that you made at last night's cocktail party? Do you tell her you were just joking? Do you talk to her again tomorrow in the hope that you can agree to disagree without animosity? Do you forget about it on the assumption that she will not let politics interfere with her evaluation of your job performance? Do you wait and see if she acts as if you really did offend her—remember you only *think* you upset her—before you do anything further? What do you do?

Fortunately, no one really expects textbook writers to answer such knotty questions but merely to discuss the general process through which we solve such problems! **Problem solving** can be defined as the cognitive process through which information is used to reach a goal that is blocked by some kind of obstacle. Let's examine that process.

## Cognitive Operations in Problem Solving

The focus of much current research is on the cognitive *operations* of problem solving. Operations remove obstacles to goals. What cognitive operations do we follow in trying to solve problems and reach our goals?

There are three major types of cognitive operations involved in problem solving that apparently must be performed in sequence. First, we have to perceive and formulate the problem to decide what kind of problem we face. Second, we need to evaluate the elements of the problem to decide what information and tools we have to work with. Finally, we often need to generate a list of solutions and evaluate them.

### Formulating the Problem

Before we begin to solve a problem, we must be able to define it in clear and specific terms. Sometimes the problem we face is obvious. For example, I want to drive to Key West, but I don't have enough cash to buy gas; what do I do? At other times, the nature of the problem is not at all clear. For example, you may know that the goal of being promoted in your job is not being reached, but you may not know what is preventing you from being promoted. Do I need to perform my job better? Do I need to get along with my superiors better? Do I need to be more assertive in requesting a promotion? To solve a problem, *you have to know what the problem is.*

As Michael Posner (1973) has pointed out, the key to effective problem solving is often our initial formulation of the problem. Take the problem illustrated in figure 8.4, for example. If you know the radius of the circle, what is the length of line *l*? See if you can figure it out. (The answer appears on page 280). The trick is in *not* thinking of it as a problem involving the triangle *l, d, x*. Formulating the problem in *that* way blocks our being able to see what solution is called for. As can be seen in figure 8.5, the problem can be easily solved by thinking of *l* as the diagonal of the rectangle with sides *x* and *d*. The radius of the circle, then, is the other diagonal of the rectangle (dashed line in fig. 8.5), and because our geometry teachers taught us that the two diagonals of a rectangle are equal, it's easy to determine that line *l* is the same length as the radius.

## Understanding and Organizing the Elements of the Problem

After formulating the problem, we must make an inventory of the elements of the problem—the information and other resources available to us. Often, effective problem solving requires that we *flexibly* interpret the meaning and utility of these elements. Many of life's problems require an insightful reorganization of the elements of the problem: When you lock your keys in your car, a bent coat hanger becomes a door opener. One of the ways in which human problem solving is rather predictably fallible, however, is that we are often *not* flexible enough in evaluating the elements in problems. Consider the following situation. Karl Duncker (1945) has provided a problem for you to solve. See in figure 8.6 that you are given three candles, some thumbtacks, and a box of matches. Your problem is to put one of the candles on the wall in such a way that it will not drip wax on the floor or table when burning. Check out figure 8.7 on page 281 when you have come up with an answer.

The limitations most of us experience in evaluating the elements of problems is that we get stuck in "mental ruts," or in psychological terms, we get stuck in mental sets. The term **mental set** refers to a habitual way of approaching or perceiving a problem. Because problems often require a novel or flexible use of their elements, a habitual way of looking at the elements of a problem can interfere with finding a solution. If you had

**problem solving**
The cognitive process through which information is used to reach a goal that is blocked by some obstacle.

**mental set**
A habitual way of approaching or perceiving a problem.

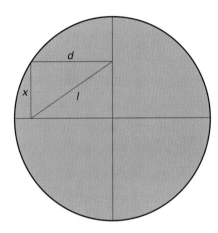

**FIGURE 8.4**

If you know the length of the radius of the circle (distance from the center to any side), what is the length of line *l*? This problem shows the importance of formulating a problem in the correct way.

Source: After W. Kohler, *The Task of Gestalt Psychology.* Copyright © 1969 by Princeton University Press.

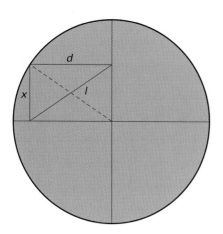

**FIGURE 8.5**
The problem given in figure 8.4 can be easily solved if it's viewed in the right way. Its solution requires you to think of line *l* as one of two diagonals of a rectangle rather than as part of a triangle. Line *l* is equal to the other diagonal (dotted line), which is the radius of the circle.
Source: After W. Kohler, *The Task of Gestalt Psychology.* Copyright © 1969 by Princeton University Press.

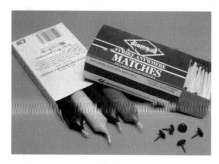

**FIGURE 8.6**
A Duncker candle problem. How can you mount the candle on the wall so that it will not drip wax on the table or floor when it's burning? See figure 8.7 for a good solution.

**trial and error**
The random application of one possible solution after another.

**algorithms**
(al′go-rith′mz) Systematic patterns of reasoning that guarantee finding a correct solution to a problem.

**heuristics**
Efficient problem-solving strategies that do not guarantee a correct solution.

**representativeness heuristic**
The strategy of making judgments about the unknown on the assumption that it is similar to what we know.

trouble with the Duncker candle problem, it was probably because you—like most people—thought of the box in the habitual way; the box is not immediately thought of as part of the solution because it is merely seen as an incidental item that holds the matches.

### Generating and Evaluating Alternative Solutions

Very often a problem has more than one solution. Our task then is to generate a list of possible solutions, evaluate each one by attempting to foresee what effects or consequences it would produce, choose the best solution, and then develop an effective way of implementing it.

## Heuristic Thinking

The cognitive strategies used to carry out the steps in the problem-solving operations just described can be of three general types: trial and error, algorithmic, or heuristic. Let's look at each of these cognitive strategies one at a time. We humans often approach problems without any cognitive strategy at all, simply trying one possible solution after another. This is usually referred to as the **trial-and-error** approach. Although common, this approach to problem solving can be very time consuming and certainly does not guarantee that a solution will be discovered.

In contrast, **algorithms** are systematic patterns of reasoning that (if followed) guarantee a correct solution. Computers generally use algorithms. Indeed, computers are especially suited for them, because they can quickly consider the many alternatives required by complex algorithms. Computers do not always use algorithms, however. For extremely complex problems, computers are sometimes programmed to use shortcuts known as **heuristics.** Heuristics are strategies that increase the probabilities of finding a correct solution. But because they do not systematically evaluate every possible solution, heuristics do not guarantee finding the correct one. Indeed, they often lead to poor solutions.

The concept of heuristic reasoning is derived partially from research that attempts to simulate human intelligence using computers. Efforts to program computers to play the game of chess, for example, were originally frustrated by the enormous number of possible solutions that would have to be considered before making each move. To avoid such extensive algorithmic programs, heuristic programs were written. For example, the program is written to maximize protection of the queen or to control the center of the board. Moves that meet these goals are executed, but the long-range consequences of each move are not considered by the artificial intelligence program. That is why excellent chess players can generally beat computers at chess.

Heuristic reasoning is very efficient but is subject to error. We need to understand the flaws inherent in heuristic reasoning because we solve problems heuristically far more often than algorithmically, largely because algorithmic reasoning takes more time and effort (Kahneman, Slovic, & Tversky, 1982). Many graduate programs in business administration devote a great deal of time to helping future managers avoid such heuristic decision making. For example, we tend to make judgments about the unknown on the assumption that it is similar to what we know (Tversky & Kahneman, 1974). This strategy is known as the **representativeness heuristic.** For example, if I describe "Lou" as shy and withdrawn, neat and tidy, and passionate about detail, what job would you guess he holds? Did an occupation come to mind—like librarian or some other occupation that you associate with those characteristics? We tend to make judgments in such situations on the basis of similarity to our stereotypes about people in different occupations. Reasoning on the basis of similarity is valid to some extent—people in different occupations do tend to differ in personality characteristics *on the average*—but it can lead to false conclusions. Not many people are librarians or accountants; that means that the vast majority of people with personalities like Lou's do something else.

phemes stand alone as words. *Word, stand,* and *fast* are each single freestanding morphemes. Other morphemes can exist only if they are bound to other morphemes. Examples are the morpheme for past tense in push*ed,* the plural morpheme in car*s,* and the prefix morpheme *anti* meaning "against" in the word *antibiotic.* The average person knows thousands of morphemes but can speak an infinite number of utterances using a finite set of morphemes and rules for combining them.

### Syntax

The rules of a language that allow an infinite number of understandable utterances to be generated are called **syntax.** There are rules for the ways in which phonemic sounds can be combined in morphemes and rules for how morphemes can be combined in utterances. For instance, in English, we learn that the suffix *-ed* communicates past tense and that the *-s* suffix denotes a plural. We learn the importance of word order. For example, we wouldn't say "this an interesting class is." These rules of syntax are the heart of generative language, for without them, only a finite number of things could be said with the finite set of morphemes. These rules allow us to make new sentences that will immediately and effortlessly be understood by all speakers who speak normally in the same language.

It is interesting to consider, however, the differences between rules of syntax and the *prescriptive rules* of grammar that are usually taught by authorities, such as parents and teachers. Everyone who speaks a language in a way that can be understood by others knows the syntax of that language, but not everyone uses "proper" grammar. Winston Churchill, an undisputed master of the English language, provided a humorous example of the artificiality of prescriptive rules when he wrote the awkward but grammatically correct "this is the kind of language up with which I will not put." It is also interesting to note that few cultures emphasize prescriptive rules of syntax as much as Western European cultures. Other cultures feel that speaking in an understandable way is all that matters.

We will discuss the way that language develops in the next chapter's section on child development, but it's interesting to note that children develop language by learning phonemes first, then morphemes, and then syntax. Children first learn to babble in the speech sounds of their language, then they use some freestanding morphemes by themselves (*mamma, milk, bye-bye*), and then they begin to acquire syntactic rules for combining morphemes into longer and more complex utterances.

### Language and Thought: The Whorfian Hypothesis

Language and thinking are closely related phenomena. Although we often think in visual images, sounds, and images of movements—and some thought may involve no conscious images at all—much of our thinking takes place in the form of silent conversations with ourselves. If this is true, does language exert any influence on our thinking? If so, it is possible that people who speak different languages might think somewhat differently.

This hypothesis was stated by Benjamin Whorf (1956) and is known as the *Whorfian* hypothesis, or **linguistic relativity hypothesis.** Although Whorf was most concerned with the impact of different languages on the thinking of people from different cultures, his concrete examples of how this might happen generally concerned the relationship between language and perception. For example, Eskimos have several words for *snow* and can discriminate among different kinds of snow better than, say, lifelong residents of Florida. Does the fact that Eskimos have more words to describe different kinds of snow—and can notice small differences among different kinds of snow—mean that their additional words improve their perception of snow? Whorf proposed that the presence of these words in the Eskimo vocabulary improved visual perception. It seems at least as plausible to assume that the Eskimos first learned to perceive slight differences among different kinds of snow and *then* invented a vocabulary for talking about them to others.

We learn language by first learning phonemes, then morphemes, followed by syntax.

"I understood each and every word you said but not the order in which they appeared."

**syntax**
(sin´taks)  The grammatical rules of a language.

**linguistic relativity hypothesis**
The idea that the structure of a language may influence the way individuals think.

These people from different cultures have different words to describe water. According to Benjamin Whorf, the vocabulary of a language can influence the way speakers of that language think.

A test of the Whorfian, or linguistic relativity, hypothesis was performed by researchers at the University of Alberta (Hoffman, Lau, & Johnson, 1986). Their experiment was based on the fact that each language contains terms referring to "personality types" that are important in each culture. For example, most of us understand that the "artistic type" is a person who is interested in the arts, imaginative, intense, moody, and unconventional. Each language contains such terms, but not every language has terms to describe the same personality types. For example, the Chinese language does not have a term for the artistic type, but it contains labels for other personality types that are not found in the English language. For example, the "shēn cáng bù lòu" type is recognized by speakers of Chinese to be a very knowledgeable person but one so shy that he or she is reluctant to reveal knowledge and skills unless it is absolutely necessary.

The Whorfian hypothesis suggests that these labels for personality types influence how we think about people. Do they? Fluent speakers of English were compared in their memories for, and reasoning about, hypothetical persons whose personality types were described by the experimenters. Individuals whose language contained a label for the particular personality type described by the experimenter were able to recall the hypothetical people more easily and thought about them in ways that were more consistent with the personality type. For example, English-speaking research participants recalled the characteristics of the hypothetical person described as artistic more often and reasoned about the artistic type in ways that reflected the description of his or her personality more accurately than Chinese-speaking participants did. The opposite was true of the shēn cáng bù lòu type. In this sense, the words in our language do seem to influence our cognition.

Linguistic relativity has led us to reexamine some of our common language usage. Persons concerned about gender equity have lobbied for the substitution of gender-neutral terms for unnecessarily masculine terms, as in the case of changing *chairman* to *chairperson*. If Whorf is correct, using *chairman* might subtly affect the way we think about the capabilities of females to serve in leadership roles. Although some of the changes seem initially odd to some people (*server* instead of *waiter* or *waitress*), they seem to be rapidly taking over common usage. Producers of *Star Trek: The Next Generation* took this trend one step further when the original "where no *man* has gone before" was changed to "where no *one* has gone before." No one is excluded now.

## Animal Languages: Can We Talk to the Animals?

Although humans have the most flexible and symbolic language for communicating propositions, we are not the only species that can communicate. Bees, for example, use a simple but elegant system to communicate messages such as *flowers containing a nectar supply are about 200 meters away on a line that is 20 degrees south of the angle of the sun.* The bee who discovers the nectar tells the other bees about it not through speech or written memos but through a symbolic dance.

If the nectar is within 100 meters of the hive, the bee does a *round dance* (see fig. 8.8), first turning a tight circle in one direction and then reversing and circling in the opposite direction. This dance does not communicate the direction of the nectar find, so it sends swarms of bees flying out in all directions within 100 meters of the hive looking for the nectar. If the nectar is 200 to 300 meters from the hive, the "speaker" bee gives better directions to his attentive audience. The bee does a *tail-wagging dance.* This dance is in the form of a tight figure eight. The direction of the nectar is communicated through the angle of the middle part of the dance relative to the sun. The distance is communicated by the rate of turning, the rate of tail wagging, and the sound made by the vibration of the wings. Distances between 100 and 200 meters are communicated through much looser figure-eight patterns in the tail-wagging dance (von Frisch, 1953).

Using these dances, bees are able to communicate rather complex messages very efficiently. Unlike humans, however, they have a limited vocabulary and can only communicate in a way that is firmly limited by inheritance. Human language, in contrast,

**FIGURE 8.8**
The language dances of honeybees. The round dance indicates that nectar is within 100 meters of the hive. The tail-wagging dance points in the direction of the nectar when it's over 200 meters away. Distances between 100 and 200 meters are signaled by a third dance.

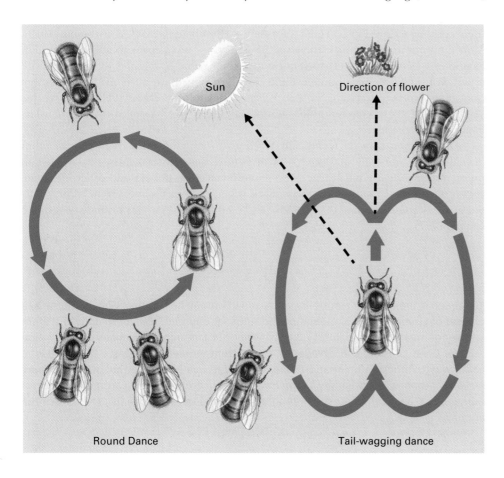

Sun   Direction of flower

Round Dance   Tail-wagging dance

must be learned through interactions with fluent speakers. In addition, human languages are more flexible. Animal communication can be varied little, whereas humans can generate an infinite number of unique and novel utterances.

These differences between human and animal languages have led some psychologists to assume that only humans can ever acquire a human language because we alone have the mental abilities needed for a generative language (Lenneberg, 1967). Until recently, this was an assumption that was difficult to challenge. Using the principles of operant conditioning, parrots have been taught to use English surprisingly well (Pepperberg, 2002). A parrot named Alex can name colors, label categories of objects (like "apples"), and refer to the number of a group of objects. Even more impressive accomplishments have been made with chimpanzees and apes. Because they are less able than parrots to learn to vocalize sounds, however, another mode of communication has been used in these studies.

Beatrix and Allen Gardner (1971) raised a young chimpanzee named Washoe to whom they taught American Sign Language (ASL), a language made up of hand signals used by the deaf. Washoe has acquired a limited but useful command of the ASL version of English. She uses more than 150 signs and uses them in such combinations as GIMME SWEET DRINK.

Washoe is not the only ape to learn a human language. Penny Patterson (1977) has taught more than 600 signs to Koko, a gorilla who may be showing even more spontaneous and generative use of language than Washoe. Koko signs THAT KOKO when she sees herself in the mirror; she once called a ring, a sign she had not been taught, a FINGER BRACELET; and she once replied to the question "How are you feeling?" by signing I WAS SAD AND CRIED THIS MORNING.

The linguistic accomplishments of even the most advanced adult chimpanzees and apes is limited compared with that of human 3-year-olds, however. Chimpanzees use language mostly to ask for something (food, tickling games, etc.). They rarely comment on their world or ask questions to gain information (Rumbaugh & Gill, 1976; Slobin, 1979). More important to scientists, their use of signs does not appear to show syntax. For example, Washoe is as likely to request a tickling game by signing ROGER TICKLE as TICKLE ROGER. To a human, these orders of signs have different meanings, but they appear to be interchangeable to Washoe (Reynolds & Flagg, 1983). This has led some researchers to conclude that chimpanzees have not mastered true human language (Terrace, 1980).

Although it may be technically accurate to conclude that Washoe and other primates have not fully mastered human syntax, this criticism misses an important point. Washoe clearly has learned to communicate with people and other chimpanzees using a form of human language. Even if her grammar is lousy, some of her statements speak volumes about the cognitive and emotional lives of our primate next-of-kin (Fouts, 1997).

## Review

Language is the efficient symbolic code used in human communication. It utilizes a finite set of sounds, units of meaning, and rules for combining them to convey a limitless set of meanings. The question of whether our language influences our cognition has not been satisfactorily answered, but current evidence suggests that it does in some ways. Although no animals have learned to use human language in the same ways as humans, surprisingly complex two-way conversations can occur between humans and apes who have been taught sign language—we can talk to some of the animals.

To be sure that you have learned the key points from the preceding section, cover the list of correct answers and try to answer each question. If you give an incorrect answer to any question, return to the page given next to the correct answer to see why your answer was not correct.

1. While *language* is the term used to describe the symbolic code used in communication, the meaning of the code is termed _____.

   a) surface structure            c) semantics

   b) heuristics                   d) syntax

2. Human language can be referred to as _____ in that an infinite set of utterances can be made using a finite set of elements and rules.

   a) divergent                    c) semantic

   b) conceptual                   d) generative

3. _____ refers to the rules of a language for the ways in which morphemes can be combined in that language to allow an infinite number of understandable utterances to be generated.

   a) Semantics                    c) Phonemics

   b) Syntax                       d) Morphemics

4. According to the _____ hypothesis, the vocabulary and structure of a language can influence the way speakers of that language think.

1. Does it make sense to you to say that apes are not capable of using language in a human way?

2. The Greek language has three different words for love. Would that influence the way Greeks think about and understand love?

**Correct Answers:**  1. c (p. 285),    2. d (p. 286),    3. b (p. 287),    4. linguistic relativity (or Whorfian) (p. 287).

## ● Intelligence: The Sum Total of Cognition

In the sense used in this book, **intelligence** refers to the cognitive abilities of an individual to learn from experience, to reason well, and to cope effectively with the demands of daily living. In short, intelligence has to do with how well a person is able to use cognition in coping with the world.

The term *intelligence* was not in widespread use until it was popularized in the late 1800s by the writings of Sir Francis Galton. Galton was a cousin of Charles Darwin, the scientist credited for developing the theory of evolution based on natural selection of inherited characteristics. Galton believed that intellectual ability was inherited, and he tried unsuccessfully to develop an intelligence test to use in his research. Although he was unsuccessful in his own research, Galton gave psychology the concept of intelligence.

### Differing Views of Intelligence

Since Galton's time, intelligence has been the subject of intensive research, theoretical pronouncements, and often heated debate. After nearly 100 years of scrutiny, however, psychologists still cannot agree on several basic issues. For example, opinions differ on

**intelligence**
(in-tel´i-jens)  The cognitive abilities of an individual to learn from experience, to reason well, and to cope with the demands of daily living.

Sir Francis Galton (1822–1911).

**g**
A broad general factor of intelligence, a concept endorsed by some investigators of intelligence.

how many kinds or dimensions of intellectual ability exist. Other psychologists believe that, instead of trying to answer that question, we should work to identify the basic cognitive components of intelligence.

### Intelligence: General or Specific Abilities?

In Galton's view, intelligence is a single *general factor* that provides the basis for the more specific abilities that each of us possesses. According to this conception, if we are generally intelligent, we are more likely to develop strong mechanical, musical, artistic, and other kinds of abilities. This view that a general factor of intelligence underlies each of our more specific abilities has been advocated in more modern times by psychologist Charles Spearman (Spearman & Wynn-Jones, 1950), who used the term **g** to refer to the general factor of intelligence. Spearman based his opinion on complex mathematical analyses of intelligence test scores that support, but do not prove, his theory of general intelligence. The concept of a g factor of intelligence is also held by David Wechsler, who is the author of the most widely used intelligence tests for children and adults in the United States today (Wechsler, 1955).

Other psychologists have argued that intelligence is not a single general factor but a collection of many separate specific abilities. These psychologists make a great deal of the fact that most of us are much better in some cognitive skills than others, rather than being generally good at everything. Louis Thurstone (1938), for example, developed an alternative to tests of general intelligence, called the *Primary Mental Abilities Test,* that measures seven intellectual abilities. J. P. Guilford (1982), taking an even more extreme position than Thurstone, suggested that some 150 different abilities make up what we call intelligence.

Howard Gardner (1983) also has argued that there are multiple types of intelligence. Gardner became convinced that there are many separate kinds of intelligence partly by studying patients who had suffered brain damage to only some parts of the cerebral cortex. He found that these individuals lost some kinds of intellectual abilities while other kinds of intelligence were left intact. This suggested to him that different types of intelligence are mediated by different parts of the brain. Gardner also studied the fascinating abilities of rare individuals with *savant syndromes.* These individuals have low general intelligence but show extraordinary splinter skills in art, music, or arithmetic computation. As a result of his investigations, Gardner has suggested that there are *seven independent types of intelligence:*

1. Linguistic (verbal)
2. Logical-mathematical
3. Musical
4. Spatial (artistic)
5. Kinesthetic (athletic)
6. Interpersonal (social skills)
7. Intrapersonal (personal adjustment)

Gardner's definition of intelligence is much broader than the traditional one, because Gardner believes that great skill in music and good emotional adjustment should be said to reflect intelligence just as much as skill in mathematics. Most tests of intelligence focus on just verbal and logical-mathematical areas of intelligence.

Most contemporary psychologists believe that there is truth to both views. That is, it is probably correct that a general factor underlies all intelligence, but people can be strong in one specific area of intelligence and weak in another (Anderson, 2001; Garlick, 2002).

### The Biological Basis of General Intelligence

Recently, a great deal has been written about the nature of g, or general intelligence. The prevailing theory is that persons with high g have a greater ability to form neural connections between axons and dendrites in the brain (Anderson, 2001; Garlick, 2002).

Howard Gardner's definition of intelligence is much broader than the traditional one. He believes great skill in music or sports reflects intelligence as much as great skill in mathematics.

That is, when stimulated by the environment, some people—those with high g—are more likely to form new neural connections than are other people. As a result, adults with higher general intelligence have better connected neurons. This greater ability to form neural connections is hypothesized to lead to better general intellectual performance in two ways. First, a greater ability to form neural connections means that a person with high g is better able to learn from experience (Anderson). Second, greater interconnectedness of the neurons means that the brain can process information more quickly (Garlick). There is evidence that the brains of persons with higher g do have more neural connections (Garlick) and that they process a variety of simple cognitive tasks more quickly (Anderson). Persons with higher g have faster reflexes, have faster reaction times, and take less time to make simple judgments (such as which of two lines is shorter). This greater speed of processing is thought to be the primary basis for greater general intelligence.

As we will see in the next section, however, the fact that more intelligent people process information more quickly does not mean that they do everything more quickly in cognitive tasks. Sometimes taking our time leads to better problem solving.

### Cognitive Components of Intelligent Behavior

A promising way of conceptualizing and studying intelligence has been proposed by psychologist Robert Sternberg (Sternberg, 1979, 1981; Sternberg & Gardner, 1982) and others. This approach suggests that the basic nature of intelligence can be illuminated

Robert Sternberg proposes six steps in reasoning. Expert chess players seem to perform the first step, encoding information about the positions of the pieces, more effectively than beginners.

by applying what we have learned in research on cognition, particularly research carried out using an information-processing model of cognition.

Sternberg has proposed a tentative theory of intelligence that specifies the cognitive steps that a person must use in reasoning and solving some kinds of problems—or in simple terms, the cognitive components of intelligence. For example, consider the following analogy problem (Sternberg, 1979):

LAWYER is to CLIENT as DOCTOR is to?

a) MEDICINE

b) PATIENT

To solve this problem, Sternberg believes that we must go through a number of cognitive steps. Among these steps, the person must

1. *Encode* (mentally represent in the memory system in some usable form) all relevant information about the problem. In this case, the person might encode information related to the term *lawyer* that includes that a lawyer knows the law, represents others before the courts, is paid fees for providing services, and so on. For the term *client,* the information that this is an individual who obtains professional assistance and pays a fee for those services would need to be encoded, and so on for all of the attributes of all of the terms in the problem.

2. *Infer* the nature of the relationships between the terms in the problem. In this case, it is essential to see that *lawyer* and *client* are related because a lawyer provides a service for a fee and a client obtains a service by paying a fee.

3. *Map* or identify common characteristics in relevant pairs of elements. In this case, the person must see that both lawyers and doctors provide services for fees and that both clients and patients obtain services by paying fees.

4. *Apply* the relationship identified between lawyer and client to the relationship between doctor and patient.

5. *Compare* the alternative answers.

6. *Respond* with an answer—in this case, "patient."

Sternberg suggests that this way of looking at intelligence does more than provide us with a convenient way of describing the steps in intelligent reasoning. It gives us a framework for discovering which components are most important in determining whether one person is "more intelligent" than another. For example, several initial studies have provided a finding that is, at least at first glance, rather surprising (Sternberg, 1979). Better reasoners take *more* time to complete the encoding component than poor reasoners, but they are *faster* at all of the other stages. Sternberg explains this finding by drawing a parallel to a lending library. A library that invests more time in carefully cataloging books (like the encoding component) will be more than repaid for this investment of time in terms of more rapid access to the books. As we have seen earlier, one of the critical differences between expert and beginning chess players is that experts encode the board positions more effectively (Chase & Simon, 1973). Such findings hold promise in identifying the key cognitive elements in effective intelligence and may even allow us to improve intelligence in the future by training people to carry out those key components more effectively (Sternberg, 1981).

### Fluid and Crystallized Intelligence

In much the same way that Sternberg distinguished among three components of intelligence, other psychologists tell us that it is important to distinguish between *fluid intelli-*

*gence* and *crystallized intelligence* (Hunt, 1995). **Fluid intelligence** is the ability to learn or invent new strategies for dealing with new kinds of problems. **Crystallized intelligence** is the ability to use previously learned skills to solve familiar problems. We began with Sternberg's way of looking at the components of intelligence, because it is helpful to see the link between intelligence and specific cognitive skills. We will use the more widely used distinction between fluid and crystallized intelligence in the rest of the book, however.

It is important to note that the distinction between fluid and crystallized intelligence is not just a logical one. It is well supported by research on how intelligence changes with age. Crystallized intelligence—the ability to use familiar skills—improves throughout the years that adults work (Garlick, 2002). That is one reason that most leadership jobs are held by persons over age 40 (Hunt, 1995). In contrast, fluid intelligence—the ability to learn new skills for new problems—declines from middle age on (Garlick; Hunt). To some extent, it really is harder to teach an old dog new tricks, but we old dogs do okay with our still-growing crystallized intelligence!

## Measures of Intelligence: The IQ Test

Intelligence would be too vague a concept to be of much use to psychologists if it were not for the reasonably accurate and meaningful tests that have been developed to measure it. A measure of intelligence makes it possible to use the concept of intelligence in both research and clinical practice. As noted in chapter 1, the first person to develop a useful measure of intelligence was Alfred Binet. In 1903, he began working on developing a test that he hoped would distinguish intellectually normal from subnormal Parisian schoolchildren. In the United States, Binet's test was refined by Lewis Terman of Stanford University, as the still widely used *Stanford-Binet Intelligence Scale*. Similar tests were also developed by David Wechsler, known as the *Wechsler Intelligence Scale for Children* (3rd ed.), or *WISC-III*, and the *Wechsler Adult Intelligence Scale, Revised*, or *WAIS-R*. Items similar to those on the WISC-III are as follows:

| *Subject* | *Examples of Items* |
| --- | --- |
| Information | "Which president signed the Emancipation Proclamation?" |
| Similarities | "How are a bell and a violin alike?" |
| Arithmetic | "If you buy five pieces of gum for 18 cents each, how much change would you get back from a dollar?" |
| Vocabulary | "What does *dissipate* mean?" |
| Comprehension | "What should you do if you see another child bitten by a dog?" |
| Picture completion | "Show me the part that is missing in this picture." (wheel of a car) |
| Picture arrangement | "Arrange the pictures on these cards so they tell a story that makes sense." |
| Block design | "Arrange these blocks so they look like the design in this picture." |
| Object assembly | "Put this puzzle together as quickly as you can." (jigsaw puzzle of a dog) |
| Coding | "Use this key that matches numbers with geometric shapes to write the shape that goes with each number in the block below it." |

How is it possible to develop a test that measures intelligence when psychologists cannot decide what intelligence is? Intelligence tests are no more than a small sample of *some* of the cognitive abilities that constitute intelligence. These tests are considered

**fluid intelligence**
The ability to learn or invent new strategies to deal with new problems.

**crystallized intelligence**
The ability to use previously learned skills to solve familiar problems.

useful not because we are sure they measure the right things but because they do a fairly good job of *predicting* how people will perform in situations that seem to require intelligence, such as in school or on the job. This state of affairs has led some psychologists to say—only slightly in jest—that intelligence should be defined as whatever intelligence tests measure. We cannot be very confident that intelligence tests are very good at measuring "intelligence," whatever that turns out to be. But intelligence tests are fairly good at picking out those individuals who perform well on tasks that seem to require intelligence.

### Construction of Intelligence Tests

We can perhaps better understand the nature of intelligence tests and the meaning of the related term *IQ* by taking a brief look at how intelligence tests were originally constructed. Binet constructed his test by looking for a large number of items related to cognitive efficiency that differentiated children of different ages. That is, he looked for items that he thought about half the children of one age could answer but that nearly all older children could answer and very few younger children could answer. He did this based on the assumption that intellectual abilities improve with age during childhood.

Once Binet had compiled a list of items, he gave them to a large number of children of different ages to determine exactly how many children at each age level could answer each question. Then he arranged the order of the questions in the test from the least to the most difficult.

In simplified terms, the score obtained on Binet's intelligence test is equal to the number of questions answered correctly, but it's expressed in terms of the age of the children for which that score is the *average*. For example, if a child correctly answers 18 items, and the average number of items answered by children 8 years and 6 months in age is 18, then the score on the test would be expressed as "8 years 6 months." Binet called this score the *mental age*. If your mental age is higher than your actual age *(chronological age)*, then you are considered bright because you answered the average number of items for older children. If your mental age is lower than your chronological age, then you are considered below average in intelligence because you could answer only the average number of questions answered by younger children. This is all that an intelligence test is: a measure that compares your performance with the performance of individuals of different ages on items believed to reflect intelligence.

Is a child with a mental age of 9 years 4 months and a chronological age of 7 years 2 months brighter than a child with a chronological age of 8 years 5 months and a mental age of 10 years 3 months? Because it's difficult to compare the mental ages of children of different chronological ages, a more easily used score than the mental age was later developed for intelligence tests. This score is called the **intelligence quotient, or IQ.** The intelligence quotient is obtained by dividing the mental age (MA) by the chronological age (CA) so that children of different chronological ages can be directly compared. To remove the decimal point, the result is multiplied by 100. Thus, IQ = MA/CA × 100. For example, if a child's MA is 6 years 6 months and his chronological age is also 6 years 6 months, then his IQ is 100.

IQs that are over 100 indicate that the person is more intelligent than average (the MA is greater than the CA). For example, if a child obtains an MA of 10 years, but her CA is only 8 years, then her IQ is 10/8 × 100 = 125. Conversely, IQs less than 100 indicate that the individual is less intelligent than average. A child who is 10 years in CA but obtains an MA of only 7 years has an IQ of 7/10 × 100 = 70.

Actually, Binet's approach to calculating the intelligence quotient from the ratio between the child's mental age and chronological age—called the **ratio IQ**—is no longer used in contemporary intelligence tests. There are several technical reasons that

Albert Einstein had uncommon intelligence. Only about 2 percent of the general population have IQs above 130.

**intelligence quotient (IQ)**
A numerical value of intelligence derived from the results of an intelligence test.

**ratio IQ**
The intelligence quotient based on the ratio between the person's mental age and chronological age.

# HUMAN DIVERSITY

## Cultural Influences on Inferential Reasoning

Why is one fish swimming ahead of the others in the accompanying photograph? I am asking you to engage in the cognitive process of **inferential reasoning**—to reach a conclusion that goes beyond the information presented by using the information that you have and what you know about fish and other creatures. Is the fish in front leading the other fish, or is the fish in front being chased by the other fish? Which do you think is more likely?

Do you think your culture played a role in your thinking about this question? Although people from different cultures are far more alike than they are different, psychological research has revealed some important ways in which people raised in different cultures think differently. Using pictures of fish like this one, Morris and Peng (1994) found that Chinese participants were more likely than North American participants to infer that the fish in front was being chased by the group. Morris and Peng suggested that this tendency may reflect the greater influence of groups on individual behavior in collectivist cultures like China. In contrast, individualistic North Americans are more likely to think of individuals—even individual fish—acting alone to take the lead. That is, Americans tend to see the lone fish as the "leader of the pack."

This kind of research has also been used to study bicultural persons. Some people are raised in two cultures at the same time. For example, because Hong Kong was a British colony for 100 years, many residents were raised in a culture containing many western and east Asian elements. Similarly, many young people who migrate from China to the United States have had the Chinese culture instilled in them, but they are influenced by their adopted American culture as well. Psychologists such as Ying-yi Hong of the Hong Kong University of Science and Technology (Hong, Morris, Chiu, & Benet-Maretinez, 2000) be-

lieve that bicultural individuals switch back and forth between their two cultural mind-sets as they move between Chinese and western cultures. For example, an immigrant to the United States might think and act in ways that fit the American culture at work, but shift to a more Chinese way of thinking at home with her husband and parents. Hong and colleagues examined this possibility by randomly dividing bicultural research participants into three groups and "priming" them to orient to either Chinese or western culture. One group was shown pictures that are representative of the United States (such as the U.S. Capitol building). The second group was shown pictures that evoke Chinese culture (such as the Great Wall of China). The third group was shown abstract geometric figures that represent neither culture. Later, in a part of the experiment that the participants thought was unrelated, they were shown the picture of the fish. The bicultural individuals who were primed to think in terms of Chinese culture were more likely to see the lone fish as being chased by the others than were the bicultural individuals who were primed to think of American culture (they were more likely to see the lone fish as the leader). Individuals who were not primed to think of either culture (those shown the geometric figures) were in between in their inferential reasoning.

Much remains to be learned about the influence of culture on cognition, but these studies suggest that culture can significantly influence this type of inferential reasoning. Such studies also help us begin to understand the complicated psychological lives of bicultural individuals who must move between cultural frames of reference on a daily basis. What do these studies suggest we must do to improve relations among the many cultures of the world? How can we constructively communicate with someone who thinks a little differently than we do? How should they communicate with us? ■

the ratio IQ is no longer used, but the most important reason to understand is that there are some significant limitations to the concept of mental age. For example, a very bright 4-year-old with an IQ of 150 has the mental age of the average 6-year-old but would not handle many situations demanding intellectual ability as well as the 6-year-old. Conversely, a child with low intelligence will often seem less competent than an average younger child with the same mental age.

For these reasons, a new approach to the measurement of intellectual ability, termed the **deviation IQ,** was developed. The deviation IQ is based on an intriguing mathematical property of measurements of many phenomena, including intellectual ability. As shown in figure 8.9, the scores of large numbers of persons on tests of

**deviation IQ**
The intelligence quotient based on the degree of deviation from average of the person's score on an intelligence test.

**FIGURE 8.9**
The normal distribution of scores on a test of intellectual ability.

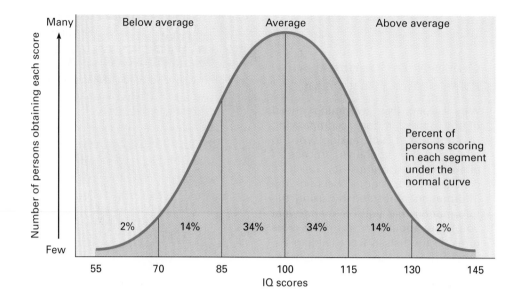

**normal distribution**
The symmetrical pattern of scores on a scale in which a majority of the scores are clustered near the center and a minority are at either extreme.

**standardization**
Administering a test in the same way to all individuals.

intelligence fall in a **normal distribution.** This means that most people will obtain the *average* score, or scores that are close to the average, on the test. As scores *deviate* from the average in either direction (either higher or lower than average), the scores become progressively less common. Thus, scores a few points above or below average are common, but scores that are many points above or below average are very uncommon.

Instead of defining an average IQ as one in which the mental age and chronological age are the same (IQ of 100), the average score on the intelligence test (the midpoint of the normal distribution) is assigned an IQ score of 100, and based on the shape of the curve, scores above the average are assigned IQ scores above 100 and below average scores are assigned IQ scores below 100. The exact IQ score is based on how much the score deviates from the average. Look carefully again at figure 8.9 to see how this works.

Deviation IQ scores work very well for adults. They also work well for children, but children's scores have to be compared with different normal distributions for each age group because their scores increase as children grow older. The same concept of deviation from the midpoint of the normal distribution is also used in many other tests of human characteristics. Scores on the tests of academic achievement that you took in school, some of the tests of specific job skills that you will take when you apply for employment, and some tests of personality are based on the same concept as the deviation IQ.

### Characteristics of Good Intelligence Tests

When you measure the size of a window with a yardstick before buying drapes, you don't have to ask how good yardsticks are for measuring length. For the purpose you are using it, yardsticks are good measuring instruments. However, for something as important, yet difficult to define, as intelligence, it makes sense for us to ask how accurate the measuring instrument is. The following is a list of criteria that an intelligence test must meet before we accept it as an adequate measuring instrument. In chapter 12, in the section on personality tests, you will see how these criteria apply equally to all psychological tests.

1. **Standardization.** Because intelligence tests are designed to compare the performance of one person with others, the test must be given in the same way to every person. If this were not so, differences in performance might be due to differences in the way the test is administered rather than to true differences in ability. For this reason, properly designed psychological tests contain detailed instructions telling the examiner how to administer the test to each person in the same *standardized* way.

2. **Norms.** To compare the individual's score with that of others, the developer of the test must give the test to a large sample of people who represent the general population. For example, you could not develop an intelligence test for adults by giving the test only to college students, because they are brighter than the general population. The sample used in evaluating the performance of individuals given the test is called the *normative sample.* It must be large enough to validly represent the general population and must contain approximately the same proportion of each subgroup in the general population to be a valid standard of comparison for anyone taking the test. For example, a normative sample that contained no Hispanic children would not have the same validity when used to evaluate young Hispanics.

3. **Objectivity.** An intelligence test must be constructed so that there is little or no ambiguity as to what constitutes a correct answer to each item. If there is ambiguity, and the scoring is subjective rather than *objective,* then factors other than the individual's performance might influence the scoring, such as the examiner's mood or prejudices.

4. **Reliability.** To be useful, an intelligence test must be *reliable.* This means that the scores obtained would be approximately the same if administered on two different occasions or by two different examiners. If the scores change a great deal from one testing to the next, no faith can be put in the scores.

5. **Validity.** Most important, an intelligence scale must be *valid;* that is, it must measure what it's supposed to measure. Validity can be evaluated in a number of different ways, but for intelligence tests, the most important issue is the degree to which the test *predicts* performance on other tasks that most people agree require intelligence. This is referred to as *predictive validity.* For example, the Wechsler and Stanford-Binet intelligence tests are considered valid in part because they are fairly good predictors of performance in school. About 25 percent of the differences in school performance among a group of students can be predicted from IQ scores. This is not a high level of predictability. As you are well aware, many factors besides intelligence, such as motivation and personality, contribute to school performance. But intelligence test scores are better predictors of school performance than any other measure that psychologists or educators now possess. So in this sense, intelligence tests are valid.

## Tacit Intelligence

We have said that intelligence tests are considered to be useful because they allow psychologists to predict how well individuals will perform in situations that require intelligence. The predictions are not very precise, but they are accurate in extreme cases. That is, children with an IQ of 120 will almost always perform better in school than children with an IQ of 80, but we could not predict with much confidence that children with an IQ of 105 will perform better than children with an IQ of 95. Still, in spite of their lack of precision, intelligence tests are useful predictors.

It is important to understand that general intelligence tests like the Stanford-Binet or the Wechsler scales are limited in what they predict. They are most useful in predicting success in school and complex occupations. General intelligence tests are not useful in predicting competence in specific areas that are generally not taught in school. For example, if a general intelligence test were given to all of the adults who live in your city, the scores would not be very useful in predicting who would be the best at fishing, growing vegetables, maintaining their cars, taking photographs, picking horses at the race track, painting with water colors, or shopping for food within a budget. Some researchers have referred to these competencies as "everyday intelligence," or **tacit intelligence,** and have developed tests to measure tacit intelligence (Galotti, 1990; Schmidt & Hunter, 1993; Sternberg & Wagner, 1993).

**norms**
Standards (created by the scores of a large group of individuals) used as the basis of comparison for scores on a test.

**objectivity**
Lack of subjectivity in a test question so that the same score is produced regardless of who does the scoring.

**reliability**
A test's ability to produce similar scores if the test is administered on different occasions or by different examiners.

**validity**
The extent to which a test measures what it's supposed to measure.

**tacit intelligence**
The practical knowledge and skills needed to deal with everyday problems that are usually not taught in school.

According to Kathleen Galotti (1990) of Carleton College, a useful test of tacit intelligence must assess practical knowledge and skills in getting things done. Sternberg and Wagner (1993) developed a measure of tacit intelligence consisting of scenarios describing work-related situations in particular areas of employment. Persons taking the test are asked to rate the quality of a number of different solutions to the problems. Because different areas of employment—from plumbing to selling insurance—pose different kinds of problems, tests of tacit intelligence that are specific to a given area are most useful in predicting who will perform well in that domain (Sternberg & Wagner, 1993).

Although tacit intelligence is rather distinct from the cognitive competencies measured by general tests of intelligence, there are three ways in which tacit intelligence is related to general intelligence. First, at very low levels of general intelligence, it is rare to find individuals with highly developed tacit intelligence. Second, it is unlikely that persons of limited general intelligence will succeed in highly complex areas of tacit knowledge, such as amateur astronomy. Third, although persons with higher general intelligence are not more likely to have highly developed knowledge and skills in any particular area of everyday functioning, persons with higher general intelligence are more likely to have good practical knowledge across *many* different areas. In one study of a representative sample of U.S. high school students, students were administered a test of practical knowledge in 25 areas that are not taught in most schools (health, fishing, art, mechanical systems, law, etc.). The high school students with the highest general intelligence scores were much more likely to possess high levels of practical knowledge across many of the areas tested (Lubinski & Humphreys, 1997). Some students with lower general intelligence scores had high levels of practical knowledge in one area (e.g., fishing or mechanical systems), but few had high levels of practical knowledge in many areas. That is, general intelligence is a better predictor of the breadth of knowledge than the depth of knowledge in any one area. Persons who are highly motivated to learn about a particular practical topic are not greatly limited by their level of general intelligence, unless the topic is very complex or their level of general intelligence is very low. Persons with higher intelligence scores are more likely to master many areas of practical knowledge, however.

## Individual Differences in Intelligence: Contributing Factors

Why is one person more intelligent than another person? After many years of research, it is now clear that both our heredity and our experiences combine to determine our level of intelligence (Plomin & Petrill, 1997; Dickens & Flynn, 2001). In chapter 3, we described how studies of twins and persons adopted at birth point to clear genetic influences on intelligence. The IQ scores of genetically identical monozygotic (identical) twins are considerably more similar than the scores of dizygotic twins, even though both kinds of twins are reared in essentially the same intellectual environment. Dizygotic twins, who are no more alike genetically than siblings born at different times, are no more similar in IQ than any other siblings. Furthermore, it makes little difference whether monozygotic twins grew up in the same home or were adopted and raised in *separate* homes. In both cases, their IQs are very similar (Erlenmeyer-Kimling & Jarvik, 1963; Hunt, 1995; Lewontin, 1982).

Adoption studies have similarly indicated that heredity is one of the more important factors determining IQ. A large number of studies have shown that the IQs of adopted children are more similar to the IQs of their biological parents with whom they never lived than those of their adoptive parents who raised them. Taken together, the twin and adoption studies make a strong case that heredity is one of the determinants of IQ.

The intellectual environment in which a child is reared is also an important factor in intelligence, however. The exposure that children have to the world of adult intelligence through interactions with their caregivers seems essential to normal intellectual development. Children who have been so severely neglected by their parents as to be deprived of this stimulation show very slow intellectual development but usually develop more rapidly when placed in good foster homes (Clarke & Clarke, 1976). Schiff and Lewontin (1986) studied a group of children of poorly educated mothers who put one of their children up for adoption but raised their other children themselves. The children were adopted shortly after birth by much better educated families. Years later, the IQs of the adopted children averaged 109, whereas those of their nonadopted siblings averaged 95.

Recent evidence suggests that it is possible to intentionally increase intelligence scores by enriching young children's intellectual environments. In a well-designed formal experiment, infants from low-income families were randomly assigned to either environmental enrichment or a control group that received no intervention (Burchinal, Campbell, Bryant, Wasik, & Ramey, 1997). The environmental enrichment program consisted of a free early educational preschool, access to a lending library of educational toys, and home visits from child development experts who taught parents how to provide responsive and stimulating child care at home. The enrichment program produced consistently higher intelligence scores from 2 years of age to 12 years of age. At age 12, 42 percent of the control group had Wechsler intelligence scores of 85 or below, compared with only 13 percent of the early enrichment group (Campbell & Ramey, 1994). At age 15, the youths who had received early intellectual enrichment scored higher on measures of reading and mathematics achievement, had failed fewer grades, and were less likely to have been assigned to special education classes (Campbell & Ramey, 1995).

The beneficial influences of the environment on intelligence test scores is not limited to early childhood, however. Well-designed studies show that increased amounts of education result in improved scores on tests of both crystallized and fluid intelligence. Both attending more years of schooling and participating in extended year-round educational programs produce increased scores on measures of intellectual ability and academic achievement (Frazier & Morrison, 1998; Williams, 1998). Thus, there is considerable evidence that both heredity and experience influence intelligence. From a practical perspective, it seems very likely that investments in improving the level of intellectual stimulation of children from low-income families by providing free educational day care and assistance in parenting and by extending schooling throughout childhood and adolescence would pay off in terms of significant improvements in both intellectual ability and school achievement.

The amount of cognitive stimulation provided to infants is one factor in determining level of intelligence.

## The Importance of Intelligence Scores in Modern Society

Intelligence test scores are important because they predict to some extent how well we will do in life. Persons with higher intelligence tend to learn more in school, get better grades, and complete more years of education (Brody, 1997; Hunt, 1995). In addition, more intelligent individuals tend to hold more complex and highly paid jobs (Brody, 1997; Hunt, 1995). The average IQ of truck drivers is a little under 100, whereas the average IQ of doctors and lawyers is 125 or higher (Hunt, 1995). At the other end of the IQ spectrum, persons with IQs below 85 (about 15 percent of the population) are very likely to have dropped out of high school, to live below the poverty line, to be unemployed for long periods, to be divorced, to receive aid for dependent children, to have health problems, and to have a criminal record. Indeed, the correlation between IQ and success in education and occupations is about as high as the correlation between people's heights and weights (Hunt, 1995).

Why does intelligence predict how well we will do in our jobs? There appear to be three major reasons:

1. Many occupations are available only to persons with college or graduate degrees, and persons with higher intelligence are more likely to qualify for advanced education (partly because admission tests largely measure intelligence) and are more likely to complete advanced degree programs once they are admitted (Brody, 1997).

2. It takes less time to train persons with higher intelligence to a high level of job knowledge and skill than persons with lower levels of intelligence (Gottfredson, 1997; Hunt, 1995). If the job skills are relatively well specified and not complex, however, level of intelligence does not influence job success very much after those skills have been learned (Hunt, 1995).

3. Persons with higher intelligence tend to perform better in complex jobs, particularly if they involve making judgments in changing situations and require constant updating of job skills (physicians, lawyers, scientists, engineers, computer programmers, etc.; Gottfredson, 1997). Even in nonprofessional occupations, persons with higher levels of intelligence are more likely to be promoted into more complex jobs than are persons with lower levels of intelligence (Wilk, Desmarais, & Sackett, 1995).

## Are People Becoming More Intelligent?

James Flynn (1998) of the University of Otago in New Zealand published provocative data on changes in average intelligence test scores over successive generations—known as the "Flynn effect." In many countries around the world, there is strong evidence that intelligence scores have risen dramatically over the past few generations. When tested at the same age using the same test, people born in earlier years answered fewer questions correctly than persons born more recently. Therefore, when the raw scores of persons born in different years are converted to deviation IQ scores using the norms for the group born in the earliest years, persons born more recently have higher average IQs than persons born earlier on the average (Flynn, 1998).

The rate of increase in scores on tests of general adult intelligence (that measure both fluid and crystallized intelligence) like the Stanford-Binet and Wechsler intelligence scales are shown in figure 8.10 (Neisser, 1998). These increases are surprisingly large, but data on tests that measure only fluid intelligence show even larger gains of about 20 points per generation (every 30 years; Neisser, 1998; Williams, 1998). The strongest evidence of changes in fluid intelligence comes from the Raven Progressive Matrices Test (Carpenter, Just, & Shell, 1990). In this test, the person is presented with a number of increasingly difficult nonverbal matrix problems to solve, like the item in figure 8.11.

The Raven test has been administered to representative samples of young adults each year in some countries over many years, with the best data coming from Holland. James Flynn (1999) asked us to imagine a Dutch woman with a score of 110 at age 25 years on the Raven test who taught teenagers in school from the time she was 25 until she was 55 years old. Her raw score (the number of questions answered correctly) on the Raven test did not change over that part of her life span, but her score's standing relative to her pupils' scores changed dramatically. In 1952, her score on the Raven was higher than those of 75 percent of her students. By 1967, however, her score was equal to the average score of her students, and by 1982, 75 percent of her students had higher Raven scores than she! Her raw score did not change over time, but the raw scores of her students increased markedly over time.

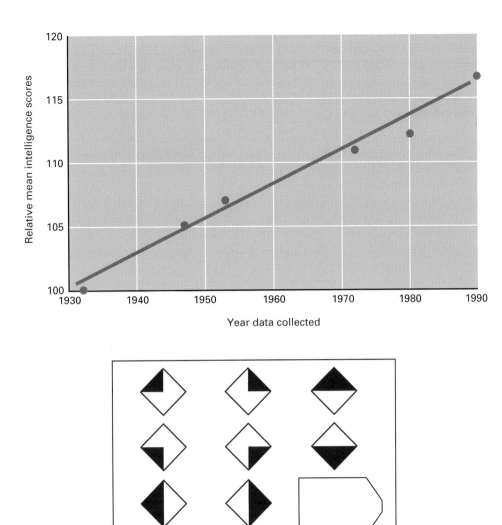

**FIGURE 8.10**
Intelligence scores of individuals born in different years (who were tested in different years when they reached the same age) when their scores are converted to intelligence scores based on 1932 norms.

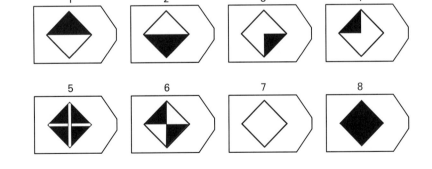

**FIGURE 8.11**
An example of an item like those on the Raven Progressive Matrices Test. Which of the eight figures presented at the bottom best completes the logic of the matrix at the top? Hint: Add the figures to one another horizontally. The correct answer is 8.

Is it really possible that the students of our hypothetical Dutch teacher surpassed her in fluid intelligence to such a great degree over a span of only 30 years? On the average, are we really that much smarter than our parents? Few psychologists doubt that large changes in intelligence test scores have occurred since the early 1900s (Hunt, 1995; Neisser, 1998; Williams, 1998), but we are all frankly shocked by these data. What do they mean? Has each generation really surpassed the previous generation so much in the wide range of competencies and cognitive skills that we call intelligence? In many ways, my grandparents seemed to be as intelligent as my children seem to be.

My grandparents were very successful, but they succeeded in a much less complex world than the present world. It is simply not possible to know if they could have not been successful in coping with today's computerized, mathematics-based world.

Are intelligence scores going up and what would the increases mean? There are at least four plausible explanations for why intelligence may have actually risen over successive generations:

1. During the same era that intelligence scores have risen, nutrition and health have improved dramatically in many parts of the world. Indeed, in the same countries that show increases in intelligence, the rates of increase in average height, weight, and life expectancy scores have been almost identical to the rate of increase in intelligence scores shown in figure 8.10 (Martorell, 1998). Women in these countries also have become more likely to receive adequate prenatal and obstetric care and are increasingly less likely to smoke and drink during pregnancy. Because nutrition and body size are positively correlated with intelligence (Alaimo & others, 2001; Sigman & Whaley, 1998), it is possible that much of the increase in intelligence scores is due to improvements in nutrition and health. Indeed, in several studies, when families of children in very poor parts of the world have been randomly assigned to an experimental group that received nutritional supplements or to a control group that did not receive supplements, the children who received nutritional supplements were found to have higher intelligence scores (Sigman & Whaley, 1998). Similarly, children with intestinal parasites are robbed of nutrition by the parasites. In economically deprived parts of the world, treating intestinal parasites (at a cost of 15 cents per child) has produced dramatic improvements in school and test performance (Williams, 1998). It seems unlikely that nutritional supplementation beyond the U.S. recommended daily allowances of nutrients improves intellectual or academic growth, however (Martorell, 1998). Vitamins are not "smart pills" for adequately nourished persons.

2. Increases in levels of education may have produced increases in intelligence test scores. This could work in two ways—indirect effects through the parents of each generation and direct effects on each generation of children. Since the beginning of the twentieth century, each successive generation has had better educated parents. Indeed, in the United States, there has been a 10-fold increase in parental education levels during this century (Greenfield, 1998). This is important because the level of education of parents is correlated with the intelligence scores of their children (Flynn, 1998). It is possible that better educated parents provide a more intellectually stimulating home environment, which increases the intelligence test scores of their children (Greenfield, 1998). At the same time, each successive generation of children has received more education than the last. In the 1930s, the mean number of years of education in the United States was 9 years; by the 1990s, the mean had risen above 14 years (Williams, 1998). It is possible these increases in education over the years are responsible for some of the increase in intelligence test scores. In particular, schools place more emphasis on teaching skills associated with fluid intelligence today than in the days of our grandparents, when memorization of facts was the focus of education (Williams, 1998). Thus, it may make sense that scores on measures of fluid intelligence have increased more than scores on tests of crystallized intelligence over time.

3. Children born in the latter part of the twentieth century are stimulated and challenged by a degree of environmental complexity that was unknown in 1930s (Neisser, 1998). Educational television, computers, learning toys, preschools, and other innovations may have increased intelligence by increasing children's levels of intellectual stimulation (Williams, 1998).

4. Large increases in intelligence test scores occurred during a period of time in which big changes occurred in the lives of persons of color in the United States. We will have much more to say about the apparently beneficial effects of the end of official segregation and other changes in the next section. Although this is probably a factor in the overall increase in intelligence and academic achievement in the United States, it could not explain the large increases in intelligence test scores found in countries such as Holland, where relatively few persons of color live and institutionalized segregation was never practiced.

On the other hand, there are important reasons we must be cautious in concluding that genuine increases in intelligence have occurred. For example, children have much more exposure to the specific kinds of problems on tests of fluid intelligence today than did children at the start of the last century (Neisser, 1998). Does the item in figure 8.11 remind you of "brain teasers" on the back of cereal boxes or in "happy meals" from your favorite restaurant in childhood? As you try to solve this problem, can you hear Bob from *Sesame Street* singing, "Which of these things is not like the others?" If scores on tests of fluid intelligence are higher only because people born more recently are more familiar with such problems, the improved test scores may not reflect actual changes in intelligence at all. Scores on intelligence tests may have risen only because people born more recently have greater familiarity with the test items. Keep in mind, though, that although the greatest increases have been found in measures of fluid intelligence like the Raven test, large increases over generations have occurred in many kinds of measures of intelligence, including aspects of intelligence not "tested" on cereal boxes or restaurant place mats (Neisser, 1998).

Some psychologists who wonder if the increase in intelligence scores actually means that people have become "smarter" have pointed to the widely publicized decline in scores on the Scholastic Assessment Test (SAT). Could intelligence really be increasing when SAT scores were decreasing (Neisser, 1998)? It appears, however, the decline in SAT scores was temporary, because SAT scores have been rising again since 1960 (Zajonc & Mullally, 1997). It is difficult to interpret changes in SAT scores, in any case, because they can be due to changes in who takes the test. The SAT is normed on people who take this test each year, and only persons applying to college take the test. In contrast, the Preliminary Scholastic Assessment Test (PSAT) covers similar material and is administered to a representative sample of U.S. high school juniors each year. Although they have not risen as fast as scores on intelligence tests, average scores on the PSAT have been steadily rising since it was first administered in 1961 (Williams & Ceci, 1997).

## Race-Ethnic Differences in Intelligence and Achievement: The Narrowing Gap

Data gathered since the 1930s have consistently shown that the average intelligence and academic achievement scores of African Americans are about 15 points lower than those of white Americans, with children of Hispanic/Latino heritage having average scores that fall between those of whites and African Americans. Asian Americans, on the other hand, have average intelligence scores that are about 5 points higher than those of whites (Williams & Ceci, 1997). If people in general have become more intelligent over successive generations, what has happened to the difference between groups that differ in race and ethnicity?

Between 1970 and 1990, more than half of the gap in reading and mathematics achievement scores between African American and non-Hispanic white 17-year-olds has closed, as measured by the National Assessment of Educational Progress (Hauser, 1998). This extremely important trend reflects greater improvements in academic achievement scores among African American youths than among white youths (Grissmer, Williamson, Kirby, & Berends, 1998). Not as much data are available on changes in race-ethnic differences on tests of general intelligence, but there is some evidence that African

**FIGURE 8.12**

Changes in scores on a measure of verbal intelligence among adults in the United States of African American and non-Hispanic white heritage who were born during different years during the 1900s.

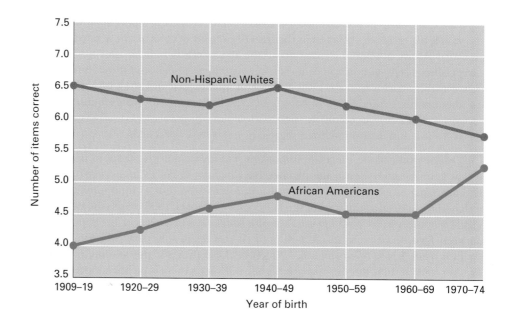

Americans have shown greater gains on tests of general intelligence over the past 50 years than whites have (Flynn, 1999). In addition, the results of a strong study of a measure of verbal ability are encouraging. Since the early 1970s, the General Social Survey administered a measure of verbal ability to representative samples of adults across the United States. As shown in figure 8.12, there was a large difference in scores between African American and white adults in the United States among adults born between 1909 and 1929. There has been steady improvement in the verbal ability scores of African Americans over time (and a slight decline in the scores for whites), however, which has nearly erased the race-ethnic gap among adults born between 1970 and 1974 (Huang & Hauser, 1998).

Why have such greater increases in average scores on intellectual and academic tests occurred among African Americans? No one knows for sure, but marked changes in the environment seem to be the most plausible answer. Since the end of official segregation in the United States, the educational experiences of African Americans have changed dramatically. The timing of changes in schooling related to desegregation in different regions of the country closely parallel gains in academic achievement made by African Americans in those regions (Grissmer & others, 1998). From 1973 to 1990, the mean educational level of adults increased among white families by 70 percent, but the mean educational level of adults in African American families increased by 350 percent during the same period (Williams, 1998). Because amount of schooling is related to scores on measures of both intellectual ability and academic achievement, the closing gap in ability and achievement may be due, in part, to the closing gap in educational opportunity.

Other factors probably also play a role in the narrowing gap between race-ethnic groups in the United States. For example, the average number of children in white families decreased from 4.7 to 2.4 from early 1970s to the mid-1990s, whereas the average number of children in African American families decreased from 6.0 to 4.2 (Huang & Hauser, 1998). Because the adverse effects of larger family size on intelligence and achievement are greatest on later-born children in larger families (Zajonc & Mullally, 1997), the marked decline in the number of larger African American

Group differences on intelligence tests, such as college entrance exams, between African Americans and white Americans appear to be dwindling as prejudice and economic barriers weaken.

## Improving Critical Thinking

It could be said that a successful person is not a person who has no problems—because all of us have problems—but is a person who is able to solve most of his or her problems. As I have discussed in this chapter, however, we human beings are not particularly good at using cognitive skills to solve problems. Our abilities to reason—as impressive as they may be compared with those of every other creature on earth—are not always equal to the problems that face us.

There is a great deal of evidence that shows that we can improve our ability to cope with the demands of life by sharpening our *critical thinking skills* (Halpern, 1998). This section provides a brief overview of a number of ways to improve critical thinking. It is not a solution by itself, however. If you are going to improve your critical thinking skills, reading this section must be only the first step in a long process.

## Increase Mental Effort

The first step in improving critical thinking skills is motivational, not cognitive. Critical thinking requires a willingness to engage in cognitive work (Halpern, 1998). It simply takes more time and effort to think carefully and critically about a problem than to make the first decision that pops into your head. On the other hand, the amount of effort needed to dig your way out of the consequences of some poor decisions is much greater. So, we either work hard to make good decisions or we work hard to clean up the messes caused by our poor decisions—it's our choice.

## Improve Problem Formulation

Most of life's problems are not simple math problems that need no formulation. They are complex situations that must be stated in the form of specific problems. Experts on critical thinking recommend that we attempt to formulate all problems in at least two different ways (Halpern, 1998). This forces us into the realization that there is more than one way to think about the prob-

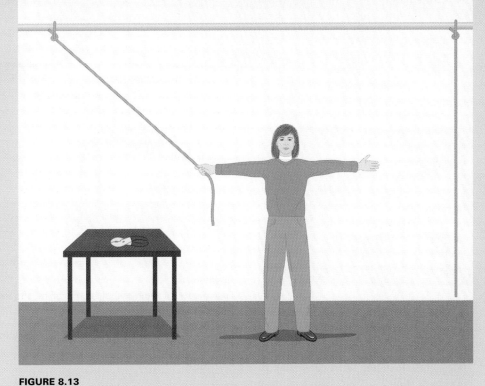

**FIGURE 8.13**

The Maier string problem. How do you tie the two strings together if you cannot reach them both at the same time? See figure 8.14 for the solution.

lem—and some of those ways lead to better problem solving than other ways. As you work to formulate the problems that face you in the best way, think about the way in which each problem has been framed (or you have framed the problem yourself). Framing the problem in different terms can lead to different decisions. The way in which a problem is formulated and framed is sometimes as important as the problem itself.

## Break Out of Unproductive Mental Sets

As discussed in this chapter, mental sets are one of the most common barriers to effective problem solving. Sometimes we must break out of our habitual ways of viewing the elements of the problem to discover a solution. One of the most troublesome of these sets has been referred to as *functional fixedness.* Before we define this term, let's look at a problem where it's encountered. Consider the Maier (1931) string problem.

Figure 8.13 shows that you are in a room where two strings are hanging from the ceiling. Your job is to tie the strings together. The problem is that, when holding onto one string, you cannot reach the other. The only other thing in the room with you is a pair of pliers, but, even holding onto one string with the pliers, you cannot reach the other string. What do you do? Look at figure 8.14 for the solution. The difficulty that most people have in solving this problem is similar to the one in Duncker's candle problem. We are simply not accustomed to using pliers as a pendulum to move a string, just as we wouldn't ordinarily use a matchbox as a candle holder. Karl Duncker (1945) referred to the difficulty we have in seeing new uses for objects as functional fixedness. It's a kind of mental set that interferes with problem solving by focusing our thinking on the habitual uses of the elements in a problem. Often the key to effective problem solving is being able

*(continued)*

to break out of functional fixedness and other interfering mental sets when appropriate.

Let's look at another famous problem that was developed to illustrate the interference of mental set. Psychologist Karl Luchins (1942) asked college students to imagine that they had three jars of different sizes. They then were asked how they would measure an amount of water that was different from that held by any single jar. For example, they might be asked to measure 5 quarts when the three jars held the quantities as shown here.

| Jar A | Jar B | Jar C |
|-------|-------|-------|
| 18 qt | 43 qt | 10 qt |

How would you solve this problem? Five quarts can be measured by filling jar B, then pouring water from it until jar A is filled, leaving 25 quarts in jar B. Then jar C is filled twice from jar B, leaving 5 quarts in jar B. It's simple when you catch on to the method. In algebraic terms, the solution can be expressed as $B - A - 2C$.

After solving five more problems using jars of different sizes, all of which could be solved using the equation $B - A - 2C$, the subjects were given a problem like this: Measure 20 quarts when jar A contains 24 quarts; jar B contains 52 quarts, and jar C contains 4 quarts. This problem could also be solved using the equation $B - A - 2C$, but did you solve it that way? Or did you see that it could be solved more simply by subtracting one jar C from jar A ($A - C$)? In Luchins' study, more than three-fourths of his students solved the problem the long way.

Why did Luchins' students make a difficult problem out of a simple one? Do people just have a tendency to do everything the hard way? Luchins ruled out that unlikely possibility in his experiment by having another group of students skip the first six $B - A - 2C$ problems and solve the seventh problem *first*. These students *all* used the simple $A - C$ solution. The students

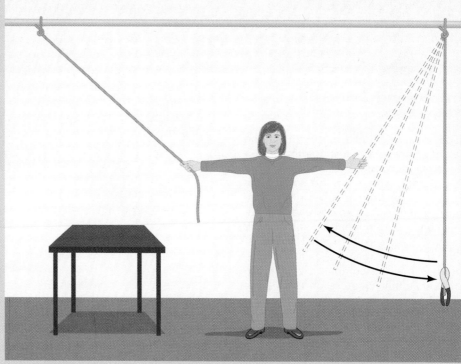

**FIGURE 8.14**

The solution to the Maier string problem is to use the pliers as a pendulum to bring the second string closer.

who took the long solution to the seventh problem after solving six $B - A - 2C$ problems simply had fallen into a "mental rut" or set.

As we look for ways to improve problem solving in everyday life, we must be careful to examine our way of understanding the elements of the problem to avoid functional fixedness, prejudice, or other mental sets that may be interfering with optimal problem solving. The problem may be solvable if you look at it the right way.

## Monitor Your Critical Thinking

People who are effective in critical thinking are aware that they are engaging in critical thinking (Halpern, 1998). That is, they are conscious of being critical thinkers and they monitor how well they are doing. When they catch themselves formulating problems in the first way that comes to mind or in getting stuck in mental ruts, they pull themselves back into a critical thinking mode.

## A General Strategy for Critical Thinking

This section integrates the suggestions I have presented here with recommen-

dations for generating and evaluating possible solutions to problems. These suggestions are presented in the form of a general strategy for critical thinking and problem solving (Goldfried & Davison, 1976; Halpern, 1998; Turkat & Calhoun, 1980). Even following this strategy will not solve all of life's problems, but it will give you a fighting chance.

You might try going through a hypothetical problem using this strategy just to see how it works. Suppose you run out of money for school—what would the best solution to this problem be for you? A loan? A part-time job? By trying this general outline for problem solving and the other ideas presented in this section, you may be better prepared to deal with the next curve ball that life throws at you.

Here is the general strategy:

1. What is the problem?
   a. Define the problem in clear, specific terms.
   b. Define the problem in at least one other way to find the best formulation.
   c. Be aware of the potential influence of framing.

d. Think flexibly about the elements of the problem and avoid mental sets.

e. Draw a diagram of the problem to see how the elements relate to one another.

f. Make a list of the additional information you need to solve the problem, and then obtain that information.

2. Generate all possible solutions.

   a. At first, do not judge any solution—just keep thinking of alternative solutions.

   b. Wild ideas are welcome.

   c. See if some of your possible solutions can be combined to make a better possible solution.

3. Now, eliminate any possible solutions that are clearly poor choices.

   a. Alternatives with no chance of success should be dropped.

   b. Intuitive solutions based on heuristic reasoning should be eliminated in situations where logical (algorithmic) reasoning is possible.

4. Examine the likely consequences of the remaining possible solutions one at a time.

   a. List all possible negative consequences of this option.

   b. List all possible positive consequences of this option.

   c. Eliminate the option if it is more likely to produce negative than positive consequences.

   d. Go on to the next option (and repeat steps a through c).

   e. Compare all remaining options in terms of likely consequences.

   f. Select the solution with the greatest likelihood of more positive consequences than negative consequences.

5. Generate all possible ways to implement the solution you have chosen. How can you best do this? Use steps 2 through 4 to select the best way to implement the solution.

6. Implement the solution. ■

## Summary

Chapter 8 discusses cognition, language, the meaning of intelligence, and the measurement of intelligence.

I. In the process of cognition, information is obtained through the senses, transformed through the interpretive processes of perception and thinking, stored and retrieved through the processes of memory, and used in the processes of problem solving and language.

II. Concepts, the basic units of thinking, are categories of things, events, or qualities linked together by some common feature or features.

    A. Some concepts are categories based on a single common feature; others are more complex.

        1. Members of categories defined by conjunctive concepts all have two or more common characteristics.

        2. Members of disjunctive concepts have either one common characteristic or another one, or both.

    B. Not all concepts are equally easy for us to learn; some are more natural and easily learned than others.

III. In problem solving, information is used to reach a goal that is blocked by an obstacle.

    A. Cognitive operations are used to solve problems. After we decide what kind of problem we face, we evaluate the elements of the problem and decide what information and tools we have to work with. Then we generate a list of solutions and evaluate them.

    B. Algorithmic and heuristic operations are two types of cognitive strategies used in solving problems.

        1. Algorithmic thinking is systematic and logical.

        2. Heuristic thinking is efficient but is not guaranteed to lead to a correct solution and often causes logic and relevant information to be ignored.

    C. Emotional factors and the way in which questions are framed can influence our decisions in ways that are unrelated to the facts or the logic of the problem.

D. The term *artificial intelligence* describes the logical operations of computers programmed to think like humans.
   1. Expert systems programs are often used to aid human decision making.
   2. Research on artificial intelligence has led to improved understanding of expertise in humans.

E. Creative problem solving requires the ability to think in flexible and unusual ways (divergent thinking); the most useful creative solutions are also thought out logically and realistically (convergent thinking).

IV. Language is a symbolic code used in human communication.

A. Semantic content is the meaning communicated through language.

B. We generate language from a set of elements and a set of rules for combining them into speech.
   1. The phoneme is the smallest unit of sound in a language. The English language has only 44 phonemes.
   2. Morphemes are the smallest units of meaning in a language.
   3. Syntax is the rules of a language through which an infinite number of understandable utterances are generated.

C. Much of our thinking is in the form of language: The Whorfian, or linguistic relativity, hypothesis states that the structure of language influences how people think.

V. *Intelligence* refers to the cognitive abilities of an individual to learn from experience, to reason well, and to cope effectively with the demands of daily living.

A. Intelligence is viewed as a single general factor by some psychologists and as many independent kinds of intellectual ability by others.

B. Intelligence tests measure a small sample of the cognitive abilities that constitute intelligence.
   1. Useful IQ tests must be standardized, objective, reliable, valid, and evaluated against proper norms.
   2. In some cases, measures of tacit intelligence (knowledge and skills specific to a task that are usually not taught in schools) predict success better in specific everyday tasks than do measures of general intelligence.

C. Intelligence test scores are important in predicting occupational success because persons with higher scores are more likely to qualify for advanced education, take less time to train to perform job skills, and perform complex jobs better.

D. Intelligence is influenced by both genetic and environmental factors working in combination.

E. Scores on tests of intelligence and academic achievement appear to have risen considerably in many countries (possibly due to improvements in health and education), and the gap between race-ethnic groups has apparently declined in recent years.

F. The lives of persons with very low levels of intelligence have improved in recent years with improved special education, services designed to assist them in living normal lives, and increased acceptance by persons of higher intelligence.

G. Contrary to widespread misperceptions, persons with very high levels of intelligence are taller, stronger, healthier, and happier than persons of average intelligence.

1. A scholarly and readable overview of cognition is Hunt, R. R., & Ellis, H. C. (1999). *Fundamentals of cognitive psychology* (6th ed.). Boston: McGraw-Hill.

2. For a clear summary of Kahnemann and Tversky's work on irrationality in human reasoning that contrasts it with the assumption of rational choice underlying economics, see Tetlock, P. E., & Mellers, B. A. (2002). The great rationality debate. *Psychological Science, 13,* 94–99.

3. For a firsthand account of Francine (Penny) Patterson's attempt to teach language to a gorilla and of Herbert Terrace's experiences with the chimpanzee Nim Chimpsky, see Patterson, F., & Linden, E. (1981). *The education of Koko.* New York: Henry Holt; and Terrace, H. S. (1980). *Nim.* New York: Knopf.

4. For differing views on the topic of ethnic differences in intelligence, see Jensen, A. R. (1980). *Bias in mental testing.* New York: Free Press; Mackenzie, B. (1984). Explaining race differences in IQ: The logic, the methodology, and the evidence. *American Psychologist, 39,* 1207–1213; Herrnstein, R. J., & Murray, C. (1994). *The bell curve: Intelligence and class structure in American life.* New York: Free Press; and Hunt, E. (1995). The role of intelligence in modern society. *American Scientist, 83,* 356–368.

5. For an excellent discussion of the fair interpretation of ability test scores in business and government for persons of different levels of socioeconomic status and persons with sensory and physical impairments, see Sandoval, J., Frisby, C. L., Geisinger, K. F., Ramos-Grenier, J., & Scheuneman, J. D. (1998). *Test interpretation and diversity: Achieving equity in assessment.* Washington, DC: American Psychological Association.

6. For good statements on intelligence, see Frederiksen, N. (1986). Toward a broader conception of human intelligence. *American Psychologist, 41,* 445–452; and Neisser, U., & others. (1996). Intelligence: Knowns and unknowns. *American Psychologist, 51,* 77–101.

**Resources**

# PART IV

# Developmental Psychology

In the first eight chapters of this book, you have learned about many psychological processes and the biological and cultural factors that influence these processes. You have learned about sensation, perception, learning, memory, thinking and problem solving, and language. In chapter 9, you will learn how these psychological processes emerge and change across the span of development from early childhood to old age.

Here is a visual overview of what you will learn in the fourth section of the text.

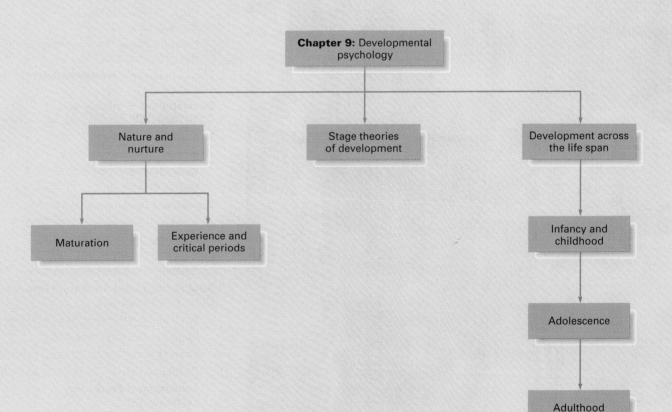

## Chapter Outline

# Developmental Psychology

## PROLOGUE

Jean Piaget was a notable Swiss scientist who studied the development of cognition in children until his death in 1980. His most important contribution was to show us that children of different ages understand the world in ways that are often very different from the way adults understand it. Indeed, young children understand their worlds in ways that are so different from adults that it is sometimes like trying to communicate with a creature from another galaxy!

A classic experiment by Piaget and his frequent collaborator Barbel Inhelder (1963) makes this point very well. Children of different ages were shown three small three-dimensional replicas of "mountains" arranged on a table top. On the other side of the table, a doll was seated. The children were asked to look at the mountains and then were asked to indicate which picture from several showed the mountains as the doll would see them. Six-year-olds could not do it at all, some 7- and 8-year-olds could, and children 9 to 11 years of age had no more trouble with the task than an adult would.

Life doesn't stand still. We are in a state of constant change throughout our lives. When we ask ourselves who we are, we think of ourselves in terms of who we are now. But we have been and will be many different people in our lifetime: an infant, a child, a teenager, a young adult, a mature person, and an aged person. The thread of continuity that runs through our lives is very real, but we change more than we realize. To understand ourselves fully, we must understand the process of

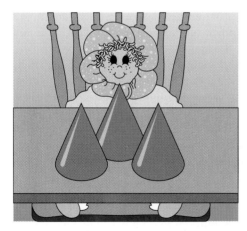
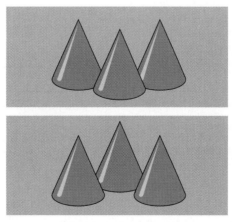

What does the doll see?

**development**
The more-or-less predictable changes in behavior associated with increasing age.

**developmental psychology**
The field of psychology that focuses on development across the life span.

**maturation**
(mach″u-rā′shun)  Systematic physical growth of the body, including the nervous system.

**development,** the more-or-less predictable changes in behavior associated with increasing age.

Why do we change as we grow older? Psychologists differ on the question of how much of our development is biologically determined or shaped by the learning environment, but most believe that development is the product of the combined forces of "nature" (biology) and "nurture" (environment). **Developmental psychology** is the field of psychology that focuses on development across the life span. This chapter on developmental psychology is about the person that you were yesterday, are today, and will become tomorrow. Just as we cannot understand butterflies without understanding their metamorphosis from caterpillars, we cannot understand human beings without understanding how they change across the life span.  ■

## ● Basic Processes of Development

What forces cause us to change as we pass through life? What factors determine whether we grow up to be baseball players or umpires, musicians or opticians? In this section, we will look at the factors that play key roles in the process of development. As you have probably already learned to expect, not all psychologists agree about these factors, so a variety of viewpoints are presented in this chapter.

Both nature and nurture work together in development. Without getting some advice (nurture), a child can't use a baseball glove correctly. But the child must be physically developed enough to use the glove (nature).

### Nature or Nurture?

Some psychological theorists believe that nearly all important developmental changes are controlled by biological factors (nature): Our behavior "unfolds" over time, like a plant growing from seed to flower. Other theorists assert that the psychological environment (nurture) is the master of our development: Our behavior is "molded" by experiences, like clay in the hands of a sculptor. The vast majority of contemporary psychologists believe, however, that both nature and nurture combine to influence our actions, thoughts, and feelings.

Language provides a good example of the rich interplay of nature and nurture in our lives. There can be no question that experience is important in language development. Children will learn to use language only if they are exposed to language, and they will learn to speak the language to which they are exposed. For example, a French child adopted by a Chinese-speaking family will grow up speaking Chinese, not French. But neither goldfish nor marmosets will learn to speak a human language when given the same amount of experience required by a human child to learn language. One must have a human brain (or, as discussed in chapter 8, an ape brain might be sufficient) to learn a human language. In the absence of the right nature, nurture can accomplish nothing.

Other examples of the blending of nature and nurture abound in child development. Children cannot use a baseball glove correctly unless they have seen others play ball (nurture). But you cannot effectively teach children to do much with a glove until age 4 or so, after considerable physical development has taken place (nature). We are creatures of complex combinations of both our nature and nurture.

### Maturation

In the study of development, the most important aspect of nature (biological factors) is **maturation.** This term refers to systematic physical growth of the nervous system and other bodily structures. A primary question for the psychologist specializing in the study

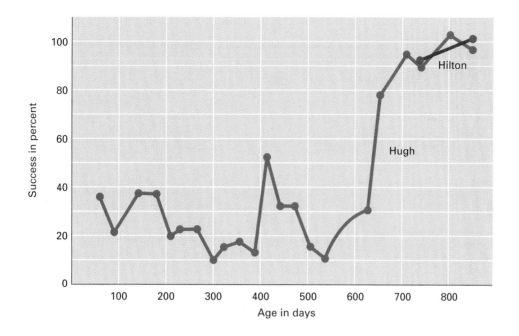

**FIGURE 9.1**
The importance of maturational readiness is shown in McGraw's (1940) study of toilet training twin boys named Hugh and Hilton. Although Hugh's training was begun at 50 days of age, no progress was achieved until he was about 650 days of age. In contrast, Hilton's progress was rapid because training was begun when he was maturationally ready.
**Source:** Data from M. B. McGraw, "Neural Maturation as Exemplified in Achievement of Bladder Control," *Journal of Pediatrics*, 16:580–590, 1940.

of development is "How much of the change that we see occurring with age is the result of physical maturation?"

Although both experience and maturation are important in most developmental changes, maturation is surprisingly important in many specific contexts. For example, experience obviously plays an important role in toilet training—children must be taught to use the toilet—but maturation also plays a key role. Successful toilet training is difficult for most children before at least the age of 24 months. They are simply not *maturationally ready* to learn that task. After 24 to 36 months of age, however, most children learn to use the toilet fairly rapidly.

An experiment using identical twin boys illustrates the idea of maturational readiness beautifully. Toilet training was begun for one boy, Hugh, when he was only 50 days old. Training for Hilton, the other twin, did not begin until 700 days of age (almost 2 years). As shown in figure 9.1, Hugh made no real progress until about 20 months of age, whereas Hilton's progress was rapid from the beginning. Both children learned, but only when they reached the proper level of maturation (McGraw, 1940).

Maturation seems to function in much the same way in intellectual, social, and other areas of development. For example, children perform cognitive tasks more quickly and accurately as they grow older, largely because the myelin coating that speeds neural transmission in the cerebral cortex (see p. 61 to refresh your knowledge about myelin) continues to grow throughout childhood (Bjorklund & Green, 1992). Perhaps partly as a result, cognition changes dramatically with age. It's unlikely that we could teach an 18-month-old to play cooperatively with other children, teach a 4-year-old the concept of physical mass, or teach the concept of justice to a 6-year-old. These behaviors and concepts generally cannot be learned until later ages, suggesting that maturation of the brain is one of the factors involved in the development of cognition.

## Early Experience and Critical Periods

When the Puritans came to America in the 1600s, they brought with them a belief about children that most of us still hold today—namely, that early childhood is the "formative period" for our personalities. We believe that the experiences that we have as young children powerfully and permanently shape our adult behavior. This is not just a belief held by laypeople; many psychologists hold it, too. But is it true that early experiences irreversibly form our personalities?

Toilet training, typical of many human behaviors, is learned more quickly when the child is maturationally ready.

Konrad Lorenz followed by some of his goslings.

## Imprinting

Supporting the view that our early experiences are of prime importance is a large body of research on nonhuman animals. German biologist Konrad Lorenz (1937), for example, has extensively studied the behavior and development of the graylag goose. During one phase of his investigations, he wanted to know why young goslings followed their mothers in the little, single-file parades that are the joy of farmers and park-visiting children everywhere. Do they follow the mother goose because of an inborn tendency or instinct (nature), or do they learn to follow (nurture) their mother? Lorenz found that goslings do have an inborn tendency to follow but that they will follow any moving, noisy object that they are exposed to after hatching, not just mother geese. Furthermore, once they begin following something, they generally will not follow anything else but that object. If their mother is out to lunch when they hatch and a rooster should happen to strut by, they will follow him until they are mature geese—presumably much to the rooster's embarrassment.

Lorenz called this special kind of early learning **imprinting.** He thought of it as a kind of learning that was highly constrained by maturation. The maturational control is seen clearly in the fact that imprinting can occur only during a brief, sensitive period of the bird's life called the **critical period.** If imprinting does not occur during the critical period, it probably will

**imprinting**
(im′print-ing)  A form of early learning that occurs in some animals during a critical period.

**critical period**
A biologically determined period in the life of some animals during which certain forms of learning can take place most easily.

## THE FAR SIDE® BY GARY LARSON

**When imprinting studies go awry**

never occur. Still, the fact that imprinting is a kind of learning —part of nurture—is obvious because the birds will learn to follow anything that meets the biological requirements. Goslings have been imprinted on quacking duck decoys and footballs pulled by squeaking pulleys. A famous photo even shows Konrad Lorenz being followed by a flock of goslings that had imprinted on him. It's not clear, however, that anything comparable to imprinting occurs in humans, although we do form attachments to our caregivers through prolonged experience with them.

Harry Harlow (1905–1981).    Margaret Harlow (1918–1971).

### Early Social Deprivation

Studies conducted with monkeys, which are closer to humans on the evolutionary ladder than geese, also show the long-lasting effects of early experience in a way that seems more relevant than imprinting to the human condition. Harry and Margaret Harlow (Harlow & Harlow, 1965; Harlow & Novak, 1973) carried out a number of studies of the role of early social experiences in development. Are our earliest social experiences especially important to the development of social behavior in childhood and adulthood? Sigmund Freud would have us believe that these **early experiences** are of the greatest significance, but until the Harlows, few researchers had experimentally tested Freud's claims.

The Harlows raised a group of infant monkeys in complete isolation for the first few months of life. Later they returned the monkeys, which had never lived with a mother, to regular group cages with other monkeys. When the monkeys reached adulthood (about 3 years of age), they were placed in breeding cages with another monkey of the other sex. It was then that the Harlows noticed that the social, sexual, and emotional behavior of these monkeys was distinctly abnormal. Females raised without early experience with a real mother appeared fearful and viciously attacked the male when a sexual advance was made. The males, on the other hand, alternated between fearfulness and overenthusiastic, clumsy sexual advances.

Although they had normal social experiences for 2½ years, these monkeys' abnormal experiences during the first 6 months of life had a continuing detrimental effect on their social behavior. Moreover, when a few of the females finally became pregnant and had offspring, the lasting effects of the early social deprivation were made more clear. When the mother-deprived monkeys

The Harlow studies of early social deprivation in monkeys revealed that abnormal experiences during the first 6 months of life have a detrimental effect on the social behavior of adult monkeys.

became mothers themselves, they rejected and even attacked their own infants. Some of the mother-deprived mothers even killed their own infants, and the rest had to be removed from the cage to prevent their deaths.

Much less is known about the effects on humans of abnormal early experiences. As a result, opinion is deeply divided among psychologists about this issue. Some believe that abnormal experiences produce irreversible damage (e.g., Bruner, 1974), whereas others believe that, under favorable conditions, the early effects may not be permanent (Kagan, 1984; Parker, Barrett, & Hickie, 1992; Paris, 2000; Thompson & Nelson, 2001). Humans may be more open to the effects of experience throughout the life span. Still, this tentative conclusion is based on only a handful of studies of children with abnormal early experiences who were placed in good homes at an early age and showed marked improvement. Children with abnormal early experiences who live in marginally stable families might be less able to recover.

**early experiences**
Experiences occurring very early in development, believed by some to have lasting effects.

## Variations in Development: Getting There at Different Times

It is very important to understand that it's normal for child development to be highly variable. This is true in two senses: (a) there are differences between children in their development and (b) children vary in the rate of their own development from one period to the next.

Different children develop at different rates. It's normal for one child to walk or talk several months before another child. When we look at charts of the normal age at which children sit, walk, speak in sentences, and so on, we must remember that variations from those norms may mean nothing at all. Deviations from the average are not unusual. Variation is the rule, not the exception, in child development. Any large variation in development should be discussed with a pediatrician or child psychologist, but small variations should not be a cause for concern.

It's also normal for children to be variable in their own development. Children who are shorter than their age-mates often shoot up suddenly to become taller than most. A fussy baby can become a calm, happy child. And it's not unusual for a child who was above average on an IQ test at age 4 to be just average at age 9 or vice versa. Discontinuities in development, again, are the rule rather than the exception.

Studies suggest that the effects of abnormal early experiences can be reversed by positive, appropriate experiences at later ages. Sometimes these positive experiences are with adoptive parents.

## Review

Children change dramatically from birth to adulthood. This fact has led some theorists in the past to assert that developmental changes in behavior are biologically programmed to "unfold" with increasing age. Other theorists have argued that changes in behavior occur because the learning environment "molds" our development. Today it's generally believed, however, that development results from a blend of both biological and environmental influences. Maturation provides an important example of this interaction between biology and environment: Some forms of learning (which clearly depend on the environment) can occur efficiently only when the child has reached a certain level of readiness through physical maturation.

Experiences during critical periods of early development can have lifelong effects on animal behavior. The Harlows' experiments with social deprivation during the infancy of monkeys also show long-lasting effects of abnormal early experiences. Studies of human infants who had abnormal early experiences, but who were adopted by normal families during childhood, however, suggest that humans may be less permanently influenced by early experience than other animals and may be more open to environmental influences throughout the entire life span.

## Check Your Learning

To be sure that you have learned the key points from the preceding section, cover the list of correct answers and try to answer each question. If you give an incorrect answer to any question, return to the page given next to the correct answer to see why your answer was not correct. Remember that these questions cover only some of the important information in this section; it is important that you make up your own questions to check your learning of other facts and concepts.

1. In developmental psychology, the term *nurture* refers to _____ factors that influence development.

    a) biological      c) both of the above

    b) environmental      d) none of the above

## HUMAN DIVERSITY

### Raising a Child Who Cannot Hear

All parents must make important decisions about raising children that can have a major impact on their child's emotional and intellectual development. The parents of children who are challenged by physical or sensory limitations, however, face a number of additional decisions. In the case of children with little or no hearing, for example, parents must first decide if the child will learn to speak orally (called "voice") or will learn sign language. The parents of Montreal Expos team member Curtis Pride felt that he would always be an outsider if he did not learn to voice (Gildea, 1993). Other parents disagree, however. They feel that the child will not be able to enter the *deaf culture* (Rutherford, 1988) if sign language is not learned. Many deaf people consider themselves as part of a distinct cultural group rather than having a physical disability. They feel that a deaf child who does not learn sign language will not fully join the only culture that will truly accept the child.

Another choice parents must make is whether to send their child to a residential school for deaf children or to send her or him to a neighborhood school with hearing children. Some parents of deaf children feel that it is best for them to learn to be part of the mainstream culture. Many deaf persons, however, feel that residential schools are better because they allow deaf children to be part of an accepting community, to communicate freely with others, and to develop more fully. Unlike some other groups who are different from the majority of the population, many deaf persons object to being "integrated" into the hearing world. No matter how hard they might try to be part of the mainstream culture, they feel that they will remain separate because few hearing people know sign language.

Jan Hafer and Ellen Richmond (1988) encourage hearing parents of deaf children to learn sign language and to

Parents of deaf children often decide to learn sign language along with their children.

learn about deaf culture and history by interacting with successful deaf persons. But many deaf children live in families where no one has learned sign language. Sign language is a complex language, and it can take parents months or years to learn it. Often, financial and time constraints make it difficult for parents to attend sign language classes, but some experts believe that not doing so can lead to isolation of the child and slow his or her language development (Dolnick, 1993, p. 48).

Technology is progressing in ways that will soon create new options for parents—and new difficult decisions to make. The television program *60 Minutes* ran a story about a deaf girl who had a device implanted in the cochlea of her ears that improved her hearing. The parents of the girl described the operation as "a miracle of biblical proportions" (Dolnick, 1993, p. 43). But some deaf persons wrote letters asserting that the surgery amounts to genocide or child abuse. For example, Roslyn Rosen, president of the National Association of the Deaf, stated that she would not prefer to be able to hear. "I'm happy with who I am, and I don't want to be 'fixed.' Would an Italian American rather be a WASP? In our society everyone agrees that whites have an easier time than blacks. But do you think a black person would undergo operations to become white?" (Dolnick, 1993, p. 38).

Do you have any characteristic that sets you apart from other persons or has created barriers for you? Are you in the minority because of your height, weight, ethnicity, sexual orientation, religion, intelligence, attractiveness, or any other feature? Some of the ways in which human beings differ from one another are more challenging or lead to greater discrimination than others, but most of us are in the minority in some way. How has this influenced you? How do you think you would be different if you had a more challenging physical characteristic? ◼

2. In the study of development, the most important biological factor is _____, the systematic physical growth of the body, including the nervous system.

    a) maturation         c) growth factors

    b) hormones          d) environment

3. A biologically determined period in the life of some animals during which certain forms of learning can take place most easily is called a _____.

   a) stage

   c) critical period

   b) milestone

   d) landmark

4. It is normal for the development of children to be _____.

---

**Thinking Critically about Psychology**

1. Is there any practical difference in implications of the "molding" and "unfolding" views of development for parents?

2. Do you think there are critical periods in human development?

---

Correct Answers: 1. b (p. 320), 2. a (p. 320), 3. c (p. 322), 4. variable (p. 324).

**stage**
One of several time periods in development that is qualitatively distinct from the periods that come before and after.

## Stage Theories of Development

Although all psychologists agree that people change over time, they disagree considerably over how to conceptualize those changes. One group sees us as changing gradually with age; the other school of thought sees people as going through a series of abrupt changes from one stage to the next. To relate this difference in opinion to our previous discussion, those who see gradual changes generally lean more toward a "molding" view by which they interpret behavior as gradually changing, mostly due to increasing experience. Those who see **stages** in development typically lean toward a view in which behavior "unfolds" over time, largely due to biological maturation.

Stage theorists believe that the changes occurring from one stage to the next make children qualitatively different (different in "kind") rather than quantitatively different (different in amount) from how they were at a previous stage. When a child learns to use simple words to express herself, for example, she has changed qualitatively; that is, she has become different from the kind of child she was when she could not use language. This qualitative change opens up new experiences and possibilities. Although stage theorists believe that changes between stages are qualitative, they believe that children also change quantitatively during each stage. For example, once the child has mastered some simple words, she will progress for a while by learning more simple words before the next qualitative change takes place (combining words syntactically).

Stage theorists also believe that all children must pass through the same qualitatively different stages in the same order. Stages are believed to be biologically programmed to unfold in a fixed sequence in all normal persons. In addition, they believe that a child cannot progress to the next stage until the current one has been mastered.

A close examination of the writings of even the staunchest stage theorists, however, shows that they recognize that the transition from one stage to the next is a gradual blending. In other words, a child may master one part of a new stage while still struggling with part of a previous stage. One gifted professor of psychology suggested to me that the stages of child development are like a rainbow: We can see that there are different colors in a rainbow, but it's not possible to see exactly where one color stops and the next one begins. Stages of development, like the colors in a rainbow, blend together.

In the sections that follow, we will discuss several major stage theories of cognitive development, moral development, and personality development. By taking a close look at each of these theories, we will better appreciate stage theories in general and will learn a little about the development of children in each of these three important areas.

**Formal operational stage: 11 years on**

By the end of the stage of childhood, most individuals have progressed to full adult cognition, including the ability to reason using abstract concepts.

**Concrete operational stage: 7–11 years**

During middle childhood, the child has the ability to reason like an adult in every way except for reasoning about abstract concepts, such as justice, infinity, or the meaning of life.

**Preoperational stage: 2–7 years**

During the preoperational stage, the child is capable of symbolic thought. Young children's thought is still quite different from that of adults, however. It is often "illogical" in numerous ways that reveal the unique nature of the preoperational child's cognition.

**Sensorimotor stage: Birth–2 years**

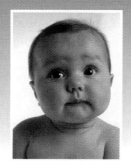

The child deals with reality in terms of sensations and motor movements. At this stage, children are unable to reason in mental symbols.

**FIGURE 9.2**
Piaget's stages of cognitive development.

## Piaget's Stage Theory of Cognitive Development

Perhaps the best-known stage theory in psychology is that of Jean Piaget. Piaget was a Swiss scholar who wrote extensively about the development of cognition in children. Piaget distinguished four major stages of cognitive development. These four stages are summarized in figure 9.2. Note that the child's cognitive capacities develop rapidly until about the time of puberty but change little after that. Note, also, the magnitude of

| Table 9.1 | Kohlberg's Levels of Moral Development | | |
|---|---|---|---|
| **Premoral Level** | **Conventional Level** | **Principled Level** |
| Young children have no sense of morality as adults understand it. They make moral judgments to obtain rewards and avoid punishment. | At this stage, children make moral decisions on the basis of what they think others will think of them, particularly parents and other persons of authority. Because society's rules, or conventions, state what is expected of them, persons at the conventional level of moral development make moral decisions based on rules. | At this stage, we judge actions on the basis of ethical principles rather than the consequences to us (as in the first two stages). The most advanced moral reasoning within this stage, according to Kohlberg, is based on one's principles of morality, even if they differ from the rules of the larger community. |

Jean Piaget (1896–1980).

Lawrence Kohlberg (1927–1987).

the changes in cognition that occur during the childhood stages. On the average, children progress from human beings who cannot reason in mental symbols to persons fully capable of adult reasoning in 11 short years, with many dramatic changes along the way.

We will look more closely at each of the stages of cognitive development as we follow the course of normal development in detail later in the chapter.

## Stage Theories of Moral Development

Two theorists have provided us with stage theories of moral development that are related to Piaget's theory of cognitive development.

### Kohlberg's Theory of Moral Development

Lawrence Kohlberg (1969) collected data for his stage theory of moral development by presenting boys with moral dilemmas and asking for evaluations of the people and actions involved. The following is an example of the type of dilemma used by Kohlberg in his research:

> In Europe, a lady was dying because she was very sick. There was one drug that the doctors said might save her. This medicine was discovered by a man living in the same town. It cost him $200 to make it, but he charged $2,000 for just a little of it. The sick lady's husband, Heinz, tried to borrow enough money to buy the drug. He went to everyone he knew to borrow the money. He told the man who made the drug that his wife was dying and asked him to sell the medicine cheaper or let him pay later. But the man said, "No, I made the drug and I'm going to make money from it." So Heinz broke into the store and stole the drug.

Did Heinz do the right thing? Kohlberg was interested in the logical process through which people arrived at their answers to moral dilemmas. He concluded that we pass through the three major levels of the development of moral reasoning shown in table 9.1. Nearly all children use only premoral reasoning at age 7, but conventional moral reasoning predominates after age 11. Thus, Kohlberg sees the first two major shifts in moral reasoning as occurring at the same times as the beginnings of the preoperational and concrete operational stages in Piaget's theory of cognitive development. According to Kohlberg, we engage in little principled moral reasoning until age 13, and very few of us ever make it to a stage in which we reason mostly in principled ways. He gives Mahatma Gandhi, Martin Luther King, and Eleanor Roosevelt as examples of persons at the principled stage of moral reasoning (Kohlberg, 1964).

Look carefully at the description of each of Kohlberg's stages of moral development and decide if Heinz did the right thing. At the premoral level, he did the wrong thing because it would get him into trouble. At the conventional stage of moral development, Heinz would be judged to be wrong because he clearly broke the law (the conventions of right and wrong). However, from the perspective of principled reasoning, it

**Table 9.2   Gilligan's Stage Theory of Moral Development**

| Morality as Individual Survival | Morality as Self-Sacrifice | Morality as Equality |
| --- | --- | --- |
| The young child's first sense of what is "right" is what is good for him or her. Young children follow rules to obtain rewards for themselves and to avoid punishment. | The next stage of moral reasoning is attained after becoming aware of the needs of others. In this stage, the person believes that, to be good and to be approved of by others, they must sacrifice their own needs and meet the needs of others. | In the most advanced stage of moral development, the person views his her own needs as equal to those of others. Persons at this stage of moral development have progressed from believing that they must always please others at the expense of their own wishes to a belief that everyone's needs should be met when possible and that sacrifices should be shared equally when the needs of different persons cannot all be met. This is a stage of advocacy of nonviolence—it is not right for anyone to be intentionally hurt, including the person himself or herself. |

could be argued that Heinz did the right thing. After trying to obtain the drug legally, he ignored the consequences of his action (imprisonment), disregarded the community's conventions (the laws against theft), and followed what he thought was the higher moral principle of saving his wife's life.

Does that evaluation bother you? Not everyone would agree that this use of principled reasoning is correct because it tends to place the individual above the law. Indeed, an individual could also explain why Heinz was wrong in terms of the principled stage of moral development. For example, an individual's personal principles might say that it is better for society as a whole to always respect the property rights of others and allow Heinz's wife to die. It is not the particular decision that differs at the different levels of moral development but the nature of moral reasoning involved.

### Gilligan's Theory of Moral Development

Because Kohlberg and others used mostly boys in the initial studies that led to Kohlberg's theory of moral development, Carol Gilligan (1982) has suggested that Kohlberg's theory does not always accurately describe moral development in girls. She argues that female children pass through somewhat different stages. Whereas male development begins with selfish self-interest and moves toward greater reliance on abstract principles of justice, females progress from self-interest toward a balanced concern for the welfare of self and others. Female moral reasoning, in other words, centers on the needs of people rather than on abstractions.

Specifically, Gilligan (1982) suggests that females progress through the three stages of moral development shown in table 9.2. How would the morality of Heinz's actions be judged at each of these stages of moral development? As in Kohlberg's premoral stage, the kind of immature moral reasoning that Gilligan terms the morality as individual survival stage would judge Heinz to be wrong simply because he would be punished. At the morality as self-sacrifice stage, Heinz might be judged to be correct in sacrificing his own welfare to save his wife. At the morality as equality stage, one would have to equally balance the benefits to everyone in making a moral judgment.

Gilligan's contribution to our understanding of moral development has been acknowledged by Kohlberg and others (Levine, Kohlberg, & Hewer, 1985). However, considerable evidence suggests that Gilligan overemphasized gender differences in moral reasoning. Indeed, reviews of research on the subject (Jaffee & Hyde, 2000; Walker, 1986) have shown that males and females are more similar in moral reasoning than they are different.

"Not guilty, because puppies do these things."

Carol Gilligan.

| Table 9.3 | Erik Erikson's Stages of Personality Development | |
|---|---|---|
| **Age** | **Name of Stage** | **Developmental Accomplishments or Failures** |
| 0–1 year | Basic trust vs. mistrust | Learns to feel comfortable and trust parents' care; or develops a deep distrust of a world that is perceived to be unsafe |
| 1–3 years | Autonomy vs. shame and doubt | Learns sense of competence by learning to feed self, use toilet, play alone; or feels ashamed and doubts own abilities |
| 3–5 years | Initiative vs. guilt | Gains ability to use own initiative in planning and carrying out plans; or, if cannot live within parents' limits, develops a sense of guilt over misbehavior |
| 5–11 years | Industry vs. inferiority | Learns to meet the demands imposed by school and home responsibilities; or comes to believe that he or she is inferior to others |
| 11–18 years | Identity vs. role confusion | Acquires sense of own identity; or is confused about role in life |
| 18–40 years | Intimacy vs. isolation | Develops couple relationship and joint identity with partner; or becomes isolated from meaningful relationships with others |
| 40–65 years | Generativity vs. stagnation | Develops a concern with helping others and leaving children, products, and ideas to future generations; or becomes self-centered and stagnant |
| 65–years on | Integrity vs. despair | Reaps benefits of earlier stages and understands and accepts meaning of a temporary life; or despairs over ever being able to find meaning in life |

Erik H. Erikson (1902–1994).

## Erikson's Stage Theory of Personality Development

Erik Erikson provides us with a very different example of a stage theory of development. Erikson's stages are turning points, or *crises*, the outcome of which will partly determine the course of future personality development. In using the term *crises*, Erikson was not suggesting that these turning points are always experienced as emotionally difficult periods, although they certainly can be for some individuals. Rather, Erikson chose this term to emphasize that they can be turning points with far-reaching implications.

The eight stages of Erikson's theory of personality development, which contain the crises, are presented in table 9.3. The name given to each stage by Erikson reflects the two possible outcomes of the stage. To a great extent, particularly in infancy and childhood, the outcome is influenced by the actions of children's parents and other significant people. For example, if infants' parents provide consistent, warm, and adequate care during their child's first year (stage of basic trust vs. mistrust), infants will learn to trust the world as a basically safe place. If infants are cared for inconsistently or are physically or emotionally abused, they will consider the world an unsafe place that cannot be trusted. Erikson believed that this basic sense of trust or mistrust is usually carried with the individual throughout life.

To take another example, the challenge of the fourth stage (industry vs. inferiority) is learning to meet the demands placed on the child by parents (to clean his or her room in a way that pleases the parents), by teachers (to read, write, and calculate), and by peers (to ride a bike, to take turns). If children master these demands, they develop a belief that effort (industry) leads to success. If they fail to meet the demands of this stage, Erikson believed that a lifelong feeling of inferiority develops.

## Review

Psychologists who lean toward a view that developmental changes "unfold" largely through maturation also see those developmental changes as occurring in distinct steps, or stages, through which all children pass in the same order. Those psychologists who lean toward a view of developmental changes as being "molded" by learning experiences tend to perceive these changes as being more gradual in nature and not marked by clear-cut stages. It's useful to think of development as occurring in something like stages, but ones that are not clearly separable from one another. Stage theorists view many aspects of human existence as unfolding in stages: cognition (Piaget), moral reasoning (Kohlberg and Gilligan), and personality (Erikson). Although stage theories tend to give us the impression that all children develop at the same rate, variation in development is normal within broad limits.

Check Your Learning

To be sure that you have learned the key points from the preceding section, cover the list of correct answers and try to answer each question. If you give an incorrect answer to any question, return to the page given next to the correct answer to see why your answer was not correct.

1. _____ distinguished four major stages of cognitive development, the sensorimotor stage, the preoperational stage, the concrete operational stage, and the formal operational stage.

   a) Jean Piaget          c) Sigmund Freud
   b) John Bowlby          d) Harry Harlow

2. Kohlberg's theory of moral development was criticized by Gilligan primarily because _____.

   a) the data did not support his conclusions          c) it was done so long ago
   b) it was based on a study of boys only          d) his subjects consisted of urban children only

3. Gilligan suggests that moral reasoning in _____ centers on the needs of people rather than on abstractions.

   a) males          c) both males and females
   b) females

4. In Erikson's stage theory of personality development, the stages are turning points, or _____, the outcome of which will partly determine the course of future personality development.

Thinking Critically about Psychology

1. What are the similarities between the most advanced stages of moral reasoning described by Kohlberg and Gilligan?

2. What are the advantages of theories like Erikson's for understanding life-span development? What are their disadvantages?

Correct Answers: 1. a (p. 327), 2. b (p. 329), 3. b (p. 329), 4. crises (p. 330).

## ● The Concept of Development across the Life Span

We now turn our attention to the normal course of development across the human life span. Our topic will be the typical physical and psychological changes that occur in people from birth to old age. Why is this important? This section is of *fundamental* importance to understanding human condition. Although we tend to think of ourselves as the persons we are right now, human lives are in a constant state of change. The person you are today is different in some ways from the person you were 10 years ago and from the person you will be 10 years from now.

Do you have any photographs that were taken of you as an infant? How about photos of you when you were in the first grade or just starting high school? If so, you can create an amazing learning experience by laying these photos out in a time line. My, how you have grown!

I thought it would help me write this chapter if I did the same thing. The six photos above show me from 5 months to my fifties. Look at the changes! The person in all the photos is me—the thread of continuity in my life is very clear—but the changes are certainly obvious, too. Look at that bewildered infant! It's amazing to me that I was ever that small—as an infant, I weighed less than 5 percent of what I weigh now—or that there was a time when I could neither walk nor talk. By the time I was 5 and was going off to kindergarten in that dashing sailor suit, I was walking, talking, and tying my shoes. But I could not yet read a book, let alone imagine that I would ever write one.

In high school, I played football and took the advice of my coach that the only proper way to cut hair was *off*. I learned how to play guitar about the same year that this photo was taken and played in some really bad high school rock bands. Later, in the sixties, I grew more hair and sang and played a lot of folk songs (very badly). By the seventies, I was a young professor and clinical child psychologist, working hard to establish a career. I worked long hours and spent a great deal of time with my children. I was so busy that I did not even own a guitar for most of the seventies. Is that a bit of gray creeping into my shaggy head of hair?

In the eighties, my hair was still long, but no longer brown. During this decade, I found time to play the guitar again. In fact, a friend of mine owned a recording studio and he let me live out a childhood fantasy of recording a song. That's me in the studio, listening intently to the advice of my bass player, who happens also to be my son. Many changes had taken place in my life by midlife, but when I listened to the recording I found that I still played the guitar badly and sang even worse! The last photo is me in my fifties—back to short hair and showing more than a few wrinkles. Once again, there is little time for the guitar, but considering my lack of talent, that's for the best.

Now, consider this question: Which picture best represents me—the real me? The answer: all of them. And that is exactly the point of this section on the life span. We are all in a constant state of change—called development—throughout our lives. If you are going to understand human lives, you must understand that fundamental point.

We will now begin to tell the story of development across the life span. We will follow the child from infancy through the stages of childhood, through adolescence, and finally through the stages of adult life.

## Development in Infancy and Childhood

### Neonatal Period: The Newborn

The first two weeks of life are termed the **neonatal period** and mark the transition from the womb to independent life. What is the world of the neonate like?

Physically, the neonate is weak and dependent on adults. It cannot raise its head or roll over by itself. It does have a repertoire of a few useful reflexive behaviors, however. When stimulated on one side of the mouth, for example, the neonate turns its head toward the stimulation and begins searching and sucking until something is in its mouth. This **rooting reflex** enables the baby to take its mother's nipple in its mouth and nurse.

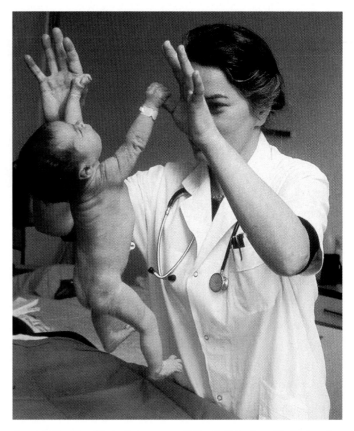

A neonate will reflexively grasp anything that is placed in its hand.

The sensory abilities of neonates are surprisingly well developed. Their hearing is fairly good, and they react differently to different odors and tastes (Santrock, 1998). However, they are distinctly nearsighted little people. They can see fairly well (but probably fuzzily) up to about 12 inches from their eyes, but the world farther away is probably a blur to them (Salapatek, 1977). It was previously believed that the skin senses of neonates were poorly developed, but it is now clear that they are quite sensitive to touch (Santrock, 1998) and that male neonates definitely react to circumcision of the penis without anesthesia as if it were painful (Gunnar, Malone, & Fisch, 1988). Few cognitive abilities are developed during the neonatal period, but neonates respond to faces in a way that suggests that they recognize that they are a conceptual class distinct from other concepts of objects (Santrock, 1998). In most ways, however, the process of cognitive development is just beginning.

The emotions of the neonate are quite diffuse. Sleep is very common in this stage, occupying about 16 hours a day (Roffwarg, Muzio, & Dement, 1966). The neonate engages in little of what could be called social behavior, except the intimate contact between neonate and parent in cuddling and nursing. At first, the neonate is a passive participant, but, as we will see in a moment, he or she soon becomes an active partner in social interactions.

### Infancy: 2 Weeks to 2 Years

#### Physical Development

At 2 weeks of age, the baby acquires the official title of infant. Much is going on developmentally during this period of rapid change. Physical development and growth are more rapid during the first year than at any other time in life. By 2 months, many infants can raise their head and chest on their arms and can grasp an object that is held directly in front of their head and shoulders. By 6 months, many can roll over from back to front, sit, and soon begin to crawl. By 1 year, many can walk alone and grasp small objects with

**neonatal period**
(ne″ō-nā′tal) The first two weeks of life following birth.

**rooting reflex**
An automatic response in which an infant turns its head toward stimulation on the cheek.

Although we think of infancy as a single stage of development, a tremendous amount of change occurs from birth to 2 years. This photo illustrates the physical differences in infants from 2 through 18 months. Notice the differences in how they sit—the 2-month-old can only lie there, whereas the 18-month-old can lounge casually on the arm of the couch.

their fingers and thumbs. By 2 years, they are "getting into everything" and walking well, but with the peculiar gait that earns them the nickname of "toddlers."

From 2 weeks to 2 months, rapid change takes place in all senses. Clear vision increases to 12 feet during this period. By 6 months of age, their vision is 20/20 (normal). Young infants amuse themselves, and their families, by staring at interesting visual stimuli. They prefer to look at patterned stimuli with sharp contours (Banks & Salapatek, 1981). Fortunately for parents, human faces fall into this category.

### Cognitive Development (Sensorimotor Stage)

**sensorimotor stage**
In Piaget's theory, the period of cognitive development from birth to 2 years.

**object permanence**
The understanding that objects continue to exist when they are not in view.

Infancy is the **sensorimotor stage,** according to Jean Piaget. During the early part of this stage, the infant moves from pure reflexive actions to the ability to coordinate sensations and motor movements, such as voluntarily taking a nipple into the mouth and sucking. From about 2 months on, the infant begins to interact actively with its environment. It no longer passively stares at objects but takes great pleasure in pushing, pulling, and mouthing them. This kind of experience, in which the infant actively changes the sensations it receives by using its hands and feet to alter the environment (sensorimotor experience), is believed to be important in the development of motor behaviors such as crawling (Held & Hein, 1963). By 4½ months, most infants respond positively to the sound of their names (Mandel, Jusczyk, & Pisoni, 1995).

From at least 2 months on, infants remember some of what they have experienced for a time (Ornstein & Haden, 2002). Psychologist Carolyn Rovee-Collier (1999) developed a clever way to study memory in infants. Infants are placed in a crib with a distinctive mobile overhead. A ribbon is connected to one ankle, but at first it is not connected to the mobile. This is done to test the babies to see how much they kick spontaneously. Then they experience a training period in which the ribbon on their ankle is connected to the mobile—kicking causes movement of the mobile that the infants find to be positively reinforcing, so they kick more frequently. Later they are tested for their memory of this simple learning experience by placing them in the crib again and seeing how much they kick with the ribbon unattached. If they kick more than in their initial test, that suggests that they remember the learning experience. Infants of 6 months show memory for the task for as long as 2 weeks on average. The memory of older infants is tested by first having them learn to press a lever to move an electric train around a track. Later they are tested on their recall of this new skill. One-year-olds show recall of the train task for up to 8 weeks on average, whereas the average 18-month-old can remember this task for over 12 weeks.

During infancy, children develop the ability to form cognitive representations of the world. For example, by 6 to 9 months of age, the child begins to understand that objects exist even when they are out of sight. This is called **object permanence.** Before that time, if an object at which the infant is looking is hidden from sight by a card, the infant will not push the card aside to look for it. It's as if the infant does not know that the object is still there—a variation of "out of sight, out of mind." After 6 to 9 months of age,

During the sensorimotor stage, infants stare at interesting visual stimuli, including human faces.

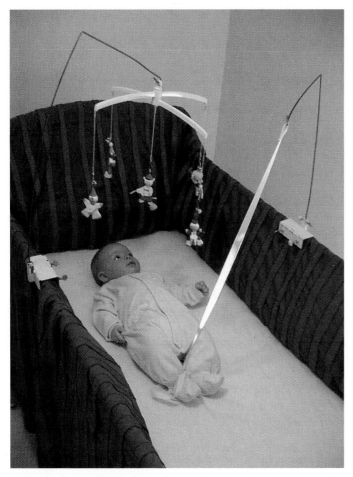
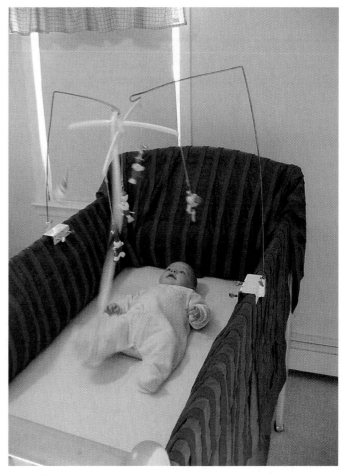

Psychologist Carolyn Rovee-Collier studies the memory of young infants using a clever adaptation of a mobile in a crib. At first (left), the infant is placed in the crib with a ribbon tied to her or his ankle to see how often the baby spontaneously kicks. Then (right) the ribbon is attached to the mobile to make it move when the baby kicks. On the average, the babies kick more often when the ribbon is attached because movement of the mobile is positively reinforcing. Later the babies are tested for their memory of this simple learning task by placing them in the crib again with the ribbon unattached. Babies who recall the task kick more than in the initial test.

however, the infant will search for the object behind the cloth, suggesting that the infant knows that it's back there somewhere. This is both a happy and a sad development for parents. Now that the 9-month-old knows that spoons still exist when thrown on the floor, the infant quickly masters the game of "dropsies" (McCall, 1979). Infants joyously fill their mealtimes with the game of throwing their spoons on the floor while Dad or Mom picks them up. But although the child can represent parts of the world in mental images, she cannot yet use those images to reason.

By 9 months, too, infants begin to understand some nouns, such as *ball* and *cookie*, and can respond to *bye-bye* and other gestures. These changes mark the beginning of a far more complex level of cognitive functioning. By 12 months, most infants can say some words, and by 18 months the infant has a speaking vocabulary of 20 words. By 18 months, the average infant can also understand prohibitions ("No, no . . . don't touch") and can respond correctly to "Show me your nose (ear, toe, mouth, etc.)." By age 2, the infant has a speaking vocabulary of 250 words and speaks in word combinations that fascinate adults in accomplishing so much by saying so little. It has often been referred to as **telegraphic speech** because it leaves out the same words that would be left out of a brief telegram. Sentences like "Milk all gone" and "Daddy silly" say all that needs to be said.

**telegraphic speech**
The abbreviated speech of 2-year-olds.

Awareness that objects still exist after they are removed from view (object permanence) emerges between the ages of 6 and 9 months.

## Emotional and Social Development

Infants enter the world with a restricted range of emotions that grows more complex as they mature. Neonates are capable of only three emotional expressions: surprise, pleasure, and distress (National Advisory Mental Health Council, 1995a). By about 2 months, they show their first true social behavior—they smile at the faces of their caregivers. By 4 months, they have added a fourth emotion to their repertoire—anger. The infant's repertoire of emotions expands again between 6 and 9 months, when shyness around strangers and fear of being separated from their caregivers emerge for the first time. Before 6 to 9 months, infants are generally comfortable with any adult who will take care of them, but after that time they are often fearful of anyone but their mother, father, or other caregiver (National Advisory Mental Health Council, 1995a). Infants also first learn to fear the sight of a hypodermic needle at about 6 to 9 months (Izard, 1978; Sroufe, 1978). The emergence of social smiling at 2 months is a nice reward for parents, who change diapers and walk the floor at night, but the appearance of anger and fear between 4 and 9 months is not always welcome. Both are signs of normal, healthy development of the infant's emotions, however.

Cornell University psychologist Eleanor Gibson developed an interesting method of studying the development of the fear of heights (Gibson & Walk, 1960). When 6- to 9-month-old infants are placed on the "visual cliff" (see fig. 9.3), they show fear and avoidance of the "deep" side. The visual cliff is made using a clear sheet of Plexiglas. Under one side, a patterned floor is right under the glass. On the other side, the pattern is several feet below the glass. When lighted properly, it appears to be a cliff from which the infant could fall. It's interesting to note that infants can *perceive* the depth of the visual cliff several months before they show any fear of it. They look puzzled when placed on the deep side of the visual cliff at 4 months but do not show fear until after they can crawl and have experienced stumbling and falling firsthand (Lewis & Rosenblum, 1978; Scarr & Salapatek, 1970),

**FIGURE 9.3**

Eleanor Gibson and Richard Walk (1960) developed the visual cliff to test infant depth perception. The visual cliff consists of a thick sheet of glass placed on a table. The "shallow" end of the visual cliff has a checkerboard surface an inch or so below the glass. The "deep" end of the visual cliff has a checkerboard surface several feet below the glass. An infant who has reached the crawling stage will crawl from the center of the table across the shallow end, but not across the deep end, to reach his or her mother. This indicates that by at least the age of 6 months infants can perceive depth.

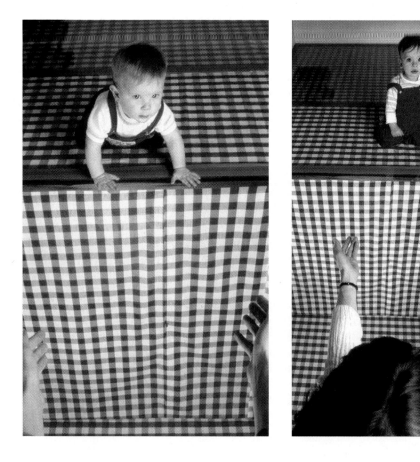

By 2 years, emotions grow even more complex. By this time, many infants act guilty after misbehavior and seem to feel ashamed after failure. Two-year-old infants are richly social creatures who have formed strong **attachments** to their parents or other caregivers (Lewis & Rosenblum, 1978). The strength of this attachment can be seen in three ways. First, infants often cling, grasp, grab, and do whatever else they can to stay close to their parents. Nothing short of the parents' physical closeness and undivided attention will suffice at times. Second, when infants 6 to 9 months or older are separated from their parents, they often show intense **separation anxiety**—the crying and fussing that baby-sitters know so well. Third, infants of this age sometimes also exhibit fear of strangers; no one but the adults to whom they are attached (parents, day-care workers, grandparents) has the same soothing effect.

## Early Childhood: 2 to 7 Years

According to Piaget, a qualitative change occurs as the child reaches the preoperational stage at about 2 years of age. Notice as you read this section how different the young child is from the infant. Early childhood is still a period of rapid growth, but growth is far less explosive than in infancy and declines in rate annually. Great improvements in the coordination of small and large muscle groups take place during this period, which sees the emergence of hopping, skipping, throwing, and the other motor behaviors that are so much a part of early childhood.

### Cognitive Development (Preoperational Stage)

The **preoperational stage** begins at 2 years of age and is a time of dramatic change in cognition. By about 2 years of age, most children are first capable of thinking in mental images. The young child's ability to think is quite different from that of adults, however.

The preoperational child's thinking is often quite illogical by adult standards. Indeed, the name of this stage comes from the fact that the child still cannot perform logical mental operations. There are a variety of other ways in which the cognition of the pre-operational child is wonderfully distinct. For example, the young child's thought is **egocentric,** or self-centered. Piaget does not mean by this term that the child is selfish, but that the child is simply not able to see things from another person's perspective. Ego-centrism also leads young children to believe that inanimate objects are alive, just as they are (known as **animism**). It's common for children of this age to believe that the moon is alive and actually follows them around when they are walking or riding in a car at night.

The child's imagination is often very active at this stage, and because of the child's egocentrism, it's difficult at times for him or her to distinguish real from imaginary. That's why imaginary friends that seem very real to the child are relatively common during this stage. Other errors of logic are quite common, too, giving young children a special kind of logic demonstrated in comments such as "Grandma, he's not your son; he's my dad!"

**Transductive reasoning**—errors in inferring cause-and-effect relationships—is also common in the preoperational child (Schlottmann, 2001). For example, a preoperational child might conclude that spiders cause the basement to be cold. Indeed, the basement *is* cold and there *are* spiders in it, but young children often confuse the cause-and-effect relationships among such facts.

By the end of this period, the preoperational child begins to grasp logical operations and makes fewer cause-and-effect errors. At age 5, the child may be able to pick out all the blue marbles from a jar or all the big marbles, but thinking about two concepts at one time is still difficult. For example, picking out all the big blue marbles may still be too much.

**attachments**
The psychological bonds between infants and caregivers.

**separation anxiety**
The distress experienced by infants when they are separated from their caregivers.

**preoperational stage**
In Piaget's theory, the period of cognitive development from ages 2 to 7.

**egocentric**
(e″gō-sen′trik) The self-oriented quality in the thinking of preoperational children.

**animism**
(a′-nə-mizm) The egocentric belief of preoperational children that inanimate objects are alive, as children are.

**transductive reasoning**
(trans-duk′tiv) Errors in understanding cause-and-effect relationships that are commonly made by preoperational children.

Strong attachments are formed between infants and caregivers during the first two years of life.

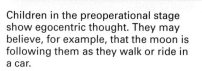
Children in the preoperational stage show egocentric thought. They may believe, for example, that the moon is following them as they walk or ride in a car.

The most notable social changes in the preoperational period are in peer relationships. Between the ages of about 2 and about 7, children go from mostly solitary play, through parallel play, and finally on to cooperative play.

In the concrete operational stage, children learn to recognize that the volume of a liquid does not change when it is poured into a glass of a different shape.

**solitary play**
Playing alone.

**parallel play**
Playing near but not with another child.

**cooperative play**
Play that involves cooperation between two or more children.

Perhaps the most impressive developmental change during the preoperational stage is the growth in language. From a speaking vocabulary of 250 words at age 2, the child reaches a vocabulary of more than 14,000 words by age 6, learning a phenomenal average of almost 9 new words per day (Carey, 1977; Santrock, 1998). From simple 2- or 3-word combinations at age 2, the child masters much of adult syntax during the same period. Seemingly, the child has finally achieved the maturational capacity to learn language and proceeds to do so without hesitation.

### Emotional and Social Development

Both positive and negative emotions are fairly well developed by age 2, but they become considerably richer and more intricate during the preoperational stage. Most of this elaboration of emotion seems to be linked to cognitive development. For example, children do not develop fears of unexperienced things—such as fires, drowning, and traffic accidents—until well into the preoperational period, when they are capable of understanding the concepts behind the fears.

The most notable social changes during this period occur in relationships with peers. At age 2, most children engage in **solitary play.** That is, they play by themselves, even if other children are present. This type of play rapidly decreases in frequency from ages 2 to 5. At first, solitary play is replaced by **parallel play,** in which children play *near* one another in similar activities, but not *with* one another. By the end of the preoperational stage, **cooperative play,** which involves a cooperative give-and-take, has become the predominant type of play (Barnes, 1971).

The shifting pattern of play seems to parallel cognitive development. In the early part of the preoperational stage, when thinking is highly egocentric, it's not surprising that selfishness and lack of cooperation should prevail. Young children may not be able to understand any other type of play. As they reach the end of the stage, however, egocentric thinking declines and cooperative play increases.

A similar shift occurs in emotional outbursts from the beginning to the end of the preoperational stage. Two- and 3-year-olds typically engage in temper tantrums that are directed at no one, whereas 4- to 7-year-olds direct their aggression at others (Sheppard & Willoughby, 1975). Although this kind of behavior is hardly "sociable," it's a more social, less egocentric form of emotion than temper tantrums.

By age 2, most boys and girls have begun to act in sex-typed ways. Males tend to play with trucks, airplanes, and blocks; girls play mostly with dolls, stuffed animals, and dress-up clothes (Fagot, 1974). At this early age, they seem to have a conscious awareness of their own sex (McConaghy, 1979) and understand the sex stereotypes of the culture concerning clothing, occupations, and recreation (Ruble & Ruble, 1980).

## Middle Childhood: 7 to 11 Years

These are the elementary school years. It's no accident that formal education begins in earnest during this period, because most children are then intellectually and socially ready for the demands of school. Physical growth proceeds at a fairly slow pace in middle childhood, but it's a healthy period in which most children experience little illness. Continued improvements in strength and coordination are the only notable advances.

## Cognitive Development (Concrete Operational Stage)

The opening of the **concrete operational stage** is marked by important cognitive changes. Children emerge as capable thinkers who use most adult concepts except those that are abstract. They can order objects (seriation) according to size, weight, and other dimensions. They understand the **reversibility** of logical operations; having added together $7 + 2 = 9$, they have little trouble reversing the operation to see that $9 - 2 = 7$.

One of the most fascinating acquisitions of the concrete operational child is the concept of **conservation.** When children younger than 7 are shown two wide beakers containing equal amounts of water, they have no trouble seeing that they contain the "same amount" of water. But, when the water from one beaker is poured into a tall, narrow beaker right in front of their eyes, they usually think the tall beaker contains "more" water because it's higher. Children over the age of 7 who are in the concrete operational period are not fooled by appearances in this way. According to Piaget, the concrete operational children are able to deal with conservation problems because their thought is more **decentered,** which means that they can think of more than one thing at a time. Consequently, the concrete operational child no longer has trouble picking out the big blue marbles from a jar; he or she can deal with both concepts at the same time. The rapid growth in cognitive ability during middle childhood is based on rapid increases in children's speed of processing information and expansions in the capacity of short-term memory (Fry & Hale, 1996).

## Emotional and Social Development

Few changes of note occur in the expression of emotions during the concrete operational stage, but social relationships are markedly different than before. Children enter this period with close ties to their parents. Although these continue to be important, relationships with peers become increasingly significant during this period. Before age 7, children have friendships, but they generally are not enduring and typically are not close. After 7, peer friendships become more important to children and tend to last longer. Friendship groups, or *cliques*, also emerge during the concrete operational stage. Most friendships are with members of the same sex, and those cross-sex friendships that do exist are generally "just friends." Although the terms *boyfriend* and *girlfriend* are freely used, they have little meaning in the adult sense.

**concrete operational stage**
In Piaget's theory, the period of cognitive development from ages 7 to 11.

**reversibility**
(re-ver′sǝbil-ǝ-tē) The concept understood by concrete operational children that logical propositions can be reversed (if $2 + 3 = 5$, then $5 - 3 = 2$).

**conservation**
The concept understood by concrete operational children that quantity (number, mass, etc.) does not change just because shape or other superficial features have changed.

**decenter**
(dē-sen′ter) To think about more than one characteristic of a thing at a time; a capacity of concrete operational children.

---

### Review

When we look back over the explosive growth of the neonate into a child, it appears that there may be some utility in discussing development in terms of stages. Interrelated changes in several behavioral systems do occur that may be dramatic enough to justify the phrase "qualitatively different stage." However, the entrance to a new stage is not marked by abrupt changes. Developmental changes are gradual and inconsistent, and they take place both within and between stages. There is value, then, in thinking of human development in terms of stages, but there are limits on that value. The detailed picture of infant and child development presented in this section shows that human growth is both a series of landmark steps and a continuous, flowing process. There are no shortcuts to describing the marvelous complexities of human development.

---

### Check Your Learning

To be sure that you have learned the key points from the preceding section, cover the list of correct answers and try to answer each question. If you give an incorrect answer to any question, return to the page given next to the correct answer to see why your answer was not correct.

1. Although an infant during the _____ (first two weeks of life) is weak and dependent on adults, it does have useful reflexive behaviors and has already begun to learn.

   a) trimester

   b) neonatal period

   c) toddler period

   d) prenatal period

2. By 6 to 9 months of age, a child begins to understand that objects exist even when they are out of sight. This is called _____.

   a) object permanence

   b) continuation

   c) constancy theory

   d) conservation

3. According to Piaget, the _____ stage (ages 2 to 7 years) is marked by a phenomenal growth in language.

   a) operational

   b) concrete operational

   c) infancy

   d) preoperational

4. _____ describes the concept understood by concrete operational children (ages 7 to 11 years) that quantity does not change just because shape or other superficial features have changed.

   a) Object permanence

   b) Conservation

   c) Quantity maintenance

   d) Continuity

## Thinking Critically about Psychology

1. If you were a teacher of kindergarten children, how would knowledge of the pre-operational stage of cognitive development influence the way you teach?

2. If you were forced to choose, would you describe development in infancy and childhood as a series of stages or as a continuous process? How would you support your choice?

Correct Answers: 1. b (p. 333), 2. a (p. 334), 3. d (p. 337), 4. b (p. 339).

## ● Adolescent Development

**adolescence**
The period from the onset of puberty until the beginning of adulthood.

**puberty**
(pū′ber-tē) The point in development at which the individual is first physically capable of sexual reproduction.

**Adolescence** is ushered in by the monumental physical changes of **puberty** through which the person who was a child only yesterday becomes sexually capable of being the parent of a child. The adolescent period is marked by rapid physical growth and change and by a heightening of sexual and romantic interest in others. And it's a time in which peers are often more important than parents in terms of attachment and influence. The adolescent is capable of reasoning in abstractions for the first time. Partly for this reason, he or she may spend a great deal of time contemplating abstract issues such as justice and equality. There is no clear-cut demarcation of the end of adolescence in our society. Rather than at any specific age, individuals pass from adolescence to adulthood when they establish adult social relationships and adult patterns of work.

### Physical Development

A number of psychologically important physical changes occur during adolescence, particularly during puberty, which is the onset of adolescence. These changes alter physical appearance so much that—in what seems like a moment—girls come to look like women and boys like men. Height and weight increase sharply, pushing adolescents quickly to adult size. A look in the mirror changes forever the adolescent's image of himself or herself.

Puberty begins with the production of sex hormones by the ovaries in females and the testes in males. These hormones trigger a series of physiological changes that lead to ovulation and menstruation in females and the production of sperm cells in males. These are the **primary sex characteristics** that indicate that the adolescent has the ability to reproduce. These physical changes are accompanied by activation of sexual desire and corresponding increases in dating, kissing, petting, masturbation, and other sexual activities.

**Menarche,** or the first menstrual period, occurs on the average at about 12 years 6 months in American females, and the production of sperm begins about two years later in males (Tanner, 1970). The age of menarche is younger today than in the past. In 1900, the average age of menarche in the United States was about 14 years (Tanner, 1970). Researchers believe that these differences are due to improved nutrition and health care in the United States over the years.

The more obvious changes occurring during puberty are the development of the **secondary sex characteristics.** In females, the first change is an accumulation of fat in the breasts, which results in a slight "budding," followed by a gradual enlargement of the breasts over a period of several years. There is also a growing accumulation of fat around the hips, resulting in a broadening that further gives the appearance of the adult female body shape. Finally, about the time of menarche, pubic hair begins to grow.

In males, the first secondary sexual change is the growth of the testes, followed by a broadening of the shoulders, lowering of the voice, and growth of the penis. Soon, pubic and facial hair grow, thus creating the physical image of an adult male.

Another outwardly obvious sign of puberty is the rapid increase in weight and height known as the **adolescent growth spurt.** Just before puberty, rapid weight gain is common, mostly in the form of fat. This can be a source of concern to both the adolescent and her or his parents, but soon most of this weight is redistributed or shed. At about the onset of puberty, the adolescent suddenly shoots up in height. As shown in figure 9.4, the rate of growth in height steadily declines after infancy, but it rises sharply for a little over a year in early adolescence. During the year of most rapid growth, many boys gain as much as 4 inches and 26 pounds, and many girls add as much as 3½ inches and 20 pounds.

Activation of sexual desire occurs during adolescence.

**primary sex characteristics**
Ovulation and menstruation in females and production of sperm in males.

**menarche**
(mĕ-nar′kē)  The first menstrual period.

**secondary sex characteristics**
Development of the breasts and hips in females; growth of the testes, broadening of the shoulders, lowered voice, and growth of the penis and facial hair in males; and growth of pubic and other body hair in both sexes.

**adolescent growth spurt**
The rapid increase in weight and height that occurs around the onset of puberty.

**FIGURE 9.4**
The adolescent growth spurt can be seen by the rapid increase in height that occurs in males and females at the beginning of puberty.
**Source:** Data from J. M. Tanner, R. H. Whitehouse and M. Takaishi, "Standards from Birth to Maturity for Height, Weight, Height Velocity and Weight Velocity" in *Archives of Diseases in Childhood*, 41:555–571, 1966.

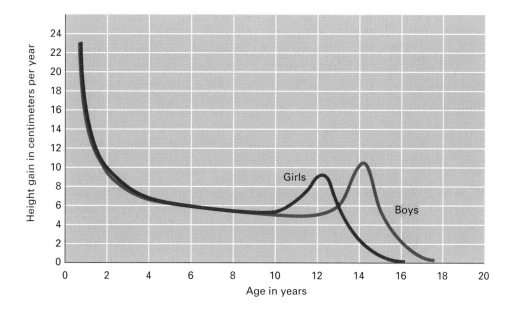

The most important physical changes that take place in adolescence, however, are changes in the brain (Spear, 2000). The structure and organization of the limbic system and frontal lobes change rapidly from childhood to adolescence in ways that promote risk taking, novelty seeking, and emotional response to stress. These changes are reversed in late adolescence as the brain takes on its adult organization (Lewis, 1997). Spear (2000) has speculated that these changes, which are typical of many species of mammals, facilitate adolescents' leaving their families and breeding with members of other families to avoid inbreeding.

## Cognitive Development (Formal Operational Stage)

At about age 11, the shift from concrete operational to formal operational thought begins in some adolescents. Other individuals do not begin the shift as early or reach this advanced level of thinking until early adulthood, and some never reach it at all (Piaget, 1972; Santrock, 1998). The **formal operational stage** is characterized by an ability to use abstract concepts. The logic of formal operational thinking goes beyond the concrete details of each incident or problem to the underlying abstract principles involved.

In a classic experiment conducted by Swiss developmental psychologists Barbel Inhelder and Jean Piaget (1958), children and adolescents of different ages were given two weights that could be hooked at different places on the arms of a scale; their job was to make the scale balance. Seven-year-olds—who were at the beginning of the concrete operational stage—were generally unable to balance the scale at all. They could understand that the two weights must be placed on opposite arms of the scale, but they did not seem to understand the importance of where the weights were hooked on the arms. By the end of the concrete operational stage, age 10, most children were able to balance the scale through trial and error, but they were not able to explain in words how it worked.

By about age 14, many of the subjects had reached the stage of formal operational thinking and were able to explain that, the farther a weight is placed from the center (fulcrum) of the scale, the more downward force it exerts. These children were able, without trial and error, to place a 5-kilogram weight twice as far from the fulcrum as a 10-kilogram weight on the other side. They could also easily deduce from this principle that weights of 3 and 6 or 2 and 4 kilograms would balance on the same hooks used by the 5- and 10-kilogram weights. They understood, in other words, the *abstract* principle that it's the *ratio* of weights and distances that matters, not the specific weights involved in any one example. They were able to think in abstract logical terms.

Individuals who have achieved formal operational thinking are able to use it in many areas of their lives. Piaget suggests, for example, that adolescents often seem preoccupied by concepts such as truth, justice, and the meaning of life partly because the capacity to think in such abstract terms is new to them.

Although most adolescents have reached the level of formal operational reasoning, their cognition at times often retains an immature quality. This is not really surprising; they have recently developed the ability to reason abstractly but have little experience on which to base their abstract thoughts. In particular, David Elkind (1967, 1981; Elkind & Bowen, 1979) has pointed out that adolescents often possess a form of egocentrism that, although different from the egocentrism of young children, similarly distorts their perception of reality. There are four primary features of **adolescent egocentrism.** As you will readily notice, the thinking of fully mature adults is not always free of these characteristics. However, the four reality-distorting qualities described by Elkind are more characteristic of the adolescent stage than any other stage, and they help explain why conversations between adolescents and adults are sometimes so frustrating to both parties.

**formal operational stage**
In Piaget's theory, the period of intellectual development usually reached by about age 11 and characterized by the ability to use abstract concepts.

**adolescent egocentrism**
The quality of thinking that leads some adolescents to believe that they are the focus of attention in social situations, to believe that their problems are unique, to be unusually hypocritical, and to be "pseudostupid."

The ability to understand abstract concepts is a characteristic of formal operational thought.

The primary characteristic of adolescent egocentrism has been termed the *imaginary audience*—an audience that adolescents believe is watching everything they do. If they stumble, stammer, or wear the wrong clothes, *everyone* will notice and talk about it. The adolescent also often lives what seems to be a *personal fable*—he or she believes that no one has similar problems or could possibly understand what he or she is going through. Adolescent egocentrism is also characterized by excessive *hypocrisy*—it's okay for the adolescent to copy someone else's homework, but a teacher who leaves class to take a short personal telephone call is irresponsible in the adolescent's eyes. Finally, adolescent egocentrism involves what Elkind (1981) calls *pseudostupidity*—oversimplified logic. For example, when adolescents say, "If alcoholics know they are going to die of cirrhosis of the liver, why don't they just stop?" they fail to consider the many factors that contribute to an addiction to alcohol. Thus, their thinking is sometimes distorted a bit by their egocentrism, making their relationships with each other and with adults more difficult at times.

By adolescence, peers have become very important. The onset of puberty usually signals a dramatic increase in conformity to the ideas and judgments of the adolescent's peer group.

## Emotional and Social Development

The shift from childhood to adolescence and from adolescence to adulthood is marked by changes in the emotional and social spheres of our lives. Until relatively recently, however, these changes have been more the subject of speculation than of research.

### Adolescent Social Development

Adolescents also show marked changes in their social relationships. Adolescence is a time of drifting away, and sometimes of breaking away, from the family. Although relationships with peers become increasingly important through late childhood, by adolescence peers often become the most important people in the individual's life. The onset of puberty particularly brings a distancing from parents (Arnett, 1999; Galambos, 1992). The shift in orientation from parents to peers can be seen in the dramatic increase in conformity to the ideas and judgments of the peer group that occurs at the beginning of puberty (ages 11 to 13) but declines from age 15 on. In addition, young adolescents spend much more time with their peers than parents, even on weekends (Santrock, 1998).

### Adolescent Emotions

Since 1904, when the first American text on adolescent psychology was published by G. Stanley Hall, a debate has continued unabated about the nature of adolescent emotions. Is it a carefree period of happiness or, as Hall would have it, a time of "storm and stress"? Like many philosophical debates that are eventually settled by scientific evidence, the truth lies somewhere between the extreme viewpoints.

Contrary to popular views of adolescence, current research suggests that about 80 percent of adolescents are relatively happy and well adjusted (Arnett, 1999; Offer & Schonert-Reichl, 1992). In most areas, adolescents are as well adjusted as children and adults, but there are three areas in which adolescents have greater problems than both younger and older individuals:

Contrary to popular views of adolescence, current research suggests that about 80 percent of adolescents experience a relatively happy youth. However, risky behavior is common, and some adolescents do experience serious emotional and behavioral problems.

1. ***Parent-child conflicts.*** Conflicts between parents and children increase during early adolescence and remain common until they decline in late adolescence (Arnett, 1999).

These conflicts typically focus on dating, how long teenagers should be away from home, where they can go, and who they can be with (which often reflect differences in parent and adolescent views on sex, alcohol, drugs, delinquency, and safety).

2. *Mood changes.* Many studies now show that, compared with childhood and adulthood, adolescents experience more shifts of mood and more extremely positive and negative moods (Arnett, 1999; Roberts, Caspi, & Moffitt, 2001). Compared with children and adults, adolescents also are much more likely to feel self-conscious, embarrassed, awkward, lonely, nervous, and ignored.

3. *Risky behavior.* During adolescence, there is a sharp increase in the amount of behavior that exposes the child to danger. There is a marked increase in drinking to become drunk, use of drugs, reckless driving (and automobile accidents and fatalities), unprotected sex, aggression, and delinquent behavior, which does not decline until early adulthood (Arnett, 1999). Rates of suicide also increase dramatically during adolescence (but are still lower than in adulthood). Approximately 18 males per 100,000 persons aged 15 through 19 years and 4 females per 100,000 in the same age range commit suicide (Holinger & Offer, 1993).

Why do these unfortunate changes take place during adolescence? No one knows for sure, but it appears that adolescence is a tough time for many youths for a combination of reasons. Changes in the brain, surges in sex hormones, increases in social stress, and conflicts over autonomy during this natural period of transition all seem to be involved (Arnett, 1999; Spear, 2000).

## Review

In the span of about a decade, each individual passes from childhood to adulthood. This adolescent period of transition begins with the adolescent growth spurt and the emergence of primary and secondary sex characteristics (puberty) and ends with the assumption of adult patterns of work, living, and relationships. It's a period of dramatic physical changes. Considerable gains are made in height, weight, and strength; body fat is redistributed; and boys and girls come to look like men and women. These physical changes are often of considerable concern to self-conscious adolescents, particularly when irregularities and sex differences in physical development are obvious. Cognitively, most adolescents develop formal operational thinking, which gives them the ability to reason abstractly, but they experience an adolescent form of egocentrism. Socially, they complete the shift from a focus on their families to a focus on peers. The great majority of adolescents are well adjusted, but adolescents are moodier and engage in more parent-child conflict and risky behavior than at any other period of their lives.

## Check Your Learning

To be sure that you have learned the key points from the preceding section, cover the list of correct answers and try to answer each question. If you give an incorrect answer to any question, return to the page given next to the correct answer to see why your answer was not correct.

1. _____ is the period from the onset of puberty until the beginning of adulthood and is marked by rapid physical growth and change, as well as by a heightening of sexual and romantic interest in others.

2. The rapid increase in weight and height that occurs around the onset of puberty is known as the _____.

   a)  maturation stage              c)  physical development stage
   b)  adolescent growth spurt       d)  menarche

3. The _____ stage is characterized by an ability to use abstract concepts.

   a)  concrete operational          c)  preoperational
   b)  formal operational            d)  operational

4. We are more likely to experience which of the following during adolescence than at any other time in our lives?

   a)  moodiness                     c)  risky behavior
   b)  parent-child conflicts        d)  all of the above

1. Although adolescence is a time when peer influence often outweighs parental influence, most adolescents continue to hold values and attitudes that are similar to those of their parents. What factors might account for this?

2. What psychological changes mark the period called adolescence? Do they seem significant enough to be treated as a separate developmental period?

**Correct Answers:** 1. Adolescence (p. 340), 2. b (p. 341), 3. b (p. 342), 4. d (pp. 343–344).

## ● Adulthood: Young Adulthood through Older Adulthood

Adulthood is the time of taking on adult responsibilities in work and social relationships. Adulthood is not a single phase of life. The challenges of adult love, work, and play change considerably during adulthood. The demands of maintaining a marriage are very different for newlyweds, parents of infants, parents of teenagers, or a couple in their seventies. Similar changes occur in the demands of work and play. In other words, adulthood is not the end of the process of development. Developmental changes *continue* throughout adulthood.

### Physical Development

The life span is a continuous process of physical change. We continue to strengthen and grow well into early adulthood, but the body begins a slow process of physical decline after early adulthood. Physical speed and endurance decline gradually from early adulthood on. More and more of us need reading glasses for near vision with increasing age and have difficulty seeing in weak light and in the periphery of vision due to a loss of rod cells in the retina after middle age. Our ability to hear high-pitched tones declines after age 20, with loss of ability to hear low-pitched sounds beginning in our sixties (Fisk & Rogers, 2002). Our sense of taste remains pretty much intact into later life, but many older adults report that food tastes more bland. This is due to marked declines in the sense of smell with aging, which plays an important role in our appreciation of foods. Overall, men are likely to suffer these declines in hearing and smell earlier than women (Steinberg, 1995). A substantial number of older adults show marked declines due to cerebral arteriosclerosis (hardening of the arteries), which results in serious loss of intellectual ability. The rate and extent of these declines differ markedly from individual to individual, depending in part on the level of healthy exercise and activity that the individual maintains during adulthood.

## Cognitive Development

It may surprise you to learn that cognitive development continues to take place during adulthood. Most of us think that cognition develops to its full potential in childhood and adolescence, then remains unchanged during adulthood. Actually, some cognitive abilities improve, some remain unchanged, and some decline during adulthood. Small but steady improvements occur from the twenties to the seventies in the components of crystallized intelligence, such as knowledge of facts and word meanings (Cornelius & Caspi, 1987; Kaufman & others, 1996; Steinberg, 1995). No declines occur before about age 75 in such fundamental aspects of intelligence as the ability to reason about everyday problems and to understand mathematical concepts, or to learn and remember meaningful information (Schulz & Ewen, 1988). Indeed, there are small increases during the adult years in our ability to solve problems of life in ways that are judged to be "wise" (Baltes & Staudinger, 1993).

On the other hand, declines do occur in fluid intelligence and short-term memory during later adulthood (Kaufman & others, 1996; Radvansky, 1999). Older adults tend to perform slightly less well than younger adults in abstract problem solving, divergent thinking, cognitive tasks that must be performed quickly, and some aspects of short-term memory (Bashore & others, 1997; Grady & others, 1995; Li, 2002; Shimamura, Berry, Mangels, Rusting, & Jurica, 1995). Therefore, older adults perform as well as younger adults on some tasks (learning and reasoning about everyday concepts), do better than younger adults on some tasks (e.g., word meaning and decision making), but perform less well than younger adults in other ways (abstract reasoning, divergent thinking, and short-term memory). The cognitive performance of older adults is also slower than that of younger adults.

Sometimes the declines in specific aspects of cognitive functioning that occur in old age have important consequences. For example, adults in their seventies are more likely than adults in their twenties to forget to take their medication, particularly when they have other cognitive demands placed on them (Einstein, McDaniel, Smith, & Shaw, 1998). In many cases, however, older adults learn to make the best use of their cognitive abilities and compensate for any small declines. In evaluating the importance of cognitive declines during old age, it is important to understand that not all adults age at the same rate. There are large differences among older individuals in their cognitive abilities. In one study of adults, 50 percent of adults in their mid eighties had scores on a verbal recall task that fell within the range of scores of 20-year-olds (Rapp & Amaral, 1992). Significant declines in cognitive abilities do occur in some older adults, especially ones who are seriously ill, but many healthy older adults show little evidence of intellectual decline through their seventies (Shimamura & others, 1995).

## Emotional and Social Development

What about changes in our emotions, social relationships, and personalities? Do we go through developmental changes in these areas, too? The answer is a very interesting "yes and no." Imagine that a group of 1,000 18-year-old women and men took a test that measures their typical ways of responding emotionally and socially (their personalities, in other words) and then took the same test every 10 years until they were 90. How consistent would their personalities be across their adult lives? In one sense, their personalities would be very consistent over time and would become increasingly consistent as they grew older. For example, people who scored higher than most other people at age 20 on a measure of emotionality would still score higher than most others at ages 30, 40, and so on. In this sense, the major dimensions of adult personality are very stable (McCrae & Costa, 1994; Moscowitz, Brown, & Cote, 1997; Roberts & others, 2001).

In another sense, however, predictable *changes* in personality occur during the adult part of the life span (McCrae & others, 1999). Although adults tend to keep their same *rank order* relative to others on most dimensions of personality over time (if they are higher or lower than others at 18, they still tend to be higher or lower than others at 40, etc.), the *average* scores of adults change over time. On average, adults become less anxious and emotional, less socially outgoing, and less creative as they grow older, but they become more dependable, agreeable, and accepting of life's hardships (Carstensen, Issacowitz, & Charles, 1999; McCrae & others, 1999; Roberts & others, 2001; Sheldon & Kasser, 2001). In addition, gender differences in personality become muted over time: Women become more assertive, confident, and independent, and men become more aware of their aesthetic needs and their need for affection (Stewart & Ostrove, 1998).

How can our personalities be both stable and changing over time? Although the average score of adults on, say, emotionality declines, people who are higher than others on emotionality at one age tend to stay higher than others at later ages, even though their emotionality declines along with the rest of the adult population. At 60, they are considerably less emotional than they were at 20 in absolute terms, but they are still more emotional than most other 60-year-olds (who have become less emotional in absolute terms, too). So, the key dimensions of our personalities change with increasing age, often in ways that make life more enjoyable, but people tend to stay in their same positions on each trait relative to other people.

It should be obvious to anyone who knows the life histories of even a few individuals, however, that most human lives are not "stable" in the strictest sense. Most of us experience periods of happiness and stability in alternation with periods of discontent and change. The woman who grows unhappy with her career in retailing after 20 years and returns to college to become a minister and the man who happily remarries after an unhappy 15-year marriage are but two examples.

There is much disagreement as to the way in which to think about such changes, however. Some psychologists believe that adulthood consists of a series of "stages of development," rather like the stages of child development proposed by Piaget and others. Erik Erikson (1963) and Daniel Levinson (1978, 1986) have each proposed a set of stages of adult life. These stages are different from the stages of infant and child development in that (a) not every adult is believed to go through every stage; (b) the order of the stages can vary for some individuals; and (c) the timing of the stages is not controlled by biological maturation. Although Erikson proposes three stages of adulthood and Levinson proposes nine stages, Levinson's theory can be thought of as an elaboration of Erikson's views. For this reason, we will discuss both stage theories together. Notice that both theorists see adulthood as a series of *alternating* periods of stability and transition.

Although personality traits remain relatively stable throughout adulthood, most adults can expect some personality changes in their middle and later years. Some of these are positive; for example, middle-age men often become more aware of their need for affection. Middle-age women often become more self-confident.

### Early Adulthood: Intimacy vs. Isolation (17 to 45 Years)

Erikson (1963) discussed his proposed stages of adult life in terms of the challenges faced at each stage and the consequences of successfully or unsuccessfully meeting those challenges. These adult stages are the continuation of the stages of child and adolescent development hypothesized by Erikson. He referred to early adulthood as the stage of *intimacy versus isolation*. The challenge of this stage is to enter into committed, loving relationships with others that partially replace the bonds with parents. If we are successful in this task, we will have the intimacy needed to progress in adult life; if not, we will become isolated and less capable of full emotional development, according to Erikson.

Levinson (1986) sees the transition to early adulthood as beginning sometime between the ages of 17 and 22 for most individuals (see fig. 9.5). Early adulthood itself consists of three briefer stages. The *entry to early adulthood* lasts until approximately age 28. This is a time of creating an adult manner of working and living independently and often a time of marriage and young children. The *age 30 transition* (28 to 33) is a time of reevaluating one's start into adult life. Is this the right job for me? The right city? The right spouse? A sense of pressure often accompanies these decisions—they must be

Era of late adulthood:
60–?

**Late adult transition: Age 60–65**

Culminating life
structure for middle
adulthood: 55–60

Age 50 transition:
50–55

Entry life structure
for middle adulthood:
45–50

**Midlife transition: Age 40–45**

Culminating life
structure for early
adulthood: 33–40

Age 30 transition:
28–33

Entry life structure
for early adulthood:
22–28

**Early adult transition: Age 17–22**

Era of preadulthood:
0–22

**FIGURE 9.5**
Daniel Levinson's periods of adult
development.

made "before it's too late." Sometimes major changes are made and sometimes the individual decides that his or her initial choices were the right ones, but either way the process of reevaluation can often be uncomfortable.

The *culmination of early adulthood* is a time of working hard toward one's goals. It extends roughly from the early thirties to about age 40. During this phase, adults sometimes join the PTA Executive Board to improve the quality of their children's school, plant trees in the yard, and work long hours for promotion to a senior position at work. The individual is often aware of feeling like a full member of the adult generation at this time.

In general, the stage of early adulthood is a demanding one. The young adult often takes on the challenges of a career, a marriage, and parenthood during the same period. Frequently, large debts are incurred in buying homes and automobiles in anticipation of greater income, which has not yet arrived. As Levinson (1986) points out, crucially important decisions must be made concerning family and occupation before one has the maturity and life experience to make them comfortably. It is, at the same time, a period of vigorous health and sexuality, rich family rewards, and the potential for occupational advancement. For most of us, it is a time when the rewards exceed the costs.

### Middle Adulthood: Generativity vs. Stagnation (40 to 65 Years)

During the transition to this phase of life, we often take stock of whom we have become. This represents a marked shift from focusing on who we are *becoming* in our twenties and thirties to thinking about who we *are* during middle age (Carstensen & others, 1999). For some people, this is a positive experience—they are happy with their adult selves at the transition to midlife. For many others, this is a time of at least some disappointment. Too many promotions have been missed, too many investments

Erikson believed that to successfully navigate middle adulthood, people must develop a sense of generativity, or a devotion to endeavors that will last beyond their own life span.

have gone bad, and too many elections have been lost to believe that we can still be the unqualified success that we once dreamed of being. As a result of this appraisal of whom we have become, many people either redefine their goals (to fit their more modest accomplishments) or change directions during the transition to midlife. For example, one study of women in the baby-boom generation who attended a selective liberal arts college found that two-thirds made major changes in their educational or occupational work lives around the age of 40 (Stewart & Vandewater, 1999). Often this involved pursuing studies or careers that had been set aside earlier in life when traditional conceptions of female roles were more dominant. In general, the women who made such changes were more content later than the women who had wanted to make changes but did not. Both men and women often make career changes, move geographically, adopt new fitness programs, divorce, or change course in other ways during the transition to middle adulthood. In many cases, this leads to an increased sense of identity, self-direction, and competence (Stewart & Ostrove, 1998).

Erikson refers to middle adulthood as the stage of *generativity versus stagnation*. The challenge is to find meaning in our "generative" activities (work, family life, community activities, religion). In part, this requires a shift away from ourselves to focus on others. People who successfully navigate middle adulthood develop a devotion to endeavors that live beyond their own life spans. This might take the form of building a family business, guiding one's children or grandchildren, or taking younger coworkers under one's wing as a mentor (Sheldon & Kasser, 2001). Generativity is a matter of "reaching out" rather than being self-centered. A person who merely works hard may only be meeting his or her own selfish needs. According to Erikson, a person who is self-absorbed will stagnate and find that life loses much of its meaning during middle adulthood.

Levinson describes four brief stages of middle adulthood. Middle adulthood opens with the *midlife transition*. This transitional stage reaches a peak in the early forties. For some individuals, this transition is quite easy, but for others it's a period of anguish and turmoil. The majority of a sample of 40 men studied by Levinson—10 executives, 10 biologists, 10 factory workers, and 10 novelists—experienced at least some turmoil during their early forties. Erikson described this stage as the early peak of the struggle between generativity and stagnation—can I find meaning in my life the way it's turning out? It's also a time to face growing evidence of biological aging and to accept or agonize over one's wrinkles and gray hair.

"Nothing serious, Bob—just a case of the forties."

"Nothing serious, Bob—just a case of the forties."
© The New Yorker Collection 1988 Robert Mankoff from cartoonbank.com. All Rights Reserved.

The *entry to middle adulthood stage*, from about 45 to 50, is a period of calm and stability for most people who have emerged from the midlife transition. Individuals who are happy with themselves following the midlife transition often find this period to be one of the most productive and creative times of their lives. The illusory ambitions that were shattered during the midlife transition have often been replaced with more attainable goals that are pursued with vigor. Individuals often feel that the painful process of reassessment during their early forties led to changes that left them a better person.

The *age 50 transition* is a stage that is similar to the age 30 transition. For many adults, this is a time to reassess the goals and lifestyle chosen during midlife and the entering middle adulthood stages. Another stable period from about age 55 to 65 follows the age 50 transition. Levinson refers to this stage as the *culmination of middle adulthood*.

### Climacteric

**climacteric**
(klī-mak′ter-ik)  The period between about ages 45 and 60 in which there is a loss of capacity to sexually reproduce in women and a decline in the reproductive capacity of men.

**menopause**
(men′o-pawz)  The cessation of menstruation and the capacity to reproduce in women.

Although most psychologists believe that the changes that characterize adult development are timed more by the "social clock" than by biological aging, one biological event that has an impact for many persons is the **climacteric.** The climacteric is a period beginning at about age 45 when a loss of the capacity to sexually reproduce in women and a decline in the reproductive capacity of men occurs.

In women, the decrease in the level of sex hormones during this period eventually leads to the end of menstruation, or **menopause.** This event, which takes place at 46 to 48 years of age on the average (but can normally take place between the ages of 36 and 60) is sometimes an uncomfortable time for women. It's sometimes accompanied by hot flashes, anxiety, and depression, but most women do not find it as difficult as they were led to expect (Stewart & Ostrove, 1998).

The changes that accompany the male climacteric are generally less notable than in women. There is a decline in the number of sperm cells produced, and slight changes in the pattern of sexual arousal, but the decrease in sex hormones that occurs during the climacteric appears to have few psychological or sexual effects.

### Later Adulthood: Integrity vs. Despair (65 Years On)

Erikson refers to the late sixties and beyond as the stage of *integrity versus despair.* Levinson devotes little of his theory to the later adult years and adds little to Erikson's ideas.

In the stage of integrity versus despair, older adults who see meaning in their lives when considered as a whole will continue to find life satisfying.

The older adult who sees meaning in her or his life when considered as a whole continues to live a satisfying existence instead of merely staying alive. The person who sees life as a collection of unmet goals and unanswered riddles may despair of ever achieving a meaningful life and will often withdraw and live out the remaining years like a prison sentence.

Far more older Americans find meaning rather than despair in their lives, however. This may come as a surprise to you. Just as most of us once thought that the process of development ended in childhood, most of us *still* think that there is little real life after age 65. Too often we think of older adults as leading colorless, joyless, passionless lives. It's surprising to some of us to learn that real *living* usually continues until death (Baltes & Staudinger, 1993).

During this century, the average life expectancy of North Americans has increased dramatically. Persons born in 1900 had a life expectancy of less than 50 years, whereas persons born in 1955 can expect to live to be 70. A child born in 1999 can expect to live to be almost 80. As life expectancy has increased, our conceptions of old age have changed dramatically, too. Today, most people can expect to have many healthy years after the traditional retirement age of 65. As a result, many plan second careers, active political involvement, writing, or other engaging activities in their sixties, seventies, and eighties. Even so, older persons increasingly have a sense that time is running out on their lives. For some older people, this is a frightening realization, but in general, it is accompanied by a positive focusing on the meaningful emotional priorities of life (Carstensen & others, 1999).

## Evaluation of Stage Theories of Adulthood

Although they are thought-provoking and appealing in some ways, stage theories of adult development can be criticized on a number of grounds:

1.  *Gender differences.* The theories of adult development offered by Erikson and Levinson clearly had men more in mind than women. Indeed, for many years, all of the participants in studies of adult development were men. It was as if women did not develop, or, if they did, it did not matter! In recent years, however, a number of studies of adult development have been conducted that suggest that there are broad similarities between the patterns of adult development in women and men (Roberts & Newton, 1987; Stewart & Ostrove, 1998).

2.  *Cultural differences and historical change.* Early theories of adult development implied that they applied universally to all people born in all times. Very few studies have been conducted, however, to determine if the same patterns of adult development are found in different cultures. Indeed, we have data on only a very limited range of kinds of peoples—mostly white, college-educated, English-speaking adults. Much remains to be learned about the rest of the human race. Even within a given culture, it appears that historical change alters the course of adult development (Stewart & Ostrove, 1998). Consider the North American baby-boom generation born in the late 1940s and early 1950s after the end of World War II. They were born into a world of traditional gender roles but were young adults during the age of feminism and rapidly changing gender roles. As children and teenagers, they experienced the civil rights movement and the assassinations of Martin Luther King, Jr., John F. Kennedy, and Robert Kennedy. Later, they took sides for or against the Vietnam War. As middle-aged adults, they lived through both the age of international terrorism and the most protracted period of economic prosperity in North American history. How have these events influenced the course of their adult development? How will the course of adult development be different for persons born in 1980 or 2000, who will have very different experiences? Until these fundamental questions are answered, we will not fully understand adult development (Stewart & Ostrove, 1998).

Michael DeBakey is a pioneer in heart surgery who, among other things, performed the first heart transplant surgery. Remarkably, this gifted surgeon, who was born in 1908, was still performing heart surgery in his nineties.

3. ***Questions about stage theories.*** Finally, it is important to note that not all developmental psychologists believe that adulthood can be thought of as a series of crises or stages. Stewart and Ostrove (1998), for example, believe that far more middle-aged adults experience positive "mid-course corrections" than "mid-life crises." Laura Carstensen believes that the processes that govern developmental change during adulthood are changeable and not tied to specific ages. Rossi (1980) similarly argues that the inevitability and negative impact of the midlife transition have been dangerously exaggerated. Indeed, theorists who oppose the idea of "stages" of adulthood have conducted studies of their own, suggesting that predictable changes do not take place at the times indicated by the stage theorists. For example, two studies found no evidence that "midlife crises" are common during the early forties (Farrell & Rosenberg, 1981).

## Causes of Aging and Predictors of Longevity

Aging is partly a biological process. Over the years, the body deteriorates—skin sags and wrinkles, artery walls become less flexible, muscular strength is lost, cardiac and respiratory efficiency declines. And there are changes in the brain as well. On the average, the total brain weight of persons in their eighties is about 8 percent less than that of a middle-aged person. For older persons with senile dementia, however, the brain weighs 20 percent less than in middle age (Emery & Oxmans, 1992).

Aging is not only a biological process; it involves many psychological aspects as well. Older people are different from younger people because they have experienced more. They have lived through eras that younger individuals have not, they have often retired from their jobs, they no longer have living parents, they often have children who are adults, and they have a host of other factors. Just as people experience biological aging at different rates, the psychological experience of aging also differs from person to person.

The key psychological variables that seem to be associated with happy aging are (a) whether one stays active and engaged in life's activities, (b) whether one believes the myths about old age, and (c) whether one avoids smoking and excessive drinking (Vaillant & Mukamal, 2001). Considerable research suggests that older individuals who continue to be actively engaged in meaningful activities are the happiest as older adults (Maddox, 1964; Neugarten & Hagestad, 1976). These activities can involve family, hobbies, sports, politics, or employment. All that matters is that they be activities that are meaningful to the individual.

The other key to a satisfactory older adulthood seems to be in ignoring the restrictive myths and stereotypes of old age so prevalent in our society. Many older adults are active in sports and creative in the arts and sciences. They sometimes attend college or throw exciting parties. In general, they do not behave like the passive, irritable "old people" of the stereotype. Philosopher Bertrand Russell, artists Marc Chagall and Pablo Picasso, political leaders Golda Meir and Mao Tse-tung, and psychologists Jean Piaget and B. F. Skinner continued to be creative and productive well into their eighties.

Not only have psychologists learned much about the factors that predict a well-adjusted older adulthood, we have recently

"I was grinding out barnyards and farmhouses and cows in the meadow, and then, suddenly, I figured to hell with it."

learned something about psychological factors that predict how long people will live. In 1921, Lewis Terman began a study of 1,528 highly intelligent schoolchildren who were studied frequently across their life spans. As of the early 1990s, about half of the subjects had died and half were still living. Psychologist Howard Friedman and his colleagues (1995) have looked back at the records of the Terman study to determine whether psychological factors predicted the subjects' longevity. Because the subjects in Terman's study were all well above average in intelligence, we cannot be sure that the conclusions apply to the U.S. population in general. On the other hand, because college students and professors tend to be above average in intelligence, the results may well be relevant to us.

Friedman found that subjects in the Terman study lived longer if they were rated as having a "conscientious, dependable, and truthful" personality during childhood—they were 30 percent less likely to die during each year of life. On the other hand, children who were rated as being "cheerful" tended to die earlier. This surprising finding is explained partly by the fact that cheerful children were more likely to take risks and were more likely to smoke and drink as adults, and early death was linked to risk taking, smoking, and drinking. In addition, conscientious and dependable children were less likely to be involved in dangerous accidents and were more likely either to have a stable marriage or to remain single—and going through a divorce was linked to early death. If the parents of the children were divorced, the risk of early death was increased even more (by an average of four years). It is not clear that divorce is still stressful enough to result in premature death today—now that it is more common—but it is clearly still a stressful event for everyone involved. When Terman's subjects reached their thirties, they were interviewed about their emotions and behavior. Those with the most emotional difficulties also were more likely to die early (Peterson & others, 1998).

So, if you were a cheerful child with divorced parents, should you take out extra life insurance? No, but if you smoke, drink, take risks, and are thinking about leaving a good marriage just for a change of scenery, you might consider changing your behavior. We will return to the relationship between psychological factors and health in chapter 13, where we will examine how to change our behavior in ways that promote better health and longevity.

Several variables affect how much we fear our own deaths. For example, highly religious people seem to have less fear of death than do nonreligious people.

## Death and Dying: The Final "Stage"

Everything has an end, including each of our lives. The life cycle begins with the life of a single cell and ends with the death of the person who unfolded from that cell. In recent years, the topic of death and dying has received some long overdue scientific attention, which has produced some interesting results.

Thoughts of death are an important part of the last stages of life for many individuals. Older adults spend more time thinking about death than do younger adults. Contemplating and planning for one's death is a normal part of old age (Kalish & Reynolds, 1976). Older adults tend to be less frightened by death than are younger adults. Older adults often come to accept its inevitability with little anguish. Indeed, it often helps them make the most out of the time remaining (Carstensen & Charles, 1998).

One's fear of death is related to other variables besides age, however. One significant factor is religious belief. Highly religious individuals experience the least fear of death. Nonreligious individuals experience moderate levels of anxiety about death, whereas religious people who do not consistently practice their faith experience the greatest fear of dying (Nelson & Nelson, 1973).

Psychiatrist Elisabeth Kübler-Ross (1969, 1974) provided us with new and important insights into the process of dying through her interviews of hundreds of terminally ill patients at the University of Chicago Hospital. From these interviews, she developed a theory that people who learn of their impending death (and sometimes the impending death of their loved ones) tend to pass through five rather distinct stages:

1. ***Denial.*** At first, the individual strongly resists the idea of death by denying the validity of the information about his or her terminal illness. It's common at this stage for the terminally ill person to accuse his or her doctor of being incompetent, to seek a more favorable diagnosis, or to look for a "miracle cure." Sometimes the denial is more subtle, however. The individual may simply act as if the news of impending death was never revealed and proceed as if nothing is wrong for a while.

2. ***Anger.*** After the initial denial, the terminally ill person reacts to the fact of her or his impending death with anger: Why me? It's not fair that this should be happening to me! There is much hostility, envy of others, and resentment during this stage. As a result, the terminally ill person is often highly irritable and frequently quarrels with nurses, doctors, and loved ones.

3. ***Bargaining.*** The anger and denial of the impending death are largely gone by this third stage, and the terminally ill person fully realizes that death is coming. But death still is not accepted as inevitable. Instead, the person tries to strike bargains to prolong his or her life. These bargains may be in the form of willingness to undergo painful treatments to extend life, but they are more often silent deals with God, such as "I'll leave most of my money to the church if I can have six more months." Interestingly, if the person does live past this bargaining stage, the bargain is usually broken—the church does not get the money.

4. ***Depression.*** Eventually, the reality of impending death leads to a loss of hope. Bargains no longer seem possible; death is coming no matter what. The person often begins to feel guilty about leaving loved ones behind, feels incapable of facing death with dignity, and feels quite depressed.

5. ***Acceptance.*** In time, the depression lifts and the person finally achieves an acceptance of death. This generally is not a happy feeling of acceptance but a state of emotional exhaustion that leaves the individual peacefully free of negative emotions.

Kübler-Ross (1974) and others point out that not every terminally ill person passes through these stages. Reactions to impending death are highly individual (Peifel, 1990). If we go through the process of dying with a loved one, we must be careful not to impose on him or her our views of how the process of accepting death should proceed.

---

### Review

Intelligence and personality remain relatively constant throughout the adult years in most healthy adults, but some change does take place. Some aspects of intellectual ability improve throughout adulthood, whereas other aspects do not change. Still, minor declines in some aspects of intelligence occur in most of us, particularly after age 70. Similarly, a few positive changes in personality seem to take place. Psychologists disagree as to whether the changes in adulthood can be thought of as a series of stages. Erikson and Levinson have outlined a series of stages of adult life, but we still have much to learn about adult development.

Although some older adults despair of ever achieving a meaningful pattern of living, many others achieve a sense of integrity and continue to find life meaningful and joyful until death. Aging is partly a biological process of physical deterioration, but aging is also a psychological process that can be slowed to some degree by staying engaged in meaningful activities and by not believing the many negative myths about old age that are so prevalent in our society. Regardless of how the individual lives out the later adult years, the final "stage" of life is always death. Older adults tend to accept their impending deaths, especially religious adults, but individuals who must face the knowledge of their impending deaths earlier in the life span generally go through several stages of anguish before reaching a state of acceptance.

Check Your Learning

To be sure that you have learned the key points from the preceding section, cover the list of correct answers and try to answer each question. If you give an incorrect answer to any question, return to the page given next to the correct answer to see why your answer was not correct.

**Check Your Learning**

1. The challenge of the _____ stage is to enter into committed, loving relationships with others that partially replace bonds with parents.

   a)   early adulthood          c)   later adulthood

   b)   middle adulthood         d)   midlife

2. According to Erikson, a person in middle adulthood must be _____ (or productive) to find meaning in life.

   a)   stagnant                 c)   generative

   b)   divergent                d)   flexible

3. Two keys to a satisfactory older adulthood seem to be ignoring the restrictive myths and stereotypes of old age and remaining actively engaged in life.

   a)   True

   b)   False

4. _____ is one significant factor related to one's fear of death.

   a)   Marital status           c)   Success in life

   b)   Local climate            d)   Religious belief

**Thinking Critically about Psychology**

1. How might the course of your adult development differ from that of your grandparents? How will your culture influence your development during adulthood?

2. Do you think that your personality has changed in the past 10 years? Do you expect it to change in the future?

Correct Answers: 1. a (p. 347),  2. c (p. 349),  3. a (p. 352),  4. d (p. 353).

# application of psychology

## Parenting

During the important early stages of development—infancy, childhood, and most of adolescence—we typically live with our parents. They give us food and shelter, protect us from danger, and provide many of our early learning experiences. Parents play a key role in giving children a healthy start in life. But although parenting is important, we as a society provide parents with no training in how to raise their children. Our schools teach reading, writing, and arithmetic, but not parenting. For this reason, we will look carefully at the topic of parenting, with an emphasis on the styles of parenting that are best for children.

## Parenting and Infant Attachment

Let's begin with a look at the parents' role in helping their infant develop a secure relationship—or attachment—with the parents. The newborn in the hospital nursery seems equally happy to be rocked by anyone who has free arms, but sometime during the first year of life (usually by about 6 to 9 months) infants typically become closely attached to one or more of their caretakers. At this point in develop-

ment, most infants develop a normal "stranger anxiety" and react fearfully and tearfully when strangers are present and cling to the safe fortress of the adult to whom they are attached (Ainsworth, 1979). By 18 to 24 months, however, most toddlers are better able to deal with stranger anxiety. They prefer to be near their primary caretaker when strangers are first encountered, but they are able to move out to explore the world and play, knowing that the safe caretaker is nearby. Infants who are able to deal with stranger anxiety in this way are said to be "securely attached."

Some infants and toddlers, however, are less securely attached to their parent. When separated from their caretaker, some "insecurely attached" toddlers cling excessively to the caretaker and become extremely upset when separated from the parent. Seemingly, the attachment is not secure enough to allow the toddler to turn her or his back on the parent for a moment. Other toddlers who are not securely attached rarely use the parent as a safe haven but, rather, seem to ignore or even avoid the parent. It is as if the attachment to the parent is too weak to be helpful to the toddler.

By age 18 to 24 months, "securely attached" toddlers are able to explore the world and play if they know a safe caregiver is nearby.

What leads to secure attachment? Part of the answer is the child's inborn temperament. Some children are simply calmer and more receptive to the parent from birth. But parents play an important role as well. Parents can help their infants form secure attachments by taking care of the infant's needs in a consistent way and by being warm, affectionate, and accepting. In this case, being an accepting parent means staying calm and loving (most of the time, at least) when the baby "acts like an infant"—crying in the middle of the night, wetting diaper after diaper, and spitting every bite of cereal back into your hand (Goldsmith & Alansky, 1987)!

It is important for parents to help their infants develop the firm foundation of a secure attachment, but how worried should the parent of an insecurely attached infant be? The best answer is that the parent should be concerned enough to look at his or her parenting to see whether healthy changes can be made, but not overly concerned. It is not uncommon for an extremely clingy 2-year-old who receives consistent and loving parenting to grow into a

Our parents care for us from infancy through adolescence and provide us with many of our most important learning experiences.

happy and secure 5-year-old—I've personally seen it happen many times.

## Parenting and Discipline Style

Discipline style is one of the most important parts of parenting. As soon as the infant can move, the adult must attempt to regulate the child's behavior to protect the child and point the child in healthy directions. In other words, the parent must provide guidance and discipline. What discipline style is the best for children? Psychologist Diana Baumrind (1983) has extensively studied the discipline styles used by parents and has divided them into three types: authoritarian, permissive, and authoritative.

The *authoritarian* parent gives strict rules to the child or adolescent with little discussion of the reasons for the rules. It is the "because I say so" approach to rules. Authoritarian parents are openly critical of their children and frequently give them instructions on how to behave. Rules are enforced by punishing a child who does not obey, sometimes quite harshly.

In contrast, the *permissive* parent gives the child or adolescent few rules and rarely punishes misbehavior. The child is given great respect and autonomy but often too much independence at too early an age.

The *authoritative* parent (notice the difference in spelling between *authoritative* and *authoritarian*) is an authority figure to the child but provides good explanations for all rules and freely discusses them with the child. In allowing their children to freely state their opinions about rules, and sometimes being persuaded to alter the rules by a logical argument from them, authoritative parents give children a greater sense of involvement in their own rules. Authoritative parents emphasize reinforcement of appropriate behavior and affectionate warmth over punishment and often do not use any physical punishment at all. They encourage independence, but within clearly defined limits to take the child's level of development into consideration. In short, authoritative parents show their children that they are loved and respected but provide the amount of authority that the child needs.

Which of these approaches to discipline works best? Research clearly indicates that children whose parents adopt an authoritative style are better behaved, more successful, and happier than the children of parents who use other styles of discipline, and their families are more harmonious (Baumrind, 1983, 1991; Querido, Warner, & Eyeberg, 2002).

## Direction of Effect in Child Rearing: The Two-Way Street

University of Virginia professor Richard Bell (1968) pointed out some time ago that we must be very careful in our interpretations of studies of parenting. I just said that children whose parents are authoritative are generally better behaved and happier than children whose parents use other styles of discipline. Does this necessarily mean that authoritative parenting causes good behavior in children? Most developmental psychologists think so, but it is very likely that something else is going on as well. It is probable that children who are happy and easy to get along with make it easier for their parents to adopt an authoritative style of discipline. A happy, reasonable child can be given a great deal of independence and needs little strict discipline. But would the same parent adopt a different style of discipline if the child were irritable, defiant, and aggressive? Several studies suggest that this might be the case—that children affect their parents as much as parents affect their children.

Hugh Lytton of the University of Calgary (Anderson, Lytton, & Romney, 1986) has compared parents of normal, well-behaved children to parents with children who were so disobedient and aggressive that they had been referred to psychologists for help. He observed these two groups of parents interacting with their children in a playroom in his laboratory. As in previous studies, Lytton found that the parents of the badly behaved children were less affectionate, less likely to reward positive behavior, more critical, and gave many more instructions to their children on how to behave than did the parents of the well-behaved children.

Generally, psychologists have concluded that it is exactly this pattern of authoritarian parenting that causes the children to behave badly (e.g., Baumrind, 1983). But Lytton provided a clever twist to his study. He exchanged parents and children—so that the parents of well-behaved children were matched with badly behaved children and vice versa—and observed their

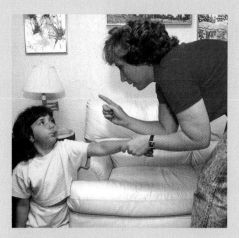

A child's temperament may have as much effect on disciplinary style as the parent's choice. Lytton found that parents who usually used the authoritative style tended to become more authoritarian when faced with an unruly child.

interactions again. When the parents of well-behaved children were faced with an aggressive, disobedient child, the formerly model parents behaved just like the parents of the badly behaved children. Quickly, they also resorted to the unpleasant, critical, authoritarian style of discipline.

So who influences whom in the family? Does the parent's discipline affect the child's behavior, or does the child's behavior influence the parent's discipline? Clearly, a great deal of both is going on. This is a very important point. Effective parenting is a very important influence on the child, but even the best parents know that different children will evoke different parenting responses from them. The parents of temperamental, difficult children will have to resist the natural tendency to make authoritarian responses to their children's provocative behavior if they are going to help their children develop optimally.

## Common Discipline Mistakes

Psychologist Susan O'Leary (1995) has made a comprehensive study of the most common discipline mistakes made by ineffective parents. Parents of poorly behaved children often make the following mistakes:

1. *Lax parenting.* Ineffective parents often fail to enforce their rules for the children and give in to their children's demands to bend the rules or avoid punishment.

*(continued)*

Effective parents are consistent in the enforcement of rules.

2. *Reinforcement of inappropriate behavior.* Parents of poorly behaved children often provide positive reinforcement for inappropriate behavior. This is sometimes unintentional—such as only paying attention to their children when they misbehave—but is sometimes intentional—as in praising their child for giving another child a black eye. Effective parents provide positive reinforcement for good behavior, but not for inappropriate behavior.

3. *Verbosity.* Ineffective parents engage in lengthy arguments with their children about their misbehavior instead of simply enforcing the rules. Effective parents know that a brief explanation of why the rule is being enforced is much more effective than a lengthy debate. "I'm sorry, but you can't watch television tonight because you did not do your homework" says all that needs to be said in most cases.

4. *Overreactivity.* Ineffective parents become angry, harsh, critical, and mean when their children misbehave. Effective parents stay cool and in control as they calmly enforce the rules.

## Sociocultural Factors in Parenting

Parents from all cultures want their children to be "well behaved," but they often define appropriate behavior differently and believe in different methods of child rearing. For this reason, we must understand cultural differences in parenting (Rubin, 1998). Consider one major difference among cultures: In collectivistic cultures, such as the Chinese, Japanese, and Indian cultures, the emphasis is on the well-being of the family and the larger culture, not on the well-being of each individual. In individualistic cultures, such as the mainstream culture in the United States, the emphasis is on the individual rather than the group.

The kinds of behavior that help a person succeed in collectivistic and individualistic cultures are different in some cases, and therefore, parents raise their children differently in some ways. For example, in the United States, most parents believe that being shy and inhibited places children at a disadvantage—they would prefer for their children to be outgoing and assertive instead. This is because the individuals who assert themselves most confidently will be most likely to succeed as individuals. In Chinese families, however, shyness and inhibition are viewed as advantages, because they help the child fit into the group and yield to its wishes. It is not surprising, then, that Chinese parents praise their shy children, whereas American parents disapprove of shy behavior and sometimes seek mental health treatment for their shy children (Rubin, 1998).

Another difference between Chinese and mainstream U.S. cultures reflects the relative emphasis on academic achievement in the two cultures and differences in how it is encouraged. In the United States, Chinese immigrant parents teach mathematics skills to their young children in more formal ways and structure their children's use of time more than European American parents do (Huntsinger, Jose, & Larson, 1998). Controlling for other factors, such as parental income and education, the parenting practices of Chinese American parents appear to lead to higher mathematics achievement among their children (Huntsinger & others, 1998). Importantly, the two groups of children do not differ in terms of personal adjustment, suggesting that the greater emphasis on academic achievement is not personally harmful to the Chinese American children. In these and many other ways, parenting reflects the varying goals and beliefs of people living in different cultures.

## Myth of the Perfect Parent

Loving and effective parenting is the greatest gift that a parent can give a child. But it is important to point out that *perfect* parenting is not as important as some of us seem to think. Many parents act as if their children are as delicate as spun glass. They are paralyzed in their attempts to be good parents by their fear that they will do the wrong thing and scar their children for life.

Actually, children are pretty resilient creatures. Within broad limits, they will grow up very well in spite of the fact that none of them have perfect parents. They will not be miserable forever if their parents sometimes lose their tempers and speak in harsh tones, and they will learn to play with other children without being coached in every step.

That is not to say that parents cannot harm their children. Unfortunately, children are hurt badly every day by neglectful and abusive parents. But most of the minor imperfections of parenting that are characteristic of every child's upbringing are of relatively little consequence.

## Day Care, Divorce, and Parenting

Until relatively recently, most children in the United States were cared for by one of their parents—almost always the mother—who stayed at home full-time to raise the children and care for the home while the other parent worked outside the home. And most of us felt that this way of raising children was the "natural" way of things. Indeed, the image of the "caretaker mother and breadwinner father" is so deeply embedded in our view of child rearing that many of us are shocked to learn that very few children are raised in that manner today. In actuality, only 7 percent of all children in the United States are raised by two married parents through their entire childhood, with the mother not working outside the home (Braverman, 1989; Silverstein, 1991).

In many families, both married parents have chosen—or have felt compelled by economic necessity—to be employed full-time outside the home. Indeed, the percentage of women with school-age children who work outside the home has risen from 40 percent in the 1970s to 75 percent in the 1990s (Silverstein, 1991). In many other cases, divorce results in the custodial parent's (usually the mother) being more likely to work outside the home. About 50 percent of all marriages now end in divorce, and divorced women are 50 percent more likely than married women to work outside the home (Scarr, Phillips, & McCartney, 1990). In addition, more children than ever before are raised now by single parents who have never married (up over 350 percent since the 1970s) (Silverstein, 1991).

All of these changes in the nature of the American family over the past quarter century have resulted in mothers' spending less time raising their children. Who cares for the children, then? It is distressing to learn that the increased entry of mothers into the labor

# Visual Review of Stage Theories of Development

The following visual reviews may help you consolidate your learning of some of the information presented in this chapter in a visual format. Be sure not to limit your review to these diagrams, but because they are key to understanding some of the important concepts of the chapter, mastering them should help you master the entire chapter.

stage:        years on

By the end of the stage of childhood, most individuals have progressed to full adult cognition, including the ability to reason using abstract concepts.

stage:       years

During middle childhood, the child has the ability to reason like an adult in every way except for reasoning about abstract concepts, such as justice, infinity, or the meaning of life.

stage:       years

During the preoperational stage, the child is capable of symbolic thought. Young children's thought is still quite different from that of adults, however. It is often "illogical" in numerous ways that reveal the unique nature of the preoperational child's cognition.

stage:        years

The child deals with reality in terms of sensations and motor movements. At this stage, children are unable to reason in mental symbols.

**FIGURE 9.6**
This is a diagram of Piaget's stage theory of child development. Fill in the missing labels for the names of the stages and the average age ranges for the stages and check them for accuracy by referring back to figure 9.2 on p. 327.

Era of late adulthood:
60–?

**transition:** Age 60–65

Culminating life
structure for middle
adulthood: 55–60

Age 50 transition:
50–55

Entry life structure
for middle adulthood
45–50

**transition:** Age 40–45

Culminating life
structure for early
adulthood: 33–40

Age 30 transition:
28–33

Entry life structure
for early adulthood:
22–28

**transition:** Age 17–22

Era of preadulthood:
0–22

**FIGURE 9.7**
This is a diagram of the stage theory of adult development proposed by Daniel Levinson. Fill in
the missing labels for the names of three major adult transitions and check them for accuracy
by referring back to Figure 9.5, page 348.

# PART V

# The Self

In this section you will learn about motives, emotions, and aggression. You will study the biological, emotional, and motivational aspects of sexuality. This section also includes important information on the elements that define us as individuals and make us different from others: gender identity and gender roles, sexual orientation, and personality. You will learn about the major psychological theories of personality and methods of assessing an individual's personality characteristics.

Here is a visual overview of what you will learn in the fifth section of the text.

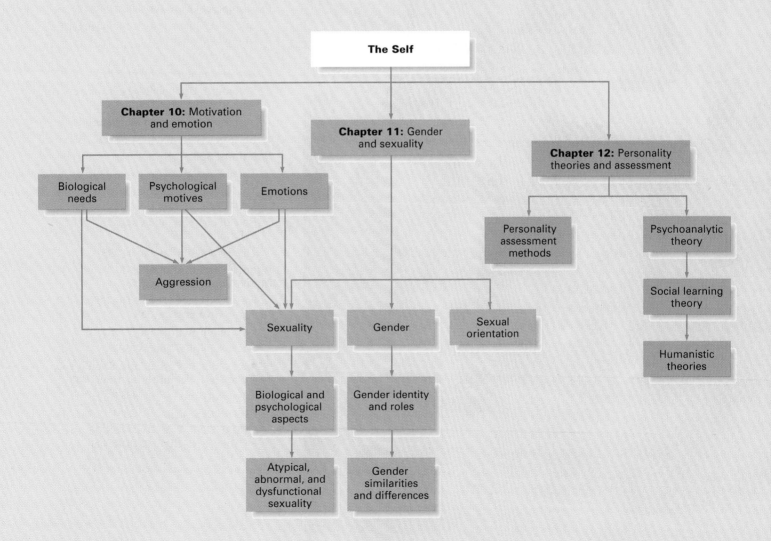

# Chapter Outline

# Motivation and Emotion

## PROLOGUE

Conducting research is one of the most consistently enjoyable parts of my career. Even if I never contribute anything really important to psychology through research, each study is an intriguing puzzle and I love finding each clue to a mystery that puts any spy novel to shame. Still, for all my love of research, I wonder if great researcher Walter Cannon could have talked me into doing for science what he persuaded his colleague A. L. Washburn to do to understand the motive of hunger.

Cannon and Washburn (1912) were trying to isolate the biological mechanism of hunger. They believed that the feeling of hunger was caused by contractions of the stomach wall. To determine whether this idea was correct, Cannon convinced Washburn to swallow a balloon that was attached to a long tube connected to an air pump. The balloon was then inflated to fill Washburn's stomach. In this way, stomach contractions could be mechanically detected because they squeezed the balloon and increased the air pressure in the tube (see fig. 10.1). While the intermittent contractions were being measured, Washburn, who could not talk because of the tube gagging his mouth and throat, indicated when he felt a conscious sensation of hunger by pressing a key connected to a recording instrument. (History does not tell us, however, whether Washburn used his other hand to signal more negative feelings to Cannon during this unpleasant experiment.)

As Cannon predicted, Washburn did feel hungry when his stomach contracted, leading them to conclude that hunger was no more than the rumbling contractions of an empty stomach. As we will see later in the chapter, such contractions are still believed to be part of the feeling of hunger for many people, but, sadly, considering Washburn's selfless contribution to science, stomach contractions are only one factor in hunger, and one of the least important factors at that.

This chapter is about our motives and our emotions. Motives are states that make us active rather than inactive and lead us to do one thing rather than another. If I have just eaten, I may take a nap or quietly read the newspaper; but if I am hungry, I will get up and fix food. The motive of hunger activates and directs my behavior. Some motives are based on the survival needs of the body for food, water, and warmth. These biological motives are regulated by intricate and sensitive mechanisms under the control of the hypothalamus that detect the body's needs.

Other motives—the so-called psychological motives—are not directly related to the survival needs of the body. The motive to maintain a moderate level of novel stimulation and activity, the motive to achieve and be successful, and the motive to have friendly relationships with others are examples of psychological motives. These motives are often strongly influenced by learning experiences and therefore differ from individual to individual and culture to culture.

Emotions are special states that often motivate us. Emotions are a complex mixture of three different but intimately related psychological processes. First, emotions involve a positive or negative conscious experience. That simply means that all emotions feel good or bad; if they were neutral, we wouldn't call them emotions. Second, emotions are accompanied by physiological arousal of the autonomic nervous system, some endocrine glands, and other physiological

## Key Terms

**FIGURE 10.1**
Diagram of the device used in the experiment by Cannon and Washburn (1912) to find out if stomach contractions caused a conscious feeling of hunger. Note the balloon swallowed by Washburn to measure the contractions.

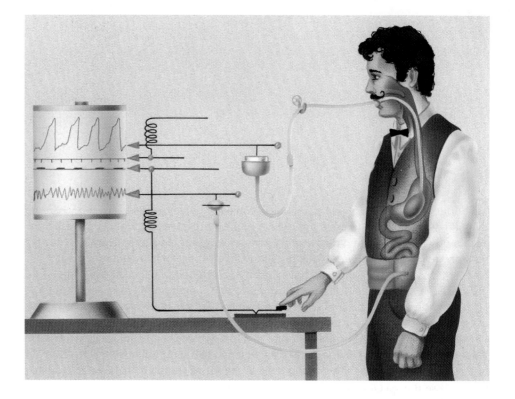

Hungry grocery shoppers are motivated shoppers who are likely to buy more food than nonhungry shoppers are.

**motivation**
The internal state or condition that activates and gives direction to our thoughts, feelings, and actions.

systems. And third, they usually involve some kind of related behavior. When you see a car driving toward you, you feel a negative conscious experience, your autonomic nervous system churns you up, and you run. As we will see, some aspects of emotions appear to be inborn, whereas other aspects are shaped by our learning experiences. ■

## ● Definitions of Motivation and Emotion

To people who are interested in human behavior, the key question is *why?* Carol wants to know why she continues to have sex with Michael when she knows she does not love him and is afraid of getting pregnant. The manager of the packing plant wants to know why two of her employees do not seem to care about doing a good job. A father wants to know why his son is not willing to work hard for good grades in school. Answers to questions like these often involve the concept of motivation—if they lead us to look *inside* the person.

The term **motivation** refers to an *internal* state that activates and gives direction to our thoughts. Meg was starting to feel a little hungry when an ad on television for tacos made her feel famished, reminded her that she had food in the refrigerator, and sent her scrambling to the kitchen. If her motive for hunger had not been activated, perhaps her motive to succeed in school might have led her in a different direction—maybe to read her psychology textbook. If no motives at all were activated, she would be doing nothing—just sitting around or maybe taking a nap. Motives are at the center of our lives—they arouse and direct what we think, feel, and do.

Some motives, such as hunger, are clearly based on internal physiological states. As we will see, several internal factors, such as the level of sugar in the blood, are important in regulating hunger. But other motives, such as the motive to succeed, are not based on simple internal physiological states. For all motives, however, *external cues* play an important role. Seeing the ad for tacos on television was an external cue that stimulated Meg's hunger motive; hearing her roommate worry aloud about passing her next psychology test would be an external cue that could have stimulated her motive to succeed.

Motivation is closely related to the topic of emotions. The term **emotion** refers to positive or negative feelings—generally reactions to stimuli—that are accompanied by physiological arousal and characteristic behavior. When we are afraid, for example, we experience an acutely unpleasant feeling: The sympathetic division of our autonomic nervous system is aroused and the fear generally shows in our behavior. The emotion of passion, on the other hand, is a conglomeration of very different feelings, biological changes, and behavior.

Motivation and emotions are closely linked concepts for three reasons: (a) The arousal of emotions activates behavior as motives do; (b) motives are often accompanied by emotions, (for example, the motive to perform well on a test is often accompanied by anxiety; sexual motivation is generally blended with the emotions of passion and love); and (c) emotions typically have motivational properties of their own—because you are in love, you are motivated to be with your special person; because you are angry, you want to strike out at the object of your anger. We will begin this chapter with a discussion of basic motives necessary for biological survival, then will move to a discussion of more "psychological" motives, and will end with a discussion of human emotions.

### ● Primary Motives: Biological Needs

Many human motives stem from the *need* for things that keep an organism alive: food, water, warmth, sleep, avoidance of pain, and so on. We consider these to be **primary motives** because we must meet these biological needs or die. The sexual motive is also considered to be a primary motive, not because we would die if it were not fulfilled, but because the species could not reproduce and survive if the sexual motive were not satisfied.

This chapter focuses on the biological motives of hunger and thirst, partly because they are the best understood of the primary motives. Information is provided on the primary motives of avoidance of pain in chapter 4 and the need for sleep in chapter 5.

### Homeostasis: Biological Thermostats

Most of the primary motives are based on the body's need to maintain a certain level of essential life elements: adequate sugar in the blood to nourish cells, sufficient water in the body, and so on. These critical levels are regulated by **homeostatic mechanisms.** These mechanisms sense imbalances in the body and stimulate actions that restore the proper balance. The homeostatic mechanisms of the body are often compared to the thermostats of home heating systems. When the temperature of the house falls below a preset level, the thermostat senses that fact and signals the heater to produce heat until the proper temperature has been restored; then it signals the heater to turn off. The body's responses to imbalances include both internal reactions and overt behavior. For instance, when the water level in body cells falls below a safe level, a signal is sent to the kidneys to reabsorb additional water from the urine. At the same time, a signal is sent to the brain that leads the animal—human or otherwise—to seek out and drink liquids. Similar homeostatic mechanisms are involved in hunger and the maintenance of body temperature.

### Hunger: The Regulation of Food Intake

The biological control center of hunger is not the rumbling stomach. It does play a minor part in the control of hunger, but a much less important one than most of us think. Instead, the **hypothalamus** plays the controlling role in the motivation of hunger (Mook, 1986; Petri, 1986; Seeley & Schwartz, 1997). This small but extremely important forebrain structure that we first discussed in chapter 3 is involved in the regulation of many motives and emotions (see fig. 10.2).

Recent advances in our understanding of the brain have revealed that hunger is regulated by three centers in the hypothalamus. Two of these hypothalamic control

**emotion**
Positive or negative feelings generally in reaction to stimuli that are accompanied by physiological arousal and related behavior.

**primary motives**
Human motives for things that are necessary for survival, such as food, water, and warmth.

**homeostatic mechanisms**
(hō″mē-ō-stat′ik) Internal body mechanisms that sense biological imbalances and stimulate actions to restore the proper balance.

**hypothalamus**
(hī′pō-thal′ah-mus) The part of the forebrain involved with motives, emotions, and the functions of the autonomic nervous system.

**FIGURE 10.2**
Three parts of the hypothalamus play a key role in the control of hunger: the lateral feeding center, the ventromedial satiety center, and the paraventricular nucleus. The lateral feeding center directly stimulates hunger and eating. The paraventricular nucleus controls hunger through the control of blood sugar. The ventromedial satiety center operates in a feedback loop with the body's adipose cells. Secretions of leptin lead to the ventromedial satiety center to directly inhibit eating, stimulate the paraventricular nucleus, and increase the metabolism of fat cells through activation of the sympathetic nervous system (Ezell, 1995; Seeley & Schwartz, 1997).

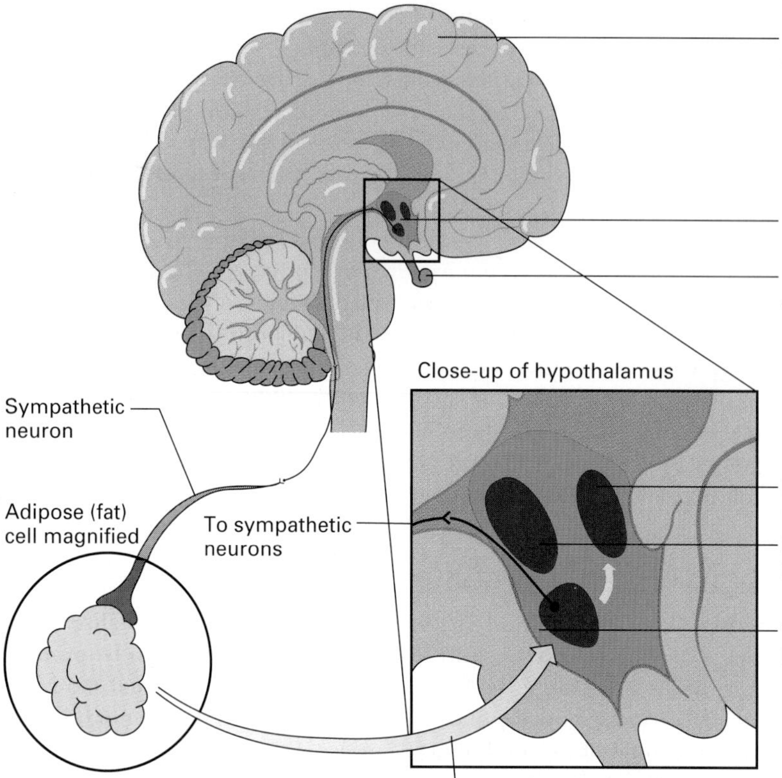

Cerebral cortex

Hypothalamus

Pituitary gland

Close-up of hypothalamus

Sympathetic neuron

Adipose (fat) cell magnified

To sympathetic neurons

Paraventricular nucleus

Lateral hypothalamus

Ventromedial hypothalamus

Adipose cell secretes leptin

Leptin stimulates the satiety center in ventromedial hypothalamus, which directly inhibits hunger, and sends message to adipose cells through sympathetic neurons and sends message to paraventricular nucleus, which controls blood-sugar levels.

**lateral hypothalamus**
A portion of the hypothalamus involved in feeling hungry and starting to eat (the feeding center).

**ventromedial hypothalamus**
A part of the hypothalamus involved in inhibiting eating when sufficient food has been consumed (the satiety center).

**hyperphagia**
(hī″per-fā′jē-ah) Excessive overeating that results from the destruction of the satiety center of the hypothalamus.

**paraventricular nucleus**
A part of the hypothalamus that plays a role in the motive of hunger by regulating the level of blood sugar.

centers operate in opposing ways. A *feeding system,* which initiates eating when food is needed, is located in the **lateral hypothalamus,** and a *satiety system,* which stops eating when enough food has been consumed, is located in the **ventromedial hypothalamus.**

Studies of laboratory rats have shown that when the lateral hypothalamus (the feeding system) is electrically stimulated, rats that are too satiated (full) to eat will begin eating again. If this part of the hypothalamus is destroyed, on the other hand, rats will stop eating altogether and will starve to death if not artificially fed. Conversely, if the ventromedial hypothalamus (the satiety system) is surgically destroyed, the rats will overeat into a startling state of obesity (excessive fat). Figure 10.3 shows a normal rat and a rat with **hyperphagia** whose body weight tripled after surgical destruction of the ventromedial satiety center. These rats do not eat more times each day than normal rats but continue eating much longer each time they eat. Apparently, the destruction of part of the satiety system eliminates the homeostatic signal to stop eating when enough food has been consumed.

Alexander Reeves and Fred Plumb (1969) reported a clinical case study of a woman with tragic damage to the satiety center in the hypothalamus that bears a striking resemblance to hyperphagic laboratory animals. A 20-year-old bookkeeper sought medical help for her suddenly abnormal appetite and weight gain. X rays identified a tumor in the hypothalamus, but it could not be surgically removed. Prior to her death three years later, she regularly consumed 10,000 calories per day in an endless attempt to satisfy her hunger.

The third part of the hypothalamus that plays a role in the regulation of hunger is the **paraventricular nucleus.** This center both increases and decreases appetite by controlling the level of sugar in the blood (Martin, White, & Hulsey, 1991).

What information do the three centers of the hypothalamus use in regulating hunger? Apparently, two cues are used to regulate hunger on a daily basis, and a third cue is used to regulate body weight on a long-term basis:

1. ***Stomach contractions.*** Cannon and Washburn, whom we discussed at the beginning of the chapter, were partly right about the role of stomach contractions. The most immediate cue in the regulation of hunger really does come from the stomach. Contractions signal the lateral hypothalamic feeding system, whereas a full stomach activates the ventromedial satiety system.

2. ***Blood-sugar levels.*** Eating is also regulated on a short-term basis by the amount of sugar (glucose) in the blood. The hypothalamus contains specialized neurons that can directly detect the level of glucose in the bloodstream, but two other organs provide most of the information to the hypothalamus. The liver, which is a storehouse for sugar, detects blood glucose levels, and the upper small intestine, or *duodenum,* detects sugar in food that has just been eaten. Both organs send chemical messages to the paraventricular nucleus of the hypothalamus, which plays a role in initiating or stopping eating (Ezell, 1995; Petri, 1986).

   The role of blood glucose in the regulation of hunger has been clearly demonstrated. Two of the experimental methods involve the two hormones secreted by the islets of Langerhans (chapter 3, p. 88). When **insulin** is injected into the bloodstream of a satiated person, it causes a drop in the level of glucose, and the person feels hungry. Conversely, when the hormone **glucagon** is injected into the bloodstream of a hungry person, it produces an increase in blood glucose, and the individual no longer feels hungry.

   Blood glucose levels are a key mechanism in the short-term control of hunger, so it is important to understand a simple fact about blood glucose and hunger. When you eat, it takes a few minutes for food to be digested and enter the bloodstream in the form of glucose. If you eat slowly, therefore, your brain will have enough time to detect the increase in blood glucose and make you feel "full" before you eat more than you need. In other words, the faster you eat, the more you will eat before you feel full.

3. ***Body fat levels.*** The long-term maintenance of body weight is managed by the ability of the hypothalamus to detect the level of fat in the body (Mook, 1986; Petri, 1986; Seeley & Schwartz, 1997). Recent research has revealed that the adipose (fat) cells that live on your waist, hips, and elsewhere secrete leptin into the bloodstream. The more full of fat the adipose cells are, the more leptin they secrete. When the circulating leptin reaches the hypothalamus, structures in and around the ventromedial hypothalamus detect it. This causes the hypothalamus to react in three ways to control body weight. First, the ventromedial satiety center sends a direct message to inhibit eating. Second, it signals the paraventricular nucleus to control hunger by regulating the level of blood sugar.

   A third action taken by the ventromedial satiety center to control body weight in response to leptin also has been discovered. It provides a new and absolutely fascinating chapter on the sublime complexity of the human body. When leptin levels are high, the ventromedial hypothalamus activates the sympathetic nervous system. Tiny branches of this nervous system actually end on the adipose cells. Stimulation of the adipose cells by the sympathetic neurons causes their metabolism to increase to burn off fat in the form of heat (Ezell, 1995).

**FIGURE 10.3**
Destruction of the part of the hypothalamus that is involved in the satiety system causes rats to eat themselves into a state of extreme obesity called hyperphagia. A normal rat is shown on the left.

**insulin**
(in´su-lin)  A hormone produced by the islets of Langerhans that reduces the amount of sugar in the bloodstream.

**glucagon**
(gloo´kah-gon)  A hormone produced by the islets of Langerhans that causes the liver to release sugar into the bloodstream.

## Body Weight and the "Set Point"

As we have just seen, increases in body fat signal the body not only to eat less but also to increase the metabolism of the cells that store fat. This feedback system must work differently for different people, however. Otherwise, we would all have more or less the same amount of body fat. This has led scientists to hypothesize that each of us has a different *set point* for body fat, which determines when the ventromedial hypothalamus will initiate actions to reduce eating and increase metabolism. It is like the point that you set on your home's thermostat to control the heater.

It appears to be very difficult to raise or lower body weight above or below this set point for very long (as we will see in the last section of this chapter, in which losing weight is discussed). It is not known which step or steps in the feedback loop determine the set point, but medical researchers are very interested in understanding why the set point is so high for highly obese persons with medical complications. Therefore, the discovery of the feedback loop shown in figure 10.2 has stimulated medical research companies to invest hundreds of millions of dollars in research to find a cure for obesity.

### Specific Hungers

Did you ever get a craving for a particular kind of food? Did you wonder if your body was trying to tell you something—that it needed a nutrient in that food? Animals that are experimentally deprived of protein, a vitamin, or fat will tend to eat greater quantities of foods containing that element when later given a choice (National Advisory Mental Health Council, 1995b; Schulkin, 1999). For example, a rat whose adrenal glands have been surgically removed—producing a fatal deficiency in the body's supply of sodium unless sodium is consumed in the form of salt—shows a preference for salty water within 15 seconds of its being offered (Nachman, 1962). Since human eating is strongly influenced by learning and other psychological factors, it's not known whether we are as good as rats at listening to the nutritional needs of our bodies. But that craving might be telling you something important.

### Psychological Factors in Hunger

Learning plays a role in eating habits. Many families encourage and model overeating.

Although hunger is clearly a motive that is tied to biological needs, psychological factors are also involved in the regulation of food intake. Through maturation and learning, we go from an infant who only drinks milk to an adult with distinct food preferences that play an important role in our lives (Rozin, 1996). If you grew up in the American South, you might adore chitlins (deep-fried pig intestines) and stewed okra. If you grew up in another part of the world, however, the very idea of these foods might be disgusting. A Catholic woman might enjoy beef, pork, and shellfish, but eating these foods might violate deeply held religious beliefs of some of her Hindu and Jewish neighbors. Learning plays a powerful role in determining *what* we eat, *when* we eat (we are often ready to eat at our customary times for eating, even if we have just had a snack), and even *how much* we eat (many families encourage and model overeating). Studies of nonhuman animals show that even rats and chimpanzees learn what to eat by watching older animals (National Advisory Mental Health Council, 1995b).

Emotions also play a role in eating. People who are anxious often eat more than usual, and people who are depressed may lose their appetite for long periods of time. Ironically, though, individuals who get depressed after starting a new regime of healthy eating and exercise often lose the will to continue. If you are temporarily depressed enough to believe that nobody cares if you live or die—even you—why would you bother to eat healthfully?

Perhaps the most troublesome psychological factors to those who are trying to control their eating, however, are **incentives.** How many times have you finished dinner at a restaurant or family gathering, feeling a bit overstuffed, only to be tempted into eating a seductive dessert? Incentives are external cues that activate motives. The smell of freshly baked bread makes you hungry; passing a fast-food joint on your way home from

**incentives**
External cues that activate motives.

school creates a craving for french fries; and the sight of the dessert creates a desire to eat even when you are way past the point of biological hunger. Incentives have their effect through the same brain mechanisms that regulate the biological aspects of hunger. The sight of food causes neurons in your hypothalamus to fire, particularly if it's a favorite food, and the smell of food triggers the release of insulin, which stimulates hunger by causing your blood sugar to drop (Rolls, Burton, & Mora, 1976). Laboratory research with animals has shown that incentives can be powerful enough under some circumstances to push weight above the natural set point. All rats will overeat to the point of obesity if they have easy access to large quantities of a variety of tasty high-calorie foods (National Advisory Mental Health Council, 1995b). Unless you are trying to gain weight, therefore, it is not a good idea to keep large quantities of a variety of tasty high-calorie foods in your kitchen.

External incentives, such as the look or smell of a food, can increase our motivation to eat.

## Thirst: The Regulation of Water Intake

Just as we must control the intake of food to survive, we must also regulate the intake of water. What is the homeostatic mechanism involved in thirst? Actually, there are several mechanisms, as in the case of hunger; like hunger also, the key regulatory centers are in the hypothalamus.

### Biological Regulation of Thirst

A *drink system* and a *stop drinking system* are regulated by different sections of the hypothalamus. Surgical destruction of the drink system causes the animal to refuse water; destruction of the stop drinking system results in excessive drinking. Although the control centers for thirst occupy much of the same areas as the centers for hunger, they operate separately by using different neurotransmitters (Grossman, 1960; Schulkin, 1999).

The hypothalamus uses three principal cues in regulating drinking: mouth dryness, loss of water by cells, and reductions in blood volume.

1.  *Mouth dryness.* Dryness of the mouth is the thirst cue of which we are most consciously aware. In the 1920s, biologist Walter Cannon studied the role of mouth dryness in thirst, this time using himself as the subject. After drinking large amounts of water to be sure he was not thirsty, he injected himself with a drug that stops the flow of saliva. Very soon, he felt thirsty. Next, he injected his mouth with a local anesthetic that blocked all sensations from his mouth. This quickly eliminated the sensation of being thirsty. Cannon concluded that mouth dryness was the cue that led to the sensation of thirst, but he was only partially correct again. We know today that other factors play more important roles.

Learning influences which beverages we drink as well as when we drink them. For example, drinking cola at breakfast is a fairly recent idea.

2.  *Cell fluid levels.* When the total amount of water in the body decreases, the concentration of salts in the fluids of the body increases. Of particular importance to the regulation of thirst are *sodium salts* that exist primarily in the fluids outside the body's cells (because salts cannot pass through the semipermeable membranes of the cells). Decreases in the total body fluids of even 1 to 2 percent produce increases in the sodium concentration that are large enough to draw water out of the cells and *dehydrate* them (Hole, 1990; Petri, 1986). This happens to cells throughout the body, but when certain specialized cells in the drink center of the hypothalamus dehydrate and shrivel, they send multiple messages to correct the situation. In particular, they chemically signal the **pituitary gland,** which is located just below the hypothalamic drink center, to secrete the **antidiuretic hormone (ADH)** into the bloodstream. When ADH reaches the kidneys, it causes them to conserve water in the body by reabsorbing it from the urine. In addition, the hypothalamic center simultaneously sends a message of thirst to the cerebral cortex, which initiates searching for and drinking liquids (Schulkin, 1999).

3.  *Total blood volume.* The third cue used by the hypothalamus to regulate thirst is total blood volume. As the volume of water in the body decreases, the volume of

**pituitary gland**
(pĭ-tu´i-tār˝ē)  The body's master gland, located near the bottom of the brain, whose hormones help regulate the activity of the other glands in the endocrine system.

**antidiuretic hormone (ADH)**
(an˝tĭ-di˝u-ret´ik)  A hormone produced by the pituitary that causes the kidneys to conserve water in the body by reabsorbing it from the urine.

blood—which is composed mostly of water—decreases as well. A decreased volume of blood is first sensed by the kidneys. The kidneys react in two ways. First, they cause blood vessels to contract to compensate for the lowered amount of blood. Second, in a series of chemical steps, they cause the creation of the substance **angiotensin** in the blood. When angiotensin reaches the hypothalamus, the drink center sends a thirst message to the cerebral cortex, which eventually leads to drinking (Schulkin, 1999).

**angiotensin**
(an″jē-ō-ten′sin) A substance in the blood that signals the hypothalamus that the body needs water.

### Psychological Factors in Thirst

Psychological factors also play a role in the regulation of drinking, although overall this role does not appear to be as large as in hunger. Learning influences *which* beverages we drink (the average citizen of Nepal prefers yak's milk to cow's milk) as well as *when* we drink them (an advertising campaign has been mounted in recent years to convince us to drink colas for breakfast). Incentives, such as the sight of a glass of beer, may activate thirst in a person who is otherwise not thirsty. Stress and emotions seem to have little effect on drinking compared with eating, except in the case of beverages that contain alcohol or stimulants (coffee, tea, colas, and so on), which alter our moods.

## Review

The term *primary motivation* refers to states based on biological needs that activate and guide behavior. Examples of primary motives include hunger, thirst, maintaining warmth, and avoiding pain. These motives must be satisfied if the organism is to survive. Primary motives are generally based on a complex number of biological factors. For example, the control centers for eating and drinking are located in the hypothalamus. The hypothalamus responds directly or indirectly to a number of body signals that food or water is needed. In the case of hunger, stomach contractions, levels of blood glucose, and levels of blood fat are all involved in the regulation of eating. Thirst is similarly regulated by a combination of mouth dryness, level of fluids in the body cells, and the total volume of blood in the body.

Although the primary motives are based on biological survival needs, psychological factors are involved in these motives as well. External stimuli, such as the sight of a highly preferred food or beverage, can act as an incentive that activates eating or drinking, even when the individual is satiated. Learning also influences what, when, and how much we eat and drink.

## Check Your Learning

To be sure that you have learned the key points from the preceding section, cover the list of correct answers and try to answer each question. If you give an incorrect answer to any question, return to the page given next to the correct answer to see why your answer was not correct. Remember that these questions cover only some of the important information in this section; it is important that you make up your own questions to check your learning of other facts and concepts.

1. The term _____ refers to an internal state or condition that activates and gives direction to our thoughts, feelings, and actions.

   a) cognition               c) motivation
   b) incentive               d) physiology

2. A _____ is an internal mechanism that senses biological imbalances and stimulates actions to restore the proper balance.

3. The hunger and thirst motives are controlled by excitatory and inhibitory brain systems, with centers in the _____ playing key roles.

   a) cerebellum              c) thalamus
   b) hypothalamus            d) hippocampus

4. _____ refers to an external cue that activates primarily hunger motivation.

a) Incentive           c) Catalyst

b) Efferent            d) Stimulus

---

1. If you were trying to help someone control his or her food intake, how would your advice be different after reading this section?

2. How have your learning experiences influenced the expression of your hunger and thirst motives?

**Correct Answers:**  1. c (p. 368),    2. homeostatic mechanism (p. 369),    3. b (p. 369),    4. a (p. 372).

**Thinking Critically about Psychology**

**psychological motives**
Motives related to the individual's happiness and well-being, but not to survival.

**novel stimulation**
New or changed experiences.

## Psychological Motives

**Psychological motives** are motives that are not directly related to the biological survival of the individual or the species. They are "needs" in the sense that the individual's happiness and well-being depend on these motives. Even more than primary motives, psychological motives vary considerably in the degree to which they are influenced by experience. Some psychological motives are found in every normal member of a species and seem to be innate, whereas others seem to be entirely learned. In this section, we will look at three psychological motives: the need for novel stimulation, the need for affiliation with others, and the need for achievement.

### Stimulus Motivation: Seeking Novel Stimulation

Did you ever come home to an empty house and flip on the radio or television just to kill the silence? Have you ever spent all day Saturday writing a term paper and then felt you *had* to get up and take a walk or talk to someone just for sheer diversion? Most people get bored easily if there is little overall stimulation or if the stimulation is unchanging. We, and other animals, have an apparently inborn motive to seek **novel stimulation.**

If you put a rat in a T-maze (see fig. 10.4) in which it must choose between turning right into an alley painted gray or turning left into one painted with complex stripes, the rat will explore the more complex, more "interesting" alley first. But the next time it will be more likely to turn into the gray alley, which it has not seen yet, apparently because it is "curious" about it (Dember, 1965).

Monkeys that are kept in boring cages will similarly work hard pressing a lever to earn a chance to look at other monkeys or even to watch a model train run (Butler, 1953). Monkeys will also work manual puzzles for hours without any reward except finally getting them apart (Harlow, Harlow, & Meyer, 1950) (see fig. 10.5). Watch a human infant play with her crib toys for a few minutes and you will see that humans, too, are motivated to manipulate, investigate, and generally shake up their environments. If you go without physical activity for a while, you will see that you have a need for activity, too.

### Optimal Arousal Theory

Although no known homeostatic mechanism accounts for our need for novel stimulation, we clearly must have a certain amount of it to feel comfortable. But, just as too little stimulation is unpleasant and will motivate us to increase stimulation, *too much* stimulation is unpleasant and will motivate us to find ways to decrease it. Too many people talking at once, too much noise, or a room that contains too many clashing colors and patterns will send a person off in search of a few minutes of peace, quiet, and reduced

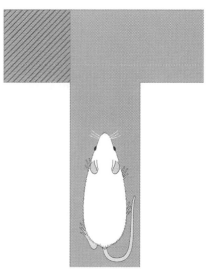

**FIGURE 10.4**
T-maze like those used to study stimulus motivation in rats.

**FIGURE 10.5**

A monkey disassembling mechanical lock puzzles for no reward other than the activity and novel stimulation involved in the process.

The need for novel stimulation motivated this monkey to learn to unlock the window that opens into the room with an electric train.

stimulation. Apparently, an optimal level of stimulation exists, and we feel uncomfortable going either above or below this level (Korman, 1974).

Our apparent "need" for an optimal level of stimulation has led psychologists to suggest that each individual strives to maintain an **optimal level of arousal** in the nervous system. *Arousal,* as used in this way, is a rather vague term, but it refers to the overall state of alertness and activation of the person. The individual who is sleeping is at a very low level of arousal; the relaxed person is at a somewhat higher level; the active, alert person is functioning at a moderate level; the anxious person is experiencing a high level of arousal; and the person in a frenzied panic is at an extremely high level. Arousal is linked to the activity of the brain's **reticular formation** and the sympathetic division of the autonomic nervous system. Optimal arousal theory does not suggest, however, that there is a biological need for a moderate or an optimal level of arousal. The individual can survive at high or low levels of arousal, but he or she is motivated to achieve a comfortable, optimal level of arousal by acting in ways that increase or decrease stimulation.

### Arousal and Performance: The Yerkes-Dodson Law

Not only is arousal an important motivational concept, but it's also linked to the efficiency of our performance in various situations. If arousal is too low, performance will be inadequate; if it's too high, performance may become disrupted and disorganized. This simple notion is often referred to as the **Yerkes-Dodson law,** but it's somewhat more complicated than it looks at first. The ideal level of arousal for different kinds of performance varies considerably. Football players "warm up" and "psych up" physically and emotionally to reach high levels of arousal for the game. It would be difficult to exceed the ideal level of arousal needed for highly physical contact sports. On the other hand, the performance of a skilled artisan applying pottery glazes by hand would be most efficient at much lower levels of arousal (see fig. 10.6). Too much arousal, as in the form of high levels of anxiety, would tend to disrupt the delicate, skilled performance of the potter.

## Affiliation Motivation

Do you usually enjoy being with friends? Do you feel lonely during periods when you do not have many friends? Human beings are social creatures. Given the opportunity, we generally prefer to have regular contact with other people. In this sense, it can be said that people have a **motive for affiliation** (Houston, 1985).

**optimal level of arousal**
The apparent human need for a comfortable level of stimulation, achieved by acting in ways that increase or decrease it.

**reticular formation**
(reh-tik′ū-lar) Sets of neurons in the medulla and pons from which neurons project down the spinal cord to play a role in maintaining muscle tone and cardiac reflexes and upward throughout the cerebral cortex where they influence wakefulness, arousal level, and attention.

**Yerkes-Dodson law**
A law stating that effective performance is more likely if the level of arousal is suitable for the activity.

**motive for affiliation**
The need to be with other people and to have personal relationships.

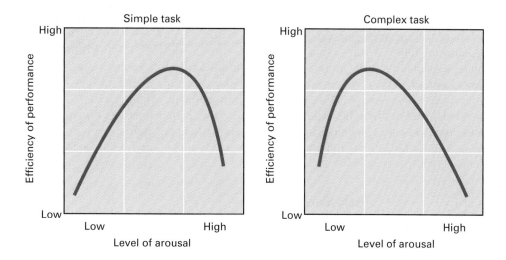

**FIGURE 10.6**
The Yerkes-Dodson law describes the relationship between the amount of arousal and the efficiency of performance. In general, either insufficient or excessive arousal results in inefficient performance, but the optimal level of arousal is higher for simple, physically active tasks than for complex, highly skilled tasks.

The need for affiliation is present in all normal humans, but most research on this topic concerns differences between individuals who have different levels of this motive. Individuals who are high in the need for affiliation, for example, tend to prefer being with others rather than satisfying other motives. When asked to perform a clerical task with a partner, individuals who are high in the need for affiliation but low in the need for achievement choose to work with a friend, regardless of how competent the friend is. In contrast, individuals who are low in the need for affiliation but high in the need for achievement choose the partner who they believe is most competent (French, 1956).

Two theories have been proposed to explain our apparent need for affiliation (Houston, 1985). Some believe that affiliation motivation is an inborn need that is based on natural selection. A stone-age human who chose to hunt alone would have been less able to kill large animals for food and to avoid being the prey of other animals, and thus to survive, than a human who felt a need to live and hunt with others. Thus, the forces of nature may have selected those humans with a need for affiliation—because they were the ones who survived. Other psychologists, however, believe that each human learns the motive to affiliate through his or her own learning experiences. Because infants experience being fed, cleaned, tickled, kept warm, and other positive forms of nurturing in the presence of another human being, other human beings may become "positive stimuli" through classical conditioning. Similarly, because our actions that lead us to be in the presence of others—smiling, stretching out our baby arms for a hug, and the like—often lead to pleasant outcomes, then affiliative behaviors are likely to be positively reinforced (Houston, 1985).

Some people always seem to need high levels of sensation. The optimal arousal theory would suggest that they are usually below their optimal level of arousal.

That motive for affiliation may be related in some way to the greater chance that humans who affiliate—flock together—will survive receives some support from the fact that affiliation motivation appears to be stronger when we are frightened about our well-being. Stanley Schachter (1959) has conducted a number of experiments on the relationship between anxiety and the need for affiliation. In a typical experiment, female university students were brought to the laboratory in small groups. There they met a man dressed in a white coat who introduced himself as Dr. Gregor Zilstein, a professor of neurology and psychiatry. He told half of the research participants that they would be participating in an experiment involving painful electric shocks—and they were shown the forbidding shock apparatus in the background. He told the other half of the participants that they would receive very mild shocks, which they would experience as a mere tickle. The first group was made far more anxious than the second group, as shown by the students' own ratings of their anxiety. Both groups were given the choice of waiting alone in individual waiting rooms or together in a group waiting room. As Schachter predicted, almost two-thirds of the subjects who were made to feel anxious chose to wait in groups, indicating a high level of need for affiliation. However, only one-third of the low anxiety group members chose to wait together.

The motive for affiliation is present in everyone to some extent, but people differ in the strength of their need to be with others.

Achievement motivation is a complex psychological process. People differ both in their definitions of success and their reasons for being motivated to seek it.

**achievement motivation**
The psychological need in humans for success.

Subsequent studies have similarly shown that everyday painful experiences—such as failing college tests—increase our motive to affiliate with others (Van Duuren & DiGiacomo, 1997). As the saying goes, "misery loves company." On the other hand, some people tend to have more affiliation motivation than others under most circumstances, and when the chips are down—such as when they are fighting cancer—they are more likely to seek emotional support from family members (Manne, Alfieri, Taylor, & Dougherty, 1999). There is considerable evidence that higher levels of affiliation motivation predict better psychological adjustment throughout life, perhaps in part because the motive for affiliation promotes social support when times are tough (McAdams & Vaillant, 1982).

## Achievement Motivation

Most high school senior classes vote on the female and male who are "mostly likely to succeed." Who was it in your high school class? Were they real go-getters who were willing to work hard to succeed? If so, they were probably high in achievement motivation. **Achievement motivation** is the psychological need to succeed in school, work, and other areas of life. Although the concept of achievement motivation has been around for a long time, a great deal of research in recent years has revitalized the topic by demonstrating that achievement motivation is more complex than originally suspected. The first scholarly works on achievement motivation portrayed it as a uniformly positive psychological force—the motivation that allowed many people to achieve the American dream of occupational and financial success. More recently, it has become clear that different people have different definitions of "success" and different motives for wanting to achieve their version of success.

We will focus our discussion of achievement motivation on a topic that is very relevant to you at this stage of your life—achievement in college—but the same ideas apply to achievement throughout life. Would you say that you are highly motivated to succeed in college? If so, how would you define success in college? Do you want to make good grades or do you want to learn a lot of new and interesting information (or both)? Andrew Elliot and Marcy Church (1997) of the University of Rochester have conducted fascinating and important studies of achievement motivation among college students. Remember that motivation activates and directs behavior. Elliot and Church distinguished three key elements in the motivation to get out of bed, go to class, pay attention, take notes, ask questions, and set aside other activities to study for tests:

1. *Mastery goals.* Persons with high mastery goals are intrinsically motivated to learn interesting and important new information. They enjoy challenging courses if those courses help them master new information, and they are disappointed by easy courses in which they get good grades but learn very little.

2. *Performance-approach goals.* Persons with high performance-approach goals are motivated to work hard to get better grades than other students to gain the respect of others.

3. *Performance-avoidance goals.* Persons with high performance-avoidance goals are motivated to work hard to avoid getting bad grades and looking unintelligent to others.

How would you rank the importance of these three sources of achievement motivation for yourself and your friends? Each of these three types of motivational goals will activate and direct work that will help you succeed, but Elliot and Church (1997) believe that they lead to rather different consequences. At the beginning of a college course on the psychology of personality, the students answered questions about their level of each of these three types of achievement motivation. At the end of the course, the students completed measures of how much they enjoyed and valued the course, and the researchers used their course grades to see how well they had performed on tests.

The different types of achievement motivation were associated with different outcomes at the end of the course. Not surprisingly, students with higher mastery goals reported enjoying the course more at the end. This was especially true if they were also low in performance-approach goals—being motivated to make good grades to impress other people interferes with enjoyment of the course. Students with higher performance-approach goals made better grades, especially if they had low mastery goals. The desire to impress other people by making good grades does lead to better grades, but sadly, wanting to learn the material for its own sake sometimes gets in the way of making good grades. The students who made the lowest grades had either low performance-approach and low mastery goals (they had little positive motivation of either type to learn the material) or they had high performance-avoidance goals (they had only negative motivation to learn the material). Students with high performance-avoidance goals at the start of the course also reported that they enjoyed the course content less than other students. Working just to avoid failure rarely makes for a positive or fruitful experience.

Thus, in order to understand one's achievement motivation for success in college, we need to understand both *what* people want and *why* they want it. Both our goals and our motives for attaining them have consequences for our success in college and enjoyment of the process. The same is true for success in other areas of life.

As if achievement motivation were not complicated enough by itself, we must also consider **fear of success** in order to understand a person's motivation to achieve. Although outperforming others often brings private feelings of satisfaction, it can invite envy that may strain social relationships (Exline & Lobel, 1999). Although this is not a concern of some people, it creates fear of success in others than can motivate them to achieve below their potential. Fear of success is more common among women than men in North America (Fried-Buchalter, 1997; Kumari, 1996), but college women with feminist, nontraditional sex-role attitudes have less fear of success than do women with more traditional sex-role attitudes (Kumari, 1996). Apparently, women who adhere to traditional sex roles fear criticism and rejection if they deviate from expected passive feminine roles. Sadly, women with the highest self-esteem are most likely to have high levels of fear of success, perhaps because they feel that they could succeed if they were to try (Kumari, 1996).

**fear of success**
The fear of the consequences of success, particularly the envy of others.

**opponent-process theory of motivation**
Solomon's theory of the learning of new motives based on changes over time in contrasting feelings.

## Solomon's Opponent-Process Theory of Acquired Motives

Richard Solomon (1980) of the University of Pennsylvania proposed a theory that has important implications for our learning of *new* motives, particularly ones that are difficult to understand in any other way. Why do some people love to fight in karate matches or parachute out of airplanes? How do some people become so "addicted" to their spouses, boyfriends, or girlfriends that they cannot leave them, even when they *do not enjoy* being with them anymore?

Solomon provided an intriguing answer to these and other questions with his **opponent-process theory of motivation** (don't confuse this with the opponent-process theory of color vision). Solomon explained craving such diverse things as parachute jumping, drugs, and dysfunctional lovers by means of two concepts: (a) Every state of positive feeling is followed by a *contrasting* negative feeling, and vice versa; and (b) any feeling—either positive or negative—that is experienced many times in succession loses some of its intensity.

The classic example is parachute jumping. Solomon summarizes data (which no one doubts!) that show that parachute jumping is frightening at first. When the novice jumper lands, he or she is generally in a mild state of shock but soon begins smiling and talking excitedly about the jump. That is, the negative state of fear is followed by the contrasting positive state of euphoria. The shift from negative fear to positive euphoria that reinforces the act of jumping is shown graphically in the left part of figure 10.7. But after

**FIGURE 10.7**
General illustration of Solomon's opponent-process theory of acquired motives as it applies to initially negative experiences, such as parachute jumping.
**Source:** Data from Richard L. Solomon, "The Opponent-Process Theory of Acquired Motivation," in *American Psychologist,* 35:691–712. Copyright © 1980 by the American Psychological Association.

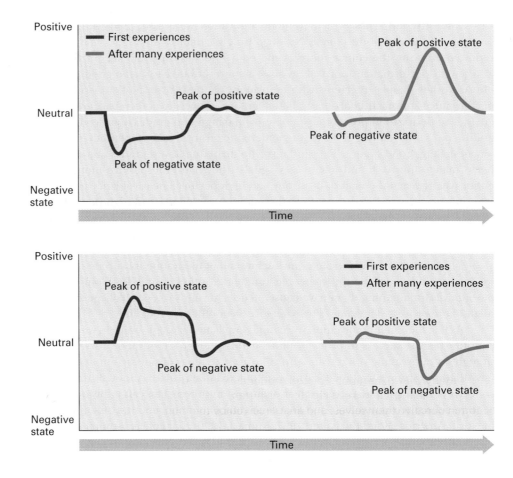

**FIGURE 10.8**
General illustration of Solomon's opponent-process theory of acquired motives as it applies to initially positive experiences, such as taking euphoric drugs.
**Source:** Data from Richard L. Solomon, "The Opponent-Process Theory of Acquired Motivation," in *American Psychologist,* 35:691–712. Copyright © 1980 by the American Psychological Association.

many jumps, the fear becomes less intense. This change is shown in the right side of figure 10.7. There is a lessening in fear from the first experiences with jumping to later jumps. However, note that the amount of reinforcing *contrast* in the two parts of figure 10.7 stays the same. This means that, as the fear is reduced, the amount of euphoria produced afterward becomes even stronger. This is Solomon's explanation of the learning of new motives like karate, motorcycle racing, and jogging—even the use of saunas. Not only does the initial negative state diminish due to repetition, but you get hooked by the contrasting shift to increasingly more intense levels of positive feeling.

The process of becoming addicted to things that feel good at first follows the opposite course. The wonderful, druglike feeling that comes from being with that new guy that you have a crush on, for example, is followed by a contrasting feeling of missing him when he is not with you. Not only is being with him positive, but getting him back is doubly reinforcing because it stops the negative feeling of missing him. Furthermore, as the positive feelings diminish, as shown in figure 10.8, the feeling of missing—even needing—the loved one becomes more intense. If you stop seeing him because the positive feeling is gone, it is this negative feeling of missing him that motivates you to go back. This is Solomon's explanation for why it's often so hard to end a loveless relationship. It's not the happiness that holds you—that is long since gone—it's the negative withdrawal symptoms that are so difficult to get through. If this sounds like a drug addiction, it's no accident. Solomon sees addictions to heroin and other drugs as forming in exactly the same way. First comes the pleasurable "rush," followed by the uncomfortable feeling of coming down. After frequent use, the pleasure of using the drug (cocaine, nicotine, etc.) in the same amount is greatly diminished, but the pain of withdrawal is much worse. It's the pain of withdrawal that powerfully motivates the addict to take more of the drug, not the diminished pleasure that the drug brings. Solomon's theory is not relevant to all motives, but it may help us understand the learning of some perplexing motives.

## HUMAN DIVERSITY

### Conflict and the First-Generation College Student

Are you the first member of your family to attend college? If so, this fact may lead to conflicting emotions in you. Let's look at the college experiences of a man named John who now works as a psychologist. He is from a poor white family and was the first of 4 siblings and 16 cousins to finish college. He knew that his family was proud of him, but he sometimes felt that he had left his family and old friends behind in his quest for higher education. Sometimes these feelings interfered with his motivation to complete school.

Many first-generation college students struggle with similar feelings (Piorkowski, 1983; Whitten, 1992). They often perceive themselves, and are perceived by their families, as moving into a new social class. This can be anxiety provoking for both the student and the family. Issues related to group loyalty arise as the student's interests, vocabulary, and worldview become different from those of his family and neighborhood friends. Family members sometimes accuse first-generation college students of "changing" or "thinking they are better" than the family. These issues are particularly challenging for members of ethnic groups that traditionally attended college infrequently. Not only do they face strained relationships with their family and friends, but they often do not fit into the college community if they attend a majority-culture institution.

Many first-generation college students handle these conflicts very successfully. They recognize that they are part of both their college and home communities and develop strategies for moving comfortably from one to the other. They speak standard English on the college campus and speak the language of their home community, which might be Spanish, Creole, or Black English, when they are among friends. They reassure their family members by word and deed that they still feel a part of their home, even though they are changing in some ways. This is important because students who are able to integrate their old and new lifestyles more successfully make higher grades than do students who experience a high degree of conflict (Whitten, 1993b).

But first-generation college students are not the only ones who experience conflicts based on their backgrounds at college. Consider Roslyn, a 38-year-old African American woman who is a third-generation college graduate. Her grandparents were college-educated teachers, and her parents both have graduate training. As a college student, she usually hid this background from her African American peers. She often had a sense of isolation because she was one of the few African American students in her dormitory whose education was being paid for entirely by her parents. She also felt guilty about having more material goods than her peers and other African Americans in her neighborhood.

What is the climate like at your institution for first-generation college students and students who do not fit the mold in other ways? How effective is your college when it comes to addressing diversity issues? How do your family and friends feel about your decision to enter college? Thinking about these questions may help you identify sources of potential conflict in yourself or understand the experience of other students better. ∎

## Intrinsic and Extrinsic Motivation

It is important to distinguish between intrinsic and extrinsic motivation. We speak of **intrinsic motivation** when people are motivated by the inherent nature of the activity, their pleasure of mastering something new, or the natural consequences of the activity. For example, the monkeys that we mentioned earlier who will take apart mechanical puzzles for no reward other than getting them apart are intrinsically motivated to solve puzzles. People who read nonfiction books that are unrelated to their work just because it is fun to learn new things are intrinsically motivated. Similarly, people who donate anonymously to charity because they wish to help people without being recognized are intrinsically motivated. **Extrinsic motivation,** on the other hand, is motivation that is external to the activity and not an inherent part of it. If a child who hates to do arithmetic

**intrinsic motivation**
(in-trin′sik) Human motives stimulated by the inherent nature of the activity or its natural consequences.

**extrinsic motivation**
(eks-trin′sik) Human motives activated by external rewards.

homework is encouraged to do so by payment of a nickel for every correct answer, he is extrinsically motivated. That is, he works for the external payment rather than because of an intrinsic interest in math. Similarly, a person who works hard to be a good employee because she wants to be admired by others—rather than because of a genuine interest in the work—is extrinsically motivated. People who are intrinsically motivated tend to work harder and respond to challenges by working even harder. They enjoy their work more and often perform more creatively and effectively than people who are extrinsically motivated (National Advisory Mental Health Council, 1995b). Intrinsic motivation is shaped by our learning experiences. For example, children from families who emphasize the joys and importance of learning have more intrinsic motivation to learn in school (Gottfried, Fleming, & Gottfried, 1998).

Perhaps the most significant issue concerning the distinction between intrinsic and extrinsic motivation is the question of when extrinsic rewards should be supplied by parents, teachers, and employers in an effort to increase motivation. When is it wise to use extrinsic motivation in the form of positive reinforcement to increase the frequency of some behavior (such as completing homework, delivering packages on time, and so on)? Considerable evidence suggests that if a behavior occurs infrequently—and its intrinsic motivation can be assumed low for that individual—then extrinsic motivation can be successful in increasing the frequency of occurrence of the behavior. Children who hate to do their math homework often will do it diligently if rewarded with additional allowance money. On the other hand, if the individual is already intrinsically motivated to perform an activity, adding extrinsic motivation may detract from the intrinsic motivation. For example, when young children who like to draw pictures in school were given certificates for good drawing, they drew pictures less often than did children who had not received certificates (Lepper, Greene, & Nisbett, 1973). This study, and many subsequent studies (Ryan & Deci, 2000; Tang & Hall, 1995), suggest that we must be careful to avoid squelching intrinsic motivation by providing unnecessary extrinsic rewards.

What about praise? When we pat a child on the back for a job well done—whether it be homework or reading a book—does our praise increase the child's intrinsic motivation? Psychologists Jennifer Henderlong and Mark Lepper (2002) suggest that it depends on what we say and how we say it.

Praise increases intrinsic motivation when the praise:

1. Implies that the child was successful because of his or her effort and not because of the child's natural talent or abilities.
2. Is sincere and does not imply that the adult is controlling the child.
3. Does not compare the child to other children.
4. Implies that the adult has standards for the child's behavior that the child believes that he or she can attain with effort.

In contrast, praise that focuses on the child's abilities rather than effort, seems controlling rather than sincere, compares the child to others, or implies that he or she must reach standards in the future that seem impossible (or too low), may undermine intrinsic motivation according to Henderlong and Lepper (2002).

For example, if a child writes a clever poem for her teacher, Henderlong and Lepper (2002) suggest that this might be effective praise that would increase the child's intrinsic motivation to write:

> "I really like this poem! I especially like the way you found so many ways to compare leaves and songs. That must have taken a lot of thought!"

On the other hand, praise like this might reduce the child's intrinsic motivation:

> "This is brilliant! See, I told you that you were the only genius in Mrs. Long's class. If you just write, write, write every night like your mother told you, you'll be great! Soon, Harvard and Yale will be fighting over you."

For many years, it was assumed that another good way to increase intrinsic motivation was to give people choices. When people have options, they will choose activities that they are intrinsically motivated to perform, and performing them will further enhance their intrinsic motivation. Recent findings suggest that this is true, but only in individualistic Western societies (Iyengar & Lepper, 1999). American children of European ancestry show more intrinsic motivation for school tasks and other activities that they choose themselves. In contrast, Asian American children from collectivistic cultures that place greater emphasis on the well-being of the group than on the well-being of the individual have more intrinsic motivation for activities that were selected for them by trusted authority figures or friends (Iyengar & Lepper, 1999). As in many aspects of psychological life, sociocultural factors are important in motivation.

## Maslow's Hierarchy of Motives

We have touched on only a few of the human motives, but it's already obvious that we are creatures of many and varied needs. Abraham Maslow (1970) put forward an interesting theory about our many motives. According to Maslow, we are not a crazy-quilt confusion of motives; rather, our motives are organized in a hierarchy arranged from the most basic to the most personal and advanced.

**Maslow's hierarchy of motives** (needs) is shown in figure 10.9. If lower needs in the hierarchy are not met for the most part, then higher motives will not operate. Higher needs lie dormant until the individual has a chance to satisfy immediately pressing lower needs, such as hunger, thirst, and safety. When the lower needs have been met, then motives to develop relationships with others, to achieve a positive self-esteem, and to realize one's full potential ethically, artistically, and philosophically (**self-actualization**) become important to the individual.

Maslow's hierarchy of motives helps explain such things as why starving peasant farmers are not particularly interested in the political philosophies of rival governments and why, throughout history, science, art, and philosophy have mostly been produced when a nation could afford to have a privileged class who did not have to work to eat. The concept of the hierarchy of motives also helps us understand why a person would give up a prestigious, but time-consuming, career to try to save a marriage with a much-loved spouse. Higher motives become unimportant when lower motives are unmet.

But, as helpful as Maslow's hierarchy of motives is, there are some obvious exceptions to it. The hierarchy does not explain why an individual would risk her or his life to rescue a friend from a burning building. Nor does it explain why imprisoned members of the Irish Republican Army intentionally starved themselves to death in 1981 to gain

**Maslow's hierarchy of motives**
The concept that more basic needs must be met before higher-level motives become active.

**self-actualization**
According to Maslow, the seldomly reached full result of the inner-directed drive of humans to grow, improve, and use their potential to the fullest.

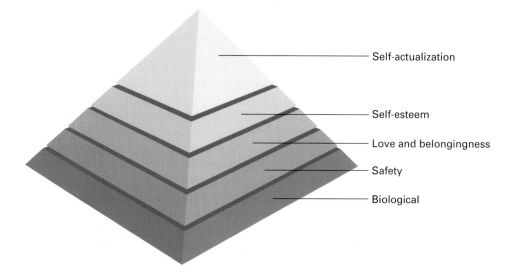

**FIGURE 10.9**
Maslow's hierarchy of motives.
**Source:** Diagram based on data from *Hierarchy of Needs from Motivation and Personality,* Third Edition, by Abraham H. Maslow. Revised by Robert Frager, et al., Harper & Row, Publishers, Inc., 1954, 1987.

Self-actualization

Self-esteem

Love and belongingness

Safety

Biological

what might be seen by outsiders as minor changes in how political prisoners were treated. Similarly, the hierarchy fails to shed light on the common occurrence of an individual's ignoring spouse and children to pursue self-esteem in a career. Obviously, humans are sometimes willing to endure unmet lower motives to pursue higher ones. Still, Maslow's hierarchy appears to explain more facets of motivation than it fails to explain.

### Self-Actualization and the American Dream

Maslow believed that the highest need was for self-actualization. Because most people are unable to fully satisfy lower-level motives, he believed that few of us achieve full self-actualization. Self-actualization is defined in terms of the following characteristics (based on Jones & Crandall, 1986):

- Being dedicated to a mission in life that transcends your selfish interests
- Believing that people are essentially good and trustworthy
- Loving others even when you do not like their behavior
- Feeling adequate to deal with life
- Being able to accept your own weaknesses
- Not being dependent on the approval of others (preferring to be yourself than popular)
- Being able to express your feelings even when they are unpopular
- Being unashamed of all of your emotions, even negative emotions
- Being unafraid of failure

To what extent would you say that you are self-actualized in Maslow's terms? How common is self-actualization in contemporary American society? In 1993, Tim Kasser and Richard Ryan wrote an influential paper entitled *A Dark Side of the American Dream*, which portrayed the American dream of financial success as antithetical to self-actualization. They showed that persons who are highly motivated to achieve financial success are typically less actualized and less well adjusted. Although they presented only correlational evidence, which cannot tell us if maladjustment leads to high achievement motivation for financial success or vice versa, they theorized that motivation leads to lack of self-actualization, anxiety, depression, and health problems (Kasser & Ryan, 1993). Similarly, Charles Carver and Eryn Baird (1998) of the University of Miami found that college students' levels of motivation for financial success and status were negatively correlated with their levels of self-actualization. In contrast, the students who were motivated to achieve a different kind of success (helping others, teaching them important information and skills, and participating in social and political movements) were more self-actualized. Thus, what you want in the future is associated with different levels of well-being and self-actualization.

Importantly, however, Carver and Baird (1998) showed that our *reasons* for wanting to achieve success are almost as important as our definition of success itself. College students who were motivated to help others because helping is inherently enjoyable and important were more self-actualized than other students. Being motivated to help others was not always associated with self-actualization, however. Students who were motivated to help others because they thought it would look good on their résumés or because other people would like them better were less self-actualized than others. Students who aspired to wealth and power were less self-actualized regardless of why they wanted that kind of success, but if they wanted financial success and power because it would provide independence and happiness, they were somewhat more actualized than were students who wanted it to impress other people. Again, both your goals and your reasons for wanting them are of great psychological importance.

Psychological motives help define and shape our lives, but unlike biological motives, they are not directly linked to the survival of the individual or the species. Some psychological motives are common to all normal members of a species and seem to be innate, whereas others appear to be primarily, if not entirely, learned. The stimulus motive—the need to maintain a moderate level of novel stimulation and activity—is an example of an apparently inborn psychological motive. The stimulus motive has led psychologists to speculate that individuals seek to maintain an optimal level of arousal in the nervous system by regulating stimulus input and activity levels. Other psychological motives appear to be influenced by social learning to a greater extent.

Most people have some need to affiliate with others, but people differ in the degree of their affiliation motivation. This motive appears to be strongest when times are tough—misery loves company, as they say. This is perhaps because people who affiliate with others during those tough times reap the benefits of social support.

Achievement motivation is the drive to be successful. This is a complex phenomenon, partly because it is a combination of desires to learn and succeed, fear of failure, and fear of the problems associated with success. In addition, people differ in both their definitions of success and their reasons for seeking success. In general, people who strongly aspire to success defined in terms of wealth and power are less well adjusted and self-actualized than are people who aspire to help and teach others. Regardless of an individual's definition of success, however, people who are motivated to achieve success to impress and please others tend to be less well adjusted than those people who are motivated to succeed by their own values.

Some people acquire powerful new motives through learning. Richard Solomon provided a theory of acquired motives that attempts to explain diverse motives, from the desire to parachute to drug addictions, in terms of the contrasting feelings during and after experiences. For example, the first parachute jump is frightening, but the rush of relief afterward is highly reinforcing. In time, the relative strength of the fear declines and the potency of the rush increases, leading to motivation to parachute.

Some motives are intrinsic—inherent in the activity—whereas others are extrinsic to the activity. Both kinds of motives play a constructive role in our lives, but the unnecessary use of extrinsic rewards for an activity can backfire by reducing a person's intrinsic motivation for that activity. Giving persons a choice of activities improves intrinsic motivation in individualistic societies, but guidance from trusted persons improves intrinsic motivation in collectivistic societies.

To be sure that you have learned the key points from the preceding section, cover the list of correct answers and try to answer each question. If you give an incorrect answer to any question, return to the page given next to the correct answer to see why your answer was not correct.

1. _____ motives are related to the individual's happiness and well-being, but not to survival.

   a)   Primary                     c)   Psychological
   b)   Hunger                      d)   Tertiary

2. The _____ law states that efficient performance is more likely if the level of arousal is suitable for the activity (neither too high nor too low).

   a)   tort                         c)   Weber-Fechner
   b)   opponent-process            d)   Yerkes-Dodson

3. Threats to our well-being generally increase our _____ (or need to be with other people).

   a) achievement motivation     c) affiliation motivation

   b) power motivation     d) intimacy motivation

4. _____ motivation is the psychological need for success in school, occupation, and other situations.

   a) Affiliation     c) Acceptance

   b) Aggression     d) Achievement

5. According to Maslow's _____, an individual moves from one level of motivation to the next after fulfilling the basic needs on the lower level.

## Thinking Critically about Psychology

1. Do you think our need for affiliation is an inborn need or a learned motive? Why?

2. What is your definition of success and what are your reasons for desiring it? Are your goals related in a positive way to your well-being and self-actualization?

*Correct Answers:* **1.** c (p. 375), **2.** d (p. 376), **3.** c (p. 376), **4.** d (p. 378), **5.** hierarchy of motives (p. 383).

## ● Emotions

What do poets write about? Of all the facets of human existence, which do they choose for their themes? It's not depth perception, neural transmission, or cognitive development; it's not classical conditioning or intelligence. They write mostly about *emotions*, the experiences that give color, meaning, and intensity to our lives. One obvious reason poets focus on emotions is that emotions are interesting. People love to mull over their feelings and passions and to learn about the real or imagined emotions of others. If we did not enjoy our emotions so much, poems, plays, novels, and soap operas might not exist.

In 1899, Charles Darwin noted that many human emotions, such as fear and rage, can also be observed in dogs, birds, and other animals. Why do animals experience emotions? What is the function of emotions in the lives of human and nonhuman animals? Since the time of Darwin, one widely held view has been that our emotions evolved over time through natural selection (Cacioppo, Gardner, & Berntson, 1999). According to this view, two general classes of emotions were "sculpted by the hammer and chisel of adaptation and natural selection to differentiate hostile from hospitable stimuli" (Cacioppo & others, 1999, p. 840). This means that animals—including humans—who react to emotionally dangerous stimuli (like poisonous snakes) and avoid them, and react emotionally to helpful stimuli (such as friends or food) and approach them are more likely to survive and reproduce (Damasio, 2001). Animal species that do not avoid danger and approach helpful things will perish and their genes will be lost, whereas animals who experience positive and negative emotions will survive. Thus, we experience negative emotion when someone threatens to hit us, and we experience positive emotion when we see a friend because these emotions are key to our survival. Emotions are not always pleasant, but under most circumstances, they protect us.

There are many different emotions, of course, but psychologists David Watson and Auke Tellegen (1985; Tellegen, Watson, & Clark, 1999) have suggested that the many varieties of emotional experience arise from different combinations of simple negative and positive emotions. Watson and Tellegen suggest that most emotions can be described in terms of their placement on the "map" of emotions presented in figure 10.10.

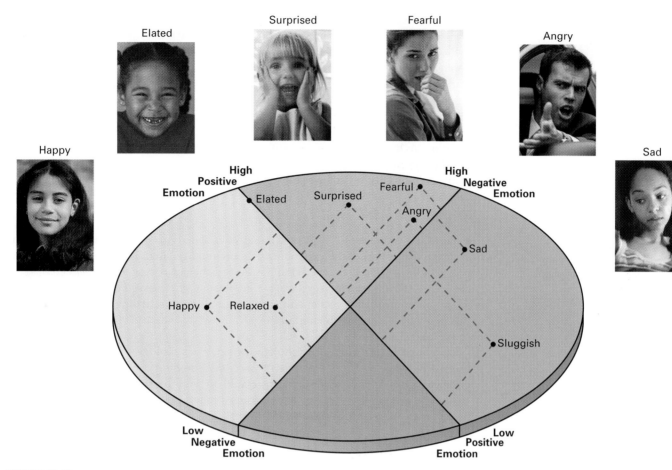

**FIGURE 10.10**
Watson and Tellegen's "map" of the structure and relationships among different emotions.

The map is created using two bipolar dimensions of emotion, much like the north-south and east-west dimensions on geographic maps. One dimension has high negative emotion at one pole and low negative emotion at the other pole. The second dimension has high positive emotion on one pole and low positive emotion on the other pole. Watson and Tellegen have used extensive research on how each much emotion is correlated with each other emotion (and whether the correlation is positive or negative) to place the various emotions on this map.

Watson and Tellegen's emotional map is more than just a good way to organize our description of emotions. The implication is that all of the varied human emotions can be thought of as different combinations of only two basic elements—positive and negative emotions. For example, elation is viewed as a high level of positive emotion in combination with a neutral level of negative emotion. Surprise is a combination of moderately high positive and negative emotions, and sadness is a combination of high negative emotion and moderately low positive emotion. Where on this emotional map would you place the way you felt during the most emotional part of the past week? What word(s) would you use to describe that emotion?

A number of important points should be made about Watson and Tellegen's emotional map. First, positive and negative emotion are not the opposites of one another. This may seem unreasonable at first, but notice that the specific emotions that we consider to be "opposites" (such as happy and sad or nervous and relaxed) are, in fact, in opposite positions on the emotional map.

Second, notice that anger and fear are very close together on the emotional map. There are many reasons to believe that fear and anger are, in many ways, variants of the same emotion. This idea dates back to the "flight or fight" syndrome described in William James' first psychology textbook published in 1890. Intense negative emotion (which involves arousal of the sympathetic nervous system and the secretion of epinephrine and other endocrine hormones) prepares the individual to either run away in fear or to fight in anger. The two emotions are essentially identical at the physiological level, but many factors (How big is the scary person in front of me? Is that a gun? Do I remember my karate?) determine whether the emotion will be experienced as fear or anger. Third, did you notice that love is not on the emotional map? Many experts consider love to be distinct from the other emotions shown in figure 10.10 (National Advisory Mental Health Council, 1995a), but the experience of romantic love often involves many emotions that are all over the emotional map!

## Three Theories of Emotion

What exactly is emotion? Most psychological explanations of emotion distinguish the same basic elements of the experience of emotion: (a) There is a *stimulus situation* that provokes the reaction; (b) there is a positively or negatively toned *conscious experience*— the "emotion" that we feel; (c) there is a bodily state of *physiological arousal* produced by the autonomic nervous system and endocrine glands; and (d) there is related *behavior* that generally accompanies emotions—the animal that is afraid cringes, trembles, then runs (Lang, 1995).

Since the founding of psychology, however, psychologists have disagreed about the order in which the four elements of emotions (stimulus, conscious experience, physiological arousal, and behavior) are related to one another. Three main theories have been proposed to explain the workings of emotions. (It may help if you refer to fig. 10.11 as you read the following theories.)

### James-Lange Theory

The commonsense view of emotions is that the stimulus of seeing a mugger makes us consciously feel afraid and that the conscious fear leads us to tremble and run. William James (1890) suggested that this view is just backward, however. He believed that the emotional stimulus is routed (by the sensory relay center known as the thalamus) directly to the limbic system, which produces the body reactions of fear through the hypothalamus and sympathetic division of the autonomic nervous system. The sensations from this body reaction are then sent back to the cortex and produce what we feel in the conscious experience of emotion. According to James, "We feel sorry because we cry, angry because we strike, afraid because we tremble." A number of years later, Danish physiologist Carl Lange (1922) independently proposed the same theory, so it's known today as the **James-Lange theory of emotion.**

Because we tend to "feel" emotions throughout our bodies rather than just in our heads, the James-Lange theory makes sense. But, several years after the death of William James, Harvard University biologist Walter Cannon (1927) published a set of strong criticisms of the James-Lange theory. His four major points were as follows:

1. People whose spinal columns have been severed in accidents still experience emotions normally, even though all feedback to the brain through the spinal cord from the organs aroused by the autonomic nervous system has been cut off. Cannon concluded that the experience of emotion cannot be based on feedback from aroused visceral organs. This criticism discouraged many supporters of the James-Lange theory at the time, but it is not actually a strong argument for two reasons. First, James actually hypothesized that feedback from both visceral organs and skeletal muscles contribute to emotional experience, and the afferent nerves that carry feedback from skeletal muscles to the brain do not all run through the spinal cord. Second, severing the spinal cord still leaves intact feedback to the brain from the viscera through the vagus nerve (LeDoux, 1996).

**James-Lange theory of emotion**
The theory that conscious emotional experiences are caused by feedback to the cerebral cortex from physiological reactions and behavior.

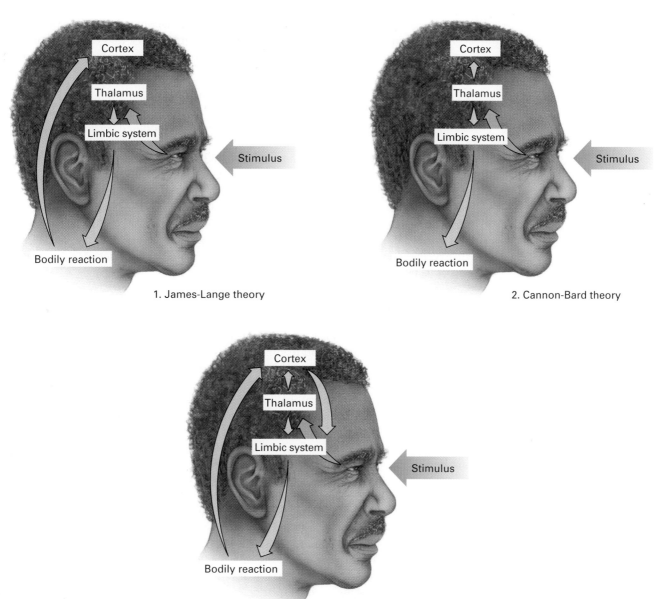

1. James-Lange theory

2. Cannon-Bard theory

3. Cognitive theory

**FIGURE 10.11**
Illustration of three major theories of emotion: (1) the James-Lange theory, (2) the Cannon-Bard theory, and (3) the cognitive theory.

2. The visceral organs respond relatively slowly to stressful situations—too slowly, according to Cannon, to provide the nearly instantaneous emotional experience involved, for example, in seeing a mugger suddenly rush at you. Again, this criticism of the James-Lange theory was off target because James did not claim that all of the body feedback involved in emotional experience comes from the visceral organs. James thought that feedback from the skeletal muscles, which respond quickly and provide instant feedback to the brain, were involved as well (LeDoux, 1996). When you see the mugger, you immediately jump and gasp—and afferent feedback about these reactions reaches the brain very quickly.

3. The physiological reactions that accompany different emotions are so similar that it's hard to see how a person could feel distinctly different emotions such as fear and rage simply from the first sensory feedback provided by autonomic arousal.

4.  Injecting human research participants with the hormone epinephrine (adrenaline) stimulates the visceral organs. The afferent feedback to the brain from the stimulated visceral organs is experienced as arousal in most circumstances, rather than as a feeling of emotion.

Cannon's criticisms of the James-Lange theory of emotion did not disprove it, but caused it to be out of favor for many years. More recently, however, contemporary psychologist Carroll Izard (1972, 1991, 1997) has revived a modified version of the James-Lange theory. Izard believes that the afferent feedback that is most important in the conscious experience of emotion does not come from the slow-reacting organs that are activated diffusely by the autonomic nervous system. Rather, the most important sensory feedback comes from the *facial muscles*. Stop reading and smile for a few seconds. Did you feel the muscles move your face around? That's the sensory feedback from your facial muscles. Now smile a big, happy smile. Did you feel a little bit happier when you smiled? Most people do—that's the idea behind Izard's version of the James-Lange theory. Part of what you feel when you have an emotional experience is just sensory feedback from your facial muscles.

Izard's updated version of the James-Lange theory effectively answered all of Cannon's criticisms of that theory. Facial reactions in emotional situations provide afferent feedback to the brain even when the spinal cord is severed (criticism 1), provide nearly instantaneous feedback to the brain (criticism 2), are different for each emotion and therefore provide afferent feedback that is specific to each emotion (criticism 3), and are not influenced by epinephrine (criticism 4). At first glance, however, the hypothesis that afferent feedback from the face is an important element in conscious emotional experience seems unreasonable to many people. Consider this fact, however: Of the 44 muscles in the human face, 40 are devoted solely to emotional expression—the other 4 are for opening the mouth, speaking, and chewing (National Advisory Mental Health Council, 1995a). If so many facial muscles are devoted to emotional expression, maybe it does make sense to hypothesize that sensory feedback from them is an important part of the experience of emotions.

More important, there is solid experimental support for Izard's version of the James-Lange theory. For example, in a classic study, individuals who were given electric shocks reported less pain when they were told to make no facial reactions to the shock than when they let their emotions show in their faces. Perhaps the sensory feedback from their facial expressions made the difference in the amount of pain they experienced (Colby, Lanzetta, & Kleck, 1977). You might try that strategy the next time you have to experience minor pain at the doctor's or dentist's office. A "stiff upper lip" (or, even better, a relaxed facial expression) reduces the pain (a little).

Another strong study (among many that support Izard's theory) was conducted by Chris Kleinke and two of his students at the University of Alaska at Anchorage (Kleinke, Peterson, & Rutledge, 1998). There were two experimental groups and one control group in this formal experiment. One experimental group of college students was asked to express negative emotions with their facial expressions in front of a video camera. Students in the second experimental group were asked to express positive moods with their faces for the camera. Students in the control group were asked to maintain neutral facial expressions. All students completed a measure of their current mood before and after making the facial expressions. On the average, the moods of students in the control group did not change, but students who made facial expressions portraying positive emotions tended to feel better afterwards, while students who expressed negative emotions felt worse afterward.

In addition, Izard's theory is supported by studies conducted in both Western and non-Western cultures that suggest that human facial expressions are surprisingly similar around the world. Six basic emotions and their characteristic facial expressions appear to be universal: anger, disgust, happiness, sadness, surprise, and fear. Even people who have been blind from birth and cannot see facial expressions of emotions in others show the six basic emotional facial expressions themselves (Ekman, 1992; Izard & others, 1997). This suggests that these patterns of emotional expression are inborn in humans and supports Izard's contention that facial expressions are important in emotions.

Currently, most experts on emotion believe that afferent feedback from the facial muscles is an important element in conscious emotional experience but that afferent feedback from other muscle groups, and even from the slow-moving and diffuse visceral organs, play a role, too (LeDoux, 1996). In addition, there is now evidence that brain activity in the somatosensory cortex (see p. 78), which is involved in the perception of feelings in the body, plays a key role in the experience of emotion (Damasio, 1999, 2001). Thus, bodily sensations are a part of the experience of emotion. As you will see in the next sections, however, many other factors play important roles.

## Cannon-Bard Theory

Walter Cannon (1927) did not just criticize the James-Lange theory; he proposed an alternative theory of his own. This theory was later revised by Philip Bard (1934) and is known as the **Cannon-Bard theory of emotion.** Cannon believed that information from the emotional stimulus goes first to the thalamus. From there, the information is simultaneously relayed *both* to the cerebral cortex, where it produces the emotional experience, and to the hypothalamus and autonomic nervous system, where it produces the physiological arousal that prepares the animal to fight, run away, or react in some other way. To Cannon and Bard, the conscious emotional experience and physiological arousal are two simultaneous and largely independent events.

## Cognitive Theory

A third, more contemporary theory of emotion views the *cognitive interpretation* of emotional stimuli—from both outside and inside the body—to be the key event in emotions. Although it is fair today to characterize the **cognitive theory of emotion** as a single theory (Lazarus, 1991; Leventhal & Tomarken, 1986; Scherer, 1997), a number of different individuals contributed different facets of the theory over many years. The key theorists in the development of the cognitive theory of emotion are Magda Arnold (1960), Albert Ellis (1962), and Stanley Schachter and Jerome Singer (1962). According to these theorists, the process of cognitive interpretation in emotions has two steps: (a) the interpretation of stimuli from the environment and (b) the interpretation of stimuli from the body resulting from autonomic arousal. We will look at each of these steps individually.

*Interpretation of Incoming Stimuli.* The cognitive perspective on the interpretation of stimuli relevant to emotions from the external world harkens back to the ancient Greek philosopher Epictetus, who said, "People are not affected by events, but by their interpretations of them." For example, if you receive a box in the mail that makes a ticking sound, will you be happy or afraid? If the return address says the box is from Violet, and Violet is your deadly enemy, you might think it contains a time bomb and feel afraid. If Violet is a loving friend, however, you would open the box feeling happy, expecting to find a clock. In this case, the interpretation of the stimulus, not the stimulus itself, causes the emotional reaction. Thus, in the cognitive theory of emotion, information from the stimulus travels first to the cerebral cortex, where it is both interpreted and experienced. Then a message is sent down to the limbic system and autonomic nervous system that results in physiological arousal.

Evidence supporting this aspect of the cognitive theory has been provided by an experiment in which four groups of college students were shown an upsetting film showing a number of crude, circumcision-like operations conducted without anesthesia as part of the puberty ceremony of an Australian aborigine tribe (Speisman, Lazarus, Mordokoff, & Davison, 1964). One group of students saw the film without a soundtrack. A

**Cannon-Bard theory of emotion**
The theory that conscious emotional experiences and physiological reactions and behavior are relatively independent events.

**cognitive theory of emotion**
The theory that the cognitive interpretation of events in the outside world and stimuli from our own bodies is the key factor in emotions.

second group heard a soundtrack that emphasized the agony experienced by the boys. A third group heard a soundtrack that described the operations in a detached intellectual way. And a fourth group heard a soundtrack that ignored the painful operation by talking about irrelevant details.

Although all of the students saw the same film, the soundtracks apparently had a big effect on their cognitive interpretation of what they saw. The group who heard the soundtrack emphasizing the agony of the operations showed much greater autonomic arousal than did the group with no soundtrack. The soundtrack that emphasized the agony led to an interpretation of the film as a more upsetting stimulus. The groups who heard soundtracks that deemphasized the emotional nature of the events, either by intellectualizing or by ignoring it, showed less autonomic arousal. Apparently, the cognitive interpretation (encouraged by the soundtrack) altered the emotional meaning of the film considerably.

***Interpretation of Body Stimuli.*** The second step in the cognitive theory of emotion is the interpretation of stimuli from within the body that results from autonomic arousal. Cognitive theory resembles the James-Lange theory in emphasizing the importance of internal body stimuli in the experience of emotion, but it goes further in suggesting that cognitive *interpretation* of these stimuli is more important than the internal stimuli themselves.

This aspect of the cognitive theory of emotion was suggested by Stanley Schachter and Jerome Singer (1962). They believe that emotional arousal is diffuse and not specific to the different emotions. That is, the autonomic nervous system and endocrine glands are activated in the same global way regardless of which emotion is being experienced. The internal stimuli from the emotional arousal of the body play an important role in the experience of the emotion, but only through a cognitive interpretation of the *source* of the arousal. For example, if you are all churned up inside after hearing gunshots in your neighborhood, you will interpret the feelings from your body as fear. But if you feel all churned up after a kiss, you will interpret the feelings as love.

Schachter and Singer's addition to cognitive theory helps explain such things as why sexual attraction is often mistaken for love and why frightened hostages often develop friendly feelings toward their captors if they are treated with even a slight amount of respect. Because the autonomic sensations produced in emotional situations are not distinctive, it's easy to misinterpret their meaning. Sexual arousal can be mistaken for love, and fear for friendship, if we interpret the arousal incorrectly.

Schachter and Singer (1962) tested this facet of cognitive theory in an important experiment. People were taken to a laboratory for what they thought would be a study of the effects of a vitamin on vision. They were given an injection of the supposed vitamin and asked to wait with another research participant for the experiment to begin. The other person was actually an actor who worked for the experimenters. The injection contained the hormone epinephrine, a substance that causes arousal of the heart and other organs. Schachter and Singer were interested in how the subjects would cognitively *interpret* this arousal under a number of different circumstances.

The actor behaved in a happy, silly manner with half of the participants; with the other half, he acted angry and walked out of the experiment. As predicted by Schachter and Singer, the behavior of the actor influenced the participants' cognitive interpretations of their own arousal. When they were with a happy actor, they rated themselves as happy; when they were with an angry actor, they interpreted their arousal as anger. Importantly, this effect was found only when the participants were not accurately informed about the true effects of the injection. When they were informed, the behavior of the actor did not influence their emotions—they simply attributed the arousal to the drug.

A much more interesting test of Schachter and Singer's hypothesis about the interpretation of internal arousal in emotions was conducted by Donald Dutton and Arthur Aron (1974). The research participants were unsuspecting males between the ages of 18 and 35 who were visiting the Capilano Canyon in British Columbia, Canada,

"David, you're denying your feelings again, aren't you?"

without a female companion. An attractive female experimenter approached the men and asked them to answer questions as part of a survey that she was supposedly conducting on reactions to scenic attractions. The key item in the study required them to make up a brief story about an ambiguous picture of a woman. Their stories were later scored for the amount of sexual content, which was considered a measure of the amount of sexual attraction that the male participants felt toward the attractive interviewer. To provide a second measure of interpersonal attraction, the interviewer tore off a piece of paper from the survey and gave her name and phone number to a participant, inviting him to call her if he wanted to talk further.

Have I mentioned where the interviews took place? Half of the interviews were conducted in such a way as to create a high level of arousal (fear) in the male, and the other half were conducted to create a low level of arousal. The high-fear interviews were conducted while the males were *on* a 450-foot-long cable and wood suspension bridge with low handrails that stretched across the Capilano Canyon some 230 feet above rocks and shallow rapids. The authors reported that the bridge had "a tendency to tilt, sway, and wobble, creating the impression that one is about to fall over the side" (p. 511). I visited Capilano Canyon a few years ago and walked the suspension bridge, and I can personally attest to the fact that it wobbles, sways, and is generally fearsome! The low-fear interviews were conducted upstream on a solid wooden bridge that is not fear arousing.

The results strongly supported Schachter and Singer's (1962) theory that the autonomic arousal that accompanies all emotions is similar and that it's our cognitive interpretation of the cause of that arousal that is important. The participants who were highly aroused (confirmed by their own later reports) while on the high-fear, swaying suspension bridge made up stories that contained significantly more sexual imagery than did the low-fear participants. The high-fear group was also more than four times as likely to call the female interviewer later. Apparently, the high-fear group interpreted their autonomic arousal as a greater degree of attraction to the interviewer.

Similar enhancement of attraction presumably occurs in other highly arousing situations, such as football games, emergency landings of airplanes, and the like. So be careful to separate all the possible sources of arousal when you are trying to decide if you are in love. On the other hand, if you really want a blind date to be attracted to you, you might arrange to meet him or her on the Capilano Canyon suspension bridge. Of course, there's always the possibility that your date will interpret the arousal as anger toward you for getting him or her up there!

Rainer Reisenzein (1983) of the Free University of Berlin reviewed the experimental evidence relevant to Schachter and Singer's contribution to the cognitive theory of emotion that had been gathered in the 20 years since it was first stated. He concluded that the most convincing support for this theory has come from studies showing that *misinterpreted* arousal can intensify emotional experiences. Recent advances in our ability to measure autonomic arousal suggest that slightly different patterns of arousal may be associated with somewhat different emotions, but these differences are quite subtle (Ekman, Levenson, & Friesen, 1983; Lang, 1995). The basic premise of Schachter and Singer's hypothesis, that the physiological arousal associated with different emotions is pretty much the same, is probably still reasonable in spite of these subtle differences. The interpretation of the arousal is apparently the critical variable in emotions.

The swaying bridge over Capilano Canyon.

The solid bridge over Capilano Canyon.

## The Physiology of Emotion and Lie Detectors

Last night on television the lawyer of a senator who was accused of committing a crime recommended that she take a private *lie-detector test* and that, if she passed it, they should announce the results in a press conference. What is a lie-detector test and how valid is it for the investigation of crimes? In a lie-detector test, the individual is asked questions about the crime while physiological measurements are taken that indicate sympathetic arousal of the autonomic nervous system—such as sweating, blood pressure, heart rate, breathing rate, and muscle tension—using a device called a *polygraph*. This test is based on the assumption that people react emotionally—and therefore autonomically—when they tell lies.

The lie-detector examination typically uses a procedure known as the *guilty knowledge test*. In this procedure, the individual is asked questions about information that

The polygraph, or lie-detector, test assumes that people react emotionally with autonomic arousal when they tell lies.

would be known only by the guilty party. For example, the examiner might ask if the person had stolen a long list of items (e.g., ring, watch, wallet). If the suspect answered no to most of the items but showed reaction in the sympathetic autonomic nervous system only to those items that were actually stolen, the results would suggest the guilt of the suspect. The guilty knowledge test is thought to be necessary because even innocent people often react emotionally to questions such as "Did you rob the Smiths' house?"

Psychologist David Lykken of the University of Minnesota has made a careful and fair-minded study of lie detection over many years. Twenty years ago, he concluded that well-trained lie-detector examiners were reasonably accurate in detecting deception but that the error rate was too high to be acceptable (Lykken, 1979). Based on the accumulation of evidence since then, however, he has more recently concluded that they are not much more accurate than tossing a coin (Lykken, 1998). Understandably, their use has been banned in federal court proceedings, but they are still used in police interrogations and by businesses to screen employees.

## Role of Learning and Culture in Emotions

Most psychologists who specialize in the study of emotions believe that at least the most basic emotions are inborn and do not have to be learned. Cats do not have to be taught how to hiss and arch their backs in rage; dogs do not have to be trained to wag their tails; and people probably do not have to learn their basic emotions, either (Izard & others, 1997). Even children who are deprived of most normal learning experiences because of being born both deaf and blind show normal emotional reactions (Eibl-Eibesfeldt, 1973).

Comparisons of different cultures, however, suggest that learning does play an important role in emotions in two ways. First, cultural learning influences the *expression* of emotions more than what is experienced. For example, some cultures encourage free emotional expression, whereas other cultures teach people, through modeling and reinforcement, to reveal little of their emotions in public. Paul Ekman (1992) of the University of California at San Francisco and his colleague conducted a clever study of the influence of cultural learning on emotional expression. They showed Japanese and American participants films of unpleasant scenes involving pain and injury and videotaped their facial expressions. When the persons from the two cultures were alone, there were no differences in their facial expressions of emotion, but when an authority figure was also present in the room, the "Japanese more than the Americans masked negative expressions with the semblance of a smile" (Ekman, 1992, p. 34). It seems likely that the Japanese cultural prohibition against the expression of negative emotions made the difference.

Culture influences the way we show emotions. For example, the Japanese culture tends to discourage the expression of negative emotions.

A colleague recently drew my attention to a deeply moving example of a similar cultural prohibition against the expression of some emotions in men. In the summer of

1993, one television network covered the evacuation of a few Muslims from war-ravaged Bosnia. As a young boy was handed up to his father on the truck, the boy began to weep. When the father saw this, tears began to roll down his own face. The father immediately turned away from the boy and rearranged the boy so that he could not see the tears on his father's face. The father then appeared to be attempting to distract himself so that he would no longer cry. Much in our cultural learning experiences influences the expression of emotions.

Second, there is accumulating evidence that people in different cultures tend to *interpret* differently those situations that create emotional reactions (Scherer, 1997). This makes perfect sense from the perspective of the cognitive theory of emotion. Recall that the same stimulus situation can elicit very different emotional reactions in two different people if they interpret the situation differently. It seems likely that these differences in our subjective interpretations are the result of different social learning experiences (Bandura, 1977, 1999). Therefore, it makes sense that people raised in different cultures might learn to interpret emotional stimuli differently.

Klaus Scherer (1997) of the University of Geneva conducted a truly international study of this topic by collecting data in 37 countries. In each country, 100 college students were asked to recall situations in which they had experienced each of seven emotions (joy, anger, fear, sadness, disgust, guilt, and shame). They were then asked a number of questions about how they interpreted the emotion-causing stimulus. For example, the following question was used to assess interpretations in terms of morality: "If the event was caused by your own or someone else's behavior, would this behavior itself be judged as improper or immoral by your acquaintances?" Scherer (1997) found many more similarities than differences across cultures, but there were some differences. For example, college students from African countries were more likely to view their negative emotions as being caused by the actions of other people and to interpret the actions that caused their negative emotions as immoral and unjust. In contrast, college students from Latin American countries were less likely to see their negative emotions as being caused by the immoral behavior of others.

Cultural differences in emotion is a new field of inquiry, but one that promises to tell us much about human emotions. If there are important cultural differences in how we interpret and give emotional meaning to the events in our lives, we must understand these differences if the citizens of the world are to fully communicate and cooperate with one another. Much research will be needed, however, to distinguish between the myths and stereotypes that we hold about one another and true cultural differences.

## The Pursuit of Happiness

The Constitution of the United States states that everyone has a right to "life, liberty, and the pursuit of happiness." What makes the pursuit of happiness successful? What factors lead a person to be happy? Is it money, love, or something else? Psychologists have only seriously studied happiness since the last decade of the twentieth century, but a great deal of valuable information has already been learned.

*Does money buy happiness?* Almost three-quarters of entering college students say that being very well off financially is very important or essential to them (Myers, 2000). Does money make you happy? The answer is yes and no. If we look at countries around the world, people in affluent countries are more likely to say that they are happy than people from poorer countries are (Myers, 2000; Plaut, Markus, & Lachman, 2002). The meaning of this correlation is not clear, however, for two reasons. First, the more affluent countries are also the countries with more stable, democratic governments that afford their citizens more rights and freedoms. So it is unclear whether happiness stems from wealth or rights—or both. Second, among the citizens of the United States and other very affluent countries, there is little correlation between a person's income and happiness. After a person's basic needs for food, shelter, and security are met, it is not clear that making a lot of money will make you happy.

*Does having friends and a romantic partner make you happy?* Again, this is not an easy question to answer. In general, people with many friends are a little more likely to say that they are happy than people with fewer friends are. Similarly, both men and women who are married or are in a committed romantic partnership are more likely to report that they are happy than are adults who never have had a partner or spouse (Myers, 2000). It is possible, of course, that happier people are more likely to attract friends and romantic partners, but it seems likely that the social support of friends and partners helps us be happy.

*Do work or hobbies make you happy?* It depends! People who become deeply involved in their daily activities (job, volunteer work, hobby, etc.), who are intrinsically motivated to engage in these activities (who are not just working for the paycheck), and who perceive the challenges as ones they can meet, are the happiest in this important aspect of their lives (Csikzentmihalyi & Csikzentmihalyi, 1988; Massimini & Delle Fave, 2000). Working at a job that is not inherently interesting, or taking up a hobby just to pass the time away, may not contribute significantly to happiness, however.

*Does religion make you happy?* The evidence here is mixed. Some studies suggest that people with strong religious faith are happier than others (Myers, 2000), but other studies suggest that this is not the case (Diener & Seligman, 2002; Lykken & Tellegen, 1996). More research is needed on this topic.

*Are some people inherently more likely to be happy?* As the old adage goes, some people see the glass as half empty, while others view the same glass as half full. Do some people just have a greater tendency to be happy regardless of their circumstances? While it is true that life could deal the most resiliently happy individuals enough tragedy to devastate their lives, there is strong evidence that some people have a knack for making the best of their lives almost regardless of the circumstances. What psychological characteristics seem to contribute to happiness? Current research suggests that four key psychological factors contribute to happiness:

1. People who say they are happy tend to compare themselves less to other people (Lyubomirsky, 2001). They are not in a competition with their friends or neighbors and mostly judge themselves by their own standards.

2. People who are happy are better at seeing the silver linings in their dark clouds (Lyubomirsky, 2001). Although happy people experience the same number of uncontrollable stressful events in their lives as less happy people, they are more likely to believe that they can learn useful lessons from negative events and better themselves. This is partly because happy people see their skills as changeable rather than fixed. If they lose a job, for example, they believe they can learn the skills required of an even better job.

3. To a considerable degree, happiness is linked to our personalities (Diener & Seligman, 2002; Lykken & Tellegen, 1996; Steel & Ones, 2002). We will study personality traits in chapter 12, but for the moment, note that people who score high on measures of "extraversion" (socially outgoing and uninhibited personality) tend to be happier than other people. Not surprisingly, people who score low on the personality trait of "neuroticism" (which means that they do not get upset easily and they recover quickly when they do get upset) also tend to be happy. This association between personality traits and happiness has been found in many cultures (Schimmack & others, 2002).

4. Data from a large and important study of 2,310 middle-aged twins (Lykken & Tellegen, 1996) suggest that about half of the differences in happiness among people is due to genetic factors. This finding implies that much of our happiness depends on our genes, probably because of the considerable influence of genetics on our personality traits. Even if it is true that half of the differences in happiness among people is the result of genetics, however, the other half is in our hands!

Emotions are fascinating psychological states that are difficult to describe and define. Most definitions of emotion, however, contain four elements: (a) the stimulus that provokes the emotion; (b) the positively or negatively toned conscious experience; (c) the state of arousal of the body produced by the autonomic nervous system and endocrine glands; and (d) the behavior that characteristically accompanies emotions. Three primary theories have been proposed to explain emotions: the James-Lange theory, the Cannon-Bard theory, and cognitive theory, each viewing a different relationship between stimulus, experience, arousal, and behavior. Many elements of emotions are apparently inborn in all humans, but learning seems to play a role in determining how much emotion will be displayed, how it will be displayed, and how the stimuli that evoke emotional reactions will be interpreted.

## Review

To be sure that you have learned the key points from the preceding section, cover the list of correct answers and try to answer each question. If you give an incorrect answer to any question, return to the page given next to the correct answer to see why your answer was not correct.

## Check Your Learning

1. _____ are the experiences that give color, meaning, and intensity to our lives.

2. The _____ theory of emotion is the theory that conscious emotional experiences are caused by afferent feedback to the cerebral cortex from visceral organs and muscles.

   a)  Izard                           c)  James-Lange
   b)  Cannon-Bard                      d)  cognitive

3. The _____ theory of emotion is the theory that the *interpretation* of the incoming stimuli and the interpretation of body stimuli together cause the emotional experience.

   a)  cognitive                       c)  Cannon-Bard
   b)  psychoanalytic                  d)  association

4. Cultural learning appears to play a role in the interpretation of emotion-causing stimuli and in the expression of emotions.

   a)  True                            b)  False

1. Think of an intense emotion you have recently experienced and explain the sequence of events according to each of the three theories discussed in the text.

2. What is important to your happiness?

## Thinking Critically about Psychology

**Correct Answers:** 1. Emotions (p. 386),  2. c (p. 388),  3. a (p. 391),  4. a (p. 394).

## ● Aggression: Emotional and Motivational Aspects

Aggression is a topic of paramount importance to the human race. We pride ourselves on being humane creatures who have left the brutal jungle to establish "civilized" societies. But the sad reality is that no other animal species even comes remotely close to our record of violent and harmful acts against members of our own species. Although fights to the death do sometimes occur over mates and territory in lower mammals, and apes do apparently "intentionally murder" other apes on rare occasions, no species rivals the frequency of human aggression. In my lifetime alone, hundreds of millions of humans have been killed by other humans in wars, revolutions, and acts of terrorism.

Violent crimes and murder have always been a part of human societies, but in recent years their frequency has reached unprecedented levels in many parts of the world. In the United States, in spite of recent declines, violence has become the second most common cause of death among 15- to 24-year-olds after accidents, and it is the leading cause of death among African American males (Lore & Schultz, 1993). Perhaps most incomprehensible is the frequency of aggression toward members of one's own family. More than a third of the murders investigated by the FBI have been committed by one family member against another and some 3 percent involve the murder of a child by a parent. Each year in the United States, 4 million husbands and wives violently attack each other, resulting in severe injuries in a quarter million of the cases. Each year, too, 2 million children are kicked, beaten, or punched by their parents.

Why are human beings so aggressive? Can we do anything to curb violence in our society? Aggression is a complex phenomenon with both motivational and emotional aspects that we should carefully examine. Like most important topics in psychology, aggression has been the focus of a great deal of research and theoretical speculation. One view holds that aggression is a natural instinct; another suggests that it's a natural reaction to adverse events such as frustration and pain; and a third viewpoint considers aggression as learned behavior. We will look at these theoretical positions one at a time.

### Freud's Instinct Theory: The Release of Aggressive Energy

Sigmund Freud suggested that all animals, humans included, are born with potent aggressive instincts. These instincts create a drive to commit aggressive acts that must be satisfied. In other words, they create an uncomfortable pressure that must be released in some way. Often, the aggressive instinct is released in an overt act of aggression. But the key to curbing violence, according to **Freud's instinct theory,** lies in finding nonviolent ways to release aggressive energy, such as competing in business or sports, watching aggressive sports, or reading about violent crimes.

Freud's central point that aggression is instinctual has been echoed in modern times by a number of biologists who suggested that violence is necessary for the "survival of the fittest" (Lorenz, 1967). Author Robert Ardrey (1966) put it this way:

> Man is a predator whose natural instinct is to kill with a weapon. The sudden addition of the enlarged brain to the equipment of an armed, already successful, predatory animal created not only the human being but also the human predicament. (p. 332)

The most controversial aspect of Freud's theory is his belief that instinctual aggressive energy must be released in some way. He calls the process of releasing instinctual energy **catharsis.** Freud's suggestion that societies should encourage the nonviolent catharsis of aggressive energy has been much debated. In particular, some psychologists believe that the ways that Freud and his followers have suggested as safe means of catharsis actually have the effect of increasing aggressions. A bit later in this section, we will look at research bearing on this topic.

Human beings are the most aggressive species on the planet, and violence has increased in recent years. What can we do to curb violence in our society?

**Freud's instinct theory**
The theory that aggression is caused by an inborn aggressive instinct.

**catharsis**
The process of releasing instinctual energy.

## Frustration-Aggression Theory

Other psychologists believe, like Freud, that aggression is an inborn part of human nature, but they do not agree that it stems from an ever-present instinctual need to aggress. Instead, they believe that aggression is a natural reaction to the frustration (blocking) of important motives. This **frustration-aggression theory** (Berkowitz, 1993; Dollard, Doob, Miller, Mowrer, & Sears, 1939) suggests, for example, that a child who takes a toy from another child may very well get a sock in the nose, or that a nation that frustrates another nation's desire for oil or for a seaport might become a target of war. People and nations who are frustrated react with anger and aggression. It is not surprising, therefore, that violence is more common among people who live in poverty, as they are chronically frustrated in their attempts to meet even the most basic human needs (Staub, 1996).

In recent years, the frustration-aggression theory has been expanded to include aversive events other than frustration. Anything aversive—from frustration to pain—is said to increase the likelihood of aggression (Berkowitz, 1989). Some of the most interesting research findings on aggression come from studies that link uncomfortable heat with aggression. Although the results of these correlational studies and formal experiments are not completely consistent, they suggest that being exposed to uncomfortable heat may increase the likelihood of aggression (Cohn & Rotton, 1997). The most ambitious and impressive study to date examined the association between higher than usual summer temperatures in the 50 largest cities in the United States and rates of serious and deadly violent crimes (Anderson, Bushman, & Groom, 1997). Controlling for other relevant variables (such as changes in violent crimes over years), the number of summer days with a high temperature exceeding 90 degrees Fahrenheit during 1950–1995 was significantly related to rates of serious and deadly assaults. Consistent with the frustration-aggression hypothesis, rates of nonviolent property crimes were not significantly related to temperature. That is, in this and other studies (Anderson, 2001; Cohn & Rotton, 1997), heat is not associated with crime in general, but only with violent crime. This suggests that heat specifically increases the likelihood of aggression.

Craig Anderson (2001) raised a cogent concern about global warming. If trends in world temperature continue upward and if violent crime is truly linked to high temperature, as it appears to be, then an increase of 8 degrees in average temperatures in North America could be associated with a 20 percent increase in serious and deadly assault.

**frustration-aggression theory**
The theory that aggression is a natural reaction to the frustration of important motives.

## Social Learning Theory

To Freud, people have a need to aggress that must be relieved. According to the frustration-aggression hypothesis, people aggress only in response to frustrating or other adverse circumstances. In contrast, Albert Bandura (1973) and other social learning theorists believe that people are aggressive only if they have *learned* that it's to their benefit to be aggressive. Social learning theorists do not deny that frustration can make us more likely to be angry and aggressive, but they state that we will act aggressively in reaction to frustration only if we have learned to do so. We must see others be successful by being aggressive, or we must win victories of our own through aggression (make someone stop bothering us or take away someone else's possession) before we will become aggressive people.

Social learning theorists directly conflict with Freud on the topic of catharsis. Freudian psychologists believe that we must find cathartic outlets for our aggressive energy to keep it from emerging as actual aggression. They recommend such things as yelling when angry, hitting a punching bag, and vicariously experiencing aggression by reading violent books or watching violence on television. Social learning theorists argue that these activities will not decrease violence but instead will *increase* it by teaching violence to the person (Bandura, 1973).

The evidence against the idea of vicarious catharsis through watching violence on television is quite clear. Televised violence does not decrease violence in those who watch it; it *increases* it. The evidence is particularly clear for children. As discussed more

Freudian psychologists believe releasing aggressive feelings in a nonharmful way, like games, reduces the chance of violent behavior. However, social learning theorists believe that watching or practicing aggressive behavior, even in nonharmful ways, can actually increase the chances for violence.

completely in chapters 2 and 6, evidence indicates that watching televised violence increases violent play, increases actual violence, and makes children less likely to intervene in the violent acts of other children (Anderson & Bushman, 2001; Bandura, 1973; Liebert & others, 1983). Because 75 percent of the television programs in the United States contain violence (compared, for example, with 10 percent in Sweden), the issue of televised violence is understandably one of national concern (Wood, Wong, & Chachere, 1991).

### Violent Youth Gangs

The United States has long had a problem with crimes committed by urban adolescents who have joined together in gangs, but there has been a recent increase in both the number of youths in gangs and the violence that they commit. Psychologist Ervin Staub (1996) has provided a plausible theory to explain the increase in gang violence in America that incorporates elements of both the frustration-aggression and social learning theories of aggression. According to Staub (1996), the problem begins in the homes of young adolescents who later join gangs. When parents use harsh physical punishment to discipline their children, they are modeling aggression for the child to imitate. In addition, the child is likely to react to the pain of the harsh punishment with even more aggressive misbehavior. This often leads the parent to write off the aggressive child as "no good" and to cease to supervise his or her activities—giving the child the freedom to spend time with older gang members.

This harsh and inadequate parenting creates children who act in aggressive ways toward their classmates at school, leading to rejection by most of their peers—most kids fear and dislike aggressive bullies. But gangs composed of other aggressive youths offer a place for aggressive kids to belong who have been rejected by their families and peers. The person most likely to respect an aggressive adolescent is another aggressive adolescent who has been rejected by family and peers.

Unfortunately, the gangs provide a place to belong at the cost of encouraging strong feelings of "us" versus "them." Gangs encourage their members to hate and demean the members of other gangs and to think of them as an "opposing army." Conflicts between rival gangs are made more frequent and intense because the sale of drugs by gangs gives poor adolescents their first opportunity to rise above the grinding frustrations of poverty.

Like all of us, youths in gangs live in a society that bombards them with the message that violence is an effective way to solve problems. They see it on television shows, at the movies, and just by observing violence in their homes and neighborhoods. If they watch the news on television, they see a nation that applauds violence when the "us" is the United States and the "them" is, for example, the army of Iraq. We give celebrations in honor of military leaders who organize the killing of hundreds of thousands of the enemy in wars, and we often encourage our war heroes to run for president. All of this provides a clear social learning experience that killing your enemies not only is okay but also is a source of great pride. Finally, the widespread availability of highly lethal automatic weapons in our society makes it easy for the small armies that we call "gangs" to be well armed. And guns in the hands of aggressive youths who believe that they are at war with other gangs often means death.

Research is desperately needed to test this and other theories of the rise of gang violence in the United States. Staub's theory is promising, but our society must be willing to invest in research on gangs, domestic violence, warfare, and other forms of violence if we are going to find ways to curb aggression.

## Review

Aggression is a topic of fear and concern to everyone. Three major theories have been proposed to explain human aggression. Sigmund Freud proposed that aggression is the result of an inborn motive to aggress that needs to be released. The frustration-aggression theory suggests that aggression is an inborn reaction to frustration and pain. Social learning theory suggests that aggression is not an inborn behavior but that people will aggress only if they have learned to do so. The most interesting conflict between these theories concerns Freud's prescription for reducing violence in society. Freudian psychologists suggest that an outlet—catharsis—must be found for the aggressive motive but that this can be a nonviolent outlet, such as hitting a punching bag or watching violence on television. Much research on this topic suggests that Freud was wrong and supports the social learning theory view that such supposed outlets merely teach people to be more violent.

## Check Your Learning

To be sure that you have learned the key points from the preceding section, cover the list of correct answers and try to answer each question. If you give an incorrect answer to any question, return to the page given next to the correct answer to see why your answer was not correct.

Match each definition with one of the following terms:

**Terms:**

  a)   social learning theory
  b)   Freud's instinct theory
  c)   frustration-aggression theory

1.  According to _____, aggression is caused by an inborn aggressive instinct.

2.  According to _____, aggression is a natural reaction to aversive events, such as frustration, pain, and heat.

3.  According to _____, people act aggressively only if they have learned to do so.

## Thinking Critically about Psychology

1.  In your opinion, which theory of aggression offers the best ideas for reducing gang violence?

2.  Does the link that has been established between aggression and violence in television prove that social learning theorists are correct? Why or why not?

Correct Answers:   1. b (p. 398),   2. c (p. 399),   3. a (p. 400).

## Should You Try to Lose Weight? If So, How?

We live in a society that values thinness. Women are told in countless subtle—and sometimes blatant—ways that you must be thin to find love, to be successful, and to be happy. And men are told that fat is the equivalent of softness, weakness, and unattractiveness. Watch television one evening this week: You will see sleek and slender women and men working as attorneys, physicians, and executives. The mechanics and secretaries are much more likely to be heavy (except for the secretary for whom the husband leaves his shrill and plump wife). Who falls in love on television or in the movies? With few exceptions, it is the slender men who fall in love with slender women, and vice versa. The chubbier ones are the humorous friends who rarely find romance and never receive the big promotion at work. Drew Carey is a welcome exception but even his television character is played for laughs.

When these shows break for a commercial, we are offered countless ways to deal with the fact that we aren't the fortunate skinny ones. Advertisements for liquid diets, artificial sweeteners, and weight-loss plans are shown many times each day.

How many of us are actually "overweight" to the extent that it poses at least a minor health risk? In the United States, 31 percent of men and 24 percent of women are overweight (about half of whom are severely overweight in medical terms). Now, how many of us think we are overweight? In the United States, 37 percent of men and 52 percent of women feel that they are overweight (Brownell & Rodin, 1994). That means that a few more men think that they are overweight than actually are overweight, but more than *twice* as many women think they are overweight than is actually the case. As a result, 24 percent of men and a whopping 40 percent of women are on a diet at any one time. Americans, especially American women, are very likely to decide we are too fat and try to do something about it

The pressure to be thin leads to unhealthy eating patterns for many people. If this celery is not part of a balanced diet, this woman's desire to be thin may harm her health.

through dieting—even if we are not actually overweight.

We are so bombarded by the message that thin is desirable that it seems to be an unquestionable truth. It is not; it is a belief that happens to have been part of American culture since the 1960s, but not all peoples during all times have considered thin to be beautiful. Take a trip to an art museum and look at the beautiful nude women painted by artists during the seventeenth and eighteenth centuries. By current U.S. standards, these women are overweight. Even looking back to the 1950s in the United States, the women that men found to be ideal sex symbols (Marilyn Monroe, Jane Russell, and Jayne Mansfield) probably would be on diets today. Furthermore, there are considerable differences among different ethnic groups in the United States today concerning ideal body weight, with whites having stricter standards than most other groups. In addition, in many contemporary non-Western cultures, much higher amounts of body fat are considered to be beautiful. For example, the Anay tribe of Nigeria encourage weight gain in women, with the ideal body weight being in excess of 400 pounds.

People in our society, however, are unquestionably prejudiced against persons who are overweight. If you are considerably heavier than is desirable in our culture, you may be less likely to land the job, get the promotion, or attract the person you wish to attract. That is certainly not to say that you will necessarily be a less successful or happy person, but you may find that you have one strike against you.

Should you try to lose weight, then, to avoid the prejudice? It is important to keep in mind that our heredity and history of eating and exercise determine how thin we can be to a great extent. Some people can eat whatever they wish and remain thin through long periods of their lives. Others will never be able to reach the cultural ideal no matter how much they diet and exercise and would have great difficulty staying there if they were to reach it (Brownell, 1991; Devlin & others, 2000).

The most important issue to consider in thinking about dieting is that it can be dangerous. The constant pressure that women, in particular, receive to be thin leads many to dangerous patterns of eating. Some starve themselves until they reach an unhealthy body weight, sometimes to the point that they are considered to exhibit *anorexia nervosa*. Others find themselves purging (inducing vomiting) after eating large amounts of calories, sometimes to the extent of being considered to exhibit *bulimia.* Although the most serious cases of these disorders involve much more than a simple desire to be thin (distorted body image, compulsively rigid eating patterns, etc.) (Ruderman & Besbeas, 1992), the pressure to be thin undoubtedly leads to unhealthy patterns of eating in many Americans.

The most common threat to health, however, is so-called *yo-yo dieting.* Many dieters lose quite a few pounds, gain it back, then diet again. At first, their weight goes down and up with their eating habits like a yo-yo, but soon dieting stops working. What has happened? The body's internal *set point* mechanism for regulating body fat does not like to allow the body to lose fat. The body seems to think that fat is necessary for survival in case a famine strikes. When you diet and lose weight once, the body thinks that a famine has struck, and it learns from the experience. The next time that you diet, the body rapidly compensates for the lost calories by slowing down the rate at which you use energy *(metabolism)*. So, instead of causing you to lose weight on your next diet, your reduced intake of food causes your metabolism to slow down enough to offset the reduced calories (Steen, Oppliger, & Brownell, 1988; Thompson, Jarvie, Lahey, & Cureton, 1982). Thus, yo-yo dieting is eventually self-defeating. More important, it is dangerous. Repeated yo-yo dieting has been found to be associated with increased heart disease in the Framingham health study, probably because it leads to fluctuations in fat levels in the bloodstream (Lissner & others, 1991). Thus, dieting can be dangerous to your health.

So, all things considered, should you diet? If you do not consider yourself to be overweight, you are probably convinced beyond a doubt that dieting is ridiculous. However, if you consider yourself to be overweight and were planning on losing a few pounds, you might be much less convinced. In fact, you may be quite confused and concerned at this point.

Fortunately, the alternatives are not simply to diet or not to diet. Instead of dieting, we have the alternative of making permanent lifestyle changes in eating and exercise. These changes will probably improve your health and will result in the loss of some weight. If you top off these changes in eating and exercise by giving up the wish to look like a star of *Friends,* you will really be ahead of the game.

Consider the following suggestions:

1. *Don't "diet."* Do not try to regulate your weight by eating less for a brief period of time than is comfortable or healthy for you. In other words, do not go on diets. Weight that is lost in that way will almost always be regained when you return to a more natural pattern of eating (Brownell, 1991). You may recall the experience with dieting of television personality Oprah Winfrey in 1990. She dieted and her weight fell from 190 to 123, but when she stopped the diet, she regained all of the lost weight and some additional weight. In 1993,

Oprah lost 60 pounds again, but regained it. Her story is not at all unusual, because the great majority of persons who lose weight through dieting regain the weight after stopping the diet, often leading to a pattern of yo-yo dieting.

2. *Eat differently.* Instead of dieting, commit yourself to a lifelong pattern of eating *differently* that you can live with. You do not have to starve yourself; you just need to choose your calories carefully. Reducing the amount of saturated fat that you eat in the form of meat and dairy products makes terrific sense, and it also reduces your chance of cardiovascular disease and some forms of cancer. Cheeseburgers are *dangerous* to your health!

Second, reducing the amount of processed sugar you eat makes sense because sugar gives you calories with very little nutrition and only briefly satisfies your hunger. When you eat sugar, you feel an immediate drop in hunger, but the sugar causes a sudden increase in insulin levels that typically purges the blood of more sugar than you ate, making you feel more hungry in an hour or two (Rodin, 1985). Most of us also think of candy and soft drinks as high-energy food that can work as a pick-me-up when we are tired. To test this idea, Robert Thayer (1987) and a group of his students conducted a study of the effects of eating a candy bar on feelings of energy and general tension. He compared the effects of eating a candy bar with taking a brisk 10-minute walk. Eating a candy bar in the morning when energy levels tend to be low did produce an increase in feelings of energy that lasted for two hours. On the other hand, eating a candy bar in the afternoon when energy levels tend to be higher led to a brief increase in energy that dissipated in an hour and was followed by a *decrease* in energy level two hours after eating the candy bar. In contrast, the 10-minute walk always led to a greater increase in energy and a reduction in feelings of tension.

Thus, eating differently means focusing on complex carbohydrates

(fruits and vegetables) and protein and reducing saturated fat and sugar intake.

One way to eat less and still feel satisfied with meals is to eat fewer foods in each meal. We need to eat a variety of foods to have a balance of nutrients, but we eat more when there are more different foods on our plate at each meal (Raynor & Epstein, 2001). Balance your selection of foods over several days, but instead of having three or four different foods on your plate, try two. You'll become satiated (full) quicker on two foods than when you have the variety of four foods to eat.

3. *Emphasize exercise.* Increased exercise is beneficial in many ways. We are told that a pound of body fat is the equivalent of 3,500 calories, so if you cut down by 500 calories a day, you should lose a pound every week (7 days × 500 calories = 3,500 calories in a week). Right? That arithmetic works only if your metabolism does not *slow down* by 500 calories a day to offset the loss of calories taken in.

As I said, *the body does not like to lose fat.* As a result, you must *increase* your metabolism by increasing your activity level (Thompson & others, 1982). If you burn calories through regular and moderate aerobic exercise, you stand a much better chance of losing weight than by restricting calories alone for two reasons. First, depending on your level of fitness and what is sensible for you, a good workout might burn 300 to 500 calories by itself. But, more important, *regular* moderate aerobic exercise keeps your metabolism from falling if you reduce your calorie intake (Wadden & others, 1997). In addition, of course, exercise is beneficial to your cardiovascular health and helps promote a relaxed sense of well-being.

4. *Do not give up because of lapses in your healthy lifestyle.* We're only human; it's easy to commit to a lifestyle change in eating, but many things can knock you off your healthy course. A week spent with your family, a vacation trip, exams, and other things can disrupt your

*(continued)*

Regular moderate aerobic exercise keeps your metabolism up and provides important cardiovascular conditioning.

plans to exercise and eat right. This is inevitable, but it need not mean that your plans to eat better and exercise more are impossible dreams. Just start exercising again.

It is very important to understand why lapses occur. First, they are caused by temptations (or incentives; see page 372). We are more likely to eat the things that we have decided not to eat if they are right there in front of us. For example, we had friends over last night, and, although I know it is not smart, we served them chocolate cake for dessert. Unfortunately, the rest of it is still in the kitchen and it is singing to me—begging and pleading, in a lovely singing voice —for me to feast on it. I am resisting now because I know you are watching me and I have to set a good example, but what will

happen when I turn off the word processor? Tempting foods are incentives that stimulate hunger— avoid them. (Excuse me for a moment while I throw out the cake.)

Second, lapses in healthy lifestyles are caused by temporary losses in self-control. These losses in self-control can be caused by a variety of things, but high on the list are boredom and bad moods (Grilo, Shiffman, & Wing, 1989). If you sit around all day watching boring television, you may find yourself eating much more than usual. Similarly, a lousy mood caused by a bad day at work, the breakup of a relationship, or some other cause often leads to an attitude of "Who cares if I eat well or exercise? What good is it doing me?" Maybe understanding this fact will help you delay your decision about ending your fitness program until after a bad mood passes. Besides, exercise is a great natural antidote to a bad mood.

In addition to knowing what causes lapses, it is essential to understand that they are almost *inevitable*. Everyone has them, and that's okay. The secret to long term fitness is understanding that one piece of cake won't wreck your improved lifestyle unless you stop your fitness program because of it. If you miss exercising for a few days or overeat on a trip, don't say, "See! I knew I couldn't stick to a healthy lifestyle! I'm a potato chips and ice cream person, and that's that!" Instead, just realize that you have suffered a minor setback and get right back on your plan. People who have lifelong patterns of

Lapses are almost inevitable when you change to a healthy eating style. It's important to remember that setbacks are only temporary and to get back to your plan as soon as you can.

healthy eating and exercise aren't people who never have lapses; they are people who never let a lapse become permanent.

I should hasten to add that there are exceptions to every rule. Some people *can* go on a diet, lose weight, and keep it off for long periods of time. In addition, there are people who should lose weight for health reasons (obesity, diabetes, etc.). For these persons, assistance from experts who have developed effective weight-control strategies would be wise (Grilo & others, 1989). ■

---

## Summary

Chapter 10 defines motivation and emotion, discusses primary motives and psychological motives, and explores three theories of emotions. The topic of aggression is included in the chapter because of its close link to both emotion and motivation.

I.  *Motivation* refers to those factors that activate behavior and give it direction. Emotions are positive or negative feelings usually accompanied by behavior and physiological arousal that are generally reactions to stimulus situations.

II. Primary motives are human motives that stem from the need for those things that keep a person alive.

    A.    Homeostatic mechanisms in the body sense imbalances of essential life elements and stimulate actions that will restore the proper balance.

    B.    Hunger is biologically regulated by three centers in the hypothalamus.

        1.    Rats will not eat if their lateral feeding center is destroyed.

        2.    Rats become hyperphagic (obese because of overeating) if the ventromedial satiety center is destroyed.

        3.    The paraventricular nucleus of the hypothalamus regulates blood sugar levels.

    C.    Cues for regulating hunger on a daily basis are stomach contractions and blood-sugar levels; body fat is apparently involved in the long-term regulation of hunger.

    D.    Learning influences when we eat, what we eat, and how much we eat. Hunger, as well as other motives, is affected by incentives—external cues that activate motives.

    E.    The hypothalamus also controls thirst. Cues used to regulate drinking are mouth dryness, loss of water by cells, and reductions in blood volume.

    F.    Learning influences drinking behavior, and incentives can activate thirst.

III.  Psychological motives are "needs" in the sense that the individual's happiness and well-being, but not survival, depend on these motives.

    A.    Humans and other animals have an inborn motive to seek an optimal level of arousal. The Yerkes-Dodson law states that if arousal is too low, performance will be poor, but if it is too high, performance may become disrupted and disorganized.

    B.    Individuals high in affiliation motivation tend to prefer being with others.

    C.    Achievement motivation is the psychological need for success. People are motivated to achieve by different combinations of:

        1.    Desire to learn and master new topics and skills.

        2.    Desire to do better than others.

        3.    Fear of failure.

    D.    Motivation to achieve is reduced by fear of success in some individuals.

    E.    Intrinsic motivation refers to motives stimulated by the inherent nature of the activity. External motivation is motivation stimulated by external rewards.

    F.    According to Maslow, motives are organized in a hierarchy arranged from the most basic to the most personal and advanced.

IV.  Emotions are the experiences that give color, meaning, and intensity to our lives.

    A.    Theories that attempt to explain emotions include the James-Lange theory, the Cannon-Bard theory, and the cognitive theory.

    B.    Most psychologists believe that many basic emotions are primarily inborn but that learning also plays an important role in emotions.

V.  Aggression is a complex phenomenon that is not yet fully understood.

    A.    Freud suggested that all people are born with potent aggressive instincts that are released through catharsis.

    B.    Other psychologists say aggression is a reaction to the frustration (blocking) of important motives or other aversive events (the frustration-aggression hypothesis).

    C.    Social learning theorists explain aggression as learned behavior.

## Resources

1. For an overview of human motivation, see Franken, R. E. (1998). *Human motivation* (4th ed.). Monterey, CA: Wadsworth.

2. For a more advanced discussion of the psychology of emotion, see Ekman, P., & Davidson, R. J. (1994). *The nature of emotion: Fundamental questions.* New York: Oxford University Press.

3. For a more advanced overview of the psychology of hunger and eating, see Capaldi, E. D. (1996). *Why we eat what we eat: The psychology of eating.* Washington, DC: American Psychological Association. Also see Devlin, M. J., Yanovski, S. Z., & Wilson, G. T. (2000). Obesity: What mental health professionals need to know. *American Journal of Psychiatry, 157,* 854–866.

4. For a wonderful book on biological and psychological aspects of emotion, see Ledoux, R. (1998). *The emotional brain.* New York: Touchstone.

5. For psychological perspectives on human aggression, see Bandura, A. (1973). *Aggression: A social learning analysis.* Englewood Cliffs, NJ: Prentice-Hall; Lore, R. K., & Schultz, L. A. (1993). Control of human aggression: A comparative perspective. *American Psychologist, 48,* 16–25; and Hamburg, D. A., George, A., & Ballentine, K. (1999). Preventing deadly conflict: The critical role of leadership. *Archives of General Psychiatry, 56,* 971–977.

## Visual Review of Theories of Motivation and Emotion

This visual review may help you consolidate your learning of some of the information presented in this chapter in a visual format. Be sure not to limit your review to these diagrams, but because they are key to understanding some of the important concepts in this chapter, mastering them should help you master the entire chapter.

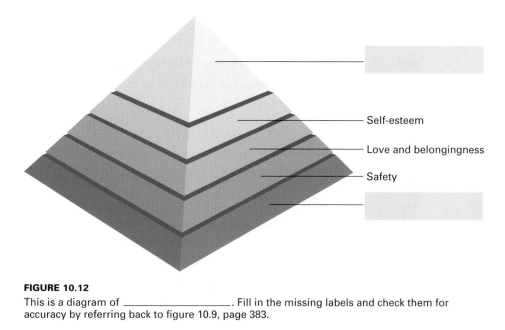

Self-esteem

Love and belongingness

Safety

**FIGURE 10.12**
This is a diagram of _____. Fill in the missing labels and check them for accuracy by referring back to figure 10.9, page 383.

**Answer:** Maslow's hierarchy of motives.

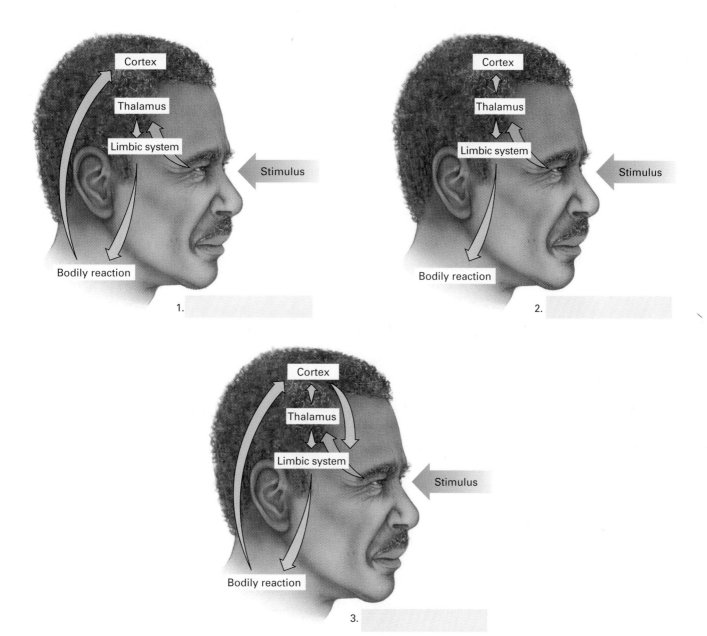

1. _____

2. _____

3. _____

**FIGURE 10.13**

These three figures illustrate each of the three theories of emotion covered in this chapter. Write the name of the theory next to each illustration and check your answers for accuracy by referring back to figure 10.11, page 389.

# Chapter Outline

# Gender and Sexuality

## PROLOGUE

What are women like? What are men like? Based on what you have observed, what psychological characteristics do you think distinguish women from men? In general, are women strong, caring, and wise? Are women less aggressive and independent than men? How about emotional and fearful—are those characteristic traits of women or men? Let me tell you how the great anthropologist Margaret Mead (who is pictured on the opposite page) answered these questions about women and men—she said the answers depend on their culture.

Mead studied many remote cultures during the 1920s to learn how cultures shape people through social learning. The topic of one of her most famous books was the differences between women and men in different cultures (Mead, 1935). She said that, among the Arapesh people of New Guinea, neither men nor women were likely to be aggressive or hostile. They showed very little competitiveness but worked together on joint projects, such as farming, that benefited everyone in the tribe equally. Mead described both men and women as maternal, gentle, and actively involved in raising their children. Jealousy, envy, and conflict, even between parents and adolescents, were almost nonexistent.

The Mundugamor people were quite different from the Arapesh, however. For example, both men and women were highly competitive and physically aggressive, and both found child rearing to be an unrewarding burden. Gentleness and caring were rare in dealing with children, who were required to be independent from an early age.

Among the Arapesh, therefore, both men and women displayed traits that would have been considered "feminine" in American culture, whereas both women and men displayed stereotypically "masculine" traits among the Mundugamor. Mead also described the Tchambuli people. Marked differences existed between men and women among these people, but they were the opposite of American culture. Women held the power in the village and were preoccupied with farming, fishing, and manufacturing, whereas the men played a passive, secondary role.

What are women and men like, then? According to Margaret Mead, it depends on the ways they have been shaped by their culture. Not everyone shares this view, however.

This chapter discusses two topics that are often referred to by the same name —sex: (a) the gender of a person—male or female—and (b) sexual behavior. Much of who you are and what you do is related to your gender and sexuality. Your experiences as a young boy or girl, the expectations that you learned from society of what it means to be a woman or a man, and how you view the sexual aspects of yourself are central to your total being.

We will first discuss gender identity, gender roles, and sexual orientation. The ways in which we view our gender and our sexual orientation are a product of both biological and psychological factors. These factors result in some differences between men and women in Western cultures, but we will find that women and men are more similar in psychological terms than they are different.

## Key Terms

Starting with a brief history of the scientific study of sexuality, we will next focus our attention on the biological and psychological aspects of sexual motivation and the sexual response cycle. We will describe some common problems of sexuality and their solutions, will discuss atypical and abnormal sexuality, and finally will turn our attention to several social problems associated with human sexuality, including sexual violence and sexually transmitted diseases. ■

## Gender and Sexual Orientation

We will begin our discussion of gender and sex with a detailed look at the psychological aspects of being a male or female. We will look at the development of the identity and behaviors associated with gender and will look at similarities and differences between women and men. We will also look at the related topic of sexual orientation—the gender to whom a person is drawn romantically and sexually.

A person's **sex** is defined by his or her male or female genitals. **Gender,** in contrast, is the psychological experience of one's sex (Gentile, 1993). In most cases, a person's sex and gender are the same, but not always. As we will see later in this chapter, it is possible for persons with male genitals to feel that their gender is female and vice versa.

It will help advance our discussion to distinguish between two important aspects of gender: gender identity and gender roles. **Gender identity** is the subjective experience of being a male or a female. As is true for all aspects of personal identity, gender identity is a part of our personalities and a central component of our self-concepts. **Gender role,** on the other hand, refers to all of the behaviors that communicate to others the degree to which we are "masculine" or "feminine" in the terms defined by our culture (Money, 1987, 1988). Thus, your gender role is the outward behavioral expression of your gender identity. Gender roles vary from culture to culture and provide a set of expectations for persons on the basis of their sex.

The term *sexuality* refers to the behaviors in which we engage to obtain sexual pleasure and to all of the feelings and beliefs that are interwoven with sexual behavior. One aspect of our psychological selves that is very much a part of both our sexuality and our gender identity is sexual orientation—our tendency to prefer romantic and sexual partners of the same or different sex. This chapter will discuss all of these aspects of gender and sex.

### Gender Identity and Gender Roles

Gender identity develops early in infancy. Immediately after the infant is born (and sometimes well before birth through ultrasound imaging) the newborn is identified as either male or female based on her or his genitals. The parents select a name appropriate to the baby's gender and greet the newborn infant with cultural expectations for the behavior of boys or girls. Children quickly learn the gender behaviors that are expected of them. Parents, other family members, peers, teachers, and others communicate their behavioral expectations for girls and boys in mostly subtle, but very effective, ways.

Gender roles are the behaviors and characteristics that a culture expects of males and females based on their biological sex. Members of a culture classify behaviors as to whether they are appropriate and expected of males and females. *Feminine* behaviors are expected of females, and *masculine* behaviors are expected of males.

Early in the study of gender roles, masculinity and femininity were thought of as discrete categories (you were either masculine or feminine) that matched exactly with a person's biological sex. More recent views, however, have conceived of gender roles as being a graded continuum, with people displaying varying degrees of *both* masculinity and femininity (Bem, 1974; Spence & Helmreich, 1978). There are two reasons for this change in thinking about gender roles. First, masculinity and femininity are not opposites of each other but, rather, are two separate dimensions. And second, both women and men can be both masculine and feminine. A person who has both masculine and

---

**sex**
The distinction between male and female based on biological characteristics.

**gender**
The psychological experience of being male or female.

**gender identity**
One's view of oneself as male or female.

**gender role**
The behaviors consistent with being male or female in a given culture.

**sexual orientation**
The tendency to prefer romantic and sexual partners of the same or different sex.

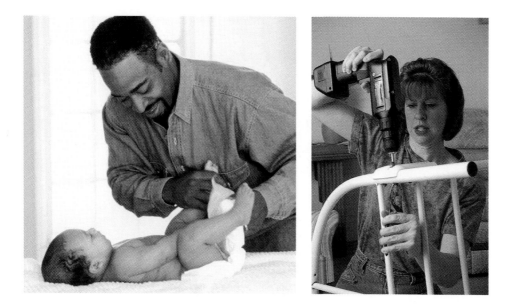

Androgynous men and women combine the best characteristics of the stereotypical masculine and feminine roles.

feminine characteristics is referred to as **androgynous.** For example, in the United States today, a woman or man who is sensitive to others, nurturing, and emotionally expressive (traditionally feminine traits) and strong, independent, and competitive (masculine traits) would be considered to be androgynous.

There is considerable evidence that people who are androgynous are more likely to adapt well to a variety of situations because they are more flexible in their approach to life's demands (Garcia, 1982; Taylor & Hall, 1982). Let's consider a simple example: A friend of mine named Kate was driving her 7-year-old friend, Kevin, to the library one afternoon when she had a sudden blowout in her car. The tire ruptured with a loud bang, and the car skidded and wobbled for a few frightening moments until Kate brought it under control. Kate heaved a sigh of relief, then spent a few minutes calming her young friend (a traditionally feminine behavior). Soon they were both belly-laughing at their inelegant halt on the side of the road. Then, she efficiently changed the tire (a traditionally masculine behavior) and drove Kevin to the library. Kate's behavior was wonderfully androgynous in that it contained the most adaptive elements of both masculine and feminine genders. Today, a growing number of men and women easily cross traditional lines of gender roles.

**androgynous**
Having both typical feminine and masculine characteristics.

## Gender Similarities and Gender Differences

Are there important psychological differences between women and men? This is not an easy question to answer for many reasons, some of which are scientific and some of which are not. Alice Eagly (1995) of Northwestern University has written, "When psychologists publish research that compares the behavior of women and men, they face political as well as scientific issues" (p. 145). The political issue is that some people—women and men alike—welcome studies that indicate that women and men are different, whereas others believe that it encourages a sexist view of women. Moreover, from a purely scientific perspective, it may be premature to reach any firm questions about psychological differences between the sexes at this point. Research is progressing at such a rapid pace that opinions are still changing.

In this section, we will summarize hundreds of well-designed studies of gender differences. Only differences that have been replicated in multiple studies are presented. After describing these gender differences, we will discuss contemporary theories of their origins. As you read this section, please note that *average* differences are described in this section. It is important, therefore, to remember that many women and men differ considerably from the "average" for their genders. For that reason, we must be careful not

**FIGURE 11.1**

The number of persons receiving each score (from the lowest on the left, to the highest on the right) on a test of mathematical ability. The mean score for males is a little higher (a little more to the right) than the mean score for females, but there is tremendous overlap in the scores of males and females. However, note that more females receive the score that is the mean for females (higher peak at the mean) than is the case for males. Similarly, the scores of females are more tightly grouped around their mean than are the scores of males. This greater spread in male scores results in more males than females receiving both extremely high scores and extremely low scores on such tests.

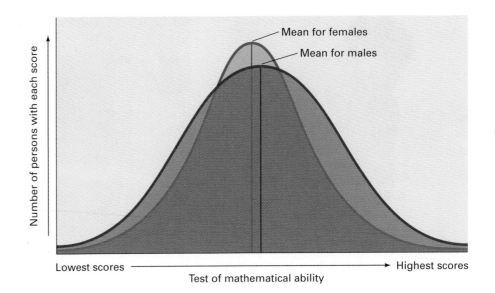

to let scientific evidence about average differences reinforce prejudicial gender stereotypes. The only fair way to deal with people is to evaluate them one at a time. Still, the study of gender differences is of great importance if kept in context.

### Gender Differences in Physical Strength and Skills

Before we consider psychological differences, we need to note some physical differences that will be important in our discussion of theories of the origins of gender differences. Only women can be pregnant, give birth, and breastfeed infants. In addition, on the average, men have greater upper-body strength than women. There is also clear evidence that men typically can throw objects farther and throw them with greater accuracy (Buss, 1995). Although these strength and throwing advantages are of little importance in contemporary life, many psychologists believe physical and reproductive differences tell us something about the origins of gender differences (Buss, 1995; Eagly & Wood, 1999; Wood & Eagly, 2002).

### Gender Differences in Cognitive Ability and Achievement

Overall, women and men are more similar in terms of cognitive ability and academic achievement than they are different. As shown in table 11.1, there are no gender differences in achievement in many school subjects, from English literature to psychology, but there are some areas in which women excel and some in which men excel. On average, women perform better than men in a range of language skills, verbal and spatial memory, perceptual speed, and fine motor skills, whereas men perform better than women in mathematics, science, and social studies (Stumpf & Stanley, 1998). Most of these gender differences are quite small, however. Only one difference in cognitive performance is moderately large: On the average, men tend to receive higher scores on tests of spatial and mechanical reasoning (Stumpf & Stanley, 1998).

Even when gender differences in average cognitive performance are small, however, the implications of that difference can be considerable. Consider the data on mathematical ability presented in figure 11.1. This figure presents the scores of many women and men arranged from the lowest to the highest score from left to right. The vertical height of the curves represents the number of women or men who received each score. Although the mean score of men is slightly higher than the mean score of women, the size of this difference is quite small compared with the range of differences *within* each gender. For example, the highest-scoring males differ from the lowest-scoring males *far more* than the average female and male differ from one another. Thus, even though the

| Table 11.1   Consistently Identified Gender Differences in Cognitive Ability and Achievement | |
| --- | --- |
| **On the average, women score higher than men on tests of:** | **On the average, men score higher than women on tests of:** |
| Language skills | Spatial and mechanical reasoning |
| Reading comprehension | Mathematics achievement |
| Spelling | Science achievement |
| Verbal and spatial memory | Computer science |
| Perceptual speed | Social studies achievement |
| Fine motor skills | Electronics, automotive, and shop skills |

**Sources:** Benbow & others, 2000; Buss, 1995; Eagly, 1995; Eagly & Wood, 1999; Halpern, 1997; Hedges & Nowell, 1995; Hyde & Plant, 1995; Keenan & Shaw, 1997; Seidlitz & Diener, 1998; Steele, 1997; Stumpf & Stanley, 1998.

mean score for men is higher than the mean score for women, many women exceed the mean score for males. Why, then, is the implication of this small difference important enough to discuss?

Note in figure 11.1 that the scores of women are also bunched more tightly around the mean score than are the scores of men (Hedges & Nowell, 1995). That is, the scores of men are spread out more in both directions from the average score. When both the small gender difference in mean scores and the small gender difference in the degree of spread of scores around the mean are considered together, the implication is important. Although scores at the highest end of the scale are uncommon for both men and women, they are much more common for men than women. Indeed, about seven times as many males as females place in the top 1 percent on tests of mathematical ability used in college applications (Benbow & others, 2000; Hedges & Nowell, 1995). This helps explain why a small difference in average performance on such tests could result in many fewer women being admitted to top science and engineering programs—they are less likely to receive the highest scores on entrance exams. On the other hand, males also receive the lowest scores.

Persons with very high mathematics scores represent only a small portion of the workforce, even in scientific and engineering fields. A more powerful reason for the greater success of men in scientific and technological fields may be prejudicial barriers erected against women, and barriers in the minds of women themselves. It is very important to note that women receive *higher* school grades in mathematics courses at all grade levels, even though their average scores on tests that measure mathematical ability are slightly lower. This suggests that women are actually *better* prepared for careers in scientific and technological fields. Women, however, tend to attribute their success in mathematics courses to hard work, whereas men are more likely to attribute their success to their intellectual ability (Kimball, 1989). This difference in the way women and men think about their success in mathematics courses may play an important role in how they approach careers that involve mathematics (Nosek, Banaji, & Greenwald, 2002).

Susan Chapman and her associates (Chapman, Krantz, & Silver, 1992) conducted a study of the career interests of women among freshmen entering Barnard College, a highly selective women's college of Columbia University. Chapman found that women's interest in careers involving mathematics was not related at all to their scores on tests of mathematics ability and achievement. On the other hand, women who reported more anxiety about their skills in mathematics were less interested in careers in science, regardless of their mathematical ability. This suggests that lack of confidence in mathematics may be a significant barrier for women.

| Table 11.2     Consistently Identified Gender Differences in Emotion and Social Behavior | |
|---|---|
| **On the average, women are more likely to** | **On the average, men are more likely to** |
| Be nurturing and sympathetic | Be competitive and dominant |
| Be sociable and friendly | Be assertive |
| Be trusting and open | Commit most kinds of crimes (especially sex crimes) |
| Be cooperative and conciliatory | Be unafraid of risks |
| Engage in indirect verbal aggression | Engage in unprovoked physical aggression |
| Be anxious or depressed | Have high self-esteem |
| Be better able to hide their emotions | |

**Sources:** Bettencourt & Miller, 1996; Bjorklund & Kipp, 1996; Byrnes, Miller, & Schafer, 1999; Dindia & Allen, 1992; Eagly, 1995; Eagly & Wood, 1999; Feingold, 1994; Hyde & Plant, 1995; Keenan & Shaw, 1997; Kling & others, 1999; Knight, Fabes, & Higgins, 1996.

It would be misleading to conclude our discussion of gender differences in cognitive ability and academic achievement without discussing the implications of differences in which women have the advantage. Although men score only slightly lower on tests of reading and spelling on the average, men are twice as likely to fall in the lowest 10 percent of reading scores. These essentially illiterate males have enormous difficulty finding employment in our information-based economy (Hedges & Nowell, 1995).

### Gender Differences in Emotion and Social Behavior

Most gender differences in social and emotional functioning tend to be greater than gender differences in cognitive performance (Bjorklund & Kipp, 1999; Eagly & Wood, 1999; Keenan & Shaw, 1997). Many studies suggest that women are more likely than men to be nurturing, friendly, helpful, open, trusting, cooperative, and able to conceal their emotions. In contrast, men are more likely to be competitive, dominant, and assertive. Women are also more likely to be anxious, to be depressed, to have slightly lower self-esteem, and to engage in indirect verbal aggression (e.g., spreading false rumors). Men, on the other hand, are more likely to engage in physical aggression and risky behavior and are more likely to commit most kinds of crimes (Bjorklund & Kipp, 1999; Eagly & Wood, 1999; Keenan & Shaw, 1997). Even though most of these gender differences are well-documented and moderately large, there are many exceptions to the rule. Even if *most* women and men have the characteristics listed in table 11.2, there are many nurturing and cooperative men and many highly competitive and aggressive women. Knowing a person's gender is not a reliable indication of his or her personality.

### Gender Differences in Mating and Sexual Behavior

As shown in table 11.3, many studies conducted in many cultures indicate that women and men also differ in ways related to sexual behavior and the selection of a mate (Bjorklund & Shackleford, 1999; Buss, 1995, 1999; Eagly & Wood, 1999). Men tend to prefer a mate who is younger and physically attractive but who has good housekeeping skills. On the average, they are sexually jealous and controlling of their partners but are more likely to feel comfortable with the idea of casual sex for themselves. Women, in contrast, tend to prefer mates who are somewhat older and who have good character

| Table 11.3    **Consistently Identified Gender Differences in Mating and Sexual Behavior** | |
| --- | --- |
| **On the average, women are more likely to** | **On the average, men are more likely to** |
| Prefer an older mate | Prefer a younger mate |
| Prefer a mate who has high earning potential | Prefer a mate who is physically attractive |
| Prefer a partner of good character | Prefer a mate with good housekeeping skills |
| Be threatened more by emotional infidelity | Be threatened more by sexual infidelity |
| Restrict sex to potential long-term partners | Feel comfortable with the idea of casual sex for themselves |
|  | Be sexually jealous and controlling of their partner |

**Sources:** Bjorklund & Kipp, 1999; Bjorklund & Shackleford, 1999; Buss, 1995; Eagly & Wood, 1999; Oliver & Hyde, 1993.

and high earning potential. On the average, women say they are more threatened by the idea of their partner's emotional infidelity (caring about someone else) than their sexual infidelity, and they are more likely to be sexually intimate only with potential long-term partners (Bjorklund & Shackleford, 1999; Buss, 1995; Eagly & Wood, 1999).

A revealing naturalistic study was conducted to test the notion that men are more comfortable with the idea of casual sex than women are (Clark & Hatfield, 1989). On a college campus, females and males of average attractiveness who worked for the researchers walked up to college students (who did not know that they were part of a study) and asked, "Would you go to bed with me?" In two different samples, 75 percent of the men agreed to have sex, but none of the women agreed. Although there are many reasons why the women may have said no (fear for their safety seems like an obvious reason), the results of this study are consistent with those of other studies. Many studies indicate large differences between women and men in willingness to have casual sex (Oliver & Hyde, 1993). For example, college-age men say they would ideally like to have three times as many sex partners in their lifetimes (average of 18) as would women (average of fewer than 5) (Buss, 1995), and adult men in the general population are three times more likely to have had 10 or more sex partners in their lifetimes than women are (Michael & others, 1994).

All of this research raises a perplexing question: If men have the characteristics listed in tables 11.2 and 11.3 (if they are aggressive, unfaithful brutes who are only interested in a woman's superficial beauty and cooking skills), how are women ever going to find men of good character? The phrase "men of good character" seems like an oxymoron after reading this section! The answer is that this research, while technically accurate, exaggerates the differences in men and women in mate selection. Although it is true that college men say that the number of different sexual partners that they would like to have over the next 30 years is higher *on average* than the number desired by college women, the preferences of men and women are not so different when examined carefully. Most college men (48%) and college women (66%) say that they want only *one* sexual partner over the next 30 years (Pederson & others, 2002). The difference in the average number of desired sex partners comes from the fact that a few men say they want (and sometimes actually have) very high numbers of different sex partners (10 or more), whereas almost no women say they want (or actually have) such high numbers of sex partners. When married or in committed relationships, moreover, the overwhelming majority (over 95%) of both men and women are monogamous. Most of the gender difference in the number of sex partners is the result of a few males who say they would prefer a very promiscuous lifestyle.

What about the assertion that men are more concerned with their partner's sexual infidelity than emotional infidelity (caring about someone else)? A study of adult men and women (both heterosexual and homosexual) found that although men *said* that emotional infidelity was less important to them, when they discussed actual acts of infidelity of their partners in the past, both women and men of both sexual orientations experienced both types of infidelity as upsetting, but were more upset by emotional than sexual infidelity (Harris, 2002; Miller & others, 2002).

Thus, although women and men differ in important ways, some of the prevailing views—even among scientists—of gender differences in mating behavior exaggerate the facts (Miller & others, 2002).

## Origins of Gender Differences

Why are women and men different in the ways previously described? Current thinking is dominated by two very different theories of gender differences. One view holds that inherited biological differences between women and men have evolved over thousands of years that are responsible for gender differences in behavior. A rival theory suggests that gender differences in behavior are the result of differences in social learning experiences associated with gender roles. We will first summarize current data on gender differences in the structure of the brain and then will turn our attention to the two major theories of gender differences.

***Gender Differences in the Brain.*** There is now consistent evidence from many brain-imaging studies demonstrating that the brain structures of men and women differ in a number of ways, in addition to the gender differences in the brain that are related to reproduction (Schulkin, 1999). Also, considerable evidence from studies of both humans and nonhuman animals indicates that differences in levels of estrogen, testosterone, and other sex hormones during gestation play an important role in the creation of gender differences in the brain that are evident during adulthood (Wisniewski, 1998). On the average, the cerebral cortex of men is about 10 percent larger than that of women from childhood through late adulthood (Collaer & Hines, 1995; Giedd & others, 1997; Hopkin, 1995; Reiss & others, 1996). This difference is due to a greater volume of white matter (myelinated axons) in men, with no gender difference in the amount of "little gray cells" (the gray matter composed of the cell bodies of neurons) (Passe & others, 1997). The right cerebral hemisphere is slightly larger than the left hemisphere to the same degree in both sexes during childhood (Reiss & others, 1996), but by adulthood the relative size of the right hemisphere is larger in men (Wisniewski, 1998). This is interesting, as most spatial abilities are mediated more by the right than the left hemisphere. Thus, the greater relative size of the right hemisphere in men is consistent with their better spatial abilities.

In addition, there are gender differences in the corpus callosum. This band of 200 million neurons connecting the two cerebral hemispheres grows in size during childhood as its neurons become fully encased in the myelin sheaths that speed neural impulses. By adulthood, the corpus callosum reaches a larger size in women than men (Collaer & Hines, 1995), possibly indicating greater integration of the two hemispheres in women (Banich, 1998). Consistent with this possibility, a fascinating gender difference has been found in cortical activity during the performance of verbal tasks (Shaywitz & others, 1995). As shown in figure 11.2, when adult women and men performed a rhyming task, there was activation only in the verbal areas of the left hemisphere in men (note that left and right are reversed in the images shown in figure 11.2). In contrast, women showed activation in both cerebral hemispheres when they performed the same task. This suggests that the cerebral hemispheres function in a more integrated manner in women during some language tasks, perhaps because of the greater connectedness of their hemispheres through the corpus callosum. This difference is consistent with the superior language skills of women.

There are also interesting gender differences in subcortical areas of the brain. As children grow older, the amygdala increases in size more rapidly in males than females (Giedd & others, 1997) and is larger in adult men (Collaer & Hines, 1995). In contrast, the hippocampus increases in size more rapidly in female children (Giedd & others, 1997) and is larger in adult women (Collaer & Hines, 1995). These differences in the amygdala and hippocampus are tantalizingly consistent with some of the gender differences previously described. Although both the amygdala and hippocampus play roles in both memory and emotion, the amygdala is more associated with the expression of aggression, whereas the hippocampus plays a key role in everyday memory and in the inhibition of previously punished behavior (Gray, 1988). Thus, the better memory performance of women and their greater inhibition and lower levels of aggression are consistent with gender differences in these key elements of the limbic system. There are also structural differences in the hypothalamus (Swaab & Hofman, 1995) that may be relevant to gender differences in emotion.

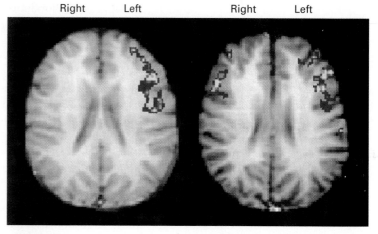

Right    Left        Right    Left

**FIGURE 11.2**

These composite magnetic resonance images show the distribution of active areas in the brains of males (left) and females during a "rhyming task." In males, activation is lateralized (confined) to the left interior frontal regions, but in females the same region is active bilaterally (on the right as well as on the left).

Although the similarities between gender differences in the brain and gender differences in behavior are provocative, we should not make too much of them. Both the human brain and human behavior are profoundly complex, and we are far from fully understanding the relationships between them. Even if the correlations between brain and behavior that are noted in this section prove to be meaningful, moreover, it is not clear what they mean. On the one hand, biological differences in the anatomy and physiology of the brain certainly could be the *cause* of gender differences in cognition and emotion. On the other hand, gender differences in the brain could be the *result* of gender differences in behavior and experience. The structure of the brain is not fixed at birth but is plastic and changing throughout the life span, and it is well established that variations in experience can create changes in brain anatomy and physiology (Greenough, Black, & Wallace, 1987). The fact that most of the differences between the brains of males and females are not evident until adulthood is consistent with the possibility that gender differences in behavior and experience produce gender differences in the brain. It is far too early to choose between these two possibilities—particularly because both could be correct to some extent. As will become obvious in the next sections, opinions about the origins of gender differences in behavior are quite divided at present.

*Evolutionary Psychology and Gender Differences.* Charles Darwin (1871) proposed that males and females in many species differ in physical appearance and behavior because past evolutionary pressures on the two sexes were different. That is, the natural forces that determine that some genes will survive (because the animal with those genes will live long enough to reproduce successfully), whereas other genes will perish, are sometimes different for females and males in Darwin's view. For example, some male hummingbirds may have long and symmetrical tails because they are sexually attractive to females (which increases the likelihood that a male's genes will be passed on to the next generation). Female hummingbirds that find long feathers attractive may have become common over countless generations because long feathers are associated with genes that confer resistance to parasites (which increase the likelihood that a female's genes will be passed on) (Geary, 1999).

Darwin's idea of different forces of natural selection on females and males has become the basis of one theory of the origin of human gender differences (Bjorklund

**evolutionary theory of gender differences**
The theory that gender differences are based on genes that resulted from different evolutionary pressures on ancestral women and men.

& Kipp, 1996; Bjorklund & Shackleford, 1999; Buss, 1995, 1999; Geary, 1998, 1999). According to the **evolutionary theory of gender differences,** gender differences arise from deep within—from genes that were selected by evolutionary pressures long ago (Geary, 1998). The principal hypothesis of evolutionary theory is that gender differences emerged because ancestral *women and men faced different evolutionary pressures* during the Pleistocene era when humans eked out a living by hunting animals and gathering wild plant foods. These different pressures ultimately result from the fact that mammalian reproduction is based on the insemination of the female by the male, followed by a long period of gestation (pregnancy) and nurturing of the immature young. According to this theory, this pattern of reproduction had several implications that led to the evolution of the gender differences previously described:

1. *Evolutionary pressures associated with hunting.* Because women were slowed by pregnancy and had to stay with the young during nursing, the work of hunting large animals fell to men. Evolutionary theorists believe that this meant that strong, fearless males who could throw weapons accurately were more likely to survive. Because throwing weapons at moving animals requires good spatial abilities, males with this attribute were also more likely to survive, and men eventually came to excel in this area. There is also some evidence that spatial ability is the basis of modern men's somewhat better performance on tests of mathematical ability (Casey & others, 1995, 1997), suggesting that the natural selection of the best hunters also led to men's somewhat stronger math skills. Thus, over many generations, men's need to excel as hunters led to several gender differences.

2. *Evolutionary selection of dominance and aggression.* Men could reproduce only if they could gain access to fertile women. One factor that increased the likelihood of mating with females during hunter-gatherer times was being stronger, more dominant, and more aggressive than male competitors (Buss, 1995). Thus, the evolutionary pressure to fend off male competitors selected these features in males. In contrast, no such pressures existed in our past that selected for aggression and dominance in females. That is, dominance and aggressiveness did not help females pass on their genes.

3. *Evolutionary pressures created by child care.* The care of young children had to fall to women during these ancestral times because nursing was the only way to nourish infants and toddlers. Evolutionary theorists suggest that the raising of young children was more successful when women banded together in groups that were large enough to scare off predators that might kill their young (Bjorklund & Kipp, 1999; Buss, 1995; Geary, 1998). Because women who were nurturing to their infants were most likely to be successful parents and because women who were sociable, cooperative, verbal, and lacking in physical aggression were most likely to be accepted in the group, women with these traits were more likely to survive and pass these genes on to future generations of females. Thus, women's need to raise children in groups created evolutionary pressures that shaped their social, emotional, and cognitive functioning.

4. *Evolutionary pressures created by gender differences in parental investment.* Because ancestral women were pregnant and nursing for long periods with each child, their level of investment in each child was very high in evolutionary terms. Because women could give birth to only a relatively small number of children, it was important that each offspring survive if their genes were to be passed on (Bjorklund & Kipp, 1999; Buss, 1995; Geary, 1998). In contrast, because the only contribution to reproduction that males were required to make was copulation, they could maximize the chances that their genes would be passed on by having sex with as many fertile females as possible. According to evolutionary theory, men tend to prefer younger, attractive women because youthfulness and the facial, hip, and breast characteristics that men find attractive are associated with reproductive health and fertility (Geary, 1999). The fact that fertilization is

hidden inside the female body also contributes to the different evolutionary pressures for the two sexes. Although females always know that they are the mother of the children they give birth to, males cannot be certain that they are the father (the female could have had sex with another male without his knowledge). These facts of reproductive life meant that the level of parental investment of males in each offspring was much lower than for females, according to evolutionary theorists (Bjorklund & Kipp, 1999; Buss, 1995; Geary, 1998). Evolutionary theorists believe that this is why modern men evolved to be sexually jealous and controlling of women (to reduce the chances that they would bear the child of another man), but to be comfortable with the idea of promiscuity for themselves (because this could increase the number of children with their genes). In addition, these theorists suggest that men spend less time caring for children in all cultures that have been studied to date because of their different levels of parental investment in children (Geary, 1998).

5. *Evolutionary pressures in mate selection.* Because women are limited in their ability to gather food during some parts of their pregnancy and child rearing, they and their offspring are most likely to survive if their mate helps support them. Thus, according to evolutionary theorists (Bjorklund & Kipp, 1999; Buss, 1995; Geary, 1998), whereas men compete for mates, women *select* mates. Women have evolved to prefer mates who have the social status and skills that come with age, who have financial resources, and who have good character (which will presumably lead them to help their mate and offspring survive). Because women depended on the help of men during ancestral times, evolutionary theory suggests that this is why they are more likely to be upset by emotional infidelity (which could mean that the male would help another female survive) than sexual infidelity.

***Critique of Evolutionary Theory.*** What do you think of the evolutionary theory of gender differences? It isn't very romantic, and some find it to be dehumanizing. Others feel that it is a self-serving attempt by men to justify their competitiveness, promiscuity, and shirking of child care. In addition, it is concerning to many that evolutionary theory implies that women and men are locked into gender differences by their genes. Evolutionary theory can be criticized on a number of scientific grounds as well. First, by their very nature, evolutionary theories differ from most other psychological theories because they can never be directly tested. We can say whatever we want about things that happened during the Pleistocene era, but we cannot conduct formal experiments to put our hypotheses to the test. Data can be gathered to see if an evolutionary theory makes sense, but such theories are better thought of as intellectual frameworks for thinking about human behavior than as testable theories per se. In addition, some of the specific arguments advanced by evolutionary theorists can be argued. For example, if women's need to group together for protection led to their greater sociability and cooperativeness, why did men's need to group together to hunt large animals not lead to the same prosocial qualities? Since greater perceptual speed is an advantage in hunting, why do women outperform men in this area? If gender differences in sexuality are inherited, why are there large differences among hunter-gatherer societies that exist today in the extent to which men control women's sexual behavior (Eagly & Wood, 1999)? Many such specific questions are left unanswered by evolutionary theory.

***Social-Role Theory of Gender Differences.*** The major alternative to evolutionary theory is the **social-role theory of gender differences** (Bussey & Bandura, 1999; Eagly & Wood, 1999; Steele, 1997; Wood & Eagly, 2000). Its primary hypothesis is that each society's division of labor, and the different social roles that it creates for women and men, are the forces that create psychological gender differences. That is, gender differences in behavior result from the different opportunities, challenges, experiences, and restrictions that social roles create for men and women.

**social-role theory of gender differences**
The theory that the opportunities and restrictions inherent in women's and men's different social roles create psychological gender differences.

In one important way, the two theories of gender differences are in agreement. Like evolutionary theory, social-role theory agrees that some biological gender differences led to a division of labor between the genders. Thousands of years ago, the biological realities of reproduction for women and the advantages of men's greater physical strength led most human societies to create social structures in which men had greater power and status. In turn, this difference in social status and roles—which still exists to varying degrees in virtually all human societies—led to social learning experiences that taught men to be dominant, assertive, and aggressive and taught women to be submissive, cooperative, and sociable. The division of labor encouraged women to acquire domestic skills and encouraged men to learn the skills of resource gathering (hunting in the past, wage earning today). Similarly, the childbearing and nursing role fostered the learning of helpful and nurturing behavior among women. As a result, women and men came to prefer mates than fit the stereotyped requirements of their respective social roles.

As each successive generation of children is socialized into gender-based social roles, these roles become internalized in the individual as the qualities that women and men expect and value in themselves (Eagly & Wood, 1999; Steele, 1997). Once gender-specific social roles are internalized, women and men evaluate themselves in terms of how well they fit the role assigned by society on the basis of their biological sex. Thus, gender roles create a powerful internalized force to maintain themselves.

Although social-role theory suggests that biological sex differences created the initial push for a gender-based division of labor in the past, gender roles are maintained today by current socialization practices, not by our genes. Now that hunting animals is no longer necessary and societies governed by laws have rendered physical aggression less advantageous (it mostly gets you put in jail), social-role theory posits that many gender differences are maintained today only by social pressures that are useless vestiges of past needs. Furthermore, as gender roles change in contemporary societies, psychological differences between women and men will also change (Eagly & Wood, 1999). Men may knowingly or unknowingly oppose social changes that threaten their position of power, and women may find patterns of behavior that are inconsistent with their internalized gender roles to be uncomfortable at first, however. Thus, although changes in outdated gender roles are to be expected, they may proceed slowly and bumpily at times.

Claude Steele (1997) of Stanford University has addressed the influence of internalized gender roles on cognitive performance. He suggests that people succeed in school subjects only when achievement is part of the person's self-definition. For example, if a woman does not believe that "I am a person who can excel in mechanical engineering courses," it is very unlikely that she will surprise herself by making good grades. Steele (1997) believes that few North American women are socialized to view themselves as competent in math and engineering, but many men are. It is these differences in socialization, rather than biological differences, that he believes create differences in performance.

Empirical support for Steele's (1997) view comes from experiments in which expectations about performance were manipulated. In one study, women and men were asked to take a difficult test of mathematics skills and concepts. Half of the participants were told that it was a test on which males outperform females, whereas the remaining participants were told that it was a test that showed no gender differences. When the participants were led to expect gender differences in performance, men correctly answered three times as many questions as women. When they were led to believe that there would be no gender differences, however, there were none—the women and men performed equally well (Steele, 1997). Thus, expectations of gender differences apparently can *create* gender differences in cognitive performance.

Additional support for social-role theory comes from studies that have asked whether differences in cognitive performance are more closely related to a person's biological sex or gender identity. Kalichman (1989) found that performance on a spatial reasoning task (on which males tend to do better) was predicted better by each participant's degree of identification with the stereotypical masculine gender role than with being a member of the male sex. That is, both males and females who were more "masculine" performed better on this task than did less masculine participants. Similarly, a number of studies show that both men and women who are characterized by androgynous gender roles (high in both masculinity and femininity) perform more accurately on a wide range of cognitive tasks (Halpern, 1992; Nash, 1975; Signorella & Jamison, 1986).

Some social-role theorists have examined gender differences in mate selection to test their hypothesis that gender differences in behavior will change as social roles for women and men change (Eagly & Wood, 1999). Among 37 cultures around the world, the degree of equality between the genders (defined in terms of the percentage of women holding high status jobs and political office and equity in incomes) varies widely. Among the cultures with the greatest degree of gender equality, the typical pattern of males preferring younger women with good domestic skills and females preferring older men with good earning potential is weakest (Eagly & Wood, 1999). Similarly, a study of 93 cultures found that girls are less likely to be socialized to be obedient and more likely to be socialized to be achievement-oriented in societies in which women can inherit property and hold political office (Low, 1989). The same study found that boys are most likely to be socialized to be competitive in societies that allow males to have multiple wives (Low, 1989). This suggests that changing social roles could produce changes in gender differences as hypothesized by social-role theory.

***Critique of Social-Role Theory.*** What do you think about the social-role theory of gender differences? Is it consistent with your intuitions about women and men? Because it has been proposed more recently, social-role theory is less well articulated than evolutionary theory at this point. For that reason, it may be premature to evaluate it in scientific terms. It is important to note, however, that it has not yet fully addressed the significance of biological differences between women and men. Social-role theorists believe that biological differences in physical strength and reproduction helped create gender differences in the division of labor long ago but downplay the influence of contemporary biological influences on current gender differences (Eagly & Wood, 1999). Social-role theory has not yet addressed the considerable amount of data indicating that there are at least some differences in the brains of women and men. It is possible that such differences could be integrated into social-role theory, however. As discussed in the section on gender differences in the brain, the differences in brain structure could be the result of differences in the behavior and experiences of women and men. That is, it is possible that gender differences in the brain are actually the result of different social roles rather than vice versa. These and other issues have not yet been fully addressed by social-role theorists, however.

## Development of Gender Identity and Roles

Although it is always important to remember that women and men are far more similar than they are different, the social roles and identities associated with gender are of great importance in human lives. How do we develop our gender identities? The process of gender development is complex and has captured the interest of many psychological theorists. By 2 or 3 years of age, children know that they are a boy or a girl and show differences in their play behavior. Children of this age already prefer to play with children of their same gender, and they play with gender-typed toys. Girls play more with "feminine" toys (tea sets and dolls), and boys play more with "masculine" toys (airplanes and guns). It is not until about age 7, however, when the concrete operational stage is reached, that children have a stable concept of what it means to be a boy or girl (Bem, 1981; Bussey & Bandura, 1992, 1999; Kohlberg, 1966). Before this stage, children recognize that boys and girls are different, but they see these differences only in terms of superficial physical features (Tavris & Wade, 1984).

"Jason, I'd like to let you play, but soccer is a girls' game."

In the section that follows, we will look at the way that two schools of thought in psychology have tried to explain the development of gender identity. Each theory is a tentative and partial explanation at best and focuses on a somewhat different aspect of the formation of gender identity. As you read about them, ask yourself if there are useful ideas in each of these theories. Consider also how these psychological theories of the development of our gender identities are similar to the social-role theory of the origins of gender differences.

### Psychoanalytic Theory of Gender Identity

Sigmund Freud suggested that young children usually take on the manners and ways of their parent of the same sex in a process called *identification*. Freud assumed that all children wish to win the approval of both parents and to avoid rejection. They adopt the gender role and act just like Mom or Dad for two reasons. First, as we will discuss more fully in later chapters, Freud believed that children are frightened by their powerful parents. One way to avoid getting into trouble with the same-sex parent is to adopt the behaviors of that parent. The second reason for adopting the gender identity of the same-sex parent, however, is to win the approval of the other-sex parent. The child sees that the intimate relationship between the parents gives the same-sex parent benefits that the child does not have. For example, the same-sex parent gets to sleep in the same bedroom with the other-sex parent. Freud believes that the child unconsciously identifies with the same-sex parent largely to be loved more by the other-sex parent. Freud's theory is interesting but does not easily explain why children develop normal gender identities even when raised in single-parent families and have little contact with their same-sex parent.

By the age of 2 or 3, children begin playing with gender-stereotyped toys. Freud suggested children learn gender by identification with their same-sex parent. Social learning theorists believe gender is learned by observing and imitating other people.

### Social Learning Theory of Gender Identity

Social learning theorist Albert Bandura (1969, 1977; Bussey & Bandura, 1992, 1999) proposed a theory of gender identity that is very different from Freud's. He suggested that children learn behavior appropriate to their gender through observations of adults and older siblings and through reinforcement and punishment of gender behaviors. According to this theory, children initially imitate the behaviors of both men and women, but parents and other members of their social world reward them for acting like a boy or girl and do not reward them (or punish them) for acting as the other sex does. For example, a little boy who dresses up like a girl will likely be told in emphatic terms that "boys don't wear those clothes!" Similarly, a little girl who cries may be given the message that it is okay to cry because girls are expected to express their emotions, whereas boys may be told that "big boys don't cry." A number of studies have suggested that parents spend a great deal of time encouraging their children to engage in gender-role behavior that is consistent with their biological sex (Bell & Carver, 1980; Hyde, 1985; Turner & Gervai, 1995). Similarly, parents of boys are three times more likely to discuss the scientific implications of natural phenomena with their children than parents of girls are (Crowley & others, 2001).

Thus, social learning theory suggests that gender roles are not an inherent part of our biological makeup but are learned from society. One implication is that gender roles could be quite different than they are today. In the United States, for example, many people believe that we should teach boys and girls to be more androgynous by rewarding assertiveness, strength, and emotionally expressive behavior in both sexes. If the social learning theory is correct, encouraging both female and male children to have the best features of the traditional male and female gender roles should result in less different gender roles in the future.

## Sexual Orientation

Close your eyes and imagine the perfect partner for you for a romantic and sexual relationship. The gender of the person that you imagine reveals a great deal about your sexual orientation. Persons who are sexually attracted to members of the other sex are termed **heterosexual.** In contrast, persons who are attracted to members of the same sex have a **homosexual** orientation. Most homosexual men use the term *gay*, whereas most

**heterosexual**
Romantically and sexually attracted to those of the different sex.

**homosexual**
Romantically and sexually attracted to those of the same sex, as distinguished from heterosexual.

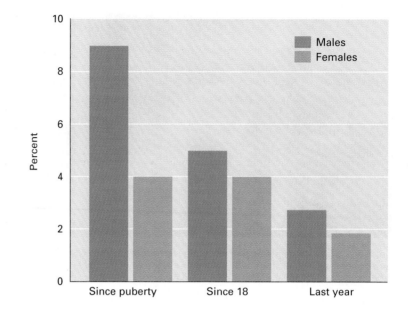

homosexual women prefer the term *lesbian.* Other people are attracted to varying extents to both members of their same sex and members of the other sex. When this is the case, the sexual orientation is termed *bisexuality.*

A national survey of more than 3,000 adults conducted by the University of Chicago (Michael, Gagnon, Laumann, & Kolata, 1994) provided the first reliable figures on sexual orientation and same-sex sexual behavior among Americans. As shown in figure 11.3, 9 percent of adult males report that they have had sex with another male since puberty. About half of these males who had an early same-sex experience continue to have homosexual experiences after age 18 (4 percent of all adult males), and 2.8 percent of males identify themselves as either gay or bisexual.

Among women, 4 percent have had sex with another woman since puberty, with these experiences almost always occurring after age 18. About 1.1 percent of all adult women in the United States identify themselves as lesbian or bisexual. Thus, fewer women have same-sex experiences than men (and women tend to have these experiences at later ages), and fewer women than men identify themselves as homosexual or bisexual. In contrast, more women than men report feeling sexually attracted to persons of both sexes (Diamond, 2000; Laumann, Gagnon, Michael, & Michaels, 1994).

Homosexual experiences and gay and lesbian orientations were found in the University of Chicago survey to be somewhat less common than suggested by Kinsey and others (1948) and other early researchers who were not able to interview samples of persons that were representative of the United States. If you live in a large city, the percentages of homosexual and bisexual orientations reported by the University of Chicago study may seem low to you. That is because gays and lesbians tend to live in larger cities rather than in suburban or rural areas. In the 12 largest U.S. cities, over 9 percent of males consider themselves to be gay or bisexual—over three times as many as in the U.S. population as a whole. Among women who live in large cities, nearly 3 percent identify themselves as lesbian or bisexual, more than twice as many as in the general population. In rural areas of the United States, only 1.3 percent of males and virtually no females identify themselves as gay, lesbian, or bisexual, often making life a lonely experience for the gay men and lesbian women who live in rural areas (Michael & others, 1994).

Many myths surround homosexuality and bisexuality. For example, it is commonly believed that homosexual persons take on the gender roles of the other sex—that gay men act feminine and lesbian women are masculine. In fact, homosexual persons, like heterosexuals, exhibit a wide range of gender roles. Another myth is that gays and lesbians try to seduce heterosexuals into becoming homosexual. Again, no evidence supports this belief.

But, as is true of myths and stereotypes about any group of people, they tend to be used to justify discrimination against members of the group. Persecution of gays and lesbians is common and has a long history. For example, homosexuals were one of the groups singled out to be killed in Nazi Germany. Still today, persecution of gays and lesbians often reaches extreme forms of violence. Acts of aggression perpetrated against gays and lesbians simply on the basis of their sexual orientation is referred to as *gay bashing*. Thousands of gays and lesbians are victimized in this way every year in the United States, making violence against homosexuals a major social problem.

### Gays and Lesbians in the Military

Less than two weeks after his inauguration in 1993, President Bill Clinton announced that he had asked the Secretary of Defense to prepare a policy that would ban discrimination against homosexual men and women in the armed forces. The existing policy prevented an admitted gay or lesbian from joining the armed services and required that openly homosexual soldiers be dismissed dishonorably if discovered while in military service. President Clinton's position was that the policy was based on unfounded prejudice against gays and lesbians and he opposed any official policy of discrimination. However, the harsh reaction from heterosexual military personnel and many people in all walks of life made this a hotly debated issue and led to only a partial change in policies regarding gays and lesbians in the military. This heated controversy continues today.

The opponents of the proposed changes in the policy banning openly homosexual men and women from military service first alleged that gays and lesbians perform their military jobs poorly, but these charges were quickly withdrawn when no evidence could be found to support them. Indeed, in testimony in congressional hearings, top military officers have stated that homosexual men and women perform their jobs as well as their heterosexual counterparts (Herek, 1993). However, the military leaders who oppose liberalization of the policy on gays and lesbians state that having admitted homosexuals in the military would be bad for the morale of heterosexuals. They argue that homosexuals have difficulties controlling their sexual urges and would sexually harass and attempt to seduce heterosexuals. They further argue that heterosexuals would not be able to adjust to having homosexuals in their units when they have to live in barracks and share showers and latrines with them (Herek, 1993).

The issue of whether to allow people who are openly homosexual to serve in the military is still controversial. What is your opinion?

Similarly, a less public debate has arisen about the government's policy to deny security clearances to many gays and lesbians on the basis of their sexual orientation. Gays and lesbians are routinely denied security clearances that are necessary for many jobs in government and private industry because they are considered to be bad security risks. Homosexual men and women are considered to be easier to blackmail and to be less likely to be loyal to the United States and keep its secrets.

When you read this list of allegations against gays and lesbians, what do you think? If your sexual orientation is heterosexual, do you think that gays and lesbians are more unstable and untrustworthy? Are they more likely to sexually harass other soldiers or sailors? Would heterosexuals have great difficulties in accepting gays and lesbians in the military? Many Americans believe that the answer to all of these questions is yes. But are these allegations based on facts?

Psychologist Gregory Herek (1990, 1993) of the University of California at Davis has reviewed the large body of research on gays and lesbians to see whether there is evidence that they are poor security risks and unfit for military service. His review suggests that there is no evidence to support any of the allegations made against homosexuals. Herek cites studies that clearly show that homosexual men and women are not more likely to have psychological disorders or to be unstable or disloyal. He similarly cites evidence that gays and lesbians are not more likely to sexually harass others or to attempt to seduce heterosexuals into homosexual behavior.

It would be difficult to deny, however, that the presence of openly gay men in the service would upset some heterosexual male soldiers and sailors. The distressing record of gay bashing by male soldiers has been tragically reinforced by recent events in which gays have been killed because of their sexual orientation. Does this mean that we could not have a military force with good morale if admitted gays and lesbians were allowed to join? Herek (1993) likens the prejudice against gays and lesbians to the prejudice against African Americans and women in the military. It has only been since 1948 that African Americans were allowed to serve in the same units as whites. Before that time, they served in segregated units commanded by white officers. Over the past 40 years, however, the military has conducted active training programs to reduce and control prejudice against ethnic minorities in the military. As a result, the American military is able to function effectively as an ethnically integrated unit. Similar strides have been made in integrating women more completely into the military. Although women's roles were greatly restricted in the past, and they still face many barriers, women and men were able to function together effectively in the Persian Gulf War of 1991. Women served well, without serious problems, in battle zones where they shared latrines, shower facilities, and tents with their male counterparts.

Herek (1993) suggests that the same programs that effectively decreased and managed prejudice against ethnic minorities and women could be used to solve morale problems that would result from allowing admitted gays and lesbians to serve in the military. He reminds us of two things: First, heterosexual and homosexual men and women have been working together effectively and sharing showers and toilets in the military without problems for many years—the heterosexuals simply did not usually know who the homosexuals were most of the time. If homosexuals managed to coexist peacefully in the past, why could they not do so in the future? Second, extensive research on the psychology of prejudice makes it clear that when people who are prejudiced against each other get to know one another by working together, the prejudice diminishes markedly (Herek, 1993). Herek (1993) believes that, if supported by active campaigns against prejudice and active campaigns to protect gays and lesbians against retaliation, this official form of prejudice on the basis of sexual orientation could be brought to an end without sacrificing the morale of the military. What do you think?

### Stigmatization, Stress, and Sexual Orientation

Although attitudes toward homosexuality are shifting toward greater acceptance, gays and lesbians are still harshly stigmatized around the world. It is undoubtedly still far more difficult to be a gay or lesbian teenager who faces the threat of prejudice and ridicule from peers (Herek, 2000). In addition, gays and lesbians often do not feel comfortable seeking social support from friends and families because it would involve admission of their sexual orientation. Gays also face a greater risk of AIDS and are far more likely than heterosexuals to experience the stress of taking care of a partner who is dying from AIDS (Irving, Bor, & Catalan, 1995). It is perhaps not surprising, therefore, that a number of well-conducted studies have found gay and lesbian teens and adults to be at greater risk for depression, suicide, and substance abuse (Fergusson, Horwood, & Beautrais, 1999; Herrell & others, 1999; Sandfort & others, 2001).

### Origins of Sexual Orientation

Why do some persons develop a homosexual orientation? I should acknowledge that I am reluctant to tackle this question for three reasons. First, I am not sure that I can

Heterosexual persons hold myths and stereotypes about gay men and lesbian women.

accurately discuss—or even should discuss—deeply personal matters about which I have no direct knowledge. Second, the very act of discussing the factors that lead to homosexuality may falsely imply that I disapprove of homosexuality. Third, although advances have been made in the past decade, the scientific evidence on this topic is still quite incomplete. I ultimately decided to include this section because the question of the origins of homosexuality is so charged by religious and political beliefs and so inflamed by misunderstanding and fear that I believe that an open discussion of even incomplete facts and tentative theories may be helpful.

Do some of us *learn* to be homosexual? Many people believe that a person's first sexual experiences are so reinforcing that they shape our sexual orientation. If our first sexual experience is with a person of the same sex, will we be more likely to develop a homosexual orientation? Anthropologist Gil Herdt (1984) of the University of Chicago has argued strongly against this idea by describing the sexual practices of the Sambian people of New Guinea. Sambian men believe that boys will become men only if they ingest the sperm of older males. Therefore, at 7 years of age, boys leave their family home and live in the men's lodge, where they are initiated into ritualized homosexuality. They regularly perform oral sex on older males for several years, and then receive oral sex from younger males when they reach sexual maturity. During this time, they have no sexual contact with females. Although Sambian males report enjoyment of their youthful homosexual activities, when they are old enough to marry, almost all Sambian males prefer to have sexual relationships exclusively with females. The experience of Sambian males suggests that one does not learn to be homosexual just by having homosexual experiences as a youth. Consistent with this view, only a minority of persons in the United States who have youthful sexual experiences with a person of the same sex develop a homosexual identity in adulthood (Michael & others, 1994).

Psychologist John Money (1987b, 1988) has hypothesized that social learning does play a role in the development of homosexuality, but in combination with biological factors that predispose some persons to homosexuality. Several kinds of studies have provided evidence that is consistent with (but does not prove) this hypothesis:

1.  Twin studies suggest that genetic factors may predispose some individuals to homosexuality (Eckert & others, 1986; Kendler & others, 2000). If one twin is homosexual, the other is more likely to also be homosexual if the twins are identical (they share the same genetic makeup) than if the twins are fraternal (they share half of their genes on average).

2.  There is substantial evidence that atypical levels of some sex hormones during prenatal development increase the likelihood of homosexuality (Meyer-Blauberg & others, 1995).

3.  Many studies indicate that gay males are more likely to have more than one older male sibling (e.g., Blanchard & others, 1996a, 1996b; Bogaert, 1998). Because later-born males are exposed to lower levels of prenatal testosterone

(Blanchard & others, 1995), this could reflect a hormonal influence on male homosexuality. Interestingly, however, birth order and the percentage of male or female siblings is apparently not related to the likelihood of female homosexuality (Bogaert, 1998).

4. There is consistent evidence that homosexuals differ from heterosexuals in the same areas of the hypothalamus and other brain structures that are different among men and women (Allen & Gorski, 1992; LeVay, 1991; Swaab & Hofman, 1990, 1995). Thus, it seems likely that, in a few limited respects, the brains of homosexuals resemble the brains of heterosexual persons of the other sex more than heterosexual persons of their own sex.

Thus, it is possible that genetic factors and prenatal hormones organize the brains of some persons in a way that increases the likelihood that they will be homosexual. Since the differences in brain structure are not evident until early puberty (Swaab & Hofman, 1995), however, it is also possible that differences in brain structure could be the result of differences in experiences.

John Money (1987b, 1988) does not believe that biological factors work alone, however, because many individuals who have these biological characteristics do not become homosexual. Rather, he believes that only some predisposed persons who have specific kinds of experiences will develop a homosexual orientation. What might those experiences be? Psychologist Daryl Bem (1996) of Cornell University has proposed a controversial theory of the interaction of predisposition and learning. Bem (1996) believes that predisposing factors lead some children to exhibit behavior more typical of the other sex and to prefer to play with children of the other sex. About half of adult gay males report such atypical sex-typed behavior as children, compared to less than 15 percent of adult heterosexual males. The difference for gay women is in the same direction, but not as strong. When boys with atypical sex-typed behavior were followed into adulthood in a half-dozen studies reviewed by Bem (1996), about two-thirds identified themselves as gay as adults, compared with about 5 percent of adult males who had shown typical sex-typed behavior as children.

Bem (1996) believes that engaging in atypical sex-typed behavior creates an opportunity for two kinds of learning experiences that lead to homosexuality. First, there is substantial evidence that people rarely develop sexual or romantic feelings for the persons they spend the most time with during childhood. For example, adults who grow up on Israeli kibbutzim, where children are raised in large communal groups, almost never marry a person from their group. Similarly, adopted siblings who grew up together almost never marry, in spite of being biologically unrelated. Familiarity breeds friendships, but not sexual attraction (Bem, 1996). Bem believes that homosexuals who preferred to play with children of the other sex when they were children became too familiar with the other sex to develop sexual attraction to them.

Second, Bem (1996) believes that children who engage in atypical sex-typed behavior find children of their own sex to be upsetting. Effeminate boys and masculine girls often dislike children of their own sex who engage in typical sex-typed behavior and find them to be emotionally arousing—frightening, threatening, or disgusting. When gender-atypical children reach the period of sexual awakening in puberty, however, Ben believes that the emotional arousal created by persons of the same sex enhances sexual attraction. Recall that the cognitive theory of emotion described in the previous chapter states that any kind of emotional arousal can be misinterpreted as romantic and sexual attraction. Thus, Bem (1996) believes that we are most likely to be sexually attracted to the class of people that we find to be unfamiliar and emotionally arousing (persons of the same sex for persons who had shown atypical sex-typed behavior as children). In Bem's (1996) terms, "the exotic becomes erotic."

Does Bem's (1996) theory seem reasonable to you? It is consistent with some evidence, but it is speculative and will be difficult to test directly. Moreover, it ignores the fact that half of gay men (and an even larger proportion of lesbian women) did *not* show atypical sex-typed behavior as children. If his speculative theory is valid, it is likely to be valid only for some individuals.

The term *sex* refers to the biological characteristics of being male or female, whereas the term *gender* refers to the identity and behaviors associated with being a male or female in a given culture. Gender identity, the internalized sense of being either male or female, is a central aspect of the personality. It gives rise to behaviors that society expects of males and females, referred to as gender roles. The achievement of gender identity and the gender role one adopts are the product of a complex developmental process. Psychoanalytic theory emphasizes the child's identification with the same- and other-sex parents in the development of gender roles. Social learning theory suggests that children initially imitate the behavior of both same- and other-sex persons but learn which gender behavior is expected for their sex from the reactions of adults and other children. Gender roles are classified as masculine or feminine, but a person may express high levels of both masculinity and femininity, a pattern referred to as androgyny. Males and females are far more similar than different in all psychological domains, but there is consistent evidence of gender differences in some aspects of cognitive performance, social and emotional behavior, sexuality, and mate selection. There also is strong evidence of gender differences in brain anatomy and physiology at both cortical and subcortical levels. Two major theories attempt to explain gender differences. Evolutionary theory posits that gender differences evolved over many generations due to different evolutionary pressures on women and men. Social-role theory suggests that psychological gender differences arise from the different opportunities, experiences, and limitations associated with the female and male gender roles. In addition to gender identity and gender roles, persons also differ in how they express their sexuality in intimate relationships. Sexual orientation directs a person's sexual arousal toward either other-sex (heterosexual) or same-sex (homosexual) partners, or both (bisexual). Researchers have not yet established what causes differences in sexual orientation, but both biological factors and learning may be important.

Check Your Learning

To be sure that you have learned the key points from the preceding section, cover the list of correct answers and try to answer each question. If you give an incorrect answer to any question, return to the page given next to the correct answer to see why your answer was not correct. Remember that these questions cover only some of the important information in this section; it is important that you make up your own questions to check your learning of other facts and concepts.

1. The set of behaviors that communicates to others the degree to which we are masculine or feminine is referred to as our _____.

   a)  sex                          c)  gender role
   b)  sexual orientation           d)  culture

2. A person who has both feminine and masculine gender characteristics is referred to as _____.

   a)  androgynous                  c)  bisexual
   b)  polygamous                   d)  heterosexual

3. Persons with a more masculine gender identity tend to score slightly higher on tests of spatial ability than do persons with a more feminine gender identity.

   a)  True                         b)  False

4.  The theory of the origin of sex differences that views psychological gender differences as more likely to change in the near future is _____.

    a)    evolutionary theory          b)    social-role theory

5.  Gays and lesbians are not more likely to be unstable or to be disloyal than heterosexuals.

    a)    True                          b)    False

## Thinking Critically about Psychology

1.  What do you think has been more important in your choice of a major and in your plans for a career—your sex or your gender identity?

2.  Are your abilities, emotions, and sexuality typical of your gender? Do you think these patterns of behavior are the product of evolution, of learned gender roles, or both?

3.  Why do you think that crimes of violence are so common against gay males ("gay bashing")? What could be done to solve this problem?

Correct Answers:  1. c (p. 410),  2. a (p. 411),  3. a (p. 412),  4. b (p. 419),  5. a (p. 426).

## Biological and Psychological Aspects of Sexuality

Sexuality is a topic that is full of both interest and emotion for most of us. It plays a pivotal role in many intimate relationships, is the subject of intense moral debates, and is plagued by misinformation more than perhaps any other natural aspect of human life. The emotional nature of sexuality may be evident to you now as you begin to read this chapter. Are you approaching the topic of sexuality in the same dispassionate manner that you read about thirst or memory? Consider this: Although the majority of college women and nearly all college men masturbate, when was the last time you spoke to a friend as openly about your enjoyment of masturbation as about your enjoyment of music, jogging, or pizza? Very few of us are completely comfortable with the topic of sexuality.

In this section, we will briefly discuss sexuality in scientific terms. In describing sexuality in this academic fashion, we will compare sexuality in human and nonhuman animals and will contrast the sexual motive to other motives. We will not begin to do justice to the importance of sexuality in human lives, but at least we may combat the misinformation to a degree.

Images and themes of sexuality appear in art and literature reaching as far back as the earliest civilizations, but the scientific study of sexuality has only recently emerged. Two European physicians working at the turn of the twentieth century were at the forefront of early studies of sexuality. Richard Von Krafft-Ebing (1840–1902), a Viennese neurologist, extensively studied variations and deviations in human sexual behavior. However, Krafft-Ebing's view of sexuality was mostly negative and his work was filled with misconceptions. For example, Krafft-Ebing believed that masturbation caused all sexual deviations and was at the root of sexual problems. Today we know that this basic premise of Krafft-Ebing's views of sexuality is false.

A second major figure in the study of human sexuality was Henry Havelock Ellis (1859–1939). An English physician, Ellis was the first to discuss extensively the role of social and cultural influences in shaping human sexual behavior and one of the first scholars to study homosexuality. He also stated for the first time that men and women experience similar sexual desires and that psychological problems such as anxiety and depression can influence physical sexual functioning.

The work of researcher Alfred C. Kinsey in the 1940s was a major turning point in the study of sexuality. Kinsey is now credited with beginning the modern era of the scientific study of sexuality.

Subsequent to the many published volumes of research by Krafft-Ebing and by Ellis in the early part of the century, there was surprisingly little scientific study of human sexuality for many years. In many ways, the scientific world was not yet prepared to discuss human sexuality objectively. A major turning point in the study of sexuality occurred, however, in the 1940s with the work of Alfred C. Kinsey (1894–1956). Kinsey became interested in human sexual behavior when he was made aware of the extremely limited amount of scientific information available on this topic. He conducted large surveys that allowed him to describe many aspects of human sexuality, including the broad range of sexual activities (Kinsey, Pomeroy, & Martin, 1948; Kinsey, Pomeroy, Martin, & Gebhard, 1953). His methods seem weak today, but he opened the door to better research that would follow.

Other modern pioneers in the study of sexual behavior include John Money of Johns Hopkins University. Money is best known for his studies in sexual development and his classic research of *gender roles,* a term that he first coined (Money, 1955). Also of great importance was the work of William Masters and Virginia Johnson. They conducted groundbreaking laboratory studies of volunteers who were observed during the sexual response cycle from the initial excitement to the moment of orgasm, while Masters and Johnson measured the physiological changes that accompany the sexual behavior. Masters and Johnson's two most important books, *Human Sexual Response* (1966) and *Human Sexual Inadequacy* (1970), helped form the basis for our understanding of human sexual functioning and sexual problems and stood as the foundation for sex therapy.

## Sexual Anatomy and Functioning

The major structures of the sexual anatomy of females and males are presented in figures 11.4 and 11.5, respectively. The **uterus** is a pear-shaped, muscular structure that carries the fetus during pregnancy. After conception, the fertilized egg implants itself in the wall of the uterus, where it grows and develops during gestation. Except during

**uterus**
The muscular structure that carries the fetus during pregnancy.

**FIGURE 11.4**
Major structures of the female sexual anatomy.

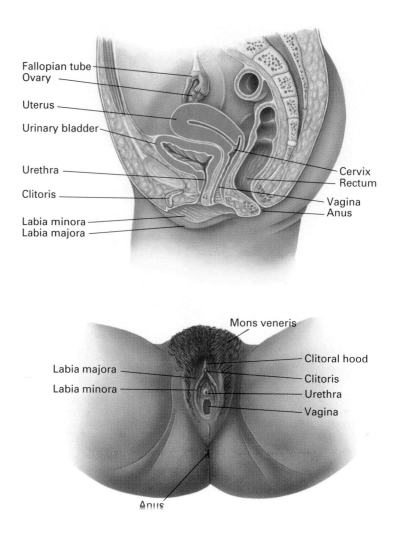

**ovaries**
Female endocrine glands that secrete sex-related hormones and produce ova, or eggs.

**fallopian tubes**
The tubes through which ova (eggs) reach the uterus.

**cervix**
The neck of the uterus that is connected to the vagina.

**vulva**
The external genital structures of the female.

**mons**
The fleshy mound that sits at the top of the vulva.

**labia majora**
The larger, outer lips of the vulva.

**labia minora**
The smaller, inner lips of the vulva.

**clitoris**
The structure at the upper part of the vagina that is most sensitive to sexual stimulation in females.

**testes**
Male endocrine glands that secrete sex-related hormones and produce sperm cells.

pregnancy, it is this inner lining of the uterus that is shed during the menstrual cycle approximately every 28 days.

The **ovaries** are the two structures that produce estrogen and other hormones and produce *ova*, or eggs, for reproduction. The **fallopian tubes** branch off from the top of the uterus, extending near, although not quite touching, the ovaries. The fallopian tubes form a passage in which ova are transported from the ovaries to the uterus. At the bottom of the uterus is the **cervix,** which is the neck of the uterus that is connected to the vagina. It is through the cervix that menstrual flow is discharged and through which the newborn is passed into the birth canal during delivery.

The female external genitals (fig. 11.4) consist of a set of structures collectively referred to as the **vulva,** made up of the mons, labia majora, labia minora, and the clitoris. The **mons,** a fleshy mound of tissue that sits at the top of the vulva, is the upper area covered with pubic hair. The **labia majora,** or large lips of the vulva, are the outer vaginal lips that surround the inner lips, or **labia minora.** The two labia provide folds that cover the opening of the vagina and are a sensitive source of pleasure during sexual stimulation. The folds of the labia minora converge at the top of the vagina to form a hood for the **clitoris,** which is the structure at the upper part of the vagina that is most highly responsive to sexual stimulation. The labia and clitoris both play critical roles in female sexual response.

The male reproductive system consists of the testes (testicles) and a related system of tubes and glands. Like the ovaries, the **testes** produce both hormones and reproductive cells. The male reproductive cells are the sperm, which carry the father's genetic information for conception. The testes are suspended below the abdomen away from the

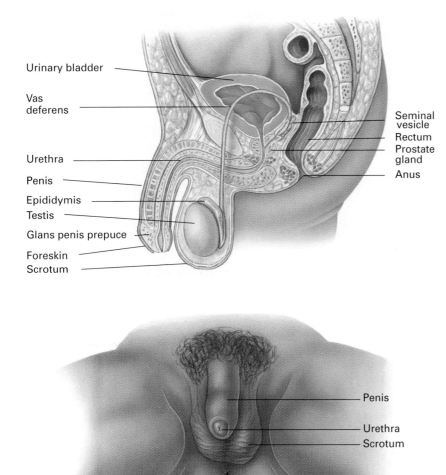

**FIGURE 11.5**
Major structures of the male sexual anatomy.

Urinary bladder

Vas deferens

Urethra

Penis

Epididymis

Testis

Glans penis prepuce

Foreskin

Scrotum

Seminal vesicle

Rectum

Prostate gland

Anus

Penis

Urethra

Scrotum

Anus

heat of the body because sperm are only produced at a temperature slightly lower than the 98.6° temperature of the rest of the body. Extending from each testicle is the **epididymis,** which holds mature sperm cells after they have been produced in the testes and connects with the vas deferens. The **vas deferens** is the tube that carries sperm from the epididymis toward the outside of the body. The sperm cells are carried in a fluid called **semen,** which is produced by the **prostate gland** and **seminal vesicle.**

The external genitals of the male and female are structured to allow sexual intercourse. The external male genitals, shown in figure 11.5, consist of the penis and scrotum. The **penis** is a tubular structure filled with three spongy tubes that fill with blood during sexual response. It is the filling of the penis with blood that causes it to become stiff and erect during sexual arousal. The **scrotum** is a loose skin structure that extends behind the penis and supports the testes. The scrotum responds to changes in temperature, contracting when cold and relaxing when warm, to ensure that the testes remain at a temperature optimal for sperm production.

### The Sexual Response Cycle

The response of humans to sexual stimuli involves a predictable biological response known as the *sexual response cycle.* Although there are substantial similarities between the sexual response cycles of women and men, there are some important differences. As shown in figure 11.6, Masters and Johnson (1966) describe four stages of the sexual response cycle:

**epididymis**
The structure that holds sperm cells until ejaculation.

**vas deferens**
The structure that carries sperm from the epididymis toward the outside of the body during ejaculation.

**semen**
The fluid that contains sperm cells.

**prostate gland**
One of the structures that produce fluid for semen.

**seminal vesicle**
One of the structures that produce fluid for semen.

**penis**
The tubular structure that becomes erect during sexual arousal and through which sperm is ejaculated.

**scrotum**
The loose skin sac that encloses the testes.

**FIGURE 11.6**
The human sexual response cycle.

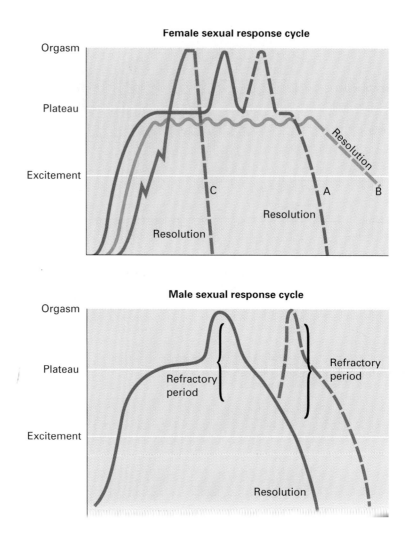

**Female sexual response cycle**

**Male sexual response cycle**

**excitement phase**
The first stage of the sexual response cycle, during which the penis becomes erect and the vagina lubricates.

**plateau phase**
High levels of sexual arousal and pleasure that are maintained for variable periods of time.

**orgasm**
The reflexive phase of the sexual response cycle accompanied by peak levels of arousal and pleasure and usually by ejaculation in males.

**resolution phase**
The stage in the sexual response cycle following orgasm when arousal and pleasure diminish.

1. *Excitement phase.* Both women and men show an initial increase in physiological arousal, called the **excitement phase.** This may begin from visual stimulation, physical contact, odors, fantasies, and the like. Blood flows to the penis and the vagina, erection and lubrication occur, the nipples become erect, the heart beats faster, blood pressure rises, and the body becomes aroused in other ways.

2. *Plateau phase.* If the sexual stimulation is intense enough, sexual arousal builds quickly to the **plateau phase,** which is characterized by high levels of arousal that are sustained for periods ranging from seconds to many minutes. The degree of sexual pleasure is very high, but not yet at a maximum.

3. *Orgasmic phase.* With sufficient stimulation, and under the proper psychological circumstances, the individual usually progresses to the reflexive stage of **orgasm.** A peak of physical arousal and pleasure is reached. Breathing is rapid, blood pressure and heartbeat reach high levels, the skin flushes, and the individual partially loses muscular control for a brief time and experiences involuntary spasms of many muscle groups. There is little variability in the orgasmic phase of men, but much more variation in the orgasms of women. Three common patterns of female orgasmic response have been distinguished (Masters & Johnson, 1966). Some women reach a single brief and intense orgasm, like that of men. Other women, depending on the circumstances, experience multiple intense orgasmic peaks. Other women experience a large number of smaller peaks of orgasm.

4. *Resolution phase.* Following orgasm, the body's level of physical arousal rapidly declines in the **resolution phase.** Within a few minutes, the body returns to a

condition much like its original state prior to the beginning of the response cycle, although heightened relaxation and tiredness are common. In males, the resolution phase is accompanied by a period of time when the male is unresponsive to further sexual stimulation, termed the **refractory period.** Although women briefly may be too sensitive to enjoy further sexual stimulation during the resolution phase, with individual preferences determining her interest in further stimulation, there is no refractory period in which women are physically incapable of resumed sexual arousal.

Research has found that some basic assumptions about differences between men and women's sexual response are not completely true. For example, contrary to earlier writings, researchers have found that a small number of men, like many women, appear to experience repeated or multiple orgasms at times (Robins & Jensen, 1978; Zilbergeld, 1978). In addition, some females expel a clear fluid into the vagina during orgasm in a way that is similar to male ejaculation (Belzer, 1981; Perry & Whipple, 1981). It is important to understand the ways in which the sexuality of women and men differ, but the more we learn, the less different they seem.

**refractory period**
The period of time following orgasm during which males are incapable of sexual arousal.

## Sexual Motivation

It will come as no surprise to you to learn that human beings have a sexual motive, much as we have motives for hunger or thirst. Without a sexual motive, humans and other animals that depend on sexual reproduction would soon be extinct. Whereas hunger, thirst, and other primary motives are necessary for the survival of the individual, sexual motivation is a primary motive that is essential to the survival of the species. The same basic biological mechanisms are involved in sexual motivation in all mammals, but the biological controls that govern sexual behavior are less significant in humans than in most other animals.

### Similarity to Other Primary Motives

We will understand sexual motivation better if we compare it with other primary motives (p. 369). The sexual motive resembles hunger, thirst, and other primary motives in a number of important respects:

1. *Hypothalamic control.* Like hunger and thirst, the sexual motive is controlled by our hardworking friend, the hypothalamus. One center in the hypothalamus and related brain structures activates motivation and sexual behavior. This system is the equivalent of the hypothalamic feeding and drinking systems. If the hypothalamus is surgically destroyed, sexual behavior will not be initiated even in the presence of sexually provocative stimuli. A second system of the hypothalamus inhibits sexual behavior. If this inhibitory system is destroyed in laboratory animals, the animals become hypersexual; that is, they engage in unusual and unrestrained amounts of sexual behavior. These two centers act in balance to regulate sexual motivation. The hypothalamus also indirectly influences female sexuality through its control of the menstrual cycle. Women are significantly more likely to initiate sex with a male partner or to masturbate when levels of estrogen peak at the time of ovulation (Adams, Gold, & Burt, 1978). This cycle of increased interest in sex may have evolved to increase the likelihood of fertilization of ova. Understandably, women who take birth control pills, which regulate estrogen levels, do not show this monthly peaking of sexual interest.

2. *Role of external stimuli.* Like hunger, which can be stimulated by external stimuli, known as incentives, such as the sights and aromas of dessert stimulating the hunger of a well-fed person, sexual motivation is highly sensitive to external stimuli. The person who initially is not sexually aroused, whether male or female, will often be aroused by a seductive partner or romantic fantasies. Indeed, external stimuli play a very important role in arousing the sexual motive (Wilson,

Kuehn, & Beach, 1963). One aspect of the role of external stimuli has been termed the *Coolidge effect.* Following intercourse, males of many animal species will have intercourse again with the same receptive female sometime after the refractory period has elapsed. Bermant (1976), for example, found that a ram (male sheep) will have sex an average of five times with the same ewe (female sheep) before seeming to lose interest. However, if a *different* receptive ewe is introduced after each mating, the ram will mate more than three times as often before losing sexual interest, and it will reach orgasm much more quickly than with the same ewe. Apparently, variety is a powerful external factor in sexual motivation for many mammalian species.

3. *Role of learning.* We have already seen that learning can play a powerful role in shaping the primary motives. What, when, and how much we eat, for example, is greatly influenced by our learning experiences. Sexual motivation is influenced by learning, at least to the same degree and probably to an even greater extent. The enormous variety in the sexual behavior of the members of any society at any point in history strongly points to the role of learning in sexuality. In North America today, for example, many individuals consider oral stimulation of the genitals to be a natural and loving part of a couple's sexual repertoire, whereas many others consider it to be a "crime against nature."

   Differences in sexuality between cultures portray the influence of learning experiences on sexual motivation. Contrast our own sexual behavior to the Polynesian residents of the island of Mangaia. Sexual pleasure is a principal concern of the Mangaians, young and old alike. Sex play among Mangaian children is common, with sexual intercourse usually beginning between the ages of 12 and 14. Most young males begin intercourse with an older, experienced woman, who teaches a variety of oral and genital sexual skills to him. Soon the frequency of masturbation drops and intercourse with age-mates becomes an every-night affair. This intense level of sexuality continues into married adulthood, with the average 20-year-old male reporting two to three orgasms per night, six nights per week. The quality of sexual intimacy is not overlooked in Mangaia, however, in spite of the quantity. There is a strong cultural emphasis on both partners' experiencing intense pleasure in intercourse. One of the worst insults that can befall a Mangaian male, in fact, is to be accused of reaching orgasm too quickly and not being interested in the pleasure of his female partner.

4. *Role of emotions.* Like the other primary motives, especially eating, sexual motivation is influenced to a great extent by our emotions. Because stress, anxiety, and depression are accompanied by increased sympathetic autonomic arousal, and because sexual arousal is mediated by parasympathetic arousal, which is in opposition to sympathetic activity, these emotions generally result in a decrease in sexual motivation. Because the balance between the sympathetic and parasympathetic systems is complicated, however, anxiety and depression sometimes result in an increase in sexual motivation. Just pointing to the obvious influence of strong negative emotions on our sexuality, however, does not begin to do justice to the intricate interplay of emotions and sexuality. Far more than any other motive, sexual passion is powerfully linked to even the delicate nuances of romantic love and other subtle emotions.

### Differences from Other Primary Motives

Although sexual motivation is similar to the other primary motives in the many ways just mentioned, there are important differences as well (Houston, 1985):

1. *Survival value.* We must satisfy the primary motives of hunger, thirst, need for warmth, and so on to survive as individuals and, collectively, to survive as a species. Although satisfaction of the sexual motive is essential to the survival of the species, it is not necessary for individual survival.

2. ***Increases and decreases in arousal.*** We are motivated to *decrease* the physiological arousal created by hunger and other primary motives. However, humans are obviously motivated to both *increase* and *decrease* their sexual arousal. The intimate behaviors that we engage in to initiate the arousal phase of the sexual response cycle ("foreplay") obviously increase arousal. Yet the fact that Americans spend many millions of dollars each year on erotic videos, erotic telephone "conversations," and topless bars is strong testimony to our motive to increase sexual arousal and then to decrease it through sexual activity.

3. ***Role of deprivation.*** Motives such as hunger and thirst rather predictably rise and fall according to the length of time since they were last satisfied. A person who has just eaten a large meal will not be hungry, but a person who has been deprived of food for eight hours will be ravenous. To an extent, the same is true for sex. If you are used to a regular sex life, the two weeks that your lover goes home to visit family may lead to a noticeable increase in sexual interest. But sexual motivation is far less linked to deprivation than the other primary motives. Except during the refractory period, humans are susceptible to sexually arousing stimuli and situations at almost all times. On the other hand, individuals without a sexual outlet report going long periods of time without the arousal of sexual longings. Indeed, it has often been observed that we don't really need sex until we have it—the more often we are sexually aroused and satisfied, the more sexual motivation we seem to have.

4. ***Decreases in energy.*** The other primary motives lead to behavior that increases the body's store of energy and other bodily needs. In contrast, sexual behavior results in a marked decrease in energy.

## Hormones and Sexual Behavior

In nonhuman animals, hormones from the endocrine system play a major role in regulating sexual motivation. Female dogs, cats, and rats are receptive to sexual intercourse only when they are ovulating—a time referred to as being "in heat." Males of these species are less influenced by hormones than females and are receptive to sexual stimulation at most times. In some species, however—mice, deer, and goats, for example—males will engage in sexual intercourse only during annual or biannual seasons ("ruts") when they are producing sperm. This means that sexual behavior in nonhuman animals is limited to those few times when fertilization and reproduction are highly likely.

The sexual motivation of humans is far less influenced by hormonal factors (Geer, Heiman, & Leitenberg, 1984). Although women tend to have somewhat more sexual interest during ovulation (Adams & others, 1978), intercourse is likely during periods in which impregnation is and is not possible. In addition, women continue to be interested in sex after menopause, when estrogen levels decline. This lack of a strong connection between sexuality and reproduction in humans is a major difference between animal and human sexual behavior, and it opens the door to the many meanings that sexuality has in our lives. Although sexual motivation is not governed by hormones in humans, sexuality and hormones are certainly related.

The sexual motive is unlike other primary motives because we are motivated not just to decrease it, as we would hunger and thirst, but to increase it as well.

## Patterns of Sexual Behavior

The large-scale national survey of sexual behavior carried out by the University of Chicago (Michael & others, 1994) was conducted to learn whom we have sex with, what we do, and how often we do it to allow experts to predict how rapidly and how far the

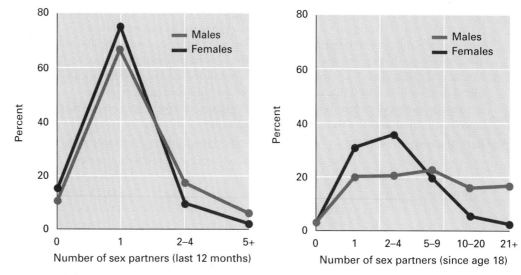

**FIGURE 11.7**

Number of sex partners in the past 12 months (left) and since age 18 (right) for males and females.

AIDS epidemic will spread. What was learned also will help us understand our own sexuality better.

Whom do we have sex with? Are we as sexually promiscuous as it seems on television and at the movies? As shown on the left side of figure 11.7, the great majority of female and male Americans over the age of 18 have had either no sex partner or only one sex partner in the past 12 months. Few Americans of either sex have had more than one sex partner in a one-year span, and many of these individuals have had more than one partner only because one relationship ended and another began during the past 12 months. Only 5 percent of males and 2 percent of females have had five or more sex partners in the past year. Among married individuals, 95 percent have had no sex partner other than their spouse in the past year. Indeed, about 85 percent of married women and 75 percent of married men never have sex with someone other than their spouse while they are married (Michael & others, 1994). Americans are much less promiscuous than we often think.

On the other hand, the average American does not have sex with only one partner in her or his lifetime. As shown on the right side of figure 11.7, less than one-fourth of adult males and less than one-third of adult females have had only one sex partner. Among females, a little more than 50 percent have had between two and nine sex partners in their lifetimes. Among males, one out of three men has had 10 or more sex partners in his lifetime. It is clear that we tend to be quite faithful when we are in a relationship but that we have many sex partners as we move from one relationship to another (Michael & others, 1994). This pattern of sexual relationships is often called *serial monogamy*.

How often do Americans have sex with their partners? As shown in figure 11.8, most adult women and men have sex with their partners a little less than once a week. A little more than a fourth of us have sex two to three times a week, with fewer than 10 percent of Americans having sex four or more times a week. Most men and women say that they spend between 15 minutes and an hour making love each time. Some of you will be surprised (and some of you will not be surprised) to learn that people who are in committed relationships have sex more often than single persons (Michael & others, 1994).

When heterosexual North Americans have sex with their partners, vaginal intercourse is by far the preferred practice, but certainly not the only sexual practice that is enjoyed. About 95 percent of both women and men report that vaginal intercourse is "appealing." Nearly two-thirds of 18- to 44-year-old women view receiving oral sex as appealing and over half enjoy performing oral sex. Both percentages were lower in

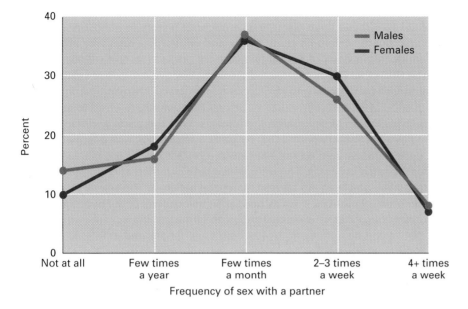

**FIGURE 11.8**
Frequency of having sex with a partner over the past year for females and males.

women over 44, however. Over 75 percent of men 18 to 44 years old find both receiving and performing oral sex to be appealing. Again, both percentages are lower for middle-aged and older men, however. Relatively few men and fewer women (less than 5 percent) find anal sex appealing. By and large, our sexual practices match our preferences: The last time that they had sex, 95 percent of men and women said that they had vaginal intercourse, about 25 percent performed oral sex, and the same percentage received oral sex. Only 1 percent of women and 2 percent of males said that anal sex was part of their last sexual encounter.

The University of Chicago sex survey found few differences in sexual behavior across levels of education, religion affiliation, or ethnic group. Hispanic men and women reported somewhat higher frequencies of sex, but the only large ethnic difference was in the age of first having sex. African American males reported an average age of first having intercourse of about 15½ years. In contrast, all other men and women reported first having intercourse at about age 17 (Michael & others, 1994). Otherwise, there were fewer sociocultural differences in sexual behavior than might have been expected.

The best news from the survey is that most people who are having sex in committed relationships are enjoying it a great deal. Among 18- to 59-year-old adults, 95 percent of men and 71 percent of women say that they usually or always have an orgasm when they have sex with a partner. About 90 percent of persons in committed relationships say that they receive "great physical pleasure," and about 85 percent say they receive "great emotional satisfaction" (Michael & others, 1994). Not surprisingly, a happy sex life is strongly related to general happiness. In the University of Chicago sex survey, nearly everyone who was generally happy was also happy with their sex life—and almost all of these happy people were in monogamous, committed relationships. Also not surprising is the finding that happy people have sex more often than unhappy people. In the University of Chicago sex survey, 72 percent of people who said they were extremely happy with their lives said that they had sex once a week or more. In contrast, only 27 percent of unhappy people had sex at least once a week. Does happiness lead to more frequent sex, or is frequent sex the secret to happiness? What do you think?

As you read about the sexual behavior of Americans, I hope you will not fall into the trap of thinking that what is "average" is "normal." If you have sex less often or more often than average, and you and your partner are happy with your sex life, what could be more normal than that? The same is true for the average time spent making love, preferred sexual practices, and so on. Learning about norms and averages is useful, but the focus should be on what is happy and healthy for each individual.

## Review

Sex and sexuality have been discussed throughout history in philosophy, literature, and the arts, but the scientific study of sex and gender is a relatively new field. The first scientific discussions of sexuality date back only to the early 1900s, and it was only in the 1940s that Kinsey conducted the first objective surveys of sexual behavior. The anatomy of both males and females is constructed to provide the most efficient means of copulation and reproduction. Sexual functioning, referred to as the sexual response cycle, is similar for males and females, with the primary differences being that men have a refractory period that requires a regeneration of energy between response cycles and women do not have such a refractory period, increasing the potential for repeated orgasms. The differences between men and women in terms of sexual response, however, are far less than once believed. The sexual motive is similar to other primary motives, such as hunger, in that centers of the hypothalamus play an important role, external sexual stimuli can stimulate the sexual motive, and the sexual motive can be influenced by learning experiences and emotions. The sexual motive is different from other primary motives, however, in that it is not necessary to the survival of the individual, it does not always lead to decreases in arousal, it is not influenced by deprivation in the same way, and it leads to a decrease rather than an increase in energy.

## Check Your Learning

To be sure that you have learned the key points from the preceding section, cover the list of correct answers and try to answer each question. If you give an incorrect answer to any question, return to the page given next to the correct answer to see why your answer was not correct.

1. The penis is the part of the male body that is most responsive to sexual stimulation. The part of the female body that is most responsive to sexual stimulation is the _____.

   a)   clitoris                    c)   cervix
   b)   mons                        d)   uterus

2. The four stages of the sexual response cycle were described by _____.

   a)   Freud                       c)   Kinsey
   b)   Krafft-Ebing                d)   Masters and Johnson

3. Hormones have a greater influence on sexual motivation in humans than in other animals.

   a)   True                        b)   False

## Thinking Critically about Psychology

1. We will study the psychology of love in a later chapter—can learning about sexual anatomy and the sexual response cycle teach us anything that is relevant to romantic love?

2. How could an understanding of sexual motivation help a person maintain a committed relationship with a partner?

Correct Answers: 1. a (p. 432), 2. d (p. 433), 3. b (p. 437).

## ● Atypical and Abnormal Sexual Behavior

Human beings differ widely in their sexual preferences and practices. In the sections that follow, we will look at the range of unusual, or **atypical, sexual behavior.** In the first section, atypical patterns of sexuality are described that are considered abnormal only if the individuals who engage in the sexual practices consider them abnormal for themselves. In the next sections, we will examine patterns of sexuality that are usually considered to be abnormal (fetishism, sexual sadism, and masochism) or always considered to be abnormal (voyeurism, exhibitionism, and forced sex).

### Transvestism and Transsexualism

These two superficially similar patterns of sexuality are often confused because they both involve dressing in the clothing of the other sex. But they have little else in common except that they are rarely harmful to anyone. **Transvestism** refers to the practice of dressing in the clothes of the other sex. Transvestites often state that they cross-dress because it is sexually stimulating, but many transvestites say they cross-dress to free themselves from confining sexual stereotypes. Transvestites are almost always males who have relatively well-adjusted sex lives.

**Transsexualism,** on the other hand, refers to a condition in which the individual feels trapped in a body of the wrong sex. For example, a person who is anatomically male feels that he is actually a woman who somehow was given the wrong body. Transsexuals may occasionally or permanently dress in clothes of the other anatomical sex, but this cross-sex dressing has nothing to do with sexual arousal. These individuals merely feel that they are dressing in the clothes of their true sex.

In some instances, these individuals undergo hormone injections and plastic surgery to change their sex organs to those of the desired sex. For example, physician Richard Raskins had a sex-change operation because he felt like a female trapped in a male body. After the operation, he adopted the name Renee Richards and briefly played on the women's professional tennis circuit. Male-to-female sex change operations are much more common than the opposite, probably in part because surgically created penises are less satisfactory than surgically created vaginas (for example, there is less genital sexual pleasure).

The sex-change clinic at Johns Hopkins Medical Center stopped doing sex-change operations during the 1970s because follow-up studies showed that their patients were no happier with their lives after surgery than before. Follow-up studies of patients from other centers, however, have shown that the patients were generally happy with their new bodies if properly selected for surgery and counseled on what to expect from it (Baker, 1969; Pauly, 1968).

Although many authorities consider the unusual patterns of sexual behavior just described to be normal under most circumstances, the following patterns range from ones that are *usually* considered to be abnormal to ones that are *always* considered to be abnormal because of the harm caused to the individual and/or others.

### Fetishism

**Fetishism** refers to the fact that some individuals are primarily or exclusively aroused by specific physical objects or types of material (such as leather or lace). In some cases, the fetish is only an exaggeration of normal interest in specific body parts. For example, some individuals are only or primarily aroused by breasts, buttocks, blue eyes, and so on. But the term *fetish* is usually reserved for cases involving inanimate objects, such as panties, shoes, or stockings. A fetish is considered to be abnormal if it interferes with the sexual adjustment of the person or his or her partner. Often, the fetishist (who is usually a male) is aroused only by "used" articles and is sexually aroused by the act of stealing them from an unknowing woman. Because this can be frightening to the victim and is dangerous and illegal, fetishism is considered abnormal when practiced in this manner.

Richard Raskins became Renee Richards after having sex-change surgery. Raskins felt before the surgery that she was trapped in the wrong body.

**atypical sexual behavior**
Sexual practice that differs considerably from the norm.

**transvestism**
(trans-ves′tizm) The practice of obtaining sexual pleasure by dressing in the clothes of the opposite sex.

**transsexualism**
(trans-seks′u-ah-lizm) A condition in which an individual feels trapped in the body of the wrong sex.

**fetishism**
(fet′ish-izm) The practice of obtaining sexual arousal primarily or exclusively from specific objects.

**sexual sadism**
(sād´izm) The practice of obtaining sexual pleasure by inflicting pain on others.

**sexual masochism**
(mas´-o-kizm) A condition in which receiving pain is sexually exciting.

**voyeurism**
(voi´yer-izm) The practice of obtaining sexual pleasure by watching members of the opposite sex undressing or engaging in sexual activities.

**exhibitionism**
(ek˝sĭ-bish´ŭ-nizm˝) The practice of obtaining sexual pleasure by exposing one's genitals to others.

**rape**
The act of forcing sexual activity on an unwilling person.

## Sexual Sadism and Masochism

**Sexual sadism** is the practice of receiving sexual pleasure from inflicting pain on others. **Sexual masochism** is the condition in which receiving pain is sexually exciting. Sometimes verbal abuse or "degradation" is substituted for physical pain. Approximately 5 to 10 percent of men and women find giving or receiving pain to be sexually exciting at times, but this is the preferred or only method of sexual arousal for very few individuals. Many individuals who practice sadism and masochism, or *S&M*, do so with a consenting partner who also enjoys the practice, and they do not inflict pain that is severe or medically dangerous—for example, mild spankings, pinching, and so on. In such cases, S&M may be considered normal if care is taken to avoid accidental harm and one's partner is *truly* willing. In some cases, however, the partner is unwillingly coerced into participation in S&M activities. In some cases, furthermore, S&M involves intense pain (such as whipping, burning, and kicking). S&M is always considered abnormal if there is any question about voluntary participation by both partners or if physical harm is inflicted. In rare cases, the sadist mutilates or even murders the victim to receive pleasure. Such practices are unquestionably abnormal.

## Voyeurism and Exhibitionism

**Voyeurism** is the practice of obtaining sexual pleasure by watching others undressing or engaging in sexual activities. Voyeurs generally find this exciting only when the person they are watching is unaware of their presence and when there is an element of danger involved. They are no more aroused than the average person while at a nudist camp, but they become very excited peeping into windows (Tollison & Adams, 1979). Because they often frighten the person they are watching, and because the activity is illegal, voyeurism is considered to be abnormal. The voyeur is generally a heterosexual male who has trouble establishing a normal sexual relationship. Some voyeurs commit rape and other serious crimes, but most are not physically dangerous.

Individuals who practice **exhibitionism** obtain sexual pleasure from exposing their genitals to others. Almost all exhibitionists are heterosexual males who typically are married but who are shy and have inhibited sex lives. Exhibitionists generally want to shock their victims but rarely are dangerous in other ways (Tollison & Adams, 1979). Because such behavior is illegal and frightening, however, exhibitionism is considered abnormal.

## Forced Sexual Behavior

Several other forms of deviant sexual behavior are clearly abnormal because they involve actual, threatened, or implied force to the victim. These acts include rape, sexual abuse of children, incest, and sexual harassment.

### Rape

In **rape,** an individual forces another person to engage in a sexual act. In the vast majority of cases, the rapist is a male and the victim is a female—a woman is raped every 6 minutes in the United States (Federal Bureau of Investigation, 1990). In the United States, 22 percent of adult women and 2 percent of adult men have been forced to do something sexual at least once since age 13. The percentage of women who have been raped is strikingly similar across different ages, ethnic groups, places of residence (city, suburban, or rural), levels of education, and marital groups. In almost every instance, women were forced by men (or by two or more persons—at least one of whom was a male—almost a third of the time). Contrary to expectations, the person who forced the women to do something sexual was a stranger only 4 percent of the time and a casual acquaintance only 19 percent of the time. When women are raped, it is almost always by someone they know well (22 percent), someone they are in love with (46 percent), or their husband (9 percent). In the much less common instances of men being forced into sex, they are forced by women two-thirds of the time.

| Table 11.4    Rape Myths and Rape Facts | |
| --- | --- |
| **Myth** | **Facts** |
| **Myth:** A woman who goes to the home of a man on their first date implies she is willing to have sex. | **Fact:** A person going anywhere does not imply that he or she wants to do anything. Rapists distort their perceptions to fit their beliefs. |
| **Myth:** One reason that women falsely report a rape is that they have a need to call attention to themselves. | **Fact:** It is very rare for a woman to falsely report a rape. Reporting a rape is a traumatic event. |
| **Myth:** Any healthy woman can resist a rapist if she really wants to. | **Fact:** Rapes are brutal and violent acts that may be worse with resistance. |
| **Myth:** Women who go around braless or wearing short skirts are asking for trouble. | **Fact:** No victim has ever asked to be raped. Rapists are responsible for their actions. |

The aftermath of rape is traumatic. Rape victims almost invariably feel that their entire life has been altered due to their assault (Nadelson, 1990). Many victims of rape experience mental anguish, often referred to as the **rape trauma syndrome,** characterized by intense feelings of anxiety and depression as well as disturbances in sleep, relationships, and daily functioning (Calhoun & Atkeson, 1989; Thornhill & Thornhill, 1990). Unfortunately, many myths in Western culture have become attached to rape victims. These myths tend to place the responsibility for the rape on the victim while absolving the offender of personal responsibility for the rape.

There is no specific psychological profile for sexual offenders. Indeed, if one thing characterizes rapists it is that they are highly heterogeneous and cannot be characterized by generalities (Kalichman, 1990). Theories of rape, however, have stated that most men who rape are driven by aggressive impulses or the need to feel powerful and dominating rather than by sexual desire (Ellis, 1989; Groth, 1979). Many rapists will have raped numerous women before they are finally apprehended (Abel, Barlow, Blanchard, & Guild, 1977).

Victims often hesitate to report a rape because the process of testifying against the rapist is often made unpleasant by the investigating officers and the rapist's defense attorney. For this reason, many communities have established rape crisis centers, which provide ongoing support for victims throughout the reporting, investigation, and prosecution processes. Rape crisis centers also provide counseling to rape victims to assist them in readjusting after their victimization. See table 11.4 for a summary of rape myths and facts.

### Sexual Abuse of Children

Many children are sexually assaulted and exploited. In a large survey (Kohn, 1987), 27 percent of women and 16 percent of men reported being sexually violated during childhood. Some statistics suggest that as many as 40 million persons in the United States were sexually victimized as children. There are a variety of types of child sexual abuse. When the sexual contact is perpetrated by a family member, the sexual abuse is termed **incest.** When there is force or threat of force used, the sexual assault is **child rape.** When there is no clear threat of force, the sexual abuse of children is referred to as **child molestation.** Even child molestation is considered to be a form of forced sexual behavior, however, because the child cannot consent in any meaningful way to the sexual behavior.

**rape trauma syndrome**
The effects of rape on the emotions, behavior, and well-being of many victims long after the rape has occurred.

**incest**
(in´sest) Sexual relations between relatives.

**child rape**
Sexual behavior with a child achieved by force or direct threat of force.

**child molestation**
Sexual behavior with a child without force or direct threat of force.

Children who have been sexually violated demonstrate a wide range of emotional and behavioral reactions. If the sexual contact is not threatening to the child, such as in sexual exploration by an older child, there are rarely serious psychological effects for the child if the parents calmly handle the occurrence with love and understanding. When the sexual abuse is upsetting to the child, as is almost invariably the case when the perpetrator is an adult or when threat of force is involved, the psychological effects on the victim can be serious.

Many of the effects of child sexual abuse are believed to be long term. Indeed, the aftermath of child sexual abuse may be similar to that of adult sexual assault, in that children tend to be traumatized and suffer traumatic reactions (Finkelhor, 1990). Children are likely to act out sexually in response to sexual victimization, experience a sense of personal betrayal by the person who violated them, feel that they are powerless and lack control, and feel stigmatized because they were assaulted (Finkelhor & Browne, 1985).

Adults who engage in **pedophilia** experience sexual pleasure primarily through sexual contact with children. They usually first gain the trust and acceptance of their victims before engaging in sexual behavior. This means that child molesters and rapists are usually known and trusted by the child victim. Indeed, the molester or rapist is a neighbor, a family member, or someone who knows the child before the incident in 90 percent of cases (Mohr, Turner, & Jerry, 1964). The child molester is typically a male heterosexual and the victim is usually a young girl. In some cases, the molester is a male homosexual or a heterosexual female and the victim is a young boy. Tragically, many child molesters will have violated hundreds of children before they are caught. Like persons who rape adults, men who rape or molest children tend to be highly heterogeneous in their psychological makeup (Finkelhor & Browne, 1985).

## Sexual Harassment

Unwanted sexual advances; requests for sexual favors; unwanted touching of the legs, breasts, or buttocks; sexually suggestive comments; and any other form of coercive sexual behavior by others constitute **sexual harassment.** As many as 60 percent of women in the United States have been subjected to one or more of these forms of sexual harassment (Hotelling, 1991). But sexual harassment also includes the leering looks and inane remarks that men often foist on women on the street, which have made nearly every woman uncomfortable (angry, frightened, disgusted) at one time or another. Although it is less common, men are also the victims of sexual harassment in colleges and in the workplace.

Many Americans first developed a clear awareness of the issue of sexual harassment when attorney Anita Hill alleged that she previously had been sexually harassed by then Supreme Court nominee, Justice Clarence Thomas. One key component of sexual harassment is that it occurs between persons with different amounts of power, often in schools or the workplace. For example, a woman who is sexually harassed by her boss may think that she cannot report the situation without risking the loss of her job. But differences in power can exist even between two students or two employees with the same job if the person engaging in the harassment is physically stronger than the other (and even if no explicit threat of force is made). There are laws (such as the Civil Rights Act of 1964), regulations, and policies that guarantee every person's right to attend school and work in a nonthreatening environment. However, because of the imbalance in power inherent in sexual harassment, it is undoubtedly still true that most incidents of sexual harassment are not reported to authorities. Every victim of sexual harassment suffers in the sense of becoming less comfortable and relaxed at school or work. In some cases, however, sexual harassment can provoke serious levels of anxiety and depression.

**pedophilia**
(pe″do-fil′ē-ah) The practice of obtaining pleasure from sexual contact with children.

**sexual harassment**
Unwanted sexual advances, comments, or any other form of coercive sexual behavior by others.

Atypical patterns of sexual behavior that involve no harm to the individual or others are considered to be normal, even though they are unusual and perceived as immoral by some members of society. Other forms of deviant sexual behavior are considered abnormal if they result in harm to anyone. The transvestite obtains sexual pleasure from dressing in clothing of the other sex. Transsexualism is the condition in which individuals consider themselves to be trapped within bodies of the other sex. Unless the individual is troubled by the condition, transvestism and transsexualism are generally not harmful to anyone. Fetishism—obtaining sexual pleasure from specific objects—need not be harmful but can be if the objects are stolen or the preference causes trouble in some other way. Sadism—sexual arousal from inflicting pain—may be harmless if practiced in a mild way with a completely willing partner but is generally considered abnormal because of the pain and medical risk involved. Masochism—sexual arousal from receiving pain—is generally considered abnormal for the same reason. Voyeurism is the practice of obtaining sexual pleasure by peeping at nude or sexually involved individuals. Exhibitionism is the practice of obtaining sexual excitement by exposing one's genitals to an unwilling person. Because of the frightening nature and illegality of these activities, both exhibitionism and voyeurism are considered abnormal. Forced sexual behaviors—including rape, sexual abuse of children, incest, and sexual harassment—are always considered abnormal because of the inherent psychological and physical harm that may occur.

To be sure that you have learned the key points from the preceding section, cover the list of correct answers and try to answer each question. If you give an incorrect answer to any question, return to the page given next to the correct answer to see why your answer was not correct.

1. Sexual behavior is considered to be abnormal if it is _____.
   a) atypical      c) harmful
   b) strange or bizarre      d) infrequent

2. A person who obtains sexual pleasure from dressing in clothing of the other sex is said to be _____.
   a) a transvestite      c) a transylvanian
   b) a transsexual      d) all of the above

3. A person who obtains sexual pleasure by watching others undressing or engaging in sexual activities is said to be _____.
   a) an exhibitionist      c) a masochist
   b) a pedophile      d) a voyeur

4. Most persons who commit child molestation are _____.
   a) homosexual females      c) homosexual males
   b) heterosexual females      d) heterosexual males

1. Have you ever experienced, engaged in, or witnessed sexual harassment? What do you think can be done to reduce the frequency of this problem?

2. Some people believe that those who practice transvestism are not psychologically healthy. What do you think?

Correct Answers:  1. c (p. 441),  2. a (p. 441),  3. d (p. 442),  4. d (p. 444).

## ● Sexual Dysfunction and Sexual Health

Several types of problems can interfere with successful and pleasurable sexual intercourse. These problems are quite common and considered abnormal only when they are prolonged. Even when prolonged, however, they do not mean that the individual has "psychological problems." Sexual problems can and usually do occur in perfectly normal individuals (Munjack & Staples, 1977).

**Sexual dysfunctions** are disturbances in any phase of the sexual response cycle. Different dysfunctions may have several different potential causes, both physical and psychological in origin. The most common physical causes of sexual dysfunction are drug or alcohol abuse, side effects of some medications, and some forms of illness. It is important, therefore, that all persons with problems with sexual functioning first be evaluated by a physician who specializes in the sexual-reproductive system, such as a gynecologist or urologist (Diokno & Hollander, 1991). Fortunately, solutions are available for sexual difficulties caused by medical problems. Many sexual dysfunctions are caused by psychological factors, however.

Sexual dysfunctions are classified according to the phases of sexual response within which they occur: sexual desire, sexual arousal, and orgasm.

### Dysfunctions of Sexual Desire

Among the most common sexual dysfunctions are those involving interest and desire in sexual relations (LoPiccolo & Friedman, 1988). It is important not to confuse sexual desire with sexual frequency, because a person can have frequent sexual encounters to please his or her partner but have very little desire for these sexual interactions. In contrast, a person may have strong sexual desire but not engage in sex for any number of reasons.

It is also important to note that everybody has a different natural level of sexual interest. A person is said to have a disorder of sexual desire only if he or she lacks almost all desire for sexual contact and is troubled by the lack of desire. Two specific types of dysfunctions involve sexual desire. First, **inhibited sexual desire** occurs when a person has sexual desire very infrequently or not at all. The second desire problem is called **sexual aversion disorder** and is characterized by a nearly complete fearful avoidance of sexual contact with others (American Psychiatric Association, 1994).

Both men and women experience disorders of sexual desire. There are numerous possible causes of these problems, including extreme anxiety about sexual intimacy or having had a sexually traumatic experience. In other cases, the person may not have a general lack of desire but may lack interest in his or her sexual partner because of problems in that relationship (Beck, 1995; Kaplan, 1983; LoPiccolo & Friedman, 1988).

Therapists who work with sexual desire problems first examine the person's overall relationship with his or her partner. If there are few relationship problems, therapy for sexual desire problems tends to focus on the anxiety that the person may experience in relation to sexual intimacy. Anxieties may block desires for sexual contact and interfere with sexual interest. Sexual inhibitions may result from experiences and characteristics of the person. These issues are examined in the context of sex therapy, where persons evaluate their anxieties and employ strategies to reduce them. Often therapy will involve both members of a couple to address specific aspects of their sexual interactions (Rosen & Leiblum, 1995).

### Dysfunctions of Sexual Arousal

Sexual arousal disorders occur when there is a lack of sufficient sexual arousal—including erection of the penis for the male and lubrication of the vagina for the female—

**sexual dysfunction**
An inability to engage successfully or comfortably in normal sexual activities.

**inhibited sexual desire**
A condition in which a person desires sex rarely or not at all.

**sexual aversion disorder**
A condition in which a person fearfully avoids sexual behavior.

Therapy can often help couples with sexual dysfunction.

during the excitement phase of sexual response. Note, however, that a person is said to have a disorder of sexual arousal only if this failure to respond occurs consistently, occurs even with adequate levels of sexual stimulation, and interferes with sexual pleasure or causes discomfort. Thus, in sexual arousal dysfunctions, an interruption of the physical processes occurs in the excitement phase of sexual response—namely, blood flow to the genital region and muscle tension. Women may develop **female sexual arousal disorder** (previously referred to unkindly as "frigidity"), which is characterized by a lack of vaginal lubrication and a minimal subjective experience of sexual excitement (American Psychiatric Association, 1994). Disruptions that occur during female sexual arousal disorder are specifically associated with the physical experiences of sexual excitement. Because most women experience transient forms of these difficulties when circumstances do not lend themselves to sexual arousal on occasion, the lack of arousal must be persistent under even favorable circumstances to be considered a sexual dysfunction.

Other less common female dysfunctions are vaginismus and dyspareunia. **Vaginismus** refers to involuntary contractions of the walls of the vagina that make it too narrow to allow the penis to enter for sexual intercourse. In **dyspareunia,** the woman experiences pain during intercourse. Often, but not always, these conditions are accompanied by orgasmic dysfunction and anxiety associated with sex. Like the male dysfunctions, the female dysfunctions can usually be eliminated with professional help.

Similar to sexual arousal disorder in women, **male sexual arousal disorders** directly reflect the physiological process of sexual excitement in the male sexual response cycle. In men, the most common sexual arousal disorder is **erectile dysfunction** (previously called "impotence"). Specifically, despite high levels of sexual stimulation, there is insufficient arousal to result in the penis's gaining an erection suitable for sexual penetration. As is the case for women, to be considered a sexual dysfunction, these difficulties must be persistent even under ideal circumstances and must be accompanied by a lack of sexual pleasure.

There are many potential causes of dysfunctions of sexual arousal, most of which represent a complex interaction between physical and psychological processes (LoPiccolo, 1985). Anxiety, fear, distractions, fatigue, relationship problems, depression, and substance abuse can all cause sexual arousal disorders. Even just worrying about having an erection can sometimes lead to prolonged erectile failure. Sex therapy, therefore, usually addresses these issues in counseling. However, specific sex therapy techniques can be used to reduce sexual anxieties and increase subjective experiences of sexual sensation. For example, a couple may be instructed in how to pay maximum attention to their senses during sexual contact to increase their pleasure experience (Masters & Johnson, 1970).

## Orgasm Dysfunctions

Orgasm dysfunctions involve the disruption of the climax phase of the sexual response cycle. Thus, although the person has a sufficient level of desire and arousal, the sexual response cycle does not progress to orgasm. In women, sexual dysfunctions of orgasm are referred to as **inhibited female orgasm.** This is defined as a persistent absence or prolonged delay of orgasm, despite sufficient sexual stimulation and arousal (American Psychiatric Association, 1994). Notice the important phrase at the end of this definition, "despite sufficient sexual stimulation and arousal." The term *inhibited female orgasm* should not be used if the sex partners do not fully understand what constitutes adequate stimulation for the woman or if the partner is not caring enough to provide sufficient stimulation. In addition, because women experience many different normal patterns of sexual response and orgasm, the delay or absence of orgasm must be dissatisfying to the woman before it is thought to be a sexual dysfunction. Still, inhibited orgasm is a common reason for women to seek sex therapy from psychologists (Heiman & LoPiccolo, 1983).

Inhibited orgasm has many potential causes, including performance anxiety, relationship difficulties, fear of abandonment, and depression. Like other sexual dysfunctions, inhibited orgasm may be the result of sexually traumatic experiences. On the

**female sexual arousal disorder**
A condition in which sexual arousal does not occur in appropriate circumstances in a female.

**vaginismus**
(vaj″i-niz′mus) A female sexual dysfunction in which the individual experiences involuntary contractions of the vaginal walls, making the vagina too narrow to allow the penis to enter comfortably.

**dyspareunia**
(dis″pah-roo′nē-ah) A sexual dysfunction in which the individual experiences pain during intercourse.

**male sexual arousal disorders**
Conditions in which sexual arousal does not occur in appropriate circumstances in a male.

**erectile dysfunction**
A condition in which the penis does not become erect enough for intercourse under sexually arousing circumstances.

**inhibited female orgasm**
A female sexual dysfunction in which the individual is unable to experience orgasm.

**premature ejaculation**
A male sexual dysfunction in which the individual reaches orgasm and ejaculates sperm too early.

**retarded ejaculation**
A condition in which a male does not ejaculate despite adequate sexual stimulation.

other hand, failure to achieve orgasm is commonly the result of a lack of adequate clitoral stimulation (Goldsmith, 1988). Many of the sex therapy techniques used to reduce fears and anxieties discussed earlier may be used to treat female inhibited orgasm. In addition, inhibited orgasm may be caused by specific aspects of a relationship or situation that can become the focus of counseling.

In men, the most common orgasm dysfunction involves ejaculating as a result of minimal levels of sexual stimulation, usually just after or even before penetration occurs. When this problem persists over time and becomes distressful, it is considered a sexual dysfunction referred to as **premature ejaculation** (American Psychiatric Association, 1994). There are many causes of premature ejaculation, including inexperience, performance anxiety, fears, and unfortunate learning experiences early in one's sexual history (Annon, 1984). A variety of potential treatments for premature ejaculation can lengthen the period of time before ejaculation occurs. One method, called the *squeeze technique,* requires either the man or his partner to apply a comfortable but firm squeeze to the penis (either just below its head or at its base) to stop the impending orgasm. The pressure from the squeeze causes a delay of ejaculation when applied several times before ejaculation occurs. With repeated use, it can be an effective treatment for premature ejaculation, as the need for squeezing diminishes over time (Masters & Johnson, 1970).

Some men, in contrast, have an orgasm dysfunction known as **retarded ejaculation.** In this case, the man is rarely able to have an orgasm in spite of adequate sexual stimulation or is able to reach orgasm only after very long periods of stimulation (American Psychiatric Association, 1994).

All sexual dysfunctions share several things in common. First, because they involve sexual behavior, it is often difficult and embarrassing to seek help or discuss the problem. Society sometimes places unrealistic and demanding expectations on the sexual performance of women and men. Second, people with sexual problems may believe that they are the only persons who have such difficulties, leading them to believe that they are psychologically abnormal. Finally, because society places limitations on discussing sexual matters, people often believe that when they do have a sexual problem they have nowhere to turn for help. This, too, is incorrect—there are many sources of help for sexual dysfunctions.

Often, the first place to seek help for a sex problem is a medical doctor who can evaluate the person for possible physical problems related to the sexual difficulty. A physician can also refer persons with sexual dysfunctions to a psychologist who specializes in sex therapy if needed. Sex therapists must be certified by the American Association of Sex Educators, Counselors, and Therapists or another similar professional organization. Before starting therapy, be sure to verify that a therapist has received the proper training and credentials for the practice of sex therapy.

## Health Problems Related to Sexual Anatomy

Several health problems related to female and male sexual anatomy require our attention. These include forms of cancer and sexually transmitted diseases, including AIDS. Although these are medical problems, they have a psychological component—namely, the behaviors that we engage in that increase or decrease our risk and opportunity for early detection.

### Cancers of Sexual Anatomy

It is important for women to have regular gynecological examinations to check for possible cancers of the cervix, uterus, and ovaries. Any unusual changes in the menstrual cycle or atypical discharges should be reported to a physician. In addition, it is important for women to perform breast self-examinations each month. Breast self-examination should be performed at the end of each menstrual period, when the breasts are least likely to be swollen or tender (in older women who have experienced menopause, self-examinations should be done on a monthly basis). Women should carefully feel and look for any changes in size, shape, or color of the breasts and nipples. Signs of breast cancer include puckering of the skin, dimples, lumps, bumps, soreness, or any unusual nipple discharge or bleeding. Any such indications should be reported immediately to a physician. Although many such bumps and changes are not dangerous, it requires a medical professional to determine this. Early detection of breast cancer offers the best hope for fighting this serious health threat. In addition to performing monthly breast self-examinations, it is also important for women to have their breasts examined by a physician after the age of 20. Further, women should also ask their doctors when they should receive a *mammogram,* a low-dose X ray that is particularly accurate at detecting cancers before they can be felt in a self-examination.

There are also health problems related to male sexual anatomy. Men, particularly over 40, should have regular examinations by a physician that include checks for abnormalities of the prostate that may indicate prostate cancer. It is important for men to learn how to perform a self-examination of their testicles to detect early signs of testicular cancer. This is particularly crucial between the ages of 16 and 35, when testicular cancers are most common. The examination should be performed once a month. After showering, when the scrotum is likely to be relaxed and the testicles are loosely suspended, men should roll each testicle gently between their thumb and forefinger, feeling carefully for any lumps, bumps, or unusual tenderness. Testicles are smooth when they are healthy, so bumps or indentations are possible signs of cancerous growths. It is, however, normal to feel the epididymis, which may seem like a bump, along the back of each testicle. Not all bumps are cancers, but it requires a medical professional to distinguish dangerous bumps from harmless ones. If detected early, testicular cancer has a very high rate of cure. However, when undetected, testicular cancer is among the most deadly forms of cancer.

## Sexually Transmitted Diseases

Diseases that are caused by microorganisms spread through sexual contact were once called venereal diseases but today are referred to as **sexually transmitted diseases (STDs).** Throughout the ages, countless occurrences of STD epidemics have ravaged people across continents. Today in the United States, several STDs threaten the health of millions of persons each year. Some are easily treated and cured if detected early in their course; others are incurable and may eventually lead to death. When untreated and unattended, all STDs can cause chronic illness and infertility, and they pose serious threats to pregnant women and their offspring. All STDs are serious health problems that require immediate medical attention. Not surprisingly, the likelihood of contracting all sexually transmitted diseases increases sharply with the number of different sex partners a person has and with the frequency of unsafe sex (Michael & others, 1994). In this section, we will discuss the most common types of STD.

**sexually transmitted diseases (STDs)**
Physical diseases, such as syphilis and AIDS, that are transmitted through sexual contact.

**syphilis**
A sexually transmitted disease caused by spirochete bacteria.

*Syphilis.* Caused by a spiral, corkscrew-shaped bacterium called a spirochete, **syphilis** has been increasing in incidence in the United States in recent years, with more than 40,000 cases occurring each year. Syphilis progresses through a series of stages of infection. The first stage is referred to as *primary syphilis,* which may last two weeks to a month after infection. Early symptoms of syphilis infection usually include the appearance of a painless sore in the area where the spirochete entered the body, most often the penis or vaginal area. This sore is called a *chancre* and may at first appear to be a pimple, but usually it will become open and appear infected. The chancre goes away, but the person still has syphilis, which then enters its secondary stage. *Secondary syphilis* is characterized by bumpy skin rashes that develop over various areas of the body

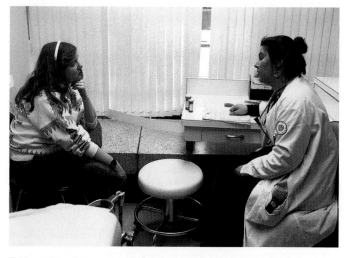

Taking steps to prevent sexually transmitted diseases is an important part of any sexual relationship.

(including the palms and soles) and that are accompanied by several common symptoms of illness, including fever, headache, nausea, swollen glands, sore throat, loss of hair, and loss of appetite. During the primary and secondary stages, syphilis can be cured in most cases with antibiotics. However, if untreated, syphilis eventually develops into its *tertiary* stage, which includes numerous serious health complications. The spirochetes may infect the tissues of the heart, brain, spinal cord, joints, and a number of other organ systems and eventually can cause death.

*Gonorrhea.* More than 700,000 cases of gonorrhea in the United States are reported to the Centers for Disease Control and Prevention each year, with actual rates of the disease estimated at over 2 million per year. Like syphilis, gonorrhea is a bacterial infection. However, the course of gonorrhea infection is quite different from syphilis. In men, gonorrhea's earliest symptoms involve the discharge of pus from the penis and painful burning and itching during urination. These symptoms usually occur within the first weeks of infection. In women, the early symptoms of gonorrhea infection usually involve a yellow-green vaginal discharge. Women may also experience vaginal itching when infected with gonorrhea, but many infected women do not detect the infection early in its course. In men and women, untreated gonorrhea can result in numerous serious health threats, including progression of the infection to the bladder, kidneys, heart, and brain. Fortunately, when detected, gonorrhea is usually cured easily with antibiotics. However, in recent years, strains of gonorrhea and syphilis that are very difficult to treat with antibiotics have become common, especially among ethnic minorities and the poor in large cities (Aral & Holmes, 1991).

*Chlamydia.* Chlamydia is the most common STD, with between 4 and 10 million cases occurring each year in the United States and with as many as 10 percent of college students being infected (Schacter, 1989). Chlamydia is caused by a small organism that invades several different types of cells in the body and uses them to multiply itself. The symptoms of chlamydia are usually vague and difficult to define. Often, there are no immediate signs of infection, with infection becoming apparent after a long period of time. Men may experience burning sensations during urination and may have a pus discharge from the penis. Chlamydia may also move into the testes and cause infertility. In women, the symptoms may include burning and itching of the vagina and burning sensations during urination. Untreated infections in women may progress to the fallopian tubes, causing infertility, and may develop into pelvic inflammatory disease, resulting in fever and serious illness. If detected, chlamydia is treated with antibiotics and is usually curable. However, chlamydia may be recurrent.

A magnified photograph of a pubic louse, or crab, which can cause itching when it bites into the skin.

*Pubic Lice.* This STD, commonly called "crabs," is caused by very small parasitic organisms that can just barely be seen that bite into the skin and feed on blood, causing skin itching. Pubic lice are treated with a variety of medicated shampoos and other applications.

*Genital Herpes.* Caused by the *herpes simplex virus (type-2),* genital herpes is treatable, but not curable. Similar to herpes simplex type-1, which causes cold sores, the symptoms of genital herpes are principally small, painful lesions that appear in the genital area. These lesions appear to be like small blisters that open and become wet. When present, herpes lesions are highly contagious and allow for the transmission of the virus to others who come in contact with them. It is also important for the infected person to avoid touching the herpes lesions or to wash thoroughly after doing so. Exposure of the herpes virus to the eyes can be particularly dangerous, potentially causing damage to the cornea. After

to the alcohol rather than their own choices. That is, alcohol can provide a means of evading responsibility for one's actions. It is easy for a person to say that he had been drinking and did not know what he was doing.

What are the implications of these findings? Is there anything that you can do to prevent date rape? The ongoing discussion of what constitutes date rape is an important positive step. Everyone understands that an intentional and forceful rape is wrong under any circumstance, but the boundaries need to be clarified for some cases of date rape. Following are some simple guidelines that may help.

## Guidelines for Men

1. *It is always rape when she says "no."* Women do not mean "yes" when they say "no." Be clear about this—"no" means "no." The research of psychologist Charlene Muehlenhard suggests that men often think that "no" means "yes" in sexual situations, especially if it is not stated emphatically (Muehlenhard & Hollabaugh, 1988). Men need to be aware of their tendency to think wishfully about women's sexual availability and to realize that even an unclear statement of "no" is a clear warning sign that he may be committing the felony of rape if he does not stop his sexual advances.

2. *If it is not clear that she has consented to sex, she has not consented.* Just learning to take "no" for an answer is not enough to avoid committing date rape. What should a male do if his date does not say "no" to a sexual advance but says something like "I really don't know if this is a good idea"? Is it rape if he continues, anyway? Sexual situations are filled with pressures that make it difficult to communicate clearly, and men tend to misinterpret subtle signals. This means that the only appropriate decision is to discontinue sexual advances when it is not perfectly clear that they are wanted. If she really wants you to continue, she will tell you more clearly later, but if she was saying "no," you will have avoided becoming a rapist.

3. *If she is drunk or high, she cannot give consent to sex.* Whether a male is intentionally trying to loosen his date's inhibitions or not, a drunken (or unconscious or stoned or high) date cannot give consent to sex. Decisions made while drunk can be tomorrow's tragedy—both to the woman who finds that she has had sex with a man with whom she had no intention of having sex and to the man who is arrested for raping a woman who he thought had given consent. And remember, a male who has been drinking is more likely to do things that he would not otherwise have done. Like drinking and driving, drinking and dating is a dangerous combination.

## Guidelines for Women

1. *Communicate your wishes about sex clearly and early.* As noted earlier, men have a tendency to hear women say "yes" about sex more often than women say it, especially if the communication from the woman is not crystal clear from the very start (Muehlenhard & Hollabaugh, 1988). This means that, to be safe, women who do not want sexual contact may need to communicate that fact in a way that leaves no room for doubt as soon as the first sexual advance is made. Our society teaches us to communicate about sexuality in subtle and indirect ways, but women who communicate their desires and limits clearly and assertively from the very beginning can reduce their chances of being the victim of a date rape.

2. *The combination of alcohol and sexual situations is dangerous.* Alcohol and other drugs bring out the worst in people. When a male has been drinking, he will be more likely to disregard a clear "no" or to become angry and violent when frustrated than when he has not been drinking. Similarly, when a female has been drinking, she may be less likely to say "no" to unwanted sex or may even be unable to make a rational decision about sex if she is intoxicated. Even moderate drinking can create serious problems, but heavy drinking is an invitation to date rape.

3. *Even "nice guys" can commit rape.* Because rapists are not characterized by any particular type of personality, it is not possible to predict who will commit rape. As stated earlier, most date rapists are men who seemed like nice guys to the victim before the rape. This is not to say that all men are potential rapists, but you should not assume that a male could not rape you under the wrong circumstances just because he seems nice. Try to avoid miscommunication and risky situations with all men.

Finally, if you or someone you know has been raped or if you are concerned that you might rape someone, help is available. Most college campuses have come to recognize date rape as a serious problem. The majority of counseling centers and student development centers have methods for addressing the date rape problem. Student organizations often assemble meetings to discuss issues of dating and dating violence. Off campus, community resources, such as mental health centers and crisis lines, offer services to persons concerned about being a victim of sexual assault or about the possibility that one could become sexually assaultive. There are many possibilities for improving the present problem of date rape, but all require open and honest communication and a willingness to evaluate one's own behavior. ■

# Summary

Chapter 11 describes the biological bases of sex, the psychological dimensions of gender and sexual orientation, and the psychological and social issues related to sex and gender.

I. The terms *sex, gender identity*, and *gender role* refer to important aspects of the human experience.

   A. A person's sex is defined by his or her male or female genitals. Gender identity is the personal experience of being a male or a female. Gender role refers to the patterns of behavior that communicate to others the degree to which we are masculine or feminine in the terms defined by our culture.

   B. Gender identity, gender roles, and sexual orientation are important aspects of our self-concepts and personalities.

      1. Gender roles are described based on how feminine or masculine the person's behavior is in terms of the expectations of his or her culture.

      2. Persons who show a healthy combination of masculine and feminine characteristics (androgyny) may be better able to cope with the complex demands of life than persons who are exclusively feminine or masculine.

   C. Although women and men are far more similar than different, some psychological differences between women and men have been consistently found in many studies.

      1. On the average, women perform slightly better than men in verbal skills, memory, perceptual speed, and fine motor skills, whereas men perform slightly better than women in mathematics, science, and social studies.

         a. Only one gender difference in cognitive functioning is even moderately large, however: On the average, men score considerably higher on tests of spatial and mechanical reasoning.

         b. These gender differences are more strongly related to gender identity (masculinity, femininity) than to biological sex.

      2. On the average, women are more likely than men to be nurturing, friendly, helpful, open, trusting, cooperative, able to conceal their emotions, anxious, or depressed; to have low self-esteem; and to engage in indirect verbal aggression. In contrast, men are more likely to be competitive, dominant, assertive, physically aggressive, risk taking, and the perpetrator of most kinds of crimes.

      3. On the average, men prefer younger mates who are physically attractive and have good housekeeping skills. Men tend to be sexually jealous and controlling of their partners but feel comfortable with the idea of casual sex for themselves. On the average, women prefer mates who are older and have good character and high earning potential. Women tend to be more threatened by their partner's emotional infidelity than their sexual infidelity and are more likely to be sexually intimate only with potential long-term partners.

      4. In spite of these differences, there is much more variation *within* each gender than *between* the genders, and many persons of each gender do not resemble the average.

      5. Two theories dominate current thinking about the origins of psychological gender differences.

   a.   The principal hypothesis of evolutionary theory is that gender differences became coded in our genes in the distant past because ancestral women and men faced different evolutionary pressures as a result of their different roles in reproduction and hunting.

   b.   The principal hypothesis of social-role theory is that gender differences in reproduction led each society to create a division of labor. The different social roles that this created for women and men—and the different opportunities, experiences, and restrictions associated with these roles—are the forces that create psychological gender differences.

D.   Two major theories of the development of gender identity have been proposed, both of which emphasize that gender identity develops from our interaction with others rather than being a simple reaction to our anatomical sex.

   1.   Psychoanalytic theory states that children usually identify with their same-sex parent to gain parental approval and to avoid rejection.

   2.   Social learning theory suggests that children imitate both females and males initially, but gender behavior that is consistent with their anatomical sex is usually learned because it is positively reinforced and other-sex behavior is punished.

E.   Sexual orientation is another key issue of our self-concept and sexuality.

   1.   Persons are considered to be heterosexual, homosexual, or bisexual on the basis of the degree of romantic and sexual attraction to members of the same or other sex.

   2.   It appears that both biological and social factors may play a role in development of sexual orientation.

II.   The scientific study of sexuality is a relatively recent event but has resulted in a good understanding of biological and psychological aspects of sexuality.

A.   The first scientific writings on sexuality were published in the early 1900s by Richard Von Krafft-Ebing and Henry Havelock Ellis.

B.   Serious scientific research on sexuality has increased since the 1940s, when Alfred Kinsey conducted groundbreaking surveys that provided the first descriptions of sexual behavior in American women and men.

C.   In the 1970s, Virginia Johnson and William Masters conducted laboratory studies that provided the first detailed description of the human sexual response cycle from initial excitement to orgasm.

III.   Although sexuality is far more than the activity of sex organs, an understanding of sexual anatomy and physiology is essential to understanding sexuality.

A.   Sexual motivation is similar to other primary motives in a variety of ways (including control by hypothalamic centers and the powerful role played by external stimuli, learning, and emotions), but it differs from other primary motives in a number of ways related to arousal and deprivation.

B.   Hormones play a less important role in the regulation of sexual behavior in humans than in other animals.

IV.   A number of uncommon patterns of sexual behavior are considered to be normal, even though they are unusual, unless they cause distress in the person. Other uncommon patterns of sexuality are usually or always harmful to the person and his or her partner.

A. Transvestism and transsexualism are atypical sexual patterns that deviate considerably from the norm but are not considered to be abnormal unless the individual is unhappy with his or her sexual pattern.

B. Abnormal patterns of atypical sexual behavior include voyeurism, exhibitionism, fetishism, sadism, masochism, rape, incest, pedophilia, and sexual harassment.

C. Sexual violence (including rape and the sexual assault and molestation of children) and sexual harassment are important social problems.

D. Sexual dysfunctions are problems that can interfere with successful and pleasurable sexual intercourse. These include

   1. Disorders of desire

   2. Disorders of arousal

   3. Orgasmic disorders

E. A number of health problems are related to sexual anatomy. These include

   1. Cancers of sexual anatomy

   2. Sexually transmitted diseases caused by bacteria (syphilis, gonorrhea, and chlamydia)

   3. Sexually transmitted lice

   4. Sexually transmitted diseases caused by viruses (genital warts, herpes, and the fatal acquired immune deficiency syndrome, or AIDS).

## Resources

1. For a summary of what is known about gender differences in cognitive abilities, see Halpern, D. F. (1997). Sex differences in intelligence: Implications for education. *American Psychologist, 52,* 1091–1102.

2. For a summary of what is known about the development of gender differences in emotion and aggression, see Keenan, K., & Shaw, D. (1997). Developmental and social influences on young girls' early problem behavior. *Psychological Bulletin, 121,* 95–113.

3. For very different views on the origins of gender differences, see Buss, D. M. (1995). Psychological sex differences: Origins through sexual selection. *American Psychologist, 50,* 164–168; Buss, D. M. (1999). Human nature and individual differences: The evolution of human personality. In L. A. Pervin & O. P. John (Eds.), *Handbook of personality: Theory and research* (2nd ed.) (pp. 31–56). New York: Guilford Press; Eagly, A. H., & Wood, W. (1999). The origins of sex differences in human behavior: Evolved dispositions versus social roles. *American Psychologist, 54,* 408–423.

4. For an excellent professional book on recovery from the trauma of rape, see Foa, E. B., & Rothbaum, B. O. (1998). *Treating the trauma of rape: Cognitive-behavioral therapy for PTSD.* New York: Guilford Press.

5. For more from the University of Chicago survey of sexual behavior, see Laumann, E. O., Gagnon, J. H., Michael, R. T., & Michaels, S. (1994). *The social organization of sexuality: Sexual practices in the United States.* Chicago: University of Chicago Press; and Michael, R. T., Gagnon, J. H., Laumann, E. O., & Kolata, G. (1994). *Sex in America: A definitive survey.* Boston: Little, Brown.

6. For more information on homosexuality, see Money, J. (1988). *Gay, straight, and in-between.* New York: Oxford University Press; and Mackey, R. A., O'Brien, B. A., & Mackey, E. F. (1997). *Gay and lesbian couples: Voices from lasting relationships.* Westport, CT: Praeger Publishers/Greenwood.

7. For information about AIDS, see Kalichman, S. J. (1996). *Answering your questions about AIDS.* Washington, DC: American Psychological Association.

8. For more on the issue of gays and lesbians in the military, see Shawver, L. (1995). *And the flag was still there: Straight people, gay people, and sexuality in the U.S. military.* New York: Harrington Park/Haworth Press.

9. For cogent discussions of feminist psychology, see Worell, J., & Johnson, N. G. (1997). *Shaping the future of feminist psychology: Education, research, and practice.* Washington, DC: American Psychological Association; and Crawford, M., & Unger, R. (2000). *Women and gender: A feminist psychology* (3rd ed.). Boston: McGraw-Hill.

10. Visit the McGraw-Hill Human Sexuality Drop-In Center at http://www.mhhe.com/socscience/sex/index.htm

# Chapter Outline

# Personality Theories and Assessment

## PROLOGUE

In psychology, we use the term *personality* to refer to the typical ways of acting, thinking, and feeling that make one person different from another. How would you describe your personality? What are you like?

There are thousands of words in the English language that we could use to describe our personalities, but many psychologists believe that an individual's personality can be summed up pretty well using just five basic concepts. How would you rate yourself on the following five dimensions of personality? On the first dimension, if you tend to be very relaxed and secure, give yourself a "1"—but, if you tend to be very tense and insecure, give yourself a "3." If you are neither very tense nor very relaxed, give yourself a "2" on this dimension. You could even give yourself 1.5 if you think that you are somewhere between a 1 and a 2. Now, rate yourself on the other four dimensions in the same way.

| 1 | 2 | 3 |
|---|---|---|
| Relaxed and secure . . . . . . . . . . . . . . . . . . . . . . . . . . . . . | | Tense and insecure |
| Quiet and not social . . . . . . . . . . . . . . . . . . . . . . . . . . . | | Talkative and sociable |
| Down-to-earth and unadventurous . . . . . . . . . . . . . . . | | Imaginative and daring |
| Irritable and ruthless . . . . . . . . . . . . . . . . . . . . . . . . . . . | | Good-natured and kind |
| Careless and unreliable. . . . . . . . . . . . . . . . . . . . . . . . . . | | Careful and reliable |

Some psychologists believe that the enormous range of variation in human personalities can be thought of as different combinations of high or low scores on these five basic dimensions of personality. How well do these five dimensions capture your personality?

In this chapter, we will discuss four approaches to the description and understanding of personality. These are trait theory, psychoanalytic theory, humanistic theory, and social learning theory. The last section summarizes several approaches to the measurement of personality.

Trait theory focuses on the best ways to describe the consistencies and organization of personality. In contrast, the other three theories are more concerned with *why* we behave as we do. Psychoanalytic theory was first stated by Sigmund Freud. Freud believed that your personality results from the struggle among opposing forces within your mind. We are born with selfish instincts, but our ability to think realistically and our values and ideals tend to hold those selfish impulses in check. The particular way in which each of us balances these forces gives us our unique personality.

Humanistic psychologists view the development of personality in an almost completely opposite way. Humanists believe that, rather than entering the world plagued with selfish instincts, we are born with a healthy, positive drive to realize our full potential. To humanists, the most important aspect of personality is the person's view of his or her self. An accurate self-concept is essential to healthy personality functioning, but humanists believe that society often sets such unrealistically high standards for what is "good" that it is difficult to see ourselves

## Key Terms

personality 462

traits 462

psychoanalytic theory 466

unconscious mind 468

repression 468

id 468

pleasure principle 468

primary process thinking 468

ego 469

reality principle 469

superego 469

ego ideal 469

displacement 469

sublimation 469

identification 469

psychosexual stages 470

Oedipus complex 471

Electra complex 471

feelings of inferiority 473

social learning theory 476

reciprocal determination 476

self-efficacy 477

self-regulation 478

situationism 478

person × situation interactionism 478

humanistic theory 480

inner-directedness 480

subjective reality 480

self-concept 480

symbolization 481

conditions of worth 481

self-actualization 482

projective test 488

accurately. The social learning theory of personality takes a simpler view of personality development. From this perspective, personality is something that is learned through our interactions with other members of society. People are not born with powerful negative or positive drives that collide with society. We simply learn our personalities from our interactions with others. ■

## Definition of Personality

**personality**
The sum total of the typical ways of acting, thinking, and feeling that makes each person unique.

**traits**
Relatively enduring patterns of behavior (thinking, acting, and feeling) that are relatively consistent across situations.

What do we mean when we use the term *personality?* It's no accident that the word *person* is in the word *personality*. Your personality defines you as a person rather than just a biological conglomeration of organs. One's **personality** is the sum total of all of the ways of acting, thinking, and feeling that are *typical* for that person and make that person *different* from all other individuals.

Notice that the two emphases in this definition are on the terms *typical* and *different*. An individual's personality is composed of all the relatively unchanging psychological characteristics that are *typical* for that person. Some people are typically generous; others are typically impulsive; others are typically shy. If people did not have at least some relatively unchanging qualities, we would never know what to expect from them. Each time we encountered a friend, it would be like dealing with a stranger. We know what to expect from our friends because of the relatively unchanging psychological characteristics that make up each person's personality.

The second emphasis in the definition of personality is on the term *different*. Each person's unique pattern of typical ways of acting, thinking, and feeling sets him or her apart from each other person. Each of us is a unique person because no one else has exactly our combination of typical psychological qualities. Even if every person were exactly identical in every physical characteristic—eye color, height, weight, tone of voice—we would be able to distinguish one person from another because of their typical ways of acting, thinking, and feeling.

## Trait Theory: Describing the Consistencies of Personality

What is the best way to *describe* an individual's personality? How can your entire personality best be reduced to a few words? Typically, we use terms like *friendly, aggressive, flirtatious,* and *fearful*. We are so fond of describing people in such terms, in fact, that there are more than 17,000 words for them in the English language (Allport & Odbert, 1936). In psychological terms, these words refer to **traits.** Traits are defined as relatively enduring patterns of behavior that are relatively consistent across situations. When we say that a person has the trait of friendliness, for example, we mean that she is friendly to most people and that her friendliness does not change much as time goes by.

Some psychologists have developed their ideas about traits to the extent that they are considered to be theories of personality. Unlike the other theories that we will discuss in this chapter, trait theories are more concerned with *describing* traits than *explaining* their origins. Although there are many important trait theories of personality, the best known are classic theories of Gordon Allport and contemporary five-factor theory.

### Allport's Trait Theory

Allport (1937, 1961) believed that the most important traits were those motivational traits related to our *values*. Allport tells us that the best way to understand people and predict how they will behave in the future is to find out what they value—the things that they will strive to attain. A person who values money more than family life, for example, can be expected to accept a promotion that would mean greater pay but would require spending more time away from home. A person who values family life over money, in contrast, could be predicted to make the opposite decision.

Howard Stern's tendency to be flamboyant is a well-known aspect of his personality.

An important topic to all trait theorists is the ways that traits are related to one another and are organized. Because humans distinguish so many different traits in one another, each trait theorist has tried to reduce this confusing complexity by showing that some traits are more important than others. Allport (1961) believed that traits could be ranked in terms of their importance as *cardinal, central,* or *secondary.* Cardinal traits are those that dominate a person's life. The quest for knowledge could be said to be one of the cardinal traits that dominated Albert Einstein's life, whereas the desire for social justice dominated Mahatma Gandhi's behavior. Allport felt that relatively few people possessed such cardinal traits. Much more common, however, are the central traits. These are important traits that influence and organize much of our behavior. For example, one person's behavior might mostly be aimed at obtaining intimacy and sexual gratification. Another person, on the other hand, may be relatively uninterested in intimacy or sex but may strongly desire power and prestige. Secondary traits are much more specific (such as being rude to door-to-door salespeople) and much less important to a comprehensive description of a person's personality.

## Five-Factor Trait Theory

Over the years, many trait models like those of Allport have been proposed, each stating that a different set of traits best describes our personalities. None of these models of personality was widely accepted in psychology, however, until recent years. Thanks in part to improvements in statistical methods and experimental strategies used to study personality traits, there is now considerable consensus among trait theorists that five basic traits provide a complete description of our personalities (Goldberg, 1993; McCrae & Costa, 1987, 1999; Wiggins & Pincus, 1992).

The so-called big five personality traits are described in table 12.1. These descriptions elaborate on the five dimensions of personality discussed in the prologue to this chapter. The most important adjectives that describe each trait are listed under the overall label of the trait. Notice that the adjectives are listed as opposites. Personality tests have been developed to measure these five traits. The goal is to use information that the

Gordon Allport (1897–1967).

| Table 12.1   Brief Description of the Big Five Personality Traits | | | |
|---|---|---|---|
| **1. Neuroticism** | | **4. Agreeableness** | |
| Calm . . . . . . versus . . . . Worrying | | Irritable . . . . . . versus . . . . Good-natured | |
| At-ease . . . . . versus . . . . Nervous | | Ruthless . . . . . . versus . . . . Soft-hearted | |
| Relaxed . . . . . versus . . . . High-strung | | Selfish . . . . . . versus . . . . Selfless | |
| Secure . . . . . versus . . . . Insecure | | Callous . . . . . . versus . . . . Sympathetic | |
| Comfortable . . . . . versus . . . . Self-conscious | | Vengeful . . . . . . versus . . . . Forgiving | |
| **2. Extraversion** | | **5. Conscientiousness** | |
| Retiring . . . . . versus . . . . Sociable | | Negligent . . . . . . versus . . . . Conscientious | |
| Sober . . . . . versus . . . . Fun-loving | | Careless . . . . . . versus . . . . Careful | |
| Reserved . . . . . versus . . . . Affectionate | | Undependable . . . . . . versus . . . . Reliable | |
| Quiet . . . . . versus . . . . Talkative | | Lazy . . . . . . versus . . . . Hardworking | |
| Loner . . . . . versus . . . . Joiner | | Disorganized . . . . . . versus . . . . Well organized | |
| **3. Openness** | | | |
| Conventional . . . . . versus . . . . Original | | | |
| Down-to-earth . . . . . versus . . . . Imaginative | | | |
| Uncreative . . . . . versus . . . . Creative | | | |
| Narrow interests . . . . . versus . . . . Broad interests | | | |
| Unadventurous . . . . . versus . . . . Daring | | | |

person taking the test gives to determine whether the person is, for example, more "calm or worrying" or more "at ease or high-strung." Then an overall score is generated from these items to yield a description of the person on that trait and the other traits. For example, a person who revealed himself or herself as worrying, nervous, high-strung, insecure, and self-conscious would be considered to be high on neuroticism. A person who answered questions on the personality test indicating that she or he was calm, at ease, relaxed, secure, and comfortable would be considered to be very low in neuroticism. Most people, of course, would be somewhere in between. As discussed in chapter 10, these five basic traits are thought to be relatively stable across the span and to be influenced by both inheritance and experiences (McRae & Costa, 1994, 1999; Zuckerman, 1995).

By the way, are people the only animal with personalities? Does your dog or cat have a personality that makes it different from other animals? Since the time of Pavlov, there has been clear evidence that mammals have personality traits like humans, and there is recent evidence that the five-factor model describes the personalities of non-human mammals pretty well (Gosling & John, 1999).

## Validation of Personality Trait Theory

Trait theorists have used a number of ingenious methods to validate the traits that they believe organize our personalities. For example, in one classic study (Eysenck & Levey, 1972), research participants were given a measure of the extraversion dimension of personality. Persons who score low on this dimension are considered to be *introverts* (quiet, reserved, loner, etc.), whereas persons who score high are considered to be *extraverts* (sociable, fun-loving, affectionate, etc.). Both groups were put through a classical conditioning procedure to condition the response of eye blinking to a neutral conditioned stimulus using puffs of air to the cornea as the unconditioned response. Why would Eysenck choose this very simple form of learning to test the validity of the trait of extraversion? He believes that introverts have higher levels of cortical arousal than extraverts and that this higher cortical arousal facilitates classical conditioning. As shown in figure 12.1, the finding that introverts showed a much higher percentage of conditioned eyeblink responses to the conditioned stimulus than extraverts supported Eysenck's prediction.

**FIGURE 12.1**

Eysenck's experimental test of the validity of the personality trait of extraversion using classical eye-blink conditioning.

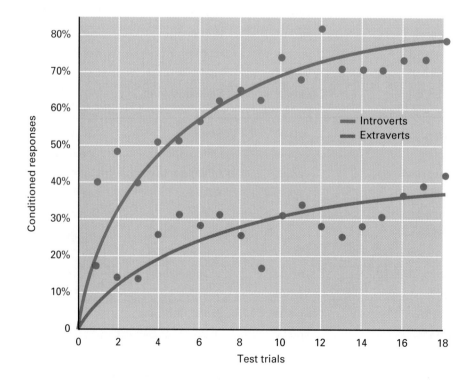

More recently, psychologists at Stanford University have used functional MRI to validate the traits of extraversion and neuroticism (Canli & others, 2001). When a group of women were shown pictures of scenes that evoke positive emotions, the brains of individuals high on the trait of extraversion showed much more activation in the amygdala and related structures than did individuals low on this trait. When the women were shown scenes that evoke negative emotions, women high on the trait of neuroticism showed much stronger response in regions of the cerebral cortex involved in processing emotions. These findings are remarkable in documenting strong correlations between personality traits and measures of brain activity. They lend important support to trait theories of personality.

---

## Review

Psychologists often describe the consistencies in personality in terms of traits. Traits are relatively enduring patterns of thinking, acting, and feeling that are relatively consistent across situations. Today, many psychologists believe that five basic dimensions of personality can be used to explain most of the variations among human— and even nonhuman mammal animal—personalities. Gordon Allport, and other psychologists have developed their ideas about traits to the extent that they can be considered theories of personality. These theories are designed to describe personality more than explain it.

---

## Check Your Learning

To be sure that you have learned the key points from the preceding section, cover the list of correct answers and try to answer each question. If you give an incorrect answer to any question, return to the page given next to the correct answer to see why your answer was not correct. Remember that these questions cover only some of the important information in this section; it is important that you make up your own questions to check your learning of other facts and concepts.

1. One's _____ is the sum total of all of the ways of acting, thinking, and feeling that are *typical* for that person and make that person *different* from all other individuals.

2. _____ are defined as relatively enduring and consistent ways of behaving.

   a)  States              c)  Characteristics
   b)  Traits              d)  Conditions

3. Trait theories are more concerned with describing the nature and operation of traits than explaining their origins.

   a)  True                b)  False

4. Allport believed that the most important traits were those motivational traits related to our _____ .

---

## Thinking Critically about Psychology

1. Does the five-factor model of personality leave out any important aspects of what makes you unique?

2. How would a police detective who was a proponent of trait theory attempt to catch a serial killer?

**Correct Answers:** 1. personality (p. 462), 2. b (p. 462), 3. a (p. 462), 4. values (p. 462).

## Psychoanalytic Theory: Sigmund Freud

Sigmund Freud was a young physician building a medical practice in Vienna in the late 1800s. He was particularly interested in treating patients with emotional problems but felt frustrated by the lack of knowledge that existed at that time. Although he had devoted many years of study in Austria and France to the disorders of the brain and nerves, Freud found that what he had learned was of little help to his patients. Thus, being a person of considerable confidence and intelligence, Sigmund Freud set out to develop his own methods of treatment. In the course of his development of treatment methods, Freud also developed a general theory of personality, an explanation for why people develop their unique patterns of typical behavior. His view is known today as **psychoanalytic theory.**

**psychoanalytic theory**
Freud's theory that the origin of personality lies in the balance among the id, the ego, and the superego.

Freud's theory of personality began with a very limited question. He wanted to understand the condition known today as *conversion disorder.* In this condition, the individual appears to have a serious medical problem, such as paralysis or deafness, for which there is no medical cause. To understand Freud's theory—which some of you will find quite shocking—we should begin with a description of one of Freud's first case studies. I think you will see the origins of his unusual ideas about what shapes our personalities in this amazing description. The young woman was not treated by Freud, but he helped her physician publish a description of her—one that had a lasting impact on his theories.

Bertha Pappenheim's unusual problems began at age 21. After 6 months of caring for her dying father each night, the formerly healthy young woman suddenly became paralyzed in her legs, arms, and neck and lost the ability to talk, except in a meaningless garble. Surprisingly, her physician could find nothing physically wrong with her. In time, her speech and muscular coordination returned, only to be followed by other strange symptoms. She was plagued by hallucinations of writhing snakes and grinning skulls; she was deaf for a time; she experienced blurred vision; and she had difficulty swallowing water for 6 weeks. But, after 18 months of frequent therapy sessions with her physician, Joseph Breuer, she was free of these bizarre maladies.

Bertha Pappenheim (1861–1936).

Dr. Breuer terminated his relationship with Ms. Pappenheim partly because of her improvement, but partly because he had developed strong emotional feelings for her, and he suspected that she had similar feelings for him. On the evening after his last session with Ms. Pappenheim, the young physician sat eating supper with his family when he was summoned back to Bertha's home by her maid. When Breuer arrived, he found Bertha writhing in bed, complaining of painful cramps in her lower abdomen. Suddenly, she shocked Breuer with the words, "Now Dr. Breuer's baby is coming! It is coming!" She was giving birth to a completely imaginary baby. Because of his complicated emotional feelings toward Ms. Pappenheim, Dr. Breuer transferred her to the care of another physician.

In 1895, Breuer and Freud jointly published an account of Bertha Pappenheim's problems, giving different interpretations of her symptoms. To protect her identity, she was given the pseudonym of "Anna O." Freud's theory was shocking: Freud believed that six months of being alone with her father while he was sick in bed heightened unconscious sexual desires for her father to the point that they threatened to become conscious. The paralysis and other symptoms, according to Freud, served the purpose of making it impossible for her to express her sexual longings; they held in check her nearly uncontrollable and wholly unacceptable desires. Later, these sexual feelings were transferred to Dr. Breuer, by whom she unconsciously wished to become pregnant.

It was only after her father died and she left Dr. Breuer's care that her unusual problems cleared up. Bertha Pappenheim's life continued to be tragic after her treatment by Dr. Breuer, however. Her new physician attempted to treat her with morphine. She soon became addicted to the drug and had to be placed in a mental institution. But by age 28, she had recovered and moved with her mother to Frankfurt. Although

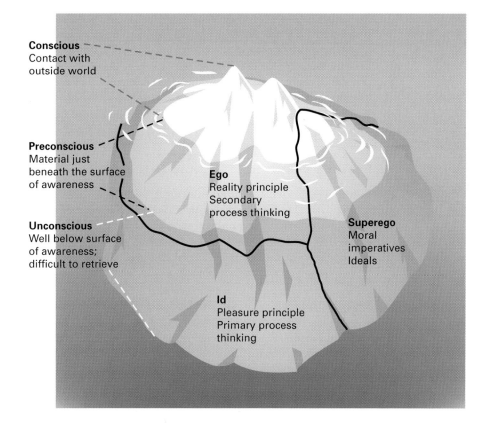

**Conscious**
Contact with
outside world

**Preconscious**
Material just
beneath the surface
of awareness

**Unconscious**
Well below surface
of awareness;
difficult to retrieve

**Ego**
Reality principle
Secondary
process thinking

**Superego**
Moral
imperatives
Ideals

**Id**
Pleasure principle
Primary process
thinking

**FIGURE 12.2**
Freud's model of personality structure. Freud theorized that we have three levels of awareness—the conscious, the preconscious, and the unconscious. To dramatize the enormous size of the unconscious, he compared it to the portion of an iceberg that lies beneath the water's surface. Freud also divided personality structure into three components—id, ego, and superego—which operate according to different principles and exhibit different modes of thinking. In Freud's model, the id is entirely unconscious, but the ego and superego operate at all three levels of awareness.

wealthy, Bertha began working in an orphanage for illegitimate children, first as a volunteer and then as its director. Gradually, the scope of her work grew to encompass educating unwed mothers, fighting anti-Semitism, and becoming an important activist for women's rights. In 1904, she founded the Federation of Jewish Women, which was successful in stopping the slave trade that exported impoverished Jewish girls to South America, where they were forced into prostitution. She also went against the orthodox religious views of her time and founded a school for Jewish women, the Beth-Jakob Seminary. Bertha Pappenheim's death in 1936 spared her from the worst of the Nazi persecution of Jews and the ultimate rape of her efforts. In 1938, the Nazis announced that the seminary would become a brothel and its students prostitutes. Rather than suffer this indignity, the 93 young women dressed in their finest clothes and swallowed poison (Freeman, 1972).

## Freud's Mind: Three Levels of Consciousness

Freud distinguished three levels of conscious awareness—the *conscious mind,* the *preconscious mind,* and the *unconscious mind.* We are presently aware of the contents of the first level of the mind, temporarily unaware of the contents of the second level, and more permanently unaware of the contents of the third.

To Freud, the mind is like an iceberg; the **conscious mind** is merely the tip visible above the surface, whereas the bulk of the important workings of the mind lurks mysteriously beneath the surface (see fig. 12.2). Just below the surface is what Freud called the **preconscious mind.** It consists of memories that are not presently conscious but can be easily brought into consciousness. You are not thinking right now about your last meal, the name of your psychology instructor, or the taste of your favorite drink, but you could quickly bring those items into conscious awareness if you wanted to. The preconscious mind is the vast storehouse of easily accessible memories. The contents of the preconscious were once conscious and can be returned to consciousness when needed.

**conscious mind**
That portion of the mind of which one is presently aware.

**preconscious mind**
That portion of the mind containing information that is not presently conscious but can be easily brought into consciousness.

"Good morning, beheaded—uh, I mean beloved."

**unconscious mind**
The part of the mind of which we can never be directly aware; the storehouse of primitive instinctual motives and of memories and emotions that have been repressed.

**repression**
Sigmund Freud's theory that unpleasant information is often pushed into unconsciousness without our being aware of it.

**id**
According to Freud, the inborn part of the unconscious mind that uses the primary process to satisfy its needs and that acts according to the pleasure principle.

**libido**
The energy of the life instincts of sex, hunger, and thirst.

**pleasure principle**
According to Freud, the attempt of the id to seek immediate pleasure and avoid pain, regardless of how harmful it might be to others.

**primary process thinking**
According to Freud, the attempt by the id to satisfy its needs by forming a wish-fulfilling mental image of the desired object.

Further down from consciousness lies the **unconscious mind.** It stores primitive instinctual motives plus memories and emotions that are so threatening to the conscious mind that they have been unconsciously pushed into the unconscious mind through the process of **repression.** The contents of the unconscious mind, unlike the preconscious mind, are not normally accessible to consciousness. They can rarely be made fully conscious, and then only with great difficulty.

## Freud's Mind: Id, Ego, and Superego

Freud also divided the mind into three parts in a different, but related, way. The best-known aspect of Freud's theory of personality is his view that the mind is composed of three parts, each with a different function: the *id,* the *ego,* and the *superego* (see fig. 12.2).

### Id: The Selfish Beast

When the infant is born, the mind has only one part, the **id.** The id is composed primarily of two sets of instincts, *life instincts* and *death instincts.* Freud wrote relatively little about the death instincts, but he believed that aggression and even suicidal urges arose from these instincts. The life instincts, termed **libido** by Freud, give rise to motives that sustain and promote life, such as hunger, self-protection, and sexual desire. To Freud, the sexual and aggressive urges are by far the most important of these motives. As strange as it may seem, sex and aggression are used by Freud to explain a vast range of personality characteristics, from kindness to shyness to cruelty. Freud believed that from birth on, every person's life is dominated by these two motives—the desire to experience sexual pleasure and the desire to harm others. Because the id operates entirely at the unconscious level of the mind, however, we are generally not aware of these motives. Only safe, watered-down versions of our true sexual and aggressive urges ever reach conscious awareness.

Freud's view of the dark side of the human mind is not an easy one for most of us to accept. Freud tells us that there lives within each of us a selfish, cruel beast. The beast—the id—operates according to the **pleasure principle.** The id wants to obtain immediate pleasure and avoid pain, regardless of how harmful it might be to others. But the id's selfishness is not its most alien characteristic to most of us. According to Freud, the id seeks to satisfy its desires in ways that are totally out of touch with reality. The id, in fact, has no conception whatsoever of reality. The id attempts to satisfy its needs using what Freud calls **primary process thinking**—by simply forming a wish-fulfilling *mental image* of the desired object. We use the primary process when we daydream about having sex, think about eating chocolate fudge cake, or angrily plan how to get revenge on the person who embarrassed us yesterday. Dreams are also a primary process means of fulfilling motives. The primary process satisfies motives through imagination rather than in reality.

But a person could not actually survive for long living by the pleasure principle (eventually you would get hurt if you fulfilled every selfish desire without regard for the feelings of others) or using only the primary process of wish fulfillment (forming a mental image of food will not meet the biological needs of the body for nutrition). Fortunately, during infancy, the period of time when we have only an id, we have adults around who see to it that our needs are realistically and safely met. As we grow up, our interactions with our parents and other parts of the real world lead us to convert part of the id into two other parts of the mind—the ego and the superego—that help us cope more effectively with the world. To borrow a phrase told to me by a skilled teacher, the ego and superego help us "keep a lid on the id."

### Ego: The Executive of Personality

The **ego** is formed because the id has to find realistic ways of meeting its needs and avoiding trouble caused by selfish and aggressive behavior. The ego operates according to the **reality principle.** This means that it holds the id in check until a safe and realistic way has been found to satisfy its motives. The ego's goal is to help the id fulfill its needs. It opposes the id's wishes only long enough to find a realistic way to satisfy them. The ego can be thought of as the *executive of the personality* because it uses its cognitive abilities to manage and control the id and balance its desires against the restrictions of reality and the superego.

### Superego: The Conscience and Ego Ideal

The id and ego have no morals. They seek to satisfy the id's selfish motives without regard for the good of others. The ego tries to be realistic about how those motives are satisfied. But as long as the needs are *safely* met, it does not care if rules are broken, lies are told, or other people are wronged. Although each of us wants our desires to be satisfied immediately, if everyone acted in this manner simultaneously, society would fall into chaos.

Restrictions are placed on the actions of the id and ego when the **superego** develops, the part of the mind that opposes the desires of the id by enforcing moral restrictions and by striving to attain a goal of "ideal" perfection. Parents are the main agents of society in creating the superego. They teach moral principles to their children by punishing transgressions and rewarding proper behavior. These experiences become incorporated into the child's mind as the two parts of the superego. According to Freud, parental punishment creates the set of moral inhibitions known as the **conscience,** whereas their rewards set up a standard of perfect conduct in the superego called the **ego ideal.** These two parts of the superego work together by punishing behavior that breaks the moral code through guilt and rewarding good behavior through pride. As the superego develops strength, children are able to control themselves and behave in ways that allow society to function smoothly. According to Freud's view, most of us do not steal, murder, and rape not because we do not want to or because our egos could not find relatively safe ways to do so but because our superegos hold these desires in check.

## Displacement and Identification: Becoming a Member of Society

The ego is not always able to find ways to satisfy id motives that avoid trouble and stay within the moral boundaries of the superego. Sometimes the ego must settle for a *substitute* for the goal of the id. A child who would really like to kick his father may have to settle for slugging his little brother instead. Or, if his superego prohibits hurting his brother, he may have to kick his teddy bear. The process of substituting a more acceptable goal is called **displacement.**

In terms of the interests of society, the best kind of displacement is called **sublimation.** In this form of displacement, a socially desirable goal is substituted for a socially harmful goal. Competing in school is a sublimation of aggressive motives, painting nude portraits is a sublimation of sexual motives, and so on. Indeed, Freud believed that all of the cultural and economic achievements of society were the result of sublimation. Thus, the individual who sublimates id energy not only is able to fit into society but contributes to its advancement as well.

Another process that allows individuals to learn to operate in society without friction is **identification.** This term refers to the fact that we tend to base the way we think, act, and feel on other individuals who are successful in gaining satisfaction from life. According to Freud, this is more than just a superficial act of imitation; we incorporate the other person's goals, actions, and values into our personalities. Thus, children come to

"Fifty is plenty," "Hundred and fifty."
© The New Yorker Collection 1987 Bill Woodman from cartoonbank.com. All Rights Reserved.

**ego**
(ē′go) According to Freud, that part of the mind that uses the reality principle to satisfy the id.

**reality principle**
According to Freud, the attempt by the ego to find safe, realistic ways of meeting the needs of the id.

**superego**
According to Freud, that part of the mind that opposes the desires of the id by enforcing moral restrictions and by striving to attain perfection.

**conscience**
According to Freud, the moral inhibitions of the superego.

**ego ideal**
According to Freud, the standard of perfect conduct of the superego.

**displacement**
(dis-plās′ment) A defense mechanism in which the individual directs aggressive or sexual feelings away from the primary object to someone or something safe.

**sublimation**
(sub″li-mā′shun) According to Freud, a form of displacement in which a socially desirable goal is substituted for a socially harmful goal; the best form of displacement for society as a whole.

**identification**
The tendency to base one's identity and actions on individuals who are successful in gaining satisfaction from life.

Competition in sports is one way of sublimating unacceptable aggressive impulses, according to Freud.

**erogenous zones**
A part of the body that releases sexual energy when stimulated.

**psychosexual stages**
In the personality theory of Sigmund Freud, developmental periods during which the sexual energy of the id finds different sources of satisfaction.

**oral stage**
According to Freud, the first psychosexual stage (from birth to 1 year), in which id gratification is focused on the mouth.

**oral dependent personality**
A personality type in which the person seeks pleasure through overeating, smoking, and other oral means.

**oral aggressive personality**
A personality type in which the person seeks pleasure by being verbally hostile to others.

**anal stage**
According to Freud, the second psychosexual stage (from 1 to 3 years), in which gratification is focused on the anus.

**anal retentive**
A personality type based on anal fixation, in which the person is stingy, obstinate, stubborn, and compulsive.

**anal expulsive**
A personality type based on anal fixation in which the person is cruel, pushy, messy, and disorderly.

**phallic stage**
(fal´ik) According to Freud, the third psychosexual stage (from 3 to 6 years), in which gratification is focused on the genitals.

behave more like the adults they identify with. In this way, identification serves an important role in socializing children. Indeed, according to Freud, identification is the key step in the development of the superego. We do not fully incorporate the morals and goals of society until we identify with the parent and internalize his or her values and ideals.

## Growing Up: The Stages of Psychosexual Development

Freud's theory of personality is a *developmental* theory. He believes that our personalities are formed as we pass through a series of developmental stages from infancy to adulthood. Events that happen as the individual passes through these stages can be critical in the formation of personality. Excessive punishment or reward from parents or traumatically stressful events experienced during a period of development can leave the person's personality "stuck," or *fixated,* at that stage. This fixation of personality development will, according to Freud, leave a lifelong mark on the personality.

To Freud, the developmental stages result from a shifting of the primary outlet of primarily sexually libido energy of the id from one part of the body to another. These parts of the body are termed **erogenous zones.** Because the developmental stages are based on changes in the release of sexual energy, Freud called them the **psychosexual stages.** According to Freud, the five stages of psychosexual development are as follows.

### Oral Stage (Birth to 1 Year)

The infant's earliest source of id gratification is the mouth. During the **oral stage,** the infant gets pleasure from sucking and swallowing. Later, when he has teeth, the infant enjoys the aggressive pleasure of biting and chewing. If the infant enjoys swallowing too much, however, she may fixate on this stage and become an **oral dependent personality** who continues to seek pleasure through the mouth by overeating and smoking and by being a gullible person who "swallows" ideas too easily.

If the infant's oral pleasures are frustrated, on the other hand, such as by a mother who sticks rigidly to a feeding schedule regardless of the infant's desire to eat, he may grow up to be a fixated **oral aggressive personality** who seeks aggressive pleasure through the mouth, for instance, by being verbally hostile to others. Similar fixations are possible at every stage of development.

### Anal Stage (1 to 3 Years)

When parents decide to toilet train their children during the **anal stage,** the children learn how much *control* they can exert over others with their anal sphincter muscles. Children can have the immediate pleasure of expelling feces, but that may cause their parents to punish them. If they delay gratification until they are on the toilet, children can gain the approval of their parents. According to Freud, excessive punishment of failures during toilet training may create a fixated personality that is either stingy, obstinate, stubborn, and compulsive (**anal retentive**) or cruel, pushy, messy, and disorderly (**anal expulsive**).

### Phallic Stage (3 to 6 Years)

During the **phallic stage,** the genitals become the primary source of pleasure. According to Freud, the child begins to enjoy touching her or his own genitals and develops a sexual attraction to the parent of the opposite sex. Freud believed that the shift to genital pleasure goes on in the unconscious mind, so we are not consciously aware of the touching or the incestuous urges. Instead, the child merely feels an intense love for the opposite-sex parent: Daughters become "daddy's girl" and sons become "mommy's boy." These sexual attractions bring about the intense unconscious conflict that Freud calls the *Oedipus complex* for boys and the *Electra complex* for girls.

Freud borrowed the term **Oedipus complex** from the ancient Greek play *Oedipus Rex* by Sophocles. It tells the mythical story of an infant who was abandoned by the king and queen of Thebes and grew up in a rival city. As a young man, not knowing who his parents are, Oedipus returns to Thebes, kills his father, and marries his mother. Freud believes that the play reveals a wish that is in all of us during the phallic stage of development.

According to Freud, all males unconsciously want to kill their fathers and sexually possess their mothers. Note that I said that this is an *unconscious* wish of which the boys are not consciously aware. Because such desires are unacceptable, they are blocked from consciousness. But the incestuous desires remain in the unconscious id, where they cause considerable discomfort. The child unconsciously senses that if these hidden impulses ever become unleashed, he will enrage his father. A fear arises in the immature mind of the boy that his father will punish his sexual desires toward his mother by removing his genitals—a fear called **castration anxiety.** This fear eventually leads the boy to repress desires for his mother and to avoid angering his father by identifying with him. As previously noted, this step of identification with the father is crucial for the development of the superego to Freud, because the boy incorporates the moral values and ideals of the father when he identifies with him in the resolution that ends the Oedipal complex.

The **Electra complex** of girls is the counterpart of the male Oedipus complex in Freud's theory. In the Greek myth, Electra has an incestuous relationship with her father. When her mother finds out, she murders the father. The enraged daughter in turn convinces her brother to murder her mother. The Electra complex is one of Freud's most controversial doctrines, as contemporary readers find that it portrays women in an outrageously negative light (Chodorow, 1989).

In Freud's theory, the Electra complex begins with the girl's "upsetting" discovery that she does not have a penis, but has an empty space instead. According to Freud, the girl unconsciously concludes that she has been castrated and blames the mother for letting this happen. As a result, she transfers her love and sexual desire from her mother to her father. In doing so, she hopes to share the father's valued penis because she has lost hers. The desire to possess a penis is termed **penis envy** by Freud.

However, the girl's sexual and emotional attachment to the father is too dangerous because of the prohibitions of society against her feelings. To resolve the Electra complex, therefore, her feelings for her father must be transformed into wholesome affection, and she must accept that she is "inferior," like her mother, and identify with her mother. In doing so, according to Freud, she will accept her role in society and develop her superego by incorporating the values of her mother.

According to Freud, failure to resolve the phallic stage results in a **phallic personality,** characterized by egocentric selfishness, impulsiveness, and lack of genuine feeling for others.

## Latency Stage (6 to 11 Years)

The **latency stage** is that period of life from about age 6 to age 11 in which sexual interest is relatively inactive. Sexual desire has been strongly repressed through the resolution of the Oedipal or Electra complex and is not a source of trouble at this time. Instead, sexual energy is being sublimated and converted into interest in doing schoolwork, riding bicycles, playing house, and participating in sports. To pass successfully through this developmental period, the child must develop a certain degree of competence in these areas.

According to Freud, we pass through five developmental stages, with the primary outlet of id energy or pleasure moving from one part of the body to another. Freud believes that, from ages 1 to 3, we are in the anal stage.

**Oedipus complex**
(ed´i-pus) According to Freud, the unconscious wish of all male children to kill their fathers and sexually possess their mothers.

**castration anxiety**
(kas-trā´shun) According to Freud, the fear of a young boy that his father will punish his sexual desire for his mother by removing his genitals.

**Electra complex**
(e-lek´-trah) According to Freud, the transfer of a young girl's sexual desires from her mother to her father after she discovers she has no penis.

**penis envy**
According to Freud, the desire of a girl to possess a penis.

**phallic personality**
(fal´ik) personality type caused by fixation in the phallic stage in which the person is selfish, impulsive, and lacking in genuine feeling for others.

**latency stage**
According to Freud, the fourth psychosexual stage (from about 6 to 11 years), during which sexual energy is sublimated and converted into socially valued activities.

### Genital Stage (11 Years On)

With the arrival of puberty and the **genital stage,** there is renewed interest in obtaining sexual pleasure through the genitals. Masturbation often becomes frequent and leads to orgasm for the first time. Sexual and romantic interest in others also becomes a central motive. But, because the parents have been successfully ruled out as sex objects through the Oedipus and Electra complexes, the new sex objects are peers of about the same age.

Although some interpersonal relationships are entered into merely to obtain selfish genital pleasure, individuals who have reached the genital stage are able to care about the welfare of the loved one as much as or more than themselves. This forms the basis for the more or less lasting relationships that characterize the genital stage and extend throughout adulthood. Sublimation continues to be important during this period as sexual and aggressive id motives become transformed into energy for marriage, occupations, and child rearing.

## Theories Derived from Psychoanalysis

Psychoanalytic thinking continues to be important in clinical and counseling psychology, but mostly through revised versions of Freud's theory of personality. Some modern psychologists adhere to an orthodox version of psychoanalysis, but far more endorse somewhat newer versions that grew out of Freudian thinking but differ on several major points. These revisions of psychoanalysis each differ from one another in some ways, but they share the view that Freud placed too much emphasis on unconscious sexual motivation and aggression, gave too little importance to positive aspects of personality, underemphasized the importance of adequate social relationships, and was highly prejudicial toward women (Westen & Gabbard, 1999).

The revisions of Freud's thinking began in a storm that took place during his own lifetime. As Freud's fame spread throughout Europe, he developed a group of followers. But when two of these followers, Carl Jung and Alfred Adler, disagreed with Freud on the issue of sexual motivation, they were angrily dismissed from the loyal fold. Freud was an authoritarian individual who tolerated little disagreement from others.

### Carl Jung

Carl Jung was a physician who had just begun his career working in a psychiatric hospital in Switzerland when he read Freud's most influential early work, *The Interpretation of Dreams.* He began to correspond with Freud and travel to Vienna for meetings. As Jung and Freud became friends, Jung joined the inner circle of Freud's followers as an influential member. Jung published a number of works that used Freud's ideas to explain aspects of severe mental illness, but gradually Jung came to question Freud's emphasis on sexual motivation. Within seven years of their first meeting, these differences in opinion led to a severing of their personal and professional relationship.

Jung felt that Freud took a one-sided negative view of the human condition. Although Jung thought that the unconscious mind did contain selfish and hostile forces, he believed that it also contained positive, even spiritual, motives. In fact, a fundamental characteristic of the human mind to Jung was that all important elements came in the form of *opposites.* We possess the potential to be both good and evil, feminine and masculine, mother and father. The question is simply how much of each we manifest in our personalities.

Among Jung's most original and lasting contributions to the understanding of personality are the concepts of *extraversion* and *introversion.* Each of us possesses a desire to be friendly, open to the things happening in the world, and concerned about others **(extraversion),** but each of us also possesses a tendency to focus our attention on ourselves, to be shy, and to meet our own needs **(introversion).** As with all of the polar opposites, Jung felt that it was important to allow a balance of these two opposing tendencies. We should not be too much of an introvert or too much of an extravert.

Carl Jung (1875–1961).

Each of us, according to Jung, is a blend of extravert and introvert. Jung felt that a balance of these two opposing tendencies is desirable.

Jung also modified Freud's view of the unconscious. He felt that we possess both a *personal unconscious* and a *collective unconscious*. The **personal unconscious** contains those motives, conflicts, and information that we have repressed into unconsciousness because they are threatening to us. The **collective unconscious** is the unconscious mind with which all humans are born. He used the term *collective* to emphasize that its contents are the same for all humans. Much of his later career was devoted to blending his interest in psychology with his childhood interest in cultures from the past. He assembled a variety of evidence to suggest that every culture expresses the same sorts of unconscious motives in very much the same symbolic ways. For example, in Jung's view the sexual symbol of the phallus (the penis) has appeared in many cultures throughout history in the form of totem poles, scepters held by kings to symbolize authority, and structures such as the Washington Monument.

### Alfred Adler

Alfred Adler was a young physician practicing medicine in Vienna when he was invited to join the Vienna Psychoanalytic Association. He soon became a favorite of Freud and was asked to be the second president of the society succeeding Freud himself. In time, however, the two argued over the publication policies of the association's journal and parted company. Differences between the psychological views of the two men had already become apparent, but they became increasingly obvious after the personal dispute.

Adler agreed with Freud that the struggle to come to grips with one's sexual and hostile impulses was important to the development of personality, but he did not feel it was the most important factor. In his early career, Adler felt that the primary struggle in personality development was the effort to overcome **feelings of inferiority** in social relationships and to develop feelings of superiority. At first, he limited this view to individuals who were born with physical defects, as was Adler himself, but later he expanded this view to include physically normal individuals as well. Because we are all small and dependent on the protection of adults as children, we all begin life with feelings of inferiority. The task of personality development, according to Adler, is to outgrow the inferiority of childhood and to see ourselves as competent adults. Adler felt that the role of parents and other caretakers was so important in this crucial process that he devoted much of his time to the development of a preschool program that he thought fostered proper personality development. Even today, "Adlerian" preschools are popular in many parts of Europe and North America.

**personal unconscious**
According to Jung, the motives, conflicts, and information that are repressed by a person because they are threatening to that individual.

**collective unconscious**
According to Jung, the content of the unconscious mind with which all humans are born.

**feelings of inferiority**
According to Adler, the feelings that result from children being less powerful than adults that must be overcome during the development of the healthy personality.

Alfred Adler (1870–1937).

Karen Horney (1885–1952).

Later in his career, Adler deemphasized the importance of struggling to outgrow childhood feelings of inferiority. In fact, he felt that the effort to achieve feelings of superiority over other individuals was an essentially unhealthy motive. Instead, he focused on two other factors as the most important elements in personality development. First, Adler felt that all human beings are born with a positive motive, *social interest,* to establish loving, helpful relationships with other people. The full development of a healthy personality requires that the individual learn to express this motive fully in his or her relationships with others. This contrasted with Freud's belief that only selfish motives are inborn. Second, Adler felt that people's lives are governed by their *goals.* Often these goals are not realistic at all, but they regulate our actions anyway, as we strive to achieve them. Adler's emphasis on goals, by giving such importance to a cognitive ego function, was also in sharp contrast to Freud's belief.

### Karen Horney

German-born physician Karen Horney became a leader in the revisions of psychoanalysis some 20 years after the first contributions of Jung and Adler. But, perhaps in part because she continued to write into the 1950s, she remains the most influential of the three. Readers today generally find her ideas more contemporary than those of Freud, Jung, or Adler. Horney considered herself to be a "Freudian" throughout her career because she agreed that unconscious conflicts were the source of most human misery and maladjustment. Like Jung and Adler, however, Horney felt that Freud placed too much importance on sexual conflicts. Moreover, she believed that conflict was not the inevitable result of inborn motives in the id. She believed instead that conflicts developed only as the result of inadequate child-rearing experiences. If the child feels loved and secure, no conflicts will develop, and positive aspects of the personality will dominate. If, however, the child loses confidence in parental love—because of the parent's indifference, harshness, or overprotection or for other reasons—the child becomes anxiously insecure. And this anxious insecurity is the source of all conflicts. For example, an insecure individual may develop a need to be "perfect" and feel tormented by all revelations that he is not. Another individual may aggressively push away the affection of others out of fear that they, too, will not consistently love her, but pushing away others is in conflict with the underlying need to be loved.

Horney was also an important critic of Freud's view of women. She rejected Freud's notion that penis envy is the central feature of the feminine psychological makeup. She felt that the issue was not envy of the penis or of masculinity per se but of the power and privilege of the male role in society.

Most contemporary psychoanalytic psychologists have continued to revise the theories of Freud in much the same directions. Writers such as Erich Fromm, Harry Stack Sullivan, and Erik Erikson (the latter theorist's views were presented in chapter 9 because of their relevance to developmental psychology) have continued to develop the neo-Freudian view of personality. They revise Freud's image of women, deemphasize the importance of sexual and aggressive motives, emphasize positive aspects of personality, and assert the importance of adequate social relationships. We will have more to say on this topic later in this chapter.

## Review

Sigmund Freud's theory of personality grew out of his early interest in the cause of the unusual symptoms of some of his patients. He decided that, since they had no conscious reason to have such symptoms, the cause must be unconscious, specifically repressed sexual or aggressive desires. Through the course of many years of treating patients with a variety of psychological problems, Freud came to believe that unconscious motives, particularly sexual and aggressive ones, were the source of most aspects of our personalities. Freud divided the mind into three levels of consciousness (conscious, preconscious, and unconscious) and into three parts with different functions (id, ego, and superego). The id is the storehouse of the unconscious sexual and aggressive instincts, and is the inborn, selfish part of the mind that operates according to the pleasure principle. The id seeks immediate satisfaction of its needs without concern for the welfare of others. The ego is the executive of the personality, which controls the id through adherence to the reality principle; it seeks to satisfy the needs of the id in ways that are both realistic and safe. The superego represents society's rules of right and wrong that often hold the id in check, not on the basis of what is realistic but on what is moral.

The process of becoming an acceptable member of society is aided by the psychological processes of displacement and identification. When it's too dangerous to directly satisfy an id motive, the motive is displaced on a safer, substitute goal. The most desirable form of displacement from society's perspective is sublimation, in which dangerous motives are transformed into socially desirable motives. The process of identification with social models further aids the individual's acceptance as a member of society by leading to the full development of the superego.

Sexual energy is transformed during the life span in yet another way. As the individual matures from infancy to adulthood, the principal means of obtaining sexual pleasure shifts from one part of the body to another. Pleasure shifts from the mouth to the anus and then to the genitals; it passes through a period when it lies more or less dormant and then reemerges as genital sexuality. Abnormal experiences at any of these stages can lead to fixations that hinder the full development of an effective personality.

Following the lead of Jung, Adler, and Horney, who broke away from orthodox psychoanalytic views during Freud's lifetime, contemporary psychoanalysts generally deemphasize the importance of sexual and aggressive motives. They have revised Freud's view of the inferiority of women, have emphasized the importance of social relationships in personality formation, and have stated that Freud overlooked important positive aspects of our personalities.

---

## Check Your Learning

To be sure that you have learned the key points from the preceding section, cover the list of correct answers and try to answer each question. If you give an incorrect answer to any question, return to the page given next to the correct answer to see why your answer was not correct.

1. The _____ mind is the part of the mind containing information that is not presently conscious but can be easily brought into consciousness.

   a) conscious                    c) unconscious
   b) preconscious                 d) suppressed

2. According to Freud, the _____ is the inborn part of the unconscious mind that uses the primary process to satisfy its needs and that acts according to the pleasure principle.

   a) id                           c) superego
   b) ego                          d) reality principle

3. To Freud, the five developmental stages represent a shifting of the primary outlet of id energy, particularly sexual energy, from one part of the body to another. For this reason, they are called _____.

4. Carl Jung disagreed with Freud's one-sided negative view of the human condition and proposed that all important elements came in the form of _____ such as introversion and extraversion.

   a) positive conditions          c) opposites
   b) synonyms                     d) matches

## Thinking Critically about Psychology

1. Does Freud's theory describe human behavior only for Europeans and Americans of his era, or does it apply to people of any generation or culture?

2. Why do you think Karen Horney and Sigmund Freud had such different views of women?

**social learning theory**
The viewpoint that the most important parts of our behavior are learned from other persons in society—family, friends, and culture.

**reciprocal determination**
(re-sip″ro-kal) Bandura's observation that the individual's behavior and the social learning environment continually influence one another.

Albert Bandura (1925–   ).

## ● Social Learning Theory: Albert Bandura

The social learning view of personality is vastly different from that of the psychoanalysts. Little or no attention is paid to topics such as instincts, the unconscious mind, or the developmental stages that are of primary importance to psychoanalysis. Instead, social learning theorists focus on a psychological process that is largely ignored by psychoanalysts, *learning*. To the social learning theorist, personality is simply something that is learned; it's the sum total of all the ways we have learned to act, think, and feel. Because personality is learned from other people in society, the term *social learning* is used.

**Social learning theory** had its origins in the behavioral writings of Ivan Pavlov, John B. Watson, and B. F. Skinner. Each of these theorists argued that personality is no more than learned behavior and that the way to understand personality is simply to understand the processes of learning. To social learning theorists, the key concepts in the study of personality are not id, ego, and superego, but classical conditioning, operant conditioning, and modeling, which were discussed in chapter 6. We will not repeat our discussion of these principles here, but it may be helpful for you to glance back over this material.

### Role of Learning in Personality

In the social learning view, a person will develop an adequate personality only if he or she is exposed to good models and is reinforced for appropriate behavior. An inadequate learning environment, on the other hand, will result in inadequate personality development.

A study by Susan Mineka of Northwestern University of the origins of fear provides a good example of the social learning position (Mineka, Davidson, Cook, & Keir, 1984). This study examined the learning of snake fears in rhesus monkeys (because researchers cannot ethically expose human children to social situations that may transmit fears), but the results may well apply to humans. Mineka and colleagues found that young monkeys who had been raised in a laboratory—and had never seen a snake—could learn to fear snakes through modeling. Although none of the monkeys showed fear of snakes when initially tested, they showed a strong and lasting fear after observing older monkeys (who had been raised in the wild and feared snakes) react fearfully to live or toy snakes. Simply seeing an adult react fearfully transmitted the fear to the younger monkeys and changed the monkey's "personality" in this specific way. To the social learning theorist, personality is formed through many such learning experiences.

The leading figure in social learning theory today and the person who gave the theory its name is Stanford University psychologist Albert Bandura (1977, 1989, 1999). In one sense, Bandura is very much a behaviorist. He agrees with the view that personality is the sum total of learned behavior. But he broke with traditional behaviorism in two main ways: (a) He sees people as playing an active role in determining their own actions, rather than being passively acted upon by the learning environment, and (b) he emphasizes the importance of cognition in personality.

Bandura (1977) portrays us as playing an active role in our own lives by stating that social learning is an example of **reciprocal determination:** Not only is a person's behavior learned, but the social learning environment is altered by the person's behavior

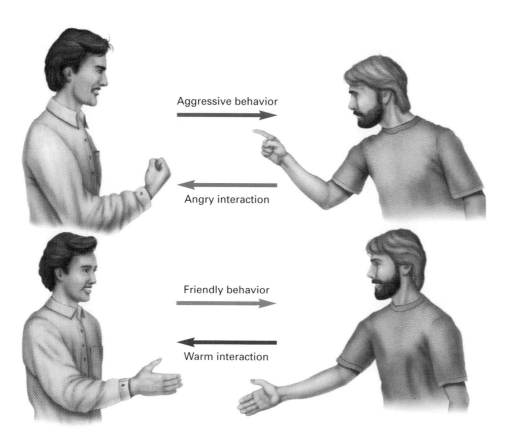

**FIGURE 12.3**
Social learning theorists believe in reciprocal determination; we learn our behavior from interactions with other persons, but our behavior influences how other persons interact with us.

(see fig. 12.3). The environment that we learn from, after all, is made up of people. If we behave toward them in a timid way, or a friendly way, or a hostile way, those people will react in very different ways to us—and will hence be teaching us very different things about social relationships. The aggressive, overconfident person will learn that the world is a cold, rejecting place; the friendly person will learn that the world is warm and loving. Personality is learned behavior, but it is also behavior that influences future learning experiences.

## Role of Cognition in Personality

According to Bandura, our learned cognitions are the prime determinant of our behavior. A person who believes that helping others makes them less self-reliant will be stingy; a person who thinks that other people find her boring will act quiet and shy. Bandura (1982, 1999) places particular emphasis on our cognitions about our ability to handle the demands of life. In his theory, **self-efficacy** is the perception that one is capable of doing what is necessary to reach one's goals—both in the sense of knowing what to do and being emotionally able to do it. People who perceive themselves as self-efficacious accept greater challenges, expend more effort, and may be more successful in reaching their goals as a result. A person with a poor sense of self-efficacy about social poise may not accept a promotion at work because it would involve giving many speeches and having to negotiate with dignitaries. Although our perceptions of self-efficacy are learned from what others say about us, from our direct experiences of success and failure, and from other sources, these cognitions continue to influence our behavior "from the inside out."

Bandura (1977, 1989) also emphasizes the learning of personal standards of reward and punishment by which we judge our own behavior. We learn our personal standards from observation of the personal standards that other people model and from the standards that others use when rewarding or punishing us. But although we are the

**self-efficacy**
According to Bandura, the perception of being capable of achieving one's goals.

**self-regulation**
According to Bandura, the process of cognitively reinforcing and punishing our own behavior, depending on whether it meets our personal standards.

**situationism**
(sit″ū-ā′shun-izm) The view that behavior is not consistent but is strongly influenced by different situations.

**person × situation interactionism**
(in″ter-ak′shun-izm) The view that behavior is influenced by a combination of the characteristics of both the person and the situation.

passive recipients of these standards in a sense, we then actively use them to govern our own behavior in the process that Bandura calls **self-regulation.** When we behave in ways that meet our personal standards, we cognitively pat ourselves on the back—we reinforce ourselves. We generally do not actually say to ourselves, "Good going; you did okay!" Rather, we feel a self-reinforcing sense of pride or happiness when we have met our standards (like Freud's ego ideal). Conversely, we punish ourselves (feel guilty, disappointed) when we fail to meet our personal standards (like Freud's conscience). In these ways, the process of self-regulation serves much the same purpose as Freud's superego.

## Situationism and Interactionism

Are you cheerful or are you gloomy? It may well depend on the situation you are in. Some situations make us cheery and some make us gloomy. Behaviorist B. F. Skinner (1953) argued strongly against the concept of traits. He suggested, instead, that behavior is determined by the situations people find themselves in, not traits inside the person. This viewpoint, known as **situationism,** suggests that our behavior is consistent only as long as our situations remain consistent. A woman might be friendly most of the time when she is with her family, but cold and distant when she is with her gossipy coworkers, and stiff and formal with her boss. According to Skinner, people behave in ways that suit their situations, and—because situations are apt to change—behavior cannot be consistent enough to be adequately described in terms of traits.

Social learning theorists have suggested a constructive compromise between the trait and situationism positions (Bandura, 1977, 1999; Mischel & Shoda, 1999). This compromise is so important to social learning theory that is impossible to fully understand it without understanding its solution to the problem of situational influences. The solution, known as **person × situation interactionism,** suggests that our behavior is influenced by a combination of characteristics of the person *and* the situation. For example, you might know somebody who is friendly and even fairly dominant when alone with you but painfully shy at parties. Or you might know somebody who is fairly quiet and dull in one-to-one conversations with you but a witty, vibrant conversationalist at parties. These two people tell us two important things about personality: First, each person's behavior is different in the two different situations (being alone with you versus being at a party). Second, the two situations influence their behavior in *different* ways. People are influenced by situations, it's true, but different individuals are influenced by the same situations in different ways.

This is the essential point of interactionism: The only way to fully describe a person's personality is in terms of "if . . . then" statements (Mischel & Shoda, 1999). "If he feels liked by others, then he is cheerful and kind. If he thinks other people don't like him, then he is gloomy and sarcastic." Such if . . . then statements provide a description of our personalities that allows a prediction of future behavior in a variety of situations. In order to understand *why* persons behave in different situations in the various ways that they do, however, requires a deeper level of analysis. To social learning theorists, the "person variables" in the person × situation interaction are the cognitive (beliefs, etc.), motivational (goals, etc.), and emotional tendencies that we have acquired through social learning and that determine how we respond to different situations (Mischel & Shoda, 1999).

The person × situation interaction is more complicated than it first appears for two reasons. First, people play a role through selective determination in selecting and even creating the situations in which they live. For example, a very shy person may avoid social situations, whereas an aggressive person would tend to seek out challenging situations and might even provoke hostile encounters with others. If we select and create our own situations based on our personal characteristics, this means that situational factors tend to play less of a day-to-day role in influencing our behavior than they otherwise might (Emmons & Diener, 1986).

Second, Darryl Bem (Bem & Allen, 1974) has added another interesting and important footnote to the concept of interactionism. He reminds us that one of the important ways in which individuals differ from one another is that some people are influenced more by situations than others. Some people are grumpy with everybody all the time, whereas other people are friendly with some people, grumpy with others, and in-between with the rest. With this in mind, a complete description of personality must also indicate the degree to which the person is influenced by different situations.

Bem's footnote about interactionism also raises an interesting question: Is it better to be a person who is strongly or weakly influenced by situations? Although it certainly would not be good to be wishy-washy and change your behavior every time the wind blows, Bem suggests that it's also not good to be too unchanging. Only individuals with serious psychological problems are rigidly insensitive to their surroundings. It's probably best to respond to changing situations to a moderate degree.

## Review

Albert Bandura is the leading proponent of social learning theory. Although this approach to personality theory grew out of the behaviorism of Pavlov, Watson, and Skinner, Bandura expanded behavioral thinking by emphasizing the importance of cognition in personality and the active role played by individuals in the social learning process (reciprocal determinism). To the social learning theorist, the process of learning is of central importance to personality development. Social learning theorists believe that people are influenced by the situations they are in too much for simple trait descriptions to be sufficient. They emphasize person × situation interactions, however, to highlight the fact that different people are influenced by situations in different ways. Thus, personality can best be conceptualized in terms of multiple if . . . then descriptions that capture both characteristics of the person (patterns of cognition, motivation, and affect) and the influence of situations on that person.

## Check Your Learning

To be sure that you have learned the key points from the preceding section, cover the list of correct answers and try to answer each question. If you give an incorrect answer to any question, return to the page given next to the correct answer to see why your answer was not correct.

1. _____ is the theory that our personalities are formed primarily through learning from other members of society and the theory in which the key concepts are classical conditioning, operant conditioning, and modeling.

2. Albert Bandura suggests that social learning is _____ : Not only is a person's behavior learned, but the social learning environment (situation) is altered by the person's behavior.

   a) bilateral                    c) bipolar
   b) reciprocally determined      d) interactive

3. According to Bandura, _____ is the perception that one is capable of doing what is necessary to reach one's goals.

   a) cognition                    c) confidence
   b) self-regulation              d) self-efficacy

4. _____ suggests that our behavior is influenced by a combination of characteristics of the person (traits) and the situation.

   a) Situationism                 c) Trait theory
   b) Learning theory              d) Person × situation interactionism

1. How might you use Bandura's theory of personality to help you better understand your own personality?

2. How would a police detective who understood person × situation interactionism attempt to catch a serial killer?

## Humanistic Theory: Maslow and Rogers

**humanistic theory**
The psychological view that human beings possess an innate tendency to improve and to determine their lives through the decisions they make.

**inner-directedness**
A force that humanists believe all people possess that internally leads them to grow and improve.

**subjective reality**
Each person's unique perception of reality that, according to humanists, plays a key role in organizing our personalities.

**self-concept**
Our subjective perception of who we are and what we are like.

The **humanistic theory** of psychology is often referred to as the *third force* in psychology. Although it has deep historical roots in philosophy, it has only been since the 1950s that humanism has become an influential movement in psychology. This approach to personality is the least unified and well defined of the three major viewpoints. This lack of unity is probably due less to the newness of humanistic psychology than to its origins. Each of the other two schools of thought began with the ideas of a single person. Although the views of the original leaders were subsequently revised by later followers, the original writings of Pavlov and Freud gave a certain unity to the theories that followed. Humanistic theory, on the other hand, emerged from the writings of a number of figures who shared only a few basic concepts.

The founders of humanistic psychology include Carl Rogers, Abraham Maslow, Victor Frankl, Virginia Satir, Fritz Perls, and Rollo May, to name only a few. It's impossible, therefore, to write a single statement that adequately summarizes the humanistic approach to personality. For this reason, we will focus primarily on the views of Carl Rogers and secondarily on the views of Abraham Maslow, emphasizing the parts of their theories that are consistent with the views of humanists in general.

### Inner-Directedness and Subjectivity

Humanists believe that humans possess an internal force, an **inner-directedness,** that pushes them to grow, to improve, and to become the best individuals they are capable of being. People have the freedom to make choices, and they are generally pretty good at making intelligent choices that further their personal growth. This inner-directedness is the primary force behind the development of personality.

Obviously, humanists have a positive view of the human species, but they are not blind to the fact that life is a struggle for everyone at some point and that many people consistently make a mess of their lives. We lose our ability to grow and to make good choices when we live with critical, rejecting people or when society tries to force us to be something that we are not. And, as Maslow has pointed out, the transition to higher motives is stunted when more basic motives are unsatisfied.

The personality that develops through the positive push of inner-directedness can only be understood "from the inside out," that is, from the perspective of the individual. To the humanist, the only reality is a **subjective reality.** Everyone views life in somewhat different, highly personal terms. What is real for you may not be real for me. You may see people as basically immoral, whereas I see them as basically moral. Each person's personality is a direct reflection of the individual's subjective view of reality. Our consistent way of acting, thinking, and feeling reflect our unique perceptions of what life is all about. And, as we will see in the next section, no subjective view of reality is more important to humanistic theorists than our subjective view of ourselves.

### The Self-Concept

The concept of the "self" is central to the personality theory of Carl Rogers and other humanists. Our **self-concept** is our subjective perception of who we are and what we are like. Of all of our subjective views of life, our view of ourselves is most important to our

Carl Rogers (1902–1987).

personalities. The concept of self is learned from our interactions with others: You might learn that you are a good athlete by seeing that you run faster than most other people or by your parents' and friends' telling you that you are a good athlete.

Rogers distinguishes between two self-concepts. There is the **self**—the person I think I am—and the **ideal self**—the person I wish I were. For example, I am pretty sure I can never be better than a "C" class racquetball player (self), but I would *love* to win tournaments in the "A" class (ideal self). On a higher plane, I see myself as a fairly nice person, but I wish I could learn to be less selfish at times. Rogers' concept of the ideal self is very similar to Freud's ego ideal.

Psychological problems can arise from three kinds of difficulties with the self and ideal self. First, excessive discrepancies between the self and the ideal self can be uncomfortable. It's okay for the ideal self to be slightly out of reach—that can stimulate us to improve ourselves. But if the ideal self is so unrealistically perfect that we know it can never be reached, then we feel like failures.

A study by Timothy Strauman (1992) at the University of Wisconsin tested this notion. Students in introductory psychology classes were interviewed and tested to determine whether there were discrepancies between the way they view themselves (their concept of self) and the way that they think they would like to be or ought to be (two aspects of the ideal self). Students who saw themselves as different from the way that they would *like* to be were more likely to experience sadness over time, and students who saw themselves as different from the way they *ought* to be were more likely to be anxious. Very similar results were found in an almost identical study conducted at the University of Iowa (Scott & O'Hara, 1993).

Second, an inaccurate self-concept can also cause problems. If our view of our "selves" is not reasonably *congruent* (similar to the way we actually act, think, and feel), then we will develop an obscured view of ourselves. For example, if I see myself as totally free from prejudice, but I feel a twinge of resentment when someone from a minority group gets preference over me in a job promotion, then my feelings of resentment will not "fit" my self-concept. According to Rogers, I might deny those feelings that are incongruent with my self-concept by not admitting them to awareness. In Rogers' terms, we are aware of feelings and information only when they are mentally **symbolized.** The failure to symbolize parts of our experience is harmful not only because it leads to inaccurate concepts of self, but also because feelings can continue to influence us, often in conflicting or anxiety-provoking ways, even when we are not aware of them.

Third, we also deny awareness to some of our feelings and experiences as a result of our parents' and society's reactions to our behavior. By reacting with warmth and praise to some of our actions (sharing a toy with little sister), but with coldness and punishment to others (hitting little sister with the toy), our parents create **conditions of worth.** They let us know that they find us "worthy" under some conditions and "unworthy" under other conditions. We internalize many of these conditions and perceive ourselves as worthwhile only when we act and feel in accordance with those conditions. Furthermore, we often deny feelings that are inconsistent with the internalized conditions of worth. The child, for example, may not symbolize her hostile feelings toward her sister, robbing herself of a valuable bit of self-awareness. Some psychologists believe that society's views of the ideal female and ideal male often create problems (Wood & others, 1997). When girls and boys internalize expectations for how they should ideally behave based on stereotypes of what females and males are like, conflict is created for those individuals whose actual behavior is different from their gender stereotype. Dominant females and gentle males, for example, could have difficulties accurately symbolizing these characteristics that are inconsistent with gender stereotypes in their self-concept.

Rogers' concept of unsymbolized feelings is similar in some ways to Freud's view of repressed feelings. Both can continue to influence the person, often in a harmful manner. But Freud views some repression as a necessary part of life, whereas Rogers believes that lack of awareness is always harmful. If we are to allow full expression to our

**self**
According to humanists, the person one thinks one is.

**ideal self**
According to humanists, the person one wishes one were.

**symbolization**
In Rogers' theory, the process of representing experience, thoughts, or feelings in mental symbols of which we are aware.

**conditions of worth**
The standards used by others or ourselves in judging our worth.

Abraham Maslow (1908–1970).

inner-directed tendency to grow, we must be fully aware of (symbolize) all of our feelings and experiences. Only in this way can we accurately understand and accept ourselves for exactly what we are (while always striving to do better).

## Self-Actualization

A major tenet of humanistic psychology is that humans possess an inner drive to grow, improve, and use their potential to the fullest. Abraham Maslow calls the ultimate in completed growth **self-actualization.** According to Maslow, the self-actualizing person is reaching the highest level of personal development and has fully realized her or his potential as a human being. What is a self-actualizing person like? Maslow (1967, 1970) gives the following description (see also page 384):

1. The self-actualizing person has reached a high level of moral development and is more concerned about the welfare of friends, loved ones, and humanity than self. The self-actualizing person is usually committed to some cause or task, rather than working for fame or money.

2. Self-actualizing people are open and honest and have the courage to act on their convictions, even if it means being unpopular. Self-actualizing individuals are not particularly interested in fads, fashion, and social customs and often appear unorthodox. They enjoy friends but are not dependent on their company or approval; they enjoy privacy and independence. On the other hand, their feelings for their close friends are intensely positive and caring.

3. They have an accurate, rather than a romanticized, view of people and life, yet they are positive about life.

4. Life is always challenging and fresh to the self-actualizing person. They are spontaneous and natural in their actions and feelings. Life is experienced in intense, vivid, absorbing ways, often with a sense of unity with nature.

**self-actualization**
According to Maslow, the seldom reached full result of the inner-directed drive of humans to grow, improve, and use their potential to the fullest.

Do not despair if you do not compare too well against Maslow's list. For one thing, self-actualization is at the end of a lifelong process of improvement, according to Maslow. You just may not have gotten there yet! Remember, too, from the chapter on motivation that *all* lower-level motives must be satisfied before a person can proceed toward self-actualization. If you are like most of us, you still have an unmet motive or

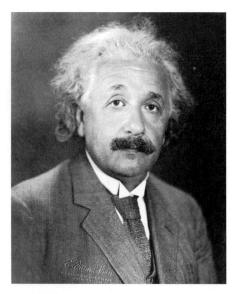

Albert Einstein (1879–1955).

Eleanor Roosevelt (1884–1962).

Ludwig van Beethoven (1770–1827).

two that is blocking your full development. Maslow felt that there are very few fully self-actualized individuals in the world. He identified a few that he thought probably were and studied them. His list included Albert Einstein, Eleanor Roosevelt, and Ludwig van Beethoven.

Maslow believed that we partially actualized souls get an occasional glimpse of what it is like to be self-actualizing in what he calls **peak experiences.** These are intensely moving, pleasurable, beautiful experiences when a person is fully absorbed in the experience, forgets his or her selfish interests, and feels a sense of unity with the world. These experiences can occur when looking at the stars, watching the birth of a baby, making love with your beloved, or even while doing something mundane, such as taking a shower. Most of us will experience some peak experiences in our lifetimes, but Maslow tells us that they are more common for self-actualizing individuals.

**peak experiences**
Intensely moving experiences in which the individual feels a sense of unity with the world.

## Humanism Compared with Classic Psychoanalysis and Social Learning Theory

Humanism, psychoanalysis, and social learning theory differ from one another in their views of the basic nature of human beings and of society. In classic psychoanalytic theory, people are seen as selfish and hostile at birth; they are nothing but id. Society is seen as a good force that instills the ego and superego into children, thus enabling them to behave realistically and morally enough to live in the social world.

To the humanist, the psychoanalytic view is exactly wrong. People possess a positive inborn drive to grow and improve. Instead of being born evil, the human is born basically good. Society, on the other hand, is seen by the humanist as a frequently destructive force that leads people to deny their true feelings (of jealousy, insecurity, passion) and creates unattainable ideal self-concepts (for example, American society tells us that we should all be attractive, athletic, sexy, famous, and rich).

Social learning theorists differ from psychoanalytic and humanistic theorists in their evaluation of the basic nature of humans and society. Social learning theorists see humans as neutral at birth, having the potential to learn to be either good or bad. Similarly, society can be either destructive or constructive. A part of society that teaches inappropriate behavior to its children is destructive, whereas a part of society that teaches appropriate behavior is constructive.

All three theories, however, believe that we internalize society's standards of what is desirable and moral and guide our behavior accordingly. Freud spoke of the conscience and ego ideal of the superego, Bandura used the concept of self-regulation, and Rogers spoke in terms of the ideal self. Although they differ in important ways, these are highly similar ideas about why we tend to obey the rules and standards of society. For a comparison of all three theories, see table 12.2.

## Contemporary Merging of the Major Theories of Personality

For many years, the three major theories of personality have shared a few ideas, even though they have disagreed in most ways. Recently, however, exponents of the three major theories of personality have made theoretical statements that sound remarkably like one another (Bandura, 1999; Mischel & Shoda, 1999; Westen & Gabbard, 1999). It is surprising but gratifying to see groups of psychologists who once bitterly criticized each another adopt the best ideas of one another. For example, both modern psychoanalysts and social learning theorists now speak of the humanists' concept of self as the core feature of personality (Bandura, 1999; Westen & Gabbard, 1999), and Maslow's positive drive to self-actualization has been incorporated into both psychoanalytic (Westen & Gabbard, 1999) and social learning (Mischel & Shoda, 1999) theories. Social learning theorists are speaking about unconscious processes (Mischel & Shoda, 1999), and psychoanalysts (Westen & Gabbard, 1999) are discussing person × situation

## Table 12.2   Comparison of Classic Psychoanalytic, Social Learning, and Humanistic Theories of Personality

| | Classic Psychoanalytic | Social Learning | Humanistic |
|---|---|---|---|
| An "unconscious" or "unsymbolized" mind exerts a powerful influence on us. | Yes | No | Yes |
| We learn what is "good" and "bad" from our families and cultures. | Yes | Yes | Yes |
| Our internalized knowledge of what is "good" and "bad" is an important part of our personalities. | Yes (superego and ego ideal) | Yes (self-regulation) | Yes (ideal self) |
| People are inherently . . . | Selfish and evil | Neither good nor bad | Good |
| Society . . . | Usually teaches us to convert our selfish nature into positive behavior | Can influence us in either positive or negative ways | Often harms or destroys our inherent tendency to be healthy and good |

interactionism in ways that closely parallel social learning theory. If these trends continue, the three major theories of personality may eventually become a single unified theory. At present, however, the three theories still remain far apart on some core issues (see table 12.2).

## Review

Humanism is the least unified of the three movements, but several basic concepts about personality are shared by nearly all humanists. The most significant factor in the development of personality is the positive inner-directed drive to grow and improve. Unless our experiences with society interfere with this drive, it can be counted on to direct personal growth in positive directions. The personality that develops from this growth can be understood only from the point of view of the individual. Personality is seen as reflecting each person's subjective view of reality. We act, think, and feel in accordance with how we view reality. And the most important aspect of that view of reality is our subjective concept of self. The ways I view both the self that I think I am and the self I would like to be are powerful determinants of my personality. If my ideal self is unattainably perfect, I will always fall painfully short of my standards. If my self-concept is inaccurate, I will not be able to deal with information about myself that is incongruent with my self-concept. Incongruent information is not admitted to consciousness, a state of affairs that humanists view as unhealthy for the personality.

Humanists, psychoanalysts, and social learning theorists take very different views of the basic nature of people and society. Psychoanalysts view humans as wholly selfish and hostile ids at birth. Society, in contrast, is seen as a positive force providing experiences that create the ego and superego that allow humans to function effectively in society. Humanists view people as essentially good but see society as a negative force that often interferes with the individual's inner-directed growth. Social learning theorists see people as having the potential to develop in either positive or negative ways, depending on whether their personalities were learned from positive or negative aspects of society. Although there are signs that the proponents of the major theories of personality are growing more similar over time, they remain far apart on such key issues.

To be sure that you have learned the key points from the preceding section, cover the list of correct answers and try to answer each question. If you give an incorrect answer to any question, return to the page given next to the correct answer to see why your answer was not correct.

1. According to _____ theory, human beings possess an innate tendency to improve and to determine their lives by the decisions they make.

   a)   social learning
   b)   psychoanalytic
   c)   humanistic
   d)   conditioning

2. According to the humanists, the _____ is the person one wishes he or she were.

   a)   real self
   b)   ideal self
   c)   new self
   d)   self

3. Our _____ is our subjective perception of who we are and what we are like.

   a)   self-concept
   b)   ideal self
   c)   self-efficacy
   d)   actualized self

4. Humanists believe that humans are born neither good nor evil.

   a)   True
   b)   False

1. If, as the humanistic perspective suggests, reality is subjective, how can individuals ever hope to agree on anything?

2. What are the best new ideas that you learned from this summary of the three theories of personality? What are the least helpful ideas to you?

**Correct Answers:** 1. c (p. 480),  2. b (p. 481),  3. a (p. 480),  4. b (p. 483).

# HUMAN DIVERSITY

## Personality and Culture

Your introduction to psychology is occurring at an exciting time in the history of the field. Increasingly, psychologists are accepting the idea that sociocultural factors such as ethnicity, race, gender, sexual preference, and physical challenges are important in understanding human personality (Betancourt & Lopez, 1993; Cross & Markus, 1999). One new focus of cross-cultural research has been on the validity of North American concepts of personality in other cultures. For example, a number of studies have confirmed the five-factor model of personality in many Western and non-Western cultures (McCrae & Costa, 1997). When correlations among items were examined using translated instruments, the same pattern of intercorrelated traits emerged in many cultures. Does this mean that these five personality traits are a human universal and equally meaningful in all cultures? There are two reasons to believe that the five-factor model and other trait approaches to personality may not be as valid in non-Western cultures as they are in North America.

First, some studies show that dimensions of personality that are specific to each culture emerge along with the five factors found in Western cultures. For example, a trait referred to as Chinese traditionalism has been found in Chinese participants along with the traits usually identified in the five-factor model. This additional trait is positively correlated with life satisfaction and negatively correlated with antisocial behavior (Zhang & Bond, 1998). Thus, personality may vary across cultures in the sense that traits that are specific to each culture may help us understand a person's personality, adjustment, and well-being.

Second, and more important, the concept of personality simply may have less meaning in some cultures than in North America. In individualistic cultures such as mainstream U.S. culture, we look for explanations for a person's behavior *within* that individual. Consider the focus of personality theories that have arisen in European and North American cultures. Trait theories focus on attributes of the individual (the traits). Psychoanalytic theories focus on conflicts within the individual. Social learning and humanistic theories highlight concepts such as self-concept, self-efficacy, and self-regulation. These theories of personality consider groups outside the individual only as positive or negative social influences on the individual. It makes perfect sense to focus on the individual in individualistic cultures, but less sense in collectivistic cultures

(Cross & Markus, 1999). In Japan, China, India, and other Asian cultures, the behavior of the individual is understood more in terms of the expectations, rights, and duties of being a member of a *group* (family, caste, country). Psychological explanations that focus on the individual ignore much of Asian thinking about the nature of people.

Susan Cross of Iowa State University and Hazel Markus (1999) of Stanford University offer the following concrete example of the vast difference between individualistic and collectivistic cultures' views of the person. These four "personal ads" were published on the same day in two California newspapers (a general readership paper and a paper that has a readership of mostly immigrant families from India):

*From the* San Francisco Chronicle:

> 28 SWM, 6'1", 160 lbs. Handsome, artistic, ambitious, seeks attractive WF, 24–29, for friendship, romance, and permanent partnership.

> Very attractive, independent SWF, 29, 5'6" 110 lbs., loves fine dining, the theater, gardening and quiet evenings at home. In search of handsome SWM 28–34 with similar interests.

*From the* India Tribune:

> Gujarati Vaishnav parents invite correspondence from never married Gujarati well settled, preferably green card holder from respectable family for green card holder daughter 29 years, 5'4", good looking, doing CPA.

> Gujarati Brahmin family invites correspondence from a well cultured, beautiful Gujarati girl for 29 years, 5'8", 145 lbs. handsome looking, well settled boy.

Notice that these ads are similar in some ways (all refer to physical appearance and age) but very different in other ways. The ads in the general readership newspaper reflect the individualistic U.S. culture. They describe only the individual's characteristics and preferences. In contrast, the ads in the *India Tribune* reflect the collectivistic Indian culture by focusing on the individual's membership in *groups.* They were placed in the name of the families rather than the individual, and they refer both to the state in India from which the families came (Gujarati) and to the caste of the family (Vaishnav and Brahmin). It is this strong emphasis on the embeddedness of the individual in groups that have more importance than the individual that

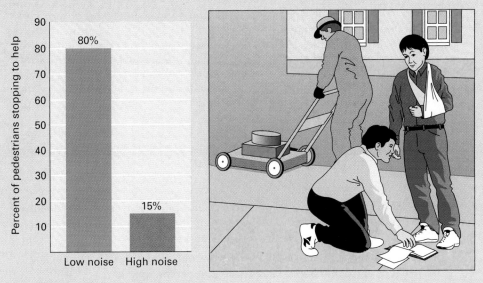

**FIGURE 12.7**

The percentage of pedestrians who stopped to help a man with an arm cast who had dropped his books was compared under conditions of low and high noise.
Source: Data for graph from K. E. Mathews and L. K. Canon, in *Journal of Personality and Social Psychology*, 32:571–577, 1975.

enced only by situations—different people react to the same situations differently—but these experiments may help you understand why many psychologists feel that describing personality only in terms of fixed traits is inadequate as well. Both a description of characteristics of the person and how these personal characteristics interact with changing situations is needed for a full description of personality.

What about happiness and general satisfaction with life? How much is that influenced by situational influences? Many survey studies have been done in recent years in almost 100 different countries that show that some situations have a powerful influence on happiness (Myers & Diener, 1995). People who live in countries with stable democracies and people who are in stable relationships are considerably more likely to be happy than people who are not. People who live in poverty are less happy than average, but above the poverty line, people with more money are only slightly more likely to be happy. Happily, people of different ages, genders, and race and ethnic groups are equally likely to be happy after income and other factors are taken into account.

For our last example, we'll go to the opposite end of the continuum of human behavior to violent aggression against others. Is aggressiveness influenced by situational influences? We often speak of regrettable acts of human

violence as being committed in the "heat of the moment" or as being acts of "hotheads." Craig Anderson (1989) has reviewed a large number of studies that make it clear that there is an unintended wisdom about situational influences on aggression in those phrases: Violent acts that are committed in "heated" emotions are more common when the physical temperature of the climate is hot. Figure 12.8 shows the relationship between the month of the year and four types of physical aggres-

sion. The four graphs are dramatically similar in showing that aggression is more common during hotter months.

It is likely that most of the persons who committed these aggressive acts tended to behave in aggressive ways in other situations, but even if that is the case, a simple aspect of the situation—temperature—clearly influenced the likelihood of aggression. Situational factors can have a marked impact on our behavior. Need more convincing? Think back to chapter 10 to the discussion of "falling in love on a swaying suspension bridge" (pages 392–393). In that section, I described a study that showed that young males were more attracted to a female interviewer when they met her on a wobbly suspension bridge high above a gorge (probably because they attributed the arousal from the bridge to the young woman). Situations also play a role in whether or not you fall in love!

Why is this point important enough for me to devote this entire section to it? We often find ourselves in the position of predicting how other people will behave. In doing so, it's important to keep the powerful influence of situations in mind. For example, think about someone you know who is in high school now (a sibling, cousin, or neighbor). Now let me ask you to use your imagination for a moment. First, imagine that you have graduated and that

*(continued)*

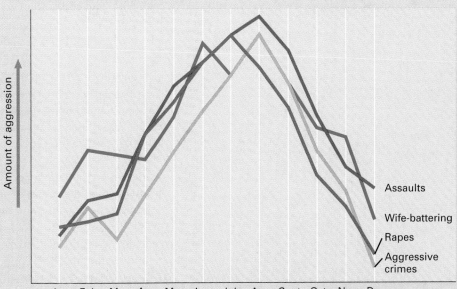

**FIGURE 12.8**

The results of four studies showing the strong relationship between the month of the year and four kinds of physical aggression. Aggression is more common in the warmer months.

you were offered a wonderful job, but you have to move across country tomorrow to start the new job. As a result of the new job, you finally are able to buy a really nice car, but it won't be ready until after you have left for the new job. Do you think the high school student is mature enough to drive your car across country alone for you? As you think about this question, you will find that it is important to keep in mind the high school student's traits but also the unusual situation that she or he will be in. The same kind of reasoning should go into predicting how you will do in the new city and in the new job. You are usually a happy, outgoing person, but will you find yourself a little moody and shy in a new city where you know no one? Situations are important influences on us all. ■

## Summary

Chapter 12 defines personality, explores four major perspectives on personality—traits theory, psychoanalytic theory, social learning theory, and humanistic theory—and discusses several approaches to personality assessment.

I. Personality is the sum total of all of the ways of acting, thinking, and feeling that are typical for that person and make that person unique.

II. Some psychologists believe that one's personality can be described in terms of traits.

    A. Traits are defined as relatively enduring ways of behaving that are relatively consistent across different situations.

    B. The five-factor model is a widely endorsed description of the basic personality traits.

III. Psychoanalytic theory was developed by Sigmund Freud in the early twentieth century.

    A. Freud distinguished three levels of conscious awareness—the conscious mind, the preconscious mind, and the unconscious mind. In his view, the mind is composed of three parts—id, ego, and superego.

        1. The id operates on the pleasure principle. It seeks to obtain immediate pleasure and avoid pain.

        2. The ego operates on the reality principle. It seeks safe and realistic ways to satisfy the id.

        3. The superego opposes the id by imposing moral restrictions and by striving for perfection.

    B. When the ego cannot find ways to satisfy the id, it seeks a substitute.

        1. The substitution of a more acceptable goal is displacement, and displacement of a socially desirable goal is called sublimation.

        2. Identification is the tendency to sublimate by modeling our actions on individuals who are successful in life.

    C. Freud's theory is developmental in that it distinguishes five stages in the development of personality: the oral stage, the anal stage, the phallic stage, the latency stage, and the genital stage. During the phallic stage, boys experience the Oedipus complex, and girls experience the Electra complex.

    D. Alfred Adler, Carl Jung, and Karen Horney broke away from Freud primarily over the issues of sexual motivation, the presence of positive aspects of personality, and the importance of adequate social relationships.

IV. To social learning theorists, the key concepts in the study of personality are learning and cognition.

    A. Our personalities are learned, but Albert Bandura says that social learning is reciprocally determined by the actions of behavior on the environment, and vice versa.

    B. Behavior is self-regulated by our internalized cognitive standards for self-reward and limited by our perception of our own self-efficacy.

C.    Behaviorist B. F. Skinner believed that people were influenced by their situations too much for trait theories to be correct. This view is known as situationism.

D.    Social learning theorists have adopted the position of person $\times$ situation interactionism. This suggests that the behavior of different people is influenced by situations in different ways because our behavior reflects both situational influences and our personal characteristics.

V.    Humanistic theory is based on a belief that humans possess an inner-directedness that pushes them to grow. To the humanist, reality is subjective.

A.    Self-concept is our subjective perception of who we are and what we are like. Carl Rogers distinguishes between the self (the person I think I am) and the ideal self (the person I wish I were).

B.    Problems result when the ideal self is unrealistic or when feelings and information that are incongruent with a person's self-concept are denied conscious awareness.

VI.    Personality assessment is the use of psychological methods to learn about a person's personality.

A.    The most widely used method is the interview.

B.    Personality is also assessed by observing the person's behavior in a natural or simulated situation. Rating scales help make observational methods more objective.

C.    Another widely used method of personality assessment is the projective test, which psychoanalysts believe reveals the motives and conflicts of the unconscious mind.

D.    Objective personality tests, such as the MMPI-2, consist of questions that measure different aspects of personality. Objective personality tests are generally better at assessing personality than projective techniques, but all personality tests are only partly accurate.

**Resources**

1.    For in-depth discussions of the major theories of personality, see Feist, J., & Feist, G. J. (1998). *Theories of personality* (4th ed.). Boston: McGraw-Hill; Hall, C. S., Lindzey, G., & Campbell, J. B. (1998). *Theories of personality* (4th ed.). New York: John Wiley.

2.    For a readable, detailed summary of Sigmund Freud's basic concepts, see Hall, C. S. (1954, 1999). *A primer of Freudian psychology*. New York: Meridian Books.

3.    For a summary of recent books that criticize the scientific basis of Freud's theory of personality, see Crews, F. (1996). The verdict on Freud. *Psychological Science, 1,* 63–68.

4.    A readable summary of Carl Jung's theory of personality is presented in Hall, C. S., & Nordby, V. J. (1973). *A primer of Jungian psychology.* New York: Taplinger.

5.    Interviews with leading humanists Carl Rogers and Abraham Maslow in the prime of their careers appear in Frick, W. B. (1971). *Humanistic psychology.* Columbus, OH: Merrill.

6.    For summaries of the evolving social learning view of personality, see Bandura, A. (1977). *Social learning theory.* Englewood Cliffs, NJ: Prentice-Hall; and Bandura, A. (1999). Social cognitive theory of personality. In L. A. Pervin & O. P. John (Eds.), *Handbook of personality: Theory and research* (2nd ed., pp. 154–196). New York: Guilford.

7. No one presents Carl Rogers' views on successful and happy lives like Carl Rogers does: Rogers, C. R. (1980). *A way of being.* Boston: Houghton Mifflin.

8. For the African American perspective in psychology, see Jones, R. (Ed.). (1992). *Black psychology* (3rd ed.). Berkeley, CA: Cobb & Henry.

9. For the Hispanic/Latino perspective in psychology, see Padilla, A. M. (1995). *Hispanic psychology: Critical issues in theory and research.* Thousand Oaks, CA: Sage.

10. For powerful discussions of the role of culture in personality, see Markus, H. R., & Kitayama, S. (1991). Culture and the self: Implications for cognition, emotion, and motivation. *American Psychologist, 93* (2), 224–253; and Cross, S. E., & Markus, H. R. (1999). The cultural constitution of personality. In L. A. Pervin & O. P. John (Eds.), *Handbook of personality: Theory and research* (2nd ed., pp. 378–396). New York: Guilford.

## Visual Review of Personality Theory

Reviewing the figure below may help you consolidate your learning of some of the information presented in this chapter in a visual format. Be sure not to limit your review to these diagrams, but because they are key to understanding some of the important concepts in this chapter, mastering them should help you master the entire chapter.

An iceberg is often used to illustrate Sigmund Freud's theoretical structure of the mind. Fill in the labels for the three levels of consciousness (along the left) and the three parts of the mind (on the iceberg).

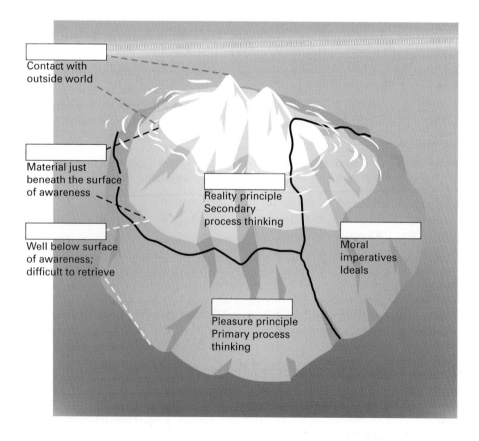

Contact with outside world

Material just beneath the surface of awareness

Well below surface of awareness; difficult to retrieve

Reality principle
Secondary process thinking

Moral imperatives
Ideals

Pleasure principle
Primary process thinking

# PART VI

# Health and Adjustment

In this section you will learn about stress and coping, psychological aspects of physical health, and mental health. The final chapter in this section provides an overview of psychological and medical therapies for mental health problems. Here is a visual overview of what you will learn in the sixth section of the text.

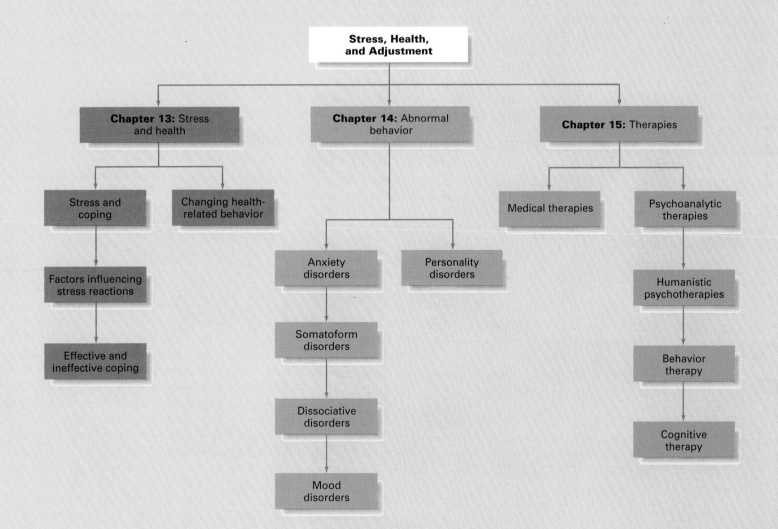

# Chapter Outline

# Stress and Health

## PROLOGUE

No one's life is free of stress. Regardless of how sensible, intelligent, or privileged you are, you will be challenged at times by frustrations, losses, changes, and conflicts. Stress comes from negative events, such as failing a college course, but stress is part of many positive events, too, such as starting a new job or having a baby. Stress is as inescapable as death and taxes.

A certain amount of stress is probably healthy—it energizes us and challenges us to grow. But stress is generally experienced as an uncomfortable, unhealthy force that most of us would be happier without. If you have experienced the death of a loved one or a divorce, you have firsthand knowledge of the emotions that such stress can bring. But don't forget that the psychological part of you exists in the biological part of you, and that what affects your "mind" also affects your body (McEwen, 1998). Consider the following landmark studies.

Bengt Arnetz of Harvard University (Arnetz & others, 1987) conducted a study of the effects of psychological stress on the body's ability to fight disease. Arnetz studied a large group of Swedish women who had lost their jobs and had remained unemployed for nine months. Compared with women with secure jobs, women who had lost their jobs had white blood cells that were less reactive to infections. Similarly, Janice Kiecolt-Glaser and colleagues (1987) of Ohio State University compared the immune system functioning of married and divorced women. The immune systems of recently divorced women functioned less well than those of married women, but with gradual improvements occurring over the first year after divorce. Within the group of married women, furthermore, immune functioning was poorest for those women with the unhappiest marriages. These findings may explain why disease and death rates are higher for recently divorced and unhappily married persons than for happily married persons (Kiecolt-Glaser & others, 1987).

In the few years since these remarkable studies were conducted, many other studies have confirmed their basic findings (summarized by Cohen, 1996, and Weisse, 1992). These studies offer strong evidence for the intimate relationship between our psychological lives and our physical health. It now seems clear that psychological stressors can diminish the body's ability to fight disease.

If stress is inevitable, and if too much stress is a threat to our psychological and physical well-being, then *coping* well with stress is of paramount importance. A healthy and happy person is someone who can enjoy the good times and cope with the bad. Sometimes we can cope with stress by removing it—by changing jobs or filing a complaint against a sexually harassing boss. But we cannot remove all the stress from our lives and will have to cope with some of it. Generally, we are better able to cope with the kinds of stress that we have had previous experience with and that we can control somewhat. Good social support also improves our ability to cope with stress. Simply disclosing our feelings to friends (or to a psychotherapist) has been shown to improve immune system functioning and reduce need for medical care (Pennebaker, Colder, & Sharp, 1990; Richards, Beal, Seagal, & Pennebaker, 2000). But there will be times when we cope ineffectively with stress. The trick, of course, is to cope as effectively as possible and not worry too much about the rest. ■

## Key Terms

## Stress: Challenges to Coping

As we noted in chapter 1, one of the goals of psychology is to *influence* your psychological functioning in beneficial ways. The specialty field of **health psychology** seeks to improve the well-being of your body as well. In this section, we will address perhaps the key factor that must be understood if psychology is to improve our health and happiness—stress. **Stress** can be thought of as any event that strains or exceeds an individual's ability to cope (Lazarus, 1999). The goal of this discussion of stress is to provide you with a new perspective on both stress and your health.

The extent to which stress is related to some of our most serious medical conditions was greatly underestimated until research dramatically altered our perceptions of our own health. Leading causes of death and disability such as heart disease and stroke are almost certainly linked to stress, and as we saw in the prologue to this chapter, immunity to infections is greatly affected by stress (Cohen & Williamson, 1991; Suinn, 2001). It is even probable that the link between stress and immunity extends to susceptibility to cancer (O'Leary, 1990; Taylor, 1986). In an era in which effective treatments are available for a wide variety of infectious diseases, the major killers are stress-related diseases and cancer. This makes the interface with psychology one of the most important frontiers in medical research today.

Frustration results when we are unable to satisfy a motive.

### Sources of Stress

We need to begin our discussion of stress by looking at its causes. Most sources of stress are obvious to us all—they rip and tear at our lives—but other sources of stress are quite surprising. Knowing what causes stress is the first step in understanding and coping with it. The major sources of stress include the following factors.

### Frustration

When we are not able to satisfy a motive, **frustration** results. You see frustration in the face of a child who cannot reach the toy he's dropped or in the exasperation of the college senior who finds that she cannot register for the one class that she needs to graduate. When frustrations are serious, as in the case of the woman who has been denied a deserved and hoped for promotion, or when they are prolonged, as when individuals living in poverty cannot obtain proper food or medical care, they can be a major source of stress.

### Conflict

Conflict is closely related to the concept of frustration. **Conflict** occurs when two or more motives cannot be satisfied because they interfere with one another. Suppose you have been invited to spend a week skiing with friends, and then your car breaks down. You check your budget and find that you can afford to either fix your car *or* go skiing—that is a conflict. Psychologists use the terms *approach* and *avoidance* in discussing conflicts. In this sense, we "approach" things that we want and "avoid" things that we do not want. There are four major kinds of conflicts involving approach and avoidance (Lewin, 1931; Miller, 1944):

1. *Approach-approach conflict.* In **approach-approach conflict,** the individual must choose between two positive goals of approximately equal value. Suppose that when you finish school you are fortunate enough to be offered two attractive jobs. Both seem to offer good working conditions, good prestige, and reasonable salary. If both jobs are so good, why do you feel so anxious? Why are you having stomachaches and trouble sleeping? Even though both goals are positive—you would be happy with either job—the choice between these two goals can be very

**health psychology**
The field of psychology that uses psychological principles to encourage healthy lifestyles and to minimize the impact of stress.

**stress**
Any event or circumstance that strains or exceeds an individual's ability to cope.

**frustration**
The result of being unable to satisfy a motive.

**conflict**
The state in which two or more motives cannot be satisfied because they interfere with one another.

**approach-approach conflict**
Conflict in which the individual must choose between two positive goals of approximately equal value.

stressful. This is an example of a hidden source of stress. Because everything looks so positive, it's often difficult to see that you are in a serious conflict. The choice between two colleges, two roommates, or two ways of spending the summer can be similarly stressful.

2. *Avoidance-avoidance conflict.* This type of conflict involves more obvious sources of stress. In **avoidance-avoidance conflict,** the individual must choose between two or more negative outcomes. The person with a toothache must choose between the pain of the tooth and the anticipated discomfort of going to the dentist.

3. *Approach-avoidance conflict.* **Approach-avoidance conflict** arises when obtaining a positive goal necessitates a negative outcome as well. A student who is accepted to college in another state will be in a stressful conflict if she knows that it will mean being separated from her serious boyfriend, who works in his family's business in her hometown. Attending the college will have both positive and negative consequences, so she may experience considerable stress, especially as the time grows nearer for beginning school.

Notice that I said the student would especially experience stress *as the time grows nearer* for her to attend college. There is an important and interesting fact about approach-avoidance conflict behind that statement. As the positive and negative outcomes grow nearer (attending college and leaving the boyfriend, respectively), either in distance or time, the relative strength of the motives to approach and avoid them changes. This change has been described graphically in terms of the gradients of approach and avoidance. Notice in figure 13.1 that the strength of the motive to avoid the negative consequence of losing the boyfriend increases quickly (has a steep gradient) as distance (or time) from the goal decreases. The strength of the motive to approach the positive goal of attending college, on the other hand, increases slowly (has a gradual gradient). At any particular distance from the goal, the effective amount of motive to approach or avoid is the remainder when the motive to avoid is subtracted from the motive to approach.

At greater distances, there is a stronger motive to approach than avoid, so the net motive is to approach. At shorter distances, the motive to avoid is stronger than the motive to approach, so there is a net motive to avoid. Let's look at what this means in terms of our example.

The student who had been accepted to college began to experience a high level of stress about the time that the strength of the approach and avoidance motives were about equal. If the motives to approach and avoid were actually about equal in strength as diagrammed in figure 13.1, she might have even changed her mind and given up her admission to college as the time to attend

**avoidance-avoidance conflict**
Conflict in which the individual must choose between two negative outcomes of approximately equal value.

**approach-avoidance conflict**
Conflict in which achieving a positive goal will produce a negative outcome as well.

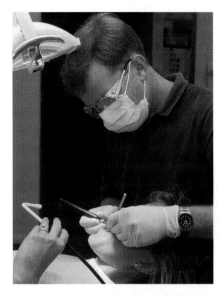

In an avoidance-avoidance conflict, the individual must choose between two or more negative outcomes, such as the pain of the tooth or the expected discomfort of going to the dentist.

**FIGURE 13.1**

Gradients of approach and avoidance in an approach-avoidance conflict.

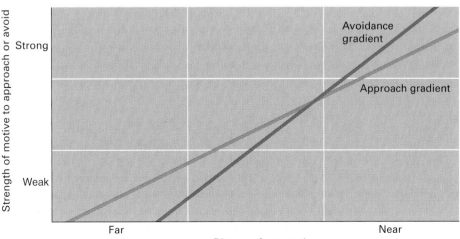

**FIGURE 13.2**
The amount of sympathetic autonomic arousal (as measured by changes in the electrical conductance of the skin caused by changes in skin sweat) in inexperienced parachutists at different "distances" from the approach-avoidance goal of jumping.
**Source:** Data from S. Epstein and W. D. Fenz, "Steepness of Approach and Avoidance Gradients in Humans as a Function of Experience: Theory and Experiment," *Journal of Experimental Psychology,* 70:1–12, 1965. Copyright 1965 by the American Psychological Association.

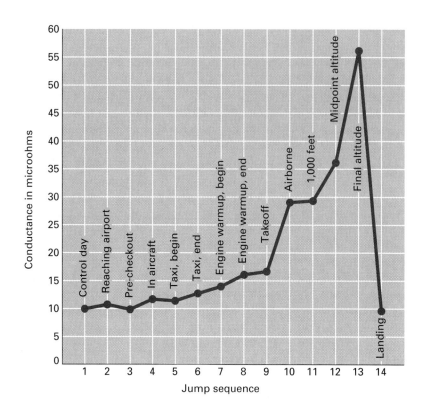

college came nearer and the net motive switched strongly in favor of avoidance. After turning down her admission, however, she would have again been at a great "distance" from college. She might again feel a motive to approach and wish she had not decided against going.

Have you ever found yourself in such a conflict? Did you find yourself going back and forth on a decision? If so, you have had a very common human experience. The actual outcome of such a conflict depends on many factors, particularly the relative strength of the two motives.

Researcher Seymour Epstein has vividly demonstrated the stressfulness of approach-avoidance conflicts in his classic study of parachute jumpers (Epstein, 1982). Epstein views parachute jumping as an approach-avoidance conflict because the jump entails both dangerous risks and exhilarating thrills. In his research, inexperienced jumpers were rigged with devices to measure the amount of sympathetic autonomic arousal by monitoring changes in skin sweat. As shown in figure 13.2, the autonomic reaction of the jumpers mounted dramatically to a peak at the moment of the jump, then returned to normal levels immediately after they landed. Although few of us face such obvious approach-avoidance conflicts, the more subtle conflicts in our lives affect us in similar ways.

**multiple approach-avoidance conflict**
Conflict that requires the individual to choose between two alternatives, each of which contains both positive and negative consequences.

4. *Multiple approach-avoidance conflict.* Sometimes the conflicts that we face are complex combinations of approach and avoidance conflicts. A **multiple approach-avoidance conflict** requires the individual to choose between alternatives that contain both positive and negative consequences. Imagine that you are a promising high school athlete and you have been offered athletic scholarships to two colleges. One is from a strong school that won its conference championship in basketball last season, but you strongly dislike the coach and several of the players on the team. The other is from a weaker school that has had an embarrassing record of performance in recent years, but you like the coach and players. What do you do? Do you go to the stronger college, where there are people you do not like, or do you go to the weaker school, where you like the people with whom you would be playing? This is a multiple approach-avoidance conflict because both choices involve both positive and negative outcomes.

**Pressure**

Does the pressure of working for good grades ever get to you? If you have been employed, was it a high-pressure job? The term **pressure** is used to describe the stress that arises from threats of negative events. In school, there is always the possibility that you will not perform well and you will fail. Some jobs are loaded with possibilities for making a mess of things and getting fired. Some unhappy marriages are sources of pressure because one spouse always seems to displease the other, no matter how hard he or she tries to avoid it. The pressure of trying to avoid these negative events can sometimes be more stressful than the negative events themselves.

**Life Events**

Major **life events** create stress because they require adjustment and coping. Interestingly, major events in our lives are often stressful whether they are positive or negative. Although we mostly discuss negative life events in this section, keep in mind that even positive life changes, such as marriage or entering graduate school, can be stressful.

Common negative life events that create stress for us include such things as the loss of employment and being in an automobile crash. The most stressful negative life events that have been studied by psychologists include the following:

1. *Crime, sexual assault, and violence.* Many studies document that being the victim of a crime, being sexually assaulted, and witnessing violence are highly stressful (Brewin & others, 1999; Gilboa-Schechtman & Foa, 2001; King, Coxell, & Mezey, 2002; Koren, Arnon, & Klein, 1999; Laor, Wolmer, & Cohen, 2001; Mayou, Bryant, & Ehlers, 2001). For example, Edna Foa and David Riggs(1995) of the Medical College of Pennsylvania interviewed a group of women who were the victims of assault. They asked the women if they were experiencing high levels of irritability and anxiety, upsetting memories or dreams about the assault, and distressing flashbacks in which they had the illusion of being assaulted again. As shown in figure 13.3 the great majority of women experienced high levels of such stress symptoms one month after the assault, with the percentage declining gradually over the course of the first year. Overall, it is clear that being a victim of sexual assault results in more severe stress reactions than other kinds of physical assault. Over 40 percent of the women in this study who had been sexually assaulted still experienced serious levels of post-traumatic stress symptoms a year after the sexual assault.

The term *pressure* is used to describe the stress that arises from threats, such as the possibility of poor performance on an exam.

**pressure**
Stress that arises from the threat of negative events.

**life events**
Psychologically significant events that occur in a person's life, such as divorce, childbirth, or change in employment.

**FIGURE 13.3**
The percentage of women who experience serious levels of stress symptoms following the traumatic stress of assault is very high one month after the assault but declines gradually over the first year. Some women still show serious levels of stress symptoms a year after being assaulted, however, particularly if the assault was sexual (Foa & Riggs, 1995).

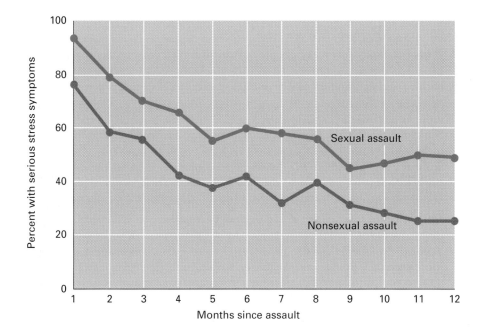

**FIGURE 13.4**

The death of a spouse is a severe stressor that leads to serious depression in some widowed men and women (Zisook & Schuchter, 1991).

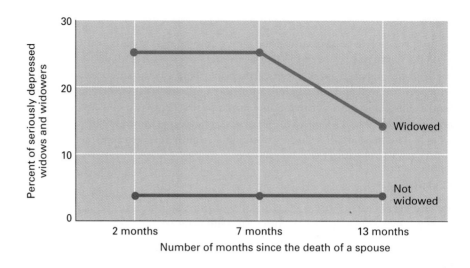

2. *Loss of a family member.* Darrin Lehman and associates (1987) of the University of Michigan interviewed individuals who had lost a spouse or a child in a fatal automobile accident. An average of five years later, people who had lost a family member still experienced more depression than a control group who had not lost a loved one. Similarly, Sidney Zisook and Stephen Schuchter (1991) examined the stressful effects of the death of a spouse in a large sample of women and men. As shown in figure 13.4, widowed women and men were more likely to exhibit serious depression during the first year after the death of their spouse than were married women and men who had not lost their partners.

3. *Natural disasters.* Natural disasters also can be potently stressful negative life events. Paul and Gerald Adams (1984) showed that the 1980 Mount Saint Helens volcanic eruption was extremely stressful to the residents of nearby Othello, Washington. Compared with the preceding year, the residents of Othello made 90 percent more emergency room visits and were diagnosed by the town's physicians and mental health workers as having 200 percent more stress-related physical illnesses and psychological disorders, and the town police responded to 45 percent more reports of family violence. The number of deaths in Othello increased by 19 percent. Similar effects have been reported for persons who were in the direct path of hurricanes, earthquakes, and other life-threatening natural disasters (Asarnow & others, 1999; Escobar, Canino, Rubio-Stipec, & Bravo, 1992; La Greca, Silverman, & Wasserstein, 1998).

4. *Terrorism.* For many years, people in many troubled parts of the world have had to cope with the stress of terroristic attacks. In recent years, terrorism has become a sadly common source of intense stress for Americans as well. The bombing of the federal building in Oklahoma City killed 148 adults and 19 children. Tragically, the attacks on the World Trade Center and the Pentagon on September 11, 2001, killed thousands more and shocked the world. Not surprisingly, studies have found that anxiety, depression, sleep problems, and intrusive flashback thoughts about the disaster were common long after the attacks, particularly for those who were near the attack or who lost loved ones or possessions (Koplewicz & others, 2002; Galea & others, 2002; LeDoux & Gorman, 2001).

5. *Daily hassles.* It is not surprising that major negative events are stressful, but Richard Lazarus (1982) of the University of California at Berkeley reminds us that the small *hassles* of daily life are also important sources of stress. Getting a speeding ticket, losing your sunglasses, having your friend arrive an hour late for dinner, and countless other microscopic irritants can grate abrasively on mind and body. Indeed, Lazarus (1984) asked a group of 100 educated, middle-class individuals to record their major life events, daily hassles, and daily positive

CHAPTER 13   Stress and Health   **505**

## Table 13.1   The Social Readjustment Rating Scale

| Life Event | Mean Value | Life Event | Mean Value |
|---|---|---|---|
| Death of spouse | 100 | Son or daughter leaving home | 29 |
| Divorce | 73 | Trouble with in-laws | 29 |
| Marital separation | 65 | Outstanding personal achievement | 28 |
| Jail term | 63 | Spouse begins or stops work | 26 |
| Death of close family member | 63 | Begin or end school | 26 |
| Personal injury or illness | 53 | Change in living conditions | 25 |
| Marriage | 50 | Revision of personal habits | 24 |
| Fired at work | 47 | Trouble with boss | 23 |
| Marital reconciliation | 45 | Change in work hours or conditions | 20 |
| Retirement | 45 | Change in residence | 20 |
| Change in health of family member | 44 | Change in schools | 20 |
| Pregnancy | 40 | Change in recreation | 19 |
| Sex difficulties | 39 | Change in church activities | 19 |
| Gain of new family member | 39 | Change in social activities | 18 |
| Business readjustment | 39 | Mortgage or loan for lesser purchase (car, TV, etc.) | 17 |
| Change in financial state | 38 | Change in sleeping habits | 16 |
| Death of close friend | 37 | Change in number of family get-togethers | 15 |
| Change to different line of work | 36 | Change in eating habits | 15 |
| Change in number of arguments with spouse | 35 | Vacation | 13 |
| Mortgage or loan for major purchase (home, etc.) | 31 | Christmas | 12 |
| Foreclosure on mortgage or loan | 30 | Minor violations of the law | 11 |
| Change in responsibilities at work | 29 | | |

Reprinted from *Journal of Psychosomatic Research, Vol. 11* by Thomas H. Holmes and R. H. Rahe, "The Social Readjustment Scale," 1967, with permission from Elsevier Science.

events for a year and found that daily hassles were the best predictors of both health and psychological well-being. Although it is probable that daily hassles are an important source of stress, we must be cautious in estimating how potent they are. If we are not happy or not feeling well, it may be that we would remember to write down more of the hassles of the day or, indeed, would be more likely to experience events like a slow drive home through traffic as a hassle. That is, hassles may be *both* a cause and a result of stress.

There is also reason to believe that *positive life events* can be stressful under some circumstances (Sarason, Johnson, & Siegel, 1978). Marriage, the birth of a child, job promotion, and the purchase of a house are examples of events that most people think of as positive, but they may also require stressful adjustments in patterns of living. Hence, positive life changes can be another source of stress of which we are typically unaware.

The relationship between stressful life events and physical illness has been the subject of a great deal of research (Dohrenwend & others, 1982; Holmes & Rahe, 1967; Rabkin & Streuning, 1976). United States Navy physicians Thomas Holmes and Richard Rahe have developed a scale to measure the amount of stress from life events in terms of the life change units. Table 13.1 shows this scale of stress of events and the amount of stressful impact that Holmes and Rahe believe each event has on our lives. The individual taking the test indicates which events have happened to him or her during the past year and adds up the units of impact. Holmes and Rahe (1967) have found that Navy personnel who had experienced unusually high levels of life stress during the past year were more likely to develop a wide range of medical problems while on sea duty than were individuals with lower life change units.

The now classic scale of life change units developed by Holmes and Rahe (1967) has stimulated a great deal of useful research, but it is important to note that it was developed using men and may not apply equally well to women. If a similar scale were developed for women, would the stressful life changes be different, or would the order be different? A colleague of mine suggested that the death of a child, violent victimization, and serious conflicts with family members would be at the top. What do you think?

One lesson from these studies of life events is to space out your life changes when you can (Lloyd, Alexander, Rice, & Greenfield, 1980). Try not to graduate from college, move to a new city, take a new job, buy a new house, get married, and have a baby all in one year. If you do, don't be surprised if you are moody, have stomachaches, and have more colds.

### Environmental Conditions

There is growing evidence that aspects of the environment in which we live (temperature, air pollution, noise, humidity, etc.) can be sources of stress (Staples, 1996). For example, urban riots have occurred much more frequently on hot (mid-80s Fahrenheit) than cool days, although they have been rare on extremely hot days, perhaps because extreme heat leads to lethargic lack of energy (Baron & Ramsberger, 1978). Similarly, visits to the psychiatric emergency room of California's Sacramento Medical Center were found to be related to environmental conditions (Briere, Downes, & Spensley, 1983). Visits for all types of psychological problems were higher during periods of high air pollution, and there were more emergency visits for depression during cloudy, humid days. These environmental sources of stress do not appear to be as potent as other stressors but apparently contribute to our overall stress levels.

## Stress Reactions

Now that we have looked at the causes of stress, let's examine our reactions to it. When we are under stress, we feel it—we *react* to it. To fully benefit from the lessons that recent psychological and medical research has taught us about stress reactions, we must understand two important insights about stress:

1. First, we react to stress *as a whole*. That is, stress usually produces *both* psychological and physiological reactions—not one or the other, but both. If we remember from chapter 3 that several key aspects of the nervous system—the hypothalamus and the autonomic nervous system—control key aspects of both psychological functioning (emotions and motives) *and* body functioning, including the endocrine glands, this concept is easier to understand. It is through these joint systems that stress affects both our physical and psychological selves.

2. Second, our psychological and bodily reactions to stress are highly similar, whether the stress is physical or psychological. Although each source of stress evokes coping reactions that are specific to it, a *general* reaction to all types of stress also occurs, based largely on the interlinked responses of the hypothalamus, the sympathetic division of the autonomic nervous system, and the adrenal glands. This rather astonishing fact is a key to the modern field of health psychology, which we will discuss throughout this chapter.

### The General Adaptation Syndrome

Let's look more closely at this general reaction to stress. Canadian medical researcher Hans Selye first gave us the insight more than 50 years ago that the body reacts in much the same general way to any threat, whether the threat is in the form of an infection, an injury, or a psychological stress. Regardless of the source of the stress, the body mobi-

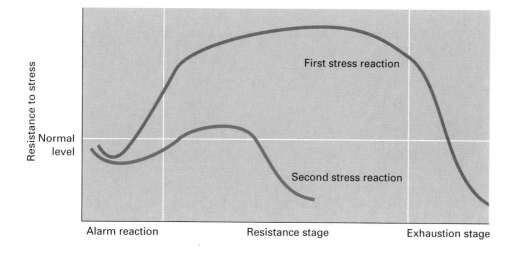

**FIGURE 13.5**
Changes in resistance to stress during the three stages of the general adaptation syndrome. Note that a second stress produces a more rapid dissipation of resistance.
**Source:** Data from H. Selye, *The Stress of Life.*
Copyright © 1976 McGraw-Hill Book Company.

lizes its defenses to ward off the threat in a pattern referred to by Selye as the **general adaptation syndrome (GAS).** Three stages can be distinguished in this syndrome (see fig. 13.5):

1. *Alarm reaction.* As shown in figure 13.6, the body's initial response to threat or other stress is to mobilize its stored resources. The sympathetic division of the autonomic nervous system increases heart rate and blood pressure, diverts blood away from digestion and into the skeletal muscles, increases perspiration, and in other ways prepares the body for a physical struggle. The endocrine glands pump epinephrine and other hormones into the bloodstream that aid the actions of the autonomic nervous system and increase levels of blood sugar. This is sometimes referred to as the *fight-or-flight* reaction, as it prepares the body to either fight with the source of stress or run away from it.

   When the stress is intense or prolonged, these body changes give rise to conscious feelings of general muscle tension, stomachaches, headaches, and other feelings of "sickness" (Maier & Watkins, 1998, 2000). In the early stages of the general adaptation syndrome, it's often difficult to distinguish between the feelings associated with catching a cold, being under psychological stress, or even falling in love. Because anything that causes an alarm reaction produces essentially the same response from the body, the differences are often relatively subtle.

   During the alarm reaction stage, the rapid mobilization of resources leaves the individual temporarily less resistant to the stress than originally. This state of affairs is quickly changed as the next stage is entered.

2. *Resistance stage.* During the second stage of the GAS, the body's resources have been fully mobilized, and resistance to the stress is high. This resistance is costly in terms of resources, however. If new stress (psychological or physical) is encountered, the body is less able to deal with it. In this way, psychological stress can leave the person more vulnerable to physical stress (disease), and vice versa. Moreover, if the stress continues, the individual's resources will eventually become depleted, leading to the third stage of the GAS.

3. *Exhaustion stage.* If the stress continues, the individual's resources may become exhausted, and resistance to the stress is lowered. In cases of prolonged exposure to severe physical stress (such as intense cold), death can occur during the exhaustion stage. Psychological stress is rarely able to precipitate death, but it can severely disrupt body functioning (Selye, 1976).

**general adaptation syndrome (GAS)**
According to Selye, the mobilization of the body to ward off threats, characterized by a three-stage pattern of the alarm reaction, the resistance stage, and the exhaustion stage.

**FIGURE 13.6**
The body mobilizes its resources for
"fight-or-flight" in the general adaptation
syndrome in response to stress.

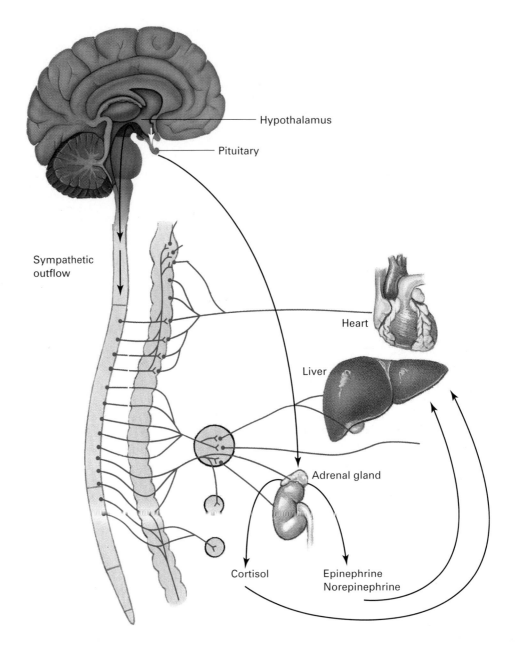

Hypothalamus

Pituitary

Sympathetic
outflow

Heart

Liver

Adrenal gland

Cortisol

Epinephrine
Norepinephrine

Notice in figure 13.5 that if a second stressor is encountered when the individual has already entered the GAS, the progress toward exhaustion is much more rapid. Keep in mind two additional points as you think about the GAS. First, not all stressors overwhelm and exhaust the body; obviously, we cope effectively with most stress. Second, emotional and other psychological reactions to stress follow roughly the same GAS pattern, sometimes resulting in "emotional exhaustion" when coping fails.

***Healthy and Unhealthy Aspects of the GAS.***   As Selye (1976) helped us see, the general adaptation syndrome is the body's protective response to dangers. Without the GAS, we humans would be very frail creatures indeed. Then the body's complex reaction to stress—the GAS—is a blessing, right? Unquestionably, but it is a very mixed blessing. The GAS can be our best defense at times but our own worst enemy at other times.

The GAS does its best work during emergencies. Whether suddenly exposed to a deadly virus or being lost on a freezing ski trail, we need our bodies to respond with an alarm reaction to such emergencies. Our physical ability to endure such threats is enhanced for a while by the GAS.

Even our ability to cope behaviorally is helped by the GAS at times. I once nearly stepped on a water moccasin, and my body responded with a full-blown GAS alarm reaction. My autonomic nervous system went into screaming sympathetic arousal and produced a multitude of changes in my body that prepared me to respond behaviorally to the snake. For purposes of simplicity let's look only at changes in my cardiac system during the moments that followed. As we know from our discussion of these topics in chapter 3, sympathetic arousal caused my adrenal glands to pump epinephrine, norepinephrine, and other stress hormones into my bloodstream. These, in turn, increased my blood pressure and caused my blood to create substances that make the blood clot faster. My heart beat faster, rushing oxygen to my muscles, and blood flow was diverted from my liver and digestive organs to the muscles in my legs and arms. Those physiological changes that we call the alarm phase of the GAS were very welcome indeed as I jumped, turned tail, and ran from the water moccasin. My legs were supplied with the necessary oxygen to run to the next county, and I didn't mind one bit that my lunch was never digested properly. Because blood flow to my liver was diminished during the GAS, it was not filtered as usual and my cholesterol levels probably rose, but I didn't mind that, either. And, if I had fallen and cut my knee, I would have been glad that hormones had prepared my blood to clot quickly.

Most of the stressors that we face in contemporary society, however, are not snakes, bears, or avalanches. More often, they are the day-to-day stresses of school, work, and families. Remember, however, that the body's reaction is much the same regardless of the source of stress. As a result, the GAS is not only unnecessary for some stressors, it can be dangerous if it is prolonged.

Take the example of preparing your income taxes—an annoying stress, but not one requiring speedy legs, high blood pressure, or fast-clotting blood. Nonetheless, a group of accountants was given repeated blood tests for several months and found to have normal levels of blood-clotting factors and cholesterol, until the April 15 deadline for filing tax returns grew near; then their cholesterol and clotting factors shot up (Friedman & Rosenman, 1974). Unfortunately, elevated levels of blood pressure, cholesterol, and blood-clotting factors are a potentially deadly combination because they cause the formation of the "clots" of cholesterol inside arteries, called *plaque*, that clog and harden blood vessels. When the affected blood vessels are those that supply the heart muscles with oxygen, a heart attack can result. Since the time of this original study, many other studies have been conducted that suggest that many kinds of stressful life events affect blood clotting, blood pressure, and other aspects of the functioning of the heart that increase the risk of heart attack (Benschop & others, 1998; Rosenberg & others, 2001; Suinn, 2001). Thus, although the GAS is a lifesaver in the face of emergencies, the GAS can paradoxically affect the cardiac system in ways that can be quite dangerous to our hearts.

Modern-day stressors, such as preparing forms for tax deadlines, call for all of the body's reactions of the general adaptation syndrome. Although the GAS is a lifesaver in emergencies, it can be life-threatening if stress is prolonged.

***Stress, the GAS, and the Immune System.*** As we saw in the prologue to this chapter, another negative aspect of stress is that it decreases the effectiveness of the body's natural disease-fighting system, the **immune system.** Many studies now show that stress reduces the effectiveness of the immune system (Maier & Watkins, 1998, 2000; Suinn, 2001). For example, Sheldon Cohen (Cohen, 1996) conducted an experiment on the effects of stress on immunity to the common cold virus. Volunteers completed questionnaires that measured stressful life events and were interviewed about a variety of health practices. Then they were exposed to live cold viruses and were watched to see who developed a

**immune system**
The complex body system of defenses to illness, such as white cells and natural killer cells of the blood.

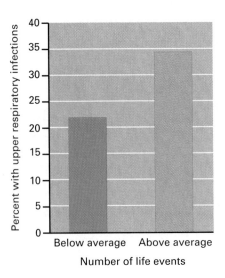

**FIGURE 13.7**
Volunteers with above-average numbers of stressful life events were more likely than volunteers with below-average numbers of life events to develop upper respiratory infections ("colds") after being experimentally exposed to live cold viruses.

cold. Even after the effects of poor health practices (smoking, drinking, poor eating, poor exercising, and poor sleeping) were considered, life events were associated with less immunity to the cold virus. As shown in figure 13.7, more volunteers with above-average numbers of life events developed upper respiratory infections than did volunteers with below-average numbers of life events. I am sorry to tell you that even the stress of studying for college examinations temporarily suppresses the immune system (Glaser & others, 1990; Suinn, 2001). Unfortunately, the older you become, the more stress takes a toll on your immune system (Kiecolt-Glaser & Glaser, 2001).

Fortunately, something positive can be done about the relationship between stress and health. Researchers have found significant increases in immune system functioning as the result of programs that teach patients to relax and cope with stress more effectively (Fawzi & others, 1990; Suinn, 2001). Thus, it works both ways: Psychological factors such as stress can harm the functioning of the immune system, but psychological treatments such as stress management can restore immune system functioning in some cases.

### Depression and Health

The negative effects of stress on our health are most evident in persons with high levels of depression. As we will discuss in chapter 14, although some individuals develop serious depression in the absence of obvious sources of stress, high levels of depression are common among individuals undergoing stress. Many studies consistently show that persons who tend to be highly depressed have impaired immune system functioning, poorer health, and higher rates of death from cardiac disease (Pennix & others, 2001; Schleifer & others, 1996; Avissar & others, 1997; Vaillant, 1998; Zorilla & others, 1996).

But let's think critically about the relationship between depression and health. It is possible that depression reduces the effectiveness of the immune system because the autonomic and endocrine systems that are disturbed during depression also control the immune system (Maier & Watkins, 1998). However, there is another possible explanation as well. People who are depressed are more likely to eat and sleep poorly and are more likely to drink excessively, smoke cigarettes, and not exercise (Windle & Windle, 2001)—all of which are also known to reduce the activity of the immune system. Which explanation is correct? Most researchers currently believe that stress and depression take a direct toll on our immune systems (Cohen, 1996; Herbert & Cohen, 1993), but the poor health practices of depressed persons harm their immunity, too. The multiple assaults on the immune system in depressed people add up to negative effects on their physical health. This means that depression should be viewed as an important and treatable health risk factor, much like high blood pressure and high blood cholesterol levels.

### Psychological Reactions to Stress

The physiological reactions to stress are usually accompanied by psychological reactions. These changes primarily involve emotions, motivations, and cognitions. Under stress, we feel anxious, depressed, and irritable (Cano & O'Leary, 2000). We experience changes in our appetite for food and may gain or lose large amounts of weight. Our interest in sex often decreases, but it may increase. Cognitive changes occur as well: We have difficulty concentrating, lose our ability to think clearly, and find that our thoughts keep returning to the source of the stress. We will have more to say on this topic in the next chapter, on abnormal behavior.

## Review

A human life that was completely free of stress would be pretty dull, but excess stress can take a toll. Stress comes from a variety of sources in our lives. Frustration over not being able to satisfy a motive, conflicts arising from mutually incompatible motives, pressure, and unpleasant environmental conditions are all sources of stress. Similarly, life events, both negative ones such as the loss of employment and positive ones such as marriage, can be potent sources of stress. These sources of stress lead to stress reactions. People react to stress in both psychological and physical ways. Stress brings anxiety, anger, and depression but also body changes such as increased appetite, headaches, and difficulty sleeping. Under some circumstances, stress even leads to high blood pressure, increased blood cholesterol, and decreased efficiency of the body's immune system. The body tends to react to all stressors, psychological and physical ones, in much the same way. This nonspecific response to stress has been called the general adaptation syndrome.

---

## Check Your Learning

To be sure that you have learned the key points from the preceding section, cover the list of correct answers and try to answer each question. If you give an incorrect answer to any question, return to the page given next to the correct answer to see why your answer was not correct. Remember that these questions cover only some of the important information in this section; it is important that you make up your own questions to check your learning of other facts and concepts.

1. _____ can be thought of as any event that strains or exceeds an individual's ability to cope.

2. In _____, the individual must choose between two or more negative outcomes. For example, a person with a toothache must choose between the pain of the tooth and the expected discomfort of going to the dentist.

   a)   approach-approach conflict   c)   approach-avoidance conflict
   b)   avoidance-avoidance conflict   d)   simple conflict

3. A _____ is a psychologically significant event that occurs in a person's life that may create stress; it can be positive, such as marriage, or negative, such as divorce.

   a)   pressure   c)   life event
   b)   repression   d)   milestone

4. When the body encounters a stress, such as the threat of injury, it mobilizes its defenses in a pattern referred to by Selye as the _____.

   a)   alarm reaction   c)   generalized stress response
   b)   stress reaction   d)   general adaptation syndrome

---

## Thinking Critically about Psychology

1. Using your knowledge of the stages of the general adaptation syndrome, what advice would you give someone who is experiencing a traumatic divorce or the breakup of a long-term relationship?

2. What are the major sources of stress in your life? Are they caused by things that you have much control over?

---

Correct Answers: 1. Stress (p. 500), 2. b (p. 501), 3. c (p. 503), 4. d (p. 507).

## ● Factors that Influence Reactions to Stress

More is involved in our reactions to stress than the stress itself. Much remains to be learned about these factors, but enough is currently known to outline some of the reasons for individual differences in reactions to stress. In addition to the sheer amount of stress, what determines how we will react to stress?

### Prior Experience with the Stress

Stress reactions are generally less severe when the individual has had some prior experience with the stress event. For example, a soldier who is going into combat for the fourth time will usually be less stressed by it than a soldier facing combat for the first time. In a sense, prior exposure to a kind of stress often "inoculates" us to that stressor.

### Developmental Factors

We saw in chapter 9 that people are often quite different psychologically at different ages and levels of development. Understandably, then, the impact of stress is frequently rather different at different ages as well. For example, younger widows and widowers (65 or younger) are more than twice as likely to still be depressed 13 months after the death of their spouse than are older widows and widowers. Perhaps the stressfulness of the death of a spouse is less during a period in life when it is more common and when the surviving spouse expects to live less time without the lost spouse. Similarly, the effects of the stress of sexual abuse are more likely to leave the victimized children with serious anxiety when the victim is younger (61 percent of preschool children compared with 8 percent of adolescents) but leads to more suicidal thinking in older children (41 percent of adolescent victims compared with no preschool victims) (Kendall-Tackett, Williams, & Finkelhor, 1993). The effects of stress depend, in part, on the developmental level of the person who is stressed.

### Predictability and Control

In general, stress events are less stressful when they are predictable than when they are not, and they are less stressful when the individual perceives that he or she can exert some degree of control over the stress (Folkman & Moskowitz, 2000). Let's look at several experiments that address the related issues of *predictability and control*.

Mild electric shocks are unpleasant stressful events that are often used in laboratory studies of stress. In one study, three groups of participants listened to a voice counting. At the count of 10, one group received an electric shock 95 percent of the time, the second group received a shock 50 percent of the time, and the third group received a shock only 5 percent of the time. A measure of sympathetic autonomic arousal (the amount of skin sweat) was taken during the counting. Which group do you think showed the strongest reaction? The shocks were least predictable for the group that received shocks only 5 percent of the time. Even though they received the fewest shocks, the higher degree of uncertainty resulted in greater sympathetic autonomic arousal than for the other two groups (Epstein & Roupenian, 1970). However, when the stress continues over long periods of time, predictable stress appears to become more stressful than unpredictable stress (Abbott, Schoen, & Badia, 1984).

A second line of research focuses on personal control over stress. In one study, two groups of participants participated in a difficult cognitive task in which errors were punished by electric shocks. One group could control this stressful situation by taking breaks whenever they wished, but the other group could take breaks only when told to do so. The amount of increase in blood pressure was significantly greater for the group that had no control over the stress (Hokanson, DeGood, Forrest, & Brittain, 1963).

The effects of uncontrollable stress on health have also been shown in an experiment using laboratory rats as subjects. Three groups of rats were placed in similar

Unpredictable events over which we have little control, such as when the fire alarm will call this firefighter into action, can be unpleasantly stressful.

Skinner boxes and electrodes were attached to their tails. One group never received any shocks and served as a standard of comparison to use in evaluating the health of the other two groups. The other two groups received occasional mild electric shocks to their tails. Group A was able to exert some control over the shocks because turning the wheel in the box allowed the rat to avoid upcoming shocks or turn off shocks that had already started. Rats in Group B had no control over the shocks. Turning the wheel in their box actually had nothing to do with the shocks; they simply received all the same shocks that their "partner" in Group A received. Again, the effects of lack of control were dramatic. The rats in Group B, which had no control over the stressful shocks, were significantly more likely to develop stomach ulcers and to lose weight than were the rats in Group A, which could exert some control (Weiss, 1972).

Furthermore, lack of control over stress has been shown to have a variety of highly important consequences for health. Rats receiving uncontrollable shocks show a suppression in the proliferation of the white blood cells, which play an important role in the body's immune response (Laudenslager, Ryan, Drugan, Hyson, & Maier, 1983) and exhibit less immunity to cancer cells (Visitainer, Volpicelli, & Seligman, 1982). Importantly, only animals that were exposed to *uncontrollable* stress showed these ill effects; controllable stress did not take a detectable toll on the body in these cases.

The results of these studies are extremely important in the lesson they provide for personal stress management. Stress events in our daily lives that are not predictable or controllable are all the more stressful. It is highly important, therefore, that we seek ways to embrace life's challenges and take control over our stressors (or to leave situations that result in uncontrollable stress). For example, working under a supervisor who often lashes out at you in unpredictable and uncontrollable ways may need to be dealt with by talking to your supervisor, by asking for assistance from your supervisor's boss, or by finding another job.

## Social Support

The magnitude of reactions to stress is considerably less for individuals with good social support from close friends and family members than for individuals with inadequate social support (Compas & Luecken, 2002). It's not yet completely clear how **social support** functions to buffer us against stress, but having someone to talk to, receive advice from, and be cheered and reassured by is an important factor determining our reactions to stress (Heller, Swindle, & Dusenbury, 1986; Kaniasty & Norris, 1995; Sutker, Uddo, Davis, & Ditta, 1995; Uchino, Cacioppo, & Kiecolt-Glaser, 1996).

**social support**
The role played by friends and relatives in providing advice, assistance, and someone in whom to confide private feelings.

Individuals with good social support are less likely to react to negative life events with depression, anxiety, and health problems. For example, persons who learn that they are infected with the human immunodeficiency virus, the virus that causes AIDS, react with less anxiety, despair, and depression if they have good social support (Dew, Ragni, & Nimorwicz, 1990). Similarly, children who have been sexually abused are less likely to experience anxiety, depression, and other symptoms of stress if they have good social support from their mothers (Kendall-Tackett & others, 1993). Likewise, a large study of elderly adults showed that men who experienced the death of a family member (who was not their spouse) were more likely to show an increase in depression if they did not have the social support of a wife or did not belong to a church or temple. Interestingly, a gender difference was found in this study. Elderly women were much less likely to become depressed than men after the death of a family member (other than a spouse), perhaps because women tend to have greater social support from friends than men do (Siegel & Kuykendall, 1990).

One aspect of social support that has been studied experimentally is the opportunity to "get it off your chest." The common belief in our culture that the simple act of telling someone else about your troubles is good for you probably is correct (Kelly, 1999). A clever experiment shows us the surprising extent to which this appears to be true (Pennebaker & Beall, 1986). College student subjects participated in a study in

The social support of friends and family helps buffer the effects of stress.

which they spent 15 minutes on each of four consecutive nights writing to the experimenter about a traumatic event in their lives—both a description of the event itself and their feelings about it. For purposes of comparison, another group of students wrote about unimportant topics assigned by the experimenter. Writing about the traumatic events, such as the death of a family member, understandably caused the students to feel sad and to have brief elevations in blood pressure immediately after venting their feelings. However, over the next six months, the students who "got it off their chest" reported being ill less often and making fewer visits to the university health center. Apparently, it is good for your health to share your negative feelings with someone else. Therefore, having someone to confide in seems to be one of the important benefits of social support. There are risks associated with getting things off your chest, however. Sometimes revealing personal information has the effect of making us or other people look bad. It is wise to be selective in what and to whom you disclose (Kelly, 1999).

Under some circumstances, the best "social support" comes from a trained psychotherapist. We will have much more to say about this process in chapter 15, but it is important to note here that receiving psychotherapy is associated with improvements in physical as well as emotional health (Mumford, Schlesinger, & Glass, 1981).

Social support can also help us make stressful decisions and successfully follow through on those decisions. Yale University psychologist Irving Janis developed a program to help cigarette smokers stop smoking—and not resume smoking. Some clients were given "buddies" who were also in the program and were instructed to keep in close contact during the first crucial weeks (they met weekly and spoke daily on the telephone for five weeks). Ten years later, almost all of these high social support clients were still total nonsmokers. In contrast, clients who were not given buddies or who contacted their buddies infrequently were averaging over a pack of cigarettes a day. Similar positive effects of buddies were found in other programs to stop smoking (Mermelstein, Cohen, Lichtenstein, Baer, & Kamarck, 1986) and to increase exercise and change eating habits (Janis, 1983; Janis & Hoffman, 1982). When we are under stress, a little help from our friends can bring out the best in us in many ways.

## Person Variables in Reactions to Stress: Cognition and Personality

We have seen that our reactions to stress are influenced by a number of factors: our prior experience with the stressor, the degree to which we can predict and control the stressor, and the availability of social support. But our personal characteristics—the so-called **person variables**—are also important in determining our responses to stress (Asarnow & others, 1999; Cui & Vaillant, 1996).

As we saw in chapter 12, many personality theorists believe that the best way to understand behavior is to acknowledge that we are influenced by both the situations in which we find ourselves *and* some key characteristics we have as individuals. This view, referred to as *person × situation interactionism*, was described on page 478. In terms of stress, it means that our reactions are partly determined by the situation (the stressor, our social support, etc.) and partly determined by some of our personal characteristics (how we think about the stressor, how "reactive" our bodies are to stress, etc.).

### Cognitive Factors in Stress Reactions

An important reason that different people react differently to the same stressor is that people *think* about these events differently (Beck, 1976; Joiner & others, 1999; Lazarus, 1999; Tomaka & others, 1997). Some individuals appear more likely than others to interpret events in stress-provoking ways. For example, suppose you are a graduate student in clinical psychology and your supervisor suggests a better way to help a client. She says, "You're doing very well with this client, but a better way to help him with his fear of automobiles might be to . . ." and she proceeds to spell out her recommendations. Some individuals would be likely to interpret her statement as a combination of a nice compliment and a helpful bit of advice from a master therapist. Other individuals would interpret the same statement as a criticism of how they are doing as a student of therapy and would expect to be dismissed from the program. As we have noted before, the interpretation of the event determines its stressfulness.

### Personality Characteristics and Stress Reactions

In addition to cognitive factors, differences among individuals in their characteristic emotions and personalities prior to stress influence their reactions to stress (Folkman & Moscowitz, 2000). For example, children and teenagers who tend to be more anxious prior to earthquakes, hurricanes, and other stressful events are more likely to react to the stressor with increased fears and worries (Asarnow & others, 1999; La Greca & others, 1998). Similarly, military recruits who were more insecure and often sought reassurance from others before the stressor of basic training were more likely to be depressed afterward (Joiner & Schmidt, 1998). Thus, the effects of stress can only be understood in terms of a person × situation interaction. Stress (a situation variable) influences people with different cognitive and emotional characteristics before the stressor (person variables) in different ways.

A personality characteristic that appears to be important in influencing the health consequences of stress has been termed the **Type A personality.** Some people simply react better than others to the stress of our pressured, competitive world. Have you ever watched a group of people play video games? For some people, it is a pleasant diversion, whereas for others it is a matter of life-or-death competition. A group of health psychologists watched subjects play a video game and took measures of the activity of their cardiovascular systems. Some subjects reacted to the game with large increases in heart rate, blood pressure, and cholesterol (Jorgensen, Nash, Lasser, Hymowitz, & Langer, 1988). What is going on here? What kind of personality reacts even to trivial competitive stress with health-threatening sympathetic arousal?

The classic work on Type A personality was done by Meyer Friedman and Ray Rosenman (1974), two physicians who specialize in heart disease. They were observant enough to look beyond their medical tests to see that many of their heart disease patients, particularly younger men aged 30 to 60, were often of the "same type" behaviorally. They were hard-driving, impatient, hostile individuals who rarely slowed down to smell the roses. This pattern of behavior they identified as *Type A personality.* The following characteristics more specifically describe the Type A personality (Diamond, 1982; Friedman & Rosenman, 1974; Matthews, 1982):

**person variables**
All characteristics of an individual that are relatively enduring, such as ways of thinking, beliefs, or physiological reactivity to stress.

**Type A personality**
The pattern of behavior characterized most by intense competitiveness, hostility, overwork, and a sense of time urgency.

1. Is highly competitive, hard-driving, and ambitious in work, sports, and games

2. Works hurriedly, always rushing, has a sense of "time urgency," and often does two things at once

3. Is a workaholic, takes little time off for relaxation or vacation

4. Speaks loudly or "explosively"

5. Is perfectionistic and demanding

6. Is hostile, aggressive, and frequently angry with others.

If this description sounds like you, keep in mind that there is a little Type A behavior in most of us, and you should be concerned only if it's excessive.

Of all the components of the Type A behavior pattern, the most important one appears to be a *particular kind of hostility*. Individuals who are hostile in the sense of reacting to frustration with verbal aggression (yelling, criticizing, insulting) or even physical aggression seem to be at slightly higher risk for coronary heart disease, but individuals who are hostile in the sense of being chronically suspicious and resentful are not (Friedman & Booth-Kewley, 1987; Miller & others, 1996; Ben-Zur, 2002; Smith & Ruiz, 2002).

Why is Type A behavior associated with increased risk of coronary heart disease? Type A behavior appears to be indirectly linked to heart disease through two major risk factors: high blood pressure and cholesterol (Matthews, 1982; Weidner & others, 1987). One theory suggests that this is because Type A individuals react physiologically more to stress than other individuals do. Researchers at Duke University Medical Center (Williams & others, 1982) classified a group of undergraduate males as Type A or normal. Both groups were asked to subtract 13 from 7,683, then subtract 13 from the answer, and so on, with a prize being given to the person with the fastest subtraction rate. In this competitive situation, the Type A individuals showed greater increases in blood flow to the skeletal muscles and in the amount of epinephrine and norepinephrine in the blood. Because these changes are associated with the formation of cholesterol plaques, as we have already seen in discussing the GAS, the greater responsiveness of the Type A individuals may indirectly lead to hardening of the arteries of the heart. Similarly, Type A individuals also have been shown to respond to stress with greater increases in blood pressure—another key risk factor for coronary disease (Haynes, Feinleib, & Kannel, 1980; Matthews, 1982; Williams & others, 1982). Fortunately, there is evidence that hostility can be reduced by a type of psychotherapy (Suinn, 2001).

## Person Variables in Reactions to Stress: Gender and Ethnicity

There is growing evidence that both gender differences and ethnic differences exist in stress and coping. As described in this section, we cannot fully understand stress and coping without understanding the role of these key person variables. When studying differences between genders or ethnic groups, however, it is important to remember that not all members of a group behave in the same way. In this section, we are speaking only of differences between groups *on average*. As we learned in chapter 11, there are sure to be large differences among both women and men, for example, in their reactions in stress that are probably larger than the average difference between women and men.

### Gender Differences in Response to Stress

Women are more likely than men to experience lasting reactions to traumatic events. That is, they are more likely to experience anxiety, depression, and sleep disturbances that begin soon after a trauma (Fullerton & others, 2001). It is likely that this finding partly reflects a greater likelihood of women being traumatized by spouse abuse, rape, and other highly stressful events. It also appears to reflect a gender difference in response to some types of traumatic events, however. For example, a study of women and men who had survived serious automobile accidents found that both women and men were affected by the trauma afterward, but women were more distressed emotionally and experienced more sleep problems than men did (Fullerton & others, 2001). Thus, when exposed to the same stressors, women on average appear to be more distressed afterward. Again, however, we are only speaking of average differences. Many women are resilient in their response to traumatic stress, and many men are seriously affected by trauma.

### Gender Differences in the Benefits of Marriage

As discussed earlier in this chapter, social support buffers us against stress. Marriage and other committed relationships are important sources of social support for both sexes. For both women and men, married people are far healthier than people who are not in committed relationships. There is a huge difference in the benefits of marriage to women and men, however (Kiecolt-Glaser & Newton, 2001). Unmarried women have 50 percent higher mortality (death) rates than do married women, but unmarried men have 250 percent higher mortality rates than do married men. Similarly, losing a spouse through divorce or death is more detrimental to the health of men than women (Kiecolt-Glaser & Newton, 2001). Why is marriage more of a benefit to men than women? Janice Kiecolt-Glaser and Tamara Newton (2001) suggest two likely reasons. First, women tend to have more social support from close friendships than men do, so women tend to have social support whether married or not. In contrast, men tend to rely exclusively on their wives for social support to buffer them from the effects of stress. Second, women are more likely than men to urge their partners to take good care of themselves medically. Thus, marriage may help men to eat well, exercise, and seek medical advice more than marriage helps women in this way. In addition, many modern marriages are still not equitable, with women having more responsibilities but less authority than men. Thus, marriage is good for both sexes, but even better for men. Keep in mind that at least part of the correlation between marriage and good health may not be based on the beneficial effects of marriage, however. It may partly be that healthier men and women are more likely to marry than less healthy persons are. Much remains to be learned about this topic.

### Fight-or-Flight and Tend-and-Befriend

William James (1897) wrote about the fight-or-flight syndrome as the central aspect of emotion. When confronted with a stressful stimulus—such as a menacing person on a dark street—we respond with arousal of the sympathetic nervous system and the adrenal glands in preparation to flee the person or fight with him. Nearly everything that James wrote about emotion was based on this syndrome. And, to a great extent, modern psychologists have followed his lead.

Psychologist Shelley Taylor and her colleagues (2000) agree that the fight-or-flight syndrome is important to both men and women, but she argues that it omits the most important aspects of responses to stress in women. Taylor believes that women are more likely than men to respond to stress with what she calls the "tend-and-befriend" response. When faced with stress, such as a fire or natural disaster, women typically respond by tending to their children. They quickly locate their children and interact with them in ways that reduce their children's physiological response to the stressor, such as by holding or touching them. In studies of employed women and men, women who have had a particularly stressful day tended to be unusually nurturing with their children in the evening. Women only withdrew from their children after work if they experienced overwhelming job stress that day. Fathers respond to stress in the workplace quite differently on average. Fathers tend to be grouchy or withdraw from family members if they have had a stressful day at work.

Taylor also hypothesized that if the threat is likely to recur, women tend to befriend others to create alliances. This process of bonding with other women serves two purposes. In some cases, the women create ways to defend against the threat, whether it is a predatory animal near their village or an unreasonable employer. In addition, creating alliances with other women provides social support to the women, which tends to reduce their own emotional and related physiological responses to the threat (Taylor, 2002; Taylor & others, 2000). Thus, according to Taylor, we cannot fully understand emotional responses to stressful events unless we recognize that there are profoundly important differences between women and men. While it may be sufficient to study the balance between fight and flight in males, who tend to deal with threats as individuals, the social nature of the emotional response to stress in females requires study of the social aspects of their tending and befriending.

**Ethnic Differences in Stress**

There is emerging evidence that members of race-ethnic groups that are in the minority in a society experiences more stress than do members of the majority culture (Contrada & others, 2000). There are a number of reasons why this may be so. First, members of ethnic minority groups tend to have fewer advantages (greater education, higher incomes, better health insurance, etc.) that shield them from stress. Second, members of minority groups often experience stressful interactions with the majority culture that are based on stereotypes, prejudice, and discrimination. Third, immigrant families often experience stress due to the more rapid acculturation of children into the new culture. Parents are sometimes stressed by their children's changing behavior, and children are sometimes stressed by pressure from their parents to maintain the language and standards of their culture. This new and important line of research for psychologists will bring many insights in the future, but it is a topic that many members of ethnic minority groups already understand very well.

## Review

The magnitude of the emotional, cognitive, and physical toll that stress takes on us varies from individual to individual and from time to time for the same individual. The factors that seem to be related to the magnitude of stress reactions are prior experience with the stress, age, gender, predictability and control over the stress, and social support.

The degree to which we react to stress also varies according to our personal characteristics. Different people react differently to stress partly because of cognitive factors. In addition, some individuals seem to react calmly to the pressures of competitive life, but the so-called Type A personality finds competitive situations to be highly stressful. The hostility that often accompanies Type A behavior seems to be a factor in the degree of wear and tear on the body, particularly cardiovascular disease.

## Check Your Learning

To be sure that you have learned the key points from the preceding section, cover the list of correct answers and try to answer each question. If you give an incorrect answer to any question, return to the page given next to the correct answer to see why your answer was not correct.

1. In general, recent stress events are _____ when they are predictable or controllable than when they are not.

   a) more stressful     c) not stressful at all

   b) less stressful     d) slightly stressful

2. Having _____, or someone to talk to, receive advice from, and be cheered and reassured by, is an important factor determining our reactions to stress.

3. _____ refers to all characteristics of an individual that are relatively enduring, such as ways of thinking, beliefs, or physiological reactivity to stress.

   a)  Identity                  c)  Individuality
   b)  Person variables          d)  Superego

4. A person who exhibits a pattern of behavior characterized by intense competitiveness, hostility, overwork, and a sense of time urgency would be identified as _____.

   a)  abnormal                  c)  Type A personality
   b)  Type B personality        d)  high-strung

5. On average, women derive more health benefits from marriage than men do.

   a)  True                      b)  False

**Thinking Critically about Psychology**

1. Is there a stressful aspect of your college life that could be eased by better social support?

2. How does our society's emphasis on monetary success and power influence the Type A personality?

Correct Answers:   1. b (pp. 512–513),   2. social support (p. 513),   3. b (p. 515),   4. c (p. 515),   5. b (p. 517).

## ● Coping with Stress

An issue of utmost importance to psychologists who work to promote both mental and physical health is that we are not all equally effective at coping with stress. What are the best ways to cope?

### Effective Coping

Effective methods of **coping** either remove the source of stress or control our reactions to it:

1. *Removing stress.* One effective way of dealing with stress is to remove the source of stress from our lives. If an employee holds a job that is stressful, discussions could be held with the employer that might lead to a reduction in the pressures of the job, or the employee could simply resign. If the stress stems from an unhappy marriage, either marriage counseling could be sought or the marriage could be ended. In a variety of ways, coping with stress can take the form of locating its source and eliminating it. Unfortunately, this is not always possible. It's not always feasible or appropriate to quit a job or leave a marriage, and some sources of stress, such as the death of a spouse, just cannot be removed.

2. *Cognitive coping.* Our cognitions are intimately linked to our reactions to stressful events. One effective method of coping, then, might be to change how we think about—or interpret—the events that push and shove our lives. For example, I know a musician who had a successful first record, but his second album was a flop—the critics panned it and the public didn't buy it. At first, he saw this as a sign that the first record was a fluke and that he had no real talent. As a result, the failure of the second album was a huge stress. However, a veteran musician convinced him that having an unsuccessful second album is a common "sophomore slump" among musicians who go on to be very successful. This

**coping**
Attempts by individuals to deal with the source of stress and/or control their reactions to it.

conversation changed his interpretation of his unsuccessful album and allowed him to view it as a challenge to do better next time. Finding an interpretation that is realistic and minimizes the stress of the events of our lives is a key part of coping with stress (Taylor, 1999).

Taylor and her colleagues (1998) have recently evaluated two cognitive strategies for coping. They evaluated a method that is widely endorsed in self-help books (imagining a positive outcome) and compared it with the cognitive strategy of imagining the steps involved in successful coping. College students were randomly assigned to two groups at the beginning of the term. One group was asked to imagine themselves beaming with success when they received high marks in the class. The second group was asked to imagine all of the practical steps involved in getting a good grade (getting the book, reading assignments, studying in advance, etc.). The group that imagined the practical steps toward success studied more, felt less anxiety, and actually received higher grades (Taylor & others 1998). This suggests that practical planning is a useful strategy in some situations.

3. ***Managing stress reactions.*** When the source of stress cannot realistically be removed or changed, another effective option is to manage our psychological and physiological reactions to the stress. For example, an individual may decide to start a new business, knowing full well that the first year or two will be hectic. She would be unwilling, then, to remove the source of the stress (the new business) but could learn to control her reactions to the stress. One strategy might be to schedule as much time as possible for relaxing activities, such as aerobic exercise, hobbies, or time with friends. Another would be to seek special training from a psychologist in controlling the body reactions to stress by learning to deeply relax the large body muscles (relaxation training is discussed more fully in a later section of this chapter).

Happily, psychological counseling that encourages all three methods of effective coping has even been successful in changing the Type A behavior pattern. Some 20 studies have demonstrated marked improvement in the behavior pattern; more important, two of the studies followed the individuals for three years after treatment to determine whether there were actual improvements in cardiac health. It is encouraging that the treated patients showed a 50 percent reduction in heart attacks and deaths compared with Type A individuals who did not receive treatment (Nunes, Frank, & Kornfeld, 1987). We will look at some of the specific treatment procedures used to modify Type A behavior later in this chapter and at others in chapter 15.

## Ineffective Coping

Unfortunately, many of our efforts to cope with stress are ineffective. They may provide temporary relief from the discomfort produced by stress but do little to provide a long-term solution and may even make matters worse. Three common, but ineffective, coping strategies are as follows:

1. ***Withdrawal.*** Sometimes we deal with stress by withdrawing from it. Many students encounter courses in college that are far more difficult than anything they had experienced in high school. Attempting to study difficult material can be highly stressful, and that stress can lead to a withdrawal from studying—by playing electronic games, talking on the telephone, partying, and the like. Similarly, a husband may ineffectively cope with the stress of an unhappy marriage by withdrawing to the refuge of a bar every day after work.

Notice that it is not *what* you do, but *how* and *why* you do it, that makes a coping strategy effective or ineffective. Spending your time playing electronic video games actually may be an effective coping strategy *if* you only do it for rea-

An ineffective method of coping with stress from an unhappy marriage is to withdraw to the refuge of a bar.

counseling in behavioral self-management skills (Meyer, Nash, McAlister, Maccoby, & Farquhar, 1980). And an in-school program in Los Angeles found that teaching the importance of low-fat diets to children who were at risk for chronic health problems produced significant changes in eating behavior (Marcus, Wheeler, Cullen, & Crane, 1987). Apparently, it is difficult to change unhealthy eating behavior, but it is not impossible (Jeffrey, 1988).

### Regular Aerobic Exercise

We all know that exercise is good for our health. But most of us would be surprised to see the large amount of evidence that links regular moderate aerobic exercise to good health (C. D. Jenkins, 1988; R. W. Jenkins, 1988). By moderate aerobic exercise, I mean at least 30 minutes of continuous exercise that raises the heart rate to 70 to 85 percent of maximum capacity at least four times each week (Taylor, 1986). Unless the individual has a preexisting medical problem that prohibits exercise, regular aerobic exercise has been shown to reduce high blood pressure, blood cholesterol levels, and the risk of coronary heart disease (Leon, 1983; Roy & Steptoe, 1991). Then why is it that so few of us exercise regularly? You know from my confessions in chapter 10 that my history of exercise is an irregular one. I have worked out three times this week, but last week I was "too busy" to exercise at all. Why do I—a person who values good health and decries hypocrisy—often fail to practice what I preach? The unfortunate fact is that I am not the exception but the rule. It has been estimated that only 21 percent of adults in the United States engage in regular aerobic exercise (White, Powell, Hogelin, Gentry, & Forman, 1987).

Part of the answer seems to be a lack of information. The number of Americans who exercise regularly has increased, but the number of us who know about the health benefits of exercise and still don't exercise regularly is very high. The real problem is *adherence* (Schwarzer, 2001). Far more of us begin exercise programs than stick with them. On the average, only half the individuals who begin a regular program of exercise are still at it only six months later (Dishman, 1982).

What, then, can a person do to help keep his or her commitment to a program of regular exercise? Psychologists are still actively working on this problem, but so far, it seems that social support from a friend who exercises with you, setting clear personal goals and providing reinforcement to yourself, finding a kind of exercise that you really *enjoy,* and avoiding excessively strenuous exercise all help long-term adherence (Taylor, 1986). A clearer belief that regular exercise really will benefit *you* also seems to help, because individuals who believe that they should take charge of their own health and those who know they are at risk for coronary heart disease for other reasons are more likely to exercise regularly (Dishman, 1982). We all need to find a reason and a way to keep exercising.

### Medical Compliance

Psychologists have also found themselves called on by physicians to help solve a surprisingly difficult and widespread problem in health care delivery. Patients with chronic health problems, such as high blood pressure and diabetes, frequently do not take their prescribed medication. This is extremely unfortunate because proper use of medication can greatly reduce the risk of stroke and heart attack associated with high blood pressure and reduce the risk of blindness, amputation of limbs, and other complications of diabetes. Reasons for failing to follow prescribed treatments include not understanding the physician's instructions, concerns about cost, not wanting to experience the side effects of some medications, and simply denying the need to continue treatment. Some health psychologists, therefore, devote a substantial amount of their time to implementing programs to help patients comply most effectively with their doctor's orders (Brownlee-Dufek & others, 1987; Taylor, 1999).

A routine of moderate exercise helps to promote good health.

## Safety Management

When we think of promoting health, we quite reasonably think of preventing diseases like cancer or heart diseases. But accidents are a major cause of disability and death. In fact, they are one of the leading causes of death for children, adolescents, and young adults. Over the past 20 years, psychologists have developed and studied methods of reducing injuries and accidental deaths, particularly in the workplace and in automobiles (Geller, 1988).

Since 2001, taxi cabs in Chicago have been required to have signs in the back seat recommending that passengers wear seat belts. Wearing seat belts greatly reduces the risk of death or injury in automobile accidents, but many people do not wear them. Does a simple reminder increase seat belt use? A classic study by Bruce Thyer and E. Scott Geller (1987) provided strong evidence in support of the use of such reminder signs. They asked 24 graduate students to wear seat belts when driving and to record for two weeks the percentage of times that passengers in the front seat of their cars wore seat belts. Then the drivers placed a sticker on the passenger-side dashboard for two weeks that said "SAFETY BELT USE REQUIRED IN THIS VEHICLE." The percentage of passengers who wore seat belts doubled—from about 35 percent to 70 percent. When the signs were removed for two weeks, seat belt use dropped to near the original level, but rose to over 70 percent when the signs were reintroduced. Something as simple as a sign reminding passengers to wear seat belts can have a *powerful* impact on safety.

Geller and others (1989) also studied the use of pledges to wear seat belts. In this study, the participants were students, faculty, and staff at Virginia Polytechnic Institute and State University. During the fall and spring quarters, over 10,000 pledge cards were made available throughout campus. Individuals who signed the pledge to wear seat belts could drop part of the card into a box, making them eligible for a lottery in which they could win prizes donated by local merchants. The top half of the card was designed to be hung from the car's rearview mirror. Observers at the entrance to university parking lots recorded whether the driver was wearing a seat belt and used parking decals to link the car to the driver's name. Among drivers who signed the pledges, use of seat belts increased from about 50 percent to about 65 percent after they pledged. This level of seat belt use was approximately twice as high as those who did not pledge.

Driving while intoxicated is a major cause of death and injury, both to the driver and to others involved in the accident. Geller, Russ, and Delphos (1987) evaluated a program in which servers in bars frequented by college students were trained to reduce excessive drinking by their customers. The servers were given information about the effects of alcohol and the risks of excessive drinking. In addition, instruction and role plays were used to teach servers techniques for reducing the drinking of customers who were beginning to drink excessively. These techniques included such things as offering food, suggesting nonalcoholic drinks, and slowing service. The intervention was evaluated by sending 32 college-aged research assistants to two bars in a college town where they posed as regular customers who tried to drink excessively. Half of the servers in each bar had been trained, but the research assistants did not know which servers had been trained. The servers who were trained were much more likely to limit drinking, and the blood alcohol levels of the research assistants who were served by the untrained servers was almost twice as high as that of research assistants served by trained servers! A brief training program for servers in bars can make a huge difference in reducing excessive drinking in college students.

Many studies have looked at simple but effective ways to reduce accidental injury and death in the workplace (Geller, 1996). Careless behavior on the job is common in many dangerous workplaces. In particular, failure to use necessary protective gear is the cause of approximately 40 percent of work-related accidents (National Safety Council, 1998). Supervisors sometimes contribute to unsafe practices, both because they, like their workers, minimize the dangers and because they believe that working safely requires working at a slower pace, making it difficult to meet production demands. Setting

# HUMAN DIVERSITY

## Psychology and Women's Health

A decade ago, psychologists Judith Rodin and Jeanette Ickovics (1990) summarized what psychologists know about the health and health care of women and issued a call for new research efforts in this area. Much still remains to be learned about the psychological factors that have an impact on women's health, but the National Institutes of Health in 2000 launched a large-scale effort to increase research on the health of women.

Women have different health concerns than men, but the medical profession is still dominated by men who are not properly trained to meet the needs of women.

haviors that greatly increase the chance of illness, such as cigarette smoking, drug use, and excessive alcohol use. As a result, the death rates for men and women are growing more similar, particularly because of a large increase in the rates of cigarette-related lung cancer. Over the past 30 years, death due to lung cancer increased 85 percent in men but over 400 percent in women (Taylor, 1999).

### Health Concerns of Women

Many important health issues are unique to women (Clifford-Walton, 1998). Breast, ovarian, and cervical cancer; hysterectomy (surgical removal of the uterus); and menstrual dysfunction are concerns only of women, and osteoporosis (thinning of the bones), eating disorders, lupus, and rheumatoid arthritis are far more common in women than men. In addition, two-thirds of all surgery in the United States is performed on women, mostly because of the high rates of cesarean deliveries and hysterectomies. Women are less likely to have medical insurance than men are, and when they are insured, their policies often do not cover essential preventive procedures such as Pap smears for early detection of cervical cancer (Taylor, 1999).

Women also have unique health concerns because they are often prescribed the hormone estrogen. Estrogen is contained in birth control pills and is sometimes prescribed for women who have reached menopause to replace the natural supply that has diminished.

In spite of these clear differences in the health concerns of women, women have been excluded from health research to a great extent in the past. This means that much of what has been learned in medical research may not apply to women. A decade ago, the National Institutes of Health mandated that women could no longer be excluded from research unless there is a strong reason. Although it took time for the new policy to affect research, there is now a greatly accelerated rate of research on the health and mental health of women.

### Changes in High-Risk Behavior

The second reason that a focus on women's health is needed is that women are behaving more like men in terms of high-risk health behavior in recent years. The last century saw marked increases among women in risky be-

### Different Equation Between Health Behaviors and Illnesses

Third, the equation relating health-related behaviors and illness is somewhat different for women than for men. For example, behaviors that create health risks for both women and men, such as cigarette smoking, moderate to excessive alcohol consumption, obesity, and high-fat diets are particularly dangerous for women who take birth control pills. Women need to be made aware of interactions among their risk factors that do not affect men.

Another way in which the health behavior equation is different for women can be seen in the example of AIDS. Men can and do acquire the HIV virus—which can lead to AIDS—from intercourse with women, but it is more common for women to acquire the virus through either vaginal or anal intercourse. Whereas only 2 percent of men with AIDS acquired HIV through heterosexual intercourse, 31 percent of women with AIDS acquired HIV in this way. Thus, the risks for contracting HIV (and AIDS) from essentially the same behaviors are quite different for women and men (Rodin & Ickovics, 1990).

A third way in which the health behavior equation is different for women concerns the effects of employment. Women who are employed are generally healthier than women who are not, but women who are employed in demeaning, low-paying, and pressured jobs have much poorer health. Interestingly, women who have satisfying jobs, are married, and have children are the healthiest of all, in spite of the pressures involved in handling all of these roles (Waldron, 1991).

### Other Sociocultural Factors in Women's Health

Gender is not the only sociocultural factor that plays a role in the health of women, of course. To understand the health behavior of women, we must also understand their ethnicity, sexual orientation, and other aspects of

*(continued)*

their sociocultural makeup (Gruskin, 1999). For example, African American women have lower rates of breast cancer than non-Hispanic white women do, but when African American women contract breast cancer, their survival rates are lower. Psychologist Beth Meyerowitz and her colleagues (1998) believe that ethnicity is related to survival from breast cancer because African American women tend to have fewer financial resources and have less access to quality health care and information about cancer. Sexual orientation also plays a role in women's health. Although lesbian women are at greatly reduced risk of contracting AIDS, they are more likely to have breast cancer. Having children reduces the risk of breast cancer, and although artificial insemination is on the rise, lesbian women are still less likely to become pregnant. In addition, lesbian women are less likely to have regular obstetric examinations and less likely to find cervical cancer early when it is most treatable. Each factor must be considered carefully in attempting to find ways to improve the health behavior of women. ■

aside the enormous human costs of workplace injuries, it is generally cost-efficient to work more safely than more quickly (because worker deaths and injuries are extremely expensive to industries in many ways). Moreover, it is not impossible to improve quality and safety at the same time (Herrero & others, 2002).

Zohar (2002) conducted an evaluation of a simple method of increasing the use of earplugs in a plant that repaired and upgraded heavy equipment. Supervisors were trained in ways to remind workers of the need to wear earplugs that would not seem insulting and were taught to positively reinforce wearing earplugs with simple thank yous and expressions of appreciation. Prior to the change in supervision, 10 percent of the workers wore earplugs. That rate steadily rose and leveled off at about 65 percent over six months.

## ● Summing Up: How Beneficial Could Health Psychology Be?

You have read a great deal in this chapter about the relationship between psychology and health. As a result, I hope that you have a better understanding of the ways in which stress, coping, and health-related behaviors can affect your physical well-being. But just how important is all this information about health psychology? You've heard me explain since chapters 1 and 3 that the mind and the body are intricately and profoundly interrelated, but how much impact could psychological factors *really* have on physical health? *A lot.* Let me try to convince you.

To understand the potential benefits of psychology to health, we need to look at what medicine has already accomplished during this century. In 1900, the leading causes of death in the United States were infectious diseases, such as tuberculosis (Levy & Moskowitz, 1982). Since that time, advances in antibiotics and other aspects of medical care have made deaths due to these causes rare.

Now the major unconquered killers, in order of their frequency as causes of death, are heart disease, cancer, and accidents (Taylor, 1999). Medical research has accomplished about all that it can in the area of bacterial infections. The next breakthroughs in medicine that save large numbers of lives will probably be more effective treatments for heart diseases, improved treatments for cancer, and treatments or vaccines for AIDS.

But notice two things: First, these expected medical breakthroughs have not happened yet and may possibly never happen; second, the number one and two killers of Americans today—heart disease and cancer—are disorders in which stress and lifestyle (eating, drinking, smoking, exercising, etc.) play a major role. And, as we just noted, although it is completely preventable, AIDS is a major cause of death. Health psychology may very well take the lead in the fight against these diseases. For example, because cigarette smoking is the leading cause of lung cancer and a prime factor in heart disease, is it more reasonable to expect medicine to cure these diseases or for us to seek more effective ways of helping smokers stop smoking and preventing nonsmokers from ever starting?

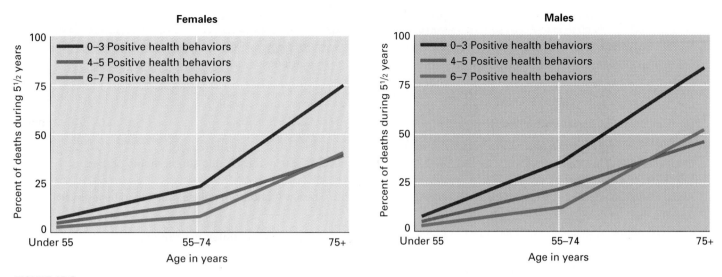

**FIGURE 13.8**

The number of positive health practices was found to be dramatically related to the percentage of deaths over a 5½-year period in the Alameda County study.

**Source:** Data from N. B. Belloc, "Relationship of Health Practices to Mortality," *Preventive Medicine* 2:67–81, 1973. Copyright © 1973 Academic Press, Orlando, FL.

So the possibilities of health psychology having a major impact on our health are quite good. Even if we accept the premise that the major causes of death in the United States are related to stress and lifestyle, however, we need to know how *much* impact psychological factors have on our health. Until we have an answer to that question, we cannot estimate the potential benefits of health psychology. A complete answer is impossible at this time, but a very impressive tentative answer can be given by looking at an extremely important study of health-related behavior.

Nearly 7,000 adults living in Alameda County, California, answered questions concerning their health, including the following questionnaire, which you can take yourself. How many of these positive health practices do you engage in?

1. Moderate or no use of alcohol

2. Sleeping seven to eight hours nightly

3. Never or rarely eating between meals

4. Being at or near your ideal weight for your height

5. Regular physical exercise

6. Never smoking cigarettes

7. Eating breakfast almost every day

Two classic studies of the health of these individuals 5½ and 9½ years later (Belloc, 1973; Breslow & Enstrom, 1980) revealed a dramatic relationship between health practices and mortality. As shown in figure 13.8, those individuals who engaged in zero to three positive health practices were considerably more likely to have died in the first 5½ years of the study than were individuals who engaged in six to seven positive health practices, particularly in middle age and beyond. After 9½ years, the death rate of the group engaged in zero to three positive health practices was, astoundingly, *twice* as high as for the group engaged in six to seven positive health practices.

Another approach to estimating the cumulative effect of changing our health-related behaviors has been offered by University of Chicago physician Michael Roizen (1999). Roizen is a respected medical school professor and expert on the prevention of health problems in older adults. During his years of trying to convince patients to adopt healthier lifestyles, he developed a clever way of convincing many people to change.

**Table 13.2 Some Healthy Behaviors Related to Feeling Younger and Living Longer**

**Eating and drinking**

Eat a low-calorie and low-fat diet of a variety of foods that are high in nutrients

Eat products made from soy beans (not including soy sauce)

Eat fish that are rich in omega 3 fatty acids, such as salmon or cod, at least once a week

Drink at least 8 glasses of water a day

Eat breakfast every day

Eat foods every day that are rich in vitamins $B_6$, C, D, E, folate, calcium, or take reasonable supplements of these nutrients

Avoid needless vitamin and mineral supplements (especially avoid vitamin A and iron, unless prescribed by a physician)

Avoid diets (eat sensibly all the time)

Drink alcohol in only moderation (about one drink per day for most people who are not at risk for alcohol abuse), if at all, but never drink in excess

**Exercising**

Exercise regularly (walking vigorously 30 minutes a day, or the equivalent)

Build stamina by engaging in aerobic exercise that breaks a sweat three times a week

Build muscle strength by lifting weights or engaging in other strength training three times a week for 10 minutes

**Health habits**

Brush your teeth and floss daily (periodontal disease harms the immune system and contributes significantly to heart disease)

Get a good night's sleep (7–8 hours a night)

Get 10–20 minutes of sun each day to produce active vitamin D (but wear sunscreen, especially for longer exposure)

Wear seat belts and have air bags in automobiles

Live in an area with clean air (low levels of ozone, hydrocarbons, and particulate matter)

**Sex**

Have safe sex (avoid casual sex and use condoms)

Have more frequent orgasms (increase from the average U.S. rate of 60 per year to 120 per year)

**Stress and social support**

Avoid high levels of stress or manage stress well

Live within your financial means and avoid bankruptcy

Develop good social support from family and friends

**Weight and cardiac health**

Maintain a steady desirable weight

Keep your blood pressure low (below 140/90 and ideally to 115/76)

Lower your cholesterol (total cholesterol below 240 mg/dl and high density or "good" cholesterol at 40 mg/dl or higher)

**Tobacco and drugs**

Don't smoke or use any type of tobacco product

Don't work or live in an environment that is filled with smoke (passive exposure is as dangerous as smoking)

Avoid use of other drugs

Based on Roizen, M. F. (1999). *Real age: Are you as young as you can be?* New York: HarperCollins.

Although most college students haven't attended a 10- or 20-year high school reunion yet, people who have are often shocked at the physical differences in their classmates. Although they are all the same chronological age, some have aged much more than others in the 10 or 20 years since graduation. Roizen uses our vanity about our physical appearance and concerns about our health to motivate us to change our health habits. His specific technique for motivating change is to convert the existing research data on the influence of a variety health practices on life expectancy into each person's "real age." According to Roizen, your real age is your chronological age minus (or plus) the number of years associated with doing (or not doing) the positive health behaviors listed in table 13.2 (this is a partial list summarized and condensed from Roizen's book). According to Roizen, a person who makes significant changes in health-related behavior can subtract 20 or more years from his or her "real age" (meaning that he or she could feel younger, be healthier, and expect to live longer).

The information summarized in this section strongly supports the idea that changes in health-related lifestyle can produce dramatic improvements in health and longevity. To date, however, health psychology has shown only modest success in actually getting large numbers of individuals who engage in few positive health behaviors to engage in more. Change is possible—many people do change their lifestyles in significant ways—but it is difficult. More remains to be learned by health psychologists about the best ways to change health-related behavior (Taylor, 1999).

## Psychology and the Cost of Health Care

One of the most pressing problems of personal economics facing all of us today is the surging cost of health care. The cost of routine health care and hospitalization has risen dramatically over the past decades. Even for those with adequate health insurance or who are members of a health maintenance organization (HMO), the increased costs are a drain through increased premiums and membership fees. For this reason, a great deal of effort has gone into the search for ways to reduce health care expenses. In particular, insurance companies and HMOs—which provide for an individual's health care needs for a flat annual fee—have been active in trying to find ways to reduce health care costs.

Surprisingly, psychology offers two of the best solutions to this problem. First, as we have seen in this chapter, health psychology has the ability to *prevent* serious health problems and to reduce recurrences of problems such as heart attacks. The savings in preventing health problems over treating them once they have developed are dramatic. Second, more traditional forms of services provided by clinical psychologists can also play a major role in the reduction of health care costs (Taylor, 1999).

Physicians have long known that 50 to 75 percent of the patients whom they see either have pains and other symptoms without any known physical cause or have genuine physical problems that are caused by stress, alcohol abuse, and other psychological factors. HMO members with such problems visit physicians twice as often as other members (Turkington, 1987). A number of studies have been conducted to see whether referring these patients actually results in a reduction in the use of medical services. These studies show that providing psychological services greatly reduces the overall cost of medical care and further benefits employers, who often pay part of the cost of insurance or HMOs, by reducing the number of days missed from work due to illness (Gabbard & others, 1997; Turkington, 1987).

---

Psychological methods have been successfully used in the prevention and treatment of medical problems. Methods have been developed to help people drink less alcohol, exercise regularly, stop smoking, lose excess weight, and make other behavioral changes that reduce the risk of heart attack and other serious diseases. Progressive relaxation training and other treatment techniques have also been successful in treating problems such as high blood pressure, headaches, epilepsy, and diabetes. The

**Review**

more that we are willing to apply to our lives the advances from the field of health psychology in understanding of illness, the more we will be able to prevent unnecessary disease and control the cost of health care.

## Check Your Learning

To be sure that you have learned the key points from the preceding section, cover the list of correct answers and try to answer each question. If you give an incorrect answer to any question, return to the page given next to the correct answer to see why your answer was not correct.

1. _____ refers to a method of learning to deeply relax the muscles of your body.

   a) Psychoanalysis      c) Aerobics

   b) Cognitive therapy      d) Progressive relaxation training

2. A surprisingly difficult and widespread problem in health care delivery is the lack of _____.

   a) pharmacies      c) medical schools

   b) drugs      d) medical compliance

3. Today the most frequent cause of death among adults in North America is _____.

   a) AIDS      c) heart disease

   b) cancer      d) accidents

4. Changes in lifestyle could produce dramatic improvements in health and longevity in North America.

   a) True      b) False

## Thinking Critically about Psychology

1. Do the members of your family exercise enough? If not, do you think there is any way that you could convince them to change?

2. Why do you think that eating breakfast every day is a sign of good health?

Correct Answers: 1. d (p. 523), 2. d (p. 525), 3. c (p. 528), 4. a (p. 531).

# application of psychology

## Prevention and Management of AIDS

Twelve years ago, the brother of one of my colleagues died of *acquired immune deficiency syndrome,* or AIDS. This tragedy brought the spectre of AIDS very much closer to home for me, as he was a decent and talented man who died unnecessarily in his twenties.

As we are all well aware, our planet is in the midst of a truly horrible fatal epidemic of AIDS. This disease, which is caused by the *human immunodeficiency virus (HIV),* has already killed over 20 million men, women, and children worldwide (World Health Organization, 2002). At the end of 2001, a total of 40 million people were infected with HIV. That reflects an increase of 9.4 million infected persons in the last 3 years, mostly in sub-Saharan Africa (World Health Organization, 2002).

Obviously, an epidemic of this magnitude demands our attention, but why bring up a medical disease in a psychology textbook? The answer is that, like most other physical diseases, there are important *psychological* aspects to the transmission and treatment of AIDS. It is extremely important that you, as an educated person, understand this point: Each individual's behavior determines his or her risk for AIDS.

To explain the role of psychological factors in AIDS, we will look first at the physical nature of the disease. AIDS is a disease that impairs the ability of the body's immune system to fight bacteria, viruses, and cancer. HIV has many effects on the immune system, but most important, the virus results in mass destruction of the immune cells known as *lymphocytes* and, indirectly, leaves the important *B-cells* of the immune system useless. HIV disables the B-cells by invading the nucleus of another type of immune cell known as *T-4 Helper cells.* The T-4 Helper cells help the B-cells identify hostile bacteria and viruses and signal the B-cells to destroy them. Unfortunately, HIV either destroys the T-4 cells or deactivates them, making the B-cells useless and leaving the body vulnerable to disease. The person with

AIDS does not actually die from the AIDS but from the other diseases, such as pneumonia and cancer, that flourish because of the weakened immune system.

AIDS is the direct result of patterns of behavior that bring persons into contact with the AIDS virus. The rates of new cases of HIV in North America have declined slightly in recent years because people are engaging in somewhat less high-risk behavior. What are these *high-risk behaviors* that increase risk for AIDS? If we know what the high-risk behaviors are, it may be possible for us all to help *prevent* AIDS by reducing high-risk behaviors.

HIV is spread through body fluids—especially blood and semen, but also by saliva and other fluids. The most common means of transmission is all forms of sexual intercourse—vaginal (contact of penis and vagina), oral (contact of penis and mouth), and anal (contact of penis and anus). Although anal intercourse is believed to create an especially high risk of transmission, vaginal intercourse is actually a more common source of transmission because it is practiced more widely. Although AIDS was first spread among homosexual men in the United States and is still more common among them, the spread of HIV by sexual acts is certainly not limited to homosexuals. Engaging in intercourse with an HIV-infected partner of either the same or the opposite sex is equally likely to result in the spread of AIDS.

The next most frequent modes of transmission are intravenous drug use and transmission from an infected mother to her infant during birth, with infection from blood transfusions and other means being much less common (Centers for Disease Control and Prevention, 2002). Persons who use drugs that are injected are at high risk for acquiring HIV through the blood if they share a needle with someone infected with HIV, but also because such drugs themselves suppress the functioning of the immune system.

AIDS is much more common in some sociocultural groups than others.

In the United States, males are five times more likely to have AIDS than women are (Centers for Disease Control and Prevention, 2002). As shown in figure 13.9, AIDS can be found in every part of the world, but it is far less common in some countries than others (World Health Organization, 2002). AIDS is relatively uncommon in Arabic countries and in Australia and New Zealand, but it is very common in Africa south of the Sahara desert, where HIV was first transmitted from monkeys to humans. In the United States, AIDS is found in all ethnic groups, but rates are higher among African Americans and Hispanics (Centers for Disease Control and Prevention, 2002).

## Prevention of AIDS Through Behavior Change

New cases of HIV infection can be prevented through programs that change high-risk sexual behaviors. What behaviors need to be changed? First, persons have virtually no chance of acquiring AIDS if (a) they are not sexually active or are involved in a monogamous sexual relationship with a partner who is not infected with HIV, and (b) they do not use intravenous drugs. AIDS is not a difficult disease to avoid if one completely avoids high-risk behaviors. Indeed, the risk of AIDS can be greatly decreased just by having fewer sex partners, engaging in "safe sex" practices such as the use of condoms, not using needle drugs, and not having sex with persons who may have been exposed to HIV.

As simple as it sounds, however, it is very difficult to convince people to change their behavior—especially their sexual behavior. College students currently have low rates of HIV infection, but because they have been slow to adopt safe sex practices, they are at risk. Needle drug users continue to share needles because it is difficult to obtain new needles, and some women who know they have HIV infection become pregnant in spite of the high risk

*(continued)*

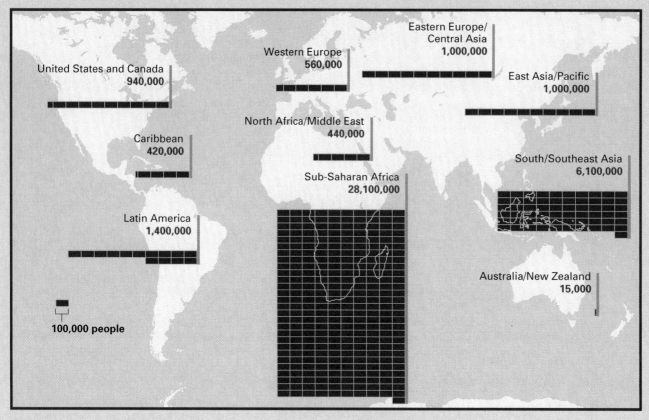

**FIGURE 13.9**

The numbers of persons living with the HIV virus or AIDS at the end of 2001 (World Health Organization, 2002). Each blue block represents 100,000 infected persons.

of transmission to their own infants (Ironson & Schneiderman, 1991).

What can health psychologists do to help prevent AIDS? A now-classic paper by Jeffrey Kelly and his colleagues (1989) provides a great example of the ways in which psychologists can help. Describing Kelly's study will involve the discussion of sexual practices that some of you may not wish to read about. But discussing these matters openly may save human lives. Certain sexual practices especially increase the risk of spreading HIV, whether practiced by homosexual or heterosexual persons. These include, but are not limited to, anal intercourse without the use of a condom for protection and stimulating the anus of the partner by finger or mouth. Decreasing these and other high-risk sexual practices, therefore, would decrease the spread of AIDS.

Kelly's research team recruited a group of 51 gay men who did not have the AIDS virus. As shown in figure 13.10, the men frequently engaged in anal intercourse and anal finger stimu-

lation and did not consistently use condoms prior to the start of counseling.

The men attended 12 weekly group counseling sessions led by clinical psychologists. These sessions provided information on AIDS that explained why high-risk behaviors should be avoided, discussed factors that led to abandoning precautions in the past (being in a depressed mood, excessive drinking, etc.), and suggested ways to better cope with these factors in the future. The sessions helped the men learn to assertively insist that their partners follow safe sex practices and counseled the men on establishing lasting monogamous relationships.

The counseling sessions led to a steady decrease in the frequency of both forms of unprotected anal sex and an increase in the use of condoms. Eight months after the counseling sessions ended, the changes in sexual behavior were still evident. Thus, such counseling offers hope in the fight against AIDS. Recently, a number of similar counseling programs have been

found to be successful, even among low-income urban populations (Kalichman, Rompa, & Coley, 1996; St. Lawrence, Crosley, Brasfield, & O'Bannon, 2002; Weinhardt, Carey, Carey, & Verdecias, 1998). Unfortunately, not enough psychologists are trained in such counseling methods, and there is too little available funding for all types of preventive programs. Partly as a result, even persons who know they have HIV often continue to engage in high-risk sexual behavior that will spread their disease (Kalichman, 2000).

## Psychological Factors in the Management of AIDS

AIDS is currently a disease with no cure. New medical treatments can greatly slow the progress of the HIV infection, but they do not cure AIDS.

A great deal of research is currently under way to find ways in which psychological interventions might be useful in helping persons with HIV adjust emotionally to their disease and even

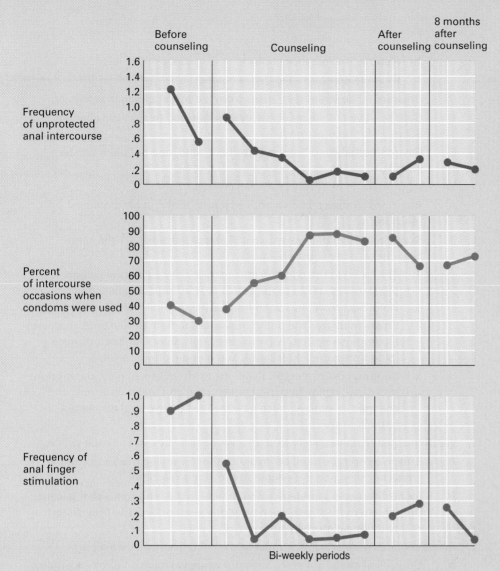

**FIGURE 13.10**

The results of a counseling program designed to reduce the frequency of sexual behaviors that increase the risk of infection with AIDS.

Source: Data from J. A. Kelly & others, "Behavioral Intervention to Reduce AIDS Risk Activities," in *Journal of Consulting and Clinical Psychology*, 57:60–67, 1989. Copyright 1989 by the American Psychological Association.

slow the progression of HIV infection. A well-controlled study has shown that persons who are HIV positive progress to AIDS faster if they experience more negative life events and cope by means of denial (Leserman & others, 2000). It may be possible, however, to develop psychological interventions that help strengthen the immune system and slow the progression of AIDS by changing health-related behavior and managing stress. Some very promising progress has been made in this area. For example, both regular aerobic exercise and stress-reduction therapy have been shown to buffer the detrimental effects of HIV on key aspects of immune functioning (Antoni & others, 1990, 2002). Unfortunately, the beneficial effects of aerobic exercise are only modest. ■

Chapter 13 describes ways in which psychological concepts are used to improve physical health.

I. Health psychology attempts to prevent health problems by helping individuals cope with stress and change health-related behavior.

II. There are many sources of stress in our lives, some obvious and some hidden.

    A. Frustration is the result of failure to satisfy a motive.

    B. Conflict is the result of two or more incompatible motives. The four major types of conflict are

        1. Approach-approach conflict

        2. Avoidance-avoidance conflict

**Summary**

3. Approach-avoidance conflict

4. Multiple approach-avoidance conflict

C. Pressure is the stress that arises from the threat of negative events.

D. Both positive and negative life events can lead to stressful changes and the need for readjustment.

E. Environmental conditions such as heat, cold, and pollution can be stressful.

III. We react to stress in relatively predictable ways.

A. Reactions to stress involve both psychological and physiological reactions.

B. Some important general aspects of stress reactions are the same regardless of the source of stress.

1. The fact that the body reacts to stress with an alarm reaction, a phase of resistance to the stress, and a stage of exhaustion if coping is not successful has been termed the general adaptation syndrome.

2. Stress mobilizes the body's resources to fight or flee but suppresses the immune system and increases risk factors for heart disease (blood pressure, cholesterol, and blood-clotting factors).

3. Common psychological reactions to stress are anxiety; depression; decreased ability to think, concentrate, and make decisions; and changes in motives, such as increased hunger and decreased interest in sex.

IV. We do not just react passively to stress; we actively attempt to cope with it.

A. Effective coping strategies involve either removing the source of the stress or managing the degree of the stress reactions.

B. Ineffective coping strategies do not help in the long run, either because they create more stress (such as aggression) or because they distort reality (defense mechanisms).

V. Stress requires greater control under some circumstances than others.

A. Sources of stress are more stressful when we have no prior experience with them.

B. Sources of stress are more stressful when they are unpredictable and when we have no control over them.

C. Stress creates more severe reactions when we have little social support.

D. Some stressors are easier to deal with when we are younger, and some are easier when we are older.

VI. Characteristics of the person also influence the magnitude of stress reactions in a person × situation interaction.

A. Differences in cognitive appraisal of potential stress events influence stress reactions.

B. Persons who tend to be anxious tend to respond more to stress.

C. Persons who procrastinate reduce their stress at first but increase their stress when deadlines arrive.

D. The Type A behavior pattern, including hostile reaction to competitive pressure, is a risk factor for heart disease.

E. Women respond more strongly to traumatic stress, on average, and derive less stress-buffering benefits than men do.

VII. Several aspects of our behavior are related to our health.

A. Learning to relax deeply can reduce health risks.

B. Abuse of substances such as alcohol and caffeine and the use of tobacco products are behaviors that create serious health risks.

C.    Health psychologists also seek to reduce health risks by helping individuals exercise properly, control their weight, and follow medical treatments properly.

D.    Simple interventions can greatly improve transportation safety and safety in the workplace.

E.    Because AIDS is usually acquired from high-risk behaviors, and because psychological factors are intimately related to immune system functioning, the science of psychology is playing a key role in the fight against the AIDS epidemic.

## Resources

1.    A sophisticated but readable discussion of stress by the father of the concept that is still very timely is Selye, H. (1976). *The stress of life.* New York: Knopf.

2.    For a discussion of the role of cognitive factors in stress by the pioneer in the field, see Lazarus, R. S. (1999). *Stress and emotion: A new synthesis.* New York: Springer.

3.    Excellent overviews of the field of health psychology appear in Taylor, S. E. (1999). *Health psychology.* (4th ed.). Boston: McGraw-Hill; and Wilson, D. K., Rodrigue, J. R., & Taylor, W. C. (1997). *Health-promoting and health-compromising behaviors among minority adolescents.* Washington, DC: American Psychological Association.

4.    An excellent description of effective methods of treating victims of rape that has not gone out of date is Calhoun, K. C., & Atkeson, B. M. (1989). *Treatment of rape victims.* New York: Pergamon Press.

5.    The classic, readable description of Type A personality can be found in Wright, L. (1988). The Type A behavior problem and coronary artery disease. *American Psychologist, 43,* 2–14.

6.    For a Web site with a great deal of useful information about HIV and AIDS, see www.cdc.gov/nchstp/hiv_aids/pubs/facts.htm

7.    Visit the Web site of the National Safety Council for more on safety promotion in the work place: http://www.nsc.org. Also see Geller, E. S. (2001). *The psychology of safety handbook.* Boca Raton, FL: CRC Press.

## Chapter Outline

# Abnormal Behavior

## PROLOGUE

Does making a speech make you nervous? How about meeting people? If these situations make you nervous, you're not alone; anxiety is quite common in these and other social situations where other people are scrutinizing you. But for some people, the level of anxiety is so intense that it disrupts their ability to function in important social situations. Let's consider the experience of a woman whom we will call Carol. Carol is an intelligent and attractive woman who is successful in her professional career. She went to a university psychological clinic specializing in anxiety disorders to learn more about her intense anxiety in social situations.

The psychologists observed Carol in three different anxiety-provoking social situations. In the first situation, a stranger played the role of a man on a first date with Carol at a restaurant. In the second scene, a woman pretended to be a new neighbor of Carol's. In the third situation, Carol delivered a brief impromptu speech to two psychologists. During these three tests, Carol wore sensors that monitored her heart rate and blood pressure, and immediately after each test she was asked to choose statements that accurately reflected her thoughts and feelings about her performance during the tests, what she thought that other people thought about her, and her ability to cope.

Carol acted very nervously in each situation. She rarely made eye contact, spoke very little, and frequently shifted her posture. Her blood pressure and her heart rate rose dramatically, particularly during the speech, but was almost as high during the first date. She felt subjectively nervous in all situations and thought that she behaved in ways that no one would like.

Carol's anxiety was intense enough that it caused serious problems in her life. It led her to turn down dates and other social invitations, and even led her to change her major to avoid taking a course in which she would have to give speeches. Because her anxiety was serious enough to cause a problem, she was considered to have a social phobia by the psychologists—one of the forms of abnormal behavior that we will study in this chapter.

Does it surprise you to learn that something as understandable as exaggerated social anxiety would be considered to be "abnormal" by psychologists and psychiatrists? Actually, most forms of abnormal behavior aren't very different from what we would consider to be normal. Abnormal behavior is simply a pattern of acting, thinking, or feeling that is harmful in some way to the individual or to others. That pattern may involve behavior that is quite unusual, but it also encompasses behavior that seems like only an exaggeration of normal behavior.

Abnormal behavior takes many forms. Excessive anxiety and depression are the most common types of abnormal behavior. Other types include alterations of perception and sudden changes in personality and identity. Other psychological disorders involve false beliefs and hallucinations that result in the individual's being "out of touch with reality." Other forms involve symptoms of health problems that have no known physical cause.

What causes abnormal behavior? Many answers have been given to this question throughout history. The earliest answer was that evil spirits caused it, but

## Key Terms

other views are more common today. Some theorists believe that abnormal behavior results from disturbances of the brain; others believe that it has psychological causes, such as excessive stress or faulty cognitions about ourselves or others. Currently, there is a movement toward explanations for abnormal behavior that combine both biological and psychological factors.  ■

**abnormal behavior**
Actions, thoughts, and feelings that are harmful to the person or to others.

**continuity hypothesis**
The view that abnormal behavior is just a more severe form of normal psychological problems.

## ● Definition of Abnormal Behavior

The term *abnormal* is one of the most elusive terms in psychology. It's not a difficult term to define in words, but it's a very difficult concept for most people to grasp. **Abnormal behavior** is defined as actions, thoughts, and feelings that are harmful to the person or to others. This harm may take many forms, including experiencing discomfort (as in feeling anxious or depressed), not being able to function in a job, not being able to relate to people well enough to have enduring friendships or family relationships, and having physical health problems that result from abnormal behavior (as when a person is too frightened of dental procedures to have needed oral surgery).

Part of the difficulty in understanding this concept is that most of us think of behavior as being abnormal only if it is very strange and unusual. That is not how psychologists and psychiatrists use the term *abnormal*. Mental health experts define the term *abnormal* broadly to include far more problems in living than most persons think of as "abnormal." As the term is defined by the mental health community today, 18 to 20 percent of all persons in the United States are considered to exhibit actions, thoughts, or feelings that are harmful enough to be considered to be abnormal (Narrow, Rae, Robins, & Regier, 2002). Thus, the term *abnormal behavior* does not refer only to rare and strange problems but also to the problems in negotiating life that are experienced by many people.

Notice that abnormality is defined in terms of *harm* to the individual or others. Even if a pattern of behavior is very unusual (statistically uncommon for that group of people), it is not necessarily considered to be abnormal. Extreme intelligence and total honesty are unusual, but they hardly are considered abnormal. On the other hand, some patterns of behavior that are quite common are clearly abnormal because they are harmful. For example, the intense prejudice against Jews that was so prevalent during the days of Hitler's Germany was both common and harmful. Similarly, psychologists consider cigarette smoking, which is still fairly common in our culture today, to be abnormal behavior because of the serious health problems that it causes.

The definition of abnormality requires subjective judgments in two ways. First, even though abnormality is defined in terms of harm rather than unusualness, it must be decided whether an individual's problems are *severe enough* to be considered "harmful." For example, almost everyone suffers some discomfort at times from shyness. How shy does a person have to be to be considered abnormally shy? Shier than 90 percent of other people? More than 95 percent of others? Clearly, psychologists must make largely arbitrary decisions about it in different ways.

Second, subjectivity is also a problem in defining what is *harmful*. That decision reflects the values of the person making the determination, and values differ greatly from one culture to another. For example, the Zuñi Indians of the southwestern United States believed it was good to be able to have hallucinations without taking drugs, for it meant that the gods were blessing you with visits. Nearly all psychologists in the United States consider hallucinations harmful, but differences of opinion exist on other issues, such as the normality or abnormality of homosexuality or cigarette smoking in our culture. There is probably no complete solution to the problem of subjectivity. The best we can do is to be aware of the problem and try to minimize the role played by our personal values in making subjective judgments about the behavior of others.

The concept of abnormal behavior is difficult to use not only because of its inherent subjectivity but also because psychologists have not been able to agree on how abnormal behavior differs from normal behavior. The **continuity hypothesis** of abnormal behavior states that abnormal behavior is just a more severe form of normal psychological problems. This hypothesis is held by many humanists and social learning theorists. The **discontinuity hypothesis,** on the other hand, suggests that abnormal behavior is entirely different from normal psychological problems. Advocates of the continuity hypothesis argue that such terms as *insanity* and *mental illness* should not be used because they imply that the individuals have *sick minds* that separate them from the rest of society. Advocates of the discontinuity hypothesis believe that only such strong terms can accurately portray the true nature of abnormal behavior.

**discontinuity hypothesis**
The view that abnormal behavior is fundamentally different from normal psychological problems.

## Historical Views of Abnormal Behavior

Before we discuss contemporary views of the causes of abnormal behavior, it's instructive to look back through history at beliefs about its cause. This historical perspective will make the important point that our ideas about the causes of abnormal behavior determine what we do to help those who experience it.

### Supernatural Theories

The oldest writings about behavior, including those of Plato, the Bible, and the tablets of Babylonian King Hammurabi (1750 B.C.), indicate that, in our earliest belief, abnormal behavior was thought to be caused by evil spirits. Although some people disagreed with this notion during every period in history, the idea that people with psychological problems are possessed by evil spirits was the most influential view during the entire 3,500-year period of history stretching from Hammurabi to shortly before the American Revolution.

During most of the time that the supernatural theory held sway, the consequences for those with psychological problems were not too severe. Treatment mostly took the form of prayer, with the most unpleasant treatment being purgatives—foul liquids that were supposed to help the person vomit out the evil spirit. During the Middle Ages (500–1500), however, these supernatural beliefs were translated into far more harmful forms of "treatment."

In medieval Europe, the Catholic Church published an official document called the *Malleus Maleficarum,* or the *Witches' Hammer.* It gave detailed descriptions of the methods of treatment, or *exorcism,* for those people acting in abnormal ways that "revealed" possession by the devil. Treatment began with a stiff regimen of prayer, fasting, and the drinking of foul concoctions that caused vomiting, but for those whose behavior did not improve, the *Malleus* recommended stronger methods. People who could not stop acting in deviant ways after exorcism were considered to be witches or warlocks (male witches). It was believed that the only way to save their souls was to destroy their bodies to drive out Satan. As a result, half a million so-called witches, mostly women, were put to death in Europe alone (Loftus, 1993). Even as late as 1692, 20 individuals were put to death as witches in Salem, Massachusetts. Nineteen were hanged for "witchcraft," whereas the twentieth victim died as a result of heavy rocks being placed on him in an effort to force him to confess (Phillips, 1933).

Fortunately, much has changed in our conceptions of abnormal behavior during the past 500 years, but the idea that mental health problems are caused by evil spirits is still held by some cultural groups in North America.

Peculiar behavior was once explained as demon possession. Here St. Catherine exorcises a demon from a woman.

### Biological Theories

An ancient voice that argued against the supernatural theory of abnormal behavior was fifth-century B.C. Greek physician Hippocrates. He believed that biological disorders of the body caused abnormal behavior. According to Hippocrates' view, the body contains four important fluids, or *humors:* blood, phlegm, black bile, and yellow bile. If these fluids get out of balance, illness and abnormal behavior is the result. An excess of black bile, for example, leads to depression; an excess of yellow bile causes irritability.

Richard von Krafft-Ebing (1840–1902).

Hippocrates' theory was inaccurate, of course, and so he was not able to punch much of a hole in the supernatural approach. But he set the stage for later developments by suggesting that abnormal behavior might have *natural* rather than supernatural causes. During the 2,000 years after Hippocrates, a number of scientists who had been influenced by Hippocrates' idea searched in vain for a biological cause of abnormal behavior. Finally, in the 1800s, medical researchers such as German physician Richard von Krafft-Ebing made discoveries that led to a resurgence of biological theory and the eventual birth of psychiatry as a discipline.

Krafft-Ebing was working with a now rare form of severe psychological disturbance called *paresis*. He and a number of independent researchers discovered that paresis was actually an advanced stage of the venereal disease *syphilis*. Syphilis is a bacterial infection that begins with a sore, or chancre, on the genitals or on another point of entry, which is later followed by a copper-colored skin rash. The untreated disease then goes through a long "invisible" period, which eventually leads to the destruction of important body organs. If the bacteria destroy brain cells, paresis is the result. Because of the long period of time between the original infection and the later paresis, it was not known that the two conditions were related until Krafft-Ebing demonstrated through inoculation tests that all individuals with paresis also had syphilis.

The discovery that paresis had a biological cause sent shock waves through the medical community. Soon physicians—who up to this time had little to do with people with abnormal behavior—were placed in charge of mental institutions, and the medical specialty of psychiatry was formed. There were high expectations that the biological causes for all the other forms of abnormal behavior would soon be discovered. But, although the discovery of penicillin and its use in the treatment of syphilis almost totally eradicated paresis, few other biological causes of abnormal behavior were discovered. In recent years, however, major advances in the medical treatment of some severe forms of abnormal behavior have been made possible by the development of effective drug therapies.

### Psychological Theories

Hippocrates was not the only ancient Greek suggesting a *natural* explanation for abnormal behavior. Pythagoras, who also gave us geometry, was very active in the treatment of psychological problems. He held the then-radical belief that psychological problems are caused by *psychological* factors such as stress. He placed individuals with problems in "temples," where they received rest, exercise, a good diet, an understanding person to talk to, and practical advice on how to straighten out their lives. Records from his temples suggest that Pythagoras' methods were highly successful. Unfortunately, the psychological ideas of Pythagoras were not able to compete with those of the supernaturalists until modern times.

Although there were many important advocates of psychological theory, it was not until Sigmund Freud published his influential views that psychological theory was able to compete with the supernatural and biological approaches. Although Freud's model of unconscious conflicts was quite different from the ideas of Pythagoras, until recent times Freud was the leading champion of the view that psychological problems had psychological causes.

## Contemporary Views of Abnormal Behavior

Today, abnormal behavior is believed to be a natural phenomenon with natural causes. As research evidence has accumulated, it has become increasingly clear that both biological and psychological factors are involved in the origins of many psychological disorders. Some disorders are solely biological in origin (such as those caused by brain injuries), and some are solely psychological in origin (such as acute grief reactions to the death of a loved one in normal individuals). But many other disorders appear to involve both kinds of causes. Inherited predispositions to certain kinds of problems, abnormal amounts of specific neurotransmitter substances in the brain, and tendencies to react autonomically to stress in an abnormal way are some of the biological factors believed to be partially responsible for a variety of psychological disorders. The psychological factors involved in these same disorders include stress, abnormal social learning histories, ineffective coping strategies, and inadequate social support. Apparently, biological and psychological factors work together to determine whether a person will experience psychological problems. For example, individuals whose autonomic nervous systems tend to react excessively to stress will have problems only if their lives are filled with considerable stress and if they cope poorly with stress. If present trends continue, we will probably see a fusion of the biological and psychological approaches into a single, naturalistic viewpoint.

## The Concept of Insanity

Now that we have closely examined the term *abnormal behavior*, let's turn to the concept of **insanity.** What does it mean to be insane? Actually, *insanity* is not a psychological or psychiatric term but a legal term. And, to make matters more complex, insanity has not one but three different legal meanings, depending on whether it's used as a criminal defense, in a hearing on competency to stand trial, or in a hearing on involuntary commitment to a mental institution:

**insanity**
A legal definition concerning a person's inability to tell right from wrong, ability to understand the trial proceedings, or whether the person is a direct danger to self or others.

1. ***Not guilty by reason of insanity.*** In some states, individuals cannot be convicted of a crime if they were legally "insane" at the time the crime was committed. There are many definitions of the term *insane* in this context, but perhaps the most influential formula was proposed by the American Law Institute and adopted by many state and federal courts in the 1970s. It states, "A person is not responsible for criminal conduct if at the time of such conduct, as a result of mental disease or defect, he lacks substantial capacity either to appreciate the wrongfulness of his conduct or to conform his conduct to the requirements of the law." This definition means that people committing crimes are considered "not guilty by reason of insanity" if they had little ability to tell right from wrong or had little ability to control their actions at the time of the crime because of serious psychological problems. Generally, juries will consider only severely psychotic or severely mentally retarded persons to be insane according to this rule, and because individuals with these problems rarely commit crimes, it's rarely a successful defense.

   John Hinckley, Jr., was found not guilty (by reason of insanity) of his attempted assassination of President Reagan.

   The controversial nature of this use of the term *insanity* in the courtroom was made clear in the public reaction to the trial of John W. Hinckley, Jr., in 1982. Hinckley admitted to having shot Ronald Reagan and others in an unsuccessful attempt to assassinate the president. The jurors found Hinckley not guilty because they believed that he was insane. As a result, Hinckley received no prison sentence for his actions but was committed to St. Elizabeth's Psychiatric Hospital in Washington, DC. If he convinces his doctors that he is sane at some point in the future, he could be released at any time. Public dissatisfaction with this verdict was intense and was partly responsible for changes in the law concerning the insanity defense. Juries in a number of states can now find defendants "guilty but mentally ill." In this case, the person receives a prison sentence but is also given psychiatric treatment.

2. ***Competence to stand trial.*** The term *insanity* is also used in hearings to determine whether the individuals are competent to stand trial. In this sense, the

question of insanity is whether the people are able to understand the proceedings of the trial sufficiently to aid in their own defense. Again, it's primarily severely psychotic and mentally retarded individuals who are considered incompetent according to this definition.

3. ***Involuntary commitment.*** A third meaning of the term *insanity* arises in hearings on the involuntary commitment of individuals to mental institutions. It's legal in most states to commit people to an institution against their will if a court finds them to be insane. The courts generally interpret this as meaning that the individuals are a direct danger—usually meaning a physical danger—to themselves or to others. Behaving in strange ways is not enough to justify involuntary commitment. There must be an element of danger.

## Review

Actions, thoughts, and feelings that are harmful to the individual or to others are considered to be abnormal. This definition is a difficult one to implement because of the subjectivity involved. How severe must an individual's problem be before he or she is considered harmful? And by whose cultural standards should harmfulness be defined? Moreover, psychologists have not been able to agree on how abnormal behavior differs from normal psychological problems. Is abnormal behavior just a more severe version of normal problems, or is it fundamentally different? Advocates of the continuity hypothesis take the former view, whereas advocates of the discontinuity hypothesis take the latter view.

Differences in perspectives among contemporary psychologists seem minor, however, when compared with differing views of abnormal behavior that have been taken throughout history. Abnormal behavior has been thought to result from supernatural causes or from biological abnormalities as well as from psychological causes. The supernatural theory is of little importance in today's psychology, but both biological and psychological factors are currently thought to be involved in the origins of abnormal behavior.

In legal terms, persons are considered to be insane if they lack the capacity to deal with the demands of life in significant ways, either to avoid danger to themselves or others, to understand the difference between right and wrong and to behave accordingly, or to safeguard themselves or others. Legal decisions concerning insanity are made in the context of trials (Is a person not guilty by reason of insanity? Is a person competent to stand trial?) and in hearings concerning involuntary commitment to mental institutions.

## Check Your Learning

To be sure that you have learned the key points from the preceding section, cover the list of correct answers and try to answer each question. If you give an incorrect answer to any question, return to the page given next to the correct answer to see why your answer was not correct. Remember that these questions cover only some of the important information in this section; it is important that you make up your own questions to check your learning of other facts and concepts.

1. _____ is defined as those actions, thoughts, and feelings that are harmful to the person or to others.

2. The discovery that paresis developed from syphilis gave support to the _____ theories of abnormal behavior.

   a) supernatural      c) psychological

   b) biological      d) cognitive

3. The writings by Sigmund Freud gave the _____ theories enough credibility to compete with the other popular theories of the time.

   a) supernatural
   c) psychological
   b) biological
   d) cognitive

4. Research supports the view that both biological factors and psychological factors are involved in the origins of many psychological disorders.

   a) True
   b) False

---

1. Could biological and psychological theories of abnormal behavior both be correct?

2. Do you think smoking cigarettes should be considered to be abnormal? How might psychologists who hold either the continuity hypothesis or discontinuity hypothesis differ on this question?

**Thinking Critically about Psychology**

---

**Correct Answers:** 1. Abnormal behavior (p. 540), 2. **b** (p. 542), 3. **c** (p. 542), 4. **a** (p. 542).

## ● Anxiety Disorders

Every life is a mixture of positive and negative emotions for everyone. But many people experience excessive levels of the kinds of negative emotions that we identify as being *nervous, tense, worried, scared,* and *anxious.* These terms all refer to anxiety. Ten to 15 million Americans experience such uncomfortable and disruptive levels of anxiety that they are said to have **anxiety disorders.** Women are more affected by anxiety disorders than men (Kessler & others, 1995). The kinds of anxiety disorders vary considerably, but all share heightened reactivity to anxiety-provoking events and increased vigilance (scanning and monitoring) for those events (Rosen & Schulkin, 1998).

### Phobias

A **phobia** is an intense, unrealistic fear. In this case, the anxiety is focused so intensely on some object or situation that the individual is acutely uncomfortable around it and will often go to great pains to avoid it. There are three types of phobias: (a) *specific phobia,* (b) *social phobia,* and (c) *agoraphobia.*

**Specific phobia** is the most specific and least disruptive of the phobias. Examples include intense fear of heights, dogs, blood, hypodermic injections, and closed spaces (Ost, 1992). Individuals with specific phobias generally have no other psychological problems, and their lives are disrupted only if the phobia creates a direct problem in daily living. For example, a fear of elevators would be highly disruptive for a person who works in a skyscraper, but it probably would not be for a vegetable farmer.

Other forms of phobia, by their very nature, frequently cause problems for the individual. The term **social phobia** is used to describe extreme anxiety about social interactions, particularly those with strangers and those in which the person might be evaluated negatively. Job interviews, public speaking, and first dates are extremely uncomfortable for individuals with social phobia (Stein & others, 2000). Persons with social phobia usually have unrealistically negative views of their social skills and attempt to

**anxiety disorders**
Psychological disorders that involve excessive levels of negative emotions, such as nervousness, tension, worry, fright, and anxiety.

**phobia**
An intense, irrational fear.

**specific phobia**
A phobic fear of one relatively specific thing.

**social phobia**
A phobic fear of social interactions, particularly those with strangers and those in which the person might be viewed negatively.

This child's fear of animals may be serious enough to be considered a specific phobia if it causes problems in her life.

**agoraphobia**
(ag″o-rah-fō′bē-ah) An intense fear of leaving one's home or other familiar places.

**generalized anxiety disorder**
An uneasy sense of general tension and apprehension for no apparent reason that makes the individual highly uncomfortable because of its prolonged presence.

**panic anxiety disorder**
A pattern of anxiety in which long periods of calm are broken by an intensely uncomfortable attack of anxiety.

avoid evaluation (Wallace & Alden, 1997). Because this kind of phobia hampers and limits social interactions, it can seriously disrupt the individual's social and occupational life.

**Agoraphobia** is the most impairing of all of the phobias. Literally meaning "fear of open spaces," agoraphobia involves an intense fear of leaving one's home or other familiar places. In extreme cases, the agoraphobic individual is totally bound to his or her home, finding a trip to the mailbox an almost intolerable experience. Other agoraphobic individuals are able to travel freely in their neighborhood but cannot venture beyond it. A 30-year-old German man recounts his experience with agoraphobia in the following passage.

> The brief trips to Bonn filled me with a surging sense of the impossible and the far . . . a feeling, especially as to distance, that could convert a half mile, or even five blocks from home, in terms of subjective need and cowardice, into an infinity of remoteness. . . . I start a little walk down the street about a hundred feet from the house, I am compelled to rush back, in horror of being so far away . . . a hundred feet away . . . from home and security. I have never walked or ridden, alone or with others, as a normal man, since that day. . . . (Leonard, 1928, pp. 238, 278)

## Generalized and Panic Anxiety Disorders

Whereas phobias are linked to specific stimulus situations, the other anxiety disorders involve a kind of anxiety that is independent of environmental triggers. Individuals with **generalized anxiety disorder** experience a vague, uneasy sense of tension and apprehension, sometimes referred to as *free-floating anxiety*. Generalized anxiety makes the individual highly uncomfortable, not because it's an intense kind of anxiety—it's generally relatively mild—but because of its relentless, almost unending presence. The person with generalized anxiety disorder does experience periods of calm, but they are often few and far between.

The individual with **panic anxiety disorder** is seized by sharp, intensely uncomfortable attacks of anxiety. Respiration increases and suddenly rapid heartbeats can be felt pounding with such intensity that the individual often feels that he or she is having a heart attack, or at the very least is going crazy.

A relatively small percentage of the population (about 5 percent of women and 2 percent of men) experience panic attacks that are frequent and severe enough to qualify as panic disorder at some point in their lifetimes (Kessler & others, 1995), but a surprisingly high percentage of adults experience occasional attacks of panic. In one survey study of 2,375 college students, 12 percent had experienced at least one panic attack at some time during their lifetimes (Telch, Lucas, & Nelson, 1989). It is important to know that such uncomfortable events are relatively common and that they should not be a source of serious concern unless they are severe or frequent enough to disrupt the individual's functioning or well-being. Persons with panic anxiety disorders are extremely sensitive to small changes in the functioning of their autonomic nervous system, especially their heart rate (Ehlers & Breuer, 1992; Schmidt, Lerew, & Trakowski, 1997), and small changes in the level of carbon dioxide in their blood (Bellodi & others, 1998; Gorman & others, 2001). More important, they interpret these minor normal fluctuations in "catastrophic" ways. That is, their attacks of anxiety are exaggerated reactions to normal body stimuli that most persons ignore.

Persons who develop panic disorder first experience spontaneous panic attacks. Current theory suggests that these are nonspecific responses to stress, but some individuals come to experience repeated panic attacks due to classical conditioning (Bouton, Mineka, & Barlow, 2001). Typically, the conditioned stimulus is a stimulus from within the body that is part of the panic attack, such as increased heart rate or shortness of breath. According to this theory, when the internal stimulus is experienced again in another context, the individual will be more likely to respond with a full-blown panic attack because of classical conditioning.

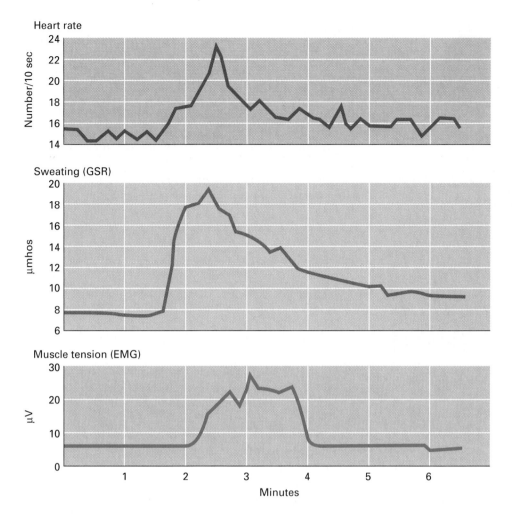

Heart rate

Sweating (GSR)

Muscle tension (EMG)

Minutes

**FIGURE 14.1**

Changes in three measures of sympathetic autonomic arousal that occurred when an individual experienced a panic attack while being studied in a laboratory.

**Source:** Data from M. Lader and A. Mathews, "Changes in Autonomic Arousal in a Woman Undergoing a Spontaneous Panic Attack," *Journal of Psychosomatic Research,* 14:377–382. Copyright 1970, Pergamon Press, Ltd.

The fact that panic attacks involve a sudden and intense increase in sympathetic autonomic arousal was demonstrated by British psychiatrist Michael Lader (Lader & Mathews, 1970). While he was studying the autonomic activity of a woman who was prone to panic attacks, she spontaneously experienced an attack in his laboratory. Figure 14.1 graphically shows the sudden changes in three measures of autonomic arousal that took place during the panic attack.

The case of Richard Benson further illustrates the experience of panic anxiety disorder.

Richard Benson, age 38, applied to a psychiatrist for therapy because he was suffering from severe and overwhelming anxiety which sometimes escalated to a panic attack. He had been treated for this problem in a private psychiatric hospital, but several weeks after his release, the severe anxiety symptoms recurred and he decided to seek outpatient therapy. During the times when he was experiencing intense anxiety, it often seemed as if he were having a heart seizure. He experienced chest pains and heart palpitations, numbness, shortness of breath, and he felt a strong need to breathe in air. He reported that in the midst of the anxiety attack, he developed a feeling of tightness over his eyes and he could only see objects directly in front of him (tunnel vision). He further stated that he feared that he would not be able to swallow.

Mr. Benson indicated that he had been anxious most of his life, but it was only since his promotion at work six months ago that the feelings of anxiety became a severe problem. The intensity of the anxiety symptoms was frightening to him and on two occasions his wife had rushed him to a local hospital because he was in a state of panic, sure that his heart was going to stop beating and he would die. (Leon, 1977, p. 113)

## Post-Traumatic Stress Disorder

Once begun, wars are never over for those who fight them. World War II ended more than 50 years ago, the last soldiers returned from Vietnam more than 25 years ago, and Operation Desert Storm war ended a little over a decade ago, yet hundreds of thousands of former soldiers continue to "fight" those wars in their minds. The men and women who served in those wars returned to safety long ago, but they are still haunted by terrible recollections of combat that intrude into their waking consciousness and fill their dreams with horror. They often feel numbed to the ordinary emotions and pleasures of life. They often feel guilt that they survived, whereas others did not, and they often feel a pervasive sense of anger and unrest. Their continuing agony has been given the unwieldy name of **post-traumatic stress disorder (PTSD).** In simple terms, they are still suffering severe stress reactions years after the traumatic stress of combat ended. Many persons who experience PTSD recover from it, but for many others it is chronic and sometimes worsens over time (Benotsch & others, 2000; Engdahl & others, 1997).

The Vietnam War appears to have produced an unprecedented 500,000 veterans with at least mild problems of PTSD (Barrett & others, 1996; Egendorf & others, 1981; Southwick & others, 1995). But many survivors of World War II still experience PTSD at a time in their lives when they should be enjoying peaceful grandparenthood (Lee, Vaillant, Torrey, & Elder, 1995). Indeed, nearly one-third of the men who had been prisoners of war of the Japanese during World War II still meet criteria for PTSD in their seventies (Engdahl & others, 1997). Similarly, many Jewish survivors of Nazi concentration camps in World War II still suffer from PTSD (Kuch & Cox, 1992; Yehuda & others, 1995).

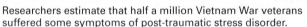

Researchers estimate that half a million Vietnam War veterans suffered some symptoms of post-traumatic stress disorder.

Not all military personnel exposed to war develop PTSD. Understandably, those Vietnam soldiers who were more directly exposed to combat or atrocities are more likely to experience PTSD (Macklin & others, 1998; Yehuda, Southwick, & Giller, 1992). The same has been found for both World War II and Gulf War veterans (Lee & others, 1995; Southwick & others, 1995; Wolfe & others, 1999). The individual's personal characteristics and social situation may also influence susceptibility to PTSD. When the level of exposure to combat is controlled statistically, soldiers with lower scores on intelligence tests upon admission to the military and more previous mental health problems are more likely to experience PTSD (Macklin & others, 1998). In addition, veterans with greater social support after the war are less likely to experience PTSD (Brewin & others, 2000; King & others, 1998).

Our awareness of PTSD grew out of efforts to assist veterans coping with the emotional aftermath of war. Psychologists soon realized, however, that PTSD is not at all limited to persons who have been exposed to war. A large national study of 8,000 adults living in the United States found that 5 percent of all adult males and 10 percent of all adult females have experienced PTSD for at least a month during their lifetimes (Kessler & others, 1995).

Among men, combat-related stress is the most common single cause of PTSD (accounting for nearly 30 percent of PTSD in males), but even for men, PTSD is often the result of other kinds of traumatic stress, such as experiencing the sudden and unexpected death of a loved one, being physically assaulted, causing automobile accidents, and witnessing violence and disasters (Andrews & others, 2000; Breslau & others, 1998; Delahanty & others, 1997; Epstein, Fullerton, & Ursano, 1998). Among women, physical assault, rape and sexual molestation, and the witnessing of violence are the leading causes of PTSD (Breslau & others, 1997; Kessler & others, 1995). The type and amount of stress encountered in everyday life depends in part on our living circumstances. Residences along the Atlantic Coast are more likely to experience hurricanes, residents of

**post-traumatic stress disorder (PTSD)**
The condition caused by extremely stressful experiences in which the person later experiences anxiety and irritability; has upsetting memories, dreams, and realistic flashbacks of the experience; and tries to avoid anything that reminds him or her of the experience.

California are more likely to experience earthquakes, and residents of inner cities are more likely to be assaulted, to be raped, or to witness violence (Breslau & others, 1997).

Most persons who experience traumatic stress in civilian life do not develop PTSD. The percentage of traumatized persons who develop PTSD depends in part on the type of stress. For example, about 15 percent of persons who experience the sudden loss of a loved one develop PTSD, and about 20 percent of victims of violent assault experience PTSD (Breslau & others, 1998). In contrast, 75 percent of women who have been raped experience PTSD for at least six months (Kessler & others, 1995). More distressingly, Burgess and Holstrom (1974) found that 6 to 10 years after the assault, approximately 25 percent of rape victims felt that they had not completely recovered. Psychologist Dean Kilpatrick's research group (1985) compared victims of rape with victims of aggravated assault and other crimes. They found substantially more mental health problems among the victims of rape. Tragically, nearly one rape victim in five had attempted suicide. Women are more likely to develop PTSD, even when the type of stress is controlled, and persons with high levels of anxiety before the stress are more likely to have serious post-traumatic stress reactions (Breslau & others, 1997, 1998; Kessler & others, 1995), but other predictors of reactions to civilian stress are not well understood.

### Obsessive-Compulsive Disorders

Also classified with anxiety disorders are the **obsessive-compulsive disorders.** Obsessions and compulsions are two separate problems, but they often occur together in the same individuals. *Obsessions* are anxiety-provoking thoughts that will not go away. They seem uncontrollable and even alien, as if they do not belong to the individual's mind. Thoughts such as a recurrent fear of losing control and killing someone or of having an incestuous sexual relationship can cause extreme anxiety.

*Compulsions* are irresistible urges to engage in behaviors such as repeatedly touching a spot on one's shoulder, washing one's hands, or checking the locks on doors. If the individual tries to stop engaging in the behavior, he or she experiences an urgent anxiety until the behavior is resumed. Obsessions and compulsions are often found in the same person, such as the person who compulsively washes his hands because he is obsessed with thoughts about germs. About 70 percent of all people with obsessive-compulsive disorders have both obsessions and compulsions, 25 percent have only obsessions, and 5 percent have only compulsions (Wilner, Reich, Robins, Fishman, & van Doren, 1976). Evidence from several studies that employed brain-imaging techniques suggests that portions of the limbic system (see page 74) function improperly in individuals with obsessive-compulsive disorders (Baxter & others, 1987).

### ● Somatoform Disorders

**Somatoform disorders** are conditions in which the individual experiences the symptoms of physical health problems that have psychological rather than physical causes. *Soma* is the Latin word for body—hence, somatoform disorders are thought to be disorders in which psychological problems "take the form" of physical problems. Although these symptoms of health problems are not physically caused, they are very real and uncomfortable to the individual. In other words, they are not faked. There are four types of somatoform disorders: *somatization disorders, hypochondriasis, conversion disorders,* and *somatoform pain disorders.* Because of similarities among them, these four disorders are discussed in pairs.

### Somatization Disorders and Hypochondriasis

**Somatization disorders** are intensely and chronically uncomfortable conditions that indirectly create a high risk of medical complications. They are far more common in women than in men (Golding, Smith, & Kashner, 1991). They take the form of chronic

**obsessive-compulsive disorders**
Disorders that involve obsessions (anxiety-provoking thoughts that will not go away) and/or compulsions (irresistible urges to engage in specific irrational behaviors).

**somatoform disorders**
(sō″mah′to-form)  Disorders in which the individual experiences the symptoms of physical health problems that have psychological rather than physical causes.

**somatization disorders**
(sō″mah-ti-zā′shun)  Intensely and chronically uncomfortable psychological conditions that involve numerous symptoms of somatic (body) illnesses without physical cause.

"He was a dreadful hypochondriac."
© Punch/Rothco. Reprinted by permission.

**hypochondriasis**
(hī´pō-kon-drī´ah-sis) A mild form of somatization disorder characterized by excessive concern about one's health.

**conversion disorders**
Somatoform disorders in which individuals experience serious somatic symptoms such as functional blindness, deafness, and paralysis.

and recurrent aches, pains, tiredness, and other symptoms of somatic (body) illness. In addition, individuals with these disorders frequently experience memory difficulties, problems with walking, numbness, blackout spells, nausea, menstrual problems, and a lack of pleasure from sex. These complaints are often expressed in dramatic ways that increase the probability of sympathy and special treatment from others.

Individuals with somatization problems also typically experience other psychological difficulties, particularly anxiety and depression. They frequently have problems with their jobs, schoolwork, or household responsibilities. The most dangerous aspect of somatization disorders, however, concerns the measures the affected individuals take to find relief from their discomfort. Many become addicted to alcohol or tranquilizers and often take medications prescribed by many different physicians, whom they are seeing simultaneously (without telling the other physicians), thus increasing the risk of dangerous chemical interactions among the drugs. Worse still, because of their frequent complaints to physicians, many are eventually the recipients of unnecessary surgery, especially unnecessary hysterectomies (removal of the uterus in women).

**Hypochondriasis** can be thought of as a milder form of somatization disorder with some special features of its own. The hypochondriac experiences somatic symptoms, but they are not as pervasive or as intense as in somatization disorders. Hypochondriacs also do not experience most of the serious side effects, such as depression, drug addiction, and unnecessary operations. Their lives, however, are dominated by their concerns about their health. They show a preoccupation with health, overreact with concern to minor coughs and pains, and go to unreasonable lengths to avoid germs, cancer-causing agents, and the like (Barsky & others, 1998).

## Conversion Disorders and Somatoform Pain Disorders

**Conversion disorders** are the most dramatic of the somatoform disorders. The name comes from the Freudian theory that anxiety has been "converted" into serious somatic symptoms in this condition rather than being directly experienced as anxiety. Individuals with this problem experience functional blindness, deafness, paralysis, fainting, seizures, inability to speak, or other serious impairments in the absence of any physical cause. In addition, these individuals appear to be generally ineffective and dependent upon others. These symptoms understandably impair the individuals' lives, particularly their ability to work. Conversion disorders can usually be distinguished from medical problems without great difficulty. In most cases, the symptoms are not medically possible. For example, in conversion disorders the areas of paralysis and loss of sensation are not shaped in the way they would be if there were actual nerve damage (see fig. 14.2). Similarly, people with conversion paralysis of the legs can be observed to move their legs normally when sleeping.

Perhaps the most interesting characteristic of conversion disorders is known as *la belle indifférence,* "beautiful indifference." Individuals with conversion disorders often are

**FIGURE 14.2**

Because of the pattern in which the sensory nerves serve the skin surface, it would only be medically possible to experience anesthesia within any of the lines shown on the hand on the right. Typical conversion anesthesias do not conform to these patterns, however.

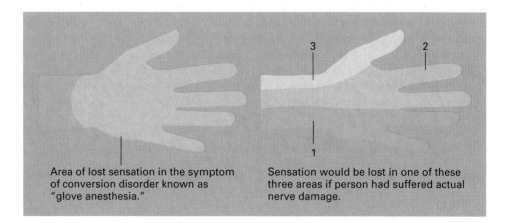

Area of lost sensation in the symptom of conversion disorder known as "glove anesthesia."

Sensation would be lost in one of these three areas if person had suffered actual nerve damage.

*not upset* by their condition. The individual with conversion disorders who wakes up paralyzed one morning may show some emotional response, but not nearly to the extent that a person who is physically paralyzed would—for example, in an automobile accident. Some psychologists believe that the conversion symptoms are welcome, in a sense, as they get these people out of responsibilities or force others to take care of them. Consider the following case:

> A 22-year-old man . . . was referred with complaints of night blindness and failing vision. His visual acuity had deteriorated rapidly and he was found to have tubular fields of vision and a gross abnormality of dark adaptation. . . .
>
> The onset of his symptoms seemed closely related to his difficulties with a girlfriend who lived some miles away from his home. In order to visit her he would have to drive at night which was made impossible by his night blindness. Soon after the relationship was broken and the girl became engaged to another man the symptoms cleared up. Visual acuity improved . . . and the visual fields showed only slight contraction. (Behrman & Levy, 1970, p. 193)*

*Reprinted from *Journal of Psychosomatic Research*, Vol. 17, J. Behrman and R. Levy, "Neurophysiological Studies on Patients with Hysterical Disturbances of Vision," p. 193. Copyright © 1970 with permission from Elsevier Science.

Conversion disorders usually begin during stress and provide some kind of benefit (i.e., reinforcement) to the individual. In the case of the 22-year-old man just described, the benefit may have been not having to admit that he did not want to visit his girlfriend.

**Somatoform pain disorders** are very similar to conversion disorders, except that the primary symptom is *pain* that has no physical cause. Sometimes somatoform pain can be distinguished from physically caused pain because it does not follow nerve pathways. But in the case of low back pain, joint pains, and chest pains, a diagnosis of somatoform pain disorder can be made only after all possible physical causes have been carefully ruled out. Like conversion disorders, somatoform pain usually occurs at times of high stress and is generally beneficial to the individual in some way, as in getting the person out of a dull job and onto disability payments.

### ● Dissociative Disorders

**Dissociative disorders** cover a broad category of loosely related rare conditions involving sudden alterations in cognition. The various types of dissociative disorders are characterized by a change in memory, perception, or "identity." These experiences are more common under stress, but can occur in the absence of stress (Morgan & others, 2001). There are four kinds of dissociative disorders: *depersonalization, dissociative amnesia, dissociative fugue,* and *dissociative identity disorder.*

### Depersonalization

The term **depersonalization** refers to experiences in which the individual feels that he or she has become distorted or "unreal," or that distortions have occurred in one's surroundings. The individual might feel that his hands have become enlarged or out of control. Or the individual might feel like a robot—even though she knows she is a real person—or that her parents are not real people. The individual knows that these feelings are not accurate, although they have an eerie reality to them. One of the more common experiences of depersonalization is the sense of leaving one's body and being able to look back at it from the ceiling.

As was mentioned when we discussed depersonalization as an altered state of consciousness in chapter 5, experiences of depersonalization are rather common, especially in young adults. Unless they are accompanied by other problems or become recurrent to the point of being uncomfortable, these experiences are not considered abnormal. Generally, they are nothing more than an unsettling experience.

**somatoform pain disorders**
(sō-ma′to-form) Somatoform disorders in which the individual experiences a relatively specific and chronic pain that has a psychological rather than a physical cause.

**dissociative disorders**
(dis-sō″sē-a-tiv) A category of conditions involving sudden cognitive changes, such as a sudden loss of memory or loss of one's identity.

**depersonalization**
(de-per″sun-al-i-zā′shun) The perceptual experience of one's body or surroundings becoming distorted or unreal in some way.

**dissociative amnesia**
A dissociative disorder that involves a loss of memory and that has a psychological rather than a physical cause.

**dissociative fugue**
(fūg) A period of "wandering" that involves a loss of memory and a change in identity.

**dissociative identity disorder**
A dissociative disorder in which the individual appears to shift abruptly and repeatedly from one "personality" to another.

## Dissociative Amnesia and Fugue

As described in chapter 7, amnesia is a loss of memory that can have either a physical or a psychological cause. **Dissociative amnesia** is psychologically caused. It most often occurs after a period of intense stress and involves loss of memory for all or part of the stressful experience itself, such as loss of memory for an automobile accident in which the individual was responsible for the death of another person. Individuals who suffer amnesia as a result of stress generally have no other psychological problems and typically recover their memories in time.

**Dissociative fugue** states resemble amnesia in that there is a loss of memory, but the loss is so complete that the individual cannot remember his or her identity or previous life. The fugue episode is also typified by a period of "wandering" that may take the individual around the corner or across the continent. In many instances, the individual takes on a new "personality" during the fugue episode, usually one that is more sociable, more fun-loving, and less conventional than the previous one. Generally these changes are transient. Consider the following case:

> When Mrs. Y. was brought to the hospital by her husband, she was dazed, confused, and weeping. Apparently aware of her surroundings and able to answer brief questions in filling out the admitting form, she could not, at the time, discuss any of her problems with the admitting physician. Her husband reported that she had left their home two weeks previously while he was at work. All the efforts of her husband and the police to trace her had failed until approximately 24 hours prior to her admission to the hospital when Mr. Y. received a report that a woman of her description had been arrested in a nearby city. When he arrived and identified her, she did not at first recognize him, did not know her own name, and could not remember what had happened to her or anything about her past. The police informed Mr. Y. that she had been arrested for "resorting" after a motel owner had called the police to complain that several different men had visited the motel room she had rented three days before in the company of a sailor. Mrs. Y. seemed unable to remember any of these alleged events. Gradually she came to recognize her husband as he talked anxiously with her whereupon she began to weep and requested to be brought home. (Goldstein & Palmer, 1963, pp. 71–72)*

---

*From *The Experience of Anxiety: A Casebook,* Expanded Edition by Michael J. Goldstein and James O. Palmer. Copyright © 1975 by Michael J. Goldstein and James O. Palmer. Reprinted by permission of Oxford University Press, Inc.

As will be obvious in the next section, dissociative fugue is quite similar to dissociative identity disorder. For that reason, all of the controversy surrounding that diagnosis applies to dissociative fugue.

## Dissociative Identity Disorder (Multiple Personality)

Individuals who exhibit **dissociative identity disorder** (formerly known as *multiple personality*) appear to shift abruptly from one "personality" to another—as if more than one person were inhabiting the same body. Generally, the two or more personalities are quite different from one another. The individual's original personality is often conventional, moralistic, and unhappy, whereas the alternative personalities tend to be quite the opposite. At least one other personality is usually sensual, uninhibited, and rebellious. In most cases, the individual reports that he or she is not aware of the other personalities when they are "in" their original personality but say that the alternative personalities "know about" their rival personalities and are often antagonistic toward the original one.

In 1977, Chris Sizemore published an autobiography revealing that she was the case of dissociative identity disorder made famous in the 1950s movie *The Three Faces of Eve*. Initially, she appeared to manifest two distinctly different personalities, referred to in the movie as Eve White and Eve Black. Eve White was depressive, anxious, conventional, and inhibited, whereas Eve Black was seductive, uninhibited, and wild. In her autobiography, Chris Sizemore reveals that she eventually went through 22 separate personalities but that in recent years she feels she has a single, well-adjusted personality. A similar pattern was reported for the case of "Sybil," a woman who believed that she had developed 16 personalities during the course of 42 years (Schreiber, 1973).

Dissociative identity disorder is a very controversial disorder today. Although there is little doubt that some people behave as if they have multiple personalities, there is great deal of debate about why they behave this way. Some mental health experts believe that dissociative identity disorder is the result of physical or sexual abuse during childhood. In this view, alternative "personalities" that do not "know" about the abuse are believed to split off from the original personality in an effort to cope with painful memories (Gleaves, 1996).

Other psychologists believe that dissociative identity disorder is the direct result of social learning (Lilienfeld & others, 1999). Sometimes, highly suggestible persons are exposed, through books or movies, to persons who are models of "multiple personalities." If they imitate these models and begin to act as if they have more than one personality, they may behave in previously unacceptable ways that are reinforced (brash, rule-breaking, or promiscuous behavior), but attribute the new behavior to "another personality" rather than accepting responsibility for the actions. Thus, in the social learning view, multiple personalities are no more than unconscious enactments of roles.

Chris Sizemore, the woman who was the subject of the book and film *The Three Faces of Eve*. Ms. Sizemore reported that she exhibited a total of 22 distinct personalities before achieving her final, permanent personality.

In most cases, social learning theorists believe that so-called multiple personalities are taught to patients by their psychotherapists, however, rather than by books or movies (Lilienfeld & others, 1999). This surprising assertion may seem far-fetched at first, but it simply means that when some well-intentioned therapists begin to suspect that a patient has been abused as a child or notice that the patient sometimes acts in ways that are inconsistent with his or her usual behavior, they may suggest to the patient that he or she has one or more "hidden personalities." A patient who is highly suggestible may accept this idea and begin to act more and more as if he or she has multiple personalities. Lilienfeld and colleagues (1999) cite evidence that most people with dissociative identity did not believe that they had multiple personalities until they began seeing a therapist who raised this possibility. Thus, therapists who look for hints of dissociative identity disorder in their patients may unwittingly teach their patients to have dissociative identity disorder. Indeed, it has been alleged that therapist influences created the multiple personalities of the person known as Sybil (Borch-Jacobsen, 1997; Rieber, 1999).

Joan Acocella (1999) has suggested that there is an alarming trend for well-meaning psychotherapists to influence their patients to believe that they have multiple personalities—particularly their female patients. She argues that this has created an epidemic of cases of dissociative identity disorder at the close of the twentieth century. Prior to 1970, dissociative identity disorder was very rarely identified, but beginning in the 1980s, tens of thousands of women developed "multiple personalities" during the course of their treatment. Lilienfeld and colleagues (1999) believe that this is not the first time in history that such an epidemic has spread among suggestible people. They hypothesize that there was an epidemic of conversion disorders (fainting, seizures, paralysis, and other physical symptoms with no known medical cause) during Freud's era in Europe, which spread through similar social learning processes.

Anxiety disorders are common problems characterized by anxiety that may be experienced as low and relatively constant levels of generalized anxiety, as sharp and intense attacks of anxiety, or as focalized phobias of various sorts, or that may be linked to obsessive thoughts or compulsive actions.

Review

In somatoform disorders, the individual experiences the symptoms of medical conditions that have psychological rather than physical causes. In some types of somatoform disorders the symptoms are dramatic and clear-cut, such as blindness, paralysis, or chronic pain. In other cases, the individual experiences multiple aches, pains, and maladies or is just excessively concerned with health.

Dissociative disorders are psychological problems involving sudden alterations in cognition. These may take the form of memory loss, changes of identity, or feelings of unreality. In rare cases, the alteration of identity is so dramatic that the individual appears to possess more than a single personality. Social learning theorists have raised concerns that dissociative disorders may often be created by the actions of well-intentioned therapists with their highly suggestible patients.

## Check Your Learning

To be sure that you have learned the key points from the preceding section, cover the list of correct answers and try to answer each question. If you give an incorrect answer to any question, return to the page given next to the correct answer to see why your answer was not correct.

1. Psychological disorders that involve excessive levels of nervousness, tension, worry, fright, and anxiety are termed _____ disorders.

    a)  panic
    b)  somatoform
    c)  behavior
    d)  anxiety

2. Individuals with _____ experience a vague, uneasy sense of tension and apprehension, sometimes referred to as free-floating anxiety, that makes the individual uncomfortable because of its prolonged presence.

    a)  panic disorder
    b)  dissociative identity disorder
    c)  generalized anxiety disorder
    d)  agoraphobia

3. _____ are conditions in which the individual experiences the symptoms of physical health problems that have psychological rather than physical causes.

    a)  Anxiety disorders
    b)  Dissociative disorders
    c)  Somatoform disorders
    d)  Social phobias

4. _____ disorders are a category of conditions involving sudden cognitive changes, such as a change in memory, perception, or identity.

    a)  Panic
    b)  Conversion
    c)  Obsessive-compulsive
    d)  Dissociative

## Thinking Critically about Psychology

1. How would a social learning theorist account for a phobic fear of snakes? How might a psychoanalyst account for the same phobia?

2. Our news media seem to highlight cases of dissociative identity disorder even though they are very rare. What role do you think the media play in our society's understanding of abnormal behavior?

**Correct Answers:** 1. d (p. 545), 2. c (p. 546), 3. c (p. 549), 4. d (p. 551).

## ● Mood Disorders

There are two primary forms of **mood disorders,** depression and mania. Depression can occur alone (a condition known as *major depression*), but mania seems to always alternate with periods of depression *(bipolar disorder)*. Both conditions produce great misery for the individual.

### Major Depression

The individual experiencing **major depression** is deeply unhappy and finds little pleasure in life. But major depression is more than merely intense sadness. The person with major depression believes that the future is bleak, holds a negative opinion of self and others, and often sees no reason to live. This is accompanied by at least some of the following: increased or decreased sleep, increased or decreased appetite, loss of interest in sex, loss of energy or excessive energy, and difficulties concentrating and making decisions. Persons who are depressed also often think about death and are far more likely than persons who are not depressed to commit suicide (Osley & others, 2001; Oquendo & others, 2001).

Fortunately, major depression is an *episodic* disorder. This means that, in 90 percent of cases, the individual experiences the symptoms for a period of time and then recovers, often returning to his or her normal self. The duration of episodes varies widely, but half of all persons with major depression recover in 12 weeks from the beginning of the depressive episode (Eaton & others, 1997; Solomon & others, 1997; Spijker & others, 2002). About one-third of all individuals who experience an episode of major depression will experience only one episode, but others will be depressed—sometimes repeatedly—during their lifetimes if not properly treated (Eaton & others, 1997; Solomon & others, 1997, 2000). In these cases, the depression comes in recurrent episodes, which last from several weeks to many months, followed by periods of relatively normal mood (Mojtabai, 2001).

Major depression is quite common, affecting 10 million or more Americans. Worldwide, as many as 100 million persons experience major depression (Gotlib, 1992). As shown in figure 14.3, the probability that an individual will develop major depression for the first time is very low until puberty, rises until a peak is reached between 45 and

**mood disorders**
Psychological disorders involving depression and/or abnormal elation.

**major depression**
An affective disorder characterized by episodes of deep unhappiness, loss of interest in life, and other symptoms.

**FIGURE 14.3**
The probability that an individual will develop major depression for the first time during a given year of life changes over the life span.
**Source:** Data from P. M. Lewinsohn, et al., "Age at First Onset for Nonbipolar Depression," *Journal of Abnormal Psychology,* 95:378–383, 1986. Copyright 1986 by the American Psychological Association.

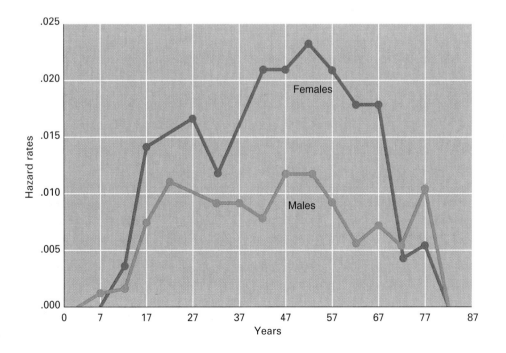

55 years of age, then declines again in old age. Overall, the risk for major depression is twice as high for women than for men, particularly during middle age (Eaton & others, 1997; Lewinsohn, Duncan, Stanton, & Hautzinger, 1986).

Major depression, despite its name, is often relatively mild. People with mild depression are very uncomfortable, but they often can cope with the demands of daily living. Severe major depression is less common but far more disabling. This is often accompanied by bizarre beliefs and perceptions that represent a psychotic distortion of reality. The following excerpt describes a case of severe depression that required the individual to be hospitalized.

> At 51 the patient suffered from a depression and was obliged to resign his position. This depression continued for about 9 months, after which he apparently fully recovered. He resumed his work but after 2 years suffered from a second depression. Again he recovered after several months and returned to a similar position and held it until 2 months before his admission. At this time he began to worry lest he was not doing his work well, talked much of his lack of fitness for his duties, and finally resigned. He spent Thanksgiving Day at his son's in a neighboring city, but while there he was sure that the water pipes in his own house would freeze during his absence and that he and his family would be "turned out into the street." A few days later he was found standing by a pond, evidently contemplating suicide. He soon began to remain in bed and sometimes wrapped his head in the bed clothing to shut out the external world. (Kolb, 1977, p. 455)[*]

[*]From L. C. Kolb, *Modern Clinical Psychiatry*, 9th ed. Copyright © 1977. Used by permission of the author.

The risk for major depression is significantly elevated in persons experiencing high levels of stress (Lewinsohn, Hoberman, & Rosenbaum, 1988; Mazure, 1998; Shrout & others, 1989). On the other hand, there is also clear evidence that some people are more vulnerable than others to depression for genetic reasons (Kendler & Prescott, 1999).

### Cognitive Factors in Depression

Aaron T. Beck (1976) and others believe that our *cognitions* are an important factor in emotional problems. For example, Beck has suggested that negative views of oneself, the world in which we live, and the future lead some persons to experience life in such negative terms that they develop depression. Much evidence is consistent with this view, particularly Beck's theory that negative views of oneself are a critical component of depression. Many studies (Alloy, Abramson, & Francis, 1999; Brown, Hammen, Craske, & Wickens, 1995) show that people who believe that they fall far short of being the persons they would like to be are more likely to experience depression. One reason that depressed persons often fall short of their ideal is that their beliefs are *perfectionistic* (Hewitt, Flett, & Ediger, 1996). Paul Hewitt and Gordon Flett (1993) found that people who believe that they should be perfect in their work are likely to develop depression if they fail even slightly at work. Similarly, people who hold out perfectionistic expectations for themselves in social relationships are often depressed if their personal relationships are not going well. In contrast, people who do not expect perfection of themselves do not become depressed when things do not go well. These findings support the basic premise of the cognitive view: It is not bad things happening to us that is upsetting; it is our *interpretation* of them that makes all the difference (Gotlib, 1992; Joiner and others, 1999).

Other studies have suggested that having a positive opinion of yourself makes depression less likely following stressful life events (Dozois & Dobson, 2001; Hammen, Marks, Mayol, & deMayo, 1985; Lewinsohn & others, 1988; Robinson, Garber, & Hilsman, 1995). Studies have also shown that a cognitive style of repressive coping (described in chapter 13) increases the risk of depression under stress (Folkman &

Lazarus, 1986; Holahan & Moos, 1987). In addition, individuals who believe that they can be happy only when they are in a close relationship are understandably more likely to respond to the loss of a relationship with depression than will individuals who do not hold this dependent belief (Hammen, Elliott, Gitlin, & Jamison, 1989; Hammen & others, 1985; Zuroff & Mongrain, 1987).

It seems clear that our beliefs about ourselves and our relationships with others make us more or less vulnerable to depression when buffeted by life's inevitable stress (Lewinsohn, Joiner, & Rohde, 2001). However, the relationship between cognition and depression is a two-way street. When persons become depressed, their cognitions change. They become more pessimistic, more critical of themselves, more likely to blame themselves for everything bad that happens, and so on. When the depression lifts, fortunately, these cognitions often return to a more positive state (Dohr, Rush, & Bernstein, 1989; Sheppard & Teasdale, 2000). Thus, although negative cognitions appear to predispose us to depression, we never think more negatively than when we are depressed.

When asked to rate their participation after a group discussion, people with major depression give more accurate ratings than do people who aren't depressed. It seems some positive "distortion" of our self-perception can be healthy.

Interestingly, the research of Peter Lewinsohn and his associates (1980) suggests that at least some aspects of the "distorted" cognitions that are characteristic of depressed individuals are not distortions at all. Lewinsohn asked individuals who were experiencing major depression to participate in a group discussion for approximately 20 minutes. During this time, they were rated by a group of judges on their friendliness, assertiveness, warmth, and other social qualities. After the group discussion, each participant also rated himself or herself on the same dimensions. Another group of people who were not depressed went through exactly the same procedure.

As would have been predicted by Beck, the depressed group rated their social skills as being less adequate than did the nondepressed participants. Is this evidence that depressed individuals distort their view of themselves? Actually, it turns out that the self-ratings of the depressed group were *quite accurate* when compared with the ratings of the judges. It was the normal participants whose view of themselves was distorted! The nondepressed persons rated themselves as being significantly more socially skilled than the judges did. Furthermore, when the depressed individuals were given treatment and became less depressed, their self-perceptions became more like the normal group: They, too, began to rate themselves in unrealistically positive terms. Perhaps having this kind of "distorted" perception of ourselves is a good thing. Maybe we would all be depressed if we saw ourselves in the realistic terms in which others see us!

## Bipolar Disorder

In the condition known as **bipolar disorder,** periods of mania alternate irregularly with periods of severe depression. **Mania** is a disturbance of mood that can be quite enjoyable to the individual in the short run but is usually damaging both to the person and to others in the long run. During the manic episode, the individual experiences a remarkable "high"—an intense euphoria in which sensory pleasures are heightened, one's self-esteem is very high, thoughts race, little sleep is needed, and unrealistic optimism prevails. Grandiose and financially damaging schemes and buying sprees are common during these periods, as are quitting jobs, getting a divorce, and engaging in sexual promiscuity. Psychotic distortions of reality are also common during manic periods. When well-meaning friends and family members try to control the manic individual, they are often rebuffed in sharp anger. Although an intensely pleasurable state, mania

**bipolar disorder**
(bī-pō'lar) A condition in which the individual experiences periods of mania that alternate irregularly with periods of severe depression.

**mania**
(mā'nē-ah) A disturbance of mood in which the individual experiences a euphoria without cause that is characterized by unrealistic optimism and heightened sensory pleasures.

# HUMAN DIVERSITY

## Ethnic and Gender Differences in Depression and Suicide

Depression afflicts every group of human beings. It is an all-too-common problem for men and women, and it is found in every ethnic group. Likewise, no human group is completely immune to the threat of suicide. There is growing evidence, however, of large differences in rates of depression and suicide between the genders and among ethnic groups. This evidence is inherently important and offers the hope of providing clues to the causes of these disorders.

Maria Oquendo and colleagues (2001) used data from two epidemiologic studies of some 20,000 adults in the United States to examine gender and ethnic differences in depression and suicide. As previously found in many studies, the likelihood of depression was approximately twice as high in women as in men. In sharp contrast, men were four to five times more likely to commit suicide than women were. Although depressed individuals are far more likely to commit suicide than are individuals who are not depressed (Osby & others, 2001), Oquendo found that depressed women are far less likely to commit suicide than depressed men are. Something about being female generally protects depressed individuals from taking their own lives.

Oquendo and colleagues (2001) also found considerable differences among a number of ethnic groups in the United States in their rates of depression and suicide. An important feature of her study was distinguishing among a number of Hispanic groups. Americans whose ancestry is in Cuba, Mexico, Puerto Rico, and other countries tend to describe themselves as being quite different. In racial terms, many Cuban Americans view themselves as white descendants of Spaniards and many Mexican Americans report that they are a blend of Spanish and native peoples. In cultural terms, these groups are similarly quite different.

Oquendo and colleagues (2001) found that among men, Mexican Americans had lower rates of depression than non-Hispanic whites, but Puerto Rican Americans had higher rates of depression than non-Hispanic whites. Among women, Puerto Rican Americans had higher rates of depression than non-Hispanic whites, but there were no other differences among ethnic groups. Among men, non-Hispanic whites had the highest suicide rates, and Mexican Americans had the lowest suicide rates. Among women, non-Hispanic whites had the highest rates of suicide, and Mexican American and Puerto Rican women had the lowest rates.

Finally, Oquendo and colleagues (2001) compared rates of suicide among depressed individuals. When depressed, Mexican Americans and Puerto Rican Americans of both genders had lower rates of suicide than non-Hispanic whites of both genders. In addition, depressed African American women had lower than expected rates of suicide compared to non-Hispanic white women.

What is it about these U.S. ethnic and gender groups that makes their rates of depression and suicide so different? First, why are rates of depression higher among Puerto Rican American women and men than other groups in the United States? One important piece of information is that rates of depression among Puerto Ricans living in Puerto Rico are *not* higher than U.S. population rates (Oquendo & others, 2001). The increased risk for depression is found only among Puerto Ricans living in the United States. This could be the result of characteristics of the individuals who migrate to the United States. Perhaps people who are happy in their lives—not prone to depression—are less likely to migrate to the United States. Alternatively, the higher rates of depression among Puerto Ricans in the United States could reflect the discrimination and hardship faced by some immigrants. This is a plausible explanation, because Puerto Ricans living in the United States clearly face economic hardships. In addition, Puerto Rican Americans may be more likely to face hardships than, say, Mexican Americans, many of whose families were residents of what is now the United States before the current 50 states were formed.

Why are depressed white women more likely than the other ethnic groups to commit suicide? Are there cultural differences that protect African American and Hispanic women from taking their lives when depressed? Are there differences in the rates at which depressed women of different cultures turn to drugs and alcohol? If so, does this play a role in rates of suicide? Does the greater involvement in community life and places of worship protect nonwhite women?

Many important questions remain to be answered. Before the complex relationships among culture, gender, and mental health can be fully understood, however, information is needed on the mental health of Asian Americans and other sizable groups living in the United States that have been understudied. In addition, future studies should take into account the fact that people of western European and African ancestry are not all the same ethnically and may differ in their rates of mental health problems as much as different Hispanic groups. For example, we know little about possible differences in the challenges faced by former slaves living in the United States compared to African Americans who are recent immigrants from Africa or the Caribbean. ■

can be quite harmful to the person's finances and personal relationships. This harm can be clearly seen in the case of "Mrs. M.":

> At 17 she suffered from a depression . . . for several months, although she was not hospitalized. At 33, shortly before the birth of her first child, the patient was greatly depressed. For a period of four days she appeared in a coma. About a month after the birth of the baby she "became excited" and was entered as a patient in an institution for neurotic and mildly psychotic patients. As she began to improve, she was sent to a shore hotel for a brief vacation. The patient remained at the hotel for one night and on the following day signed a year's lease on an apartment, bought furniture, and became heavily involved in debt. Shortly thereafter Mrs. M. became depressed and returned to the hospital. . . . After several months she recovered and, except for relatively mild fluctuations of mood, remained well for approximately 2 years.
>
> She then became overactive and exuberant in spirits and visited her friends, to whom she outlined her plans for reestablishing different forms of lucrative business. She purchased many clothes, bought furniture, pawned her rings, and wrote checks without funds. She was returned to a hospital. Gradually her manic symptoms subsided, and after four months she was discharged. For a period thereafter she was mildly depressed. In a little less than a year Mrs. M. again became overactive, played her radio until late in the night, smoked excessively, and took out insurance on a car that she had not yet bought. Contrary to her usual habits, she swore frequently and loudly . . . and instituted divorce proceedings. On the day prior to her second admission to the hospital, she purchased 57 hats. (Kolb, 1977, pp. 455–456)*

*From L. C. Kolb, *Modern Clinical Psychiatry*, 9th ed. Copyright © 1977. Used by permission of the author.

Mania usually returns in multiple episodes (Halgin & Whitbourne, 2000). When mania is recurrent, it alternates irregularly with episodes of depression. Some affected individuals shift frequently between mania and depression, while others shift infrequently. The average number of shifts from mania to depression among persons with bipolar disorder is three to four times per year (Judd & others, 2002). This alternating disorder was formerly known as *manic-depressive psychosis* and is now known as bipolar disorder. Bipolar disorder is a relatively uncommon problem; only 15 percent of individuals with affective disorder show this alternating pattern of intense highs and lows. Bipolar disorder is equally common among women and men (Kessler & others, 1995). Fortunately, bipolar disorder generally can be treated effectively with medication.

## ● Schizophrenia and Delusional Disorder

### Schizophrenia

PSYCHOLOGIST: "Why do you think people believe in God?"

PATIENT: Uh, let's, I don't know why, let's see, balloon travel. He holds it up for you, the balloon. He don't let you fall out, your little legs sticking out down through the clouds. He's down to the smokestack, looking through the smoke trying to get the balloon gassed up you know. Way they're flying on top that way, legs sticking out, I don't know, looking down on the ground, heck, that'd make you so dizzy you just stay and sleep you know, hold down and sleep there. The balloon's His home you know up there. I used to sleep outdoors, you know, sleep outdoors instead of going home. He's had a home but His not tell where it's at you know. (Chapman & Chapman, 1973, p. 3)

The person giving this confused and confusing answer has a serious problem known as **schizophrenia.** Schizophrenia is an uncommon disorder that affects about 1 percent of the general population. Approximately equal numbers of men and women are affected by schizophrenia (Kessler & others, 1993). However, it's a dramatic form of abnormality that, unless successfully treated, often renders normal patterns of living impossible.

**schizophrenia**
(skiz″o-fren′-ē-ah) A psychological disorder involving cognitive disturbance (delusions and hallucinations), disorganization, and reduced enjoyment and interests.

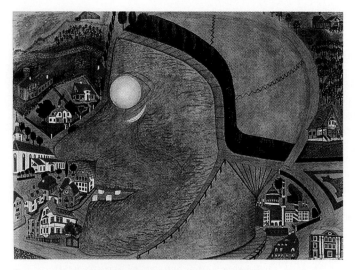

German psychiatrist Hans Prinzhorn has assembled the most extensive collection of artwork by mental patients available. This painting from the collection, by August Neter, illustrates the hallucinations and the paranoid fantasies from which many schizophrenic patients suffer. In reviewing a showing of artwork by schizophrenic patients, such as the painting shown here, poet John Ashby wrote: "The lure of the work is strong, but so is the terror of the unanswerable riddles it proposes."

**delusions**
False beliefs that distort reality.

**hallucinations**
False perceptual experiences that distort reality.

**paranoid schizophrenia**
(par′-ah-noid) A subtype of schizophrenia in which the individual holds delusions of persecution and grandeur that seriously distort reality.

Catatonic individuals sometimes exhibit a state of catatonic stupor, during which they may maintain a single posture for several hours.

Schizophrenia is characterized by three types of serious problems (Andreasen, Arndt, Alliger, Miller, & Flaum, 1995; Halgin & Whitbourne, 2000):

1. *Delusions and hallucinations.* The central feature of schizophrenia is distortions of cognition that put the individual "out of touch with reality." Persons with schizophrenia often hold strange false beliefs (**delusions**) and have distorted and bizarre false perceptual experiences (**hallucinations**). We will discuss these distortions of cognition in greater detail in discussing the subtypes of schizophrenia.

2. *Disorganized thinking, emotions, and behavior.* As is clear in the preceding example, persons with schizophrenia often think in fragmented and disorganized ways. Their emotions and behavior are similarly disorganized and illogical at times. A person with schizophrenia might laugh when told sad news or shift rapidly from happiness to sadness and back again for no apparent reason. As a result, most of us find it very difficult to have conversations with persons with schizophrenia.

3. *Reduced enjoyment and interests.* Persons with schizophrenia often show what is called "blunted affect." They find less pleasure in life than most persons and have fewer interests and goals that are important to them. Although their emotions change in unpredictable ways, both their positive and their negative emotions lack normal intensity. In many ways, they just do not care about things as much as other people. Often, this includes not being as interested in having close friendships.

Long-term studies of persons with schizophrenia show that their reduced enjoyment and interests is usually chronic and does not improve, but their delusions, hallucinations, and disorganization may improve for a while between episodes of worsened symptoms (Arndt & others, 1995; Breier, Schreiber, Dyer, & Pickar, 1991; Loebel & others, 1992). Schizophrenia is a broad class of psychotic disorders that is broken down into three major subtypes in the 1994 edition of the American Psychiatric Association's *Diagnostic and Statistical Manual of Mental Disorders (DSM-IV): paranoid, disorganized,* and *catatonic schizophrenia.* A fourth category, *undifferentiated schizophrenia,* is used to classify individuals who do not fit into the other three categories.

**Paranoid Schizophrenia**

A person with **paranoid schizophrenia** holds *false beliefs,* or *delusions,* that seriously distort reality. Most often, these are beliefs in the exceptional importance of oneself, so-called *delusions of grandeur*—such as being Jesus Christ, a CIA agent, or the inventor of a cure for war. These are often accompanied by delusions that, because one is so important, others are "out to get me" in attempts to thwart the individual's important mission. These are known as *delusions of persecution,* or *paranoia.*

If I were schizophrenic and believed that I were an agent of the CIA who alone had the ability to save the president from assassination by terrorists, I might also believe that my students were terrorists who were trying to confuse and poison me. Think for a moment how bizarre I would seem to others who learned of my paranoid delusions. Think, too, about the terrifying, bewildering existence I would live if I believed those things. It would be small wonder that my emotions would seem unpredictable and strange and that I would withdraw from social contact.

Unfortunately, the cognitive disturbances of the paranoid schizophrenic do not stop with delusions. Many individuals with this disorder also experience false perceptual experiences, or *hallucinations*. Their perceptions are either strangely distorted or they may hear, see, or feel things that are not there. These bizarre experiences further add to the terrifying, perplexing unreality of the paranoid schizophrenic's existence.

### Disorganized Schizophrenia

**Disorganized schizophrenia** resembles paranoid schizophrenia in that delusions and hallucinations are present, but the cognitive processes of the disorganized schizophrenic, as the name implies, are so disorganized and fragmented that the delusions and hallucinations have little recognizable meaning. The central features of this type of schizophrenia are extreme withdrawal from normal human contact and a shallow "silliness" of emotion. The disorganized schizophrenic acts in childlike ways, reacts inappropriately to both happy and sad events, and generally presents a highly bizarre picture to others.

### Catatonic Schizophrenia

**Catatonic schizophrenia** is quite different in appearance from other forms of schizophrenia. Although catatonics sometimes experience delusions and hallucinations, their most obvious abnormalities are in social interaction, posture, and body movement. There are long periods of catatonic stupor, an inactive, statuelike state in which the individuals seem locked into a posture. Catatonic schizophrenics are often said to exhibit "waxy flexibility" during these stupors—they passively let themselves be placed into any posture and maintain it. Often the individual ceases to talk, appears not to hear what is spoken to him or her, and may no longer eat without being fed.

Frequently, however, the stupor is abruptly broken by periods of agitation. The person may pace and fidget nervously or may angrily attack others. Both of these patterns may alternate with periods of relative normality.

### Delusional Disorder

**Delusional disorder** is a rare disorder that is characterized by paranoid delusions of grandeur and persecution. It's not a form of schizophrenia, however, and can be distinguished from paranoid schizophrenia because the delusions in delusional disorder are less illogical and are not accompanied by hallucinations. The paranoid schizophrenic might think that he is Napoleon and that he is currently working as a disc jockey for the CIA. The person with delusional disorder, on the other hand, might believe that she can see a truth that no one else has seen and that it's essential that she lead Americans away from reliance on machines. The delusions are more subtle and more believable.

Often it's the believability of these delusions that makes them so dangerous. The Reverend Jim Jones was a frightening case in point. Jones was a minister who had an impressive record of working for the poor when he came to believe that he was a prophet of God, perhaps even a new Messiah. He convinced a large number of people of the truth of his delusion and founded a new religious sect. When he began to feel that his sect was being persecuted by the government, he took his followers to the South American country of Guyana and founded the People's Temple Jonestown Settlement. There, he ruled as an absolute master over his flock, at one point decreeing that only he was fit to have sex with and impregnate the women of Jonestown. When a task force from the

Aftermath of the mass suicide at Jonestown. How do cultlike groups recruit new devotees?

Cult leader David Koresh's refusal to surrender a stockpile of illegal weapons eventually led to the death of Koresh and many of his followers.

**disorganized schizophrenia**
A subtype of schizophrenia characterized by shallow silliness, extreme social withdrawal, and fragmented delusions and hallucinations.

**catatonic schizophrenia**
(kat″ah-ton′ik) A subtype of schizophrenia in which the individual spends long periods in an inactive, statuelike state.

**delusional disorder**
A nonschizophrenic disorder characterized by delusions of grandeur and persecution that are more logical than those of paranoid schizophrenics in the absence of hallucinations.

United States flew to Jonestown to investigate rumors of human rights violations, his followers killed members of that group. Realizing that trouble was ahead and believing that he had the wisdom of God, Jones ordered all of his followers to commit suicide by drinking a poison that was always on hand for just such a situation. Believing that they were told to take their lives by the new Messiah, hundreds of men, women, and children drank the poison and died.

The man who took the name David Koresh and created a religious community during the 1990s in Waco, Texas, also exhibited qualities that suggested that he may have had delusional disorder. His alleged religious delusions, the physical abuse of the children living in his compound, and the collection of a massive and illegal arsenal of weapons may have set the stage for the confrontation that killed many of his followers. Individuals with delusional disorder are not always dangerous, but they can be when they act on their delusions.

## ● Personality Disorders

**personality disorders**
Psychological disorders that are believed to result from personalities that developed improperly during childhood.

**schizoid personality disorder**
(skiz'oid) A personality disorder characterized by blunted emotions, lack of interest in social relationships, and withdrawal into a solitary existence.

**antisocial personality disorder**
A personality disorder characterized by smooth social skills and a lack of guilt about violating social rules and laws and taking advantage of others.

To this point, we have been talking about psychological problems that develop in individuals who were once considered to be normal. To oversimplify the case, schizophrenia and the other disorders that we have considered are "breakdowns" in relatively normal persons. In contrast, the **personality disorders** discussed in this section are believed to result from personalities that developed improperly in the first place.

A number of personality disorders differ widely from one another but share several characteristics: (a) All personality disorders begin early in life; (b) they are disturbing to the person or to others; and (c) they are very difficult to treat. We will first look at two very different personality disorders to provide examples of this type of problem, then will provide brief descriptions of the other personality disorders.

### Schizoid Personality Disorder

The suffix *-oid* means "like"—hence, *schizoid personality disorder* is like schizophrenia, particularly in that blunted emotions and social withdrawal are exhibited. Unlike true schizophrenia, however, this condition is not characterized by serious cognitive disturbances.

Individuals with **schizoid personality disorder** have little or no desire to have friends and indeed are not interested in even casual social contact. They are classic "loners." Usually, they are very shy as children but are not abnormally withdrawn until later childhood or adolescence. Gradually, they seem to lose interest in friends, family, and social activities and retreat more and more into a solitary existence.

They display little emotion and appear cold and aloof. Later in life, people with schizoid personality disorder often lose interest in personal appearance, hygiene, and other polite social conventions. Often they do not work, and they may even fall into homelessness or work as streetwalking prostitutes.

### Antisocial Personality Disorder

People with antisocial personality disorder frequently violate social laws and rules, while feeling little guilt about it. The disorder begins in childhood, when the person is usually highly aggressive.

Individuals with **antisocial personality disorder** have a personality disorder quite different from the schizoid group. They frequently violate social rules and laws, take advantage of others, and feel little guilt about it. These individuals often have smooth social skills: They are sweet-talking con artists who are very likable at first. But they experience great difficulties in maintaining close personal relationships. They enter into marriages and other intimate relationships easily, but they tend to break up quickly.

People with antisocial personalities have a low tolerance for frustration. They act on impulse, lose their tempers quickly, and lie easily and skillfully. They are often hardened criminals. In childhood, they are often bullies who fight, lie, cheat, steal, and are truant from school. They blame others for their misdeeds, feel picked on by their parents and teachers, and never seem to learn from their mistakes.

Individuals with antisocial personality disorder are often unemotional and guiltless—they are calm, cool characters. They are highly uncomfortable, however, when they are kept from excitement. They have an abnormal need for stimulation, novelty, and thrills. Because many turn to alcohol and drugs for excitement, they frequently become addicts. The primary harmfulness of the antisocial personality disorder is in the damage that is done to others. Individuals with antisocial personality disorder often leave a trail of victims—victims of their lies, their crimes, their violent outbursts, and their broken intimate relationships.

The case of antisocial personality disorder described below illustrates these problems well:

> Donald's misbehavior as a child took many forms including lying, cheating, petty theft, and the bullying of smaller children. As he grew older he became more and more interested in sex, gambling, and alcohol. When he was 14 he made crude sexual advances toward a younger girl, and when she threatened to tell her parents he locked her in a shed. It was about 16 hours before she was found. Donald at first denied knowledge of the incident, later stating that she had seduced him and that the door must have locked itself. He expressed no concern for the anguish experienced by the girl and her parents, nor did he give any indication that he felt morally culpable for what he had done.
>
> When he was 17, Donald left the boarding school, forged his father's name to a large check, and spent about a year traveling around the world. He apparently lived well, using a combination of charm, physical attractiveness, and false pretenses to finance his way. During subsequent years he held a succession of jobs, never staying at any one for more than a few months. Throughout this period he was charged with a variety of crimes, including theft, drunkenness in a public place, assault, and many traffic violations. In most cases he was either fined or given a light sentence.
>
> His sexual experiences were frequent, casual, and callous. When he was 22 he married a 41-year-old woman whom he had met in a bar. Several other marriages followed, all bigamous. In each case the pattern was the same: he would marry someone on impulse, let her support him for several months, and then leave. (Lahey & Ciminero, 1980, pp. 326–327)

## Other Personality Disorders

The following are brief descriptions of the other eight types of personality disorders listed in *DSM-IV*. Be careful not to diagnose yourself or your friends while reading this list. The pattern must be extreme and consistent to qualify for a diagnosis.

1. *Schizotypal personality disorder:* few friendships, suspiciousness, strange ideas, such as belief that his or her mind can be read by others and that messages are being received in strange ways

2. *Paranoid personality disorder:* high degree of suspiciousness and mistrust of others, extreme irritability and sensitivity, coldness and lack of tender feelings

3. *Histrionic personality disorder:* self-centered, frequently seeking to be the center of attention, manipulating others through exaggerated expression of emotions and difficulties, superficially charming and seductive but lacking genuine concern for others, frequent angry outbursts

4. *Narcissistic personality disorder:* unrealistic sense of self-importance, preoccupied with fantasies of future success, requires constant attention and praise, reacts very negatively to criticism or is indifferent to criticism, exploits others, feels entitled to special consideration, lack of genuine concern for others

5. *Borderline personality disorder:* impulsive and unpredictable, unstable personal relationships, angry, almost constantly needs to be with others, lack of clear identity, feelings of emptiness

6. *Avoidant personality disorder:* extreme shyness or social withdrawal in spite of a desire for friendships, extremely sensitive to rejection, very low self-esteem

7. ***Dependent personality disorder:*** passive dependence on others for support and decisions; has low self-esteem, and puts needs of others before self

8. ***Obsessive-compulsive personality disorder:*** perfectionistic, dominating, poor ability to express affection, excessive devotion to work, indecisive when faced with major decisions

## Review

Major depression involves one or more episodes of this negative mood state. These episodes range from mild to severe, with severe episodes sometimes being accompanied by bizarre perceptions and beliefs that distort reality. In bipolar disorder, the episodes of depression alternate irregularly with periods of the mood disturbance known as mania. Although this is an intensely pleasurable state, it's harmful in that it can lead to financial difficulties, can destroy personal relationships, and can often be accompanied by reality-distorting perceptions and beliefs.

Schizophrenia is a broad range of psychotic disorders characterized by disturbances of cognition that grossly distort reality, by distortions of emotions, and by withdrawal from social relationships. There are three major subtypes of schizophrenia. Paranoid schizophrenia is characterized by delusions of grandeur and persecution, often accompanied by hallucinations. Disorganized schizophrenia resembles paranoid schizophrenia but is typified by even more fragmented cognition and by shallow, silly emotions. Catatonic schizophrenia is quite different from the other types, being marked by stupors in which the individual may maintain postures for long periods of time. Biological factors—genetics, cortical deterioration, and abnormal prenatal development—are believed to be important in the origins of schizophrenia, but stress may be the immediate cause that triggers episodes. Delusional disorder is characterized by delusions that are less bizarre and more believable than in paranoid schizophrenia. Because they are more believable, persons with delusional disorder often convince many others that they have divine powers or are important religious figures, often with tragic results.

Whereas other kinds of psychological disorders are thought to result from the "breakdown" of a normal personality, personality disorders are thought to result from faulty personality development during childhood. These disorders begin early in life, are disturbing to the individual or to others, and are difficult to treat. For example, individuals with schizoid personality disorder are very shy children who increasingly lose interest in social relationships as they grow older. Eventually, they lose interest in proper dress and social conditions, display little emotion, and rarely hold regular jobs. Antisocial personality disorder is characterized by rule-violating behavior as a child that develops into irresponsibility, dishonesty, and violence as an adult. Such individuals are often con artists who are smooth and likable at first but who have great difficulties maintaining normal relationships. They also have an abnormal need for stimulation and do not seem to learn from punishment.

## Check Your Learning

To be sure that you have learned the key points from the preceding section, cover the list of correct answers and try to answer each question. If you give an incorrect answer to any question, return to the page given next to the correct answer to see why your answer was not correct.

1. The individual experiencing _____ is deeply unhappy, finds little pleasure in life, and experiences other symptoms such as sleeping and eating problems and loss of energy.

    a) hypochondriasis

    b) major depression

    c) delusional disorder

    d) somatoform pain disorders

2. In the condition known as _____, periods of mania alternate irregularly with periods of severe depression.

   a)   major depression          c)   unipolar depression

   b)   mania disorder            d)   bipolar disorder

3. The three major areas of abnormality in schizophrenia are (a) _____;
   (b) _____; and (c) _____.

4. Strange and false perceptual experiences are termed _____.

   a)   delusions                 c)   hallucinations

   b)   paranoia                  d)   social withdrawal

5. The type of schizophrenia characterized by stupor and "waxy flexibility" is
   called _____.

   a)   catatonic                 c)   disorganized

   b)   paranoid                  d)   stuporous

6. _____ personality disorder is similar to schizophrenia, particularly
   in that blunted emotions and social withdrawal are exhibited, but unlike
   true schizophrenia, this condition is not characterized by serious cognitive
   disturbances.

   a)   Antisocial                c)   Dependent

   b)   Schizoid                  d)   Histrionic

---

1. What are some possible explanations for the higher incidence of major depression in women?

2. Why do you think personality disorders are generally difficult to treat?

**Thinking Critically
about Psychology**

---

**Correct Answers:   1. b** (p. 555),   **2. d** (p. 557),   **3.** delusions and hallucinations; disorganized thinking, emotions and behavior; and reduced enjoyment and interests (p. 560),   **4. c** (p. 560),   **5. a** (p. 561),   **6. b** (p. 562).

# application of psychology

## Psychology and Civil Liberties

The goal of clinical psychology, psychiatry, and the other mental health professions is to help persons with mental disorders. In most cases, this means offering services to persons who come to the office or hospital and request professional services. In other cases, mental health professionals play more of an activist role. I am never more proud to be a psychologist than when I see members of my profession attempting to prevent abnormal behavior in the community, offering services to the indigent, and attempting to bring a scientific perspective to debates about important social issues. No mental health profession does enough in these areas, but these efforts are often significant.

In some cases, these outreach efforts are relatively uncomplicated matters. If enough psychologists and psychiatrists volunteer their time, and if funding can be obtained from public or private sources to rent space and pay the heating bill, it is a simple matter to set up a free clinic in an area where homeless persons live. As long as the persons who receive services voluntarily seek them, there is no conflict with the laws that protect civil liberties. In other cases, the attempt to provide assistance raises difficult legal and ethical issues.

In this section, we will discuss two important social issues to which psychology and psychiatry have recently turned their attention: homelessness and physician-assisted suicide. We will see that psychological concepts lie at the heart of these complicated issues. We will also see that important questions concerning civil liberties must be resolved before psychology will be able to play an effective role.

## Abnormal Psychology and Homelessness

It has become commonplace in large cities in the United States to see homeless people sleeping on heating vents next to their bags of belongings. Who are these unfortunate persons? How

Many homeless people want psychiatric or psychological help. However, some mental health professionals argue that the right of some homeless people to refuse treatment must be respected as well.

have they fallen between the cracks in the world's most affluent society?

The primary factors associated with the increases in homelessness are government policies that have greatly reduced the amount of low-cost housing available to the poor, old-fashioned prejudice against ethnic minorities, and changes in vagrancy laws that, in many cases, give people the legal right to be homeless (to sleep on the street, to panhandle, etc.). Another reason for the increase in homeless persons is the inability of psychiatric hospitals and mental health centers to provide adequate services due to massive cuts in funding.

Most homeless persons—but certainly not all—have serious psychological disorders. As funding for mental health service programs is cut, the number of the homeless rises. A study of homeless individuals in inner-city Los Angeles (Koegel, Burnam, & Farr, 1988) found 62.2 percent to have a serious chronic mental disorder and/or alcohol or drug dependence. In the same city, very high rates of symptoms of schizophrenia were found among homeless adolescents (Mundy, Robertson, Robertson, & Greenblatt, 1990). A similar study in New York (Susser, Struening, & Conner, 1989) found serious

mental and substance abuse disorders in 71 percent of homeless men.

We can see the role played by mental disorders in the true stories of Karen and Kevin, two homeless persons in New York City (Brosnahan & Giffen, 1993). In the words of 38-year-old Karen, "I was one of those people you see on street corners screaming at imaginary people, completely out of my mind." She was homeless for 13 years, periodically being treated in mental hospitals. But she was lucky and found her way into a program that provided consistent medication and therapy and found her affordable housing. As a result, Karen has been employed almost continuously for the past 3 years and has regained custody of her 14-year-old son.

Contrast her story to that of Kevin McKiever, the homeless man who was charged in 1991 with murdering a former Radio City Rockette with a knife. He had gone to Bellevue Psychiatric Hospital a few weeks before the stabbing, seeking treatment, but he was turned away because the hospital had no openings in its underfunded community-care program. Between 1975 and 1991, 52 persons were pushed in front of subway trains in New York by strangers, mostly by psychotic homeless persons

# Therapies

## PROLOGUE

David had always been a neat and orderly person. During his first session with the therapist, he described with a half-hearted smile an incident in which he slipped and fell in mud on the way to his elementary school and returned home sobbing. But David's cleanliness caused only minor problems until his daughter was diagnosed with pinworms. David became intensely anxious when he heard the doctor describe how pinworms are spread through their eggs and recommend that the clothes of everyone in the family be boiled to prevent contagion.

David immediately went home and boiled the family's clothes and sheets. After he finished, he washed his hands. But as soon as he did, he thought that there might still be pinworm eggs on them and he washed them again. Soon David began worrying about germs, dirt, and feces that might be on his hands. Within days, he was washing his hands 200 times a day.

David's worst times were at night: He would lie in bed after washing his hands and try to resist the urge to get up and wash them again, only to fail over and over. When his wife became worried about his sanity, and his hands began to crack and bleed because of the constant washing, he decided to contact a therapist (based on Prochaska, 1984, pp. 268–271).

David had developed a form of abnormal behavior called obsessive-compulsive disorder. We will see in this chapter that, fortunately, several forms of treatment are effective for this and other psychological problems. One remedy for obsessive-compulsive disorder that often helps is medication, but a simple form of psychological therapy is also effective. In this therapy, the person agrees to be prevented from washing and to endure the anxiety that being unable to wash produces. In time, the anxiety usually drops to normal levels if the individual does not give in to the urge to wash (Baxter & others, 1992; Piacentini, 1999).

Psychotherapy is a process of people helping people. In psychotherapy, a trained professional seeks to help a person with a psychological problem by using methods based on psychological theories of the nature of the problem. These therapy methods include everyday activities such as asking questions, making suggestions, and demonstrating alternative ways of behaving, but psychotherapy differs from commonsense attempts to help because of the theories that determine what is asked and what is suggested. Several different forms of psychotherapy are based on the theories of personality that we studied in chapter 12.

Psychoanalysts feel that abnormal behavior is the result of unconscious conflicts among the id, ego, and superego. These conflicts remain hidden from consciousness because the ego and superego see them as dangerous and block them out. The process of psychoanalysis, then, is a process of relaxing the censorship exerted by the conscious mind and bringing unconscious conflicts into awareness, where they can be intelligently resolved. Because the contents of the unconscious are revealed only in disguised, symbolic ways, however, the psychoanalyst must help the individual interpret glimpses of the hidden side of the mind.

## Key Terms

psychotherapy 572

psychoanalysis 573

free association 574

dream interpretation 575

resistance 575

transference 575

catharsis 576

interpersonal psychotherapy 576

client-centered psychotherapy 580

reflection 580

Gestalt therapy 581

behavior therapy 583

systematic desensitization 583

social skills training 584

assertiveness training 585

cognitive therapy 588

feminist psychotherapy 592

group therapy 593

family therapy 593

drug therapy 595

electroconvulsive therapy (ECT) 596

psychosurgery 596

Humanistic psychologists also believe that the goal of psychotherapy is to help the person achieve greater self-awareness, but in ways that differ from those of psychoanalysts. Humanists believe that feelings that conflict with a person's self-concept are often denied conscious awareness. The humanistic psychotherapist seeks to help the person allow this information into his or her consciousness and thus achieve fuller self-awareness.

Behavior therapy is an approach to psychotherapy that is associated with the social learning view of personality. Because psychological problems are believed to be the result of unfortunate learning experiences, the behavior therapist plays the role of a teacher helping the person *unlearn* abnormal ways of behavior. Cognitive therapy is a related approach to therapy that is also based on social learning theory. Cognitive therapists believe that we have learned illogical ways of thinking that cause abnormal behavior. They attempt to change these faulty cognitions primarily by pointing out their irrationality.

Help for abnormal behavior is not delivered only in one-to-one psychotherapy, however. It's sometimes provided in the form of group or family therapy, and it often takes the form of medication and other kinds of medical treatment. ■

## Definition of Psychotherapy

**psychotherapy**
(sī-kō-ther′ah-pē) A form of therapy in which a trained professional uses methods based on psychological theories to help a person with psychological problems.

People with the serious kinds of psychological problems described in chapter 14 generally need professional help. Many forms of help are available for psychological disorders from psychologists, psychiatrists, clinical social workers, and counselors. In this chapter, the major forms of therapy are described and related to the differing theories of personality (chapter 12) and differing views of abnormal behavior (chapter 14).

In general terms, **psychotherapy** can be defined as a specialized process in which a trained professional uses psychological methods to help a person with psychological problems. The term *psychological methods* can refer to almost any kind of human interaction (such as talking or demonstrating) that is based on a psychological theory of the problem, but it does *not* include medical treatment methods such as medication.

Different forms of psychotherapy associated with psychoanalytic, humanistic, and social learning theories of personality involve very different psychological methods. The approach to psychotherapy associated with social learning theory, known as behavior therapy, views the process of helping as a form of teaching. The therapist helps the person learn not to engage in harmful behaviors and to learn adaptive behaviors to take their place. The approaches to psychotherapy associated with psychoanalytic and humanistic views of personality see their goal as providing insight—that is, bringing feelings (or conflicts of information) of which the person is unaware into conscious awareness. Although the methods of psychoanalysis and humanistic therapy differ greatly, they both view the therapist not as a teacher but as a catalyst, an agent who makes change possible but does not actually cause or enter into the change. Therapies that strive for increased awareness view the person with problems as the agent of his or her own improvement.

## Ethical Standards for Psychotherapy

The relationship between client and psychotherapist is a unique one. The patient divulges large amounts of personal information in an emotion-laden setting and places her or his future in the hands of the psychotherapist. Because this places the therapist in a position of power relative to the client, it's essential that the highest ethical standards be followed in the practice of psychotherapy. The following discussion of ethical principles is based on the policies developed by the American Psychological Association (1990, 1993) and the Association for Advancement of Behavior Therapy (1978).

Psychotherapy is considered to be ethical only under the following circumstances:

1. The goals of treatment must be carefully considered with the client. These goals should be in the best interest of the client and society and they must be fully understood by the client.

2. The choices for alternative treatment methods should be carefully considered.

3. The therapist must only treat problems that she or he is qualified to treat. No therapist is trained to use all forms of therapy or to handle all types of problems (adults, children, marital problems, etc.). Therefore, the therapist must refer cases that fall outside his or her expertise to qualified therapists.

4. The effectiveness of treatment must be evaluated in some way. The best way of doing this is to use meaningful measures of the problem and progress in treating it.

5. The rules and laws regarding the confidentiality of all information obtained about the client during treatment must be fully explained to the client. Under most circumstances it is unethical and illegal for the therapist to reveal any information about the person (even the fact that a person is a client in therapy) to anyone without the written permission of the client. However, there are exceptions to that rule. First, sometimes other psychologists in a practice will cover for the therapist in emergencies and will need to learn about the client. Second, if the therapist is still in training and being supervised by a licensed therapist, it is essential that the client be told of that fact and the name of the supervisor. Third, in some circumstances regarding court matters, the courts can require the therapist to reveal confidential information. Fourth, if the therapist learns that the client is in immediate danger of harm or of harming anyone else, the therapist is obligated to report that information to the proper authorities.

Psychotherapists must respect the rules and laws regarding the confidentiality of information about their clients.

6. The therapist must not use the power of the intense relationship with the client to exploit the client in sexual or other ways. Sexual or romantic intimacies with clients have long been strictly forbidden, but, in contrast to novels and movies in which therapists and current or former clients fall in love and marry, ethical regulations even forbid romantic or sexual relationships with former clients under virtually all circumstances. Sexual harassment of clients is similarly strictly forbidden.

7. The therapist must treat human beings with dignity and must understand and respect differences based on gender, ethnicity, sexual orientation, and other sociocultural factors. To the greatest extent possible, therapists must understand and respect human differences and not try to sway clients to their own beliefs and ways. For example, this means that a traditional male therapist must not try to influence a woman who identifies with the feminist philosophy to adopt a more subservient feminine role. Similarly, a therapist who believes that homosexuality is immoral must not attempt to convince a homosexual who is comfortable with her or his sexual orientation to change. If the therapist cannot respect the beliefs and ways of the client, the therapist must refer that person to another therapist.

## ● Psychoanalysis

**Psychoanalysis** is the approach to psychotherapy founded by Sigmund Freud. It's based on Freud's belief that the root of all psychological problems is unconscious conflicts among the id, ego, and superego. Conflicts inevitably exist among these three competing forces, but they can cause problems if they get out of hand. If too much of the

**psychoanalysis**
(sī′kō-ah-nal′i-sis) A method of psychotherapy developed by Freud based on his belief that the root of all psychological problems is unconscious conflicts among the id, the ego, and the superego.

A patient and therapist in a session of psychoanalysis.

energy of the superego and ego is devoted to holding the selfish desires of the id in check, or, if these prohibitions are weak and the id threatens to break free, psychological disturbances result. According to Freud, these conflicts must be brought into consciousness if they are to be solved.

Bringing unconscious conflicts into consciousness is not an easy matter, though. Recall from chapter 12 that the id is completely unconscious. Even the sexual and aggressive motives that we consciously experience have been transformed by the ego into safe and socially acceptable versions of the id's true desires. According to Freud, the ego operates as if the raw, selfish desires of the id were too dangerous to allow into consciousness, so it works diligently to dam up the id in the recesses of our unconscious mind. Special therapy methods must be used, therefore, to allow information about unconscious id conflicts to slip past the censorship of the ego.

It's generally possible to bring information out of the unconscious only when the ego's guard is temporarily relaxed, and even then, the id is able to reveal itself only in disguised, symbolic forms. Thus, the job of the psychoanalyst is (a) to create conditions in which the censorship of the ego is relaxed and (b) to interpret the disguised, symbolic revelations of the unconscious mind to the patient.

## Techniques of Psychoanalytic Psychotherapy

Most contemporary psychoanalysts do not practice an orthodox version of psychoanalysis but, rather, practice versions based on the revisions of Jung, Adler, Horney, and more contemporary psychoanalysts. Still, many of the specific techniques of therapy used by Freud are still in use today. These include free association, dream interpretation, interpretation of resistance, and interpretation of transference.

### Free Association

**free association**
A tool used by Freud in which the patient is encouraged to talk about whatever comes to mind, allowing the contents of the unconscious mind to slip past the censorship of the ego.

Freud's primary tool of therapy was the method of **free association.** In this method, the individual talks in a loose and undirected way about whatever comes to mind. No thought or feeling is to be withheld, no matter how illogical, trivial, unpleasant, or silly it might seem. Freud hoped that this technique would lead to a "turning off" of the intellectual control of the ego and allow for glimpses of the unconscious. Occasionally, as the mind wanders, the id slips out. To make this more likely to happen, Freud had his patients lie on a couch, facing the ceiling. He sat out of sight, behind them, so they would feel like they were talking to themselves rather than revealing forbidden information to another.

Incidentally, contemporary research suggests that Freud's choice of a reclining position for his patients may have had an important effect on his approach to psychotherapy. After working with many patients, Freud came to believe that he must help the patient achieve insight primarily about events that happened in childhood. Interestingly, Pope (1978) found that when individuals are asked to let their "mind wander" aloud, reclining people speak significantly more about the past than people who are sitting. Freud's choice of a reclining posture for his patients may have led them to focus on the past and led him to think of the past as being of prime importance in therapy.

The "glimpses of the unconscious" revealed during free association have hidden, symbolic meaning that must be translated or interpreted to the patient by the psychoanalyst. For example,

In traditional psychoanalysis, the therapist sits out of the patient's sight. Freud had his patients lie on a couch while he sat in a chair to the left.

the patient might mention during the course of free association that he wanted to go hunting with his father but that he never asked him to go hunting because he was afraid that his father was too old and might get hurt. To the psychoanalyst, this statement might be about phallic symbols (guns) and the son's unresolved Oedipus conflict (see chapter 12, pages 470–471) that has left him with an unacceptable desire to shoot his father. When interpreted to the patient, Freud believed, this information about the unconscious would help the person consciously solve his or her problems.

### Dream Interpretation

**Dream interpretation** was used by Freud in much the same manner as free association. As we mentioned in chapter 5, the obvious, or manifest, content of dreams is believed by psychoanalysts to symbolically mask the true, or latent, content of dreams. By asking patients to recall dreams, Freud believed he had obtained another "window" on the unconscious.

For example, a recurrent dream of an adolescent boy in which he was drifting through a slimy swamp on a raft, reaching down repeatedly into the dirty water and pulling up shoes might have no meaning at all to the adolescent. The psychoanalyst might translate it to mean that the boy was experiencing conflicts over his heterosexual desires. Shoes are commonly taken to symbolize vaginas in psychoanalytic thinking, and the dirty, forbidding water from which he was attempting to possess these vaginas might represent his guilt feelings about sex.

### Interpretation of Resistance

Freud also placed heavy emphasis on the interpretation of what he called resistance in therapy. **Resistance** is any form of opposition of the patient to the process of psychoanalysis. Resistance can occur in two ways. It might take vague forms, such as missing appointments with the therapist or questioning the value of psychoanalysis. Or it might be a specific resistance to the interpretations of the therapist. In either case, resistance meant to Freud that he had located a conflict in the patient that was so laden with anxiety that the patient wanted to avoid talking about it. This avoidance of a topic made Freud all the more interested in pursuing it.

Angrily telling a psychoanalyst that he or she is wrong for suggesting that you ever wanted to have casual sex with a person you did not love may convince your therapist that this is something that you actually want to do but that you consider morally unacceptable. To give you better insight into your own motives, your psychoanalyst might interpret this resistance to you. The analyst would believe that if you erroneously continue to think you do not want casual sex, you will not be able to understand and deal with the anxiety that you experience. If, on the other hand, you become aware that you do want casual sex but that you feel that it would be immoral to do so, you can make more rational, informed choices about your behavior.

### Interpretation of Transference

The relationship that forms between patient and therapist can also be a source of information about the unconscious to the psychoanalyst. Because the patient comes to the therapist in need of help, reveals a great deal of private information, and receives acceptance and support, it's not surprising that a rather intense relationship often develops. This relationship is not like the one you have with your dentist, but more like a close parent-child relationship.

Because of the intensity of the relationship in therapy, psychoanalysts believe that the kind of relationship the patient has with the therapist reveals a great deal about the way the patient relates to his or her parents and other significant authority figures. Psychoanalysts call this phenomenon **transference.** When patients repeatedly ask for reassurance that they will not be dropped as clients, argue about fees, or make sexual

"Mr. Prentice is *not* your father. Alex Binster is *not* your brother. The anxiety you feel is *not* genuine. Dr. Froelich will return from vacation September 15th. Hang on."
© The New Yorker Collection 1973 Lee Lorenz from cartoonbank.com. All Rights Reserved.

**dream interpretation**
A method developed by Freud in which the symbols of the manifest content of dreams that are recalled by the patient are interpreted to reveal their latent content.

**resistance**
Any form of patient opposition to the process of psychoanalysis.

**transference**
(trans-fer′ens) The phenomenon in psychoanalysis in which the patient comes to feel and act toward the therapist in ways that resemble how he or she feels and acts toward other significant adults.

advances, they are believed to be transferring to the therapist feelings that they have for other significant adults in their lives. That is, they are feeling and acting toward the therapist in the same basic ways that they feel and act toward their parents, employers, and so on. When interpreted to the patients, psychoanalysts believe that transference can serve as another valuable source of insight.

### Catharsis

In addition to the interpretation of symbolic revelations of unconscious conflicts, psychoanalysis allows the patient to release some of the emotion that is pent up with unconscious conflicts. All forms of psychotherapy can be very emotional experiences that at times involve talking about highly upsetting topics. Letting these emotions out—a process psychoanalysts call **catharsis**—provides a temporary relief from discomfort. Catharsis is not a technique of psychoanalysis; rather, it is one of its benefits.

This relief does not solve problems in and of itself, but it does make the patient feel better. Catharsis may facilitate the process of psychoanalysis, however, because a patient who feels better will generally be better able to make more intelligent decisions about discoveries from the unconscious.

### Excerpt from Psychoanalytic Psychotherapy

In the following excerpt from a session of psychoanalytic psychotherapy, the therapist attempts to get the client to reinterpret his anxiety:

CLIENT: We had a salesmen's meeting, and a large group of us were cramped together in a small room and they turned out the lights to show some slides, and I got so jumpy and anxious I couldn't stand it.

THERAPIST: So what happened?

C: I just couldn't stand it. I was sweating and shaking, so I got up and left, and I know I'll be called on the carpet for walking out.

T: You became so anxious and upset that you couldn't stand being in the room even though you knew that walking out would get you into trouble.

C: Yeah. . . . What could have bothered me so much to make me do a dumb thing like that?

T: You know, we've talked about other times in your life when you've become upset in close quarters with other men, once when you were in the army and again in your dormitory at college.

C: That's right, and it was the same kind of thing again.

T: And, if I'm correct, this has never happened to you in a group of men and women together, no matter how closely you've been cramped together.

C: Uh. . . . Yes, that's right.

T: So it appears that something especially about being physically close to other men, and especially in the dark, makes you anxious, as if you're afraid bad things might happen in that kind of situation.

C: (Pause) I think you're right about that . . . and I know I'm not physically afraid of other men. Do you think I might get worried about something homosexual taking place?[*]

---

[*]Source: I. B. Weiner, *Principles of Psychotherapy*. Copyright © 1975 John Wiley & Sons. This material is used by permission of John Wiley & Sons, Inc.

### Interpersonal Psychotherapy for Depression

In recent years, a new form of psychotherapy, known as **interpersonal psychotherapy,** has emerged from the psychoanalytic tradition, particularly the theories of neo-Freudian Harry Stack Sullivan (Brody & others, 2001; Harkness & others, 2002; Klerman &

---

**catharsis**
The release of emotional energy related to unconscious conflicts.

**interpersonal psychotherapy**
A form of psychological therapy, based on the theories of neo-Freudian Harry Stack Sullivan, that focuses on the accurate identification and communication of feelings and the improvement of current social relationships.

Weissman, 1993; Weissman, 1999). As discussed in chapter 12, contemporary neo-Freudian theories emphasize the importance of interpersonal relationships in our lives more than unconscious sexual motivation. Therefore, interpersonal therapy is quite different from classical Freudian psychoanalysis. Interpersonal psychotherapy ignores unconscious motivation, minimizes discussion of the past, and does not involve interpretation of the individual's relationship with the therapist (transference). Instead, interpersonal psychotherapy focuses on the "here and now." Interpersonal psychotherapy is a brief form of psychotherapy that is usually completed in 12 to 16 weeks. Unlike other forms of Freudian therapies, interpersonal therapy is highly focused and structured, with therapists following detailed treatment manuals.

To date, interpersonal therapy has been developed only to treat depression. In general, interpersonal therapists believe that depression can be treated by improving our understanding of our feelings and improving how we relate and communicate to the important people in our lives. Interpersonal therapists believe that there are *four kinds of problems that cause depression:*

1. Grief over the loss of an important relationship through the breakup of a relationship, a divorce, or the death of a loved one

2. Conflicts with people who are significant to us

3. Life events that are stressful or that create threats to our self-esteem

4. Lack of social skills for establishing healthy interpersonal relationships

How does interpersonal therapy attempt to deal with depression created by these four causes? In interpersonal psychotherapy, therapists attempt to reach *seven goals* to treat depression:

1. Help the individual feel that the therapist understands his or her feelings and considers them to be important

2. Help the individual understand how his or her feelings are related to what is going on in his or her life, particularly to his or her current social relationships. The interpersonal therapist allows discussion of past social relationships (e.g., relationships with parents, former romantic partners, etc.) only to reach an understanding of how "emotional baggage" from past relationships can influence current relationships

3. Help the individual learn to express his or her feelings to other persons in constructive ways

4. Identify relationships that are too unhealthy to fix, end them appropriately, and move on to healthier relationships with others

5. Help the individual develop a sense of mastery of the new roles that are created by life events, such as dating again after divorce or entering a new occupation

6. Improve the individual's skills for creating healthy new relationships and maintaining them

7. Help the individual develop an optimistic focus on current opportunities for change instead of on the past

To reach these goals, the therapist keeps every session focused on the individual's feelings, his or her current life circumstances, and current options for change. For example, Charles has felt very depressed for the past few months. He has a stable job as a waiter, and he has many friends and a long-term relationship with a woman whom he hopes to marry. For the past few months, he has been having many fights with his girlfriend, who recently entered college. The interpersonal psychotherapy sessions may reveal that Charles feels unimportant to his girlfriend, now that she studies during most evenings and weekends and has less time for him than in the past. When they do have time to spend together, they often fight because Charles treats her with anger and sarcasm. The therapist would first help Charles see that his feelings involve worry that he is no longer important to her, rather than anger that she has entered college. Then the therapist would help Charles learn to calmly express his feelings of worry to his girlfriend without anger or sarcasm. This would make it easier for her to respond with nurturing and reassurance. These changes, in turn, could be expected to help reduce his feelings of depression.

The most important thing about interpersonal therapy is that it is *effective* in treating depression. A number of large and well-controlled studies have shown that it is at least as effective as the most effective forms of psychotherapy (and more effective than some types of psychotherapy) and is often as effective as antidepressant medication, with far fewer side effects (Klerman & others, 1995; Mufson, Weissman, Moreau, & Garfinkel, 1999; Rosello & Bernal, 1999; Swartz, 1999). Relatively few therapists have been trained to use this new method of psychotherapy, but because it is effective and detailed treatment manuals are available, its availability is increasing rapidly. Because it is effective in a short period of time, the use of interpersonal therapy is advocated by many managed care organizations as an economical way of effectively treating depression (Weissman, 1999).

## Review

Psychoanalysis is the method of psychotherapy based on Freud's theory of personality. The therapist attempts to help the patient by bringing unconscious conflicts into consciousness so they can be intelligently resolved. Because the ego works to block from consciousness the contents of the unconscious mind (including conflicts among the id, ego, and superego), the psychoanalyst must create conditions to relax the censorship of the ego. Even when the unconscious mind reveals itself at these times, however, it does so in disguised, symbolic ways. This means that a second function of the psychoanalyst is to interpret the disguised information revealed during psychoanalysis to the patient. The method most commonly used by the psychoanalyst to relax the ego's censorship is free association. Comments made by the patient during these wandering, unguided conversations are believed to symbolically reveal hidden conflicts. In addition, the psychoanalyst interprets information from dreams, resistance to the process of therapy, and the way the patient acts toward the psychoanalyst (transference) to reveal further the unconscious mind to the patient. Psychoanalysis is believed to provide temporary relief by allowing the patient to vent some of the emotion tied up in unconscious conflicts (catharsis). A new form of psychodynamic psychotherapy, called interpersonal therapy, has been found to be effective in the treatment of depression. Unlike classical psychoanalysis, this form of psychotherapy focuses on the "here and now" and helps the individual accurately identify feelings, communicate feelings constructively, and improve social relationships.

## Check Your Learning

To be sure that you have learned the key points from the preceding section, cover the list of correct answers and try to answer each question. If you give an incorrect answer to any question, return to the page given next to the correct answer to see why your answer was not correct. Remember that these questions cover only some of the important information in this section; it is important that you make up your own questions to check your learning of other facts and concepts.

1. In general terms, _____ can be defined as a specialized process in which a trained professional uses psychological methods to help a person with psychological problems.

2. _____ is based on Freud's belief that the root of all psychological problems is unconscious conflicts among the id, ego, and superego that must be brought into conscious awareness.

a) Behavior therapy          c) Psychoanalysis

b) Client-centered therapy   d) Cognitive therapy

3. Freud's primary tool of therapy was the method of _____, in which the individual talks in a loose and undirected way about whatever comes to mind.

   a) free association          c) dream interpretation

   b) transference              d) resistance

4. _____ describes the release of emotional energy related to unconscious conflicts.

   a) Emotional cleansing       c) Liberation

   b) Catharsis                 d) Outletting

5. The new form of psychotherapy based on neo-Freudian theories that avoids focus on the past and emphasizes the accurate identification of feelings, constructive communication, and improvement of social relationships is called _____.

---

1. Give a brief personality description of the type of patients who you believe would benefit most from psychoanalysis. Would you include women? How about members of ethnic groups different from Freud's?

2. What would you consider to be the strengths of psychoanalysis? What might be its weaknesses?

**Thinking Critically about Psychology**

---

**Correct Answers:** 1. psychotherapy (p. 572), 2. c (p. 573), 3. a (p. 574), 4. b (p. 576), 5. interpersonal psychotherapy (p. 576).

## ● Humanistic Psychotherapy

The humanistic and psychoanalytic schools of thought both believe that the primary goal of therapy is to bring forth feelings of which the individual is unaware into conscious awareness. Recall from chapter 12 that Carl Rogers gives us an alternative way of thinking about feelings and information of which we are not consciously aware. Unlike Freud, Rogers does not believe that we are born with an unconscious mind. Rather, we deny awareness to information and feelings that differ too much from our concepts of self and ideal self (by not symbolizing them).

Using the same example that we used to illustrate Freud's concept of the unconscious, suppose you were a person who wanted casual sex. If your ideal self (the one you think you should ideally be) were the kind of person who would never have casual sex, you might deny conscious awareness to that desire. The desire for casual sex did not arise from an unconscious id, according to Rogers, but the end result is the same: When a feeling is denied awareness, it can create anxiety until it's brought into the open. That is, it creates trouble until the individual achieves full awareness of his or her feelings. Because humanists view full self-awareness as necessary for the complete realization of our inner-directed potential, they speak of the process of therapy in terms of "growth in awareness" rather than insight.

The methods used by humanistic therapists differ considerably from those used in psychoanalytic psychotherapy. A description of methods of humanistic therapy is complicated by the fact that a number of different approaches are grouped together under the name of humanism. We can get a perspective on these therapies, however, by looking at the methods of two leaders of the humanistic psychotherapy movement, Carl Rogers and Fritz Perls.

Carl Rogers (top right) facilitating the discussion during a group therapy session.

## Client-Centered Psychotherapy

Rogers refers to his humanistic approach as **client-centered psychotherapy** (he prefers the term *client* to the more medically oriented term *patient*) because the client, not the therapist, is at the center of the process of psychotherapy (Rogers, 1951). More recently, the term *person-centered psychotherapy* has come into vogue. The emphasis is on the ability of clients to help themselves rather than on the ability of the therapist to help the clients. The job of the therapist in client-centered therapy is not to employ specific therapy techniques or to interpret the client's behavior, but to create an atmosphere that is so emotionally safe for the clients that they will feel free to express to the therapist (and to themselves) the feelings they have denied awareness. Growth in awareness comes not from interpretations but from the client's feeling safe enough to explore hidden emotions in the therapy sessions. Rogers believes that the creation of this safe atmosphere requires three elements from the therapist. The therapist (a) must be warm; (b) must genuinely be able to like the clients and unconditionally accept everything they think, feel, or do without criticism; and (c) must have empathy—an accurate understanding and sharing of the emotions of the client. A number of studies have shown that the degree of warmth and empathy of the therapist is an important determinant of the effectiveness of psychotherapy, even when the method of psychotherapy is not client-centered therapy (Brent & Kolko, 1998; Rounsaville & others, 1987).

The closest thing to a specific "technique" in client-centered therapy is the process of **reflection.** The therapist helps the clients clarify the feelings expressed in their statements by reflecting back the emotions of the client. Sometimes the therapists ask questions, but, other than reflections, client-centered therapists say relatively little in therapy. In particular, they strictly avoid giving advice to clients. They feel that clients can easily learn to solve their own problems after they have gained awareness, but that they will remain dependent on the therapist if the therapist solves their problems for them.

## Excerpt from Client-Centered Psychotherapy

The following is an excerpt from a conversation between humanistic psychologist Carl Rogers and a client, a depressed young man. Notice the complete, nonjudgmental acceptance of the client's feelings.

ROGERS:  Everything's lousy, huh? You feel lousy? (Silence of 39 seconds)

ROGERS:  Want to come in Friday at 12 at the usual time?

CLIENT:  [Yawns and mutters something unintelligible.] (Silence of 48 seconds)

ROGERS:  Just kind of feel sunk way down deep in these lousy, lousy feelings, hm? Is that something like it?

CLIENT:  No.

ROGERS:  No? (Silence of 20 seconds)

CLIENT:  No. I just ain't no good to nobody, never was, and never will be.

ROGERS:  Feeling that now, hm? That you're just no good to yourself, no good to anybody. Just that you're completely worthless, huh? Those really are lousy feelings. Just feel that you're no good at all, hm?

[From a session three days later]

CLIENT:  I just want to run away and die.

**client-centered psychotherapy**
Carl Rogers' approach to humanistic psychotherapy, in which the therapist creates an atmosphere that encourages clients to discover feelings of which they were unaware.

**reflection**
(re-flek'shun) A technique in humanistic psychotherapy in which the therapist reflects the emotions of the client to help clients clarify their feelings.

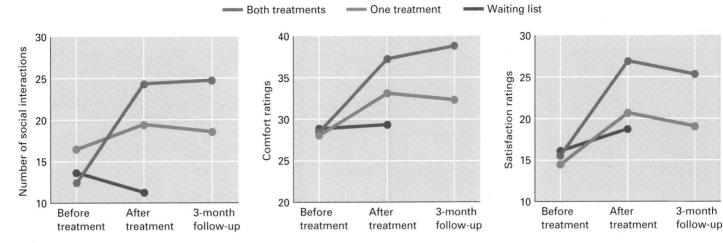

**FIGURE 15.1**

The degree of improvement in three groups of extremely shy individuals. One group received only systematic desensitization; another group received both systematic desensitization and social skills training; and a third group waited to begin treatment until the other two groups were completed.

**Source:** Data from R. F. Cappe and L. E. Alden, "A Comparison of Treatment Strategies for Clients Functionally Impaired by Extreme Shyness and Social Avoidance," *Journal of Consulting and Clinical Psychology,* 54:796–801. Copyright 1986 by the American Psychological Association.

ual constructed a list of social situations that were arranged in order from the least anxiety provoking (e.g., "saying good morning to a waitress in a restaurant") to the most anxiety provoking (e.g., "asking a person for a date"). The person then practiced these social situations with the therapist, beginning with the least anxiety-provoking scenes and working up to the most difficult ones until he or she could perform these role-play scenes with little or no anxiety.

The second group received not only systematic desensitization but also a form of *social skills training* (see the beginning of this section) in which they were taught social skills to make them better conversationalists.

The third group did not receive any treatment during the same period in which the first two treatments were evaluated. Rather, this group, known as the *wait list control group,* was given the better of the other two treatments *after* the experiment was over. This group was used to rule out the unlikely possibility that simply meeting with the therapist about their shyness would be enough to make it go away. In doing so, the researchers could be more confident that it was their treatment that actually made the individuals get better.

The results of the study are shown in figure 15.1. Both treatments resulted in significant improvement in the frequency of social interactions in which the persons engaged, the comfort level (lack of anxiety) that they experienced during social interactions, and the degree of satisfaction that they derived from these social interactions. Furthermore, the group that received both systematic desensitization and social skills training improved the most on all three measures.

Behavior therapists have paid particular attention to the widespread social skill problem of unassertiveness. Many people—both "normal" individuals and people with problems—have a difficult time expressing their true feelings, asking questions, disagreeing, and standing up for their rights. Sometimes these individuals continuously hold their feelings in and let others take advantage of them, partly because other people do not know what they want. In most cases, however, unassertive people keep their feelings inside until they become so angry that they pour them out in an angry outburst.

**Assertiveness training** is used to develop assertive rather than angry ways of expressing feelings to others. This is usually done by role playing, as in other forms of social skills training. For example, the client might initially take the role of a friend who

**assertiveness training**
A method of behavior therapy that teaches individuals assertive rather than passive or aggressive ways of dealing with problematic situations.

asks the therapist for a loan of $50 even though he knows that the therapist is short on money and that he has owed the therapist $60 for the past three months. The therapist would model an assertive way of handling the request ("I wish I could help you, but I don't have enough money to do it, and I really don't think it would be a good idea for me to lend you more money until you're able to pay me back what you already owe me"). Then they would reverse roles and let the client try to handle a similarly difficult situation. After considerable practice with the therapist, the client should possess enough skills and feel comfortable enough to handle real-life situations in an assertive way.

## Excerpt from Behavior Therapy

In the following excerpt from a session of behavior therapy, the therapist is persuading the client to practice behaving in more effective ways in a role-playing session in the therapist's office, so that the therapist can shape and reinforce the more effective behavior. The statements in brackets are comments of the therapist that were not stated during the therapy session.

CLIENT: The basic problem is that I have the tendency to let people step all over me. I don't know why, but I just have difficulty in speaking my mind.

THERAPIST: [My immediate tendency here is to reflect and clarify what the client said, adding a behavioral twist. In paraphrasing what she has already said, I can cast it within a behavioral framework by introducing such terms as *situation, respond,* and *learn*.] So you find yourself in a number of different situations where you don't respond the way you would really like to. And if I understand correctly, you would like to learn how to behave differently.

CLIENT: Yes. But you know, I have tried to handle certain situations differently, but I just don't seem to be able to do so.

THERAPIST: [Not a complete acceptance of my conceptualization, seemingly because she has tried to behave differently in the past and nothing has happened. What I should do, then, is somehow provide some explanation of why previous attempts may have failed, and use this to draw a contrast with a potentially more effective treatment strategy that we'll be using in our sessions.] It's almost as if there is a big gap between the way you react and the way you would like to react.

CLIENT: It seems that way, and I don't know how to overcome it.

THERAPIST: Well, maybe you've tried to do too much too fast in the past, and consequently weren't very successful. Maybe a good way to look at the situation is to imagine yourself at the bottom of a staircase, wanting to get to the top. It's probably too much to ask to get there in one gigantic leap. Perhaps a better way to go about changing your reaction in these situations is to take it one step at a time.

CLIENT: That would seem to make sense, but I'm not sure if I see how that could be done.

THERAPIST: Well, there are probably certain situations in which it would be less difficult for you to assert yourself such as telling your boss that he forgot to pay you for the past four weeks.

CLIENT: (Laughing.) I guess in that situation, I would say something. Although I must admit, I would feel uneasy about it.

THERAPIST: But not as uneasy as if you went in and asked him for a raise.

CLIENT: No. Certainly not.

THERAPIST: So, the first situation would be low on the staircase, whereas the second would be higher up. If you can learn to handle easier situations, then the more difficult ones would present less of a problem. And the only way you can really learn to change your reactions is through practice.

CLIENT: In other words, I really have to go out and actually force myself to speak up more, but taking it a little bit at a time?

THERAPIST: [This seems like an appropriate time to introduce the function of behavior rehearsal. I won't say anything about the specific procedure yet, but instead will talk about it in general terms and maybe increase its appeal by explaining that any failures will not really "count." If the client goes along with the general description of the treatment strategy, she should be more likely to accept the details as I spell them out.] Exactly. And as a way of helping you carry it off in the real-life situation, I think it would be helpful if we reviewed some of these situations and your reactions to them beforehand. In a sense, going through a dry run. It's safer to run through some of these situations here, in that it really doesn't "count" if you don't handle them exactly as you would like to. Also, it can provide you an excellent opportunity to practice different ways of reacting to these situations, until you finally hit on one which you think would be best.

CLIENT: That seems to make sense.

THERAPIST: In fact, we could arrange things so that you can actually rehearse exactly what you would say, and how you would say it.

CLIENT: That sounds like a good idea.*

---

*Excerpt reprinted by permission of the authors from *Clinical Behavior Therapy* by M. R. Goldfried and G. C. Davison. Copyright 1976 Holt, Rinehart & Winston, Inc.

## Review

The approach to psychotherapy associated with the social learning theory of personality is known as behavior therapy. Abnormal behavior is viewed as learned behavior. It's simply behavior that results from inappropriate learning experiences. The role of the behavior therapist is to serve as a teacher who helps the client unlearn abnormal behavior and learn adaptive ways of behaving to take its place. In systematic desensitization, for example, the behavior therapist teaches clients no longer to fear phobic stimuli by first teaching them to relax deeply and then exposing them to graduated versions of the phobic stimulus in their imagination until the full stimulus does not disturb the state of relaxation. In this way, relaxation, rather than fear, becomes the response to the formerly phobic stimulus. Other behavior therapy methods use principles of operant conditioning to teach specific skills.

## Check Your Learning

To be sure that you have learned the key points from the preceding section, cover the list of correct answers and try to answer each question. If you give an incorrect answer to any question, return to the page given next to the correct answer to see why your answer was not correct.

1. A _____ plays the role of teacher, a person who helps the client unlearn abnormal ways of behaving and learn more adaptive ways to take their place.

   a) psychoanalyst
   b) behavior therapist
   c) humanistic therapist
   d) group therapist

2. _____ is a behavior therapy method in which the client is taught not to fear phobic stimuli by learning to relax deeply in the presence of successively more threatening stimuli.

   a) Progressive relaxation training
   b) Meditation
   c) Reflection
   d) Systematic desensitization

3. In _____, people with social deficiencies are taught social skills through operant conditioning.

---

## Thinking Critically about Psychology

1. How could social skills training and graded exposure be used together to create a severe fear of meeting new people?

2. If you needed it, do you think you would prefer graded exposure or systematic desensitization to overcome a fear of heights?

---

Correct Answers: **1.** b (p. 583), **2.** d (p. 583), **3.** social skills training (p. 584).

## ● Cognitive Therapy

**cognitive therapy**
An approach to therapy that teaches individuals new cognitions—adaptive beliefs, expectations, and ways of thinking—to eliminate abnormal emotions and behavior.

**Cognitive therapy** is an important approach to therapy that rests on the assumption that faulty cognitions—maladaptive beliefs, expectations, and ways of thinking—are the cause of abnormal behavior. Cognitive therapy originated in the cognitive emphasis of contemporary social learning theorists (Bandura, 1977; Ellis, 1962) and contemporary psychoanalysts (Kelly, 1955). Because a great deal of carefully designed research has supported the effectiveness of cognitive therapy for anxiety and depression, it has become one of the most widely used therapy approaches.

### Relationship between Cognition and Behavior

Early in the development of behavior therapy, it was assumed that cognitions were relatively unimportant in the origins and treatment of abnormal behavior. For example, if a client were to go to a behavior therapist because she was unassertive, the conversations with the therapist might reveal that she believed (a cognition) that her friends would stop liking her if she expressed her true feelings to them. The behavior therapist would feel that it would be unnecessary to change this faulty belief directly, however. The behavior therapist would assume that if the client were taught assertive ways of expressing feelings, then she would see for herself that her friends still like her and, therefore, would change her faulty cognition herself. The cognitive therapy movement, on the other hand, suggests that behavior therapists can be more effective if they directly teach both more adaptive behavior and cognition.

Moreover, cognitive therapists believe that problems do not always stem from inappropriate overt actions. For example, some socially anxious people behave in appropriate, even charming ways in social situations, but they still experience anxiety because they inaccurately think of themselves as dull, awkward, and unlikable. Trying to modify their already appropriate overt actions would be fruitless in such cases. Instead, it's necessary to modify their maladaptive cognitions.

### Maladaptive Cognitions

Psychologist Albert Ellis (1962; 1999) and psychiatrist Aaron T. Beck (Beck, 1976, 1999; Beck, Rush, Shaw, & Emery, 1979) have described a number of patterns of cognition that they believe contribute greatly to abnormal behavior and emotions.

To better understand the cognitive therapy approach, we should look more closely at one of the most widely used versions, Aaron Beck's cognitive therapy program for depression. Beck believes that depression is caused primarily by the following erroneous patterns of thinking (do not be upset if you see some of your own ways of thinking here—we all think in these erroneous ways to some extent):

1. *Selective abstraction.* Let's say you ask the woman with whom you have had a committed relationship for three years if she has kissed another man since she started dating you. She answers, "Never, not once. I've never even flirted with

Aaron T. Beck.

another man. I'm not blind and I can still tell that a guy is cute, but I'm not romantically interested in anybody but you." Most persons would be reassured by the message of commitment in that statement, but would you go into a raging fit because she said she notices that some other men are attractive? If so, that is selective abstraction—basing your thinking on a small detail taken out of context and given an incorrect meaning.

2. ***Overgeneralization.*** This is the process of reaching a general conclusion based on a few specific bits of evidence. The young scientist who gets a harsh rejection of the first article she submits to a scientific journal is overgeneralizing if she concludes that no journal will ever publish her research.

3. ***Arbitrary inference.*** This is the error of reaching a conclusion based on little or no logical evidence—as the name says, the conclusion is arbitrary. For example, if you were to receive an invitation to have lunch with your boss, would you conclude that the boss was going to gently break the news to you that you will be fired? Some people reason in this arbitrary way, concluding that everything means something bad.

4. ***Magnification/minimization.*** When the guy sitting next to you says that your ears have an interesting point at the top, do you magnify this statement out of proportion? ("No wonder everybody hates me—I have grotesque Mr. Spock ears!") Or, if you receive a heartfelt compliment from a friend, do you minimize it to nothing? ("Lynne just says nice things to me because she feels sorry for me.") These examples illustrate the process of magnification/minimization.

5. ***Personalization.*** Suppose you drove to the beach with your friends and it rained all weekend. Did you become gloomy and really mean it when you complained to your friends, "Nothing ever works out for me—every time I try to have fun it turns into a nightmare!" Some people would falsely conclude that it rained just because they were at the beach. Personalization is the erroneous pattern of reasoning in which external events are seen as being related to you when there is no logical reason for doing so.

6. ***Absolutistic thinking.*** The person who did not have good enough grades to get into medical school but who has made an excellent living as a highly respected hospital administrator tells a former classmate at his 25-year high school reunion, "Ever since college, my life has been a total failure." Although it might be realistic to say that he failed in an important arena, he certainly has not been a total failure. His absolutistic thinking in all-or-nothing terms—either everything is absolutely wonderful or everything is absolutely terrible—is erroneous and maladaptive.

Albert Ellis.

It should come as no surprise that many people who think in these maladaptive ways are miserable because of it. In cognitive therapy, the therapist uses a variety of techniques of persuasion to help the client change her or his faulty patterns of thinking (Kuyken & others, 2001).

Cognitive therapy has been shown to be quite effective with post-traumatic stress disorder (Resick & others, 2002), a variety of anxiety disorders (Barlow, 1996; Borkovec & Costello, 1993; Bruce, Spiegel, Gregg, & Nuzzarello, 1995; Chambless & Gillis, 1993; Heimberg & others, 1998), the eating disorder bulimia (Garner & others, 1993; Thackwray, Smith, Bodfish, & Meyers, 1993), and major depression (Ackerson & others, 1998; Clarkin, Pilkonis, & Magruder, 1996; Ravindran & others, 1999; Simons, Gordon, Thase, & Monroe, 1995). Indeed, in many studies, cognitive therapy has been found to be more effective than more traditional psychodynamic or humanistic therapies. Comparisons with psychiatric medication have yielded slightly more complicated findings. In the case of depression, there is evidence that cognitive therapy is equally as effective as antidepressant medications in the treatment of depression (DeRubeis & others, 1999). But cognitive therapy has been shown to be more than twice as effective as medication in preventing *future* episodes of depression (Evans & others, 1992; Hollon & others, 1993; Jarrett & others, 2001; Teasdale & others, 2001). In addition, unlike medication, cognitive therapy can be used to *prevent* depression in persons who are predisposed to it by heredity (Furmark & others, 2002). For the eating disorder bulimia, cognitive therapy combined with medication appears to be superior to either single treatment alone (Agras & others, 1992).

## Excerpt from Cognitive Therapy

In the following excerpt from a session of cognitive therapy, see how the therapist uses a series of probing questions to get the client to contradict her own absolutistic thinking and arbitrary inference.

THERAPIST: Why do you want to end your life?

PATIENT: Without Raymond, I am nothing . . . I can't be happy without Raymond. . . . But I can't save our marriage.

T: What has your marriage been like?

P: It has been miserable from the very beginning . . . Raymond has always been unfaithful . . . I have hardly seen him in the past five years.

T: You say that you can't be happy without Raymond. . . . Have you found yourself happy when you are with Raymond?

P: No, we fight all the time and I feel worse.

T: Then why do you feel that Raymond is essential for your living?

P: I guess it's because without Raymond I am nothing.

T: Would you please repeat that?

P: Without Raymond I am nothing.

T: What do you think of that idea?

P: . . . Well, now that I think about it, I guess it's not completely true.

T: You said you are "nothing" without Raymond. Before you met Raymond, did you feel you were "nothing"?

P: No, I felt I was somebody.

T: Are you saying then that it's possible to be something without Raymond?

P: I guess that's true. I *can* be something without Raymond.

T: If you were somebody before you knew Raymond, why do you need him to be somebody now?

P: (puzzled) Hmmm . . .

T: You seemed to imply that you couldn't go on living without Raymond.

P: Well, I just don't think that I can find anybody else like him.

T: Did you have male friends before you knew Raymond?

P: I was pretty popular then.

T: If I understand you correctly then, you were able to fall in love before with other men and other men have fallen in love with you.

P: Uh huh.

T: Why do you think you will be unpopular without Raymond now?

P: Because I will not be able to attract any other man.

T: Have any men shown an interest in you since you have been married?

P: A lot of men have made passes at me but I ignore them.

T: If you were free of the marriage, do you think that men might be interested in you—knowing that you were available?

P: I guess that maybe they would be.

T: Is it possible that you might find a man who would be more constant than Raymond?

P: I don't know, . . . I guess it's possible.

T: Do you think there are other men as good as Raymond around?

P: I guess there are men who are better than Raymond because Raymond doesn't love me.*

---

*From A. T. Beck, & others, *Cognitive Theory of Depression*. Copyright 1979 The Guilford Press, New York, NY. Reprinted by permission of the authors.

## Review

Cognitive therapy is a therapeutic approach that has grown out of both contemporary psychoanalytic theories of personality and social learning theory, but it has become subsumed by, and has contributed to the expansion of, behavior therapy. Whereas behavior therapists originally believed that the irrational beliefs and ways of thinking (cognitions) that generally accompany abnormal behavior and emotions would simply change when the behavior and emotions changed, cognitive therapists have emphasized the value in sometimes changing cognitions first. They believe that behavior and emotional problems will improve when maladaptive cognitions are changed. Consequently, cognitive therapists conduct psychotherapy in an attempt to change cognitions by demonstrating their irrationality to clients.

## Check Your Learning

To be sure that you have learned the key points from the preceding section, cover the list of correct answers and try to answer each question. If you give an incorrect answer to any question, return to the page given next to the correct answer to see why your answer was not correct.

1. _____ is an important approach to therapy that rests on the assumption that faulty cognitions—maladaptive beliefs, expectations, and ways of thinking—are the cause of abnormal behavior.

   a) Cognitive therapy          c) Anticipation therapy

   b) Psychoanalysis             d) Reflection

2. _____ refers to the cognitive distortion of basing your thinking on a small detail taken out of context and given an incorrect meaning.

   a) Selective abstraction      c) Personalization

   b) Overgeneralization         d) Absolutistic thinking

3. If a person loses her job because the company has laid off a thousand workers and then gets depressed because "I knew they thought I was awful at my job," she is engaging in _____.

   a) selective abstraction      c) personalization

   b) overgeneralization         d) absolutistic thinking

4. In the excerpt from cognitive therapy in the preceding section, the suicidal client says, "Without Raymond, I am nothing." This person is engaging in _____.

   a) selective abstraction      c) personalization

   b) overgeneralization         d) absolutistic thinking

## Thinking Critically about Psychology

1. We have seen that cognitive therapy is effective in treating several kinds of disorders. Can you think of other human ailments for which cognitive therapy might be effective?

2. Reexamine each of Aaron Beck's list of erroneous thinking patterns associated with depression. Can you think of any characters in novels or on television who think in these ways?

Correct Answers: **1.** a (p. 588),   **2.** a (p. 588),   **3.** c (p. 589),   **4.** d (p. 589).

## ● Other Approaches and Models of Therapy

We will now look at an approach to psychotherapy that focuses on the sometimes unique difficulties faced by women in society and their needs in psychotherapy. Therapy is not always conducted on an individual basis, however. Some methods of therapy are carried out with groups or entire families, and some programs are designed to prevent rather than treat problems. Moreover, some treatments for psychological problems use medical rather than psychological methods. In this section, we will survey these alternative approaches to the solution of human problems.

### Feminist Psychotherapy

Over the past 25 years, feminist psychotherapy has evolved as an approach to understanding and treating the psychological problems of women. It has increasingly been integrated into broader views of psychotherapy.

Over the past 25 years, an approach to understanding the psychological problems of women and providing treatment for them has evolved from the philosophical foundation of feminism. Some see **feminist psychotherapy** as a radical approach to therapy; others see the principles that underlie the feminist approach to psychotherapy as eminently reasonable ideas that should have always been a part of psychotherapy for women (Weiner, 1999). You may see these ideas as radical if you believe that women are placed on a pedestal in society and given an easier, more privileged place in life than men. On the other hand, you will find feminist psychotherapy to be reasonable and long overdue if you believe that women are treated as second-class citizens in many ways (personally, politically, and economically) and that even placing them on the pedestal of femininity contributes to their second-class citizenship by treating them more like Barbie dolls than people.

The fundamental concepts of feminist psychotherapy are the following (based on Worrell, 1980):

1. Feminist psychotherapy advocates an equal relationship between the client and therapist. The therapist avoids treating the client as someone who must be told what is best for her and encourages the client to trust her own ability to make good decisions. This therapy is designed to counteract the sexist view of women as needing guidance from their fathers and husbands. Sometimes this is aided by conducting therapy with groups of similar women to afford them the opportunity to make constructive suggestions to one another and minimize the role of the therapist.

2. Women clients are encouraged to see the ways in which society has limited their development and has pushed them into dependent roles. To counter these forces, women are encouraged to view themselves as powerful human beings who can effectively use their power in the personal, economic, and political spheres of life.

**feminist psychotherapy**
An approach to psychotherapy that encourages women to confront issues created by living in a sexist society as part of their psychotherapy.

3. Another goal of feminist psychotherapy is to encourage women to become aware of the anger that they feel over living as second-class citizens in a sexist society and to find constructive ways of expressing that anger.

4. Feminist psychotherapy helps women define themselves in ways that are independent of their roles as wife, mother, and daughter. It also seeks to assist women in dealing with the natural anxiety that they may experience about leaving or redefining these expected traditional roles.

5. Women are encouraged to consider their own needs to be as valid and as worthy of taking care of as those of others. The goal is to help women increase their sense of worth and self-esteem.

6. Finally, women are encouraged to develop skills that are not traditionally encouraged in women. These include assertiveness, career skills, and the skills to deal effectively with traditional persons who oppose such changes.

It is important to understand that feminist psychotherapy isn't just for women. Its guiding principles of equality, independence, and assertiveness are healthy for everyone. As a result, the concepts of feminist psychotherapy are increasingly integrated into all forms of psychotherapy rather than considered as a separate approach to therapy.

## Group Therapy

Psychotherapy is usually conducted on a one-to-one basis, but sometimes it's carried out with groups of clients in **group therapy.** One or two therapists typically work with four to eight clients at a time. Group therapy is believed to offer therapeutic experiences that cannot be obtained in individual therapy (Clarke & others, 2001; Yalom, 1995). Some of these advantages are (a) receiving encouragement from other group members, (b) learning that a person is not alone in his or her problems, (c) learning from the advice offered by others, and (d) learning new ways to interact with others. In addition, providing therapy in a group can sometimes make more efficient use of the therapist's time.

The format of group therapy differs widely, depending on the approach taken by the therapist (psychoanalytic, humanistic, cognitive, or behavioral), but all provide an opportunity for the client to interact with other clients and to learn from these interactions with the help of the therapist. Each approach to psychotherapy has adapted its own methods for use in groups. Psychoanalysts play the role of interpreter in group therapy, just as they do in individual therapy. They avoid becoming part of the interactions of the group members, except to offer interpretations of what these interactions reveal. Humanists use group interactions to help clients develop more accurate self-perceptions through the actions and reactions of other group members toward them. Behavior therapists use groups to facilitate the teaching of adaptive behavior. For example, groups of individuals with problems in social interactions are given instructions in how to relate more effectively, are allowed to practice interacting with one another, and then are given feedback and reinforcement from the therapist and other group members.

Psychotherapists from all of these orientations generally believe that interaction with other group members offers special therapeutic advantages to some clients. Individuals with complex problems that require the full attention of the therapist, or who do not wish to discuss their personal problems in front of others, however, will benefit more from individual psychotherapy.

## Family Therapy

Another important variation of psychotherapy in which the therapist works with groups of individuals is **family therapy.** In this case, the group is the family composed of parents, children, and any

**group therapy**
Psychotherapy conducted in groups, typically of four to eight clients at a time.

**family therapy**
An approach to psychotherapy that emphasizes an understanding of the roles of each of the members of the family system, usually conducted with all members of the family present.

An advantage of group therapy is the opportunity for clients to learn from interacting with other members of the group.

Family therapy emphasizes an understanding of the roles of each of the members of the family system.

other family members living in the home. Although family therapy is conducted by therapists who take psychoanalytic, humanistic, and behavioral approaches, the approach that we most often associate with family therapy is the family systems approach of Jay Haley (1976) and Salvador Minuchin (1974).

The family systems view takes the position that it's not possible to understand adequately the psychological problems of an individual without knowing the role of that individual in the family system. This is thought to be true for two reasons. First, the problem of the individual is often caused by problems within the family. For example, a depressed mother or an aggressive child may be reacting to the unhappy, conflict-laden relationship of the mother and father. Although the mother or child may be brought to the clinic identified as "the problem," and no mention is initially made of the marital problems, neither the depression nor the aggression can be helped until the marriage problems are resolved.

The second reason that Haley and Minuchin give for needing to understand the operation of the entire family system in order to understand the problems of an individual family member is that the individual's problems may serve a *function* in the family system. For example, the teenage girl who refuses to eat until she has reached a dangerously low weight may be doing so (consciously or unconsciously) to focus concern on her and keep her parents from divorcing. Similarly, parents who blame all of the family's problems on the supposedly wild behavior of their son may be using him as a scapegoat to shift attention away from the fact that they are both unemployed alcoholics. Without working with all of the members of the family system, these factors in the origins of the problems of the individual would be difficult, if not impossible, to uncover.

The family therapist attempts to solve the problems of all of the family members by improving the functioning of the family system as a whole. The therapist attempts to reach this goal in four primary ways. The family therapist works (a) to give the family members insights into the workings of family systems in general and to correct any dysfunctions in their family, (b) to increase the amount of warmth and intimacy among family members, (c) to improve communication among family members, and (d) to help family members establish a reasonable set of rules for the regulation of the family. In this way, it's hoped that the family will become a system that provides each member with an accurate view of self, a positive opinion of self, and a sense of belonging.

## Medical Therapies

**medical therapies**
Those therapies—including drug therapy, electroconvulsive therapy, and psychosurgery—generally designed to correct a physical condition that is believed to be the cause of a psychological disorder.

In addition to psychotherapy, medical therapies are commonly used in the treatment of abnormal behavior. **Medical therapies** are generally designed to correct a physical condition that is believed to be the cause of the psychological disorder. There are three general types of medical therapy: drug therapy, in which medication is used; electro-convulsive therapy, in which seizures are electrically induced in the brain; and psychosurgery, in which brain tissue is surgically destroyed.

## Drug Therapy

By far, the most widely used medical treatment is **drug therapy,** in which medications are used to treat abnormal behavior. The idea that chemicals can be used to treat abnormal behavior dates back at least to the special diets used by Pythagoras around 490 B.C. But the widespread use of effective psychiatric drugs has come about only in the past 40 years. The era of modern drug therapy began in 1954 with the introduction of the phenothiazine drugs, such as Thorazine for the treatment of schizophrenia. Thorazine gave physicians a tool that for the first time in history substantially improved the lives of schizophrenic persons. So effective is this drug that it's given partial credit for reversing the growth in the number of patients in mental institutions during the 1960s. Other drugs were also introduced during the 1960s that are effective in the treatment of depression (antidepressants) and anxiety (tranquilizers).

How do medications help persons with psychological problems? Recall from chapter 3 that our biology and our psychological lives are intimately related. Modern psychiatric medications are designed to improve psychological functioning by influencing a specific neurotransmitter in the brain. For example, Prozac causes axons that secrete serotonin to reabsorb the serotonin more slowly. This keeps the serotonin active in the synapse longer, giving it more time to stimulate the dendrite of the next neuron. Because neural transmission using serotonin is believed not to operate optimally in individuals with high levels of anxiety, depression, and other problems, this medication often helps "normalize" serotonin transmission in the brain. Although many people view psychiatric medications as a way of "drugging" people with psychological problems to keep them quiet, the goal is to help their brains operate more *normally*. Because most medications do not influence only one neurotransmitter, however, and because most neurotransmitters play other roles in the brain unrelated to emotional problems, psychiatric medications often have side effects that result from their impact on other neural systems. For example, prolonged use of some antipsychotic medications can result in impaired control of the body's muscles if not carefully monitored. Similarly, some antidepressant medications cause the individual to have a dry mouth and gain weight.

Today the use of these drugs is widespread. Some examples of the most commonly used psychiatric drugs are given in table 15.1. In spite of the effectiveness and general acceptance of drugs, they are not without shortcomings. Prolonged use of antipsychotic medications, for example, can result in impairment of walking and other serious side effects. Other medications can lead to considerable weight gains.

**drug therapy**
A medical therapy that uses medications to treat abnormal behavior.

### Table 15.1   Some Commonly Used Psychiatric Drugs

Physicians have a variety of medications at their disposal for use in the treatment of temporary stress reactions and psychological disorders. Some examples of these medications and their benefits are given here. Some of these medications have several uses and may be prescribed by a physician for reasons other than psychological problems.

| Trade Name | Generic Name | For Relief of |
| --- | --- | --- |
| Paxil | paroxetine | Depression |
| Prozac | fluoxetine | Depression |
| Xanax | alprazolam | Anxiety |
| Risperdal | risperidone | Psychotic symptoms |
| Haldol | haloperidol | Psychotic symptoms |
| Navane | thiothixene | Psychotic symptoms |
| Eskalith | lithium | Bipolar disorder |

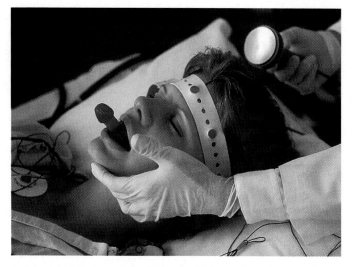

Although electroconvulsive therapy, which was introduced in the 1930s, continues to be used with some severely depressed individuals, it's not endorsed universally by the mental health profession.

**electroconvulsive therapy (ECT)**
(e-lek″tro-con-vul′siv) A medical therapy that uses electrical current to induce controlled convulsive seizures that alleviate some types of mental disorders.

**psychosurgery**
(si″kō-ser′jer-ē) A medical therapy that involves operating on the brain in an attempt to alleviate some types of mental disorders.

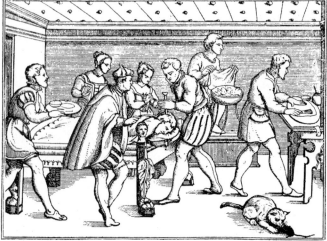

Trephining operations were apparently performed in the Middle Ages to treat abnormal behavior.

## Electroconvulsive Therapy

The idea that people can be "shocked" out of their psychological problems has been around in one form or another for 2,400 years. Hippocrates recommended the use of the herb hellebore to induce seizures that supposedly restored balance to the body's four humors. Several different kinds of "shock" treatment were popular in mental institutions during the 1800s: patients were thrown in tubs full of eels, spun in giant centrifuges, and nearly drowned by dropping them into lakes through trapdoors in bridges, a treatment known as "surprise baths" (Altschule, 1965).

Other forms of shock therapy have also been used, particularly ones in which seizures are intentionally induced. In the 1930s, it was noticed that people with epilepsy rarely developed schizophrenia. Several psychiatrists experimented with chemicals that caused seizures to see if they would cure schizophrenia, but camphor, insulin, and other chemicals were found to be of little use with schizophrenics. Italian physicians first used the method of passing an electric current through two metal plates held to the sides of the head to induce convulsive brain seizures. This method, known as **electroconvulsive therapy (ECT),** continues in widespread use today. Although ineffective with most disorders, it's believed by many psychiatrists to be useful with severely depressed individuals. ECT is believed to alter the same neurotransmitters as those affected by antidepressants, but to this day no one knows for sure how ECT works.

Although ECT has been used successfully for 50 years, the procedure is surrounded by considerable controversy. In large part, this controversy is a holdover from the primitive methods that were used when the procedure was first introduced. The shocks were given without anesthesia, and the seizures were so violent that broken bones were not uncommon. Today, the use of anesthesia and muscle relaxants makes ECT a far less unpleasant experience, but mild temporary or permanent memory loss (mostly for relatively unimportant facts) are still relatively common side effects (Campbell, 1961; Lisanby & others, 2000). The use of ECT is also controversial because, even after extended use, little adequate research has been conducted to evaluate its effectiveness. Many well-designed studies have been carried out, however, that suggest that it is effective in treating depression (Barton, 1977; McCall & others, 2000).

## Psychosurgery

Undoubtedly the most controversial medical treatment for abnormal behavior is **psychosurgery,** a therapy in which the brain is operated on to try to alleviate the behavior. As with the other medical therapies, there is a historical precedent for the idea that people with psychological disorders can be helped by operating on their brains. In fact, the precedent for psychosurgery is perhaps the oldest of all. Archaeologists have found Stone Age skulls in which holes called *trephines* had been "surgically" cut with crude stone knives. These trephining operations—signs of healing indicate that some of these poor souls actually survived the procedure—were apparently performed in an attempt to treat abnormal behavior.

Surgical operations on the brain to treat psychological disorders came into vogue in the 1940s and 1950s. In the most common version, the prefrontal lobotomy, a double-edged, butter knife–shaped instrument is inserted through holes drilled in the temple region of the skull. Neural fibers that connect the frontal region of the cerebral cortex with the limbic system are cut. The theory is that the operation will prevent disturbing thoughts and perceptions from reaching the subcortical brain structures, where they would be translated into emotional outbursts. Lobotomies are not successful in most cases, however, and loss of intellectual functioning and seizures are common side effects (Barahal, 1958). Because of their ineffectiveness and because of the success of drug therapies with schizophrenics, the use of lobotomies and other forms of psychosurgery has declined considerably (Swayze, 1995). However, as late as 1973, some 500 prefrontal lobotomies were performed in the United States each year (Holden, 1973).

More recently, the development of more precise methods of operating on the brain with needle-thin electrical instruments has revived interest in psychosurgery (Martuza, Chiocca, Jenike, Giriunas, & Ballantine, 1990). These instruments are used to operate directly on the parts of the brain associated with emotional control. For example, a type of precise psychosurgery called **cingulotomy** is sometimes performed on persons with severe obsessive-compulsive disorder who have not responded to repeated attempts to treat the disorder with behavior therapy and medication. In cingulotomy, the part of the limbic system called the *cingulate cortex* (chapter 3, page 74) is partially destroyed by electrical probes. Researchers have evaluated individuals with obsessive-compulsive disorder two to three years after their cingulotomies to see whether they had been helpful. They found significant improvement in about one-fourth of the patients, but most cases did not benefit from the surgery (Baer & others, 1995; Doughterty & others, 2002). Such operations are performed infrequently and are used only as a last resort. Even in such cases, psychosurgery is still a hotly debated procedure.

**cingulotomy**
A type of psychosurgery for severe and otherwise untreatable obsessive-compulsive disorder; it involves surgical destruction of part of the cingulate cortex.

## Review

One-to-one psychotherapy is not the only approach taken to solve psychological problems. For one thing, each method of psychotherapy is sometimes practiced with groups of clients rather than individual clients. Group therapy is practiced primarily because the presence of other people with problems offers advantages to some clients. Other clients provide encouragement, give advice, show the client that he or she is not alone in having problems, and provide opportunities for learning new ways of interacting with others. Group therapy also often makes efficient use of the therapist's time. Individuals with complex problems, or who have sensitive problems that they do not want to discuss in front of others, may be better served by individual psychotherapy, however. Entire families are also often worked with as a group by therapists who believe that the faulty operation of some family systems can cause psychological problems. Family therapy seeks to reestablish proper functioning in these families.

In addition to psychological treatments for psychological problems, physicians often use biological methods. The most widely used medical treatments are drugs. Drugs introduced since the 1950s have been partially responsible for the progress in treating psychological problems, which has resulted in a decrease in the number of institutionalized mental patients in the United States. Electroconvulsive therapy—in which an electric current produces controlled brain seizures—is sometimes used in the treatment of severe depression. The controversial method of psychosurgery in which parts of the brain are destroyed to prevent excessive emotional reactions is no longer widely used in the United States, but newer, more precise methods are still used in some cases as a last resort.

## Check Your Learning

To be sure that you have learned the key points from the preceding section, cover the list of correct answers and try to answer each question. If you give an incorrect answer to any question, return to the page given next to the correct answer to see why your answer was not correct.

1. _____, or psychotherapy conducted in groups, is believed to offer therapeutic experiences that cannot be obtained in individual therapy, such as learning from the advice offered by others.

2. _____ emphasizes an understanding of the roles of each of the members of a family system with the hope that the family will become a system that provides each member with an accurate view of self, a positive opinion of self, appropriate behavioral guidelines, and a sense of belonging.

3. _____, such as drug treatment or psychosurgery, is generally designed to correct a physical condition that is believed to be the cause of the psychological disorder.

## Thinking Critically about Psychology

1. Which type of psychotherapy makes the most sense to you? Why?

2. If you were seeking treatment for a psychological problem, would you be more likely to try group therapy or individual psychotherapy? Why?

**Correct Answers:** 1. Group therapy (p. 593). 2. Family therapy (p. 593). 3. Medical therapy (p. 594).

Chapter 15 outlines the major forms of therapy through which individuals are helped with psychological problems.

**Summary**

I.   Psychotherapy is the use of methods, such as talking, demonstrating, and reinforcing, that are based on a theory of psychological disorders to solve human problems.

   A.   Freud is the founder of the form of psychotherapy known as psychoanalysis, which helps the patient bring unconscious conflict into consciousness. The principal techniques of psychoanalysis are

      1.   Free association, which is used to relax the censorship of the ego.

      2.   Dream interpretation, which allows the therapist to obtain another "window" on the unconscious.

      3.   Resistance, which is any form of opposition of the patient to the process of psychoanalysis.

      4.   Transference, which occurs when there is a relatively intense relationship between patient and therapist during therapy; this can be interpreted to give insights to the patient.

   B.   Catharsis is the release of some of the emotion that is pent up with unconscious conflicts in psychoanalysis.

   C.   A new form of psychotherapy based on neo-Freudian theories, called interpersonal psychotherapy, has been found to be effective in treating depression.

II.   Humanistic psychotherapies strive to help the person achieve full self-awareness, so that the person's inner-directed tendency to growth can be realized. Client-centered psychotherapy and Gestalt therapy are two major types of humanistic psychotherapy.

   A.   Client-centered psychotherapy helps the client explore unsymbolized feelings and information by providing a safe emotional climate. Self-awareness, in turn, is thought to promote healthy growth.

   B.   Gestalt therapy helps the individual achieve greater self-awareness by using directive techniques, such as pointing out inconsistencies in behavior.

III.   Behavior therapists use a form of psychotherapy in which they help the client unlearn abnormal behavior and learn adaptive ways of thinking, feeling, and acting.

   A.   Systematic desensitization and graded exposure are widely used methods of fear reduction.

   B.   Social skills training is an example of teaching new adaptive skills using methods derived from operant conditioning.

   C.   Cognitive therapy rests on the assumption that the faulty cognitions that cause abnormal emotions and actions can be changed in therapy.

IV.   Some methods of therapy are carried out with groups or entire families, and some are designed to enhance personal growth rather than treat problems.

   A.   Group therapy makes efficient use of therapists' time, and the presence of other people with problems offers advantages to some clients.

   B.   Family therapy seeks to reestablish proper functioning within families.

   C.   Medical therapies are designed to correct a physical condition believed to be the cause of a psychological disorder.

# Resources

1. Descriptions of the major methods of psychotherapy are presented in Nietzel, M. T., Bernstein, D. A., & Milich, R. (1998). *Introduction to clinical psychology* (5th ed.). Englewood Cliffs, NJ: Prentice-Hall; Dryden, W., & Mytton, J. (1999). *Four approaches to counseling and psychotherapy.* New York: Routledge.

2. Group psychotherapy is discussed in depth in Yalom, I. D. (1995). *The theory and practice of group psychotherapy.* New York: Basic Books.

3. More on interpersonal psychotherapy can be found in Markowitz, J. C. (1999). Developments in interpersonal psychotherapy. *Canadian Journal of Psychiatry, 44,* 556–561.

4. Two excellent applications of the cognitive theory of emotion can be found in Beck, A. T. (1999). *Prisoners of hate: The cognitive basis of anger, hostility, and violence.* New York: HarperCollins; Ellis, A. (1999). *How to make yourself happy and remarkably less disturbable.* Atascadero, CA: Impact.

5. Four helpful booklets on depression are available from the Superintendent of Documents, Government Printing Office, Washington, DC 20402-9325:
   *Depressive illness: Treatments bring new hope* (017-024-01370-6).
   *Bipolar disorder* (017-024-01368-4).
   *Plain talk about . . . depression* (017-024-01382-0).
   *What do you do when a friend is depressed?* (017-024-01376-5).

6. For more on the ethical practice of psychotherapy, see Division 44/Committee on Lesbian, Gay, and Bisexual Concerns Joint Task Force on Guidelines for Psychotherapy with Lesbian, Gay, and Bisexual Clients (2000). Guidelines for Psychotherapy with lesbian, gay, and bisexual clients. *American Psychologist, 55,* 1440–1451.

7. If you would like help in finding affordable mental health services in your area or need to speak with a counselor in confidence about any mental health problem, call the National Mental Health Hotline of Boy's Town. Although the name of the organization is Boy's Town, it provides help to males and females of all ages. It has an extensive computerized national database that can help you find help for yourself or someone else. Its toll-free, 24-hour hot line numbers are 1-800-448-3000 and TDD (hearing impaired) 1-800-448-1833.

8. An excellent source of accurate information about the psychological and treatment of mental disorders is http://www.mentalhealth.com

9. The Web site of the American Psychological Association is an excellent resource for information about getting help for mental health problems: http://www.apa.org

# PART VII

# Social Context

In the preceding chapters, we have studied the psychology of the individual. Although social and cultural factors were often mentioned in these chapters, we have mostly been studying psychology one person at a time until now. In this section you will learn about the profound importance of the social context, and you will be introduced to important applications of psychology to the social environments of business, the legal system, and education and to the architectural environments in which we work, live, and enjoy life.

Here is a visual overview of what you will learn in the final section of the text.

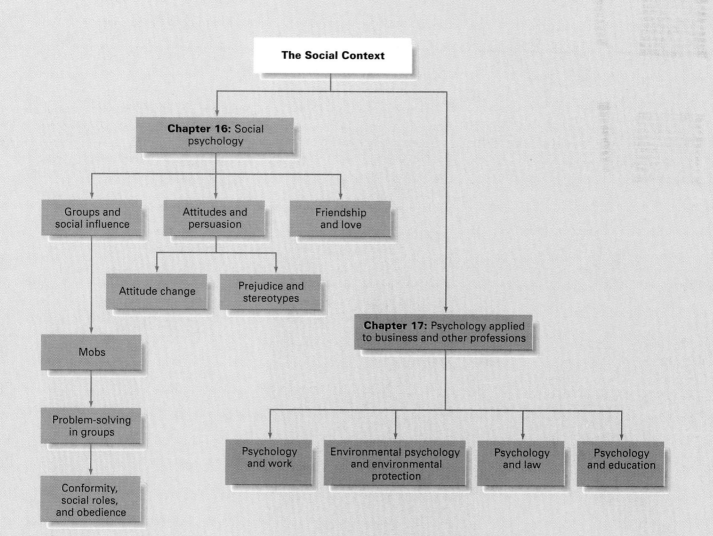

## Chapter Outline

# Social Psychology

## PROLOGUE

Human beings are social animals: We enjoy people, need people, and are profoundly influenced by them. Indeed, we often behave a bit like sheep in a flock. We are likely to dress and act like other people even when we are not asked to conform, and we are often influenced by persuasive arguments—even illogical ones.

For most of us, our most important interactions are with the people we like and love. We like to walk with them, talk with them, and snuggle with them. Whom do you like and why? Other things being equal, we are attracted to people who are similar to us (or whose opposite characteristics are good for us), who are reasonably competent (but not perfect), who are physically attractive, and who like us, too. Once mutual attraction leads to a relationship, our likelihood of staying in that relationship is determined by (a) how well our expectations of what the person is like are met and (b) how fairly balanced the relationship is.

The process of liking or disliking others is based on a complex combination of the positive and negative qualities that we see in them. Some of our reasons for liking a person have little to do with the other person at all, however. Let's look at one extraneous factor that influences the process of liking by looking at a well-known experiment (Curtis & Miller, 1987). You walk to the psychology department to take part in a study. You are introduced to another student whom you have never met and spend five minutes in a "get to know one another" conversation. Then you are separated and taken to separate cubicles. The experimenter talks with the other student for a while, then comes to your cubicle. She tells you that the study is about the ways in which people get to know one another. She also tells you that the other student has been misled into thinking that you are not a very likable person (by showing the other student a bogus "personality test" that made you look bad). To prove it, the experimenter shows you what the other student's initial ratings of you are, and they are not very positive.

The experimenter explains that she wants to know how the other student will act toward you after being given this initial negative opinion. You and the other research participant are brought together for a 10-minute conversation. Then you and the other student rate each other on likeability, warmth, and a number of other similar dimensions.

Half of the students who participated in the study were told that the other person was given *positive* information about them and half were told that the other person was given *negative* information about them. Actually, the experimenters didn't give either positive or negative information to the other students. The social psychologists who conducted this study wanted to know if we act differently toward people who we *think* like or dislike us. The experimenters observed the students through a one-way mirror and rated their behavior. You and the other research participants who thought the other students did not like them were rated as less warm and less open. In addition, the other person rated you and the other individuals in your group as less likable at the end of the study, too. The other person who you *thought* did not like you actually *didn't* like you very much in the end because of how you behaved toward that person. Human relationships can be maddeningly complex! ■

Social psychology is the branch of psychology that studies individuals as they interact with others.

**social psychology**
The branch of psychology that studies individuals as they interact with others.

**deindividuation**
State in which people in a group can feel anonymous and unidentifiable and therefore feel less concerned with what others think of their behavior.

People who feel unidentifiable, or deindividuated, because they are in a large group are more likely to behave aggressively or in other unacceptable ways.

# Definition of Social Psychology

**Social psychology** is a branch of psychology that studies individuals as they interact with others. Up to this point in this course, we have studied people as individuals removed from the social context in which they live. But people live with other people. Their most important learning comes from others, their most important motives are social motives, and so on.

People are almost always with others. It's part of human nature to be social. Social psychologist Elliot Aronson (1995) reminds us that this insight is among the oldest in psychology. In 328 B.C., Aristotle wrote, "Man is by nature a social animal. . . . Anyone who either cannot lead the common life or is so self-sufficient as not to need to, and therefore does not partake of society, is either a beast or a god." People need, like, and are profoundly influenced by people. Social psychologists study these attractions, needs, and influences.

It is not sufficient to study human beings in isolation; we must examine the psychology of the individual in the context of the social situations in which they live. To fully understand people, we must see how they are influenced by their social context.

# Groups and Social Influence

Let's begin our study of social influence with a look at the effects of being a member of a group. Although some of what you will learn will make you embarrassed to be a member of the human race, you can understand the power of social influence only by looking at both its negative and positive faces.

## Lynch Mobs

Near the start of the twentieth century, an African American man named William Carr was arrested and charged with killing the cow of a white family in southern Louisiana. A mob of solid citizens took him from the sheriff, who did not resist them, and hanged him without a trial. During the era in which this hanging took place, an average of two African Americans were lynched each week in the United States. These lynchings say much about racial prejudice—a topic we will turn to later in the chapter—but they also say a great deal about the effects of groups on the behavior of individuals. The members of lynch mobs were almost never men who had murdered before when alone or who would murder alone afterward. Something about being in a group transformed individual men who were incapable of murder into a mob that was very capable of murder (Postmes & Spears, 1998).

In some situations, being in a group can make a person feel anonymous and unidentifiable. This feeling can lead to a process known as **deindividuation** (Zimbardo, 1969). In this state, people are less aware of their own behavior and less concerned with what others think of their behavior. The result can be an increased likelihood of performing actions that you typically wouldn't do. Think about your own behavior at a crowded ball game or at a large rock concert. You might have screamed vulgar insults at the opposing team or behaved less than prim and proper. The weakened restraints that result from deindividuation can have more serious effects as well. When people are unidentifiable, they are more aggressive (Zimbardo, 1969). Similarly, an analysis of lynchings occurring over a 47-year period found that the worst atrocities occurred in larger groups, where, presumably, people felt more anonymous (Mullen, 1986).

## Uninvolved Bystanders

Let's look at another negative outcome of being in groups. I vividly remember reading in a magazine about the death of Kitty Genovese some years ago. I was more than a little disappointed in the human race when I read that she had been beaten and stabbed to death in a residential area of New York City over the course of 30 minutes while 38 of her neighbors came to their windows and watched. Incredibly, no one went out to help her; no one even called the police.

How could such a thing have happened? Did Kitty just happen to live in a neighborhood of uncaring cowards? Social psychologists don't think that is the answer. For example, Bibb Latané, John Darley, and Judith Rodin carried out a series of experiments in an attempt to understand the lack of action by bystanders like these. In one experiment (Latané & Rodin, 1969), a female experimenter asked college students to fill out a questionnaire, and while they worked, she went behind a curtain, where she staged a fake accident. The students heard her climbing and then falling from a chair. She moaned as if in great pain and begged for someone to help her get her foot out from under a heavy object. When students were alone in the other part of the room, 70 percent went to help her. But when they were paired with one other student who did not respond to the woman's pleas, only 7 percent tried to help.

In a similar experiment (Darley & Latané, 1968), college students "overheard" a staged epileptic seizure through an intercom. Eighty-five percent of the students tried to find help for the seizure victim when they thought they alone had heard it, but when they thought that others were also listening, only 30 percent sought help. Social psychologists do not think that bystanders who fail to help in an emergency are lacking in some personal quality; rather, they are influenced by being in a group. Many studies have shown that the larger the group, the less likely any particular person is to offer to help a person in distress (Latané & Nida, 1981).

To understand why people fail to help in such situations, we must understand that the decision to help or not help is complex. Latané and Darley (1970) propose that the decision to help can be best understood as a *decision tree* with many steps (see figure 16.1). First, a person must *notice* that something is out of the ordinary. A drowning victim who is screaming for help might not be noticed because everyone else at the beach is screaming and yelling in fun. If the victim is noticed, though, the person still might not help unless the situation is *interpreted* as an emergency. The bystander might think that the drowning victim is yelling and thrashing in the water for fun. A man slumped over in the street could just be drunk and not have had a heart attack. If the situation is not interpreted as an emergency, the victim will not receive help from that bystander.

Once the event is interpreted as an emergency, the bystander must decide whether she or he should *assume responsibility* for helping. If a lifeguard is present, or if others are around to help, a bystander might not assume the responsibility for helping. Even if the bystander assumes responsibility for helping, the bystander might not help if he or she does *not know how to help*. Finally, the bystander still might *decide not to help* for some reason. For example, you might notice a commotion in the water, interpret that situation as one in which a person is drowning, assume responsibility to help the victim, and know how to swim out and rescue the person, but if you are afraid that the person is so heavy that you would be drowned trying to help, you still might decide not to help. As you can see, the decision to help is only the last step in a complex process.

What social factors influence the decision tree? Latané and Darley have suggested that being in the presence of other people primarily affects the second and third stage of the decision process—interpreting the event as an emergency and assuming responsibility for helping. When we notice an event and try to interpret it, we look to others for information. If nobody else is making an effort to help, then it's less likely that we will help, because it looks as if there is no reason to help: "No one looks worried, so there must not be a problem." As mentioned in the Latané and Rodin "woman in distress" experiment, 70 percent of the individuals who were alone went to find help for the person who had fallen, but that number was reduced to 7 percent when they were paired with another person (actually a confederate of the experimenter) who made no effort at all to offer help. In other bystander experiments in which the confederate tried to find a way to help, the research participants were more likely to help, too.

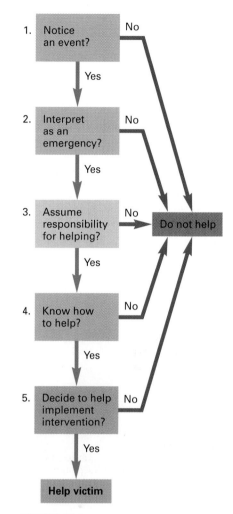

**FIGURE 16.1**
Latané & Darley's decision model of helping (1970).

**diffusion of responsibility**
The effect of being in a group that apparently reduces the sense of personal responsibility of each group member to act appropriately.

**social facilitation**
An effect in which working in a group improves one's performance on individual projects.

**social loafing**
The tendency of members of groups to work less hard when group performance is measured than when individual performance is measured.

The second stage that the presence of other bystanders is most likely to affect is assuming responsibility for helping. Groups create a **diffusion of responsibility.** If everyone in the group is responsible for a lynching, then no one person is individually responsible: "I didn't do it; we all just got worked up and did it." In emergencies, a person who is alone is clearly responsible for helping the person in need; however, in a group of bystanders, the reasoning is that I do not need to help because someone else will.

## Working and Solving Problems in Groups

We humans often gather together to perform work in groups. We sometimes study together, raise barns together, and hold meetings to discuss solutions to problems in our colleges, businesses, and cities. Is this a good thing? Does working together in groups bring out the best in us? Sometimes yes, and sometimes no.

Being in a group improves the performance of the individual members of the group in some cases. When this is the case, **social facilitation** is said to occur (Levine, Resnick, & Higgins, 1993). In one of the earliest experiments in social psychology, Triplett (1898) found that teenagers wound fishing reels faster in the presence of other teenagers doing the same thing than when they were alone.

Working as part of a group can affect how hard we work and how well we get the job done.

Often, however, being in a group results in reduced effort by group members. Suppose you convince your instructor to use the next class period to have a tug-of-war among members of your class. Do you think that you would pull harder on the rope if you were tugging alone against one classmate, or if you were part of a team of four persons tugging against four classmates? As the number of people involved in a tug-of-war increases, the average amount of force exerted by each person *declines* (Kravitz & Martin, 1986). The diminished effort of each individual in a group of tug-of-war is partly the result of lack of coordination among members of the group—some rest while others pull, resulting in less average effort. But even persons who are blindfolded and led to believe that others are pulling with them exert less effort than when they think they are pulling alone (Ingham, Levinger, Graves, & Peckham, 1974). Similarly, if you are asked to clap as loudly as you can, you will make more noise if you think your clap is being measured individually than if you think the loudness of a group of clappers is being measured together (Latané, Williams, & Harkins, 1979). Social psychologist Bibb Latané of Florida Atlantic University calls this phenomenon **social loafing.**

Social loafing also often occurs when groups solve problems and make decisions. That is, individual members of the group often exert less effort in a group than they would when working alone. When does being in a group influence our performance in negative ways? Two key variables are (a) the size of the group, and (b) the nature of the task. The larger the group, the more likely individual members are to reduce their individual contributions to the group effort (Sorkin, Hays, & West, 2001). They may loaf in larger groups because they believe that other people can make better contributions, because other members do not respond positively to their initial attempts to contribute, or because they feel that no one would notice if they slacked off.

The nature of the task is an important factor in individual performance in groups because being in the presence of other people is arousing and some tasks are performed better at different levels of arousal (Zajonc, 1965). For example, Markus (1978) asked research participants to dress in preparation for a later phase in an experiment. This task of dressing was either easy, putting on everyday shoes and socks, or difficult, involving dressing in strange, unfamiliar clothes. Participants performed this dressing task alone, with a confederate who observed them, or with a confederate who was busy repairing equipment on the other side of the room. When individuals performed the easy dressing task, they dressed *more quickly* when there was another person present in the room, compared with when they dressed alone. When the research participants had to perform the difficult dressing task, they dressed *more slowly* in the presence of others than they did when they were alone. Why does this happen?

If you recall the discussion of *optimal levels of arousal* in chapter 10 (page 375), easy tasks are easier to do when people are aroused, but difficult tasks are more difficult when people are aroused. High levels of arousal, such as that produced by performing in front of an audience, may promote social facilitation for easy or skilled tasks and social impairment for difficult or unfamiliar tasks. Professional athletes, musicians, and other performers often do their best work in the presence of an audience, because they are performing skills that have been practiced over and over again. In contrast, amateur performers who lack practice and skill are likely to perform more poorly when an audience is present.

### Groupthink

In general, people solve problems better in groups than they do when working alone (Sorkin & others, 2001). Even if the individual members of the group engage in some degree of social loafing, it is true that "two heads are better than one" and that the knowledge and skills of more than one person may be needed to solve a problem. Sometimes, however, making decisions in groups leads to disastrously bad decisions, even when the members of the group are very capable people. How does this happen?

Psychologist Irving Janis (1982) has studied the factors involved in group problem solving by knowledgeable and sophisticated decision makers. He proposed that some of the most significant and disastrous decisions made in history—such as President Kennedy's ill-fated decision to send Cuban expatriots to defeat in the Bay of Pigs invasion of Castro's Cuba, and NASA's fatal decision in 1986 to launch the space shuttle *Challenger* despite warnings from engineers about defective O-rings (Kruglanski, 1986) —were the result of faulty group decision making. Janis calls the faulty decision-making processes that occur in these groups **groupthink.**

What causes group decision making to result in groupthink? There are three key factors: (a) the process of polarization, (b) the cohesiveness of the members of the group, and (c) the size of the group. Suppose a friend asks you for advice about the following dilemma:

> I want to go to graduate school in filmmaking, but to get in I have to make an impressive grade in undergraduate scriptwriting. I could take the course from a famous instructor who is respected by the graduate school, but the famous instructor is so hard that hardly anyone gets an *A* or a *B*. Or I could take the course from an easier, less famous instructor that the graduate school might not be impressed by. What should I do?

What would you recommend? Would you tell your friend to go for broke and take the course from the famous but tough instructor, even though the chances of getting a good grade are very low? Studies have shown that most of us do *not* recommend such risky options *when we are alone with the person asking for advice.* However, when *groups* of persons discuss such dilemmas, they are much more likely to take extreme positions and recommend risky options (Stoner, 1961). The discussion of issues in groups often leads to the **polarization** of thinking by pushing our opinions toward one extreme "pole" of the issue.

For example, suppose you are a person with mildly prejudiced views about other ethnic groups. You are with a group of people and someone makes a *very* prejudicial remark about an ethnic group. You may find yourself taking a more extreme position against prejudice than you typically would—and meaning what you say. You have been pushed toward the nonprejudiced pole of the argument, and your statements have probably driven the other person to an even more prejudiced position. A classic study of polarization of attitudes occurring in group discussions found exactly these results during a discussion of ethnic attitudes among high school students (Myers & Bishop, 1970).

**groupthink**
The faulty decision-making processes that may occur in groups.

**polarization**
The tendency for group discussion to make beliefs and attitudes more extreme.

Groupthink also is more likely to occur in tightly knit, cohesive groups. The members of cohesive groups prefer to agree with one another and discourage dissent. For that reason, contradictory evidence and opinions often are not presented, leaving the group with a false sense of the correctness of their decision. It is easy to see how unsound decisions could be made under these conditions. To guard against groupthink, at least one member of the group should be asked to take the role of the "devil's advocate," regularly challenging the group's thinking.

Finally, the size of the group is important because the nature of interactions among group members changes as the size of the group increases (Fay, Garrod, & Carletta, 2000). In small groups, people influence each other's ideas through a process of *interactive dialogues*. They speak to one another and ask each other questions in reciprocal and connected ways. In larger groups, however, members are more likely to engage in *serial monologues*. They take turn giving "speeches" that present their views, but they do not integrate or respond to the views of their fellow group members in their monologues. As a result, there is less constructive give-and-take in larger groups, and the opinion held by the dominant member of the group before the discussion began is likely to prevail (Fay & others, 2000). If the dominant person's opinion is incorrect, it is less likely to be corrected in large groups.

## Conformity, Social Roles, and Obedience

I hope that you are beginning to have a new appreciation for the powerful influence of social situations on the behavior of the individual. Clearly, social situations influence us every day in important ways. But there is still a great deal more to the story of social influence. Next, we will consider our tendency to conform to the expectations of our peer groups and our cultures, the influence of socially prescribed roles and norms on our behavior, and our tendency to obediently follow the instructions of authority figures.

### Conformity

When we are members of a group, we tend to behave as others do in the group—we tend to conform. **Conformity** is yielding to group pressure to act as everyone else does, even when no direct request has been made. A most informative and now classic study of conformity was conducted by Solomon Asch (1956). He asked college students to serve as research participants in an experiment that he said concerned visual perception. Each student participated in a group with other "research participants," all of whom were actually confederates of the experimenter. The group was shown four straight lines, depicted in figure 16.2. The task was to tell which of the three lines on the right side of the figure was the same length as line *A*.

The task was intentionally made easy, with line *Y* being the obvious correct choice. But the real participant was the last one in line as each student was asked to state his or her choice out loud. One by one, the confederates playing the part of real research participants chose line *X*. The distress of the real participant was immediately apparent. He seemed to be asking, "Am I crazy or are they?" But, in an amazing 74 percent of the cases, the participants conformed to the pressure of the group and gave the wrong answer at least part of the time.

How "deep" was this conformity? Did the research participants know that they were just going along with the group's opinion, or did the group actually change their judgment? People may conform for two reasons: to gain rewards and avoid punishments (such as social approval or disapproval) or to gain information. In the Asch situation, people seemed to conform for the former reason, to seek approval and avoid disapproval. How do we know? When the same line-judging experiment was conducted in a slightly different way that allowed the research participants to make their judgments privately, almost no conformity to the erroneous judgments of other individuals occurred. Apparently, we are able to make up our minds privately even in the face of pressure from others but often go along with the crowd in terms of outward behavior.

**conformity**
Yielding to group pressure even when no direct request to comply has been made.

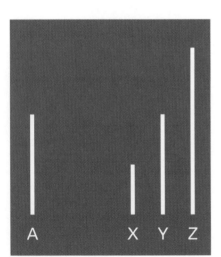

**FIGURE 16.2**
Stimuli like those used in Asch's study of conformity.

Sometimes, however, we conform to the behavior of others at a much deeper level. This happens when the "correct" judgment is less clear than in Asch's line-judging experiment. Sherif (1936) conducted a study that took advantage of a perceptual phenomenon called the *autokinetic effect*. When a person is placed in a completely darkened room with no reference points, a fixed point of light on a wall will appear to move. Because the movement of light is not real, and the distance that it seems to move differs from person to person, this is an extremely ambiguous situation (as compared with Asch's line-judging task, which was very clear-cut). Sherif placed individuals in a room with confederates and asked them to estimate the distance that a fixed light had moved. The confederates gave either extremely low or extremely high estimates of movement, and the research participants tended to agree with the confederates. In this ambiguous situation, however, they still tended to agree with the confederates even when they could report their estimates of the movement of the light in private. When the appropriate response in a situation is not clear, we look to others for information and will not only go along with them but may actually change our judgments.

Several factors increase the likelihood of conformity to the group:

1. *Size of the group.* Up to a point, the more people there are in a group, the more likely we are to go along. When the group gets too large, however, conformity drops off.

2. *Unanimous groups.* Conformity is highest when we face a group who all feel the same way about a topic—the group is unanimous. But conformity is greatly reduced when even one other person in the group feels as we do (Nail, MacDonald, & Levy, 2000).

3. *Culture and conformity.* An article by British psychologists Rod Bond and Peter Smith (1996) shows us that culture is an important factor that influences conformity. The experiment showing conformity in the judgment of the length of lines originally conducted by Solomon Asch in 1956 has now been conducted 133 times in 17 different cultures. Conformity occurs in all cultures, but persons from individualistic cultures, which place an emphasis on the welfare of the individual—as in North America—are less conforming on the Asch task than are persons from collectivistic cultures, which emphasize the welfare of society as a whole rather than the individual.

4. *Gender and conformity?* What about gender? According to our stereotypes, males are more independent and less likely to conform than females. Research conducted before the mid-1950s suggested that females were more likely to conform than males were at that time. More recent research, however, has shown that this is no longer the case (Eagly, 1978; Eagly & Johnson, 1990). Maybe our stereotypes will eventually catch up with the changing realities of gender.

In terms of outward behavior, we tend to conform to group norms.

"All those in favor say 'Aye.'"
"Aye." "Aye." "Aye."
"Aye." "Aye."

## Social Roles and Social Norms

When people work together in groups, the efforts of each individual need to be coordinated with those of others to avoid chaos. In response to this need, every culture has evolved many **social roles** and **social norms** to give guidelines as to what is expected of us (Levine & others, 1993). Just like actors in a play who have scripts for their roles, social roles tell us how we are expected to behave. In this course, you play the role of the student, and the nice person who tells you interesting things about psychology plays the role of the instructor. Each social role gives the person a different set of expectations for appropriate behavior. You are not surprised when the person in the role of instructor stands in the front of the classroom and lectures, but you would be surprised if the student sitting next to you were to stand up and deliver a 45-minute lecture on the importance of classical conditioning to our understanding of romantic love.

Social roles have a powerful impact on the behavior of individuals. When we are placed in a new role, our behavior often changes to fit the role. In a dramatic example

**social roles**
Culturally determined guidelines that tell people what behavior is expected of them.

**social norms**
Guidelines provided by every culture for judging acceptable and unacceptable behavior.

In Zimbardo's prison experiment, volunteers assigned to the social roles of guard and prisoner dramatically conformed to those roles.

of the power of social roles in influencing behavior, social psychologist Philip Zimbardo of Stanford University looked at the social roles that exist in prisons. Zimbardo was interested in these particular roles because he felt that they lead to the mistreatment of convicts in a way that worsens their behavior (Haney & Zimbardo, 1998). The following is Zimbardo's description of what was learned:

> We carefully screened over 70 volunteers who answered an ad in a Palo Alto city newspaper and ended up with about two dozen young men who were selected to be part of this study. Half were arbitrarily designated as prisoners by a flip of a coin, the others as guards. These were the roles they were to play in our simulated prison. The guards were made aware of the potential seriousness and danger of the situation and their own vulnerability. They made up their own formal rules for maintaining law, order, and respect, and were generally free to improvise new ones during their eight-hour, three-man shifts. The prisoners were unexpectedly picked up at their homes by a city policeman in a squad car, searched, handcuffed, fingerprinted, booked at the Palo Alto station house, and taken blindfolded to our jail. There they were stripped, deloused, put into a uniform, given a number, and put into a cell with two other prisoners where they expected to live for the next two weeks. The pay was good . . . and their motivation was to make money. . . . At the end of only six days we had to close down our mock prison because what we saw was frightening. It was no longer apparent to most of the subjects (or to us) where reality ended and their roles began. The majority had indeed become prisoners or guards, no longer able to clearly differentiate between role playing and self. There were dramatic changes in virtually every aspect of their behavior, thinking, and feeling. In less than a week the experience of imprisonment undid (temporarily) a lifetime of learning; human values were suspended, self-concepts were challenged, and the ugliest, most base, pathological side of human nature surfaced. We were horrified because we saw some boys (guards) treat others as if they were despicable animals, taking pleasure in cruelty, while other boys (prisoners) became servile, dehumanized robots who thought only of escape, of their own individual survival, and of their mounting hatred for the guards. We had to release three prisoners in the first four days because they had such acute situational traumatic reactions as hysterical crying, confusion in thinking, and severe depression. Others begged to be paroled, and all but three were willing to forfeit all the money they had earned if they could be paroled.*

*Reprinted by permission of Transaction Publishers. Excerpt from *Pathology of Imprisonment* by Phillip G. Zimbardo. Copyright © 1972 by Transaction Publishers. All Rights Reserved.

It is clear that social roles can influence our behavior. What is not always clear is that we play numerous roles in our lives and that each role influences us whether we are aware of it or not. I play the roles of man, spouse, father, middle-aged person, person of Irish ancestry, heterosexual, brother, son, and psychology professor, to name only the most obvious ones. Each role is a source of social influence on my behavior whether I like it or not. I can work hard at not being the typical male or the typical father, but these roles inevitably influence me. How about you? What roles do you play and how do they make you different from me?

In addition to conforming to our social roles, we also behave according to the spoken and unspoken rules known as *social norms*. The social norms of our culture tell us how we should behave in particular situations. We avoid making eye contact with other people in an elevator and cover our mouths when we cough because these are widely held social norms for Americans. Most people conform to the social norms of their culture most of the time.

The influence of roles and norms is not all bad. I have emphasized the extent to which social roles can be harmful because I want to alert you to the fact that they can detract from your individuality, but it is important to recognize that social roles and norms play an essential positive function in society. Without social roles and norms, you would not know what to expect of your psychology instructor, to take but one example. Being a student would be much more difficult if you did not know that the person who plays the role of the instructor will give lectures on which you are supposed to take notes, and that she or he will give tests and will give you a grade at the end of the term. Understanding the roles of others—and those of ourselves—greatly facilitates our ability to work together in society for the common good. But they are potent sources of influence that must be understood.

### Obedience: Direct Influence by Authority Figures

One of the most fascinating, and often frightening, lines of inquiry in social psychology has been research on **obedience,** doing what we are told to do by people in authority. This research was prompted in part by the behavior of soldiers in World War II, and other wars, who committed unthinkable atrocities when ordered to do so. What kind of person would help abuse and murder 6 million Jews during the Holocaust? What kind of person would not refuse to obey such an order? The disturbing answer from research is that most of us are that kind of person.

Stanley Milgram (1963, 1965) conducted a series of studies that cast a glaring light on the subject of obedience. To get the full impact of his findings, try to imagine that you are a research participant in one of his experiments. You have volunteered for a study of memory. When you arrive at the appointed time, you and another person, a middle-aged man, meet a somewhat stern, authoritarian experimenter wearing a white lab coat. The experimenter chooses you to be the "teacher" in the experiment and the other participant to be the "learner." The learner will have to memorize a list of word pairs, but you have to test him and operate the equipment. The "equipment" is a console labeled "SHOCK GENERATOR" with a bank of switches marked from 15 to 450 volts.

You help strap the learner into something that looks like an electric chair, and you attach electrodes to him that are connected to the shock generator in the other room. The learner asks whether the experiment could be dangerous to his heart condition, but the experimenter assures him that, although the shocks could be extremely painful, they should cause no physical harm. You return to the next room, take your seat at the console, and are told how you should use the shocks to "help" the learner memorize the list.

You are to listen to him attempt to recite the list over the intercom and shock him by throwing one of the switches after each error. You are to begin with the weakest shock and increase the intensity each time he makes a mistake. You are even given a 45-volt shock so you can see what it feels like (it's unpleasant) and the experiment begins. The learner recalls the list fairly accurately but makes a few mistakes, and you shock him as you have been instructed to do.

What you do not know is that the learner is not really getting shocked. He is a confederate of the experimenter who is acting a role. He is not even talking over the intercom; you are hearing a tape recording instead. But the important thing is that you *believe* that a man with a heart condition is strapped into an electric chair in the next room and that you are giving him shocks every time he makes a mistake.

The learner groans after an intensity of 75 volts has been reached. At 150 volts, he says that his heart is bothering him and asks to be let out of the experiment. The experimenter denies the request and tells you to give him the shock when he makes a mistake. When the learner has been given the 180-volt shock, the learner screams that he cannot stand the pain, and, as you are told to turn the shock apparatus to 300 volts—the level marked "Danger: Extreme Shock"—he refuses to recite the list of word pairs any more. When you look toward the experimenter, expecting him to stop the proceedings, he firmly tells you to administer the next shock.

What would you do? Would you give the extremely dangerous shock, even though the learner was begging you to stop? Or would you refuse to continue? Milgram asked a panel of psychiatrists how many research participants they thought would continue giving shocks at this point, and they predicted that less than 5 percent would continue. What percentage would you predict? Milgram found that an incredible 65 percent not only gave the next shock but also continued participating until they had given the highest shock (450 volts).

**obedience**
Doing what one is told to do by people in authority.

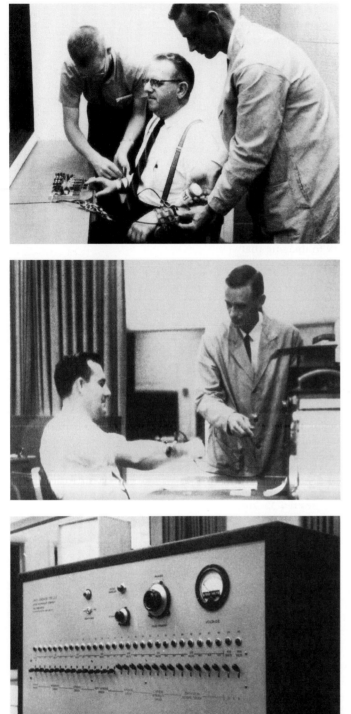

In Milgram's classic obedience experiments, the "learner" was strapped to a chair while participants were instructed to use what they believed was an electric shock generator to shock him after errors in learning.

Milgram's findings were astonishing, even to other social psychologists who understood the power of social situations. Could his results have been a fluke? Did Milgram just happen to recruit a group of sadistic individuals? To find out, Milgram repeated his study and found the same results with men and women from many different walks of life: students, blue-collar workers, white-collar workers, and professionals. He conducted his study in laboratories at prestigious Yale University and in an office space in downtown Bridgeport, Connecticut. This study has been replicated in other countries as well. The results of these studies are a painful reminder of the power of social situations and a warning of the ease with which misguided authorities can use ordinary people like you and me to obediently carry out their wishes.

It is somewhat comforting that later studies found that individuals were less likely to obey the instruction to give the high-voltage shocks when their victim was in the same room with them, acting distressed by the shocks. In addition, when the prestige of the experimenter was reduced, the percentage of obedient persons fell to about 50 percent. When the experimenter gave instructions by telephone rather than in person, the percentage fell to about 25 percent. Furthermore, when the research participant was in the presence of two other participants who refused to give the high-intensity shocks, only 10 percent obeyed the experimenter's instructions to the end. Obedience is also reduced when individuals are led to feel more personal responsibility for their actions and when it is obvious that authorities have self-serving goals. These last facts are somewhat encouraging, but they do not lessen the impact of Milgram's findings: The power of social situations over human behavior can be terrifying and must be guarded against.

A final comment is in order about Milgram's study of obedience. Although this study was of great value in exploring an important aspect of human nature, this study would not be considered ethical by today's standards. At a minimum, the experimenter would not be allowed to command the research participant to continue against her or his will—participants may leave an experiment at any time.

## The Positive Side of Groups

Has this discussion of social loafing, polarization, and groupthink convinced you that people should never work together on anything, or that the only way to remain a good person is to live in a cave as a hermit? It shouldn't at all. Think of the benefits that being in groups give us. There are many things that a single person working alone could not accomplish. Although it is true that people pull harder alone than when pulling in a group, four people working together could pull hard enough to pull a heavy boat ashore that a single person could never pull. In Milgram's obedience study, you saw that individuals in the presence of others who refused to obey the experimenter's instructions were more likely to disobey the authority figure as well.

Groups also can be therapeutic—think of support groups and group therapies—and can provide emotional support and comfort. Recall that you learned in chapter 13 that the effects of stress can be reduced considerably by strong social support (page 513). Therefore, we must be aware of the negative effects of groups on our behaviors, not so that we will avoid groups but so that we can make the best advantage of being in them.

Because we are social animals, we are almost always in the company of others. This is a fundamentally important observation because people can be fully understood only if our social nature is understood. Other people influence our behavior and we must understand that process of influence. We all need to be more aware of the power of social situations in influencing behavior. Ironically, ignoring the power of social situations only makes us more vulnerable to their influence.

The very fact of being with others can influence behavior; people often behave differently when they are in groups than when they are alone. Mobs commit crimes that the individuals alone would not commit, and groups of bystanders fail to help people in distress even though most members of that group would have done so if alone.

Groups influence individual behavior through our strong tendency to conform with the group even when not asked to do so. We may conform in terms of outward behavior and, in some instances, may change our inner judgments and attitudes as well. Groups also influence us through the expectations for our behavior that are inherent in social roles and social norms. Frighteningly, we are likely to be persuaded to obey even inappropriate requests from a prestigious authority figure, especially when we face the authority figure alone. When working in groups, individual effort declines under some circumstances and group problem solving can become distorted.

Despite these negative effects, groups can accomplish what an individual could never do when working alone; individual performance improves under some conditions; and the impact of stress can be softened by social support. The effects of our tendency to band together in groups can be positive, especially if we are aware of the potentially negative effects of groups on individual behavior. We are social animals whether we like it or not; as such we must understand the influence of groups on our behavior.

To be sure that you have learned the key points from the preceding section, cover the list of correct answers and try to answer each question. If you give an incorrect answer to any question, return to the page given next to the correct answer to see why your answer was not correct. Remember that these questions cover only some of the important information in this section; it is important that you make up your own questions to check your learning of other facts and concepts.

1.  Social psychology is the branch of psychology that studies _____.

2.  People may behave as they do in lynch mobs and at ball games because of a process called _____.

3.  In a situation where the solution is not obvious, we are most likely to conform _____.

    a)   publicly in terms of outward behaviors

    b)   privately in terms of judgments and attitudes

    c)   neither a nor b

    d)   both a and b

4. When workers exert less effort in a group than they would when working alone, the result is called _____.

   a) social loafing      c) groupthink

   b) group polarization      d) social facilitation

---

## Thinking Critically about Psychology

1. How much do you conform to others? When are you most likely to conform?

2. What do you think is the significance of Stanley Milgram's studies? What does it say about individual responsibility to behave ethically in a society?

---

**Correct Answers:**   **1.** individuals as they interact with others (p. 606),   **2.** deindividuation (p. 606),   **3. d** (p. 610),   **4. a** (p. 608).

## ● Attitudes and Persuasion

Attitudes are a pivotal concept in social psychology. They are of special interest because other people attempt to influence our attitudes through persuasion, and our attitudes are often reflected in our behavior toward others. If I give a speech to parents that changes their attitudes toward discipline practices (such as it's more important to praise children for their good behavior than to punish them for their bad behavior), they may tend to change the way they actually rear their children, too. As we will see, however, attitudes and social behavior are not perfectly correlated by any means. But there is enough relationship between the two to make attitudes a favorite topic of study of social psychologists, especially attitudes related to important aspects of social behavior such as prejudice based on a person's gender, ethnicity, age, sexual preference, or other factors.

Social psychologists define **attitudes** as beliefs that predispose us to act and feel in certain ways. Note that this definition has three components: (a) *beliefs*, such as the belief that door-to-door salespeople are generally dishonest; (b) *feelings*, such as a strong dislike for door-to-door salespeople; and (c) *dispositions to behave*, such as a readiness to be rude to them when they come to the door. Where do our attitudes come from, and what causes them to change?

**attitudes**
Beliefs that predispose one to act and feel in certain ways.

### Origins of Attitudes

The origins of most of our attitudes are fairly obvious: We learn them directly from our experiences, and we learn them from others (Olson & Zanna, 1993). Some of our attitudes are learned from firsthand experience. Children who are bitten by dogs often carry negative attitudes toward dogs for the rest of their lives, especially toward the kind of dog that bit them. In contrast, the sweet crunch of chocolate chip cookies generally leads to a favorable attitude toward them. In other words, some attitudes appear to be *classically conditioned*. If a stimulus (dogs or cookies) is paired with a positive or negative experience, the attitude will be similarly positive or negative (de Houwer, Thomas, & Baeyens, 2001; Olson & Fazio, 2001).

Attitudes are also commonly learned from others. Parents who model positive attitudes toward their Hispanic neighbors are likely to have children who have positive attitudes toward Hispanics. Children whose best friends think baseball is awful may pick up this attitude through modeling. Similarly, children who are reinforced by their parents and friends for prejudicial attitudes are likely to have these attitudes strengthened. In sum, other people instill attitudes in us through their modeling and reinforcement.

## Persuasion and Attitude Change

Attitudes are not chiseled in granite; they can change after they have been formed. Indeed, the earliest known writings on social psychology were about changing people's attitudes through **persuasion.** Aristotle's *Rhetoric* was an essay on factors that make for persuasive arguments when orators debate. You probably do not listen to many orators debate, but you are on the receiving end of other kinds of persuasive communications nearly every day. Commercials on the radio and television and advertisements in newspapers and magazines are designed to change your attitude about the sponsors' products. Political speeches and billboards are intended to persuade you how to vote. Your friend who wants to borrow your car tries to persuade you. And, when you ask your professor to let you take an exam early, you try to persuade him or her. Persuasion is a natural and necessary part of our interactions with other members of society. But because of the potentially important consequences of persuasive communications (your friend might actually talk you into lending her your car!), it's important to know something about their nature. The persuasiveness of a communication is not determined merely by the logical quality of the argument. Logic may, in fact, be one of the *least important* factors. That's a scary thought, because we would like to believe that we live in a world where logic and truth win out. But if you know what makes an argument persuasive, you can at least be on your guard. Notice that the qualities of persuasive communication fall into three general categories: characteristics of the *speaker,* of the *communication* itself, and of the *people who hear it.*

### Characteristics of the Speaker

Several characteristics of the speaker are important in determining how persuasive a communication will be:

1. *Credibility.* If you were to listen to a speech on the value of arithmetic, do you think you would be more persuaded if the speech were given by a noted engineer or a dishwasher? Elliot Aronson and Burton Golden (1962) conducted exactly this experiment and found that the engineer swayed opinions considerably more than the dishwasher, even though they gave exactly the same speech. In fact, the same person gave the same speech each time; just the introduction identifying his job differed. Many other studies have reached the same conclusion (Aronson, 1995). Our perception of the credibility of the speaker has a great deal to do with the persuasiveness of the communication.

   But credibility should not be confused in the previous example with being highly educated, intelligent, high in status, or even nice. The key is whether the speaker is a credible source of information *about the specific argument being presented.* Elaine Walster and her colleagues performed a clever experiment that forcefully makes this point (Walster, Aronson, & Abrahams, 1966). Individuals were given newspaper clippings of interviews with either a mobster or a politician. Half of the research participants read clippings that argued for more lenient treatment of criminals by the courts, and half read arguments for stricter treatment. When the mobster argued for more lenient treatment, he was completely ineffective and, in fact, slightly swayed attitudes in the opposite direction. When the mobster argued for *stricter* treatment, however, he was as persuasive as the politician. Apparently, the reasoning was that if a criminal (who knows about crime and would not personally benefit from stricter enforcement) thinks we need stricter enforcement of the laws, then it must be so.

   In general, the more credible the speaker, the more persuasive the message. But Carl Hovland has qualified this conclusion with the identification of what he called **sleeper effects** (Hovland & Weiss, 1951). Although attempts at persuasion by speakers who are low in credibility are ineffective at first, their messages may

**persuasion**
The process of changing another person's attitudes through arguments and other related means.

**sleeper effects**
According to Hovland, the potential for low-credibility speakers to influence opinion after a period of time.

Attractive, popular, or famous speakers tend to be more persuasive than unattractive speakers. But their persuasiveness seems to be limited to relatively unimportant issues.

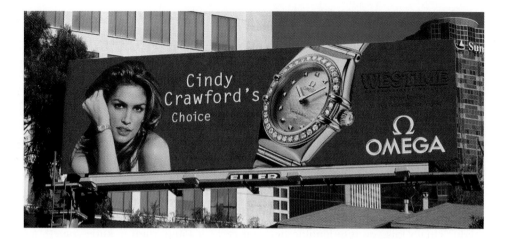

have an effect later. This is because people tend to forget what speaker presented what message. If you forget that a low-credibility speaker presented a certain message, then later that message will not seem so unbelievable.

2. *Attractiveness.* Other things being equal, a speaker who is attractive, popular, famous, and likable will be more effective in changing our opinions than an unattractive speaker. That is why Cindy Crawford is paid enormous sums to endorse products in commercials and I am not. Fortunately, the persuasiveness of attractive speakers seems to be limited to relatively unimportant issues—but that includes almost everything that advertisers want us to buy (Aronson, 1994; Chaiken & Eagly, 1983).

3. *Intent.* Speakers are generally less persuasive if they obviously intend to change your opinion, particularly if the speaker has something to gain by changing your opinion (Aronson, 1995). If a real estate agent tells you that a lot she wants you to buy is going to rise dramatically in value, you might not believe her. On the other hand, if you overhear two realtors at a cocktail party say the same thing, the message would probably be more persuasive because no one is trying to convince you or make a commission from the sale. That is the rationale behind the "hidden camera" testimonials that are included in some television commercials. Since the people supposedly do not know they are on camera, they do not seem to be trying to sell us anything.

### Characteristics of the Message

In addition to the qualities of the speaker, the characteristics of the message are also important determinants of persuasiveness:

1. *Fear appeals.* Are messages that arouse fear more persuasive than unemotional ones? Adolf Hitler appealed strongly to the fears and frustrations of the German people in the speeches he gave to rally support behind his Nazi party. Were the emotions he aroused part of the reason for his success? The American Cancer Society uses scare tactics in some of their ads to convince people to stop smoking. Are they going about it in the right way?

   Considerable evidence suggests that communications that arouse fear—such as graphic pictures of rotten teeth and gums in messages urging proper dental care—are more effective than the same messages without the fear-provoking images. Fear can enhance the persuasiveness of a communication, but only under certain circumstances (Mewborn & Rogers, 1979; Rogers, 1975). Listeners will respond favorably to a fear-inducing persuasive communication only if (a) the emotional appeal is a relatively strong one (but not too strong), (b) the listeners think that the fearful outcome (such as rotten teeth or lung cancer) is likely to happen to them, and (c) the message offers an effective way of avoiding the fearful outcome (such as an easy way to stop smoking). If all of these elements are present, emotional appeals can be highly persuasive.

2. ***Two-sided arguments.*** There are two sides to most arguments. If, for example, we use more coal in generating electric power, we will reduce our dependence on foreign oil and may be able to keep oil prices from rising. That is good. But if we burn more coal, we will also increase pollution of the atmosphere, which will hurt people's health, damage land and water in the process of strip mining, and lose lives during the mining process. That is obviously bad. If you were trying to convince Congress to support the use of less coal, would it be more effective to state just the positive side of the argument, or both sides?

There is no simple answer to this question. In part, it depends on how favorable the audience is to your position before you start talking. If the audience is leaning in your favor or has information only about your position, your message will be more persuasive if you just tell them about the benefits of not burning coal. Telling them about the negative side to the argument may lose you some supporters. But if audience members are initially unfavorable to your position or are knowledgeable about both sides of the issue, it's generally better to give them both sides of the argument. That will make you seem more credible and less biased (Baron & Byrne, 1982). So the next time somebody does an admirable job of presenting both sides of an issue, you may be dealing with a strong believer in honesty and the democratic process, but you may just be listening to a shrewd operator who is trying to change your mind.

3. ***Message framing.*** If you will recall from chapter 8 on cognition (page 274), the way in which problems are presented to us in words—or *framed*—strongly influences how we solve those problems (Rothman & Salovey, 1997). Humans are so influenced by the wording of problems that we often reach very different solutions to exactly the same problem if it is framed differently. New research suggests that the same appears to be true of persuasive communications—framing the same message in different ways can sometimes make all the difference.

An excellent and inherently important example has been provided by psychologists Beth Meyerowitz and Shelly Chaiken (1987). They compared the persuasiveness of two messages designed to encourage college-age women to conduct breast self-examinations. Two groups of women read a three-page pamphlet on breast cancer and self-examinations. Their pamphlets were identical, except for several statements. One group read statements framed to emphasize the *gains* of breast self-examination:

> By doing breast self-examination now, you can learn what your normal healthy breasts feel like so that you will be better prepared to notice any small, abnormal changes that might occur as you get older. Research shows that women who do breast self-examination have an increased chance of finding a tumor in the early, more treatable stage of the disease. (p. 504)

The other group read statements framed to emphasize the *loss* involved in not conducting breast self-examination:

> By not doing breast self-examination you will not learn what your normal, healthy breasts feel like so that you will be ill-prepared to notice any small, abnormal changes that might occur as you get older. Research shows that women who do not do breast self-examination have a decreased chance of finding a tumor in the early, more treatable stage of the disease. (p. 504)

## Breast Health Action Plan

***Mammography:***

Annual mammograms are the best way to find breast cancer early.

Have a mammogram every year if you are age 40 or older.

If you have a history of breast cancer in your family, discuss a personal mammography screening schedule with your health care provider.

***Clinical Breast Examination:***

After age 40, have a clinical breast exam by your health care provider every year.

Between ages 20 and 39, have a clinical breast exam by your health care provider at least every three years.

***Breast Self-Examination:***

Ask your health care provider to teach you the proper way to do a thorough breast self-exam. Beginning at age 20, examine your own breasts monthly.

Do messages persuade women to conduct breast self-examination? It depends on how the message is framed.

Four months later, the women were interviewed to determine if the messages had had any positive effects. The results showed that the second message, framed in terms of potential loss, was more effective than the first version. Women reading the loss-framed message had much more positive attitudes toward breast self-examination and were almost twice as likely to have practiced it. Women reading the pamphlet framed in terms of potential gains were no more likely to engage in breast self-examination than was a group who had not read either pamphlet. Interestingly, the two pamphlets did not arouse different amounts of fear, so we cannot conclude that this is just another example of the greater effects of fear-arousing communications. Although a great deal has been learned about the best ways to frame messages to encourage breast self-examination in recent years, health professionals infrequently frame appeals in the most effective ways (Kline & Mattson, 2000). Understanding framing helps us make the point that effective persuasion is not just the result of *what* you say but also *how* you say it.

### Characteristics of the Listeners

In addition to qualities of the speaker and the message, certain characteristics of the listeners help determine how persuasive an argument will be:

1. *Intelligence.* Less intelligent people are generally easier to persuade. The exception is when the message is complex and difficult to understand; under this condition, more intelligent listeners are easier to persuade (Rhodes & Wood, 1992).

2. *Need for social approval.* Some people have a greater need for social approval (a need to be approved of or liked by others) than other people do. People with a high need for social approval are generally easier to persuade than people who are low in this need (Baron & Byrne, 1982).

3. *Self-esteem.* Individuals whose self-esteem is moderate (who have opinions of themselves that are about as positive as most people's) are generally easier to convince than people with either high self-esteem or low self-esteem (Rhodes & Wood, 1992; Zellner, 1970). Persons with high self-esteem are generally very confident of their opinions and difficult to influence. Persons with low self-esteem, in contrast, tend not to pay attention to the communication enough to be swayed. For example, a person with a very low opinion of himself might hear a speech on financing public schools and become lost in his own thoughts about his own poor educational performance (Rhodes & Wood, 1992).

4. *Audience size.* People are generally easier to persuade when they are listening to the message in a group rather than alone. And bigger crowds lead to greater persuasion than smaller ones (Newton & Mann, 1980).

5. *Gender.* Early studies on persuasion suggested that women are more persuadable than men. However, these studies were biased, using messages that were of greater interest to men. Later studies controlling for this interest variable show that there are no differences in persuadability between men and women (Eagly, 1978).

### Techniques of Persuasion

Some people are better at persuasion than other people are. This is partly because they have the characteristics of persuasive speakers, and partly because they understand the characteristics of the message and the audience—they know how to pitch the most persuasive argument to their audience. But many persuasive people—from politicians to salespeople—also know and use some simple *techniques of persuasion.* As you read, try to recall if these techniques have been used on you by salespeople.

A classic technique of persuasion is the *foot-in-the-door technique.* The person first makes a small, reasonable request. After you agree to that request, however, he or she follows up with a larger request. If someone were to call you at home and say that she was a researcher at another university who would like to come over and inspect your home, would you agree to let her in? Most people would be reluctant to agree, but people who first agree to answer a few questions over the telephone are more likely to allow researchers to inspect their homes. Agreeing to one small request makes us more likely to agree to a second, larger request.

The *low-ball technique* is similar to the foot-in-the-door. First, you are offered a very reasonable deal. When you accept it, the deal is changed—for the worse. This is a favorite of some auto salespeople. First, they get you to commit to a particular car for a fair price. While you're dreaming of driving this wonderful car, you get the bad news that the salesperson forgot to figure in the delivery charge and the undercoating. Now the car costs more than you thought—do you still buy it? This technique of persuasion works more often than not—most people don't walk away from the deal (Burger, 1986).

## Behavior and Attitude Change: Cognitive Dissonance Theory

As we have seen, persuasion is an important source of attitude change, but the discrepancy that often exists between our attitudes and behavior is another key cause of changed attitudes. Even though attitudes are partially defined in terms of a disposition to behave, there is sometimes a great difference between our attitudes and our behavior. For example, during the Vietnam War, many men who held attitudes that were strongly opposed to the war obeyed their draft orders and became a part of the war. Similarly, opinion pollsters know that not everyone who has a favorable attitude toward a product will actually buy it.

An interesting point is that when behavior and attitudes are inconsistent, the attitudes often change to match the behavior *rather than the other way around.* Leon Festinger (1957) proposed the theory of **cognitive dissonance** to explain the tendency of attitudes to sometimes shift to be consistent with behavior. This theory, which has sparked some of the greatest controversy and most interesting research in social psychology, states that inconsistencies between attitudes and behavior are uncomfortable. This discomfort motivates people to do what they can to reduce the discomfort, or *dissonance.*

For example, if you smoke cigarettes (behavior), and you know that cigarette smoking is the leading cause of lung cancer and other serious diseases (attitude), your behavior and attitude are inconsistent, which produces dissonance. Dissonance theory predicts that either your attitude or your behavior will change to reduce the dissonance (Gibbons, Eggleston, & Benthin, 1997) (see figure 16.3). You could change the behavior and quit smoking, but that is often very difficult for smokers. Unfortunately, human beings usually reduce dissonance in the easiest way possible. In this case, it might be easier to change your attitude toward smoking. How many smokers do you know who say that the research linking cancer and smoking is faulty or who say, "So what if smoking causes cancer; I'll die of something, anyway"? These are irrational and self-defeating arguments, but they are effective ways of reducing dissonance.

Festinger and other social psychologists have tested the theory of cognitive dissonance in a large number of

**cognitive dissonance**
(dis´so-nans) The discomfort that results from inconsistencies between attitudes and behavior.

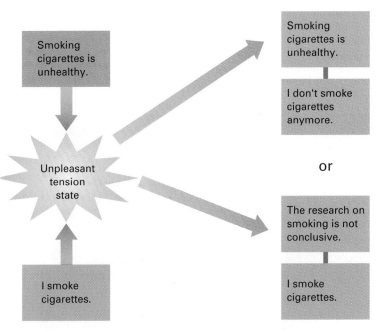

**FIGURE 16.3**
If attitudes and behavior are inconsistent, cognitive dissonance is created. To reduce this unpleasant state, either attitudes or behaviors change to be consistent with one another.

experiments. One of the best known (Festinger & Carlsmith, 1959) involved asking research participants to perform a boring spool-stacking and peg-turning task for an hour. Afterward, the participants were each asked to tell the next participant that the task was an interesting one. Half of the individuals were offered $20 to say that the task was interesting, and half were offered $1. A third group of individuals stacked spools but were not asked to say anything to the next research participant. Later, all of the participants were asked how interesting they really thought the task was.

Which group do you think reported the most favorable attitude toward the task? Perhaps surprisingly—but just as predicted by cognitive dissonance theory—the most positive attitudes were expressed by the group offered only $1. The group offered $20 was not placed in a state of dissonance: "The task was really boring, but I'll lie to the next person to get the $20." The group offered $1 was placed in a state of dissonance, however; there was no good explanation for their stating an opinion about the task that was inconsistent with their attitudes, so their attitudes improved to be more consistent with their behavior.

Cognitive dissonance is relevant to more than just our attitudes about stacking spools (Cooper & Mackie, 1983). For example, an interesting study was conducted following the 1980 presidential election. University students who supported Ronald Reagan in the election were the research participants in this experiment. They were asked to write an essay favoring an issue that Ronald Reagan opposed (federally sponsored health care) or an essay supporting the candidacy of Reagan's Democratic opponent, Jimmy Carter. Half of the students were given very little choice about writing the essays. This group could be expected to experience little cognitive dissonance ("I wrote an essay that was contrary to what I believe, but I had to do it"). The other group of students was given much more choice as to whether or not to write the essay. These students were likely to experience considerable cognitive dissonance, because they wrote an essay favoring something that they opposed, even though they did not have to do so. As Festinger would have predicted, attitudes toward Jimmy Carter and federally sponsored health care changed very little in the low–cognitive dissonance group (the individuals given little choice about writing the essays) but changed significantly more in the high–cognitive dissonance group (the ones given more choice). When the behavior of writing the essays created cognitive dissonance, attitudes changed to be more consistent with the behavior.

It's a little scary, isn't it? You probably thought your attitudes were always thoughtfully arrived at and based on reality. If Festinger is right, they may sometimes reflect nothing more than an escape from cognitive dissonance.

**prejudice**
A harmful attitude based on inaccurate generalizations about a group of people.

**stereotype**
An inaccurate generalization on which a prejudice is based.

## Prejudice and Stereotypes

Of all the attitudes that we hold about other people, the kind that is most worthy of improved understanding is prejudice. **Prejudice** is a harmful attitude based on inaccurate generalizations about a group of people based on their skin color, religion, sex, age, or any other noticeable difference. In some way, however, the difference is believed by the prejudiced person to imply something negative about the entire group. They're all lazy, or hysterical, or pushy.

The inaccurate generalization on which the prejudice is based is called a **stereotype.** We all hold stereotypes of other groups of people. How does a "rock star" look and act? If you were producing a movie, would you cast Bob Dole or Barbara Walters in the role of a rock star? You wouldn't, because neither of them fits the stereotyped image of rock stars. What are Russians like? Do you have a stereotyped view of them? Think about it for a second.

Stereotyping people, such as the "typical" salesperson, detracts from our ability to treat members of a group as individuals and leads to faulty attributions.

Would you cast Goldie Hawn as a Russian army officer in a serious dramatic film? Do you hold stereotypes of women, men, Cambodians, African Americans, old people, Cubans?

Stereotypes can be either negative or positive (you might believe that all psychology textbook authors are charming, witty, and attractive), but all stereotypes, positive or negative, are inherently harmful for three reasons:

1. *Stereotypes take away our ability to treat each member of a group as an individual.* When we hold a stereotyped view of a group, we tend to treat each member of that group as if the person has the exact characteristics of the stereotype, whether or not he or she really has those characteristics. Even when the stereotype is partially based on fact, many members of the group will differ from the stereotype in significant ways. Take the view that many of us have of Chinese Americans: One aspect of the stereotype is that they are highly intelligent. Although it's true that *on the average* Chinese Americans score slightly higher than whites on some specific measures of intelligence, not all Chinese are highly intelligent. If a teacher's expectations for a Chinese child of below-average intelligence were based on this stereotype, the child might be criticized for not living up to his or her supposed high intelligence when the child is, in fact, performing up to his or her ability. Stereotyped beliefs that an ethnic group is low in intelligence can have even more serious consequences in limiting the educational and occupational opportunities of members of that group.

2. *Stereotypes lead to narrow expectations for behavior.* Our stereotypes lead us to expect the members of the stereotyped group to behave in certain ways. For example, we expect women to be gentle, nurturing, caring, and cooperative, but we expect men to be competitive, ambitious, aggressive, and strong. Individuals of either sex who do not conform to these expectations are viewed as abnormal and are often the objects of anger or ridicule. Thus, stereotypes can be a limiting force for persons who do not conform to the narrow expectations for their group (gender, ethnicity, age, etc.).

3. *Stereotypes lead to faulty attributions.* **Attribution theory** is based on the idea that humans tend to try to explain why things happen—that is, attribute them to a cause. One of the things that we are most fond of doing is explaining behavior, both others and our own. One of your friends has just invited herself over for dinner for the third time this month. Why? Is she broke? Is she a moocher? Does she just like your company? According to attribution theory, we tend to attribute all behavior to a cause.

    Our stereotypes influence the attributions that we make about other people's behavior. As Elliot Aronson (1995) points out, if a prejudiced white man sees an overturned trash can and garbage strewn around the yard of a white family, he is apt to attribute the mess to a stray dog looking for food. But, if he sees the same thing in the yard of an African American family, he would more likely attribute it to their supposed lazy, slovenly ways.

    These faulty attributions have the effect of deepening and strengthening our prejudices as we keep "seeing" evidence that "supports" our stereotypes and rejecting evidence that is contrary to them. For more on the harmful effects of stereotypes, see *Application of Psychology:* "Stereotypes and Discrimination in the Workplace" at the end of this chapter.

**attribution theory**
(ah-tri-bu′shun)  The theory that people tend to look for explanations for their own behavior and that of others.

## Causes of Stereotypes and Prejudice

If we are to have any hope of reducing prejudice, it is essential to understand the causes of these harmful attitudes. Social psychologists have proposed four explanations for why prejudice arises:

1. ***Realistic conflict.*** The *realistic conflict theory* suggests that people who are competing for scarce resources, such as jobs, food, and territory, come to view others in increasingly negative ways (White, 1977). Although this theory may explain some instances of prejudice, prejudice often exists when there is no conflict over resources.

2. ***Us versus them.*** Another source of prejudice is the tendency people have to divide the world into two groups—*us versus them* (Turner & others, 1987). Our group becomes the "in-group," and those who are excluded become the "out-group." In a classic study, Sherif and Sherif (1953) randomly divided middle-class 11- and 12-year-old boys of the same race into two groups: the Rattlers and the Eagles. After a series of activities designed to promote in-group solidarity and between-group competition, the rival groups began to engage in fighting and name calling—they developed prejudices about one another, even though the groups had been created randomly.

   Social psychologists believe that "us versus them" prejudice is common partly because it strengthens the prejudiced individuals' self-esteem. Consider the following illustrative studies (Fein & Spencer, 1997): Introductory psychology students were asked to participate in two experiments in sequence. In the first experiment, the students were asked to choose one term from a list of values (honesty, thriftiness, etc.) and write a few paragraphs saying why that value is important. Half of the students (randomly determined) were asked to choose the value that is most important to them personally and half were asked to choose the value that is least important to them. Previous studies have shown that writing about a value that is important to the individual is an effective way of strengthening his or her self-image, but writing about an unimportant value is not.

   Therefore, as the second experiment began, half of the group had just gone through an exercise that strengthened their self image. The second experiment was presented as a study of the evaluation of job applicants. The students all read the résumé and watched the same videotape of a young female job applicant's interview for a management position. Half of the students (randomly determined) were given information indicating that the applicant was Jewish, and half of the students were given information that the applicant was not Jewish. The students then rated the applicant in terms of her personality and job qualifications. The personality and qualifications of the woman were rated more negatively by non-Jewish students when she was presented as Jewish. Because the résumé and the videotape were of the same woman, these differences in ratings clearly reflect anti-Jewish prejudice. There was significantly less prejudice, however, in the ratings of students whose self-image had just been strengthened in the preceding experiment. Other follow-up studies by the same investigators showed that college students become more prejudiced in their evaluations of others when their self-images are threatened, but that having a chance to say negative things about a member of another ethnic group increases their self-esteem (Fein & Spencer, 1997). Thus, "us versus them" prejudice appears to be perpetuated partly because it bolsters the self-esteem of persons with weak self-images.

3. ***Social learning.*** Like any other kind of attitude, it is clear that prejudice can be learned from others. When we observe the stereotypes and prejudices expressed by parents, friends, teachers, and the media, we are likely to adopt the same prejudices.

### Combating Prejudice

Prejudice is harmful to the human race. But is there anything that can be done about it? There are some effective antidotes:

# HUMAN DIVERSITY

## Stereotypes about College Students with Physical Challenges

Most Americans are "able-bodied" persons with no serious limitations on our ability to see, hear, speak, or move about. Many of us, however, are challenged by physical conditions that make these everyday activities more difficult or impossible. Like any group that is *different* from most of the people in society, persons with physical challenges are the subject of stereotypes, prejudices, limitations, and stigma. These factors can profoundly influence their lives.

An important study by Catherine Fichten and her colleagues at Dawson College found that able-bodied students' perceptions of peers with disabilities are quite different from these students' perceptions of themselves (Fichten, Robillard, Judd, & Amsel, 1989). Three groups of students participated in the study: wheelchair users, students with a visual impairment, and able-bodied students. They completed several questionnaires that measured self-concept, dating behavior, and anxiety in social situations. First they completed these questionnaires about themselves and then they completed the same measures in the way that they thought the other groups would respond.

Fichten and her colleagues found that able-bodied students and students with physical challenges viewed each other in stereotyped ways. For example, the able-bodied students believed that the students with physical challenges were more anxious about dating and dated less frequently than able-bodied students. In addition, the able-bodied students viewed the students who had physical challenges as nervous, unaggressive, insecure, dependent, and unhappy. The stereotyping was not all negative, however. Able-bodied students also viewed students with physical challenges as quiet, honest, softhearted, nonegotistical, and undemanding. The students with physical challenges held stereotypes about able-bodied students, too. They viewed the able-bodied students as demanding, argumentative, overconfident, phony, and complaining.

In most instances, however, the stereotyped perceptions were based on myths. For example, Fichten and her colleagues found no differences in either the number of dates or anxiety about dating reported by students with physical challenges and able-bodied students, even though the able-bodied students thought that students with physical challenges were less satisfied with their dating. Similarly, although able-bodied students believed that the self-esteem scores of students with physical challenges were lower than their own, there were no actual differences in the self-esteem of able-bodied students, students who were visually impaired, and students who used wheelchairs. It is striking that even the students with physical challenges themselves sometimes believed the same myths about students with other physical challenges. Both able-bodied students and students with physical challenges attributed more "handicapped" stereotypes to students with physical challenges than to able-bodied students in the Fichten study.

The Americans with Disabilities Act of 1990 brought the needs of persons with physical challenges into the consciousness of people in the United States. It was designed to enable persons with physical challenges to gain access to public facilities and to the workplace. As is the case with other civil rights legislation, societal changes require more than just the passage of laws, however. If the stereotypes are to be reduced, able-bodied persons and persons with physical challenges must learn more about each other through extended contact under conditions of equal status. It is hoped, however, that the laws that guarantee the rights of persons with physical challenges to education, employment, and recreation will create conditions under which persons with and without physical challenges can get to know each other as individuals. In time, such interactions may improve the degree to which people with disabilities will be able to participate fully in society without stereotypes and discrimination.

If you are not physically challenged yourself, what kinds of exposure have you had to persons who are? As you walk around your campus and your community today, notice how you react when you see a person with physical challenges. Do you react in the same way as to able-bodied persons? Can you see the influence of stereotypes in these reactions? How could you make it easier for persons with physical challenges at your school to interact with able-bodied students on an equal basis?

It is important to note that use of the term "physical disability" has been discouraged to emphasize the fact that the physical condition often does not disable the person in any absolute sense. Many persons prefer the more neutral term of "physically challenged." But some persons reject the newer term "physically challenged" as well, stating that they alone should decide whether or not their physical condition is "challenging" (Bregante, Martinez, & O'Toole, 1993). ■

Although prejudice can sometimes be reduced through increasing contact among ethnic groups, simple direct contact, such as attending a multiethnic school, is not enough.

1. ***Recognize prejudice.*** Most people believe that they are not prejudiced. We tend to view any negative attitudes we hold as true and justifiable. The first and most important step in reducing prejudice is to become aware of our own prejudices and their harmful consequences (Aronson, 1995).

2. ***Control automatic responses.*** It is not easy to rid yourself of prejudices that took a lifetime to acquire, even if you sincerely want to. It is possible to control our automatic prejudicial reactions, however (Devine, 1996; Fiske, 2002; Monteith & others, 2002). Imagine that a classmate asks you if she can borrow your notes from the last class. She says that she missed the class because she was sick. If she were a member of an ethnic group that your parents always said was lazy, you might immediately think, "I'll bet she was just too lazy to come to class." People who are genuinely trying to reject prejudice, however, control those immediate prejudice reactions and deal with others on their own merits—not on the basis of automatic prejudice.

3. ***Increase contact among prejudiced groups.*** Prejudice can sometimes be reduced by increasing direct contact with people from other groups (Dovidio & Gaertner, 1999; Stephan, 1987). As most people who attended multiethnic schools can tell you, however, simple direct contact with other ethnic groups is not enough to reduce prejudice. For the direct contact to work, it must occur under certain conditions.

First, the two groups must be approximately *equal in status*. For example, if two groups of accountants from two different ethnic groups spend time together, their prejudice may decrease, but if accountants from one ethnic group spend time with unskilled laborers from another ethnic group, there is little likelihood that the prejudice will diminish. Similarly, the environment in which the two groups interact should be one that encourages group equality. The interactions that occur between managers of one race and employees of another race will not decrease prejudice.

Second, prejudice between groups will decline only if the group members *view each other as typical of their respective groups*—not as exceptions to the rule. There will be no improvement in relations if the members of one group think "This person is pretty darn smart—not like the others."

Third, when two groups who are prejudiced against one another interact, their prejudice will decrease if they are engaged in *cooperative rather than competitive tasks*. If a city is trying to decrease prejudice among teenagers of two different ethnic groups by bringing them together in a basketball league, the ethnic groups should be mixed on the same teams, not put on opposing teams. Cooperation builds respect; competition maintains prejudice.

Finally, *the contact should be informal*, so that one-on-one interactions can occur. Formal interactions among employees of different ethnic groups are not as beneficial as the informal time spent together on breaks or after work.

## Review

Attitudes are a focus of research for social psychologists because they play a key role in the interactions among people: People influence our attitudes, and those attitudes, in turn, are reflected to some extent in the way that we interact with others. Attitudes are defined in terms of three components: beliefs, feelings, and dispositions to behave. Attitudes appear to be learned, sometimes through direct experience with the object of our attitude and sometimes from others.

Attitudes are subject to change after they have been formed. One common form of attitude change is through direct persuasion by others. Nearly every day someone tries to persuade us to change our attitudes or behavior. The effectiveness of these attempts to influence depends on qualities of the speaker, the message, and the listener. Speakers are more influential when they appear credible, are attractive, and do not appear to be trying to influence us for their own personal gain. We are most likely to be influenced by fear-inducing messages if the fear appeal is moderately strong, if the listener thinks the fearful outcome is likely, and if reasonable ways of avoiding the fearful outcome are presented. Messages that present some information favoring both sides of the argument are more persuasive to listeners who are knowledgeable about both sides of an issue and are initially opposed to the message. The way that a message is framed can affect persuasion. And listeners tend to be more easily persuaded when they are less intelligent, have a high need for social approval, are somewhat low in self-esteem, and are in large groups. Gender is not related to persuadability, however.

Discrepancies between our behavior and attitudes provide another potent source of attitudes. Sometimes there is a big difference between the attitudes that we express and the way we behave. Under some circumstances, changes in behavior that create a discrepancy between behavior and attitudes are followed by a change in attitudes that makes the attitudes consistent with behavior again. This is most likely to occur when there is no obvious external cause of the change in behavior. Cognitive dissonance theory explains this change in attitude by stating that the discrepancy between behavior and attitudes creates an uncomfortable state. This discomfort is reduced when the attitudes change to fit the behavior.

Prejudice is a negative attitude based on inaccurate generalizations about a group of people. These inaccurate generalizations, called stereotypes, are inherently harmful because they make it difficult to evaluate members of that group on an individual basis and lead to faulty generalizations about their behavior. At times prejudice can be reduced if people become aware of their prejudices, control automatic prejudicial reactions, and interact more under positive conditions with members of groups against whom they are prejudiced. Increased interaction will decrease prejudice only when the interactions are among persons of equal status, when those involved in the interactions view each other as typical of their respective groups, when the interactions are cooperative rather than competitive, and when the interactions are informal.

---

To be sure that you have learned the key points from the preceding section, cover the list of correct answers and try to answer each question. If you give an incorrect answer to any question, return to the page given next to the correct answer to see why your answer was not correct.

**Check Your Learning**

1. Attitudes consist of three components: _____ , _____ , and _____ .

2. Which of the following speakers would be the least persuasive?

   a)   a speaker who intends to persuade you, and you know it
   b)   a credible speaker
   c)   an attractive speaker
   d)   all of the above

3. Two-sided arguments are most persuasive when _____ .

   a)   the audience knows only one side of the issue
   b)   the audience knows both sides of the issue
   c)   the audience is unfavorable to your side of the argument
   d)   both b and c

4. Prejudices are harmful attitudes based on inaccurate generalizations known as
_____.

a) attributions

c) negativities

b) stereotypes

d) all of the above

## Thinking Critically about Psychology

1. If you were trying to convince others to donate money to your favorite cause, how would you use the information contained in this section?

2. Design a program that might reduce racial prejudice in the high school you attended.

Correct Answers: 1. beliefs, feelings, dispositions to behave (p. 616), 2. a (p. 617), 3. d (p. 619), 4. b (p. 622).

## Interpersonal Attraction: Friendship and Love

Who are your friends? Why do you suppose you became friends with them rather than with other people you know? Are you in love with someone, or have you ever been in love? What attracted you to him or her and made you experience such intense feelings? Friendship and love are powerful social phenomena that touch all of our lives in one way or another. As such, they have been of special interest to social psychologists. In this section, we will look at variables that influence our perception of others, the role played by attribution processes in person perception, the qualities of others that make them attractive to us, and the factors involved in maintaining personal relationships.

### Person Perception

**person perception**
The process of forming impressions of others.

The first step toward understanding why we are attracted to one person rather than another is to understand something about the process of **person perception.** What factors are important in the way we perceive others? We seem to go through a complex process of "cognitive algebra" to reach an average of all the many factors that enter into our perceptions of others—with some factors contributing more to the average than others (Fiske, 1993; Kaplan, 1975). We sum up a person as if we assign a weight to each person's positive and negative characteristics in accordance with how important that characteristic is to us, and then we add them all together to arrive at a total perception of the person. But, as the following sections show, the process of person perception is complicated further by the ways we gather and use information about others.

#### Negative Information: The Bad Outweighs the Good

Other things being equal, we tend to assign higher weights to negative than to positive information (Hamilton & Zanna, 1972). Put yourself in this situation: You are a person who values warmth, physical attractiveness, and honesty in others. You meet a person in class whom you find extremely warm and attractive; you have an enjoyable conversation with him after class, but during the course of the conversation he asks you to help him think of a lie to tell his girlfriend explaining where he has been. Your opinion of him will probably become quite negative if honesty is really important to you. The fact that he is being dishonest with his girlfriend will overshadow his positive characteristics. Most of us will pass up a delicious-looking cake if we know it contains even a small amount of rat poison.

#### Primacy Effects: The Importance of First Impressions

Our first impressions are usually very important in the person perception process. When you pause for a moment and think about this, it's quite disturbing. A factor that is irrelevant to the nature of the person we are perceiving—the order in which we learn

First impressions are often given greater weight than later information in the person perception process.

information about that person—can greatly influence our perception of that person. All of us have our good days and bad days, and it's a shame that the perception that others form of us is influenced so much by whether they form their first impression of us on a good or a bad day.

The first information that we are exposed to about a person tends to be given greater weight than later information (Asch, 1946; Belmore, 1987; Hovland, 1957). This is called the **primacy effect.** If you were introduced to Barbara right after you heard her deliver a polished and interesting talk to your sales group on the importance of ethics in business, your impression would probably be quite positive. Later, if you were to run into her in a bar, sitting alone, looking forlorn, disheveled, and half-drunk, you would be seeing a very different side of Barbara. But because your initial impression of her was favorable, there would be a strong tendency for you to ignore or "explain away" this new information ("Something awful must have happened to Barbara to make her act this way").

Suppose, however, that seeing Barbara in the bar was your *first* exposure to her. In that case, your first impression of her would be negative and would tend to dominate your perception of her, even after you were exposed to more positive information about her later. If your second meeting with her was hearing her lecture on business ethics, you would tend to discount the positive impression she was giving in that encounter ("She's holding herself together pretty well today—I bet most people here don't know she's really a drunken slob.").

First impressions (primacy effects) are not always of overriding importance, however. Their impact is greatly reduced under three conditions:

1. *Prolonged exposure.* Prolonged exposure to a person tends to reduce the importance of your first impression of that person. Although it's important to try to make a favorable first impression on the first day of your new job, do not worry too much about it if you do not. Eventually, your fellow employees will get to know the real you. Information about you gathered over a long period of time will erase any first impressions. Working in favor of prolonged exposure's correcting any inaccuracies in our first impressions is the fact that we are more likely to notice and remember information that is inconsistent with our first impression of a person (Belmore, 1987; Belmore & Hubbard, 1987).

2. *Passage of time.* Like anything else, first impressions tend to be forgotten over time. If a substantial period of time passes between first and subsequent impressions, the more recent impression will be of greater importance. Thus, if you flubbed your first attempt to favorably impress that gorgeous person, wait awhile and try again later.

3. *Knowledge of primacy effects.* When people are warned to avoid being influenced by first impressions, the primacy effect can be reduced (Hovland, 1957). Personnel managers and others to whom accurate person perception is important are educated to the dangers of primacy effects and may be able to reduce the importance of primacy in their perceptions.

**primacy effect**
The tendency for first impressions to heavily influence opinions about other people.

### Emotions and Person Perception

Another important factor in person perception that can be irrelevant to the nature of the person about whom we are forming an impression is our emotions. The emotional state that we are in when we meet a person has a great deal to do with our liking that person (Foster & others, 1998). Positive emotional states lead to greater attraction to others than negative emotions do. William Griffith and Russell Veitch (1971) had a radio news broadcast turned on as individuals waited for an experiment in interpersonal attraction to begin. The broadcast was actually taped beforehand, so that half of the participants heard a depressing broadcast and half heard happy news. Afterward, the participants hearing the sad news did not like the strangers they had met in the experiment as well as did the persons who had heard the good news. These findings were confirmed in a well-designed study by Joseph Forgas and Gordon Bower (1987), who also found that we are better able to remember positive information about another person when we meet him or her while we are in a good mood, and we are better able to remember negative information when we meet another person while we are in a bad mood. The effects of mood on person perception are likely, then, to be relatively enduring.

### Attribution Processes in Person Perception

We have a strong tendency to evaluate other people both on the basis of *what* they do and *why* we think they do it. Unfortunately, when we judge the reasons that other people behave as they do, we typically *underestimate* the effects of the social situation and *overestimate* the importance of their personal characteristics (Aronson, 1995; Ross, 1977). If you meet a man at a party who is acting sullen and depressed, you are more likely to assume that he is an unhappy person in general than to assume that he is usually happy but that something happened recently to make him feel lousy.

In contrast, we are more likely to see the influence of social situations on our *own* behavior. For example, a few years ago I was invited to a large party hosted by an association of African American woman attorneys in Los Angeles. Although I usually do not think of myself as shy, I found myself quite shy in the company of these women, nearly all of whom seemed more intelligent, self-secure, and stylish than I. It was easy for me to see the effect of this social situation on my own behavior, but if I had seen another male behaving shyly at the same party, I probably would have just assumed he was an inherently shy person without thinking about it.

Social psychologist Fritz Heider (1958) has termed this the **fundamental attribution error,** meaning our tendency to underestimate the impact of situations on others while more readily seeing its impact on ourselves. In simple terms, **attribution** is the process of making judgments about what causes people to behave the way they do. The most important aspect of the attribution process is deciding whether a person is behaving in a particular way because of some external cause (**situational attribution**) or because of an internal motive or trait (**dispositional attribution**). Unless we can see that someone's behavior *consistently* changes in a situation, we tend to attribute that person's behavior to dispositional causes (Kelley, 1973). Because we often lack information on the extent to which another person's behavior is consistently influenced by situations, we make dispositional attributions too often.

People in all cultures make the fundamental attribution error, but people living in East Asian collectivistic cultures are less likely to do so than people living in individualistic Western cultures (Choi, Nisbett, & Norenzayan, 1999). The Chinese and Japanese, for example, are less likely than North Americans to attribute the behavior of other people to dispositional causes (to their personal characteristics) and more likely to perceive situational influences on their behavior. This makes sense, because collectivistic cultures emphasize the importance of the social context and deemphasize the importance of the individual. This encourages people to think in terms of social influences rather than personal characteristics as causes of actions.

The East Asian view of the importance of situational influences on human behavior is often quite correct. As we saw in chapter 12, social situations can exert powerful influences on our behavior.

## General Determinants of Interpersonal Attraction

Through the complicated process of person perception, a unique impression of each person is formed. But although person perception is a highly personal process, some *general* factors influence whether one person will be attracted to another. These include proximity, similar and complementary characteristics, competence, physical attractiveness, and mutual liking.

---

**fundamental attribution error**
The tendency to underestimate the impact of situations on others while overestimating the impact on oneself.

**attribution**
The process of trying to explain why things happen—that is, attribute them to some cause.

**situational attribution**
An explanation for behavior that is based on an external cause.

**dispositional attribution**
(dis′po-zish′un-al) An explanation for behavior that is based on a personal characteristic of the individual.

## Proximity

An important, but not very romantic, cause of attraction is proximity, or geographical closeness. It's difficult to fall in love with someone you hardly ever spend time with. Physical closeness and the resulting interpersonal contact are essential to the development of attraction. You are more friendly with people who live next door to you than with people who live farther away. Why does this happen? Physical proximity increases interactions, and repeated exposure to people tends to increase liking (Zajonc, 1968). Perhaps you can remember a song you didn't like at first but learned to like after hearing it played on the radio many times—it's the same with people.

## Similar and Complementary Characteristics

In terms of interpersonal attraction, do "birds of a feather flock together" or do "opposites attract"? Are you more likely to be attracted to someone as a friend or lover who is similar to you in many ways or quite different from you? The answer is *both,* in different ways (Bem, 1996).

Jennifer probably values people who have an interest in exercise, nutrition, and philosophy because she is also interested in those things. It's enjoyable to have a friend who jogs with you, who pats you on the back for the healthy way you eat, and who shares long, delicious philosophical discussions with you. In general, similarity is highly important in attractiveness. We tend to be most attracted to those people who have similar values, interests, and attitudes (Caspi & Herbener, 1990; Feingold, 1988).

Opposites can also attract, however. Sometimes the attractiveness of persons unlike us is purely erotic (Bem, 1996). But opposites also attract when the opposite characteristic *complements,* or advantageously "fits" with, one of our own characteristics. Jennifer might also be attracted to the fellow at the party tonight in part because he has an outgoing personality, whereas she is more reserved. She may feel that she is a good listener who gets along better with talkative people than with those who are quiet like herself. And she may feel that, when she is with an outgoing person at social gatherings, he makes it easier for her to interact with other couples than a quiet man does. Similarly, a dominant person might prefer a submissive person, and a person who likes to "take care of" others might prefer someone who likes to be taken care of (Winch, 1958).

Another condition under which opposites attract is when people who are different from you *like* you (Aronson, 1995). It's often more flattering and attractive to be liked by someone who holds opposite values and opinions than by someone who holds similar ones (Jones, Bell, & Aronson, 1971). But take note that opposites usually do not attract; instead, opposites usually repel in personal relationships. A person who intensely advocates liberal causes probably would not like a person who vocally supports conservative causes. And a highly religious person probably would not be attracted to someone who disdained religion.

## Competence

We tend to be more attracted to competent than to incompetent people. Intelligence, strength, social skill, education, and athletic prowess are generally thought of as attractive qualities. But people who are seen as *too* competent may suffer a loss in attractiveness, perhaps because it makes us uncomfortable to compare ourselves unfavorably with them. Elliot Aronson and associates conducted a clever experiment that demonstrates that it's best to be a *little* less than perfect (Aronson, Willerman, & Floyd, 1966). Participants listened to one of four audiotapes of people who were supposedly trying out to be members of their university's College Bowl quiz team. Two of the people scored over 90 percent correct on difficult questions and were portrayed as being honor students, athletes, and people active in student activities. The other two answered 30 percent of the questions and were portrayed as average, unathletic students. Near the end of the tape, one of the superior students and one of the average students blundered—each

Physical attractiveness seems to be the most important factor in the early stages of attraction between people.

spilled a cup of coffee on himself. Whom from this group do you think the participants rated as most attractive? The two superior students were rated higher than the two average students, but the superior student who committed the blunder was rated as most attractive of all. Apparently, the slightly clumsy pratfall made him more endearing to others. However, the blunder did not have the same positive effect for the average student: The average student who blundered was rated least attractive of all.

**Physical Attractiveness**

Other things equal, people tend to be more attracted to physically beautiful people. In the absence of other information, we tend to like beautiful people more and think of them as nicer, better adjusted, more sexual, and more intelligent (Feingold, 1992b; Langlois & others, 2000). Not only is physical attractiveness important, but it also seems to be the *most* important factor in the early stages of attraction (Myers, 1999).

Elaine Walster and colleagues randomly paired male and female college students for blind dates. They rated each student's physical attractiveness and gave them tests to measure attitudes, intelligence, and personality characteristics. After the blind dates, the students were asked how much they liked each other and whether they intended to go out on other dates with one another. The overwhelmingly important variable in determining attraction was physical attractiveness—more so than intelligence, personality, and attitudes. The couples who were most likely to like each other well enough to continue dating were the ones in which both the male and the female rated each other as attractive (Walster, Aronson, Abrahams, & Rottman, 1966).

One of the key ways that physical attractiveness influences interpersonal attraction was demonstrated in an ingenious experiment (Snyder, Tauke, & Berscheid, 1977). Male and female college students played somewhat different roles in the study. Males were asked to participate in a study of how people get acquainted. They were asked to speak to a woman over a telephone (to rule out nonverbal communication), but each male was given written information describing the woman he was speaking to and a photograph of her.

The females in the study were paired randomly with the males on the other end of the telephone, but the information sheets and pictures had nothing to do with them. All of the information sheets seen by the males were the same, but half of the males saw a picture of a very attractive woman and half saw a picture of a much less attractive woman. After they had talked with her on the telephone, the men who thought they were talking to a beautiful woman rated her as being more sociable, poised, and humorous than did the men who thought they were talking to an unattractive woman. As in previous studies, greater physical attractiveness led to greater likeability. But that's not the only interesting finding of this study.

When observers rated tape recordings of the males' conversations, they found that males who *thought* they were talking to a beautiful woman spoke to her in a more sociable way (e.g., warm, outgoing, interesting) and were rated as enjoying themselves more in the conversation. Thus, perceiving the woman as beautiful led the men to be more charming to her.

The females' recorded conversations were even more interesting. The women knew nothing about the pictures that the men were seeing, but when the men thought that the women were beautiful, the women spoke in a more charming, confident manner and were rated as seeming to like the men more. Apparently, thinking the woman was beautiful led the man to treat her in a way that *induced her to act in a more likable way*. If Alan thinks he will like Eileen because she is pretty, he will probably speak to her in ways that will bring out her most likable side. It's a lovely self-fulfilling prophecy, *if* you happen to be physically attractive.

But don't despair; there is hope for the rest of us! Although we might all prefer to be dating someone who looks like Antonio Banderas or Cameron Diaz, people actually tend to choose dates and mates who closely match themselves in degree of physical attractiveness (Berscheid, Dion, Walster, & Walster, 1971). What is more, physical beauty is a highly subjective quality. Thus, even if you do not think your next-door neighbor is much to look at, chances are that someone else will come along who thinks he or she is just beautiful.

Perhaps the nicest thing about physical attractiveness and liking, though, is that the relationship goes both ways. Not only is it true that we tend to like people better when we think they are beautiful, but as we get to like people better, we begin to think they are more beautiful (Langlois & Stephan, 1981). Thus, to a certain extent, love *is* blind and beauty *is* in the eye of the beholder—and nothing could be nicer.

### Mutual Liking

Let's end this discussion of factors involved in interpersonal attractiveness on an upbeat note. Liking often leads to liking in return. If Vicki likes Neal, she has made herself more attractive to Neal simply by liking him. Neal, if he is like almost everyone else, will be more attracted to people who like him than to people who do not like him. Liking someone will not turn you into an irresistible beauty, but it will help.

One reason this seems to be so is that liking someone actually makes you seem more *physically* attractive, especially if a little lust is thrown in. You have heard people say that a person is more beautiful when in love, and it's true. Your eyes are more attractive. The pupils are more dilated (opened) when you look at someone you find sexually attractive, and others find large pupils more attractive sexually (Hess, 1975). And your posture and movements are more attractive and seductive. In subtle ways, you are more physically alluring when you are attracted to another person.

Another reason that liking tends to lead to liking is that you are nicer to the people whom you like, and being nicer makes you more attractive to them. A number of studies show, for example, that we tend to like people more when they praise us or when they have done favors for us. Favors and praise feel nice, and we like the giver better for having given them to us. Thus, send him flowers or give her a compact disc—it might just tip the balance of love in your favor. As you might expect, there are limits on the impact of praise and favors. If they are excessive, and especially if the other person thinks you are insincere and have selfish motives for giving them, praise and gifts will not lead to increased liking and may even lessen the liking (Aronson, 1995).

### Gender Differences in Interpersonal Attraction

It's a commonly held belief in our culture that men are not very interested in romantic love but, rather, enter into long-term relationships for the sex and the domestic help (cooking, cleaning, and mending). Women, in contrast, are viewed in our society as approaching relationships in a more emotional, romantic way. The results of surveys conducted during the 1960s, however, suggested that this popular stereotype not only was incorrect but had reality reversed. Men rated falling in love as being a more important reason for beginning a relationship than did women. Women saw other qualities of the relationship, such as respect and support, as being more important. In one survey, two-thirds of male unmarried college students said they would not marry unless they felt romantic love for their prospective wife, whereas less than one-fourth of college women felt that romantic love was a prerequisite for marriage (Hill, Rubin, & Peplau, 1976; Kephart, 1967).

However, more recent surveys suggest that things have changed in the United States concerning gender differences in valuing romantic love (Simpson, Campbell, & Berscheid, 1986). Today, the great majority of both women and men feel that being in love is necessary for marriage. Perhaps as women have come to feel less dependent on marriage for financial support, they have felt able to enter into marriage only when they are in love with their future partner.

This does not mean that men and women fall in love for all the same reasons, however. The evidence is clear that women place more emphasis on their romantic partner's intelligence, character, education, occupational status, ambition, and income than do men (Feingold, 1990, 1992a; Myers, 1999). These qualities are not unimportant to men, but they are comparatively more important to women. In contrast, there are no gender differences in how much sense of humor and a pleasant personality are valued in romantic relationships, but men place greater emphasis on physical attractiveness than do women. Again, it is not that physical attractiveness does not play a role in romantic attraction for women (it does), but women place considerably less emphasis on physical attractiveness than do men. Interestingly, these same results have been found in different generations in the United States and across a number of cultures (Feingold, 1992a).

It is important to keep in mind, however, that there are large differences among the members of both genders. Perhaps the most striking thing about the cognitive algebra of person perception is that different people often seem to be using different equations! Whether a characteristic is considered positive or negative and how much weight it will carry in person perception differ markedly from individual to individual. Jennifer may feel that an interest in exercise, nutrition, and philosophy and an outgoing personality are all highly positive characteristics. Angela may feel that these characteristics are not very important one way or another. And Lydia might find them all to be highly negative characteristics. If Jennifer, Angela, and Lydia were to meet a man with these characteristics at a party, they would each form a very different perception of him. It's like that for everyone. Because different people evaluate the same characteristics in different ways, some people are going to love you, some are going to dislike you, and the rest will find you so-so.

## Maintaining Relationships

We have talked about some of the factors that determine whether you will be attracted to another person. But how about the factors that are involved in maintaining relationships? Assuming that one of the people whom you are attracted to becomes your friend, lover, or spouse, what things determine whether you and your partner will stay in the relationship? So many relationships that begin in joy end in a long cry. Why? Two of the major factors are (a) the difference between what you expect to find in a relationship and what you actually find and (b) the degree to which the relationship is fairly balanced or equitable.

### Expectations Versus Reality in Relationships

When you begin a relationship with someone you do not know very well, part of what you fall in love with is what you *expect* the person to be like. Some of these expectations may be based on good evidence. One of his friends has told you that he is an especially nice and fair person, so it's reasonable to expect him to be fair and nice to you. You know that he is in the same profession as you, so you can expect to be able to share your workday experiences easily with him. Other expectations are based on less evidence. He has behaved in a strong, self-assured way so far, so you assume that he will always be this way, even though the biggest challenge you have seen him handle is the waiter's mistake of bringing tomato soup instead of minestrone. You *know* that he is a wonderful lover, even though he has only just kissed you goodnight once. He dresses like an outdoorsman, so you expect him to love backpacking as much as you do. And he is well educated, so you feel sure he will share your love of serious literature.

The point is that, even when your expectations are fairly well grounded, some of them will turn out to be incorrect. He will not be exactly as you expect him to be before the relationship begins. This is one primary reason relationships end. If the other person turns out to be significantly different from the person you expected, you may be unwilling to stay in the relationship. This disappointment may not lead directly to an end of the relationship; it may affect the relationship indirectly. Disappointment can lead you to be an unenthusiastic or irritable partner, which can lead to discord and an unhappy ending of the relationship (Graziano & Musser, 1982). This is especially true when a person becomes disappointed in his or her partner's level of caring and responsiveness (Huston, Niehuis, & Smith, 2001).

Even when you know a person well before beginning a serious relationship, differences between expectations and reality can be a problem. One common source of unfulfilled expectations is the predictable shift from **passionate love** to **companionate love** (Hatfield, 1988; Myers, 1999). When two people first fall in love, they often feel intense passions that are a heady and magnificent mixture of romantic, sexual, and other feelings. Even in the most healthy and enduring relationships, however, passionate love gradually becomes companionate love—a less intense but wonderful blend of friendship, intimacy, commitment, and security. Although romantic and sexual emotions often continue to be an important part of companionate love, these feelings almost inevitably become less intense over time.

If one or both of the partners does not expect passionate love to change, or if the change takes place before expected, the reality of passionate love's blending into companionate love can be difficult. On the other hand, if both partners truly want a long-term relationship (many people stay in relationships only as long as the passionate love remains, then leave feeling unfulfilled or hurt), and if the disappointment that often surrounds the lessening of romantic love is handled with compassion on both sides, the transition usually can be managed.

Finally, expectations about a love relationship can fail to match its reality because partners change over time. Sometimes, the outdoor person becomes a happy couch potato, and the party animal becomes a health-conscious, jogging vegetarian. If children arrive, and if promotions are received (or not received), these and other changes can alter the reality of the relationship as well. If these changes in one's partner are not welcome, the reality of the changed relationship can be upsetting. Sometimes, however, a change in a partner can make a good relationship even better.

### Equity in Relationships

Relationships are more likely to endure when the good things that we give to our partner are about equal to what our partner gives us. These good "things" that partners give to one another are many and varied. They include compliments, back rubs, help with homework, a day off without the kids, flowers, jokes, love making, a willingness to listen about a bad day, interesting meals, kisses, and interesting conversations. They also include things like physical attractiveness (a nice-looking person is enjoyable to look at), honesty, faithfulness, and integrity.

The commonsense idea that enduring relationships are ones in which the partners give and receive in equal proportion has been formalized and improved by social psychologists (Adams, 1965; Myers, 1999; Walster & Walster, 1978) under the name of **equity theory**. Equity theory states that partners will be comfortable in their relationship only when the ratio between their perceived contributions and benefits is equal. Equity theory is often summarized by the following equation:

$$\frac{\text{Perceived benefits of person X}}{\text{Perceived contributions of person X}} = \frac{\text{Perceived benefits of person Y}}{\text{Perceived contributions of person Y}}$$

These benefits and contributions cannot be easily translated into numerical terms, but suppose for a moment that person X perceives that she "gives" 10 things to the

**passionate love**
The mixture of romantic, sexual, and other feelings of love.

**companionate love**
The blend of friendship, intimacy, commitment, and security that generally develops after passionate love.

**equity theory**
The theory that partners will be comfortable in their relationship only when the ratio between their perceived contributions and benefits is equal.

Relationships that last tend to be based on realistic expectations and on the perception of equity in the relationship.

relationship, whereas person Y perceives that he gives only 5 things. Is this an equitable relationship? It is if person X perceives 10 benefits from the relationship, whereas person Y perceives 5 benefits, because the equation is in balance:

$$\frac{10}{10} = \frac{5}{5}$$

There are two important points to notice in the equity theory equation: First, the benefits that the two people receive from one another do not have to be equal, but the *ratio* between their benefits and contributions must be equal. A person who both gives and receives a lot can be in an equitable relationship with a person who gives and receives much less.

Second, notice that the equation is written in terms of *perceived* benefits and contributions. The only person who can judge how much he or she is giving and receiving is that person. An outside observer might see a relationship as being highly inequitable when the partners themselves are very happy with it. Tender love making might be highly important to one person but much less important than good cooking to someone else. Unfortunately, people tend to believe that the amount of "good things" that we ourselves should fairly receive is higher than the amount that we think that others should fairly receive (Messick & Sentis, 1979). If we are not careful to compensate for this natural perceptual distortion, it can lead us to perceive an inequity in our relationships when there is none at all.

If either member of a relationship perceives the relationship to be inequitable, that partner will either take steps to restore equity or will leave the relationship. Interestingly, we become uncomfortable in relationships either when we feel that we receive *too little* compared with what we give *or* when we receive *too much* compared with what we give. In either case, we will be motivated to restore equity by giving more or less or by asking (or in some other way inducing) the other person to give more or less.

---

## Review

What determines which people we will like or love? Our perceptions of others can be thought of as being based on a complex cognitive algebra in which we reach a weighted average of all of the positive and negative characteristics we see in others. Person perception is complicated by several factors, however: Different people evaluate the same characteristics in a person in different ways, and our emotional state influences person perception; negative information about a person carries more weight than positive information; and first impressions usually are more important than later impressions.

Attribution plays an important role in our perceptions of others. We want to know what a person's enduring traits and motives are. We attribute the behavior of others to external causes (situational attributions) when it consistently occurs in only one kind of situation and they consistently react in the same way. Otherwise, we tend to attribute the behavior of others to their supposed traits and motives (dispositional attributions). We also tend to attribute our own behavior to dispositional causes, but mostly our desirable behavior. We tend to attribute our undesirable behavior to situational causes.

Although person perception is a highly complex and personal process, some general factors determine whether one person will be attracted to another. Other things being equal, you are more likely to be attracted to a person who has characteristics similar to yours or who has opposite characteristics that complement your own. Other factors in attractiveness include the other person's being competent (but not excessively competent), looking physically attractive, and liking and being nice to you.

Once two people are attracted to each other, a number of other factors are involved in whether the relationship will endure. We enter into relationships partly because of our expectations as to what the other person will be like. Because those expectations are generally based on partial information, they are sometimes not met and the relationship fails. Relationships generally fail, too, when they are not equitable. In happy relationships, each person perceives a balance between what each person puts into the relationship and what each person gets out of it.

## Check Your Learning

To be sure that you have learned the key points from the preceding section, cover the list of correct answers and try to answer each question. If you give an incorrect answer to any question, return to the page given next to the correct answer to see why your answer was not correct.

1. The process of forming impressions of others is known as _____.

   a)   person perception
   b)   the primacy effect
   c)   attribution theory
   d)   the fundamental attribution error

2. The impact of the primacy effect can be reduced under three conditions: _____, _____, and _____.

3. The fundamental attribution error refers partly to our tendency to give greater weight to _____ causes of behavior in others and to neglect _____ causes when forming perceptions of others.

   a)   positive; negative
   b)   negative; positive
   c)   dispositional; situational
   d)   situational; dispositional

## Thinking Critically about Psychology

1. To what extent has it been true that "first impressions are lasting impressions" in your life?

2. What are the most important relationships in your life? Have you learned anything in this chapter that could help you enhance and prolong them?

Correct Answers:   1. a (p. 628),   2. prolonged exposure, passage of time, knowledge of primacy effects (p. 629),   3. c (p. 630).

## Stereotypes and Discrimination in the Workplace

In 1982, Ann Hopkins was a successful consultant working for Price Waterhouse, one of the nation's "big eight" accounting firms, and she was up for possible promotion to a partnership in the firm. She had brought in $25 million in business and had billed for more hours than any of the other 87 accountants who had been proposed for partner that year, all of whom were males. She had the praise of her clients and recommendations of supporters within the company, who described her as hardworking, demanding, exacting, independent, self-confident, outspoken, assertive, and courageous. The decision regarding her partnership was postponed for a year, and the following year she was told that she would not be considered further for partnership.

Ms. Hopkins' detractors at Price Waterhouse portrayed her as being overbearing, arrogant, self-centered, and abrasive. In more specific terms, those who voted against her criticized her for being "macho" and suggested that she needed a "course at charm school." Indeed, one partner who favored her promotion suggested that her chances would improve if she would "walk more femininely, talk more femininely, dress more femininely, wear make-up, have her hair styled, and wear jewelry" (*Hopkins v. Price Waterhouse*, 1985, p. 1117).

In 1984, Ann Hopkins sued Price Waterhouse for violation of her civil rights under Title VII of the 1964 Civil Rights Act, which prohibits sex discrimination. Her former firm countered that she had not been denied a partnership because of her gender, but because she had problems in interpersonal skills. Nevertheless, she won her suit in federal court, and the decision was confirmed in both the Federal Court of Appeals and the U.S. Supreme Court. Federal Judge Gerhard Gesell stated in his 1990 opinion, "The firm of Price Waterhouse refused to make Ann Hopkins a partner. Gender-based stereotyping played a role in this decision" (*Hopkins v. Price Waterhouse*, 1990, p. 1).

Psychologist Susan T. Fiske testified on behalf of Ann Hopkins in this case, and because it was the first sex discrimination case in which psychological evidence on gender stereotyping had been introduced as evidence, the American Psychological Association filed a "friend of the court" brief that summarized what is known about gender discrimination. A full description of the court case and the brief have been published and make fascinating reading for anyone interested in the application of social psychology to real-world problems (Fiske, Bersoff, Borgida, Deaux, & Heilman, 1991).

If you recall from this chapter (pages 622–624), stereotypes are harmful because they lead us to treat all members of a group as the same, lead to narrow expectations for the behavior of members of the group, and lead to inaccurate attributions. The courts found that these aspects of gender stereotyping led to discrimination in the partnership decision of Ann Hopkins.

The evidence presented by Susan Fiske as an expert witness pointed to the following three sources of gender-based job discrimination. First, in studies that simulated hiring and promotion decisions in the workplace, job performances tended to be influenced by the stereotyped beliefs that we hold about the two genders. Males were viewed as

Psychologist Susan T. Fiske testified as an expert on gender discrimination issues in the U.S. Supreme Court case involving Ann Hopkins and Price Waterhouse Accounting Firm.

more confident, influential, and deserving of respect than females, *even when the behavior of the females was exactly the same as that of the males* (Fiske & others, 1991). People see what they expect to see based on gender stereotypes in the workplace.

Second, the narrow expectations for appropriate behavior that gender stereotypes encourage can play a role in discrimination in the workplace. In other job simulation studies, women in leadership roles were given lower marks than males if their leadership was carried out in ways that fit the stereotype for males—directive or authoritarian leadership. In addition, the ratings of women were lower when they were in roles that are more typically held by men than women. Thus, violating the expectations for your gender can be dangerous in the workplace (Eagly & Karau, 2002).

Third, a number of studies have shown that faulty attributions based on gender stereotypes operate in the workplace. The supervisors of male employees tend to attribute their successes to

With the help of psychological research as evidence, Ann Hopkins successfully sued her employer for gender discrimination.

competence and ability, but they are more likely to attribute the successes of females to good luck, to their physical attractiveness, or at best, to hard work (Fiske & others, 1991).

Dr. Fiske also presented evidence that the kind of gender discrimination that was alleged in Ms. Hopkins' suit is more likely to occur when the number of women is few, the criteria for evaluation are ambiguous, and the amount of factual information on the employee is small. The attorney for Ann Hopkins was able to argue successfully that all three of these conditions were true for Ann Hopkins.

The courts found that these negative aspects of gender stereotyping played at least some part in Ann Hopkins' being denied a partnership. The evidence suggested to the court that her detractors gave her low marks because her behavior violated the expectations for women and that these same traits would not have been grounds for denying a partnership to a male. The decision of the Supreme Court put it this way:

> An employer who objects to aggressiveness in women but whose positions require this trait places women in an intolerable Catch-22: out of a job if they behave aggressively and out of a job if they don't. Title VII [of the Civil Rights Act] lifts women out of this bind. (*Price Waterhouse v. Hopkins,* 1989, pp. 1790–1791) It takes no special training to discern sex stereotyping in a description of an aggressive female employee as requiring "a course at charm school." Nor . . . does it require expertise in psychology to know that, if an employee's flawed "interpersonal skills" can be corrected by a soft-hued suit or a new shade of lipstick, perhaps it is the employee's sex and not her interpersonal skills that has drawn the criticism. (p. 1793)

The decision of the court and its affirmation by the Supreme Court should be encouraging for everyone, men and women alike, because everyone benefits when the best employees are hired and promoted. Perhaps the most encouraging aspect of the decision was that it held Price Waterhouse accountable for its failure to prevent gender discrimination from playing a role in Ann Hopkins' partnership decision. The courts concluded that the firm should have had a clearly stated and vigorously enforced partnership policy that prohibited discrimination on the basis of gender (its policy prohibited discrimination on the basis of age or health but did not mention gender or ethnicity). The firm should have investigated the criticisms against Ann Hopkins to see if they were based on gender bias, and the firm should have encouraged interactions within the firm that would decrease gender stereotyping, such as having men and women work together on mutually beneficial projects. These three points would be a good starting point for any firm that wishes to discourage discrimination on the basis of gender, ethnicity, age, disability, sexual orientation, or any other characteristic. And the *Hopkins v. Price Waterhouse* decision is a warning that firms will be held accountable if they fail to deal with discrimination based on gender and other stereotypes in the workplace.

More recent studies (Biernat & Kobrynowicz, 1997) have suggested that prejudicial stereotypes can have paradoxical effects in the workplace—they usually make life more difficult for persons experiencing prejudice but sometimes help them. In the United States, negative stereotypes about both women and African Americans are common—both are often believed by employers to be less competent in managerial positions. When female and African American managers are evaluated for raises or promotions on the basis of relatively little hard evidence, they tend to be rated in a way that is consistent with the rater's prejudice. On the other hand, when there is clear evidence that women or African American managers are doing a good job, they tend to be rated as even more competent than they actually are. Perhaps that glowing evaluation is largely deserved, because they have had to overcome prejudice to get where they are. The real moral of this story, however, is this: If you are in a job that is unusual for your gender or ethnic group and are doing a good job, help your employer accumulate a great deal of *objective* evidence of your competence to avoid being judged more by stereotypes about your group than by your actual performance. ■

Chapter 16 defines social psychology and explores the influence people have on other people, the nature of attitudes and persuasion, and interpersonal attraction.

## Summary

I. Social psychology is the branch of psychology that studies individuals as they interact with others.

II. Behavior is often influenced powerfully by its social context.

    A. Deindividuation may be responsible for some behavior in mob situations.

    B. The failure to help when in a group is a complex process. The presence of others affects the interpretation of an event as an emergency and creates a diffusion of responsibility.

    C. Individual effort may decline when people work in groups, group problem solving may lead to bad decisions when opinions become polarized, and even groups of sophisticated decision makers may be susceptible to the effects of groupthink.

D. Conformity is yielding to group pressure even when no direct request to comply has been made. Conformity can be seen in outward behavior only or can be seen in actual changes in beliefs.

E. Social roles and social norms are important ways in which social factors can influence the behavior of individuals.

F. Research by Stanley Milgram indicates that authority figures can command substantial obedience from individuals.

    1. Obedience is greatest when we are instructed to do something by a person who is high in status and who is physically present.

    2. Obedience is less likely to occur when we are in the presence of other disobedient individuals.

G. Although groups can have a harmful effect, it is important to remember that groups can sometimes accomplish what no single person can and that social support can soften the impact of stress.

III. Attitudes are beliefs that predispose us to act and feel in certain ways.

A. Attitudes are learned from direct experience and from others.

B. Attitude change through persuasion is determined by the characteristics of the speaker, the communication itself, and the people who hear it.

    1. Three characteristics of the speaker are important: credibility, attractiveness, and intent.

    2. Characteristics of the message that are important determinants of persuasiveness are fear appeals and message framing. Sometimes it helps to present both sides of the argument.

    3. Characteristics of listeners that help determine how persuasive an argument will be include their intelligence, their need for social approval, their self-esteem, and the size of the audience.

    4. Techniques of persuasion, such as the "foot-in-the-door" and "low-balling," are often used by persuasive individuals.

C. Attitudes sometimes change to become more consistent with our behavior, according to Leon Festinger's cognitive dissonance theory.

D. Prejudice is a harmful attitude based on inaccurate generalizations about a group of people. These generalizations are called stereotypes.

E. Stereotypes are harmful because they take away our ability to treat each member of a group as an individual and because they lead to faulty attributions.

IV. Friendship and love are social phenomena based on the process of person perception.

A. The process of person perception can be said to involve a "complex algebra" in which we combine and evaluate information about others to form an impression.

    1. Negative information is generally weighted more than positive information in person perception.

    2. First impressions (the primacy effect) generally influence person perception more than information learned later. The primacy effect is lessened under three conditions.

        a. The person has prolonged exposure to the individual about whom the first impression was formed.

        b. Time has passed since the first impression was formed, even if there has been no further exposure.

        c. The person who formed the first impression understands the primacy effect and tries to minimize it.

CHAPTER 16 Social Psychology **641**

    3.   Person perception is influenced by the emotional state of the perceiver.

B.   People often underestimate the power of social situations in influencing the behavior of other people and overemphasize a person's internal attributes when explaining their behavior. This bias is termed the fundamental attribution error.

C.   Although many factors ensure that each individual's perception of another individual will be unique, some general factors partly determine to whom we will be attracted.

    1.   In general, we tend to be attracted to persons who

        a.   Have characteristics that are similar or complementary to our own

        b.   Are competent but not perfect

        c.   Are physically attractive

        d.   Also like us

    2.   Women are more likely to be attracted to a person's intelligence, character, education, occupational status, ambition, and income than are men.

    3.   Men are more likely to be attracted by physical attractiveness than are women.

    4.   Within each gender, however, different people perceive the same individual differently because of differences in the weight assigned to the same characteristics and even the perception of them as positive or negative.

D.   Two major factors in determining if a relationship will last are the difference between what you expect to find in a relationship and what you actually find, and the degree to which the relationship is fairly balanced or equitable. The most enduring love relationships are able to make the transition from primarily passionate love to primarily companionate love.

---

## Resources

1. Two wonderfully readable yet scholarly overviews of social psychology are Aronson, E. (1998). *The social animal* (6th ed.). San Francisco: W. H. Freeman; and Myers, D. (2000). *Exploring social psychology* (2nd ed.). Boston: McGraw-Hill.

2. For a social psychologist's perspective on gender, see Burn, S. (1996). *The social psychology of gender.* Boston: McGraw-Hill.

3. For a recently revised classic on the psychology of racial prejudice, see Jones, J. M. (1999). *Prejudice and racism.* Boston: McGraw-Hill.

4. Attitude change is discussed in scholarly but understandable terms in Zimbardo, P. G., & Leippe, M. R. (1991). *The psychology of attitude change and social influence* (3rd ed.). Boston: McGraw-Hill.

5. To learn more about the psychology of persuasion, see Cialdini, R. (1996). *Influence: Science and practice.* New York: Talman.

## Chapter Outline

# Psychology Applied to Business and Other Professions

## PROLOGUE

Since the early 1970s, the number of women and ethnic minorities in business management positions has risen dramatically. This increase has resulted in part from the realization that good managers are good for business, regardless of their gender or race. Initially, however, the influx of women and minorities into higher-level business positions was stimulated by federal laws. These laws require that equally qualified women and minorities be given preference in hiring to remedy past discrimination against them. These regulations were successful in providing qualified women and minorities greater access to jobs that had been denied to them previously. Equal opportunity programs also provided more successful role models to younger women and minorities, encouraging a wider selection of career choices for these groups.

Psychologist Madeline Heilman of New York University (Heilman, Simon, & Repper, 1987) used the tools of psychological research to raise an important concern about equal opportunity hiring programs: Did the first group of women pay a price to be the role models for future generations of women? In one study, female undergraduates were asked to take a leadership role in a simulated management experiment. All of the research participants first took a test that they were told measured their "communication skills." Some of the women were told that they were given the leadership role on the basis of their high score on the test of communication skills. Other women, however, were told that they were given the leadership role because "there just haven't been enough female subjects signing up"—in other words, because of their gender rather than their qualifications.

After the task, the women who believed that they had been selected for the leadership role on the basis of their gender thought that they had not been good leaders, took less credit for successful outcomes of the group, and were less interested in being a leader in the future. The women who believed that they had been selected on the basis of merit, however, did not undervalue themselves as leaders (Heilman & others, 1987).

Other studies similarly have shown that the performance of women managers is valued less highly by coworkers when it is believed that they obtained their position on the basis of gender rather than qualifications (Heilman & Herlihy, 1984; Jacobsen & Koch, 1977). We should not assume that all women managers and their fellow employees believe that they were chosen on the basis of their gender, however. The qualifications of most successful women are clear to everyone, including to themselves. Still, some of the first wave of women managers who were less sure of why they were hired may have paid a personal price for equality.

Psychology is both a scientific and an applied field. The job of many psychologists is to apply the principles and methods of psychology to the solution of human problems. Psychologists working in business seek to increase the satisfaction we derive from our jobs and to improve our productivity in those jobs. They do so by using their knowledge of psychological assessment to find the right person for the right job, by using knowledge of social relationships to improve methods of managing workers, and by designing the physical characteristics of the

## Key Terms

job to fit the psychological characteristics of people. Psychologists have long been involved in the courtroom practice of law as expert witnesses on questions of insanity, but in recent years they have also studied the behavior of the people involved in the trial process—jurors, witnesses, attorneys, and others. Psychologists working in the field of education have used their knowledge of learning and cognition to develop improved ways of educating children. And we have already seen that psychologists working in the field of health psychology attempt to influence people to live healthier lives. Whenever a profession involves the welfare of *people*—and what profession doesn't?—psychology has the potential to help that profession meet its goals better. ■

## Applied Fields of Psychology

Now that you have reached the last chapter of this text, take a moment to think back to chapter 1. We noted on page 5 that the four goals of psychology are to *describe, predict, understand,* and *influence* behavior and mental processes. This chapter focuses on the last of these goals—the use of psychological principles to influence and improve the lives of human beings. In other words, it is about the *application* of psychology to the solution of human concerns. Most of our attention until now has been on the basic principles of psychology—facts and concepts about perception, learning, memory, problem solving, emotion, and many other topics. But we have already covered a great deal of information about the applications of psychology. Within each chapter, many examples of new concepts were illustrated by describing applications of those ideas. Moreover, the chapters on abnormal behavior and therapies covered the heart of the applied fields of clinical and counseling psychology, and the chapter on stress and health gave us a description of the field of health psychology.

We will turn now to other important applications of psychology—to the worlds of business, architecture, law, and education. Fewer psychologists are employed in these applied settings than in clinical, counseling, and health psychology, but they are significant and growing fields of application.

## Psychology and Work: Employees and Managers Are People

When you think of the word *work,* do the words *happiness* and *quality of life* come to mind? They should, because work is linked to the quality of our lives in important ways. The standard of living that we enjoy in terms of material goods and services is the product of business. Your car, clothes, haircut, compact discs, and newspaper would not exist without the multifaceted business sector. Moreover, our quality of life is also linked to the satisfaction that comes from our work. Most men and women spend a major part of their lives working for pay. Our sense of well-being depends in part on whether our jobs are boring and demeaning or meaningful and rewarding.

**industrial-organizational (I/O) psychologists**
Psychologists who study organizations and seek ways to improve the functioning and human benefits of business.

Psychologists who work with businesses are known as **industrial-organizational (I/O) psychologists.** They attempt to improve the human benefits of work in a number of ways. For example, they seek ways to help businesses and government organizations produce more goods and services, to increase job satisfaction by changing methods of management and training, and to find "the right person for the right job" by improving methods of employee selection. To be sure, psychological principles are sometimes used to improve profits rather than human lives—such as by developing advertisements that are more persuasive than informative—but such abuses are the exception rather than the rule for professional psychologists in business today.

Personnel departments are where industrial-organizational psychologists can be found most frequently, because employee selection and training is the primary responsibility of these departments. Some large companies employ one or more psychologists to work in personnel. Other companies use the services of industrial-organizational psychologists who work for independent consulting firms. They teach both personnel and general managers to put the principles of psychology to work in helping people contribute more effectively and happily to the goals of the business.

Other industrial-organizational psychologists work for consumers rather than businesses. They are employed by government or public-interest groups performing such jobs as helping consumers make more informed choices in their purchases.

## Employee Selection and Evaluation

Recall from chapters 1 and 8 that at the start of the twentieth century France's Alfred Binet gave us the first practical way of measuring intelligence. Since Binet's time, numerous useful ways of measuring intelligence and other psychological attributes have been used in educational, clinical, and business settings. In business, the most significant uses of psychological measurements have been in selecting and hiring new employees and in evaluating the performance of current employees. The measures most commonly used in employee decisions include interviews, paper-and-pencil tests, performance tests, job performance ratings, and the evaluation of simulated job performance. Employee selection and evaluation is an essential part of business. Finding the right person for the right job not only improves employee morale and productivity but decreases employee turnover and absenteeism as well.

### Interviews

Interviews are the heart of the process of evaluating job applicants and play a significant role in the assessment of current employees for possible promotion. Interviews are more or less structured conversations in which the employee or job applicant is questioned about her or his training, experience, and future goals. The suitability of the individual for the job is evaluated partly in terms of factual answers to questions, but also in terms of the individual's personality, spoken language, potential for leadership, and other personal factors.

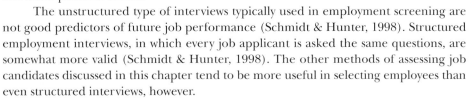

Psychologists have learned that applicants with average qualifications are rated higher if they are interviewed after two poorly qualified candidates than if they are interviewed after two highly qualified candidates.

The unstructured type of interviews typically used in employment screening are not good predictors of future job performance (Schmidt & Hunter, 1998). Structured employment interviews, in which every job applicant is asked the same questions, are somewhat more valid (Schmidt & Hunter, 1998). The other methods of assessing job candidates discussed in this chapter tend to be more useful in selecting employees than even structured interviews, however.

### Tests of Intelligence

Tests of general intelligence, like those discussed in chapter 8, are frequently used to select employees, especially for complex jobs (Gottfredson, 1997). Intellectual tests are used for this purpose by governments, the military, and private industry. Furthermore, because tests of intellectual ability are used to select applicants to medical school, law school, and graduate school, they also play a key role in determining who enters such professions. As a result, persons holding different kinds of jobs tend to be highly segregated in North America and other industrialized societies (Gottfredson, 1997). Figure 17.1 shows the range of intelligence test scores of the middle half of applicants for a wide range of jobs. Note that a person with an intelligence score of 115 would have many choices: He or she could be a competitive applicant for any type of job. On the other

**FIGURE 17.1**

The range of intelligence scores of the middle half of applicants for various occupations (25 percent had intelligence scores above each range and 25 percent had intelligence scores lower than each range).

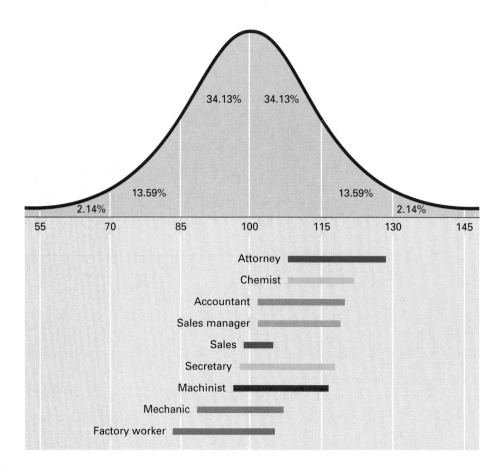

hand, a person with an intelligence score below 80 would not be competitive for any type of position (Gottfredson, 1997). This raises questions of fairness that will be discussed later in the chapter, after we have considered other methods of selecting employees.

### Tests of Specific Abilities, Skills, and Job Knowledge

Employers use a variety of measures of specific abilities, job skills, and job knowledge to evaluate potential employees. For example, spelling and reading tests are often given to applicants for secretarial and clerical jobs because applicants who are more skilled in

**FIGURE 17.2**

Sample items from a test designed to measure an individual's ability to visualize spatial relationships. Which form (A through E) can be constructed from the shapes in the upper left-hand corner (5 and 7)?

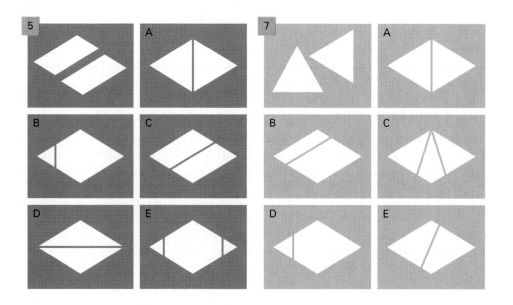

**FIGURE 17.3**
Sample items from a paper-and-pencil
test designed to measure an individual's
mechanical comprehension.

Example X
Which person has the heavier
load? (If equal, mark C.)

Example Y
Which weighs more? (If
equal, mark C.)

these areas generally perform better on jobs such as typing and proofreading. Applicants for mechanical and engineering jobs are given tests such as those pictured in figures 17.2 and 17.3. These tests tap a person's abilities to mentally visualize spatial relationships and to understand mechanical concepts. And applicants for sales positions are frequently given tests of sales aptitude. These tests describe problematic situations that often arise in sales work and require the applicant to choose the best course of action from a number of options.

**performance tests**
Employee selection tests that resemble
the actual manual performance required
on a job.

## Performance Tests

Tests that measure actual manual performance are often used in selecting employees such as assembly-line workers or equipment repair specialists. **Performance tests** are based on the assumption that the only valid way to find out if applicants can work with their hands is to evaluate them while they are actually working. The Purdue Pegboard is an example of this kind of performance test (see fig. 17.4). In this test, pins, collars, and washers are fitted together in ways specified by the tester to evaluate the applicant's manual speed and accuracy. Other types of performance tests more closely resemble the job to be performed. Applicants for typist jobs are asked to type in timed tests; forklift operators are asked to drive forklifts in a prescribed path; and potential recruits for professional baseball teams are given a chance to bat against professional pitchers. Each performance test provides a sample of behavior that can be used to predict actual performance on the job.

## Ratings of Job Performance

Not all evaluation methods are used to select the best job applicants; some are designed to evaluate current employees. Such evaluations determine raises, promotions, and even whether the individual will continue to be employed. The most widely used

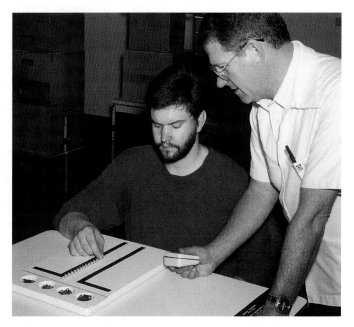

**FIGURE 17.4**
An example of a performance test that might be used to select
employees for a job assembling small machine parts.

**Dependability**

| ❑ **Unsatisfactory** | ❑ **Below average** | ❑ **Average** | ❑ **Above average** | ❑ **Outstanding** |
|---|---|---|---|---|
| Requires constant supervision to ensure that directions are followed | Requires considerable supervision; does not always follow directions | Requires average to normal supervision | Can usually be depended upon to complete assignments | Needs virtually no supervision; completely reliable |

**Quantity of work**

| ❑ **Unsatisfactory** | ❑ **Below average** | ❑ **Average** | ❑ **Above average** | ❑ **Outstanding** |
|---|---|---|---|---|
| Consistently below job requirements | Frequently below job requirements | Meets job requirements | Frequently exceeds job requirements | Consistently exceeds job requirements |

**Job knowledge**

| ❑ **Unsatisfactory** | ❑ **Below average** | ❑ **Average** | ❑ **Above average** | ❑ **Outstanding** |
|---|---|---|---|---|
| Unsatisfactory | Below average | Average | Knows job well | Thorough knowledge |

**FIGURE 17.5**

Examples of items from a multiple-step rating scale like those used to evaluate employee performance. The rater marks one category for each item.

**job performance ratings**
Ratings of the actual performance of employees in their jobs by supervisors.

method of assessing current employees is **job performance ratings.** Ratings are usually done by supervisors, but information may also be obtained from subordinates, customers, coworkers, and the employee himself or herself. If you fill out student evaluations of your professor at the end of a term, you are participating in one type of job performance rating. There are a number of different types of performance ratings, but each is designed by industrial-organizational psychologists to transform a rating of the employee's actual job performance into a numerical evaluation. This numerical information is used to track an employee's progress over time, or to compare the performances of a group of employees.

In job performance ratings, the employee is rated on a number of dimensions of job performance. The evaluator checks the statement that best describes the employee from most to least desirable. Three job dimensions from a hypothetical multiple-step rating scale are shown in figure 17.5. The statements are each assigned a value (5, 4, 3, 2, 1), so the ratings can be summed across all of the dimensions to obtain an overall evaluation of the employee.

*Checklists* provide numerical evaluations of job performance in a somewhat different way. Evaluators are asked to read a series of statements such as the following:

_____ Doesn't repeat same mistakes

_____ Orderly in work habits

_____ Effective leader

_____ Has good judgment

_____ Has creative ideas

The evaluator checks those items that are characteristic of the employee. Each characteristic is assigned a numerical value according to how important it is for the job, with the sum of these values giving the overall evaluation of the employee. Many varieties of job performance ratings are used to assess different types of employees when numerical evaluations are needed.

Performance evaluations, like interviews, are less than perfect. In both methods, evaluators may be influenced by the same principles of person perception we discussed in chapter 16. However, supervisors can be trained to identify potential biases, to attend to job-relevant behaviors, and to use rating scales effectively (Hedge & Kavanagh, 1988).

### Assessment Centers

Decisions on the hiring or promotion of managers in large companies are often based in part on evaluations made in **assessment centers.** Assessment centers are usually staffed by a team of upper managers and outside psychological consultants. Several candidates for the same position are brought together in the assessment center, so they can be intensively evaluated outside of the usual work environment. This technique was developed during World War II to evaluate candidates for undercover spy assignments and has continued to be a popular method of management selection (Bray, Campbell, & Grant, 1974).

Assessment centers use traditional methods of evaluating the candidates for promotion, such as interviews and tests, but the distinctive feature of the approach is the evaluation of candidates while they are carrying out a **simulated management task** (Thornton & Cleveland, 1990). A frequently used simulation is the **in-basket exercise.** The candidate is given a problem that might show up in the "in-basket" of the new management position. Candidates would be asked to indicate the actions they would take, such as calling a meeting, obtaining additional information, and communicating a decision. Ratings of the candidate's performance in these simulation exercises would be used in the hiring or promotion decision.

### Validity of Job Selection Measures

One major purpose of all employee selection measures is to increase the productivity of industry and government by selecting the best employees for each job. But just how good are these methods in improving employee selection? To use a term introduced in our discussion of intelligence tests in chapter 8, how *valid* are these measures?

A great deal of evidence shows that tests of intellectual ability are the best predictors of later job performance and success in job-training programs. The use of intellectual ability tests considerably improves the selection of employees (Schmidt & Hunter, 1998). For example, Hunter (1979) calculated that if the city of Philadelphia, Pennsylvania, were to stop using an intellectual ability test for the selection of police officers, it would lose $170 million over a 10-year period. These dollar losses would result from the increased cost of training officer candidates who could not pass the course or had to be fired later, needing more officers to complete the same amount of work, and the like.

Hunter and Hunter (1984) also found that performance tests and assessment centers were valid measures but were less useful than intellectual ability tests in selecting employees for most jobs. For example, Hunter (1981) indicated that the federal government's use of intellectual ability tests in its hiring of approximately 460,000 new employees each year saves the government $15.6 billion compared with hiring at random. Finally, of the methods that we discussed, unstructured interviews have been found to be the least valid method of selecting more productive employees, but projective personality tests and handwriting analyses have been found not to be valid at all for employee selection (Reilly & Chao, 1982; Schmidt & Hunter, 1998).

Why is intellectual ability important to job performance? Frank Schmidt and John Hunter (1992) proposed a model of how intellectual ability and other factors lead to superior job performance. It will sound familiar, as it is consistent with Earl Hunt's (1995) views on intelligence that we discussed in chapter 8. In this model, knowledge of the job is the most important factor in job performance. Job knowledge, in turn, is the

**assessment centers**
Programs for the evaluation of employees that use simulated management tasks as their primary method of evaluation.

**simulated management task**
A contrived task requiring managerial skills that is given to candidates for management positions to evaluate their potential as managers.

**in-basket exercise**
A type of management simulation task in which the individual attempts to solve a problem that is typical of the ones that appear in a manager's "in-basket."

**FIGURE 17.6**
Employees who know the skills and information needed to perform a job well tend to perform their jobs better. Employees with higher intellectual ability perform their jobs better mostly because they learn job knowledge faster. Similarly, more experienced employees perform better mostly because they have greater job knowledge. Employees who are higher on the personality trait of conscientiousness also tend to learn job knowledge better. To a smaller extent, all three factors (high intelligence, experience, and conscientiousness) also contribute to better job performance in ways that are unrelated to the learning of job knowledge.

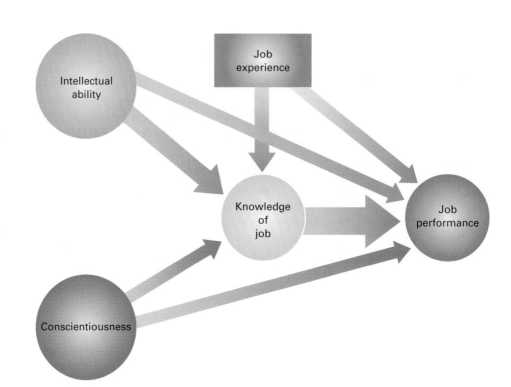

result of both the employee's job experience and intellectual ability (see fig. 17.6). Schmidt and Hunter (1992) found that employees steadily gain job knowledge over the first five years; then the benefits of on-the-job experience level off. Intellectual ability mostly influences how quickly the employee gains this job knowledge when he or she starts the job. Higher intellectual ability does improve job performance somewhat after it has been learned (by leading to better solutions to complex problems that arise on the job), but the main reason that more intelligent employees perform better is that they learn the job more quickly. Therefore, the benefits of high intelligence are most obvious in the first five years on the job, when job knowledge is still being learned. After five years on the job, that advantage of higher intelligence is smaller, because experience tends to equalize the job knowledge of employees. For this reason, tests of job knowledge are as valid as tests of intelligence in selecting experienced workers (Schmidt & Hunter, 1998).

Intellectual ability tests are the most valid method of selecting new workers for a wide range of jobs, but they are less useful for some jobs than others (Schmidt & Hunter, 1992). Intellectual ability tests are very useful in selecting employees for more complex jobs (sales, managerial, etc.) but less useful when the job is less complex (vehicle operator, semiskilled factory worker, etc.). For these jobs, performance tests of job knowledge are more useful than intellectual ability tests.

Schmidt and Hunter (1992) also found that one of the "big five" personality traits that we discussed in chapter 12 (page 463) is important in predicting job success in many occupations. Employees who are more conscientious learn job knowledge more quickly and perform their jobs better. In part, this is because employees who are low in conscientiousness are more likely to miss work and to develop conflicts with supervisors and other employees. Thus, intelligence is not the only psychological dimension that is associated with good job performance; conscientiousness is important as well.

## Fairness in Employee Selection

Some kinds of jobs are more prestigious, lucrative, and influential than other kinds of jobs. One important role of the industrial-organizational psychologist is to alert employers to the many possible biases in employee selection. Knowledge of these biases may promote greater fairness in the selection of employees for the most desirable jobs. These are highly complicated issues, however, and there are no easy solutions.

### Gender Biases in Employee Selection

Psychologist Felicia Pratto and her colleagues (1997) at Stanford University have studied differences in the numbers of women and men who work in occupations that give the individual high financial rewards, power over others, or both (attorneys, politicians, business executives, police officers, and members of the military). Approximately two-thirds of such occupations are filled by men in the United States (Pratto & others, 1997). In contrast, jobs that involve helping others (psychologists, social workers, and teachers) are mostly held by women. What forces contribute to men's holding most of the most powerful jobs?

Pratto and her colleagues believe that two factors are involved in this unequal distribution of powerful occupations. First, women and men in United States tend to *want* different kinds of jobs. In particular, women are more likely than men to seek jobs that involve helping other people (Pratto & others, 1997). Second, when women do seek powerful jobs, they are less likely to be hired. According to Pratto and her colleagues, this is because potential employers tend to view female applicants as not holding the values consistent with working in powerful occupations, mostly based on prejudicial views of women (Konrad & others, 2000; Pratto & others, 1997). It has long been known that female applicants for managerial positions tend to be rated lower than male applicants with equal qualifications (Dipboye, Fromkin, & Wilback, 1975). Such prejudice tends to unfairly exclude women from the most powerful occupational roles.

### Race-Ethnic Biases in Employee Selection

Just as the most powerful and highly paid occupations tend to be held by men rather than women, they also tend to be held by members of the majority culture rather than members of racial and ethnic minority groups. The huge disparities in occupational achievement among ethnic groups in the United States is undoubtedly the result, in large part, of prejudice. Clearly, the majority group has tended to directly and indirectly intentionally exclude minority groups from positions of power.

Psychologists John Dovidio and Samuel Gaertner (2000) studied changes both in the expression of racial prejudice and in the biased selection of minority employee applicants over a 10-year period. In studies conducted in 1989 and 1999, samples of college students studied using the same procedures. In one part of the studies, the participants were asked about racial attitudes. Consistent with trends in the United States over this period, the participants were less likely to express racial prejudice in 1999 than in 1989. In another part of the studies, the participants chose among applicants in a simulated employee selection exercise. In both 1989 and 1999, there was no racial bias in the selection of applicants whose credentials were clearly strong or clearly weak. At both times, however, members of racial minority groups were less likely to be selected for the job than whites when both applicants had average credentials. Although the overt expression of racial prejudice is declining, prejudice remains an important barrier to fair employment for members of some race-ethnic groups.

A great deal of attention has been focused on the unintended role of intelligence tests in possibly continuing to exclude members of ethnic minority groups from prestigious occupations, however. Because African Americans and Hispanics, on the average, still score somewhat lower on intellectual ability tests than whites, the use of such tests in employee selection means that a smaller proportion of applicants from these ethnic groups are selected on the basis of the test (Sackett & others, 2001; Schmidt & Ones, 1992; Wagner, 1997). For example, if an intellectual ability test were used that selects 50 percent of the white applicants, it would select an average of only 16 percent of African American applicants (Hunter & Hunter, 1984; Wagner, 1997).

Some psychologists have argued that some ethnic minority groups score, on the average, lower than whites on intelligence tests because intelligence tests are *biased* against minority groups (e.g., Williams, 1972). They believe that the bias results from basing test items on information and skills that are emphasized only in the majority culture. Other psychologists have argued that intelligence tests are equally valid for all groups (e.g., Schmidt & Hunter, 1998). In their view, the differences in intelligence tests scores reflect the disadvantages and prejudice faced by ethnic minority groups in our society more than cultural bias in the tests.

Richard Wagner (1997) of Florida State University has used data to point out a serious flaw in the argument that intelligence tests are equally valid predictors of future job performance for whites and members of ethnic minority groups. The actual size of differences between ethnic groups in actual job performance is noticeably smaller than their difference in intelligence scores. This means that a smaller percentage of ethnic minority workers with good job potential would be selected at every level of intelligence than whites. If Wagner's (1997) interpretation of the data is correct—and it appears to be—then intelligence tests are biased against members of ethnic minority groups when used in employee selection.

How should we, the members of a democratic society, respond to this potential ethnic bias inherent in the use of intelligence tests for employee selection? One obvious solution would be to place greater emphasis on tests of job knowledge and skills, which allow each person to demonstrate directly his or her fitness for the job. One can use such tests only with *experienced* workers, however, who have already learned the information and skills required by the job. For the selection of *new* employees, tests of intelligence are usually the best predictor of job success. One could minimize the ethnic bias inherent in intelligence tests by setting different minimum qualifying scores for differ-

Job satisfaction is not directly related to productivity. But it's good for both the business and the employees because it reduces employee turnover and absenteeism.

ent ethnic groups, but the 1991 U.S. Civil Rights Act made this practice illegal. It may be very difficult for our society to find a fair and acceptable solution to this problem. Richard Wagner (1997) pointed out that banning intelligence tests from employee selection might only make matters worse. If we were to substitute a less valid employee selection test, it would be *more* biased against ethnic minorities (Wagner, 1997). The better a measure predicts future job performance, the less biased it is against ethnic minority groups. And for the selection of new workers for complex jobs, intelligence tests are still the most valid employee selection measure for all groups. Thus, until more valid methods of selecting new employees that are not biased against ethnic minorities are found, we must work to find ways to use intelligence tests in ways that are fairer to everyone.

## Job Satisfaction, Happiness, and Productivity

Psychologists working in business have two inherently important goals: to improve the happiness and satisfaction of employees and to improve their productivity. The goals of improving job satisfaction and productivity can be met in two principal ways. As we have just discussed, one is to use methods of employee selection to match the right person with the right job. The other way is to improve working conditions, including the ways in which employees are managed and supervised. We will first look at the relationship among job satisfaction, happiness, and productivity; then we will examine the ways in which supervisory style and managerial, organizational, and physical conditions are related to these goals.

Are satisfied workers productive workers? That has been the assumption of industrial-organizational psychologists for many years, but research suggests that it may not always be the case (Iaffaldano & Muchinsky, 1985). Job satisfaction is only modestly associated with productivity (Judge & others, 2001). On the other hand, workers who are more than just satisfied and are *happy* at work tend to be very productive (Cote, 1999). Employers who want productive employees should create work conditions that not only satisfy their employees but also allow them to be happy at work.

But although job satisfaction is not directly related to *individual* productivity, it has a positive effect on the performance of the organization as a whole (Ostroff, 1992). Job satisfaction improves the performance of organizations in the following ways:

1. Reducing employee turnover—the rate at which employees quit and seek new jobs

2. Reducing absenteeism—the frequency with which employees fail to show up for work

3. Improving relations between labor and management

4. Improving the ability of organizations to recruit good employees

5. Improving the reputation that employees give to an organization by what they say about it in the community (Anastasi, 1987).

Still, happy employees are more productive than merely satisfied employees.

### Management Strategies to Improve Job Satisfaction, Happiness, and Productivity

Three major management strategies are widely used to improve job satisfaction, happiness, and productivity:

1. *Improving management supervisory style.* The most effective managers and supervisors are *considerate* (warm, friendly, and concerned in dealing with employees) and *communicative* (can clearly tell employees what is expected of them and how they will be evaluated on their performance). In addition, the most effective supervisors are also often high in **structuring** (spending a great deal of time organizing and directing the work of their employees). However, being high in structuring is an advantage only when the supervisor is also highly considerate. It may even be a disadvantage when less considerate supervisors closely structure their employees' activities (Anastasi, 1987).

2. *Improving managerial organization.* A great deal of attention has been paid to how the efforts of management are organized. Do messages always come down from top management, or are employees involved in decision making to some extent? Are employees told specifically how to work, or are they best organized in teams that are given specific production goals but allowed freedom in the ways they meet those goals? Does it make any difference? Two strategies of managerial organization that appear to make a significant difference in promoting job satisfaction and productivity are *participative management* and *management by objectives.*

In the **participative management** method, teams of employees at every level of the organization are actively involved in decision making (Hollander & Offermann, 1990; Ilgen, 1999; Turnage, 1990). For instance, when a dressmaking plant must change over to making a new line of clothes, teams of sewing machine operators work out the most efficient ways to do this in discussions with their supervisors. The supervisors link this decision-making process to higher management by participating in decision-making conferences with their supervisors, who then participate in decisions with the next level of management, and so on up to the top. In a classic example of the benefits of participative management, employees of the Weldon Pajama Factory showed an almost 50 percent increase in productivity and earning when such a system was introduced (Likert, 1967). Interestingly, research suggests that female managers are more likely than male managers to adopt the effective participative management strategy (Eagly & Johnson, 1990).

Another effective strategy of managerial organization is **management by objectives** (Locke & Latham, 1990; 2002). In this approach, teams of employees are given a specific goal to accomplish—anything from producing 1,000 dishes per month, to reducing air pollution from the factory by 80 percent, to reducing

**structuring**
The activities of managers that organize and direct the work of employees.

**participative management**
The practice of involving employees at all levels in management decisions.

**management by objectives**
The strategy of giving employees specific goals but giving them considerable freedom in deciding how to reach those goals.

corporate taxes by 20 percent—but the teams are given considerable freedom in *how* they meet those objectives (Ilgen, 1999). This method benefits the company because it ensures that management focuses on what is really important to the company (its objectives). But management by objectives also gives employees a greater sense of independence and an easier way to tell whether they are doing a good job of meeting their goals. It is an especially good management strategy when employees believe that the goals are reasonable and appropriate (Locke & Latham, 1990). Management by objectives is often used along with a participative management strategy, allowing employees at all levels to participate in setting and reviewing goals. Increasingly, too, meeting and exceeding the goals is often tied to bonuses, thus giving the employee positive reinforcement for greater productivity in the form of greater monetary income (McCormick & Ilgen, 1980).

3. ***Improving physical conditions.*** Considerable research has been done by industrial-organizational psychologists on the influence of physical conditions (such as lighting, noise, and temperature) on productivity and job satisfaction. For example, psychologists have found that working in 95-degree temperatures produces significant increases in perceptual and decision-making errors after four to five hours on the job (Fine & Kobrick, 1978). Considerable attention has also been paid to the design of machines that fit well with the psychological characteristics of the human beings who will be operating them.

A good working environment improves productivity and job satisfaction.

### Management Strategies to Minimize Social Loafing

Recall from chapter 16, on social psychology, that when people work together on a joint project some people usually work less hard than they would if they were working on an individual project—termed *social loafing* (Latané & others, 1979). Because organizations often need their employees to work together as a group—on group projects ranging from building automobiles to writing governmental regulations—it is important to understand what encourages social loafing and what minimizes it. University of Florida psychologist James Shepard (1995) has summarized research on this topic. According to Shepard, social loafing is the result of low motivation to work on the group project. Low motivation, in turn, results from individuals' perceiving their contributions to be unrewarded, unnecessary, or too costly to the individual.

Social loafing can be minimized, therefore, by reducing its causes:

1. If the individual believes that his or her contribution to the group effort will not be recognized or rewarded even if the group goal is met, the solution is to provide clear incentives to each individual's contribution to the group effort. This incentive could be anything from a good performance evaluation to bonuses that are tied *not to the effort of the group as a whole* but to the effort of the individual.

2. If the individual mistakenly believes that the group goal will be achieved just as well, regardless of how much he or she contributes as an individual, the solution is to show the individual that his or her contribution is indispensable. This can be accomplished by dividing up the task so that each individual contributes something that is both unique and important.

3. Sometimes individuals feel that their contributions to the group effort will cost more than they are worth. For example, a young salesperson might feel that time spent working on a new group retirement plan could be better devoted to earning commissions from sales.

    Paradoxically, some hard workers start to loaf on group tasks if they think that *other* members of the group are exploiting them by loafing.

These causes of social loafing can be combated by making the task easier (e.g., by getting a consultant to write the first draft of a new retirement plan) or by discouraging social loafing in every member of the group, so that no one will feel exploited by others.

Interestingly, studies of social loafing in different cultures have found that social loafing is universal—it happens in all cultures to some extent (Shepard, 1995). Group effort seems to be motivated by different factors in different cultures, however. The Japanese tend to motivate contributions to group work by mutually monitoring the performance of group members and responding positively to good effort and shaming poor effort. Americans, on the other hand, comment less on each other's performance and rely more on each individual's sense of duty to the group. As a result, Japanese workers are more likely than American workers to withdraw from groups where social loafing is going on (Shepard, 1995).

## Leadership

The success of any organization also depends on the quality of its leadership. Leadership is the influence of one group member on the others as they work toward shared goals. Psychologists have studied the *traits* of successful leaders. Traits such as drive, honesty, flexibility, leadership motivation, intelligence, and creativity contribute to a person's leadership potential. Effective leaders understand that leadership styles must be adapted to each situation. Some leaders seem especially capable of inspiring their followers to reach a common goal. Whether the goal is positive, as in the case of Martin Luther King, or negative, as in the case of Adolf Hitler, these leaders share the traits of charisma, clear vision, inspiration, and personalized attention to their followers (Chemers, 1997; Northouse, 1997; Shamir & Howell, 1999).

### Leadership among Women and Minorities

Women appear to approach organizational leadership in ways that are different from men, yet equally effective. Eagly and Johnson (1990) analyzed more than 150 studies of gender and leadership and concluded that women are as task-oriented as men. However, women tend to be more democratic—interacting more with their subordinates, sharing information and power, and developing extensive networks (Helgesen, 1990). In spite of their effectiveness, women tend to be undervalued in leadership positions, especially when their leadership style appears "masculine" or when they are in a traditionally "masculine" occupation (Eagly & others, 1992).

Minorities may experience difficulty obtaining leadership positions because of subtle racism in the workplace. Irons and Moore (1985) found that African Americans in the banking industry were not well networked and often lacked the mentoring necessary for moving up in the organization.

Women and minorities continue to experience the glass ceiling in American organizations. They can rise to a certain level of leadership, but the top positions usually elude them (Morrison & Von Glinow, 1990).

## Psychology of the Entrepreneur

Entrepreneurs are people who turn ideas into new businesses. They are widely thought to play an important role in free market economies by generating wealth for themselves and investors and jobs for their employees. Each year, many new businesses are launched, but most fail. What are the characteristics of persons who are successful entrepreneurs? Robert Baron (2000) and other psychologists have conducted studies of successful entrepreneurs. Persons who succeed as entrepreneurs have been found to differ from others in a number of ways (Baron, 2000):

1. ***Entrepreneurs engage in less counterfactual thinking.*** Successful entrepreneurs are less likely than other people to spend time thinking about how things *might* have been. They do not spend their time thinking about how failed opportunities might have been different; they get on with the job at hand.

2. ***Entrepreneurs have excellent social skills.*** Successful entrepreneurs have the social skills to sell their ideas to potential investors and new customers. In partic-

ular, they are adept at person perception—accurately sizing up other people (see chapter 16, page 628). They also feel comfortable in a wide range of social situations.

3. ***Entrepreneurs tend to be physically attractive.*** We saw in chapter 16 (page 618) that physical attractiveness is an advantage in social situations, and not surprisingly, successful entrepreneurs tend to be attractive. Not all successful entrepreneurs are attractive, but even among entrepreneurs, the most attractive entrepreneurs make considerably more money than the least attractive entrepreneurs do.

Do you have dreams of a successful entrepreneurial life? Do you have the characteristics listed here? Do not despair if you do not—there have been some very successful entrepreneurs who are quite different from the picture just painted. If you do not have the qualities of the typical entrepreneur, however, it may be wise to think about ways to minimize these disadvantages. And if you do have the qualities of a successful entrepreneur, remember that thinking and looking like a successful tycoon does not guarantee that you will become one!

## Human Factors Engineering

We live in a technological society in which more and more of our work is done by machines. But machines must be operated by people, so increasingly the work of people has become the operation of machines. For this reason, one branch of industrial-organizational psychology, known as **human factors engineering,** has as its goal the design of machines that can be more easily and efficiently operated by human beings.

For example, airplane pilots must operate a number of different manual controls while their eyes are occupied looking at radar, reading gauges, and watching where the plane is going. The job of the human factors engineer is to design manual controls in a way that will make them easier and safer to use. In this case, the controls would probably be designed in a way that makes use of the pilot's sense of touch, because controls do not have to be seen to be perceived. Controls of different shapes can be easily distinguished by touch and are particularly easy to use if their shape is related to their function, as shown in figure 17.7. Human factors research has also found that controls are more easily operated when they are located next to the dial that they influence rather than in separate clusters (see fig. 17.8) and when the direction of turning a control matches the direction of the corresponding dial (see fig. 17.9).

Taking a different approach to improving the interface between people and machines, human factors engineers have found that short rest periods greatly improve efficiency in many tasks. For example, workers who need to detect infrequent visual signals, such as an air traffic controller has to do, have been found to maintain nearly perfect accuracy over an hour and a half when

**human factors engineering**
The branch of industrial-organizational psychology interested in the design of machines to be operated by human beings.

 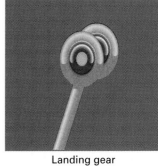

Landing flap          Landing gear

**FIGURE 17.7**
An example of controls that are designed to be easily distinguished by touch and related in form to their function.

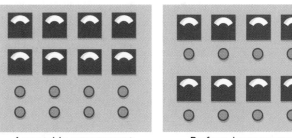

Acceptable arrangement          Preferred arrangement

**FIGURE 17.8**
Examples of controls and dials arranged to fit the cognitive characteristics of human operators.

**FIGURE 17.9**
Examples of controls designed to operate in a way that is compatible with the direction of operation of the corresponding dial.

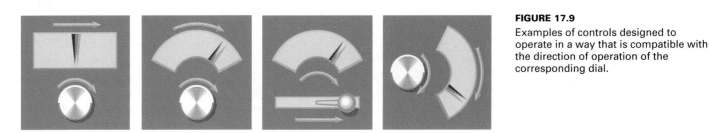

The risk of cardiovascular disease is twice as high for people with sedentary lifestyles as for those who exercise regularly.

they take a 10-minute break every 30 minutes. When the workers do not take breaks, however, their accuracy in detecting the signals falls below 75 percent after being on the job for more than 30 minutes (Bergum & Lehr, 1962).

Human factors engineering was in the spotlight in the 1980s after serious accidents at nuclear power plants at Three Mile Island and Chernobyl released large amounts of radioactivity. Although the causes of these accidents were complex, investigations suggested that the plant operators were asked to deal with too much information that was presented in confusing ways. The design of the operating system and its computer displays of information overloaded the cognitive capacities of the operators, and fatal mistakes were made (Wickens, 1992). Human factors engineers have been working to simplify computer displays of information in many work settings (Howell, 1993).

Human factors engineers have also turned their attention to consumer safety issues. For example, some kinds of automobile safety belts pose a danger to children and smaller adults because the shoulder strap is close to the neck. In response to this concern, human factors engineers developed a type of shoulder harness that can be easily and effectively adjusted to fit the height of the passenger using only one hand (Tillman & Tillman, 1991). Such efforts by human factors engineers make the marriage between people and machines happier, safer, and more efficient.

As more is learned about both biology and psychology, a future direction for human factors engineering is in the development of ways to overcome human frailties. The largest market for such innovative human engineering is older persons. Of all humans aged 65 years or older who have ever lived, half of them are alive today! As these individuals grow older, they will be increasingly likely to make errors and experience limitations due to their growing motor, sensory, and memory limitations. In most cases, these problems will be minor—forgetting to watch a television program—but in other cases, the errors will be serious, as in taking too few or too many doses of medication each day. In other cases, the elderly will experience unnecessary restrictions on the quality of their lives, such as not being able to learn to use e-mail to keep up with the grandchildren. Psychologists Arthur Fisk and Wendy Rogers (2002) suggest that research could lead to minimal changes in instruction manuals, operating controls, medicine labels, and the like that could make huge differences to older people. But it is not just the elderly that need help with these things. Fisk and Rogers report that the majority of diabetics make errors in monitoring their glucose levels. This kind of simple human engineering of labels and instructions through research that is based in an understanding of human perception and memory could make an enormous difference.

Other areas of human factors research focus on persons with far less common, but more serious limitations. For example, persons who are totally paralyzed are often fully aware of their surroundings and able to think clearly, but have no way of communicating with others. This situation has been referred to as the "locked-in" syndrome. Recent research suggests that it will some day be possible to use computer-analyzed brain activity recordings to drive artificial speech generators to allow these individuals to "speak" freely (Kubler & others, 2001).

## Health Psychology in the Workplace

We first discussed the field of *health psychology* in chapter 13. We learned about the growing awareness among both medical professionals and the general public that stress and unhealthy patterns of behavior (such as overwork, poor diet, and lack of exercise) are extremely important threats to good health. There is an increasing understanding in the business world, too, that good health among employees is good business (Ilgen, 1990). Healthy employees are more productive, miss fewer days of work, make fewer claims for health benefits, and are less likely to die or become disabled during their most valuable and productive years. The cost of poor health to business is enormous.

Fortunately, many American businesses have concluded that programs to improve employee health are good for everyone—and profitable as well. Consider, for example, programs to increase the cardiovascular fitness of employees. The Centers for Disease

Control and Prevention have determined that the risk of cardiovascular disease is *twice* as high for sedentary persons as for persons who exercise regularly—making it a risk factor as important as high blood pressure, high serum cholesterol, and smoking (Powell, Thompson, Caspersen, & Kendrick, 1987). Thus, some 50,000 businesses in the United States have instituted some type of program to increase the fitness of their employees.

Suppose you are offered two jobs after graduation with identical work requirements, salaries, and opportunities for advancement—but one gives you the option of a free membership in the health club of your choice or a locker in the company gym (and time during the day to take an exercise break). The same company prohibits smoking in the workplace and has fruit juice rather than soft drinks in the vending machines. Assuming you are health conscious, which job would you take?

If you took the job with the company that makes exercise easy, would you be working for a company that made a profitable decision in this case? Yes, indeed. First, your company would tend to attract healthier employees who were excited about the opportunity to exercise and who would incur fewer health-related costs. Second, the company would likely save money by *keeping* its employees healthy through exercise. For example, the Johnson & Johnson Corporation studied the costs of such a health plan for 11,000 of its employees and found that it saved the company almost a quarter of a million dollars per year in direct health care claims (Bly, Jones, & Richardson, 1986). In these and other ways, psychologists are beginning to show business that a healthy work environment yields not only employee well-being, but healthy profits, too.

## Other Applications of Psychology to the Workplace

We have sampled a few of the ways in which psychology has been applied to business, but there are many others. For example, psychological principles and methods have been used in developing methods of *training* new employees and in developing the potential of current employees through continued education (Tannenbaum & Yukl, 1992). When a new person is hired by IBM to repair computers, she or he must first be trained to do it. When a salesperson is promoted to a sales management position by Prudential, he or she must be taught how to manage sales. When a new management trainee is hired by McDonald's, she or he must be trained in purchasing, hiring, safely storing foods, and so on. When the number of employees who need training is multiplied by the number of jobs they must learn, it's easy to see why the efficiency of business depends in part on the efficiency of training programs (Wagner, 1997).

In many areas of the workplace, computers play an increasingly large role in training. Computer-assisted instruction can be used to teach basic information, from

Computerized flight simulators allow new pilots to "fly" aircraft in the safety of the training laboratory until they develop the skill for real flying.

insurance underwriting to telephone repair, in ways that are more efficient for both the employer and the employee. It is in the area of *computer simulation*, however, that computers offer their greatest advantages in training. It is neither ethical nor feasible to teach sailors to operate multimillion-dollar submarines or jet aircraft by allowing them to "learn from their mistakes." One error during the training process could result in loss of life and the destruction of enormously expensive vehicles. In response to this need, extremely realistic computerized simulators allow new pilots to "fly" aircraft in the safety of the training laboratory until they develop the skills to handle the real thing. Similar computer simulations allow physicians to practice medical diagnosis and investment managers to test their decision-making skills in the stock market.

Psychologists have also contributed to the advertising and marketing end of business. Advertising is almost as old as civilization itself. Excavation of the ruins of the ancient city of Pompeii, for example, found announcements of the availability of products and services painted on the walls of buildings (Anastasi, 1987). And psychologists have been trying to find ways to improve the effectiveness of advertising almost as long as there has been a field of psychology. The first book on the psychology of advertising was published by Walter Scott in 1908.

Psychologists have found that a number of perceptual factors such as size, color, repetition, and spatial position influence the effectiveness of advertisements. For example, half-page magazine ads are noticed by readers only half as often as full-page ads, and full-color ads are read by 50 percent more readers than are black-and-white ads (Anastasi, 1987).

Attempts to improve advertising effectiveness often involve emotional appeals. Recall from chapter 16 that fear appeals are sometimes effective in making communications more persuasive. Advertisers of mouthwash, toothpaste, hair dye, and the like would have us believe that if we do not use their products we will be coldly rejected by the people we care about. Manufacturers of boots, bathing suits, perfumes, and sports cars similarly imply in their ads that if we would only buy their goods we would be adored by others for our sexiness.

Psychologists in industry also work to determine the preferences of consumers. Others conduct research to determine the best ways to convey information about the contents of foods and drugs to consumers. Still others concentrate on reducing prejudice and other barriers to equal opportunities for minority groups in business. The roles for psychologists in business are as varied as the business sector of society.

## Review

The quality of our lives is linked to business in terms of both our enjoyment of the goods and services that business produces and the satisfaction that we derive from our jobs. Industrial-organizational psychologists help business improve its productivity, improve worker safety and health, and help workers obtain more meaning and enjoyment from their jobs. Psychologists most frequently work through personnel departments because they have responsibility for selecting and training employees.

Industrial-organizational psychologists also help managers improve managerial style (how they relate to their employees), the organizational structure of management (such as through participative management or management by objectives), and the physical and health conditions of work. Through these and many other methods, psychologists are able to contribute to worker satisfaction, happiness, and productivity.

## Check Your Learning

To be sure that you have learned the key points from the preceding section, cover the list of correct answers and try to answer each question. If you give an incorrect answer to any question, return to the page given next to the correct answer to see why your answer was not correct. Remember that these questions cover only some of the important information in this section; it is important that you make up your own questions to check your learning of other facts and concepts.

1. A(n) _____ is a psychologist who seeks ways to improve the functioning and human benefits of business.

   a)  developmental psychologist
   b)  industrial-organizational psychologist
   c)  clinical psychologist
   d)  Gestalt psychologist

2. A dimension of personality that has been shown to predict job performance in a variety of types of jobs is _____.

3. _____ are the most valid selection measures for most complex jobs.

   a)  Projective tests
   b)  Performance tests
   c)  Biodata
   d)  Intellectual ability tests

4. _____, or spending a great deal of time organizing and directing the work of employees, is most effective when the supervisor is also considerate of others.

   a)  Structuring
   b)  Authoritative direction
   c)  Decentralizing
   d)  Categorizing

5. _____ refers to the branch of industrial-organizational psychology interested in the design of machines to be operated by human beings.

   a)  Mechanical engineering
   b)  Architectural engineering
   c)  Graphic design
   d)  Human factors engineering

---

1. If interviews are the least valid method for selecting employees, why do they continue to be such a popular technique?

2. What questions might you ask a potential employer about working conditions to determine your likelihood of achieving a high level of job happiness?

**Thinking Critically about Psychology**

**Correct Answers:   1.** b (p. 644),   **2.** conscientiousness (p. 651),   **3.** d (p. 651),   **4.** a (p. 654),   **5.** d (p. 657).

## ● Environmental Psychology

**Environmental psychologists** study two important and fascinating topics: (1) the effects of the environment on our behavior and mental processes, and (2) the effects of our behavior on the environment. We begin by summarizing what has been learned about the ways in which environments influence us and then move to our effects on the environment.

Architects and interior designers strive to create environments where people can live and work more happily, healthfully, and productively (Stokols, 1995). Environmental psychologists are actively involved in the study of psychological reactions to different aspects of the physical environment. Most findings to date have been interesting but perhaps not surprising. For example, people perceive others in less positive ways and are less interested in socializing in drab, ugly rooms than in attractive rooms (Maslow & Mintz, 1956; Russell & Mehrabian, 1978). Adding touches such as potted plants and an aquarium to professors' offices makes students feel more welcome (Campbell, 1978).

**environmental psychologists**
Psychologists who study the effects of the environment on our behavior and mental processes, and the effects of our behavior on the environment.

Psychologists have helped architects design workspaces that are conducive to both job satisfaction and productivity. Do these workers have enough private space?

And people are less positive toward others in hot rooms than in comfortable rooms (Griffith & Veitch, 1971). Other findings have been less expected and have contributed more to architecture and interior design.

## Office and Workspace Design

A great deal of effort has gone into the design of workspaces to make them enjoyable and safe for employees and to promote productive performance. For example, a popular trend today is to design office space in the so-called *office landscape* format. In this format, offices are laid out in large open spaces and separated from one another only by low movable partitions, desks, and file cabinets. This creates a space that can be flexibly rearranged, is inexpensive to construct, and is attractive in appearance. Contrary to expectation, however, studies of the psychological effects of office landscapes have not painted a positive picture. One study was conducted after a number of workers moved from a building with traditional separate offices into a new building that was equally divided into traditional offices and an office landscape area. After six months, workers who had moved into the office landscape area were considerably less satisfied with their surroundings. They reported that they interacted more with each other, but they cooperated less. In addition, they found the new office area less private and noisier and reportedly accomplished less work (Hundert & Greenfield, 1969).

Greg Oldham and Yitzhak Fried (1987) have also examined characteristics of favorable and unfavorable work environments. Studying clerical employees from different departments in the same large university, they found that the physical nature of the environment explained many of the differences between the departments in terms of employee turnover and satisfaction. Workers were most likely to be dissatisfied and to resign from their jobs when the office was poorly lighted, when few enclosures provided privacy to the workers, when employees were seated close together, and when many employees occupied the same office. Clerical workers like well-lighted, private space.

## Architectural Design of Living Units

Psychologists have increasingly played a role in the design of living units. Perhaps because psychologists tend to work in universities, college dormitories have been a frequent subject of such research. Traditional plans for college dormitories call for one long corridor into which a number of small rooms open. Typically, the residents of these rooms share a single common lounge and bathroom, which are also located off the corridor. In contrast to this traditional single-corridor design is the suite design. In this concept, three or four rooms are clustered around a small lounge and bathroom shared only by the residents of that one suite. Proponents of the suite-design concept suggest that although the same number of people can be housed per square foot in this design (see fig. 17.10), it's a far more "human" approach to dense housing. In this case, psychological studies have rather strongly supported the suite-design concept. Residents of single-corridor dorms spend less time in the dorms, express greater desire to avoid interaction with other residents, and feel that they have less control over what happens in their dormitory than do residents of suite-design dorms (Baum & Valins, 1977).

Even more impressive is the finding that the effects of living in a single-corridor dorm extend outside of the dorm setting. Freshmen living in both types of dorms were taken to a laboratory, where they were asked to wait with other students in a waiting room. Residents of single-corridor dorms initiated fewer conversations, sat at greater physical distance from the other students, and spent less time looking at the faces of other students. Apparently, their unsatisfactory living environment led them to be some-

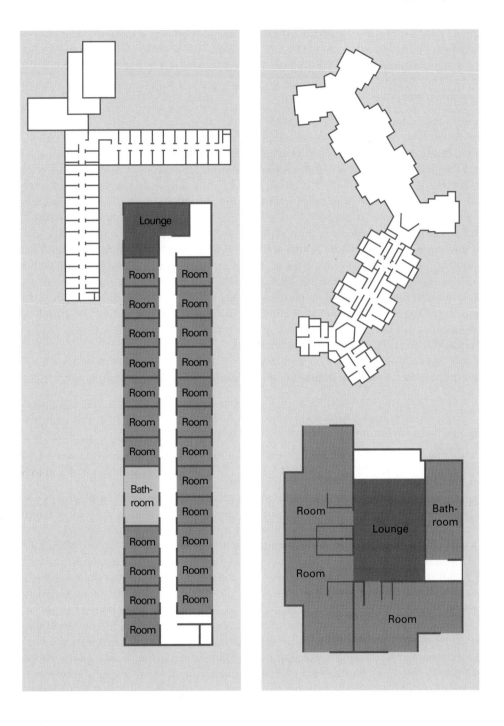

**FIGURE 17.10**
Examples of the single corridor and
suite design floor plans for college
dormitories.

what less sociable even outside of the dormitory (Baum, Harpin, & Valins, 1975). If you live in a single-corridor dorm, you should not be concerned about lasting damage to your social life, but it may have some minor effect on your current behavior.

Duncan Case (1981) has also provided evidence that the architecture of college dormitories influences friendship patterns over long periods of time. According to Case, the key element in dormitories is "shared required paths"—shared elevators, drinking fountains, and the like. College students who lived in dormitories were studied. During their sophomore year, over 80 percent of these students shared a room with someone with whom they had shared a required path during their freshman year. Even during their senior year, 50 percent of the roommates had met through shared required paths during their freshman year. Because the students reported that their best friend was one of their roommates 73 percent of the time, it is clear that friendships are dictated in part by architecture.

## Environmental Protection

It is no secret that the life-support system that we call earth is in serious jeopardy. There are broad categories of assaults on our planet: (a) overpopulation, (b) resource depletion, and (c) pollution and waste management. What are the causes of these threats to our life-giving environment? In the area of pollution, for example, are the culprits the dangerous gases and particles that are emitted by automobiles, buses, trucks, and power plants? What about the pollutants that industries still dump into our rivers, lakes, and oceans? In one sense, these *are* the culprits (and many sources of pollution like them). But in a more important sense, things (machines, factories, etc.) are not the root causes of environmental destruction, *people* are. It is people who build the factories and machines and decide how to operate them. Therefore, protecting the environment will require *changing the behavior of people.* That is why the topic of environmental protection is an important part of a course on psychology. As we will see, the people whose behavior must be changed if the planet is to continue to support human life are the people in government, the people who own and operate businesses, and the people who are consumers (Geller, 1995). All of us, in other words.

### Overpopulation, Resource Depletion, and Pollution and Waste Management

In this section, we will describe the main threats to the environment that result from human behavior. In the next section, we will look at the attempts of psychologists to change these environmentally destructive behaviors.

Mismanagement of the earth's resources can have tragic effects for both the environment and the people of the world. Approximately one-fifth of the world's population lives in extreme poverty, which puts them at risk for death and disease. Every day, more than 50,000 infants and children die of starvation or nutrition-related problems.

*Overpopulation.* It took about 3 million years to reach a population of 1 billion people on the planet. Now, with the addition of approximately 97 million people to the planet every year, another billion of us are added every 8 years. The current population of over 6 billion will *double* in about 47 years, putting the world's population at 10 to 12 billion near the middle of the twenty-first century! At the current rate, we are adding close to 184 additional mouths to feed every minute! There is no question that the human behavior of reproducing at these high rates is a major threat to the environment.

Of the over 6 billion people currently on earth, over 1 billion of them live in absolute poverty, which puts them at high risk of death or serious health problems due to malnutrition and disease. Each day an average of 50,000 infants and children die as a result of starvation and nutrition-related illness. Many of these people live in developing, or "third world," countries. Not surprisingly, people show little concern for preserving the environment when daily survival of self and family is in jeopardy. As a result, people in many developing countries are forced into behaviors that are harmful to the environment. Examples include exhausting natural resources for export to industrial nations (such as the ongoing destruction of the hardwood forests of Indonesia and South America), degrading the soil through poor farming techniques, and polluting water supplies through poor agricultural, industrial, and sanitation practices. In developing nations throughout the world, these problems are multiplied as the increasing populations become concentrated in large cities. Although it is still possible to find experts who deny it, the earth's carrying capacity for human beings is quickly reaching its limit (many would say that it has already been surpassed).

*Resource Depletion.* A second major environmental problem involves the rate at which humankind is depleting the earth's natural resources. Some of those resources are only necessary to our modern lifestyles—for example, we must have oil and coal (fossil fuels) to maintain our electrified and automobile-driven way of life. But other resources are essential to our very survival (clean air, clean water, topsoil that can be farmed, etc.). It is the rare American who is not generally aware of the shrinking supply of usable fossil fuels. We consume millions of barrels of oil each day, a thirst that has already resulted in the depletion of half of the earth's total oil supply. America has about 200 years worth of coal left, but its use creates other problems (e.g., air pollution and global warming) that will make this alternative unfeasible.

Water and soil are resources that are already in short supply throughout much of the world. In our own country, primarily in the West and Southwest, demands have surpassed the region's ability to provide adequate amounts of fresh water. Amazingly, the Colorado River, the great provider of water for the Southwest, no longer reaches its former final destination of the Pacific Ocean—it is completely exhausted by humanity along the way. Still, the competition among western states for water is already fierce. In developing nations, only about half the people have access to safe drinking water today, and the problem will only grow worse in the future. As the population continues to increase, more and more water will be needed for agricultural, industrial, and personal uses. It is essential that ways be found to preserve and protect the earth's limited water resources. In addition, the amount of land that is available for agriculture is diminishing. Each year erosion, urban sprawl, and other factors create a net loss of tillable land for growing crops.

Similar stories could be told about the loss of other resources such as precious metals, the oceans' supply of fish, the forests, the rapid extinction of plants and animal species, and numerous other gifts that are supplied by earth's life-support system. They all point to a pattern of excessive consumption that is surpassing the earth's ability to sustain itself.

Our electrified and automobile-driven way of life is fast depleting the earth's irreplaceable resources.

***Pollution and Waste Management.*** The third major insult to the environment comes from the pollution of earth's air, land, and water and difficulties disposing of both routine and hazardous waste. We have all heard about the problems of acid rain; smog and high ozone levels; toxic waste; and polluted rivers, lakes, and saltwater bays. We have also heard about the threats of *global warming* and the *greenhouse effect,* which refer to the fact that average temperatures are increasing because of pollutants (primarily excessive carbon dioxide and methane) trapping the earth's heat and not letting it escape into space. Although scientists disagree about the extent of this threat, most experts predict that even a relatively small overall warming could have devastating effects on the earth's ability to sustain its current population. The great American "breadbasket" in the Midwest, for example, could become much less suitable for agriculture. The climate most appropriate for farming would move north to Canada, which would allow that country to become the new "breadbasket," were it not for the fact that it generally lacks the topsoil necessary for the task.

Pollution of our fresh water resources is another problem that must be addressed soon. Not only are some of our aquifers (underground water supplies) shrinking, but our waters are being polluted by numerous sources such as industrial and mining wastes, agricultural pesticides and fertilizers, and acid rain. Even now, it is estimated that more than 25 million people die in third world countries each year as a result of polluted water. As with other environmental problems, the extent of humankind's polluting behaviors is surpassing the earth's ability to clean and renew itself.

### Psychological Approaches to Environmental Protection

Part of the solution to environmental problems will come from technological innovations, such as the development of automobiles that use less fossil fuel and create less air pollution. The primary hope for preserving our global life-support system, however, is that we will change our environmentally destructive behavior. Staying within the earth's carrying capacity will require us to both control population growth and reduce our rate of depleting natural resources. Because the people of the United States consume *vastly* more than our fair share of natural resources, changes in our behavior are particularly important. There are two theoretical approaches to changing environmentally sensitive behavior: the behavioral approach and an approach derived from humanistic and cognitive psychology. As you will see, however, recent trends are to use the best of each approach.

***Behavioral Approach.*** The behavioral approach to changing behavior to protect the environment is defined by two key characteristics:

1. The behavioral approach mostly uses the principles of learning to change behavior. After all, learning is a change in behavior due to experience (chapter 6, page 198). Therefore, it is natural to attempt to change behavior using the principles of learning.

2. Because contemporary behaviorism was largely defined by the rigorous experimental approach of B. F. Skinner (chapter 1, page 12), behaviorists are careful to gather data to evaluate everything they do. When they attempt to use what they have learned in the laboratory to solve problems in the real world, they evaluate the effectiveness of their real-world solutions as rigorously as they would if it were a laboratory experiment. This "experimental approach" to real-world problems allows psychologists to quickly abandon ineffective strategies and adopt more effective solutions. Sometimes, the experimental approach means adopting methods that someone else suggested but that we were sure would not work. Data should provide the ultimate checks and balances on psychologists' theories.

An excellent example of a behavioral approach to changing the behavior of consumers is provided by Van Houwelingen and Van Raaij (1989). They tested a method based on operant conditioning (chapter 6, page 206) for reducing the consumption of natural gas in the home. The principle of operant conditioning states that behavior that is reinforced by its consequences will be more likely, whereas behavior that is punished by its consequences will decrease in frequency. These researchers installed special gas meters in 50 homes so the occupants could easily see how much gas they were using (and how much it cost). If feedback on the amount and costs of gas use "punishes" excessive gas consumption, it should decline. Van Houwelingen and Van Raaij (1989) found that providing the meters reduced gas consumption by about 10 percent. They further found that having immediate feedback was essential, because gas consumption went back to its original wasteful levels when the meters were removed. The consumers had not permanently learned more economical behavior. This finding suggests that operant feedback must be kept in place to yield long-term changes in behavior. Another, similar, successful application of operant feedback is increasing the number of miles that truck drivers achieve per gallon of fuel by publicly displaying each driver's miles per gallon figures (Geller, 1995).

Reminders to engage in pro-environmental behavior can help improve people's habits, but rewards for appropriate behavior have a stronger effect.

***Cognitive and Humanistic Approaches.*** Many psychologists attempt to change environmentally relevant behavior by changing people's attitudes or by appealing to their "higher motives." Such approaches are based in the theories that guide humanistic psychology, cognitive psychology, and the social psychology of attitude change. For example, an effective cognitive technique for changing behavior is to ask people to make a *pledge* to change their behavior. Cognitive dissonance theory (see chapter 16, page 621) predicts that people who make such a pledge would feel uncomfortable if they did not make good on their pledge. This approach has been found to be successful in producing lasting changes in recycling (Geller, 1995).

Recently, psychologists have begun to study the behavior of industrial managers in attempt to understand why they often engage in behavior that damages the environment. Nearly all large industrial companies employ *environmental managers*, people whose job it is to reduce the pollution released by their company. They are generally people like you and me—indeed, some of you will soon join their ranks. Some of them work effectively to reduce pollution (by changing to less dangerous raw materials, filtering pollutants out of air and water, etc.), but many do not. Why would intelligent and well-educated industrial managers knowingly damage the environment in which they and their families live? Cordano and Frieze (2000) have found that two kinds of attitudes predict how effectively environmental managers will act to prevent pollution. First, effective environmental managers believe that it is important to protect the environment, both for the company and the public. Second, environmental managers who do their jobs well believe that other significant people in the company support environmental protection.

Stern (2000) similarly hypothesizes that such attitudes are important determinants of the behavior of both managers and consumers, but adds other elements to the equation. People who act to protect the environment not only believe that it is important to protect the environment but also have an emotional commitment to the environment, feel sympathy for others, believe that they are able to make a difference (refer back to Bandura's concept of self-efficacy in chapter 12, page 477), and operate in circumstances that allow them to act (they are not prevented by restrictive regulations, etc.). Finally, Stern (2000) points to the strong negative impact of habit on environmentally sensitive behavior. It is difficult to motivate people to change their habitual ways of doing things, even when it is clear to them that the world can no longer tolerate the levels of pollution and waste that it could in the past.

***Integrating the Behavioral, Cognitive, and Humanistic Approaches to Environmental Protection.***   Psychologists E. Scott Geller (1995) and Paul Stern (2000) argued for an integration of the various approaches to environmental protection. One reason for such an integration is that the most effective interventions come from a range of theoretical perspectives and our efforts should not be limited by our theoretical blinders. A second reason is that the techniques derived from different theoretical perspectives often work best in combination.

Consider the following combination of behavioral and attitude change techniques: In some cases, power companies have an economic incentive to help consumers reduce energy consumption. For example, in some parts of the country, it is very costly to electric companies to have residential electric use increase dramatically in the summer, because they either need to invest in generating capacity that is unneeded during most of the year or buy electricity at inflated prices from the power grid during times of high demand. What if an electric company offered to pay 93 percent of the cost of improving the insulation of existing homes? That offer would provide a strong economic incentive to homeowners to reinsulate, because a small investment in insulation would save them a considerable amount on their future electric bills. Such incentives are helpful but are dramatically more effective when combined with informative and persuasive communications from the power company (Stern, 2000). See chapter 16, page 617, for a refresher on what constitutes persuasive communication.

Environmental psychologists conduct research on the psychological impact of our physical environment. They have found that some aspects of the interior design of rooms, such as the drabness of colors or the presence of plants, influence the mood of the persons in those rooms and their interest in socializing. Similarly, the physical characteristics of the room also influence emotions and social behavior. Friendship patterns have been found to be affected by the architecture of living units in that individuals who share "required paths" are more likely to develop friendships in a dormitory than those who do not. By studying environments such as these and the environments of workspaces, environmental psychologists can offer information to architects and interior designers that helps them design spaces with optimal psychological impact.

Review

The earth's environment has been seriously, and perhaps catastrophically, damaged by overpopulation, resource depletion, and pollution and the mismanagement of waste. Ultimately, the cause of environmental damage is the behavior of humans. Psychologists continue to develop and evaluate methods of changing environmentally sensitive behavior at the level of the individual, the business, and the government, with most research focusing on the individual consumer. Techniques for changing environmentally sensitive behavior have come from two broad traditions within psychology. The behavioral approach is characterized mostly by the use of principles of learning to change behavior and the rigorous evaluation of the effectiveness of techniques in the real world. The second approach is based on cognitive and humanistic traditions and focuses on changing attitudes, values, beliefs, and circumstances. In addition, this approach draws heavily on social psychology research on persuasive communication to change attitudes and beliefs. Recently, psychologists from both traditions have recognized the importance of combining the best of both approaches.

## Check Your Learning

To be sure that you have learned the key points from the preceding section, cover the list of correct answers and try to answer each question. If you give an incorrect answer to any question, return to the page given next to the correct answer to see why your answer was not correct.

1. A(n) _____ studies the effects of the physical environment on behavior and mental processes and studies ways to protect the environment.

   a) developmental psychologist    c) clinical psychologist

   b) environmental psychologist    d) psychoanalyst

2. College students who live in dormitories tend to meet other students with whom they have _____.

3. The two main psychological approaches to changing behavior that impacts the natural environment are (a) _____ and (b) _____.

4. The behavioral approach is characterized by a focus on (select two):

   a) attitudes, values, beliefs, and circumstances    c) persuasive communication

   b) principles of learning    d) rigorous testing of methods

5. The cognitive and humanistic approach is characterized by a focus on (select two):

   a) attitudes, values, beliefs, and circumstances    c) persuasive communication

   b) principles of learning    d) rigorous testing of methods

## Thinking Critically about Psychology

1. Does the physical environment of your home, apartment, or dormitory make it easy or difficult to meet your neighbors? In what ways?

2. What do you do to protect the environment?

**Correct Answers: 1. b** (p. 661), **2.** shared required paths (p. 663), **3.** behavioral approach; cognitive and humanistic approach (p. 666), **4. b** and **d** (p. 666), **5. a** and **c** (p. 666).

## ● Psychology and Law: The Behavior of Juries and Witnesses

Psychology and the legal profession have been working together for many years. Psychologists frequently testify regarding an individual's sanity or competency to stand trial. Moreover, attorneys are necessarily involved in hearings on the involuntary commitment of patients to mental hospitals and in the protection of the rights of psychiatric patients. In recent years, however, psychologists have begun to apply their methods and principles to the *practice* of law in the courtroom. When you think about it, this application of psychology to the practice of law is not surprising. The administration of justice is a process that involves *people*—attorneys, defendants, witnesses, and judges. Any understanding of the profession of law that ignores the human element—the psychology of the people involved—would be an incomplete understanding.

To date, the most extensive psychological study of the legal process has focused on the criminal trial. The findings suggest that, unless they are better understood and controlled, psychological factors in the trial process pose a serious threat to our constitutional guarantee of a fair trial. In addition to the quality of the evidence, the likelihood of conviction depends in part on personal characteristics of the defendant and on characteristics of the jury members. Psychological factors can even influence the quality and convincingness of the evidence itself. Psychologists are increasingly serving the role of consultant on procedures such as jury selection and the presentation of evidence.

### Characteristics of Defendants and Plaintiffs

Although we would like to believe that all of us would be treated equally in court, it is not always the case. Your chance of being acquitted in a criminal trial in the United States is better if you are physically attractive, wealthy, and white. Poor people are more likely than affluent ones to be convicted of crimes when charged with similar assault and larceny charges (Haney, 1980). Physically attractive defendants are less likely to be convicted than unattractive ones, unless the attractiveness seemed to play a part in the crime (as in a swindle) (Nemeth, 1981). And racially prejudiced white jury members are more likely to vote to convict African Americans than whites (Haney, 1980).

The same characteristics of the defendants also play a role in the harshness of the sentence. In first-degree murder cases, blue-collar workers are more likely to be sentenced to death than white-collar workers are. And from 1930 to 1979, 2,066 African Americans were executed, compared with 1,751 whites, even though there are four times as many whites in the United States as African Americans (Haney, 1980). These findings suggest that justice is not equal for different kinds of defendants in criminal cases, probably because of the prejudices held by jury members about different groups of people. Since characteristics such as income, attractiveness, and race have nothing to do with one's guilt or innocence, these person perception variables make it difficult for all people to receive equal protection under the law.

Psychologists have also studied the behavior of juries in civil suits, in which monetary damage awards are sought to compensate for injuries caused by alleged negligence or other wrongdoing. Do the characteristics of the plaintiff (the person seeking a damage award) and the defendant influence the financial awards made by jurors—independently of the facts of the case? The answer is yes. In mock trials, younger plaintiffs and male plaintiffs were awarded much larger financial settlements when injured than older and female plaintiffs were (Greene & Loftus, 1998). Participants on the mock juries explained that these prejudicial differences in sizes of awards were made because they believed that younger males who were injured would have made more money in their careers than older or female plaintiffs, placing less emphasis on their needs for compensation. Juries awarded larger settlements when the defendant was a corporation rather than an individual, independently of the other facts of the case (Greene & Loftus, 1998). As in criminal cases, irrelevant psychological factors influence the decisions of jurors in civil cases.

## Characteristics of Jury Members

Certain types of jury members are more likely to vote for conviction and recommend harsher sentences than other types. Jurors who are more conviction-prone and punitive in sentencing are those who are white, older, better educated, higher in social status, and more conservative and who believe more strongly that authority and law should be respected (Nemeth, 1981). There is mixed evidence as to whether men are more likely than women to vote for conviction, but there is clear-cut evidence of gender differences in cases of rape. Women are more likely to convict and to be harsher in sentencing than male jurors, whereas males are more likely to believe that the female victim encouraged the rapist (Nemeth, l981). Overall, juries tend to be "kinder to their own kind." Affluent, educated, white jurors tend to be harsher in their treatment of less affluent, less educated, minority defendants.

There is also evidence that jurors who believe in the death penalty are more likely to convict than those who do not. Prior to 1968, individuals who had strong objections to the death penalty were routinely barred from serving on juries in cases involving a possible death penalty. In a landmark ruling in 1968, however, an appeals judge commuted a death penalty to life imprisonment in the case of *Witherspoon v. Illinois* on the grounds that the jury was composed only of persons who favored the death penalty and was not, therefore, a fair and "representative" jury. In making this ruling, the judge cited a Gallup poll conducted at that time that found that only about 55 percent of the people surveyed favored the death penalty. The judge ruled that prospective jurors could be excluded only when they were so opposed to the death penalty that they would vote against it regardless of the evidence.

Was this a good decision? Was the judge in *Witherspoon v. Illinois* correct in assuming that a jury composed only of individuals who favor the death penalty—a "death-qualified" jury—might not give the defendant a fair trial? Actually, a number of studies support the judge's decision (Nemeth, 1981). For example, a study was conducted on the relationship between attitudes toward the death penalty and the tendency to convict in a sample of 207 industrial workers. They were initially asked to fill out a number of questionnaires including the following:

---

# Capital Punishment Attitude Questionnaire

*Directions.* Assume you are on a jury to determine the sentence for a defendant who has already been convicted of a very serious crime. If the law gives you a *choice* of death or life imprisonment, or some other penalty: (check *one* only)

1. I could not vote for the death penalty regardless of the facts and circumstances of the case.

2. There are some kinds of cases in which I know I could not vote for the death penalty even if the law allowed me to, but others in which I would be willing to consider voting for it.

3. I would consider all of the penalties provided by the law and the facts and circumstances of the particular case.

4. I would usually vote for the death penalty in a case where the law allows me to.

5. I would always vote for the death penalty in a case where the law allows me to.

From G. L. Jurow, "New Data on the Effects of a 'Death-Qualified' Jury on the Guilt Determination Process," *Harvard Law Review* 84:59. ©1971 Harvard Law Review Association. Used by permission.

| Table 17.1 | Number of Jurors in a Simulated Trial Who Voted to Convict or Acquit, Divided According to Their Willingness to Impose the Death Penalty | |
|---|---|---|
| **Willingness to Impose Death Penalty If Serving as a Juror** | **Number Voting to** | |
| | **Convict** | **Acquit** |
| Low (1 and 2) | 19 | 40 |
| Medium (3) | 59 | 73 |
| High (4 and 5) | 14 | 2 |

From G. L. Jurow, "New Data on the Effects of a 'Death-Qualified' Jury on the Guilt Determination Process," *Harvard Law Review* 84:59. © 1971 Harvard Law Review Association. Used by permission.

As these workers did, try to imagine that you have been selected to serve on the jury in a murder trial in a state that imposes the death penalty. Which alternative would you choose? All of the participants were shown two videotapes of mock murder trials that contained all of the standard elements of procedure and evidence. The first concerned a robbery of a liquor store in which the proprietor of the store was killed in the process. The second case was of a man charged with robbing, raping, and killing a college student in her apartment. After each videotaped trial, the "jurors" voted to convict or acquit the defendant.

The jurors in this experiment were divided into three groups on the basis of their responses to the questionnaire concerning capital punishment. Jurors scoring low in willingness to impose the death penalty (who checked item 1 or 2) were far more likely to vote for acquittal than conviction in the first trial (see table 17.1). Conversely, jurors who were high in willingness to impose the death penalty (who checked item 4 or 5) were much more likely to vote for conviction. The same pattern was shown in the voting after the second trial, although not as strongly.

Thus, this and other studies finding similar differences suggest that juries composed only of jurors who are in favor of the death penalty (who are also more likely to be conservative, high status, authoritarian males) are biased in favor of conviction of defendants (Nemeth, 1981). This means that the current practice of excluding only those jurors who are most strongly opposed to the death penalty or of using separate juries for the trial and the sentencing may make good psychological sense.

## Psychological Factors in Presenting Evidence

It's somewhat reassuring to learn that several studies have suggested that although characteristics of the defendants and jurors are important in determining conviction or acquittal, the evidence is several times more important (Nemeth, 1981). Unfortunately, facts are not the only important aspect of courtroom evidence; psychological factors in *presenting* the facts are involved as well.

Criminal trials are "adversarial proceedings." The attorneys for the prosecution and defense attempt to convince the jury of the guilt or innocence of the defendant as if they were competing in a debate. Because both attorneys cannot talk at the same time, they obviously must make their presentations one at a time. Unfortunately, the *order* in which evidence is presented appears to make a difference in the outcome of the trial. One study investigated the effect of order of presentation in a simulated trial in which law students played the roles of attorneys for the defense and prosecution and undergraduate students served as jurors. The simulated case concerned a man who was charged with murder but claimed he had acted in self-defense. Half of the time, the prosecutor went first, and half of the time the defense attorney went first. The results showed that the attorney who went second held a decided advantage (Thibaut & Walker, 1975). This is not good news if you are falsely accused of a crime, since tradition has it that the prosecutor is allowed to make the last statement to the jury.

"Your Honor, the jury finds the defendant weakly developed as a central character, overshadowed by the principal witnesses, unconvincingly portrayed as a victim of society, and guilty as charged."

© The New Yorker Collection 1988 Thom Cheney from cartoonbank.com. All Right Reserved.

Recall from chapter 16 that information you encounter first when getting to know a stranger ("first impressions") is stronger in determining your overall impression of that person *unless* a relatively long time elapses between the first and subsequent information. That last qualification may help explain the findings about the order of presentation of courtroom evidence. It may be that, because courtroom arguments are lengthy and complex, recently presented information is more easily remembered and potent. This interpretation is strengthened by the finding that the advantage of presenting in the second position is increased further if an attorney states the most convincing points at the very end of the second presentation rather than at the beginning (Thibaut & Walker, 1975).

## Interrogating Criminal Suspects

Social psychologist Craig Haney (1980) has analyzed the standard American method of police interrogation to examine its psychological aspects. Police use a number of psychological techniques to increase the probability of a confession. Imagine that you have been taken to a barren interrogating room. You are alone with the interrogators—the room does not even have a telephone—giving you a feeling of being completely cut off from the outside world. The interrogator often stands very close to you, violating your personal space, and giving you a feeling of powerlessness.

The interrogator begins the questioning by pointing out your apparent guilt. But the crime is discussed in such a way as to make it seem so understandable—almost morally justifiable—that you feel that the interrogator would not shame you if you were to confess. If the crime is not a big deal, why not just admit to doing it? But the interrogator soon grows impatient with you for not admitting to the crime and storms out of the room. A second officer in the room steps over, though, and asks you to excuse the behavior of the first interrogator—it's been a long and frustrating day. This second officer is very sympathetic to your situation and emphasizes how much easier the court would be on you if you were to confess. This officer really seems to feel genuine concern for you. Just then, the first interrogator enters the room again and asks you for a confession. You see anger beginning to build, and you blurt out a confession just to avoid the angry outburst. This kind of scene is repeated many times a day in police stations across the country, although not always with favorable results. Individuals who have been interrogated many times by the police know the routine as well as the police and tend not to be influenced by it. The cases in which police interrogations lead to false confessions are an even greater concern, however. Persons with poor intellectual and emotional resources are sometimes coerced into making false confessions by the pressures of police interrogations (Gudjonsson, 2001; Santilla & others, 1999)

Recent research on police interrogations of suspects has also looked for ways to help police investigators detect lying by suspects. All such methods are far from perfectly reliable, but may help investigators in their work. For example, these studies do not support the notion that people who are lying fidget nervously and fail to make eye contact with their interrogator. On the other hand, this research suggests that liars blink less often and pause their speech longer than persons telling the truth (Mann, Vrij, & Bull, 2002).

## Review

Criminal trials are conducted by people, so it's not surprising to learn that psychological factors play a role. What may be more surprising—and disturbing—is to see how strong a role they can play. Having different types of people involved in the trial process is likely to produce different outcomes. Poor, uneducated, minority defendants are more likely to be convicted and receive harsher sentences. Jurors who are white, older, higher in social status, more conservative, and more authoritarian than average, as well as those who believe in capital punishment, are more likely to vote for conviction and impose harsh punishments. The quality of the evidence presented in criminal trials is more important in determining the jury's decision than the psychological characteristics of the defendant and jurors, but psychological factors are also involved in courtroom evidence. Even the order in which evidence is presented can influence the outcome of a trial. Obviously, these factors must be understood and controlled as much as possible if the judicial system is to be fair for all concerned.

**Check Your Learning**

To be sure that you have learned the key points from the preceding section, cover the list of correct answers and try to answer each question. If you give an incorrect answer to any question, return to the page given next to the correct answer to see why your answer was not correct.

*Answer each question with True or False.*

1. Other things being equal, you have a greater chance of being acquitted in a criminal trial by a white, middle-class jury if you are physically attractive, high in social status, and white.

2. Jurors who believe in the death penalty are less likely to vote for the conviction of a defendant.

3. The attorney who speaks last in a trial has an advantage in persuading the jury.

**Thinking Critically about Psychology**

1. In what ways might a psychologist be able to assist a defendant in preparing for a criminal trial? What are the ethical issues involved in giving such assistance?

2. Based on the information presented, can someone get a "fair" trial? Why or why not?

**Correct Answers:** 1. True (p. 669), 2. False (p. 670), 3. True (pp. 671–672).

## Psychology and Education: Better Teaching and Testing

Like industrial-organizational psychology, **educational psychology** is almost as old as the discipline of psychology itself. Binet's development of a useful intelligence test for schoolchildren laid the foundation for educational testing. Others, such as Edward Lee Thorndike of Columbia University, conducted research during the early 1900s on factors that influence school learning and memory. But although educational psychology is an old field, its current excitement stems from relatively new developments. These innovations show particular promise in improving the education of children with special educational needs. Psychologists serve education as professors who help train teachers in the psychology of education, as consultants on the development of testing programs, and as specialists employed by school systems (**school psychologists**) to consult with teachers and to test children who may need special educational programs.

Public education was established to implement Thomas Jefferson's philosophy that every American citizen should have equal educational as well as political opportunities. Because citizens need an education to govern themselves through democratic institutions, it was decided that education should be available to every American child rather than as a privilege of the rich. The most important recent innovations in educational psychology have been ones that help more children benefit fully from their time in school: the mastery learning approach, effective methods of educating economically disadvantaged children, the development of more meaningful tests of achievement, and the integration of children with psychological and physical challenges into the normal classroom environment, known as mainstreaming.

**educational psychology**
The field in which principles of learning, cognition, and other aspects of psychology are applied to improve education.

**school psychologists**
Psychologists who aid schools by testing children to determine eligibility for placement in special education programs and who consult with teachers and parents.

## Mastery Learning and Intelligent Tutoring Systems

If you were a teacher, would you try to teach a child to add and subtract before she had learned to count? Would you teach trigonometry to a child before he had mastered the basics of plane geometry? It does not make much sense to try to teach a child a new skill before she or he has learned the basic skills that are the foundation for further learning, yet it happens every day in American education—children are pushed from one subject to another before they are ready to progress. Why? The reason is that, in many schools, education is conducted according to group schedules. A certain amount of time is allotted for the group to learn to count, and then the group moves on to addition. Students take plane geometry in the fall semester and then trigonometry in the spring. If an individual child is not ready to progress, he or she must usually move on with the group anyway.

Educational psychologist Benjamin Bloom has been an outspoken critic of this approach and has proposed the **mastery learning** concept to take its place (Bloom, 1974). Quite simply, Bloom insists that children should never progress from one learning task to another until they have fully mastered the first one. If this rule is followed, Bloom suggests, learning will be far more effective in the long run. For example, a group of high school students who were enrolled in a course on automobile mechanics took part in an evaluation of the mastery learning approach. The course was divided into eight units that built on one another in succession. Half of the students progressed through the units as a group according to a prearranged schedule. The other students—the mastery learning group—moved at their own pace and did not begin the next unit until they had passed a test on the previous unit. At the end of the course, the mastery learning group had learned far more in the same amount of time (Wentling, 1973).

Bloom suggests that the mastery learning approach is particularly effective for slow-learning children, but it does not penalize brighter children. In the traditional approach of group scheduling, the top fifth of American students learns three times as much as the bottom fifth by the time they graduate from high school. When students use a mastery learning approach, however, the learning of the bottom fifth improves so much as to cut this difference in half (Bloom, 1974).

More recently, the availability of inexpensive computers that can be used in the classroom has made possible an improvement on the mastery learning approach called **intelligent tutoring systems** (or ITS) (Atkinson, 2002; Snow & Swanson, 1992). In the ITS approach, a computer is programmed to serve as an individualized tutor to the student. In the case of arithmetic, the animated computer program would tell the student about a new rule of, say, subtraction (visually on the screen and orally through headphones) and then ask the student to solve some problems based on the new rule. As in mastery learning, the computer does not allow the student to progress to the next rule until the current one is mastered. But ITS can also respond to any errors that the student makes and adapt the instruction accordingly. Let's say the student is learning to "borrow" when subtracting two-digit numbers and makes a mistake. The computer might see that the mistake was based on a misunderstanding of the rule for borrowing and would then repeat the rule—possibly in simpler language. On the other hand, the computer might detect that the mistake was based on forgetting how to subtract single-digit numbers and go back to a brief review of that material. Not only does ITS make it easier for teachers to work with children who are at different levels of mastery in the same classroom, but it also allows individual remediation of any "gaps" in the learning process. Increasingly, ITS programs are available to students even after school over the Internet (Dedic & others, 2001).

**mastery learning**
The concept that children should never progress from one learning task to another until they have mastered the more basic one.

**intelligent tutoring systems**
An approach to learning in which computers provide tutoring to students.

The availability of inexpensive classroom computers lets intelligent tutoring systems tailor lessons to each student's level of mastery.

## Project Follow Through: Educating Economically Disadvantaged Children

One of the harshest realities of American life is that millions of people live in extreme poverty despite the overall affluence of the nation. Who are the poor? Where do they come from? Most of the people living in poverty today are the children of the previous generation of poor people and will be the parents of the next generation of the poor. Poverty tends to run in families.

A key element in the development of a lifestyle of poverty is educational failure. People who do not learn enough in school to be employable have little chance of rising above poverty. The cycle of educational failure in economically disadvantaged children is an all too familiar story. Each year in school, children from disadvantaged families learn about two-thirds of what the average child learns. This means that they fall further behind their classmates each successive year in a dangerous downward spiral, which often ends in dropping out of school (Becker & Carnine, 1980).

In the mid-1960s, a massive experiment was conceived by the U.S. Office of Education to test new ways of educating economically disadvantaged children. Nine groups of researchers were given funds to design and implement what they thought would be ideal educational programs, and independent research organizations were contracted to evaluate their effectiveness. This massive educational experiment—involving tens of thousands of children across the country—was named **Project Follow Through.** This program followed children through the crucial years of kindergarten through third grade, in contrast to the earlier attempts to help disadvantaged children that had stopped at the kindergarten level.

**Project Follow Through**
A federally sponsored program designed to help educate economically disadvantaged children.

The nine Follow Through projects differed considerably in educational philosophy, and most were clearly unsuccessful in improving educational progress. The most successful of the projects was consistently able, however, to bring disadvantaged children to the national average or above. This project, designed by Wesley Becker and Siegfried Engelmann, known as the Direct Instruction Project, made simple but powerful use of what is now known about the psychology of education. Becker and Engelmann designed a curriculum based on a knowledge of the cognitive skills needed in reading and other subjects. They also designed a teaching method based on the principles of learning—particularly positive reinforcement—and used practice methods designed to enhance memory for what had been learned. The success of this program is an impressive testimony to the value of the accumulated knowledge of educational psychology (Doernberger & Zigler, 1993).

## Person × Situation Interaction in the Classroom

We learned in chapter 12 that our traits and the situations we find ourselves in work together to influence our behavior—the *person × situation interaction.* This concept is highly important in understanding and evaluating efforts to improve teaching and the school environment. For example, one of the recurrent debates among American educators concerns how structured the classroom should be. Should the classroom be open and unfettered by walls, with relatively relaxed rules concerning student behavior, or are small rooms and firm rules best? The answer to this question, in part, is that different students tend to react better to different school environments. The school achievement of children in structured classrooms is generally better than in unstructured classrooms, but a child's tendency to be anxious interacts with this characteristic of the environment. As shown in figure 17.11, anxious children perform slightly better than less anxious children in structured classrooms, but the performance of anxious children takes a nosedive in unstructured classrooms (Grimes & Allinsmith, 1961). In evaluating new educational approaches, we must remember to take into account the person × situation interaction.

**FIGURE 17.11**
In unstructured classrooms, the academic achievement of anxious children is much poorer than that of less anxious children. But, in structured classrooms, children's anxiety does little damage to their school performance. In evaluating different approaches to education, we must remember to consider the person × situation interaction.
Source: J. W. Grimes and W. Allinsmith, "Compulsivity, Anxiety, and School Achievement" in *Merrill-Palmer Quarterly,* 7:247–271, © 1961 Wayne State University Press, Detroit, MI.

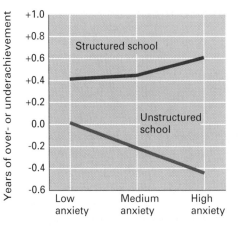

**criterion-referenced testing**
Testing designed to determine whether a child can meet the minimum standards of a specific educational objective.

**mainstreaming**
The practice of integrating children with special needs into regular classrooms.

Mainstreaming provides children with special needs a public education in the least restrictive environment. Public Law 94-142 helped get many such children into regular classrooms.

## Criterion-Referenced Testing

The renewed interest in finding better ways to prepare students to lead successful adult lives has also led to the development of an approach to evaluating how much students have learned in school. In traditional approaches to educational testing, children are compared with one another. For example, a traditional test of computational skills in arithmetic would require children to work a large number of problems. A child who correctly solved the same number of problems as the average for children in her or his grade would be considered to be "on grade level." The goal of **criterion-referenced testing,** however, is not to compare children but to determine whether a given child can meet the minimum criteria for a specific educational objective (Sprinthal, Sprinthal, & Oja, 1998). These are usually practical objectives. For example, one criterion-referenced test asks children to fill in a personal information form like the ones required by most employment applications. The issue in this kind of testing is not how well a child can fill in the form compared with other children but simply whether the child can *do* it appropriately. This is a skill well worth teaching to students, because adults who cannot fill out employment forms stand little chance of being hired. One study showed that only 61 percent of American 17-year-olds could fill out an employment application form without errors, however (Mellon, 1975).

Criterion-referenced testing provides the kind of information that teachers need to improve education. If the items accurately reflect the goals of education, then criterion-referenced test scores can provide feedback to teachers on how well they are teaching. If Mary cannot fill out a personal information blank, then the teacher knows that Mary needs more instruction on that skill. If most of the students in a school cannot fill out such forms, then the school administration knows that a better teaching method must be implemented. Thus, criterion-referenced tests play an important role in evaluating and improving teaching methods.

## Mainstreaming: Education for Persons with Special Needs

During the 1970s, enormous strides were made in the legal standing of children with challenging conditions such as mental retardation, emotional problems, and physical challenges. Federal legislation—famous as *Public Law 94-142*—established that *every* child has a *right* to a public education, regardless of his or her special needs. This means that many more children with severe challenges are being served by public schools than ever before.

Furthermore, Public Law 94-142, and its successor, the Individuals with Disabilities Education Act (IDEA), states that the child is entitled to receive her or his education in the *least restrictive environment.* This legal phrase means that children must receive educational and psychological assistance in circumstances that are as similar as possible to the normal day-to-day environment of nonhandicapped children. Thus, it's no longer legal to isolate children with special needs in separate schools *if* it's possible to educate them in regular schools and allow them to interact with other children. Whenever possible, in fact, children with special needs must be kept in the regular classroom for as large a part of the school day as possible and removed for special assistance only when necessary. This practice is known as **mainstreaming,** because it keeps such children within the mainstream of normal social and educational development.

In addition to protecting the legal rights of people with special needs, the IDEA law offers some important benefits to all concerned. First, it gives students with special needs an opportunity to learn how to fit into the world of youngsters without disabilities. Equally important, it gives children without special needs a chance to learn firsthand that children with special needs are fully human and well worth having as friends (Augustine, Gruber, & Hanson, 1990; Sprinthall & others, 1998).

---

Educational psychologists have long sought to improve ways of teaching and testing schoolchildren, but the recent excitement in educational psychology stems from new concepts and methods of teaching and testing that promise to help more children benefit fully from the opportunities offered by the educational system. The mastery learning approach provides a way to both enhance learning and decrease the gap between the most and least successful learners; the Project Follow Through experiment has identified effective methods for educating disadvantaged children; and the shift toward criterion-referenced testing provides us with a more meaningful way of evaluating success in teaching necessary skills and knowledge to children. In a different way, the mainstreaming approach assures children with special needs of their rightful place in the educational system.

**Review**

---

To be sure that you have learned the key points from the preceding section, cover the list of correct answers and try to answer each question. If you give an incorrect answer to any question, return to the page given next to the correct answer to see why your answer was not correct.

**Check Your Learning**

1. _____ psychology is the field in which principles of learning, cognition, and other aspects of psychology are applied to improve teaching and learning.

   a)   Developmental            c)   Environmental
   b)   School                   d)   Educational

2. _____ is the concept that children should never progress from one learning task to another until they have mastered the more basic one.

   a)   Stage theory             c)   Step learning
   b)   Mastery learning         d)   Progression theory

3. _____ testing is designed to determine whether a child has met the minimum standards of a specific educational program.

   a)   Intelligence             c)   Criterion-referenced
   b)   Aptitude                 d)   Personality

4. The practice of integrating children with special needs into regular classrooms is called _____.

   a)   integration              c)   combining
   b)   assimilation             d)   mainstreaming

---

1. How could the mastery learning approach provide a greater degree of equality of opportunity to all people?

**Thinking Critically about Psychology**

2. This textbook was designed to increase your ease of learning. What could be done to make it better?

## Summary

Chapter 17 describes the applications of psychology to business, architecture, law, education, and the environment.

I. Psychologists who work for businesses are known as industrial-organizational psychologists. They help businesses design better methods of selecting and promoting employees, help managers organize and manage employees more effectively, and design machines that can be used more efficiently and safely by employees (human factors engineering).

   A. The best predictor of the success of new employees in complex jobs is intelligence, but it is less valid for less complex jobs. Over time, the advantage of high intelligence in less complex jobs declines as employees acquire job knowledge and skills.

   B. Structured interviews are more valid for the selection of employees than unstructured interviews are.

   C. Tests of job knowledge and performance tests are valid methods for hiring experienced workers.

   D. The dimension of personality known as conscientiousness is a good nonintellectual predictor of job success.

   E. It is important for industrial-organizational psychologists to alert employers to gender and ethnic biases in hiring and promoting employees to reduce discrimination in access to desirable jobs.

   F. Several methods exist for assessing performance of currently employed workers.

      1. Worker performance is evaluated using job performance ratings, such as multiple-step rating scales and checklists.

      2. Assessment centers are frequently used to evaluate applicants or currently employed candidates for management positions in companies.

   G. The overall goals of psychologists working in business are to improve the satisfaction of employees and to improve their productivity. They can accomplish these goals by

      1. Selecting the right person for the job

      2. Improving supervisory style

      3. Improving managerial organization

      4. Improving physical conditions

   H. Employee health programs can also improve job satisfaction while reducing both the direct costs of health benefits and the indirect costs due to poor health and premature death of valuable employees.

II. The field of environmental psychology uses the methods of experimental psychology to evaluate human reactions to architectural spaces and to study the effects of our behavior on the environment.

III. Psychologists apply their methods to the practice of the law in the courtroom.

   A. They have found that the characteristics of defendants affect the likelihood of conviction and the harshness of the sentence. The characteristics of plaintiffs and defendants also affect the decisions of juries in civil cases independently of the merits of the case.

    B.    They have also found that certain types of jury members are more likely than other types to vote for conviction and to recommend harsher sentences.

    C.    The order in which evidence is presented appears to affect the outcome of the trial.

IV.  The behavior of humans has seriously damaged the earth's environment through overpopulation, resource depletion, and pollution and the mismanagement of waste.

    A.    Saving the environment from catastrophic damage will require changes in behavior at the level of the individual, the business, and the government.

    B.    Psychologists working in two theoretical traditions have developed techniques for changing environmentally sensitive behavior.

        1.    The behavioral approach is characterized by the use of principles of learning to change behavior and the rigorous evaluation of the effectiveness of techniques in the real world.

        2.    The cognitive and humanistic approach focuses on changing attitudes, values, beliefs, and circumstances.

        3.    Recently, psychologists from both traditions have recognized the importance of combining the best of both approaches.

V.  Psychologists serve the field of education as professors who help train teachers, as consultants on testing programs, and as school psychologists employed by school systems.

    A.    One successful approach is mastery learning, based on Benjamin Bloom's belief that children should never progress from one learning task to another until they have fully mastered the previous one.

    B.    Another helpful approach is criterion-referenced testing, a form of testing designed to determine if a given child can meet the minimum criteria for a specific educational objective.

    C.    The Individuals with Disabilities Education Act (IDEA) states that every child has a right to public education, regardless of his or her disability. The law states that the education must take place in the least restrictive environment possible.

## Resources

1.  An excellent overview of industrial-organizational psychology is Aamodt, M. G. (1999). *Applied Industrial/Organizational Psychology* (3rd ed.). Belmont, CA: Wadsworth.

2.  For a fascinating commentary on human engineering and other applications of psychology, see Norman, D. A. (1990). *The design of everyday things.* New York: Doubleday; and Norman, D. A. (1993). *Things that make us smart: Defending human attributes in the age of the machine.* New York: Addison-Wesley.

3.  For extremely well-written summaries of the teaching methods that educational psychologists have found make important differences in how much children learn, see Brophy, J. (1986). Teacher influences on student achievement. *American Psychologist, 41,* 1069–1077; and Brophy, J. (1996). *Teaching problem students.* New York: Guilford.

4.  For more on the psychology of juries, see Bull, R. H., & Carson, D. (1995). *Handbook of psychology in legal contexts.* Orlando: Wiley.

5. A nice summary of the past and future of environmental psychology is provided by Stokols, D. (1995). The paradox of environmental psychology. *American Psychologist, 50,* 821–837.

6. For a very readable discussion of reducing social loafing in work settings, see Shepard, J. A. (1995). Remedying motivation and productivity losses in collective settings. *Current Directions in Psychological Science, 4,* 131–139.

7. For an eye-opening description of pollution in an American city, see Adeola, F. O. (2000). Endangered community, enduring people: Toxic contamination, health, and adaptive responses in a local context. *Environment and Behavior, 32,* 209–249.

# Appendix:
## Measurement and Statistics

**Richard E. Mayer**  University of California, Santa Barbara

In chapter 2, you were introduced to the basic concepts of research design in psychology. This appendix builds on that foundation by discussing the basic concepts of measurement and statistics that are used in psychological research. This appendix shows you how psychological characteristics are measured in quantitative (numerical) terms and how statistics are used to summarize quantitative findings and reach conclusions based on them. Even if you never conduct a psychological study, you need to learn about statistics and measurements in psychology for two reasons. First, the ability to read and evaluate the research that is presented in this textbook or discussed in class helps you avoid being intimidated by the research data of "experts"; it helps you assess the soundness of an experiment; and it helps you interpret the results. Second, a basic understanding of psychological statistics and measurement is rapidly becoming a "survival skill" for every educated member of our society. You need to avoid being fooled by "scientific" surveys, advertisers' evidence, and the like. You need to be able to recognize the difference between a useful study and one that is seriously flawed. Finally, you may need to be able to use basic statistics in your business or occupation. Thus, this appendix is designed to help you as a student and as an educated citizen.

For example, suppose you come across the following article in your local newspaper:

### TV Viewing Linked to School Failure

*Garden City*— Researchers at State University have found that students who watch in excess of three hours of television per day get lower grades than other students. The study was based on a survey of students at Garden Valley School. The average student watched approximately two hours of TV per day. Efforts to discourage TV watching have been announced by the school's principal, Mr. George Elliot. "We must get our kids to stop watching TV," Mr. Elliot stated.

As you read this summary of a research study, you should ask yourself such questions as, Is this a sound study? and How should I interpret the results? After reading this appendix, you will be better able to answer questions like these concerning research studies that you read about.

## Descriptive Statistics

One of the basic uses for statistics in psychological studies is to *describe behavior* in an understandable way. This is called *descriptive statistics*. Two common examples of descriptive statistics are as follows:

*Describing behavior concerning one variable.*  For example, a study may report that the "average" student watches two hours of TV per day.

*Describing the relation between two variables.*  For example, a study may report that students who watch more television tend to score lower on tests of school achievement than those who watch less.

| Use | Situation | Example | Typical statistics |
|-----|-----------|---------|--------------------|
| Describing one variable | There is one score for each subject. | Each of 20 students in Mrs. Perkins's class tells how many hours he or she watched TV yesterday. | Frequency distribution Mean, median, or mode Standard deviation, variance, or range |
| Describing the relation between two variables | There are two scores for each subject—one score on variable X and one score on variable Y. | Each of 20 students in Mrs. Perkins's class tells how many hours he or she watched TV yesterday, and each student gets a score on the school achievement test. | Correlation |

As you can see, descriptive statistics summarize the data for a group of subjects. Figure A.1 summarizes these two uses of statistics that are discussed in the remainder of this part of the appendix.

In the Garden Valley study, the researchers obtained data on only a small number of schoolchildren from just one school; however, the researchers want to generalize their data to all schoolchildren in the United States. Thus, it is important for you to understand the distinction between a *parameter* and a *statistic* as they are used here:

> *Parameter.* Parameters are numbers that describe the behavior of an *entire population*. A population consists of all possible subjects, objects, or cases, such as all schoolchildren in the United States. For example, if we were to ask every schoolchild in the United States how many hours he or she watches TV each day, then we could develop parameters such as the average number of hours of TV viewing.

> *Statistic.* Statistics are numbers that describe the behavior of only a *sample* drawn out of a larger population. A sample is a portion of an entire population, such as some of the schoolchildren at one school.

Sample statistics—such as the average number of hours of TV watching of some students at Garden Valley School—are rarely identical to population parameters—such as the average number of hours of TV viewing of all U.S. schoolchildren.

Another distinction that you need to understand is the difference between a *variable* and a *score:*

> *Variable.* A variable is a measurable characteristic or behavior, such as age, sex, weight, height, or shoe size. In the Garden Valley study, one variable is the number of hours of TV viewing per day.

> *Score.* A score is the value a given person has for a given variable, such as Joe's age being 27 years or his shoe size being 8½. In the Garden Valley study, Mary watched three hours of TV per day, so her score is 3 on the variable "hours of TV viewing per day."

The data for a study consist of all the scores obtained for each variable that is used.

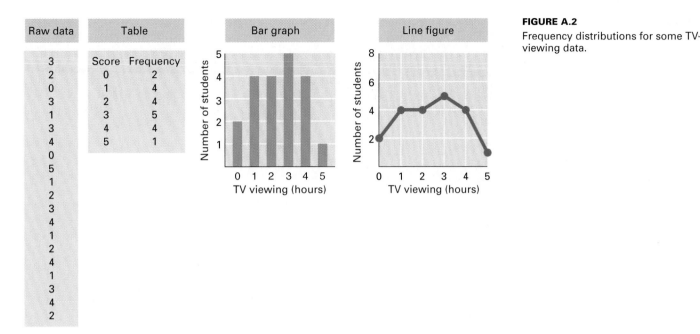

**FIGURE A.2**
Frequency distributions for some TV-viewing data.

## Describing Behavior Concerning One Variable

### Problem

One of the major uses of statistics in psychology is to describe the behavior of a group on one variable. For example, the Garden Valley study attempted to describe the TV-viewing behavior of schoolchildren. Let's suppose that we go to Garden Valley School and ask 20 students from Mrs. Perkins's class to tell us how many hours they watched TV yesterday. Suppose that we get one answer from each student, as listed in the left panel of figure A.2.

### Frequency Distribution

What are the TV-viewing habits of school students? One way to provide data for this question is simply to list the number of hours that each of 20 students reported watching TV. However, because it's hard to make much sense out of a long list of numbers, researchers often organize their data into a *frequency distribution*. A frequency distribution is a table or graph that shows the relationship between a score (such as number of hours of TV watching) and frequency (such as the number or percentage of students who gave each score).

Figure A.2 shows some frequency distributions for the TV-viewing data using the formats of a table, bar graph, and line figure. In the table, the first column gives the possible scores (0, 1, 2, 3, 4, or 5) for hours of TV viewing per day, and the second column gives the frequency of each score (that is, how many of the 20 students fell into that category). In the bar graph and line figure, the horizontal X-axis gives the possible scores and the vertical Y-axis gives the frequency.

Although the frequency distribution helps you organize data, you may want to summarize the description even further. You could summarize the frequency distribution by giving two numbers—a measure of *central tendency* and a measure of *dispersion*. A measure of central tendency tells where the middle of the distribution is, such as how many hours, on the average, do school students watch TV? A measure of dispersion tells you how spread out the scores are, such as how different are the school students in the number of hours they view TV? These numbers are discussed in the next two subsections.

**FIGURE A.3**
Measures of central tendency for some TV-viewing data.

| Mean | Median | | Mode | |
|------|--------|--|------|--|
| $\Sigma X = 3 + 2 + 0 + 3 + 1 + 3 + 4 +$ $0 + 5 + 1 + 2 + 3 + 4 + 1 +$ $2 + 4 + 1 + 3 + 4 + 2 = 48$ $n = 20$ $\overline{X} = \dfrac{\Sigma X}{n} = \dfrac{48}{20} = 2.4$ | Ranking | Scores in order | Score | Frequency |
| | 1st | 0 | 0 | 2 |
| | 2nd | 0 | 1    Most    4 | |
| | 3rd | 1 | 2    frequent    4 | |
| | 4th | 1 | 3 | 5 |
| | 5th | 1 | 4 | 4 |
| | 6th | 1 | 5 | 1 |
| | 7th | 2 | | |
| | 8th | 2 | Mode = 3 | |
| | 9th   Middle of 2 | | | |
| | 10th   rankings   2 | | | |
| | 11th | 3 | | |
| | 12th | 3 | | |
| | 13th | 3 | | |
| | 14th | 3 | | |
| | 15th | 3 | | |
| | 16th | 4 | | |
| | 17th | 4 | | |
| | 18th | 4 | | |
| | 19th | 4 | | |
| | 20th | 5 | | |
| | Median = point midway between 2 and 3 (i.e., 2.5) | | | |

*Central Tendency.* How many hours per day does the "average student" watch TV? There are three major measures of central tendency: mean, median, and mode.

The *mean* is the arithmetic average of all the scores. To compute the mean, you simply add all the scores and divide the sum by the number of scores. The formula for finding the mean is $\overline{X} = \Sigma X / n$, where $\overline{X}$ is the mean, $\Sigma X$ is the sum or total of the scores, and n is the number of scores. The left portion of figure A.3 shows that the sum of the scores is 48, the number of scores is 20, and the mean is 2.4 hours. One problem with using mean as a measure of central tendency is that it's sensitive to extreme scores. For example, if the only student who reported watching 5 hours per day were to change his answer to 24 hours, the mean would increase considerably, from 2.4 to 3.35.

The *median* is the score that divides the distribution in the middle, so that half of the frequency is greater than the median and half is less than the median. To determine the median, list the scores in ascending (or descending) order, and count down until you reach the score in the middle. An example is given in the middle panel of figure A.3. As you can see, the median is not as sensitive to extreme scores. If the student who watched 5 hours were replaced by a student who watched 24 hours, the median would remain the same.

The *mode* is the score that occurs most often. For example, the mode in figure A.3 is 3 because five people watched TV for three hours while fewer than five watched TV for each other score. There can be ties among modes; for example, the scores 3, 1, 2, 1, 3, 0, 4, 1, 3, 5 have two modes—1 and 3. This is called a *bimodal distribution* because there are two modes. If there is a tie among several scores, such as 1, 1, 2, 2, 3, 3, 4, 4, 0, 0, then there can be several modes—such as 5 modes in the preceding example. This is called a *multimodal distribution*. Although the mode is not often used in research studies, in some cases it may be preferred. For example, the designer of apartments will find it is *more useful* to know that the "modal" family unit is either 1 or 4 than to know that the mean family is 2.5. The builder who includes one-bedroom apartments for single adults is likely to rent the available space faster than the builder who believes that only two-bedroom apartments are needed for families with an average of 2.5 people.

| | Standard deviation | | Range | |
|---|---|---|---|---|
| Raw data | Deviation $(X - \overline{X})$ | Square of deviation $(X - \overline{X})^2$ | 0 | Lowest |
| 3 | .6 | .36 | 0 | |
| 2 | −.4 | .16 | 1 | |
| 0 | −2.4 | 5.76 | 1 | |
| 3 | .6 | .36 | 1 | |
| 1 | −1.4 | 1.96 | 1 | |
| 3 | .6 | .36 | 2 | |
| 4 | 1.6 | 2.56 | 2 | |
| 0 | −2.4 | 5.76 | 2 | |
| 5 | 2.6 | 6.76 | 2 | |
| 1 | −1.4 | 1.96 | 3 | |
| 2 | −.4 | .16 | 3 | |
| 3 | .6 | .36 | 3 | |
| 4 | 1.6 | 2.56 | 3 | |
| 1 | −1.4 | 1.96 | 3 | |
| 2 | −.4 | .16 | 4 | |
| 4 | 1.6 | 2.56 | 4 | |
| 1 | −1.4 | 1.96 | 4 | |
| 3 | .6 | .36 | 4 | |
| 4 | 1.6 | 2.56 | 5 | Highest |
| 2 | −.4 | .16 | | |
| | | $\Sigma(X - \overline{X})^2 = 38.80$ | | |

Range = (highest − lowest) + 1
Range = 5 − 0 + 1 = 6

$$S = \sqrt{\frac{\Sigma(X - \overline{X})^2}{n}} = \sqrt{\frac{38.8}{20}} = 1.39$$

*Dispersion.* How different are the scores from one another? There are two major measures of dispersion from the central tendency: standard deviation and range.

The *standard deviation* is a sort of average difference between each score and the mean. It's a statistic that indicates how widely or narrowly scores are spread around the mean on the average. To compute the standard deviation, subtract the mean score from each score, square each of these differences, divide by the number of scores, and then take the square root. The formula for standard deviation is

$$s = \sqrt{\frac{\Sigma(X - \overline{X})^2}{n}}$$

where s is the standard deviation, $\Sigma(X - \overline{X})^2$ is the sum of the square of the differences, and n is the number of scores. The left panel of figure A.4 shows how to compute the standard deviation for TV-viewing scores.

The *range* is the distance between the highest score and the lowest score. To compute the range, simply subtract the lowest score from the highest and add 1. The right panel of figure A.4 shows that if the lowest score is 0 and the highest score is 5, then the range is 6; that is, the distance between 0 and 5 is 6 units. The range is rarely used as a measure of dispersion because it's so sensitive to extreme scores. For example, if the student who watched 5 hours of TV were replaced by a student who watched 24 hours, the range would jump to 25.

*Normal Curve.* The scores for any frequency distribution can be plotted on a graph, as in the right panel of figure A.2, and they can take a multitude of shapes. One important frequency distribution is the normal curve. It has fascinated scientists and statisticians because many different characteristics in nature tend to be normally distributed—such

**FIGURE A.5**
The normal curve.

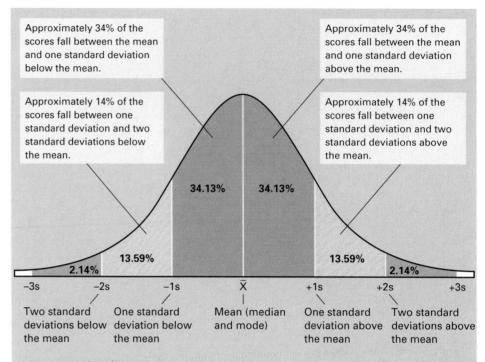

Approximately 34% of the scores fall between the mean and one standard deviation below the mean.

Approximately 14% of the scores fall between one standard deviation and two standard deviations below the mean.

Approximately 34% of the scores fall between the mean and one standard deviation above the mean.

Approximately 14% of the scores fall between one standard deviation and two standard deviations above the mean.

34.13%  34.13%

13.59%  13.59%

2.14%  2.14%

| −3s | −2s | −1s | X̄ | +1s | +2s | +3s |

Two standard deviations below the mean

One standard deviation below the mean

Mean (median and mode)

One standard deviation above the mean

Two standard deviations above the mean

If the mean is 3.0 (X = 3.0) and the standard deviation is 1.0 (s = 1.0) the scores are as follows:

| 0.0 | 1.0 | 2.0 | 3.0 | 4.0 | 5.0 | 6.0 |
| (−3s) | (−2s) | (−1s) | (X̄) | (+1s) | (+2s) | (+3s) |

as adult height, weight, and intelligence. This does not mean that these characteristics will have the same mean and standard deviation; rather, they all have the same general *shape* of frequency distribution. An example of a normal curve is given in figure A.5.

The normal curve is a frequency distribution that has the following characteristics:

*Symmetrical.* The right side is a mirror image of the left side.

*Bell shaped.* The most common scores are near the mean, with scores becoming less common as you move away from the mean in either direction.

*68-95-99 density.* The area on the normal curve that is within one standard deviation above the mean and one standard deviation below the mean contains 68.26 percent of the cases; within two standard deviations there are 95.42 percent of the cases; and within three standard deviations there are 99.74 percent of the cases.

To make sure that you understand the shape of the normal curve, let's try some examples. Look at the percentages of cases in each area of the normal curve in figure A.5. Suppose that Susan scored one standard deviation above the mean on a test. If the scores are normally distributed, she performed better than _____ percent of the class. Try another one: Tom scored one standard deviation below the mean, so he did better than _____ percent of the class. Finally, try this one: Mary scored better than 98 percent of the other students, so she scored _____ standard deviations (*above/below*) the mean. Look at figure A.6 for the answers.

### Describing the Relation between Two Variables

#### Problem

So far you have learned how to describe scores on one variable using statistics such as mean and standard deviation. However, your goal might be to describe the relation between two variables. For example, in the Garden Valley study, you might want to know

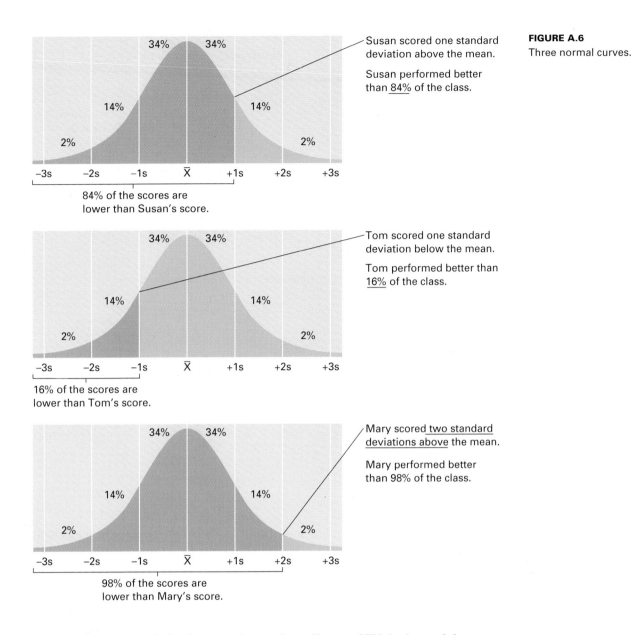

**FIGURE A.6**
Three normal curves.

whether there is any relation between the number of hours of TV viewing and the score on a school achievement test. Let's suppose that we go to Garden Valley School and ask 10 students from Mrs. Perkins's class to tell us how many hours they watched TV yesterday and that we get test scores for each student's performance on a school achievement test. Thus, we will have two scores for each of 10 students, as listed in the left panel of figure A.7.

## Scatter Plot

What is the relation between TV viewing and school achievement? One way to examine this question is to draw a scatter plot of the scores. A scatter plot is a graph consisting of two axes—such as hours of TV viewing on the X-axis and achievement score on the Y-axis—with one dot corresponding to each score on the two variables. An example for the Garden Valley study is shown in the right panel of figure A.7. As you can see, there seems to be a pattern in which a score on one axis is negatively, or inversely, related to a score on the other; in other words, the higher your TV-watching score, the lower your achievement score.

Figure A.8 shows five scatter plots, ranging from a strong positive correlation between the variables to no correlation to a strong negative correlation. Although scatter

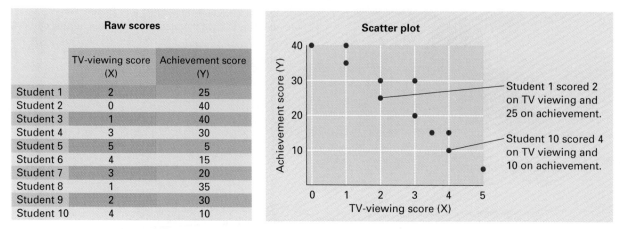

**FIGURE A.7**
Correlation between TV-viewing and achievement scores for 10 students.

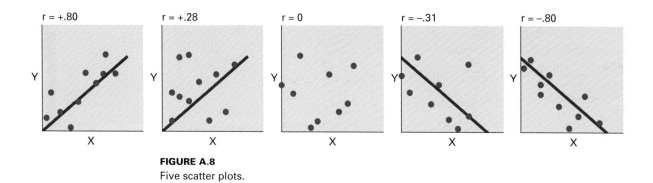

**FIGURE A.8**
Five scatter plots.

plots provide a general description of the relation between two variables, you may want to summarize the data even further. You could mathematically summarize your scatter plot by giving a quantitative measure of correlation.

### Correlation

As you first learned in chapter 2, the *correlation coefficient* is a number between $-1$ and $+1$ that indicates the degree of correlation between two variables. A strong positive correlation (such as r $= +.8$) indicates that TV viewing is strongly related to school achievement, with more TV viewing corresponding to higher achievement. A strong negative correlation (such as r $= -.8$) indicates that TV viewing is strongly related to school achievement, with more TV viewing corresponding to lower achievement. A neutral correlation (coefficients close to r $= .0$) indicates that no relation exists between the two variables.

Figure A.8 shows the correlation coefficients for five scatter plots. You can think of correlation in the following way. First, draw a scatter plot. Then, draw a straight line through the scatter plot so that the distance between each dot and the line is minimized. The closer the dots are to the line, the stronger the relationship between the two variables—in either a positive correlation or a negative correlation. If the dots are spread across the whole graph, as in the middle panel of figure A.8, no correlation exists between the variables.

The formula for computing the correlation coefficient is

$$r = \frac{\Sigma xy}{\sqrt{\Sigma x^2 \cdot \Sigma y^2}}$$

| Subject | TV-viewing score (X) | Deviation (X − X̄) | Squared deviation (X − X̄)² | Achievement score (Y) | Deviation (Y − Ȳ) | Squared deviation (Y − Ȳ)² | Cross product (X − X̄)·(Y − Ȳ) |
|---|---|---|---|---|---|---|---|
| 1 | 2 | −.5 | .25 | 25 | 0 | 0 | 0 |
| 2 | 0 | −2.5 | 6.25 | 40 | 15 | 225 | −37.5 |
| 3 | 1 | −1.5 | 2.25 | 40 | 15 | 225 | −22.5 |
| 4 | 3 | .5 | .25 | 30 | 5 | 25 | 2.5 |
| 5 | 5 | 2.5 | 6.25 | 5 | −20 | 400 | −50.0 |
| 6 | 4 | 1.5 | 2.25 | 15 | −10 | 100 | −15.0 |
| 7 | 3 | .5 | .25 | 20 | −5 | 25 | −2.5 |
| 8 | 1 | −1.5 | 2.25 | 35 | 10 | 100 | −15.0 |
| 9 | 2 | −.5 | .25 | 30 | 5 | 25 | −2.5 |
| 10 | 4 | 1.5 | 2.25 | 10 | −15 | 225 | −22.5 |
| | X̄ = 2.5 | | Σ(X − X̄)² = 22.50 | X̄ = 25 | | Σ(Y − Ȳ)² = 1350 | Σ[(X − X̄)·(Y − Ȳ)] = −165 |

$$r = \frac{\Sigma xy}{\sqrt{\Sigma x^2 \cdot \Sigma y^2}} = \frac{\Sigma[(X - \bar{X}) \cdot (Y - \bar{Y})]}{\sqrt{\Sigma(X - \bar{X})^2 \cdot \Sigma(Y - \bar{Y})^2}} = \frac{-165}{\sqrt{(22.50)(1350)}} = -.95$$

**FIGURE A.9**
How to compute a correlation coefficient.

where x is the difference between each X variable minus the mean; y is the difference between each Y variable and the mean; $\Sigma xy$ is the sum of the cross products (each x score multiplied by its corresponding y score); $\Sigma x^2$ is the sum of the squares of the x scores; and $\Sigma y^2$ is the sum of the squares of the y scores. Figure A.9 shows how to compute the value of r (that is, the correlation coefficient) for the Garden Valley data.

Correlation coefficients are very useful ways of summarizing the relation between variables, but they can lead to errors in interpretation. Whenever you are presented with a correlation coefficient, you should ask yourself "How should I interpret this correlation?" Some of the most common errors in interpretation follow:

*Failure to recognize curvilinear trends.* If you obtain a low correlation, this may be because no relation exists between the two variables, or it may be due to other factors. A correlation coefficient looks only for a straight-line relation between two variables; more of one variable is related to more (or less) of another variable. But some relationships between variables change as scores change, producing a curvilinear line that will not be reflected in the coefficient of correlation. Hence, a strong curvilinear relation may exist without producing a strong linear correlation coefficient. An example is shown in figure A.10. In this case, TV viewing up to three hours seems to be related positively with school achievement; thereafter, increased viewing is negatively related with school achievement.

*Use of restricted range.* A low correlation may also be due to using only a small range of scores along one of the variables. This is because there must be both high and low scores on each variable to see what is related to these scores. For example, if you do a separate correlation for heavy viewers (that is, three or more hours) and a separate correlation for light viewers (that is, zero to two hours), the correlation coefficients may be lowered because you included only high scores the first time and only low scores the second time. Because accurate correlations depend on the use of scores distributed across the entire range of both variables, restricting the range of one of the variables will artificially lower the correlation coefficient. Similarly, when conducting experiments using college students to see what is correlated with IQ, the experimenter may find low correlation coefficients, because most college students have high IQs and very few have low IQs.

**FIGURE A.10**

A curvilinear relation between two variables.

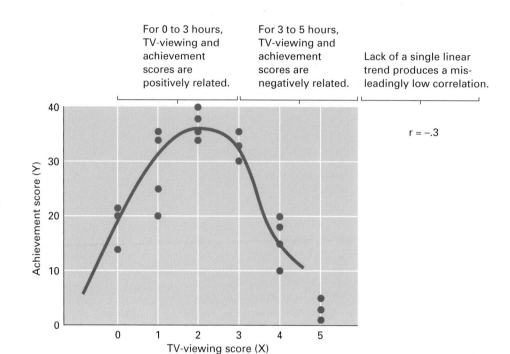

For 0 to 3 hours, TV-viewing and achievement scores are positively related.

For 3 to 5 hours, TV-viewing and achievement scores are negatively related.

Lack of a single linear trend produces a misleadingly low correlation.

$r = -.3$

*Inferred causation.* If you obtain a high correlation (either negative or positive), you may want to make an inference concerning which variable *caused* the values of the other. For example, if TV viewing and school achievement are strongly negatively correlated, you might want to conclude that TV viewing causes poor school achievement. However, such a conclusion is not justified based on correlation coefficients.

*Correlation does not mean causation.* Correlation does not necessarily indicate that one variable caused the other. Although it's possible that TV viewing causes poor school achievement, it's just as logical to argue that lower school achievement causes increased TV viewing. (Students who do poorly in school are "turned off" to school, so they turn on the TV.) A third possibility is that both TV viewing and low school achievement are caused by a third variable not included in the study, such as the degree of family stability or student health.

## ● Inferential Statistics

Thus far you have learned how behavior can be described using statistics. In many cases, however, description of behavior is just the first step. The second basic use of statistics is to draw conclusions regarding hypotheses based on data. This is called *inferential statistics* because it involves making inferences about causes of behavior that can apply to the entire population from which the sample was taken.

### Problem

In the Garden Valley study, we might want to know whether TV viewing causes poor school performance. To test this idea, we could ask 20 students from Mrs. Perkins's class to volunteer for a study of TV viewing and school achievement. We can divide our 20 students into two groups: those who are *asked* to watch two hours or less ("light group") and those who are *asked* to watch three hours or more ("heavy group"). This will provide us with two sets of achievement scores that can be analyzed with statistical tests. Figure A.11 shows the score on a school achievement test two weeks later for each of the students in the light group and each of the students in the heavy group.

| Group | Achievement scores | Mean |
|-------|-------------------|------|
| Light | 40, 35, 25, 30, 35, 40, 15, 20, 25, 35 | $\overline{X}_1 = 30$ |
| Heavy | 15, 10, 20, 5, 15, 20, 25, 0, 5, 35 | $\overline{X}_2 = 15$ |

The independent variable is amount of TV viewing.

The dependent variable is achievement score.

**FIGURE A.11**
Achievement scores for 10 heavy and 10 light TV viewers.

## Research Design

In the preceding example, we have conducted a formal experiment. To understand the nature of formal experiments, let's review the following ideas that were introduced in chapter 2:

*Independent variable.* The independent variable is what the experimenter tries to manipulate or to control the value of in the groups (or conditions or treatments). In the Garden Valley study, the independent variable is how much TV viewing the students were asked to do, and the two groups (or conditions or treatments) are heavy versus light.

*Dependent variable.* The dependent variable is the measurement that is taken as a result of the manipulations—that is, the score that each research participant gives as an outcome. In the Garden Valley study, the dependent variable is the score on the achievement test.

*Hypothesis.* The hypothesis is a prediction concerning the specific results of the study, in terms of the independent and dependent variables. For example, in the Garden Valley study, the hypothesis might be that heavy and light groups will not differ on school achievement scores.

For any formal experiment that is limited to two variables, you should be able to identify the independent variable, the dependent variable, and the hypothesis.

## Tests for Significance

Researchers will calculate the mean achievement score for each of the two groups and compare the results. In the Garden Valley study, the mean achievement score for the heavy TV viewers is 15, whereas the mean achievement score for the light TV viewers is 30. This does not necessarily mean that heavy TV viewers have lower scores than light viewers. Although it looks as if the heavy group scores lower than the light group, in this experiment the difference could be due to chance. For example, if you were to roll a die six times with your left hand, you might get 1, 2, 4, 3, 4, 1 for a mean of 2.5; then, if you were to roll the same die six times with your right hand, you might get 4, 6, 2, 5, 4, 3 for a mean of 4.0. This does not mean that your right hand is a better die roller than your left. The difference between 2.5 versus 4.0 is due to chance; in this case, if you had rolled the die 1,000 times with your left hand and then 1,000 times with your right, you probably would have gotten both means to average very near 3.5. Thus, in formal experiments it's possible to obtain a difference between the groups that is just due to chance. A statistical test can be performed to determine whether a difference between two means is *statistically significant*—in other words, a difference that is probably not due to chance.

A test of significance is used when each research participant has one score, and the researcher wants to determine whether the mean for one group is different from the mean for another group. The test will reveal whether the difference between the means is probably due to chance or to an actual difference between the groups. The researcher will report the results and include a *p-value,* which represents the level of significance. A p-value of .01 means that the difference in mean scores would be expected to occur by chance only 1 time out of every 100 trials, and a p-value of .05 means that the difference would be expected on the basis of chance 5 times out of 100. Usually, if a p-value is less than .05, then the differences obtained are tentatively accepted as genuine ones—that is, probably not due to chance.

## Misinterpretations

As with any statistical test, there are many ways to misinterpret the results. The following are some common mistakes:

*Multiple tests.* If the researcher obtains a significant result, this does not automatically guarantee that the difference is not due to chance. For example, let's suppose that we gave 20 different ability and achievement tests to our heavy and light groups and then looked for differences between the groups on each test. If we use a p-value of .05, this means that 5 percent of the time (or 1 out of 20) we would expect to find a significant difference that is due to chance. With 20 such tests, we could expect one of them to show a significant result just by chance. Thus, when an experimenter performs many statistical tests, you should be leery of the one or two tests that come out to be significant. To be on the safe side, you might like to see a replication—that is, a repeat of the same experiment with different participants.

*Low sample size.* If the researcher fails to obtain significant results, this does not guarantee that there is really no difference between the groups. When very low sample sizes are used (such as below 15 per group), one or two extreme scores can throw off the results. In general, small sample sizes require a larger difference between the means for the difference to be statistically significant. Thus, before you decide for sure that the difference is not significant, you should allow for a fair test—with several replications and adequate sample size.

# Glossary

**abnormal behavior:** Actions, thoughts, and feelings that are harmful to the person or to others. (p. 540)

**absolute threshold:** The smallest magnitude of a stimulus that can be detected half the time. (p. 115)

**acetylcholine (a˝suh-teel´koh˝leen):** A neurotransmitter used by somatic neurons that contract the body's large muscles. Acetylcholine also plays a role in memory and is thought to help regulate dreaming. (p. 63)

**achievement motivation:** The psychological need in humans for success. (p. 378)

**acquired immune deficiency syndrome (AIDS):** A viral disease spread by blood and other body fluids that eventually destroys the body's immune system. (p. 451)

**action potential:** A brief electrical signal that travels the length of the axon. (p. 61)

**adolescence:** The period from the onset of puberty until the beginning of adulthood. (p. 340)

**adolescent egocentrism:** The quality of thinking that leads some adolescents to believe that they are the focus of attention in social situations, to believe that their problems are unique, to be unusually hypocritical, and to be "pseudostupid." (p. 342)

**adolescent growth spurt:** The rapid increase in weight and height that occurs around the onset of puberty. (p. 341)

**adrenal glands (ah-drē´nal):** Two glands on the kidneys that are involved in physical and emotional arousal. (p. 88)

**afferent neurons (af´er-ent):** Neurons that transmit messages from sense organs to the central nervous system. (p. 65)

**agoraphobia (ag˝o-rah-fō´bē-ah):** An intense fear of leaving one's home or other familiar places. (p. 546)

**algorithms (al´go-rith´mz):** Systematic patterns of reasoning that guarantee finding a correct solution to a problem. (p. 280)

**all-or-none principle:** The principle that once a neural action potential is produced, its magnitude is always the same. (p. 61)

**amphetamine psychosis (sī-kō´sis):** A prolonged reaction to the excessive use of stimulants, characterized by disordered thinking, confused and rapidly changing emotions, and intense suspiciousness. (p. 184)

**amphetamines (am-fet´ah-mīnz):** Powerful stimulants that produce a conscious sense of increased energy and euphoria. (p. 184)

**amygdala (ah-mig´dah-lah):** A part of the limbic system that plays a role in emotion. (p. 74)

**anal expulsive:** A personality type based on anal fixation in which the person is cruel, pushy, messy and disorderly. (p. 470)

**anal retentive:** A personality type based on anal fixation, in which the person is stingy, obstinate, stubborn, and compulsive. (p. 470)

**anal stage:** According to Freud, the second psychosexual stage (from 1 to 3 years), in which gratification is focused on the anus. (p. 470)

**androgynous:** Having both typical feminine and masculine characteristics. (p. 411)

**angiotensin (an˝jē-ō-ten´sin):** A substance in the blood that signals the hypothalamus that the body needs water. (p. 374)

**animism (an´i-mizm):** The egocentric belief of preoperational children that inanimate objects are alive, as children are. (p. 337)

**anterograde amnesia (an´ter-ō-grād):** Disorder of memory characterized by an inability to store and/or retrieve new information in long-term memory. (p. 259)

**antidiuretic hormone (ADH) (an˝tī-dī˝´u-ret´ik):** A hormone produced by the pituitary that causes the kidneys to conserve water in the body by reabsorbing it from the urine. (p. 373)

**antisocial personality disorder:** A personality disorder characterized by smooth social skills and a lack of guilt about violating social rules and laws and taking advantage of others. (p. 562)

**anxiety disorders:** Psychological disorders that involve excessive levels of negative emotions, such as nervousness, tension, worry, fright, and anxiety. (p. 545)

**applied psychologists:** Psychologists who use knowledge of psychology to solve and prevent human problems. (p. 22)

**approach-approach conflict:** Conflict in which the individual must choose between two positive goals of approximately equal value. (p. 500)

**approach-avoidance conflict:** Conflict in which achieving a positive goal will produce a negative outcome as well. (p. 501)

**artificial intelligence:** Computers that are programmed to think like human brains. (p. 282)

**assertiveness training:** A method of behavior therapy that teaches individuals assertive rather than passive or aggressive ways of dealing with problematic situations. (p. 585)

**assessment centers:** Programs for the evaluation of employees that use simulated management tasks as their primary method of evaluation. (p. 649)

**association areas:** Areas within each lobe of the cerebral cortex believed to play general rather than specific roles. (p. 79)

**astral projection (as´tral):** Depersonalization that includes the illusion that the mind has left the body. (p. 180)

**attachments:** The psychological bonds between infants and caregivers. (p. 337)

**attitudes:** Beliefs that predispose one to act and feel in certain ways. (p. 616)

**attribution:** The process of trying to explain why things happen—that is, attribute them to some cause. (p. 630)

**attribution theory (ah-tri-bu´shun):** The theory that people tend to look for explanations for their own behavior and that of others. (p. 623)

**atypical sexual behavior:** Sexual practice that differs considerably from the norm. (p. 441)

**audition (aw-dish´un):** The sense of hearing. (p. 126)

**autonomic nervous system (aw˝´to-nom´ik):** The division of the peripheral nervous system that regulates the actions of internal body organs, such as heartbeat. (p. 67)

**avoidance-avoidance conflict:** Conflict in which the individual must choose between two negative outcomes of approximately equal value. (p. 501)

**avoidance conditioning:** Operant conditioning in which the behavior is reinforced because it prevents something negative from happening (a form of negative reinforcement). (p. 212)

**axons (ak´sonz):** Neuron branches that transmit messages to other neurons. (p. 59)

**basilar membrane (bas´i-lar):** One of the membranes that separates the two tubes of the cochlea and on which the organ of Corti rests. (p. 130)

**basket cells:** Sensory receptor cells at the base of hairs that detect pressure. (p. 133)

**behavior:** Directly observable and measurable actions. (p. 5)

**behavior therapy:** Psychotherapy based on social learning theory in which the therapist helps the client unlearn abnormal ways of behaving and learn more adaptive ways to take their place. (p. 583)

**behaviorism (be-hāv´yor-izm):** The school of psychology that emphasizes the process of learning and the measurement of overt behavior. (p. 12)

**binocular cues (bīn-ok´ū-lar):** Two visual cues that require both eyes to allow us to perceive depth. (p. 147)

**bipolar disorder (bī-pō´lar):** A condition in which the individual experiences periods of mania that alternate irregularly with periods of severe depression. (p. 557)

**blind experiment:** A formal experiment in which the researcher who measures the dependent variable does not know which participants are in the experimental group or the control group. In double-blind experiments, the participants also do not know if they are in the experimental or the control group. (p. 45)

**blind spot:** The spot where the optic nerve attaches to the retina; it contains no rods or cones. (p. 120)

**bone conduction hearing:** Hearing accomplished through sounds transmitted through the bones of the head directly to the cochlear fluid. (p. 130)

**brain:** The complex mass of neural cells and related cells encased in the skull. (p. 58)

**Broca's area:** An area of the frontal lobe of the left cerebral hemisphere that plays a role in speaking language. (p. 76)

## C

**Cannon-Bard theory of emotion:** The theory that conscious emotional experiences and physiological reactions and behavior are relatively independent events. (p. 391)

**castration anxiety (kas-trā´shun):** According to Freud, the fear of a young boy that his father will punish his sexual desire for his mother by removing his genitals. (p. 471)

**catatonic schizophrenia (kat˝ah-ton´ik):** A subtype of schizophrenia in which the individual spends long periods in an inactive, statuelike state. (p. 561)

**catharsis (kah-thar´sis):** The release of emotional energy related to unconscious conflicts. (pp. 398, 576)

**cell body:** The central part of the neuron that includes the nucleus. (p. 58)

**cell membrane:** The covering of a neuron or another cell. (p. 60)

**central nervous system:** The brain and the spinal cord. (p. 65)

**cerebellum (ser˝ē-bel´um):** Two rounded structures behind the pons involved in the coordination of muscle movements, learning, and memory. (p. 72)

**cerebral cortex (ser´ē-bral):** The largest structure in the forebrain, controlling conscious experience and intelligence and being involved with the somatic nervous system. (p. 74)

**cerebral hemispheres:** The two main parts of the cerebral cortex, divided into left and right hemispheres. (p. 80)

**cervix:** The neck of the uterus that is connected to the vagina. (p. 432)

**child molestation:** Sexual behavior with a child without force or direct threat of force. (p. 443)

**child rape:** Sexual behavior with a child achieved by force or direct threat of force. (p. 443)

**chromosomes (kro´mo-somz):** Strands of DNA (deoxyribonucleic acid) in cells. (p. 91)

**chunks:** Units of memory. (p. 239)

**ciliary muscle (sil´ē-ar˝e):** The muscle in the eye that controls the shape of the lens. (p. 119)

**cingulate cortex:** A part of the limbic system lying in the cerebral cortex that processes cognitive information in emotion. (p. 74)

**cingulotomy:** A type of psychosurgery for severe and otherwise untreatable obsessive-compulsive disorder; it involves surgical destruction of part of the cingulate cortex. (p. 597)

**circadian rhythm (sur-ka´de-un):** Internally generated cycles lasting about 24 hours a day that regulate sleepiness and wakefulness, body temperature, and the secretion of some hormones. (p. 168)

**classical conditioning:** A form of learning in which a previously neutral stimulus (CS) is paired with an unconditioned stimulus (UCS) to elicit a conditioned response (CR) that is identical to or very similar to the unconditioned response (UCR). (p. 202)

**client-centered psychotherapy:** Carl Rogers' approach to humanistic psychotherapy, in which the therapist creates an atmosphere that encourages clients to discover feelings of which they were unaware. (p. 580)

**climacteric (klī-mak´ter-ik):** The period between about ages 45 and 60 in which there is a loss of capacity to sexually reproduce in women and a decline in the reproductive capacity of men. (p. 350)

**clinical method:** The method of studying people while they are receiving psychological help from a mental health professional. (p. 37)

**clitoris:** The structure at the upper part of the vagina that is most sensitive to sexual stimulation in females. (p. 432)

**closure principle (klo´zhur):** The Gestalt principle of perception that states that incomplete figures of familiar objects will tend to be perceived as wholes. (p. 145)

**cochlea (cok´lē-ah):** A spiral structure of the inner ear that is filled with fluid and contains the receptors for hearing. (p. 128)

**coefficient of correlation:** The numerical expression of the strength and direction of a relationship between two variables. (p. 39)

**cognition (kog-nish´un):** The intellectual processes through which information is obtained, transformed, stored, retrieved, and otherwise used. (pp. 11, 274)

**cognitive dissonance (dis´so-nans):** The discomfort that results from inconsistencies between attitudes and behavior. (p. 621)

**cognitive map (kog´ni-tiv):** An inferred mental awareness of the structure of a physical space or related elements. (p. 222)

**cognitive psychology:** The viewpoint in psychology that emphasizes the importance of cognitive processes, such as perception, memory, and thinking. (p. 11)

**cognitive theory of emotion:** The theory that the cognitive interpretation of events in the outside world and stimuli from our own bodies is the key factor in emotions. (p. 391)

**cognitive therapy:** An approach to therapy that teaches individuals new cognitions—adaptive beliefs, expectations, and ways of thinking—to eliminate abnormal emotions and behavior. (p. 588)

**collective unconscious:** According to Jung, the content of the unconscious mind with which all humans are born. (p. 473)

**companionate love:** The blend of friendship, intimacy, commitment, and security that generally develops after passionate love. (p. 635)

**concepts (kon´septs):** Categories of things, events, and qualities that are linked together by a common feature or features in spite of their differences. (p. 274)

**concrete operational stage:** In Piaget's theory, the period of cognitive development from ages 7 to 11. (p. 339)

**conditioned response (CR):** A response that is similar or identical to the unconditioned response that comes to be elicited by a conditioned stimulus. (p. 201)

**conditioned stimulus (CS):** A stimulus that comes to elicit responses as a result of being paired with an unconditioned stimulus. (p. 201)

**conditions of worth:** The standards used by others or ourselves in judging our worth. (p. 481)

**cones:** The 6 million receptor cells located mostly in the center of the retina that transduce light waves into neural impulses, thereby coding information about light, dark, and color. (p. 119)

**conflict:** The state in which two or more motives cannot be satisfied because they interfere with one another. (p. 500)

**conformity:** Yielding to group pressure even when no direct request to comply has been made. (p. 610)

**conjunctive concepts (kon-junk˝tiv´):** Concepts defined by the simultaneous presence of two or more common characteristics. (p. 275)

**conscience:** According to Freud, the moral inhibitions of the superego. (p. 469)

**conscious mind:** That portion of the mind of which one is presently aware. (p. 467)

**consciousness (kon´shus-nes):** A state of awareness. (p. 162)

**conservation:** The concept understood by concrete operational children that quantity (number, mass, etc.) does not change just because shape or other superficial features have changed. (p. 339)

**continuity hypothesis:** The view that abnormal behavior is just a more severe form of normal psychological problems. (p. 540)

**continuity principle (kon´ti-noo´´i-tee):** The Gestalt principle of perception that states that lines or patterns that follow a smooth contour will be perceived as part of a single unit. (p. 144)

**control group:** The group in simple experiments that is not exposed to any level of the independent variable and is used for comparisons with the treatment group. (p. 44)

**convergent thinking:** Thinking that is logical and conventional and that focuses on a problem. (p. 283)

**conversion disorders:** Somatoform disorders in which individuals experience serious somatic symptoms such as functional blindness, deafness, and paralysis. (p. 550)

**cooperative play:** Play that involves cooperation between two or more children. (p. 338)

**coping:** Attempts by individuals to deal with the source of stress and/or control their reactions to it. (p. 519)

**cornea (kor´ne-ah):** The protective coating on the surface of the eye through which light passes. (p. 119)

**corpus callosum (kor´pus kah-lo´sum):** The major neural structure connecting the left and right cerebral hemispheres. (p. 80)

**correlational method (kor´´e-la´shun-al):** A research method that measures the strength of the relation between variables. (p. 38)

**cortisol:** A hormone produced by the adrenal glands. (p. 88)

**counterconditioning:** The process of eliminating a classically conditioned response by pairing the conditioned stimulus (CS) with an unconditioned stimulus (UCS) for a response that is stronger than the conditioned response (CR) and that cannot occur at the same time as the CR. (p. 204)

**creativity:** The ability to make human products and ideas (such as symphonies or solutions to social problems) that are both novel and valued by others. (p. 283)

**cretinism (kre´tin-izm):** A type of mental retardation in children caused by a deficiency of thyroxin. (p. 89)

**criterion-referenced testing:** Testing designed to determine if a child can meet the minimum standards of a specific educational objective. (p. 676)

**critical period:** A biologically determined period in the life of some animals during which certain forms of learning can take place most easily. (p. 322)

**criticism trap:** An increase in the frequency of a negative behavior that often follows the use of criticism, reinforcing the behavior it is intended to punish. (p. 214)

**crystallized intelligence:** The ability to use previously learned skills to solve familiar problems. (p. 295)

**cultural relativity:** The perspective that promotes thinking of different cultures in relative terms rather than judgmental terms. (p. 19)

**culture:** The patterns of behavior, beliefs, and values shared by a group of people. (p. 17)

**cupula (ku´pu-lah):** A gelatin-like structure containing a tuft of hairlike sensory receptor cells in the semicircular canals. (p. 132)

## D

**dark adaptation:** Increased sensitivity of the eye in semidarkness following reduction in overall illumination. (p. 121)

**day residue:** Dream content that is similar to events in the person's waking life. (p. 172)

**daydreams:** Relatively focused thinking about fantasies. (p. 162)

**decay theory:** The theory that forgetting occurs as the memory trace fades over time. (p. 249)

**decenter (de-sen´ter):** To think about more than one characteristic of a thing at a time; a capacity of concrete operational children. (p. 339)

**decibel (db) (des´i-bel):** Measurement of the intensity of perceived sound. (p. 127)

**declarative memory:** Semantic and episodic memory. (p. 241)

**deep structure:** The underlying structure of a statement that holds its meaning. (p. 286)

**defense mechanisms:** According to Freud, the unrealistic strategies used by the ego to discharge tension. (p. 521)

**deindividuation:** State in which people in a group can feel anonymous and unidentifiable and therefore feel less concerned with what others think of their behavior. (p. 606)

**delay of reinforcement:** The passage of time between the response and the positive reinforcement that leads to reduced efficiency of learning. (p. 208)

**delusional disorder:** A nonschizophrenic disorder characterized by delusions of grandeur and persecution that are more logical than those of paranoid schizophrenics in the absence of hallucinations. (p. 561)

**delusions:** False beliefs that distort reality. (p. 560)

**dendrites (den´drits):** Extensions of the cell body that usually serve as receiving areas for messages from other neurons. (p. 59)

**dependent variable:** The variable whose quantitative value is expected to depend on the effects of the independent variable. (p. 44)

**depersonalization (de-per´´sun-al-i-za´shun):** The perceptual experience of one's body or surroundings becoming distorted or unreal in some way. (pp. 180, 551)

**depolarization:** The process during which positively charged ions flow into the axon, making it less negatively charged inside. (p. 61)

**depressants:** Drugs that reduce the activity of the central nervous system, leading to a sense of relaxation, drowsiness, and lowered inhibitions. (p. 186)

**descriptive studies:** Methods of observation used to describe predictable behavior and mental processes. (p. 36)

**development:** The more-or-less predictable changes in behavior associated with increasing age. (p. 320)

**developmental psychology:** The field of psychology that focuses on development across the life span. (p. 320)

**deviation IQ:** The intelligence quotient based on the degree of deviation from average of the person's score on an intelligence test. (p. 297)

**difference threshold:** The smallest difference between two stimuli that can be detected half the time. (p. 115)

**diffusion of responsibility:** The effect of being in a group that apparently reduces the sense of personal responsibility of each group member to act appropriately. (p. 608)

**discontinuity hypothesis:** The view that abnormal behavior is fundamentally different from normal psychological problems. (p. 541)

**disinhibition (dis´´in-hi-bish´un):** A temporary increase in the strength of an extinguished response caused by an unrelated stimulus event. (p. 220)

**disjunctive concepts (dis-junk´´tiv´):** Concepts defined by the presence of one of two common characteristics or both. (p. 275)

**disorganized schizophrenia:** A subtype of schizophrenia characterized by shallow silliness, extreme social withdrawal, and fragmented delusions and hallucinations. (p. 561)

**displacement (dis-plas´ment):** A defense mechanism in which the individual directs aggressive or sexual feelings away from the primary object to someone or something safe. (p. 469)

**dispositional attribution (dis´´po-zish´un-al):** An explanation for behavior that is based on a personal characteristic of the individual. (p. 630)

**dissociative amnesia:** A dissociative disorder that involves a loss of memory and that has a psychological rather than a physical cause. (p. 552)

**dissociative disorders (dis-so´´se-a-tiv):** A category of conditions involving sudden cognitive changes, such as a sudden loss of memory or loss of one's identity. (p. 551)

**dissociative fugue (fug):** A period of "wandering" that involves a loss of memory and a change in identity. (p. 552)

**dissociative identity disorder:** A dissociative disorder in which the individual appears to shift abruptly and repeatedly from one "personality" to another. (p. 552)

**divergent thinking:** Thinking that is loosely organized, only partially directed, and unconventional. (p. 283)

**divided consciousness:** The splitting off of two conscious activities that occur simultaneously. (p. 163)

**dizygotic twins (dī˝zī-got´ik):** Twins formed from the fertilization of two ova by two sperm. (p. 95)

**DNA (deoxyribonucleic acid):** Structures in cells in the form of two curved rails of a ladder type connected at intervals by base pairs of adenine, thymine, guanine, and cystine that code genetic information. (p. 91)

**dominant gene:** The gene that produces a trait in an individual even when paired with a recessive gene. (p. 93)

**dopamine (do˝păh´ meen):** A neurotransmitter substance used by neurons in the brain that control large muscle movements and by neurons in pleasure and reward systems in the brain. (p. 63)

**Down syndrome:** An abnormality caused by the presence of an additional 21st chromosome. (p. 94)

**dream interpretation:** A method developed by Freud in which the symbols of the manifest content of dreams that are recalled by the patient are interpreted to reveal their latent content. (p. 575)

**dreaming:** Conscious awareness during sleep that primarily occurs during rapid-eye-movement (REM) sleep. (p. 165)

**drug therapy:** A medical therapy that uses medications to treat abnormal behavior. (p. 595)

**dyspareunia (dis˝pah-roo´nē-ah):** A sexual dysfunction in which the individual experiences pain during intercourse. (p. 447)

**E**

**eardrum:** A thin membrane that sound waves cause to vibrate; a structure of the middle ear. (p. 128)

**early experiences:** Experiences occurring very early in development, believed by some to have lasting effects. (p. 323)

**educational psychology:** The field in which principles of learning, cognition, and other aspects of psychology are applied to improve education. (p. 673)

**efferent neurons (ef´er-ent):** Neurons that transmit messages from the central nervous system to organs and muscles. (p. 65)

**ego (ē´go):** According to Freud, that part of the mind that uses the reality principle to satisfy the id. (p. 469)

**ego ideal:** According to Freud, the standard of perfect conduct of the superego. (p. 469)

**egocentric (ē˝go-sen´trik):** The self-oriented quality in the thinking of preoperational children. (p. 337)

**elaboration (e-lab˝o-rā´shun):** The process of creating associations between a new memory and existing memories. (p. 247)

**Electra complex (e-lek´trah):** According to Freud, the transfer of a young girl's sexual desires from her mother to her father after she discovers she has no penis. (p. 471)

**electroconvulsive therapy (ECT) (e-lek˝trō-con-vul´siv):** A medical therapy that uses electrical current to induce controlled convulsive seizures that alleviate some types of mental disorders. (p. 596)

**electroencephalogram (EEG) (e-lek˝trō-en-sef´ah-lo-gram):** A recording of the electrical activity of the brain obtained through electrodes placed on the scalp. (pp. 71, 165)

**electromagnetic radiation (e-lek˝trō-mag-net´ik):** A form of energy, including electricity, radio waves, and X rays, of which visible light is a part. (p. 118)

**emotion:** Positive or negative feelings generally in reaction to stimuli that are accompanied by physiological arousal and related behavior. (p. 369)

**empirical evidence:** Evidence based on observations of publicly observable phenomena, such as behavior, that can be confirmed by other observers. (p. 34)

**encode (en´cōd):** To represent information in some form in the memory system. (p. 236)

**endocrine system (en´dō-krin):** The system of glands that secretes hormones. (p. 86)

**engram (en´gram):** The partially understood memory trace in the brain that is the biological basis of memory. (p. 257)

**environmental psychologists:** Psychologists who study the effects of the physical environment on behavior and mental processes. (p. 661)

**epididymis:** The structure that holds sperm cells until ejaculation. (p. 433)

**epinephrine (ep˝i-nef´rin):** A hormone produced by the adrenal glands. (p. 88)

**episodic memory (epĭ-sod-ik):** Memory for specific experiences that can be defined in terms of time and space. (p. 241)

**equity theory:** The theory that partners will be comfortable in their relationship only when the ratio between their perceived contributions and benefits is equal. (p. 635)

**erectile dysfunction:** A condition in which the penis does not become erect enough for intercourse under sexually arousing circumstances. (p. 447)

**erogenous zone:** A part of the body that releases sexual energy when stimulated. (p. 470)

**escape conditioning:** Operant conditioning in which the behavior is reinforced because it causes a negative event to cease (a form of negative reinforcement). (p. 212)

**estrogen (es´tro-jen):** A female sex hormone. (p. 89)

**ethnic group:** A group of persons who are descendants of a common group of ancestors. (p. 17)

**ethnic identity:** Each person's sense of belonging to a particular ethnic group. (p. 17)

**evolutionary psychology:** The perspective in psychology that the psychological characteristics of human and nonhuman animals arose through natural selection. (p. 20)

**evolutionary theory of gender differences:** The theory that gender differences are based on genes that resulted from different evolutionary pressures on ancestral women and men. (p. 418)

**excitement phase:** The first stage of the sexual response cycle, during which the penis becomes erect and the vagina lubricates. (p. 434)

**exhibitionism (ek˝sĭ-bish´ŭ-nizm˝):** The practice of obtaining sexual pleasure by exposing one's genitals to others. (p. 442)

**experimental control:** The requirement that all explanations for differences in the dependent variable are controlled in formal experiments, except for differences in conditions of the independent variable. (p. 44)

**experimental group:** The group in an experiment that receives some value of the independent variable. (p. 44)

**experimenter bias:** Subtle but potentially powerful unintentional influences on the dependent variable caused by experimenters' interacting differently with participants in the experimental and control groups. (p. 45)

**expert systems:** Problem-solving computer programs that operate in specific areas such as diagnosis and treatment of medical disorders. (p. 282)

**expressive aphasia (ah-fa´ze-ah):** An impairment of the ability to generate spoken language, but not in the comprehension of language. (p. 76)

**external auditory canal:** The tube connecting the pinna to the middle ear. (p. 128)

**extinction (eks-ting´shun):** The process of unlearning a learned response because of the removal of the original source of learning. (p. 219)

**extraversion (eks˝tro-ver´zhun):** According to Jung, the tendency of some individuals to be friendly and open to the world. (p. 472)

**extrinsic motivation (eks-trin´sik):** Human motives activated by external rewards. (p. 381)

**F**

**fallopian tubes:** The tubes through which ova (eggs) reach the uterus. (p. 432)

**false memory:** Remembering an event that did not occur or that occurred in a way that was substantially different from the memory of the event. (p. 254)

**family therapy:** An approach to psychotherapy that emphasizes an understanding of the roles of each of the members of the family system, usually conducted with all members of the family present. (p. 593)

**fear of success:** The fear of the consequences of success, particularly the envy of others. (p. 379)

**feelings of inferiority:** According to Adler, the feelings that result from children being less powerful than adults that must be overcome during the development of the healthy personality. (p. 473)

**female sexual arousal disorder:** A condition in which sexual arousal does not occur in appropriate circumstances in a female. (p. 447)

**feminist psychotherapy:** An approach to psychotherapy that encourages women to confront issues created by living in a sexist society as part of their psychotherapy. (p. 592)

**fertilization (fer´tĭ-li-zā´shun):** The uniting of sperm and ovum, which produces a zygote. (p. 92)

**fetishism (fet´ish-izm):** The practice of obtaining sexual arousal primarily or exclusively from specific objects. (p. 441)

**figure-ground principle:** The Gestalt principle of perception that states that part of a visual stimulus will be the center of our attention (figure) and the rest will be the indistinct ground. In many cases, the figure and ground can be reversed in our perception of the same stimulus. (p. 144)

**fixed interval schedule:** A reinforcement schedule in which the reinforcer is given following the first response occurring after a predetermined period of time. (p. 209)

**fixed ratio schedule:** A reinforcement schedule in which the reinforcer is given only after a specified number of responses. (p. 209)

**fluid intelligence:** The ability to learn or invent new strategies to deal with new problems. (p. 295)

**forebrain:** The parts of the brain, including the thalamus, hypothalamus, and cerebral cortex, that cover the hindbrain and midbrain and fill much of the skull. (p. 72)

**formal experiment:** A research method that allows the researcher to manipulate the independent variable to study its effect on the dependent variable. (p. 42)

**formal operational stage:** In Piaget's theory, the period of intellectual development usually reached by about age 11 and characterized by the ability to use abstract concepts. (p. 342)

**fovea (fō´vē-ah):** The central spot of the retina, which contains the greatest concentration of cones. (p. 120)

**framing:** The way in which a problem or question is presented. (p. 281)

**free association:** A tool used by Freud in which the patient is encouraged to talk about whatever comes to mind, allowing the contents of the unconscious mind to slip past the censorship of the ego. (p. 574)

**free nerve endings:** Sensory receptor cells in the skin that detect pressure, temperature, and pain. (p. 133)

**frequency of cycles:** The rate of vibration of sound waves; determines pitch. (p. 126)

**Freud's instinct theory:** The theory that aggression is caused by an inborn aggressive instinct. (p. 398)

**frontal lobes:** The part of the cerebral cortex in the front of the skull involved in planning, organization, thinking, decision making, memory, voluntary motor movements, and speech. (p. 76)

**frustration:** The result of being unable to satisfy a motive. (p. 500)

**frustration-aggression theory:** The theory that aggression is a natural reaction to frustration of important motives. (p. 399)

**functional MRI:** A type of MRI that measures the activity of parts of the brain by measuring the use of oxygen by groups of neurons. (p. 72)

**functionalism (funk´shun-al-izm):** The nineteenth-century school of psychology that emphasized the useful functions of consciousness. (p. 9)

**fundamental attribution error:** The tendency to underestimate the impact of situations on others while overestimating the impact on oneself. (p. 630)

## G

**g:** A broad general factor of intelligence, a concept endorsed by some investigators of intelligence. (p. 292)

**gamete (gam´ēt):** A sex cell, which contains 23 chromosomes instead of the normal 46. (p. 92)

**ganglia (gang´glē-ah):** Clusters of cell bodies of neurons outside of the central nervous system. (p. 69)

**gender:** The psychological experience of being male or female. (p. 410)

**gender identity:** One's view of oneself as male or female. (pp. 17, 410)

**gender role:** The behaviors consistent with being male or female in a given culture. (p. 410)

**general adaptation syndrome (GAS):** According to Selye, the mobilization of the body to ward off threats, characterized by a three-stage pattern of the alarm reaction, the resistance stage, and the exhaustion stage. (p. 507)

**generalized anxiety disorder:** An uneasy sense of general tension and apprehension for no apparent reason that makes the individual highly uncomfortable because of its prolonged presence. (p. 546)

**generative (jen´e-ra´´tiv):** The ability to create an infinite set of utterances using a finite set of elements and rules. (p. 286)

**genes (jēnz):** Segments of chromosomes made up of sequences of base pairs of adenine, thymine, guanine, and cystine that are the basic biological units of inheritance because they contain all the coded genetic information needed to influence some aspect of a structure or function of the body. (pp. 21, 92)

**genital stage (jen´i-tal):** According to Freud, the psychosexual stage (from 11 years through adulthood) in which sexual and romantic interest is directed toward one's peers. (p. 472)

**gestalt (ges-tawlt´):** An organized or unified whole. (p. 8)

**Gestalt psychology:** The school of thought based on the belief that human consciousness cannot be broken down into its elements. (pp. 8, 581)

**Gestalt therapy:** A humanistic therapy in which the therapist takes an active role (questioning and challenging the client) to

help the client become more aware of his or her feelings. (p. 581)

**glands:** Structures in the body that secrete substances. (p. 86)

**glucagon (gloo´kah-gon):** A hormone produced by the islets of Langerhans that causes the liver to release sugar into the bloodstream. (pp. 88, 371)

**glutamate (gloo-tuh-mât):** The most widespread excitatory neurotransmitter in the brain. (p. 64)

**gonads (gō´nadz):** The glands that produce sex cells and hormones important in sexual arousal and that contribute to the development of secondary sex characteristics. (p. 88)

**graded exposure:** A behavior therapy technique in which a person with a phobia is first exposed to a stimulus that is mildly fear provoking. Once the client has mastered his or her anxiety in that situation, he or she is exposed to a graded series of more fearful situations. (p. 583)

**group therapy:** Psychotherapy conducted in groups, typically of four to eight clients at a time. (p. 593)

**groupthink:** The faulty decision-making processes that may occur in groups. (p. 609)

**gustation (gus-tā´shun):** The sense of taste. (p. 140)

## H

**hallucinations:** False perceptual experiences that distort reality. (p. 560)

**hallucinogens (hah-lū´si´´no-jenz):** Drugs that alter perceptual experiences. (p. 187)

**hammer, anvil, stirrup:** Three linked bones of the middle ear, which pass sound waves to the inner ear. (p. 128)

**health psychology:** The field of psychology that uses psychological principles to encourage healthy lifestyles and to minimize the impact of physical illness. (p. 500)

**hertz (Hz):** The measurement of the frequency of sound waves in cycles per second. (p. 126)

**heterosexual:** Romantically and sexually attracted to those of the different sex. (p. 423)

**heuristics:** Efficient problem-solving strategies that do not guarantee a correct solution. (p. 280)

**hindbrain:** The lowest part of the brain, located at the rear base of the skull. (p. 72)

**hippocampus (hip´´o-kam´pus):** The part of the limbic system that plays a role in emotional arousal and memory. (pp. 74, 260)

**homeostatic mechanisms (hō´´mē-ō-stat´ik):** Internal body mechanisms that sense biological imbalances and stimulate actions to restore the proper balance. (p. 369)

**homosexual:** Romantically and sexually attracted to those of the same sex, as distinguished from heterosexual. (p. 423)

**hormones (hor´mōnz):** Chemical substances, produced by endocrine glands, that influence internal organs. (p. 86)

**human factors engineering:** The branch of industrial-organizational psychology interested in the design of machines to be operated by human beings. (p. 657)

**humanistic psychology:** The psychological view that human beings possess an innate tendency to improve and determine their lives by the decisions they make. (p. 14)

**humanistic theory:** The psychological view that human beings possess an innate tendency to improve and to determine their lives through the decisions they make. (p. 480)

**hyperphagia (hī˝per-fā´jē-ah):** Excessive overeating that results from the destruction of the satiety center of the hypothalamus. (p. 370)

**hypnagogic state (hip˝nah-goj´ik):** A relaxed state of dreamlike awareness between wakefulness and sleep. (p. 165)

**hypnosis (hip-nō´sis):** An altered state of consciousness in which the individual is highly relaxed and susceptible to suggestions. (p. 178)

**hypochondriasis (hī˝pō-kon-drī´ah-sis):** A mild form of somatization disorder characterized by excessive concern about one's health. (p. 550)

**hypothalamus (hī˝pō-thal´ah-mus):** The small part of the forebrain involved with motives, emotions, and the functions of the autonomic nervous system. (pp. 74, 369)

**hypothesis:** A prediction based on a theory that is tested in a study. (p. 35)

**I**

**id:** According to Freud, the inborn part of the unconscious mind that uses the primary process to satisfy its needs and that acts according to the pleasure principle. (p. 468)

**ideal self:** According to humanists, the person one wishes one were. (p. 481)

**identification:** The tendency to base one's identity and actions on individuals who are successful in gaining satisfaction from life. (p. 469)

**immune system:** The complex body system of defenses to illness, such as white cells and natural killer cells of the blood. (p. 509)

**imprinting (im´print-ing):** A form of early learning that occurs in some animals during a critical period. (p. 322)

**in-basket exercise:** A type of management simulation task in which the individual attempts to solve a problem that is typical of the ones that appear in a manager's "in-basket." (p. 649)

**incentives:** External cues that activate motives. (p. 372)

**incest (in´sest):** Sexual relations between relatives. (p. 443)

**independent variable:** The variable whose quantitative value is independently controlled by the researcher. (p. 44)

**industrial-organizational (I/O) psychologists:** Psychologists who study organizations and seek ways to improve the functioning and human benefits of business. (p. 644)

**inhalants (in-hā´lants):** Toxic substances that produce a sense of intoxication when inhaled. (p. 187)

**inhibited female orgasm:** A female sexual dysfunction in which the individual is unable to experience orgasm. (p. 447)

**inhibited sexual desire:** A condition in which a person desires sex rarely or not at all. (p. 446)

**inner-directedness:** A force that humanists believe all people possess that internally leads them to grow and improve. (p. 480)

**insanity:** A legal definition concerning a person's inability to tell right from wrong, ability to understand the trial proceedings, or whether the person is a direct danger to self or others. (p. 543)

**insight (in´sīt):** A form of cognitive change that involves recognition of previously unseen relationships. (p. 224)

**insomnia:** A disorder in which the person has difficulty falling asleep or staying asleep. (p. 175)

**insulin (in´su-lin):** A hormone produced by the islets of Langerhans that reduces the amount of sugar in the bloodstream. (pp. 88, 371)

**intelligence (in-tel´i-jens):** The cognitive abilities of an individual to learn from experience, to reason well, and to cope with the demands of daily living. (p. 291)

**intelligence quotient (IQ):** A numerical value of intelligence derived from the results of an intelligence test. (p. 296)

**intelligent tutoring systems:** An approach to learning in which computers provide tutoring to students. (p. 674)

**intensity:** The density of vibrating air molecules, which determines the loudness of sound. (p. 127)

**interference theory:** The theory that forgetting occurs because similar memories interfere with the storage or retrieval of information. (p. 250)

**interneuron:** Neurons in the central nervous system that connect other neurons. (p. 65)

**interpersonal psychotherapy:** A form of psychological therapy, based on the theories of neo-Freudian Harry Stack Sullivan, that focuses on the accurate identification and communication of feelings and the improvement of current social relationships. (p. 576)

**interview:** A subjective method of personality assessment that involves questioning techniques designed to reveal the personality of the client. (p. 488)

**intrinsic motivation (in-trin´sik):** Human motives stimulated by the inherent nature of the activity or its natural consequences. (p. 381)

**introspection (in˝tro-spek´shun):** The process of looking inward at one's own consciousness. (p. 7)

**introversion (in-tro-ver´zhun):** According to Jung, the tendency of some individuals to be shy and to focus their attention on themselves. (p. 472)

**ions (i´ons):** Electrically charged particles. (p. 60)

**iris (ī´ris):** The colored part of the eye behind the cornea that regulates the amount of light that enters. (p. 119)

**islets of Langerhans (i´lets of lahng´er-hanz):** Endocrine cells in the pancreas that regulate the level of sugar in the blood. (p. 88)

**J**

**James-Lange theory of emotion:** The theory that conscious emotional experiences are caused by feedback to the cerebral cortex from physiological reactions and behavior. (p. 388)

**job performance ratings:** Ratings of the actual performance of employees in their jobs by supervisors. (p. 648)

**K**

**kinesthetic receptors (kin˝es-thet´ik):** Receptors in the muscles, joints, and skin that provide information about movement, posture, and orientation. (p. 132)

**Korsakoff's syndrome (Kor-sak´ofs):** A disorder involving both anterograde and retrograde amnesia caused by excessive use of alcohol. (p. 261)

**L**

**labia majora:** The larger, outer lips of the vulva. (p. 432)

**labia minora:** The smaller, inner lips of the vulva. (p. 432)

**language:** A symbolic code used in communication. (p. 285)

**latency stage:** According to Freud, the fourth psychosexual stage (from about 6 to 11 years) during which sexual energy is sublimated and converted into socially valued activities. (p. 471)

**latent content:** According to Freud, the true meaning of dreams that is found in the symbols in their manifest content. (p. 173)

**lateral hypothalamus:** A portion of the hypothalamus involved in feeling hungry and starting to eat (the feeding center). (p. 370)

**learned taste aversion (ah-ver´shun):** Negative reaction to a particular taste that has been associated with nausea or other illness. (p. 228)

**learning:** Any relatively permanent change in behavior brought about through experience. (p. 198)

**learning set:** Improvement in the rate of learning to solve new problems through practice solving similar problems. (p. 225)

**lens:** The transparent portion of the eye that adjusts to focus light on the retina. (p. 119)

**levels of processing model:** An alternative to the stage theory of memory stating that the distinction between short-term and long-term memory is a matter of degree rather than different kinds of memory and is based on how incoming information is processed. (p. 247)

**libido:** The energy of the life instincts of sex, hunger, and thirst. (p. 468)

**life events:** Psychologically significant events that occur in a person's life, such as divorce, childbirth, or change in employment. (p. 503)

**light adaptation:** Regaining sensitivity of the eye to bright light following an increase in overall illumination. (p. 122)

**limbic system:** A complex brain system, composed of the amygdala, hippocampus, septal area, and cingulate cortex, that works with the hypothalamus in emotional arousal. (p. 74)

**linguistic relativity hypothesis:** The idea that the structure of a language may influence the way individuals think. (p. 287)

**long-term memory (LTM):** The third stage of memory, involving the storage of information that is kept for long periods of time. (p. 240)

## M

**magnetic resonance imaging (MRI):** An imaging technique using magnetic resonance to obtain detailed views of brain structure and function. (p. 72)

**mainstreaming:** The practice of integrating children with special needs into regular classrooms. (p. 676)

**major depression:** An affective disorder characterized by episodes of deep unhappiness, loss of interest in life, and other symptoms. (p. 555)

**male sexual arousal disorders:** Conditions in which sexual arousal does not occur in appropriate circumstances in a male. (p. 447)

**management by objectives:** The strategy of giving employees specific goals but giving them considerable freedom in deciding how to reach those goals. (p. 654)

**mania (mā´nē-ah):** A disturbance of mood in which the individual experiences a euphoria without cause that is characterized by unrealistic optimism and heightened sensory pleasures. (p. 557)

**manifest content:** According to Freud, the literal meaning of dreams. (p. 173)

**mantras (man´trahz):** Words or sounds containing religious meaning that are used during meditation. (p. 178)

**Maslow's hierarchy of motives:** The concept that more basic needs must be met before higher-level motives become active. (p. 383)

**mastery learning:** The concept that children should never progress from one learning task to another until they have mastered the more basic one. (p. 674)

**maturation (mach˝u-rā´shun):** Systematic physical growth of the body, including the nervous system. (p. 320)

**medical therapies:** Those therapies—including drug therapy, electroconvulsive therapy, and psychosurgery—generally designed to correct a physical condition that is believed to be the cause of a psychological disorder. (p. 594)

**meditation (med˝i-tā-shun):** Several methods of focusing concentration away from thoughts and feelings and generating a sense of relaxation. (p. 177)

**medulla (mĕ-dul´ah):** The swelling just above the spinal cord within the hindbrain responsible for controlling breathing and a variety of reflexes. (p. 72)

**menarche (me-nar´kē):** The first menstrual period. (p. 341)

**menopause (mĕn´o-pawz):** The cessation of menstruation and the capacity to reproduce in women. (p. 350)

**mental processes:** Private psychological activities that include thinking, perceiving, and feeling. (p. 5)

**mental set:** A habitual way of approaching or perceiving a problem. (p. 279)

**metabolism (me-tab´o-lizm):** The process through which the body uses energy. (p. 89)

**midbrain:** The small area at the top of the hindbrain that serves primarily as a reflex center for orienting the eyes and ears. (p. 72)

**modeling:** Learning based on observation of the behavior of another. (p. 225)

**monocular cues (mon-ok´ū-lar):** Eight visual cues that can be seen with one eye and that allow us to perceive depth. (p. 146)

**monozygotic twins (mon˝ō-zī-got´ik):** Twins formed from a single ovum; they are identical in appearance because they have the same genetic structure. (p. 94)

**mons:** The fleshy mound that sits at the top of the vulva. (p. 432)

**mood disorders:** Psychological disorders involving depression and/or abnormal elation. (p. 555)

**morphemes (mor´fēm):** The smallest units of meaning in a language. (p. 286)

**motivated forgetting:** Forgetting that is believed to be based on the upsetting or threatening nature of the information that is forgotten. (p. 255)

**motivation:** The internal state or condition that activates and gives direction to our thoughts, feelings, and actions. (p. 368)

**motive for affiliation:** The need to be with other people and to have personal relationships. (p. 376)

**motives:** Internal states or conditions that activate behavior and give it direction. (p. 13)

**multiple approach-avoidance conflict:** Conflict that requires the individual to choose between two alternatives, each of which contains both positive and negative consequences. (p. 502)

**myelin sheath (mī´e-lin):** The insulating fatty covering wrapped around the axon that speeds the transmission of neural messages. (p. 61)

**myoclonia (mī˝o-klō´nē-ah):** An abrupt movement that sometimes occurs during the hypnagogic state in which the sleeper often experiences a sense of falling. (p. 165)

## N

**narcolepsy:** A sleep disorder in which the person suddenly falls asleep during

activities usually performed when fully awake, even when the person has had adequate sleep. (p. 175)

**narcotics:** Powerful and highly addictive depressants. (p. 187)

**naturalistic observation:** A research method based on recording behavior as it occurs in natural life settings. (p. 37)

**negative reinforcement:** Reinforcement that comes about when the removal or avoidance of a negative event is the consequence of behavior. (p. 212)

**neonatal period (ne˝ō-nā´tal):** The first two weeks of life following birth. (p. 333)

**nerve:** A bundle of long neurons outside the brain and spinal cord. (p. 59)

**neural pruning:** The normal process of selective loss of gray matter in the brain over time, which is thought to improve the efficiency of neural systems by eliminating unnecessary cells. (p. 84)

**neurogenesis (nu´ro jen˝i sis):** The hypothesized growth of new neurons in adult mammals. (p. 84)

**neuron (nu´ron):** An individual nerve cell. (p. 58)

**neuropeptides (nur-o-pep-tidz):** A large group of neurotransmitters sometimes referred to as neuromodulators, because they appear to broadly influence the action of the other neurotransmitters. (p. 64)

**neuroscience perspective:** The viewpoint in psychology that focuses on the nervous system in explaining behavior and mental processes. (p. 16)

**neurotransmitters (nu˝rō-tranz´-mit-erz):** Chemical substances, produced by axons, that transmit messages across the synapse. (p. 62)

**night terrors:** Upsetting nocturnal experiences that occur most often in preschool-age children during deep non-REM sleep. (p. 175)

**nightmares:** Dreams that occur during REM sleep and whose content is exceptionally frightening, sad, angry, or in some other way uncomfortable. (p. 174)

**nocioceptors:** Receptors for stimuli that are experienced as painful. (p. 134)

**norepinephrine (nor´ep-i-nef´rin):** A neurotransmitter believed to be involved in vigilance and attention and released by sympathetic autonomic neurons and the adrenal glands. (p. 64)

**normal distribution:** The symmetrical pattern of scores on a scale in which a majority of the scores are clustered near the center and a minority are at either extreme. (p. 298)

**norms:** Standards (created by the scores of a large group of individuals) used as the basis of comparison for scores on a test. (p. 299)

**novel stimulation:** New or changed experiences. (p. 375)

## O

**obedience:** Doing what one is told to do by people in authority. (p. 613)

**object permanence:** The understanding that objects continue to exist when they are not in view. (p. 334)

**objectivity:** Lack of subjectivity in a test question so that the same score is produced regardless of who does the scoring. (p. 299)

**observational methods:** Methods of personality assessment that involve watching a person's actual behavior in a natural or simulated situation. (p. 488)

**obsessive-compulsive disorders:** Disorders that involve obsessions (anxiety-provoking thoughts that will not go away) and/or compulsions (irresistible urges to engage in specific irrational behaviors). (p. 549)

**occipital lobes (ok-sip´ĭ-tal):** The part of the cerebral cortex, located at the base of the back of the head, that plays an essential role in the processing of sensory information from the eyes. (p. 79)

**Oedipus complex (ed´i-pus):** According to Freud, the unconscious wish of all male children to kill their fathers and sexually possess their mothers. (p. 471)

**olfaction (ol-fak´shun):** The sense of smell. (p. 140)

**olfactory epithelium (ōl-fak´to-rē ep´i-thē´lē-um):** The sheet of receptor cells at the top of the nasal cavity. (p. 141)

**operant conditioning (op´e-rant):** Learning in which the consequences of behavior lead to changes in the probability of its occurrence. (p. 206)

**operational definition:** A definition used in science that is explicitly based on the procedures, or operations, used to measure a scientific phenomenon, including behavior. (p. 34)

**opiates (ō´pē-ats):** Narcotic drugs derived from the opium poppy. (p. 187)

**opponent-process theory of color vision:** The theory of color vision contending that the visual system has two kinds of color processors, which respond to light in either the red-green or yellow-blue ranges of wavelength. (p. 124)

**opponent-process theory of motivation:** Solomon's theory of the learning of new motives based on changes over time in contrasting feelings. (p. 379)

**optic chiasm:** The area in the brain where half of the optic nerve fibers from each eye cross to the opposite side of the brain. (p. 120)

**optic nerve:** The nerve that carries neural messages about vision to the brain. (p. 120)

**optimal level of arousal:** The apparent human need for a comfortable level of stimulation, achieved by acting in ways that increase or decrease it. (p. 376)

**oral aggressive personality:** A personality type in which the person seeks pleasure by being verbally hostile to others. (p. 470)

**oral dependent personality:** A personality type in which the person seeks pleasure through overeating, smoking, and other oral means. (p. 470)

**oral stage:** According to Freud, the first psychosexual stage (from birth to 1 year), in which id gratification is focused on the mouth. (p. 470)

**organ of Corti (kor´tē):** A sensory receptor in the cochlea that transduces sound waves into coded neural impulses. (p. 130)

**orgasm:** The reflexive phase of the sexual response cycle accompanied by peak levels of arousal and pleasure and usually by ejaculation in males. (p. 434)

**oval window:** The membrane of the inner ear that vibrates in response to movement of the stirrup, creating waves in the fluid of the cochlea. (p. 128)

**ovaries (o´vah-rēz):** Female endocrine glands that secrete sex-related hormones and produce ova, or eggs. (pp. 88, 432)

## P

**pancreas (pan´krē-as):** The organ near the stomach that contains the islets of Langerhans. (p. 88)

**panic anxiety disorder:** A pattern of anxiety in which long periods of calm are broken by an intensely uncomfortable attack of anxiety. (p. 546)

**papillae (pah-pil´ē):** Clusters of taste buds on the tongue. (p. 140)

**parallel play:** Playing near but not with another child. (p. 338)

**paranoid schizophrenia (par´ah-noid):** A subtype of schizophrenia in which the individual holds delusions of persecution and grandeur that seriously distort reality. (p. 560)

**parasympathetic nervous system (par˝uh-sim˝-pa-thet´ik):** The division of the autonomic nervous system that promotes bodily maintenance and energy conservation and storage under nonstressful conditions. (p. 69)

**parathormone (par´ah-thor´mōn):** A hormone that regulates ion levels in neurons and controls excitability of the nervous system. (p. 89)

**parathyroid glands (par˝ah-thī´roid):** Four glands embedded in the thyroid that produce parathormone. (p. 89)

**paraventricular nucleus:** A part of the hypothalamus that plays a role in the motive of hunger by regulating the level of blood sugar. (p. 370)

**parietal lobes (pah-rī´e-tal):** The part of the cerebral cortex that is located behind the frontal lobes at the top of the skull and that contains the somatosensory area. (p. 78)

**partial reinforcement effect:** The phenomenon that responses that have been reinforced on variable ratio or variable interval schedules are more difficult to extinguish than responses that have been continuously reinforced. (p. 219)

**participative management:** The practice of involving employees at all levels in management decisions. (p. 654)

**passionate love:** The mixture of romantic, sexual, and other feelings of love. (p. 635)

**peak experiences:** Intensely moving experiences in which the individual feels a sense of unity with the world. (p. 483)

**pedophilia (pe˝do-fil´ē-ah):** The practice of obtaining pleasure from sexual contact with children. (p. 444)

**penis:** The tubular structure that becomes erect during sexual arousal and through which sperm is ejaculated. (p. 433)

**penis envy:** According to Freud, the desire of a girl to possess a penis. (p. 471)

**perception (per-sep´-shun):** The process of organizing and interpreting information received from the outside world. (p. 114)

**perceptual constancy:** The tendency for perceptions of objects to remain relatively unchanged in spite of changes in raw sensations. (p. 146)

**performance tests:** Employee selection tests that resemble the actual manual performance required on a job. (p. 647)

**peripheral nervous system (pĕ-rif´er-al):** The network of nerves that branches from the brain and spinal cord to all parts of the body. (p. 65)

**person perception:** The process of forming impressions of others. (p. 628)

**person × situation interactionism (in˝ter-ak´shun-izm):** The view that behavior is influenced by a combination of the characteristics of both the person and the situation. (p. 478)

**person variables:** All characteristics of an individual that are relatively enduring, such as ways of thinking, beliefs, or physiological reactivity to stress. (p. 515)

**personal unconscious:** According to Jung, the motives, conflicts, and information that are repressed by a person because they are threatening to that individual. (p. 473)

**personality:** The sum total of the typical ways of acting, thinking, and feeling that make each person unique. (p. 462)

**personality disorders:** Psychological disorders that are believed to result from personalities that developed improperly during childhood. (p. 562)

**persuasion:** The process of changing another person's attitudes through arguments and other related means. (p. 617)

**phallic personality (fal´ik):** A personality type caused by fixation in the phallic stage in which the person is selfish, impulsive, and lacking in genuine feeling for others. (p. 471)

**phallic stage (fal´ik):** According to Freud, the third psychosexual stage (from 3 to 6 years), in which gratification is focused on the genitals. (p. 470)

**pheromones:** Chemicals that stimulate receptors in the vomeronasal organ in some animals, influencing some aspects of reproductive behavior. (p. 142)

**phi phenomenon (fī fe-nom´ĕ-non):** The perception of apparent movement between two stationary stimuli. (p. 9)

**phobia:** An intense, irrational fear. (p. 545)

**phonemes (fō´nēm):** The smallest units of sound in a language. (p. 286)

**pineal gland (pin´ē-al):** The endocrine gland that is largely responsible for the regulation of biological rhythms. (p. 89)

**pinna (pin´nah):** The external part of the ear. (p. 128)

**pitch:** The experience of sound vibrations sensed as high or low. (p. 127)

**pituitary gland (pĭ-tu´i-tār´´ē):** The body's master gland, located near the bottom of the brain, whose secretions help regulate the activity of the other glands in the endocrine system. (pp. 87, 373)

**placebo effect:** Changes in behavior produced by a condition in a formal experiment thought to be inert or inactive, such as a placebo pill. (p. 45)

**plasticity:** The ability of parts of the brain, particularly the cerebral cortex, to acquire new functions that partly or completely replace the functions of a damaged part of the brain. (p. 84)

**plateau phase:** High levels of sexual arousal and pleasure that are maintained for variable periods of time. (p. 434)

**pleasure principle:** According to Freud, the attempt of the id to seek immediate pleasure and avoid pain, regardless of how harmful it might be to others. (p. 468)

**polarization:** The tendency for group discussion to make beliefs and attitudes more extreme. (p. 609)

**polarized (pō´lar-īz´d):** The resting state of a neuron, when more negative ions are inside and more positive ions are outside the cell membrane. (p. 60)

**pons (ponz):** The part of the hindbrain that is involved in balance, hearing, and some parasympathetic functions. (p. 72)

**positive reinforcement (rē´in-fors´ment):** Any consequence of behavior that leads to an increase in the probability of its occurrence. (p. 206)

**positron emission tomography (PET):** An imaging technique that reveals the functions of the brain. (p. 71)

**post-traumatic stress disorder (PTSD):** The condition caused by extremely stressful experiences in which the person later experiences anxiety and irritability; has upsetting memories, dreams, and realistic flashbacks of the experience; and tries to avoid anything that reminds him or her of the experience. (p. 548)

**preconscious mind:** That portion of the mind containing information that is not presently conscious but can be easily brought into consciousness. (p. 467)

**prejudice:** A harmful attitude based on inaccurate generalizations about a group of people. (p. 622)

**premature ejaculation:** A male sexual dysfunction in which the individual reaches orgasm and ejaculates sperm too early. (p. 448)

**preoperational stage:** In Piaget's theory, the period of cognitive development from ages 2 to 7. (p. 337)

**pressure:** Stress that arises from the threat of negative events. (p. 503)

**primacy effect:** The tendency for first impressions to heavily influence opinions about other people. (p. 629)

**primary motives:** Human motives for things that are necessary for survival, such as food, water, and warmth. (p. 369)

**primary process thinking:** According to Freud, the attempt by the id to satisfy its needs by forming a wish-fulfilling mental image of the desired object. (p. 468)

**primary reinforcers:** Innate positive reinforcers that do not have to be acquired through learning. (p. 208)

**primary sex characteristics:** Ovulation and menstruation in females and production of sperm in males. (p. 341)

**proactive interference (prō-ak´tiv):** Interference created by memories from prior learning. (p. 250)

**problem solving:** The cognitive process through which information is used to reach a goal that is blocked by some obstacle. (p. 279)

**procedural memory:** Memory for motor movements and skills. (p. 241)

**progressive relaxation training:** A method of learning to deeply relax the muscles of the body. (pp. 523, 583)

**Project Follow Through:** A federally sponsored program designed to help educate economically disadvantaged children. (p. 675)

**projective test:** A test that uses ambiguous stimuli designed to reveal the contents of the client's unconscious mind. (p. 488)

**prostate gland:** One of the structures that produce fluid for semen. (p. 433)

**proximity principle (prok´sim´´-i-tee):** The Gestalt principle of perception that states that parts of a visual stimulus that are close together will be perceived as belonging together. (p. 144)

**psychoanalysis (sī´´kō-ah-nal´i-sis):** A method of psychotherapy developed by Freud based on his belief that the root of all psychological problems is unconscious conflicts among the id, the ego, and the superego. (p. 573)

**psychoanalytic theory:** Freud's theory that the origin of personality lies in the balance among the id, the ego, and the superego. (pp. 13, 466, 573)

**psychological motives:** Motives related to the individual's happiness and well-being, but not to survival. (p. 375)

**psychology:** The science of behavior and mental processes. (p. 5)

**psychometrics:** The perspective in psychology founded by Binet that focuses on the measurement of mental functions. (p. 11)

**psychophysics (sī´´kō-fiz´iks):** A specialty area of psychology that studies sensory limits, sensory adaptation, and related topics. (p. 115)

**psychosexual stages:** In the personality theory of Sigmund Freud, developmental periods during which the sexual energy of the id finds different sources of satisfaction. (p. 470)

**psychosurgery (sī´´kō-ser´jer-ē):** A medical therapy that involves operating on the brain in an attempt to alleviate some types of mental disorders. (p. 596)

**psychotherapy (sī-kō-ther´ah-pē):** A form of therapy in which a trained professional uses methods based on psychological theories to help a person with psychological problems. (p. 572)

**psychotropic drugs:** The various classes of drugs, including stimulants, depressants, and hallucinogens, that alter conscious experience. (p. 181)

**puberty (pū´ber-tē):** The point in development at which the individual is first physically capable of sexual reproduction. (p. 340)

**punishment:** A negative consequence of a behavior, which leads to a decrease in the frequency of the behavior that produces it. (p. 213)

**pupil (pyoo´pil):** The opening of the iris. (p. 119)

**Q**

**quantitative measures (kwon´ti-tā-tiv):** Capable of being measured in numerical terms. (p. 38)

**R**

**random assignment:** The requirement that participants be assigned randomly to experimental conditions in formal experiments rather than in a systematic way. (p. 44)

**rape:** The act of forcing sexual activity on an unwilling person. (p. 442)

**rape trauma syndrome:** The effects of rape on the emotions, behavior, and well-being of many victims long after the rape has occurred. (p. 443)

**ratio IQ:** The intelligence quotient based on the ratio between the person's mental age and chronological age. (p. 296)

**reality principle:** According to Freud, the attempt by the ego to find safe, realistic ways of meeting the needs of the id. (p. 469)

**recall method:** A measure of memory based on the ability to retrieve information from long-term memory with few cues. (p. 244)

**receptor sites:** Sites on the neuron that receive the neurotransmitter substance. (p. 63)

**recessive gene:** The gene that produces a trait in an individual only when the same recessive gene has been inherited from both parents. (p. 93)

**reciprocal determination (re-sip´´ro-kal):** Bandura's observation that the individual's behavior and the social learning environment continually influence one another. (p. 476)

**recognition method:** A measure of memory based on the ability to select correct information from among the options provided. (p. 244)

**reconstruction (schema) theory:** The theory that information stored in LTM sometimes changes over time to become more consistent with our beliefs, knowledge, and expectations. (p. 251)

**reflection (re-flek-shun):** A technique in humanistic psychotherapy in which the therapist reflects the emotions of the client to help clients clarify their feelings. (p. 580)

**refractory period:** The period of time following orgasm during which males are incapable of sexual arousal. (p. 435)

**rehearsal:** Mental repetition of information for retention in short-term memory. (p. 238)

**relearning method:** A measure of memory based on the length of time it takes to relearn forgotten material. (p. 244)

**reliability:** A test's ability to produce similar scores if the test is administered on different occasions or by different examiners. (p. 299)

**REM sleep:** Rapid-eye-movement sleep, characterized by movement of the eyes under the lids; often accompanies dreams. (p. 167)

**replication:** Repeating studies based on the scientific principle that the results of studies should be doubted until the same results have been found in similar studies by other researchers. (p. 35)

**representativeness heuristic:** The strategy of making judgments about the unknown on the assumption that it is similar to what we know. (p. 280)

**repression:** Sigmund Freud's theory that forgetting occurs because the conscious mind often deals with unpleasant information by pushing it into unconsciousness. (pp. 255, 468)

**resistance:** Any form of patient opposition to the process of psychoanalysis. (p. 575)

**resolution phase:** The stage in the sexual response cycle following orgasm when arousal and pleasure diminish. (p. 434)

**response prevention:** The prevention of avoidance responses to ensure that the individual sees that the negative consequence will not occur to speed up the extinction of avoidance responses. (p. 220)

**retarded ejaculation:** A condition in which a male does not ejaculate despite adequate sexual stimulation. (p. 110)

**reticular formation (reh-tik´ū-lur´):** Sets of neurons in the medulla and pons from which neurons project down the spinal cord to play a role in maintaining muscle tone and cardiac reflexes and upward throughout the cerebral cortex where they influence wakefulness, arousal level, and attention. (pp. 72, 376)

**retina (ret´i-nah):** The area at the back of the eye on which images are formed and that contains the rods and cones. (p. 119)

**retroactive interference (ret˝rō-ak´tiv):** Interference created by memories from later learning. (p. 250)

**retrograde amnesia (ret´rō-grād):** A memory disorder characterized by an inability to retrieve old long-term memories, generally for a specific period of time extending back from the beginning of the disorder. (p. 261)

**reversibility (re-ver´sĭ-bil-ĭ-tē):** The concept understood by concrete operational children that logical propositions can be reversed (if 2 + 3 = 5, then 5 − 3 = 2). (p. 339)

**rods:** The 125 million cells located outside the center of the retina that transduce light waves into neural impulses, thereby coding information about light and dark. (p. 119)

**role playing:** A therapeutic technique in which the therapist and client act as if they were people in problematic situations. (p. 584)

**rooting reflex:** An automatic response in which an infant turns its head toward stimulation on the cheek. (p. 333)

**round window:** The membrane that relieves pressure from the vibrating waves in the cochlear fluid. (p. 129)

## S

**saccule, utricle (sak´ūl ū´tre-k´l):** Fluid-filled sacs of the vestibular organ that inform the brain about the body's orientation. (p. 132)

**sample:** A group of human or nonhuman research participants studied to learn about an entire population of human beings or animals. (p. 35)

**schizoid personality disorder (skiz´oid):** A personality disorder characterized by blunted emotions, lack of interest in social relationships, and withdrawal into a solitary existence. (p. 562)

**schizophrenia (skiz˝o-fren´e-ah):** A psychological disorder involving cognitive disturbance (delusions and hallucinations), disorganization, and reduced enjoyment and interests. (p. 559)

**school psychologists:** Psychologists who aid schools by testing children to determine eligibility for placement in special education programs and who consult with teachers and parents. (p. 673)

**science:** Approach to knowledge based on systematic observation. (p. 5)

**scientific method:** Method of studying nature based on systematic observation and rules of evidence. (p. 34)

**serotonin:** The loose skin sac that encloses the testes. (p. 433)

**secondary reinforcers:** Learned positive reinforcers. (p. 208)

**secondary sex characteristics:** Development of the breasts and hips in females; growth of the testes, broadening of the shoulders, lowered voice, and growth of the penis and facial hair in males; and growth of pubic and other body hair in both sexes. (p. 341)

**sedatives:** Depressants that in mild doses produce a state of calm relaxation. (p. 187)

**self:** According to humanists, the person one thinks one is. (p. 481)

**self-actualization:** According to Maslow, the seldomly reached full result of the inner-directed drive of humans to grow, improve, and use their potential to the fullest. (pp. 383, 482)

**self-concept:** Our subjective perception of who we are and what we are like. (p. 480)

**self-efficacy:** According to Bandura, the perception of being capable of achieving one's goals. (p. 477)

**self-regulation:** According to Bandura, the process of cognitively reinforcing and punishing our own behavior, depending on whether it meets our personal standards. (p. 478)

**semantic content:** The meaning in symbols, such as language. (p. 285)

**semantic memory (se-man´tik):** Memory for meaning without reference to the time and place of learning. (p. 241)

**semen:** The fluid that contains sperm cells. (p. 433)

**semicircular canals (sem˝ē-ser´kū-lar):** Three nearly circular tubes in the vestibular organ that inform the brain about tilts of the head and body. (p. 132)

**seminal vesicle:** One of the structures that produce fluid for semen. (p. 433)

**semipermeable (sem˝e-per´mē-ah-b´l):** A surface that allows some, but not all, particles to pass through. (p. 60)

**sensation (sen-sā´shun):** The process of receiving, translating, and transmitting messages from the outside world to the brain. (p. 114)

**sense organs:** Organs that receive stimuli. (p. 114)

**sensorimotor stage:** In Piaget's theory, the period of cognitive development from birth to 2 years. (p. 334)

**sensory adaptation:** Weakened magnitude of a sensation resulting from prolonged presentation of the stimulus. (p. 115)

**sensory receptor cells:** Cells in sense organs that translate messages into neural impulses that are sent to the brain. (p. 114)

**sensory register:** The first stage of memory, in which an exact image of each sensory experience is held briefly until it can be processed. (p. 237)

**separation anxiety:** The distress experienced by infants when they are separated from their caregivers. (p. 337)

**septal area:** A part of the limbic system that processes cognitive information in emotion. (p. 74)

**serial position effect:** The fact that immediate recall of items listed in a fixed order is often better for items at the beginning and end of the list than for those in the middle. (p. 244)

**serotonin (ser´ uh-to˝ nin):** A neurotransmitter used by systems of neurons believed to regulate sleep, dreaming, appetite, anxiety, depression, and the inhibition of violence. (p. 63)

**sex:** The distinction between male and female based on biological characteristics. (p. 410)

**sexual aversion disorder:** A condition in which a person fearfully avoids sexual behavior. (p. 446)

**sexual dysfunction:** Inability to engage successfully or comfortably in normal sexual activities. (p. 446)

**sexual harassment:** Unwanted sexual advances, comments, or any other form of coercive sexual behavior by others. (p. 444)

**sexual masochism (mas´o-kizm):** A condition in which receiving pain is sexually exciting. (p. 442)

**sexual orientation:** The tendency to prefer romantic and sexual partners of the same or different sex. (p. 410)

**sexual sadism (sād´izm):** The practice of obtaining sexual pleasure by inflicting pain on others. (p. 442)

**sexually transmitted diseases (STDs):** Physical diseases, such as syphilis and AIDS, that are transmitted through sexual contact. (p. 449)

**shaping:** A strategy of positively reinforcing behaviors that are successively more similar to desired behaviors. (p. 211)

**short-term memory (STM):** The second stage of memory, in which five to nine bits of information can be stored for brief periods of time. (p. 237)

**similarity principle:** The Gestalt principle of perception that states that parts of a visual stimulus that are similar will be perceived as belonging together. (p. 144)

**simulated management task:** A contrived task requiring managerial skills that is given to candidates for management positions to evaluate their potential as managers. (p. 649)

**situational attribution:** An explanation for behavior that is based on an external cause. (p. 630)

**situationism (sit˝ū-ā´shun-izm):** The view that behavior is not consistent but is strongly influenced by different situations. (p. 478)

**Skinner box:** A cage for animals, equipped with a response lever and a food tray dispenser, used in research on operant conditioning. (p. 211)

**sleep apnea:** The sudden interruption of breathing during sleep. (p. 175)

**sleep disorders:** Disturbances of sleep. (p. 175)

**sleeper effects:** According to Hovland, the potential for low-credibility speakers to influence opinion after a period of time. (p. 617)

**sleep-inhibiting system:** An area of the brain that inhibits sleep. (p. 173)

**sleep-promoting systems:** Two areas of the brain that lead to sleep. (p. 173)

**sleeptalking:** Talking during any phase of the sleep cycle. (p. 175)

**sleepwalking:** Walking and carrying on complicated activities during the deepest part of non-REM sleep. (p. 175)

**social facilitation:** An effect in which working in a group improves one's performance on individual projects. (p. 608)

**social learning theory:** The viewpoint that the most important parts of our behavior are learned from other persons in society—family, friends, and culture. (pp. 13, 476)

**social loafing:** The tendency of members of groups to work less hard when group performance is measured than when individual performance is measured. (p. 608)

**social norms:** Guidelines provided by every culture for judging acceptable and unacceptable behavior. (p. 611)

**social phobia:** A phobic fear of social interactions, particularly those with strangers and those in which the person might be viewed negatively. (p. 545)

**social psychology:** The branch of psychology that studies individuals as they interact with others. (p. 606)

**social roles:** Culturally determined guidelines that tell people what behavior is expected of them. (p. 611)

**social-role theory of gender differences:** The theory that the opportunities and restrictions inherent in women's and men's different social roles create psychological gender differences. (p. 419)

**social skills training:** The use of techniques of operant conditioning to teach social skills to persons who lack them. (p. 584)

**social support:** The role played by friends and relatives in providing advice, assistance, and someone in whom to confide private feelings. (p. 513)

**sociocultural perspective:** The theory of psychology that states that it is necessary to understand one's culture, ethnic identity, and other sociocultural factors to fully understand a person. (p. 17)

**solitary play:** Playing alone. (p. 338)

**somatic nervous system (sō-mat´ik):** The division of the peripheral nervous system that carries messages from the sense organs to the central nervous system and from the central nervous system to the skeletal muscles. (p. 66)

**somatization disorders (sō˝mah-ti-zā´shun):** Intensely and chronically uncomfortable psychological conditions that involve numerous symptoms of somatic (body) illnesses without physical cause. (p. 549)

**somatoform disorders (sō˝mah´to-form):** Disorders in which the individual experiences the symptoms of physical health problems that have psychological rather than physical causes. (p. 549)

**somatoform pain disorders:** Somatoform disorders in which the individual experiences a relatively specific and chronic pain that has a psychological rather than physical cause. (p. 551)

**somatosensory area:** The strip of parietal cortex running parallel to the motor area of the frontal lobes that plays a role in body senses. (p. 78)

**sound waves:** Cyclical changes in air pressure that constitute the stimulus for hearing. (p. 126)

**specialized end bulbs:** Sensory receptor cells that detect pressure. (p. 133)

**specific phobia:** A phobic fear of one relatively specific thing. (p. 545)

**spinal cord:** The nerve fibers in the spinal column. (p. 58)

**spontaneous recovery:** A temporary increase in the strength of a conditioned response, which is likely to occur during extinction after the passage of time. (p. 220)

**stage:** One of several time periods in development that is qualitatively distinct from the periods that come before and after. (p. 326)

**stage theory of memory:** A model of memory based on the idea that we store information in three separate but linked memories. (p. 236)

**standardization:** Administering a test in the same way to all individuals. (p. 298)

**stereochemical theory:** The theory that different odor receptors can be stimulated only by molecules of a specific size and shape that fit them like a key in a lock. (p. 142)

**stereotype:** An inaccurate generalization on which a prejudice is based. (p. 622)

**stimulants:** Drugs that increase the activity of motivational centers in the brain, providing a sense of energy and well-being. (p. 184)

**stimulus (stim´ū-lus):** Any aspect of the outside world that directly influences our behavior or conscious experience. (p. 114)

**stimulus discrimination:** The tendency for responses to occur more often in the presence of one stimulus than others. (p. 216)

**stimulus generalization:** The tendency for similar stimuli to elicit the same response. (p. 217)

**stimulus incorporation:** Stimuli that occur during sleep that are incorporated into dreams either directly or in altered form. (p. 172)

**stress:** Any event or circumstance that strains or exceeds an individual's ability to cope. (p. 500)

**stroke:** A rupture or blockage of a blood vessel in the brain that interrupts blood flow and often results in the destruction of a part of the brain. (p. 76)

**structuralism (struk´tūr-al-izm):** The nineteenth-century school of psychology that sought to determine the structure of the mind through controlled introspection. (p. 8)

**structuring:** The activities of managers that organize and direct the work of employees. (p. 654)

**subjective reality:** Each person's unique perception of reality that, according to humanists, plays a key role in organizing our personalities. (p. 480)

**sublimation (sub˝li-mā´shun):** According to Freud, a form of displacement in which a socially desirable goal is substituted for a socially harmful goal; the best form of displacement for society as a whole. (p. 469)

**superego:** According to Freud, that part of the mind that opposes the desires of the id by enforcing moral restrictions and by striving to attain perfection. (p. 469)

**surface structure:** The superficial spoken or written structure of a statement. (p. 286)

**survey method:** A research method that uses interviews and questionnaires with individuals. (p. 36)

**symbolization:** In Rogers' theory, the process of representing experience, thoughts, or feelings in mental symbols of which we are aware. (p. 481)

**sympathetic nervous system (sim˝pa-thet´ik):** The division of the autonomic nervous system that prepares the body to respond to psychological or physical stress. (p. 67)

**synapse (sin-aps´):** The space between the axon of one neuron and another neuron. (p. 62)

**synaptic facilitation:** The process by which neural activity causes structural changes in the synapses that facilitate more efficient learning and memory. (p. 257)

**synaptic gap:** The small space between two neurons at a synapse. (p. 62)

**synaptic knobs (si-nap´tik):** The knoblike tips of axons. (p. 62)

**synaptic vesicles:** Tiny vessels containing stored quantities of the neurotransmitter substance held in the synaptic knobs of the axon. (p. 62)

**syntax (sin´taks):** The grammatical rules of a language. (p. 287)

**syphilis:** A sexually transmitted disease caused by spirochete bacteria. (p. 449)

**systematic desensitization:** A behavior therapy method in which the client is taught not to fear phobic stimuli by learning to stay relaxed in the presence of successively more threatening stimuli. (p. 583)

### T

**tacit intelligence:** The practical knowledge and skills needed to deal with everyday problems that are usually not taught in school. (p. 299)

**tactile discs (tak´til):** Sensory receptor cells that detect pressure. (p. 133)

**taste cells:** The sensory receptor cells for gustation located in the taste buds. (p. 140)

**telegraphic speech:** The abbreviated speech of 2-year-olds. (p. 335)

**temporal lobes:** The part of the cerebral cortex that extends back from the area of the temples beneath the frontal and parietal lobes and that contains areas involved in the sense of hearing and understanding language. (p. 78)

**testes (tes´tēz):** Male endocrine glands that secrete sex-related hormones and produce sperm cells. (pp. 88, 432)

**testosterone (tes-tos´ter-ōn):** A male sex hormone. (p. 89)

**thalamus (thal´ah-mus):** The part of the forebrain that primarily routes sensory messages to appropriate parts of the brain. (p. 74)

**theories:** Tentative explanations of facts and relationships in sciences. (pp. 5, 34)

**thyroid gland (thī´roid):** The gland below the voice box that regulates metabolism. (p. 89)

**thyroxin (thī-rok´sin):** A hormone produced by the thyroid that is necessary for proper mental development in children and helps determine weight and level of activity in adults. (p. 89)

**timbre (tim´ber, tam´br):** The characteristic quality of a sound as determined by the complexity of the sound wave. (p. 127)

**traits:** Relatively enduring patterns of behavior (thinking, acting, and feeling) that are relatively consistent across situations. (p. 462)

**transcendental state:** An altered state of consciousness, sometimes achieved during meditation, that is said to transcend normal human experience. (p. 178)

**transduction (trans-duk´shun):** The translation of energy from one form to another. (p. 114)

**transductive reasoning (trans-duk´tiv):** Errors in understanding cause-and-effect relationships that are commonly made by preoperational children. (p. 337)

**transference (trans-fer´ens):** The phenomenon in psychoanalysis in which the patient comes to feel and act toward the therapist in ways that resemble how he or she feels and acts toward other significant adults. (p. 575)

**transsexualism (trans-seks´u-ah-lizm):** A condition in which an individual feels trapped in the body of the wrong sex. (p. 441)

**transvestism (trans-ves´tizm):** The practice of obtaining sexual pleasure by dressing in the clothes of the opposite sex. (p. 441)

**trial and error:** The random application of one possible solution after another. (p. 280)

**trichromatic theory (trī˝krō-mat´ik):** The theory of color vision contending that the eye has three different kinds of cones, each of which responds to light of one range of wavelength. (p. 122)

**Type A personality:** The pattern of behavior characterized most by intense competitiveness, hostility, overwork, and a sense of time urgency. (p. 515)

### U

**unconditioned response (UCR):** An unlearned, inborn reaction to an unconditioned stimulus. (p. 201)

**unconditioned stimulus (UCS):** A stimulus that can elicit a response without any learning. (p. 201)

**unconscious mind:** The part of the mind of which we can never be directly aware; the storehouse of primitive instinctual motives and of memories and emotions that have been repressed. (pp. 13, 163, 468)

**uterus:** The muscular structure that carries the fetus during pregnancy. (p. 431)

### V

**vaginismus (vaj˝i-niz´mus):** A female sexual dysfunction in which the individual experiences involuntary contractions of the vaginal walls, making the vagina too narrow to allow the penis to enter comfortably. (p. 447)

**validity:** The extent to which a test measures what it's supposed to measure. (p. 299)

**variable:** A factor whose numerical value can vary. (p. 38)

**variable interval schedule:** A reinforcement schedule in which the reinforcer is given following the first response occurring after a variable amount of time. (p. 210)

**variable ratio schedule:** A reinforcement schedule in which the reinforcer is given after a varying number of responses have been made. (p. 209)

**vas deferens:** The structure that carries sperm from the epididymis toward the outside of the body during ejaculation. (p. 433)

**ventromedial hypothalamus:** A part of the hypothalamus involved in inhibiting eating when sufficient food has been consumed (the satiety center). (p. 370)

**vestibular organ (ves-tib´ū-lar):** The sensory structures in the inner ear that provide the brain with information about orientation and movement of the head and body. (p. 132)

**vicarious punishment:** Observed punishment of the behavior of a model, which also decreases the probability of the same behavior in the observer. (p. 227)

**vicarious reinforcement (vī-kar´ē-us):** Observed reinforcement of the behavior of a model, which also increases the probability of the same behavior in the observer. (p. 227)

**visual acuity (vizh´u-al ah-ku´i-tē):** Clarity and sharpness of vision. (p. 120)

**visual illusion:** Visual stimuli in which the cues used in visual perception create a false perception. (p. 149)

**vomeronasal organ:** An organ in the nasal cavity of many animals that contains receptors for pheromones. (p. 142)

**voyeurism (voi´yer-izm):** The practice of obtaining sexual pleasure by watching members of the opposite sex undressing or engaging in sexual activities. (p. 442)

**vulva:** The external genital structures of the female. (p. 432)

### W

**wavelength:** The frequency of light waves, which determines the hue we perceive. (p. 119)

**Weber's law:** A law stating that the amount of change in a stimulus needed to detect a difference is in direct proportion to the intensity of the original stimulus. (p. 116)

**Wernicke's aphasia:** A form of aphasia in which persons can speak fluently (but nonsensically) and cannot make sense out of language spoken to them by others. (p. 79)

**Wernicke's area:** The language area of the cortex that plays an essential role in understanding spoken language. (p. 78)

### Y

**Yerkes-Dodson law:** A law stating that effective performance is more likely if the level of arousal is suitable for the activity. (p. 376)

### Z

**zygote (zī´gōt):** The stable cell resulting from fertilization; in humans, it has 46 chromosomes—23 from the sperm and 23 from the ovum. (p. 92)

# References

## A

Abbey, A. (1982). Sex differences in attributions for friendly behavior: Do males misperceive females' friendliness? *Journal of Personality and Social Psychology, 42,* 830–838.

Abbey, A., & Melby, C. (1986). The effects of nonverbal cues on gender differences in perceptions of sexual intent. *Sex Roles, 15,* 283–298.

Abbott, B. B., Schoen, L. S., & Badia, P. (1984). Predictable and unpredictable shock: Behavioral measures of aversion and physiological measures of stress. *Psychological Bulletin, 96,* 45–71.

Abel, G., Barlow, D., Blanchard, E., & Guild, D. (1977). Components of rapists' arousal. *Archives of General Psychiatry, 34,* 895–908.

Abhold, J. (1992). Unpublished doctoral dissertation, University of Arkansas, cited in Loftus, E. F. (1993). The reality of repressed memories. *American Psychologist, 48,* 518–537.

Ackerman, D. (1991). *A natural history of the senses.* New York: Vintage Books.

Ackerson, J., Scogin, F., McKendree-Smith, N., & Lyman, R. D. (1998). Cognitive bibliotherapy for mild and moderate adolescent depressive symptomatology. *Journal of Consulting and Clinical Psychology, 66,* 685–690.

Acocella, J. (1999). *Creating hysteria: Women and multiple personality disorder.* San Francisco: Jossey-Bass.

Adams, D. B., Gold, A. R., & Burt, A. D. (1978). Rise in female-initiated sexual activity at ovulation and its suppression by oral contraceptives. *New England Journal of Medicine, 299,* 1145–1150.

Adams, J. (1965). Inequity in social exchange. In L. Berkowitz (Ed.), *Advances in experimental social psychology* (Vol. 2). New York: Academic Press.

Adams, P. R., & Adams, G. R. (1984). Mount Saint Helens' ashfall: Evidence for a disaster stress reaction. *American Psychologist, 39,* 252–260.

Adelson, J. (1979, February). Adolescence and the generalization gap. *Psychology Today,* pp. 33–38.

Ader, R. (Ed.). (1981). *Psychoneuroimmunology.* New York: Academic Press.

Ader, R., & Cohen, N. (1981). Conditioned immunopharmacologic responses. In R. Ader (Ed.), *Psychoneuroimmunology.* New York: Academic Press.

Ader, R., & Cohen, N. (1993). Psychoneuroimmunology: Conditioning and stress. *Annual Review of Psychology, 44,* 53–85.

Adolphs, R., Damasio, H., Tranel, D., Cooper, G., & Damasio, A. R. (2000). The role of somatosensory cortices in the visual recognition of emotion as revealed by three-dimensional lesion mapping. *Journal of Neuroscience, 20,* 2683–2690.

Adolphs, R., Tranel, D., & Denburg, N. (2000). Impaired emotional declarative memory following unilateral amygdala damage. *Learning and Memory, 7,* 180–186.

Agras, W. S., & others. (1992). Pharmacologic and cognitive-behavioral treatment for bulimia nervosa: A controlled comparison. *American Journal of Psychiatry, 149,* 82–87.

Ainsworth, M. D. S. (1979). Infant-mother attachment. *American Psychologist, 34,* 932–937.

Aizawa, M. (1994). Molecular interfacing for protein molecular devices and neurodevices. *IEEE Engineering in Medicine and Biology Magazine, 13*(1), 94.

Alaimo, K., Olson, C., & Frongillo, E. A. (2001). Food insufficiency and American school-aged children's cognitive, academic, and psychological development. *Pediatrics, 108,* 44–53.

Albert, K. A., Hemmings, H. C., Adamo, A. I. B., Potkin, S. G., Akbarian, S., Sandman, C. A., Cotman, C. W., Bunney, W. E., & Greengard, P. (2002). Evidence for decreased darpp-32 in the prefrontal cortex of patients with schizophrenia. *Archives of General Psychiatry, 59,* 705–712.

Allen, J. J., Iacono, W. G., Laravuso, J. J., & Dunn, L. A. (1995). An event-related potential investigation of posthypnotic recognition amnesia. *Journal of Abnormal Psychology, 104,* 421–430.

Allen, K. E., Hart, R. M., Buell, J. S., Harris, F. R., & Wolf, M. M. (1964). Effects of social reinforcement on isolate behavior of a nursery school child. *Child Development, 35,* 511–518.

Allen, L. S., & Gorski, R. A. (1992). Sexual orientation and the size of the anterior commissure in the human brain. *Proceedings of the National Academy of Sciences USA, 89,* 7199–7202.

Alloy, L. B., Abramson, L. Y., & Francis, E. L. (1999). Do negative cognitive styles confer vulnerability to depression? *Current Directions in Psychological Science 8,* 128–132.

Allport, G. W. (1937). *Personality: A psychological interpretation.* New York: Holt, Rinehart & Winston.

Allport, G. W. (1961). *Pattern and growth in personality.* New York: Holt, Rinehart & Winston.

Allport, G. W., & Odbert, H. S. (1936). Trait names: A psycholexical study. *Psychological Monographs, 47* (211), 1–171.

Altschule, M. D. (1965). *Roots of modern psychiatry* (2nd ed.). New York: Grune & Stratton.

American Psychiatric Association. (1994). *Diagnostic and statistical manual of mental disorders* (4th ed.). Washington, DC: Author.

American Psychological Association. (1982). *Ethical principles in the conduct of research with human participants.* Washington, DC: Author.

American Psychological Association. (1990). Ethical principles of psychologists. *American Psychologist, 45,* 390–395.

American Psychological Association. (1993). Guidelines for providers of psychological services to ethnic, linguistic, and culturally diverse populations. *American Psychologist, 48,* 45–48.

Amoore, J. E., Johnston, J. W., & Rubin, M. (1964, February). The stereo-chemical theory of odor. *Scientific American.*

Anastasi, A. (1987). *Psychological testing* (6th ed.). New York: Macmillan.

Ancoli-Israel, S., Kripke, D. F., & Mason, W. (1987). Characteristics of obstructive and central sleep apnea in the elderly: An interim report. *Biological Psychiatry, 22,* 741–750.

Anderson, C. A. (1989). Temperature and aggression: Ubiquitous effects of heat on occurrence of human violence. *Psychological Bulletin, 106,* 74–96.

Anderson, C. A. (2001). Heat and violence. *Psychological Science, 10,* 33–38.

Anderson, C. A., & Bushman, B. J. (2001). Effects of violent video games on aggressive behavior, aggressive cognition, aggressive affect, physiological arousal, and prosocial behavior: A meta-analytic review of the scientific literature. *Psychological Science, 12,* 353–359.

Anderson, C. A., Bushman, B. J., & Groom, R. W. (1997). Hot years and serious and deadly assault: Empirical tests of the heat hypothesis. *Journal of Personality and Social Psychology, 73,* 1213–1223.

Anderson, C. A., Lindsay, J. J., & Bushman, B. J. (1999). Research in the psychological laboratory: Truth or triviality? *Current Directions in Psychological Science, 8,* 3–9.

Anderson, D., Huston, A., Althea, C., Schmitt, K., Linebarger, D., & Wright, J. (2001). Early childhood television viewing and adolescent behavior: The recontact study. *Monographs of the Society for Research in Child Development, 66,* 1–158.

Anderson, K. E., Lytton, H., & Romney, D. M. (1986). Mother's interactions with normal and conduct-disordered boys: Who affects whom? *Developmental Psychology, 22,* 604–609.

Anderson, M. (2001). Annotation: Conceptions of intelligence. *Journal of Child Psychology and Psychiatry, 42,* 287–298.

Andreasen, N. C. (1999). A unitary model of schizophrenia: Bleuler's "fragmented phrene" as schizoencephaly. *Archives of General Psychiatry, 56,* 781–787.

Andreasen, N. C., Arndt, S., Alliger, R., Miller, D., & Flaum, M. (1995). Symptoms of schizophrenia: Methods, meanings, and mechanisms. *Archives of General Psychiatry, 52,* 341–351.

Andrews, B., Brewin, C. R., Rose, S., & Kirk, M. (2000). Predicting PTSD symptoms in victims of violent crime: The role of shame, anger, and childhood abuse. *Journal of Abnormal Psychology, 109,* 69–73.

**Angoff, W. H.** (1988). The nature-nurture debate, aptitudes, and group differences. *American Psychologist, 43,* 713–720.

**Annon, J.** (1984). Simple behavioral treatment of sexual problems. In J. M. Swanson & K. Forrect (Eds.), *Men's reproductive health.* New York: Springer.

**Antoni, M. H., & others.** (1990). Psychoneuroimmunology and HIV-1. *Journal of Consulting and Clinical Psychology, 58,* 38–49.

**Antoni, M. H., Cruess, D. G., Cruess, S., Lutgendorf, S., Kumar, M., Ironson, G., Klimas, N., Fletcher, M. A., & Schneiderman, N.** (2000). Cogitive-behavioral stress management intervention effects on anxiety, 24-hr urinary norepinephrine output, and T-cytotoxic suppressor cells over time among symptomatic HIV-infected gay men. *Journal of Consulting and Clinical Psychology, 68,* 31–45.

**Aral, S. O., & Holmes, K. K.** (1991). Sexually transmitted diseases in the AIDS era. *Scientific American,* pp. 62–70.

**Ardrey, R.** (1966). *The territorial imperative.* New York: Atheneum.

**Arndt, S., Andreasen, N. C., Flaum, M., Miller, D., & Nopoulos, P.** (1995). A longitudinal study of symptom dimensions in schizophrenia: Prediction and patterns of change. *Archives of General Psychiatry, 52,* 352–360.

**Arnett, J. J.** (1999). Adolescent storm and stress, reconsidered. *American Psychologist, 54,* 317–326.

**Arnetz, B., & others.** (1987). Immune function in unemployed women. *Psychosomatic Medicine, 49,* 3–18.

**Arnold, M. B.** (1960). *Emotion and personality* (2 Vols.). New York: Columbia University Press.

**Aronson, E.** (1995). *The social animal* (6th ed.). San Francisco: W. H. Freeman.

**Aronson, E., & Golden, B.** (1962). The effect of relevant and irrelevant aspects of communicator credibility on opinion change. *Journal of Personality, 30,* 135–146.

**Aronson, E., Willerman, B., & Floyd, J.** (1966). The effect of a pratfall on increasing interpersonal attractiveness. *Psychonomic Science, 4,* 227–228.

**Asarnow, J., Glynn, S., Pynoos, R. S., Nahum, J., Guthrie, D., Cantwell, D. P., & Franklin, B.** (1999). When the earth stops shaking: Earthquake sequelae among children diagnosed for pre-earthquake psychopathology. *Journal of the American Academy of Child and Adolescent Psychiatry, 38,* 1016–1023.

**Asch, S.** (1946). Forming impressions of personality. *Journal of Abnormal and Social Psychology, 41,* 258–290.

**Asch, S.** (1956). Studies of independence and conformity. A minority of one against a unanimous majority. *Psychological Monographs, 70* (9, Whole No. 416).

**Aschoff, J.** (1981). *Handbook of behavioral neurobiology: Vol. 4. Biological rhythms.* New York: Plenum.

**Association for Advancement of Behavior Therapy.** (1978). *Ethical issues for human services* (pamphlet). New York: Author.

**Astin, A. W., Korn, W. S., & Berz, E. R.** (1991). *The American freshman: National norms for 1990.* Los Angeles: American Council on Education.

**Atkeson, B. M., Forehand, R. L., & Rickard, K. M.** (1982). The effects of divorce on children. In B. B. Lahey & A. E. Kazdin (Eds.),

*Advances in clinical child psychology* (Vol. 5). New York: Plenum.

**Atkinson, R. C., & Shiffrin, R. M.** (1968). Human memory: A proposed system and its control processes. In K. W. Spence & J. T. Spence (Eds.), *The psychology of learning and motivation* (Vol. 2). New York: Academic Press.

**Atkinson, R. K.** (2002). Optimizing learning from examples using animated pedagogical agents. *Journal of Educational Psychology, 94,* 416–427.

**Augustine, D. K., Gruber, K. D., & Hanson, L. R.** (1990). Cooperation works. *Educational Leadership, 47,* 4–11.

**Ausubel, D. P.** (1960). The use of advance organizers in the learning and retention of meaningful verbal material. *Journal of Educational Psychology, 51,* 267–272.

**Avissar, S., Nechamkin, Y., Roitman, G., & Schreiber, G.** (1997). Reduced G protein functions and immunoreactive levels in mononuclear leukocytes of patients with depression. *Archives of General Psychiatry, 154,* 211–217.

**Ayllon, T., & Haughton, E.** (1964). Modification of the symptomatic verbal behaviour of mental patients. *Behaviour Research and Therapy, 2,* 87–97.

**B**

**Baare, W., van Oel, C., Hulshoff Pol, H., Schnack, H., Durston, S., Sitskoorn, M., & Kahn, R.** (2001). Volumes of brain structures in twins discordant for schizophrenia. *Archives of General Psychiatry, 58,* 33–40.

**Baddeley, A.** (1992). Working memory. *Science, 255,* 550–559.

**Baddeley, A.** (1998). Recent developments in working memory. *Current Opinion in Neurobiology, 8,* 234–238.

**Baddeley, A.** (2001). Is working memory still working? *American Psychologist, 56,* 851–864.

**Baddeley, A. D.** (1999). *Essentials of human memory.* Hove, England: Psychology Press/Taylor & Francis.

**Baer, L., Rauch, S. L., Ballantine, T., Martuza, R., Cosgrove, R., Cassem, E., Giriunas, I., Manzo, P. A., Domino, C., & Jenike, M. A.** (1995). Cingulotomy for intractable obsessive-compulsive disorder. *Archives of General Psychiatry, 52,* 384–392.

**Bahrick, H. P.** (1984). Semantic memory content in permastore: 50 years of memory for Spanish learned in school. *Journal of Experimental Psychology: General, 113,* 1–29.

**Bahrick, H. P., Bahrick, L. E., Bahrick, A. S., & Bahrick, P. E.** (1993). Maintenance of foreign language vocabulary and the spacing effect. *Psychological Science, 4,* 316–321.

**Bahrick, H. P., Bahrick, P. O., & Wittlinger, R. P.** (1975). Fifty years of memory for names and faces: A cross-sectional approach. *Journal of Experimental Psychology, 104,* 54–75.

**Bailey, J. M., Dunne, M. P., & Martin, N. G.** (2000). Genetic and environmental influences on sexual orientation and its correlates in an Australian twin sample. *Journal of Personality and Social Psychology, 78,* 524–536.

**Bailey, J. M., & Pillard, R. C.** (1995). Genetics of human sexual orientation. *Annual Review of Sex Research, 6,* 126–150.

**Baker, H.** (1969). Transsexualism—problems in treatment. *American Journal of Psychiatry, 125,* 118–124.

**Baltes, P. B., & Staudinger, U. M.** (1993). The search for a psychology of wisdom. *Current Directions in Psychological Science, 2,* 75–80.

**Banaji, M. R., & Bhaskar, R.** (1999). Implicit stereotypes and memory: The bounded rationality of social beliefs. In D. L. Schachter & E. Scarry (Eds.), *Memory, brain, and belief.* Cambridge, MA: Harvard University Press.

**Bandelow, B., Wedekind, D., Pauls, J., Broocks, A., Hajak, G., & Ruther, E.** (2000). Salivary cortisol in panic attacks. *American Journal of Psychiatry, 157,* 454–456.

**Bandura, A.** (1969). *Principles of behavior modification.* New York: Holt, Rinehart & Winston.

**Bandura, A.** (1973). *Aggression: A social learning analysis.* Englewood Cliffs, NJ: Prentice-Hall.

**Bandura, A.** (1977). *Social learning theory.* Englewood Cliffs, NJ: Prentice-Hall.

**Bandura, A.** (1982). Self-efficacy mechanism in human agency. *American Psychologist, 37,* 122–147.

**Bandura, A.** (1989). Human agency in social cognitive theory. *American Psychologist, 44,* 1175–1184.

**Bandura, A.** (1999a). Social cognitive theory of personality. In D. Cervone & others (Eds.), *The coherence of personality: Social cognitive bases of consistency, variability, and organization* (pp. 185–241). New York: Guilford Press.

**Bandura, A.** (1999b). Social cognitive theory of personality. In L. A. Pervin & O. P. John (Eds.), *Handbook of personality: Theory and research* (2nd ed., pp. 154–196). New York: Guilford.

**Bandura, A., Blanchard, E. B., & Ritter, B.** (1969). The relative efficacy of desensitization and modeling approaches for inducing behavioral, affective, and attitudinal changes. *Journal of Personality and Social Psychology, 13,* 173–199.

**Bandura, A., Ross, D., & Ross, S. A.** (1963). Imitation of film-mediated aggressive models. *Journal of Abnormal and Social Psychology, 66,* 3–11.

**Banich, M. T.** (1998). Integration of information between the two cerebral hemispheres. *Current Directions in Psychological Science, 7,* 32–37.

**Banich, M. T., & Heller W.** (1998). Evolving perspectives on lateralization of function. *Current Directions in Psychological Science, 7,* 1–2.

**Banks, M., & Salapatek, P.** (1981). Infant pattern vision: A new approach based on the contrast sensitivity function. *Journal of Experimental Child Psychology, 31,* 1–45.

**Barahal, H. S.** (1958). 1000 prefrontal lobotomies. Five- to ten-year follow-up study. *Psychiatric Quarterly, 32,* 653–678.

**Barber, T. X., & Wilson, S. C.** (1977). Hypnosis, suggestions, and altered states of consciousness. Experimental evaluation of the new cognitive behavioral theory and the traditional trance-state theory of hypnosis. In W. E. Edmundson (Ed.), *Conceptual and investigative approaches to hypnosis and hypnotic phenomena.* New York: New York Academy of Sciences.

**Bard, P.** (1934). Emotion I: The neurohumoral basis of emotional reactions. In C. Murchison (Ed.), *Handbook of general experimental psychology.* Worcester, MA: Clark University Press.

**Barlow, D. H.** (1996). Health care policy, psychotherapy research, and the future of psychotherapy. *American Psychologist, 51,* 1050–1058.

**Barlow, D. H., & Lehman, C. L.** (1996). Advances in the psychosocial treatment of anxiety disorders: Implications for national health care. *Archives of General Psychiatry, 53,* 727–735.

**Barnes, K. E.** (1971). Preschool play norms: A replication. *Developmental Psychology, 5,* 99–103.

**Baron, J. B., & Sternberg, R. J.** (Eds.). (1987). *Teaching thinking skills.* San Francisco: W. H. Freeman.

**Baron, R., & Byrne, D.** (1982). *Exploring social psychology* (2nd ed.). Boston: Allyn & Bacon.

**Baron, R. A.** (2000). Psychological perspectives on entrepreneurship: Cognitive and social factors in entrepreneurs' success. *Current Directions in Psychological Science, 9,* 15–18.

**Baron, R. A., & Ramsberger, V. M.** (1978). Ambient temperature and the occurrence of collective violence: The "long hot summer" revisited. *Journal of Personality and Social Psychology, 36,* 351–360.

**Barr, C. E., Mednick, S. A., & Munk-Jorgensen, P.** (1990). Exposure to influenza epidemics during gestation and adult schizophrenia. *Archives of General Psychiatry, 47,* 869–874.

**Barrett, D. H., Resnick, H. S., Foy, D. W., & Dansky, B. S.** (1996). Combat exposure and adult psychosocial adjustment among U.S. army veterans serving in Vietnam, 1965–1971. *Journal of Abnormal Psychology, 105*(4), 575–581.

**Barsky, A. J., Fama, J. M., Bailey, E. D., & Ahern, D. K.** (1998). A prospective 4- to 5-year study of DSM-III-R hypochondriasis. *Archives of General Psychiatry, 55,* 737–744.

**Bartels, M., Rietveld, M. J. H., Van Baal, G. C. M., & Boomsma, D. I.** (2002). Genetic and environmental influences on the development of intelligence. *Behavior Genetics, 32,* 237–249.

**Bartlett, F. C.** (1932). *Remembering: A study in experimental and social psychology.* New York: Cambridge University Press.

**Barton, J. L.** (1977). ECT in depression: The evidence of controlled studies. *Biological Psychiatry, 12,* 687–695.

**Bartoshuk, L.** (1988). Taste. In R. C. Atkinson, R. J. Herrnstein, G. Lindzey, & R. D. Luce (Eds.), *Stevens' handbook of experimental psychology: Vol. 1. Perception and motivation.* New York: Wiley-Interscience.

**Bartzokis, G., Beckson, M., Lu, P., Nuechterlein, K., Edwards, N., & Mintz, J.** (2001). Age-related changes in frontal and temporal lobe volumes in men. *Archives of General Psychiatry, 58,* 461–465.

**Bashore, T. R., Ridderinkhof, R., & van der Molen, M. W.** (1997). The decline of cognitive processing speed in old age. *Current Directions in Psychological Science, 6,* 163–169.

**Basoglu, M., Marks, I., Livanou, M., & Swinson, R.** (1997). Double-blindness procedures, rater blindness, and ratings of outcome: Observations from a controlled trial. *Archives of General Psychiatry, 54,* 744–748.

**Batsell, W.** (2000). Augmentation: Synergistic conditioning in taste-aversion learning. *American Psychological Society, 9,* 164–168.

**Baum, A., Harpin, R. E., & Valins, S.** (1975). The role of group phenomena in the experience of crowding. *Environment and Behavior, 7,* 185–198.

**Baum, A., & Valins, S.** (1977). *Architecture and social behavior: Psychological studies of social density.* Hillsdale, NJ: Erlbaum.

**Baumrind, D.** (1972). An exploratory study of socialization effects on Black children: Some Black-White comparisons. *Child Development, 43,* 261–267.

**Baumrind, D.** (1983). Rejoinder to Lewis's reinterpretation of parental firm control effects: Are authoritative families really harmonious? *Psychological Bulletin, 94,* 132–142.

**Baumrind, D.** (1991). Parenting styles and adolescent development. In J. Brooks-Gunn, R. Lerner, & A. Peterson (Eds.), *The encyclopedia of adolescence.* New York: Garland.

**Baxter, L. R., Phelps, M. E., Maziotta, J. C., Guze, B. H., Schwartz, J. M., & Selin, C. E.** (1987). Local cerebral glucose metabolic rates in obsessive-compulsive disorder. *Archives of General Psychiatry, 44,* 211–218.

**Baxter, L. R., Schwartz, J. M., Bergman, K. S., & Szuba, M. P.** (1992). Caudate glucose metabolic rate changes with both drug and behavior therapy for obsessive-compulsive disorder. *Archives of General Psychiatry, 49,* 681–689.

**Beatty, J.** (1995). *Principles of behavioral neuroscience.* Madison, WI: Brown & Benchmark.

**Beck, A. T.** (1976). *Cognitive therapy and the emotional disorders.* New York: International Universities Press.

**Beck, A. T.** (1999). *Prisoners of hate: The cognitive basis of anger, hostility, and violence.* New York: HarperCollins.

**Beck, A. T., Rush, A. J., Shaw, B. F., & Emery, G.** (1979). *Cognitive therapy of depression.* New York: Guilford Press.

**Beck, J. G.** (1995). Hypoactive sexual desire disorder: An overview. *Journal of Consulting and Clinical Psychology, 63,* 919–927.

**Becker, W. C., & Carnine, D.** (1980). Direct instruction: An effective approach to educational intervention with the disadvantaged and low performers. In B. B. Lahey & A. E. Kazdin (Eds.), *Advances in clinical child psychology* (Vol. 3). New York: Plenum.

**Beeman, M. J., & Chiarello, C.** (1998). Complementary right- and left-hemisphere language comprehension. *Current Directions in Psychological Science, 7,* 2–8.

**Behrman, J., & Levy, R.** (1970). Neurophysiological studies on patients with hysterical disturbances of vision. *Journal of Psychosomatic Research, 14,* 187–194.

**Beiman, I., Majestic, H., Johnson, S. A., Puente, A., & Graham, L.** (1976). *Transcendental meditation versus behavior therapy: A controlled investigation.* Paper presented to the Association for the Advancement of Behavior Therapy.

**Bell, N. J., & Carver, W.** (1980). A reevaluation of gender label effects: Expectant mothers' responses to infants. *Child Development, 51,* 925–927.

**Bell, R. Q.** (1968). A reinterpretation of the direction of effects in studies of socialization. *Psychological Review, 75,* 81–95.

**Belloc, N. B.** (1973). Relationship of health practices to mortality. *Preventive Medicine, 2,* 67–81.

**Bellodi, L., Perna, G., Caldirola, D., Arancio, C., Bertani, A., & Di Bella, D.** (1998). $CO_2$-induced panic attacks: A twin study. *American Journal of Psychiatry, 155*(9), 1184–1188.

**Belmore, S. M.** (1987). Determinants of attention during impression formation. *Journal of Experimental Psychology: Learning, Memory, and Cognition, 13,* 480–489.

**Belmore, S. M., & Hubbard, M. L.** (1987). The role of advance expectancies in person memory. *Journal of Personality and Social Psychology, 53,* 61–70.

**Belzer, E. G.** (1981). Orgasmic expulsions of women: A review and heuristic inquiry. *Journal of Sex Research, 17,* 1–12.

**Bem, D. J.** (1996). Exotic becomes erotic: A developmental theory of sexual orientation. *Psychological Review, 103,* 320–335.

**Bem, D. J., & Allen, A.** (1974). On predicting some of the people some of the time: The search for cross-situational consistencies in behavior. *Psychological Review, 81,* 506–520.

**Bem, S.** (1974). The measurement of psychological androgyny. *Journal of Consulting and Clinical Psychology, 42,* 155–162.

**Bem, S.** (1981). Gender schema theory: A cognitive account of sex typing. *Psychological Review, 88,* 354–364.

**Benedict, R. F.** (1934). *Patterns of culture.* Boston: Houghton Mifflin.

**Benes, F. M.** (1998). Images in neuroscience: Brain development, VIII. *American Journal of Psychiatry, 155,* 1489.

**Benotsch, E. G., Brailey, K., Vasterling, J. J., & Sutker, P. B.** (2000). War zone stress, personal and environmental resources, and PTSD symptoms in Gulf War veterans: A longitudinal perspective. *Journal of Abnormal Psychology, 109,* 205–213.

**Benschop, R. J., Geenen, R., Mills, P. J., Naliboff, B. D., Kiecolt-Glaser, J. K., Herbert, T. B., van der Pompe, G., Miller, G. E., Matthews, K. A., Godaert, G. L., Gilmore, S. L., Glaser, R., Heijnen, C. J., Dopp, J. M., Bijlsma, J. W. J., Solomon, G. F., & Cacioppo, J. T.** (1998). Cardiovascular and immune responses to acute psychological stress in young and old women: A meta-analysis. *Psychosomatic Medicine, 60,* 29–296.

**Benson, H.** (1975). *The relaxation response.* New York: Morrow.

**Ben-Sur, H.** (2002). Associations of Type A behavior with the emotional traits of anger and curiosity. *Anxiety, Stress, and Coping, 15,* 95–104.

**Benton, D., & Sargent, J.** (1992). Breakfast, blood glucose and memory. *Biological Psychology, 33,* 207–210.

**Bergum, B. O., & Lehr, D. J.** (1962). Vigilance performance as a function of interpolated rest. *Journal of Applied Psychology, 46,* 425–427.

**Berkowitz, L.** (1989). Frustration-aggression hypothesis: Examination and reformulation. *Psychological Bulletin, 106,* 59–73.

**Berkowitz, L.** (1993). *Aggression: Its causes, consequences, and control.* New York: McGraw-Hill.

**Berman, K. F., Illowsky, B. P., & Weinberger, D. R.** (1988). Physiological dysfunction of dorsolateral prefrontal cortex in schizophrenia: Further evidence for regional and behavioral specificity. *Archives of General Psychiatry, 45,* 616–622.

**Bermant, G.** (1976). Sexual behavior: Hard times with the Coolidge effect. In M. H. Siegel & H. P. Ziegler (Eds.), *Psychological research: The inside story.* New York: Harper & Row.

**Bernstein, I. L.** (1978). Learned taste aversions in children receiving chemotherapy. *Science, 200,* 1302–1309.

**Bernstein, I. L.** (1985). Learned food aversions in the progression of cancer and its treatment. In N. S. Braverman & P. Bernstein (Eds.), *Experimental assessments and clinical applications of conditioned food aversions. Annals of the New York Academy of Sciences, 443.*

**Bernstein, I. L., Webster, M. M., & Bernstein, P.** (1982). Food aversions in children receiving chemotherapy for cancer. *Cancer, 50,* 2961–2963.

**Berry, J. W., & Bennett, J. A.** (1992). Cree conceptions of cognitive competence. *International Journal of Psychology, 27, 1,* 73–88.

**Berscheid, E., Dion, K. K., Walster, E., & Walster, G. W.** (1971). Physical attractiveness and dating choice: A test of the matching hypothesis. *Journal of Experimental Social Psychology, 7,* 173–189.

**Betancourt, H., & Lopez, S. R.** (1993). The study of culture, ethnicity, and race in American psychology. *American Psychologist, 48, 6,* 629.

**Bettencourt, B. A., & Miller, N.** (1996). Gender differences in aggression as a function of provocation: A meta-analysis. *Psychological Bulletin, 119,* 422–447.

**Biernat, M., & Kobrynowicz, D.** (1997). Gender- and race-based standards of competence: Lower minimum standards but higher ability standards for devalued groups. *Journal of Personality and Social Psychology, 72,* 544–557.

**Bigelow, H. J.** (1850). Dr. Harlow's case of recovery from the passage of an iron bar through the head. *American Journal of Medical Science, 20,* 13–22.

**Birch, H. C.** (1945). The relation of previous experience to insightful problem solving. *Journal of Comparative Psychology, 38,* 367–383.

**Bjorklund, D. F., & Green, B. L.** (1992). The adaptive nature of cognitive immaturity. *American Psychologist, 47,* 46–54.

**Bjorklund, D. F., & Kipp, K.** (1999). Parental investment theory and gender differences in the evolution of inhibition mechanisms. *Psychological Bulletin, 120,* 163–188.

**Bjorklund, D. F., & Pellegrini, A. D.** (2002). *The origins of human nature: Evolutionary Developmental Psychology.*

**Bjorklund, D. F., & Shackleford, T. K.** (1999). Differences in parental investment contribute to differences between men and women. *Current Directions in Psychological Science, 8,* 86–89.

**Blanchard, R., & others.** (1996a). Birth order and sibling sex ratio in homosexual male adolescents and probably pre-homosexual feminine boys. *Developmental Psychology, 31,* 22–30.

**Blanchard, R., & others.** (1996b). Birth order and sibling sex ratio in two samples of Dutch gender-dysphoric homosexual males. *Archives of Sexual Behavior, 25,* 495–514.

**Blonder, L. X., Bowers, D., & Heilman, K. M.** (1991). The role of the right hemisphere in emotional communication. *Brain, 114,* 1115–1127.

**Bloom, B. S.** (1974). Time and learning. *American Psychologist, 29,* 681–688.

**Bly, J., Jones, R., & Richardson, T.** (1986). Impact of worksite health promotion on healthcare costs and utilization: Evaluation of Johnson and Johnson's Life for Life program. *Journal of the American Medical Association, 256,* 3235–3240.

**Bock, M.** (1986). The influence of emotional meaning on the recall of words processed for form or self-reference. *Psychological Research, 48,* 107–112.

**Bock, M., & Klinger, E.** (1986). Interaction of emotion and cognition in word recall. *Psychological Research, 48,* 99–100.

**Bogaert, A. F.** (1998). Birth order and sibling sex ratio in homosexual and heterosexual non-white men. *Archives of Sexual Behavior, 27,* 467–473.

**Bolm-Andorff, U., Schwämmle, J., Ehlenz, K., Koop, H., & Kaffarnik, H.** (1986). Hormonal and cardiovascular variations during a public lecture. *European Journal of Applied Physiology, 54,* 669–674.

**Bond, R., & Smith, P. B.** (1996). Culture and conformity: A meta-analysis of studies using Asch's (1952b, 1956) line judgment task. *Psychological Bulletin, 119,* 111–137.

**Bondareff, W., Raval, J., Woo, B., Hauser, D. L., & Colletti, P. M.** (1990). Magnetic resonance imaging and the severity of dementia in older adults. *Archives of General Psychiatry, 47,* 47–51.

**Borch-Jacobsen, M.** (1997). Sybil—The making and marketing of a disease: An interview with Herbert Spiegel. In T. Dufresne (Ed.), *Freud under analysis: History, theory, practice. Essays in honor of Paul Roazen.* Northvale, NJ: Jason Aronson.

**Borden, R. J.** (1986). Ecology and identity. In J. F. G. Grosser & F. Schmeidler (Eds.), *Proceedings of ecosystems and new energetics* (pp. 25–41). Academia Cosmologica Nova, Munich, Germany: Man and Space.

**Borkovec, T. D., & Costello, E.** (1993). Efficacy of applied relaxation and cognitive-behavioral therapy in the treatment of generalized anxiety disorder. *Journal of Consulting and Clinical Psychology, 61,* 611–619.

**Bouchard, T. J., & McGue, M.** (1981). Familial studies of intelligence: A review. *Science, 212,* 1055–1059.

**Bourne, L. E.** (1966). *Human conceptual behavior.* Boston: Allyn & Bacon.

**Bousfield, W. A.** (1953). The occurrence of clustering in recall of randomly arranged associates. *Journal of General Psychology, 49,* 229–240.

**Bousfield, W. A., & Sedgwick, C. H.** (1944). An analysis of sequences of restricted associative responses. *Journal of General Psychology, 30,* 149–165.

**Bouton, M. E., Mineka, S., & Barlow, D. H.** (2001). A modern learning theory perspective on the etiology of panic disorder. *Psychological Review, 108,* 4–32.

**Bower, G. H.** (1973). Educational applications of mnemonic devices. In K. O. Doyle (Ed.), *Interaction: Readings in human psychology.* Boston: D. C. Heath.

**Bower, G. H., & Clark, M. C.** (1969). Narrative stories as mediators for serial learning. *Psychonomic Science, 14,* 181–182.

**Bowers, K. S.** (1976). *Hypnosis for the seriously curious.* Monterey, CA: Brooks/Cole.

**Bracha, H. S., Torrey, E. F., Gottesman, I. I., Bigelow, L. B., & Cunniff, C.** (1992). Second-trimester markers of fetal size in schizophrenia: A study of monozygotic twins. *American Journal of Psychiatry, 149,* 1355–1361.

**Bransford, J. D., & Franks, J. J.** (1971). The abstraction of linguistic ideas. *Cognitive Psychology, 2,* 331–350.

**Braverman, L. B.** (1989). Beyond the myth of motherhood. In M. McGoldrick, C. M. Anderson, & F. Walsh (Eds.), *Women and families.* New York: Free Press.

**Bray, D. W., Campbell, R. J., & Grant, D. L.** (1974). *Formative years in business: A long-term AT&T study of managerial lives.* New York: Wiley.

**Bregante, J. L., Martinez, K., & O'Toole, C. J.** (1993). *New bridges: Building community between disabled and nondisabled women.* Presentation at the Fifth International Interdisciplinary Conference on Women.

**Breier, A., Schreiber, J. L., Dyer, J., & Pickar, D.** (1991). National Institute of Mental Health longitudinal study of chronic schizophrenia: Prognosis and predictors of outcome. *Archives of General Psychiatry, 48,* 239–246.

**Brent, D. A., & Kolko, D. J.** (1998). Psychotherapy: Definitions, mechanisms of action, and relationship to etiological models. *Journal of Abnormal Child Psychology, 26,* 17–25.

**Breslau, N., Davis, G. C., Peterson, E. L., & Schultz, L.** (1997). Psychiatric sequelae of posttraumatic stress disorder in women. *Archives of General Psychiatry, 54,* 81–87.

**Breslau, N., Johnson, E., Hiripi, E., & Kessler, R.** (2001). Nicotine dependence in the United States—prevalence, trends, and smoking persistence. *Archives of General Psychiatry, 58,* 810–816.

**Breslau, N., Kessler, R. C., Chilcoat, H. D., Schultz, L. R., Davis, G. C., & Andreski, P.** (1998). Trauma and posttraumatic stress disorder in the community. *Archives of General Psychiatry, 55,* 626–632.

**Breslow, L., & Enstrom, J. E.** (1980). Persistence of health habits and their relationship to mortality. *Preventive Medicine, 9,* 469–483.

**Brewin, C. R., Andrews, B., Rose, S., & Kirk, M.** (1999). Acute stress disorder and posttraumatic stress disorder in victims of violent crime. *American Journal of Psychiatry, 156,* 360–366.

**Brewin, C. R., Andrews, B., & Valentine, J. D.** (2000). Meta-analysis of risk factors for posttraumatic stress disorder in trauma-exposed adults. *Journal of Consulting and Clinical Psychology, 68,* 748–766.

**Briere, J., Downes, A., & Spensley, J.** (1983). Summer in the city: Urban weather conditions and psychiatric emergency-room visits. *Journal of Abnormal Psychology, 92,* 77–80.

**Briggs, G. C., Freeman, R. K., & Yaffe, S. J.** (1986). *Drugs in pregnancy and lactation.* Baltimore: Williams & Wilkins.

**Brody, A. L., Saxena, S., Stoessel, P., Gillies, L. A., Fairbanks, L. A., Alborzian, S., Phelps, M. E., Huang, S. C., Wu, H. M., Ho, M. L., Ho, M. K., Au, S. C., Maidment, K., & Baxter, L. R.** (2001). Regional brain metabolic changes in patients with major depression treated with either paroxetine or interpersonal therapy. *Archives of General Psychiatry, 58,* 631–640.

**Brody, N.** (1997). Intelligence, schooling, and society. *American Psychologist, 52,* 1046–1050.

**Brooks, C. M.** (1988). The history of thought concerning the hypothalamus and its functions. *Brain Research Bulletin, 20,* 657–667.

**Brosnahan, M., & Giffen, D.** (1993). Out of hospitals, left on the streets. *New York Times,* No. 49, 416, pp. 7–11.

**Brown, G. P., Hammen, C. L., Craske, M. G., & Wickens, T. D.** (1995). Dimensions of dysfunctional attitudes as vulnerabilities to depressive symptoms. *Journal of Abnormal Psychology, 104,* 431–435.

**Brown, R., & Kulik, J.** (1977). Flashbulb memories. *Cognition, 5,* 73–99.

**Brown, R. W., & McNeil, D.** (1966). The "tip of the tongue" phenomenon. *Journal of Verbal Learning and Verbal Behavior, 5,* 325–337.

**Brownell, K. D.** (1991). Dieting and the search for the perfect body: Where physiology and culture collide. *Behavior Therapy, 22,* 1–12.

**Brownell, K. D., & Rodin, J.** (1994). The dieting maelstrom: Is it possible and advisable to lose weight? *American Psychologist, 49,* 781–791.

**Brownlee-Dufek, M., Peterson, L., Simonds, J. F., Goldstein, D., Kilo, C., & Hoette, S.** (1987). The role of health beliefs in the regimen adherence and metabolic control of adolescents and adults with diabetes mellitus. *Journal of Consulting and Clinical Psychology, 55,* 139–144.

**Bruce, T. J., Spiegel, D. A., Gregg, S. F., & Nuzzarello, A.** (1995). Predictors of alprazolam discontinuation with and without cognitive behavior therapy in panic disorder. *American Journal of Psychiatry, 152,* 1156–1160.

**Bruner, J. S.** (Ed.). (1974). *The growth of competence.* New York: Academic Press.

**Bruner, J. S., & Goodman, C. C.** (1947). Value and need as organizing factors in perception. *Journal of Abnormal and Social Psychology, 42,* 33–44.

**Buchsbaum, M.** (1983). The mind readers. *Psychology Today,* pp. 58–62.

**Buckhout, R.** (1974). Eyewitness testimony. *Scientific American,* pp. 23–33.

**Buckner, R. L., & Barch, D.** (1999). Memory, 1: Episodic memory retrieval. *American Journal of Psychiatry, 156,* 1311.

**Budney, A., Hughes, J., Moore, B., & Novy, P.** (2001). Marijuana abstinence effects in marijuana smokers maintained in their environment. *Archives in General Psychiatry, 58,* 917–924.

**Buenker, J. D., & Ratner, L.** (1992). *Multiculturalism in the United States: A comparative guide to acculturation and ethnicity.* Westport, CT: Greenwood.

**Burchinal, M. R., Campbell, F. A., Bryant, D. M., Wasik, B. H., & Ramey, C. T.** (1997). Early intervention and mediating processes in cognitive performance of children of low-income African American families. *Child Development, 68,* 935–954.

**Burger, J. M.** (1986). Temporal effects on attributions: Actor and observer differences. *Social Cognition, 4,* 377–387.

**Burgess, A. W., & Holstrom, K. L.** (1974). Rape trauma syndrome. *American Journal of Psychiatry, 131,* 981–986.

**Burling, T. A., & others.** (1989). Computerized smoking cessation program for the worksite: Treatment outcome and feasibility. *Journal of Consulting and Clinical Psychology, 57,* 619–622.

**Buss, A.** (1989). Personality as traits. *American Psychologist, 44,* 1378–1388.

**Buss, D. M.** (1995). Psychological sex differences: Origins through sexual selection. *American Psychologist, 50,* 164–168.

**Buss, D. M.** (1999). Human nature and individual differences: The evolution of human personality. In L. A. Pervin & O. P. John (Eds.), *Handbook of personality: Theory and research* (2nd ed.), (pp. 31–56). New York: Guilford.

**Buss, D. M.** (2001). Cognitive biases and emotional wisdom in the evolution of conflict between the sexes. *Psychological Science, 10,* 219–223.

**Bussey, K., & Bandura, A.** (1992). Self-regulatory mechanisms governing gender development. *Child Development, 63,* 1236–1250.

**Bussey, K., & Bandura, A.** (1999). Social cognitive theory of gender development and differentiation. *Psychological Review, 106,* 676–713.

**Butcher, H. J.** (1968). *Human intelligence: Its nature and assessment.* New York: Harper Torchbooks.

**Butler, R. A.** (1953). Discrimination learning by rhesus monkey by visual-exploration motivation. *Journal of Comparative and Physiological Psychology, 46,* 95–98.

**Byne, W., Buchsbaum, M., Kemether, E., Hazlett, E., Shinwari, A., Mitropoulou, V., & Siever, L.** (2001). Magnetic resonance imaging of the thalamic mediodorsal nucleus and pulvinar in schizophrenia and schizotypal personality disorder. *Archives in General Psychiatry, 58,* 133.

**Byrnes, J. P., Miller, D. C., & Schafer, W. D.** (1999). Gender differences in risk taking: A meta-analysis. *Psychological Bulletin, 125,* 367–383.

**C**

**Cacioppo, J. T., Gardner, W. L., & Berntson, G. G.** (1999). The affect system has parallel and integrative processing components: Form follows functions. *Journal of Personality and Social Psychology, 76,* 839–855.

**Cain, W. S.** (1988). Olfaction. In R. C. Atkinson, R. J. Herrnstein, G. Lindzey, & R. D. Luce (Eds.), *Stevens' handbook of experimental psychology: Vol. 1. Perception and motivation.* New York: Wiley-Interscience.

**Calabrese, J. R., Kling, M. A., & Gold, P. W.** (1987). Alterations in immunocompetence during stress, bereavement, and depression: Focus on neuroendocrine regulators. *American Journal of Psychiatry, 144,* 1123–1134.

**Calahan, D.** (1970). *Problem drinkers.* San Francisco: Jossey-Bass.

**Calahan, D., & Room, R.** (1974). *Problem drinking among American men.* New Brunswick, NJ: Rutgers Center of Alcohol Studies.

**Calhoun, K. S., & Atkeson, B. M.** (1989). *Treatment of rape victims.* New York: Pergamon Press.

**Calkins, M. W.** (1893). Statistics of dreams. *American Journal of Psychology, 5,* 311–343.

**Campbell, D. E.** (1961). The psychological effects of cerebral electroshock. In H. J. Eysenck (Ed.), *Handbook of abnormal psychology.* New York: Basic Books.

**Campbell, D. E.** (1978). *Interior office design and visitor response.* Paper presented to the American Psychological Association, Toronto.

**Campbell, F. A., Pungello, E. P., Miller-Johnson, S., Burchinal, M., & Ramey, C. T.** (2001). The development of cognitive and academic abilities: Growth curves from an early childhood educational experiment. *Developmental Psychology, 37,* 231–242.

**Campbell, F. A., & Ramey, C. T.** (1994). Effects of early intervention on intellectual and academic achievement: A follow-up study of children from low-income families. *Child Development, 65,* 684–698.

**Campbell, F. A., & Ramey, C. T.** (1995). Cognitive and school outcomes for high-risk African American students at middle adolescence: Positive effects of early intervention. *American Educational Research Journal, 32,* 743–772.

**Canli, T., Zhao, Z., Desmond, J., Kang, E., Gross, J., & Gabrieli, J. D. E.** (2001). An fMRI study of personality influences on brain reactivity to emotional stimuli. *Behavioral Neuroscience, 115,* 33–42.

**Cannon, T. D., Mednick, S. A., Parnas, J., Schulsinger, F., Praestholm, J., & Vestergaard, A.** (1993). Developmental brain abnormalities in the offspring of schizophrenic mothers: I. Contributions of genetic and perinatal factors. *Archives of General Psychiatry, 50,* 551–564.

**Cannon, T. D., van Erp, T. G. M., Huttunen, M., Lonnqvist, J., Salonen, O., Valanne, L., Poutanen, V. P., Standertskjold-Nordenstam, C. G., Gur, R. E., & Yan, M.** (1998). Regional gray matter, white matter, and cerebrospinal fluid distributions in schizophrenic patients, their siblings, and controls. *Archives of General Psychiatry, 55,* 1084–1091.

**Cannon, W. B.** (1927). The James-Lange theory of emotions: A critical examination and an alternative theory. *American Journal of Psychology, 39,* 106–124.

**Cannon, W. B., & Washburn, A. L.** (1912). An explanation of hunger. *American Journal of Physiology, 29,* 441–454.

**Cano, A., & O'Leary, K. D.** (2000). Infidelity and separations precipitate major depressive episodes and symptoms of nonspecific depression and anxiety. *Journal of Consulting and Clinical Psychology, 68,* 774–781.

**Cappe, R. F., & Alden, L. E.** (1986). A comparison of treatment strategies for clients functionally impaired by extreme shyness and social avoidance. *Journal of Consulting and Clinical Psychology, 54,* 796–801.

**Carey, S.** (1977). The child as a word learner. In M. Halle, J. Bresnan, & G. A. Miller (Eds.), *Linguistic theory and psychological reality.* Cambridge, MA: MIT Press.

**Carmichael, L., Hogan, H. P., & Walter, A. A.** (1932). An experimental study of the effect of language on the reproduction of visually perceived form. *Journal of Experimental Psychology, 15,* 73–86.

**Carpenter, P. A., Just, M. A., & Shell, P.** (1990). What one intelligence test measures: A theoretical account of the processing in the Raven Progressive Matrices Test. *Psychological Review, 97,* 404–431.

**Carroll, C. R.** (1989). *Drugs in modern society* (2nd ed.). Dubuque, IA: Wm. C. Brown.

**Carroll, C. R.** (2000). *Drugs in modern society* (5th ed.). Boston: McGraw-Hill.

**Carstensen, L. L., & Charles, S. T.** (1998). Emotion in the second half of life. *Current Directions in Psychological Science, 7,* 144–149.

**Carstensen, L. L., Isaacowitz, D. M., & Charles, S. T.** (1999). Taking time seriously.

A theory of socioemotional selectivity. *American Psychologist, 54,* 165–181.

**Carver, C. S., & Baird, W.** (1998). The American dream revisited: Is it what you want or why you want that matters. *Psychological Science, 9,* 289–292.

**Case, F. D.** (1981). Dormitory architecture influences: Patterns of student social relations over time. *Environment and Behavior, 13,* 23–41.

**Casey, M. B., Nuttall, R., & Pezaris, E.** (1997). Mediators of gender differences in mathematics college entrance test scores: A comparison of spatial skills with internalized beliefs and anxieties. *Developmental Psychology, 33,* 669–680.

**Casey, M. B., Nuttall, R., Pezaris, E., & Benbow, C. P.** (1995). The influence of spatial ability on gender differences in mathematics college entrance test scores across diverse samples. *Developmental Psychology, 31,* 697–705.

**Caspi, A., & Herbener, E. S.** (1990). Continuity and change: Assortative marriage and the consistency of personality in adulthood. *Journal of Personality and Social Psychology, 58,* 250–258.

**Castelluci, V., & Kandel, E. R.** (1976). Presynaptic facilitation as a mechanism for behavioral sensitization in *Aplysia. Science, 194,* 1176–1178.

**Ceci, S. J., & Bruck, M.** (1995). *Jeopardy in the courtroom.* Washington, DC: American Psychological Association.

**Ceci, S. J., & Williams, W. M.** (1997). Schooling, intelligence, and income. *American Psychologist, 52,* 1051–1058.

**Chaiken, S., & Eagly, A. H.** (1983). Communication modality as a determinant of persuasion: The role of communicator salience. *Journal of Personality and Social Psychology, 45,* 241–256.

**Chambless, D. L., & Gillis, M. M.** (1993). Cognitive therapy of anxiety disorders. *Journal of Consulting and Clinical Psychology, 61,* 248–260.

**Chapman, L. J., & Chapman, J. P.** (1973). *Disordered thought in schizophrenia.* New York: Appleton-Century-Crofts.

**Chapman, L. J., Krauss, D. H., & Silver, R.** (1992). Mathematics anxiety and science careers among able college women. *Psychological Science, 3,* 292–295.

**Chase, W. G., & Simon, H. A.** (1973). The mind's eye in chess. In W. G. Chase (Ed.), *Visual information processing.* New York: Academic Press.

**Chemers, M. M.** (1997). *An integrative theory of leadership.* Mahwah, NJ: Lawrence Erlbaum.

**Chochinov, H. M., Wilson, K. G., Enns, M., Mowchun, N., Lander, S., Levitt, M., & Clinch, J. J.** (1995). Desire for death in the terminally ill. *American Journal of Psychiatry, 152,* 8.

**Chodorow, N. J.** (1989). Family structure and feminine personality. In *Feminism and psychoanalytic theory.* New Haven: Yale University Press.

**Choi, I., Nisbett, R. E., & Norenzayan, A.** (1999). Causal attribution across cultures: Variation and universality. *Psychological Bulletin, 125,* 47–63.

**Chomsky, N.** (1957). *Syntactic structures.* The Hague: Mouton.

**Chruschel, T. L.** (1982). General pharmacology and toxicology of alcohol. In F. Hoffmeister & G. Stille (Eds.), *Psychotropic agents. Part III: Alcohol and Psychotomimetics* (Vol. 55). New York: Springer-Verlag.

**Church, R. M.** (1969). Response suppression. In B. A. Campbell & R. M. Church (Eds.), *Punishment and aversive behavior.* New York: Appleton-Century-Crofts.

**Clancy, S. A., Schacter, D. L., Lensenweger, M. F., & Pitman, R. K.** (2002). Memory distortion in people reporting abduction by aliens. *Journal of Abnormal Psychology, 111,* 455–461.

**Clancy, S. A., Schacter, D. L., McNally, R. J., & Pitman, R. K.** (2000). False recognition in women reporting recovered memories of sexual abuse. *Psychological Science, 11,* 26–31.

**Clark, K. B., & Clark, M. P.** (1939). The development of self and the emergence of racial identification in Negro preschool children. *Journal of Social Psychology, 10,* 591–599.

**Clark, R. D., & Hatfield, E.** (1989). Gender differences in receptivity to sexual offers. *Journal of Psychology & Human Sexuality, 2,* 39–55.

**Clarke, A. M., & Clarke, A. B. D.** (Eds.). (1976). *Early experience: Myth and science.* New York: Appleton-Century-Crofts.

**Clarke, G. N., Hornbrook, M., Lynch, F., Polen, M., Gale, J., Beardslee, W., O'Connor, E., & Seeley, J.** (2001). A randomized trial of a group cognitive intervention for preventing depression in adolescent offspring of depressed parents. *Archives of General Psychiatry, 58,* 1127–1134.

**Clarkin, J. F., Pilkonis, P. A., & Magruder, K. M.** (1996). Psychotherapy of depression: Implications for reform of the health care system. *Archives of General Psychiatry, 53,* 717–723.

**Clifford-Walton, V. A.** (1998). Feminist perspectives on women's health research. In S. E. Romans & others (Eds.), *Folding back the shadows: A perspective on women's mental health.* Dunedin, New Zealand: University of Otago Press.

**Cohen, L. G., Celnik, P., Pascual-Leone, A., Corwell, B., Falz, L., Dambroasia, J., Honda, M., Sadato, N., Gerloff, C., & Catala, M. D.** (1997). Functional relevance of cross-model plasticity in blind humans. *Nature, 389,* 180–183.

**Cohen, S.** (1996). Psychological stress, immunity, and upper respiratory infections. *Current Directions in Psychological Science, 5,* 86–90.

**Cohen, S., & Williamson, G.** (1991). Stress and infectious disease in humans. *Psychological Bulletin, 109,* 5–24.

**Cohn, E. G., & Rotton, J.** (1997). Assault as a function of time and temperature: A moderator-variable time-series analysis. *Journal of Personality and Social Psychology, 72,* 1322–1334.

**Colby, C. Z., Lanzetta, J. T., & Kleck, R. E.** (1977). Effects of the expression of pain on autonomic and pain tolerance responses to subject controlled pain. *Psychophysiology, 14,* 537–540.

**Collaer, M. L., & Hines, M.** (1995). Human behavioral sex differences: A role for gonadal hormones during early development? *Psychological Bulletin, 118,* 55–107.

**Collins, A. M., & Loftus, E. F.** (1975). A spreading activation theory of semantic processing. *Psychological Review, 82,* 407–428.

**Comas-Diaz, L.** (2000). An ethnopolitical approach to working with people of color. *American Psychologist, 55,* 1319–1325.

**Committee on Lesbian, Gay, and Bisexual Concerns.** (2000). Guidelines for psychotherapy with lesbian, gay, and bisexual clients. *American Psychologist, 55,* 1440–1451.

**Compas, B. E., & Luecken, L.** (2002). Psychological adjustment. *Psychological Science, 11,* 111–114.

**Conklin, H. M., & Iacono, W. G.** (2002). Schizophrenia: A neurodevelopmental perspective. *Psychological Science, 11,* 33–37.

**Contrada, R. J., Ashmore, R. D., Gary, M. L., Coups, E., Egeth, J. D., Sewell, A., Ewell, K., Goyal, T. M., & Chasse, V.** (2000). Ethnicity-related sources of stress and their effects on well-being. *Psychological Science, 9,* 136–143.

**Cook, E. W., Hodes, R. L., & Lang, P.** (1986). Preparedness and phobia: Effects of stimulus content on human visceral learning. *Journal of Abnormal Psychology, 95,* 195–207.

**Cook, M., & Mineka, S.** (1990). Selective association in the observational learning of fear in monkeys. *Journal of Abnormal Psychology, 98,* 448–459.

**Cooper, J., & Mackie, D.** (1983). Cognitive dissonance in an intergroup context. *Journal of Personality and Social Psychology, 44,* 536–544.

**Cooper, J. R., Bloom, F. E., & Roth, R. H.** (1986). *The biochemical basis of neuropharmacology* (5th ed.). New York: Oxford University Press.

**Cooper, J. R., Bloom, F. E., & Roth, R. H.** (1996). *The biochemical basis of neuropharmacology* (7th ed.). New York: Oxford University Press.

**Cope, J. G., & Geller, E. S.** (1984). Community-based interventions to increase the use of automobile litterbags. *Journal of Resource Management and Technology, 13,* 127–132.

**Cordano, M., & Hanson-Frieze, I.** (2000). Pollution reduction preferences of U.S. environmental managers: Applying Ajzen's theory of planned behavior. *Academy of Management Journal, 43,* 627–643.

**Coren, S., & Girgus, J. S.** (1978). *Seeing is deceiving: The psychology of visual illusions.* Hillsdale, NJ: Erlbaum.

**Cornelius, S. W., & Caspi, A.** (1987). Everyday problem solving in adulthood and old age. *Psychology and Aging, 2,* 144–153.

**Cote, S.** (1999). Affect and performance in organizational settings. *Current Directions in Psychological Science 8,* 65–68.

**Cowan, N.** (1987). Auditory sensory storage in relation to the growth of sensation and acoustic information extraction. *Journal of Experimental Psychology, 13,* 204–215.

**Cowan, N.** (1988). Evolving conceptions of memory storage, selective attention, and their mutual constraints within the human information-processing system. *Psychological Bulletin, 104,* 163–191.

**Craik, F., Moroz, T. M., Moscovitch, M., Stuss, D. T., Winocur, G., Tulving, E., & Kapur, J.** (1999). In search of the self: A positron emission tomography study. *Psychological Science, 10,* 26–34.

**Craik, F. I. M., & Lockhart, R. S.** (1972). Levels of processing. A framework for memory research. *Journal of Verbal Learning and Verbal Behavior, 11,* 671–684.

**Croft, R., Klugman, A., Baldeweg, T., & Gruzelier, J.** (2001). Electrophysiological evidence of serotonergic impairment in long-term MDMA ("ecstasy") users. *American Journal of Psychiatry, 158,* 1687–1692.

Cross, S. E., & Markus, H. R. (1999). The cultural constitution of personality. In L. A. Pervin & O. P. John (Eds.), *Handbook of personality: Theory and research* (2nd ed., pp. 378–396). New York: Guilford.

Crowley, K., Callanan, M. A., Tenenbaum, H. R., & Allen, E. (2001). Parents explain more often to boys than to girls during shared scientific thinking. *Psychological Science, 12,* 258–261.

Csikzentmihalyi, M., & Csikzentmihalyi, I. (1988). *Optimal experience: Psychological studies of flow in consciousness.* New York: Cambridge University Press.

Cui, X., & Vaillant, G. E. (1996). Antecedents and consequences of negative life events in adulthood: A longitudinal study. *American Journal of Psychiatry, 153,* 1.

Curtis, R. C., & Miller, K. (1987). Believing another person likes or dislikes you: Behaviors making the beliefs come true. *Journal of Personality and Social Psychology, 51,* 284–290.

**D**

Dale, N., & Kandel, E. R. (1990). Facilitatory and inhibitory transmitters modulate spontaneous transmitter release at cultured Aplysia sensorimotor synapses. *Journal of Physiology, 421,* 203–222.

Dalman, C., Allebeck, P., Cullberg, J., Grunewald, C., & Köster, M. (1999). Obstetric complications and the risk of schizophrenia. *Archives of General Psychiatry, 56,* 234–240.

Damasio, A. (1999). *The feeling of what happens: Body and emotion in the making of consciousness.* San Diego: Harcourt.

Damasio, A. (2001). Fundamental feelings. *Nature, 413,* 781.

Darley, J., & Latané, B. (1968). Bystander intervention in emergencies. Diffusion of responsibility. *Journal of Personality and Social Psychology, 8,* 377–383.

Darling, N., & Steinberg, L. (1993). Parenting style as context: An integrative model. *Psychological Bulletin, 113,* 487–496.

Darwin, C. (1871). *The descent of man and selection in relation to sex* (Vols. 1 and 2). London: Murray.

Darwin, C. (1899). *The expression of the emotions in man and animals.* New York: Appleton.

Dash, P. K., Hochner, B., & Kandel, E. R. (1990). Injection of the cAMP-responsive element into the nucleus of Aplysia sensory neurons blocks long-term facilitation. *Nature, 345,* 718–721.

Davidson, R. J. (1992). Emotion and affective style: Hemispheric substrates. *Psychological Science,* 39–43.

Davidson, R. J., Ekman, P., Saron, C. D., Senulis, J. A., & Friesen, W. V. (1990). Approach-withdrawal and cerebral asymmetry: Emotional expression and brain physiology. *Journal of Personality and Social Psychology, 58,* 330–341.

Dawson, D. A. (2000). Alcohol consumption, alcohol dependence, and all-cause mortality. *Alcoholism: Clinical & Experimental Research, 24,* 72–81.

Dedic, H., Rosenfield, S., Cooper, M., & Fuchs, M. (2001). "Do I really hafta?"; Webcal, a look at the use of livemath software in Web-based materials that provide interactive engagement in a collaborative learning environment for differential calculus. *Educational Research and Evaluation, 7,* 285–312.

Deese, J., & Deese, E. K. (1979). *How to study* (3rd ed.). New York: McGraw-Hill.

Deikman, A. J. (1980). De-automization and the mystic experience. In J. R. Tisdale (Ed.), *Growing edges in the psychology of religion* (pp. 201–217). Chicago: Nelson-Hall.

Delahanty, D. L., Herberman, H. B., Craig, K. J., Hayward, M. C., Fullerton, C. S., & Ursano, R. J. (1997). Acute and chronic distress and posttraumatic stress disorder as a function of responsibility for serious motor vehicle accidents. *Journal of Consulting and Clinical Psychology, 65(4),* 560–567.

Delgado, J. M. R. (1969). *Physical control of the mind: Toward a psycho-civilized society.* New York: Harper & Row.

Dember, W. N. (1965). The new look in motivation. *American Scientist, 53,* 409–427.

Denmark, F. (1998). Women and psychology: An international perspective. *American Psychologist, 53,* 465–473.

DeRubeis, R. J., Gelfand, L. A., Tang, T. Z., & Simons, A. D. (1999). Medications versus cognitive behavior therapy for severely depressed outpatients: Mega-analysis of four randomized comparisons. *American Journal of Psychiatry, 156,* 1107–1013.

D'Esposito, M. (2000). Functional imaging of neurocognition. *Seminars in Neurology, 20,* 487–498.

Devine, P. G. (1996, January/February). Breaking the prejudice habit. *Psychological Science Agenda,* pp. 10–11.

Dew, M. A., Ragni, M. V., & Nimorwicz, P. (1990). Infection with human immunodeficiency virus and vulnerability to psychological distress. *Archives of General Psychiatry, 47,* 437–445.

Dewsbury, D. A. (1990). Early interactions between animal psychologists and animal activists and the founding of the APA Committee on Precautions in Animal Experimentation. *American Psychologist, 45,* 315–327.

Diamond, E. L. (1982). The role of anger and hostility in essential hypertension and coronary heart disease. *Psychological Bulletin, 92,* 410–433.

Diamond, L. M. (2000). Sexual identity, attractions, and behavior among young sexual-minority women over a 2-year period. *Developmental Psychology, 36,* 241–250.

Dick , D., Rose, R., Viken, R., Kaprio, J., & Koskenvuo, M. (2001). Exploring gene-environment interactions: Socioregional moderation of alcohol use. *Journal of Abnormal Psychology, 110,* 625–632.

Dickens, W. T., & Flynn, J. R. (2001). Heritability estimates versus large environmental effects: The IQ paradox resolved. *Psychological Review, 108,* 346–369.

Diener, E., & Seligman, M. E. P. (2002). Very happy people. *Psychological Science, 13,* 81–84.

Dierker, L., Avenevoli, S., Merikangas, K., Flaherty, B., & Stolar, M. (2001). Association between psychiatric disorders and the progression of tobacco use behaviors. *Journal of American Academy of Child & Adolescent Psychiatry, 40,* 1159–1167.

Dindia, K., & Allen, M. (1992). Sex differences in self-disclosure: A meta-analysis. *Psychological Bulletin, 112,* 106–124.

Diokno, A. C., & Hollander, J. B. (1991). Diagnosis of erectile dysfunction. In J. F. Leyson (Ed.), *Sexual rehabilitation of the spinal cord patient.* Clifton, NJ: Humana Press.

Dipboye, R. L., Fromkin, Il. L., & Wilback, K. (1975). The importance of applicant sex, attractiveness, and scholastic standing in evaluation of job application resumes. *Journal of Applied Psychology, 60,* 39–43.

Dishman, R. K. (1982). Compliance/adherence in health-related exercise. *Health Psychology, 1,* 237–267.

Doernberger, C., & Zigler, E. (1993). Project Follow Through: Intent and reality. In E. Zigler & S. J. Styfco (Eds.), *Head Start and beyond: A national plan for extended childhood intervention* (p. 155). New Haven: Yale University Press.

Dohr, K. B., Rush, A. J., & Bernstein, I. H. (1989). Cognitive biases and depression. *Journal of Abnormal Psychology, 98,* 263–267.

Dohrenwend, B., Pearlin, L., Clayton, P., Hamburg, B., Dohrenwend, B., Riley, M., & Rose, R. (1982). Report on stress and life events. In G. R. Elliott & C. Eisdorfer (Eds.), *Stress and human health: Analysis and implications on research.* New York: Springer-Verlag.

Dollard, J., Doob, L. W., Miller, N. E., Mowrer, O. H., & Sears, R. R. (1939). *Frustration and aggression.* New Haven: Yale University Press.

Dolnick, E. (1993). Deafness as culture. *Atlantic Monthly, 272,* 37–53.

Dougherty, D. D., Baer, L., Cosgrove, G. R., Cassem, E. H., Price, B. H., Nierenberg, A. A., Jenike, M. A., & Rauch, S. L. (2002). Prospective long-term follow-up of 44 patients who received cingulotomy for treatment-refractory obsessive-compulsive disorder. *American Journal of Psychiatry, 159,* 269–275.

Dovidio, J. F., & Gaertner, S. L. (1999). Reducing prejudice: Combating intergroup biases. *Current Directions in Psychological Science 8,* 101–105.

Dovidio, J. F., & Gaertner, S. L. (2000). Aversive racism and selection decisions: 1989 and 1999. *American Psychological Society, 11,* 315–319.

Dozois, D. J. A., & Dobson, K. S. (2001). Information processing and cognitive organization in unipolar depression: Specificity and comorbidity issues. *Journal of Abnormal Psychology, 110,* 236–246.

Dragoi, V., & Staddon, J. E. R. (1999). The dynamics of operant conditioning. *Psychological Review, 106,* 20–61.

Dravnieks, A. (1983). Odor character profiling. *Journal of the Air Pollution Control Association, 33,* 752–755.

Duncker, K. (1945). On problem solving. *Psychological Monographs, 58(5).*

Durston, S., Hulshoff, H., Casey, B. J., Giedd, J., Buitelaar, J., & van Engeland, H. (2001). Anatomical MRI of the developing human brain: What have we learned? *Journal of American Academy of Child & Adolescent Psychiatry, 40,* 1012–1019.

Dutton, D. G., & Aron, A. P. (1974). Some evidence for heightened sexual attraction under conditions of high anxiety. *Journal of Personality and Social Psychology, 30,* 510–517.

Dwyer, W. O., Leeming, F. C., Cobern, M. K., Porter, B. E., & Jackson, J. M. (1993). Critical review of behavioral interventions to preserve the environment: Research since 1980. *Environment and Behavior, 25,* 275–321.

**Dyck, D. G., Greenberg, A. H., & Osachuk, T. A.** (1986). Tolerance to drug-induced (Poly I:C) natural killer cell activation: Congruence with a Pavlovian conditioning model. *Journal of Experimental Psychology: Animal Behavior Processes, 12,* 25–31.

**Dywan, J., & Bowers, K.** (1983). The use of hypnosis to enhance recall. *Science, 222,* 184–185.

### E

**Eagly, A. H.** (1978). Sex differences in influenceability. *Psychological Bulletin, 85,* 86–116.

**Eagly, A. H.** (1995). The science and politics of comparing women and men. *American Psychologist, 50,* 145–158.

**Eagly, A. H., & Johnson, B. T.** (1990). Gender and leadership style. *Psychological Bulletin, 108,* 233–256.

**Eagly, A. H., & Karau, S. J.** (2002). Role congruity theory of prejudice toward female leaders. *Psychological Review, 109,* 573–598.

**Eagly, A. H., Makhijani, M. G., & Klonsky, B. G.** (1992). Gender and the evaluation of leaders: A meta-analysis. *Psychological Bulletin, 111,* 3–22.

**Eagly, A. H., & Wood, W.** (1999). The origins of sex differences in human behavior: Evolved dispositions versus social roles. *American Psychologist, 54,* 408–423.

**Eaton, W. W., Anthony, J. C., Gallo, J., Cai, G., Tien, A., Romanoski, A., Lyketsos, C., & Chen, L.** (1997). Natural history of diagnostic interview schedule/DSM-IV major depression. *Archives of General Psychiatry, 54,* 993–999.

**Ebert, P. D., & Hyde, J. S.** (1976). Selection for agonistic behavior in wild female *Mus musculus. Behavior Genetics, 6,* 291–304.

**Eckert, E. D., Bouchard, T. J., Bohlen, J., & Heston, L. L.** (1986). Homosexuality in monozygotic twins reared apart. *British Journal of Psychiatry, 148,* 421–425.

**Egendorf, A., Kaduschin, C., Laufer, R. S., Rothbart, G., & Sloan, L.** (1981). *Legacies of Vietnam: Comparative adjustment of veterans and their peers.* (Publication No. V101 134P-630). Washington, DC: U.S. Government Printing Office.

**Ehlers, A., & Breuer, P.** (1992). Increased cardiac awareness in panic disorder. *Journal of Abnormal Psychology, 101,* 371–382.

**Eibl-Eibesfeldt, I.** (1973). The expressive behavior of the deaf and blind-born. In M. von Cranach & I. Vine (Eds.), *Social communication and movement.* New York: Academic Press.

**Einstein, G. O., McDaniel, M. A., Smith, R. E., & Shaw, P.** (1998). Habitual prospective memory and aging; Remembering intentions and forgetting actions. *Psychological Science, 9,* 284–288.

**Ekman, P.** (1992). Facial expressions of emotion: New findings, new questions. *Psychological Science, 3,* 34–38.

**Ekman, P., Levenson, R. W., & Friesen, W. V.** (1983). Autonomic nervous system activity distinguishes among emotions. *Science, 221,* 1208–1210.

**Elkind, D.** (1967). *Children and adolescents: Interpretive essays on Jean Piaget.* New York: Oxford University Press.

**Elkind, D.** (1981). Understanding the young adolescent. In L. D. Steinberg (Ed.), *The life cycle: Readings in human development.* New York: Columbia University Press.

**Elkind, D., & Bowen, R.** (1979). Imaginary audience behavior in children and adolescents. *Developmental Psychology, 15,* 38–44.

**Elliot, A. J., Chirkov, V. I., Kim, Y., & Sheldon, K. M.** (2001). A cross-cultural analysis of avoidance (relative to approach) personal goals. *Psychological Science, 12,* 505–510.

**Elliot, A. J., & Church, M. A.** (1997). A hierarchical model of approach and avoidance achievement motivation. *Journal of Personality and Social Psychology, 72,* 218–232.

**Elliott, D. M.** (1997). Traumatic events: Prevalence and delayed recall in the general population. *Journal of Consulting and Clinical Psychology, 65,* 811–820.

**Ellis, A.** (1962). *Reason and emotion in psychotherapy.* New York: Lyle Stuart.

**Ellis, A.** (1999). *How to make yourself happy and remarkably less disturbable.* Atascadero, CA: Impact.

**Ellis, H. C.** (1987). Recent developments in human memory. In V. Mokosky (Ed.), *The G. Stanley Hall Series.* Washington, DC: American Psychological Association.

**Ellis, H. C., & Hunt, R. R.** (1993). *Fundamentals of cognitive psychology.* Madison, WI: Brown & Benchmark.

**Ellis, L.** (1989). *Theories of rape: Inquiries into causes of sexual aggression.* New York: Hemisphere.

**Emery, V. O., & Oxmans, T. E.** (1992). Update on the dementia spectrum of depression. *American Journal of Psychiatry, 149,* 305–317.

**Emmons, R. A., & Diener, E.** (1986). Situation selection as a moderator of response consistency and stability. *Journal of Personality and Social Psychology, 51,* 1013–1019.

**Engdahl, B., Dikel, T. N., Eberly, R., & Blank, A.** (1997). Posttraumatic stress disorder in a community group of former prisoners of war: A normative response to severe trauma. *American Journal of Psychiatry, 154*(11), 1576–1581.

**Engle, S. A.** (1999). Using neuroimaging to measure mental representations: Finding color-opponent neurons in visual cortex. *Current Directions in Psychological Science, 8,* 23–27.

**Eppley, K. R., Abrams, A. I., & Spear, J.** (1989). Differential effects of relaxation techniques on trait anxiety: A meta-analysis. *Journal of Clinical Psychology, 45,* 957–973.

**Epstein, R. S., Fullerton, C. S., & Ursano, R. J.** (1998). Posttraumatic stress disorder following an air disaster: A prospective study. *American Journal of Psychiatry, 155*(7), 934–938.

**Epstein, S.** (1982). Conflict and stress. In L. Goldberger & S. Breznitz (Eds.), *Handbook of stress.* New York: Free Press.

**Epstein, S., & Roupenian, A.** (1970). Heart rate and skin conductance during experimentally induced anxiety. *Journal of Personality and Social Psychology, 16,* 20–28.

**Erel, O., Oberman, Y., & Yirmiya, N.** (2000). Maternal versus nonmaternal care and seven domains of children's development. *Psychological Bulletin, 126,* 727–747.

**Ericsson, K. A., Krampe, R. T., & Teschmer, R. C.** (1993). The role of deliberate practice in the acquisition of expert performance. *Psychological Review, 100,* 383–406.

**Erikson, E.** (1963). *Childhood and society.* New York: Norton.

**Erlenmeyer-Kimling, L., & Jarvik, L. F.** (1963). Genetics and intelligence: A review. *Science, 142,* 1477–1479.

**Escobar, J. I., Canino, G., Rubio-Stipec, M., & Bravo, M.** (1992). Somatic symptoms after a natural disaster: A prospective study. *American Journal of Psychiatry, 149,* 965–967.

**Evans, M. D., & others.** (1992). Differential relapse following cognitive therapy and pharmacotherapy for depression. *Archives of General Psychiatry, 49,* 802–808.

**Evers, S. E., Bass, M., Donner, A., & McWhinney, I. R.** (1987). Lack of impact on salt restriction advice on hypertensive patients. *Preventive Medicine, 16,* 213–220.

**Exline, J. J., & Lobel, M.** (1999). The perils of outperformance: Sensitivity about being the target of a threatening upward comparison. *Psychological Bulletin, 125,* 307–337.

**Exner, J.** (1986). *The Rorschach: A comprehensive system: Vol. 2. Current research and advanced interpretation.* New York: Wiley.

**Eysenck, H. J.** (1997). Personality and experimental psychology: The unification of psychology and the possibility of a paradigm. *Journal of Personality and Social Psychology, 73,* 1224–1237.

**Eysenck, H. J., & Levey, A.** (1972) Conditioning, introversion-extraversion and the strength of the nervous system. In V. Nebylitsyn & J. Gray (Eds.), *Biological basis of individual behavior.* (pp. 206–220). New York: Academic Press.

**Eysenck, M. W., Mogg, K., May, J., Richards, A., & Mathews, A.** (1991). Bias in interpretation of ambiguous sentences related to threat in anxiety. *Journal of Abnormal Psychology, 100,* 144–150.

**Ezell, C.** (1994). The long and short of short- and long-term memory. *Journal of NIH Research, 6,* 56–61.

**Ezell, C.** (1995). Fat times for obesity research: Tons of new information, but how does it all fit together? *Journal of NIH Research, 7,* 39–43.

### F

**Fagot, B. I.** (1974). Sex differences in toddlers' behavior and parental reaction. *Developmental Psychology, 10,* 554–558.

**Farquhar, J. W.** (1979). *The American way of life need not be hazardous to your health.* New York: Norton.

**Farrell, M. P., & Rosenberg, S. D.** (1981). *Men at midlife.* Boston: Auburn House.

**Fawzi, F. I., & others.** (1990). A structured psychiatric intervention for cancer patients: 2. Changes over time in immunological measures. *Archives of General Psychiatry, 47,* 729–736.

**Fay, N., Garrod, S., & Carletta, J.** (2000). Group discussion as interactive dialogue. *Psychological Science, 11,* 481–486.

**Federal Bureau of Investigation.** (1990). *Crime in the United States.* Washington, DC: Author.

**Feifel, H.** (1990). Psychology and death: Meaningful rediscovery. *American Psychologist, 45,* 537–543.

**Feig, S. L., & Lozsadi, D. A.** (1998). Paying attention to the thalamic reticular nucleus. *Trends in Neuroscience, 21,* 28–32.

**Fein, S., & Spencer, S. J.** (1997). Prejudice as self-image maintenance: Affirming the self through derogating others. *Journal of Personality and Social Psychology, 73,* 31–44.

**Feingold, A.** (1988). Matching for attractiveness in romantic partner and same-sex friends: A meta-analysis and theoretical critique. *Psychological Bulletin, 104,* 226–235.

**Feingold, A.** (1990). Gender differences in effects of physical attractiveness on romantic attraction: A comparison across five research paradigms. *Journal of Personality and Social Psychology, 59,* 981–993.

**Feingold, A.** (1992a). Gender differences in mate selection processes: A test of the parental investment model. *Psychological Bulletin, 112,* 125–139.

**Feingold, A.** (1992b). Good-looking people are not what we think. *Psychological Bulletin, 111,* 304–341.

**Feingold, A.** (1994). Gender differences in personality: A meta-analysis. *Psychological Bulletin, 116,* 429–456.

**Fergusson, D. M., Horwood, L. J., & Beautrais, A. L.** (1999). Is sexual orientation related to mental health problems and suicidality in young people? *Archives of General Psychiatry, 56,* 876–880.

**Ferster, C. B., & Skinner, B. F.** (1957). *Schedules of reinforcement.* New York: Appleton-Century-Crofts.

**Festinger, L. A.** (1957). *A theory of cognitive dissonance.* Evanston, IL: Harper & Row, Peterson.

**Festinger, L. A., & Carlsmith, L. M.** (1959). Cognitive consequences of forced compliance. *Journal of Abnormal and Social Psychology, 58,* 203–210.

**Fichten, C. S., Robillard, K., Judd, D., & Amsel, R.** (1989). College students with physical disabilities: Myths and realities. *Rehabilitation Psychology, 34,* 243–257.

**Fine, B. J., & Kobrick, J. L.** (1978). Effects of altitude and heat on complex cognitive tasks. *Human Factors, 20,* 115–122.

**Finkelhor, D.** (1990). Early and long-term effects of child sexual abuse: An update. *Professional Psychology: Research and Practice, 21,* 325–330.

**Finkelhor, D., & Browne, A.** (1985). The traumatic impact of child sexual abuse. *American Journal of Orthopsychiatry, 55,* 530–541.

**Fisher, R. P., & Geiselman, R. E.** (1988). Enhancing eyewitness memory with the cognitive interview. In M. M. Gruneberg, P. E. Morris, & R. N. Sykes (Eds.), *Practical aspects of memory: Current research and issues: Vol. 1. Memory in everyday life* (pp. 34–39). Chichester, England: Wiley.

**Fisk, A. D., & Rogers, W. A.** (2002). Psychology and aging: Enhancing the lives of an aging population. *American Psychological Society, 11,* 107–110.

**Fiske, S. T.** (1993). Social cognition and social perception. *Annual Review of Psychology, 44,* 155–194.

**Fiske, S. T.** (2002). What we know now about bias and intergroup conflict, the problem of the century. *Current Directions in Psychological Science, 11,* 123–128.

**Fiske, S. T., Bersoff, D. N., Borgida, E., Deaux, K., & Heilman, M. E.** (1991). Social science research on trial: Use of sex stereotyping research in *Price Waterhouse v. Hopkins. American Psychologist, 46,* 1049–1060.

**Flor, H., Elbert, T., Knecht, S., Wienbruch, C., Pantev, C., Birbaumer, N., Larbig, W., & Taub, E.** (1995). Phantom-limb pain as a perceptual correlate of cortical reorganization following arm amputation. *Nature, 375,* 482–490.

**Flynn, J. R.** (1998). IQ gains over time: Towards finding the causes. In U. Neisser (Ed.), *The rising curve: Long-term gains in IQ and related measures* (pp. 25–66). Washington, DC: American Psychological Association.

**Flynn, J. R.** (1999). Searching for justice: The discovery of IQ gains over time. *American Psychologist, 54,* 5–20.

**Foa, E. B., & Riggs, D. S.** (1995). Posttraumatic stress disorder following assault: Theoretical considerations and empirical findings. *Current Directions in Psychological Science, 4,* 61–65.

**Folkman, S., & Lazarus, R. S.** (1986). Stress processes and depressive symptomatology. *Journal of Abnormal Psychology, 95,* 107–113.

**Foreyt, J. P., Scott, L. W., Mitchell, R. E., & Gotto, A. M.** (1979). Plasma lipid changes in the normal population following behavioral treatment. *Journal of Consulting and Clinical Psychology, 47,* 440–452.

**Forgas, J. P., & Bower, G. H.** (1987) Mood effects on person-perception judgments. *Journal of Personality and Social Psychology, 53,* 53–60.

**Forster, J. L., Jeffrey, R. W., & Snell, M. K.** (1988). One-year follow-up study to a worksite weight control program. *Preventive Medicine, 17,* 129–133.

**Foster, C. A., Witcher, B. S., Campbell, W. K., & Green, J. D.** (1998). Arousal and attraction: Evidence for automatic and controlled processes. *Journal of Personality and Social Psychology, 74,* 86–101.

**Foulkes, D.** (1989, December). Understanding our dreams. *Natural Science,* pp. 296–301.

**Foulkes, D., & Schmidt, M.** (1983). Temporal sequence and unit composition in dream reports from different stages of sleep. *Sleep, 6,* 265–280.

**Foulkes, W. D.** (1962). Dream reports from different stages of sleep. *Journal of Abnormal and Social Psychology, 65,* 14–25.

**Fouts, R.** (1997). *Next of kin: What chimpanzees have taught me about who we are.* New York: William Morrow.

**Fowles, D. C.** (1992). Schizophrenia: Diathesis-stress revisited. *Annual Review of Psychology, 43,* 303–336.

**Foxx, R., & Rubinoff, A.** (1981). A behavioral treatment of caffeinism. *Journal of Applied Behavior Analysis, 14,* 21–30.

**Frankel, F. H.** (1995). Discovering new memories in psychotherapy—Childhood revisited, fantasy, or both? *New England Journal of Medicine,* 591–594.

**Franz, E. A., Waldie, K. E., & Smith, M. J.** (2000) The effect of callostomy on novel versus familiar bimanual actions: A neural dissociation between controlled and automatic processes? *Psychological Science, 11,* 82–85.

**Frazier, J. A., & Morrison, F. J.** (1998). The influence of extended-year schooling on growth of achievement and perceived competence in early elementary school. *Child Development, 69,* 495–517.

**Freeman, L.** (1972). *The story of Anna O.* New York: Walker.

**French, E. G.** (1956). Motivation as a variable in work-partner selection. *Journal of Abnormal and Social Psychology, 53,* 96–99.

**Fried-Buchalter, S.** (1997). Fear of success, fear of failure, and the imposter phenomenon among male and female marketing managers. *Sex Roles, 37,* 847–859.

**Friedman, H. S., & Booth-Kewley, S.** (1987). The "disease-prone" personality: A meta-analytic view of the construct. *American Psychologist, 42,* 539–555.

**Friedman, H. S., Tucker, J. S., Schwartz, J. E., Tomlinson-Keasey, C., Martin, L. R., Wingard, D. L., & Criqui, M. H.** (1995). Psychosocial and behavioral predictors of longevity: The aging and death of the "termites." *American Psychologist, 50,* 69–78.

**Friedman, M., & Rosenman, R. H.** (1974). *Type A behavior and your heart.* New York: Knopf.

**Fry, A. F., & Hale, S.** (1996). Processing speed, working memory, and fluid intelligence: Evidence for a developmental cascade. *Psychological Science, 7,* 237–241.

**Fullerton, C. S., Ursano, R. J., Epstein, R. S., Crowley, B., Vance, K., Kao, T. C., Dougall, A., & Baum, A.** (2001). Gender differences in posttraumatic stress disorder after motor vehicle accidents. *American Journal of Psychiatry, 158,* 1486–1491.

**Furomoto, L.** (1992). Joining separate spheres—Christine Ladd-Franklin, woman-scientist (1847–1930). *American Psychologist, 47,* 174–182.

**Furomoto, L., & Scarborough, E.** (1986). Placing women in the history of psychology: The first women psychologists. *American Psychologist, 41,* 35–42.

**Fuster, J. M.** (1995). *Memory in the cerebral cortex.* Cambridge, MA: MIT Press.

**G**

**Gabbard, G. O., Lazar, S. G., Hornberger, J., & Spiegel, D.** (1997). The economic impact of psychotherapy: A review. *American Journal of Psychiatry, 154,* 147–155.

**Galambos, N. L.** (1992). Parent-adolescent relations. *Current Directions in Psychological Science, 1,* 146–149.

**Galanter, E.** (1962). *New directions in psychology.* New York: Holt, Rinehart & Winston.

**Galea, S., Ahern, J., Resnick, H., Kilpatrick, D., Bucuvalas, M., Gold, J., & Vlahov, D.** (2002). Psychological sequelae of the September 11 terrorist attacks in New York City. *New England Journal of Medicine, 346,* 982–987.

**Gallup, G., & Proctor, W.** (1982). *Adventures in immortality.* New York: McGraw-Hill.

**Galotti, K.** (1990). Approaches to studying formal and everyday reasoning. *Psychological Bulletin, 105,* 331–351.

**Garb, H. N., Florio, C. M., & Grove, W. M.** (1998). The validity of the Rorschach and Minnesota Multiphasic Personality Inventory: Results from meta-analyses. *Psychological Science, 9,* 402–404.

**Garcia, J., Hankins, W. G., & Rusiniak, K. W.** (1974). Behavioral regulation of the *milieu interne* in man and rat. *Science, 185,* 824–831.

**Garcia, L. T.** (1982). Sex-role orientation and stereotypes about male-female sexuality. *Sex Roles, 8,* 863–876.

**Garcia-Herrero, S., Saldana, M. A. M., Manzanedo del Campo, M. A., & Ritzed, D. O.** (2002). From the traditional concept of safety management to safety integrated with quality. *Journal of Safety Research, 33,* 1–20.

**Garcia-Vera, M. P., Labrador, F. J., & Sanz, J.** (1997). Stress-management training for essential hypertension: A controlled study. *Applied Psychophysiology and Biofeedback, 22,* 261–283.

**Gardner, B. T., & Gardner, R. A.** (1971). Two-way communication with an infant chimpanzee. In A. M. Schrier & F. Stollnitz (Eds.), *Behavior of nonhuman primates* (Vol. 4). New York: Academic Press.

**Gardner, H.** (1983). *Frames of mind: The theory of multiple intelligence.* New York: Basic Books.

**Garlick, D.** (2002). Understanding the nature of the general factor of intelligence: The role of individual differences in neural plasticity as an explanatory mechanism. *Psychological Review, 109,* 116–136.

**Garner, D. M., Rockert, W., Davis, R., Garner, M. V., Olmsted, M. P., & Eagle, M.** (1993). Comparison of cognitive-behavioral and supportive-expressive therapy for bulimia nervosa. *American Journal of Psychiatry, 150,* 37–46.

**Garraghty, P. E., Churchill, J. D., & Banks, M. K.** (1998). Adult neural plasticity: Similarities between two paradigms. *Current Directions in Psychological Science, 7,* 87–91.

**Garro, L. C.** (1990). Culture, pain and cancer. *Journal of Palliative Care, 6,* 34–44.

**Gates, A. I.** (1917). Experiments as the relative efficiency of men and women in memory and reasoning. *Psychological Review, 24,* 139–146.

**Gazzaniga, M.** (1992). *Nature's mind: The biological roots of thinking, emotion, sexuality, language, and intelligence.* Boston: Houghton Mifflin.

**Gazzaniga, M. S.** (1967). The split brain in man. *Scientific American,* pp. 24–29.

**Gazzaniga, M. S.** (1983). Right hemisphere language following brain bisection: A 20-year perspective. *American Psychologist, 38,* 525–537.

**Gazzaniga, M. S.** (1998, July). The split brain revisited. *Scientific American,* pp. 50–55.

**Gazzaniga, M. S.** (2000). *Cognitive neuroscience: A reader.* Malden, MA: Blackwell.

**Geary, D. C.** (1998). *Male, female: The evolution of human sex differences.* Washington, DC: American Psychological Association.

**Geary, D. C.** (1999). Evolution and developmental sex differences. *Current Directions in Psychological Science, 8,* 115–120.

**Geen, R. G., & Quanty, M. B.** (1977). The catharsis of aggression: An evaluation of a hypothesis. In L. Berkowitz (Ed.), *Advances in experimental social psychology* (Vol. 10). New York: Academic Press.

**Geer, J., Heiman, J., & Leitenberg, H.** (1984). *Human sexuality.* Englewood Cliffs, NJ: Prentice-Hall.

**Geller, E. S.** (1988). A behavioral science approach to transportation safety. *Bulletin of the New York Academy of Medicine, 64,* 632–661.

**Geller, E. S.** (1995). Integrating behaviorism and humanism for environmental protection. *Journal of Social Issues, 51,* 179–195.

**Geller, E. S.** (1996). *The psychology of safety: How to improve behaviors and attitudes on the job.* Boca Raton, FL: CLC Press.

**Geller, E. S., Kalsher, M. J., Rudd, J. R., & Lehman, G. R.** (1989). Promoting safety belt use on a university campus: An integration of commitment and incentive strategies. *Journal of Applied Social Psychology, 19,* 3–19.

**Geller, E. S., Ross, N. W., & Delphos, W. A.** (1987). Does server intervention training make a difference: An empirical field evaluation. *Alcohol, Health & Research World,* 64–69.

**Gentile, D. A.** (1993). Just what are sex and gender, anyway? A call for a new terminological standard. *Psychological Science, 4,* 120–126.

**Gershon, E. S., & Rieder, R. O.** (1992, September). Major disorders of mind and brain. *Scientific American,* pp. 126–133.

**Ghetti, S., Qin, J., & Goodman, G. S.** (2002). False memories in children and adults: Age, distinctiveness, and subjective experience. *Developmental Psychology, 38,* 705–718.

**Gibbons, F. X., Eggleston, T. J., & Benthin, A. C.** (1997). Cognitive reactions to smoking relapse: The reciprocal relation between dissonance and self-esteem. *Journal of Personality and Social Psychology, 72,* 184–195.

**Gibson, E., & Walk, R.** (1960). The "visual cliff." *Scientific American,* pp. 64–71.

**Giedd, J. N., Castellanos, F. X., Rajapakse, J. C., Vaituzis, A. C., & Rapoport, J. L.** (1997). Sexual dimorphism of the developing human brain. *Progress in Neuro-Psychopharmacology & Biological Psychiatry, 21,* 1185–1201.

**Gilbertini, M., Graham, C., & Cook, M. R.** (1999). Self-report of circadian type reflects phase of the melatonin rhythm. *Biological Psychology, 50,* 19–33.

**Gilboa-Schechtman, E., & Foa, E. B.** (2001). Patterns of recovery from trauma. The use of intraindividual analysis. *Journal of Abnormal Psychology, 110,* 392–400.

**Gildea, W.** (1993, August 29). Seeing pride in his accomplishments. *Washington Post,* pp. 7, 2.

**Gilligan, C.** (1982). *In a different voice,* Cambridge, MA: Harvard University Press.

**Glanzer, M., & Cunitz, A. R.** (1966). Two storage mechanisms in free recall. *Journal of Verbal Learning and Verbal Behavior, 5,* 351–360.

**Glaser, R., & Chi, M. T. H.** (1988). Overview. In M. T. H. Chi, R. Glaser, & M. J. Farr (Eds.), *The nature of expertise.* Hillsdale, NJ: Erlbaum.

**Glaser, R., & others.** (1990). Psychological stress-induced modulation of interleukin 2 receptor gene expression and interleukin 2 production in peripheral blood leukocytes. *Archives of General Psychiatry, 47,* 707–712.

**Gleaves, D. H.** (1996). The sociocognitive model of dissociative identity disorder: A reexamination of the evidence. *Psychological Bulletin, 120,* 42–59.

**Goldberg, L. R.** (1993). The structure of phenotypic personality traits. *American Psychologist, 48,* 26–34.

**Goldfried, M., & Davison, G.** (1976). *Clinical behavior therapy.* New York: Holt, Rinehart & Winston.

**Golding, J. M., Smith, R., & Kashner, T. M.** (1991). Does somatization disorder occur in men? *Archives of General Psychiatry, 48,* 231–235.

**Goldman-Rakic, P. S.** (1992). Working memory and the mind. *Scientific American,* pp. 111–117.

**Goldsmith, H. H., & Alansky, J. A.** (1987). Maternal and infant temperamental predictors of attachment: A meta-analytic review. *Journal of Consulting and Clinical Psychology, 55,* 805–816.

**Goldsmith, L.** (1988). Treatment of sexual dysfunction. In E. Weinstein & E. Rosen (Eds.), *Sexuality counseling: Issues and implications.* Monterey, CA: Brooks/Cole.

**Goldstein, M. J., & Palmer, J. O.** (1963). *The experience of anxiety.* New York: Oxford University Press.

**Gorman, J. M., Kent, J., Martinez, J., Browne, S., Coplan, J., & Papp, L. A.** (2001). Physiological changes during carbon dioxide inhalation in patients with panic disorder, major depression, and premenstrual dysphoric disorder. *Archives of General Psychiatry, 58,* 125–131.

**Gosling, S. D., & John, O. P.** (1999). Personality dimensions in nonhuman animals: A cross-species review. *Current Directions in Psychological Science 8,* 69–75.

**Gotlib, I.** (1992). Interpersonal and cognitive aspects of depression. *Current Directions in Psychological Science, 1,* 149–154.

**Gottesman, I. I.** (2001). Psychopathology through a life span-genetic prism. *American Psychologist, 56,* 861–878.

**Gottfredson, L. S.** (1997). Why *g* matters: The complexity of everyday life. *Intelligence, 24,* 79–132.

**Gottfried, A. E., Fleming, J. S., & Gottfried, A. W.** (1998). Role of cognitively stimulating home environment in children's academic intrinsic motivation: A longitudinal study. *Child Development, 69,* 1448–1460.

**Gould, E., Beylin, A., Tanapat, P., Reeves, A., & Shors, T.** (1999). Learning enhances adult neurogenesis in the hippocampal formation. *Nature Neuroscience, 2,* 260–265.

**Gould, E., Reeves, A., Graziano, M., & Cross, C.** (1999). Neurogenesis in the neocortex of adult primates. *American Association for the Advancement of Science, 286,* 548–552.

**Gould, E., Tanapat, P., Rydel, T., & Hastings, N.** (2000). Regulation of hippocampal neurogenesis in adulthood. *Biological Psychiatry, 48,* 715–720.

**Grady, C. L., McIntosh, A. R., Horwitz, B., Maisog, J. M., Ungerleider, L. G., Mentis, M. J., Pietrini, P., Schapiro, M. B., & Haxby, J. V.** (1995). Age-related reductions in human recognition memory due to impaired encoding. *Science, 269,* 218–220.

**Graf, P., Squire, L. R., & Mandler, G.** (1984). The information that amnesic patients do not forget. *Journal of Experimental Psychology, Learning, Memory, and Cognition, 10,* 164–178.

**Gray, J. A.** (1988). The neuropsychological basis of anxiety. In C. G. Last & M. Hersen (Eds.), *Handbook of anxiety disorders.* Elmsford, NY: Pergamon Press.

**Graziano, W. G., & Musser, L. M.** (1982). The going and parting of the ways. In S. Duck (Ed.), *Personal relationships 4: Dissolving personal relationships.* London: Academic Press.

**Greden, J. F.** (1974). Anxiety or caffeinism: A diagnostic dilemma. *American Journal of Psychiatry, 131,* 1089–1092.

**Greene, E., & Loftus, E. F.** (1998). Psycholegal research on jury damage awards. *Current Directions in Psychological Science 7,* 50–54.

**Greenfield, P.** (1998). The cultural evolution of IQ. In U. Neisser (Ed.), *The rising curve: Long-*

*term gains in IQ and related measures* (pp. 81–124). Washington, DC: American Psychological Association.

**Greenough, W. T., Black, J. E., & Wallace, C. S.** (1987). Experience and brain development. *Child Development, 58,* 539–559.

**Griffith, W., & Veitch, R.** (1971). Influences of population density on interpersonal affective behavior. *Journal of Personality and Social Psychology, 17,* 92–98.

**Grilo, C. M., Shiffman, S., & Wing, R. R.** (1989). Relapse crises and coping among dieters. *Journal of Consulting and Clinical Psychology, 57,* 488–495.

**Grimes, J. W., & Allinsmith, W.** (1961). Compulsivity, anxiety, and school achievement. *Merrill-Palmer Quarterly, 7,* 247–269.

**Grissmer, Williamson, Kirby, & Berends.** (1998). Exploring the rapid rise in Black achievement scores in the United States (1970–1990). In U. Neisser (Ed.), *The rising curve: Long-term gains in IQ and related measures* (pp. 251–286). Washington, DC: American Psychological Association.

**Grosser, B., Monti-Bloch, L., Jennings-White, C., & Berliner, D.** (2000). Behavioral and electrophysiological effects of androstadienone, a human pheromone. *Psychoneuroendocrinology, 25,* 289–300.

**Grossman, S. P.** (1960). Eating and drinking elicited by direct adrenergic and cholinergic stimulation of hypothalamus. *Science, 132,* 301–302.

**Groth, N.** (1979). *Men who rape: The psychology of the offender.* New York: Plenum.

**Groves, P. M., & Rebec, C. V.** (1988). *Introduction to biological psychology* (3rd ed.). Dubuque, IA: Wm. C. Brown.

**Gruskin, E. P.** (1999). *Treating lesbians and bisexual women: Challenges and strategies for health professionals.* Thousand Oaks, CA: Sage

**Gudjonsson, G.** (2001). False confessions. *Psychologist, 14,* 588–591.

**Guilford, J. P.** (1950). Creativity. *American Psychologist, 5,* 444–454.

**Guilford, J. P.** (1967). *The nature of human intelligence.* New York: McGraw-Hill.

**Guilford, J. P.** (1982). Cognitive psychology's ambiguities: Some suggested remedies. *Psychologist Review, 89,* 48–59.

**Gunnar, M. R., Malone, S., & Fisch, R. O.** (1988). The psychobiology of stress and coping in the human neonate: Studies of adrenocortical activity in response to stress in the first week of life. In T. Field, P. McCabe, & N. Schneiderman (Eds.), *Stress and coping.* Hillsdale, NJ: Lawrence Erlbaum.

**Gustavson, C. R., Garcia, J., Hankins, W. G., & Rusiniak, K. W.** (1974). Coyote predation control by aversive conditioning. *Science, 184,* 581–584.

**Guyatt, G. H., Cook D. J., King, D., Norman, G. R., Kane, S. L., & van Ineveld, C.** (1999). Effect of framing of questionnaire items regarding satisfaction with training on residents' responses. *Academic Medicine, 74,* 192–194.

**H**

**Haan, N.** (1976). "... Change and sameness ..." reconsidered. *International Journal of Aging and Human Development, 7,* 59–65.

**Hafer, J. C., & Richmond, E. D.** (1988). What hearing parents should learn about deaf culture. *Perspectives for Teachers of the Hearing Impaired, 7,* 2–5.

**Haimov, I., & Lavie, P.** (1996). Melatonin— A soporific hormone. *Current Directions in Psychological Science, 5,* 106–111.

**Haley, J.** (1976). *Problem-solving therapy.* San Francisco: Jossey-Bass.

**Halgin, R., & Whitbourne, S. K.** (2000). *Abnormal psychology: Clinical perspectives on psychological disorders.* Boston: McGraw-Hill.

**Hall, C. S.** (1951). What people dream about. *Scientific American,* pp. 60–63.

**Halpern, D.** (1992). *Sex differences in cognitive abilities* (2nd ed.). Hillsdale, NJ: Erlbaum.

**Halpern, D. F.** (1997). Sex differences in intelligence: Implications for education. *American Psychologist, 52,* 1091–1102.

**Halpern, D. F.** (1998). Teaching critical thinking for transfer across domains: Dispositions, skills, structure training, and metacognitive monitoring. *American Psychologist, 53,* 449–455.

**Hamann, S. B., Ely, T. D., Grafton, S. T., & Kilts, C. D.** (1999). Amygdala activity related to enhanced memory for pleasant and aversive stimuli. *Nature Neuroscience, 2,* 289–293.

**Hamann, S. B., Ely, T. D., Hoffman, J. M., & Kilts, C. D.** (2002). Ecstasy and agony: Activation of the human amygdala in positive and negative emotion. *Psychological Science, 13,* 135–141.

**Hamilton, D. L., & Zanna, M. P.** (1972). Differential weighting of favorable and unfavorable attributes in impressions of personality. *Journal of Experimental Research in Personality, 6,* 204–212.

**Hammen, C., Elliott, A., Gitlin, M., & Jamison, K. R.** (1989). Sociotropy/autonomy and vulnerability to specific life events in patients with unipolar depression and bipolar disorders. *Journal of Abnormal Psychology, 98,* 154–160.

**Hammen, C., Marks, T., Mayol, A., & deMayo, R.** (1985). Depressive self-schema, life stress, and vulnerability to depression. *Journal of Abnormal Psychology, 94,* 308–319.

**Hanawalt, H. F., & Demarest, I. H.** (1939). The effect of verbal suggestion in the recall period upon the reproduction of visually perceived forms. *Journal of Experimental Psychology, 25,* 159–174.

**Haney, C.** (1980). Social psychology and the criminal law. In P. W. Middlebrook (Ed.), *Social psychology and modern life* (2nd ed.). New York: Knopf.

**Haney, C., & Zimbardo, P.** (1998). The past and future of U.S. prison policy: Twenty-five years after the Stanford prison experiment. *American Psychologist, 53,* 709–727.

**Harkness, K. L., Frank, E., Anderson, B., Houck, P. R., Luther, J., & Kupfer, D. J.** (2002). Does interpersonal psychotherapy protect women from depression in the face of stressful life events? *Journal of Consulting and Clinical Psychology, 70,* 908–915.

**Harlow, H. F.** (1949). The formation of learning sets. *Psychological Review, 56,* 51–56.

**Harlow, H. F., & Harlow, M. K.** (1965). The affectional systems. In A. M. Schrier, H. F. Harlow, & F. Stollnitz (Eds.), *Behavior of nonhuman primates* (Vol. 2). London: Academic Press.

**Harlow, H. F., Harlow, M. K., & Meyer, D. R.** (1950). Learning motivated by a manipulation drive. *Journal of Experimental Psychology, 40,* 228–234.

**Harlow, H. F., & Novak, M. A.** (1973). Psychopathological perspectives. *Perspectives in Biology and Medicine, 16,* 461–478.

**Harmon, T. M., Hyan, M. T., & Tyre, T. E.** (1990). Improved obstetric outcomes using hypnotic analgesia and skill mastery combined with childbirth education. *Journal of Consulting and Clinical Psychology, 58,* 525–530.

**Harris, C. R.** (2002). Sexual and romantic jealousy in heterosexual and homosexual adults. *Psychological Science, 13,* 7–12.

**Harris, T. G.** (1973, July). As far as heroin is concerned, the worst is over. *Psychology Today,* pp. 68–79.

**Harte, J. L., Eifert, G. H., & Smith, R.** (1995). The effects of running and meditation on beta-endorphin, corticotropin-releasing hormone and cortisol in plasma, and on mood. *Biological Psychology, 40,* 251–265.

**Hartmann, E., Russ, D., Oldfield, M., Sivian, I., & Cooper, S.** (1987). Who has nightmares? The personality of the lifelong nightmare sufferer. *Archives of General Psychiatry, 44,* 49–56.

**Hatfield, E.** (1988). Passionate and companionate love. In R. J. Sternberg & M. L. Barnes (Eds.), *The psychology of love.* New Haven: Yale University Press.

**Hauser, R. M.** (1998). Trends in Black-White test-score differentials: I. Uses and misuses of NAEP/SAT data. In U. Neisser (Ed.), *The rising curve: Long-term gains in IQ and related measures* (pp. 219–249). Washington, DC: American Psychological Association.

**Haynes, S. G., Feinleib, M., & Kannel, W. B.** (1980). The relationship of psychosocial factors to coronary heart disease in the Framingham Study. Part III: Eight-year incidence of CHD. *American Journal of Epidemiology, 3,* 37–58.

**Hazlett, E. A., & others.** (1999). Three-dimensional analysis with MRI and PET of the size, shape, and function of the thalamus in the schizophrenia spectrum. *American Journal of Psychiatry, 156,* 1190–1199.

**Hebb, D. O.** (1949). *Organization of behavior.* New York: Wiley.

**Hedge, J. W., & Kavanagh, M. J.** (1988). Improving the accuracy of performance evaluations: Comparison of three methods of performance appraiser training. *Journal of Applied Psychology, 73,* 68–73.

**Hedges, L. V., & Nowell, A.** (1995). Sex differences in mental test scores, variability, and numbers of high-scoring individuals. *Science, 269,* 41–45.

**Heider, F.** (1958). *The psychology of interpersonal relations.* New York: Wiley.

**Heien, D. M., & Pittman, D. J.** (1993). The external costs of alcohol abuse. *Journal of Studies on Alcohol, 54,* 302–307.

**Heilman, M. E., & Herlihy, J. M.** (1984). Affirmative action, negative reaction? Some moderating conditions. *Organizational Behavior and Human Performance, 33,* 204–213.

**Heilman, M. E., Simon, M. C., & Repper, D. P.** (1987). Intentionally favored, unintentionally harmed? Impact of sex-based preferential selection on self-perceptions and self-evaluations. *Journal of Applied Psychology, 72,* 62–68.

**Heiman, J. R., & LoPiccolo, J.** (1983). Clinical outcome of sex therapy: Effects of daily versus weekly treatment. *Archives of General Psychiatry, 40,* 443–449.

**Heimberg, R. G., Liebowitz, M. R., Hope, D. A., Schneier, F. R., Holt, C. S., Welkowitz, L. A., Juster, H. R., Campeas, R., Bruch, M. A., Cloitre, M., Fallon, B., & Klein, D. F.** (1998). Cognitive behavioral group therapy vs. phenelzine therapy for social phobia. *Archives of General Psychiatry, 55,* 1133–1141.

**Held, R., & Hein, A.** (1963). Movement-produced stimulation in the development of visually guided behavior. *Journal of Comparative and Physiological Psychology, 56,* 23–44.

**Helgesen, S.** (1990). *The female advantage: Women's ways of leadership.* New York: Doubleday Currency.

**Heller, K., Swindle, R. W., & Dusenbury, L.** (1986). Components of social support processes. *Journal of Consulting and Clinical Psychology, 54,* 466–470.

**Heller, W., Nitscke, J. B., & Miller, G. A.** (1998). Lateralization in emotion and emotional disorders. *Current Directions in Psychological Science, 7,* 26–32.

**Henderlong, J., & Lepper, M. R.** (2002). The effects of praise on children's intrinsic motivation: A review and synthesis. *Psychological Bulletin, 128,* 774–795.

**Hendin, H., & Klerman, G.** (1993). Physician-assisted suicide: The dangers of legalization. *American Journal of Psychiatry, 150,* 143–145.

**Hennekens, C. H., Rosner, B., & Cole, D. S.** (1978). Daily alcohol consumption and fatal coronary heart disease. *American Journal of Epidemiology, 107,* 196–200.

**Herbert, T. B., & Cohen, S.** (1993). Depression and immunity: A meta-analytic review. *Psychological Bulletin, 113,* 472–486.

**Herdt, G.** (1984). *Ritualized homosexuality in Melanesia.* Berkeley: University of California Press.

**Herek, G. M.** (1990). Gay people and government security clearance. *American Psychologist, 45,* 1035–1042.

**Herek, G. M.** (1993). Sexual orientation and military service: A social science perspective. *American Psychologist, 48,* 538–549.

**Herek, G. M.** (2000). The psychology of sexual prejudice. *Psychological Science, 9,* 19–22.

**Herrell, R., Goldberg, J., True, W. R., Ramakrishnan, V., Lyons, M., Eisen, S., & Tsuang, M. T.** (1999). Sexual orientation and suicidality. *Archives of General Psychiatry, 56,* 867–874.

**Herrnstein, R.** (1971). IQ. *The Atlantic Monthly, 228,* 43–64.

**Hess, E. H.** (1975, November). The role of pupil size in communication. *Scientific American,* pp. 110–119.

**Hetherington, E. M., Bridges, M., & Insabella, G. M.** (1998). What matters? What does not? Five perspectives on the association between marital transitions and children's adjustment. *American Psychologist, 53,* 167–184.

**Hetherington, M.** (1979). Divorce: A children's perspective. *American Psychologist, 34,* 851–858.

**Hewitt, P. L., & Flett, G. L.** (1993). Dimensions of perfectionism, daily stress, and depression: A test of the specific vulnerability hypothesis. *Journal of Abnormal Psychology, 102,* 58–65.

**Hewitt, P. L., Flett, G. L., & Ediger, E.** (1996). Perfectionism and depression: Longitudinal

assessment of a specific vulnerability hypothesis. *Journal of Abnormal Psychology, 105,* 276–280.

**Hilgard, E. R.** (1975). Hypnosis. *Annual Review of Psychology, 26,* 19–44.

**Hilgard, E. R.** (1978). Hypnosis and pain. In R. A. Sternbach (Ed.), *The psychology of pain.* New York: Raven Press.

**Hilgard, E. R., & Hilgard, J. R.** (1975). *Hypnosis in the relief of pain.* Los Altos, CA: William Kaufmann.

**Hill, C., Rubin, Z., & Peplau, L.** (1976). Breakups before marriage: The end of 103 affairs. *Journal of Social Issues, 32,* 147–168.

**Hirst, W.** (1982). The amnesic syndrome: Descriptions and explanations. *Psychological Bulletin, 91,* 435–460.

**Hobson, J. A.** (1989). *Sleep.* New York: Scientific American Library.

**Hochberg, J.** (1988). Visual perception. In R. C. Atkison, R. J. Herrnstein, G. Lindzey, & R. D. Luce (Eds.), *Stevens' handbook of experimental psychology: Vol. 1. Perception and motivation.* New York: Wiley-Interscience.

**Hoffman, C., Lau, L., & Johnson, D. R.** (1986). The linguistic relativity of person cognition: An English-Chinese comparison. *Journal of Personality and Social Psychology, 51,* 1097–1105.

**Hogan, R., Mankin, D., Conway, J., & Fox, S.** (1970). Personality correlates of undergraduate marijuana use. *Journal of Consulting and Clinical Psychology, 35,* 58–63.

**Hokanson, J. E., DeGood, D. E., Forrest, M. S., & Brittain, T. M.** (1963). Availability of avoidance behaviors for modulating vascular-stress responses. *Journal of Personality and Social Psychology, 67,* 60–68.

**Holahan, C. J., & Moos, R. H.** (1987). Risk, resistance, and psychological distress: A longitudinal analysis with adults and children. *Journal of Abnormal Psychology, 96,* 3–13.

**Holahan, C. K., Holahan, C., & Wonacott, N. L.** (1999). Self-appraisal, life satisfaction, and retrospective life choices across one and three decades. *Psychology & Aging, 14,* 238–244.

**Holahan, C. K., Sears, R. R., & Cronbach, L. J.** (1995). *The gifted group in later maturity.* Stanford, CA: Stanford University Press.

**Holden, C.** (1973). Psychosurgery: Legitimate therapy or laundered lobotomy? *Science, 179,* 1109–1112.

**Hole, J. W.** (1990). *Human anatomy and physiology* (5th ed.). Dubuque, IA: Wm. C. Brown.

**Holinger, P. C., & Offer, D.** (1993). *Adolescent suicide.* New York: Guilford Press.

**Hollander, E. P., & Offermann, L. R.** (1990). Power and leadership in organizations: Relations in transition. *American Psychologist, 45,* 179–189.

**Hollon, S. D., Shelton, R. C., & Davis, D. D.** (1993). Cognitive therapy for depression: Conceptual issues and clinical efficacy. *Journal of Consulting and Clinical Psychology, 61,* 270–275.

**Holmes, D. S.** (1984). Meditation and somatic arousal: A review of experimental evidence. *American Psychologist, 39,* 1–10.

**Holmes, T. H., & Rahe, R. H.** (1967). The social readjustment rating scale. *Journal of Psychosomatic Research, 11,* 213–218.

**Honeck, R. P.** (1973). Interpretive vs. structural effects on semantic memory. *Journal of Verbal Learning and Verbal Behavior, 12,* 448–455.

**Hopkin, K.** (1995). Sugar 'n spice vs. puppy-dog tails: Sex differences in the brain. *Journal of NIH Research, 7,* 39–43.

**Hopkins, K.** (1997). Show me where it hurts: Tracing the pathways of pain. *Journal of NIH Research, 9,* 37–43.

**Horgan, J.** (1993, June). Eugenics revisited. *Scientific American,* pp. 122–131.

**Horne, J.** (1988). *Why we sleep: The functions of sleep in humans and other mammals.* New York: Oxford University Press.

**Hotelling, K.** (1991). Sexual harassment: A problem shielded by silence. *Journal of Consulting and Clinical Psychology, 69,* 487–501.

**Hough, R. L., & others.** (1987). Utilization of health and mental health services by Los Angeles Mexican-Americans and non-Hispanic whites. *Archives of General Psychiatry, 44,* 702–709.

**Houston, J. P.** (1985). *Motivation.* New York: Macmillan.

**Houwer, J. D., Thomas, S., & Baeyens, F.** (2001). Associative learning of likes and dislikes: A review of 25 years of research on human evaluative conditioning. *Psychological Bulletin, 127,* 853–869.

**Hovland, C. I.** (Ed.). (1957). *The order of presentation in persuasion.* New Haven: Yale University Press.

**Hovland, C. I., & Weiss, W.** (1951). The influence of source credibility on communication effectiveness. *The Public Opinion Quarterly, 15,* 635–650.

**Howell, W. C.** (1993). Engineering psychology in a changing world. *Annual Review of Psychology, 44,* 231–263.

**Huang, M., & Hauser, R. M.** (1998). Trends in Black-White test-score differentials: II. The WORDSUM Vocabulary Test. In U. Neisser (Ed.), *The rising curve: Long-term gains in IQ and related measures* (pp. 303–334). Washington, DC: American Psychological Association.

**Huddy, L., Billig, J., Bracciodieta, J., Hoeffler, L., Moynihan, P. J., & Pugliani, P.** (1997). The effect of interviewer gender on the survey response. *Political Behavior, 19,* 197–220.

**Huesmann, L. R., Moise, J. F., & Podolski, C. L.** (1997). The effects of media violence on the development of antisocial behavior. In D. M. Stoff, J. Breiling, & J. D. Maser (Eds.), *Handbook of antisocial behavior* (pp. 181–193). New York: John Wiley.

**Hugdahl, K., & Karker, A. C.** (1981). Biological versus experiential factors in phobic conditioning. *Behaviour Research and Therapy, 16,* 315–321.

**Hughes, J. R., Oliveto, A. H., Helzer, J., Higgins, S. R., & Bickel, W. K.** (1992). Should caffeine abuse, dependence, or withdrawal be added to DSM-IV and ICD-10? *American Journal of Psychiatry, 149,* 33–40.

**Hundert, A. J., & Greenfield, N.** (1969). *Physical space and organizational behavior: A study of an office landscape.* Paper presented to the American Psychological Association, Los Angeles.

**Hunt, E.** (1995). The role of intelligence in modern society. *American Scientist, 83,* 356–368.

**Hunter, J. E.** (1979). *An analysis of the validity, test fairness, and utility for the Philadelphia Police Officers Selection Examination prepared by Educational Testing Service.* Report to the Philadelphia Federal District Court, Alvarez v. City of Philadelphia.

**Hunter, J. E.** (1981). *The economic benefits of personnel selection using ability tests: A state-of-the-art review including a detailed analysis of the dollar* *benefit of U.S. Employment Office placements and a critique of the low-cutoff method of test use.* Washington, DC: U.S. Employment Service, U.S. Department of Labor.

**Hunter, J. E., & Hunter, R. F.** (1984). Validity and utility of alternative predictors of job performance. *Psychological Bulletin, 96,* 72–98.

**Huntsinger, C. S., Jose, P. E., & Larson, S. L.** (1998). Do parent practices to encourage academic competence influence the social adjustment of young European American and Chinese American children? *Developmental Psychology, 34,* 747–756.

**Huston, T. L., Niehuis, S., & Smith, S. E.** (2001). The early marital roots of conjugal distress and divorce. *Current Directions in Psychological Science, 10,* 116–119.

**Hyde, J. S.** (1985). *Half the human experience: The psychology of women.* Lexington, MA: D. C. Heath.

**Hyde, J. S., & Plant, E. A.** (1995). Magnitude of psychological gender differences: Another side to the story. *American Psychologist, 50,* 159–161.

**Hyman, I. E., & Billings, F. J.** (1998). Individual differences in the creation of false childhood memories. *Memory, 6,* 1–20.

**Hyman, I. E., & Loftus, E. F.** (1998). Errors in autobiographical memory. *Clinical Psychology Review, 18,* 933–947.

**Hyman, I. E., & Pentland, J.** (1996). The role of mental imagery in the creation of false memories. *Journal of Memory and Language, 35,* 101–117.

**I**

**Iaffaldano, M. T., & Muchinsky, P. M.** (1985). Job satisfaction and job performance. A meta-analysis. *Psychological Bulletin, 97,* 251–273.

**Ilgen, D. R.** (1990). Health issues at work: Opportunities for industrial/organizational psychologists. *American Psychologist, 45,* 273–283.

**Ilgen, D. R.** (1999). Teams embedded in organizations: Some implications. *American Psychologist, 54,* 129–139.

**Ingham, A. G., Levinger, B., Graves, J., & Peckham, V.** (1974). The Ringelmann effect: Studies of group size and group performance. *Journal of Experimental Social Psychology, 10,* 371–384.

**Inhelder, B., & Piaget, J.** (1958). *The growth of logical thinking from childhood to adolescence.* New York: Basic Books.

**Irons, E. D., & Moore, G. W.** (1985). *Black managers: The case of the banking industry.* New York: Praeger.

**Ironson, G., & Schneiderman, N.** (1991). Psychoimmunology and HIV-1: Scope of the problem. In N. Schneiderman (Ed.), *Psychoimmunology and HIV-1.* Geneva: World Health Organization.

**Irving, G. A., Bor, R., & Catalan, J.** (1995). Psychological distress among gay men supporting a lover or partner with AIDS: A pilot study. *AIDS Care, 7,* 605–617.

**Isen, A. M., & Levin, P. F.** (1972). The effect of feeling good on helping: Cookies and kindness. *Journal of Personality and Social Psychology, 21,* 384–388.

**Iverson, L. L.** (1979). The chemistry of the brain. *Scientific American,* pp. 134–149.

**Iyengar, S. S., & Lepper, M. R.** (1999). Rethinking the value of choice: A cultural

perspective on intrinsic motivation. *Journal of Personality and Social Psychology, 76,* 349–366.

**Izard, C. E.** (1972). *Patterns of emotions: A new analysis of anxiety and depression.* New York: Academic Press.

**Izard, C. E.** (1977). *Human emotions.* New York: Plenum.

**Izard, C. E.** (1978). Emotions as motivations: An evolutionary-developmental perspective. In H. E. Howe & R. A. Dienstbeier (Eds.), *Nebraska Symposium on Motivation* (Vol. 26). Lincoln: University of Nebraska Press.

**Izard, C. E.** (1991). *The psychology of emotions.* New York: Plenum Press.

**Izard, C. E.** (1997). Emotions and facial expressions: A perspective from Differential Emotions Theory. In J. A. Russell & others, (Eds.), *The psychology of facial expression: Studies in emotion and social interaction* (pp. 57–77). New York: Cambridge University Press.

**Izard, C. E., & others.** (1997). The ontogeny and significance of infants' facial expressions in the first 9 months of life. *Developmental Psychology, 31,* 997–1013.

**Izquierdo, I., & Medina, J. H.** (1997). The biochemistry of memory formation and its regulation by hormones and neuromodulators. *Psychobiology, 15,* 1–9.

**J**

**Jacob, S., Kinnunen, L., Metz, J., Cooper, M., & McClintock, M.** (2001). Sustained human chemosignal unconsciously alters brain function. *Neuroreport: An International Journal for the Rapid Communication of Research in Neuroscience, 12,* 2391–2394.

**Jacobsen, M. B., & Koch, W.** (1977). Women as leaders: Performance evaluation as a function of the method of leader selection. *Organizational Behavior and Human Performance, 20,* 149–157.

**Jacobson, E.** (1938). *Progressive relaxation.* Chicago: University of Chicago Press.

**Jaffee, S., & Shibley-Hyde, J.** (2000). Gender differences in moral orientation: A meta-analysis. *Psychological Bulletin, 126,* 703–726.

**James, W.** (1890). *The principles of psychology.* New York: Holt, Rinehart & Winston.

**Janis, I. L.** (1982). *Groupthink: Psychological studies of policy decisions and fiascoes.* Boston: Houghton Mifflin.

**Janis, I. L.** (1983). The role of social support in adherence to stressful decisions. *American Psychologist, 38,* 143–160.

**Janis, I. L., & Hoffman, D.** (1982). Effective partnerships in a clinic for smokers. In I. L. Janis (Ed.), *Counseling on personal decisions: Theory and research on short-term helping relationships.* New Haven: Yale University Press.

**Jarrett, R. B., Kraft, D., Doyle, J., Foster, B. M., Eaves, G. G., & Silver, P. C.** (2001). Preventing recurrent depression using cognitive therapy with and without a continuation phase. *Archives of General Psychiatry, 58,* 381–388.

**Jeffrey, K. J., & Reid, I. A.** (1997). Modifiable neuronal connections: An overview of psychiatrists. *American Journal of Psychiatry, 154,* 156–164.

**Jeffrey, R. W.** (1988). Risk behaviors and health: Contrasting individual and population perspectives. *American Psychologist, 44,* 1194–1202.

**Jenkins, C. D.** (1988). Dietary risk factors and their modification in cardiovascular disease. *Journal of Consulting and Clinical Psychology, 56,* 350–357.

**Jenkins, R. W.** (1988). Epidemiology of cardiovascular diseases. *Journal of Consulting and Clinical Psychology, 56,* 324–332.

**Johnson, M. K., Bransford, J. P., & Solomon, S.** (1973). Memory for tacit implications of sentences. *Journal of Experimental Psychology, 98,* 203–205.

**Johnston, T. D., & Edwards, L.** (2002). Genes, environments, and the development of behavior. *Psychological Review, 109,* 26–34.

**Joiner, T. E., Metalsky, G. I., Lew, A., & Klocek, J.** (1999). Testing the causal mediation component of Beck's theory of depression: Evidence for specific mediation. *Cognitive Therapy & Research, 23,* 401–412.

**Joiner, T. E., & Schmidt, N. B.** (1998). Excessive reassurance-seeking predicts depressive but not anxious reactions to acute stress. *Journal of Abnormal Psychology, 107,* 533–537.

**Jones, A., & Crandall, R.** (1986). Validation of a short index of self-actualization. *Personality and Social Psychology Bulletin, 12,* 63–73.

**Jones, E., Bell, L., & Aronson, E.** (1971). The reciprocation of attraction from similar and dissimilar others: A study in person perception and evaluation. In C. McClintock (Ed.), *Experimental social psychology.* New York: Holt, Rinehart & Winston.

**Jones, G. V.** (1983). Identifying basic categories. *Psychological Bulletin, 94,* 423–428.

**Jones, M. C.** (1924). A laboratory study of fear: The case of Peter. *Pedagogical Seminary, 31,* 308–315.

**Jorgensen, R. S., Nash, J. K., Lasser, N. L., Hymowitz, N., & Langer, A. W.** (1988). Heart rate acceleration and its relationship to total serum cholesterol, triglycerides, and blood pressure. *Psychophysiology, 25,* 39–44.

**Josephson, W. L.** (1987). Television violence and children's aggression: Testing the priming, social script, and disinhibition predictions. *Journal of Personality and Social Psychological, 53,* 882–890.

**Judd, L. L., Akiskal, H. S., Schettler, P. J., Endicott, J., Maser, J., Solomon, D. A., Leon, A., Rice, J. A., & Keller, M. B.** (2002). The long-term natural history of the weekly symptomatic status of bipolar I disorder. *Archives of General Psychiatry, 59,* 530–537.

**Judge, T. A., Thoresen, C. J., Bono, J. E., & Patton, G. K.** (2001). The job satisfaction-job performance relationship: A qualitative and quantitative review. *Psychological Bulletin, 127,* 376–407.

**Jurow, G. L.** (1971). New data on the effects of a "death-qualified" jury on the guilt determination process. *Harvard Law Review, 84,* 567–611.

**K**

**Kagan, J.** (1984). *The nature of the child.* New York: Basic Books.

Kahneman, D., & Tversky, A. (1982). The psychology of preferences. *Scientific American,* pp. 160–173.

Kahneman, D., & Tversky, A. (1996). On the reality of cognitive illusions. *Psychological Review, 103,* 582–591.

Kahneman, D., Slovic, P., & Tversky, A. (1982). *Judgment under uncertainty: Heuristics and biases.* New York: Cambridge University Press.

Kalichman, S. C. (1989). Sex roles and sex differences in adult spatial performance. *Journal of Genetic Psychology, 150,* 93–100.

Kalichman, S. C. (1990). Affective and personality characteristics of replicated MMPI profile subgroups of incarcerated adult rapists. *Archives of Sexual Behavior, 19,* 443–459.

Kalichman, S. C. (2000). HIV transmission risk behaviors of men and women living with HIV-AIDS: Prevalence, predictors, and emerging clinical interventions. *Clinical Psychology: Science and Practice, 7,* 32–47.

Kalichman, S. C., Rompa, D., & Coley, B. (1996). Experimental component analysis of a behavioral HIV-AIDS prevention intervention for inner-city women. *Journal of Consulting and Clinical Psychology, 64* (4), 687–693.

Kalish, R. A., & Reynolds, D. K. (1976). *Death and ethnicity: A psychocultural study.* Los Angeles: University of Southern California Press.

Kandel, E., & Abel, T. (1995). Neuropeptides, adenyl cyclase, and memory storage. *Science, 268,* 825–826.

Kandel, E. R. (1999). Biology and the future of psychoanalysis: A new intellectual framework for psychiatry revisited. *American Journal of Psychiatry, 156,* 505–524.

Kandel, E. R., & Hawkins, R. D. (1992). The biological basis of learning and individuality. *Scientific American,* pp. 79–80.

Kandel, E. R., & Schwartz, J. H. (1982). Molecular biology of learning: Modulation of transmitter release. *Science, 218,* 433–443.

Kandel, E. R., Schwartz, J. H., & Jessel, T. M. (1995). *Essentials of neural science and behavior.* East Norwalk, CT: Appleton & Lange.

Kaniasty, K., & Norris, F. H. (1995). Mobilization and deterioration of social support following natural disasters. *Current Directions in Psychological Science, 4,* 94–98.

Kaplan, H. S. (1983). *The evaluation of sexual disorders.* New York: Brunner/Mazel.

Kaplan, M. F. (1975). Information integration in social judgment: Interaction of judge and informational components. In M. F. Kaplan & S. Schwartz (Eds.), *Human judgment and decision processes.* New York: Academic Press.

Kaplan, R. M. (2000). Two pathways to prevention. *American Psychologist, 55,* 382–396.

Kapur, N. (1999). Syndromes of retrograde amnesia: A conceptual and empirical synthesis. *Psychological Bulletin, 125,* 800–825.

Kasper, S., Wehr, T. A., Bartko, J. J., Gaist, P. A., & Rosenthal, N. E. (1989). Epidemiological findings of seasonal changes in mood and behavior. *Archives of General Psychiatry, 46,* 823–833.

Kasser, T., & Ryan, R. M. (1993). A dark side of the American dream: Correlates of financial success as a central life aspiration. *Journal of Personality and Social Psychology, 65,* 410–422.

Kassin, S., Tubb, V., Hosch, H., & Memon, A. (2001). On the general acceptance of eyewitness testimony research. *American Psychologist, 56,* 405–416.

Kassin, S. M., Ellsworth, P. C., & Kassin, S. M. (1989). The "general acceptance" of psychological research on eyewitness testimony: A survey of experts. *American Psychologist, 44,* 1089–1098.

Kaufman, A. S., Kaufman, J. C., Chen, T. H., & Kaufman, N. L. (1996). Differences on six horn abilities for 14 age groups between 15–16 and 75–94 years. *Psychological Assessment, 8,* 161–171.

Kearins, J. (1986). Visual spatial memory in aboriginal and white Australian children. *Australian Journal of Psychology, 38*(3), 203–214.

Keefe, F. J., & France, C. R. (1999). Pain: Biopsychosocial mechanisms and management. *Current Directions in Psychological Science, 5,* 137–141.

Keenan, K., & Shaw, D. (1997). Developmental and social influences on young girls' early problem behavior. *Psychological Bulletin, 121,* 95–113.

Kehoe, P., & Bass, E. M. (1986). Conditioned aversions and their memories in 5-day-old rats during suckling. *Journal of Experimental Psychology: Animal Behavior Processes, 12,* 40–47.

Kelley, H. H. (1973). The processes of causal attribution. *American Psychologist, 28,* 107–128.

Kelly, A. E. (1999). Revealing personal secrets. *Current Directions in Psychological Science 8,* 105–109.

Kelly, G. A. (1955). *The psychology of personal constructs.* New York: Norton.

Kelly, J. A., St. Lawrence, J. S., Hood, H. V., & Brasfield, T. L. (1989). Behavioral intervention to reduce AIDS risk activities. *Journal of Consulting and Clinical Psychology, 57,* 60–67.

Kendall-Tackett, K. A., Williams, L. M., & Finkelhor, D. (1993). Impact of sexual abuse on children: A review and synthesis of recent empirical studies. *Psychological Bulletin, 113,* 164–180.

Kendler, K. (2001). Twin studies of psychiatric illness. *Archives of General Psychiatry, 58,* 1005–1014.

Kendler, K. S., & Prescott, C. A. (1999). A population-based twin study of lifetime major depression in men and women. *Archives of General Psychiatry, 56,* 39–44.

Kendler, K. S., Thornton, L. M., Gilman, S. E., & Kessler, R. C. (2000). Sexual orientation in U.S. national sample of twin and nontwin sibling pairs. *American Journal of Psychiatry, 157,* 1843–1846.

Kephart, W. (1967). Some correlates of romantic love. *Journal of Marriage and the Family, 29,* 470–474.

Kessler, R. C., McGonagle, Z. S., Nelson, C. B., Hughes, M., Eshelman, S., Wittchen, H. U., & Kendler, K. S. (1993). Lifetime and 12-month prevalence of DSM-III-R psychiatric disorders in the United States: Results from the National Comorbidity Survey. *Archives of General Psychiatry, 51,* 8–19.

Kessler, R. C., Sonnega, A., Bromet, E., Hughes, M., & Nelson, C. B. (1995). Posttraumatic stress disorder in the national comorbidity survey. *Archives of General Psychiatry, 52,* 1048–1060.

Kiecolt-Glaser, J. K., Fisher, L. D., Orgrocki, P., Stout, J. C., Speicher, C. E., & Glaser, R. (1987). Marital quality, marital disruption, and immune function. *Psychosomatic Medicine, 49,* 13–30.

Kiecolt-Glaser, J. K., & Glaser, R. (2001). Stress and immunity: Age enhances the risks. *Psychological Science, 10,* 18–21.

Kiecolt-Glaser, J. K., & Newton, T. L. (2001). Marriage and health: His and hers. *Psychological Bulletin, 127,* 472–503.

Kilic, C., Noshirvani, H., Basoglu, M., & Marks, I. (1997). Agoraphobia and panic disorder: 3.5 years after alprazolam and/or exposure treatment. *Psychotherapy & Psychosomatics, 66,* 175–178.

Kilpatrick, D. G., Best, C. L., Veronen, L. J., Amick, A. E., Villeponteaux, L. A., & Ruff, G. A. (1985). Mental health correlates of criminal victimization: A random community survey. *Journal of Consulting and Clinical Psychology, 53,* 866–873.

Kimball, M. M. (1989). A new perspective on women's math achievement. *Psychological Bulletin, 105,* 198–214.

Kimberg, D. Y., Esposito, M. D., & Farah, M. J. (1998). Cognitive functions in the prefrontal cortex: Working memory and executive control. *Current Directions in Psychological Science, 6,* 185–192.

King, L. A., King D. W., Keane, T. M., Fairbank, J. A., & Adams, G. A. (1998). Resilience-recovery factors in post-traumatic stress disorder among female and male Vietnam veterans: Hardiness, postwar social support, and additional stressful life events. *Journal of Personality and Social Psychology, 74*(2), 420–434.

King, M., Coxell, A., & Mezey, G. (2002). Sexual molestation of males: Association with psychological disturbance. *British Journal of Psychiatry, 181,* 153–157.

Kinney, D. K., Levy, D. L., Todd-Yurgelun, D. A., Tramer, S. J., & Holzman, P. S. (1998). Inverse relationship of perinatal complications and eye tracking dysfunction in relatives of patients with schizophrenia: Evidence of a two-factor model. *American Journal of Psychiatry, 15,* 976–978.

Kinsbourne, M. (1988). *Cerebral dysfunction in depression.* Washington, DC: American Psychiatric Association Press.

Kinsey, A. C., Pomeroy, W. B., & Martin, C. E. (1948). *Sexual behavior in the human male.* Philadelphia: W. B. Saunders.

Kinsey, A. C., Pomeroy, W. B., Martin, C. E., & Gebhard, P. H. (1953). *Sexual behavior in the human female.* Philadelphia: W. B. Saunders.

Kirkpatrick B., Ran, R., Amador, X. F., Buchanan, R. W., McGlashan, T., Tohen, M., & Bromet, E. (1998). Summer birth and the deficit syndrome of schizophrenia. *American Journal of Psychiatry, 155,* 1221–1226.

Kirsch, I., & Braffman, W. (2001). Imaginative suggestibility and hypnotizability. *American Psychological Society, 10,* 57–61.

Kirsch, I., & Lynn, S. J. (1995). The altered state of hypnosis: Changes in the theoretical landscape. *American Psychologist, 50,* 846–858.

Kitayama S., Markus, H. R., Matsumoto, H., & Norasakkunkit, V. (1997). Individual and collective processes in the construction of the self: Self-enhancement and self-criticism in Japan. *Journal of Personality and Social Psychology, 72,* 1245–1267.

Klatzky, R. L. (1980). *Human memory: Structures and processes.* San Francisco: W. H. Freeman.

Kleinke, C. L., Peterson, T. R., & Rutledge, T. R. (1998). Effects of self-generated facial expressions on mood. *Journal of Personality and Social Psychology, 74,* 272–279.

**Kleitman, N.** (1960). The nature of dreaming. In G. E. W. Wolstenholme & M. O'Connor (Eds.), *Ciba Foundation symposium on the nature of sleep.* Boston: Little, Brown.

**Klerman, G. L., & Weissman, M. M.** (1993). *New applications of interpersonal psychotherapy.* Washington DC: American Psychiatric Press.

**Klerman, G. L., Weissman, M. M., Rounsaville, B., & Chevron, E. S.** (1995). Interpersonal psychotherapy for depression. *Journal of Psychotherapy Practice & Research, 4,* 342–351.

**Kline, K. N., & Mattson, M.** (2000). Breast self-examination pamphlets: A content analysis grounded in fear appeal research. *Health Communication, 12,* 1–21.

**Kling, K. C., Hyde, J. S., Showers, C. J., & Buswell, B. N.** (1999). Gender differences in self-esteem. *Psychological Bulletin, 125,* 470–500.

**Knight, G. P., Fabes, R. A., & Higgins, D. A.** (1996). Concerns about drawing causal inferences from meta-analyses: An example in the study of gender differences in aggression. *Psychological Bulletin, 119,* 410–421.

**Koegel, P., Burnam, A., & Farr, R. K.** (1988). The prevalence of specific psychiatric disorders among homeless individuals in the inner city of Los Angeles. *Archives of General Psychiatry, 45,* 1085–1092.

**Kohlberg, L.** (1964). The development of moral character. In M. L. Hoffman & L. W. Hoffman (Eds.), *Review of child development research* (Vol. I, p. 400). New York: Russell Sage Foundation.

**Kohlberg, L.** (1966). A cognitive-developmental analysis of children's sex-role concepts and attitudes. In E. E. Maccoby (Ed.), *The development of sex differences.* Stanford, CA: Stanford University Press.

**Kohlberg, L.** (1969). Stage and sequence: The cognitive-developmental approach to socialization. In D. A. Goslin (Ed.), *Handbook of socialization theory and research.* Chicago: Rand McNally.

**Köhler, W.** (1969). *The task of gestalt psychology.* Princeton, NJ: Princeton University Press.

**Kohn, A.** (1987). Shattered innocence. *Psychology Today,* pp. 54–58.

**Kolb, L. C.** (1977). *Modern clinical psychiatry* (9th ed.). Philadelphia: W. B. Saunders.

**Konrad, A. M., Ritchie Jr., J. E., Lieb, P., & Corrigall, E.** (2000). Sex differences and similarities in job attribute preferences: A meta-analysis. *American Psychological Association, Inc., 126,* 593–641.

**Koplewicz, H. S., Vogel, J. M., Solanto, M. V., Morrissey, R. F., Alonso, C. M., Abikoff, H., Gallagher, R., & Novick, R. M.** (2002). Child and parent response to the 1993 World Trade Center bombing. *Journal of Traumatic Stress, 15,* 77–85.

**Koren, D., Arnon, I., & Klein, E.** (1999). Acute stress response and posttraumatic stress disorder in traffic accident victims: A one-year prospective follow-up study. *American Journal of Psychiatry, 156,* 367–373.

**Korman, A. K.** (1974). *The psychology of motivation.* Englewood Cliffs, NJ: Prentice-Hall.

**Koss, M., Leonard, K., Beezley, D., & Oros, C.** (1985). Nonstranger sexual aggression: A discriminant analysis of the psychological characteristics of undetected offenders. *Sex Roles, 12,* 981–992.

**Koss, M., & Oros, C.** (1982). Sexual experiences survey: A research instrument investigating sexual aggression and victimization. *Journal of Consulting and Clinical Psychology, 50,* 455–457.

**Kosslyn, S., Thompson, W., Costantini-Ferrando, M., Alpert, N., & Spiegel, D.** (2000). Hypnotic visual illusion alters color processing in the brain. *American Journal of Psychiatry, 157,* 1279–1285.

**Kravitz, D. A., & Martin, B.** (1986). Ringelmann rediscovered: The original article. *Journal of Personality and Social Psychology, 50,* 936–941.

**Kripke, D., Garfinkel, L., Wingard, D., Klauber, M., & Marler, M.** (2002). Mortality associated with sleep duration and insomnia. *Archives of General Psychiatry, 59,* 131–136.

**Kroger, W. S., & Douce, R. G.** (1979). Hypnosis in criminal investigation. *International Journal of Clinical and Experimental Hypnosis, 27,* 358–384.

**Krueger, R. W. C. F.** (1929). The effect of overlearning on retention. *Journal of Experimental Psychology, 12,* 71–78.

**Kruglanski, A. W.** (1986, August). Freeze-think and the *Challenger. Psychology Today,* pp. 48–49.

**Kubler, A., Kotchoubey, B., Kaiser, J., Wolpaw, J. R., & Birbaumer, N.** (2001). Brain-computer communication: Unlocking the locked in. *American Psychological Association, Inc., 127,* 358–375.

**Kübler-Ross, E.** (1969). *On death and dying.* New York: Macmillan.

**Kübler-Ross, E.** (1974). *Questions and answers on death and dying.* Englewood Cliffs, NJ: Prentice-Hall.

**Kuch, K., & Cox, B. J.** (1992). Symptoms of PTSD in 124 survivors of the Holocaust. *American Journal of Psychiatry, 149,* 337–340.

**Kumari, R.** (1996). Relationship of sex role attitudes and self-esteem to fear of success among college women. *Psychological Studies, 40,* 82–86.

**Kunugi, H., & others.** (1995). Schizophrenia following in utero exposure to the 1957 influenza epidemics in Japan. *American Journal of Psychiatry, 152,* 450–452.

**Kuyken, W., Kurzer, N., DeRubeis, R. J., Beck, A. T., & Brown, G. K.** (2001). Response to cognitive therapy in depression: The role of maladaptive beliefs and personality disorders. *Journal of Consulting and Clinical Psychology, 69,* 560–566.

**Kwon, H., Menon, V., Eliez, S., White, C., Dyer-Friedman, J., Taylor, A., Glover, G., & Reiss, A.** (2001). Functional neuroanatomy of visuospatial working memory in fragile X syndrome: Relation to behavioral and molecular measures. *American Journal of Psychiatry, 158,* 1040–1051.

**L**

**LaCroix, A. Z., Mead, L. A., Liang, K., Thomas, C. B., & Pearson, T. P.** (1986). Coffee consumption and the incidence of coronary heart disease. *New England Journal of Medicine, 315,* 977–982.

**Lader, M. H., & Mathews, A.** (1970). Physiological changes during spontaneous panic attacks. *Journal of Psychosomatic Research, 14,* 377–382.

**La Greca, A. M., Silverman, W. K., & Wasserstein, S. B.** (1998). Children's predisaster functioning as a predictor of posttraumatic stress following Hurricane Andrew. *Journal of Consulting and Clinical Psychology, 66,* 883–892.

**Lahey, B. B., & Ciminero, A. R.** (1980). *Maladaptive behavior.* Glenview, IL: Scott, Foresman.

**Lahey, B. B., Hartdagen, S. E., Frick, P. J., McBurnett, K., Connor, R., & Hyrd, G. W.** (1988). Conduct disorder: Parsing the confounded relation to parental divorce and antisocial personality. *Journal of Abnormal Psychology, 97,* 334–337.

**Lahey, B. B., Loeber, R., Quay H. C., Applegate, B., Shaffer, D., Waldman, I., Hart, E. L., McBurnett, K., Frick, P. J., Jensen, P., Dulcan, M., Canino, G., & Bird, H.** (1998). Validity of DSM-IV subtypes of conduct disorder based on age of onset. *Journal of the American Academy on Child and Adolescent Psychiatry, 37,* 435–442.

**Lamb, H. R., & Weinberger, L. E.** (1992). Conservatorship for gravely disabled psychiatric patients: A four-year follow-up study. *American Journal of Psychiatry, 149,* 909–913.

**Lang, P. J.** (1995). The emotion probe: Studies of motivation and attention. *American Psychologist, 5,* 372–385.

**Lange, C. G.** (1922). *The emotions.* Baltimore: Williams & Williams.

**Langlois, J. H., Kalakanis, L., Rubenstein, A. J., Larson, A., Hallam, M., & Smoot, M.** (2000). Maxims or myths of beauty? A meta-analytic and theoretical review. *Psychological Bulletin, 126,* 390–423.

**Langlois, J. H., & Stephan, C. W.** (1981). Beauty and the beast: The role of physical attractiveness in the development of peer relations and social behavior. In S. S. Brehm, S. M. Kassin, & F. X. Gibbons (Eds.), *Developmental social psychology.* New York: Oxford University Press.

**Laor, N., Wolmer, L., & Cohen, D. J.** (2001). Mother's functioning and children's symptoms 5 years after a SCUD missile attack. *American Journal of Psychiatry, 158,* 1020–1026.

**Latané, B., & Darley, J.** (1970). *The unresponsive bystander: Why doesn't he help?* New York: Appleton-Century-Crofts.

**Latané, B., & Nida, S.** (1981). Ten years of research on group size and helping. *Psychological Bulletin, 89,* 308–324.

**Latané, B., & Rodin, J.** (1969). A lady in distress: Inhibiting effects of friends and strangers on bystander intervention. *Journal of Experimental Social Psychology, 5,* 189–202.

**Latané, B., Williams, K., & Harkins, S.** (1979). Too many hands make light the work: The causes and consequences of social loafing. *Journal of Personality and Social Psychology, 37,* 822–832.

**Laudenslager, M. L., Ryan, S. M., Drugan, R. C., Hyson, R. L., & Maier, S. F.** (1983). Coping and immunosuppression: Inescapable but not escapable shock suppresses lymphocyte proliferation. *Science, 221,* 568–570.

**Lauer, C., Riemann, D., Lund, D., & Berger, M.** (1987). Shortened REM latency: A consequence of psychological strain? *Psychophysiology, 24,* 263–271.

Laumann, E. O., Gagnon, J. H., Michael, R. T., & Michaels, S. (1994). *The social organization of sexuality: Sexual practices in the United States.* Chicago: University of Chicago Press.

Lazarus, R. S. (1982). Thoughts on the relations between emotion and cognition. *American Psychologist, 37,* 1019–1024.

Lazarus, R. S. (1984). On the primacy of cognition. *American Psychologist, 39,* 117–123.

Lazarus, R. S. (1991). *Emotion and adaptation.* New York: Oxford University Press.

Lazarus, R. S. (1999). *Stress and emotion: A new synthesis.* New York: Springer.

LeDoux, J. (1996). *The emotional brain.* New York: Simon & Schuster.

LeDoux, J. E., & Gorman, J. M. (2001). A call to action: Overcoming anxiety through active coping. *American Journal of Psychiatry, 158,* 1953–1955.

Lee, K. A., Vaillant, G. E., Torrey, W. C., & Elder, G. H. (1995). A 50-year prospective study of the psychological sequelae of World War II combat. *American Journal of Psychiatry, 152,* 4.

Lehman, D. R., Wortman, C. B., & Williams, A. F. (1987). Long-term effects of losing a spouse or child in a motor vehicle crash. *Journal of Personality and Social Psychology, 52,* 218–231.

Lenneberg, E. H. (1967). *Biological foundations of language.* New York: Wiley.

Leon, A. S. (1983). Exercise and coronary heart disease. *Hospital Medicine, 19,* 38–59.

Leon, G. R. (1977). *Case histories of deviant behavior: An interactional perspective* (2nd ed.). Boston: Holbrook Press.

Leonard, W. E. (1928). *The locomotive god.* London: Chapman & Hall.

Lepper, M. R., Greene, D., & Nisbett, R. E. (1973). Undermining children's intrinsic interest with extrinsic reward: A test of the "overjustification" hypothesis. *Journal of Personality and Social Psychology, 28,* 129–137.

Leserman, J., Petitto, J. M., Golden, R. N., Gaynes, B. N., Gu, H., Perkins, D. O., Silva, S. G., Folds, J. D., & Evans, D. L. (2000). Impact of stressful life events, depression, social support, coping and cortisol on progression to AIDS. *American Journal of Psychiatry, 157,* 1221–1228.

LeVay, S. (1991). A difference in hypothalamic structure between heterosexual and homosexual men. *Science, 253,* 1034–1037.

Leventhal, H., & Tomarken, A. J. (1986). Emotion: Today's problem. *Annual Review of Psychology, 37,* 565–610.

Levin, D. T., & Simons, D. J. (1997). Failure to detech changes to attended objects in motion pictures. *Psychonomic Bulletin & Review, 4,* 501–506.

Levine, C., Kohlberg, L., & Hewer, A. (1985). The current formulation of Kohlberg's theory in response to critics. *Human Development, 28,* 94–100.

Levine, J. D., Gordon, N. C., & Fields, H. C. (1979). The role of endorphin in placebo analgesia. In J. J. Bonica, J. G. Liebeskind, & D. Albe-Fressard (Eds.), *Advances in pain research and therapy* (Vol. 3). New York: Raven Press.

Levine, J. M., Resnick, L. B., & Higgins, E. T. (1993). Social foundations of cognition. *Annual Review of Psychology, 44,* 585–612.

Levinson, D. J. (1978). *The seasons of a man's life.* New York: Knopf.

Levinson, D. J. (1986). A conception of adult development. *American Psychologist, 41,* 3–13.

Levy, R., & Moskowitz, J. (1982). Cardiovascular research: Decades of progress, a decade of promise. *Science, 217,* 121–128.

Lewin, K. (1931). Environmental forces in child behavior and development. In C. Murchison (Ed.), *A handbook of child psychology.* Worcester, MA: Clark University Press.

Lewinsohn, P. M., Duncan, E. M., Stanton, A. K., & Hautzinger, M. (1986). Age at first onset for nonbipolar depression. *Journal of Abnormal Psychology, 95,* 378–383.

Lewinsohn, P. M., Hoberman, H. M., & Rosenbaum, M. (1988). A prospective study of risk factors for major depression. *Journal of Abnormal Psychology, 97,* 251–264.

Lewinsohn, P. M., Joiner, T. E., & Rohde, P. (2001). Evaluation of cognitive diathesis-stress models in predicting major depressive disorder in adolescents. *Journal of Abnormal Psychology, 110,* 203–215.

Lewinsohn, P. M., Mischel, W., Chaplin, W., & Barton, R. (1980). Social competence and depression: The role of illusory self-perceptions. *Journal of Abnormal Psychology, 89,* 203–212.

Lewis, D. (2000). Neural systems IV: Prefrontal cortex. *American Journal of Psychiatry, 157,* 1752.

Lewis, D. A. (1997). Development of the prefrontal cortex during adolescence: Insights into vulnerable neural circuits in schizophrenia. *Neuropsychopharmacology, 16,* 385–398.

Lewis, M., & Rosenblum, L. A. (Eds.). (1978). *The development of affect.* New York: Plenum.

Lewontin, R. (1982). *Human diversity.* New York: Scientific American Library.

Leyens, J. P., Camino, L., Parke, R. D., & Berkowitz, L. (1975). Effects of movie violence on aggression in a field setting as a function of group dominance and cohesion. *Journal of Personality and Social Psychology, 32,* 346–360.

Li, S. C. (2002). Connecting the many levels and facets of cognitive aging. *Psychological Science, 11,* 38–43.

Liebert, R. M., Neale, J. M., & Davidson, E. S. (1983). *The early window: The effects of television on children and youth.* New York: Pergamon Press.

Likert, R. (1967). *The human organization: Its management and value.* New York: McGraw-Hill.

Lilienfeld, S. O., Kirsch, I., Sarbin, T. R., Lynn, S. J., Chaves, J. F., Ganaway, G. K., & Powell, R. A. (1999). Dissociative identity disorder and the sociocognitive model: Recalling the lessons of the past. *Psychological Bulletin, 125,* 507–523.

Lilienfeld, S. O., Wood, J. M., & Garb, H. N. (2000). The scientific status of projective techniques. *Journal of the American Psychological Society, 1,* 27–66.

Lindsey, K. P., & Paul, G. L. (1989). Involuntary commitment to public mental institutions: Issues involving the overrepresentation of blacks as assessment of relevant functioning. *Psychological Bulletin, 106,* 171–183.

Lisanby, S. H., Maddox, J. H., Prudic, J., Devanand, D. P., & Sackeim, H. A. (2000). The effects of electroconvulsive therapy on memory of autobiographical and public events. *Archives of General Psychiatry, 57,* 581–590.

Lissner, L., & others. (1991). Variability of body weight and health outcomes in the Framingham population. *New England Journal of Medicine, 324,* 1839–1844.

Lloyd, C., Alexander, A. A., Rice, D. G., & Greenfield, N. S. (1980). Life change and academic performance. *Journal of Human Stress, 6,* 15–25.

Locke, E. A., & Latham, G. P. (1990). *A theory of goal setting and task performance.* Englewood Cliffs, NJ: Prentice-Hall.

Loebel, A. D., Lieberman, J. A., Alvir, J. M. J., Mayerhoff, D. I., Geisler, S. H., & Szymanski, S. R. (1992). Duration of psychosis and outcome in first-episode schizophrenia. *American Journal of Psychiatry, 149,* 1183–1188.

Loehlin, J. C., Lindzey, G., & Spuhler, J. N. (1975). *Race differences in intelligence.* San Francisco: Freeman.

Loftus, E. F. (1992). When a lie becomes memory's truth: Memory distortion after exposure to misinformation. *Current Directions in Psychological Science, 1,* 121–123.

Loftus, E. F. (1993). The reality of repressed memories. *American Psychologist, 48,* 518–537.

Loftus, E. F. (1997). Creating false memories. *Scientific American,* pp. 70–75.

Loftus, E. F., & Palmer, J. C. (1974). Reconstruction of automobile destruction: An example of the interaction between language and memory. *Journal of Verbal Learning and Verbal Behavior, 13,* 585–589.

Loftus, E. F., Polonsky, S., & Fullilove, M. T. (1993). *Memories of childhood sexual abuse: Remembering and repressing.* Unpublished manuscript, Columbia University, cited in Loftus, E. F. (1993). The reality of repressed memories. *American Psychologist, 48,* 518–537.

London, E. D., & others. (1990). Morphine-induced metabolic changes in the human brain: Studies with positron emission tomography and [fluorine 18] fluorodeoxyglucose. *Archives of General Psychiatry, 47,* 73–81.

LoPiccolo, J. (1985). Diagnosis and treatment of male sexual dysfunction. *Journal of Sex and Marital Therapy, 11,* 215–232.

LoPiccolo, J., & Friedman, J. M. (1988). Blood-spectrum treatment of low sexual desire: Integration of cognitive, behavioral, and systematic therapy. In S. R. Leiblum & R. C. Rosen (Eds.), *Sexual desire disorders.* New York: Guilford.

Lore, R. K., & Schultz, L. A. (1993). Control of human aggression: A comparative perspective. *American Psychologist, 48,* 16–25.

Lorenz, K. (1937). The companion in the bird's world. *Auk, 54,* 245–273.

Lorenz, K. (1967). *On aggression.* New York: Bantam.

Low, B. S. (1989). Cross-cultural patterns in the training of children: An evolutionary perspective. *Journal of Comparative Psychology, 103,* 311–319.

Lubinski, D., & Humphreys, L. G. (1997). Incorporating general intelligence into epidemiology and the social sciences. *Intelligence, 24,* 159–202.

Luchins, K. S. (1942). Mechanization in problem solving: The effects of "Einstellung." *Psychometric Monographs, 54*(6).

Lykken, D., & Tellegen, A. (1996). *Happiness is a stochastic phenomenon* (Vol. 7): Blackwell Publishers.

Lykken, D. T. (1979). The detection of deception. *Psychological Bulletin, 86,* 47–53.

Lykken, D. T. (1998). *A tremor in the blood: Uses and abuses of the lie detector.* New York: Plenum

Lynn, S. J., Lock, T. G., Myers, B., & Payne, D. G. (1997). Recalling the unrecallable: Should hypnosis be used to recover memories in psychotherapy? *Current Directions in Psychological Science, 6,* 79–83.

Lyubomirsky, S. (2001). Why are some people happier than others? *American Psychologist, 56,* 239–249.

**M**

Macklin, M. L., Metzger, L. J., Litz, B. T., McNally, R. J., Lasko, N. B., Orr, S. P., & Pitman, R. K. (1998). Lower precombat intelligence is a risk factor for posttraumatic stress disorder. *Journal of Consulting and Clinical Psychology, 66,* 323–326.

Maddox, G. L. (1964). Disengagement theory: A critical evaluation. *The Gerontologist, 4,* 80–83.

Madigan, S., & O'Hara, R. (1992). Short-term memory at the turn of the century: Mary Whiton Calkins's memory research. *American Psychologist, 47,* 170–174.

Madsen, C. H., Becker, W. C., & Thomas, D. R. (1968). Rules, praise, and ignoring: Elements of elementary classroom control. *Journal of Applied Behavioral Analysis, 1,* 139–150.

Maier, N. R. F. (1931). Reasoning in humans: II. The solution of a problem and its appearance in consciousness. *Journal of Comparative and Physiological Psychology, 12,* 181–194.

Maier, S. F., & Watkins, L. R. (1998). Cytokines for psychologists: Implications of bidirectional immune-to-braincommunication for understanding behavior, mood, and cognition. *Psychological Review, 105,* 83–107.

Maier, S. F., & Watkins, L. R. (2000). The immune system as a sensory system: Implications for psychology. *Psychological Science, 9,* 98–102.

Mandel, D. R., Jusczyk, P. W., & Pisoni, D. B. (1995). Infants' recognition of the sound patterns of their own names. *Psychological Science, 6,* 314–317.

Mann, S., Vrij, A., & Bull, R. (2002). Suspects, lies and videotape: An analysis of authentic high-stake liars. *Lay and Human Behavior, 26,* 365–376.

Manne, S., Alfieri, T., Taylor, K., & Dougherty, J. (1999). Preferences for spousal support among individuals with cancer. *Journal of Applied Social Psychology, 29,* 722–749.

Marce, L. V. (1858). *Treatise on the madness of pregnant women, recently delivered women, and nursing women.* Paris: J. B. Baillere et Fils.

Marcus, A. C., Wheeler, R. C., Cullen, J. W., & Crane, L. A. (1987). Quasi-experimental evaluation of the Los Angeles Know Your Body program: Knowledge, beliefs, and self-reported behaviors. *Preventive Medicine, 16,* 803–815.

Marenco, S., & Weinberger, D. (2000). The neurodevelopmental hypothesis of schizophrenia: Following a trail of evidence from cradle to grave. *Developmental and Psychopathology, 12,* 501–527.

Markus, H. (1978). The effect of mere presence on social facilitation: An unobtrusive test. *Journal of Experimental Social Psychology, 14,* 389–397.

Marlatt, G. A., & Rose, F. (1980). Addictive disorders. In A. E. Kazdin, A. S. Bellack, & M. Hersen (Eds.), *New perspectives in abnormal psychology* (pp. 298–324). New York: Oxford University Press.

Martell, D. A., & Dietz, P. E. (1992). Mentally disordered offenders who push or attempt to push victims onto subway tracks in New York City. *Archives of General Psychology, 49,* 472–475.

Martin, R. J., White, B. D., & Hulsey, M. G. (1991). The regulation of body weight. *American Scientist, 79,* 528–541.

Martorell, R. (1998). Nutrition and the worldwide rise in IQ scores. In U. Neisser (Ed.), *The rising curve: Long-term gains in IQ and related measures* (pp. 183–206). Washington, DC: American Psychological Association.

Martuza, R. L., Chiocca, E. A., Jenike, M. A., Giriunas, I. E., & Ballantine, H. T. (1990). Stereotactic radiofrequency thermal cingulotomy for obsessive compulsive disorder. *Journal of Neuropsychiatry, 2,* 331–336.

Maslow, A. (1967). A theory of metamotivation: The biological rooting of the value-life. *Journal of Humanistic Psychology, 7,* 93–127.

Maslow, A. (1970). *Motivation and personality* (2nd ed.). New York: Harper & Row.

Maslow, A. H., & Mintz, N. L. (1956). Effects of aesthetic surroundings: I. Initial effects of three aesthetic conditions upon perceiving "energy" and "well-being" in faces. *Journal of Psychology, 41,* 247–254.

Massimini, F., & Fave, A. D. (2000). Individual development in a biocultural perspective. *American Psychologist, 55,* 24–33.

Masters, W. H., & Johnson, V. E. (1966). *Human sexual response.* Boston: Little, Brown.

Masters, W. H., & Johnson, V. E. (1970). *Human sexual inadequacy.* Boston: Little, Brown.

Matefy, R. E., & Kroll, R. G. (1974). An initial investigation of psychedelic drug flashback phenomena. *Journal of Consulting and Clinical Psychology, 42,* 854–860.

Mathalon, D., Sullivan, E., Lim, K., & Pfefferbaum, A. (2001). Progressive brain volume changes and the clinical course of schizophrenia in men. *Archives in General Psychiatry, 58,* 148–157.

Mathews, A., & MacLeod, C. (1986). Discrimination of threat cues without awareness in anxiety states. *Journal of Abnormal Psychology, 95,* 131–138.

Matlin, M. (1983). *Cognition.* New York: Holt, Rinehart & Winston.

Matlin, M. W. (1988). *Sensation and perception* (2nd ed.). Boston: Allyn & Bacon.

Matthews, D. B., Best, P. J., White, A. M., Vandergriff, L., & Simpson, P. E. (1996). Ethanol impairs spatial cognitive processing: New behavioral and electrophysiological findings. *Current Directions in Psychological Science, 5,* 111–115.

Matthews, E. L. (1982). Psychological perspectives on the Type A behavior pattern. *Psychological Bulletin, 91,* 293–323.

Matthews, K. E., & Canon, L. K. (1975). Environmental noise level as a determinant of helping behavior. *Journal of Personality and Social Psychology, 32,* 571–577.

Mavromatis, A. (1987). *Hypnogogia.* London: Routledge.

Mayou, R., Bryant, B., & Ehlers, A. (2001). Prediction of psychological outcomes one year after a motor vehicle accident. *American Journal of Psychiatry, 158,* 1231–1238.

Mazure, C. M. (1998). Life stressors as risk factors in depression. *Clinical Psychology: Science and Practice, 5,* 291–313.

McAdams, D. P., & Vaillant, G. E. (1982). Intimacy motivation and psychosocial adjustment: A longitudinal study. *Journal of Personality Assessment, 46,* 586–593.

McCall, R. B. (1979). *Infants.* Cambridge, MA: Harvard University Press.

McClelland, D. C., & Atkinson, J. W. (1948). The projective expression of needs: I. The effect of different intensities of the hunger drive on perception. *Journal of Psychology, 25,* 205–222.

McCloskey, M., Wible, C. G., & Cohen, N. J. (1988). Is there a special flashbulb-memory mechanism? *Journal of Experimental Psychology: General, 117,* 171–181.

McConaghy, M. J. (1979). Gender permanence and the genital basis of gender: Stages in the development of constancy of gender identity. *Child Development, 50,* 1223–1226.

McCormick, E. J., & Ilgen, D. (1980). *Industrial psychology* (7th ed.). Englewood Cliffs, NJ: Prentice-Hall.

McCrae, R. R., & Costa, P. T. (1987). Validation of the five-factor model of personality across instruments and observers. *Journal of Personality and Social Psychology, 52,* 81–90.

McCrae, R. R., & Costa, P. T. (1990). *Personality in adulthood.* New York: Guilford Press.

McCrae, R. R., & Costa, P. T. (1997). Personality trait structure as a human universal. *American Psychologist, 52,* 509–516.

McCrae, R. R., & Costa, P. T. (1999). A five-factor theory of personality. In L. A. Pervin & O. P. John (Eds.), *Handbook of personality: Theory and research* (2nd ed., pp. 139–153). New York: Guilford.

McCrae, R. R., & Costa, P. T., Jr. (1994). The stability of personality: Observations and evaluations. *Current Directions in Psychological Science, 3,* 173–175.

McCrae, R. R., Costa, P. T., Jr., de Lima, M. P., Simones, A., Ostendorf, F., Angleitner, A., Marusic, I., Bratko, D., Caprara, G. V., Barbaranelli, C., Chae, J. H., & Piedmont, R. L. (1999). Age differences in personality across the adult life span: Parallels in five cultures. *Developmental Psychology, 35,* 466–477.

McEwen, B. S. (1998). Protective and damaging effects of stress mediators. *The New England Journal of Medicine, 338,* 171–179.

McGaugh, J. L. (1983). Preserving the presence of the past. Hormonal influences on memory storage. *American Psychologist, 38,* 161–174.

McGaugh, J. L. (1990). Significance and remembrance: The role of neuromodulatory systems. *Psychological Science, 1,* 15–25.

McGaugh, J. L., & Dawson, R. G. (1971). Modification of memory storage processes. In W. K. Honig & P. H. R. James (Eds.), *Animal memory.* New York: Academic Press.

McGlashan, T., & Hoffman, R. (2000). Schizophrenia as a disorder of developmentally reduced synaptic connectivity. *Archives in General Psychiatry, 57,* 637–648.

McGraw, M. B. (1940). Neural maturation as exemplified in achievement of bladder control. *Journal of Pediatrics, 16,* 580–590.

McWilliams, S. A., & Tuttle, R. J. (1973). Long-term psychological effects of LSD. *Psychological Bulletin, 79,* 341–351.

Mead, M. (1935). *Sex and temperament in three primitive societies.* New York: Morrow.

Meck, W. H., Smith, R. A., & Williams, C. L. (1989). Organizational changes in cholinergic activity and enhanced visuospatial memory as a function of choline administered prenatally or postnatally or both. *Behavioral Neuroscience, 103,* 1234–1241.

Mednick, S. A., Machon, R. A., Huttunen, M. O., & Bonett, D. (1988). Adult schizophrenia following prenatal exposure to an influenza epidemic. *Archives of General Psychiatry, 45,* 189–192.

Mellon, J. C. (1975). *National assessment and the teaching of English.* Urbana, IL: National Council of Teachers of English.

Melzack, R. (1992, April). Phantom limbs. *Scientific American,* pp. 120–126.

Melzack, R., & Wall, P. D. (1983). *The challenge of pain.* New York: Basic Books.

Mercklebach, H., van den Hout, M., Jansen, A., & van der Molen, G. M. (1988). Many stimuli are frightening, but some are more frightening: The contributions of preparedness, dangerousness, and unpredictability to making a stimulus fearful. *Journal of Psychopathology and Behavioral Assessment, 10,* 355–366.

Mermelstein, R., Cohen, S., Lichtenstein, E., Baer, J. S., & Kamarck, T. (1986). Social support and smoking cessation and maintenance. *Journal of Consulting and Clinical Psychology, 54,* 447–453.

Messick, D. M., & Sentis, K. P. (1979). Fairness and preference. *Journal of Experimental Social Psychology, 15,* 418–434.

Mesulam, M. M. (1995). Cholinergic pathways and the ascending reticular activating system of the human brain. *Annals of the New York Academy of Sciences, 757,* 169–179.

Mewborn, C. R., & Rogers, R. W. (1979). Effects of threatening and reassuring components of fear appeals on physiological and verbal measures of emotion and attitudes. *Journal of Experimental Social Psychology, 15,* 242–253.

Meyer, A. J., Nash, J. D., McAlister, A. L., Maccoby, N., & Farquhar, J. W. (1980). Skills training in a cardiovascular health education campaign. *Journal of Consulting and Clinical Psychology, 48,* 129–142.

Meyer, D. E., & Schvaneveldt, R. W. (1971). Facilitation in recognizing pairs of words: Evidence of a dependence between retrieval operations. *Journal of Experimental Psychology, 90,* 227–234.

Meyer-Bahlburg, H. F. L., & others. (1995). Prenatal estrogens and the development of homosexual orientation. *Developmental Psychology, 31,* 12–21.

Meyerowitz, B. E., & Chaiken, S. (1987). The effect of message framing on breast self-examination attitudes, intentions, and behavior. *Journal of Personality and Social Psychology, 52,* 500–510.

Meyerowitz, B. E., Richardson, J., Hudson, S., & Leedham, B. (1998). Ethnicity and cancer outcomes: Behavioral and psychosocial considerations. *Psychological Bulletin, 123,* 47–70.

Meyers, C. A., Berman, S. A., Scheibel, R. S. & Hayman, A. (1992). Case report: Acquired antisocial personal disorder associated with unilateral left orbital frontal lobe damage. *Journal of Psychiatry and Neuroscience, 17,* 121–125.

Michael, R. T., Gagnon, J. H., Laumann, E. O., & Kolata, G. (1994). *Sex in America: A definitive survey.* Boston: Little, Brown.

Milgram, S. (1963). Behavioral study of obedience. *Journal of Abnormal and Social Psychology, 67,* 371–378.

Milgram, S. (1965). Some conditions of obedience and disobedience to authority. *Human Relations, 18,* 57–76.

Miller, G. A. (1956). The magic number seven, plus or minus two. Some limits on our ability to process information. *Psychological Review, 63,* 81–97.

Miller, J. G. (1999). Cultural psychology: Implications for basic psychological theory. *Psychological Science, 10,* 85–91.

Miller, L. C., Putcha-Bhagavatula, A., & Pedersen, W. C. (2002). Men's and women's mating preferences: Distinct evolutionary mechanisms? *Psychological Science, 11,* 88–93.

Miller, M. E., & Bowers, K. S. (1993). Hypnotic analgesia: Dissociated experience or dissociated control? *Journal of Abnormal Psychology, 102,* 29–38.

Miller, N. E. (1944). Experimental studies of conflict. In J. McV. Hunt (Ed.), *Personality and the behavior disorders* (Vol. 1). New York: Ronald Press.

Miller, T. Q., Smith, T. W., Turner, C. W., Guijarro, M. L., & Hallet, A. J. (1996). A meta-analytic review of research on hostility and physical health. *Psychological Bulletin, 119,* 322–348.

Milner, B. (1974). Hemispheric specialization: Scope and limits. In F. O. Schmitt & F. G, Worden (Eds.), *The neurosciences: Third study program* (pp. 75–89). Cambridge, MA: MIT Press.

Milner, B., Corkin, S., & Teuber, H. L. (1968). Further analysis of the hippocampal amnesic syndrome: 14-year follow-up study of H. M. *Neuropsychologia, 6,* 215–234.

Milner, B., Squire, L. R., & Kandel, E. R. (1998). Cognitive neuroscience and the study of memory. *Neuron, 20,* 445–468.

Mineka, S., Davidson, M., Cook, M., & Keir, R. (1984). Observational conditioning of snake fears in rhesus monkeys. *Journal of Abnormal Psychology, 93,* 355–372.

Mineka, S., & Sutton, S. K. (1992). Cognitive biases and the emotional disorders. *Psychological Science, 3,* 65–69.

Minton, H. (2000). Psychology and gender at the turn of the century. *American Psychologist, 55,* 613–615.

Minuchin, S. (1974). *Families and family therapy.* Cambridge, MA: Harvard University Press.

Mischel, W. (1968). *Personality and assessment.* New York: Wiley.

Mischel, W., & Shoda, Y. (1999). Integrating dispositions and processing dynamics within a unified theory of personality: The cognitive-affective personality system. In L. A. Pervin & O. P. John (Eds.), *Handbook of personality: Theory and research* (2nd ed., pp. 197–218). New York: Guilford.

Modigliani, V., & Hedges, D. G. (1987). Distributed rehearsals and the primacy effect in single-trail free recall. *Journal of Experimental Psychology: Learning, Memory, and Cognition, 13,* 426–436.

Moffitt, T. E. (1993). Adolescence-limited and life-course-persistent antisocial behavior: A developmental taxonomy. *Psychological Review, 100,* 674–701.

Mogil, J. S., Sternberg, W. F., Kest, B., Marek, P., & Liebeskind, J. C. (1993). Sex differences in the antagonism of swim-stress induced analgesia: Effects of gonadectomy and estrogen replacement. *Pain, 53,* 17.

Mohr, J. W., Turner, R. E., & Jerry, M. B. (1964). *Pedophilia and exhibitionism.* Toronto: University of Toronto Press.

Mohs, R. C., Breitner, J. C. S., Silverman, J. M., & Davis, K. L. (1987). Alzheimer's disease: Morbid risk among first-degree relatives. *Archives of General Psychiatry, 44,* 405–408.

Mojtabai, R. (2001). Residual symptoms and impairment in major depression in the community. *American Journal of Psychiatry, 158,* 1645–1651.

Monahan, J., Murphy, S., & Zajonc, R. B. (2000). Subliminal mere exposure: Specific, general, and diffuse effects. *Psychological Science, 11,* 462.

Money, J. (1955). Linguistic resources and psychodynamic theory. *British Journal of Medical Psychology, 20,* 264–266.

Money, J. (1987). Sin, sickness, or status: Homosexual gender identity and psychoneuroendocrinology. *American Psychologist, 42,* 384–389.

Money, J. (1988). *Gay, straight, and in-between.* New York: Oxford University Press.

Monteith, M. J., Ashburn-Nardo, L., Voils, C. I., & Czopp, A. M. (2002). Putting the brakes on prejudice: On the development and operation of cues for control. *Journal of Personality and Social Psychology, 83,* 1029–1050.

Mook, D. G. (1986). *Motivation: The organization of action.* New York: W. W. Norton.

Moore-Ede, M. C., Sulzman, F. M., & Fuller, C. A. (1982). *The clocks that time us.* Cambridge: Harvard University Press.

Morell, P., & Norton, W. T. (1980, May). Myelin. *Scientific American,* pp. 88–118.

Morgan, C. A., Hazlett, M. G., Wang, S., Richardson, E. G., Schnurr, P., & Southwick, S. M. (2001). Symptoms of dissociation in humans experiencing acute, uncontrollable stress: A prospective investigation. *American Journal of Psychiatry, 158,* 1239–1247.

Morris, M. W., & Peng, K. (1994). Culture and cause: American and Chinese attributions for social physical events. *Journal of Personality and Social Psychology, 67,* 949–971.

Morris, N. (1986). A working memory, 1974–1984. A review of a decade of research. *Current Psychological Research and Reviews, 5,* 281–295.

Morrison, A. M., & Von Glinow, M. A. (1990). Women and minorities in management. *American Psychologist, 45,* 200–208.

Moscovitch, M., & Olds, J. (1982). Asymmetries in emotional facial expressions and their possible relation to hemisphere specialization. *Neuropsychologia, 20,* 71–81.

Moscowitz, D. S., Brown, K. W., & Cote, S. (1997). Reconceptualizing stability: Using time as a psychological dimension. *Current Directions in Psychological Science, 6,* 127–132.

Mossman, D., & Perlin, M. L. (1992). Psychiatry and the homeless: A reply to Dr. Lamb. *American Journal of Psychiatry, 149,* 951–957.

**Muehlenhard, C., & Hollabaugh, L.** (1988). Do women sometimes say no when they mean yes? The prevalence and correlates of women's token resistance to sex. *Journal of Personality and Social Psychology, 54,* 872–879.

**Mufson, L., Weissman, M. M., Moreau, D., & Garfinkel, R.** (1999). Efficacy of interpersonal psychotherapy for depressed adolescents. *Archives of General Psychiatry, 57,* 573–579.

**Mullen, B.** (1986). Atrocity as a function of lynch mob composition: A self-attention perspective. *Personality and Social Psychology Bulletin, 12,* 187–197.

**Muller, E. E., & Nistico, G.** (1989). *Brain messengers and the pituitary.* Orlando: Academic Press.

**Mumford, E., Schlesinger, H. J., & Glass, G. V.** (1981). Reducing medical cost through mental health treatment: Research problems and recommendations. In A. Broskowski, E. Marks, & S. H. Budman (Eds.), *Linking health and mental health.* Beverly Hills, CA: Sage.

**Mundy, P., Robertson, M., Robertson, J., & Greenblatt, M.** (1990). The prevalence of psychotic symptoms in homeless adolescents. *Journal of the American Academy of Child and Adolescent Psychiatry, 29,* 724–731.

**Munjack, D. J., & Staples, F. R.** (1977). Psychological characteristics of women with sexual inhibition (frigidity) in sex clinics. *Journal of Nervous and Mental Diseases, 163,* 117–129.

**Murphy, M. T., Michelson, L. K., Marchione, K., Marchione, N., & Testa, S.** (1998). The role of self-directed in vivo exposure in combination with cognitive therapy, relaxation training, or therapist-assisted exposure in the treatment of panic disorder with agoraphobia. *Journal of Anxiety Disorders, 12,* 117–138.

**Murray, H.** (1938). *Exploration in personality.* New York: Oxford University Press.

**Murray, H.** (1951). Uses of the T.A.T. *American Journal of Psychiatry, 107,* 577–581.

**Myers, D.** (1999). *Social psychology* (6th ed.). Boston: McGraw-Hill.

**Myers, D. G.** (2000). The funds, friends, and faith of happy people. *American Psychologist, 55,* 56–67.

**Myers, D. G., & Bishop, G. D.** (1970). Discussion effects on racial attitudes. *Science, 169,* 778–779.

**Myers, D. G., & Diener, E.** (1995). Who is happy? *Psychological Science, 6,* 10–18.

**Myers, D. H., & Grant, G. A.** (1972). A study of depersonalization in students. *British Journal of Psychiatry, 121,* 59–65.

### N

**Nachman, M.** (1962). Taste preference for sodium salts in adrenolectomized rats. *Journal of Comparative and Physiological Psychology, 55,* 1124–1129.

**Nadel, L., & Jacobs, W. J.** (1998). Traumatic memory is special. *Current Directions in Psychological Science, 7,* 154–157.

**Nadelson, C. C.** (1990). Consequences of rape: Clinical and treatment aspects. *Psychotherapy and Psychosomatics, 51,* 187–192.

**Nail, P. R., MacDonald, G., & Levy, D.** (2000). Proposal of a four-dimensional model of social response. *Psychological Bulletin, 126,* 454–470.

**Narrow, W. E., Rae, D. S., Robins, L. N., & Reiger, D. A.** (2002). Revised prevalence estimates of mental disorders in the United States. *Archives of General Psychiatry, 59,* 115–123.

**Nash, M.** (1987). What, if anything, is regressed about hypnotic age regression? A review of the empirical literature. *Psychological Bulletin, 102,* 42–52.

**Nash, M. R., Drake, S. D., Wiley, S., Khalsa, S., & Lynn, S. J.** (1986). The accuracy of recall by hypnotically age-regressed subjects. *Journal of Abnormal Psychology, 95,* 298–300.

**Nash, S. C.** (1975). The relationship among sex-role stereotyping, sex-role performance, and sex differences in spatial visualization. *Sex Roles, 1,* 15–32.

**Nathan, P. E., & Gorman, J. M.** (2001). *A guide to treatments that work* (2nd ed.). New York: Oxford University Press.

**National Advisory Mental Health Council.** (1995a). *Basic behavioral research for mental health: A national investment.* Rockville, MD: National Institute of Mental Health.

**National Advisory Mental Health Council.** (1995b). Basic behavioral science research for mental health: A national investment (emotion and motivation). *American Psychologist, 50,* 838–845.

**National Institute on Alcohol Abuse and Alcoholism.** (1987). *Report.* Washington, DC: U.S. Government Printing Office.

**National Safety Council.** (1996). *Accident facts: 1995 edition.* Washington, DC.

**National Safety Council.** (1998). *Accident facts.* Itasca, IL: National Safety Council.

**National Victim Center.** (1992). *Rape in America: A report to the nation.* Fort Worth, TX: Author.

**Neisser, U.** (1998). Rising test scores and what they mean. In U. Neisser (Ed.), *The rising curve: Long-term gains in IQ and related measures* (pp. 3–24). Washington, DC: American Psychological Association.

**Nelson, L. P., & Nelson, V.** (1973). *Religion and death anxiety.* Paper presented at the Society for the Scientific Study of Religion, San Francisco.

**Nemeth, C. J.** (1981). Jury trials. Psychology and law. In L. Berkowitz (Ed.), *Advances in experimental social psychology* (Vol. 14). New York: Academic Press.

**Neugarten, B. L.** (1964). *Personality in middle and late life.* New York: Atherton Press.

**Neugarten, B. L., & Hagestad, G. O.** (1976). Age and the life course. In R. H. Binstock & E. Shanas (Eds.), *Handbook of aging and the social sciences.* New York: Van Nostrand Reinhold.

**Newcomer, J. W., Selke, G., Melson, A. K., Hershey, T., Craft, S., Richards, K., & Alderson, A. L.** (1999). Decreased memory performance in healthy humans induced by stress-level cortisol treatment. *Archives of General Psychiatry, 56,* 527–533.

**Newton, J. W., & Mann, L.** (1980). Crowd size as a factor in the persuasion process: A study of religious crusade meetings. *Journal of Personality and Social Psychology, 39,* 874–883.

**Neyland, T. C., & others.** (1998). Sleep disturbances in the Viet Nam generation: Findings from a nationally representative sample of male veterans. *American Journal of Psychiatry, 155,* 929–933.

**NICHD Early Child Care Research Network.** (2002). Child care structure, process, outcome: Direct and indirect effects of child care quality on young children's development. *Psychological Science, 13,* 199–206.

**Nisbett, R., Choi, I., Peng, K., & Norenzayan, A.** (2001). Culture and systems of thought: Holistic versus analytic cognition. *Psychological Review, 108,* 291–310.

**Nogrady, H., McConkey, K. M., & Perry, C.** (1985). Enhancing visual memory: Trying hypnosis, trying imagination, and trying again. *Journal of Abnormal Psychology, 94,* 195–204.

**Northouse, P. G.** (1997). *Leadership: Theory and practice.* Thousand Oaks, CA: Sage.

**Nosek, B. A., Banaji, M. R., & Greenwald, A. G.** (2002). Math = Male, Me = Female, Therefore Math =/ Me. *Journal of Personality and Social Psychology, 83,* 44–59.

**Nunes, E. V., Frank, K. A., & Kornfeld, D. S.** (1987). Psychologic treatment for the Type A behavior pattern and for coronary heart disease: A meta-analysis of the literature. *Psychosomatic Medicine, 48,* 159–166.

### O

**Ochsner, K. N., & Lieberman, M. D.** (2001). The emergence of social cognitive neuroscience. *American Psychologist, 56,* 9.

**Offer, D., & Schonert-Reichl, K. A.** (1992). Debunking the myths of adolescence: Findings from recent research. *Journal of the American Academy of Child and Adolescent Psychiatry, 31,* 1003–1014.

**Öhman, A., Erixon, G., & Löfberg, I.** (1975). Phobias and preparedness: Phobic versus neutral pictures as conditioned stimuli for human autonomic responses. *Journal of Abnormal Psychology, 84,* 41–45.

**Öhman, A., & Mineka, S.** (2001). Fears, phobias, and preparedness: Toward an evolved module of fear and fear learning. *Psychological Review, 108,* 483–522.

**O'Leary, A.** (1990). Stress, emotion, and human immune function. *Psychology Bulletin, 108,* 363–382.

**O'Leary, S. G.** (1995). Parental discipline mistakes. *Current Directions in Psychological Science, 4,* 11–13.

**Oldham, G. R., & Fried, Y.** (1987). Employee reactions to workplace characteristics. *Journal of Applied Psychology, 72,* 75–80.

**Olds, J., & Milner, P.** (1954). Positive reinforcement produced by electrical stimulation of septal area and other regions of rat brain. *Journal of Comparative and Physiological Psychology, 47,* 419–427.

**Oliver, M. B., & Hyde, J. S.** (1993). Gender differences in sexuality: A meta-analysis. *Psychological Bulletin, 114,* 29–51.

**Olson, J. M., & Zanna, M. P.** (1993). Attitudes and attitude change. *Annual Review of Psychology, 44,* 117–154.

**Olson, M. A., & Fazio, R. H.** (2001). Implicit attitude formation through classical conditioning. *American Psychological Society, 12,* 413–417.

**Oquendo, M. A., Ellis, S. P., Greenwald, S., Malone, K. M., Weissman, M. M., & Mann, J. J.** (2001). Ethnic and sex differences in suicide rates relative to major depression in the United States. *American Journal of Psychiatry, 158,* 1652–1658.

**Orme-Johnson, D.** (1987). Medical care utilization and the transcendental meditation program. *Psychosomatic Medicine, 49,* 493–507.

Ornstein, P. A., & Haden, C. A. (2001). Memory development or the development of memory. *Psychological Science, 10,* 202–205.

Osby, U., Brandt, L., Correia, N., Ekbom, A., & Sparen, P. (2001). Excess mortality in bipolar and unipolar disorder in Sweden. *Archives in General Psychiatry, 58,* 844–850.

Ost, L. G. (1992). Blood and injection phobia: Background and cognitive, physiological, and behavioral variables. *Journal of Abnormal Psychology, 101,* 68–74.

Ostroff, C. (1992). The relationship between satisfaction, attitudes and performance: An organizational level analysis. *Journal of Applied Psychology, 77,* 963–974.

**P**

Pahnke, W. N. (1980). Drugs and mysticism. In J. R. Tisdale (Ed.), *Growing edges in the psychology of religion* (pp. 183–200). Chicago: Nelson-Hall.

Paik, H., & Comstock, G. (1994). The effects of television violence on antisocial behavior: A meta-analysis. *Communication Research, 21,* 516–546.

Palmer, S. E. (2002). Perceptual grouping: It's later than you think. *Psychological Science, 11,* 101–106.

Panskepp, J. (1993). Neurochemical control of moods and emotions: Amino acids to neuropeptides. In M. Lewis & others (Eds.), *Handbook of emotions* (pp. 87–107). New York: Guilford.

Parker, G. B., Barrett, E. A., & Hickie, I. B. (1992). From nurture to network: Examining links between perceptions of parenting received in childhood and social bonds in adulthood. *American Journal of Psychiatry, 149,* 877–885.

Parrott, A. C. (1999). Does cigarette smoking cause stress? *American Psychologist, 54,* 817–820.

Passe, T. J., Rajagopalan, P., Tupler, L. A., Byrum, C. E., MacFall, J. R., & Krishnan, K. R. R. (1997). Age and sex effects on brain morphology. *Progress in Neuro-Psychopharmacology & Biological Psychiatry, 21,* 1231–1237.

Patterson, F. (1977). The gestures of a gorilla: Language acquisition in another primate species. In J. Hambrug, J. Goodall, & L. McCown (Eds.), *Perspectives in human evolution* (Vol. 4). Menlo Park, CA: W. A. Benjamin.

Pauly, I. (1968). The current status of the change of sex operation. *Journal of Nervous and Mental Disorders, 147,* 460–471.

Pearlson, G. D., Jeffrey, P. J., Harris, G. J., Ross, C. A., Fischman, M. W., & Camargo, E. E. (1993). Correlation of acute cocaine-induced changes in local cerebral bloodflow with subjective effects. *American Journal of Psychiatry, 150,* 495–497.

Pedersen, W. C., Miller, L. C., Putcha-Bhagavatula, A. D., & Yang, Y. (2002). Evolved sex differences in the number of partners desired: The long and short of it. *Psychological Science, 13,* 157–161.

Pennebaker, J. W., & Beall, J. K. (1986). Confronting a traumatic event: Toward an understanding of inhibition and disease. *Journal of Abnormal Psychology, 95,* 274–281.

Pennebaker, J. W., Colder, M., & Sharp, L. K. (1990). Accelerating the coping process. *Journal of Personality and Social Psychology, 58,* 528–537.

Pennebaker, J. W., Kiecolt-Glaser, J. K., & Glaser, R. (1988). Disclosure of traumas and immune function: Health implications for psychotherapy. *Journal of Consulting and Clinical Psychology, 56,* 239–245.

Pennix, B. W. J. H., Beekman, A. T. F., Honig, A., Deeg, D. J. H., Schoevers, R. A., van Eijk, J. T. M., & van Tilburg, W. (2001). Depression and cardiac mortality. *Archives of General Psychiatry, 58,* 221–227.

Pepperberg, I. M. (2002). Cognitive and communicative abilities of grey parrots. *Psychological Science, 11,* 83–87.

Perls, F. S., Hefferline, R. F., & Goodman, P. (1951). *Gestalt therapy.* New York: Julian Press.

Perry, J. D., & Whipple, B. (1981). Pelvic muscle strength of female ejaculators: Evidence in support of a new theory of orgasm. *Journal of Sex Research, 17,* 22–39.

Persson-Benbow, C., Lubinski, D., Shea, D. L., & Eftekhari-Sanjuani, H. (2000). Sex differences in mathematical reasoning ability at age 13: Their status 20 years later. *Psychological Science, 11,* 474–480.

Petersen, A. C. (1979, January). Can puberty come any faster? *Psychology Today,* pp. 45–56.

Petersen, R. C., & Stillman, R. C. (1978). *Phencyclidine (PCP) abuse: An appraisal* (National Institute on Drug Abuse Monograph No. 21). Washington, DC: U.S. Government Printing Office.

Peterson, C., Seligman, M. E. P., Yurko, K. H., Martin, L. R., & Friedman, H. S. (1998). Catastrophizing and untimely death. *Psychological Science, 9,* 127–130

Peterson, L., Brown, D., & Aronson, H. (1998). Faculty gender, status, roles, and privileges in applied doctoral programs *The Clinical Psychologist, 51,* 11–16.

Peterson, L. R., & Peterson, M. J. (1959). Short-term retention of individual items. *Journal of Experimental Psychology, 58,* 193–198.

Petitto, J. M., Gariepy, J.-L., Gendreau, P. L., Rodriguez, R., & Lewis, M. H. (1999). Differences in NK cell function in mice bred for high and low aggression: Genetic linkage between complex behavioral and immunological traits. *Brain, Behavior, and Immunity, 13,* 175–186.

Petri, H. L. (1986). *Motivation: Theory and research* (3rd ed.). Belmont, CA: Wadsworth.

Pfefferbaum, B., Nixon, S. J., Tucker, P. M., Tivis, R. D., Moore, V. L., Gurwitch, R. H., Pynoos, R. S., & Geis, H. (1999). Posttraumatic stress responses in bereaved children after the Oklahoma City bombing. *Journal of the American Academy of Child and Adolescent Psychiatry, 38,* 1016–1023.

Phillips, J. D. (1933). *Salem in the seventeenth century.* Cambridge, MA: Riverside Press.

Phinney, J. (1996). When we talk about American ethnic groups, what do we mean? *American Psychologist, 51,* 918–927.

Piacentini, J. (1999). Cognitive behavioral therapy of childhood OCD. *Child and Adolescent Psychiatric Clinics of North America, 8,* 599–616.

Piaget, J. (1972). Intellectual development from adolescence to adulthood. *Human Development, 15,* 1–12.

Piaget, J., & Inhelder, B. (1963). *The child's conception of space.* London: Routledge and Paul.

Pietrini, P., Guazzelli, M., Basso, G., Jaffe, K., & Grafman, J. (2000). Neural correlates of imaginal aggressive behavior assessed by positron emission tomography in healthy subjects. *American Journal of Psychiatry, 157,* 1772–1781.

Pincomb, G. A., Lovallo, W. R., Passey, R. B., Brackett, D. J., & Wilson, M. F. (1987). Caffeine enhances the physiological response to occupational stress in medical students. *Health Psychology, 6,* 101–112.

Piorkowski, G. (1983). Survivor guilt in the university setting. *Personnel and Guidance Journal, 61,* 620–622.

Plaut, V. C., Markus, H. R., & Lachman, M. E. (2002). Place matters: Consensual features and regional variation in American well-being and self. *Journal of Personality and Social Psychology, 83,* 160–184.

Plomin, R. (1989). Environment and genes: Determinants of behavior. *American Psychologist, 44,* 105–111.

Plomin, R. (1994). Genetics and experience: The interplay between nature and nurture. Thousand Oaks, CA: Sage.

Plomin, R. (1995). Molecular genetics and psychology. *Current Directions in Psychological Science, 4,* 114–117.

Plomin, R. (1999). Genetics of childhood disorders: III. Genetics and intelligence. *Journal of the American Academy of Child and Adolescent Psychiatry, 38,* 786–788.

Plomin, R., & Petrill, S. A. (1997). Genetics and intelligence: What's new? *Intelligence, 24,* 53–77.

Pope, H., Gruber, A., Hudson, J., Huestis, M., & Yurgelun-Todd, D. (2001). Neuropsychological performance in long-term cannabis users. *Archives in General Psychiatry, 58,* 909–915.

Pope, K. S. (1978). The flow of consciousness. In K. S. Pope & J. L. Singer (Eds.), *The stream of consciousness: Scientific investigations into the flow of human experience.* New York: Plenum.

Pope, K. S. (1996). Memory, abuse, and science: Questioning claims about the false memory syndrome epidemic. *American Psychologist, 51,* 957–974.

Pope, K. S., & Singer, J. L. (Eds.). (1978). *The stream of consciousness.* New York: Plenum.

Pope, K. S., & Singer, J. L. (1980). The waking stream of consciousness. In J. M. Davidson & R. J. Davidson (Eds.), *The psychobiology of consciousness* (pp. 169–191). New York: Plenum.

Porter, S., Birt, A., Yuille, J., & Lehman, D. (2000). Negotiating false memories: Interviewer and rememberer characteristics related to memory distortion. *Psychological Science, 11,* 507–510.

Posner, M. I. (1973). *Cognition: An introduction.* Glenview, IL: Scott, Foresman.

Postmes, T., & Spears, R. (1998). Deindividuation and anti-normative behavior: A meta-analysis. *Psychological Bulletin, 123,* 238–259.

Powell, K. E., Thompson, P. D., Caspersen, C. J., & Kendrick, J. S. (1987). Physical activity and incidence of coronary heart disease. *American Review of Public Health, 8,* 253–287.

Pratto, F., Stallworth, L. M., Sidanius, J., & Siers, B. (1997). The gender gap in occupational role attainment: A social dominance approach. *Journal of Personality and Social Psychology, 72,* 37–53.

Prentice, W. C. H. (1954). Visual recognition of verbally labeled figures. *American Journal of Psychology, 67,* 315–320.

**Preston, S. H.,** (1998). Differential fertility by IQ and the IQ distribution of a population. In U. Neisser (Ed.), *The rising curve: Long-term gains in IQ and related measures* (pp. 377–388). Washington, DC: American Psychological Association.

**Price, D. D.** (1988). *Psychological and neural mechanisms of pain.* New York: Raven Press.

**Price, D. D., & Barber, J.** (1987). An analysis of factors that contribute to the efficiency of hypnotic analgesia. *Journal of Abnormal Psychology, 96,* 46–51.

**Prinzmetal, W.** (1995). Visual feature integration in a world of objects. *Current Directions in Psychological Science, 4,* 90–94.

**Prochaska, J. O.** (1984). *Systems of psychotherapy: A transtheoretical analysis* (2nd ed.). Pacific Grove, CA: Brooks/Cole.

**Pugh, E. N.** (1988). Vision: Physics and retinal physiology. In R. C. Atkinson, R. J. Herrnstein, G. Lindzey, & R. D. Luce (Eds.), *Stevens' handbook of experimental psychology: Vol. 1. Perception and Motivation.* New York: Wiley Interscience.

**Q**

**Querido, J. G., Warner, T. D., & Eyberg, S. M.** (2002). Parenting styles and child behavior in African American families of preschool children. *Journal of Clinical Child Psychology, 31,* 272–277.

**R**

**Raaheim, K., & Kaufmann, G.** (1972). Level of activity and success in solving an unfamiliar task. *Psychological Reports, 30,* 271–274.

**Raaijmakers, J. G. W., & Shiffrin, R. M.** (1992). Models for recall and recognition. *Annual Review of Psychology, 43,* 205–234.

**Rabkin, J. G., & Streuning, E. L.** (1976). Life events, stress, and illness. *Science, 194,* 1013–1019.

**Rachman, S.** (1966). Sexual fetishism: An experimental analogue. *Psychological Record, 16,* 293–296.

**Radvansky, G. A.** (1999). Aging, memory, and comprehension. *Current Directions in Psychological Science, 8,* 49–53.

**Ramsey, J., & Hungerford, H. R.** (1989). The effects of issue investigation and action training on environmental behavior in seventh grade students. *Journal of Environmental Education, 20,* 29–34.

**Ranken, H. B.** (1963). Language and thinking: Positive and negative effects of naming. *Science, 141,* 48–50.

**Rapp, P. R., & Amaral, D. G.** (1992). Individual differences in the cognitive and neurobiological consequences of normal aging. *Trends in Neuroscience, 15,* 340–344.

**Raugh, M. R., & Atkinson, R. C.** (1975). A mnemonic method for learning a second-language vocabulary. *Journal of Educational Psychology, 67,* 1–16.

**Ravindran, A. V., Anisman, H., Merali, Z., Charbonneau, Y., Telner, J., Bialik, R. J., Wiens, A., Ellis, J., & Griffiths, J.** (1999). Treatment of primary dysthymia with group cognitive therapy and pharmacotherapy:

Clinical symptoms and functional impairments. *American Journal of Psychiatry, 156,* 1608–1617.

**Ray, O. S.** (1974). *Drugs, society, and human behavior* (2nd ed.). St. Louis: C. V. Mosby.

**Raynor, H. A., & Epstein, L. H.** (2001). Dietary variety, energy regulation, and obesity. *Psychological Bulletin, 127,* 325–341.

**Rechtschaffen, A., & Buchignami, C.** (1983). Visual dimensions and correlates of dream images. *Sleep Research, 12,* 189.

**Redd, W. H., Jacobsen, P. B., Die-Trill, M., Dermatis, H., McEvoy, M., & Holland, J. C.** (1987). Cognitive/attentional distraction in the control of conditioned nausea in pediatric cancer patients receiving chemotherapy. *Journal of Consulting and Clinical Psychology, 55,* 391–395.

**Reed, C. F.** (1984). Terrestrial passage theory of the moon illusion. *Journal of Experimental Psychology: General, 113,* 489–516.

**Reeves, A., & Plumb, F.** (1969). Hyperphagia, rage, and dementia accompanying a ventromedial hypothalamic neoplasm. *Archives of Neurology, 20,* 616–624.

**Reilly, R. R., & Chao, G. T.** (1982). Validity and fairness of some alternative employee selection procedures. *Personnel Psychology, 35,* 1–62.

**Rein, S., & Spencer, S. J.** (1997). Prejudice as self-image maintenance: Affirming the self through derogating others. *Journal of Personality and Social Psychology, 73,* 31–44.

**Reisenzein, R.** (1983). The Schachter-Singer theory of emotion: Two decades later. *Psychological Bulletin, 94,* 239–264.

**Reiss, A. L., & others.** (1996). Brain development, gender and IQ in children: A volumetric imaging study. *Brain, 119,* 1763–1774.

**Reneman, L., Lavalaye, J., Schmand, B., de Wolff, F., van den Brink, W., den Heeten, G., & Booij, J.** (2001). Cortical serotonin transporter density and verbal memory in individuals who stopped using 3, 4-ethylenedioxymethamphetamine (MDMA or "Ecstasy"). *Archives in General Psychiatry, 58,* 901–906.

**Rescorla, R. A.** (1967). Pavlovian conditioning and its proper control procedures. *Psychological Review, 74,* 71–80.

**Rescorla, R. A.** (1988). Pavlovian conditioning: It's not what you think it is. *American Psychologist, 43,* 151–160.

**Resick, P. A., Nishith, P., Weaver, T. L., Astin, M. C., & Feuer, C. A.** (2002). A comparison of cognitive-processing therapy with prolonged exposure and a waiting condition for the treatment of chronic posttraumatic stress disorder in female rape victims. *Journal of Consulting & Clinical Psychology, 70,* 867–879.

**Reynolds, A. G., & Flagg, P. W.** (1983). *Cognitive psychology* (2nd ed.). Boston: Little, Brown.

**Rhodes, N., & Wood, W.** (1992). Self-esteem and intelligence affect influenceability: The mediating role of message reception. *Psychological Bulletin, 111,* 156–171.

**Ribeiro, S., Goyal, V., Mello, C., & Pavlides, C.** (1999). Constantine. brain gene expression during REM sleep depends on prior waking experience. *Learning and Memory, 6,* 500–508.

**Richards, J. M., Beal, W. E., Seagal, J. D., & Pennebaker, J. W.** (2000). Effects of disclosure of traumatic events on illness behavior among psychiatric prison inmates. *Journal of Abnormal Psychology, 109,* 156–160.

**Rieber, R. W.** (1999). Hypnosis, false memory and multiple personality: A trinity of affinity. *History of Psychiatry, 10,* 3–11.

**Rimm, D. C., & Masters, J.** (1979). *Behavior therapy* (2nd ed.). New York: Academic Press.

**Roberts, B. W., Caspi, A., & Moffitt, T. E.** (2001). The kids are alright: Growth and stability in personality development from adolescence to adulthood. *Journal of Personality and Social Psychology, 81,* 670–683.

**Roberts, P., & Newton, P. M.** (1987). Levinsonian studies of women's adult development. *Psychology and Aging, 2,* 154–163.

**Robins, M. B., & Jensen, G. G.** (1978). Multiple orgasm in males. *Journal of Sex Research, 13,* 21–26.

**Robins, R. W., Gosling, S. D., & Clark, K. H.** (1999). An empirical analysis of trends in psychology. *American Psychologist, 54,* 117–128.

**Robinson, N. S., Garber, J., & Hilsman, R.** (1995). Cognitions and stress: Direct and moderating effects on depressive versus externalizing symptoms during the junior high school transition. *Journal of Abnormal Psychology, 104,* 3.

**Robinson, R. G., & Starkstein, S. E.** (1990). Current research in affective disorders following stroke. *Journal of Neuropsychiatry and Clinical Neurosciences, 2,* 1–14.

**Rock, I., & Kaufman, L.** (1972). The moon illusion. In R. Held & W. Richards (Eds.), *Perception: Mechanisms and models.* San Francisco: W. H. Freeman.

**Rodin, J.** (1985). Insulin levels, hunger, and food intake: An example of feedback loops in body weight regulation. *Health Psychology, 4,* 1–18.

**Rodin, J., & Ickovics, R.** (1990). Women's health: Review and research agenda as we approach the 21st century. *American Psychologist, 45,* 1018–1034.

**Roe, A.** (1946). The personality of artists. *Educational Psychology Measurement, 6,* 401–408.

**Roe, A.** (1953). *The making of a scientist.* New York: Dodd, Mead.

**Roediger, H., & McDermott, K.** (2000). Tricks of memory. *American Psychological Society, 9,* 123–127.

**Roffwarg, H. P., Muzio, J. N., & Dement, W. C.** (1966). Ontogenetic development of the human sleep-dream cycle. *Science, 152,* 604–619.

**Rogers, C. R.** (1951). *Client-centered therapy: Its current practice, implications, and theory.* Boston: Houghton Mifflin.

**Rogers, R. W.** (1975). A protection motivation theory of fear appeals and attitude change. *Journal of Psychology, 91,* 93–114.

**Roizen, M. F.** (1999). *Real age: Are you as young as you can be?* New York: HarperCollins.

**Rolls, E. T., Burton, M. J., & Mora, F.** (1976). Hypothalamic neuronal responses associated with the sight of food. *Brain Research, 111,* 53–66.

**Romer, D., Gruder, C. L., & Lizardo, T.** (1986). A person-situation approach to altruistic behavior. *Journal of Personality and Social Psychology, 51,* 1001–1012.

**Rorschach, H.** (1953). *Psychodiagnostics* (5th ed.). New York: Grune & Stratton.

**Rosch, E.** (1973). Natural categories. *Cognitive Psychology, 4,* 328–350.

**Rosch, E.** (1975). Cognitive representations of semantic categories. *Journal of Experimental Psychology: General, 104,* 192–233.

Rosch, E. H., Mervis, C. B., Gray, W. B., Johnson, D. M., & Boyes-Braem, P. (1976). Basic objects in natural categories. *Cognitive Psychology, 8*, 382–439.

Rosello, J., & Bernal, G. (1999). The efficacy of cognitive-behavioral and interpersonal treatments for depression in Puerto Rican adolescents. *Journal of Consulting and Clinical Psychology, 67*, 734–745.

Rosen, J. B., & Schulkin, J. (1998). From normal fear to pathological anxiety. *Psychological Review, 105*(2), 325–350.

Rosen, R. C., & Leiblum, S. R. (1995). Treatment of sexual disorders in the 1990s: An integrated approach. *Journal of Consulting and Clinical Psychology, 63*, 877–890.

Rosenberg, E. L., Ekman, P., Jiang, W., Babyak, M., Coleman, E., Hanson, M., O'Connor, C., Waugh, R., & Blumenthal, J. A. (2001). Linkages between facial expressions of anger and transient myocardial ischemia in men with coronary artery disease. *Emotion, 1*, 107–115.

Rosenzweig, M. R. (1984). *Cognition.* New York: Holt, Rinehart & Winston.

Ross, L. (1977). The intuitive psychologist and his shortcomings: Distortions in the attribution process. In L. Berkowitz (Ed.), *Advances in experimental social psychology* (Vol. 10, pp. 173–220). New York: Academic Press.

Rossi, A. S. (1980). Aging and parenthood in the middle years. In P. B. Balter & O. G. Brim (Eds.), *Life-span development and behavior* (Vol. 3). New York: Academic Press.

Rothbaum, B. O., Hodges, L. F., Kooper, R., Opdyke, D., Williford, J. S., & North, M. (1995). Effectiveness of computer-generated (virtual reality) graded exposure in the treatment of acrophobia. *American Journal of Psychiatry, 152*, 626–628.

Rothman, A. J., & Salovey, P. (1997). Shaping perceptions to motivate healthy behavior: The role of message framing. *Psychological Bulletin, 121*, 3–19.

Rounsaville, B. J., Chevron, E. S., Prusoff, B. A., Elkin, I., Imber, S., Sotsky, S., & Watkins, J. (1987). The relation between specific and general dimensions of the psychotherapy process in interpersonal psychotherapy of depression. *Journal of Consulting and Clinical Psychology, 55*, 379–384.

Rovee-Collier, C. (1999). The development of infant memory. *Current Directions in Psychological Science, 8*, 80–85.

Roy, M., & Steptoe, A. (1991). The inhibition of cardiovascular responses to mental stress following aerobic exercise. *Psychophysiology, 28*, 689–700.

Rozin, P. (1996). Towards a psychology of food and eating: From motivation to model to marker, morality, meaning, and metaphor. *Current Directions in Psychological Science, 5*, 18–24.

Rubin, K. H. (1998). Social and emotional development from a cultural perspective. *Developmental Psychology, 34*, 611–615.

Ruble, D. N., & Ruble, T. L. (1980). Sex stereotypes. In A. G. Miller (Ed.), *In the eye of the beholder: Contemporary issues in stereotyping.* New York: Holt, Rinehart & Winston.

Ruderman, A. J., & Besbeas, M. (1992). Psychological characteristics of dieters and bulimics. *Journal of Abnormal Psychology, 101*, 383–390.

Rumbaugh, D. M., & Gill, T. V. (1976). The mastery of language-type skills by the chimpanzee (*Pan*). In S. Harnad, H. Steklis, & J. Lancaster (Eds.), *Origins and evolution of language and speech.* New York: New York Academy of Sciences.

Rumelhart, D. E., & McClelland, J. L. (Eds.). (1986). *Parallel distributed processing: Explorations in the microstructure of cognition, Vol. 1: Foundations.* Cambridge, MA: MIT Press.

Russell, J. A., & Mehrabian, A. (1978). Approach-avoidance and affiliation as functions of the emotion-eliciting equality of an environment. *Environment and Behavior, 10*, 355–387.

Russell, M. A. H. (1971). Cigarette smoking: Natural history of a dependence disorder. *British Journal of Medical Psychology, 44*, 1–16.

Russo, N. F. (1990). Overview: Forging research priorities for women's mental health. *American Psychologist, 45*, 368–373.

Rutherford, S. D. (1988). The culture of American deaf people. *Sign Language Studies, 59*, 129–147.

Ryan, R. M., & Deci, E. L. (2000). Self-determination theory and the facilitation of intrinsic motivation, social development, and well-being. *American Psychologist, 55*, 68–78.

**S**

Sachs, J. D. S. (1967). Recognition memory for syntactic and semantic aspects of connected discourse. *Perception and Psychophysics, 2*, 437–442.

Sackett, P. R., Schmitt, N., Ellingson, J. E., & Kabin, M. B. (2001). High-stakes testing in employment, credentialing, and higher education: Prospects in a post-affirmative-action world. *American Psychologist, 56*, 302–318.

Sagan, C. (1979). *Broca's brain.* New York: Random House.

Salapatek, P. (1977). Stimulus determinants of attention in infants. In B. Wolman (Ed.), *International encyclopedia of psychiatry, psychology, psychoanalysis, and neurology* (Vol. 10). New York: Aesculapis.

Sales, B., & Folkman, S. (2000). *Ethics in research with human participants.* Washington: American Psychological Association.

Sandfort, T. G. M., de Graaf, R., Bijl, R. V., & Schnabel, P. (2001). Same-sex sexual behavior and psychiatric disorders. *Archives of General Psychiatry, 58*, 85–91.

Santrock, J. W. (1995). *Children* (4th ed.). Madison, WI: Brown & Benchmark.

Santrock, J. W. (1998). *Children* (5th ed.). Boston: McGraw-Hill.

Santilla, P., Alkiora, P., Ekholm, M., & Niemi, P. (1999). False confession to robbery: The rules of suggestibility, anxiety, memory disturbance and withdrawal symptoms. *Journal of Forensic Psychiatry, 10*, 399–415.

Sarason, I. G., Johnson, J. H., & Siegel, J. M. (1978). Assessing the impact of life change: Development of the life experiences survey. *Journal of Consulting and Clinical Psychology, 46*, 932–946.

Sargent, C. (1984). Between death and shame: Dimensions of pain in Bariba culture. *Social Science and Medicine, 19*, 1299–1304.

Scarr, S. (1990). Mother's proper place: Children's needs and women's rights. *Journal of Social Behavior and Personality, 15*, 507–515.

Scarr, S., & Eisenberg, M. (1993). Child care research: Issues, perspectives, and results. *Annual Review of Psychology, 44*, 613–644.

Scarr, S., Philips, D., & McCartney, K. (1990). Facts, fantasies, and the future of childcare in the United States. *Psychological Science, 1*, 26–35.

Scarr, S., & Salapatek, P. (1970). Patterns of fear development during infancy. *Merrill-Palmer Quarterly, 16*, 53–90.

Schachter, D. L. (1999). The seven sins of memory: Insights from psychology and cognitive neuroscience. *American Psychologist, 54*, 182–203.

Schachter, S. (1959). *The psychology of affiliation. Experimental studies of sources of gregariousness.* Stanford, CA: Stanford University Press.

Schachter, S., & Singer, J. E. (1962). Cognitive, social and physiological determinants of emotional state. *Psychological Review, 69*, 379–399.

Schacter, J. (1989). Why we need a program for the control of *Chlamydia trachomatis. New England Journal of Medicine, 320*, 802–803.

Scherer, K. R. (1997). The role of culture in emotion-antecedent appraisal. *Journal of Personality Assessment, 73*, 902–922.

Schiff, M., & Lewontin, R. (1986). *Education and class: The irrelevance of IQ genetic studies.* Oxford, England: Clarendon.

Schiffman, H. R. (1976). *Sensation and perception. An integrated approach.* New York: Wiley.

Schiffman, S. S., Graham, B. G., Sattely-Miller, E. A., & Warwick, Z. S. (1998). *Current Directions in Psychological Science, 7*, 137–143.

Schimmack, U., Oishi, S., Radhakrishnan, P., & Dzokoto, V. (2002). Culture, personality, and subjective well-being: Integrating process models of life satisfaction. *Journal of Personality and Social Psychology, 82*, 582–593.

Schleifer, S. J., Keller, S. E., Bartlett, J. A., Eckholdt, H. M., & Delaney, B. R. (1996). Immunity in young adults with major depressive disorder. *American Journal of Psychiatry, 153*, 4.

Schmidt, F. L., & Hunter, J. E. (1992). Development of a causal model of processes determining job performance. *Current Directions in Psychological Science, 1*, 89–92.

Schmidt, F. L., & Hunter, J. E. (1993). Tacit knowledge, practical intelligence, general mental ability, and job knowledge. *Current Directions in Psychological Science, 2*, 8–9.

Schmidt, F. L., & Hunter, J. E. (1998). The validity and utility of selection methods in personnel psychology: Practical and theoretical implications of 85 years of research findings. *Psychological Bulletin, 124*, 262–274.

Schmidt, F. L., & Ones, D. S. (1992). Personnel selection. *Annual Review of Psychology, 43*, 627–670.

Schmidt, N. B., Lerew, D. R., & Trakowski, J. H. (1997). Body vigilance in panic disorder: Evaluating attention to bodily perturbations. *Journal of Consulting and Clinical Psychology, 65*(2), 214–220.

Schmolck, H., Buffalo, E. A., & Squire, L. A. (2000). Memory distortions develop over time: Recollections of the O. J. Simpson trial verdict after 15 and 32 months. *Psychological Science, 11*, 39–45.

Scholttman, A. (2001). Perception versus knowledge of cause and effect in children:

When seeing is believing. *Psychological Science, 10,* 111–115.

Schreiber, F. R. (1973). *Sybil.* New York: Henry Regnery.

Schulkin, J. (1999). *The neuroendocrine regulation of behavior.* New York: Cambridge University Press.

Schulz, R., & Ewen, R. B. (1988). *Adult development and aging: Myths and emerging realities.* New York: Macmillan.

Schwarz, N. (1999). Self-reports: How the questions shape the answer. *American Psychologist, 54,* 93–105.

Schwarzer, R. (2001). Social-cognitive factors in changing health-related behaviors. *Psychological Science, 10,* 47–51.

Scott, L., & O'Hara, M. W. (1993). Self-discrepancies in clinically anxious and depressed university students. *Journal of Abnormal Psychology, 102,* 282–287.

Scoville, W. B., & Milner, B. (1957). Loss of recent memory after bilateral hippocampal lesions. *Journal of Neurology, Neurosurgery, and Psychiatry, 20,* 11–21.

Seeley, R. J., & Schwartz, M. W. (1997). The regulation of energy balance: Peripheral hormonal signals and hypothalamic neuropeptides. *Current Directions in Psychological Science, 6,* 39–44.

Seidlitz, L., & Diener, E. (1998). Sex differences in the recall of affective experiences. *Journal of Personality and Social Psychology, 74,* 262–271.

Seligman, M. E. P. (1975). *Helplessness: On depression, development, and death.* San Francisco: W. H. Freeman.

Selye, H. (1976). *The stress of life.* New York: Knopf.

Shamir, B., & Howell, J. M. (1999). Organizational and contextual influences on the emergency and effectiveness of charismatic leadership. *Leadership Quarterly, 10,* 257–283.

Shadish, W. R., Matt, G. E., Navarro, A., & Phillips, G. (2000). The effects of psychological therapies under clinically representative conditions: A meta-analysis. *Psychological Bulletin, 126,* 512–529.

Shaywitz, B. A., Shaywitz, S. E., Pugh, K. R., Constable, R. T., Skudlarski, P., Fulbright, R. K., Bronen, R. A., Fletcher, J. M., Shankweiler, D. P., Katz, L., & Gores, J. C. (1995). Sex differences in the functional organization of the brain for language. *Nature, 373,* 607–609.

Sheldon, K. M., & Kasser, T. (2001). Getting older, getting better? Personal strivings and psychological maturity across the life span. *Developmental Psychology, 37,* 491–501.

Shepard, J. A. (1995). Remedying motivation and productivity losses in collective settings. *Current Directions in Psychological Science, 4,* 131–139.

Sheppard, L. C., & Teasdale, J. D. (2000). Dysfunctional thinking in major depressive disorder: A deficit in metacognitive monitoring. *Journal of Abnormal Psychology, 109,* 768–776.

Sheppard, W. C., & Willoughby, R. H. (1975). *Child behavior.* Chicago: Rand McNally.

Sherif, M. (1936). *The psychology of social norms.* New York: Harper.

Sherif, M., & Sherif, C. W. (1953). *Groups in harmony and tension; An integration of studies of intergroup relations.* New York: Harper.

Shimamura, A. P., Berry, J. M., Mangels, J. A., Rusting, C. L., & Jurica, P. J. (1995). Memory and cognitive abilities in university professors:

Evidence for successful aging. *Psychological Science, 6,* 271–277.

Shortliffe, E. H., Axline, S. G., Buchanan, B. G., Merigan, T. C., & Cohen, N. S. (1973). An artificial intelligence program to advise physicians regarding antimicrobial therapy. *Computers and Biomedical Research, 6,* 544–560.

Shrout, P. E., Link, B. G., Dohrenwend, B. P., Skodol, A. E., Stueve, A., & Mirotznik, J. (1989). Characterizing life events as risk factors for depression: The role of fateful loss events. *Journal of Abnormal Psychology, 96,* 460–467.

Siegel, J. M., & Kuykendall, D. H. (1990). Loss, widowhood, and psychological distress among the elderly. *Journal of Consulting and Clinical Psychology, 58,* 519–524.

Siegler, R. S. (2000). Unconscious insights. *Psychological Sciences, 9,* 79–83.

Sigman, M., & Whaley, S. E. (1998). In U. Neisser (Ed.), *The rising curve: Long-term gains in IQ and related measures* (pp. 155–182). Washington, DC: American Psychological Association.

Signorella, M., & Jamison, W. (1986). Masculinity, femininity, androgyny, and cognitive performance: A meta-analysis. *Psychological Bulletin, 100,* 207–228.

Silverstein, L. B. (1991). Transforming the debate about child care and maternal employment. *American Psychologist, 46,* 1025–1032.

Silverstein, L. B., & Auerbach, C. F. (1999). Deconstructing the essential father. *American Psychologist, 54,* 397–407.

Simons, A. D., Gordon, J. S., Thase, M. E., & Monroe, S. M. (1995). Toward an integration of psychologic, social, and biological factors in depression: Effects on outcome and course of cognitive therapy. *Journal of Consulting and Clinical Psychology, 63,* 369–377.

Simons, D. J., & Levin, D. T. (1998). Failure to detect changes to people during a real-world interaction. *Psychonomic Bulletin & Review, 4,* 644–649.

Simpson, J. A., Campbell, B., & Berscheid, E. (1986). The association between romantic love and marriage: Kephart (1967) twice revisited. *Personality and Social Psychology Bulletin, 12,* 363–372.

Skinner, B. F. (1953). *Science and human behavior.* New York: Macmillan.

Skolnik, A. (1966). Stability and interrelations of thematic test imagery over 20 years. *Child Development, 37,* 389–396.

Slobin, D. I. (1979). *Psycholinguistics.* Glenview, IL: Scott, Foresman.

Smith, E. (2000). Neural bases of human working memory. *American Psychological Society, 9,* 45–49.

Smith, M. L., & Glass, G. V. (1977). Meta-analysis of psychotherapy outcome studies. *American Psychologist, 32,* 752–760.

Smith, T., & Ruiz, J. (2002). Psychosocial influences on the development and course of coronary heart disease: Current status and implications for research and practice. *Journal of Consulting & Clinical Psychology, 70*(3), 548–568.

Smith, V. L., & Ellsworth, P. C. (1987). The social psychology of eyewitness accuracy: Misleading questions and communicator expertise. *Journal of Applied Psychology, 72,* 294–300.

Smyth, J. M., Soefer, M. H., Hurewitz, A., & Stone, A. A. (1999). The effect of tape recorded relaxation training on well-being, symptoms, and peak expiratory flow rate in adult asthmatics: A pilot study, *Psychology and Health, 14,* 487–501.

Snow, R. E., & Swanson, J. (1992). Instructional psychology: Aptitude, adaptation, and assessment. *Annual Review of Psychology, 43,* 583–626.

Snowden, L. R., & Cheung, F. K. (1990). Use of inpatient mental health services by members of ethnic minority groups. *American Psychologist, 45,* 347–355.

Snyder, M., Tauke, E. D., & Berscheid, E. (1977). Social perception and interpersonal behavior: On the self-fulfilling nature of social stereotypes. *Journal of Personality and Social Psychology, 35,* 656–666.

Snyder, S. H. (1974). *Madness and the brain.* New York: McGraw-Hill.

Solomon, D. A., Keller, M. B., Leon, A. C., Mueller, T. I., Shea, M. T., Warshaw, M., Maser, J. D., Coryell, W., & Endicott, J. (1997). Recovery from major depression. *Archives of General Psychiatry, 54,* 1001–1006.

Solomon, D. A., Keller, M. B., Leon, A. C., Mueller, T. I., Lavori, P. W., Shea, T., Coryell, W., Warshaw, M., Turvey, C., Maser, J. D., & Endicott, J. (2000). Multiple recurrences of major depressive disorder. *American Journal of Psychiatry, 157,* 229–233.

Solomon, R. L. (1980). The opponent-process theory of acquired motivation. *American Psychologist, 35,* 691–712.

Sorkin, R. D., Hays, C. J., & West, R. (2001). Signal-detection analysis of group decision making. *Psychological Review, 108,* 183–203.

Southwick, S. M., Morgan, C. A., III, Darnell, A., Bremner, D., Nicolaou, A. L., Nagy, L. M., & Charney, D. S. (1995). Trauma-related symptoms in veterans of Operation Desert Storm: A 2-year follow-up. *American Journal of Psychiatry, 152,* 8.

Spanos, N. P. (1996). *Multiple identities and false memories: A sociocognitive perspective.* Washington, DC: American Psychological Association Press.

Spear, L. P. (2000). Neurobehavioral changes in adolescence. *Psychological Science, 9,* 111–114.

Spearman, C. E., & Wynn-Jones, L. (1950). *Human ability.* London: Macmillan.

Speisman, J. C., Lazarus, R. S., Mordokoff, A. M., & Davison, L. (1964). Experimental reduction of stress based on ego-defense theory. *Journal of Abnormal and Social Psychology, 68,* 367–380.

Spence, J. T., & Helmreich, R. L. (1978). *Masculinity and femininity: Their psychological dimensions, correlates, and antecedents.* Austin: University of Texas Press.

Sperling, G. (1960). The information available in brief visual presentations. *Psychological Monographs, 74,* 1–29.

Spiegler, M. D., & Guevremont, D. C. (1998). *Contemporary behavior therapy* (3rd ed.). Pacific Grove, CA: Brooks/Cole.

Spijker, J., De Graaf, R., Bijl, R. V., Beekman, A. T. F., Ormel, J., & Nolen, W. A. (2002). Duration of major depressive episodes in the general population: Results from the Netherlands Mental Health Survey and Incidence Study (NEMESIS). *British Journal of Psychiatry, 181,* 208–213.

Spitzer, R. L., Terman, M., Williams, J. B. W., Terman, J. S., Malt, U. F., Singer, F., & Lewy, A. J. (1999). Jet lag: Clinical features, validation of a new syndrome-specific scale, and lack of response to melatonin in a randomized, double-blind trial. *American Journal of Psychiatry, 156,* 1392–1396.

Sprinthal, R. C., Sprinthal, N. A., & Oja, S. N. (1998). *Educational psychology: A developmental approach* (7th ed.). Boston: McGraw-Hill.

Squire, L. R. (1987). *Memory and the brain.* New York: Oxford University Press.

Squire, L. R., Knowlton, B., & Musen, G. (1993). The structure and organization of memory. *Annual Review of Psychology, 44,* 453–495.

Sroufe, L. A. (1978). The ontogenesis of emotion. In J. Osofoslay (Ed.), *Handbook of infancy.* New York: Wiley.

St. Lawrence, J. S., Crosby, R. A., Brasfield, T. L., & O'Bannon, R. E., III. (2002). Reducing STD and HIV risk behavior of substance-dependent adolescents: A randomized controlled trial. *Journal of Consulting and Clinical Psychology, 70,* 1010–1021.

Staples, S. L. (1996). Human response to environmental noise: Psychological research and public policy. *American Psychologist, 51,* 143–150.

Stark, E. (1984, October). To sleep, perchance to dream. *Psychology Today.*

Starkstein, S. E., & Robinson, R. G. (1988). Lateralized emotional response following stroke. In M. Kinsbourne (Ed.), *Cerebral dysfunction in depression.* Washington, DC: American Psychiatric Association Press.

Starkstein, S. E., Robinson, R. G., & Price, T. R. (1988). Comparison of patients with and without poststroke major depression matched for size and the location of lesion. *Archives of General Psychiatry, 45,* 247–252.

Staub, E. (1996). Cultural-societal roots of violence: The examples of genocidal violence and of contemporary youth violence in the United States. *American Psychologist, 51,* 117–132.

Steel, P., & Ones, D. S. (2002). Personality and happiness: A national-level analysis. *Journal of Personality and Social Psychology, 83,* 767–781.

Steele, C. M. (1997). A threat in the air: How stereotypes shape intellectual identity and performance. *American Psychologist, 52,* 613–629.

Steele, C. M., & Josephs, R. A. (1990). Alcohol myopia: Its prized and dangerous effects. *American Psychologist, 45,* 921–933.

Steen, S., Oppliger, R., & Brownell, K. D. (1988). Metabolic effects of repeated weight loss and regain in adolescent wrestlers. *Journal of the American Medical Association, 260,* 47–50.

Stein, E. A., & others. (1998). Nicotine-induced activation in the human brain: A functional MRI study. *American Journal of Psychiatry, 155,* 1009–1015.

Stein, M. B., Torgrud, L. J., & Walker, J. R. (2000). Social phobia symptoms, subtypes, and severity. *Archives of General Psychiatry, 57,* 1046–1052.

Steinberg, J. (1995). The graying of the senses. *Journal of NIMH Research, 7,* 32–33.

Steketee, G., & Cleere, L. (1990). Obsessive-compulsive disorders. In A. S. Bellack, M. Hersen, & A. E. Kazdin (Eds.), *International handbook of behavior modification and therapy* (2nd ed., pp. 307–332). New York: Plenum.

Stephan, W., Berscheid, E., & Walster, E. (1971). Sexual arousal and heterosexual perception. *Journal of Personality and Social Psychology, 20,* 93–101.

Stephan, W. G. (1987). The contact hypothesis in intergroup relations. In C. Hendrick (Ed.), Group processes and intergroup relations. *Review of Personality and Social Psychology, 9,* 41–67.

Stern, K., & McClintock, M. K. (1998). Regulation of ovulation by human pheromones. *Nature, 392,* 177–179.

Stern, P. C. (2000). Toward a coherent theory of environmentally significant behavior. *Journal of Social Issues, 56,* 407–424.

Stern, R. M., & Koch, K. L. (1996). Motion sickness and differential susceptibility. *Current Directions in Psychological Science, 4,* 115–120.

Sternbach, R. A. (Ed.). (1978). *The psychology of pain.* New York: Raven Press.

Sternberg, R. J. (1979). The nature of mental abilities. *American Psychologist, 34,* 214–230.

Sternberg, R. J. (1981). Testing and cognitive psychology. *American Psychologist, 36,* 1181–1189.

Sternberg, R. J. (1997). The concept of intelligence and its role in lifelong learning and success. *American Psychologist, 52,* 1030–1037.

Sternberg, R. J., & Gardner, M. K. (1982). A componential interpretation of the general factor in human intelligence. In J. J. Eysenck (Ed.), *A model for intelligence.* Berlin: Springer.

Sternberg, R. J., & Wagner, R. K. (1993). The egocentric view of intelligence and job performance is wrong. *Current Directions in Psychological Science, 2,* 1–5.

Sternberg, S. (1969). Memory scanning: Mental processes revealed by reaction time experiments. *Acta Psychologica, 30,* 276–315.

Stewart, A. J., & Ostrove, J. M. (1998). Women's personality in middle age: Gender, history, and midcourse corrections. *American Psychologist, 55,* 1185–1194.

Stewart, A. J., & Vadewater, E. A. (1999). "If I had it to do over again…": Midlife review, midcourse corrections, and women's well-being in midlife. *Journal of Personality and Social Psychology, 76,* 270–283.

Stickgold, R., Hobson, J. A., Fosse, R., & Fosse, M. (2001). Sleep, learning, and dreams: Off-line memory reprocessing. *Science, 294,* 1052–1057.

Stokols, D. (1995). The paradox of environmental psychology. *American Psychologist, 50,* 821–837.

Stoner, J. A. F. (1961). *A comparison of individual and group decisions involving risk.* Unpublished master's thesis, Massachusetts Institute of Technology, Cambridge.

Strauch, I., & Meier, B. (1996). *In search of dreams: Experimental dream research.* Albany: State University of New York Press.

Strauman, T. J. (1992). Self-guides, autobiographical memory, and anxiety and dysphoria: Toward a cognitive model of vulnerability to emotional distress. *Journal of Abnormal Psychology, 101,* 87–95.

Strayer, D. L., & Johnston, W. A. (2001). Driven to distraction: Dual-task studies of simulated driving and conversing on a cellular phone. *American Psychological Society, 12,* 462–466.

Stumpf, H., & Stanley, J. C. (1998). Stability and change in gender-related differences on the College Board Advanced Placement and Achievement Tests. *Current Directions in Psychological Science, 7,* 192–196.

Subotnik, R., Kassan, L., Summers, E., & Wasser, A. (1993). *Genius revisited: High IQ children grown up.* Norwood, NJ: Ablex.

Suinn, R. M. (2001). The terrible twos—anger and anxiety. *American Psychologist, 56,* 27–36.

Suomi, S. (1988). *Genetic and environmental influences on social-emotional development in rhesus monkeys.* Presentation to the Fourth Annual Colloquium of the Center of Family Research, University of Georgia.

Susser, E., & others. (1996). Schizophrenia after prenatal famine: Further evidence. *Archives of General Psychiatry, 53,* 25–31.

Susser, E., Struening, E. L., & Conner, S. (1989). Psychiatric problems in homeless men. *Archives of General Psychiatry, 46,* 845–850.

Susser, E. S., & Lin, S. P. (1992). Schizophrenia after prenatal exposure to the Dutch hunger winter of 1944–45. *Archives of General Psychiatry, 49,* 983–988.

Sutker, P. B., Uddo, M., Davis, J. M., & Ditta, S. R. (1995). War zone stress, personal resources, and PTSD in Persian Gulf war returnees. *Journal of Abnormal Psychology, 104,* 444–452.

Swaab, D. F., & Hofman, M. A. (1990). An enlarged superchiasmatic nucleus in homosexual men. *Brain Research, 537,* 141.

Swaab, D. F., & Hofman, M. A. (1995). Sexual differentiation of the human hypothalamus in relation to gender and sexual orientation. *Trends in Neurosciences, 18,* 264–270.

Swartz, H. A. (1999). Interpersonal psychotherapy. In M. Hersen & A. Bellack (Eds.), *Handbook of comparative interventions for adult disorders* (2nd ed., pp. 139–155). New York: John Wiley.

Swayze, V. W. (1995). Frontal leukotomy and related psychosurgical procedures in the era before antipsychotics (1935–1954): A historical overview. *American Journal of Psychiatry, 152,* 505–515.

Swendsen, J. D., Tennen, H., Carney, M. A., Affleck, G., Willard, A., & Hromi, A. (2000). Mood and alcohol consumption: An experience sampling test of the self-medication hypothesis. *Journal of Abnormal Psychology, 109,* 198–204.

Symons, C. S., & Johnson, B. T. (1997). The self-reference effect in memory: A meta-analysis. *Psychological Bulletin, 121,* 371–394.

**T**

Tamminga, C. A. (1996). Images in neuroscience: Neuroimaging, XIII. *American Journal of Psychiatry, 153,* 1249.

Tang, S.-H., & Hall, V. C. (1995). The overjustification effect: A meta-analysis. *Applied Cognitive Psychology, 9,* 365–404.

Tannenbaum, S. I., & Yukl, G. (1992). Training and development in work organizations. *Annual Review of Psychology, 43,* 399–441.

Tanner, J. M. (1970). Physical growth. In P. H. Mussen (Ed.), *Carmichael's manual of child psychology* (Vol. 1). New York: Wiley.

Tarpy, R. M., & Mayer, R. E. (1978). *Foundations of learning and memory.* Glenview, IL: Scott, Foresman.

Tart, C. T. (1975). *States of consciousness.* New York: Dutton.

Tavris, C., & Wade, C. (1984). *The longest war: Sex differences in perspective* (2nd ed.). San Diego: Harcourt Brace Jovanovich.

Taylor, M. L., & Hall, J. A. (1982). Psychological androgyny: Theories, methods, and conclusions. *Psychological Bulletin, 92,* 347–366.

Taylor, S. E. (1986). *Health psychology.* New York: Random House.

Taylor, S. E. (1999). *Health psychology* (4th ed.). Boston: McGraw-Hill.

Taylor, S. E. (2002). *The tending instinct.* Times Books.

Taylor, S. E., Cousino Klein, L., Lewis, B. P., Gruenewald, T. L., Gurung, R. A. R., & Updegraff, J. A. (2000). Biobehavioral responses to stress in females: Tend-and-befriend, not fight-or-flight. *Psychological Review, 107,* 411–429.

Taylor, S. E., Pham, L. B., Rivkin, I. D., & Armor, D. A. (1998). Harnessing the imagination, mental simulation, self-regulation, and coping. *American Psychologist, 53,* 429–439.

Teasdale, J. D., Scott, J., Moore, R. G., Hayhurst, H., Pope, M., & Paykel, E. S. (2001). How does cognitive therapy prevent relapse in residual depression? Evidence from a controlled trial. *Journal of Consulting and Clinical Psychology, 69,* 347–357.

Telch, M. J., Lucas, J. A., & Nelson, P. (1989). Nonclinical panic in college students: An investigation of prevalence and symptomology. *Journal of Abnormal Psychology, 98,* 300–306.

Tellegen, A., Watson, D., & Clark, L. A. (1999). On the dimensional and hierarchical structure of affect. *Psychological Science, 10,* 297–303.

Terman, L. M. (1925). Mental and physical traits of a thousand gifted children. In M. Terman (Ed.), *Genetic studies of genius.* Stanford, CA: Stanford University Press.

Terrace, H. S. (1980). *Nim.* New York: Knopf.

Thackwray, D. E., Smith, M. C., Bodfish, J. W., & Meyers, A. W. (1993). A comparison of behavioral and cognitive-behavioral interventions for bulimia nervosa. *Journal of Consulting and Clinical Psychology, 61,* 639–645.

Thayer, R. E. (1987). Energy, tiredness, and tension effects of a sugar snack versus moderate exercise. *Journal of Personality and Social Psychology, 52,* 119–125.

Thibaut, J., & Walker, L. (1975). *Procedural justice: A psychological analysis.* Hillsdale, NJ: Erlbaum.

Thomas, M. H., & Drabman, R. S. (1975). Toleration of real-life aggression as a function of exposure to televised violence and age of subject. *Merrill-Palmer Quarterly, 21,* 227–232.

Thompson, J. K., Jarvie, G. J., Lahey, B. B., & Cureton, K. J. (1982). Exercise and obesity: Etiology, physiology, and intervention. *Psychological Bulletin, 91,* 55–79.

Thompson, R. A., & Nelson, C. A. (2001). Developmental science and the media. *American Psychologist, 56,* 5–15.

Thomson, D. M. (1988). Context and false recognition. In G. M. Davies & D. M. Thomson (Eds.), *Memory in context: Context in memory* (pp. 285–304). Chichester, England: Wiley.

Thorndike, E. L. (1911). *Animal intelligence: Experimental studies.* New York: Macmillan.

Thornhill, N. W., & Thornhill, R. (1990). An evolutionary analysis of psychological pain following rape. *Ethology and Sociobiology, 11,* 155–193.

Thornton, G. C., & Cleveland, J. N. (1990). Developing managerial talent through simulation. *American Psychologist, 45,* 190–199.

Thurstone, L. L. (1938). Primary mental abilities. *Psychometric Monographs* (1).

Tillfors, M., Furmark, T., Marteinsdottir, I., Fischer, H., Pissiota, A., Langstrom, B., & Fredikson, M. (2001). Cerebral blood flow in subjects with social phobia during stressful speaking tasks: A pet study. *American Journal of Psychiatry, 158,* 1220–1226.

Tillman, P., & Tillman, B. (1991). *Human factors essentials.* New York: McGraw-Hill.

Tollison, C. D., & Adams, H. E. (1979). *Sexual disorders: Treatments, theory, research.* New York: Gardner Press.

Tolman, E. C., & Honzik, C. H. (1930). Introduction and removal of reward, and maze performance in rats. *University of California Publications in Psychology, 4,* 257–276.

Tolman, E. C., Ritchie, B. F., & Kalish, D. (1946). Studies in spatial learning. I: Orientation and the shortcut. *Journal of Experimental Psychology, 36,* 13–25.

Tomaka, J., Blascovich, J., Kibler, J., & Ernst, J. M. (1997). Cognitive and physiological antecedents of threat and challenge appraisal. *Journal of Personality and Social Psychology, 73,* 63–72.

Tomasello, M. (2000). Culture and cognitive development. *American Psychological Society, 9,* 37–40.

Triandis, H. (1991). *Training for diversity.* Paper presented to the annual meeting of the American Psychological Association, San Francisco.

Triplett, N. (1898). The dynamogenic factors in peacemaking and competition. *American Journal of Psychology, 9,* 507–533.

Tulving, E. (1972). Episodic and semantic memory. In E. Tulving & W. Donaldson (Eds.), *Organization and memory.* New York: Academic Press.

Tulving, E. (1985). How many memory systems are there? *American Psychologist, 40,* 385–398.

Tulving, E. (1987). Multiple memory systems and consciousness. *Human Neurobiology, 6,* 67–80.

Turkat, I. D., & Calhoun, J. F. (1980). The problem-solving flow chart. *The Behavior Therapist, 3,* 21.

Turkington, C. (1987, August). Help for the worried well. *Psychology Today,* pp. 44–48.

Turnage, J. J. (1990). The challenge of new workplace technology for psychology. *American Psychologist, 45,* 171–178.

Turnbull, C. (1962). *The forest people.* New York: Simon & Schuster.

Turner, J. C., Hogg, M. A., Oakes, P. J., Richer, S. D., & Wetherell, M. S. (1987). *Rediscovering the social group: A self-categorization theory.* Oxford, England: Blackwell.

Turner, P. J., & Gervai, J. (1995). A multidimensional study of gender typing in preschool children and their parents: Personality, attitudes, preferences, behavior, and cultural differences. *Developmental Psychology, 31,* 759–779.

Tversky, A., & Kahneman, D. (1974). Judgment under uncertainty: Heuristics and biases. *Science, 185,* 1124–1131.

Tversky, A., & Kahneman, D. (1983). Extensional versus intuitive reasoning: The conjunction fallacy in probability judgment. *Psychological Review, 90,* 293–315.

Tyler, L. E. (1965). *The psychology of human differences.* New York: Appleton-Century-Crofts.

Uchino, B. N., Cacioppo, J. T., & Kiecolt-Glaser, J. K. (1996). The relationship between social support and physiological processes: A review with emphasis on underlying mechanisms and implications for health. *Psychological Bulletin, 119,* 488–531.

**V**

Vaillant, G. E. (1998). Natural history of male psychological health, XIV: Relationship of mood disorder vulnerability to physical health. *American Journal of Psychiatry, 155,* 184–191.

Vaillant, G. E., & Mukamal, K. (2001). Successful aging. *American Journal of Psychiatry, 158,* 839–847.

Van Duuren, F., & DiGiacomo, J. P. (1997). Degrading situations, affiliation, and social dependency. *European Journal of Social Psychology, 27,* 495–510.

Van Erp, T. G. M., Saleh, P. A., Rosso, I. M. R., Huttunen, M., Lonnqvist, J., Pirkola, T., Salonen, O., Valanne, L., Poutanen, V. P., Stanertskjold-Nordenstam, C. G., & Cannon, T. D. (2002). Contributions of genetic risk and fetal hypoxia to hippocampal volume in patients with schizophrenia or schizoaffective disorder, their unaffected siblings and healthy unrelated volunteers. *American Journal of Psychiatry, 159,* 1514–1520.

Van Houwelingen, J. H., & Van Raaij, W. F. (1989). The effect of goal-setting and daily electronic feedback on in-home energy use. *Journal of Consumer Research, 16,* 98–105.

Vataja, R., Pohjasvaara, T., Leppavuoir, A., Mantyla, R., Aronen, H., Salonen, O., Kaste, M., & Erkinjuntti, T. (2001). Magnetic resonance imaging correlates of depression after ischemic stroke. *Archives in General Psychiatry, 58,* 925–931.

Veleber, D. M., & Templer, D. I. (1984). Effects of caffeine on anxiety and depression. *Journal of Abnormal Psychology, 93,* 120–122.

Ventura, J., Neuchterlein, K. H., Lukoff, D., & Hardesty, J. P. (1989). A prospective study of stressful life events and schizophrenic relapse. *Journal of Abnormal Psychology, 98,* 407–411.

Vikas, M., & Ross, W. T. (1998). The impact of positive and negative affect and issue framing on issue interpretation and risk taking. *Organizational Behavior and Human Decision Processes, 76,* 298–324.

Visitainer, M. A., Volpicelli, J. R., & Seligman, M. E. P. (1982). Tumor rejection in rats after inescapable or escapable shock. *Science, 216,* 437–439.

Voelz, Z. R., Gencoz, F., Gencoz, T., Pettit, J., Perez, M., & Joiner, T. E. (2001). Patterns of hemispheric perceptual asymmetries: Left hemispatial biases predict changes in anxiety and positive affect in undergraduate women. *Emotion, 1,* 339–347.

von Frisch, K. (1953). *The dancing bees: An account of the life and senses of the honeybee.* New York: Harcourt, Brace, & World.

## W

Wadden, T. A., Vogt, R. A., Anderson, R. E., Bartlett, S. J., Foster, G. D., Kuehnel, R. H., Wilk, J., Weinstock, R., Buckenmeyer, Berkowitz, R. I., & Steen, S. N. (1997). Exercise in the treatment of obesity: Effect of four interventions on body composition, resting energy expenditure, appetite, and mood. *Journal of Consulting and Clinical Psychology, 65,* 269–277.

Waenke, M., Schwarz, N., & Noelle-Neumann, E. (1995). Asking comparative questions: The impact of the direction of the comparison. *Public Opinion Quarterly, 59,* 347–372.

Wagner, R. K. (1997). Intelligence, training, and employment. *American Psychologist, 52,* 1059–1069.

Waldron, I. (1991). Gender and health-related behavior. In D. S. Goodman (Ed.), *Health behavior: Emerging research perspectives.* New York: Plenum.

Walker, L. (1986). Cognitive processes in moral development. In G. L. Sapp (Ed.), *Handbook of moral development: Models processes, techniques, and research.* Birmingham: Religious Education Press.

Wallace, B., & Fisher, L. E. (1983). *Consciousness and behavior.* Boston: Allyn & Bacon.

Wallace, R. K., & Benson, H. (1972). The physiology of meditation. *Scientific American,* pp. 85–90.

Wallace, S. T., & Alden, L. E. (1997). Social phobia and positive social events: The price of success. *Journal of Abnormal Psychology, 106*(3), 416–424.

Wallas, G. (1926). *The art of thought.* New York: Harcourt Brace.

Walster, E., Aronson, V., & Abrahams, D. (1966). On increasing the persuasiveness of a low prestige communicator. *Journal of Experimental Social Psychology, 2,* 325–343.

Walster, E., Aronson, V., Abrahams, D., & Rottman, L. (1966). Importance of physical attractiveness in dating behavior. *Journal of Personality and Social Psychology, 5,* 508–516.

Walster, E. W., & Walster, G. W. (1978). *Equity: Theory and research.* Boston: Allyn & Bacon.

Watson, D., & Tellegen, A. (1985). Toward a consensual structure of mood. *Psychological Bulletin, 98,* 219–235.

Watson, J. B., & Rayner, R. (1920). Conditioned emotional reactions. *Journal of Experimental Psychology, 3,* 1–4.

Watson, R. I. (1971). *The great psychologists* (4th ed.). Philadelphia: J. B. Lippincott.

Webb, W. B. (1968). *Sleep: An experimental approach.* New York: Macmillan.

Webb, W. B. (1975). *Sleep, the gentle tyrant.* Englewood Cliffs, NJ: Prentice-Hall.

Webb, W. B. (1982). Sleep and biological rhythms. In W. B. Webb (Ed.), *Biological rhythms, sleep, and performance* (pp. 87–110). New York: Wiley.

Webb, W. B., & Bonnet, M. H. (1979). Sleep and dreams. In M. E. Meyer (Ed.), *Foundations of contemporary psychology.* New York: Oxford University Press.

Wechsler, D. (1955). *Manual for the Wechsler Adult Intelligence Scale.* New York: Psychological Corporation.

Weddington, W. W., & others. (1990). Changes in mood, craving, and sleep during short-term abstinence reported by male cocaine addicts. *Archives of General Psychiatry, 47,* 861–868.

Wehr, T. A., Duncan, W. C., Sher, L., Aeschbach, D., Schwartz, P. J., Turner, E., Postolache, T. T., & Rosenthal, N. E. (2001). A circadian signal of change of season in patients with seasonal affective disorder. *Archives of General Psychiatry, 58,* 1108–1114.

Weidner, G., Sexton, G., McLellarn, R. M., Connor, S. L., & Matarazzo, J. D. (1987). The role of Type A behavior and hostility in an elevation of plasma lipids in adult women and men. *Psychosomatic Medicine, 49,* 136–145.

Weiner, K. M. (1999). Morality and responsibility: Necessary components of feminist therapy. *Women & Therapy, 22,* 105–115.

Weinhardt, L. S., Carey, M. P., Carey, K. B., & Verdecias, R. N. (1998). Increasing assertiveness skills to reduce HIV risk among women living with a severe and persistent mental illness. *Journal of Consulting and Clinical Psychology, 66,* 680–684.

Weiss, T. M. (1972). Psychological factors in stress and disease. *Scientific American,* pp. 226–240.

Weisse, C. S. (1992). Depression and immunocompetence: A review of the literature. *Psychological Bulletin, 111,* 475–489.

Weissman, M. M. (1999). Interpersonal psychotherapy and the health care scene. In D. S. Janowsky (Ed.), *Psychotherapy indications and outcomes* (pp. 213–231). Washington DC: American Psychiatric Press.

Wells, G. L. (1993). What do we know about eyewitness identification? *American Psychologist, 48,* 553–571.

Wells, G. L., & Bradfield, A. L. (1999). Distortions in eyewitnesses' recollections: Can the postidentification-feedback effect be moderated? *Psychological Science, 10,* 138–144.

Wells, G. L., Malpass, R. S., Linday, R. C. L., Fisher, R. P., Turtle, J. W., & Fulero, S. M. (2000). From the lab to the police station: A successful application of eyewitness research. *American Psychologist, 55,* 581–598.

Wells, G. L., Small, M., Penrod, S., Malpass, R. S., Fulero, S. M., & Brimacombe, C. A. E. (1998). Eyewitness identification procedures: Recommendations for lineups and photospreads. *Law and Human Behavior, 22,* 603–647.

Wentling, T. (1973). Mastery versus nonmastery instruction with varying test item feedback treatments. *Journal of Educational Psychology, 65,* 50–58.

Westen, D. (1998). The scientific legacy of Sigmund Freud: Toward a psychodynamically informed psychological science. *Psychological Bulletin, 124,* 333–371.

Westen, D., & Gabbard, G. O. (1999). Psychoanalytic approaches to personality. In L. A. Pervin & O. P. John (Eds.), *Handbook of personality: Theory and research* (2nd ed., pp. 57–101). New York: Guilford.

Wheeler, M. A., Stuss, D. T., & Tulving, E. (1997). Toward a theory of episodic memory: The frontal lobes and autonoetic consciousness. *Psychological Bulletin, 121,* 331–354.

White, C. C., Powell, K. E., Hogelin, G. C., Gentry, E. M., & Forman, M. R. (1987). The behavioral risk factor surveys: IV. The descriptive epidemiology of exercise. *Preventive Medicine, 3,* 304–310.

White, K. G. (2002). Psychophysics of remembering: The discrimination hypothesis. *Current Directions in Psychological Science, 11,* 141–145.

White, R. K. (1977). Misperception in the Arab-Israeli conflict. *Journal of Social Issues, 25,* 41–78.

Whitten, L. (1992). Survival guilt and survival conflict in African-American college students. In M. Lang & C. Ford (Eds.), *Strategies for retaining minority students in higher education.* Springfield, IL: Charles C Thomas.

Whitten, L. (1993). Survival conflict, coping style and perception of the college classroom: Factors in the academic success of African-American college students in three colleges in the New York/New Jersey metropolitan area. *Afro-Americans in New York Life and History, 17,* 41–55.

Whorf, B. L. (1956). Science and linguistics. In J. B. Carroll (Ed.), *Language, thought and reality: Selected writings of Benjamin Lee Whorf.* Cambridge, MA: MIT Press.

Wickens, C. D. (1992). *Engineering psychology and human performance.* New York: HarperCollins.

Wickens, D. D., Born, D. G., & Allen, C. K. (1963). Proactive inhibition item similarity in short-term memory. *Journal of Verbal Learning and Verbal Behavior, 2,* 440–445.

Wiens, A., Ellis, J., & Griffiths, J. (1999). Treatment of primary dysthymia with group cognitive therapy and pharamacotherapy: Clinical symptoms and functional impairments. *American Journal of Psychiatry, 156,* 1608–1617.

Wiggins, J. S., & Pincus, A. L. (1992). Personality: Structure and assessment. *Annual Review of Psychology, 43,* 473–504.

Wilk, S. L., Desmarais, L. B., & Sackett, P. R. (1995). Gravitation to jobs commensurate with ability: Longitudinal and cross-sectional tests. *Journal of Applied Psychology, 80,* 79–85.

Wilkinson, R., Allison, S., Feeney, M., & Kaminska, Z. (1989). Alertness of night nurses: Two shift systems compared. *Ergonomics, 32,* 281–292.

Williams, G. V., & Goldman-Rakic, P. S. (1995). Modulation of memory fields by dopamine D1 receptors in prefrontal cortex. *Nature, 376,* 572–575.

Williams, R. B., Lane, J. D., Kunn, C. M., Melosh, W., White, A. D., & Schanberg, S. M. (1982). Type A behavior and elevated physiological and neuroendocrine responses to cognitive tasks. *Science, 218,* 483–485.

Williams, R. L. (1972). Abuses and misuses in testing black children. *Journal of Black Psychology, 4,* 77–92.

Williams, W. M. (1998). Are we raising smarter children today? School- and home-related influences on IQ. In U. Neisser (Ed.), *The rising curve: Long-term gains in IQ and related measures* (pp. 125–154). Washington, DC: American Psychological Association.

Williams, W. M., & Ceci, S. J. (1997). Are Americans becoming more or less alike? Trends in race, class, and ability differences in intelligence. *American Psychologist, 52,* 1126–1235.

Wilner, A., Reich, T., Robins, I., Fishman, R., & van Doren, T. (1976). Obsessive-compulsive neurosis. *Comprehensive Psychiatry, 17,* 527–529.

Wilson, J. R., Kuehn, R. E., & Beach, F. A. (1963). Modification in the sexual behavior of male rats produced by changing the stimulus female. *Journal of Comparative and Physiological Psychology, 56,* 636–644.

**Winch, R. F.** (1958). *Mate-selection.* New York: Harper & Row.

**Windle, M., & Windle, R. C.** (2001). Depressive symptoms and cigarette smoking among middle adolescents: Prospective associations and intrapersonal and interpersonal influences. *Journal of Consulting and Clinical Psychology, 69,* 215–226.

**Winett, R. A.** (1995). A framework for health promotion and disease prevention programs. *American Psychologist, 50,* 341–350.

**Winner, E.** (2000). Giftedness: Current theory and research. *Psychological Science, 9,* 153–156.

**Wisniewski, A. B.** (1998). Sexually-dimorphic patterns of cortical asymmetry, and the role for sex steroid hormones in determining cortical patterns of lateralization. *Psychoneuroendocrinology, 23,* 519–547.

**Wolpe, J.** (1958). *Psychotherapy by reciprocal inhibition.* Stanford, CA: Stanford University Press.

**Wood, J. M., Bootzin, R. R., Rosenhan, D., Nolen-Hoeksema, S., & Jourdan, F.** (1992). Effects of the 1989 San Francisco earthquake on frequency and content of nightmares. *Journal of Abnormal Psychology, 101,* 219–224.

**Wood, W., Christensen, P. N., Hebl, M. R., & Rothgerber, H.** (1997). Conformity to sex-typed norms, affect, and the self-concept. *Journal of Personality and Social Psychology, 73,* 523–535.

**Wood, W., & Eagly, A. H.** (2002). A cross-cultural analysis of the behavior of women and men: Implications for the origins of sex differences. *Psychological Bulletin, 128,* 699–727.

**Wood, W., Wong, F. Y., & Chachere, J. G.** (1991). Effects of media violence on viewers' aggression in unconstrained social interaction. *Psychological Bulletin, 109,* 371–383.

**Woodruff-Pak, D. S.** (1999). New directions for a classical paradigm: Human eyeblink conditioning. *Psychological Science, 10,* 1–3.

**World Health Organization.** (2002). *Current and future directions of the HIV/AIDS pandemic.* Geneva.

**Worrell, J.** (1980). New directions in counseling women. *Personnel and Guidance Journal, 58,* 477–484.

**Wyatt, R. J.** (1996). Neurodevelopment abnormalities and schizophrenia: A family affair. *American Journal of Psychiatry, 53,* 11–15.

### Y

**Yalom, I. D.** (1995). *The theory and practice of group psychotherapy* (4th ed.). New York: Basic Books.

**Yehuda, R., Kahana, B., Schmeidler, J., Southwick, S. M., Wilson, S., & Giller, E. L.** (1995). Impact of cumulative lifetime trauma and recent stress on current posttraumatic stress disorder symptoms in Holocaust survivors. *American Journal of Psychiatry, 152,* 12.

**Yehuda, R., Southwick, S. M., & Giller, E. L.** (1992). Exposure to atrocities and severity of chronic posttraumatic stress disorder in Vietnam veterans. *American Journal of Psychiatry, 149,* 333–336.

**Yuille, J. C., & Tollestrup, D. A.** (1990). Some effects of alcohol on eyewitness memory. *Journal of Applied Psychology, 75,* 268–273.

### Z

**Zajonc, R. B.** (1965). Social facilitation. *Science, 149,* 269–274.

**Zajonc, R. B.** (1968). Attitudinal effects of mere exposure. *Journal of Personality and Social Psychology Monograph Supplement, 9,* 1–27.

**Zajonc, R. B.** (2001). Mere exposure: A gateway to the subliminal. *Psychological Science, 10,* 224–228.

**Zajonc, R. B., & Mullally, P. R.** (1997). Birth order: Reconciling conflicting effects. *American Psychologist, 52,* 685–699.

**Zamble, E., Mitchell, J. B., & Findlay, H.** (1986). Pavlovian conditioning of sexual arousal: Parametric and background manipulations. *Journal of Experimental Psychology: Animal Behavior Processes, 12,* 403–411.

**Zaragoza, M. S., & Mitchell, K. J.** (1996). Repeated exposure to suggestion and the creation of false memories. *Psychological Science, 1,* 294–300.

**Zeki, S.** (1992, September). The visual image in mind and brain. *Scientific American,* pp. 69–76.

**Zellner, M.** (1970). Self-esteem, reception, and influenceability. *Journal of Personality and Social Psychology, 15,* 87–93.

**Zhang, J., & Bond, M. H.** (1998). Personality and filial piety among college students in two Chinese societies: The added value of indigenous constructs. *Journal of Cross-Cultural Psychology, 29,* 402–417.

**Zilbergeld, B.** (1978). *Male sexuality: A guide to sexual fulfillment.* Boston: Little, Brown.

**Zimbardo, P.** (1969). The human choice: Individuation, reason, and order versus deindividuation, impulse, and chaos. In W. Arnold and D. Levine (Eds.), *Nebraska Symposium on Motivation, 17,* 237–307.

**Zimbardo, P. G.** (1972). The pathology of imprisonment. *Society, 9*(6), 4.

**Zisook, S., & Shuchter, S. R.** (1991). Depression through the first year after the death of a spouse. *American Journal of Psychiatry, 148,* 1346–1352.

**Zlotnick, C., Elkin, I. & Shea, M. T.** (1998). Does the gender of a patient or the gender of a therapist affect the treatment of patients with major depression? *Journal of Consulting and Clinical Psychology, 66,* 655–659.

**Zohar, D.** (2002). Modifying supervisory practices to improve subunit safety: A leadership-based intervention model. *Journal of Applied Psychology, 87,* 156–163.

**Zorrilla, E. P., McKay, J. R., Luborsky, L., & Schmidt, K.** (1996). Relation of stressors and depressive symptoms to clinical progression of viral illness. *American Journal of Psychiatry, 153,* 5.

**Zuckerman, M.** (1995). Good and bad humors: Biochemical bases of personality and its disorders. *Psychological Science, 6,* 325–332.

**Zuroff, D. C., & Mongrain, M.** (1987). Dependency and self-criticism: Vulnerability factors for depressive affective states. *Journal of Abnormal Psychology, 96,* 14–22.

# Credits

## Photographs

### Study Skills

**pg. xxvii:** © Mark Lewis/Stone/Getty; **pg. xxix (top):** © David Young-Wolff/PhotoEdit; **pg. xxix (bottom):** © Bill Losh/FPG/Getty

### Chapter 1

**Opener:** © PhotoDisc/Getty; **pg. 4:** © Bettman/Corbis; **pg. 5 (top):** © Mike Brinson/Getty; **pg. 5 (bottom):** © David Young-Wolff/PhotoEdit; **pg. 7 (top):** © National Library of Medicine; **pg. 7 (bottom):** © Dictionary of American Portraits, Dover Publications, Inc.; **pg. 9 (top):** © Archives of the History of American Psychology—The University of Akron; **pg. 9 (bottom):** © National Library of Medicine; **pg. 10 (top):** © Bettman/Corbis; **pg. 10 (bottom):** © Archives of the History of American Psychology—The University of Akron; **pg. 11:** © Bettman/Corbis; **pg. 12 (left):** © Underwood & Underwood/Corbis; **pg. 12 (middle):** © Archives of the History of American Psychology—The University of Akron; **pg. 12 (right):** © Christopher Johnson/Stock Boston; **pg. 13 (left):** © Bettman/Corbis; **pg. 13 (right):** © Carl Rogers Memorial Library; **pg. 16:** © The Harvard Medical Library in the Francis A. Countway Library of Medicine; **pg. 17:** © Steve Leonard; **pg. 18:** © Walter Bibikow/Getty; **pg. 19:** © The Institute of Texan Cultures; **pg. 20 (top):** © Kenneth Clarke, Northside Center for Child Development, Inc.; **pg. 20 (bottom):** © The Institute of Texan Cultures; **pg. 26 (top):** © Lee Snider/The Image Works, Inc.; **pg. 26 (middle):** © Daniel Sheehan/The Image Works; **pg. 26 (bottom):** © A. Ramey/PhotoEdit; **pg. 27 (top):** © Dan Bosler/Getty; **pg. 27 (middle):** © Bob Thomas/Getty; **pg. 27 (bottom):** © Bill Aron/PhotoEdit; **pg. 28 (top):** © David R. Frazier Photolibrary; **pg. 28 (middle):** © Val Corbett/Getty; **pg. 28 (bottom):** © Klaus Lahnstein/Getty

### Chapter 2

**Opener:** © Ray Stott/The Image Works; **pg. 37:** © Penelope Breese/Liaison/Getty; **pg. 49:** © Martin Rogers/Getty

### Chapter 3

**Opener:** © Lester Lefkowitz/Corbis; **pg. 58:** © Lewis-Everhart-Zeevid/Visuals Unlimited; **pg. 59:** © Manfred Kage/Peter Arnold, Inc.; **Fig 3.8:** © Monte S. Buchsbaum, M.D., Mt. Sinai School of Medicine, New York, NY; **Fig. 3.9:** © Edythe D. London; **Fig. 3.10:** © David N. Levin, University of Chicago; **Fig. 3.14:** © Dr. Nancy Andreasen; **Fig. 3.16:** © National Library of Medicine; **Fig. 3.17:** © Meyers, Berman, Schiebel, Hayman; **Fig. 3.19:** © Dr. Marcus Raichle; **pg. 81 (top):** © Stock Montage; **pg. 81 (bottom):** © Musee du Louvre/Paris/Giraudon/SuperStock International; **Fig. 3.24A:** © Science Photo Library/Photo Researchers; **pg. 94 (top):** © Science Photo Library/Photo Researchers; **pg. 94 (bottom):** © Manfred Kage/Peter Arnold, Inc.; **pg. 95:** © Ian O'Leary/Getty; **Fig. 3.27:** Drs. E. F. Torrey and D. R. Weinberger/NIMH Neuroscience Center; **Fig. 3.28:** © Dr. Nancy Andreasen; **Fig. 3.29:** © Monte S. Buchsbaum, M.D., Mt. Sinai School of Medicine, New York, NY; **pg. 102:** © Alan Oddie/PhotoEdit; **Fig. 3.31:** © Richard Anderson, M.D., Ph.D.

### Chapter 4

**Opener:** © Matt Suess/Getty Images; **pg. 114:** © Michael Newman/PhotoEdit; **pg. 122:** © Bob Coyle/The McGraw-Hill Companies; **pg. 130:** © Hein von Horsten; Gallo Images/Corbis; **pg. 133 (top):** © Chad Slattery/Getty; **pg. 133 (bottom):** © David Lampe/MIT; **pg. 136:** © AP/Wide World Photos; **pg. 137:** © Image 100/Royalty-Free/Corbis; **pg. 138:** © TROPIX; **Fig. 4.23:** © Kaiser Porcelain LTD. England; **pg. 146:** © Bob Coyle/The McGraw-Hill Companies; **Fig. 4.29 (top left):** © Bob Daemmrich/The Image Works; **Fig. 4.29 (top middle):** © Corbis; **Fig. 4.29 (top right):** © Grant Heilman Photography; **Fig. 4.29 (bottom left):** © Tui de Roy/Minden Pictures—All rights reserved; **Fig. 4.29 (bottom right):** © George Hunter/H. Armstrong Stock Photography; **Fig. 4.31 (left):** © Bettman/Corbis; **Fig. 4.31 (right):** © Bettman/Corbis; **Fig. 4.37:** © David Wells/The Image Works; **Fig 4.43:** © Eric Lessing/Art Resource; **Fig. 4.44:** The Royal Collection © 2002 Her Majesty Queen Elizabeth II; **Fig. 4.45:** © 1997 Succession H. Matisse, Paris/Artists Rights Society; **Fig. 4.46:** © Dr. Claribel Cone and Miss Etta Cone/The Baltimore Museum of Art: The Cone Collection/Artists Rights Society

### Chapter 5

**Opener:** © Jon Feingersh/Corbis; **pg. 167:** © Renee Lynn/Photo Researchers; **pg. 168:** © Jonathan Nourok/PhotoEdit; **pg. 172:** © Reuters/Bettman News Photos; **pg. 175:** © Tim Brown/Getty; **pg. 178:** © Jim Craigmyle/Corbis; **pg. 179:** © Francoise Sauze/SPL/Photo Researchers, Inc.; **pg. 180:** © Catherine Bushnell/McGill University; **pg. 184 (left):** © Dr. Robert B. Innis/V.A. Medical Center; **pg. 184 (right):** © Dr. Roy Morsch/Corbis; **pg. 186:** © Michael Newman/PhotoEdit; **pg. 188:** © Sonda Dawes/The Image Works; **pg. 190:** © Eric K. K. Yu/Corbis; **pg. 191:** © Tom & Dee Ann McCarthy/Corbis; **Fig. 5.8 (left):** © Karen Moskowitz/Getty; **Fig. 5.8 (right):** Benelux Press/Getty

### Chapter 6

**Opener:** © Corbis; **pg. 198:** PhotoDisc/Getty; **pg. 200:** © Bettman/Corbis; **pg. 204:** © Courtesy of Prof. Benjamin Harris, Ph.D., University of New Hampshire; **pg. 208:** © Zefa-Motions Emotions/Index Stock; **pg. 209:** © AFP/Corbis; **pg. 210:** © Leif Skoogfors/Corbis; **pg. 211:** © Dan Bossler/Getty; **pg. 216:** © Tony Freeman/PhotoEdit; **pg. 222:** © David Young-Wolff/PhotoEdit; **pg. 224:** © SuperStock International; **pg. 225:** © Tony Freeman/PhotoEdit; **pg. 227:** © Dr. Albert Bandura; **pg. 230:** © Jerry Wachter/Photo Researchers

### Chapter 7

**Opener:** © International Stock/ImageState; **pg. 236:** © David Young-Wolff/PhotoEdit; **pg. 237:** © Richard Hutchings/Photo Researchers; **pg. 239:** © Alan Levenson/Getty; **pg. 240:** © Jose Luis Pelaez, Inc./Corbis; **pg. 242:** © Tom Stewart/Corbis; **pg. 245:** © Ken Huang/Getty; **pg. 246:** © Stock Boston/Cary Wolinsky; **pg. 247:** © Stock Boston/Joseph Giannetti; **pg. 250:** © David Young-Wolff/PhotoEdit; **pg. 255:** © Chris Cheadle/Getty; **pg. 257:** © Dr. Eric Kandel/Peter Arnold, Inc.; **Fig. 7.10:** © NYT Pictures; **pg. 264:** © David Young-Wolff/PhotoEdit; **pg. 267 (left):** © Tony Freeman/PhotoEdit; **pg. 267 (right):** © SW Production/Index Stock

### Chapter 8

**Opener:** © Jose Luis Pelaez, Inc./Corbis; **pg. 274:** © Bob Krist/Leo de Wys; **pg. 275:** © McGraw-Hill; **pg. 276:** © Bobby Kingsley/Photo Researchers, Inc.; **Fig. 8.6:** © Bob Coyle/The McGraw-Hill Companies; **Fig. 8.7:** © Bob Coyle/The McGraw-Hill Companies; **pg. 281:** © SuperStock; **pg. 282:** © Bruce Ayers/Getty; **pg. 284:** © Michael Newman/PhotoEdit; **pg. 287:** © Deborah Davis/PhotoEdit; **pg. 288 (left):** © Ed Bock/Corbis; **pg. 288 (right):** © Jon Spaull/Corbis; **pg. 290:** © Dr. R. Allen Gardner; **pg. 292:** © Bettman/Corbis; **pg. 293 (left):** © Robbie Jack/Corbis; **pg. 293 (right):** © AFP/Corbis; **pg. 294:** © Image 100/Royalty-Free/Corbis; **pg. 296:** © Bettman/Corbis; **pg. 297:** Hong, Y., Morris, M. W., Chiue, C., & Benet-Martinez, V., "Multicultural Minds: A Dynamic Constructivist Approach to Culture and Cognition," *American Psychologist, 55*:709–720. **pg. 301:** © Laura Dwight/PhotoEdit; **pg. 306:** © Ian Shaw/Getty

### Chapter 9

**Opener:** © Tom Stewart/Corbis; **pg. 320:** © Jim Cummins/Corbis; **pg. 321:** © Margaret Miller/Photo Researchers; **pg. 322:** © Raika Po'ndorf/Austria; **pg. 323 (top left):** © Archives of the History of American Psychology—The University of Akron; **pg. 323 (top right):** © Harlow Primate Laboratory, University of Wisconsin; **pg. 323 (bottom):** © Harlow Primate Laboratory, University of Wisconsin; **pg. 324:** © Dennis O'Clair/Getty; **pg. 325:** © Spencer Grant/PhotoEdit; **Fig. 9.2a:** © Tony Freeman/PhotoEdit; **Fig. 9.2b:** © Laura Dwight/Laura Dwight Photography; **Fig. 9.2c:** © Michael Newman/PhotoEdit; **Fig. 9.2d:** © Laura Dwight/PhotoEdit; **Fig. 9.2e:** © Stephen Marks Inc./Getty; **Fig. 9.2f:** © David Young-Wolff/PhotoEdit; **Fig. 9.2g:** © Stuart McClymont/Getty; **Fig. 9.2h:** © Vincent Oliver/Getty; **pg. 328 (top):** © Bettman/Corbis; **pg. 328 (bottom):** © Harvard University Office of News and Public Affairs; **pg. 329:** © Ilene Perlman/Stock Boston LLC; **pg. 330:** © Bettman/Corbis; **pg. 332:** Courtesy of Benjamin B. Lahey; **pg. 333:** © Petit Format/Photo Researchers, Inc.; **pg. 334 (top):** © Carolyn Rovee-Collier/Rutgers University; **pg. 334 (bottom):** © Bruce Ayres/Getty; **pg. 335:** © Carolyn Rovee-Collier/Rutgers University; **pg. 336 (top):** © Michael Siluk; **Fig. 9.3:** © Enrico Ferorelli; **pg. 337 (top):** © Blair Seitz/Photo Researchers, Inc.; **pg. 337 (bottom):** © SuperStock International; **pg. 338 (top):** © Roy Morsch/Corbis; **pg. 338 (bottom):** © Tony Freeman/PhotoEdit; **pg. 341:** © Justin Pumfrey/Getty; **pg. 342:** © Jim Cummins/Getty; **pg. 343 (top):** Tom Wurl/Stock Boston, LLC; **pg. 343 (bottom):** Mary Kate Denny/PhotoEdit; **pg. 347:** © Brian Bailey/ImageState; **Fig. 9.5a:** © Brad Martin/Getty; **Fig. 9.5b:** © Kay Chernush/Getty; **Fig. 9.5c:** © Jerome Tisne/Getty; **Fig. 9.5d:** © CLEO/PhotoEdit; **Fig. 9.5e:** © Michael Newman/PhotoEdit; **Fig. 9.5f:** © Walter Hodges/Corbis; **Fig. 9.5g:** © Jose Luis Pelaez, Inc./Corbis; **Fig. 9.5h:** © Michael Newman/PhotoEdit; **pg. 349:** © Michael Newman/PhotoEdit; **pg. 350:** © Denis Boissavy/Getty; **pg. 352:** © David J. Phillip/AP/Wide World Photos; **pg. 353:** © Oliver Benn/Getty; **pg. 356 (top):** © Lawrence Migdale/Getty; **pg. 356 (bottom):** © Bruce Ayres/Getty; **pg. 357:** © Robert Brenner/PhotoEdit; **pg. 359:** © Ed Bock/Corbis

### Chapter 10

**Opener:** © Michael Krasowitz/Getty; **pg. 368:** © Tom Stewart/Corbis; **Fig. 10.3:** © Dr. Philip Teitelbaum; **pg. 372:** © Dex Images, Inc./Corbis; **pg. 373 (top):** © Steve Leonard; **pg. 373 (bottom):** © Michael Newman/PhotoEdit; **Fig. 10.5 (left):** © Harlow Primate Laboratory, University of Wisconsin; **Fig. 10.5 (right):** © Harlow Primate Laboratory, University of Wisconsin; **pg. 377:** © Andy Belcher/ImageState; **pg. 378 (top):** © Robert Daly/Getty; **pg. 378 (bottom):** © Elena Rooraid/PhotoEdit; **pg. 381:** © Jose Luis Pelaez, Inc./Corbis; **Fig. 10.10 (happy):** © Don Smetzer/Getty; **Fig. 10.10 (elated):** © Matthew McVay/PNI; **Fig. 10.10 (surprised):** © Francisco Villaflor/Corbis; **Fig. 10.10 (fearful):** © Larry Williams/Corbis; **Fig. 10.10 (angry):** © Color Day Production/Getty; **Fig. 10.10 (sad):** © Image 100/Royalty-Free/Corbis; **pg. 393:** © Thomas Kitchin; **pg. 394 (top):** © Wolfgang Spunbarg/PhotoEdit; **pg. 394 (bottom):** © Anne Rippy/Getty; **pg. 398:** © Bill Aron/PhotoEdit; **pg. 400:** © Tony Freeman/PhotoEdit; **pg. 402:** © Susan Van Etten/PhotoEdit; **pg. 404 (left):** © Joe Patronite/Getty; **pg. 404 (right):** © Walter Hodge/Getty

### Chapter 11

**Opener:** © Hulton Archives/Getty Images; **pg. 411 (left):** © Ariel Skelley/Corbis; **pg. 411 (right):** © Myrleen Ferguson Cate/PhotoEdit; **Fig. 11.2:** © Shaywitz, et al/NMR Research/Yale Medical School; **pg. 423 (left):** © Dennis Degnan/Corbis; **pg. 423 (right):** © Ariel Skelley/Corbis; **pg. 425:** © Anna Clopet/Corbis; **pg. 427 (left):** © StockImage/ImageState; **pg. 427 (right):** © Deborah Davis/PhotoEdit; **pg. 431:** © UPI/Bettman/Corbis; **pg. 437:** © Carl & Ann Purcell/Corbis; **pg. 441 (top):** © AP/Wide World; **pg. 441 (bottom):** © Bettman/Corbis; **pg. 446:** © Zigy Kaluzny/Getty; **pg. 449:** © Robert Brenner/PhotoEdit; **pg. 450:** © Science Photo Library/Photo Researchers, Inc.; **pg. 454:** © Stewart Cohen/Getty

### Chapter 12

**Opener:** © David Young-Wolff/PhotoEdit; **pg. 462:** AP Photo/Kathy Willens; **pg. 463:** © Archives of the History of American Psychology—The University of Akron; **pg. 466:** © Sigmund Freud Copyrights/Mary Evans Picture Library; **pg. 470:** © Pete Saloutos/Corbis; **pg. 471:** Laura Dwight/Corbis; **pg. 472:** © Bettman/Corbis; **pg. 473 (top left):** © David Young-Wolff/PhotoEdit; **pg. 473 (top right):** © Corbis; **pg. 473 (bottom):** © Stock Montage; **pg. 474:** © Bettman/Corbis; **pg. 476:** © Albert Bandura; **pg. 480:** © Carl Rogers Memorial Library; **pg. 482 (top):** © Bettman/Corbis; **pg. 482 (bottom left):** © Stock Montage; **pg. 482 (bottom middle):** © Bettman/Corbis; **pg. 482 (bottom right):** © Stock Montage; **pg. 486:** © Michael Newman/PhotoEdit; **Fig. 12.4:** Reprinted by permission of the publishers from Henry A. Murry, Thematic Apperception Test, Plate 12F, Cambridge, Mass.; Harvard University Press, Copyright © 1943 by the President and Fellows of Harvard College, © 1971 by Henry A. Murry; **pg. 492:** © Steve Skjold/PhotoEdit; **Fig. 12.6:** © Michelle Bridwell/PhotoEdit

### Chapter 13

**Opener:** © Larry Dale Gordon/Getty; **pg. 500:** © Steve Prezant/Corbis; **pg. 501:** © Craig Newbauer/Peter Arnold, Inc.; **pg. 503:** © T. Rosenthal/SuperStock International; **pg. 509:** © Jon Riley/Getty; **pg. 512:** © Blair Seitz/Photo Researchers, Inc.; **pg. 514:** © Ken Chernus/Getty; **pg. 520:** © Michael Siluk; **pg. 524:** © Michael Newman/PhotoEdit; **pg. 525:** © Wojnarowicz/The Image Works, Inc.; **pg. 527:** © International Stock/ImageState

### Chapter 14

**Opener:** © Ghislain & Marie David de Lossy/Getty; **pg. 541:** © Giraudon/Art Resource; **pg. 542:** © Bettman/Corbis; **pg. 543:** © AP/Wide World; **pg. 545:** © Willie Hill/The Image Works; **pg. 548:** © Bettman/Corbis; **pg. 553:** © Gerald Martineau/The Washington Post; **pg. 555:** © David de Lossy/Getty; **pg. 557:** © Bruce Ayres/Getty; **pg. 558:** © Frank Siteman/PhotoEdit; **pg. 560 (top):** © Collection Prinzhorn, Psychiatric Clinic of the University of Heidelberg; **pg. 560 (bottom):** © Grunnitus/Monkmeyer; **pg. 561 (top):** © UPI/Bettman/Corbis; **pg. 561 (bottom):** © Reuters/Bettman/Corbis; **pg. 562:** © Ellen Senisi/The Image Works; **pg. 566:** © Peter M. Wilson/Corbis; **pg. 567:** © Reuters/Bettman/Corbis

### Chapter 15

**Opener:** © Dion Ogust/The Image Works; **pg. 573:** © James L. Shaffer; **pg. 574 (top):** © Bruce Ayres/Getty Images; **pg. 574 (bottom):** © Freud Museum, London; **pg. 580:** © Michael Rougier/Life Magazine/Time Warner, Inc.; **pg. 581:** © Paul B. Herbert/Esalen Institute; **pg. 583:** © Bob Mahoney/The Image Works; **pg. 584:** © John Griffin/The Image Works; **pg. 588:** © Aaron Beck; **pg. 589:** © Institute for Rational-Emotive Therapy; **pg. 592:** © Zigy Kaluzny/Getty; **pg. 593:** © David Harry Stewart/Getty; **pg. 594:** © Bruce Ayres/Getty Images; **pg. 596:** © Will & Deni McIntyre/Photo Researchers, Inc.; **pg. 599:** © Jim Whitmer/Stock Boston

### Chapter 16

**Opener:** © David Madison/Getty; **pg. 606 (top):** © Chuck Savage/Corbis; **pg. 606 (bottom):** © Jake Rajs/The Image Bank; **pg. 608:** © David Young-Wolff/PhotoEdit; **pg. 611:** © Pictor; **pg. 612:** P.G. Zimbardo, Inc.; **pg. 614:** © 1965 by Stanley Milgram. From the film "Obedience" distributed by Pennsylvania State University; **pg. 618:** © Gary Conner/PhotoEdit; **pg. 619:** Reprinted by the permission of the American Cancer Society, Inc. All rights reserved; **pg. 622:** © Willie Hill, Jr./The Image Works; **pg. 625:** © David Young-Wolff/PhotoEdit; **pg. 626:** © Daemmrich/The Image Works; **pg. 628:** © Jon Feingersh/Corbis; **pg. 632:** © Esbin Anderson/The Image Works; **pg. 635:** © Ron Chapple/FPG International/Getty; **pg. 638 (left):** © Cynthia Johnson/Time Magazine; **pg. 638 (right):** © Courtesy Susan T. Fiske

### Chapter 17

**Opener:** © Jose Luis Pelaez, Inc./Corbis; **pg. 645:** © Bill Varie/Corbis; **Fig. 17.4:** © James L. Shaffer; **pg. 650 (top left):** © Marc Romanelli/Getty; **pg. 650 (top right):** SuperStock International: **pg. 650 (bottom left):** © Steven Rubin/The Image Works; **pg. 650 (bottom middle):** © Dag Sundberg/Getty; **pg. 650 (bottom right):** A. Ramey/Stock Boston; **pg. 653:** © Jose Luis Pelaez, Inc./Corbis; **pg. 655:** © Rob Gage/Getty; **pg. 658:** © Jeff Greenberg/Visuals Unlimited; **pg. 659:** © Museum of Flight/Corbis; **pg. 662:** © Chuck Keeler/Getty; **pg. 664:** © Reuters/Bettman/Corbis; **pg. 665:** © Steve Allen/Image Bank/Getty; **pg. 666:** © Frank Cezus/Getty; **pg. 674:** © Julie Houck/Corbis; **pg. 676:** © Mug Shots/Corbis

## Line Art

### Chapter 1

**Fig 1.4:** Data from R.M. Tarpy and R.E. Mayer, *Foundations of Learning and Memory*, 1978, Scott, Foresman & Company. **Fig. 1.6:** Data from 1997 Doctorate Employment Survey, American Psychological Association Research Office. www.apa.org

### Chapter 2

**Fig 2.1:** Data from S. Kasper, et al., "Epidemiological Findings of Seasonal Changes in Mood and Behavior," in *Archives of General Psychiatry*, 46-833. **Fig 2.6:** Adapted from J.P. Leyens, L. Camino, R.D. Parke, and L. Berkowitz,"Effects of Movie Violence on Aggression in a Field Setting as a Function of Group Dominance and Cohesion," *Journal of Personality and Social Psychology, 32*:346–360. Copyright © 1975 by the American Psychological Association.

### Chapter 3

**Fig 3.18:** Data from W. Penfield and T. Rasmussen, *The Cerebral Cortex of Man*. Copyright © 1950 Macmillan Publishing Co., New York. **Fig 3.22:** From *Archives of General Psychiatry, 45*:247–252. Copyright © 1988 American Medical Association. **Fig 3.23:** Data from V. Bolm-Andorff, et al., "Hormonal and Cardiovascular Variations During a Public Lecture," in *European Journal of Applied Physiology, 54*:669–674. Copyright 1986 Springer-Verlag, New York. **Fig 3.30:** Data from C.E. Barr, S.A. Mednick, and P. Munk-Jorgensen, "Exposure to Influenza Epidemics During Gestation and Adult Schizophrenia," in *Archives of General Psychiatry, 47*:869–874, 1990.

### Chapter 5

**Fig 5.2:** Records provided by T. E. LeVere. Used by permission. **Fig 5.3:** Data based in part on J. Puig-Antich, et al., "Cortisol Secretion in Prepubertal Children with Major Depressive Disorder," *Archives of General Psychiatry, 46*:801–812, 1989. **Fig 5.4:** "Data from M.C. Moore-Ede, F.M. Sulzman, and C.A. Fuller, *The Clocks That Time Us*. Copyright 1982 Harvard University Press. **Fig 5.7:** Data from D.M. Veleber and D. Templer, "Effects of Caffeine on Anxiety and Depression," *Journal of Abnormal Psychology, 93*:120–122, 1984. Copyright © 1984 by the American Psychological Association.

### Chapter 6

**Fig 6.4:** Data from K. Eileen, et al., "Effects of Social Reinforcement Isolate Behavior of a Nursery School Child," in *Child Development 35*:511–518, 1974. Copyright 1964 The Society for Research in Child Development. **Figs 6.12 and 6.13:** E.C. Tolman, B.F. Ritchie, and D. Kalish, "Studies in Spatial Learning I: Orientation and the Short-Cut," in *Journal of Experimental Psychology, 36*:13–25, 1946. **Figs 6.14 and 6.15:** E.C. Tolman and C.H. Honzik, "Introduction and Removal of the Reward, and Maze Performance in Rats," *University of California Publications in Psychology, 4*:257–275, 1930. **Fig 6.17:** H.F. Harlow, "The Formation of Learning Sets" in *Psychological Review, 56*:51–56, 1949.

### Chapter 7

**Fig 7.3:** R.L. Peterson and M.J. Peterson, "Short Term Retention of Individual Items," in *Journal of Experimental Psychology, 58*:193–198, 1959. **Fig 7.6:** Data from M. Glanzer and A.R. Cunitz, "Two Storage Mechanisms in Free Recall," *Journal of Verbal Learning and Verbal Behavior, 5*:351–360, 1966 Academic Press; and R.M. Tarpy and R.F. Mayer, *Foundations of Learning and Memory*, 1978 Scott Foresman. **Fig 7.7:** Data from D.D. Wickens, D.G. Born, and C.K. Allen, "Proactive Inhibition Item Similarity in Short Term Memory," in *Journal of Verbal Learning and Verbal Behavior, 2*:440–445, 1963. © 1963 Academic Press. **Fig 7.8:** Redrawn from L. Carmichael, H.P. Hogan, and A.A. Walter, "An Experimental Study of the Effect of Language on the Reproduction of Visually Perceived Form," in *Journal of Experimental Psychology, 15*:78–86, 1932.

### Chapter 8

**Figs 8.4 and 8.5:** After W. Kohler, *The Task of Gestalt Psychology*. Copyright 1960 by Princeton University Press. **Fig** [illegible] Adapted from U. Neisser "Rising Test Scores and What They Mean." In U. Neisser (Ed.), *The Rising Curve: Long-Term Gains in IQ and Related Measures*, p. 303–334. Copyright © 1998 by the American Psychological Association. **Fig 8.11:** Adapted from P.A. Carpenter, M.A. Just, and P. Shall "What One Intelligence Test Measures: A Theoretical Account of the Processing in the Ravens Progressive Matrices Test," *Psychological Review, 97*:404–432. Copyright © 1990 by the American Psychological Association. Adapted with permission. **Fig 8.12:** Adapted from M. Huang & R.M. Hauser, "Trends in Black-White Test-Score Differentials: II. The WORDSUM Vocabulary Test." In U. Neisser (Ed.) *The Rising Curve: Long-Term Gains in IQ and Related Measures*, p. 303–334. Copyright © 1998 by the American Psychological Association.

### Chapter 9

**Fig 9.1:** Data from M.B. McGraw, "Neural Maturation as Exemplified in Achievement of Bladder Control," *Journal of Pediatrics, 16*:580–590, 1940. **Fig 9.4:** Data from J.M. Tanner, R.H. Whitehouse and M. Takaishi, "Standards from Birth to Maturity for Height, Weight, Height Velocity and Weight Velocity," in *Archives of Diseases in Childhood, 41*:555–571, 1996. **Fig 9.5:** From *The Seasons of a Man's Life* by Daniel J. Levinson, et al. Copyright © 1978 by Daniel J. Levinson. Used by permission of Alfred A. Knopf, a division of Random House, Inc.

### Chapter 10

**Figs 10.7 and 10.8:** Data from Richard L. Solomon, "The Opponent-Process Theory of Acquired Motivation," in *American Psychologist 35*:691–712. Copyright © 1980 by the American Psychological Association. **Fig 10.9:** Diagram based on data from *Hierarchy of Needs from Motivation and Personality*, 3rd edition, by Abraham H. Maslow. Revised by Robert Frager, et al., Harper & Row Publishers, Inc., 1954, 1987. **Fig 10.10:** Adapted from Figure 2 of A. Tellegen, D. Watson, and L.A. Clark, "On the Dimensional and Hierarchical Structure of Affect," *Psychological Science 10*:297–303, 1999. Cambridge University Press. **Fig 10.12:** Diagram based on data from *Hierarchy of Needs from Motivation and Personality*, 3rd edition, by Abraham H. Maslow. Revised by Robert Frager, et al., Harper & Row Publishers, Inc., 1954, 1987.

### Chapter 11

**Fig 11.3:** From *Sex in America: A Definitive Survey* by Robert T. Michael, et al., Copyright © 1994 by CSG Enterprises, Inc., Edward O. Laumann, Robert T. Michael, and Gina Kolata. By permission of Little, Brown & Company, Inc. **Fig 11.6:** Used by permission of Masters and Johnson Institute. **Figs 11.7 and 11.8:** From *Sex in America: A Definitive Survey* by Robert T. Michael, et al., Copyright © 1994 by CSG Enterprises, Inc., Edward O. Laumann, Robert T. Michael, and Gina Kolata. By permission of Little, Brown & Company, Inc. **Fig 11.9:** Centers for Disease Control and Prevention, 1998.

### Chapter 12

**Fig 12.6:** Data from A.M. Isen and P.F. Levin, "The Effect of Feeling Good on Helping: Cookies and Kindness," *Journal of Personality and Social Psychology, 21*:384–388, 1972.

### Chapter 13

**Fig 13.2:** Data from S. Epstein and W.D. Fenz, "Steepness of Approach and Avoidance Gradients in Humans as a Function of Experience: Theory and Experiment," *Journal of Experimental Psychology 70*:1–12, 1965. Copyright © 1965 by the American Psychological Association. **Fig 13.4:** Based on Figure 1, from F.G. Foa and D.S. Riggs, "Post Traumatic Stress Disorder Following Assault: Theoretical & Empirical Findings," *Current Directions in Psychological Science 4*:61–65, 1995. **Table 13.1:** Reprinted from *Journal of Psychosomatic Research*, Vol. 11, Thomas H. Holmes and R.H. Rahe, "The Social Readjustment Scale." Copyright © 1967 with permission of Elsevier Science. **Fig 13.5:** Data from H. Selye, *The Stress of Life*. Copyright © 1976 McGraw-Hill Book Company. **Fig 13.7:** Based on S. Cohen, "Psychological Stress Immunity, and Upper Respiratory Infections," *Current Directions in Psychological Science 5*:86–90, 1996. **Fig 13.8:** Data from N.B. Belloc, "Relationship of Health Practices to Mortality," *Preventive Medicine 2*:67–81, 1973. Copyright 1973 Academic Press, Orlando, FL. **Table 13.2:** Based on Michael Roizen, *Real Age: Are You as Young as You Can Be?* Copyright © 1999 New York: HarperCollins. **Fig 13.10:** Data from J.A. Kelley, et al., "Behavioral Intervention to Reduce AIDS Risk Activities," in *Journal of Consulting and Clinical Psychology, 57*:60–67, 1989. Copyright © 1989 by the American Psychological Association.

### Chapter 14

**Fig 14.1:** Data from M. Lader and A. Matthews, "Changes in Autonomic Arousal in a Woman Undergoing a Spontaneous Panic Attack," *Journal of Psychosomatic Research, 14*:377–382. Copyright 1970, Pergamon Press, Ltd. **Fig 14.3:** Data from P.M. Lewinsohn, et al., "Age at First Onset for Nonbipolar Depression," *Journal of Abnormal Psychology, 95*:378–383, 1986. Copyright © 1986 by the American Psychological Association.

### Chapter 15

**Fig 15.1:** Data from R.F. Cappe and L.E. Alden "A Comparison of Treatment Strategies for Clients Functionally Impaired by Extreme Shyness and Social Avoidance," *Journal of Consulting and Clinical Psychology, 54*:796–801. Copyright © 1986 by the American Psychological Association. **Table 15.2:** Data from M.L. Smith and G.V. Glass, "Meta-Analysis of Psychotherapy Outcome Studies," *American Psychologist, 32*:752–760. Copyright © 1977 by the American Psychological Association.

### Chapter 17

**Fig 17.1:** Based on Wonderlic Personnel Tests, Inc. (1992). *Wonderlic Personnel Test and Scholastic Level Exam: User's Manual*, (pp. 20, 26, 27). Libertyville, IL. **Fig 17.2:** Sample items redrawn from the *Revised Minnesota Paper Form Board*. Copyright 1941, renewed 1969 by the Psychological Corporation. Used by permission. **Fig 17.3:** Sample items from the *Differential Aptitude Tests, Forms V and W, Mechanical Reasoning*. Copyright 1972, 1982 by the Psychological Corporation. All rights reserved. **Fig 17.10:** Modified from A. Baum and S. Valins, *Architecture and Social Behavior: Psychological Studies of Social Density*, 1977 Lawrence Erlbaum Associates, Inc. Used by permission of the author. **Table 17.1:** From G.L. Jurow, "New Data on the Effects of a 'Death-Qualified' Jury on the Guilt Determination Process." *Harvard Law Review 84*:59. Copyright © 1971 by the Harvard Law Review Association. **Fig 17.11:** J.W. Grimes and W. Allinsmith, "Compulsivity, Anxiety, and School Achievement," in *Merrill-Palmer Quarterly, 7*:247–271, © 1961 Wayne State University Press, Detroit, MI.

# Name Index

# Subject Index

*Italic type* indicates illustrations.
Researchers, authors, and other
    people are listed in the
    accompanying Name Index.

## A

Abnormal behavior, 538–567
    anxiety disorders, 545–549
    definition, 540
    dissociative disorders, 551–554
    insanity, 543–544
    as learned behavior, 583
    mood disorders, 555–559
    personality disorders, 562–564
    schizophrenia, 559–562
    somatoform disorders, 549–551
    views of, 541–543
Absolute threshold, 115, *Fig. 4.2*
Absolutistic thinking, 589
Abstraction, selective, 588–589
Accommodation, visual, 147
Acetylcholine
    Alzheimer's disease, 258
    definition, 63
    neuropeptides and, *Tab. 3.1*
    reticular formation and, 72
Achievement motivation, 378–379
Acoustic codes in short-term
    memory, 238
Acquired immune deficiency
    syndrome (AIDS); *see* HIV/AIDS
Acquired motives theory, 379–380
Act-alike drugs, 188–189
Action potential, 61
Acupuncture, 136–137
ADA (Americans with Disabilities Act
    of 1970), 625
Adaptation, 27
ADD (attention-deficit disorder),
    *Tab. 3.1*
Addiction, 183, 380
Adenine (A), 91–93
ADH (antidiuretic hormone), 373
ADHD (attention-deficit hyperactivity
    disorder), *Tab. 3.1*
Adlerian personality theory, 473–474
Adolescence, 340–344
Adolescent egocentrism, 342
Adolescent growth spurt, 341
Adoptees, inheritance research on, 96
Adrenal glands, 88, *Fig. 3.22, Fig. 3.23*
Adrenaline, 390
Adulthood, development in, 345–354
Aerial perspective, 147
Afferent feedback, 389–391
Afferent neurons, 65, *Fig. 3.6*
Affiliation motivation, 376–378
Afterimages, 123
Age regression under hypnosis, 179
Aggression
    amygdala and, 74
    motivation and, 398–401
    research, 493
    stress reactions and, 521

Aging, 352–353
Agoraphobia, 546
AIDS (acquired immune deficiency
    syndrome); *see* HIV/AIDS
Alcohol, 191–192, *Tab. 5.1*
    date rape and, 454–455
Alcoholism, 261, 380
Alex (parrot), 290
Algorithms, 280
All-or-none principle, 61
Allport's trait theory of personality,
    462–463
Alprazolam, 187, *Tab. 5.1*
Altered states of consciousness,
    176–192
    characteristics, 177
    depersonalization, 180
    drug-induced, 181–192
    hypnosis, 178–180
    meditation, 177–178
Alzheimer's disease
    acetylcholine, 258
    the brain and, 102–103
    hippocampus and, 74
    MRI image, *Fig. 3.31*
The American dream, 384
American Psychological Association
    (APA), 572, 600, *Fig. 5.7*
American Sign Language (ASL), 290
Americans with Disabilities Act
    of 1970, 625
Ames room illusion, 150, *Fig. 4.37,
    Fig. 4.38*
Amnesia, 259–261
Amobarbital, *Tab. 5.1*
Amphetamines, 101, 184, *Tab. 5.1*
Ampulla, *Fig. 4.16*
Amygdala, 74, *Fig. 3.13*
    emotional memory, 258–259
    gender differences, 417
Anal expulsive, 470
Anal retentive, 470
Anal stage, 470
Analgesia, 179–180
Anay people (Nigeria), 402
Androgynous, 411
Angel dust (PCP), 188, *Tab. 5.1*
Angiotensin, 374
Animals
    languages, 289–290
    personality, 464
Animism, 337
Anorexia nervosa, 402
Anterograde amnesia, 259
Antidiuretic hormone (ADH), 373
Antisocial personality disorder, 562
Anvil, 128
Anxiety disorders, 545–549
    cognitive therapy and, 589
    diagnosing, 539
Anxiety, neurotransmitters and,
    *Tab. 3.1*
APA; *see* American Psychological
    Association
Aphasia, 76, 79

Appetite and serotonin, *Tab. 3.1*
Applied psychologists, 22
Applied psychology, 642–677
    educational psychology, 673–676
    entrepreneurs, 656–657
    environmental psychology,
        661–667
    hiring, 645–653
    human factors engineering,
        657–658
    job satisfaction, 653–656
    legal psychology, 668–672
    mainstreaming, 676–677
    testing, 673–676
Approach-approach conflict, 500
Approach-avoidance conflict, 501
Approval, need for, 620
Arapesh people (New Guinea), 409
Arbitrary inference, 589
Architectural design, 662–664
Arguments, 619
Artificial intelligence, 282–283
ASL (American Sign Language), 290
Assertiveness training, 585
Assessment centers, 649
Association, *Fig. 6.2*
Association areas, 79–80
Association for Advancement of
    Behavior Therapy, 572
Associative network, 243, 254
Astral projection, 180, 551
Attachments, 337, 356–357
Attention-deficit hyperactivity
    disorder (ADHD), *Tab. 3.1*
Attention, reticular formation and, 72
Attitudes in groups, 616–627
Attractiveness and persuasion, 618;
    *see also* Interpersonal attraction
Attribution, 630
Attribution theory, 623
Atypical sexual behavior, 441
Audition, 126
Authoritarian parenting, 357
Authoritative parenting, 357
Authority figures, 613–614
Autokinetic effect in group
    dynamics, 611
Autonomic nervous system, 67–69
    anatomy, *Fig. 3.7*
    hypothalamus and, 74
    meditation and, 178
    norepinephrine and, *Tab. 3.1*
Autonomic storm, 167, 169
Autonomy, 357, *Tab. 9.3*
Avoidance-avoidance conflict, 501
Avoidance conditioning, 212
Avoidant personality disorder, 563
Axons, 58, *Fig. 3.1, Fig. 3.2, Fig. 3.3,
    Fig. 3.4*

## B

B-cells, 533
Barbital, *Tab. 5.1*
Barbiturates, *Tab. 5.1*

Bariba people (Benin, West
    Africa), 138
Basic concepts, 275–277
Basilar membrane, 130, *Fig. 4.15*
Basket cells, 133
Bee dances, *Fig. 8.8*
Behavior; *see also* Abnormal behavior;
    Biology; *entries at Social*
    basic constructs, 25–28
    definition, 5
    frontal lobe regulation, 77
    genetic influences, 91–97, *Fig. 3.25*
    high-risk and AIDS, 533–535
    operant conditioning, 206–217
    patterns and health, 523–531
Behavior therapy, 583–587
Behaviorism, 11–13
    environmental protection,
        666–667
    in evolution of psychology, *Fig. 1.5*
Bell curve, 298, A-5–A-6
*The Bell Curve*, 307–308
Benzedrine, *Tab. 5.1*
Beth-Jakob Seminary, 467
Bimodal distribution, A-4
Binocular cues, 147–150
Biology
    basis of intelligence, 292–293
    brain, 70–86, 99–103
    endocrine system, 86–90
    factors in learning, 227–229
    gender differences, 416–419
    genetics, 91–97
    memory and, 257–261
    nervous system, 58–70
    primary motives and, 369–374
    psychology and, 26
    sexuality and, 430–439
Bipolar disorder, 557
Bisexuality, 424
Blind experiments, 45–46
    double-blind experiments, 52–53
Blind people, dreams of, 161
Blind spot, 120
Body clock, 90, 168–170
Body functions, essential, 67
Body image, 402–404
Body senses, 131–140
Body temperature, 169
Bone conduction hearing, 130
Borderline personality disorder, 563
Braille alphabet, *Fig. 4.18*
Brain, 70–86
    anatomy, *Fig. 3.11, Fig. 3.12,
        Fig. 3.13*
    brain imaging, 70–72
    definition, 58
    development in adolescence, 342
    gender differences, 416–417
    memory, 240–241
    schizophrenic activity, *Fig. 3.29*
Brain imaging, 70–72
Brightness constancy, 146
Brightness, vision, 119
Broca's area, 76, *Fig. 3.19*